Computer Architecture A Quantitative Approach

SECOND EDITION

Order Form

Purchase of this beta-test manuscript and participation in the testing program entitles you to a 50% discount on the first edition of *Computer Architecture: A Quantitative Approach,* Second Edition (available in the summer of 1995). Purchase may only be made directly from the publisher. Your order must be accompanied by this page; photocopies or facsimiles can not be accepted.

Please complete the following form:

Enclosed is my check or money order for one copy of Hennessy and Patterson's *Computer Architecture,* Second Edition, including shipping and any applicable tax:

1 copy of Hennessy and Patterson, ISBN 1-55860-352-2	$64.95	US
-50% beta discount	($32.48)	US
Subtotal	= $32.47	US
California deliveries must include 8.25% sales tax	= $ _____	
Shipping	= $ 3.50	
Total enclosed	= $ _____	

Please ship to:

_____
NAME

_____
STREET ADDRESS OR P.O. ADDRESS

_____

_____
CITY/STATE/ZIP CODE

Mail this page to:

Morgan Kaufmann Publishers, Inc.
340 Pine Street, Sixth Floor
San Francisco, CA 94104-3205

This offer expires October 1, 1995

Computer
Architecture
A
Quantitative
Approach

SECOND EDITION

David A. Patterson
UNIVERSITY OF CALIFORNIA AT BERKELEY

John L. Hennessy
STANFORD UNIVERSITY

With a Contribution by
David Goldberg
Xerox Palo Alto Research Center

MORGAN KAUFMANN PUBLISHERS, INC.
SAN FRANCISCO, CALIFORNIA

Executive Editor Bruce M. Spatz
Production Manager Yonie Overton
Assistant Editor Douglas Sery
Editorial Coordinator Julie Pabst
Text Design Gary Head
Cover Design David Lance Goines
Composition Nancy Logan
Two-color Art Tech Graphics Corporation
Printer IPC Software Services

Uncorrected Preliminary Manuscript

Morgan Kaufmann Publishers, Inc.
Editorial Office:
340 Pine Street, Sixth Floor
San Francisco, CA 94104-3205

ADVICE, PRAISE, & ERRORS: Any correspondence related to this publication or intended for the authors should be addressed to the editorial offices of Morgan Kaufmann Publishers, Inc., Dept. HP2 APE. Information regarding error sightings is encouraged. Any error sightings that are accepted for correction in subsequent printings will be rewarded by the authors with a payment of $1.00 (U.S.) per correction upon availability of the new printing. Electronic mail can be sent to arc2bugs@mkp.com. (Please include your full name and permanent mailing address.)

INSTRUCTOR SUPPORT: For information on classroom software and other instructor materials available to adopters, please contact the editorial offices of Morgan Kaufmann Publishers, Inc. (415) 392-2665.

ISBN 1-55860-352-2

A Note from the Publisher

Thank you very much for participating in the beta testing for the second edition of *Computer Architecture: A Quantitative Approach*. The original publication of this book represented a landmark in education—one that was acknowledged by practitioners from industry as well as colleges and universities. The beta testing of the first edition played an enormous role in the ultimate acceptance and usefulness of that book. This new edition has been almost completely rewritten, and we are once again making the preliminary version of the manuscript available to a select group of courses for beta testing. Your involvement will be influential to the character of the final publication.

The draft manuscript in this special printing has not yet benefitted from the many stages of editing, proofing, typesetting, and design that the book will undergo before publication. Some chapters will read more smoothly than others. In fact, this is a manuscript that under normal circumstances would be seen by only a small group of experienced instructors, researchers, and developers. We apologize in advance for any inconvenience or frustration this may cause you, our first reader. However, we hope that you will also have significant personal gain from your use of this book by having access to information and discussion that will not be generally available for another year. If you accept the discount offer in this Beta copy, you will receive a dramatically improved final publication that would not have been possible without your help and you will be credited $32.48 for your Beta purchase (the amount of our suggested retail price).

We are eager for your comments and we can guarantee that any bug reports, suggestions, or criticisms you may have will be carefully considered by the authors. When you submit comments to your instructor or to the internet address that follows, they will be forwarded to the authors in your name. During previous Beta programs, the authors made substantial revisions to the presentation based on student suggestions, in addition to correcting the bugs that were noted by our readers.

Here's what we need: Please let us know of any errors, inconsistencies, or incomprehensible sentences. In particular, your careful reading of the text, figures, and exercises will point to many technical problems that could not be found by even the most careful of proofreaders. It is not a good use of your time to report problems of grammar, punctuation, or standard English word usage—these things will all be handled by professional editors in the next stage of publication. We are relying on you to be the content expert.

Reward: For the first reported instance of each bug or other technical advisory that is accepted by the authors, we will send you a check of $1.00 per bug, signed by the authors.

Please submit your bugs and technical advisories to arc2bugs@mkp.com.

Thank you very much for your help. We hope you enjoy your course and the added challenge of the bug hunt.

Trademarks

The following trademarks are the property of the following organizations:

Alliant is a trademark of Alliant Computers.

AMD 29000 is a trademark of AMD.

TeX is a trademark of American Mathematical Society.

AMI 6502 is a trademark of AMI.

Apple I, Apple II, and Macintosh are trademarks of Apple Computer, Inc.

ZS-1 is a trademark of Astronautics.

UNIX and UNIX F77 are trademarks of AT&T Bell Laboratories.

Turbo C is a trademark of Borland International.

The Cosmic Cube is a trademark of California Institute of Technology.

Warp, C.mmp, and Cm* are trademarks of Carnegie-Mellon University.

CP3100 is a trademark of Conner Peripherals.

CDC 6600, CDC 7600, CDC STAR-100, CYBER-180, CYBER 180/990, and CYBER-205 are trademarks of Control Data Corporation.

Convex, C-1, C-2, and C series are trademarks of Convex.

CRAY-3 is a trademark of Cray Computer Corporation.

CRAY-1, CRAY-1S, CRAY-2, CRAY X-MP, CRAY X-MP/416, CRAY Y-MP, CFT77 V3.0, CFT, and CFT2 V1.3a are trademarks of Cray Research.

Cydra 5 is a trademark of Cydrome.

CY7C601, 7C601, 7C604, and 7C157 are trademarks of Cypress Semiconductor.

Nova is a trademark of Data General Corporation.

HEP is a trademark of Denelcor.

CVAX, DEC, DECsystem, DECstation, DECstation 3100, DECsystem 10/20, fort, LP11, Massbus, MicroVAX-I, MicroVAX-II, PDP-8, PDP-10, PDP-11, RS-11M/IAS, Unibus, Ultrix, Ultrix 3.0, VAX, VAXstation, VAXstation 2000, VAXstation 3100, VAX-11, VAX-11/780, VAX-11/785, VAX Model 730, Model 750, Model 780, VAX 8600, VAX 8700, VAX 8800, VS FORTRAN V2.4, and VMS are trademarks of Digital Equipment Corporation.

BINAC is a trademark of Eckert-Mauchly Computer Corporation.

Multimax is a trademark of Encore Computers.

ETA 10 is a trademark of the ETA Corporation.

SYMBOL is a trademark of Fairchild Corporation.

Pegasus is a trademark of Ferranti, Ltd.

Ferrari and Testarossa are trademarks of Ferrari Motors.

AP-120B is a trademark of Floating Point Systems.

Ford and Escort are trademarks Ford Motor Co.

Gnu C Compiler is a trademark of Free Software Foundation.

M2361A, Super Eagle, VP100, and VP200 are trademarks of Fujitsu Corporation.

Chevrolet and Corvette are trademarks of General Motors Corporation.

HP Precision Architecture, HP 850, HP 3000, HP 3000/70, Apollo DN 300, Apollo DN 10000, and Precision are trademarks of Hewlett-Packard Company.

S810, S810/200, and S820 are trademarks of Hitachi Corporation.

Hyundai and Excel are trademarks of the Hyundai Corporation.

432, 960 CA, 4004, 8008, 8080, 8086, 8087, 8088, 80186, 80286, 80386, 80486, iAPX 432, i860, Intel, Multibus, Multibus II, and Intel Hypercube are trademarks of Intel Corporation.

Inmos and Transputer are trademarks of Inmos.

Clipper C100 is a trademark of Intergraph.

IBM, 360, 360/30, 360/40, 360/50, 360/65, 360/85, 360/91, 370, 370/135, 370/138, 370/145, 370/155, 370/158, 370/165, 370/168, 370-XA, ESA/370, System/360, System/370, 701, 704, 709, 801, 3033, 3080, 3080 series, 3080 VF, 3081, 3090, 3090/100, 3090/200, 3090/400, 3090/600, 3090/600S, 3090 VF, 3330, 3380, 3380D, 3380 Disk Model AK4, 3380J, 3390, 3880-23, 3990, 7030, 7090, 7094, IBM FORTRAN, ISAM, MVS, IBM PC, IBM PC-AT, PL.8, RT-PC, SAGE, Stretch, IBM SVS, Vector Facility, and VM are trademarks of International Business Machines Corporation.

FutureBus is a trademark of the Institute of Electrical and Electronic Engineers.

Lamborghini and Countach are trademarks of Nuova Automobili Ferrucio Lamborghini, SPA.

Lotus 1-2-3 is a trademark of Lotus Development Corporation.

MB8909 is a trademark of LSI Logic.

NuBus is a trademark of Massachusetts Institute of Technology.

Miata and Mazda are trademarks of Mazda.

MASM, Microsoft Macro Assembler, MS DOS, MS DOS 3.1, and OS/2 are trademarks of Microsoft Corporation.

MIPS, MIPS 120, MIPS/120A, M/500, M/1000, RC6230, RC6280, R2000, R2000A, R2010, R3000, and R3010 are trademarks of MIPS Computer Systems.

Delta Series 8608, System V/88 R32V1, VME bus, 6809, 68000, 68010, 68020, 68030, 68882, 88000, 88000 1.8.4m14, 88100, and 88200 are trademarks of Motorola Corporation.

Multiflow is a trademark of Multiflow Corporation.

National 32032 and 32x32 are trademarks of National Semiconductor Corporation.

Ncube is a trademark of Ncube Corporation.

SX/2, SX/3, and FORTRAN 77/SX V.040 are trademarks of NEC Information Systems.

NYU Ultracomputer is a trademark of New York University.

VAST-2 v.2.21 is a trademark of Pacific Sierra.

Wren IV, Imprimis, Sabre, Sabre 97209, and IPI-2 are trademarks of Seagate Corporation.

Sequent, Balance 800, Balance 21000, and Symmetry are trademarks of Sequent Computers.

Silicon Graphics 4D/60, 4D/240, and Silicon Graphics 4D Series are trademarks of Silicon Graphics.

Stellar GS 1000, Stardent-1500, and Ardent Titan-1 are trademarks of Stardent.

Sun 2, Sun 3, Sun 3/75, Sun 3/260, Sun 3/280, Sun 4, Sun 4/110, Sun 4/260, Sun 4/280, SunOS 4.0.3c, Sun 1.2 FORTRAN compiler, SPARC, and SPARCstation 1 are trademarks of Sun Microsystems.

Synapse N+1 is a trademark of Synapse.

Tandem and Cyclone are trademarks of Tandem Computers.

TI 8847 and TI ASC are trademarks of Texas Instruments Corporation.

Connection Machine and CM-2 are trademarks of Thinking Machines.

Burroughs 6500, B5000, B5500, D-machine, UNIVAC, UNIVAC I, UNIVAC 1103 are trademarks of UNISYS.

Spice and 4.2 BSD UNIX are trademarks of University of California, Berkeley.

Illiac, Illiac IV, and Cedar are trademarks of University of Illinois.

Ada is a trademark of the U.S. Government (Ada Joint Program Office).

Weitek 3364, Weitek 1167, WTL 3110, and WTL 3170 are trademarks of Weitek Computers.

Alto, Ethernet, PARC, Palo Alto Research Center, Smalltalk, and Xerox are trademarks of Xerox Corporation.

Z-80 is a trademark of Zilog.

Contents

5

Advanced Pipelining   244

6

Memory-Hierarchy Design   388

7

Storage Systems   506

And now for something completely different.

Monty Python's Flying Circus

1 Fundamentals of Computer Design

1.1 | Introduction

Computer technology has made incredible progress in the past half century. In 1945, there were no stored-program computers. Today, a few thousand dollars will purchase a personal computer that has more performance, more main memory, and more disk storage than a computer bought in 1965 for a million dollars. This rapid rate of improvement has come both from advances in the technology used to build computers and from innovation in computer designs. The increase in performance of machines is plotted in Figure 1.1. While technological improvements have been fairly steady, progress arising from better computer architectures has been much less consistent. During the first 25 years of electronic computers, both forces made a major contribution; but for the last 20 years, computer designers have been largely dependent upon integrated circuit technology. Growth of performance during this period ranges from 18% to 35% per year, depending on the computer class.

More than any other line of computers, mainframes indicate a growth rate due chiefly to technology—most of the organizational and architectural innovations were introduced into these machines many years ago. Supercomputers have grown both via technological enhancements and via architectural enhancements (see Chapter 7). Minicomputer advances have included innovative ways to implement architectures, as well as the adoption of many of the mainframe's techniques. Performance growth of microcomputers has been the fastest, partly because these machines take the most direct advantage of improvements in integrated circuit technology. Also, since 1980, microprocessor technology has been the technology of choice for both new architectures and new implementations of older architectures.

Two significant changes in the computer marketplace have made it easier than ever before to be commercially successful with a new architecture. First, the virtual elimination of assembly language programming has dramatically reduced the need for object-code compatibility. Second, the creation of standardized, vendor-independent operating systems, such as UNIX, has lowered the cost and risk of bringing out a new architecture. Hence, there has been a renaissance in computer design: There are many new companies pursuing new architectural directions, with new computer families emerging—mini-supercomputers, high-performance microprocessors, graphics supercomputers, and a wide range of multiprocessors—at a higher rate than ever before.

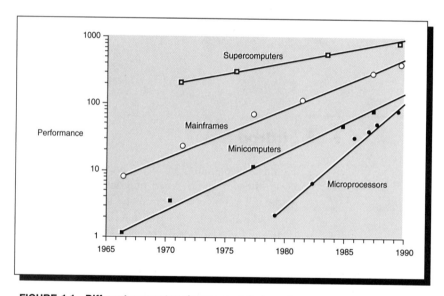

FIGURE 1.1   Different computer classes and their performance growth shown over the past ten or more years. The vertical axis shows relative performance and the horizontal axis is year of introduction. Classes of computers are loosely defined, primarily by their cost. *Supercomputers* are the most expensive—from over one million to tens of millions of dollars. Designed mostly for scientific applications, they are also the highest performance machines. *Mainframes* are high-end, general-purpose machines, typically costing more than one-half million dollars and as much as a few million dollars. *Minicomputers* are midsized machines costing from about 50 thousand dollars up to ten times that much. Finally, *microcomputers* range from small personal computers costing a few thousand dollars to large powerful workstations costing 50 thousand or more. The performance growth rates for supercomputers, minicomputers, and mainframes have been just under 20% per year, while the performance growth rate for microprocessors has been about 35% per year.

Starting in 1985, the computer industry saw a new style of architectures taking advantage of this opportunity and initiating a period in which performance has increased at a much more rapid rate. By bringing together advances in integrated circuit technology, improvements in compiler technology, and new architectural ideas, designers were able to create a series of machines that improved in performance by a factor of almost 2 every year. These ideas are now providing one of the most significant sustained performance improvements in over 20 years. This improvement was only possible because a number of important technological advances were brought together with a much better empirical understanding of how computers were used. From this fusion has emerged a style of computer design based on empirical data, experimentation, and simulation. It is this style and approach to computer design that are reflected in this text.

Sustaining the improvements in cost and performance of the last 25 to 50 years will require continuing innovations in computer design, and the authors believe such innovations will be founded on this quantitative approach to computer architecture. Hence, this book has been written not only to document this design style, but also to stimulate the reader to contribute to this field.

1.2 | Definitions of Performance

To familiarize the reader with the terminology and concepts of this book, this chapter introduces some key terms and ideas. Examples of the ideas mentioned here appear throughout the book, and several of them—pipelining, memory hierarchies, CPU performance, and cost measurement—are the focus of entire chapters. Let's begin with definitions of relative performance.

When we say one computer is faster than another, what do we mean? The computer user may say a computer is faster when a program runs in less time, while the computer center manager may say a computer is faster when it completes more jobs in an hour. The computer user is interested in reducing *response time*—the time between the start and the completion of an event—also referred to as *execution time* or *latency*. The computer center manager is interested in increasing *throughput*—the total amount of work done in a given time—sometimes called *bandwidth*. Typically, the terms "response time," "execution time," and "throughput" are used when an entire computing task is discussed. The terms "latency" and "bandwidth" are almost always the terms of choice when discussing a memory system. All of these terms will appear throughout the text.

Example   Do the following system performance enhancements increase throughput, decrease response time, or both?

1. Faster clock cycle time

2. Multiple processors for separate tasks (handling the airlines reservations system for the country, for example)

3. Parallel processing of scientific problems

Answer   Decreasing response time usually improves throughput. Hence, both 1 and 3 improve response time and throughput. In 2, no one task gets work done faster, so only throughput increases.

Sometimes these measures are best described with probability distributions rather than constant values. For example, consider the response time to complete an I/O operation to disk. The response time depends on a number of nondeterministic factors, such as what the disk is doing at the time of the I/O request and how many other tasks are waiting to access the disk. Because these values are not fixed, it makes more sense to talk about the average response time of a disk access. Likewise, the effective disk throughput—how much data actually goes to or from the disk per unit time—is not a constant value. For most of this text, we will treat response time and throughput as deterministic values, though this will change in Chapter 9 when we discuss I/O.

In comparing design alternatives, we often want to relate the performance of two different machines, say X and Y. The phrase "X is faster than Y" is used here to mean that the response time or execution time is lower on X than on Y for the given task. In particular, "X is n% faster than Y" will mean

$$\frac{\text{Execution time}_Y}{\text{Execution time}_X} = 1 + \frac{n}{100}$$

Since execution time is the reciprocal of performance, the following relationship holds:

$$1 + \frac{n}{100} = \frac{\text{Execution time}_Y}{\text{Execution time}_X} = \frac{\dfrac{1}{\text{Performance}_Y}}{\dfrac{1}{\text{Performance}_X}} = \frac{\text{Performance}_X}{\text{Performance}_Y}$$

Some people think of a performance increase, n, as the difference between the performance of the faster and slower machine, divided by the performance of the slower machine. This definition of n is exactly equivalent to our first definition, as we can see:

$$n = 100 \left(\frac{\text{Performance}_X - \text{Performance}_Y}{\text{Performance}_Y} \right)$$

$$\frac{n}{100} = \frac{\text{Performance}_X}{\text{Performance}_Y} - 1$$

$$1 + \frac{n}{100} = \frac{\text{Performance}_X}{\text{Performance}_Y} = \frac{\text{Execution time}_Y}{\text{Execution time}_X}$$

The phrase "the throughput of X is 30% higher than Y" signifies here that the number of tasks completed per unit time on machine X is 1.3 times the number completed on Y.

Example   If machine A runs a program in 10 seconds and machine B runs the same program in 15 seconds, which of the following statements is true?

- A is 50% faster than B.

- A is 33% faster than B.

Answer   Machine A is n% faster than machine B can be expressed as

$$\frac{\text{Execution time}_B}{\text{Execution time}_A} = 1 + \frac{n}{100}$$

or

$$n = \frac{\text{Execution time}_B - \text{Execution time}_A}{\text{Execution time}_A} * 100$$

Thus,

$$\frac{15 - 10}{10} * 100 = 50$$

A is therefore 50% faster than B.

To help prevent misunderstandings—and because of the lack of consistent definitions for "faster than" and "slower than"—we will never use the phrase "slower than" in a quantitative comparison of performance.

Because performance and execution time are reciprocals, increasing performance decreases execution time. To help avoid confusion between the terms "increasing" and "decreasing," we usually say "improve performance" or "improve execution time" when we mean *increase* performance and *decrease* execution time.

Throughput and latency interact in a variety of ways in computer designs. One of the most important interactions occurs in pipelining. *Pipelining* is an implementation technique that improves throughput by overlapping the execution of multiple instructions; pipelining is discussed in detail in Chapter 6. Pipelining of instructions is analogous to using an assembly line to manufacture cars. In an assembly line it may take eight hours to build an entire car, but if there are eight steps in the assembly line, a new car is finished every hour. In the assembly line, the latency to build one car is not affected, but the throughput increases proportionally to the number of stages in the line if all the stages are of the same length. The fact that pipelines in computers have some overhead per stage increases the latency by some amount for each stage of the pipeline.

1.3 | Quantitative Principles of Computer Design

This section introduces some important rules and observations that arise time and again in designing computers.

Make the Common Case Fast

Perhaps the most important and pervasive principle of computer design is to make the common case fast: In making a design tradeoff, favor the frequent case over the infrequent case. This principle also applies when determining how to spend resources since the impact on making some occurrence faster is higher if the occurrence is frequent. Improving the frequent event, rather than the rare event, will obviously help performance, too. In addition, the frequent case is often simpler and can be done faster than the infrequent case. For example, when adding two numbers in the *central processing unit* (CPU), we can expect overflow to be a rare circumstance and can therefore improve performance by optimizing the more common case of no overflow. This may slow down the case when overflow occurs, but if that is rare, then overall performance will be improved by optimizing for the normal case.

We will see many cases of this principle throughout this text. In applying this simple principle, we have to decide what the frequent case is and how much performance can be improved by making that case faster. A fundamental law, called *Amdahl's Law*, can be used to quantify this principle.

Amdahl's Law

The performance gain that can be obtained by improving some portion of a computer can be calculated using Amdahl's Law. *Amdahl's Law* states that the performance improvement to be gained from using some faster mode of execution is limited by the fraction of the time the faster mode can be used.

Amdahl's Law defines the speedup that can be gained by using a particular feature. What is speedup? Suppose that we can make an enhancement to a machine that will improve performance when it is used. *Speedup* is the ratio

$$\text{Speedup} = \frac{\text{Performance for entire task using the enhancement when possible}}{\text{Performance for entire task without using the enhancement}}$$

Alternatively:

$$\text{Speedup} = \frac{\text{Execution time for entire task without using the enhancement}}{\text{Execution time for entire task using the enhancement when possible}}$$

Speedup tells us how much faster a task will run using the machine with the enhancement as opposed to the original machine.

Example

Consider the problem of going from Nevada to California over the Sierra Nevada mountains and through the desert to Los Angeles. You have several types of vehicles available, but unfortunately your route goes through ecologically sensitive areas in the mountains where you must walk. Your walk over the mountains will take 20 hours. The last 200 miles, however, can be done by high-speed vehicle. There are five ways to complete the second portion of your journey:

1. Walk at an average rate of 4 miles per hour.

2. Ride a bike at an average rate of 10 miles per hour.

3. Drive a Hyundai Excel in which you average 50 miles per hour.

4. Drive a Ferrari Testarossa in which you average 120 miles per hour.

5. Drive a rocket car in which you average 600 miles per hour.

How long will it take for the entire trip using these vehicles, and what is the speedup versus walking the entire distance?

Vehicle for second portion of trip	Hours for second portion of trip	Speedup in the desert	Hours for entire trip	Speedup for entire trip
Feet	50.00	1.0	70.00	1.0
Bike	20.00	2.5	40.00	1.8
Excel	4.00	12.5	24.00	2.9
Testarossa	1.67	30.0	21.67	3.2
Rocket car	0.33	150.0	20.33	3.4

FIGURE 1.2 The speedup ratios obtained for different means of transport depend heavily on the fact that we have to walk across the mountains. The speedup in the desert—once we have crossed the mountains—is equal to the rate using the designated vehicle divided by the walking rate; the final column shows how much faster our entire trip is compared to walking.

Answer

We can find the answer by determining how long the second part of the trip will take and adding that time to the 20 hours needed to cross the mountains. Figure 1.2 shows the effectiveness of using the enhanced mode of transportation.

Amdahl's Law gives us a quick way to find speedup, which depends on two factors:

1. The fraction of the computation time in the original machine that can be converted to take advantage of the enhancement. In the example above, the fraction is $\frac{50}{70}$. This value, which we will call Fraction$_{enhanced}$, is always less than or equal to 1.

2. The improvement gained by the enhanced execution mode; that is, how much faster the task would run if *only* the enhanced mode were used. In the above example this value is given in the column labeled "speedup in the desert." This value is the time of the original mode over the time of the enhanced mode and is always greater than 1. We call this value Speedup$_{enhanced}$.

The execution time using the original machine with the enhanced mode will be the time spent using the unenhanced portion of the machine plus the time spent using the enhancement:

$$\text{Execution time}_{new} = \text{Execution time}_{old} * \left((1 - \text{Fraction}_{enhanced}) + \frac{\text{Fraction}_{enhanced}}{\text{Speedup}_{enhanced}} \right)$$

The overall speedup is the ratio of the execution times:

$$\text{Speedup}_{overall} = \frac{\text{Execution time}_{old}}{\text{Execution time}_{new}} = \frac{1}{(1 - \text{Fraction}_{enhanced}) + \frac{\text{Fraction}_{enhanced}}{\text{Speedup}_{enhanced}}}$$

Example   Suppose that we are considering an enhancement that runs 10 times faster than the original machine but is only usable 40% of the time. What is the overall speedup gained by incorporating the enhancement?

Answer   Fraction$_{enhanced}$ $= 0.4$

Speedup$_{enhanced}$ $= 10$

$$\text{Speedup}_{overall} \quad = \frac{1}{0.6 + \frac{0.4}{10}} = \frac{1}{0.64} \approx 1.56$$

Amdahl's Law expresses the law of diminishing returns: The incremental improvement in speedup gained by an additional improvement in the performance of just a portion of the computation diminishes as improvements are added. An important corollary of Amdahl's Law is that if an enhancement is only usable for a fraction of a task, we can't speed up the task by more than the reciprocal of 1 minus that fraction.

A common mistake in applying Amdahl's Law is to confuse "fraction of time converted to use an enhancement" and "fraction of time after enhancement is in use." If, instead of measuring the time that **could use** the enhancement in a computation, we measure the time **after** the enhancement is in use, the results will be incorrect! (Try Exercise 1.8 to see how wrong.)

Amdahl's Law can serve as a guide to how much an enhancement will improve performance and how to distribute resources to improve cost/performance. The goal, clearly, is to spend resources proportional to where time is spent.

Example

Suppose we could improve the speed of the CPU in our machine by a factor of five (without affecting I/O performance) for five times the cost. Also assume that the CPU is used 50% of the time, and the rest of the time the CPU is waiting for I/O. If the CPU is one-third of the total cost of the computer, is increasing the CPU speed by a factor of five a good investment from a cost/performance viewpoint?

Answer

The speedup obtained is

$$\text{Speedup} = \frac{1}{0.5 + \dfrac{0.5}{5}} = \frac{1}{0.6} = 1.67$$

The new machine will cost

$$\frac{2}{3} * 1 + \frac{1}{3} * 5 = 2.33 \text{ times the original machine}$$

Since the cost increase is larger than the performance improvement, this change does not improve cost/performance.

Locality of Reference

While Amdahl's Law is a theorem that applies to any system, other important fundamental observations come from properties of programs. The most important program property that we regularly exploit is *locality of reference*: Programs tend to reuse data and instructions they have used recently. A widely held rule of thumb is that a program spends 90% of its execution time in only 10% of the code. An implication of locality is that based on the program's recent past, one can predict with reasonable accuracy what instructions and data a program will use in the near future.

To examine locality, several programs were measured to determine what percentage of the instructions were responsible for 80% and for 90% of the instructions executed. The data are shown in Figure 1.3, and the programs are described in detail in the next chapter.

Locality of reference also applies to data accesses, though not as strongly as to code accesses. There are two different types of locality that have been observed. *Temporal locality* states that recently accessed items are likely to be accessed in the near future. Figure 1.3 shows one effect of temporal locality. *Spatial locality* says that items whose addresses are near one another tend to be referenced close together in time. We will see these principles applied later in this chapter, and extensively in Chapter 8.

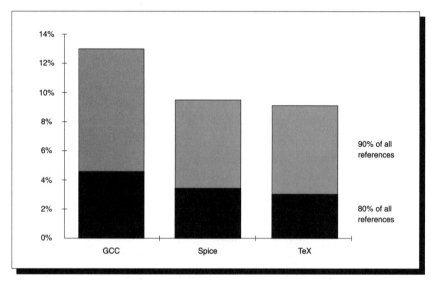

FIGURE 1.3   This plot shows what percentage of the instructions are responsible for 80% and for 90% of the instruction executions. For example, just under 4% of Spice's program instructions (also called the *static* instructions) represent 80% of the dynamically executed instructions, while just under 10% of the static instructions account for 90% of the executed instructions. Less than half the static instructions are executed even once in any one run—in Spice only 30% of the instructions are executed one or more times. Detailed descriptions of the programs and their inputs appear in Figure 2.17 (page 67).

1.4 | The Job of a Computer Designer

A computer architect designs machines to run programs. If you were going to design a computer, your task would have many aspects, including instruction set design, functional organization, logic design, and implementation. The implementation may encompass integrated circuit (IC) design, packaging, power, and cooling. You would have to optimize a machine design across these levels. This optimization requires familiarity with a very wide range of technologies, from compilers and operating systems to logic design and packaging.

Some people have used the term *computer architecture* to refer only to instruction set design. They refer to the other aspects of computer design as "implementation," often insinuating that implementation is uninteresting or less challenging. The authors believe this view is not only incorrect, but is even responsible for mistakes in the design of new instruction sets. The architect's or designer's job is much more than instruction set design, and the technical hurdles in the other aspects of the project are certainly as challenging as those encountered in doing instruction set design.

In this book the term *instruction set architecture* refers to the actual programmer-visible instruction set. The instruction set architecture serves as the boundary between the software and hardware, and that topic is the focus of Chapters 3 and 4. The implementation of a machine has two components: organization and hardware. The term *organization* includes the high-level aspects of a computer's design, such as the memory system, the bus structure, and the internal CPU design. For example, two machines with the same instruction set architecture but different organizations are the VAX-11/780 and the VAX 8600. *Hardware* is used to refer to the specifics of a machine. This would include the detailed logic design and the packaging technology of the machine. This book focuses on instruction set architecture and on organization. Two machines with identical instruction set architectures and nearly identical organizations that differ primarily at the hardware level are the VAX-11/780 and the 11/785; the 11/785 used an improved integrated circuit technology to obtain a faster clock rate and made some small changes in the memory system. In this book the word "architecture" is intended to cover all three aspects of computer design.

Functional Requirements

Computer architects must design a computer to meet functional requirements as well as price and performance goals. Often, they also have to determine what the functional requirements are, and this can be a major task. The requirements may be specific features, inspired by the market. Application software often drives the choice of certain functional requirements by determining how the machine will be used. If a large body of software exists for a certain instruction set architecture, the architect may decide that a new machine should implement an existing instruction set. The presence of a large market for a particular class of applications might encourage the designers to incorporate requirements that would make the machine competitive in that market. Figure 1.4 (see page 15) summarizes some requirements that need to be considered in designing a new machine. Many of these requirements and features will be examined in depth in later chapters.

Many of the requirements in Figure 1.4 represent a minimum level of support. For example, modern operating systems use virtual memory and protection. This requirement establishes a minimum level of support, without which the machine would not be viable. Any additional hardware above such thresholds can be evaluated from the viewpoint of cost/performance.

Most of the attributes of a computer—hardware support for different data types, performance of different functions, and so on—can be evaluated on the basis of cost/performance for the intended marketplace. The next section discusses how one might make these tradeoffs.

Balancing Software and Hardware

Once a set of functional requirements has been established, the architect must try to optimize the design. Which design choices are optimal depends, of course, on the choice of metrics. The most common metrics involve cost and performance. Given some application domain, one can try to quantify the performance of the machine by a set of programs that are chosen to represent that application domain. (We will see how to measure performance and what aspects affect cost and price in the next chapter.) Other measurable requirements may be important in some markets; reliability and fault tolerance are often crucial in transaction processing environments.

Throughout this text we will focus on optimizing machine cost/performance. This optimization is largely a question of where is the best place to implement some required functionality? Hardware and software implementations of a feature have different advantages. The major advantages of a software implementation are the lower cost of errors, easier design, and simpler upgrading. Hardware offers performance as its sole advantage, though hardware implementations are not always faster—a superior algorithm in software can beat an inferior algorithm implemented in hardware. Balancing hardware and software will lead to the best machine for the applications of interest.

Sometimes a specific requirement may effectively necessitate the inclusion of hardware support. For example, a machine that is to run scientific applications with intensive floating-point calculations will almost certainly need hardware for floating-point operations. This is not a question of functionality, but rather of performance. Software-based floating point could be used, but it is so much slower that the machine would not be competitive. Hardware-supported floating point is a de facto requirement for the scientific marketplace. By comparison, consider building a machine to support commercial applications written in COBOL. Such

Functional requirements	Typical features required or supported
Application area	Target of computer
Special purpose	Higher performance for specific applications (Ch. 10)
General purpose	Balanced performance for a range of tasks
Scientific	High-performance floating point (Appendix A)
Commercial	Support for COBOL (decimal arithmetic), support for data bases and transaction processing
Level of software compatibility	Determines amount of existing software for machine (Ch. 10)
At programming language	Most flexible for designer, need new compiler
Object code or binary compatible	Architecture is completely defined—little flexibility—but no investment needed in software or porting programs
Operating system (OS) requirements	Necessary features to support chosen OS
Size of address space	Very important feature (Ch. 8); may limit applications
Memory management	Required for modern OS; may be flat, paged, segmented (Ch. 8)
Protection	Different OS and application needs: page vs. segment protection (Ch. 8)
Context switch	Required to interrupt and restart program; performance varies (Ch. 5)
Interrupts and traps	Types of support impact hardware design and OS (Ch. 5)
Standards	Certain standards may be required by marketplace
Floating point	Format and arithmetic: IEEE, DEC, IBM (Appendix A)
I/O bus	For I/O devices: VME, SCSI, NuBus, Futurebus (Ch. 9)
Operating systems	UNIX, DOS or vendor proprietary
Networks	Support required for different networks: Ethernet, FDDI (Ch. 9)
Programming languages	Languages (ANSI C, Fortran 77, ANSI COBOL) affect instruction set

FIGURE 1.4   Summary of some of the most important functional requirements an architect faces. The left-hand column describes the class of requirement, while the right-hand column gives examples of specific features that might be needed. We will look at these design requirements in more detail in later chapters.

applications make heavy use of decimal and string operations; thus, many architectures have included instructions for these functions. Other machines have supported these functions using a combination of software and standard integer and logical operations. This is a classic example of a tradeoff between hardware and software implementation, and there is no single correct solution.

In choosing between two designs, one factor that an architect must consider is design complexity. Complex designs take longer to complete, prolonging time to market. This means a design that takes longer will need to have higher performance to be competitive. In general, it is easier to deal with complexity in software than in hardware, chiefly because it is easier to debug and change software.

Thus, designers may choose to shift functionality from hardware to software. On the other hand, design choices in the instruction set architecture and in the organization can affect the complexity of the implementation as well as the complexity of compilers and operating systems for the machine. The architect must be constantly aware of the impact of his design choices on the design time for both hardware and software.

Designing to Last Through Trends

If an architecture is to be successful, it must be designed to survive changes in hardware technology, software technology, and application characteristics. The designer must be especially aware of trends in computer usage and in computer technology. After all, a successful new instruction set architecture may last tens of years—the core of the IBM 360 has been in use since 1964. An architect must plan for technology changes that can increase the lifetime of a successful machine.

To plan for the evolution of a machine, the designer must be especially aware of rapidly occurring changes in implementation technology. Figure 1.5 shows some of the most important trends in hardware technology. In writing this book, the emphasis is on design principles that can be applied with new technologies and on accounting for ongoing technology trends.

These technology changes are not continuous but often occur in discrete steps. For example, DRAM (dynamic random-access memory) sizes are always increased by factors of 4 due to the basic design structure. Thus, rather than doubling every year or two, DRAM technology quadruples every three or four years. This stepwise change in technology leads to thresholds that can enable an implementation technique that was previously impossible. For example, when MOS technology reached the point where it could put between 25,000 and 50,000 transistors on a single chip, it became possible to build a 32-bit microprocessor on a single chip. By eliminating chip crossings within the CPU, a dramatic increase in cost/performance was possible. This design was simply infeasible until the technology reached a certain point. Such technology thresholds are not rare and have a significant impact on a wide variety of design decisions.

The architect will also need to be aware of trends in software and how programs will use the machine. One of the most important software trends is the increasing amount of memory used by programs and their data. The amount of memory needed by the average program has grown by a factor of 1.5 to 2 per year! This translates to a consumption of address bits at a rate of 1/2 bit to 1 bit per year. Underestimating address-space growth is often the major reason why an instruction set architecture must be abandoned. (For a further discussion, see Chapter 8 on memory hierarchy.)

Another important software trend in the past 20 years has been the replacement of assembly language by high-level languages. This trend has resulted in a larger role for compilers and in the redirection of architectures toward the support of the compiler. Compiler technology has been steadily improving. A designer must understand this technology and the direction in which it is evolving since compilers have become the primary interface between user and machine. We will talk about the effects of compiler technology in Chapter 3.

A fundamental change in the way programming is done may demand changes in an architecture to efficiently support the programming model. But the emergence of new programming models occurs at a much slower rate than improvements in compiler technology: As opposed to compilers, which improve yearly, significant changes in programming languages occur about once a decade.

Technology	Density and performance trend
IC logic technology	Transistor count on a chip increases by about 25% per year, doubling in three years. Device speed increases nearly as fast.
Semiconductor DRAM	Density increases by just under 60% per year, quadrupling in three years. Cycle time has improved very slowly, decreasing by about one-third in ten years.
Disk technology	Density increases by about 25% per year, doubling in three years. Access time has improved by one-third in ten years.

FIGURE 1.5 Trends in computer implementation technologies show the rapid changes that designers must deal with. These changes can have a dramatic impact on designers when they affect long-term decisions, such as instruction set architecture. The cost per transistor for logic and the cost per bit for semiconductor or disk memory decrease at very close to the rate at which density increases. Cost trends are considered in more detail in the next chapter. In the past, DRAM (dynamic random-access memory) technology has improved faster than logic technology. This difference has occurred because of reductions in the number of transistors per DRAM cell and the creation of specialized technology for DRAMs. As the improvement from these sources diminishes, the density growth in logic technology and memory technology should become comparable.

When an architect has understood the impact of hardware and software trends on machine design, he can then consider the question of how to balance the machine. How much memory do you need to plan for the targeted CPU speed? How much I/O will be required? To try to give some idea of what would constitute a balanced machine, Case and Amdahl coined two rules of thumb that are now usually combined. The combined rule says that a 1-MIPS *(million instructions per second)* machine is balanced when it has 1 megabyte of memory and 1-megabit-per-second throughput of I/O. This rule of thumb provides a reasonable starting point for designing a balanced system, but should be refined by measuring the system performance of the machine when it is executing the intended applications.

1.5 | Putting It All Together: The Concept of Memory Hierarchy

In the "Putting It All Together" sections that appear near the end of every chapter, we show real examples that use the principles in that chapter. In this first chapter, we discuss a key idea in memory systems that will be the sole focus of our attention in Chapter 8.

To begin this section, let's look at a simple axiom of hardware design: *smaller is faster*. Smaller pieces of hardware will generally be faster than larger pieces. This simple principle is particularly applicable to memories for two different reasons. First, in high-speed machines, signal propagation is a major cause of delay; larger memories have more signal delay and require more levels to decode addresses. Second, in most technologies one can obtain smaller memories that are faster than larger memories. This is primarily because the designer can use more power per memory cell in a smaller design. The fastest memories are generally available in smaller numbers of bits per chip at any point in time, but they cost substantially more per byte.

Increasing memory bandwidth and decreasing the latency of memory access are both crucial to system performance, and many of the organizational techniques we discuss will focus on these two metrics. How can we improve these two measures? The answer lies in combining the principles we discussed in this chapter together with the rule that smaller is faster.

The principle of locality of reference says that the data most recently used is likely to be accessed again in the near future. Favoring accesses to such data will improve performance. Thus, we should try to keep recently accessed items in the fastest memory. Because smaller memories will be faster, we want to use smaller memories to try to hold the most recently accessed items close to the CPU and successively larger (and slower) memories as we move further away from the

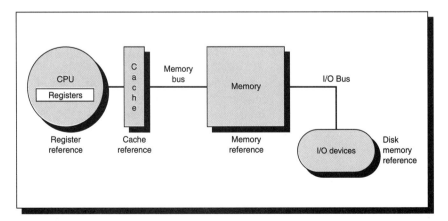

FIGURE 1.6   These are the levels in a typical memory hierarchy. As we move further away from the CPU, the memory in the level becomes larger and slower.

CPU. This type of organization is called a *memory hierarchy*. In Figure 1.6, a typical multilevel memory hierarchy is shown. Two important levels of the memory hierarchy are the cache and virtual memory.

A *cache* is a small, fast memory located close to the CPU that holds the most recently accessed code or data. When the CPU does not find a data item it needs in the cache, a *cache miss* occurs, and the data is retrieved from main memory and put into the cache. This usually causes the CPU to pause until the data is available.

Likewise, not all objects referenced by a program need to reside in main memory. If the computer has *virtual memory*, then some objects may reside on disk. The address space is usually broken into fixed-size blocks, called *pages*. At any time, each page resides either in main memory or on disk. When the CPU references an item within a page that is not present in the cache or main memory, a *page fault* occurs, and the entire page is moved from the disk to main memory. The cache and main memory have the same relationship as the main memory and disk.

Level	1	2	3	4
Called	Registers	Cache	Main memory	Disk storage
Typical size	< 1 KB	< 512 KB	< 512 MB	> 1 GB
Access time (in ns)	10	20	100	20,000,000
Bandwidth (in MB/sec.)	800	200	133	4
Managed by	Compiler	Hardware	Operating system	Operating system/user
Backed by	Cache	Main memory	Disk	Tape

FIGURE 1.7   The typical levels in the hierarchy slow down and get larger as we move away from the CPU. Sizes are typical for a large workstation or minicomputer. The access time is given in nanoseconds. Bandwidth is given in MB per second, assuming 32-bit paths between levels in the memory hierarchy. As we move to lower levels of the hierarchy, the access times increase, making it feasible to manage the transfer less responsively. The values shown are typical in 1990 and will no doubt change over time.

Machine	Register size	Register access time	Cache size	Cache access time
VAX-11/780	16 32-bit	100 ns	8 KB	200 ns
VAXstation 3100	16 32-bit	40 ns	1 KB on chip, 64 KB off chip	125 ns
DECstation 3100	32 32-bit integer; 16 64-bit floating point	30 ns	64 KB instruction; 64 KB data	60 ns

FIGURE 1.8   Sizes and access times for the register and cache levels of the hierarchy vary dramatically among three different machines.

Typical sizes of each level in the memory hierarchy and their access times are shown in Figure 1.7. While the disk and main memory are usually configurable, the register count and cache size are typically fixed for an implementation. Figure 1.8 shows these values for three machines discussed in this text.

Because of locality and the higher speed of smaller memories, a memory hierarchy can substantially improve performance.

Example Suppose we have a computer with a small, high-speed memory that holds 2000 instructions. Assume that 10% of the instructions are responsible for 90% of the instruction accesses and that the accesses to that 10% are uniform. (That is, each of the instructions in the heavily used 10% is executed an equal number of times.) If we have a program with 50,000 instructions and we know which 10% of the program is most heavily used, what fraction of the instruction accesses can be made to go to high-speed memory?

Answer Ten percent of 50,000 is 5000. Hence, we can fit 2/5 of the 90%, or 36% of the instructions fetched.

How significant is the impact of memory hierarchy? Let's do a simplified example to illustrate its impact. Though we will evaluate memory hierarchies in a much more precise fashion in Chapter 8, this rudimentary example illustrates the potential impact.

Example Suppose a cache is five times faster than main memory, and suppose that the cache can be used 90% of the time. How much speedup do we gain by using the cache?

Answer This is a simple application of Amdahl's Law.

$$Speedup = \frac{1}{(1 - \% \text{ of time cache can be used}) + \dfrac{\% \text{ of time cache can be used}}{\text{Speedup using cache}}}$$

$$Speedup = \frac{1}{(1 - 0.9) + \dfrac{0.9}{5}}$$

$$Speedup = \frac{1}{0.28} \approx 3.6$$

Hence, we obtain a speedup from the cache of about 3.6 times.

1.6 | Fallacies and Pitfalls

The purpose of this section, which will be found in every chapter, is to explain some commonly held misbeliefs or misconceptions that one could acquire. We call such misbeliefs *fallacies*. When discussing a fallacy, we try to give a counter-example. We also discuss *pitfalls*—easily made mistakes. Often pitfalls are generalizations of principles that are true in a limited context. The purpose of these sections is to help you avoid making these errors in machines that you design.

Pitfall: Ignoring the inexorable progress of hardware when planning a new machine.

Suppose you plan to introduce a machine in three years, and you claim the machine will be a terrific seller because it's twice as fast as anything available today. Unfortunately, the machine will probably not sell well, because the performance growth rate for the industry will yield machines of the same performance. For example, assuming a 25% yearly growth rate in performance, a machine with performance x today can be expected to have performance $1.25^3x=1.95x$ in three years. Your machine would have essentially no performance advantage! Many projects within computer companies are canceled, either because they do not pay attention to this rule or because the project slips and the performance of the delayed machine is below the industry average. While this phenomenon can occur in any industry, the rapid improvements in cost/performance make this a major concern in the computer industry.

Fallacy: Hardware is always faster than software.

While a hardware implementation of a well-defined and necessary feature is faster than a software implementation, the functionality provided by the hardware is often more general than the needs of the software. Thus, a compiler may be able to choose a sequence of simpler instructions that accomplishes the required work more efficiently than the more general hardware instruction. A good example is the MVC (move character) instruction in the IBM 360 architecture. This instruction is very general and will move up to 256 bytes of data between two arbitrary addresses. The source and destination may begin at any byte address—and may even overlap. In the worst case, the hardware must move one byte at a time; determining whether the worst case exists requires significant analysis when the instruction is decoded.

Because the MVC instruction is very general, it incurs overhead that is often unnecessary. A software implementation can be faster if it can eliminate this overhead. Measurements have shown that nonoverlapped moves are 50 times more frequent than overlapped moves and that the average nonoverlapped move is only 8 bytes long. In fact, more than half of the nonoverlapped moves move only a single byte! A two-instruction sequence that loads a byte into a register and then stores it in memory is at least twice as fast as MVC when moving a single byte. This illustrates the rule of making the frequent case fast.

1.7 | Concluding Remarks

The task the computer designer faces is a complex one: Determine what attributes are important for a new machine, then design a machine to maximize performance while staying within cost constraints. Performance can be measured as either throughput or response time; because some environments favor one over the other, this distinction must be borne in mind when evaluating alternatives. Amdahl's Law is a valuable tool to help determine what performance improvement an architectural enhancement can have. In the next chapter we will look at how to measure performance and what properties have the biggest impact on cost.

Knowing what cases are the most frequent is critical to improving performance. In Chapters 3 and 4, we will look at instruction set design and use, watching for common properties of instruction set usage. Based on measurements of instruction sets, tradeoffs can be made by deciding which instructions are the most important and what cases to try to make fast.

In Chapters 5 and 6 we will examine the fundamentals of CPU design, starting with a simple sequential machine and moving to pipelined implementations. Chapter 7 focuses on applying these ideas to high-speed scientific computation in the form of vector machines. Amdahl's Law will be our guiding light throughout Chapter 7.

We have seen how a fundamental property of programs—the principle of locality—can help us build faster computers by allowing us to make effective use of small, fast memories. In Chapter 8, we will return to memory hierarchies, looking in depth at cache design and support for virtual memory. The design of high-performance memory hierarchies has become a key component of modern computer design. Chapter 9 deals with a closely allied topic—I/O systems. As we saw when using Amdahl's Law to evaluate a cost/performance tradeoff, it is not sufficient to merely improve CPU time. To keep a balanced machine, we must also boost I/O performance.

Finally, in Chapter 10, we will look at current research directions focusing on parallel processing. How these ideas will affect the kinds of machines designed and used in the future is not yet clear. What is clear is that an empirical and experimental approach to designing new computers will be the basis for continued and dramatic performance growth.

1.8 | Historical Perspective and References

If ... history ... teaches us anything, it is that man in his quest for knowledge and progress, is determined and cannot be deterred.

John F. Kennedy, Address at Rice University, September 12, 1962.

A section of historical perspectives closes each chapter in the text. This section provides some historical background on some of the key ideas presented in the chapter. The authors may trace the development of an idea through a series of machines or describe some important projects. This section will also contain references for the reader interested in examining the initial development of an idea or machine or interested in further reading.

The First Electronic Computers

J. Presper Eckert and John Mauchly at the Moore School of the University of Pennsylvania built the world's first electronic general-purpose computer. This machine, called ENIAC (Electronic Numerical Integrator and Calculator), was funded by the United States Army and became operational during World War II, but was not publicly disclosed until 1946. ENIAC was a general-purpose machine used for computing artillery firing tables. One hundred feet long by eight-and-a-half feet high and several feet wide, the machine was enormous—far beyond the size of any computer built today. Each of the 20, 10-digit registers was two feet long. In total, there were 18,000 vacuum tubes.

While the size was two orders of magnitude bigger than machines built today, it was more than three orders of magnitude slower, with an add taking 200 microseconds. The ENIAC provided conditional jumps and was programmable, which clearly distinguished it from earlier calculators. Programming was done manually by plugging up cables and setting switches. Data was provided on punched cards. Programming for typical calculations required from a half-hour to a whole day. The ENIAC was a general-purpose machine limited primarily by a small amount of storage and tedious programming.

In 1944, John von Neumann was attracted to the ENIAC project. The group wanted to improve the way programs were entered and discussed storing programs as numbers; von Neumann helped crystallize the ideas and wrote a memo proposing a stored-program computer called EDVAC (Electronic Discrete Variable Automatic Computer). Herman Goldstine distributed the memo and put von Neumann's name on it, much to the dismay of Eckert and Mauchly, whose names were omitted. This memo has served as the basis for the commonly used term "von Neumann computer." The authors and several early inventors in the computer field believe that this term gives too much credit to von Neumann, who wrote up the ideas, and too little to the engineers, Eckert and Mauchly, who worked on the machines. For this reason, this term will not appear in this book.

In 1946, Maurice Wilkes of Cambridge University visited the Moore School to attend the latter part of a series of lectures on developments in electronic computers. When he returned to Cambridge, Wilkes decided to embark on a project to build a stored-program computer named EDSAC, for Electronic Delay Storage Automatic Calculator. The EDSAC became operational in 1949 and was the world's first full-scale, operational, stored-program computer [Wilkes, Wheeler, and Gill 1951; Wilkes 1985]. (A small prototype called the Mark I, which was built at the University of Manchester and ran in 1948, might be called the first operational stored-program machine.) The EDSAC was an accumulator-based architecture. This style of machine remained popular until the early 1970s, and the instruction sets looked remarkably similar to the EDSAC. (Chapter 3 starts with a brief summary of the EDSAC instruction set.)

In 1947, Eckert and Mauchly applied for a patent on electronic computers. The dean of the Moore School, by demanding the patent be turned over to the university, may have helped Eckert and Mauchly conclude they should leave. Their departure crippled the EDVAC project, which did not become operational until 1952.

Goldstine left to join von Neumann at the Institute for Advanced Study at Princeton in 1946. Together with Arthur Burks, they issued a report (1946) based on the memo written earlier. The paper led to the IAS machine built by Julian Bigelow at Princeton's Institute for Advanced Study. It had a total of 1024, 40-bit words and was roughly 10 times faster than ENIAC. The group thought about uses for the machine, published a set of reports, and encouraged visitors. These reports and visitors inspired the development of a number of new computers. The paper by Burks, Goldstine, and von Neumann was incredible for the period. Reading it today, one would never guess this landmark paper was written more than 40 years ago, as most of the architectural concepts seen in modern computers are discussed there.

Recently, there has been some controversy about John Atanasoff, who built a small-scale electronic computer in the early 1940s [Atanasoff 1940]. His machine, designed at Iowa State University, was a special-purpose computer that was never completely operational. Mauchly briefly visited Atanasoff before he built ENIAC. The presence of the Atanasoff machine, together with delays in filing the ENIAC patents (the work was classified and patents could not be filed until after the war) and the distribution of von Neumann's EDVAC paper, were used to break the Eckert-Mauchly patent [Larson 1973]. Though controversy still rages over Atanasoff's role, Eckert and Mauchly are usually given credit for building the first working, general-purpose, electronic computer [Stern 1980]. Another early machine that deserves some credit was a special-purpose machine built by Konrad Zuse in Germany in the late 1930s and early 1940s. This machine was electromechanical and, due to the war, was never extensively pursued.

In the same time period as ENIAC, Howard Aiken was building an electro-mechanical computer called the Mark-I at Harvard. He followed the Mark-I by a relay machine, the Mark-II, and a pair of vacuum tube machines, the Mark-III and Mark-IV. The Mark-III and Mark-IV were being built after the first stored-program machines. Because they had separate memories for instructions and data, the machines were regarded as reactionary by the advocates of stored-program computers. The term *Harvard architecture* was coined to describe this type of machine. Though clearly different from the original sense, this term is used today to apply to machines with a single main memory but with separate instruction and data caches.

The Whirlwind project [Redmond and Smith 1980] was begun at MIT in 1947 and was aimed at applications in real-time radar signal processing. While it led to several inventions, its overwhelming innovation was the creation of magnetic core memory. Whirlwind had 2048, 16-bit words of magnetic core. Magnetic cores served as the main memory technology for nearly 30 years.

Commercial Developments

In December 1947, Eckert and Mauchly formed Eckert-Mauchly Computer Corporation. Their first machine, the BINAC, was built for Northrop and was shown in August 1949. After some financial difficulties, they were acquired by Remington-Rand, where they built the UNIVAC I, designed to be sold as a general-purpose computer. First delivered in June 1951, the UNIVAC I sold for $250,000 and was the first successful commercial computer—48 systems were built! Today, this early machine, along with many other fascinating pieces of computer lore, can be seen at the Computer Museum in Boston, Massachusetts.

IBM, which earlier had been in the punched card and office automation business, didn't start building computers until 1950. The first IBM computer, the IBM 701, shipped in 1952 and eventually sold 19 units. In the early 1950s, many people were pessimistic about the future of computers, believing that the market and opportunities for these "highly specialized" machines were quite limited.

Several books describing the early days of computing have been written by the pioneers [Wilkes 1985; Goldstine 1972]. There are numerous independent histories, often built around the people involved [Slater 1987; Shurkin 1984], as well as a journal, *Annals of the History of Computing,* devoted to the history of computing.

The history of some of the computers invented after 1960 can be found in Chapters 3 and 4 (the IBM 360, the DEC VAX, the Intel 80x86, and the early RISC machines), Chapter 6 (the pipelined processors, including the CDC 6600), and Chapter 7 (vector processors including the TI ASC, CDC Star, and Cray processors).

Computer Generations—
A Capsule Summary of Computer History

Since 1952, there have been thousands of new computers, using a wide range of technologies and having widely varying capabilities. In an attempt to get a perspective on the developments, the industry has tended to group computers into generations. This classification is often based on the implementation technology used in each generation, as shown in Figure 1.9. Typically, each computer generation is eight to ten years in length, though the length and start times—especially of recent generations—is debated. By convention, the first generation is taken to be commercial electronic computers, rather than the mechanical or electromechanical machines that preceded them.

Generation	Dates	Technology	Principal new product	New companies and machines
1	1950-1959	Vacuum tubes	Commercial, electronic computer	IBM 701, UNIVAC I
2	1960-1968	Transistors	Cheaper computers	Burroughs 6500, NCR, CDC 6600, Honeywell
3	1969-1977	Integrated circuit	Minicomputer	50 new companies: DEC PDP-11, Data General Nova
4	1978-199?	LSI and VLSI	Personal computers and workstations	Apple II, Apollo DN 300, Sun 2
5	199?-	Parallel processing?	Multiprocessors?	??

FIGURE 1.9   Computer generations are usually determined by the change in dominant implementation technology. Typically, each generation offers the opportunity to create a new class of computers and for new computer companies to be created. Many researchers believe that parallel processing using high-performance microprocessors will be the basis for the fifth computer generation.

Development of Principles
Discussed in This Chapter

What is perhaps the most basic principle was originally stated by Amdahl [1967] and concerned the limitations on speedup in the context of parallel processing:

A fairly obvious conclusion which can be drawn at this point is that the effort expended on achieving high parallel processing rates is wasted unless it is accompanied by achievements in sequential processing rates of very nearly the same magnitude. [p. 485]

Amdahl stated his law focusing on the implications of speeding up only a portion of the computation. The basic equation can be used as a general technique for measuring the speedup and cost-effectiveness of any enhancement.

Virtual memory first appeared on a machine called Atlas, designed in England in 1962 [Kilburn, et al. 1982]. The IBM 360/85, introduced in the late 1960s, was the first commercial machine to use a cache, but it seems that the idea was discussed for several machines being built in England in the early 1960s (see the discussion in Chapter 8).

Knuth [1971] published the original observations about program locality:

Programs typically have a very jagged profile, with a few sharp peaks. As a very rough approximation, it appears that the nth most important statement of a program from the point of view of execution time accounts for about $(a-1)a^{-n}$ of the running time, for some 'a' and for small 'n'. We also found that less than 4 per cent of a program generally accounts for more than half of its running time. [p. 105]

References

AMDAHL, G. M. [1967]. "Validity of the single processor approach to achieving large scale computing capabilities," *Proc. AFIPS 1967 Spring Joint Computer Conf. 30* (April), Atlantic City, N.J., 483–485.

ATANASOFF, J. V. [1940]. "Computing machine for the solution of large systems of linear equations," Internal Report, Iowa State University.

BELL, C. G. [1984]. "The mini and micro industries," *IEEE Computer* 17:10 (October) 14–30.

BURKS, A. W., H. H. GOLDSTINE, AND J. VON NEUMANN [1946]. "Preliminary discussion of the logical design of an electronic computing instrument," Report to the U.S. Army Ordnance Department, p. 1; also appears in *Papers of John von Neumann,* W. Aspray and A. Burks, eds., The MIT Press, Cambridge, Mass. and Tomash Publishers, Los Angeles, Calif., 1987, 97–146.

GOLDSTINE, H. H. [1972]. *The Computer: From Pascal to von Neumann,* Princeton University Press, Princeton, N.J.

KILBURN, T., D. B. G. EDWARDS, M. J. LANIGAN, AND F. H. SUMNER [1982]. "One-level storage system," reprinted in D. P. Siewiorek, C. G. Bell, and A. Newell, *Computer Structures: Principles and Examples* (1982), McGraw-Hill, New York.

KNUTH, D. E. [1971]. "An empirical study of FORTRAN programs," *Software Practice and Experience,* Vol. 1, 105–133.

LARSON, JUDGE E. R. [1973]. "Findings of Fact, Conclusions of Law, and Order for Judgment," File No. 4–67, Civ. 138, *Honeywell v. Sperry Rand and Illinois Scientific Development,* U.S. District Court for the District of Minnesota, Fourth Division (October 19).

REDMOND, K. C. AND T. M. SMITH [1980]. *Project Whirlwind—The History of a Pioneer Computer,* Digital Press, Boston, Mass.

SHURKIN, J. [1984]. *Engines of the Mind: A History of the Computer*, W. W. Norton, New York.

SLATER, R. [1987]. *Portraits in Silicon,* The MIT Press, Cambridge, Mass.

STERN, N. [1980]. "Who invented the first electronic digital computer," *Annals of the History of Computing* 2:4 (October) 375–376.

WILKES, M. V. [1985]. *Memoirs of a Computer Pioneer,* The MIT Press, Cambridge, Mass.

WILKES, M. V., D. J. WHEELER, AND S. GILL [1951]. *The Preparation of Programs for an Electronic Digital Computer*, Addison-Wesley Press, Cambridge, Mass.

E X E R C I S E S

1.1 [10/10/10/12/12/12] <1.1,1.2> Here are the execution times in seconds for the Linpack benchmark and 10,000 iterations of the Dhrystone benchmark (see Figure 2.5, page47) on VAX models:

Model	Year shipped	Linpack execution time (seconds)	Dhrystone execution time (10,000 iterations) (seconds)
VAX-11/780	1978	4.90	5.69
VAX 8600	1985	1.43	1.35
VAX 8550	1987	0.695	0.96

a. [10] How much faster is the 8600 than the 780 using Linpack? How about using Dhrystone?

b. [10] How much faster is the 8550 than the 8600 using Linpack? How about using Dhrystone?

c. [10] How much faster is the 8550 than the 780 using Linpack? How about using Dhrystone?

d. [12] What is the average performance growth per year between the 780 and the 8600 using Linpack? How about using Dhrystone?

e. [12] What is the average performance growth per year between the 8600 and the 8550 using Linpack? How about using Dhrystone?

f. [12] What is the average performance growth per year between the 780 and the 8550 using Linpack? How about using Dhrystone?

1.2–1.5 For the next four questions, assume that we are considering enhancing a machine by adding a vector mode to it. When a computation is run in vector mode it is 20 times faster than the normal mode of execution. We call the percentage of time that could be spent using vector mode the *percentage of vectorization.*

1.2 [20] <1.3> Draw a graph that plots the speedup as a percentage of the computation performed in vector mode. Label the y axis "Net Speedup" and label the x axis "Percent Vectorization."

1.3 [10] <1.3> What percent of vectorization is needed to achieve a speedup of 2?

1.4 [10] <1.3> What percentage of vectorization is needed to achieve one-half the maximum speedup attainable from using vector mode?

1.5 [15] <1.3> Suppose you have measured the percentage of vectorization for programs to be 70%. The hardware design group says they can double the speed of the vector rate with a significant additional engineering investment. You wonder whether the compiler crew could increase the use of vector mode as another approach to increasing performance. How much of an increase in the percentage of vectorization (relative to current usage) would you need to obtain the same performance gain? Which investment would you recommend?

1.6 [12/12] <1.1, 1.4> There are two design teams at two different companies. The smaller and more aggressive company's management demands a two-year design cycle for their products. The larger and less aggressive company's management settles for a four-year design cycle. Assume that today the market they will be selling to demands 25 times the performance of a VAX-11/780.

a. [12] What should the performance goals for each product be, if the growth rates need to be 30% per year?

b. [12] Suppose that the companies have just switched to using 4-megabit DRAMS. Assuming the growth rates in Figure 1.5 (page 17) hold, what DRAM sizes should be planned for use in these projects? Note that DRAM growth is discrete, with each generation being four times larger than the previous generation.

1.7 [12] <1.3> You are considering two alternative designs for an instruction memory: using expensive and fast chips or cheaper and slower chips. If you use the slow chips you can afford to double the width of the memory bus and fetch two instructions, each one word long, every two clock cycles. (With the more expensive fast chips, the memory bus can only fetch one word every clock cycle.) Due to spatial locality, when you fetch two words you often need both. However, in 25% of the clock cycles one of the two words you fetched will be useless. How do the memory bandwidths of these two systems compare?

1.8 [15/10] <1.3> Assume—as in the Amdahl's Law example at the bottom of page 10— that we make an enhancement to a computer that improves some mode of execution by a factor of 10. Enhanced mode is used 50% of the time, measured as a percentage of the execution time when the enhanced mode is in use, rather than as defined in this chapter: the percentage of the running time **without** the enhancement.

a. [15] What is the speedup we have obtained from fast mode?

b. [10] What percentage of the original execution time has been converted to fast mode?

1.9 [15/15] <1.5> Assume we are building a machine with a memory hierarchy for instructions (don't worry about data accesses!). Assume that the program follows the 90-10 rule and that accesses within the top 10% and bottom 90% are uniformly distributed; that is, 90% of the time is spread evenly over 10% of the code and the other 10% of the time is spread evenly over the other 90% of the code. You have three types of memory for use in your memory hierarchy:

Memory type	Access time	Cost per word
Local, fast	1 clock cycle	$0.10
Main	5 clock cycles	$0.01
Disk	5,000 clock cycles	$0.0001

You have exactly 100 programs, each is 1,000,000 words, and all the programs must fit on disk. Assume that only one program runs at a time, and that the whole program must be loaded in main memory. You can spend $30,000 dollars on the memory hierarchy.

a. [15] What is the optimal way to allocate your budget assuming that each word must be statically placed in fast memory or main memory?

b. [15] Ignoring the time for the first loading from disk, what is the average number of cycles for a program to make a memory reference in your hierarchy? (This important measure is called the average memory-access time in Chapter 8.)

1.10 [30] <1.3,1.6> Find a machine that has both a fast and slow implementation of a feature—for example, a system with and without hardware floating point. Measure the speedup obtained when using the faster implementation with a simple loop that uses the feature. Find a real program that makes some use of the feature and measure the speedup. Using this data, compute the percentage of the time the feature is used.

1.11 [Discussion] <1.3,1.4> Often ideas for speeding up processors take advantage of some special properties that certain classes of applications have. Thus, the speedup obtained by an enhancement may be available to only certain applications. How would you decide to make such an enhancement? What factors would be most relevant in the decision? Could these factors be measured or estimated reasonably?

Remember that time is money.

Ben Franklin, *Advice to a Young Tradesman*

2 Performance and Cost

2.1 Introduction

Why do engineers design different computers? Why do people use them? How do customers decide on one computer versus another? Is there a rational basis for their decisions? If so, can engineers use that basis to design better computers? These are some of the questions this chapter addresses.

One way to approach these questions is to see how they have been used in another design field and then apply those solutions by analogy to our own. The automobile, for example, can provide a useful source of analogies for explaining computers: We could say that CPUs are like engines, supercomputers are like exotic race cars, and fast CPUs with slow memories are like hot engines in poor chassis.

Standard measures of performance provide a basis for comparison, leading to improvements of the object measured. Races helped determine which car and driver were faster, but it was hard to separate the skills of the driver from the performance of the car. A few standard performance tests eventually evolved, such as

- Time until the car reaches a given speed, typically 60 miles per hour

- Time to cover a given distance, typically 1/4 mile

- Top speed on a level surface

Standard measures allow designers to select between alternatives quantitatively, which enables orderly progress in a field.

Make and model	Month tested	Price (as tested)	Sec (0-60)	Sec (1/4 mi.)	Top speed	Brake (80-0)	Skidpad g	Fuel MPG
Chevrolet Corvette	2-88	$34,034	6.0	14.6	158	225	0.89	17.5
Ferrari Testarossa	10-89	$145,580	6.2	14.2	181	261	0.87	12.0
Ford Escort	7-87	$5,765	11.2	18.8	95	286	0.69	37.0
Hyundai Excel	10-86	$6,965	14.0	19.4	80	291	0.73	29.9
Lamborghini Countach	3-86	$118,000	5.2	13.7	173	252	0.88	10.0
Mazda Miata	7-89	$15,550	9.2	16.8	116	270	0.83	25.5

FIGURE 2.10   **Quantitative automotive cost/performance summary.** These data were taken from the October 1989 issue of Road and Track, page 26. "Road Test Summary" is found in every issue of the magazine.

Cars proved so popular that magazines were developed to feed the interest in new cars and to help readers decide which car to purchase. While these magazines have always carried articles describing the impressions of driving a new car—the qualitative experience—over time they have expanded the quantitative basis for comparison, as Figure 2.1 illustrates.

Performance, cost of purchase, and cost of operation dominate these summaries. Performance and cost also form the rational basis for deciding which computer to select. Thus, computer designers must understand both performance and cost if they want to design computers people will consider worth selecting.

Just as there is no single target for car designers, so there is no single target for computer designers. At one extreme, *high-performance design* spares no cost in achieving its goal. Supercomputers from Cray as well as sports cars from Ferrari and Lamborghini fit into this category. At the other extreme is *low-cost design*, where performance is sacrificed to achieve lowest cost. Computers like the IBM PC clones along with their automotive equivalents, such as the Ford Escort and the Hyundai Excel, belong here. In between these extremes is *cost/performance design* where the designer balances cost versus performance. Examples from the minicomputer or workstation industry typify the kinds of tradeoffs with which designers of the Corvette and Miata would feel comfortable.

It is on this middle ground, where neither cost nor performance is neglected, that we will focus our discussion. We begin by looking at performance, the measure of the designer's dream, before going on to describe the accountant's agenda—cost.

2.2 | Performance

Time is the measure of computer performance: the computer that performs the same amount of work in the least time is the fastest. Program *execution time* is measured in seconds per program. Performance is frequently measured as a rate of some number of events per second, so that lower time means higher performance. We tend to blur this distinction and talk about performance as either time or a rate, reporting refinements as improved performance rather than using adjectives higher (for rates) or lower (for time).

But time can be defined in different ways depending on what we count. The most straightforward definition of time is called wall-clock time, response time, or *elapsed time*. This is the latency to complete a task, including disk accesses, memory accesses, input/output activities, operating system overhead—everything. However, since with multiprogramming the CPU works on another program while waiting for I/O and may not necessarily minimize the elapsed time of one program, there needs to be a term to take this activity into account. *CPU time* recognizes this distinction and means the time the CPU is computing **not** including the time waiting for I/O or running other programs. (Clearly the response time seen by the user is the elapsed time of the program, not the CPU time.) CPU time can be further divided into the CPU time spent in the program, called *user CPU time*, and the CPU time spent in the operating system performing tasks requested by the program, called *system CPU time*.

These distinctions are reflected in the UNIX time command, which returned the following:

```
90.7u 12.9s 2:39 65%
```

User CPU time is 90.7 seconds, system CPU time is 12.9 seconds, elapsed time is 2 minutes and 39 seconds (159 seconds), and the percentage of elapsed time that is CPU time is (90.7+12.9)/159 or 65%. More than a third of the elapsed time in this example was spent waiting for I/O or running other programs or both. Many measurements ignore system CPU time because of the inaccuracy of operating systems' self-measurement and the inequity of including system CPU time when comparing performance between machines with differing system codes. On the other hand, system code on some machines is user code on others and no program runs without some operating system running on the hardware, so a case can be made for using the sum of user CPU time and system CPU time.

In the present discussion, a distinction is maintained between performance based on elapsed time and that based on CPU time. The term *system performance* is used to refer to elapsed time on an **unloaded** system, while *CPU performance* refers to **user** CPU time. We will concentrate on CPU performance in this chapter.

CPU Performance

Most computers are constructed using a clock running at a constant rate. These discrete time events are called ticks, clock ticks, clock periods, clocks, cycles, or *clock cycles*. Computer designers refer to the time of a clock period by its length (e.g., 10 ns) or by its rate (e.g., 100 MHz).

CPU time for a program can then be expressed two ways:

$$\text{CPU time} = \text{CPU clock cycles for a program} * \text{Clock cycle time}$$

or

$$\text{CPU time} = \frac{\text{CPU clock cycles for a program}}{\text{Clock rate}}$$

Note that it wouldn't make sense to show elapsed time as a function of CPU clock cycle time since the latency for I/O devices is normally independent of the rate of the CPU clock.

In addition to the number of clock cycles to execute a program, we can also count the number of instructions executed—the instruction path length or *instruction count*. If we know the number of clock cycles and the instruction count we can calculate the average number of *clock cycles per instruction* (CPI):

$$\text{CPI} = \frac{\text{CPU clock cycles for a program}}{\text{Instruction count}}$$

This CPU figure of merit provides insight into different styles of instruction sets and implementations.

By transposing instruction count in the above formula, clock cycles can be defined as instruction count * CPI. This allows us to use CPI in the execution time formula:

$$\text{CPU time} = \text{Instruction count} * \text{CPI} * \text{Clock cycle time}$$

or

$$\text{CPU time} = \frac{\text{Instruction count} * \text{CPI}}{\text{Clock rate}}$$

Expanding the first formula into the units of measure shows how the pieces fit together:

$$\frac{\text{Instructions}}{\text{Program}} * \frac{\text{Clock cycles}}{\text{Instruction}} * \frac{\text{Seconds}}{\text{Clock cycle}} = \frac{\text{Seconds}}{\text{Program}} = \text{CPU time}$$

As this formula demonstrates, CPU performance is dependent upon three characteristics: clock cycle (or rate), clock cycles per instruction, and instruction count. You can't change one of these in isolation from others because the basic technologies involved in changing each characteristic are also interdependent:

Clock rate—Hardware technology and organization

CPI—Organization and instruction set architecture

Instruction count—Instruction set architecture and compiler technology

Sometimes it is useful in designing the CPU to calculate the number of total CPU clock cycles as

$$\text{CPU clock cycles} = \sum_{i=1}^{n} (\text{CPI}_i * I_i))$$

where I_i represents number of times instruction i is executed in a program and CPI_i represents the average number of clock cycles for instruction i. This form can be used to express CPU time as

$$\text{CPU time} = \sum_{i=1}^{n} (\text{CPI}_i * I_i) * \text{Clock cycle time}$$

and overall CPI as

$$\text{CPI} = \frac{\sum\limits_{i=1}^{n}(\text{CPI}_i * I_i)}{\text{Instruction count}}) = \sum_{i=1}^{n} \left(\text{CPI}_i * \frac{I_i}{\text{Instruction count}}\right))$$

The latter form of the CPI calculation multiplies each individual CPI_i by the fraction of occurrences in a program.

CPI_i should be measured and not just calculated from a table in the back of a reference manual since it must include cache misses and any other memory system inefficiencies.

Always bear in mind that the real measure of computer performance is time. Changing the instruction set to lower the instruction count, for example, may lead to an organization with a slower clock cycle time that offsets the improvement in instruction count. When comparing two machines, you must look at all three components to understand relative performance.

Example

Suppose we are considering two alternatives for our conditional branch instructions, as follows:

CPU A. A condition code is set by a compare instruction and followed by a branch that tests the condition code.

CPU B. A compare is included in the branch.

On both CPUs, the conditional branch instruction takes 2 cycles, and all other instructions take 1 clock cycle. (Obviously, if the CPI is 1.0 for everything but branches in this simple example we are ignoring losses due to the memory system in this decision; see the fallacy on page 72.) On CPU A, 20% of all instructions executed are conditional branches; since every branch needs a compare, another 20% of the instructions are compares. Because CPU A does not have the compare included in the branch, its clock cycle time is 25% faster than CPU B's. Which CPU is faster?

Answer   Since we are ignoring all systems issues, we can use the CPU performance formula: CPI_A is $((.20*2) + (.80*1))$ or 1.2 since 20% are branches taking 2 clock cycles and the rest take 1. Clock cycle time$_B$ is $1.25 *$ Clock cycle time$_A$ since A is 25% faster. The performance of CPU A is then

$$CPU\ time_A \quad = Instruction\ count_A * 1.2 * Clock\ cycle\ time_A$$

$$= 1.20 * Instruction\ count_A * Clock\ cycle\ time_A$$

Compares are not executed in CPU B, so 20%/80% or 25% of the instructions are now branches, taking 2 clock cycles, and the remaining 75% of the instructions take 1. CPI_B is then $((.25*2) + (.75*1))$ or 1.25. Because CPU B doesn't execute compares, Instruction count$_B$ is $.80*$Instruction count$_A$. The performance of CPU B is

$$CPU\ time_B \quad = (.80*Instruction\ count_A) * 1.25 * (1.25*Clock\ cycle\ time_A)$$

$$= 1.25 * Instruction\ count_A * Clock\ cycle\ time_A$$

Under these assumptions, CPU A, with the shorter clock cycle time, is faster than CPU B, which executes fewer instructions.

Example   After seeing the analysis, a designer realized that by reworking the organization the difference in clock cycle times can easily be reduced to 10%. Which CPU is faster now?

Answer   The only change from the answer above is that Clock cycle time$_B$ is now $1.10 *$ Clock cycle time$_A$ since A is just 10% faster. The performance of CPU A is still

$$CPU\ time_A \quad = 1.20 * Instruction\ count_A * Clock\ cycle\ time_A$$

The performance of CPU B is now

$$CPU\ time_B \quad = (.80*Instruction\ count_A) * 1.25 * (1.10*Clock\ cycle\ time_A)$$

$$= 1.10 * Instruction\ count_A * Clock\ cycle\ time_A$$

With this improvement CPU B, which executes fewer instructions, is now faster.

Example

Suppose we are considering another change to an instruction set. The machine initially has only loads and stores to memory, and then all operations work on the registers. Such machines are called *load/store* machines (see Chapter 3). Measurements of the load/store machine showing the frequency of instructions, called an *instruction mix*, and clock cycle counts per instruction are given in Figure 2.2.

Operation	Frequency	Clock cycle count
ALU ops	43%	1
Loads	21%	2
Stores	12%	2
Branches	24%	2

FIGURE 2.11   An example of instruction frequency. The CPI for each class of instruction is also given. (This frequency comes from the GCC column of Figure C.4 in Appendix C, rounded up to account for 100% of the instructions.)

Let's assume that 25% of the *arithmetic logic unit* (ALU) operations directly use a loaded operand that is not used again.

We propose adding ALU instructions that have one source operand in memory. These new *register–memory instructions* have a clock cycle count of 2. Suppose that the extended instruction set increases the clock cycle count for branches by 1, but it does not affect the clock cycle time. (Chapter 6, on pipelining, explains why adding register–memory instructions might slow down branches.) Would this change improve CPU performance?

Answer

The question is whether the new machine is faster than the old machine. We use the CPU performance formula since we are again ignoring systems issues. The original CPI is calculated by multiplying together the two columns from Figure 2.2:

$$CPI_{old} = (.43*1 + .21*2 + .12*2 + .24*2) = 1.57$$

The performance of CPU_{old} is then

$$CPU\ time_{old} = Instruction\ count_{old} * 1.57 * Clock\ cycle\ time_{old}$$

$$= 1.57 * Instruction\ count_{old} * Clock\ cycle\ time_{old}$$

Let's give the formula for CPI_{new} first and then explain the components:

$$CPI_{new} = \frac{(.43 - (.25*.43))*1 + (.21 - (.25*.43))*2 + (.25*.43)*2 + .12*2 + .24*3}{1 - (.25*.43)}$$

25% of ALU instructions (which are 43% of all instructions executed) become register–memory instructions, changing the first 3 components of the numerator. There are (.25*.43) fewer ALU operations, (.25*.43) fewer loads, and (.25*.43) new register–memory ALU instructions. The rest of the numerator remains the same except the branches take 3 clock cycles instead of 2. We divide by the new instruction count, which is .25*43% smaller than the old one. Simplifying this equation:

$$\text{CPI}_{\text{new}} = \frac{1.703}{.893} = 1.908$$

Since the clock cycle time is unchanged, the performance of the new CPU is

$$\text{CPU time}_{\text{new}} = (.893 * \text{Instruction count}_{\text{old}}) * 1.908 * \text{Clock cycle time}_{\text{old}}$$

$$= 1.703 * \text{Instruction count}_{\text{old}} * \text{Clock cycle time}_{\text{old}}$$

Using these assumptions, the answer to our question is no: It's a bad idea to add register–memory instructions, because they do not offset the increased execution time of slower branches.

MIPS and What Is Wrong with Them

A number of popular measures have been adopted in the quest for a standard measure of computer performance, with the result that a few innocent terms have been shanghaied from their well-defined environment and forced into a service for which they were never intended. The authors' position is that the only consistent and reliable measure of performance is the execution time of real programs, and that all proposed alternatives to time as the metric or to real programs as the items measured have eventually led to misleading claims or even mistakes in computer design. The dangers of a few popular alternatives to our advice are shown first.

One alternative to time as the metric is MIPS, or *million instructions per second*. For a given program, MIPS is simply

$$\text{MIPS} = \frac{\text{Instruction count}}{\text{Execution time} * 10^6} = \frac{\text{Clock rate}}{\text{CPI} * 10^6}$$

Some find this rightmost form convenient since clock rate is fixed for a machine and CPI is usually a small number, unlike instruction count or execution time. Relating MIPS to time,

$$\text{Execution time} = \frac{\text{Instruction count}}{\text{MIPS} * 10^6}$$

Since MIPS is a rate of operations per unit time, performance can be specified as the inverse of execution time, with faster machines having a higher MIPS rating.

The good news about MIPS is that it is easy to understand, especially by a customer, and faster machines means bigger MIPS, which matches intuition. The problem with using MIPS as a measure for comparison is threefold:

- MIPS is dependent on the instruction set, making it difficult to compare MIPS of computers with different instruction sets;

- MIPS varies between programs on the same computer; and most importantly,

- MIPS can vary inversely to performance!

The classic example of the last case is the MIPS rating of a machine with optional floating-point hardware. Since it generally takes more clock cycles per floating-point instruction than per integer instruction, floating-point programs using the optional hardware instead of software floating-point routines take less time but have a **lower** MIPS rating. Software floating point executes simpler instructions, resulting in a higher MIPS rating, but it executes so many more that overall execution time is longer.

We can even see such anomalies with optimizing compilers.

Example

Assume we build an optimizing compiler for the load/store machine described in the previous example. The compiler discards 50% of the ALU instructions, although it cannot reduce loads, stores, or branches. Ignoring systems issues and assuming a 20-ns clock cycle time (50-MHz clock rate), what is the MIPS rating for optimized code versus unoptimized code? Does the ranking of MIPS agree with the ranking of execution time?

Answer

From the example above $CPI_{unoptimized} = 1.57$, so

$$MIPS_{unoptimized} = \frac{50 \text{ MHz}}{1.57 * 10^6} = 31.85$$

The performance of unoptimized code is

$$CPU \text{ time}_{unoptimized} = \text{Instruction count}_{unoptimized} * 1.57 * (20*10^{-9})$$

$$= 31.4*10^{-9} * \text{Instruction count}_{unoptimized}$$

For optimized code

$$CPI_{optimized} = \frac{(.43/2)*1 + .21*2 + 12*2 + .24*2}{1 - (.43/2)} = \frac{.215 + .42 + .24 + .48}{.785} = 1.73$$

since half the ALU instructions are discarded (.43/2) and the instruction count is reduced by the missing ALU instructions. Thus,

$$\text{MIPS}_{\text{optimized}} = \frac{50 \text{ MHz}}{1.73*10^6} = 28.90$$

The performance of optimized code is

$$\text{CPU time}_{\text{optimized}} = (.785 * \text{Instruction count}_{\text{unoptimized}}) * 1.73 * (20 * 10^{-9})$$

$$= 27.2 * 10^{-9} * \text{Instruction count}_{\text{unoptimized}}$$

Optimized code is 13% faster, but its MIPS rating is lower!

As examples such as this one show, MIPS can fail to give a true picture of performance in that it does not track execution time. To compensate for this weakness, another alternative to execution time is to use a particular machine, with an agreed-upon MIPS rating, as a reference point. *Relative MIPS*—as distinguished from the original form, called *native MIPS*—is then calculated as follows:

$$\text{Relative MIPS} = \frac{\text{Time}_{\text{reference}}}{\text{Time}_{\text{unrated}}} * \text{MIPS}_{\text{reference}}$$

where

$Time_{reference}$ = execution time of a program on the reference machine

$Time_{unrated}$ = execution time of the same program on machine to be rated

$MIPS_{reference}$ = agreed-upon MIPS rating of the reference machine

Relative MIPS only tracks execution time for the given program and input. Even when they are identified, it becomes harder to find a reference machine on which to run programs as the machine ages. (In the 1980s the dominant reference machine was the VAX-11/780, which was called a 1-MIPS machine; see pages 77–78 in Section 2.7.) The question also arises whether the older machine should be run with the newest release of the compiler and operating system, or whether the software should be fixed so the reference machine does not get faster over time. There is also the temptation to generalize from a relative MIPS rating using one benchmark to relative execution time, even though there can be wide variations in relative performance.

In summary, the advantage of relative MIPS is small since execution time, program, and program input still must be known to have meaningful information.

MFLOPS and What Is Wrong with Them

Another popular alternative to execution time is *million floating-point operations per second*, abbreviated megaFLOPS or MFLOPS, but always pronounced "megaflops." The formula for MFLOPS is simply the definition of the acronym:

$$\text{MFLOPS} = \frac{\text{Number of floating-point operations in a program}}{\text{Execution time} * 10^6}$$

Clearly, a MFLOPS rating is dependent on the machine and on the program. Since MFLOPS were intended to measure floating-point performance, they are not applicable outside that range. Compilers, as an extreme example, have a MFLOPS rating near nil no matter how fast the machine since compilers rarely use floating-point arithmetic.

This term is less innocent than MIPS. Based on operations rather than instructions, MFLOPS is intended to be a fair comparison between different machines. The belief is that the same program running on different computers would execute a different number of instructions but the same number of floating-point operations. Unfortunately, MFLOPS is not dependable because the set of floating-point operations is not consistent across machines. For example, the Cray-2 has no divide instruction, while the Motorola 68882 has divide, square root, sine, and cosine. Another perceived problem is that the MFLOPS rating changes not only on the mixture of integer and floating-point operations but also on the mixture of fast and slow floating-point operations. For example, a program with 100% floating-point adds will have a higher rating than a program with 100% floating-point divides. The solution for both problems is to give a canonical number of floating-point operations in the source-level program and then divide by execution time. Figure 2.3 shows how the authors of the "Livermore Loops" benchmark calculate the number of normalized floating-point operations per program according to the operations actually found in the source code. Thus, the *native MFLOPS* rating is not the same as the *normalized MFLOPS* rating reported in the supercomputer literature, which has come as a surprise to a few computer designers.

Real FP operations	Normalized FP operations
ADD, SUB, COMPARE, MULT	1
DIVIDE, SQRT	4
EXP, SIN, ...	8

FIGURE 2.12   Real versus normalized floating-point operations. The number of normalized floating-point operations per real operation in a program used by the authors of the Livermore FORTRAN Kernels, or "Livermore Loops," to calculate MFLOPS. A kernel with one ADD, one DIVIDE, and one SIN would be credited with 13 normalized floating-point operations. Native MFLOPS won't give the results reported for other machines on that benchmark.

<table>
<tr><td>**Example**</td><td>The Spice program runs on the DECstation 3100 in 94 seconds (see Figures 2.16 to 2.18 for more details on the program, input, compilers, machine, and so on). The number of floating-point operations executed in that program are listed below:</td></tr>
</table>

ADDD	25,999,440
SUBD	18,266,439
MULD	33,880,810
DIVD	15,682,333
COMPARED	9,745,930
NEGD	2,617,846
ABSD	2,195,930
CONVERTD	1,581,450
TOTAL	109,970,178

What is the native MFLOPS for that program? Using the conversions in Figure 2.3, what is the normalized MFLOPS?

Answer

Native MFLOPS is easy to calculate:

$$\text{Native MFLOPS} = \frac{\text{Number of floating-point operations in a program}}{\text{Execution time} * 10^6}$$

$$\approx \frac{110M}{94 * 10^6} \approx 1.2$$

The only operation in Figure 2.3 that is changed for normalized MFLOPS and is in the list above is divide, raising the total of (normalized) floating-point operations, and therefore MFLOPS, almost 50%:

$$\text{Normalized MFLOPS} \approx \frac{157M}{94 * 10^6} \approx 1.7$$

Like any other performance measure, the MFLOPS rating for a single program cannot be generalized to establish a single performance metric for a computer. Since normalized MFLOPS is really just a constant divided by execution time for a specific program and specific input (like relative MIPS), MFLOPS is redundant to execution time, our principal measure of performance. And unlike execution time, it is tempting to characterize a machine with a single MIPS or MFLOPS rating without naming the program. Finally, MFLOPS is not a useful measure for all programs.

Choosing Programs to Evaluate Performance

Dhrystone does not use floating point. Typical programs don't ...

Rick Richardson, *Clarification of Dhrystone,* 1988

This program is the result of extensive research to determine the instruction mix of a typical Fortran program. The results of this program on different machines should give a good indication of which machine performs better under a typical load of Fortran programs. The statements are purposely arranged to defeat optimizations by the compiler.

Anonymous, from comments in the Whetstone benchmark

A computer user who runs the same programs day in and day out would be the perfect candidate to evaluate a new computer. To evaluate a new system he would simply compare the execution time of his *workload*—the mixture of programs and operating system commands that users run on a machine. Few are in this happy situation, however. Most must rely on other methods to evaluate machines and often other evaluators, hoping that these methods will predict performance for their usage of the new machine. There are four levels of programs used in such circumstances, listed below in decreasing order of accuracy of prediction.

1. *(Real) Programs*—While the buyer may not know what fraction of time is spent on these programs, he knows that some users will run them to solve real problems. Examples are compilers for C, text-processing software like TeX, and CAD tools like Spice. Real programs have input, output, and options that a user can select when running the program.

2. *Kernels*—Several attempts have been made to extract small, key pieces from real programs and use them to evaluate performance. Livermore Loops and Linpack are the best known examples. Unlike real programs, no user would run kernel programs, for they exist solely to evaluate performance. Kernels are best used to isolate performance of individual features of a machine to explain the reasons for differences in performance of real programs.

3. *(Toy) Benchmarks*—Toy benchmarks are typically between 10 and 100 lines of code and produce a result the user already knows before he runs the toy program. Programs like Sieve of Erastosthenes, Puzzle, and Quicksort are popular because they are small, easy to type, and run on almost any computer. The best use of such programs is beginning programming assignments.

4. *Synthetic Benchmarks*—Similar in philosophy to kernels, synthetic benchmarks try to match the average frequency of operations and operands of a large set of programs. Whetstone and Dhrystone are popular synthetic benchmarks. (Figures 2.4 and 2.5 on pages 46 and 47 show pieces of the benchmarks.) Like their cousins, the kernels, no user runs synthetic benchmarks because they don't compute anything a user could use. Synthetic benchmarks are, in fact, even fur-

ther removed from reality because kernel code is extracted from real programs, while synthetic code is created artificially to match an average execution profile. Synthetic benchmarks are not even **pieces** of real programs, while all the others might be.

If you're not sure how to classify a program, first check to see if there is any input or very much output. A program without input calculates the same result every time it is invoked. (Few buy computers to act as copying machines.) While some programs, notably simulation and numerical analysis applications, use negligible input, every real program has some input.

```
        I = ITER
        ...
        N8 = 899 * I
        ...
        N11 = 93 * I
        ...
        X = 1.0
        Y = 1.0
        Z = 1.0
        IF (N8) 89,89,81
81      DO 88 I = 1, N8, 1
88              CALL P3(X,Y,Z)
89      CONTINUE
        ...
        X = 0.75
        IF (N11) 119,119,111
111     DO 118 I = 1, N11, 1
118             X = SQRT(EXP(ALOG(X)/T1))
119     CONTINUE
        ...
        SUBROUTINE P3 (X,Y,Z)
        COMMON T, TT1, T2
        X1 = X
        Y1 = Y
        X1 = T * (X1 + Y1)
        Y1 = T * (X1 + Y1)
        Z = (X1 + Y1) / T2
        RETURN
        END
        ...
```

FIGURE 2.13 Two loops of the Whetstone synthetic benchmark. Based on the frequency of Algol statements in programs submitted to a university batch operating system in the early 1970s, a synthetic program was created to match that profile. (See Curnow and Wichmann [1976].) The statements at the beginning (e.g., N8 = 899*I) control the number of iterations of each of the 12 loops (e.g., the DO loop at line 81). The program was later converted to Fortran and became a popular benchmark in marketing literature. (The line labeled 118 is the subject of a fallacy on pages 73–74 in Section 2.5.)

Because computer companies thrive or go bust depending on price/performance of their products relative to others in the marketplace, tremendous resources are available to improve performance of programs widely used in evaluating performance. Such pressures can skew hardware and software engineering efforts to add optimizations that improve performance of synthetic programs, toy programs, or kernels, but not real programs.

An extreme instance of such targeted engineering employed compiler optimizations that were benchmark sensitive. Rather than perform the analysis so that the compiler could properly decide if the optimization could be applied, a person at one startup company used a preprocessor that scanned the text for keywords to try to identify benchmarks by looking for the name of the author and the name of a key subroutine. If the scan confirmed that this program was on a predefined list, the special optimizations were performed. This machine made a sudden jump in

```
...
for(Run_Index = 1; Run_Index<=Number_Of_Runs; ++Run_Index)
{
        Proc_5();
        Proc_4();
        Int_1_Loc = 2;
        Int_2_Loc = 3;
        strcpy(Str_2_Loc,"DHRYSTONE PROGRAMS, 2'ND STRING");
        ...
}
...
Proc_4()
{
        Boolean Bool_Loc;

        Bool_Loc = Ch1_1_Glob == 'A';
        Bool_Glob = Bool_Loc | Bool_Glob;
        Ch1_2_Glob = 'B';
} /* Proc_4 */

Proc_5()
{
        Ch1_1_Glob = 'A';
        Bool_Glob = false;
} /* Proc_5 */
...
```

FIGURE 2.14 A section of the Dhrystone synthetic benchmark. Inspired by Whetstone, this program was an attempt to characterize CPU and compiler performance for a typical program. It was based on the frequency of high-level language statements from a variety of publications. The program was originally written in Ada and later converted to C and Pascal (see Weicker [1984]). Note the small size and simple-minded nature of these procedures makes it trivial for an optimizing compiler to avoid procedure-call overhead by expanding them inline. The `strcpy()` on the eighth line is the subject of a fallacy on pages 73–74 in Section 2.5.

performance—at least according to those benchmarks. Yet these optimizations were not only invalid to programs not on the list, they were useless to the identical code with a few name changes.

The small size of programs in the last three categories makes them vulnerable to such efforts. For example, despite the best intentions, the initial SPEC benchmark suite (page 79) includes a small program. 99% of the execution time of Matrix300 is in a single line (see SPEC [1989]). A minor enhancement of the MIPS FORTRAN compiler (which improved the induction variable elimination optimization—see Section 3.7 in Chapter 3) resulted in a performance increase of 56% on a M/2000 and 117% on an RC 6280. This concentration of execution time led Apollo down the path of temptation: The performance of the DN 10000 is quoted with this line changed to a call to a hand-coded library routine. If the industry adopts real programs to compare performance, then at least resources expended to improve performance will help real users.

So why doesn't everyone run real programs to measure performance? Kernels and toy benchmarks are attractive when beginning a design since they are small enough to easily simulate, even by hand. They are especially tempting when inventing a new machine because compilers may not be available until much later. Small benchmarks are also more easily standardized while large programs are difficult, hence there are numerous published results for small benchmark performance but few for large ones.

While there are rationalizations for use early in the design, there is no current valid rationale for using benchmarks and kernels to evaluate working computer systems. In the past, programming languages were inconsistent among machines, and every machine had its own operating system; so real programs could not be ported without pain and agony. There was also a lack of important software whose source code was freely available. Finally, programs had to be small because the architecture simulator had to run on an old, slow machine.

The popularity of standard operating systems like UNIX and DOS, freely distributed software from universities and others, and faster computers available today remove many of these obstacles. While kernels, toy benchmarks, and synthetic benchmarks were an attempt to make fair comparisons among different machines, use of anything less than real programs after initial design studies is likely to give misleading results and lead the designer astray.

Reporting Performance Results

The guiding principle of reporting performance measurements should be *reproducibility*—list everything another experimenter would need to duplicate the results. Let's compare descriptions of computer performance found in refereed scientific journals to descriptions of car performance found in magazines sold at supermarkets. Car magazines, in addition to supplying 20 performance metrics, list all optional equipment on the test car, the types of tires used in the performance test, and the date the test was made. Computer journals may have only seconds of execution labeled by the name of the program and the name and model of the computer—Spice takes 94 seconds on a DECstation 3100. Left to the reader's imagination are program input, version of the program, version of compiler, optimizing level of compiled code, version of operating system, amount of main memory, number and types of disks, version of the CPU—all of which make a difference in performance.

Car magazines have enough information about the measurement to allow readers to duplicate results or to question the options selected for measurements, but computer journals often do not.

Comparing and Summarizing Performance

Comparing performance of computers is rarely a dull event, especially when the designers are involved. Charges and countercharges fly across an electronic network; one is accused of underhanded tactics and the other of misleading statements. Since careers sometimes depend on the results of such performance comparisons, it is understandable that the truth is occasionally stretched. But more frequently discrepancies can be explained by differing assumptions or lack of information.

We would like to think that if we can just agree on the programs, the experimental environments, and the definition of "faster," then misunderstandings will be avoided, leaving the networks free for scholarly intercourse. Unfortunately, the outcome is not such a happy one, for battles are then fought over what is the fair way to summarize relative performance of a collection of programs. For example, two articles on summarizing performance in the same journal took opposing points of view. Figure 2.6, taken from one of the articles, is an example of the confusion that can arise.

	Computer A	Computer B	Computer C
Program 1 (secs)	1	10	20
Program 2 (secs)	1000	100	20
Total time (secs)	1001	110	40

FIGURE 2.15 Execution times of two programs on three machines. Taken from Figure I of Smith [1988].

Using our definition in Chapter 1 (page 6), the following statements hold:

A is 900% faster than B for program 1.

B is 900% faster than A for program 2.

A is 1900% faster than C for program 1.

C is 4900% faster than A for program 2.

B is 100% faster than C for program 1.

C is 400% faster than B for program 2.

Taken individually, any one of these statements may be of use. Collectively, however, they present a confusing picture—the relative performance of computers A, B, and C is unclear.

Total Execution Time: A Consistent Summary Measure

The simplest approach to summarizing relative performance is to use total execution time of the two programs. Thus

B is 810% faster than A for programs 1 and 2.

C is 2400% faster than A for programs 1 and 2.

C is 175% faster than B for programs 1 and 2.

This summary tracks execution time, our final measure of performance. If the workload consisted of running programs 1 and 2 an equal number of times, the statements above would predict the relative execution times for the workload on each machine.

An average of the execution times that tracks total execution time is the *arithmetic mean*

$$\frac{1}{n} \sum_{i=1}^{n} \text{Time}_i$$

where Time_i is the execution time for the ith program of a total of n in the workload. If performance is expressed as a rate (such as MFLOPS), then the average that tracks total execution time is the *harmonic mean*

$$\frac{n}{\displaystyle\sum_{i=1}^{n} \frac{1}{\text{Rate}_i}}$$

where Rate_i is a function of $1/\text{Time}_i$, the execution time for the ith of n programs in the workload.

Weighted Execution Time

The question arises what is the proper mixture of programs for the workload: Are programs 1 and 2 in fact run equally in the workload as assumed by the arithmetic mean? If not, then there are two approaches that have been tried for summarizing performance. The first approach when given a nonequal mix of programs in the workload is to assign a weighting factor w_i to each program to indicate the relative frequency of the program in that workload. If, for example, 20% of the tasks in the workload were program 1 and 80% of the tasks in the workload were program 2, then the weighting factors would be 0.2 and 0.8. (Weighting factors add up to 1.) By summing the products of weighting factors and execution times, a clear picture of performance of the workload is obtained. This is called the *weighted arithmetic mean*:

$$\sum_{i=1}^{n} \text{Weight}_i * \text{Time}_i$$

where Weight_i is the frequency of the ith program in the workload and Time_i is the execution time of that program. Figure 2.7 shows the data from Figure 2.6 with three different weightings, each proportional to the execution time of a workload with a given mix. The *weighted harmonic mean* of rates will show the same relative performance as the weighted arithmetic means of execution times. The definition is

$$\cfrac{1}{\displaystyle\sum_{i=1}^{n} \cfrac{\text{Weight}_i}{\text{Rate}_i}}$$

	A	B	C	W(1)	W(2)	W(3)
Program 1 (secs)	1.00	10.00	20.00	0.50	0.909	0.999
Program 2 (secs)	1000.00	100.00	20.00	0.50	0.091	0.001
Arithmetic mean :W(1)	500.50	55.00	20.00			
Arithmetic mean :W(2)	91.82	18.18	20.00			
Arithmetic mean :W(3)	2.00	10.09	20.00			

FIGURE 2.16 Weighted arithmetic mean execution times using three weightings. W(1) equally weights the programs, resulting in a mean (row 3) that is the same as the nonweighted arithmetic mean. W(2) makes the mix of programs inversely proportional to the execution times on machine B; row 4 shows the arithmetic mean for that weighting. W(3) weights the programs in inverse proportion to the execution times of the two programs on machine A; the arithmetic mean is given in the last row. The net effect of the second and third weightings is to "normalize" the weightings to the execution times of programs running on that machine, so that the running time will be spent evenly between each program for that machine. For a set of n programs each taking T_i time on one machine, the equal-time weightings on that machine are

$$w_i = \cfrac{1}{T_j * \displaystyle\sum_{j=1}^{n} \left(\cfrac{1}{T_j}\right)}.$$

Normalized Execution Time and the Pros and Cons of Geometric Means

A second approach to nonequal mixture of programs in the workload is to normalize execution times to a reference machine and then take the average of the normalized execution times, similar to the relative MIPS rating discussed above. This measurement gives a warm fuzzy feeling, because it suggests that performance of new programs can be predicted by simply multiplying this number times its performance on the reference machine.

Average normalized execution time can be expressed as either an arithmetic or *geometric* mean. The formula for the geometric mean is

$$\sqrt[n]{\prod_{i=1}^{n} \text{Execution time ratio}_i}$$

where *Execution time ratio$_i$* is the execution time, normalized to the reference machine, for the *i*th program of a total of *n* in the workload. Geometric means also have the nice property that

$$\frac{\text{Geometric mean} (X_i)}{\text{Geometric mean} (Y_i)} = \text{Geometric mean}\left(\frac{X_i}{Y_i}\right)$$

meaning that taking either the ratio of the means or the means of the ratios gets the same results. In contrast to arithmetic means, geometric means of normalized execution times are consistent no matter which machine is the reference. Hence, the arithmetic mean should **not** be used to average normalized execution times. Figure 2.8 shows some variations using both arithmetic and geometric means of normalized times.

| | Normalized to A | | | Normalized to B | | | Normalized to C | | |
	A	B	C	A	B	C	A	B	C
Program 1	100%	1000%	2000%	10%	100%	200%	5%	50%	100%
Program 2	100%	10%	2%	1000%	100%	20%	5000%	500%	100%
Arithmetic mean	100%	505%	1001%	505%	100%	110%	2503%	275%	100%
Geometric mean	100%	100%	63%	100%	100%	63%	158%	158%	100%
Total time	100%	11%	4%	910%	100%	36%	2503%	275%	100%

FIGURE 2.17   Execution times from Figure 2.6 normalized to each machine. The arithmetic mean performance varies depending on which is the reference machine—column 2 says B's execution time is 5 times longer than A's while column 4 says just the opposite; column 3 says C is slowest while column 9 says C is fastest. The geometric means are consistent independent of normalization—A and B have the same performance, and the execution time of C is 63% of A or B (100%/ 158% is 63%). Unfortunately total execution time of A is 9 times longer than B, and B in turn is about 3 times longer than C. As a point of interest, the relationship between the means of the same set of numbers is always harmonic mean ≤ geometric mean ≤ arithmetic mean.

Because weightings of weighted arithmetic means are set proportionate to execution times on a given machine, as in Figure 2.7, they are influenced not only by frequency of use in the workload, but also by the peculiarities of a particular machine and the size of program input. The geometric mean of normalized execution times, on the other hand, is independent of the running times of the individual programs, and it doesn't matter which machine is used to normalize. If a situation arose in comparative performance evaluation where the programs were fixed but the inputs were not, then competitors could rig the results of weighted arithmetic means by making their best performing benchmark have the largest input and therefore dominate execution time. In such a situation the geometric mean would be less misleading than the arithmetic mean.

The strong drawback to geometric means of normalized execution times is that they violate our fundamental principle of performance measurement—they do not predict execution time. The geometric means from Figure 2.8 suggest that for programs 1 and 2 the performance of machines A and B is the same, yet this would only be true for a workload that ran program 1 100 times for every occurrence of program 2 (see Figure 2.6 on page 49). The total execution time for such a workload suggests that machines A and B are about 50% faster than machine C, in contrast to the geometric mean, which says machine C is faster than A and B! In general there is **no workload** for three or more machines that will match the performance predicted by the geometric means of normalized execution times. Our original reason for examining geometric means of normalized performance was to avoid giving equal emphasis to the programs in our workload, but is this solution an improvement?

The ideal solution is to measure a real workload and weight the programs according to their frequency of execution. If this can't be done, then normalizing so that equal time is spent on each program on some machine at least makes the relative weightings explicit and will predict execution time of a workload with that mix (see Figure 2.7 on page 51). The problem above of unspecified inputs is best solved by specifying the inputs when comparing performance. If results must be normalized to a specific machine, first summarize performance with the proper weighted measure and then do the normalizing. Section 2.4 gives an example.

2.3 | Cost

While there are computer designs where costs tend to be ignored—specifically supercomputers—cost-sensitive designs are of growing importance. Textbooks have ignored the cost half of cost/performance because costs change, thereby dating books. Yet an understanding of cost is essential for designers to be able to make intelligent decisions about whether or not a new feature should be included in designs where cost is an issue. (Imagine architects designing skyscrapers without any information on costs of steel beams and concrete.) We therefore cover in this section fundamentals of cost that will not change for the life of the book and provide specific examples using costs that, though they may not hold up over time, demonstrate the concepts involved.

The rapid change in cost of electronics is the first of several themes in cost-sensitive designs. This parameter is changing so fast that good designers are basing decisions not on costs of today, but on projected costs at the time the product is shipped. The underlying principle that drives costs down is the *learning curve*—manufacturing costs decrease over time. The learning curve itself is best measured by change in *yield*—the percentage of manufactured devices that survive the testing procedure. Whether it is a chip, a board, or a system, designs that have twice the yield will have basically half the cost. Understanding how the learning curve will improve yield is key to projecting costs over the life of the product.

Lowering cost, however, does not necessarily lower price; it may just increase profits. But when the product is available from multiple sources and demand does not exceed supply, competition does force prices to fall with costs. For the remainder of this discussion we assume that normal competitive forces are at work with a reasonable balance between supply and demand.

As an example of the learning curve in action, the cost per megabyte of DRAM drops over the long term by 40% per year. A more dramatic version of the same information is shown in Figure 2.9, where the cost of a new DRAM chip is depicted over its lifetime. Between the start of a project and the shipping of a product, say two years, the cost of a new DRAM drops by nearly a factor of four. Since not all component costs change at the same rate, designs based on projected costs result in different cost-performance tradeoffs than those using current costs.

A second important theme in cost-sensitive designs is the impact of packaging on design decisions. A few years ago the advantages of fitting a design on a single board meant there was no backplane, no card cage, and a smaller and cheaper box—all resulting in much lower costs and even higher performance. In a few years it will be possible to integrate all the components of a system, except main memory, onto a single chip. The overriding issue will be making the system fit on the chip, thereby avoiding the speed and cost penalties of having multiple chips, which means more interfaces, more pins to interfaces, larger boards, and so forth. The density of integrated circuits and packaging technology determine the resources available at each cost threshold. The designer must know where these thresholds are—or blindly cross them.

Cost of an Integrated Circuit

Why would a computer architecture book have a section on integrated circuit costs? In an increasingly competitive computer marketplace where standard parts—disks, DRAMs, and so on—are becoming a significant portion of any system's cost, integrated circuit costs are becoming a greater portion of the cost that varies between machines, especially in the high volume, cost-sensitive portion of the market. Thus computer designers must understand the costs of chips to understand the costs of current computers. We follow here the American accounting approach to the cost of chips.

While the costs of integrated circuits have dropped exponentially, the basic procedure of silicon manufacture is unchanged: A *wafer* is still tested and chopped into *dies* that are packaged (see Figures 2.10a, b, and c). Thus the cost of a packaged integrated circuit is

$$\text{Cost of integrated circuit} = \frac{\text{Cost of die} + \text{Cost of testing die} + \text{Cost of packaging}}{\text{Final test yield}}$$

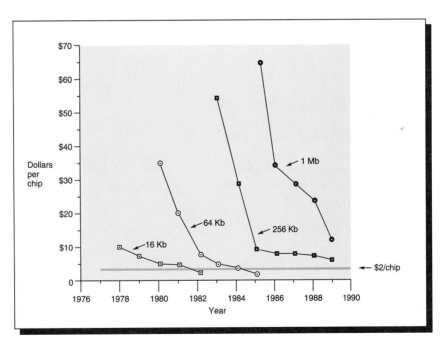

FIGURE 2.18 Prices of four generations of DRAMs over time, showing the learning curve at work. While the longer average is 40% improvement per year, each generation drops in price by nearly a factor of ten over its lifetime. The DRAMs drop to about $1 to $2 per chip over time, independent of capacity. Prices are **not** adjusted for inflation—if they were the graph would show an even greater drop in cost. For a time in 1987–1988, prices of both 256Kb and 1Mb DRAMs were higher than indicated by earlier learning curves due to what seems to have been a temporary excess of demand relative to available supply.

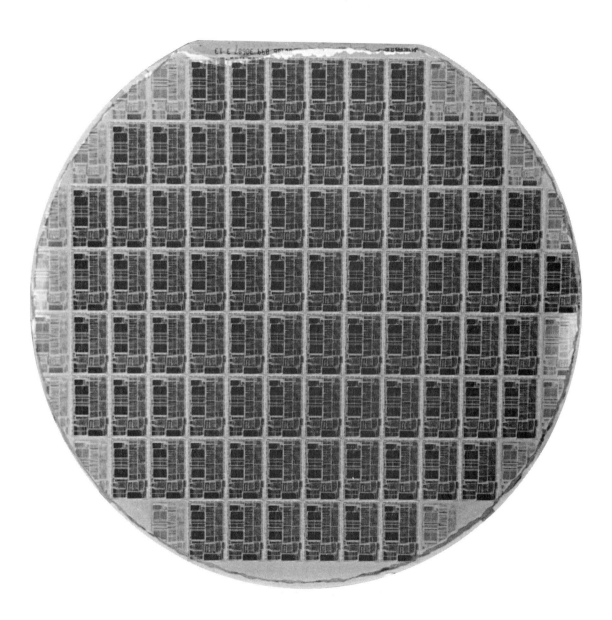

FIGURE 2.19a   Photograph of a 6-inch wafer containing Intel 80486 microprocessors. There are 80 1.6 cm x 1.0 cm dies, although four dies are so close to the edge that they may or may not be fully functional. There are no separate test dies; instead, the electrical and parametric test circuits are placed **between** the dies. The 80486 includes a floating point unit, a small cache, and a memory management unit in addition to the integer unit.

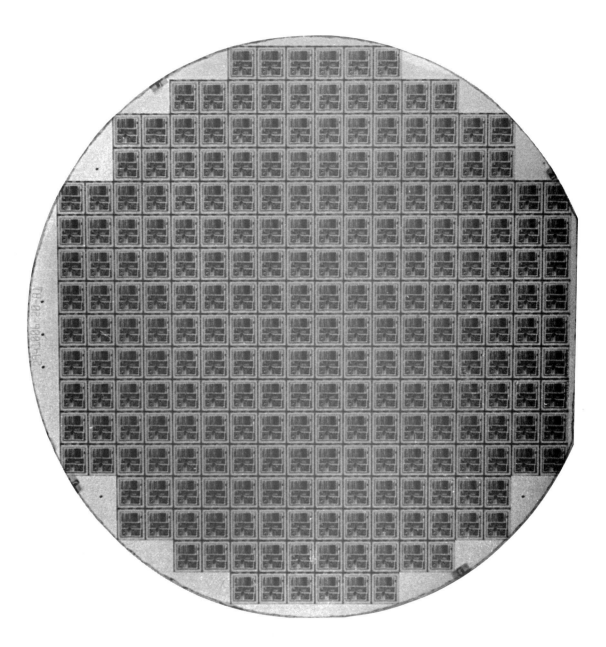

FIGURE 2.10b Photograph of a 6-inch wafer containing Cypress CY7C601 microprocessors. There are 246 full 0.8 cm x 0.7 cm dies, although again four dies are so close to the edge it is hard to tell if they are complete. Like Intel, Cypress places the electrical and parametric test circuits between the dies. These test circuits are removed when the wafer is diced into chips. In contrast to the 80486, the CY7C601 contains the integer unit only.

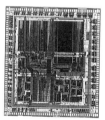

FIGURE 2.10c   At the top left is the Intel 80486 die, and the Cypress CY7C601 die is on the right, shown at their actual sizes. Below the dies are the packaged versions of each microprocessor. Note that the 80486 has three rows of pins (168 total) while the 601 has four rows (207 total). The bottom row shows a close-up of the two dies, shown in proper relative proportions.

Cost of Dies

To learn how to predict the number of good chips per wafer requires first learning how many dies fit on a wafer and then how to predict the percentage of those that will work. From there it is simple to predict cost:

$$\text{Cost of die} = \frac{\text{Cost of wafer}}{\text{Dies per wafer} * \text{Die yield}}$$

The most interesting feature of this first term of the chip cost equation is its sensitivity to die size, shown below.

The number of dies per wafer is basically the area of the wafer divided by the area of the die. It can be more accurately estimated by

$$\text{Dies per wafer} = \frac{\pi * (\text{Wafer diameter}/2)^2}{\text{Die area}} - \frac{\pi * \text{Wafer diameter}}{\sqrt{2} * \text{Die area}} - \text{Test dies per wafer}$$

The first term is the ratio of wafer area (πr^2) to die area. The second compensates for the "square peg in a round hole" problem–rectangular dies near the periphery of round wafers. Dividing the circumference (πd) by the diagonal of a square die is approximately the number of dice along the edge. The last term is for test dies that must be strategically placed to control manufacturing. For example, a 15-cm ($\approx$6-inch) diameter wafer with 5 test dies produces $3.14*225/4 - 3.14*15/\sqrt{2} - 5$ or 138 1-cm-square dies. Doubling die area—the parameter that a computer designer controls—would cut dies per wafer to 59.

But this only gives the maximum number of dies per wafer, and the critical question is what is the fraction or percentage of good dies on a wafer number, or the *die yield*. A simple model of integrated circuit yield assumes defects are randomly distributed over the wafer:

$$\text{Die yield} = \text{Wafer yield} * \left\{ 1 + \frac{\text{Defects per unit area} * \text{Die area}}{\alpha} \right\}^{-\alpha}$$

where *wafer yield* accounts for wafers that are completely bad and so need not be tested and α is a parameter that corresponds roughly to the number of masking levels critical to die yield. α depends upon the manufacturing process. Generally $\alpha = 2.0$ for simple MOS processes and higher values for more complex processes, such as bipolar and BiCMOS. As an example, wafer yield is 90%, *defects per unit area* is 2 per square centimeter, and die area is 1 square centimeter. Then die yield is $90\%*(1 + (2*1)/2.0)^{-2.0}$ or 22.5%.

The bottom line is the number of good dies per wafer, which comes from multiplying dies per wafer by die yield. The examples above predict $138*.225$ or 31 good 1-cm-square dies per 15-cm wafer. As mentioned above, both dies per wafer and die yield are sensitive to die size—doubling die area knocks die yield down to 10% and good chips per wafer to just $59*.10$, or 6! Die size depends on the technology and gates required by the function on the chip, but it is also limited by the number of pins that can be placed on the border of a square die.

A 15-cm-diameter wafer processed in two-level metal CMOS costs a semi-conductor manufacturer about $550 in 1990. The cost for a 1-cm-square die with two defects per square cm on a 15-cm wafer is $550/(138∗.225) or $17.74.

What should a computer designer remember about chip costs? The manufacturing process dictates the wafer cost, wafer yield, α, and defects per unit area, so the sole control of the designer is die area. Since α is usually 2 or larger, die costs are inversely proportional to the third (or higher) power of the die area:

$$\text{Cost of die} = f\,(\text{Die area}^3)$$

The computer designer affects die size, and hence cost, both by what functions are included on or excluded from the die and by the number of I/O pins.

Cost of Testing Die and Cost of Packaging

Testing is the second term of the chip-cost equation, and the success rate of testing (die yield) affects the cost of testing:

$$\text{Cost of testing die} = \frac{\text{Cost of testing per hour} * \text{Average die test time}}{\text{Die yield}}$$

Since bad dies are discarded, die yield is in the denominator in the equation—the good must shoulder the costs of testing those that fail. Testing costs about $150 per hour in 1990 and die tests take about 5 to 90 seconds on average, depending on the simplicity of the die and the provisions to reduce testing time included in the chip. For example, at $150 per hour and 5 seconds to test, the die test cost is $0.21. After factoring in die yield for a 1-cm-square die, the costs are $0.93 per good die. As a second example, let's assume testing takes 90 seconds. The cost is $3.75 per untested die and $16.67 per good die. The bill so far for our 1-cm-square die is $18.67 to $34.41, depending on how long it takes to test. These two testing-time examples illustrate the importance of reducing testing time in reducing costs.

Cost of Packaging and Final Test Yield

The cost of a package depends on the material used, the number of pins, and the die area. The cost of the material used in the package is in part determined by the ability to dissipate power generated by the die. For example, a *plastic quad flat pack* (PQFP) dissipating less than one watt, with 208 or fewer pins, and containing a die up to one cm on a side costs $3 in 1990. A ceramic *pin grid array* (PGA) can handle 300 to 400 pins and a larger die with more power, but it costs $50. In addition to the cost of the package itself is the cost of the labor to place a die in the package and then bond the pads to the pins. We can assume that costs $2. Burn-in exercises the packaged die under power for a short time to catch chips that would fail early. Burn-in costs about $0.25 in 1990 dollars.

We are not finished with costs until we have figured in failure of some chips during assembly and burn-in. Using the estimate of 90% for final test yield, the successful must again pay for the cost of those that fail, so our costs are $26.58 to $96.29 for the 1-cm-square die.

While these specific cost estimates may not hold, the underlying models will. Figure 2.11 shows the dies per wafer, die yield, and their product against the die area for a typical fabrication line, this time using programs that more accurately predict die per wafer and die yield. Figure 2.12 plots the change in area and cost as one dimension of a square die changes. Changes to small dies make little cost difference while 30% increases to large dies can double costs. The wise silicon designer will minimize die area, testing time, and pins per chip and understand the costs of projected packaging options when considering using more power, pins, or area for higher performance.

Cost of a Workstation

To put the costs of silicon in perspective, Figure 2.13 shows the approximate costs of components in a 1990 workstation. Costs of a component can be halved going from low volume to high volume; here we assume high-volume purchasing of 100,000 units. While costs for units like DRAMs will surely drop over time from those in Figure 2.13, units whose prices have already been cut, like displays and cabinets, will change very little.

The processor, floating-point unit, memory-management unit, and cache are only 12% to 21% of the cost of the CPU board in Figure 2.13. Depending on the options included in the system—number of disks, color monitor, and so on—the processor components drop to 9% and 16% of the cost of a system, as Figure 2.14 illustrates. In the future two questions will be interesting to consider: What costs can an engineer control? And what costs can a computer engineer control?

Cost Versus Price—Why They Differ and by How Much

Costs of components may confine a designer's desires, but they are still far from representing what the customer must pay. But why should a computer architecture book contain pricing information? Cost goes through a number of changes before it becomes price, and the computer designer must understand these to determine the impact of design choices. For example, changing cost by $1,000 may change price by $4,000 to $5,000. Without understanding the relationship of cost to price the computer designer may not understand the impact on price of adding, deleting, or replacing components.

Area (sq. cm)	Side (cm)	Die/ wafer	Die yield/ wafer	Cost of die	Cost to test die	Packaging costs	Total cost after final test
0.06	0.25	2778	79.72%	$0.25	$0.63	$5.25	$6.81
0.25	0.50	656	57.60%	$1.46	$0.87	$5.25	$8.42
0.56	0.75	274	36.86%	$5.45	$1.36	$5.25	$13.40
1.00	1.00	143	22.50%	$17.09	$2.22	$5.25	$27.29
1.56	1.25	84	13.71%	$47.76	$3.65	$52.25	$115.18
2.25	1.50	53	8.52%	$121.80	$5.87	$52.25	$199.91
3.06	1.75	35	5.45%	$288.34	$9.17	$52.25	$388.62
4.00	2.00	23	3.60%	$664.25	$13.89	$52.25	$811.54

FIGURE 2.11   Costs for several die sizes. Costs for a working chip are shown in columns 5 through 7. Column 8 is the sum of columns 5 through 7 divided by the final test yield. Figure 2.12 presents this information graphically. This figure assumes a 15.24-cm (6-inch) wafer costing $550, with 5 test die per wafer. The wafer yield is 90%, the defect density is 2.0 per square cm, and α is 2.0. It takes 12 seconds on average to test a die, the tester costs $150 per hour, and the final test yield is 90%. (The numbers differ a little from the text for a 1-cm-square die because the wafer size is calculated at the full 15.24 cm rather than rounded to 15 cm and because of the difference in testing time.)

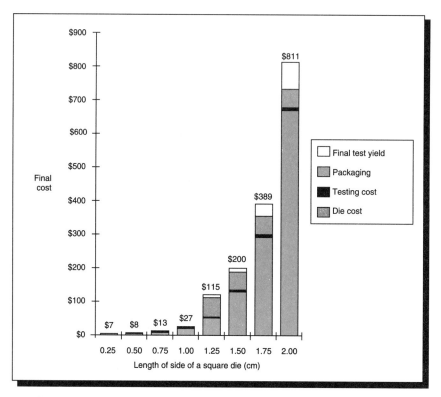

FIGURE 2.12   The costs of a chip from Figure 2.11 presented graphically. Using the parameters given in the text, packaging is a major percentage of the cost of dies of size 1.25-cm square and smaller, with die cost dominating final costs for larger dies.

		Rule of thumb	Lower cost	% Mono WS	Higher cost	% Color WS
CPU cabinet	Sheet metal, plastic		$50	2%	$50	1%
	Power supply and fans	$0.80/watt	$55	3%	$55	1%
	Cables, nuts, bolts		$30	1%	$30	1%
	Shipping box, manuals		$10	0%	$10	0%
	Subtotal		$145	7%	$145	3%
CPU board	IU, FPU, MMU, cache		$200	9%	$800	16%
	DRAM	$150/MB	$1200	56%	$2400	48%
	Video logic (frame buffer, DAC, mono/color)	Mono Color	$100	5%	$500	10%
	I/O interfaces (SCSI, Ethernet, floppy, PROM, time-of-day clock)		$100	5%	$100	2%
	Printed circuit board	8 layers $1.00/sq. in.				
		6 layers $0.50/sq. in.	$50	2%	$50	1%
		4 layers $0.25/sq. in.				
	Subtotal		$1650	77%	$3850	76%
I/O devices	Keyboard, mouse		$50	2%	$50	1%
	Display monitor	Mono	$300	14%		
		Color			$1,000	20%
	Hard disk	100 MB	$400			
	Tape drive	150 MB	$400			
Mono workstation	(8 MB, Mono logic & display, keyboard, mouse, diskless)		$2,145	100%	$2,745	
Color workstation	(16 MB, Color logic & display, keyboard, mouse, diskless)		$4,445		$5,045	100%
File server	(16 MB, 6 disks+tape drive)		$5,595		$6,195	

FIGURE 2.13   Estimated cost of components in a 1990 workstation assuming 100,000 units. IU refers to integer unit of the processor, FPU to floating-point unit, and MMU to memory-management unit. The lower cost column refers to the least expensive options, listed as a Mono workstation in the third row from the bottom. The higher cost column refers to the more expensive options, listed as a Color workstation in the second row from the bottom. Note that about half the cost of the systems is in the DRAMs. Courtesy of Andy Bechtolsheim of Sun Microsystems, Inc.

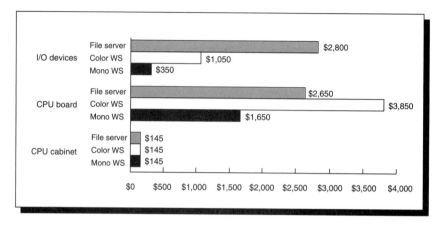

FIGURE 2.14 The costs of each machine in Figure 2.13 divided into the three main categories, assuming the lower cost estimate. Note that I/O devices and amount of memory account for major differences in costs.

The categories that make up price can be shown either as a tax on cost or as a percentage of the price. We will look at the information both ways. Figure 2.15 shows the increasing price of a product from left to right as we add each kind of overhead.

Direct costs refer to the costs directly related to making a product. These include labor costs, purchasing components, scrap (the leftover from yield), and warranty, which covers the costs of systems that fail at the customer's site during the warranty period. Direct cost typically adds 25% to 40% to component cost. Service or maintenance costs are not included because the customer typically pays those costs.

The next addition is called the *gross margin*, the company's overhead that cannot be billed directly to one product. This can be thought of as indirect cost. It includes the company's research and development (R&D), marketing, sales, manufacturing equipment maintenance, building rental, cost of financing, pretax profits, and taxes. When the component costs are multiplied by the direct cost and gross margin we reach the *average selling price*—ASP in the language of MBAs—the money that comes directly to the company for each product sold. The gross margin is typically 45% to 65% of the average selling price.

List price and average selling price are not the same. One reason for this is that companies offer volume discounts, lowering the average selling price. Also, if the product is to be sold in retail stores, as personal computers are, stores want to keep 40% of the list price for themselves. Thus, depending on the distribution system, the average selling price is typically 60% to 75% of the list price. The formula below ties the four terms together:

$$\text{List price} = \frac{(\text{Cost} * (1 + \text{Direct costs})}{(1 - \text{Average discount}) * (1 - \text{Gross margin})}$$

Figure 2.16 demonstrates the abstract concepts of Figure 2.15 using dollars and cents by turning the costs of Figure 2.13 into prices. This is done using two business models. Model A assumes 25% (of cost) direct costs, 50% (of ASP) gross margin, and a 33% (of list price) average discount. Model B assumes 40% direct costs, 60% gross margin, and the average discount is dropped to 25%.

Pricing is sensitive to competition. A company striving for market share can therefore adjust to average discount or profits, but must live with its component cost and direct cost, plus the rest of the costs in the gross margin.

Many engineers are surprised to find that most companies spend only 8% to 15% of their income on R&D, which includes all engineering (except for manufacturing and field engineering). This is a well-established percentage that is reported in companies' annual reports and tabulated in national magazines, so this percentage is unlikely to change over time.

The information above suggests that a company uniformly applies fixed-overhead percentages to turn cost into price, and this is true for many companies. But another point of view is R&D should be considered an investment, and so an investment of 8% to 15% of income means every $1 spent on R&D must generate $7 to $13 in sales. This alternative point of view then suggests a different gross margin for each product depending on number sold and the size of the investment.

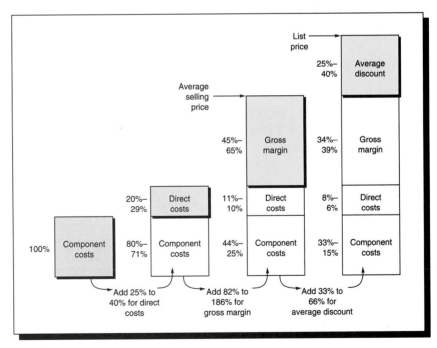

FIGURE 2.15 Starting with component costs, the price increases as we allow for direct costs, gross margin, and average discount, until we arrive at the list price. Each increase is shown along the bottom as a tax on the prior price. On the left of each column are shown the percentages of the new price for all elements.

	Model A	As % of costs	As % of list price	Model B	As % of costs	As % of list price
Component costs	$2,145	100%	27%	$2,145	100%	21%
Component costs + direct costs	$2,681	125%	33%	$3,003	140%	30%
Average selling price (adds gross margin)	$5,363	250%	67%	$7,508	350%	75%
List price	$8,044	375%	100%	$10,010	467%	100%

FIGURE 2.16   The diskless workstation in Figure 2.13 priced using two different business models. For every dollar of increased component cost the average selling price goes up between $2.50 and $3.50, and the list price increases between $3.75 and $4.67.

Large expensive machines generally cost more to develop—a machine costing 10 times as much to manufacture may cost many times as much to develop. Since large expensive machines generally do not sell as well as small ones, the gross margin must be greater on the big machines for the company to maintain a profitable return on its investment. This investment model places large machines in double jeopardy—because there are fewer sold **and** they require larger R&D costs—and gives one explanation for a higher ratio of price to cost versus smaller machines.

2.4 | Putting It All Together: Price/Performance of Three Machines

Having covered performance and costs, the next step is to measure performance of real programs on real machines and list the costs of those machines. Alas, costs are hard to come by so prices are used instead. We start with the more controversial half of price/performance.

Figure 2.17 lists the programs chosen by the authors for performance measurement in this book. Two of the programs have almost no floating-point operations, and one has a moderate amount of floating-point operations. All three programs have input, output, and options—what you would expect from real programs. Each program has, in fact, a large user community that cares how fast these programs run. (In measuring performance of machines we would like to have a larger sample, but we keep the limit at three throughout the book to make tables and graphs legible.)

Figure 2.18 shows the characteristics of three machines we measure, including the list price as tested and the relative performance as calculated by marketing.

Figure 2.19 (page 69) shows the CPU time and elapsed time measured for these programs. We include total times and several weighted averages, with the weights shown in parentheses. The first weighted arithmetic mean is assuming a workload of just the integer programs (GCC and TeX). The second is the weightings for a floating-point workload (Spice). The next three weighted means give three workloads for equal time spent on each program on one of the machines (see Figure 2.7 on page 51). The only means that are significantly different are the integer and floating-point means for VAXstation 2000 and 3100. The rest of the means for each machine are within 8% of each other, as can be seen in Figure 2.20 on page 69, which plots the weighted means.

Program name	Gnu C Compiler for 68000	Common TeX	Spice
Version	1.26	2.9	2G6
Lines	79,409	23,037	18,307
Options	-O	'&latex/lplain'	transient analysis, 200 ps steps, for 40 ns
Input	i*.c	bit-set.tex, compiler. tex,...	digsr - digital shift register
Lines/bytes of input	28,009/373,688	10,992/698,914	233/1294
Lines/bytes of output	47,553/664,479	758/524,728	656/4172
% floating-point operations (on the DECstation 3100)	0.01%	0.05%	13.58%
Programming language	C	C	FORTRAN 66
Purpose	Publicly licensed, portable, optimizing C compiler	Document formatting	Computer-aided circuit analysis

FIGURE 2.17   Programs used in this book for performance measurements. The Gnu C compiler is a product of the Free Software Foundation and, for reasons not limited to its price, is preferred by some users over the compilers supplied by the manufacturer. Only 9,540 of the 79,409 lines are specific to the 68000, and versions exist for the VAX, SPARC, 88000, MIPS, and several other instruction sets. The input for gcc are the source files of the compiler that begin with the letter "i." Common TeX is a C version of the document-processing program originally written by Prof. Donald Knuth of Stanford. The input is a set of manual pages for the Stanford SUIF compiler. Spice is a computer-aided circuit-analysis package distributed by the University of California at Berkeley. (These programs and their inputs are available as part of the software package associated with this book. The Preface mentions how to get a copy.)

	VAXstation 2000	**VAXstation 3100**	**DECstation 3100**
Year of introduction	1987	1989	1989
Version of CPU/FPU	μVAX II	CVAX	MIPS R2000A/R2010
Clock rate	5 MHz	11.11 MHz	16.67 MHz
Memory size	4 MB	8 MB	8 MB
Cache size	none	1 KB on chip, 64-KB second level	128 KB (split 64-KB instruction and 64-KB data)
TLB size	8 entries fully associative	28 entries fully associative	64 entries fully associative
Base list price	$4,825	$7,950	$11,950
Optional equipment	19" monitor, extra 10 MB	(model 40) extra 8 MB	19" monitor, extra 8 MB
List price as tested	$15,425	$14,480	$17,950
Performance according to marketing	0.9 MIPS	3.0 MIPS	12 MIPS
Operating system	Ultrix 3.0	Ultrix 3.0	Ultrix 3.0
C compiler version	Ultrix and VMS	Ultrix and VMS	1.31
Options for C compiler	-O	-O	-O2 -Olimit 1060
C library	libc	libc	libc
FORTRAN 77 compiler version	fort (VMS)	fort (VMS)	1.31
Options for FORTRAN 77 compiler	-O	-O	-O2 -Olimit 1060
FORTRAN 77 library	lib∗77	lib∗77	lib∗77

FIGURE 2.18   The three machines and software used to measure performance in Figure 2.19. These machines are all sold by Digital Equipment—in fact, the DECstation 3100 and VAXstation 3100 were announced the same day. All three are diskless workstations and run the same version of the UNIX operating system, called Ultrix. The VMS compilers ported to Ultrix were used for TeX and Spice on the VAXstations. We used the native Ultrix C compiler for gcc because gcc would not run using the VMS C compiler. The compilers for the DECstation 3100 are supplied by MIPS Computer Systems. (The "-Olimit 1060" option for the DECstation 3100 tells the compiler not to try to optimize procedures longer than 1060 lines.)

The bottom line for many computer customers is the price they pay for performance. This is graphically depicted in Figure 2.21 (page 70), where arithmetic means of CPU time are plotted against price of each machine.

	VAXstation 2000		VAXstation 3100		DECstation 3100	
	CPU time	**Elapsed time**	**CPU time**	**Elapsed time**	**CPU time**	**Elapsed time**
Gnu C Compiler for 68000	985	1108	291	327	90	159
Common TeX	1264	1304	449	479	95	137
Spice	958	973	352	395	94	132
Arithmetic mean	1069	1128	364	400	93	143
Weighted AM—integer only (50% gcc, 50% TeX, 0% Spice)	1125	1206	370	403	93	148
Weighted AM—floating point only (0% gcc, 0% TeX, 100% Spice)	958	973	352	395	94	132
Weighted AM—equal CPU time on V2000 (35.6% gcc, 27.8% TeX, 36.6% Spice)	1053	1113	357	394	93	143
Weighted AM—equal CPU time on V3100 (40.4% gcc, 26.2% TeX, 33.4% Spice)	1049	1114	353	390	93	144
Weighted AM—equal CPU time on D3100 (34.4% gcc, 32.6% TeX, 33.0% Spice)	1067	1127	363	399	93	143

FIGURE 2.19   Performance of the programs in Figure 2.17 on the machines in Figure 2.18. The weightings correspond to integer programs only, and then equal CPU time running on each of the three machines. For example, if the mix of the three programs were proportionate to the weightings in the row "equal CPU time on D3100," the DECstation 3100 would spend a third of its CPU time running Gnu C Compiler, a third running TeX, and a third running Spice. The actual weightings are in parentheses, calculated as shown in Figure 2.7 on page 51.

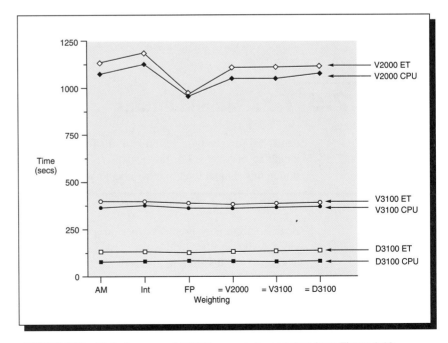

FIGURE 2.20   Plot of means of CPU time and elapsed time from Figure 2.19.

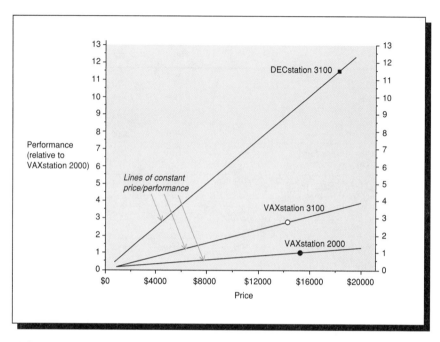

FIGURE 2.21   Price versus performance of VAXstation 2000, VAXstation 3100, and DECstation 3100 for Gnu C Compiler, TeX, and Spice. Based on Figures 2.18–2.19, this figure plots the list price **as tested** of a machine versus performance, where performance is the inverse of the ratio to the arithmetic mean of CPU time on a VAXstation 2000. The lines through the three machines show lines of constant price/performance. For example, a machine at the right end of the VAXstation 3100 line costs $20,000. Since it would cost 30% more, it must have 30% more performance than the VAXstation 3100 to have the same price performance.

2.5 | Fallacies and Pitfalls

Cost/performance fallacies and pitfalls have ensnared many computer architects, including ourselves. For this reason, more space is devoted to the warning section in this chapter than in other chapters of this text.

Fallacy: Hardware-independent metrics predict performance.

Because accurately predicting performance is so difficult, the folklore of computer design is filled with suggested shortcuts. These are frequently employed when comparing different instruction sets, especially instruction sets that are paper designs.

One such shortcut is "Code Size = Speed," or the architecture with the smallest program is fastest. Static code size is important when memory space is at a premium, but it is not the same as performance. As we shall see in Chapter 6, larger programs composed of instructions that are easily fetched, decoded, and executed may run faster than machines with extremely compact instructions that are difficult to decode. "Code Size=Speed" is especially popular with compiler writers, for while it can be difficult to decide if one code sequence is faster than another, it is easy to see which is shorter.

Evidence of the "Code Size=Speed" fallacy can be found on the cover of the book *Assessing the Speed of Algol 60* in Figure 2.22. The CDC 6600's programs are over twice as big, yet the CDC machine runs Algol 60 programs almost six times **faster** than the Burroughs B5500, a machine designed for Algol 60.

Pitfall: Comparing computers using only one or two of three performance metrics: clock rate, CPI, and instruction count.

The CPU performance equation shows why this can mislead. One example is that given in Figure 2.22: The CDC 6600 executes almost 50% more instructions than the Burroughs B5500, yet it is 550% faster. Another example comes from increasing the clock rate so that some instructions execute fast—sometimes called *peak performance*—but making design decisions that also result in a high overall CPI that offsets the clock rate advantage. The Intergraph Clipper C100 has a clock rate of 33 MHz and a peak performance of 33 native MIPS. Yet the Sun 4/280, with half the clock rate and half the peak native MIPS rating, runs programs faster [Hollingsworth, Sachs, and Smith 1989, 215]. Since the Clipper's instruction count is about the same as Sun's, the former machine's CPI must be more than double that of the latter.

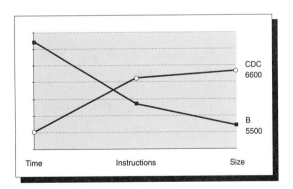

FIGURE 2.22   As found on the cover of *Assessing the Speed of Algol 60* by B. A. Wichmann, the graph shows relative execution time, instruction count, and code size of programs written in Algol 60 for the Burroughs B5500 and the CDC 6600. The results are normalized to a reference machine, with a higher number being worse. This book had a profound effect on one of the authors (DP). Seymour Cray, the designer of the CDC 6600, may not even have known of the existence of this programming language, while Robert Barton, architect of the B5500, designed the instruction set specifically for Algol 60. While the CDC 6600 executes 50% more instructions and has 220% larger code, the CDC 6600 is 550% faster than the B5500.

Fallacy: When calculating relative MIPS, the versions of the compiler and operating system of the reference machine make little difference.

Figure 2.19 shows the VAXstation 2000 taking 958 seconds of CPU time when running Spice with a standard input. Instead of Ultrix 3.0 with the VMS F77 compiler, many systems use Ultrix 3.0 with the standard UNIX F77 compiler. This compiler increases Spice CPU time to 1604 seconds. Using the standard evaluation of 0.9 relative MIPS for the VAXstation 2000, the DECstation 3100 is either 11 or 19 relative MIPS for Spice depending on the compiler of the reference machine.

Fallacy: CPI can be calculated from the instruction mix and the execution times of instructions found in the manual.

Current machines are too complicated to estimate performance from a manual. For example, in Figure 2.19 Spice takes 94 seconds of CPU time on the DECstation 3100. If we calculate the CPI from the DECstation 3100 manual—ignoring memory hierarchy and pipelining inefficiencies for this Spice instruction mix—we get 1.41 for the CPI. When multiplied by the instruction count and clock rate we get only 73 seconds. The missing 25% of CPU time is due to the estimate of CPI based only on the manual. The actual measured value, including all memory-system inefficiencies, is 1.87 CPI.

Pitfall: Summarizing performance by translating throughput into execution time.

The SPEC benchmarks report performance by measuring the elapsed time of each of 10 benchmarks. The sole dual processor workstation in the initial benchmark report ran these benchmarks no faster since the compilers didn't automatically parallelize the code across the two processors. The benchmarker's solution was to run a copy of each benchmark on each processor and record elapsed time for the two copies. This would not have helped if the SPEC release had only summarized performance using elapsed times, since the times were slower due to interference of the processors on memory accesses. The loophole was the initial SPEC release reported geometric means of performance relative to a VAX-11/780 in addition to elapsed times, and these means are used to graph the results. This innovative benchmarker interpreted ratio of performance to a VAX-11/780 as a **throughput** measure, so doubled his measured ratios to the VAX! Figure 2.23 shows the plots as found in the report for the uniprocessor and the multiprocessor. This technique almost doubles the geometric means of ratios, suggesting the mistaken conclusion that a computer that runs two copies of a program simultaneously has the same response time to a user as a computer that runs a single program in half the time.

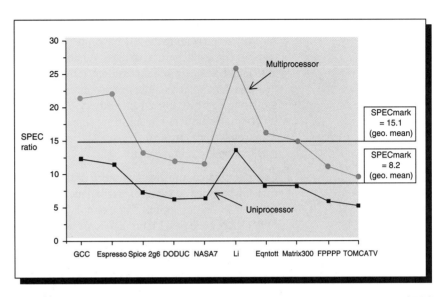

FIGURE 2.23 Performance of uniprocessor and multiprocessor as reported in SPEC Benchmark Press Release. Performance is plotted relative to a VAX-11/780. The ratio for the multiprocessor is really the ratio of elapsed time multiplied by the number of processors.

Fallacy: Synthetic benchmarks predict performance.

The best known examples of such benchmarks are Whetstone and Dhrystone. These are not real programs and, as such, may not reflect program behavior for factors not measured. Compiler and hardware optimizations can artificially inflate performance of these benchmarks but not of real programs. The other side of the coin is that because these benchmarks are not natural programs, they don't reward optimizations of behavior that occur in real programs. Here are some examples:

- Optimizing compilers can discard 25% of the Dhrystone code; examples include loops that are only executed once, making the loop overhead instructions unnecessary. To address these problems the authors of the benchmark "require" both optimized and unoptimized code to be reported. In addition, they "forbid" the practice of inline-procedure expansion optimization. (Dhrystone's simple procedure structure allows elimination of all procedure calls at almost no increase in code size; see Figure 2.5 on page 47.)

- All Whetstone floating-point loops make optimizations via vectorization essentially useless. (The program was written before computers with vector instructions were popular. See Chapter 7.)

- Dhrystone has a long history of optimizations that skew its performance. The most recent comes from a C compiler that appears to include optimizations just for Dhrystone (Figure 2.5). If the proper option flag is set at compile time, the compiler turns the portion of the C version of this benchmark that copies a variable length string of bytes (terminated by an end-of-string symbol) into a loop that transfers a fixed number of words assuming the source and destination of the string is word-aligned in memory. Although it is estimated that between 99.70% to 99.98% of typical string copies could **not** use this optimization, this single change can make a 20% to 30% improvement in overall performance— if Dhrystone is your measure.

- Compilers can optimize a key piece of the Whetstone loop by noting the relationship between square root and exponential, even though this is very unlikely to occur in real programs. For example, one key loop contains the following FORTRAN code (see Figure 2.4 on page 46):

$$X \ = \ \mathrm{SQRT(} \ \mathrm{EXP(ALOG(X)/T1)} \ )$$

- It could be compiled as if it were

$$X \ = \ \mathrm{EXP(} \ \mathrm{ALOG(X)/(2{*}T1)} \ )$$

- since

$$\mathrm{SQRT(EXP(X))} \ = \ \sqrt[2]{e^x} = \ e^{x/2} \ = \ \mathrm{EXP(X/2)}$$

It would be surprising if such optimizations were ever invoked except in this synthetic benchmark. (Yet one reviewer of this book found several compilers that performed this optimization!) This single change converts all calls to the square root function in Whetstone into multiplies by 2, surely improving performance— if Whetstone is your measure.

Fallacy: Peak performance tracks observed performance.

One definition of peak performance is performance a machine is "guaranteed not to exceed." The gap between peak performance and observed performance is typically a factor of 10 or more in supercomputers. (See Chapter 7 on vectors for an explanation.) Since the gap is so large, peak performance is not useful in predicting observed performance unless the workload consists of small programs that normally operate close to the peak.

As an example of this fallacy, a small code segment using long vectors ran on the Hitachi S810/20 at 236 MFLOPS and on the Cray X-MP at 115 MFLOPS. Although this suggests the S810 is 105% faster than the X-MP, the X-MP runs a

	Cray X-MP	Hitachi S810/20	Performance
A(i)=B(i)*C(i)+D(i)*E(i) (vector length 1000 done 100,000 times)	2.6 secs	1.3 secs	Hitachi 105% faster
Vectorized FFT (vector lengths 64, 32,...,2)	3.9 secs	7.7 secs	Cray 97% faster

FIGURE 2.24   Measurements of peak performance and actual performance for the Hitachi S810/20 and the Cray X-MP. From Lubeck, Moore, and Mendez [1985, 18-20]. Also see the pitfall in the Fallacies and Pitfalls section of Chapter 7.

Machine	Peak MFLOPS rating	Harmonic mean MFLOPS of the Perfect benchmarks	Percent of peak MFLOPS
Cray X-MP/416	940	14.8	1%
IBM 3090-600S	800	8.3	1%
NEC SX/2	1300	16.6	1%

FIGURE 2.25   Peak performance and harmonic mean of actual performance for the Perfect Benchmarks. These results are for the programs run unmodified. When tuned by hand performance of the three machines moves to 24.4, 11.3, and 18.3 MFLOPS, respectively. This is still 2% or less of peak performance.

program with more typical vector lengths 97% faster than the S810. These data are shown in Figure 2.24.

Another good example comes from a benchmark suite called the Perfect Club (see page 80). Figure 2.25 shows the peak MFLOPS rating, harmonic mean of the MFLOPS achieved for 12 real programs, and the percentage of peak performance for three large computers. They achieve only 1% of peak performance.

While the use of peak performance has been rampant in the supercomputer business, recently this metric spread to microprocessor manufacturers. For example, in 1989 a microprocessor was announced as having the performance of 150 million "operations" per second ("MOPS"). The only way this machine can achieve this performance is for one integer instruction and one floating-point instruction to be executed each clock cycle **and** for the floating-point instruction to perform both a multiply operation and an add. For this peak performance to predict observed performance a real program would have to have 66% of its operations be floating point and no losses for the memory system or pipelining. In contrast to claims, typical measured performance of this microprocessor is under 30 "MOPS."

The authors hope that peak performance can be quarantined to the supercomputer industry and eventually eradicated from that domain; but in any case, approaching supercomputer performance is not an excuse for adopting dubious supercomputer marketing habits.

2.6 | Concluding Remarks

Having a standard of performance reporting in computer science journals as high as that in car magazines would be an improvement in current practice. Hopefully, that will be the case as the industry moves toward basing performance evaluation on real programs. Perhaps arguments about performance will even subside.

Computer designs will always be measured by cost and performance, and finding the best balance will always be the art of computer design. As long as technology continues to rapidly improve, the alternatives will look like the curves in Figure 2.26. Once a designer selects a technology, he can't achieve some performance levels no matter how much he pays and, conversely, no matter how much he cuts performance there is a limit to how low the cost can go. It would be better in either case to change technologies.

As a final remark, the number of machines sold is not always the best measure of cost/performance of computers, nor does cost/performance always predict number sold. Marketing is very important to sales. It is easier, however, to market a machine with better cost/performance. Even businesses with high gross margins need to be sensitive to cost/performance, otherwise the company cannot lower prices when faced with stiff competition. Unless you go into marketing, your job is to improve cost/performance!

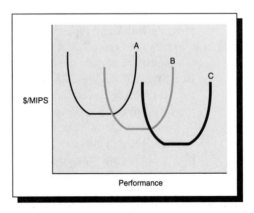

FIGURE 2.26 The cost per MIPS goes up on the y axis, and system performance increases on the x axis. A, B, and C are three technologies, let us say three different semiconductor technologies, to build a processor. Designs in the flat part of the curves can offer varieties of performance at the same cost/performance. If performance goals are too high for a technology it becomes very expensive, and too cheap a design makes the performance too low (cost per MIPS expensive for low MIPS). At either extreme it is better to switch technologies.

2.7 | Historical Perspective and References

The anticipated degree of overlapping, buffering, and queuing in the [IBM 360] Model 85 [first computer with a cache] appeared to largely invalidate conventional performance measures based on instruction mixes and program kernels.

Conti, Gibson, and Pitkowsky [1968]

In the earliest days of computing, designers set performance goals—ENIAC was to be 1000 times faster than the Harvard Mark I, and the IBM Stretch (7030) was to be 100 times faster than the fastest machine in existence. What wasn't clear, though, was how this performance was to be measured. In looking back over the years, it is a consistent theme that each generation of computers obsoletes the performance evaluation techniques of the prior generation.

The original measure of performance was time to perform an individual operation, such as addition. Since most instructions took the same execution time, the timing of one gave insight into the others. As the execution times of instructions in a machine became more diverse, however, the time for one operation was no longer useful for comparisons. To take these differences into account, an *instruction mix* was calculated by measuring the relative frequency of instructions in a computer across many programs. The Gibson mix [1970] was an early popular instruction mix. Multiplying the time for each instruction times its weight in the mix gave the user the *average instruction execution time*. (If measured in clock cycles, average instruction execution time is the same as average CPI.) Since instruction sets were similar, this was a more accurate comparison than add times. From average instruction execution time, then, it was only a small step to MIPS (as we have seen, the one is the inverse of the other). MIPS has the virtue of being easy for the layman to understand, hence its popularity.

As CPUs became more sophisticated and relied on memory hierarchies and pipelining, there was no longer a single execution time per instruction; MIPS could not be calculated from the mix and the manual. The next step was benchmarking using kernels and synthetic programs. Curnow and Wichmann [1976] created the Whetstone synthetic program by measuring scientific programs written in Algol 60. This program was converted to FORTRAN and was widely used to characterize scientific program performance. An effort with similar goals to Whetstone, the Livermore FORTRAN Kernels, was made by McMahon [1986] and researchers at Lawrence Livermore Laboratory in an attempt to establish a benchmark for supercomputers. These kernels, however, consisted of loops from real programs.

The notion of relative MIPS came along as a way to resuscitate the easily understandable MIPS rating. When the VAX-11/780 was ready for announcement in 1977, DEC ran small benchmarks that were also run on an IBM 370/158. IBM marketing referred to the 370/158 as a 1-MIPS computer, and since the programs ran at the same speed, DEC marketing called the VAX-11/780 a 1-MIPS computer. (Note that this rating included the effectiveness of the compilers on both machines at the moment the comparison was made.) The popularity of the VAX-11/780 made it a popular reference machine for relative MIPS, especially since relative MIPS for a 1-MIPS computer is easy to calculate: If a machine was five times faster than the VAX-11/780, for that benchmark its rating would be 5 relative MIPS. The 1-MIPS rating was unquestioned for four years until Joel Emer of DEC measured the VAX-11/780 under a timesharing load. He found that the VAX-11/780 native MIPS rating was 0.5. Subsequent VAXes that run 3 native MIPS for some benchmarks were therefore called 6-MIPS machines because they run 6 times faster than the VAX-11/780.

Although other companies followed this confusing practice, pundits have redefined MIPS as "Meaningless Indication of Processor Speed" or "Meaningless Indoctrination by Pushy Salespersons." At the present time, the most common meaning of MIPS in marketing literature is not native MIPS but "number of times faster than the VAX-11/780" and frequently includes floating-point programs as well. The exception is IBM, which defines MIPS relative to the "processing capacity" of an IBM 370/158, presumably running large system benchmarks (see Henly and McNutt, [1989, 5]). In the late 1980s DEC began using *VAX units of performance* (VUP), meaning ratio to VAX-11/780, so 6 relative MIPS became 6 VUPs.

The 1970s and 1980s marked the growth of the supercomputer industry, which was defined by high performance on floating-point–intensive programs. Average instruction time and MIPS were clearly inappropriate metrics for this industry, and hence the invention of MFLOPS. Unfortunately customers quickly forget the program used for the rating, and marketing groups decided to start quoting peak MFLOPS in the supercomputer performance wars.

A variety of means have been proposed for averaging performance. McMahon [1986] recommends the harmonic mean for averaging MFLOPS. Flemming and Wallace [1986] assert the merits of the geometric mean in general. Smith's reply [1988] to their article gives cogent arguments for arithmetic means of time and harmonic means of rates. (Smith's arguments are the ones followed in "Comparing and Summarizing Performance" under Section 2.2, above.)

As the distinction between architecture and implementation pervaded the computing community (see Chapter 1), the question arose whether the performance of an architecture itself could be evaluated, as opposed to an implementation of the architecture. A study of this question performed at Carnegie-Mellon University is summarized in Fuller and Burr [1977]. Three quantitative measures were invented to scrutinize architectures:

S   Number of bytes for program code

M   Number of bytes transferred between memory and the CPU during program execution for code and data (S measures size of code at compile time, while M is memory traffic during program execution.)

R   Number of bytes transferred between registers in a canonical model of a CPU

Once these measures were taken, a weighting factor was applied to them to determine which architecture was "best." Yet there has been no formal effort to see if these measures really matter—do the implementations of an architecture with superior S, M, and R measures outperform implementations of lesser architectures? The VAX architecture was designed in the height of popularity of the Carnegie-Mellon study, and by those measures it does very well. Architectures created since 1985, however, have poorer measures than the VAX, yet their implementations do well against the VAX implementations. For example, Figure 2.27 compares S, M, and CPU time for the VAXstation 3100, which uses the VAX instruction set, and the DECstation 3100, which doesn't. The DECstation 3100 is 300% to almost 500% faster even though its S measure is 35% to 70% worse and its M measure is 5% to 15% worse. The effort to evaluate architecture independent of implementation was a valiant one, it seems, if not a successful one.

	S (code size in bytes)		M (megabytes code + data transferred)		CPU Time (in seconds)	
	VAX 3100	**DEC 3100**	**VAX 3100**	**DEC 3100**	**VAX 3100**	**DEC 3100**
Gnu C Compiler	409,600	688,128	18	21	291	90
Common TeX	158,720	217,088	67	78	449	95
Spice	223,232	372,736	99	106	352	94

FIGURE 2.27   Code size and CPU time of the VAXstation 3100 and DECstation 3100 for Gnu C Compiler, TeX, and Spice. The programs and machines are described in Figures 2.17 and 2.18. Both machines were announced the same day by the same company and run the same operating system. The difference is in the instruction sets, compilers, clock cycle time, and organization. The *M* measure comes from Figure 3.33 (page 123) for smaller inputs than those in Figure 2.17 (page 67), but the relative performance is unchanged. Code size includes libraries.

A promising development in performance evaluation is the formation of the System Performance Evaluation Cooperative, or SPEC, group in 1988. SPEC contains representatives of many computer companies—the founders being Apollo/Hewlett-Packard, DEC, MIPS, and Sun—who have agreed on a set of real programs and inputs that all will run. It is worth noting that SPEC couldn't have happened before portable operating systems and the popularity of high-level languages. Now compilers, too, are accepted as a proper part of the performance of computer systems and must be measured in any evaluation. (See Exercises 2.8–2.10 on pages 83–84 for more on SPEC benchmarks.)

History teaches us that while the SPEC effort is useful with current computers, it will not be able to meet the needs of the next generation. An effort similar to SPEC, called the Perfect Club, binds together universities and companies interested in parallel computation [Berry et al. 1988]. Rather than being forced to run the existing sequential programs' code, the Perfect Club includes both programs and algorithms, and allows members to write new programs in new languages, which may be needed for the new architectures. Perfect Club members may also suggest new algorithms to solve important problems.

While papers on performance are plentiful, little is available on computer cost. Fuller [1976] wrote the first paper comparing price and performance for the Annual International Symposium on Computer Architecture. This was also the last price/performance paper at this conference. Phister's book [1979] on costs of computers is exhaustive, and Bell, Mudge, and McNamara [1978] describe the computer construction process from DEC's perspective. In contrast, there is a good deal of information on die yield. Strapper [1989] surveys the history of yield modeling, while technical details on the die-yield model used in this chapter are found in Strapper, Armstrong, and Saji [1983].

References

BELL, C. G., J. C. MUDGE, AND J. E. McNAMARA [1978]. *A DEC View of Computer Engineering,* Digital Press, Bedford, Mass.

BERRY, M., D. CHEN, P. KOSS, D. KUCK [1988]. "The Perfect Club benchmarks: Effective performance evaluation of supercomputers," CSRD Report No. 827 (November), Center for Supercomputing Research and Development, University of Illinois at Urbana-Champaign.

CONTI, C. J., D. H. GIBSON, AND S. H. PITKOWSLI [1968]. "Structural aspects of the System/360 Model 85:I general organization," *IBM Systems J.* 7:1, 2–11.

CURNOW, H. J. AND B. A. WICHMANN [1976]. "A synthetic benchmark," *The Computer J.* 19:1.

FLEMMING, P. J. AND J. J. WALLACE [1986]. "How not to lie with statistics: The correct way to summarize benchmarks results," *Comm. ACM* 29:3 (March) 218–221.

FULLER, S. H. [1976]. "Price/performance comparison of C.mmp and the PDP-11," *Proc. Third Annual Symposium on Computer Architecture* (Texas, January 19–21), 197–202.

FULLER, S. H. AND W. E. BURR [1977]. "Measurement and evaluation of alternative computer architectures," *Computer* 10:10 (October) 24–35.

GIBSON, J. C. [1970]. "The Gibson mix," Rep. TR. 00.2043, IBM Systems Development Division, Poughkeepsie, N.Y. (Research done in 1959.)

HENLY, M. AND B. McNUTT [1989]. "DASD I/O characteristics: A comparison of MVS to VM," Tech. Rep. TR 02.1550 (May), IBM, General Products Division, San Jose, Calif.

HOLLINGSWORTH, W., H. SACHS AND A. J. SMITH [1989]. "The Clipper processor: Instruction set architecture and implementation," *Comm. ACM* 32:2 (February), 200–219.

LUBECK, O., J. MOORE, AND R. MENDEZ [1985]. "A benchmark comparison of three supercomputers: Fujitsu VP-200, Hitachi S810/20, and Cray X-MP/2," *Computer* 18:12 (December) 10–24.

McMAHON, F. M. [1986]. "The Livermore FORTRAN kernels: A computer test of numerical performance range," Tech. Rep. UCRL-55745, Lawrence Livermore National Laboratory, Univ. of California, Livermore, Calif. (December).

PHISTER, M., JR. [1979]. *Data Processing Technology and Economics,* 2nd ed., Digital Press and Santa Monica Publishing Company.

SMITH, J. E. [1988]. "Characterizing computer performance with a single number," *Comm. ACM* 31:10 (October) 1202–1206.

SPEC [1989]. "SPEC Benchmark Suite Release 1.0," October 2, 1989.

STRAPPER, C. H. [1989]. "Fact and fiction in yield modelling," Special Issue of the *Microelectronics Journal* entitled *Microelectronics into the Nineties*, Oxford, UK; Elsevier (May).

STRAPPER, C. H., F. H. ARMSTRONG, AND K. SAJI, [1983]. "Integrated circuit yield statistics," *Proc. IEEE* 71:4 (April) 453–470.

WEICKER, R. P. [1984]. "Dhrystone: A synthetic systems programming benchmark," *Comm. ACM* 27:10 (October) 1013–1030.

WICHMANN, B. A. [1973]. *Algol 60 Compilation and Assessment*, Academic Press, New York.

EXERCISES

2.1 [20] <2.2> After graduating, you are asked to become the lead computer designer. Your study of usage of high-level–language constructs suggests that procedure calls are one of the most expensive operations. You have invented a scheme that reduces the loads and stores normally associated with procedure calls and returns. The first thing you do is run some experiments with and without this optimization. Your experiments use the same state-of-the-art optimizing compiler that will be used with either version of computer.

Your experiments reveal the following information:

- The clock cycle time of the unoptimized version is 5% faster.

- 30% of the instructions in the nonoptimized version are loads or stores.

- The optimized version executes 1/3 fewer loads and stores than the nonoptimized version. For all other instructions the dynamic execution counts are unchanged.

- All instructions (including load and store) take one clock cycle.

Which is faster? Justify your decision quantitatively.

2.2 [15/15/10] <2.2> Assume the two programs in Figure 2.6 on page 49 each execute 100,000,000 floating-point operations during execution.

a. [15] Calculate the (native) MFLOPS rating of each program.

b. [15] Calculate the arithmetic, geometric, and harmonic mean (native) MFLOPS for each machine.

c. [10] Which of the three means matches the relative performance of total execution time?

Questions 2.3–2.7 require the following information.

The Whetstone benchmark contains 79,550 floating-point operations, not including the floating-point operations performed in each call to the following functions:

- arctangent, invoked 640 times

- sine, invoked 640 times

- cosine, invoked 1920 times

- square root, invoked 930 times

- exponential, invoked 930 times

- and logarithm, invoked 930 times

The basic operations for a single iteration (not including floating-point operations to perform the above functions) are broken down as follows:

Add	37,530
Subtract	3,520
Multiply	22,900
Divide	11,400
Convert integer to fp	4,200
TOTAL	79,550

The total number of floating-point operations for a single iteration can also be calculated by including the floating-point operations needed to perform the functions arctangent, sine, cosine, square root, exponential, and logarithm:

Add	82,014
Subtract	8,229
Multiply	73,220
Divide	21,399
Convert integer to fp	6,006
Compare	4,710
TOTAL	195,578

Whetstone was run on a Sun 3/75 using the F77 compiler with optimization turned on. The Sun 3/75 is based on a Motorola 68020 running at 16.67 MHz, and it includes a floating-point coprocessor. (Assume the coprocessor does not include arctangent, sine, cosine, square root, exponential, and logarithm as instructions.) The Sun compiler allows the floating-point to be calculated with the coprocessor or using software routines, depending on compiler flags. A single iteration of Whetstone took 1.08 seconds using the coprocessor and 13.6 seconds using software. Assume that the CPI using the coprocessor was measured to be 10 while the CPI using software was measured to be 6.

2.3 [15] <2.2> What is the (native) MIPS rating for both runs?

2.4 [15] <2.2> What is the **total** number of instructions executed for both runs?

2.5 [8] <2.2> On the average, how many integer instructions does it take to perform each floating-point operation in software?

2.6 [18] <2.2> What is the native and normalized MFLOPS for the Sun 3/75 with the floating-point coprocessor running Whetstone? (Assume convert counts as a single floating-point operation and use Figure 2.3 for normalized operations.)

2.7 [20] <2.2> Figure 2.3 on page 43 suggests how many floating-point operations it takes to perform the six functions above (arctangent, sine, and so on). From the data above you can calculate the average number of floating-point operations per function. What is the ratio between the estimates in Figure 2.3 and the floating-point operation measurements for the Sun 3? Assume the coprocessor implements only Add, Subtract, Multiply, Divide, and Convert.

Questions 2.8–2.10 require the information in Figure 2.28.

The SPEC Benchmark Release 1.0 Summary [SPEC 89] lists performance as shown in Figure 2.28.

Program Name	VAX-11/780 Time	DECstation 3100 Time	DECstation 3100 Ratio	Delta Series 8608 Time	Delta Series 8608 Ratio	SPARCstation 1 Time	SPARCstation 1 Ratio
GCC	1482	145	10.2	193	7.7	138.9	10.7
Espresso	2266	194	11.7	197	11.5	254.0	8.9
Spice 2g6	23951	2500	9.6	3350	7.1	2875.5	8.3
DODUC	1863	208	9.0	295	6.3	374.1	5.0
NASA7	20093	1646	12.2	3187	6.3	2308.2	8.7
Li	6206	480	12.9	458	13.6	689.5	9.0
Eqntott	1101	99	11.1	129	8.5	113.5	9.7
Matrix300	4525	749	6.0	520	8.7	409.3	11.1
FPPPP	3038	292	10.4	488	6.2	387.2	7.8
TOMCATV	2649	260	10.2	509	5.2	469.8	5.6
Geometric mean	3867.7	381.4	10.1	496.5	7.8	468.5	8.3

FIGURE 2.28 SPEC performance summary 1.0. The four integer programs are GCC, Espresso, Li, and Eqntott, with the rest relying on floating-point hardware. The SPEC report does not describe the version of the compilers or operating system used for the VAX-11/780. The DECstation 3100 is described in Figure 2.18 on page 68. The Motorola Delta Series 8608 uses a 20-MHz MC88100, 16-KB instruction cache, and 16-KB data cache using two M88200s (see Exercise 8.6 in Chapter 8), the Motorola Sys. V/88 R32V1 operating system, the C88000 1.8.4m14 C compiler, and the Absoft SysV88 2.0a4 Fortran compiler. The SPARCstation 1 uses a 20-MHz MB8909 integer unit and 20-MHz WTL3170 floating-point unit, a 64-KB unified cache, SunOS 4.0.3c operating system and C compiler, and Sun 1.2 Fortran compiler. The size of main memory in these three machines is 16 MB.

2.8 [12/15] <2.2> Compare the relative performance using total execution times for the 10 programs versus using geometric means of ratios of the speed of the VAX-11/780.

a. [12] How do the results differ?

b [15] Compare the geometric mean of the ratios of the four integer programs (GCC, Espresso, Li, and Eqntott) versus the total execution time for these four programs. How do the results differ from each other and from the summaries of all ten programs?

2.9 [15/20/12/10] <2.2> Now let's compare performance using weighted arithmetic means.

a. [15] Calculate the weights for a workload so that running times on the VAX-11/780 will be equal for each of the ten programs (see Figure 2.7 on page 51).

b. [20] Using those weights, calculate the weighted arithmetic means of the execution times of the ten programs.

c. [12] Calculate the ratio of the weighted means of the VAX execution times to the weighted means for the other machines.

d. [10] How do the geometric means of ratios and the ratios of weighted arithmetic means of execution times differ in summarizing relative performance?

2.10 [Discussion] <2.2> What is an interpretation of the geometric means of execution times? What do you think are the advantages and disadvantages of using total execution times versus weighted arithmetic means of execution times using equal running time on the VAX-11/780 versus geometric means of ratios of speed to the VAX-11/780?

Questions 2.11–2.12 require the information in Figure 2.29.

Microprocessor	Size (cm)	Pins	Package	Clock rate	List price	Year available
Cypress CY7C601	0.8×0.7	207	Ceramic PGA	33 MHz	$500	1988
Intel 80486	1.6×1.0	168	Ceramic PGA	33 MHz	$950	1989
Intel 860	1.2×1.2	168	Ceramic PGA	33 MHz	$750	1989
MIPS R3000	0.8×0.9	144	Ceramic PGA	25 MHz	$300	1988
Motorola 88100	0.9×0.9	169	Ceramic PGA	25 MHz	$695	1989

FIGURE 2.29   Characteristics of microprocessors. List prices were quoted as of 7/15/89 at quantity 1000 purchases.

2.11 [15] <2.3> Pick the largest and smallest microprocessors from Figure 2.29, and use the values found in Figure 2.11 (page 62) for yield parameters. How many good chips do you get per wafer?

2.12 [15/10/10/15/15] <2.3> Let's calculate costs and prices of the largest and smallest microprocessors from Figure 2.29. Use the assumptions on manufacturing found in Figure 2.11 (page 62) unless specifically mentioned otherwise.

a. [15] There are wide differences in defect densities between semiconductor manufacturers. What are the costs of untested dies assuming: (1) 2 defects per square cm; and (2) 1 defect per square cm.

b. [10] Assume that testing costs $150 per hour and the smaller chip takes 10 seconds to test and the larger chip takes 15 seconds, what is the cost of testing each die?

c. [10] Making the assumptions on packaging in Section 2.3, what is the cost of packaging and burn-in?

d. [15] What is the final cost?

e. [15] Given the list price and the calculated cost from the questions above, calculate the gross margin. Assume the direct cost is 40% and average selling discount is 33%. What percentage of the average selling price is the gross margin for both chips?

2.13–2.14 A few companies claim they are doing so well that the defect density is vanishing as the reason for die failures, making wafer yield responsible for the vast majority. For example, Gordon Moore of Intel said in a talk at MIT in 1989 that defect density is improving to the point that some companies have been quoted as producing a 100% yield over the whole run. In fact, he has a 100% yield wafer on his desk.

2.13 [20] <2.3> To understand the impact of such claims, list the costs of the largest and smallest dies in Figure 2.29 for defect densities per square centimeter of 3, 2, 1, and 0. For the other parameters use the values found in Figure 2.11 (page 62). Ignore the costs of testing time, packaging, and final test.

2.14 [Discussion] <2.3> If the statement above becomes true for most semiconductor manufacturers, how would that change the options for the computer designer?

2.15 [10/15] <2.3,2.4> Figure 2.18 (page 68) shows the list price as tested of the DECstation 3100 workstation. Start with the costs of the "higher cost" model in Figure 2.13 on page 63, (assuming a color), workstation but change the cost of DRAM to $100/MB for the full 16 MB of the 3100.

a. [10] Using the average discount and overhead percentages of Model B in Figure 2.16 on page 66, what is the gross margin on the DECstation 3100?

b. [15] Suppose you replace the R2000 CPU of the DECstation 3100 with the R3000, and that this change makes the machine 50% faster. Use the costs in Figure 2.29 for the R3000, and assume the R2000 costs a third as much. Since the R3000 does not require much more power, assume that both the power supply and the cooling of the DECstation 3100 are satisfactory for the upgrade. What is the cost/performance of a diskless black-and-white (mono) workstation with an R2000 versus one with an R3000? Using the business model from the answer to part a, how much must the price of the R3000-based machine be increased?

2.16 [30] <2.2,2.4> Pick two computers and run the Dhrystone benchmark and the Gnu C Compiler. Try running the programs using no optimization and maximum optimization. (Note: gcc is a benchmark, so use the appropriate C compiler to compile both programs. Don't try to compile gcc and use it as your compiler!) Then calculate the following performance ratios:

1. Unoptimized Dhrystone on machine A versus unoptimized Dhrystone on machine B.

2. Unoptimized GCC on A versus unoptimized GCC on B.

3. Optimized Dhrystone on A versus optimized Dhrystone on B.

4. Optimized GCC on A versus optimized GCC on B.

5. Unoptimized Dhrystone versus optimized Dhrystone on machine A.

6. Unoptimized GCC versus optimized GCC on A.

7. Unoptimized Dhrystone versus optimized Dhrystone on B.

8. Unoptimized GCC versus optimized GCC on B.

The benchmarking question is how well the benchmark predicts performance of real programs.

If benchmarks do predict performance, then the following equations should be true about the ratios:

(1) = (2) and (3) = (4)

If compiler optimizations work equally as well on real programs as on benchmarks, then

(5) = (6) and (7) = (8)

Are these equations true? If not, try to find the explanation. Is it the machines, the compiler optimizations, or the programs that explain the answer?

2.17 [30] <2.2,2.4> Perform the same experiment as in question 2.16, except replace Dhrystone by Whetstone and replace GCC by Spice.

2.18 [Discussion] <2.2> What are the pros and cons of synthetic benchmarks? Find quantitative evidence—such as data supplied by answering questions 2.16 and 2.17—as well as listing the qualitative advantages and disadvantages.

2.19 [30] <2.2,2.4> Devise a program in C or Pascal that gets the peak MIPS rating for a computer. Run it on two machines to calculate the peak MIPS. Now run GCC and TeX on both machines. How well do peak MIPS predict performance of GCC and TeX?

2.20 [30] <2.2,2.4> Devise a program in C or FORTRAN that gets the peak MFLOPS rating for a computer. Run it on two machines to calculate the peak MFLOPS. Now run Spice on both machines. How well do peak MFLOPS predict performance of Spice?

2.21 [Discussion] <2.3> Use the cost information in Section 2.3 as a basis for the merits of timesharing a large computer versus a network of workstations. (To determine the potential value of workstations versus timesharing, see Section 9.2 in Chapter 9 on user productivity.)

A n   *Add the number in storage location n into the accumulator*

E n   *If the number in the accumulator is greater than or equal to
zero execute next the order which stands in storage location;
otherwise proceed serially.*

Z   *Stop the machine and ring the warning bell.*

Selection from the list of 18 machine instructions for the EDSAC
from Wilkes and Renwick [1949]

3 | Instruction Set Examples and Measurements

3.1 | Introduction

Between 1970 and 1985 many thought the primary job of the computer architect was to design of instruction sets. As a result, textbooks of that era emphasize instruction set design, much as computer architecture textbooks of the 1950s and 1960s emphasized computer arithmetic. The educated architect was expected to have strong opinions about the strengths and especially the weaknesses of the popular machines. The importance of binary compatibility in quashing innovations in instruction set design was unappreciated by many researchers and textbook writers, giving the impression that many architects would get a chance to design an instruction set.

The definition of computer architecture today has been expanded to include design and evaluation of the full computer system–not just the definition of the instruction set–and hence there are plenty of topics for the architect to study. (As you might have guessed the first time you lifted this book.) The widespread agreement on instruction set design since 1985 has reduced interest in instruction set design.

Nonetheless, the instruction set is the vocabulary that software must use to command the hardware, and hence architects must be familiar with the popular vocabularies. In this chapter we present the two popular vocabularies of our times: the Intel 80x86 and everyone else. This later category is dominated by instruction sets invented since 1985, which are so similar that we can use a generic example called DLX to represent the whole class. To introduce the general ideas of instruction set design, we picked an older architecture that includes nearly every feature ever found in a computer: VAX. It has a sophisticated elegance that allows these features to be defined concisely, and we build on this background to introduce the other two.

After introducing the three instruction sets, we review compiler issues in instruction set design and then present a raft of measurements. These measurements depend on the programs measured and on the compilers used in making the measurements. The results should not be interpreted as absolute, and you might see different data if you did the measurement with a different compiler or a different set of programs. The authors believe that the measurements shown in this chapters are reasonably indicative of a class of typical applications. All the measurements shown are *dynamic*—that is, the frequency of a measured event is weighed by the number of times that event occurs during execution of the measured program.

Now, we begin by exploring how instruction set architectures can be classified and analyzed.

3.2 | Classifying Instruction Set Architectures

The type of internal storage in the CPU is the most basic differentiation, so we will focus on the alternatives for this portion of the architecture in this section. The major choices are a stack, an accumulator, or a set of registers. Operands may be named explicitly or implicitly: the operands in a *stack architecture* are implicitly on the top of the stack; in an *accumulator architecture* one operand is implicitly the accumulator; *General-purpose register architectures* have only explicit operands—either registers or memory locations. Depending on the architecture, the explicit operands to an operation may be accessed directly from memory or they may need to be first loaded into temporary storage, depending on the class of instruction and choice of specific instruction. Figure 3.1 shows how the code sequence C = A + B would typically appear on these three classes of instruction sets. As Figure 3.1 shows, there are really two classes of register machines. One can access memory as part of any instruction, called *register-memory* architecture, and one can access memory only with load and store instructions, called *load-store* architecture.

While most early machines used stack or accumulator-style architectures, every machine designed in the past ten years uses a general-purpose register architecture. The major reasons for the emergence of general-purpose register machines are twofold. First, registers—like other forms of storage internal to the CPU—are faster than memory. Second, registers are easier for a compiler to use and can be used more effectively than other forms of internal storage. For example, on a register machine the expression (A∗B) – (C∗D) – (E∗F) may be evaluated by doing the multiplications in any order, which may be more efficient due to the location of the operands or because of pipelining concerns (see Chapter 4). But on a stack machine the expression must be evaluated left to right, unless special operations or swaps of stack positions are done.

More importantly, registers can be used to hold variables. When variables are allocated to registers, the memory traffic is reduced, the program is sped up (since registers are faster than memory), and the code density improves (since a register can be named with fewer bits than can a memory location). Compiler writers would prefer that all registers be equivalent and unreserved. Many machines compromise this desire—especially older machines with many dedicated registers—effectively decreasing the number of general-purpose registers. If the number of truly general-purpose registers is too small, trying to allocate variables to registers will not be profitable. Instead, the compiler will reserve all the uncommitted registers for use in expression evaluation.

How many registers are sufficient? The answer of course depends on how they are used by the compiler. Most compilers reserve some registers for expression evaluation, use some for parameter passing, and allow the remainder to be allocated to hold variables.

The VAX and DLX are general purpose register machines: VAX is a register-memory machines and DLX is a load-store machine. The Intel 80x86 has the unusual distinction of covering all three models: the original 8086 announced in 1978 was an extended accumulator machine; a floating point stack was added in a 1980 coprocessor; and general purpose registers were added in 1985 as part of the 80386. We'll start our instruction set tour with the earliest machine.

Stack	Accumulator	Register (register-memory)	Register (load-store)
Push A	Load A	Load R1,A	Load R1,A
Push B	Add B	Add R1,B	Load R2,A
Add	Store C	Store C, R1	Add R3,R1,R2
Pop C			Store C, R3

FIGURE 3.1 The code sequence for C = A + B for four instruction sets. It is assumed that A, B, and C all belong in memory and that the values of A and B cannot be destroyed.

3.3 | The VAX Architecture

The DEC VAX was introduced with its first model, the VAX-11/780, in 1977. The VAX was designed to be a 32-bit extension of an earlier 16-bit architecture, called the PDP-11. Among the goals of the VAX, two stand out as both important and having had a substantial impact on the VAX architecture.

First, the designers wanted to make the existing PDP-11 customer base feel comfortable with the VAX architecture and view it as an extension of the PDP-11. This motivated the name VAX-11/780, the use of a very similar assembly language syntax, inclusion of the PDP-11 data types, and emulation support for the PDP-11. (Its interesting that the Alpha, the successor to the VAX, includes emulation support but none of the cosmetic concessions to its predecessor.) Second, the designers wanted to ease the task of writing compilers and operating systems. This translated to a set of goals that included defining interfaces between languages, the hardware, and OS; and supporting a highly orthogonal architecture.

In terms of addressing modes and operations supported in instructions, the other instruction sets discussed in this chapter are largely subsets of the VAX. The reader should be aware that there are entire books devoted to the VAX architecture as well as a number of papers reporting instruction set measurements. Our summary of the VAX instruction set—like the other instruction set summaries in this chapter—focuses on the general principles of the architecture and on the portions of the architecture most relevant to understanding the measurements examined here. A list of the full VAX instruction set is included in Appendix C.

The VAX is a general-purpose register machine with a large orthogonal instruction set. Figure 3.2 shows the registers of the VAX. The VAX provides 16 general-purpose registers, but four registers are effectively claimed by the instruction set architecture. Sixteen registers is the total register state for integer and floating point data, including pointers to the arguments, stack frame, and top of stack, and even the PC. This dedicated use means the VAX has just 12 32-bit registers that can be used for integer and floating point data. For example, R14 is the stack pointer and R15 is the PC (program counter). Hence, R15 cannot be used as a general-purpose register, and using R14 is very difficult because it interferes with instructions that manipulate the stack frame.

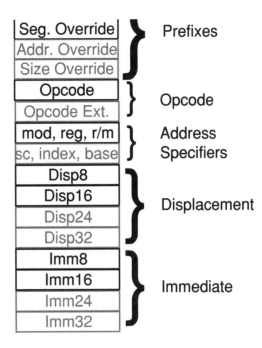

FIGURE 3.2 **shows the 16, 32-bit registers of the VAX, with four dedicated to special purposes so that they cannot be used as general purpose registers.** Unlike the other machines in this chapter, the floating point data uses the same registers as the integer data. Data longer than 32 bits is kept in adjacent registers: for example, 64-bit data could be placed in R3 and R4 and 128-bit data could be placed in R8, R9, R10, and R11.

Figure 3.3 shows the data types supported. The VAX uses the name "word" to refer to 16-bit quantities, while in this text we use the convention that a *word* is 32 bits. Be careful when reading the VAX instruction mnemonics, as they often refer to the names of the VAX data types. Figure 3.3 shows the conversion between the data type names used in this text and the VAX names. In addition to the data types in Figure 3.3, the VAX provides support for fixed- and variable-length bit strings, up to 32 bits in length.

Bits	Data type	Our name	DEC's name
8	Integer	Byte	Byte
16	Integer	Halfword	Word
32	Integer	Word	Long word
32	Floating point	Single precision	F_floating
64	Integer	Doubleword	Quad word
64	Floating point	Double precision	D_floating or G_floating
128	Integer	Quadword	Octaword
128	Floating point	Huge	H_floating
8n	Character string	Character	Character
4n	Binary-coded decimal	Packed	Packed
8n	Numeric string	Unpacked	Numeric strings: Trailing and leading separate

FIGURE 3.3   VAX data types, their lengths, and names. The first letter of the DEC type (B, W, L, F, Q, D, G, O, H, C, P, T, S) is often used to complete an opcode name. As examples, the move opcodes include MOVB, MOVW, MOVL, MOVF, MOVQ, MOVD, MOVG, MOVO, MOVH, MOVC3, MOVP. Each move instruction transfers an operand of the data type indicated by the letter following MOV. (There is no difference between moves of character and numeric strings, so only move character operations are needed.) The length fields that appear as Xn indicate that the length may be any multiple of X in bits. The packed data type is special in that the length for operations on this type is always given in digits, each of which is four bits. The packed objects are still allocated and addressed in units of bytes. For any string data type the starting address is the low-order address of the string.

How is a memory address interpreted? That is, what object is accessed as a function of the address and the length? All the machines discussed in this chapter are byte addressed and provide access for bytes (8 bits), halfwords (16 bits), and words (32 bits). Most of the machines also provide access for doublewords (64 bits).

There are two different conventions for ordering the bytes within a word. *Little Endian* byte order puts the byte whose address is "x...x00" at the least significant position in the word (the little end). *Big Endian* byte order puts the byte whose address is "x...x00" at the most significant position in the word (the big end). In Big Endian addressing, the address of a datum is the address of the most significant byte; while in Little Endian, the address of a datum is the least significant byte. The VAX is a little Endian machine.

When operating within one machine, the byte order is often unnoticeable—only programs that access the same locations as both words and bytes can notice the difference. However, byte order is a problem when exchanging data among machines with different orderings. (The byte orders used by a number of different machines are listed inside the front cover.)

VAX Addressing Modes

We now look at addressing modes—how architectures specify the address of an object they will access. In general purpose register machines, an addressing mode can specify a constant, a register, or a location in memory. When a memory location is used, the actual memory address specified by the addressing mode is called the *effective address*. The VAX includes nearly every addressing mode ever found in a computer, and Figure 3.4 shows the modes. Immediates or literals are usually considered a memory addressing mode (even though the value they access is in the instruction stream), while registers are often separated. We have kept addressing modes that depend on the program counter, called *PC-relative addressing*, separate. PC-relative addressing is used primarily for specifying code addresses in control transfer instructions.

Figure 3.4 shows the most common names for the addressing modes, though the names differ among architectures. In this figure and throughout the book, we will use an extension of the C programming language as a hardware description notation. In this figure, only two non-C features are used. First, the left arrow (←) is used for assignment. Second, the array M is used as the name for memory. Thus, M[R1] refers to the contents of the memory location whose address is given by the contents of R1. Later, we will introduce extensions for accessing and transferring data smaller than a word.

Addressing modes have the ability to significantly reduce instruction counts; they also add to the complexity of building a machine. Thus, the usage of various addressing modes is quite important in helping the architect choose what to include.

Figure 3.5 shows the results of measuring addressing mode usage patterns on the VAX, which supports all the modes shown in Figure 3.4. These major addressing modes account for all but a few percent (0% to 3%) of the memory-accesses. First, we break the references into three broad classes: register, immediate (including short literal), and memory addressing modes. In all three programs, more than half the operand references are to registers.

Addressing mode	Example instruction	Meaning	When used
Register	Add R4,R3	R4←R4+R3	When a value is in a register.
Immediate or literal	Add R4,#3	R4←R4+3	For constants. In the VAX, literal and immediate are two different addressing modes.
Displacement or based	Add R4,100(R1)	R4←R4+M[100+R1]	Accessing local variables.
Register deferred or indirect	Add R4,(R1)	R4←R4+M[R1]	Accessing using a pointer or a computed address.
Indexed	Add R3,(R1 + R2)	R3←R3+M[R1+R2]	Sometimes useful in array addressing— R1=base of array; R2=index amount.
Direct or absolute	Add R1,(1001)	R1←R1+M[1001]	Sometimes useful for accessing static data; address constant may need to be large.
Memory indirect or memory deferred	Add R1,@(R3)	R1←R1+M[M[R3]]	If R3 is the address of a pointer p, then mode yields $*p$.
Auto-increment	Add R1,(R2)+	R1←R1+M[R2] R2←R2+d	Useful for stepping through arrays within a loop. R2 points to start of array; each reference increments R2 by size of an element, d.
Auto-decrement	Add R1,-(R2)	R2←R2-d R1←R1+M[R2]	Same use as autoincrement. Autoincrement/decrement can also be used to implement a stack as push and pop.
Scaled or indexed	Add R1,100(R2)[R3]	R1← R1+M[100+R2+R3*d]	Used to index arrays. May be applied to any base addressing mode in some machines.

FIGURE 3.4 Selection of addressing modes with examples, meaning, and usage. The extensions to C used in the hardware descriptions are defined above. In autoincrement/decrement and scaled or index addressing modes, the variable d designates the size of the data item being accessed (i.e., whether the instruction is accessing 1, 2, 4, or 8 bytes); this means that these addressing modes are only useful when the elements being accessed are adjacent in memory. In our measurements, we use the first name shown for each mode. A few machines, such as the VAX, encode some of these addressing modes as PC-relative.

About one-third of the operands on the VAX are memory references. How are those memory locations specified? The VAX memory addressing modes fall into three separate classes: PC-based addressing, scaled addressing, and the other addressing modes (sometimes called the general addressing modes). The primary use of PC-based addressing is to specify branch targets, rather than data operands; thus, we do not include this addressing mode here. Scaled mode is counted as a separate addressing mode, and the based mode on which it is built is counted as well. Figure 3.6 shows the use of addressing modes in the three benchmark programs. Not surprisingly, displacement mode dominates. Taken together, displacement and register deferred, which is essentially a special case of displacement with a zero constant value, constitute from 70% to 96% of the dynamically occurring addressing modes.

As these figures show, immediate and displacement addressing dominate addressing mode usage. Let's look at some properties of these two heavily used modes.

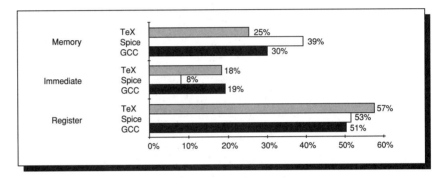

FIGURE 3.5 Breakdown of basic operand types for the three benchmarks on the VAX. The frequencies are very similar across programs, except for the low usage of immediates by Spice and its correspondingly higher use of memory operands. This probably arises because few floating-point constants are stored as immediates, but are instead accessed from memory. An operand is counted by the number of times it appears in an instruction, rather than by the number of references. Thus, the instruction ADDL2 R1,45(R2) counts as one memory reference and one register reference. The memory address modes in Figure 3.6 are counted in the same fashion. Wiecek [1982] reports that about 90% of the operand accesses are either a read or a write, and only about 10% of the accesses both read and write the same operand (such as R1 in the ADDL2).

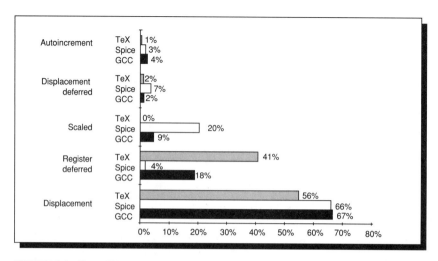

FIGURE 3.6   Use of VAX memory addressing modes, which account for about 31% of the operand references, in the three programs. Spice again stands out because of the low frequency of register deferred. In Spice, non-zero displacement values occur much more frequently. The use of arrays rather than pointers probably influences this. Likewise, Spice uses the scaled mode to access array elements. The displacement deferred mode is used to access actual parameters in a FORTRAN subroutine. Remember that PC-based addressing is not included here—use of PC-based addressing can be measured by branch frequency.

Displacement or Based Addressing Mode

The major question that arises for a displacement-style addressing mode is that of the range of displacements used. Based on the use of various displacement sizes, a decision of what sizes to support can be made. Choosing the displacement field sizes is important because they directly affect the instruction length. Measurements taken on the data access on a load/store architecture using our three benchmark programs are shown in Figure 3.7. We will look at branch offsets in the next subsection—data accessing patterns and branches are so different, little is gained by combining them.

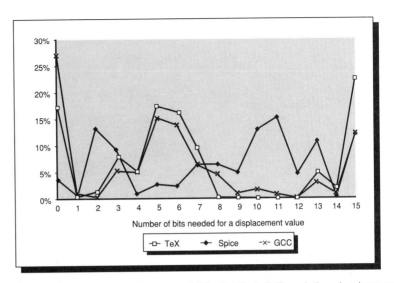

FIGURE 3.7 Displacement values are widely distributed. Though there is a large number of small values, there is also a fair number of large values. The wide distribution of displacement values is due to multiple storage areas for variables and different displacements used to access them. The different storage areas and their access patterns are discussed further in Section 3.7. The chart shows only the magnitude of the displacement and not the sign, which is heavily affected by the storage layout. The entry corresponding to 0 on the x axis shows the percentage of displacements of value 0. The vast majority of the displacements are positive, but a majority of the largest displacements (14+ bits) are negative. Again, this is due to the overall addressing scheme used by the compiler and might change with a different compilation scheme. Since this data was collected on a machine with 16-bit displacements, it cannot tell us anything about accesses that might want to use a longer displacement. Such accesses are broken into two separate instructions—the first of which loads the upper 16 bits of a base register. By counting the frequency of these "load immediate" instructions, which have limited use for other purposes, we can bound the number of accesses with displacements potentially larger than 16 bits. Such an analysis indicates GCC, Spice, and TeX may actually require a displacement longer than 16 bits for up to 5%, 13%, and 27% of the memory references, respectively. Furthermore, if the displacement is larger than 15 bits, it is likely to be quite a bit larger since most constants being loaded are large. To evaluate the choice of displacement length, we might also want to examine a cumulative distribution, as shown in Exercise 3.1 (see Figure 3.44).

Immediate or Literal Addressing Mode

Immediates can be used in arithmetic operations, in comparisons (primarily for branches), and in moves in which a constant is wanted in a register. The last case occurs for constants written in the code, which tend to be small, and for address constants, which can be large. For the use of immediates it is important to know whether they need to be supported for all operations or for only a subset. The chart in Figure 3.8 shows the frequency of immediates for the general classes of operations in an instruction set.

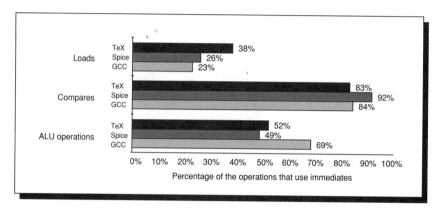

FIGURE 3.8   We see that for ALU operations about half the operations have an immediate operand, while for compares more than 85% of the occurrences use an immediate operand. (For ALU operations, shifts by a constant amount are included as operations with immediate operands.) For loads, the load immediate instructions load 16 bits into either half of a 32-bit register. These load immediates are not loads in a strict sense because they do not reference memory. In some cases, a pair of load immediates may be used to load a 32-bit constant, but this is rare. The compares include comparisons against zero that are done in conditional branches based on this comparison. These measurements were taken on a MIPS R2000 architecture with full compiler optimization. The compiler attempts to use simple compares against zero for branches whenever possible because these branches are efficiently supported in the architecture.

Another important instruction set measurement is the range of values for immediates. Like displacement values, the sizes of immediate values affect instruction lengths. As Figure 3.9 shows, immediate values that are small are most heavily used. However, large immediates are sometimes used, most likely in addressing calculations. The data in Figure 3.9 was taken on a VAX, which provides many instructions that have zero as an implicit operand. These include instructions to compare against zero and to store zero into a word. Because of the use of these instructions, the measurements show relatively infrequent use of zero.

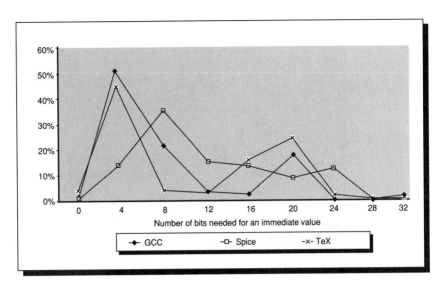

FIGURE 3.9   The distribution of immediate values is shown. The x axis shows the number of bits needed to represent the magnitude of an immediate value—0 means the immediate field value was 0. The vast majority of the immediate values are positive: Overall, less than 6% of the immediates are negative. These measurements were taken on a VAX, which supports a full range of immediates and sizes as operands to any instruction. The measured programs are the standard set—GCC, Spice, and TeX.

Register is an addressing mode no different from any other in the VAX. Thus, a 3-operand VAX instruction may include from zero to three operand memory references, each of which may be any of the memory addressing modes. Since the memory indirect modes require an additional memory access, up to 6 memory accesses may be required for a 3-operand instruction. When the addressing modes are used with R15 (the PC), only a few are defined, and their meaning is special. The defined addressing modes with R15 are as follows:

- *Immediate*—an immediate value is in the instruction stream; this mode is encoded as autoincrement on PC.

- *Absolute*—a 32-bit absolute address is in the instruction stream; this mode is encoded as autoincrement deferred with PC as the register.

- *Byte/word/long displacement*—the same as the general mode, but the base is the PC, giving PC-relative addressing.

- *Byte/word/long displacement deferred*—the same as the general mode, but the base is the PC, giving addressing that is indirect through a memory location that is PC-relative.

Encoding of VAX Addressing Modes

How the addressing modes of operands are encoded depends on the range of addressing modes and the degree of independence between opcodes and modes. For a small number of addressing modes or opcode/addressing mode combinations, the addressing mode can be encoded in the opcode. For a large number of combinations, such as the VAX, typically a separate *address specifier* is needed for each operand. The address specifier tells what addressing mode the operand is using.

When encoding the instructions, the number of registers and the number of addressing modes both have a significant impact on the size of instructions. This is because the addressing mode field and the register field may appear many times in a single instruction. In fact, for most instructions many more bits are consumed encoding addressing modes and register fields than in specifying the opcode. The architect must balance several competing forces when encoding the instruction set:

1.   The desire to have as many registers and addressing modes as possible.

2.   The impact of the size of the register and addressing mode fields on the average instruction size and hence on the average program size.

3.   A desire to have instructions encode into lengths that will be easy to handle in the implementation. As a minimum, the architect wants instructions to be in multiples of bytes, rather than an arbitrary length. Many architects have chosen to use a fixed-length instruction to gain implementation benefits while sacrificing average code size.

Since the addressing modes and register fields make up such a large percentage of the instruction bits, their encoding will significantly affect how easy it is for an implementation to decode the instructions. The importance of having easily decoded instructions is discussed in Chapter 4.

A VAX instruction consists of an opcode followed by zero or more operand specifiers. The opcode is almost always a single byte that specifies the operation, the data type, and the operand count. Almost all operations are fully orthogonal with respect to addressing modes—any combination of addressing modes works with nearly every opcode, and many operations are supported for all possible data types.

Operand specifiers may vary in length from one byte to many, depending on the information to be conveyed. The first byte of each operand specifier consists of two 4-bit fields: the type of address specifier and a register that is part of the addressing mode. If the operand specifier requires additional bytes to specify a displacement, additional registers, or an immediate value, it is extended in 1-byte increments. The name, assembler syntax, and number of bytes for each operand specifier are shown in Figure 3.3.9. The total instruction length and format are easy to state: Simply add up the sizes of the operand specifiers and include one byte (or rarely two) for the opcode.

Example

How long is the following instruction?

```
ADDL3 R1,737(R2),#456
```

Answer

The opcode length is 1 byte, as is the first operand specifier (R1). The second operand specifier has two parts: the first part is a byte that specifies the addressing mode and base register; the second part is the 2-byte long displacement. The third operand specifier also has two parts: the first byte specifies immediate mode, and the second part contains the immediate. Because the data type is long (ADDL3), the immediate value takes 4 bytes.

Thus, the total length of the instruction is 1 + 1 + (1+2) + (1+4) = 10 bytes.

The size of a VAX instruction is almost always one byte for the opcode plus the number of bytes in the addressing modes. From these data the average size of an instruction can be estimated. Architects often do this type of estimating when they do not have exact measurements available. This is particularly true when data collection is expensive. Collecting the VAX data in this chapter, for example, took from one to several days of running time for each program.

Example

The average VAX instruction has 1.8 operands. Assume that the percentage of memory operands is 31%, immediates is 15%, and registers is 54%. Use these facts and the data on displacement sizes in Figure 3.9 to estimate the average size of a VAX instruction. Such an estimate is useful for determining memory bandwidth per instruction, a critical design parameter.

Answer

From the above data we know that literal and register modes, which each take 1 byte, dominate the mix. The most heavily used addressing mode, displacement mode, can vary from 2 bytes to 5 bytes—the register byte plus 1 or more offset bytes. Based on the length information in Figure 3.9 we guess that the average displacement is 1.5 bytes, for a total size of 2.5 bytes for the addressing mode. For this example, we assume that literal, register, and displacement modes make up all the accesses.

This means there is 1 byte for the opcode, 1 byte for register or literal mode, and about 2.5 bytes for displacement mode. Using 1.8 operands per instruction and the average frequencies of accesses, we obtain $1 + 1.8 * (0.54 + 0.15 + 0.31 * 2.5)$ or 3.64 bytes.

Wiecek [1982] measured 3.8 bytes per instruction. Direct measurements of three programs showed the average sizes to be 3.6, 4.9, and 4.2 for GCC, Spice, and TeX, respectively.

Addressing mode	Syntax	Length in bytes
Literal	#value	1 (6-bit signed value)
Immediate	#value	1 + length of the immediate
Register	Rn	1
Register deferred	(Rn)	1
Byte/word/long displacement	Displacement (Rn)	1 + length of the displacement
Byte/word/long displacement deferred	@displacement (Rn)	1 + length of the displacement
Scaled (Indexed)	Base mode [Rx]	1 + length of base addressing mode
Autoincrement	(Rn)+	1
Autodecrement	– (Rn)	1
Autoincrement deferred	@(Rn)+	1

FIGURE 3.10 Length of the VAX operand specifiers. The length of each addressing mode is 1 byte plus the length of any displacement or immediate field that is in the mode. Literal mode uses a special 2-bit tag and the remaining 6 bits encode the constant value. The data in Figure 3.9 shows the heavy use of small constants; the same observation motivated this optimization. The length of an immediate is dictated by the data type indicated in the opcode, not the value of the immediate.

VAX Instructions for Control Flow

We can distinguish four different types of control-flow change:

1. Conditional branches

2. Jumps

3. Procedure calls

4. Procedure returns

We want to know the relative frequency of these events, as each event is different, may use different instructions, and may have different behavior. The frequencies of these control-flow instructions for a load/store machine running our benchmarks is shown in Figure 3.18.

The destination address of a branch must always be specified. This destination is specified explicitly in the instruction in the vast majority of cases; procedure return is the major exception, since the target of return is not known at compile time. The most common way to specify the destination is to supply a displacement that is added to the *program counter*, or PC. Branches of this sort are called *PC-relative* branches. PC-relative branches are advantageous because the branch target is often near the current instruction, and specifying the position relative to the current PC requires fewer bits. Using PC-relative addressing also permits the code to run independent of where it is loaded. This property, called *position-inde-pendence*, can eliminate some work when the program is linked and is also useful in programs linked during execution. The VAX uses PC-relative branches.

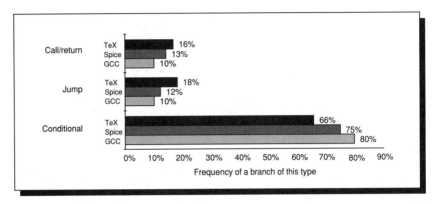

FIGURE 3.11 Breakdown of branches into three classes. Each branch is counted in one of three bars. Conditional branches clearly dominate. On average 90% of the jumps are PC-relative.

To implement returns and indirect branches in which the target is not known at compile time, a method other than PC-relative addressing is required. Here, there must be a way to specify the target dynamically, so that it can change at run-time. This may be as simple as naming a register that contains the target address. Alternatively, the branch may permit any addressing mode to be used to supply the target address, as with the VAX.

Program	Percentage of backward branches	Percentage taken branches	Percentage of all control instructions that actually branch
GCC	26%	54%	63%
Spice	31%	51%	63%
TeX	17%	54%	70%
Average	25%	53%	65%

FIGURE 3.12 Branch direction, branch-taken frequency, and frequency that the PC is changed. The first column shows what percentage of all branches (both taken and untaken) are backward-going. The second column shows what percentage of all branches (remember that a branch is always conditional) are taken. The final column shows what percentage of all control-flow instructions actually cause a non-sequential transfer in the flow.

We will say that a branch is *taken* if the condition tested by the branch is true and the next instruction to be executed is the target of the branch. All jumps, therefore, are taken. Figure 3.20 shows the branch-direction distribution, the frequency of taken (conditional) branches, and the percentage of control-flow instructions that change the PC. Most backward-going branches are loop branches, and typically loop branches are taken with about 90% probability. Many programs have a higher percentage of loop branches, thus boosting the frequency of taken branches over 60%. Overall, branch behavior is application- dependent and sometimes compiler-dependent. Compiler dependencies arise because of changes to the control flow made by optimizing compilers to improve the execution time of loops.

Example

Assuming that 90% of the backward-going branches are taken, find the probability that a forward-going branch is taken using the averaged data in Figure 3.12.

Answer

The average frequency of taken branches is the sum of the backward-taken and forward-taken times their respective frequencies:

$$\% \text{ taken branches} = (\% \text{ taken backward} * \% \text{ backward}) +$$
$$(\% \text{ taken forward} * \% \text{ forward})$$

$$53\% = (90\% * 25\%) + (\% \text{ taken forward} * 75\%)$$

$$\% \text{ taken forward} = \frac{53\% - 22.5\%}{75\%}$$

$$\% \text{ taken forward} = 40.7\%$$

It is not unusual to see the majority of forward branches be untaken. The behavior of forward-going branches often varies among programs.

The VAX branch instructions are related to the arithmetic instructions because the branch instructions rely on condition codes. Condition codes are set as a side-effect of an operation, and they indicate whether the result is positive, negative, zero, or if an overflow occurred. Most instructions set the VAX condition codes according to their result; instructions without results, such as branches, do not. The VAX condition codes are N (Negative), Z (Zero), V (oVerflow), and C (Carry). There is also a compare instruction just to set the condition codes for a subsequent branch.

The VAX branch instructions include all conditions. Popular branch instructions include beql(=), bneq(≠), blss(<), bleq(≤), bgtr(>), and bgeq(≥), which do just what you would expect. There are also unconditional branches whose name is determined by the size of the PC-relative offset. Thus brb (branch byte) has an 8-bit displacement and brw (branch word) has a 16-bit displacement.

The final major category we cover here is the procedure call and return instructions. Procedure calls and returns include control transfer and possibly some state saving; at a minimum the return address must be saved somewhere. Some architectures provide a mechanism to save the registers, while others require the compiler to generate instructions. There are two basic conventions in use to save registers. *Caller-saving* means that the calling procedure must save the registers that it wants preserved for access after the call. *Callee-saving* means that the called procedure must save the registers it wants to use. There are times when caller save must be used due to access patterns to globally visible variables in two different procedures. For example, suppose we have a procedure P1 that calls procedure P2, and both procedures manipulate the global variable x. If P1 had allocated x to a register it must be sure to save x to a location known by P2 before the call to P2. A compiler's ability to discover when a called procedure may access register-allocated quantities is complicated by the possibility of separate compilation, and situations where P2 may not touch x, but P2 can call another procedure, P3, that may access x. Because of these complications, most compilers will conservatively caller save **any** variable that **may be** accessed during a call.

In the cases where either convention could be used, some will be more optimal with callee-save and some will be more optimal with caller-save. As a result, the most sophisticated compilers use a combination of the two mechanisms, and the register allocator may choose which register to use for a variable based on the convention.

The VAX has elaborate versions of call and return, taking dozens of clock cycles to execute. The argument pointer, R12, points to the base of the list of arguments or parameters in memory that are passed to the procedure. The frame pointer, R13, points to the base of the local variables of the procedure that are kept in memory (the stack frame). The VAX call and return instructions manipulate these pointers plus the stack pointer (R14) to maintain the stack in proper condition across procedure calls and to provide convenient base registers to use when accessing memory operands. Call and return also save and restore the general purpose registers as well as the program counter: the first 16 bits of the procedure is used as a mask that determines which registers will be saved and restored; the pitfall on page 146 describes the VAX call in more detail.

Operations on the VAX

The operators supported by most instruction set architectures can be categorized, as in Figure 3.13. Because the instructions used to implement control flow are largely independent of other instruction set choices and because the measurements of branch and jump behavior are also fairly independent of other measurements, we examine the use of control-flow instructions next.

What types of operators does the VAX provide? VAX operations can be divided into classes, as shown in Figure 3.14 (Detailed lists of the VAX instructions are included in Appendix C.) Figure 3.15 gives examples of typical VAX instructions and their meanings.

Type	Example	Instruction meaning
Data transfers		**Move data between byte, halfword, word, or doubleword operands; * is the data type**
	MOV*	Move between two operands
	MOVZB*	Move a byte to a halfword or word, extending it with zeroes
	MOVA*	Move address of operand; data type is last
	PUSH*	Push operand onto stack
Arithmetic, logical		**Operations on integer or logical bytes, halfwords (16 bits), words (32 bits); * is the data type**
	ADD*_	Add with 2 or 3 operands
	CMP*	Compare and set condition codes
	TST*	Compare to zero and set condition codes
	ASH*	Arithmetic shift
	CLR*	Clear
	CVTB*	Sign extend byte to size of data type
Control		**Conditional and unconditional branches**
	BEQL, BNEQ	Branch equal/not equal
	BCS, BCC	Branch carry set, branch carry clear
	BRB, BRW	Unconditional branch with an 8-bit or 16-bit offset
	JMP	Jump using any addressing mode to specify target
	AOBLEQ	Add one to operand; branch if result ≤ second operand
	CASE_	Jump based on case selector
Procedure		**Call/return from procedure**
	CALLS	Call procedure with arguments on stack (see Section 3.9)
	CALLG	Call procedure with FORTRAN-style parameter list
	JSB	Jump to subroutine, saving return address
	RET	Return from procedure call
Bit-field character decimal		**Operate on variable-length bit fields, character strings, and decimal strings, both in character and BCD format**
	EXTV	Extracts a variable-length bit field into a 32-bit word
	MOVC3	Move a string of characters for given length
	CMPC3	Compare two strings of characters for given length
	MOVC5	Move string of characters with truncation or filling
	ADDP4	Add decimal string of the indicated length
	CVTPT	Convert packed-decimal string to character string

FIGURE 3.13 continued on next page

Floating point		Floating-point operations on D, F, G, and H formats
	ADDD_	Add double-precision D-format floating numbers
	SUBD_	Subtract double-precision D-format floating numbers
	MULF_	Multiply single-precision F-format floating point
	POLYF	Evaluate a polynomial using table of coefficients in F format
System		**Change to system mode, modify protected registers**
	CHMK, CHME	Change mode to kernel/executive
	REI	Return from exception or interrupt
Other		**Special operations**
	CRC	Calculate cyclic redundancy check
	INSQUE	Insert a queue entry into a queue

FIGURE 3.13 (Adjoining page) Classes of VAX instructions with examples. The asterisk stands for multiple data types—B, W, L, and usually D, F, G, H, and Q; remember how these VAX data types relate to the names used in the text (see Figure 3.3 on page 94). For example, MOVW moves the VAX data-type word, which is 16 bits and is called a halfword in this text. The underline, as in ADDD_, means there are 2-operand (ADDD2) and 3-operand (ADDD3) forms of this instruction. The operand count is explicit in the opcode.

Operator type	Examples
Arithmetic and logical	Integer arithmetic and logical operations: add, and, subtract, or
Data transfer	Loads/stores (move instructions on machines with memory addressing)
Control	Branch, jump, procedure call and return, traps
System	Operating system call, virtual memory management instructions
Floating point	Floating-point operations: add, multiply
Decimal	Decimal add, decimal multiply, decimal-to-character conversions
String	String move, string compare, string search

FIGURE 3.14 Categories of instruction operators and examples of each. All machines generally provide a full set of operations for the first three categories. The support for system functions in the instruction set varies widely among architectures, but all machines must have some instruction support for basic system functions. The amount of support in the instruction set for the last three categories may vary from none to an extensive set of special instructions. Floating-point instructions will be provided in any machine that is intended for use in an application that makes much use of floating point. These instructions are sometimes part of an optional instruction set. Decimal and string instructions are sometimes primitives, as in the VAX, or may be synthesized by the compiler from simpler instructions.

Example assembly instruction	Length	Meaning
`MOVL @40(R4),30(R2)`	5	$M[M[40+R4]]\leftarrow_{32} M[30+R2]$
`MOVAW R2,(R3)[R4]`	4	$R2\leftarrow_{32} R3+(R4*2)$
`ADDL3 R5,(R6)+,(R6)+`	4	$i\leftarrow M[R6]; R6\leftarrow R6+4; R5\leftarrow i+M[R6]; R6\leftarrow R6+4$
`CMPL -(R6),#100`	7	$R6\leftarrow R6-4;$ Set the condition code using: $M[R6]-10$
`CVTBW R10,(R8)`	3	$R10_{16..31}\leftarrow_{16} (M[R8]_0)^8 \,\#\#\, M[R8]$
`BEQL name`	2	if equal(CC) {PC$\leftarrow$name} PC$-128 \leq$ name $<$ PC$+128$
`BRW name`	3	PC$\leftarrow$name PC$-32768 \leq$ name $<$ PC$+32768$
`EXTZV (R8),R5,R6,-564(R7)`	7	$t\leftarrow_{40} M[R7-564+(R5>>3)];$ $i\leftarrow R5 \,\&\, 7; j\leftarrow$if R6>=32 then 32 else if R6<0 then 0 else R6; $M[R8]\leftarrow_{32} 0^{32-j} \,\#\#\, t_{39-i-j+1..39-i};$
`MOVC3 @36(R9),(R10),35(R11)`	6	$R1\leftarrow 35+R11; R3\leftarrow M[36+R9];$ for (R0$\leftarrow$M[R10];R0!=0;R0--) {$M[R3]\leftarrow_8 M[R1]; R1++; R3++$} R2=0; R4=0; R5=0
`ADDD3 R0,R2,R4`	4	$(R0\#\#R1)\leftarrow_{64} (R2\#\#R3)+(R4\#\#R5)$ register contents are type D floating point.

FIGURE 3.15 Some examples of typical VAX instructions. VAX assembly language syntax puts the result operand last; we have put it first for consistency with other machines. Instruction length is given in bytes. The conditional(CC) is true if the condition-code setting reflects equality after a compare. Remember that most instructions set the condition code; the only function of compare instructions is to set the condition code. The names i, j are used as a temporaries in the instruction descriptions; t is 40 bits in length, while i and j are 32 bits. The EXTZV instruction may appear mysterious. Its purpose is to extract a variable-length field (0 to 32 bits) and zero extend it to 32 bits. The source operands to the EXTZV are the starting bit position (which may be any distance from the starting byte address), the length of the field, and the starting address of the bit string to extract the field from. The VAX numbers its bits from low order to high order, but we number bits in the reverse order. Thus, the subscripts adjust the bit offsets accordingly (which makes EXTZV look more mysterious!). Although the result of the variable bit string operations are always 32 bits, the MOVC3 changes the values of registers R0 through R5 as shown (although any of R0, R2, R4, and R5 could be used to hold the count).

3.4 | The 80x86 Architecture

The VAX was the vision of a single architect; the pieces of this sophisticated architecture fit nicely together and the whole architecture can be described succinctly. Such is not the case of the 80x86; it is the product of several independent groups who evolved the architecture over almost 10 years, adding new features to the original instruction set as one might add clothing to a packed bag. Here are important 80x86 milestones:

1978: The Intel 8086 architecture was announced as an upward-compatible extension of the then-successful 8080, an 8-bit microprocessor. The 8086 is a 16-bit architecture, with all internal registers 16 bits wide. Whereas the 8080 was a straightforward accumulator machine, the 8086 extended the architecture with additional registers. Because nearly every register has a dedicated use, the 8086 falls somewhere between an accumulator machine and a general-purpose register machine, and can fairly be called an *extended accumulator* machine.

1980: The Intel 8087 floating point coprocessor is announced. This architecture extends the 8086 with about 60 floating point instructions. Its architects rejected extended accumulators to go with a hybrid of stacks and registers, essentially an *extended stack* architecture: A complete stack instruction set is supplemented by a limited set of register-memory instructions.

1982: The 80286, introduced in 1982, extended the 8086 architecture by creating an elaborate memory-mapping and protection model and by extending the address space to 24 bits plus a few instructions to round out the instruction set and to manipulate the protection model. Because it was important to run 8086 programs without change, the 80286 offered a real addressing mode to make the machine look just like an 8086.

1985: The 80386 extended the 80286 architecture to 32 bits. In addition to a 32-bit architecture with 32-bit registers and a 32-bit address space, the 80386 added a new addressing modes and additional operations. The added instructions make the 80386 nearly a general-purpose register machine. The 80386 also adding paging support in addition to segmented addressing (see Chapter 6). Like the 80286, the 80386 has a mode to execute 8086 programs without change.

This history illustrates the impact of the "golden handcuffs" of compatibility on the 80x86, as the existing software base at each step was too important to jeopardize with significant architectural changes. Fortunately, the subsequent 80486 in 1989 and Pentium in 1992 were aimed at higher performance, with only three instructions added to the user visible instruction set to help with multiprocessing.

Whatever the artistic failures of the 80x86, keep in mind that there are more instances of this architectural family than of any other in the world. Nevertheless, this checkered ancestry has led to an architecture that is difficult to explain and impossible to love. We start our explanation with the registers and addressing modes, move on to the integer operations, then cover the floating point operations, and conclude with an examination of instruction encoding.

80x86 Registers and Data Addressing Modes

The evolution of the instruction set can be seen in the registers of the 80x86 (Figure 3.17). Original registers are shown in black, with the extensions of the 80386 shown in color, a coloring scheme followed in subsequent figures. The 80386 basically extended all 16-bit registers (except the segment registers) to 32-bits, prefixing an "E" to their name to indicate the 32-bit version. The arithmetic, logical, and data-transfer instructions are two-operand instructions that allow the combinations shown in Figure 3.16.

Source/destination operand type	Second source operand
Register	Register
Register	Immediate
Register	Memory
Memory	Register
Memory	Immediate

FIGURE 3.16   Instruction types for the arithmetic, logical, and data-transfer instructions. The 80x86 allows the combinations shown. Immediates may be 8, 16, or 32 bits in length; a register is any one of the 14 major registers in Figure 3.17 (not IP or FLAGS). The only restriction is the absence of a memory–memory mode.

To explain the addressing modes we need to keep in mind whether we are talking about both the 16-bit mode used by the 8086 and 80286 and the 32-bit mode available on the 80386 and its successors. The memory addressing modes supported are absolute, register indirect, based, indexed, based indexed with displacement, based with scaled indexed, and based with scaled indexed and displacement. Displacements can be 8 bits or 32 bits in 32-bit mode, and 8 bits or 16 bits in 16-bit mode. Although a memory operand can use any addressing mode, there are restrictions on what registers can be used in a mode. The subsection below on 80x86 instruction encodings gives the full set of restrictions on registers, but the following description of addressing modes gives the basic register options:

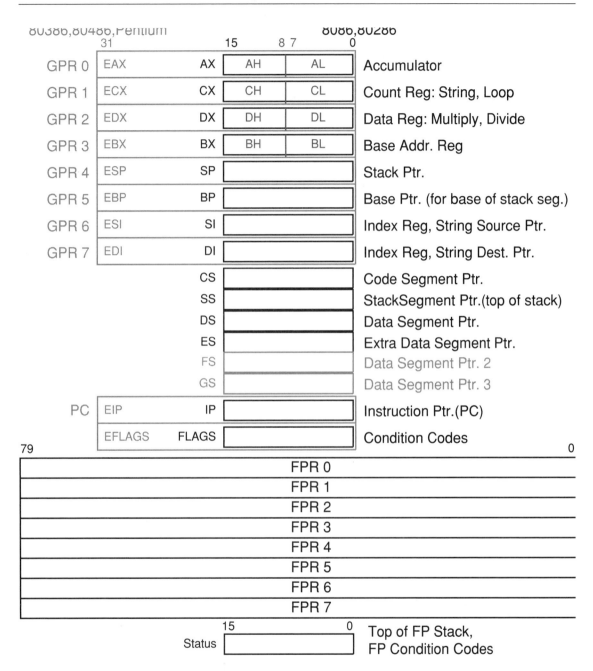

FIGURE 3.17 The 80x86 has evolved over time, and so has it register set. The original set is shown in black, and the extended set in color. The 8086 divided the first four register in half so that they could be used either as one 16-bit register or as two 8b-it registers. Starting with the 80386, the top 8 registers were extended to 32 bits and could also be used as general purpose registers. The floating point registers on the bottom are 80 bits wide, and although they look like regular registers they are not: they implement a stack, with the top of stack pointed to by the status register. One operand must be the top of stack, and the other can be any of the other 7 registers below the top of stack.

- *Register indirect*—BX, SI, DI in 16-bit mode and EAX, ECX, EDX, EBX, ESI, and EDI in 32-bit mode.

- *Based mode with 8-bit or 16-bit/32-bit displacement*—BP, BX, SI, DI in 16-bit mode and EAX, ECX, EDX, EBX, ESI, and EDI in 32-bit mode. The displacement is either 8 bits or the size of the address mode: 16 or 32 bits. (Intel gives two names to this addressing mode, Based and Indexed, but they are essentially identical and we combine them.)

- *Indexed*—address is sum of two registers. The allowable combinations are BX+SI, BX+DI, BP+SI, and BP+DI. This mode is called Based Indexed on the 8086. (The 32-bit mode uses a different addressing mode to get the same effect).

- *Based indexed with 8-bit or 16-bit displacement*—the address is sum of displacement and contents of two registers. The same restrictions on registers apply as in indexed mode.

- *Base plus Scaled Indexed*—This addressing mode and the next was added in the 80386, and is only available in 32-bit mode. The address calculation is

$$Base\ register + 2^{Scale} \times Index\ register$$

- where *Scale* has the value 0, 1, 2, or 3 and *Index register* can be any of the 8 32-bit general registers except ESP and Base register can any of the 8 32-bit general registers.

- *Base plus Scaled index with 8-bit or 32-bit displacement*—the address is sum of displacement and address calculated by the scaled mode immediately above. The same restrictions on registers apply.

The final address generated by the 80x86 is little Endian.

Ideally we would postpone discussion of 80x86 logical and physical addresses until Chapter 6, as we do for the VAX, but the segmented address space prevents us from hiding that information. Figure 3.18 shows the memory mapping options on the generations of 80x86 machines; Chapter 6 describes the segmented protection scheme in greater detail.

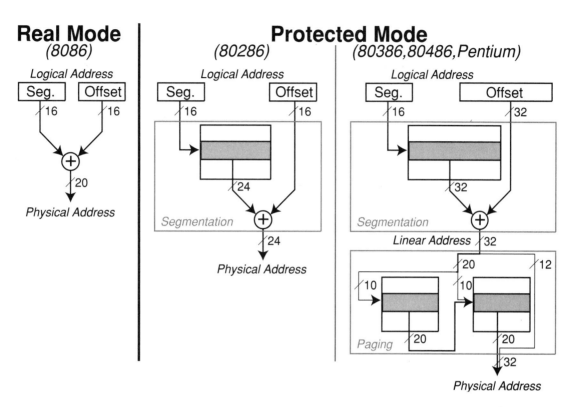

Real Mode
(8086)

Logical Address

| Seg. | | Offset |

16   16

⊕

20

Physical Address

Protected Mode

(80286)

Logical Address

| Seg. | | Offset |

16   16

24

Segmentation   ⊕

24

Physical Address

(80386,80486,Pentium)

Logical Address

| Seg. | | Offset |

16   32

32

Segmentation   ⊕

Linear Address 32

20   12

10   10

Paging 20   20

32

Physical Address

FIGURE 3.18 The original segmented scheme of the 8086 is shown on the left. All 80x86 processors support this style of addressing, called "real mode." It simply takes the contents of a segment register, shifts it left 4 bits, and adds it to the 16-bit offset, forming a 20-bit physical address. The 80286 used the contents of the segment register to select a segment descriptor, which includes a 24-bit base address among other items (see Chapter 6). It is added to the 16-bit offset to form the 24-bit physical address. The 80386 and successors expand this base address in the segment descriptor to 32 bits and also add an optional paging layer below segmentation. A 32-bit linear address is first formed from the segment and offset, and then this address is divided into two 10-bit fields and a 12-bit page offset (see Chapter 6). The first 10-bit field selects the entry in the first level page table, and then this entry is used in combination the second 10-bit field to access the second -level page table to select the upper 20 bits of the physical address. Prepending this 20-bit address to the final 12-bit field gives the 32-bit physical address. Paging can be turned off, redefining the 32-bit linear as the physical address. Note that a "flat" 80x86 address space comes simply by loading the same value in all the segment registers.; that is, it doesn't matter which segment register is selected.

The assembly language programmer clearly must specify which segment register should be used with an address, no matter which address mode is used. To save space in the instructions, segment registers are selected automatically depending on which address register is used. The rules are simple: references to instructions (IP) use the Code Segment register (CS); references to the stack (BP or SP) use the Stack Segment register (SS); and the default segment register for the other registers is the Data Segment register (DS). The next subsection explains how they can be overridden.

80x86 Integer Operations

The 8086 provides support for both 8-bit (byte) and 16-bit (called word) data types. The data type distinctions apply to register operations as well as memory accesses. The 80386 adds 32-bit addresses and data, called double words. Almost every operation works on both 8-bit data and on one longer data size. That size is determined by the mode, and is either 16-bits or 32-bits.

Clearly some programs want to operate on data of all three sizes, so the 80x86 architects needed to provide a convenient way to specify each version, ideally without expanding code size significantly. They decided that most programs would by dominated by either 16-bit or 32-bit data, and so it made sense to be able to set a default large size. This default size is set in the code segment. To override the default size, an 8-bit *prefix* is attached to the instruction to tell the machine to use the other large size for this instruction.

The prefix solution was borrowed from the 8086, which allows multiple prefixes to modify instruction behavior. The three original prefixes override the default segment register, lock the bus so to perform a semaphore (see Chapter 9), or repeat the following instruction until CX counts down to zero. This later prefix was intended to by paired with a byte move instruction to move a variable number of bytes. The 80386 also added a prefix to override the default address size.

The 80x86 integer operations can be divided into four major classes:

1. Data movement instructions, including move, push, and pop;

2. Arithmetic and logic instructions, including logical operations, test, shifts, and integer and decimal arithmetic operations;

3. Control flow, including conditional and unconditional branches, calls, and returns;

4. String instructions, including string move and string compare.

Figure 3.19 shows some typical 80x86 instructions and their functions.

Instruction	Function
JE name	if equal(CC) {IP←name}; IP-128 ≤ name < IP+128
JMP name	IP←name
CALLF name, seg	SP←SP-2; M[SS:SP]←IP+5; SP←SP-2; M[SS:SP]←CS; IP←name; CS←seg;
MOVW BX,[DI+45]	BX←$_{16}$M[DS:DI+45]
PUSH SI	SP←SP-2; M[SS:SP]←SI
POP DI	DI←M[SS:SP]; SP←SP+2
ADD AX,#6765	AX←AX+6765
SHL BX,1	BX←BX$_{1..15}$ ## 0
TEST DX,#42	Set CC flags with DX & 42
MOVSB	M[ES:DI]←$_8$M[DS:SI]; DI←DI+1; SI←SI+1

FIGURE 3.19   Some typical 80x86 instructions and their functions. A list of frequent operations appears in Figure 3.20. We use the abbreviation SR:X to indicate the formation of an address with segment register SR and offset X. This effective address corresponding to SR:X is (SR<<4)+X. The CALLF saves the IP of the next instruction and the current CS on the stack.

The data transfer, arithmetic, and logic instructions are unremarkable, except that the arithmetic and logic instructions operations allow the destination to either be a register or a memory location.

Control-flow instructions must be able to address destinations in another segment. This is handled by having two types of control-flow instructions: "near" for intrasegment (within a segment) and "far" for intersegment (between segments) transfers. In far jumps, which must be unconditional, two 16-bit quantities follow the opcode in 16-bit mode. One of these is used as the instruction pointer, while the other is loaded into CS and becomes the new code segment. In 32-bit mode the first field is expanded to 32 bits to match the 32-bit EIP.

Calls and returns work similarly—a far call pushes the return instruction pointer and return segment on the stack and loads both the instruction pointer and code segment. A far return pops both the instruction pointer and the code segment from the stack. Programmers or compiler writers must be sure to always use the same type of call **and** return for a procedure—a near return does not work with a far call, and vice versa.

Instruction	Meaning
Control	**Conditional and unconditional branches**
JNZ, JZ	Jump if condition to IP + 8-bit offset; JNE (for JNZ), JE (for JZ) are alternative names
JMP, JMPF	Unconditional jump—8-bit or 16-bit offset intrasegment (near), and intersegment (far) versions
CALL, CALLF	Subroutine call—16-bit offset; return address pushed; near and far versions
RET, RETF	Pops return address from stack and jumps to it; near and far versions
LOOP	Loop branch—decrement CX; jump to IP + 8-bit displacement if CX ≠0
Data transfer	**Move data between registers or between register and memory**
MOV	Move between two registers or between register and memory
PUSH	Push source operand on stack
POP	Pop operand from stack top to a register
LES	Load ES and one of the GPRs from memory
Arithmetic, logical	**Arithmetic and logical operations using the data registers and memory**
ADD	Add source to destination; register–memory format
SUB	Subtract source from destination; register–memory format
CMP	Compare source and destination; register–memory format
SHL	Shift left
SHR	Shift logical right
RCR	Rotate right with Carry as fill
CBW	Convert byte in AL to word in AX
TEST	Logical AND of source and destination sets flags
INC	Increment destination; register–memory format
DEC	Decrement destination; register–memory format
OR	Logical OR; register–memory format
XOR	Exclusive OR; register–memory format
String instructions	**Move between string operands; length given by a repeat prefix**
MOVS	Copies from string source to destination; may be repeated
LODS	Loads a byte or word of a string into the A register

FIGURE 3.20   Some typical operations on the 80x86. Many operations use register–memory format, where either the source or the destination may be memory and the other may be a register or immediate operand.

String instructions are part of the 8080 ancestry of the 80x86, and are not commonly executed in most programs.

Figure 3.20 lists some of the integer 80x86 instructions. Many of the instructions are available in both byte and word formats. A full listing of instructions appears in Appendix C.

80x86 Floating Point Operations

Intel provided a stack architecture with its floating point instructions: loads push numbers onto the stack, operations find operands in the two top elements of the stacks, and stores can pop elements off the stack, just as the stack example in Figure 3.1 suggests.

Intel supplemented this stack architecture with instructions and addressing modes that allow the architecture to have some of the benefits of a register-memory model. In addition to finding operands in the top two elements of the stack, one operand can be in memory or in one of the seven registers below the top of the stack. This hybrid is still a restricted register-memory model, however, in that loads always move data to the top of the stack while incrementing the top of stack pointer and stores can only move the top of stack to memory. Intel uses the notation ST to indicate the top of stack, and ST(i) to represent the i-th register below the top of stack.

One novel feature of this architecture is that the operands are wider in the register stack than they are stored in memory, and all operations are at this wide internal precision. Numbers are automatically converted to the internal 80-bit format on a load and converted back to the appropriate size on a store. Memory data can be 32-bit (single precision) or 64-bit (double precision) floating point numbers, called *real* by Intel. The register-memory version of these instructions will then convert the memory operand to this Intel 80-bit format before performing the operation. The data transfer instructions also will automatically convert 16-bit and 32-bit integers to reals, and vice versa, for integer loads and stores.

The 80x86 floating point operations can be divided into four major classes:

1. Data movement instructions, including load, load constant, and store

2. Arithmetic instructions, including add, subtract, multiply, divide, square root, and absolute value

3. Comparison, including instructions to send the result to the integer CPU so that it can branch

4. Transcendental instructions, including sine, cosine, log, and exponentiation

Figure 3.21 shows some of the 60 floating point operations. We use the curly brackets { } to show optional variations of the basic operations: {I} means there is an integer version of the instruction, {P} means this variation will pop one operand off the stack after the operation, and {R} means reverse the sense of the operands in this operation. Not all combinations are provided. Hence

$$F\{I\}SUB\{R\}\{P\}$$

represents these instructions found in the 80x86:

FSUB

FISUB

FSUBR

FISUBR

FSUBP

FSUBRP

There are no pop or reverse pop versions of the integer subtract instructions.

Note that we get even more combinations when including the operand modes for these operations. The floating point add has these options, ignoring the integer and pop versions of the instruction:

FADD   ; both operands in stack, result replaces top of stack

FADD   ST(i)   ; one source operand is i-th register below the top of stack, and the result replaces the top of stack

FADD   ST(i),ST   ; one source operand is the top of stack, and the result replaces i-th register below the top of stack

FADD   mem32   ; one source operand is a 32-bit location in memory, and the result replaces the top of stack

FADD   mem64   ; one source operand is a 64-bit location in memory, and the result replaces the top of stack

Data Transfer	Arithmetic	Compare	Trancendental
F{I}LD mem/ST(i)	F{I}ADD{P} mem/ /ST(i)	F{I}COM{P}{P}	FPATAN
F{I}ST{P} mem/ST(i)	F{I}SUB{R}{P} mem/ /ST(i)	F{I}UCOM{P}{P}	F2XM1
FLDPI	F{I}MUL{P} mem/ ST(i)	FSTSW AX/mem	FOOS
FLD1	F{I}DIV{R}{P} MEM/ /ST(i)		FPTAN
	FSQRT		FPREM
	FABS		FSIN
	FRNDINT		FYL2X

FIGURE 3.21   The floating point instructions of the 80x86. The first column shows the data transfer instructions, which moves data to memory or to one of the registers below the top of the stack. The last three operations push constants on the stack: pi, 1.0, and 0.0. The second column contains the arithmetic operations described above. Note that the last three operate only on the top of stack. The third column is the compare instructions. Since there are no special floating point branch instructions, the result of the compare must be transferred to the integer CPU via the FSTSW instruction, either into the AX register or into memory. The floating point comparison can then be tested using integer branch instructions. The final column give the higher level floating point operations.

80x86 Instruction Encoding

Saving the worst for last, the encoding of instructions in the 8086 is complex, with many different instruction formats. Instructions may vary from one byte, when there are no operands, up to six bytes, when the instruction contains a 16-bit immediate and uses 16-bit displacement addressing. Prefix instructions increase 8086 instruction length beyond the obvious sizes.

The 80386 additions expand the instruction size even further, as Figure 3.22 shows. Both the displacement and immediate fields can be 32-bits long; two more prefixes are possible; the opcode can be 16 bits long; and the scaled index mode specifier adds another 8 bits. The maximum 80386 instruction size is limited to 15 bytes.

Figure 3.23 shows the instruction format for several of the example instructions in Figure 3.19. The opcode byte usually contains a bit saying whether the operand is a byte wide or the larger size, 16 bits or 32 bits depending on the mode. For some instructions the opcode may include the addressing mode and the register; this is true in many instructions that have the form "register←register op immediate." Other instructions use a "postbyte" or extra opcode byte, labeled "mod, reg, r/m" in Figure 3.22, which contains the addressing mode information. This postbyte is used for many of the instructions that address memory. The based with scaled index uses a second postbyte, labeled "sc, index, base" in Figure 3.22.

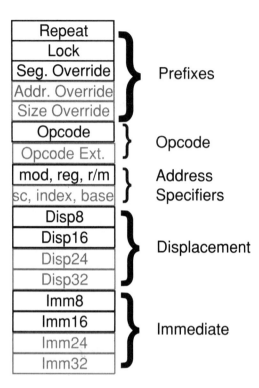

FIGURE 3.22   The instruction format of the 8086 (in black) and the extensions for the 80386 (in color). Every field is optional except the opcode.

The floating point instructions are encoded in the escape opcode of the 8086 and the postbyte address specifier. The memory operations reserve two bits to decide if the operand is a 32-bit or 64-bit real or a 16-bit or 32-bit integer. Those same 2 bits are used in versions that do not access memory to decide if the stack should be popped after the operation and whether the top of stack or a lower register should get the result.

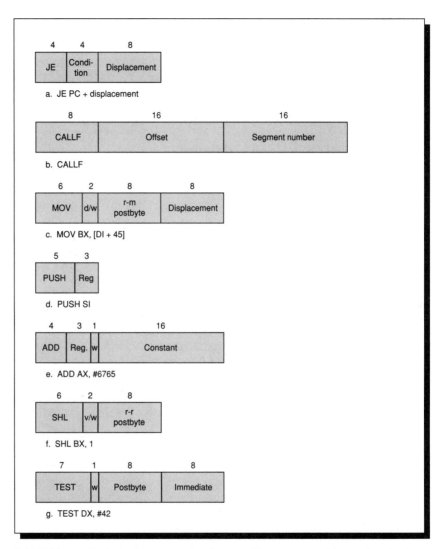

FIGURE 3.23 Typical 8086 instruction formats. The encoding of the postbyte is shown in Figure 3.24. Many instructions contain the 1-bit field w, which says whether the operation is a byte or word. Fields of the form v/w or d/w are a d-field or v-field followed by the w-field. The d-field in MOV is used in instructions that may move to or from memory and shows the direction of the move. The field v in the SHL instruction indicates a variable-length shift; variable-length shifts use a register to hold the shift count. The ADD instruction shows a typical optimized short encoding usable only when the first operand is AX. Overall instructions may vary from one to six bytes in length.

Alas, you cannot separate the restrictions on registers from the encoding of the addressing modes in the 80x86. Hence Figures 3.24 and 3.25 show the encoding of the two postbyte address specifiers for both 16-bit and 32-bit mode.

reg	w=0	w=1		r/m	mod=0		mod=1		mod=2		mod=3
		16b	32b		16b	32b	16b	32b	16b	32b	
0	AL	AX	EAX	0	addr=BX+SI	=EAX	*same*	*same*	*same*	*same*	*same*
1	CL	CX	ECX	1	addr=BX+DI	=ECX	*addr as*	*addr as*	*addr as*	*addr as*	*as*
2	DL	DX	EDX	2	addr=BP+SI	=EDX	*mod=0*	*mod=0*	*mod=0*	*mod=0*	*reg*
3	BL	BX	EBX	3	addr=BP+SI	=EBX	*+ disp8*	*+ disp8*	*+ disp16*	*+ disp32*	*field*
4	AH	SP	ESP	4	addr=SI	=(sib)	SI+disp8	(sib)+disp8	SI+disp8	(sib)+disp32	"
5	CH	BP	EBP	5	addr=DI	=disp32	DI+disp8	EBP+disp8	DI+disp16	EBP+disp32	"
6	DH	SI	ESI	6	addr=disp16	=ESI	BP+disp8	ESI+disp8	BP+disp16	ESI+disp32	"
7	BH	DI	EDI	7	addr=BX	=EDI	BX+disp8	EDI+disp8	BX+disp16	EDI+disp32	"

FIGURE 3.24   The encoding of the first address specifier of the 80x86, "*mod, reg, r/m*". The first four columns show the encoding of the 3-bit *reg* field, which depends on the *w* bit from the opcode and whether the machine is in 16-bit or 32-bit mode. The remaining columns explain the *mod* and *r/m* fields. The meaning of the 3-bit *r/m* field depends on the value in the 2-bit *mod* field and the address size. Basically the registers used in the address calculation are listed in the sixth and seventh columns, under *mod*=0, with *mod*=1 adding a 8-bit displacement and *mod*=2 adding a 16-bit or 32-bit displacement, depending on the address mode. The exceptions are: *r/m*=6 when *mod*=1 or *mod*=2 in 16-bit mode selects BP plus the displacement;   *r/m*=5 when *mod*=1 or *mod*=2 in 32-bit mode selects EBP plus displacement.; and *r/m*=4 i n 32-bit mode when *mod*≠3 (*sib*) means scaled index mode shown in Figure 3.25. When *mod*=3, the *r/m* field indicates a register, using the same encoding as the *reg* field.

	Index	Base
0	EAX	EAX
1	ECX	ECX
2	EDX	EDX
3	EBX	EBX
4	no index	ESP
5	EBP	if mod=0, disp32 if mod≠0, EBP
6	ESI	ESI
7	EDI	EDI

FIGURE 3.25   Based plus scaled index mode address specifier found in the 80386. This mode is indicated by the *(sib)* notation in Figure 3.24. Note that this mode expands the list of registers to be used in other modes: register indirect using ESP comes from Scale=0, Index=4, and Base=4, and base displacement with EBP comes from Scale=0, Index=5, and mod=0. The two bit scale field is used in this formula of the effective address:

$$Base\ register + 2^{Scale} \times Index\ register$$

80x86 Summary

Beauty is in the eye of the beholder.

American saying

As we have seen, "orthogonal" is not a term found in the Intel architectural dictionary. To fully understand which registers and which addressing modes are available you need to see the encoding of all addressing modes and sometimes the encoding of the instructions to see which addressing modes are available. For better or worse, Intel had a 16-bit microprocessor years before its competitors' more elegant architectures, and this head start led to the selection of the 8086 as the CPU for the IBM PC. What it lacks in style is made up in quantity, making the 80x86 beautiful from the right perspectives.

The saving grace is the 80x86 architectural components are not too difficult to implement, as Intel has demonstrated by rapidly improving performance over the last 15 years.

3.5 | The DLX Architecture

In many places throughout this book we will have occasion to refer to a computer's "machine language." The machine we use is a mythical computer called "MIX." MIX is very much like nearly every computer in existence, except that is, perhaps, nicer ... MIX is the world's first polyunsaturated computer. Like most machines, it has an identifying number—the 1009. This number was found by taking 16 actual computers which are very similar to MIX and on which MIX can be easily simulated, then averaging their number with equal weight:

$$\lfloor(360 + 650 + 709 + 7070 + U3 + SS80 + 1107 + 1604 + G20 + B220 + S2000 + 920 + 601 + H800 + PDP\text{-}4 + 11)/16\rfloor = 1009.$$

The same number may be obtained in a simpler way by taking Roman numerals.

Donald Knuth, *The Art of Computer Programming. Volume I: Fundamental Algorithms*

In this section we will describe a simple load/store architecture called DLX (pronounced "Deluxe"). The authors believe DLX to be the world's second polyunsaturated computer—the average of a number of recent experimental and commercial machines that are very similar in philosophy to DLX. Like Knuth, we derived the name of our machine from an average expressed in Roman numerals:

(AMD 29K, DECstation 3100, HP 850, IBM 801, Intel i860, MIPS M/120A, MIPS M/1000, Motorola 88K, RISC I, SGI 4D/60, SPARCstation-1, Sun-4/110, Sun-4/260) / 13 = 560 = DLX.

The architecture of DLX was chosen based on observations about the most frequently used primitives in programs. More sophisticated (and less performance-critical) functions are implemented in software with multiple instructions. In Section 3.10 we discuss how and why these architectures became popular.

Like most recent load/store machines, DLX emphasizes

- A simple load/store instruction set

- Design for pipelining efficiency (discussed in Chapter 4)

- An easily decoded instruction set

- Efficiency as a compiler target

DLX provides a good architectural model for study, not only because of the recent popularity of this type of machine, but also because it is an easy architecture to understand.

DLX—Our Generic Load/Store Architecture

In this section, the DLX instruction set is defined. We will use this architecture again in Chapters 4 and 5, and it forms the basis for a number of exercises and programming projects.

- Figure 3.26 shows that DLX has thirty-two 32-bit general-purpose registers (GPRs); the value of R0 is always 0. Additionally, there are a set of floating-point registers (FPRs), which can be used as 32 single-precision (32-bit) registers, or as even-odd pairs holding double-precision values. Thus, the 64-bit floating-point registers are named F0, F2, ..., F28, F30. Both single- and double-precision floating-point operations are provided. There are a set of special registers used for accessing status information. The FP status register is used for both compares and FP exceptions. All movement to/from the status register is through the GPRs; there is a branch that tests the comparison bit in the FP status register.

31	0
Zero/GPR 0	
GPR 1	
GPR 2	
GPR 3	
GPR 4	
GPR 5	
GPR 6	
GPR 7	
GPR 8	
GPR 9	
GPR 10	
GPR 11	
GPR 12	
GPR 13	
GPR 14	
GPR 15	
GPR 16	
GPR 17	
GPR 18	
GPR 19	
GPR 20	
GPR 21	
GPR 22	
GPR 23	
GPR 24	
GPR 25	
GPR 26	
GPR 27	
GPR 28	
GPR 29	
GPR 30	
Return Addr./GPR 31	

31	0
FPR 0	
FPR 1	
FPR 2	
FPR 3	
FPR 4	
FPR 5	
FPR 6	
FPR 7	
FPR 8	
FPR 9	
FPR 10	
FPR 11	
FPR 12	
FPR 13	
FPR 14	
FPR 15	
FPR 16	
FPR 17	
FPR 18	
FPR 19	
FPR 20	
FPR 21	
FPR 22	
FPR 23	
FPR 24	
FPR 25	
FPR 26	
FPR 27	
FPR 28	
FPR 29	
FPR 30	
FPR 31	

31	0
PC	

FIGURE 3.26 DLX has 32, 32-bit registers for registers, 32-32bit register for single precision floating point, and one 32-bit PC. GPR 0 always contains 0 and GPR 31 is used by the return instruction, so there are really 30 general purpose registers. The 32 floating point registers form 16 double precision floating point registers in even-odd pairs.

- The data types are 8-bit bytes, 16-bit half words, and 32-bit word for integer data and 32-bit single precision and 64-bit double precision for floating point.

- All instructions are 32 bits.

- Memory is byte addressable in Big Endian mode with a 32-bit address. All memory references are through loads or stores between memory and either the GPRs or the FPRs. Accesses involving the GPRs can be to a byte, to a half-word, or to a word. The FPRs may be loaded and stored with single-precision or double-precision words (using a pair of registers for DP). All memory accesses must be aligned. There are also instructions for moving between a FPR and a GPR.

- The only data addressing modes are immediate and indexed. The branch addressing modes are PC relative and register indirect.

- There are also a few special registers that can be transferred to and from the integer registers. An example is the floating-point status register, used to hold information about the results of floating-point operations.

DLX Operations

There are four classes of instructions: loads and stores, ALU operations, branches and jumps, and floating-point operations.

Any of the general-purpose or floating-point registers may be loaded or stored, except that loading R0 has no effect. There is a single addressing mode, base register + 16-bit signed offset. Halfword and byte loads place the loaded object in the lower portion of the register. The upper portion of the register is filled with either the sign extension of the loaded value or zeros, depending on the opcode. Single-precision floating-point numbers occupy a single floating-point register, while double-precision values occupy a pair. Conversions between single and double precision must be done explicitly. The floating-point format is IEEE 754 (see Appendix A). Figure 3.27 examples of the load and store instructions. A complete list of the instructions appears in Figure 3.30 (page 132).

All ALU instructions are register–register instructions. The operations include simple arithmetic and logical operations: add, subtract, AND, OR, XOR, and shifts. Immediate forms of all these instructions, with a 16-bit sign-extended immediate, are provided. The operation LHI (load high immediate) loads the top half of a register, while setting the lower half to 0. This allows a full 32-bit constant to be built in two instructions. (We sometimes use the mnemonic LI, standing for Load Immediate, as an abbreviation for an add immediate where one of the source operands is R0; likewise, the mnemonic MOV is sometimes used for an ADD where one of the sources is R0.)

Example instruction	Instruction name	Meaning
LW R1,30(R2)	Load word	$R1 \leftarrow_{32} M[30+R2]$
LW R1,1000(R0)	Load word	$R1 \leftarrow_{32} M[1000+0]$
LB R1,40(R3)	Load byte	$R1 \leftarrow_{32} (M[40+R3]_0)^{24} \#\# M[40+R3]$
LBU R1,40(R3)	Load byte unsigned	$R1 \leftarrow_{32} 0^{24} \#\# M[40+R3]$
LH R1,40(R3)	Load halfword	$R1 \leftarrow_{32} (M[40+R3]_0)^{16} \#\#M[40+R3]\#\#M[41+R3]$
LF F0,50(R3)	Load float	$F0 \leftarrow_{32} M[50+R3]$
LD F0,50(R2)	Load double	$F0\#\#F1 \leftarrow_{64} M[50+R2]$
SW 500(R4),R3	Store word	$M[500+R4] \leftarrow_{32} R3$
SF 40(R3),F0	Store float	$M[40+R3] \leftarrow_{32} F0$
SD 40(R3),F0	Store double	$M[40+R3] \leftarrow_{32} F0; \ M[44+R3] \leftarrow_{32} F1$
SH 502(R2),R3	Store half	$M[502+R2] \leftarrow_{16} R3_{16..31}$
SB 41(R3),R2	Store byte	$M[41+R3] \leftarrow_8 R2_{24..31}$

FIGURE 3.27 The load and store instructions in DLX. All use a single addressing mode and require that the memory value be aligned. Of course, both loads and stores are available for all the data types shown.

There are also compare instructions, which compare two registers $(=,\neq,<,>,\leq,\geq)$. If the condition is true, these instructions place a 1 in the destination register (to represent true); otherwise they place the value 0. Because these operations "set" a register they are called set-equal, set-not-equal, set-less-than, and so on. There are also immediate forms of these compares. Figure 3.28 gives some examples of the arithmetic/logical instructions.

Control is handled through a set of jumps and a set of branches. The four jump instructions are differentiated by the two ways to specify the destination address and by whether or not a link is made. Two jumps use a 26-bit signed offset added to the program counter (of the instruction sequentially following the jump) to determine the destination address; the other two jump instructions specify a register that contains the destination address. There are two flavors of jumps: plain jump, and jump and link (used for procedure calls). The latter places the return address in R31.

Example instruction	Instruction name	Meaning
ADD R1,R2,R3	Add	R1←R2+R3
ADDI R1,R2,#3	Add immediate	R1←R2+3
LHI R1,#42	Load high immediate	R1←42##0^{16}
SLL R1,R2,#5	Shift left logical	R1←R2<<5
SLT R1,R2,R3	Set less than	if (R2<R3) R1←1 else R1←0

FIGURE 3.28 Examples of arithmetic/logical instructions on DLX, both with and without immediates.

Example instruction	Instruction name	Meaning
J name	Jump	PC←name; ((PC+4)-2^{25}) ≤ name < ((PC+4)$+2^{25}$)
JAL name	Jump and link	R31←PC+4; PC←name; ((PC+4)-2^{25}) ≤ name < ((PC+4)$+2^{25}$)
JALR R2	Jump and link register	R31←PC+4; PC←R2
JR R3	Jump register	PC←R3
BEQZ R4,name	Branch equal zero	if (R4==0) PC←name; ((PC+4)-2^{15}) ≤ name < ((PC+4)$+2^{15}$)
BNEZ R4,name	Branch not equal zero	if (R4!=0) PC←name; ((PC+4)-2^{15}) ≤ name < ((PC+4)$+2^{15}$)

FIGURE 3.29 Typical control-flow instructions in DLX. All control instructions, except jumps to an address in a register, are PC-relative. If the register operand is R0, the branch is unconditional, but the compiler will usually prefer to use a jump with a longer offset over this "unconditional branch."

All branches are conditional. The branch condition is specified by the instruction, which may test the register source for zero or non-zero; this may be a data value or the result of a compare. The branch target address is specified with a 16-bit signed offset that is added to the program counter. Figure 3.29 gives some typical branch and jump instructions.

Floating-point instructions manipulate the floating-point registers and indicate whether the operation to be performed is single or double precision. The operations MOVF and MOVD copy a single-precision (MOVF) or double-precision (MOVD) floating-point register to another register of the same type. The operations MOVFP2I and MOVI2FP move data between a single floating-point register and an integer register; moving a double-precision value to two integer registers require two instructions. Integer multiply and divide that work on 32-bit floating-point registers are also provided, as are conversions from integer to floating point and vice versa.

The floating-point operations are add, subtract, multiply, and divide; a suffix D is used for double precision and a suffix F is used for single precision (e.g., AD-DD, ADDF, SUBD, SUBF, MULTD, MULTF, DIVD, DIVF). Floating-point compares set a bit in the special floating-point status register that can be tested with a pair of branches: BFPT and BFPF, branch floating point true and branch floating point false.

Figure 3.30 contains a list of all operations and their meaning.

Instruction type / opcode	Instruction meaning
Data transfers	**Move data between registers and memory, or between the integer and FP or special registers; only memory address mode is 16-bit displacement + contents of a GPR**
LB,LBU,SB	Load byte, load byte unsigned, store byte
LH,LHU,SH	Load halfword, load halfword unsigned, store halfword
LW,SW	Load word, store word (to/from integer registers)
LF,LD,SF,SD	Load SP float, load DP float, store SP float, store DP float
MOVI2S, MOVS2I	Move from/to GPR to/from a special register
MOVF, MOVD	Copy one floating-point register or a DP pair to another register or pair
MOVFP2I,MOVI2FP	Move 32 bits from/to FP registers to/from integer registers
Arithmetic / Logical	**Operations on integer or logical data in GPRs; signed arithmetic trap on overflow**
ADD,ADDI,ADDU,ADDUI	Add, add immediate (all immediates are 16 bits); signed and unsigned
SUB,SUBI,SUBU,SUBUI	Subtract, subtract immediate; signed and unsigned
MULT,MULTU,DIV,DIVU	Multiply and divide, signed and unsigned; operands must be floating-point registers; all operations take and yield 32-bit values
AND,ANDI	And, and immediate
OR,ORI,XOR,XORI	Or, or immediate, exclusive or, exclusive or immediate
LHI	Load high immediate—loads upper half of register with immediate
SLL, SRL, SRA, SLLI, LI, SRAI	Shifts: both immediate (S__I) and variable form (S__); shifts are shift left logical, right logical, right arithmetic
S__,S__I	Set conditional: "__" may be LT,GT,LE,GE,EQ,NE
Control	**Conditional branches and jumps; PC-relative or through register**
BEQZ,BNEZ	Branch GPR equal/not equal to zero; 16-bit offset from PC+4
BFPT,BFPF	Test comparison bit in the FP status register and branch; 16-bit offset from PC+4
J, JR	Jumps: 26-bit offset from PC (J) or target in register (JR)
JAL, JALR	Jump and link: save PC+4 to R31, target is PC-relative (JAL) or a register (JALR)
TRAP	Transfer to operating system at a vectored address; see Chapter 5
RFE	Return to user code from an exception; restore user mode; see Chapter 5
Floating point	**Floating-point operations on DP and SP formats**
ADDD,ADDF	Add DP, SP numbers
SUBD,SUBF	Subtract DP, SP numbers
MULTD,MULTF	Multiply DP, SP floating point
DIVD,DIVF	Divide DP, SP floating point
CVTF2D, CVTF2I, CVTD2F, CTD2I, CVTI2F, CVTI2D	Convert instructions: CVT x2y converts from type x to type y, where x and y are one of I (Integer), D (Double precision), or F (Single precision). Both operands are in the FP registers
___D,___F	DP and SP compares: "__" may be LT,GT,LE,GE,EQ,NE; sets comparison bit in FP status register

FIGURE 3.30   Complete list of the instructions in DLX. The formats of these instructions are shown in Figure 3.31 This list can also be found in the back inside cover.

Instruction Format

All instructions are 32 bits with a 6-bit primary opcode. Figure 3.31 shows the instruction layout.

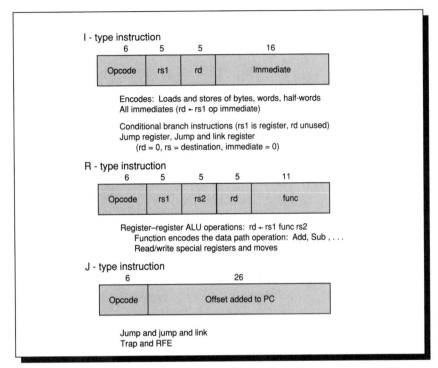

FIGURE 3.31 Instruction layout for DLX. All instructions are encoded in one of three types.

3.6 | Cross Cutting Issues: The Role of Compilers

Today most programming is done in high-level languages. This means that since most instructions executed are the output of a compiler, an instruction set architecture is essentially a compiler target. In earlier times, architectural decisions were often made to ease assembly language programming. Because performance of a computer will be significantly affected by the compiler, understanding compiler technology today is critical to designing and efficiently implementing an instruction set. In earlier days it was popular to try to isolate the compiler technology and its effect on hardware performance from the architecture and its performance, just as it was popular to try to separate an architecture from its implementation. This is essentially impossible with today's compilers and machines. Architectural choices affect the quality of the code that can be generated for a machine and the complexity of building a good compiler for it. Isolating the compiler from the hardware is likely to be misleading. In this section we will discuss the critical goals in the instruction set primarily from the compiler viewpoint. What features will lead to high-quality code? What makes it easy to write efficient compilers for an architecture?

The Structure of Recent Compilers

To begin, let's look at what optimizing compilers are like today. The structure of recent compilers is shown in Figure 3.32.

A compiler writer's first goal is correctness—all valid programs must be compiled correctly. The second goal is usually speed of the compiled code. Typically, a whole set of other goals follow these first two, including fast compilation, debugging support, and interoperability among languages. Normally, the passes in the compiler transform higher-level, more abstract representations into progressively lower-level representations, eventually reaching the instruction set. This structure helps manage the complexity of the transformations and makes writing a bug-free compiler easier.

The complexity of writing a correct compiler is a major limitation on the amount of optimization that can be done. Although the multiple-pass structure helps reduce compiler complexity, it also means that the compiler must order and perform some transformations before others. In the diagram of the optimizing compiler in Figure 3.32, we can see that certain high-level optimizations are performed long before it is known what the resulting code will look like in detail. Once such a transformation is made, the compiler can't afford to go back and revisit all steps, possibly undoing transformations. This would be prohibitive, both in compilation time and in complexity. Thus, compilers make assumptions about the ability of later steps to deal with certain problems. For example, compilers usually have to choose which procedure calls to expand inline before they know the exact size of the procedure being called. Compiler writers call this problem the *phase-ordering problem*.

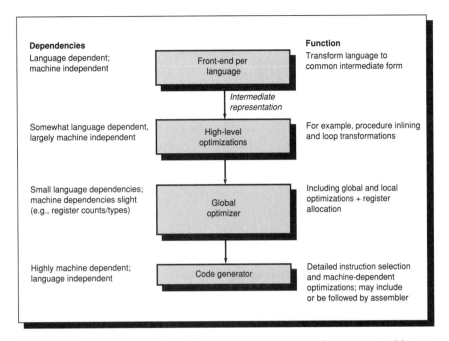

Dependencies

Language dependent;
machine independent

Somewhat language dependent,
largely machine independent

Small language dependencies;
machine dependencies slight
(e.g., register counts/types)

Highly machine dependent;
language independent

Front-end per
language

*Intermediate
representation*

High-level
optimizations

Global
optimizer

Code generator

Function

Transform language to
common intermediate form

For example, procedure inlining
and loop transformations

Including global and local
optimizations + register
allocation

Detailed instruction selection
and machine-dependent
optimizations; may include
or be followed by assembler

FIGURE 3.32 Current compilers typically consist of two to four passes, with more highly optimizing compilers having more passes. A *pass* is simply one phase in which the compiler reads and transforms the entire program. (The term "phase" is often used interchangeably with "pass.") The optimizing passes are designed to be optional and may be skipped when faster compilation is the goal and lower quality code is acceptable. This structure maximizes the probability that a program compiled at various levels of optimization will produce the same output when given the same input. Because the optimizing passes are also separated, multiple languages can use the same optimizing and code-generation passes. Only a new front end is required for a new language. The high-level optimization mentioned here, procedure inlining, is also called *procedure integration*.

How does this ordering of transformations interact with the instruction set architecture? A good example occurs with the optimization called *global common subexpression elimination*. This optimization finds two instances of an expression that compute the same value and saves the value of the first computation in a temporary. It then uses the temporary value, eliminating the second computation of the expression. For this optimization to be significant, the temporary must be allocated to a register. Otherwise, the cost of storing the temporary in memory and later reloading it may negate the savings gained by not recomputing the expression. There are, in fact, cases where this optimization actually slows down code when the temporary is not register allocated. Phase ordering complicates this problem, because register allocation is typically done near the end of the global optimization pass, just before code generation. Thus, an optimizer that performs this optimization **must** assume that the register allocator will allocate the temporary to a register.

Because of the central role that register allocation plays, both in speeding up the code and in making other optimizations useful, it is one of the most important—if not the most important—optimizations. Recent register allocation algorithms are based on a technique called *graph coloring*. The basic idea behind graph coloring is to construct a graph representing the possible candidates for allocation to a register and then to use the graph to allocate registers. Although the problem of coloring a graph is NP-complete, there are heuristic algorithms that work well in practice.

Graph coloring works best when there are at least 16 (and preferably more) general-purpose registers available for global allocation for integer variables and additional registers for floating point. Unfortunately, graph coloring does not work very well when the number of registers is small because the heuristic algorithms for coloring the graph are likely to fail. The emphasis in the approach is to achieve 100% allocation of active variables.

Optimizations performed by modern compilers can be classified by the style of the transformation, as follows:

1. High-level optimizations—often done on the source with output fed to later optimization passes.

2. Local optimizations—optimize code only within a straight-line code fragment (called a *basic block* by compiler people).

3. Global optimizations—extend the local optimizations across branches and introduce a set of transformations aimed at optimizing loops.

4. Register allocation.

5. Machine-dependent optimizations—attempt to take advantage of specific architectural knowledge.

Optimization name	Explanation	Percent of the total number of optimizing transforms
High-level	**At or near the source level; machine-independent**	
Procedure integration	Replace procedure call by procedure body	N.M.
Local	**Within straight-line code**	
Common subexpression elimination	Replace two instances of the same computation by single copy	18%
Constant propagation	Replace all instances of a variable that is assigned a constant with the constant	22%
Stack height reduction	Rearrange expression tree to minimize resources needed for expression evaluation	N.M.
Global	**Across a branch**	
Global common subexpression elimination	Same as local, but this version crosses branches	13%
Copy propagation	Replace all instances of a variable A that has been assigned X (i.e., $A=X$) with X	11%
Code motion	Remove code from a loop that computes same value each iteration of the loop	16%
Induction variable elimination	Simplify/eliminate array-addressing calculations within loops	2%
Machine-dependent	**Depends on machine knowledge**	
Strength reduction	Many examples, such as replace multiply by a constant with adds and shifts	N.M.
Pipeline scheduling	Reorder instructions to improve pipeline performance	N.M.
Branch offset optimization	Choose the shortest branch displacement that reaches target	N.M.

FIGURE 3.33   Major types of optimizations and examples in each class. The third column lists the static frequency with which some of the common optimizations are applied in a set of 12 small FORTRAN and Pascal programs. The percentage is the portion of the static optimizations that are of the specified type. These data tell us about the relative frequency of occurrence of various optimizations. There are nine local and global optimizations done by the compiler included in the measurement. Six of these optimizations are covered in the figure, and the remaining three account for 18% of the total static occurrences. The abbreviation "N.M." means that the number of occurrences of that optimization was not measured. Machine-dependent optimizations are usually done in a code generator, and none of those were measured in this experiment. The data are from Chow [1983], and were collected using the Stanford UCODE compiler.

It is sometimes difficult to separate some of the simpler optimizations—local and machine-dependent optimizations—from transformations done in the code generator. Examples of typical optimizations are given in Figure 3.33. The last column of Figure 3.33 indicates the frequency with which the listed optimizing transforms were applied to the source program. Data on the effect of various optimizations on program run-time are shown in Figure 3.34. The data in Figure 3.34 demonstrate the importance of register allocation, which adds the largest single improvement. We will look at the overall effect of optimization on our three benchmarks later in this section.

Optimizations performed	Percent faster
Procedure integration only	10%
Local optimizations only	5%
Local optimizations + register allocation	26%
Global and local optimizations	14%
Local and global optimizations + register allocation	63%
Local and global optimizations + procedure integration + register allocation	81%

FIGURE 3.34 Performance effects of various levels of optimization. Performance gains are shown as what percent faster the optimized programs were compared to the unoptimized programs. When register allocation is turned off, data are loaded into, or stored from, the registers on every individual use. These measurements are also from Chow [1983] and are for 12 small FORTRAN and Pascal programs.

The Impact of Compiler Technology on the Architect's Decisions

The interaction of compilers and high-level languages significantly affects how programs use an instruction set. To better understand this interaction, three important questions to ask are:

1. How are variables allocated and addressed? How many registers are needed to allocate variables appropriately?

2. What is the impact of optimization techniques on instruction mixes?

3. What control structures are used and with what frequency?

To address the first questions, we must look at the three separate areas in which current high-level languages allocate their data:

- The *stack*—used to allocate local variables. The stack is grown and shrunk on procedure call or return, respectively. Objects on the stack are addressed relative to the stack pointer and are primarily scalars (single variables) rather than arrays. The stack is used for activation records, **not** as a stack for evaluating expressions. Hence values are almost never pushed or popped on the stack.

- The *global data area*—used to allocate statically declared objects, such as global variables and constants. A large percentage of these objects are arrays or other aggregate data structures.

- The *heap*—used to allocate dynamic objects that do not adhere to a stack discipline. Objects in the heap are accessed with pointers and are typically not scalars.

Register allocation is much more effective for stack-allocated objects than for global variables, and register allocation is essentially impossible for heap-allocated objects because they are accessed with pointers. Global variables and some stack variables are impossible to allocate because they are *aliased*, which means that there are multiple ways to refer to the address of a variable making it illegal to put it into a register. (All heap variables are effectively aliased.) For example, consider the following code sequence (where & returns the address of a variable and * dereferences a pointer):

```
p = &a      -- gets address of a in p
a = ...      -- assigns to a directly
*p = ...      -- uses p to assign to a
...a...      -- accesses a
```

The variable "a" could not be register allocated across the assignment to *p without generating incorrect code. Aliasing causes a substantial problem because it is often difficult or impossible to decide what objects a pointer may refer to. A compiler must be conservative; many compilers will not allocate **any** local variables of a procedure in a register when there is a pointer that may refer to **one** of the local variables.

After register allocation, memory traffic consists of five types of references:

1. Unallocated reference—a potentially allocatable memory reference that was not assigned to a register.

2. Global scalar—a reference to a global scalar variable not allocated to a register. These variables are usually sparsely accessed and thus rarely allocated.

3. Save/restore memory reference—a memory reference made to save or restore a register (during a procedure call) that contains an allocated variable and is not aliased.

4. A required stack reference—a reference to a stack variable that is required due to aliasing possibilities. For example, if the address of the stack variable were taken, then that variable cannot usually be register allocated. Also included in this category are any data items that were caller saved due to aliasing behavior—such as a potential reference by a called procedure.

5. A computed reference—any heap reference or any reference to a stack variable via a pointer or array index.

Our second question concerns how an optimizer affects the mix of instructions executed. Figure 3.35 addresses this issue for the benchmarks used here. The data was taken on a load/store machine using full global optimization that includes all of the global and local optimizations listed in Figure 3.33 (page 137). Differences between optimized and unoptimized code are shown in both absolute and relative terms. The most obvious effect of optimization—besides decreasing the total instruction count—is to increase the relative frequency of branches by decreasing the number of memory references and ALU operations more rapidly than the number of branches (which are decreased only slightly).

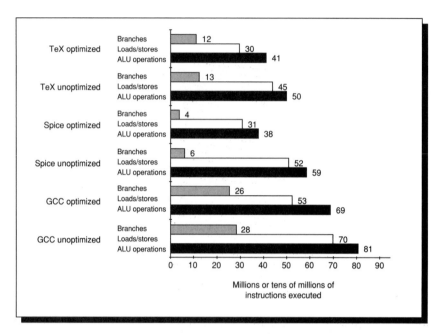

FIGURE 3.35   The effects of optimization in absolute instruction counts. The x axis is the number of instructions executed in millions for GCC and TeX and in tens of millions for Spice. The unoptimized programs execute 21%, 58%, and 30% more instructions for GCC, Spice, and TeX, respectively. This data was taken on a DECstation 3100 using –O2 optimization. Optimizations that do not affect instruction count, but may affect instruction cycle counts, are not measured here. This data was collected for the first edition of this book using different inputs and compilers than the figures in the next section.

3.7 | Putting It All Together: Measurements of Instruction Set Usage

In this section we examine the dynamic use of the instruction sets presented in this chapter. We present detailed measurements for 80x806 and DLX, the architectures that are popular today. To facilitate comparisons among dynamic instruction set measurements, we use a subset of the SPEC92 programs:

Gcc: the gnu C compiler;

Espresso: the Computer Aided Circuit Design system for logic minimization;

Spice: the Computer Aided Circuit Design system, which has some floating
point calculations;

NASA7: a collection of NASA kernels, this collect of programs is floating
point intensive.

The VAX measurements were taken in 1990 on a VAX 8700 using VAX Fortran
V5.0-1 and VAX C V3.1 on the VMS operating system. The 80x86 results were
taken in 1994 using the Sun Solaris Fortran and C compilers V2.0 and executed
in 32-bit mode. The DLX results were based on the MIPS Fortran and C compilers for the R4000 processor taken in 1994.

Remember that these measurements depend on the benchmarks chosen and
the compiler technology used. While the authors feel that the measurements in
this section are reasonably indicative of the usage of these four architectures, other programs may behave differently from any of the benchmarks here, and different compilers may yield different results. In doing a real instruction set study, the
architect would want to have a much larger set of benchmarks, spanning as wide
an application range as possible, and consider the operating system and its usage
of the instruction set. Single-user benchmarks like those measured here do not
necessarily behave in the same fashion as the operating system.

Instruction Count Measurements

Figure 3.36 shows the number of instructions executed for each benchmark. The
VAX uniformly executes fewer instructions. VAX advantages include operands
can be left in memory and the rich addressing modes. The 80x86 and DLX are
surprisingly close in instruction count, except for the floating point intensive
NASA7.

SPEC pgm	VAX	x86	DLX	86÷V	D÷V	D÷86
gcc	N.A.	3,771,327,742	3,892,063,460			1.03
espresso	1,664,002,614	2,216,423,413	2,801,294,286	1.33	1.68	1.26
spice	11,146,129,316	15,257,026,309	16,965,928,788	1.37	1.52	1.11
nasa7	4,743,859,295	15,603,040,963	6,118,740,321	3.29	1.29	0.39

FIGURE 3.36   Number of instructions executed for four SPEC programs.

	gcc		espresso		spice		nasa7	
	x86	*DLX*	*x86*	*DLX*	*x86*	*DLX*	*x86*	*DLX*
load	939	853	485	641	3,122	3,469	3,662	28
load imm	65	296	29	31	7	118	3	14
store	575	507	168	142	2,013	345	1,267	10
Total data tran.	**1,579**	**1,656**	**683**	**813**	**5,142**	**3,932**	**4,931**	**52**
add (including lea)	288	623	189	746	3,279	4.195	2,719	1,095
sub	110	308	78		174	1,280	1,348	226
mul	3		0		19		803	
div	1		0		0		0	
compare	510	93	338	105	1,441	102	176	
mov rr	158		110		311		587	
Total int. arith.	**1,070**	**1,024**	**706**	**851**	**5,224**	**5,577**	**5,632**	**1,321**
cond. branch	655	532	420	362	1,819	1,680	233	216
uncond branch	82	40	19		288	166	22	
call	56	41	15		40		181	8
return, jmp indirect	56	61	15		40		181	8
Total control	**849**	**673**	**469**	**362**	**2,186**	**1,846**	**616**	**233**
shift	63	156	54	234	335	2,481	336	55
and	171	55	194	235	277		58	12
or	16	186	61	132	0		2	21
other (xor,,not,..)	13		49	51	0		0	11
Total logical	**264**	**397**	**358**	**652**	**611**	**2,481**	**395**	**87**
load fp					567	1,046	1,212	1,413
store fp					521	364	780	608
Total fp data tran	**0**	**0**	**0**	**0**	**1,087**	**1,410**	**1,992**	**2,021**
add					131	203	397	456
sub					204	222	586	602
mul					245	335	978	1,077
div					76	79	14	
compare					71		1	
mov					22		37	237
other (abs, sqrt....)					186		8	
Total fp arith	**0**	**0**	**0**	**0**	**934**	**839**	**2,021**	**2,372**
Misc	**10**	**142**	**0**	**123**	**72**	**881**	**15**	**26**
Total	**3,771**	**3,892**	**2,216**	**2,801**	**15,257**	**16,966**	**15,603**	**6,113**

FIGURE 3.37   Number of instructions (in millions) executed by category for 80x86 and DLX for the four SPEC programs. The apparent lack of move register-register instructions in DLX is due to their folding into existing logical instructions, most likely the OR instruction.

For the 80x86 and DLX we have much more detailed instruction statistics on the four programs. Figure 3.37 shows the actual instruction counts and Figure 3.38 shows the percentage in each category. Figure 3.37 shows many fewer compares for DLX due to the branching on register contents rather than the condition codes of the 80x86. The fewer shifts on the 80x86 are likely due to the scaled addressing mode, which is accomplished in DLX by a shift of 1, 2, or 3 bits before the index calculation. Presumably the 80x86 executes fewer of the floating point additions, subtracts, multiplies and divides due to the built-in higher level operations such as square root and cosine. Some combination of compiler technology and more floating point registers account for the dramatically fewer instructions in NASA7.

	gcc		espresso		spice		nasa7	
	x86	DLX	x86	DLX	x86	DLX	x86	DLX
Total data tran.	42%	43%	31%	29%	34%	23%	32%	1%
Total int. arith.	28%	26%	32%	30%	34%%	33%	36%	22%
Total control	23%	17%	21%	13%	14%	11%	4%	4%
Total logical	7%	10%	16%	23%	4%	5%	3%	1%
Total fp data tran.	0%	0%	0%	0%	7%	8%	13%	33%
Total fp arith.	0%	0%	0%	0%	6%	5%	13%	39%
Misc	0%	4%	0%	4%	0%	5%	0%	0%

FIGURE 3.38   Percentage of instructions executed by category for 80x86 and DLX for the four SPEC programs of Figure 3.37.

Measurements of 80x86 Usage

The given a the single addressing mode and single instruction size of DLX, there is little more to report for DLX. The 80x86 is another matter. We start with addressing modes. Figure 3.39 shows the distribution of the operand types in the 80x86. These measurements cover the "second" operand of the operation; for example,

```
mov EAX, [45]
```

counts as a single memory operand. If registers were counted, the average distribution would be approximately 63%, 7%, and 30%, respectively. The memory operands are divided into their respective addressing modes in Figure 3.40. Probably the biggest surprise is the popularity of the addressing modes added by the 80386, the last four rows of the figure. They account for half of all the memory accesses. On the VAX and DLX, the equivalent of the direct addressing mode is rare. Perhaps the segmented address space of the 80x86 makes direct addressing more useful, since the address is relative to a base address from the segment register.

	Gcc	Espresso	NASA7	Spice	Average
register	31%	30%	19%	21%	25%
immediate	21%	19%	9%	6%	14%
memory	48%	52%	71%	73%	61%

FIGURE 3.39   Operand type distribution by program.

Addressing Mode	Gcc%	Espresso %	NASA7 %	Spice %	Average
Register indirect	10%	10%	6%	2%	7%
Base + 8-bit disp.	46%	43%	32%	4%	31%
Base + 32-bit disp.	2%	0%	24%	10%	9%
Indexed	1%	0%	1%	0%	1%
Based indexed + 8-bit disp.	0%	0%	4%	0%	1%
Based indexed + 32-bit disp.	0%	0%	0%	0%	0%
Base + Scaled Indexed	12%	31%	9%	0%	13%
Base + Scaled Index + 8-bit disp.	2%	1%	2%	0%	1%
Base + Scaled Index + 32-bit disp.	6%	2%	2%	33%	11%
32-bit Direct	19%	12%	20%	51%	26%

FIGURE 3.40   Operand type distribution by program. This chart does not include addressing modes used by branches or control instructions.

These addressing modes largely determine the size of the Intel instructions. Figure 3.42 shows the distribution of instruction sizes for the four programs. The average number of bytes per instructions is 2.9 for Gcc, 2.8 for Espresso, 3.2 for NASA7, and 3.8 for Spice.

Given that the floating point instructions have aspects of both stacks and registers, how are they used? Figure 3.41 shows that at least for the compilers used in this measurement, the stack model of execution is followed infrequently.

	NASA&	Spice
stack (2nd opernd ST (1))	0.3%	2.0%
register (2nd operand ST(i), i≥1	23.3%	8.3%
memory	76.3%	89.7%

FIGURE 3.41   The percentage of instructions for the floating point operations (add, sub, mul, div) that use the strict stack model of implicit operands on the stack, register version naming an explicit operand that is not the top of stack or the one below, and memory operand.

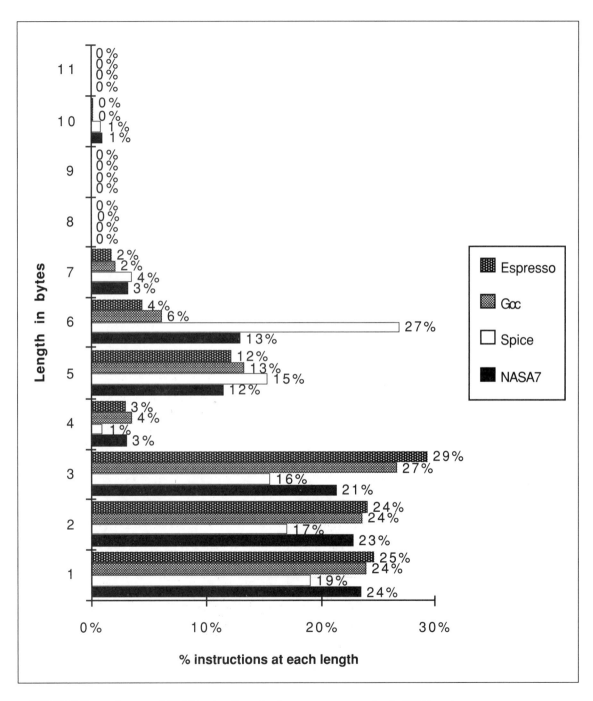

FIGURE 3.42 Histogram of 80x86 instructions for four programs running in 32-bit mode.

3.8 | Fallacies and Pitfalls

Time and again architects have tripped on common, but erroneous, beliefs. In this section we look at a few of them.

Pitfall: Designing a "high-level" instruction set feature specifically oriented to supporting a high-level language structure.

Attempts to incorporate high-level language features in the instruction set have led architects to provide powerful instructions with a wide range of flexibility. But often these instructions do more work than is required in the frequent case or don't match the requirements of the language exactly. Many such efforts have been aimed at eliminating what in the 1970s was called the "semantic gap." While the idea is to supplement the instruction set with additions that bring the hardware up to the level of the language, the additions can generate what Wulf [1981] has called a "semantic clash":

... by giving too much semantic content to the instruction, the machine designer made it possible to use the instruction only in limited contexts. [p. 43]

More often the instructions are simply overkill—they are too general for the most frequent case, resulting in unneeded work and a slower instruction. Again, the VAX CALLS is a good example. CALLS uses a callee-save strategy (the registers to be saved are specified by the callee) **but** the saving is done by the call instruction in the caller. The CALLS instruction begins with the arguments pushed on the stack, and then takes the following steps:

1. Align the stack if needed.

2. Push the argument count on the stack.

3. Save the registers indicated by the procedure call mask on the stack (as mentioned in Section 3.7). The mask is kept in the called procedure's code—this permits callee-save to be done by the caller even with separate compilation.

4. Push the return address on the stack, then push the top and base of stack pointers for the activation record.

5. Clear the condition codes, which sets the trap enables to a known state.

6. Push a word for status information and a zero word on the stack.

7. Update the two stack pointers.

8. Branch to the first instruction of the procedure.

The vast majority of calls in real programs do not require this amount of overhead. Most procedures know their argument counts and a much faster linkage convention can be established using registers to pass arguments rather than the stack. Furthermore, the call instruction forces two registers to be used for linkage, while many languages require only one linkage register. Many attempts to support procedure call and activation stack management have failed to be useful either because they do not match the language needs or because they are too general, and hence too expensive to use.

The VAX designers provided a simpler instruction, JSB, that is much faster since it only pushes the return PC on the stack and jumps to the procedure (see Exercise 3.11). However, most VAX compilers use the more costly CALLS instructions. The call instructions were included in the architecture to standardize the procedure linkage convention. Other machines have standardized their calling convention by agreement among compiler writers and without requiring the overhead of a complex, very general procedure call instruction.

*Fallacy: There is such a thing as **a** typical program.*

Many people would like to believe that there is a single "typical" program that could be used to design an optimal instruction set. For example, see the synthetic benchmarks discussed in Section 2.2. The data in this chapter clearly show that programs can vary significantly in how they use an instruction set. For example, the frequency of control-flow instructions on DLX varied from 5% to 23%. The variations are even larger on an instruction set that has specific features for supporting a class of applications, such as decimal or floating-point instructions that are unused by other applications. There is a related pitfall.

Fallacy: An architecture with flaws cannot be successful.

The 80x86 provides a dramatic example; the architecture is one only its creators could love. Succeeding generations of Intel engineers have tried to correct unpopular architectural decisions: 80x86 supported segmentation when all others picked paging; the 80x86 uses extended accumulators for integer data when all others use general purpose registers; and it uses a stack for floating point data when everyone else abandoned execution stacks long before. Despite these major difficulties, the 8086 architecture—because of its selection as the microprocessor in the IBM PC—has been enormously successful.

Fallacy: One can design a flawless architecture.

All architecture design involves tradeoffs made in the context of a set of hardware and software technologies. Over time those technologies are likely to change, and decisions that may have been correct at the time they were made look like mistakes. For example, in 1975 the VAX designers overemphasized the importance of code-size efficiency and underestimated how important ease of decoding and pipelining would be ten years later. Almost all architectures eventually succumb to the lack of sufficient address space. However, avoiding this problem in the long run would probably mean compromising the efficiency of the architecture in the short run.

3.9 | Concluding Remarks

The earliest architectures were limited in their instruction sets by the hardware technology of that time. As soon as the hardware technology permitted, architects began looking for ways to support high-level languages. This search led to three distinct periods of thought about how to support programs efficiently. In the 1960s, stack architectures became popular. They were viewed as being a good match for high-level languages—and they probably were, given the compiler technology of the day. In the 1970s, the main concern of architects was how to reduce software costs. This concern was met primarily by replacing software with hardware, or by providing high-level architectures that could simplify the task of software designers. The result was both the high-level–language computer architecture movement and powerful architectures like the VAX, which has a large number of addressing modes, multiple data types, and a highly orthogonal architecture. In the 1980s, more sophisticated compiler technology and a renewed emphasis on machine performance has seen a return to simpler architectures, based mainly on the load/store style of machine. Continuing changes in how we program, the compiler technology we use, and the underlying hardware technology will no doubt make another direction more attractive in the future.

3.10 | Historical Perspective and References

One's eyebrows should rise whenever a future architecture is developed with a stack- or register-oriented instruction set.

Meyers [1978, 20]

The earliest computers, including the UNIVAC I, the EDSAC, and the IAS machines, were accumulator-based machines. The simplicity of this type of machine made it the natural choice when hardware resources were very constrained. The first general-purpose register machine was the Pegasus, built by Ferranti, Ltd. in 1956. The Pegasus had eight general-purpose registers, with R0 always being zero. Block transfers loaded the eight registers from the drum.

In 1963, Burroughs delivered the B5000. The B5000 was perhaps the first machine to seriously consider software and hardware-software tradeoffs. Barton and the designers at Burroughs made the B5000 a stack architecture (as described in Barton [1961]). Designed to support high-level languages such as ALGOL, this stack architecture used an operating system (MCP) written in a high-level language. The B5000 was also the first machine from a US manufacturer to support virtual memory. The B6500, introduced in 1968 (and discussed in Hauck and Dent [1968]), added hardware-managed activation records. In both the B5000 and B6500, the top two elements of the stack were kept in the CPU and the rest of the stack was kept in memory. The stack architecture yielded good code density, but only provided two high-speed storage locations. The authors of both the original IBM 360 paper [Amdahl et al. 1964] and the original PDP-11 paper [Bell et al. 1970] argue against the stack organization. They cite three major points in their arguments against stacks:

1. Performance is derived from fast registers, not the way they are used.

2. The stack organization is too limiting and requires many swap and copy operations.

3. The stack has a bottom, and when placed in slower memory there is a performance loss.

Stack-based machines fell out of favor in the late 1970s and, except for the Intel 80x86 floating point architecture, essentially disappeared.

The term "computer architecture" was coined by IBM in 1964 for use with the IBM 360. Amdahl, Blaauw, and Brooks [1964] used the term to refer to the programmer-visible portion of the instruction set. They believed that a family of machines of the same architecture should be able to run the same software. Although this idea may seem obvious to us today, it was quite novel at that time. IBM, even though it was the leading company in the industry, had **five** different architectures before the 360. Thus, the notion of a company standardizing on a single architecture was a radical one. The 360 designers hoped that six different divisions of IBM could be brought together by defining a common architecture. Their definition of architecture was

... the structure of a computer that a machine language programmer must understand to write a correct (timing independent) program for that machine.

The term "machine language programmer" meant that compatibility would hold, even in assembly language, while "timing independent" allowed different implementations.

The IBM 360 was the first machine to sell in large quantities with both byte-addressing using 8-bit bytes and general purpose registers. The 360 also had register–memory and limited memory–memory instructions.

In 1964, Control Data delivered the first supercomputer, the CDC 6600. As discussed in Thornton [1964], he, Cray, and the other 6600 designers were the first to explore pipelining in depth. The 6600 was the first general-purpose, load/store machine. In the 1960s, the designers of the 6600 realized the need to simplify architecture for the sake of efficient pipelining. This interaction between architectural simplicity and implementation was largely neglected during the 1970s by microprocessor and minicomputer designers, but was brought back in the 1980s.

In the late 1960s and early 1970s, people realized that software costs were growing faster than hardware costs. McKeeman [1967] argued that compilers and operating systems were getting too big and too complex and taking too long to develop. Because of inferior compilers and the memory limitations of machines, most systems programs at the time were still written in assembly language. Many researchers proposed alleviating the software crisis by creating more powerful, software-oriented architectures. Tanenbaum [1978] studied the properties of high-level languages. Like other researchers, he found that most programs are simple. He then argued that architectures should be designed with this in mind and should optimize program size and ease of compilation. Tanenbaum proposed a stack machine with frequency-encoded instruction formats to accomplish these goals. However, as we have observed, program size does not translate directly to cost/performance, and stack machines faded out shortly after this work.

Strecker's article [1978] discusses how he and the other architects at DEC responded to this by designing the VAX architecture. The VAX was designed to simplify compilation of high-level languages. Compiler writers had complained about the lack of complete orthogonality in the PDP-11. The VAX architecture was designed to be highly orthogonal and to allow the mapping of a high-level–language statement into a single VAX instruction. Additionally, the VAX designers tried to optimize code size because compiled programs were often too large for available memories.

In 1977, DEC introduced the VAX, and called "a Virtual Address eXtension of the PDP-11." In the mid-1970s, DEC realized that the PDP-11 was running out of address space. However, as Strecker and Bell [1976] observed, the small address space was a problem that could not be overcome, but only postponed. One of DEC's primary goals was to keep the installed base of PDP-11 customers. Thus, the customers were to think of the VAX as a 32-bit successor to the PDP-11. A 32-bit PDP-11 was possible—there were three designs—but Strecker reports that they were "overly compromised in terms of efficiency, functionality, programming ease." The chosen solution was to design a new architecture and include a PDP-11 compatibility mode that would run PDP-11 programs without change. This mode also allowed PDP-11 compilers to run and to continue to be used. The VAX-11/780 was made similar to the PDP-11 in many ways. These are among the most important:

1. Data types and formats are mostly equivalent to those on the PDP-11. The F and D floating formats came from the PDP-11. G and H formats were added later. The use of the term "word" to describe a 16-bit quantity was carried from the PDP-11 to the VAX.

2. The assembly language was made similar to the PDP-11's.

3. The same buses were supported (Unibus and Massbus).

4. The operating system, VMS, was "an evolution" of the RSX-11M/IAS OS (as opposed to the DECsystem 10/20 OS, which was a more advanced system).

5. The file system was basically the same.

The VAX-11/780 was the first machine announced in the VAX series. It is one of the most successful and heavily studied machines ever built. The cornerstone of DEC's strategy was a single architecture, VAX, running a single operating system, VMS. This strategy worked well for over ten years. The large number of papers reporting instruction mixes, implementation measurements, and analysis of the VAX make it an ideal case study.

Wiecek [1982] reported on the use of various architectural features in running a workload consisting of six compilers. Emer did a set of measurements (reported by Clark and Levy [1982]) on the instruction set utilization of the VAX when running four very different programs and when running the operating system. A good detailed description of the architecture, including memory management and an examination of several of the VAX implementations, can be found in Levy and Eckhouse [1989]. Bhandarkar and Clark [1992] give a quantitative analysis of the disadvantages of the VAX versus a RISC machine, essentially a technical explanation for the demise of the VAX.

The first microprocessors were produced late in the first half of the 1970s. The Intel 4004 and 8008 were extremely simple 4-bit and 8-bit accumulator-style machines. Morse et al. [1980] describe the evolution of the 8086 from the 8080 in the late 1970s in an attempt to provide a 16-bit machine with better throughput. At that time almost all programming for microprocessors was done in assembly language—both memory and compilers were in short supply. Intel wanted to keep its base of 8080 users, so the 8086 was designed to be "compatible" with the 8080. The 8086 was **never** object-code compatible with the 8080, but the machines were close enough that translation of assembly language programs could be done automatically.

In early 1980, IBM selected a version of the 8086 with an 8-bit external bus, called the 8088, for use in the IBM PC. (They chose the 8-bit version to reduce the cost of the machine.) This choice, together with the tremendous success of the IBM PC and its clones (made possible because IBM opened the architecture of the PC), has made the 8086 architecture ubiquitous. While the 68000 was chosen for the popular Macintosh, the Macintosh was never as pervasive as the PC (partly because Apple did not allow clones), and the 68000 did not acquire the same software leverage that the 8086 enjoys. The Motorola 68000 may have been more significant **technically** than the 8086, but the impact of the selection by IBM and IBM's open architecture strategy dominated the technical advantages of the 68000 in the market. As discussed in Section 3.4, the 80286, 80386, 80486, and Pentium have extended the architecture and provided a series of performance enhancements.

There are numerous descriptions of the 80x86 architecture that have been published—Wakerly's [1989] is both concise and easy to understand. Crawford and Gelsinger [1988] is a thorough description of the 80386.

Studies of instruction set usage began in the late 1950s. The Gibson mix, described in the last chapter, was derived as a study of instruction usage on the IBM 7090. There were several studies in the 1970s of instruction set usage. Among the best known are Foster et al. [1971] and Lunde [1977]. Most of these early studies used small programs because the techniques used to collect data were expensive. Starting in the late 1970s, the area of instruction set measurement and analysis became very active.

While the VAX was being designed, a more radical approach, called *High-Level Language Computer Architecture* (HLLCA), was being advocated in the research community. This movement aimed to eliminate the gap between high-level languages and computer hardware—what Gagliardi [1973] called the "semantic gap"—by bringing the hardware "up to" the level of the programming language. Meyers [1982] provides a good summary of the arguments and a history of high-level–language computer architecture projects. HLLCA never had a significant commercial impact. The increase in memory size on machines and the use of virtual memory eliminated the code-size problems arising from high-level languages and operating systems written in high-level languages. The combination of simpler architectures together with software offered greater performance and more flexibility at lower cost and lower complexity.

In the early 1980s, the direction of computer architecture began to swing away from providing high-level hardware support for languages. Ditzel and Patterson [1980] analyzed the difficulties encountered by the high-level–language architectures and argued that the answer lay in simpler architectures. In another paper [Patterson and Ditzel 1980], these authors first discussed the idea of reduced instruction set computers (RISC) and presented the argument for simpler architectures. Their proposal was rebutted by Clark and Strecker [1980].

The simple load/store machines from which DLX is derived are commonly called RISC *(reduced instruction set computer)* architectures. The roots of RISC architectures go back to machines like the 6600, where Thornton, Cray, and others recognized the importance of instruction set simplicity in building a fast machine. Cray continued his tradition of keeping machines simple in the CRAY-1. However, DLX and its close relatives are built primarily on the work of three research projects: the Berkeley RISC processor, the IBM 801, and the Stanford MIPS processor. These architectures have attracted enormous industrial interest because of claims of a performance advantage of anywhere from two to five times over other machines using the same technology.

Begun in the late 1970s, the IBM project was the first to start but was the last to become public. The IBM machine was designed as an ECL minicomputer, while the university projects were both MOS-based microprocessors. John Cocke is considered to be the father of the 801 design. He received both the Eckert-Mauchly and Turing awards in recognition of his contribution. Radin [1982] describes the highlights of the 801 architecture. The 801 was an experimental project, but was never designed to be a product. In fact, to keep down cost and complexity, the machine was built with only 24-bit registers.

In 1980, Patterson and his colleagues at Berkeley began the project that was to give this architectural approach its name (see Patterson and Ditzel [1980]). They built two machines called RISC-I and RISC-II. Because the IBM project was not widely known or discussed, the role played by the Berkeley group in promoting the RISC approach was critical to the acceptance of the technology. In addition to a simple load/store architecture, this machine introduced register windows—an idea that has been adopted by several commercial RISC machines (this concept is discussed further in Chapter 8). The Berkeley group went on to build RISC machines targeted toward Smalltalk, described by Ungar et al. [1984], and LISP, described by Taylor et al. [1987].

In 1981, Hennessy and his colleagues at Stanford published a description of the Stanford MIPS machine. Efficient pipelining and compiler-assisted scheduling of the pipeline were both key aspects of the original MIPS design.

These three early RISC machines had much in common. Both the university projects were interested in designing a simple machine that could be built in VLSI within the university environment. All three machines—the 801, MIPS, and RISC-II—used a simple load/store architecture, fixed-format 32-bit instructions, and emphasized efficient pipelining. Patterson [1985] describes the three machines and the basic design principles that have come to characterize what a RISC machine is. Hennessy [1984] is another view of the same ideas, as well as other issues in VLSI processor design.

In 1985, Hennessy published an explanation of the RISC performance advantage and traced its roots to a substantially lower CPI—under two for a RISC machine and over ten for a VAX-11/780 (though not with identical workloads). A paper by Emer and Clark [1984] characterizing VAX-11/780 performance was instrumental in helping the RISC researchers understand the source of the performance advantage seen by their machines.

Since the university projects finished up, in the 1983-84 timeframe, the technology has been widely embraced by industry. Many of the early computers (before 1986) laid claim to being RISC machines. However, these claims were often born more of marketing ambition than of engineering reality.

In 1986, the computer industry began to announce processors based on the technology explored by the three RISC research projects. Moussoris et al. [1986] describe the MIPS R2000 integer processor; while Kane [1987] is a complete description of the architecture. Hewlett-Packard converted their existing minicomputer line to RISC architectures; the HP Precision Architecture is described by Lee [1989]. IBM never directly turned the 801 into a product. Instead, the ideas were adopted for a new, low-end architecture that was incorporated in the IBM RT-PC and is described in a collection of papers [Waters 1986]. In 1990, IBM announced a new RISC architecture (the RS 6000), which is the first super scalar RISC machine (see chapter 6). In 1987, Sun Microsystems began delivering machines based on the SPARC architecture, a derivative of the Berkeley RISC-II machine; SPARC is described in Garner et al. [1988]. The PowerPC, joining the forces of Apple, IBM, and Motorola, promises to be important in the marketplace. Figure 3.43 summarizes several RISC architectures.

Prior to the RISC architecture movement, the major trend had been highly microcoded architectures aimed at reducing the semantic gap. DEC, with the VAX, and Intel, with the iAPX 432, were among the leaders in this approach. Today it is hard to find a computer company without a RISC product. With the announcement of Hewlett Packard and Intel in 1994 that they will eventually have a common architecture, the end of the non-RISC architectures draws near.

Machine	Registers	Addressing modes	Operations
DLX	32 integer; 16 DP or 32 SP FP	16-bit displacement; 16-bit immediates	See Figure 3.6.
AMD 29000	192 integer with stack cache; 8 DP FP	Register deferred only; 8-bit immediates	Integer multiply/divide trap to software. Branches =,≠ 0 only.
HP Precision Architecture	32 GPRs	5-bit, 14-bit, and 32-bit displacements; scaled mode (load only); autoincrement; autodecrement	Every ALU operation can skip the next instruction. Many special bit-manipulation instructions. 32-bit immediates; decimal-support instructions: integer multiply/divide not single instructions. Stores of partial word. 64-bit addresses possible through segmentation.
Intel i860	32 integer; 16 DP or 32 SP FP	16-bit displacement; indexed mode; autoincrement; 16-bit immediates	Branch compares two registers for equality. Conditional traps are supported. FP reciprocal rather than divide. Some support for 128-bit loads and stores.
MIPS R2000 / R3000	32 integer; 16 FP	16-bit displacement; 16-bit immediates	Floating-point load/store moves 32 bits to one register in the pair. Branch condition can compare two registers. Integer multiply/divide in GPRs. Special instructions for partial word load/store.
Motorola 88000	32 GPRs	16-bit displacement; indexed mode	Special bit-manipulation instructions. Branches can test for zero and also test bits set by compares.
SPARC	Register windows with 32 integer registers available per procedure; 16 DP or 32 SP FP	13-bit offset and 13-bit immediates; indexed addressing mode	Branches use condition code, set selectively by instructions. Integer multiply/divide not instructions. No moves between integer and FP registers.

FIGURE 3.43   Comparison of the major features of a variety of recent load/store architectures. All the machines have a basic instruction size of 32 bits, though some provisions for shorter or longer are supported. For example, the Precision Architecture uses 2-word instructions for long immediates. Register windows and stack caches, which are used in the SPARC and AMD 29000 architectures, are discussed in Chapter 8. The MIPS R2000 is used in the DECstation 3100, the machine benchmarked in Chapter 2, and used as the load/store machine in Chapter 3. The number of double-precision floating-point registers is indicated if they are separate from the integer registers. Appendix E has a detailed comparative description of DLX, the MIPS R2000, SPARC, the i860, and the 88000 architectures. Both the MIPS and SPARC architectures have extensions that were not supported in hardware in the first implementation.

References

AMDAHL, G. M., G. A. BLAAUW, AND F. P. BROOKS, JR. [1964]. "Architecture of the IBM System 360," *IBM J. Research and Development* 8:2 (April) 87–101.

BARTON, R. S. [1961]. "A new approach to the functional design of a computer," *Proc. Western Joint Computer Conf.,* 393–396.

BELL, C. G. ET AL [1970]. "A new architecture for minicomputers: the DEC PDP-11," *Proc. AFIPS SJCC,* 667-675.

BHANDARKAR, D., AND D. W. CLARK [1991]. "Performance from architecture: comparing a RISC and a CISC with similar hardware organizations," Proc. Fourth Conf. on Architectural Support for Programming Languages and Operating Systems, IEEE/ACM (April), Palo Alto, 310–19.BELL, G., R. CADY, H. MCFARLAND, B. DELAGI, J. O'LAUGHLIN, R. NOONAN, AND W. WULF [1970]. "A new architecture for mini-computers: The DEC PDP-11," *Proc. AFIPS SJCC,* 657–675.

CLARK, D. AND H. LEVY [1982]. "Measurement and analysis of instruction set use in the VAX-11/780," *Proc. Ninth Symposium on Computer Architecture* (April), Austin, Tex., 9–17.

CRAWFORD, J. AND P. GELSINGER [1988]. *Programming the 80386,* Sybex Books, Alameda, Calif.

FOSTER, C. C., R. H. GONTER, AND E. M. RISEMAN [1971]. "Measures of opcode utilization," *IEEE Trans. on Computers* 13:5 (May) 582–584.

GAGLIARDI, U. O. [1973]. "Report of workshop 4–software-related advances in computer hardware," *Proc. Symposium on the High Cost of Software*, Menlo Park, Calif., 99–120.

GARNER, R., A. AGARWAL, F. BRIGGS, E. BROWN, D. HOUGH, B. JOY, S. KLEIMAN, S. MUNCHNIK, M. NAMJOO, D. PATTERSON, J. PENDLETON, AND R. TUCK [1988]. "Scalable processor architecture (SPARC)," *COMPCON, IEEE* (March), San Francisco, 278–283.

HENNESSY, J. [1984]. "VLSI processor architecture," *IEEE Trans. on Computers* C-33:11 (December) 1221–1246.

HENNESSY, J. [1985]. "VLSI RISC processors," *VLSI Systems Design* VI:10 (October) 22–32.

HENNESSY, J., N. JOUPPI, F. BASKETT, AND J. GILL [1981]. "MIPS: A VLSI processor architecture," *Proc. CMU Conf. on VLSI Systems and Computations* (October), Computer Science Press, Rockville, Md.

LEVY, H. AND R. ECKHOUSE [1989]. *Computer Programming and Architecture: The VAX,* Digital Press, Boston.

LUNDE, A. [1977]. "Empirical evaluation of some features of instruction set processor architecture," *Comm. ACM* 20:3 (March) 143–152.

MCKEEMAN, W. M. [1967]. "Language directed computer design," *Proc. 1967 Fall Joint Computer Conf.,* Washington, D.C., 413–417.

MEYERS, G. J. [1978]. "The evaluation of expressions in a storage-to-storage architecture," *Computer Architecture News* 7:3 (October), 20–23.

MEYERS, G. J. [1982]. *Advances in Computer Architecture*, 2nd ed., Wiley, N.Y.

MORSE, S., B. RAVENAL, S. MAZOR, AND W. POHLMAN [1980]. "Intel Microprocessors—8008 to 8086," *Computer* 13:10 (October).

PATTERSON, D. [1985]. "Reduced Instruction Set Computers," *Comm. ACM* 28:1 (January) 8–21.

PATTERSON, D. A. AND D. R. DITZEL [1980]. "The case for the reduced instruction set computer," *Computer Architecture News* 8:6 (October) 25–33.

RADIN, G. [1982]. "The 801 minicomputer," *Proc. Symposium Architectural Support for Programming Languages and Operating Systems* (March), Palo Alto, Calif. 39–47.

STRECKER, W. D. [1978]. "VAX-11/780: A virtual address extension of the PDP-11 family," *Proc. AFIPS National Computer Conf.* 47, 967–980.

STRECKER, W. D. AND C. G. BELL [1976]. "Computer structures: What have we learned from the PDP-11?," *Proc. Third Symposium on Computer Architecture.*

TAYLOR, G., P. HILFINGER, J. LARUS, D. PATTERSON, AND B. ZORN [1986]. "Evaluation of the SPUR LISP architecture," *Proc. 13th Symposium on Computer Architecture (*June), Tokyo.

THORNTON, J. E. [1964]. "Parallel operation in Control Data 6600," *Proc. AFIPS Fall Joint Computer Conf.* 26, part 2, 33–40.

UNGAR, D., R. BLAU, P. FOLEY, D. SAMPLES, AND D. PATTERSON [1984]. "Architecture of SOAR: Smalltalk on a RISC," *Proc. 11th Symposium on Computer Architecture* (June), Ann Arbor, Mich., 188–197.

WAKERLY, J. [1989]. *Microcomputer Architecture and Programming,* J. Wiley, New York.

WATERS, F., ED. [1986]. *IBM RT Personal Computer Technology,* IBM, Austin, Tex., SA 23-1057.

WIECEK, C. [1982]. "A case study of the VAX 11 instruction set usage for compiler execution," *Proc. Symposium on Architectural Support for Programming Languages and Operating Systems* (March), IEEE/ACM, Palo Alto, Calif., 177–184.

EXERCISES

3.1 [20/15/10] <3.3, 3.8> We are designing instruction set formats for a load/store architecture and are trying to decide whether it is worthwhile to have multiple offset lengths for branches and memory references. We have decided that the offsets will be the same for these two classes of instructions. The length of an instruction would be equal to 16 bits + offset length in bits. ALU instructions will be 16 bits. Figure 3.44 contains the data in cumulative form. Assume an additional bit is needed for the sign on the offset.

For instruction set frequencies, use the data for DLX from the average of the four benchmarks for the load/store machine in Figure 3.38.

Offset bits	Cumulative data references	Cumulative branches
0	16%	0%
1	16%	0%
2	21%	10%
3	29%	27%
4	32%	47%
5	44%	66%
6	55%	79%
7	62%	89%
8	66%	94%
9	68%	97%
10	73%	99%
11	78%	100%
12	80%	100%
13	86%	100%
14	87%	100%
15	100%	100%

FIGURE 3.44 The second and third columns contain the cumulative percentage of the data references and branches, respectively, that can be accommodated with the corresponding number of bits of magnitude in the displacement.

a. [20] Suppose offsets were permitted to be 0, 8, or 16 bits in length including the sign-bit. Suppose the, what is the average length of an executed instruction?

b. [15] Suppose we wanted a fixed-length instruction and we chose a 24-bit instruction length (for everything, including ALU instructions). For every offset of longer than 8 bits, an additional instruction is required. Determine the number of instruction bytes fetched in this machine with fixed instruction size versus those fetched with a variable-sized instruction.

c. [10] What if the offset length were 16 and we never required an additional instruction? How would instruction bytes fetched compare to the choice of only an 8-bit offset? Assume ALU instructions will be 16 bits.

3.2 [15/10] <3.2> Several researchers have suggested that adding a register–memory addressing mode to a load/store machine might be useful. The idea is to replace sequences of

```
LOAD    R1,O(Rb)
ADD     R2,R2,R1
```

by

```
ADD     R2,O(Rb)
```

Assume the new instruction will cause the clock cycle to increase by 10%. Use the instruction frequencies for the GCC benchmark on the load/store machine from Figure 3.38 and assume that two-thirds of the moves are loads and the rest are stores. The new instruction affects only the clock speed and not the CPI.

a. [15] What percentage of the loads must be eliminated for the machine with the new instruction to have at least the same performance?

b. [10] Show a situation in a multiple instruction sequence where a load of R1 followed immediately by a use of R1 (with some type of opcode) could not be replaced by a single instruction of the form proposed, assuming that the same opcode exists.

3.3 [15/20] <3.1–3.3> For the next two parts of this question, your task is to compare the memory efficiency of four different styles of instruction sets for two code sequences. The architecture styles are:

Accumulator

Memory–Memory—All three operands of each instruction are in memory.

Stack—All operations occur on top of the stack. Only push and pop access memory, and all other instructions remove their operands from stack and replace them with the result. The implementation uses a stack for the top two entries; accesses that use other stack positions are memory references.

Load/store—All operations occur in registers, and register-to-register instructions have three operands per instruction. There are 16 general-purpose registers, and register specifiers are 4 bits long.

To measure memory efficiency, make the following assumptions about all four instruction sets:

■ The opcode is always 1 byte (8 bits).

■ All memory addresses are 2 bytes (16 bits).

- All data operands are 4 bytes (32 bits).

- All instructions are an integral number of bytes in length.

There are no other optimizations to reduce memory traffic, and the variables   A, B, C, and D are initially in memory.

Invent your own assembly language mnemonics and write the best equivalent assembly language code for the high-level–language fragments given.

a.   [15] Write the four code sequences for

$$A = B + C;$$

For each code sequence, calculate the instruction bytes fetched and the memory-data bytes transferred. Which architecture is most efficient as measured by code size? Which architecture is most efficient as measured by total memory bandwidth required (code + data)?

b.   [20] Write the four code sequences for

$$A = B + C;$$
$$B = A + C;$$
$$D = A - B;$$

For each code sequence, calculate the instruction bytes fetched and the memory-data bytes transferred (read or written). Which architecture is most efficient as measured by code size? Which architecture is most efficient as measured by total memory bandwidth required (code + data)? If the answers are different from part a, why are they different?

3.4 [Discussion] <3.2–3.8> What are the **economic** arguments (i.e., more machines sold) **for and against** changing instruction set architecture?

3.5 [25] <3.1–3.3> Find an instruction set manual for some older machine (libraries and private bookshelves are good places to look). Summarize the instruction set with the discriminating characteristics used in Figures 3.1 and 3.5 (pages 91 and 97). Does the machine fit nicely into one of the categories shown in Figures 3.4 and 3.6 (pages 96 and 98)? Write the code sequence for this machine for the statements in both parts of Exercise 3.5.

3.6 [30] <3.7, 3.9> Find a machine that has a powerful instruction set feature, such as the CALLS instruction on the VAX. Replace the powerful instruction with a simpler sequence that accomplishes what is needed. Measure the resultant running time. How do the two compare? Why might they be different? In the early 1980s, engineers at DEC did a quick experiment to evaluate the impact of replacing   CALLS. They found a 30% improvement in run time on a very call-intensive program when the   CALLS was simply replaced (parameters remained on the stack). How do your results compare?

3.7 [20/22/22] <4.2,4.3,4.5> Consider the following fragment of C code:

```
for (i=1; i<=100; i++)
    {A[i] = B[i] + C;}
```

Assume that A are B are arrays of 32-bit integers, and   C and i are 32-bit integers. Assume that all data values are kept in memory (at addresses 0, 5000, 1500, and 2000 for A, B, C, and i, respectively) except when they are operated on.

a. [20] Write the code for DLX; how many instructions are required dynamically? How many memory data references will be executed? What is the code size?

b. [22] Write the code for the VAX; how many instructions are required dynamically? How many memory data references will be executed? What is the code size?

c. [22] Write the code for the 80x86; how many instructions are required dynamically? How many memory data references will be executed? What is the code size?

3.8 [20/22/22] <4.2,4.3,4.5> For this question use the code sequence of problem 4.2, but put the scalar data—the value of i and the address of the array variables (but not the actual array)—in registers and keep them there whenever possible.

a. [20] Write the code for DLX; how many instructions are required dynamically? How many memory-data references will be executed? What is the code size?

b. [22] Write the code for the VAX; how many instructions are required dynamically? How many memory data references will be executed? What is the code size?

c. [22] Write the code for the 80x86; how many instructions are required dynamically? How many memory data references will be executed? What is the code size?

3.9 [15] <4.6> When designing memory systems it becomes useful to know the frequency of memory reads versus writes and also accesses for instructions versus data. Using the average instruction-mix information for DLX in Figure 3.38, find

■ the percentage of all memory accesses that are for data

■ the percentage of data accesses that are reads

■ the percentage of all memory accesses that are reads

Ignore the size of a datum when counting accesses.

3.10 [18] <4.5,4.6> Compute the effective CPI for DLX. Suppose we have made the following measurements of average CPI for instructions:

All R–R instructions		1 clock cycle
Loads/stores		1.4 clock cycles
Conditional branches		
	taken	2.0 clock cycles
	not taken	1.5 clock cycles
Jumps		1.2 clock cycles

Assume that 60% of the conditional branches are taken. Average the instruction frequencies of GCC and Espresso to obtain the instruction mix.

3.11 [20/10] <4.5,4.6> Consider adding a new index addressing mode to DLX. The addressing mode adds two registers and an 11-bit signed offset to get the effective address.

Our compiler will be changed so that code sequences of the form

```
ADD R1, R1, R2
LW  Rd, O(R1)        (or store)
```

will be replaced with a load (or store) using the new addressing mode. Use the overall average instruction frequencies in evaluating this addition.

a.   [20] Assume that the addressing mode can be used for 10% of the displacement loads and stores (accounting for both the frequency of this type of address calculation and the shorter offset). What is the ratio of instruction count on the enhanced DLX compared to the original DLX?

b.   [10] If the new addressing mode lengthens the clock cycle by 5%, which machine will be faster and by how much?

3.12 [25/15] <4.2–4.5> Find a C compiler and compile the code shown in Exercise 4.2 for a load/store machine or one of the machines covered in this chapter. Compile the code both optimized and unoptimized.

a.   [25] Find the instruction count, dynamic instruction bytes fetched, and data accesses done for both the optimized and unoptimized versions.

b.   [15] Try to improve the code by hand, and compute the same measures as in Part a for your hand-optimized version.

3.13 [30/30] <4.6, 4.7> Small synthetic benchmarks can be very misleading when used for measuring instruction mixes. This is particularly true when these benchmarks are optimized. In these exercises we want to explore these differences. These programming exercises can be done with a VAX, any load/store machine, or using the DLX compiler and simulator.

a.   [30] Compile Whetstone with optimization for a VAX, or a load/store machine similar to DLX (e.g., a DECstation or a SPARCstation), or the DLX simulator. Compute the instruction mix for the top twenty instructions. How do the optimized and unoptimized mixes compare? How does the optimized mix compare to the mix for Spice on the same or a similar machine?

b.   [30] Compile Dhrystone with optimization for a VAX, or a load/store machine similar to DLX (e.g., a DECstation or a SPARCstation), or the DLX simulator. Compute the instruction mix for the top twenty instructions. How do the optimized and unoptimized mixes compare? How does the optimized mix compare to the mix for TeX on the same or a similar machine?

3.14 [30] <4.6> Many computer manufacturers now include tools or simulators that allow you to measure the instruction set usage of a user program. Among the methods in use are machine simulation, hardware-supported trapping, and a compiler technique that instruments the object-code module by inserting counters. Find a processor available to you that includes such a tool. Use it to measure the instruction set mix for one of TeX, GCC, or Spice. Compare the results to those shown in this chapter.

315 [30] <4.5,4.6> DLX has only three operand formats for its register–register operations. Many operations might use the same destination register as one of the sources. We could introduce a new instruction format into DLX called R_2 that has only two operands and is a total of 24 bits in length. By using this instruction type whenever an operation had only two different register operands, we could reduce the instruction bandwidth required for a program. Modify the DLX simulator to count the frequency of register–register operations with only two different register operands. Using the benchmarks that come with the simulator, determine how much more instruction bandwidth DLX requires than DLX with the R_2 format.

3.16 [25] <E> How much do the instruction set variations among the RISC machines discussed in Appendix E affect performance. Choose at least three small programs (e.g., a sort), and code these programs in DLX and two other assembly languages. What is the resulting difference in instruction count?

It is quite a three-pipe problem.

Sir Arthur Conan Doyle, *The Adventures of Sherlock Holmes*

4 Pipelining

4.1 What Is Pipelining?

Pipelining is an implementation technique whereby multiple instructions are overlapped in execution. Today, pipelining is the key implementation technique used to make fast CPUs.

A pipeline is like an assembly line. In an automobile assembly line, there are many steps each contributing something to the construction of the car. Each step operates in parallel with the other steps, though on a different car. In a computer pipeline, each step in the pipeline completes a part of an instruction. Like the assembly line, different steps are completing different parts of different instructions in parallel. Each of these steps is called a *pipe stage* or a *pipe segment*. The stages are connected one to the next to form a pipe—instructions enter at one end, are processed through the stages, and exit at the other end, just as cars would in an assembly line.

In our assembly line, *throughput* is defined as the number of cars per hour and is determined by how often a completed car exits the assembly line. Likewise, the throughput of an instruction pipeline is determined by how often an instruction exits the pipeline. Because the pipe stages are hooked together, all the stages must be ready to proceed at the same time, just as we would require in an assembly line. The time required between moving an instruction one step down the pipeline is a *machine cycle*. Because all stages proceed at the same time, the length of a machine cycle is determined by the time required for the slowest pipe stage, just as in an auto assembly line, the longest step would determine the time between advancing the line. In a computer, this machine cycle is often one clock cycle (sometimes it is two, or rarely more), though the clock may have multiple phases.

The pipeline designer's goal is to balance the length of the pipeline stage, just as the designer of the assembly line tries to balance the time for each step in the process. If the stages are perfectly balanced, then the time per instruction on the pipelined machine—assuming ideal conditions (i.e., no stalls)—is equal to

$$\frac{\text{Time per instruction on nonpipelined machine}}{\text{Number of pipestages}}$$

Under these conditions, the speedup from pipelining equals the number of pipe stages, just as an assembly line with n stages can ideally produce cars n times as fast. Usually, however, the stages will not be perfectly balanced; furthermore, pipelining does involve some overhead. Thus, the time per instruction on the pipelined machine will not have its minimum possible value, though it can be close (say within 10%).

Pipelining yields a reduction in the average execution time per instruction. This reduction can be obtained by decreasing the clock cycle time of the pipelined machine or by decreasing the number of clock cycles per instruction, or by both. Typically, the biggest impact is in the number of clock cycles per instruction, though the clock cycle is often shorter in a pipelined machine (especially in pipelined supercomputers).

Pipelining is an implementation technique that exploits parallelism among the instructions in a sequential instruction stream. It has the substantial advantage that, unlike some speedup techniques (see Chapter 9 and Appendix C), it is not visible to the programmer. In this chapter we will first cover the concept of pipelining using DLX and a simplified version of its pipeline. We will then look at the problems pipelining introduces and the performance attainable under typical situations. We use DLX largely because its simplicity makes it easy to demonstrate the principles of pipelining. In fact to further simplify the diagrams, we do not include the jump instructions; adding them does not involve new concepts–only bigger diagrams. The same principles apply to more complex instruction sets, though the corresponding pipelines are more complex. Our PIAT section concludes with the MIPS R4000 pipeline. The next chapter looks at the advanced pipelining techniques being used in the highest performance processors. Before we precede to basic pipelining, we need to review a simple implementation of an unpipelined version of DLX.

A Simple Implementation of DLX

To understand how DLX can be pipelined, we need to understand how it is implemented without pipelining. This section shows a simple implementation where every instruction takes exactly one clock cycle. We will extend this basic implementation single-cycle implementation to a pipelined version, resulting in a much higher clock rate. Alternatively, we could start with a machine with a higher clock rate but that did not overlap any instructions. In such a case, pipelining would improve the CPI rather than the clock rate. For a simple instruction set like DLX, it is easier to pipeline the simple single-cycle datapath than to pipeline the more complex control needed for a datapath that takes multiple cycles per instruction.

Every DLX instruction can be implemented in five steps, though in a single-cycle implementation, all five steps occur in one clock cycle. For simplicity, we will introduce a set of names for results that are computed in one step and used on a later step. In the single-cycle version these names are simply labels on outputs of logic blocks; when we pipeline the machine, they will need to be registers. The five steps are:

1. Instruction fetch step (IF):

$$IR \leftarrow Mem[PC]$$
$$NPC \leftarrow PC + 4$$

Operation: Send out the PC and fetch the instruction from memory into the instruction register (IR). The IR is just a name used to designate the output of the instruction cache and need not be a real register. Also, compute the New PC (NPC).

2. Instruction decode/register fetch step (ID):

$$A \leftarrow Regs[IR_{6..10}];$$
$$B \leftarrow Regs[IR_{11..16}];$$

Operation: Decode the instruction and access the register file to read the registers. The names A and B are used as names of the operands and need not be real registers.

Decoding is done in parallel with reading registers, which is possible because these fields are at a fixed location in the DLX instruction format (Figure 4.19 on page 194). This technique is known as *fixed-field decoding*. Note that we may read a register we don't use, but that doesn't hurt. Because the immediate portion of an instruction is also identical in every DLX format, the sign-extended immediate is also calculated during this step in case it is needed in the next step.

3. Execution/effective address step (EX):

The ALU is operating on the operands prepared in the prior step, performing one of three functions depending on the DLX instruction type.

Memory reference:

$$\text{ALUOutput} \leftarrow \text{A} + (\text{IR}_{16})^{16}\#\#\text{IR}_{16..31} \;;$$
$$\text{SMD} \leftarrow \text{B};$$

Operation: The ALU is adding the operands to form the effective address and places the result into ALUOutput. For a store instruction the second register operand, which is the data to be stored, is placed into SMD (Store Memory Data)

Register-Register ALU instruction

$$\text{ALUOutput} \leftarrow \text{A } op \text{ B}$$

Operation: The ALU is performing the operation specified by the opcode on the value in A (Rs1) and on the value in B (Rs2).

Register-Immediate ALU instruction:

$$\text{ALUOutput} \leftarrow \text{A } op \text{ } ((\text{IR}_{16})^{16}\#\#\text{IR}_{16..31})$$

Operation: The ALU is performing the operation specified by the opcode on the value in A (Rs1) and on the value of the sign-extended immediate.

Branch/Jump:

$$\text{ALUOutput} \leftarrow \text{NPC} + (\text{IR}_{16})^{16}\#\#\text{IR}_{16..31};$$

$$\text{cond} \leftarrow (\text{A } op \text{ } 0)$$

Operation: The ALU is adding the PC to the sign-extended immediate value (16-bit for branch and 26-bit for jump) to compute the address of the branch target. For conditional branches, a register, which has been read in the prior step, is checked to decide if this address should be inserted into the PC. The comparison operation *op* is the relational operator determined by the opcode; for example, *op* is "==" for the instruction BEQZ.

The load/store architecture of DLX means that effective address and execution steps can be combined into a single step, since no instruction needs to both calculate a data address, calculate an instruction address, and perform an operation on the data. The other integer instructions not included above are JAL and TRAP. These are similar to branches or jumps, except JAL stores the return address in R31 and TRAP stores it in interrupt address register (IAR).

4. Memory access/branch completion step (MEM): The only DLX instructions active in this step are loads, stores, branches, and jumps.

Memory reference:

$$LMD \leftarrow Mem[ALUOutput] \ or$$
$$Mem[ALUOutput] \leftarrow SMD;$$

Operation: Access memory if needed. If instruction is a load, data returns from memory and is called LMD (Load Memory Data); if it is a store, then the data from SMD is written into memory. In either case the address used is the one computed during the prior step and stored in ALUOutput.

Branch:

$$if \ (cond) \ PC \leftarrow ALUOutput \ else \ PC \leftarrow$$
$$NPC$$

Operation: If the instruction branches, the PC is replaced with the branch destination address; otherwise, it is replaced with the incremented PC. For jumps the condition is always true.

5. Write-back step (WB):

Register-Register ALU instruction:

$$Regs[IR_{16..20}] \leftarrow ALUOutput;$$

Register-Immediate ALU instruction:

$$Regs[IR_{11..15}] \leftarrow ALUOutput;$$

Load instruction:

$$Regs[IR_{11..15}] \leftarrow MD;$$

Operation: Write the result into the register file, whether coming from the memory system or from the ALU; the Rd field is also in one of two positions.

These five steps represent how values flow through the datapath as shown in Figure 4.1. In this implementation, each DLX instruction is executed in one clock cycle (CPI=1). Thus, any register or memory values are effectively read at the start of the instruction and written at the end. Communication from one instruction to the next is via the PC, the register file, and the data memory. Writing a value into one or more of these state devices is done at the end of the clock cycle. In a multicycle implementation, we would use a shorter clock cycle and break the instruction into multiple clock cycles. If we chose to break the cycle into clock cycles corresponding to the five phases shown in Figure 4.1, then we would need registers to hold the data values at the end of one cycle and the start of the next. These registers will be required in the pipelined version as well, but it is easier to understand the pipeline from the viewpoint of the single-cycle unpipelined implementation.

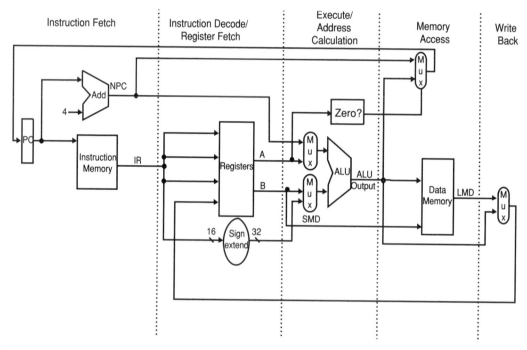

FIGURE 4.1   The implementation of the DLX datapath allows every instruction to be executed in one clock cycle.

4.2 | The Basic Pipeline for DLX

We can pipeline the datapath of Figure 4.1 simply by breaking the execution into the five phases, making each phase take a separate clock cycle, and starting a new instruction on each clock cycle. Each of the steps from the previous section becomes a *pipe stage:*a step in the pipeline. This results in the execution pattern shown in Figure 4.5, which is the typical way a pipeline structure is drawn. While each instruction still takes five clock cycles, during each clock cycle the hardware will be executing some part of five different instructions.

Instruction	Clock number								
number	1	2	3	4	5	6	7	8	9
Instruction i	IF	ID	EX	MEM	WB				
Instruction i+1		IF	ID	EX	MEM	WB			
Instruction i+2			IF	ID	EX	MEM	WB		
Instruction i+3				IF	ID	EX	MEM	WB	
Instruction i+4					IF	ID	EX	MEM	WB

FIGURE 4.2   Simple DLX pipeline. On each clock cycle, another instruction is fetched and begins its five-step execution. If an instruction is started every clock cycle, the performance will be five times that of a machine that is not pipelined.

Your instinct is right if you find it hard to believe that pipelining is as simple as this, because it's not. In this and the following sections, we will make our DLX pipeline "real" by dealing with problems that pipelining introduces.

To begin with, we have to determine what happens on every clock cycle of the machine and make sure we don't overcommit the datapath resources by overlapping instructions. For example, a single ALU cannot be asked to compute an effective address and perform a subtract operation at the same time. Fortunately, the simplicity of the DLX instruction set makes resource evaluation relatively easy. Figure 4.3 shows a simplified version of the DLX datapath drawn is pipeline fashion. As we can see the major functional units are used in different cycles and hence overlapping the execution of multiple instructions introduces relatively few conflicts. There are three observations on which this fact rests.

First, the basic datapath of the last section already used separate instruction and data memories, which we could implement with separate instruction and data caches. The use of separate caches eliminates a conflict for a single memory that would arise between instruction fetch and data memory access. If our pipelined machine has a clock cycle that is five time faster than the unpipelined version, the memory system must deliver five times the bandwidth.

Second, the register file is used in the two stages: RF for reading and WB for writing. These uses are distinct, so we simply show the register file in two places. This does mean that we need to perform two reads and one write every clock cycle. What if the read and write are to the same register? For now, we ignore this problem, but we will focus on it in the next section.

Third, Figure 4.3 does not deal with the PC. To start a new instruction every clock, we increment and store the PC every clock, and this must be done during the IF stage in preparation for the next instruction. The problem arises when we consider the effect of branches, which change the PC also, but not until the MEM stage. This is not a problem in our single-cycle datapath, since the PC is written once in MEM. For now, we will organize our pipelined datapath to write the PC in IF, and in MEM if the instruction is a branch. This introduces a conflict because a later instruction in IF will try to write the PC at the same time as the branch. We'll ignore this problem for now and return to it in Section 4.5.

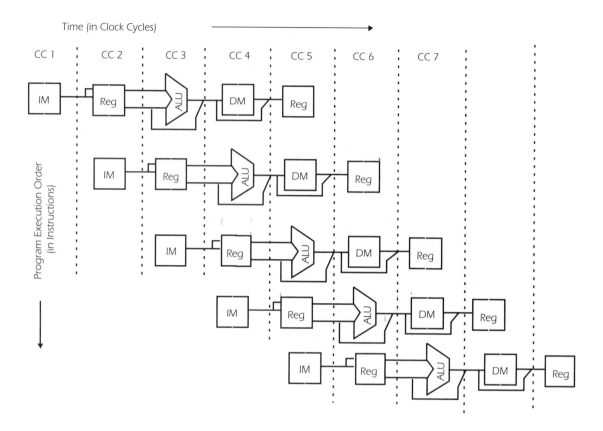

FIGURE 4.3 The pipeline can be thought of as a series of datapaths shifted in time. This shows the overlap among the parts of the datapath. Because the register file is used as a source in the EX stage and as a destination in the WB stage, it appears twice. We show that it is read in one stage and written in another by using dashed lines, on the left or right, respectively.

Because every pipe stage is active on every clock cycle, all operations in a pipe stage must complete in one clock cycle and any combination of operations to be able to occur at once. Furthermore, pipelining the datapath requires that values passed from one pipestage to the next must be placed in registers. Figure 4.4 shows the DLX pipeline with the appropriate registers, called *pipeline registers* or *pipeline latches*, between each pipeline stage. The registers are labeled with the names of the stages they connect. Figure 4.4 is drawn so that connections through the pipeline registers from one stage to another are clear. All of the registers needed to hold values are subsumed into this pipeline registers. The fields of the instruction register (IR), which is part of the IF/ID register are labeled when they are used to supply register names. Notice that the field of a register operand used for a write on a load or ALU operation is supplied from the MEM/WB pipe-line register rather than from the IF/ID register. This is because we want a load or ALU operation to write the register designated by that operation, not the register field of the instruction currently transitioning from IF to ID! The pipeline registers carry both data and control (since the register destination is really control information) from one pipeline stage to the next. Any value needed on a later pipeline stage must be placed in such a register. In the case of the destination register field that value is simply copied from one register to the next, until it is needed during the EX stage.

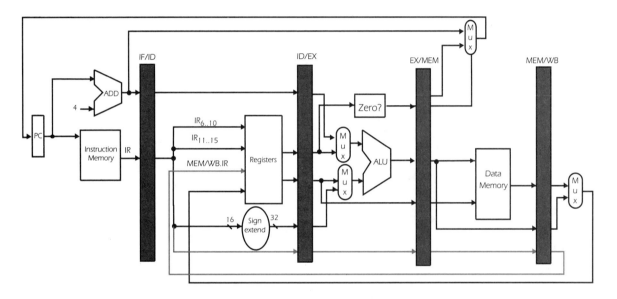

FIGURE 4.4 The datapath is pipelined by adding a set of registers, one between each pair of pipestages. The registers serve to convey values and control information from one stage to the next. We can also think of the PC as part of a pipeline register, which sits before the IF stage of the pipeline.

Any instruction is active in exactly one stage of the pipeline at a time; therefore, any actions taken on behalf of an instruction occur between a pair of pipeline registers. Thus, we can also look at the activities of the pipeline by examining what has to happen on any pipeline stage depending on the instruction type. Figure 4.5 shows this view. Fields of the pipeline registers are named so as to show the flow of data from one stage to the next. Notice that the actions in the first two stages are independent of the instruction type, which they must be because the instruction is not decoded until the end of the ID stage. The fixed position encoding of the register source operands is critical to allowing the registers to be fetched during ID.

Stage	ALU instruction	Load or store instruction	Branch instruction
IF	IF/ID.IR ← Mem[PC]; IF/ID.NPC,PC ← PC+4;		
ID	ID/EX.A ← Regs[IF/ID.IR$_{6..10}$]; ID/EX.B ← Regs[IF/ID.IR$_{11..16}$]; ID/EX.NPC ← IF/ID.NPC; ID/EX.IR ← IF/ID.IR ID/EX.Imm ← (IR$_{16}$)^{16}##IR$_{16..31}$		
EX	EX/MEM.IR ← ID/EX.IR EX/MEM.ALUOutput←ID/ EX.A op ID/EX.B; or EX/MEM.ALUOutput ← ID/ EX.A op ID/EX.Imm;	EX/MEM.ALUOutput ← ID/ EX.A + ID/EX.Imm; EX/MEM.SMD← ID/EX.B; EX/MEM.IR← ID/EX.IR	EX/MEM.ALUOutput ← ID/ EX.NPC + ID/EX.Imm; EX/MEM.cond ← (ID/EX.A op 0);
MEM	MEM/WB.ALUOutput ← EX/ MEM.ALUOutput MEM/WB.IR ← EX/MEM.IR	MEM/WB.IR ← EX/MEM.IR MEM/WB.LMD ← Mem[EX/ MEM.ALUOutput]; or Mem[EX/MEM.ALUOutput] ← EX/MEM.SMD;	if (EX/MEM.cond) PC←EX/ MEM.ALUOutput;
WB	Regs[MEM/WB.IR$_{16..20}$] ← MEM/WB.ALUOutput; or Regs[MEM/WB.IR$_{11..15}$] ← MEM/WB.ALUOutput;	Regs[MEM/WB.IR$_{11..15}$] ← MEM/WB.LMD	

FIGURE 4.5 Events on every pipe stage of the DLX pipeline. Let's review the actions in the stages that are specific to the pipeline organization. In IF, in addition to fetching the instruction and computing the new PC, we store the incremented PC (NPC) into a pipeline register for later use in computing the branch target address. In ID, we fetch the registers, extend the sign of the lower 16-bits of the IR, and pass along the IR and NPC. During EX, we perform an ALU operation or an address calculation; we pass along the IR and the B register (if the instruction is a store). During the MEM phase, we cycle the memory, make a branch decision and write the PC if needed, and pass along values needed in the final pipestage. Finally, during WB, we update the register field from either the loaded value or the ALU output.

To control this simple pipeline we need only determine how to set the control for the four multiplexers in the datapath of Figure 4.4. The two multiplexers in the ALU stage are set depending on the instruction type, which is dictated by the IR field of the ID/ALU register. The top ALU input multiplexer is set by whether the instruction is a branch or not, and the bottom multiplexer is set by whether the instruction is a register-register ALU operation or any other type of operation. The multiplexer in the MEM stage chooses whether to write back the branch target PC or the current PC and is controlled by the field EX/MEM.cond. The fourth multiplexer is controlled by whether the instruction in the WB stage is a load or a ALU operation. In addition to these four multiplexers, there is one additional multiplexer needed that is not drawn in Figure 4.4, but whose existence is clear from looking at the WB stage of an ALU operation. The register destination field is in one of two different places depending on the instruction type (register-register ALU versus either ALU immediate or load). Thus, we will need a multiplexer to choose the correct portion of the IR in the MEM/WB register to specify the register destination field.

Basic Performance Issues in Pipelining

Pipelining increases the CPU instruction throughput—the number of instructions completed per unit of time—but it does not reduce the execution time of an individual instruction. In fact, it usually slightly increases the execution time of each instruction due to overhead in the control of the pipeline. The increase in instruction throughput means that a program runs faster and has lower total execution time, even though no single instruction runs faster!

The fact that the execution time of each instruction remains unchanged puts limits on the practical depth of a pipeline, as we will see in the next section. In addition to limitations arising from pipeline latency, there are limits that arise from imbalance among the pipestages and from pipelining overhead. The clock can run no faster than the time needed for the slowest pipeline stage. Pipeline overhead arises from the combination of pipeline register or latch delay and clock skew. The pipeline registers or latches add setup time plus propagation delay to the clock cycle. Clock skew also contributes to the lower limit on the clock cycle. Once the clock cycle is as small as the sum of the clock skew and latch overhead, no further pipelining is useful, since there is no time left in the cycle for useful work.

Example

Consider an unpipelined machine with five execution steps of lengths 50 nS, 50 nS, 60 nS, 50 nS, and 50 nS. Suppose that due to clock skew and setup, pipelining the machine adds 5 nS of overhead to each execution stage. Ignoring any latency impact, how much speedup in the instruction execution rate will we gain from a pipeline?

Answer

Figure 4.6 shows the execution pattern on the unpipelined machine and on the pipelined machine.

The average instruction execution time on the unpipelined machine is:

Average instruction execution time = 50+50+60+50+50 nS = 260 nS

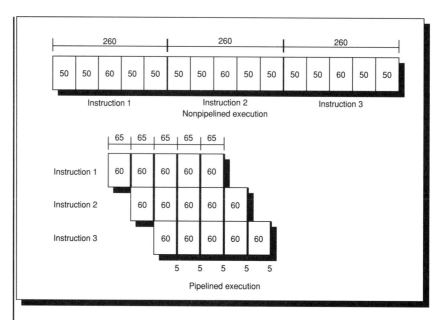

FIGURE 4.6 The execution pattern for three instructions shown for both the unpipelined and pipelined versions. In the unpipelined version, the three instructions are executed sequentially. In the pipelined version, the shaded areas represent the overhead of 5 nS per pipestage. The length of the pipestages must all be the same: 60 nS plus the 5-nS overhead. The latency of an instruction increases from 260 nS in the unpipelined machine to 325 nS in the pipelined machine.

In the pipelined implementation, the clock must run at the speed of the slowest stage plus overhead, which will be 60 + 5 or 65 nS; this is the average instruction execution time. Thus, the speedup from pipelining is

$$\text{Speedup from pipelining} = \frac{\text{Average instruction time unpipelined}}{\text{Average instruction time pipelined}}$$

$$= \frac{260 \text{ ns}}{65 \text{ ns}} = 4 \text{ times}$$

The 5-nS overhead essentially establishes a limit on the effectiveness of pipelining. If the overhead is not affected by changes in the clock cycle, Amdahl's Law tells us that the overhead limits the speedup.

Because the latches in a pipelined design can have a significant impact on the clock speed, designers have looked for latches that permit the highest possible clock rate. The Earle latch (invented by J. G. Earle [1965]) has three properties that make it especially useful in pipelined machines. First, it is relatively insensitive to clock skew. Second, the delay through the latch is always a constant two-gate delay, avoiding the introduction of skew in the data passing through the latch. Finally, two levels of logic can be performed in the latch without increasing the latch delay time. This means that two levels of logic in the pipeline can be overlapped with the latch, so the majority of the overhead from the latch can be hidden. We will not be analyzing the pipeline designs in this chapter at this level of detail. The interested reader should see Kunkel and Smith [1986].

The pipeline we now have for DLX would function just fine for integer instructions if every instruction were independent of every other instruction in the pipeline. In reality, instructions in the pipeline can depend on one another; this is the topic of the next section. The complications that arise in the floating-point pipeline will be treated in Section 4.5, and the Putting It All Together section will look at an complete real pipeline.

4.3 | The Major Hurdle of Pipelining— Pipeline Hazards

There are situations, called *hazards*, that prevent the next instruction in the instruction stream from executing during its designated clock cycle. Hazards reduce the performance from the ideal speedup gained by pipelining. There are three classes of hazards:

1. *Structural hazards* arise from resource conflicts when the hardware cannot support all possible combinations of instructions in simultaneous overlapped execution.

2. *Data hazards* arise when an instruction depends on the results of a previous instruction in a way that is exposed by the overlapping of instructions in the pipeline.

3. *Control hazards* arise from the pipelining of branches and other instructions that change the PC.

Hazards in pipelines can make it necessary to *stall* the pipeline. The major difference between stalls in a pipelined machine and stalls in an unpipelined machine occurs because there are multiple instructions under execution at once. A stall in a pipelined machine often requires that some instructions be allowed to proceed, while others are delayed. For the pipelines we discuss in this chapter, when an instruction is stalled, all instructions later in the pipeline than the stalled instruction are also stalled. Instructions earlier than the stalled instruction can continue, but no new instructions are fetched during the stall. We will see several examples of how stalls operate in this section—don't worry, they aren't as complex as they might sound!

A stall causes the pipeline performance to degrade from the ideal performance. Let's look at a simple equation for finding the actual speedup from pipelining, starting with the formula from the previous section.

$$\text{Speedup from pipeling} = \frac{\text{Average instruction time unpipelined}}{\text{Average instruction time pipelined}}$$

$$= \frac{\text{CPI unpipelined} \times \text{Clock cycle unpipelined}}{\text{CPI pipelined} \times \text{Clock cycle pipelined}}$$

$$= \frac{\text{CPI unpipelined}}{\text{CPI pipelined}} \times \frac{\text{Clock cycle unpipelined}}{\text{Clock cycle pipelined}}$$

Remember that pipelining can be thought of as decreasing the CPI or the clock cycle time. Because it is somewhat more natural to deal with the CPI, it is traditional to use the CPI to compare pipelines. The ideal CPI on a pipelined machine is usually

$$\text{Ideal CPI} = \frac{\text{CPI unpipelined}}{\text{Pipeline depth}}$$

Rearranging this and substituting into the speedup equation yields:

$$\text{Speedup} = \frac{\text{Ideal CPI} \times \text{Pipeline depth}}{\text{CPI pipelined}} \times \frac{\text{Clock cycle unpipelined}}{\text{Clock cycle pipelined}}$$

If we confine ourselves to pipeline stalls,

$$\text{CPI pipelined} = \text{Ideal CPI} + \text{Pipeline stall clock cycles per instruction}$$

We can substitute and obtain:

$$\text{Speedup} = \frac{\text{Ideal CPI} \times \text{Pipeline depth}}{\text{Ideal CPI} + \text{Pipeline stall cycles per instruction}} \times \frac{\text{Clock cycle unpipelined}}{\text{Clock cycle pipelined}}$$

While this gives a general formula for pipeline speedup (ignoring stalls other than from the pipeline), in most instances a simpler equation can be used. Often, we choose to ignore the potential increase in clock rate due to pipelining overhead. This makes the clock rates equal and allows us to drop the second term. In addition, most pipelines are designed to have an Ideal CPI of 1, allowing additional simplification:

$$\text{Speedup} = \frac{\text{Pipeline depth}}{1 + \text{Pipeline stall cycles per instruction}}$$

If the Ideal CPI is 1 but the clock rates differ, we can use:

$$\text{Speedup} = \frac{\text{Pipeline depth}}{1 + \text{Pipeline stall cycles per instruction}} \times \frac{\text{Clock cycle unpipelined}}{\text{Clock cycle pipelined}}$$

Structural Hazards

When a machine is pipelined, the overlapped execution of instructions requires pipelining of functional units and duplication of resources to allow all possible combinations of instructions in the pipeline. If some combination of instructions cannot be accommodated due to resource conflicts, the machine is said to have a *structural hazard*. The most common instances of structural hazards arise when some functional unit is not fully pipelined. Then a sequence of instructions that all use that functional unit cannot be sequentially initiated in the pipeline. Another common way that structural hazards appear is when some resource has not been duplicated enough to allow all combinations of instructions in the pipeline to execute. For example, a machine may have only one register-file write port, but under certain circumstances, the pipeline might want to perform two writes in a clock cycle. This will generate a structural hazard. When a sequence of instructions encounters this hazard, the pipeline will stall one of the instructions until the required unit is available. If some combinations of instructions, but not all, generate structural hazards, it is useful to assume the ideal pipeline CPI is one, and add in the hazards. If, however, the machine can never execute instructions at a rate of one every clock, it is simpler to change the ideal CPI and treat only those sequences that cannot achieve the higher ideal CPI as stalls.

Some pipelined machines share a single memory pipeline for data and instructions. As a result, when an instruction contains a data-memory reference, it will conflict with the instruction reference for a later instruction, as shown in Figure 4.7. To resolve this, we stall the pipeline for one clock cycle, when the data memory access occurs. Figure 4.8 shows our pipeline datapath figure with the stall cycle added. A stall is commonly called a *pipeline bubble* or just *bubble*, .since it floats through the pipeline taking space but carrying no useful work. We will see another type of stall when we talk about data hazards.

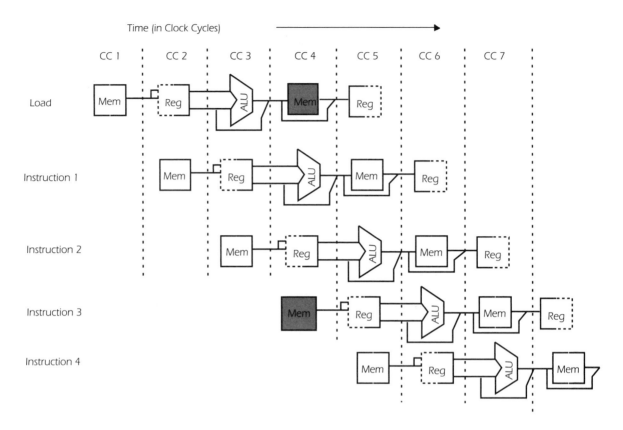

FIGURE 4.7   A machine with only one memory port will generate a conflict whenever a memory reference occurs. In this example the load instruction uses the memory for a data access at the same time Instruction 4 wants to do an instruction fetch access.

Rather than draw the pipeline datapath every time, designers often just indicate stall behavior using a simpler diagram with only the pipestage names, as in Figure 4.9. The form of Figure 4.9 shows the stall by indicating the cycle when no action occurs and simply shifting instruction 3 to the right (which delays its execution start and finish by one cycle). The effect of the pipeline bubble is actually to occupy the resources for that instruction slot as it travels through the pipeline, just as Figure 4.8 shows. Although Figure 4.8 shows how the stall is actually implemented the performance impact indicated by the two figures is the same, because instruction 3 does not complete until clock cycle 9 and no instruction completes during clock cycle 8.

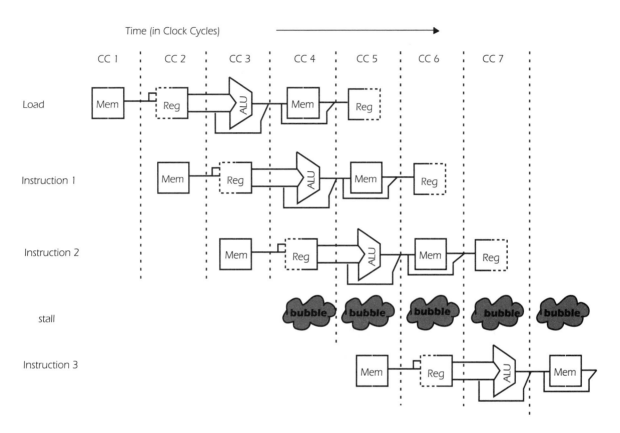

FIGURE 4.8 The structural hazard cause pipeline bubbles to be inserted. The effect is that no instruction will finish during clock cycle 8, when instruction 4 would normally have finished.

Instruction	Clock cycle number									
	1	2	3	4	5	6	7	8	9	10
Load instruction	IF	ID	EX	MEM	WB					
Instruction 1		IF	ID	EX	MEM	WB				
Instruction 2			IF	ID	EX	MEM	WB			
Instruction 3				stall	IF	ID	EX	MEM	WB	
Instruction 4						IF	ID	EX	MEM	WB
Instruction 5							IF	ID	EX	MEM
Instruction 6								IF	ID	EX

FIGURE 4.9 A pipeline stalled for a structural hazard—a load with one memory port. As shown here, the load instruction effectively steals an instruction-fetch cycle, causing the pipeline to stall—no instruction is initiated on clock cycle 4 (which normally would be instruction $i+3$). Because the instruction being fetched is stalled, all other instructions in the pipeline before the stalled instruction can proceed normally. The stall cycle will continue to pass through the pipeline, so that no instruction completes on clock cycle 8. The stall is also sometimes drawn across an entire horizontal row with Instruction 3 being moved to the next row.

Example

Let's see how much the load structural hazard might cost. Suppose that data references constitute 40% of the mix, and that the ideal CPI of the pipelined machine, ignoring the structural hazard, is 1. Assume that machine with the structural hazard has a clock rate that is 1.05 times higher. Disregarding any other performance losses, is the pipeline with or without the structural hazard faster and by how much?

Answer

First, let's compute the pipeline speedup for each machine using:

$$\text{Speedup} = \frac{\text{Pipeline depth}}{1 + \text{Pipeline stall cycles per instruction}} \times \frac{\text{Clock cycle unpipelined}}{\text{Clock cycle pipelined}}$$

Since the ideal machine has no stalls, and we can assume its clock rate is the same as the unpipelined version, its speedup is simply the Pipeline depth. The speedup of the machine with the structural hazard is

$$\text{Speedup} = \frac{\text{Pipeline depth}}{1 + 0.4 \times 1} \times \frac{\text{Clock cycle unpipelined}}{\left(\dfrac{\text{Clock cycle unpipelined}}{1.05}\right)} = 0.75 \times \text{Pipeline depth}$$

Clearly, the machine without the structural hazard is faster; we can use the ratio of the speedups to determine how much:

$$\frac{\text{Speedup}_{\text{no hazard}}}{\text{Speedup}_{\text{hazard}}} = \frac{\text{Pipeline depth}}{0.75 \times \text{Pipeline depth}} = 1.33$$

So the machine without the structural hazard is 1.33 times faster.

Example

Answer

If all other factors are equal, a machine without structural hazards will always have a lower CPI. Why, then, would a designer allow structural hazards? There are two reasons: to reduce cost and to reduce the latency of the unit. Pipelining all the functional units may be too costly. Machines that support one-clock-cycle memory references require twice as much total memory bandwidth and often have higher bandwidth at the pins. Likewise, fully pipelining a floating-point multiplier consumes lots of gates. If the structural hazard would not occur often, it may not be worth the cost to avoid it. It is also usually possible to design an unpipelined unit, or one that isn't fully pipelined, with a shorter total delay than a fully pipelined unit. For example, both the CDC 7600 and the MIPS R2010 floating-point unit choose shorter latency (fewer clocks per operation) versus full pipelining. As we will see shortly, reducing latency has other performance benefits and may overcome the disadvantage of the structural hazard.

Many recent machines do not have fully pipelined floating-point units. For example, suppose we had an implementation of DLX with a 5-clock-cycle latency for floating-point multiply, but no pipelining. Will this structural hazard have a large or small performance impact on Spice running on DLX? For simplicity, assume that the floating-point multiplies are uniformly distributed.

From Chapter 3 we find that floating-point multiply has a frequency of 2% in Spice. Our proposed pipeline can handle up to a 20% frequency of floating-point multiplies—one every five clock cycles. This means that the performance benefit of fully pipelining the floating-point multiply on Spice is likely to be low, as long as the floating-point multiplies are not clustered but are distributed uniformly. If they are clustered, the impact could be larger. Of course, other benchmarks make much heavier use of floating point multiply, and some would show significant impact.

The next two sections cover the topics of data and control hazards.

4.4 | Data Hazards

A major effect of pipelining is to change the relative timing of instructions by overlapping their execution. This introduces data and control hazards. Data hazard*s* occur when the pipeline changes the order of accesses to operands so that the order differs from the order seen by sequentially executing instructions on an unpipelined machine. Consider the pipelined execution of these instructions:

```
ADD    R1,R2,R3
SUB    R4,R1,R5
AND    R6,R1,R7
OR     R8,R1,R9
XOR    R10,R1,R11
```

All the instructions after the ADD use the result of the ADD instruction. As shown in Figure 4.10, the ADD instruction writes the value of R1 in the WB pipe stage, but the SUB instruction reads the value during its ID stage. This problem is called a *data hazard.*Unless precautions are taken to prevent it, the SUB instruction will read the wrong value and try to use it. In fact, the value used by the SUB instruction is not even deterministic: Though we might think it logical to assume that SUB would always use the value of R1 that was assigned by an instruction prior to ADD, this is not always the case. If an interrupt should occur between the ADD and SUB instructions, the WB stage of the ADD will complete, and the value of R1 at that point will be the result of the ADD. This unpredictable behavior is obviously unacceptable.

The two other instructions in the sequence after the SUB (i.e., AND and OR) are also affected by this hazard. As we can see from Figure 4.10, the write of R1 does not complete, until the end of clock cycle 5, so the AND and OR instructions that read the registers during clock cycles 4 and 5, respectively, will receive the wrong results. The XOR instruction operates properly, because its register read occurs in clock cycle 6, after the register write.

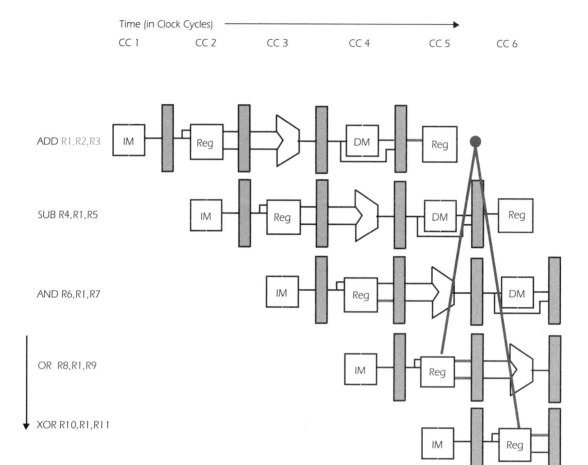

FIGURE 4.10   The use of the result of the ADD instruction in the next three instructions causes a hazard, since the register is not written until after those instructions read it.

Minimizing Data Hazard Stalls By Forwarding

The problem posed in this example can be solved with a simple hardware technique called *forwarding* (also called *bypassing* and sometimes *short-circuiting*). This technique works as follows: The ALU result from the EX/MEM register is always fed back to the ALU input latches. If the forwarding hardware detects that the previous ALU operation has written the register corresponding to a source for the current ALU operation, control logic selects the forwarded result as the ALU input rather than the value read from the register file. Notice that with forward-ing, if the SUB is stalled, the ADD will be completed, and the bypass will not be activated. This is also true for the case of an interrupt between the two instruc-tions.

As the example in Figure 4.10 shows, we need to forward results not only from the immediately previous instruction, but possibly from an instruction that started three cycles earlier. To reduce the amount of forwarding logic slightly, a simple technique is used in the register file: the register file reads are performed in the second half of the cycle, while the writes are performed in the first half. This allows an OR instruction in the example in Figure 4.10 to execute correctly. In essence, the value is being forwarded through the registers. We will still need to forward a result to the AND instruction. That result will come from the MEM/ WB register, which holds the result of the ADD instruction when the AND reaches EX. Figure 4.11 shows our example with the bypass paths in place and highlight-ing the timing of the register read and writes. This code sequence can be executed without stalls.

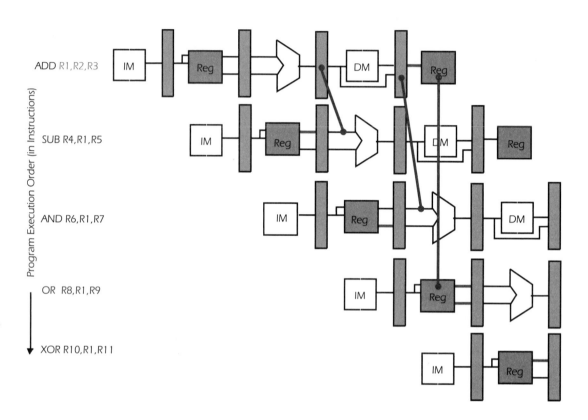

FIGURE 4.11 **A set of instructions that depend on the ADD result use forwarding paths to avoid the data hazard.** The SUB and AND instructions forward from the EX/MEM pipeline register to the first ALU input, while the OR receives its result by "forwarding" through the register file. The forwarding through the register file is easily accomplished by reading the registers in the second half of the cycle and writing in the first half, as the highlighting on the registers indicates.

Forwarding can be generalized to include passing a result directly to the functional unit that requires it: A result is forwarded from the output of one unit to the input of another, rather than just from the result of a unit to the input of the same unit. Take, for example, the following sequence:

```
ADD    R1,R2,R3
LW     R4,0(R1)
SW     12(R1),R1
SW     20(R4),R4
```

To prevent a stall in this sequence, we would need to forward the values of R1 and R4 from the pipeline registers to the ALU and data memory inputs. Figure 4.12 shows all the forwarding paths for this example. In DLX, we may require a forwarding path from any pipeline register to the input of any functional unit. Because the ALU and data memory both accept operands, forwarding paths are needed to their inputs from the ALU/MEM and MEM/EX registers. In addition, DLX uses a zero detection unit that operates during the MEM cycle and forwarding to that unit will be needed as well. Later in this section we will explore all the necessary forwarding paths and the control of those paths.

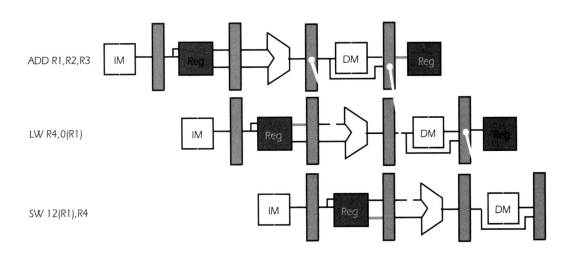

FIGURE 4.12 Forwarding is also needed to the data memory unit and from the output of the data memory unit in the MEM/WB register. These additional forwarding paths arise for loads and stores.

Data Hazard Classification

A hazard is created whenever there is a dependence between instructions, and they are close enough that the overlap caused by pipelining would change the order of access to an operand. Our example hazards have all been with register operands, but it is also possible for a pair of instructions to create a dependence by writing and reading the same memory location. In our DLX pipeline, however, memory references are always kept in order, preventing this type of hazard from arising. Cache misses could cause the memory references to get out of order if we allowed the processor to continue working on later instructions, while an earlier instruction that missed the cache was accessing memory. For DLX's pipeline we just stall the entire pipeline, effectively making the instruction that contained the miss run for multiple clock cycles. In the next chapter, we will discuss machines that allow loads and stores to be executed in an order different from that in the program, which will introduce new problems. All the data hazards discussed in this chapter involve registers within the CPU.

Data hazards may be classified as one of three types, depending on the order of read and write accesses in the instructions. By convention, the hazards are named by the ordering in the program that must be preserved by the pipeline. Consider two instructions i and j, with i occurring before j. The possible data hazards are:

- RAW *(read after write)* — j tries to read a source before i writes it, so j incorrectly gets the old value. This is the most common type of hazard and the kind we used forwarding to overcome in Figure 4.11 and 4.12.

- WAR *(write after read)* — j tries to write a destination before it is read by i, so i incorrectly gets the new value. This cannot happen in our example pipeline because all reads are early (in ID) and all writes are late (in WB). This hazard occurs when there are some instructions that write results early in the instruction pipeline, and other instructions that read a source late in the pipeline. For example, autoincrement addressing can create a WAR hazard. In the next chapter, we will see how these hazards occur when instructions are executed out of order.

- WAW *(write after write)* — j tries to write an operand before it is written by i. The writes end up being performed in the wrong order, leaving the value written by i rather than the value written by j in the destination. This hazard is present only in pipelines that write in more than one pipe stage (or allow an instruction to proceed even when a previous instruction is stalled). The DLX integer pipeline writes a register only in WB and avoids this class of hazards. When we discuss the DLX FP pipeline, we will see how this can occur.

Note that the RAR *(read after read)* case is not a hazard.

Data Hazards Requiring Stalls

Unfortunately, not all potential data hazards can be handled by bypassing. Consider the following sequence of instructions:

```
LW     R1,0(R1)
SUB    R4,R1,R5
AND    R6,R1,R7
OR     R8,R1,R9
```

The pipelined datapath with the bypass paths for this example is shown in Figure 4.13. This case is different from the situation with back-to-back ALU operations. The LW instruction does not have the data until the end of the MEM cycle, while the SUB instruction needs to have the data by the beginning of that clock cycle. Thus, the data hazard from using the result of a load instruction cannot be completely eliminated with simple hardware. As Figure 4.13 shows such a forwarding path would have to operate backwards in time–a capability not yet available to computer designers. We *can* forward the result immediately to the ALU from the MEM/WB registers for use in the AND operation, which begins two clock cycles after the load. Likewise, the OR instruction has no problem, since it receives the value through the register file. For the ADD instruction, the forwarded result arrives too late—at the end of a clock cycle, when it is needed at the beginning.

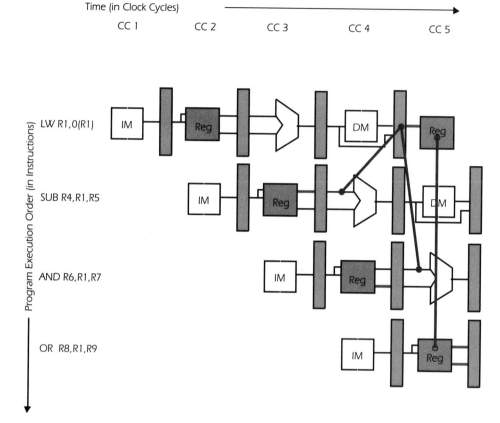

FIGURE 4.13   The load instruction can bypass its results to the AND and OR instructions, but not to the SUB, since that would mean forwarding the result in negative time.

The load instruction has a delay or latency that cannot be eliminated by forwarding alone. Instead, we need to add hardware, called a *pipeline interlock*, to preserve the correct execution pattern. In general, a *pipeline interlock* detects a hazard and stalls the pipeline until the hazard is cleared. In this case, the interlock stalls the pipeline beginning with the instruction that wants to use the data until the sourcing instruction produces it. This pipeline interlock introduces a stall or bubble, just as it did for the structural hazard in Section 4.3. The CPI for the stalled instruction increases by the length of the stall (one clock cycle in this case). The pipeline with the stall and the legal forwarding is shown in Figure 4.14. Because the stall causes the instructions starting with the SUB to move one cycle later in time, the forwarding to the AND instruction now goes through the register file, and no forwarding at all is needed for the OR instruction. The insertion of the bubble causes the number of cycles to complete this sequence to grow by one. No instruction is started during the fourth clock cycle (and none finishes during cycle six). Figure 4.15 shows the pipeline before and after the stall using a diagram containing only the pipeline stages. We will make extensive use this more concise form for showing interlocks and stalls in this chapter and the next.

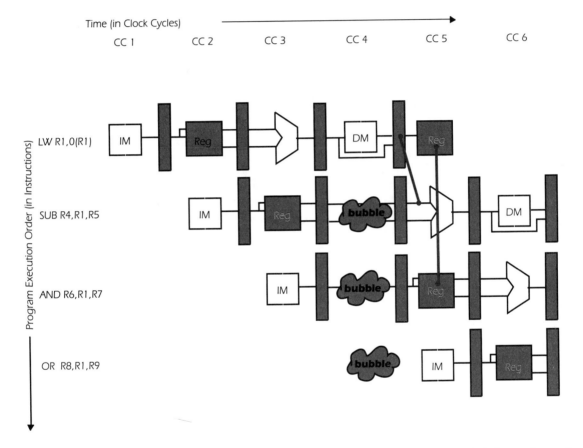

FIGURE 4.14   The load interlock causes a stall to be inserted at clock cycle 4, delaying the SUB instruction and those that follow by one cycle. This delay allows the value to be successfully forwarded on the next clock cycle.

LW R1,0(R1)	IF	ID	EX	MEM	WB				
SUB R4,R1,R5		IF	ID	EX	MEM	WB			
AND R6,R1,R7			IF	ID	EX	MEM	WB		
OR R8,R1,R9				IF	ID	EX	MEM	WB	

LW R1,0(R1)	IF	ID	EX	MEM	WB				
SUB R4,R1,R5		IF	ID	stall	EX	MEM	WB		
AND R6,R1,R7			IF	stall	ID	EX	MEM	WB	
OR R8,R1,R9				stall	IF	ID	EX	MEM	WB

FIGURE 4.15   In the top diagram, we can see why a stall is needed: the MEM cycle of the load produces a value that is needed in the EX cycle of the SUB, which occurs at the same time. This problem is solved by inserting a stall, as shown in the bottom diagram.

Example

Suppose that 30% of the instructions are loads, and half the time the instruction following a load instruction depends on the result of the load. If this hazard creates a single-cycle delay, how much faster is the ideal pipelined machine (with a CPI of 1) that does not delay the pipeline, compared to the real pipeline? Ignore any stalls other than pipeline stalls.

Answer

The ideal machine will be faster by the ratio of the CPIs. The CPI for an instruction following a load is 1.5, since they stall half the time. Because loads are 20% of the mix, the effective CPI is $(0.7 \times 1 + 0.3 \times 1.5) = 1.15$. This means that the ideal machine is 1.15 times faster.

In the next section we consider compiler techniques to reduce these penalties. After that, we look at how to implement hazard detection, forwarding, and interlocks.

Compiler Scheduling for Data Hazards

Many types of stalls are quite frequent. The typical code-generation pattern for a statement such as A=B+C produces a stall for a load of the second data value (B). Figure 4.16 shows that the store of A need not cause another stall, since the result of the addition can be forwarded to the data memory for use by the store. Machines where the arithmetic operands may come from memory will need to stall the pipeline in the middle of the instruction to wait for memory to complete its access.

LW R1,B	IF	ID	EX	MEM	WB			
LW R2,C		IF	ID	EX	MEM	WB		
ADD R3,R1,R2			IF	ID	stall	EX	MEM	WB
SW A,R3				IF	stall	ID	EX	MEM	WB

FIGURE 4.16 The DLX code sequence for A=B+C. The ADD instruction must be stalled to allow the load of C to complete. The SW need not be delayed further because the forwarding hardware passes the result from the ALU directly to the MDR for storing.

Rather than just allow the pipeline to stall, the compiler could try to schedule the pipeline to avoid these stalls, by rearranging the code sequence to eliminate the hazard. For example, the compiler would try to avoid generating code with a load followed by the immediate use of the load destination register. This technique, called *pipeline scheduling* or *instruction scheduling,* was first used in the 1960s and became an area of major interest in the 1980s, as pipelined machines became more widespread.

Example

Generate DLX code that avoids pipeline stalls for the following sequence:

```
a = b + c;
d = e - f;
```

Assume loads have a latency of one clock cycle.

Answer

Here is the scheduled code:

```
LW    Rb,b
LW    Rc,c
LW    Re,e      ; swap instructions to avoid stall
ADD   Ra,Rb,Rc
LW    Rf,f
SW    a,Ra      ; store/load exchanged to avoid stall
SUB   Rd,Re,Rf
SW    d,Rd
```

Both load interlocks (LW Rc,c to ADD Ra, Rb, Rc and LW Rf, f to SUB Rd, Re, Rf) have been eliminated. There is a dependence between the ALU instruction and the store, but the pipeline structure allows the result to be forwarded. Notice that the use of different registers for the first and second statements was critical for this schedule to be legal. In particular, if the variable e was loaded into the same register as b or c, this schedule would not be legal. In general, pipeline scheduling can increase the register count required. In the next chapter, we will see that this increase can be substantial for machines that can issue multiple instructions in one clock.

Many modern compilers try to use instruction scheduling to improve pipeline performance. In the simplest algorithms, the compiler simply schedules from other instructions in the same basic block. A *basic block* is a straightline code sequence with no jumps in or out, except at the beginning or end. Scheduling such code sequences is easy, since we know that every instruction in the block is executed if the first one is, and we can simply make a graph of the dependences among the instructions and order them to minimize the stalls. For a simple pipeline like the DLX integer pipeline with only short latencies (the only delay is one cycle on loads), a scheduling strategy focusing on basic blocks is adequate. Figure 4.17 shows that scheduling can eliminate the majority of these delays. It is clear from this figure that load delays in GCC are significantly harder to schedule than in Spice or TeX. As pipelining becomes more extensive, and the effective pipeline latencies grow, more ambitious scheduling schemes are needed; these are discussed in detail in the next chapter.

We will add additional benchmark measurements to this data for the final version.

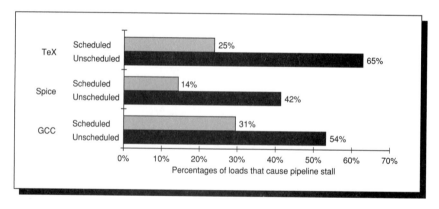

FIGURE 4.17   Percentage of the loads that result in a stall with the DLX pipeline. The black bars show the amount without compiler scheduling; the gray bars show the effect of a good, but simple, scheduling algorithm. These data show scheduling effectiveness after global optimization. Global optimization actually makes scheduling relatively harder because there are fewer candidates available for scheduling into delay slots, as we discuss in the Fallacies and Pitfalls. The pipeline slot after a load is often called the *load delay* or *delay slot*.

Implementing the Control for the DLX Pipeline

The process of letting an instruction move from the instruction decode stage (ID) into the execution stage (EX) of this pipeline is usually called *instruction issue*;

an instruction that has made this step is said to have *issued*. For the DLX integer pipeline, all the data hazards can be checked during the ID phase of the pipeline. If a data hazard exists, the instruction is stalled before it is issued. Likewise, we can determine what forwarding will be needed during ID and set the appropriate controls then. Detecting interlocks early in the pipeline reduces the hardware complexity because the hardware never has to suspend an instruction that has updated the state of the machine, unless the entire machine is stalled. Alternatively, we can detect the hazard or forwarding at the beginning of a clock cycle that uses an operand (EX and MEM for this pipeline). To show the differences in these two approaches, we will show how the load hazard can be implemented by a check in ID, while the forwarding can be implemented more locally. Figure 4.18 shows the variety of circumstances that we must handle.

Situation	Example code sequence	Action

No dependence	LW **R1**,45(R2)
	ADD R5,R6,R7
	SUB R8,R6,R7
	OR R9,R6,R7
		No hazard possible because no dependence exists on R1 in the immediately following three instructions.

Dependence requiring stall	LW **R1**,45(R2)
	ADD R5,**R1**,R7
	SUB R8,R6,R7
	OR R9,R6,R7
		Comparators detect the use of R1 in the ADD and stall the ADD (and SUB and OR) before the ADD begins EX.

Dependence overcome by forwarding	LW **R1**,45(R2)
	ADD R5,R6,R7
	SUB R8,**R1**,R7
	OR R9,R6,R7
		Comparators detect use of R1 in SUB and forward result of load to ALU in time for SUB to begin EX.

Dependence with accesses in order	LW **R1**,45(R2)
	ADD R5,R6,R7
	SUB R8,R6,R7
	OR R9,**R1**,R7
		No action required because the read of R1 by OR occurs in the second half of the ID phase, while the write of the loaded data occurred in the first half..

FIGURE 4.18 Situations that the pipeline hazard detection hardware can see by comparing the destination and sources of adjacent instructions. This table indicates that the only comparison needed is between the destination and the sources on the two instructions following the instruction that wrote the destination. In the case of a stall, the pipeline dependences will look like the third case, once execution continues.

Let's start with implementing the load hazard. If there is a load hazard, the load instruction will be in the EX stage when an instruction that needs the load data will be in the ID stage. Thus, we can describe all the possible hazard situations with a small table, which can be directly translated to an implementation. Figure 4.19 shows a table that detects all load hazards.

Opcode Field of EX/MEM (EX/MEM.IR$_{0..5}$)	Opcode Field of ID/EX (ID/EX.IR$_{0..5}$)	Matching Operand Fields
load	register-register ALU	EX/MEM.IR$_{11..15}$ = ID/EX.IR$_{6..10}$
load	register-register ALU	EX/MEM.IR$_{11..15}$ = ID/EX.IR$_{11..16}$
load	load, store, ALU immediate, or branch	EX/MEM.IR$_{11..15}$ = ID/EX.IR$_{6..10}$

FIGURE 4.19 The logic to detect load hazards must perform three comparisons. Lines 1 and 2 of the table test whether the load destination register is one of the source registers for a register-register operation. Line 3 of the table determines if the load destination is one the source operand for a load or store effective address, an ALU immediate, or a branch test.

Once a hazard has been detected, the control unit must insert the pipeline stall and prevent the instructions in the IF and ID stages from advancing. As we said in Section 4.2, all the control information is carried in the pipeline registers (Carrying the instruction along is enough, since all control is derived from that.) Thus, when we detect a hazard we need only change the control portion of the pipeline register to all 0s, which happens to be a noop. In addition, we simply recirculate the contents of the ID/EX and IF/ID registers to hold the two instructions stalled. In a pipeline with more complex hazards, the same ideas would apply; we can detect the hazard by comparing some set of pipeline registers and shift in noops to prevent erroneous execution.

Implementing the forwarding logic is similar, though there are more cases to consider. The key observation needed to implement the forwarding logic is that the pipeline registers contain both the data to be forwarded, as well as the source and destination register fields. All forwarding happens from the ALU or data memory output to the ALU input, the data memory input, or the zero detection unit. Thus, we can implement the forwarding by a comparison of the destination registers of the IR contained in the EX/MEM and MEM/WB stages against the source registers of the IR contained in the ID/EX and EX/MEM registers. Figure 4.20 shows the comparisons and possible forwarding operations where the destination is an ALU input. The exercises ask you to add the entries when the result is forwarded to the data memory. The last possible forwarding destination is the zero detect unit, whose forwarding paths look the same as those that are needed when the destination instruction is an ALU immediate.

Pipeline register sourcing instruction	Opcode sourcing instruction	Pipestage destination instruction	Opcode destination instruction	Destination forwarded result	Comparison
EX/MEM	register-register ALU	ID/EX	register-register ALU, ALU immediate, load, store, branch	Top ALU input	$EX/MEM.IR_{16..20} = IF/ID.IR_{6..10}$
EX/MEM	register-register ALU	ID/EX	register-register ALU	Bottom ALU input	$EX/MEM.IR_{16..20} = IF/ID.IR_{11..15}$
MEM/WB	register-register ALU	ID/EX	register-register ALU, ALU immediate, load, store, branch	Top ALU input	$MEM/WB.IR_{16..20} = IF/ID.IR_{6..10}$
MEM/WB	register-register ALU	ID/EX	register-register ALU	Bottom ALU input	$MEM/WB.IR_{16..20} = IF/ID.IR_{11..15}$
EX/MEM	ALU immediate	ID/EX	register-register ALU, ALU immediate, load, store, branch	Top ALU input	$EX/MEM.IR_{11..15} = IF/ID.IR_{6..10}$
EX/MEM	ALU immediate	ID/EX	register-register ALU	Bottom ALU input	$EX/MEM.IR_{11..15} = IF/ID.IR_{11..15}$
MEM/WB	ALU immediate	ID/EX	register-register ALU, ALU immediate, load, store, branch	Top ALU input	$MEM/WB.IR_{11..15} = IF/ID.IR_{6..10}$
MEM/WB	ALU immediate	ID/EX	register-register ALU	Bottom ALU input	$MEM/WB.IR_{11..15} = IF/ID.IR_{11..15}$
MEM/WB	load	ID/EX	register-register ALU, ALU immediate, load, store, branch	Top ALU input	$MEM/WB.IR_{11..15} = IF/ID.IR_{6..10}$
MEM/WB	load	ID/EX	register-register ALU	Bottom ALU input	$MEM/WB.IR_{11..15} = IF/ID.IR_{11..15}$

FIGURE 4.20 Forwarding of data to the two ALU inputs can occur from the ALU result (in EX/MEM or in MEM/WB) or from the load result in MEM/WB. There are ten separate comparisons needed to tell whether a forwarding operation should occur.

In addition to the comparators and combinational logic we need to determine when a forwarding path needs to be enabled, we also need to enlarge the multiplexers at the ALU inputs and add the connections from the pipeline registers that are used to forward the results. Figure 4.21 shows the relevant segments of the pipelined datapath with the additional multiplexers and connections in place.

ID/EX   EX/MEM   MEM/WB

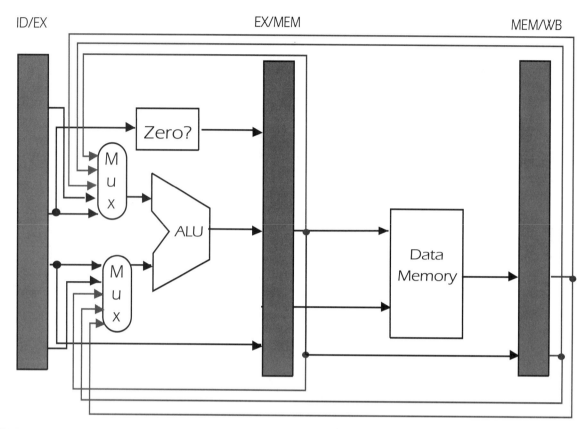

FIGURE 4.21   Forwarding of results to the ALU requires the addition of three extra inputs on each ALU multiplexer and the addition of three paths to the new inputs. The paths correspond to the ALU output at the end of the EX and the MEM stage and the memory output at the end of the MEM stage.

For DLX, the hazard detection and forwarding hardware is reasonably simple; we will see that things become much more complicated when we extend this pipeline to deal with floating point. Before we do that, we need to handle branches.

4.5 | Control Hazards

Control hazards can cause a greater performance loss for our DLX pipeline than do data hazards. When a branch is executed, it may or may not change the PC to something other than its current value plus 4. (Recall that if a branch changes the PC to its target address, it is a *taken* branch; if it falls through, it is *not taken,* or *untaken.*) If instruction *i* is a taken branch, then the PC is normally not changed until the end of MEM, after the completion of the address calculation and comparison, as shown in Figure 4.4 (page 171) and Figure 4.5 (page 172).

The simplest method of dealing with branches is to stall the pipeline as soon as we detect the branch, until we reach the MEM stage, which determines the new PC. Of course, we do not want to stall the pipeline until we know that the instruction is a branch; thus, the stall does not occur until after the ID stage, and the pipeline behavior looks like that shown in Figure 4.22. This control hazard stall must be implemented differently from a data hazard stall, since the IF cycle of the instruction following the branch must be repeated, as soon as we know the branch outcome. Thus, the first IF cycle is essentially a stall, because it never performs useful work. This stall can be implemented by setting the IF/ID register to zero for the three cycles. You may have noticed that if the branch is untaken, then the repetition of the IF stage is unnecessary since the correct instruction was indeed fetched. We will develop several schemes to take advantage of this fact shortly, but first, let's examine how we could reduce the worst case branch penalty.

Branch instruction	IF	ID	EX	MEM	WB					
Branch successor		IF	stall	stall	IF	ID	EX	MEM	WB	
Branch successor +1			stall	stall	stall	IF	ID	EX	MEM	WB
Branch successor +2				stall	stall	stall	IF	ID	EX	MEM
Branch successor +3					stall	stall	stall	IF	ID	EX
Branch successor +4						stall	stall	stall	IF	ID
Branch successor +5							stall	stall	stall	IF

FIGURE 4.22   A branch causes a three cycle stall in the DLX pipeline. Instruction i+1 is fetched, but the instruction is ignored, and the fetch is restarted once the branch target is known. It is probably obvious that if the branch is not taken, the second IF for instruction i+1 is redundant. This will be addressed shortly.

Three clock cycles wasted for every branch is a significant loss. With a 30% branch frequency and an ideal CPI of 1, the machine with branch stalls achieves only about *half* the ideal speedup from pipelining! Thus, reducing the branch penalty becomes critical. The number of clock cycles in a branch stall can be reduced in two steps:

1. Find out whether the branch is taken or not taken earlier in the pipeline.

2. Compute the taken PC (i.e., the address of the branch target) earlier.

To optimize the branch behavior, *both* of these must be done—it doesn't help to know the target of the branch without knowing whether the next instruction to execute is the target or the instruction at PC+4. Both steps should be taken as early in the pipeline as possible.

In DLX, the branches (BEQZ and BNEZ) require testing a register for equality to zero. Thus, it is possible to complete this decision by the end of the ID cycle by moving the zero test into that cycle. To take advantage of an early decision on whether the branch is taken, both PCs (taken and untaken) must be computed early. Computing the branch target address during ID requires an additional adder, because the main ALU, which has been used for this function so far, is not usable until EX. Figure 4.23 shows the revised pipelined datapath. With the separate adder and a branch decision made during ID, there is only a one-clock-cycle stall on branches. Figure 4.24 shows the branch portion of the revised pipeline table from Figure 4.3 (page 170).

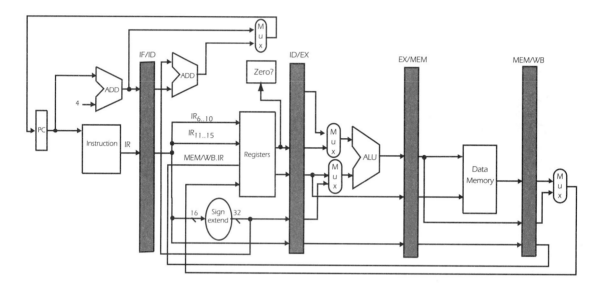

FIGURE 4.23   The stall from branch hazards can be reduced by moving the zero test and branch target calcula-tion into the ID phase of the pipeline.

Pipe stage	Branch instruction
IF	IF/ID.IR←Mem[PC]; IF/ID.NPC,PC ← PC+4;
ID	ID/EX.A ← Regs[IF/ID.IR$_{6..10}$]; ID/EX.B ← Regs[IF/ID.IR$_{11..16}$]; ID/EX.IR ← IF/ID.IR; ID/EX.Imm ← (IR$_{16}$)^{16}##IR$_{16..31}$ **if(Regs[IF/ID.IR$_{6..10}$]op0)PC←IF/ID.NPC+(IR$_{16}$)^{16}##IR$_{16..31}$**
EX	
MEM	
WB	

FIGURE 4.24   This revised pipeline structure is based on the original in Figure 4.5, page 172. It includes a separate adder, as in Figure 4.23, to compute the branch target address. The operations that are new or have changed are in bold. Because the branch target address addition happens during ID, it will happen for all instructions; the branch condition (Regs[IF/ID.IR$_{6..10}$] op 0) will also be done for all instructions. The last operation in ID is to replace the PC. We must know that the instruction is a branch before we perform this step. This requires decoding the instruction before the end of ID, or doing this operation at the very beginning of EX when the PC is sent out. Because the branch is done by the end of ID, the EX, MEM, and WB stages are unused for branches. An additional complication arises for jumps that have a longer offset than branches. We can resolve this by using an additional adder that sums the PC and lower 26 bits of the IR. Alter-natively, by decoding the jump opcodes early, we could attempt a clever scheme that does a 16-bit add in the first half of the cycle and determines whether to add in 10 bits from IR in the second half of the cycle.

In some machines, branch hazards are even more expensive in clock cycles than in our example, since the time to evaluate the branch condition and compute the destination can be even longer. For example, a machine with separate decode and register fetch stages will probably have a *branch delay*—the length of the control hazard—that is at least one clock cycle longer. The branch delay, unless it is dealt with, turns into a branch penalty. Many VAXs have branch delays of four clock cycles or more, and large, deeply pipelined machines often have branch penalties of six or seven. In general, the deeper the pipeline, the worse the branch penalty in clock cycles. Of course, the relative performance effect of a longer branch penalty depends on the overall CPI of the machine. A high CPI machine can afford to have more expensive branches because the percentage of the machine's performance that will be lost from branches is less.

Before talking about methods for reducing the pipeline penalties that can arise from branches, let's take a brief look at the dynamic behavior of branches.

Branch Behavior in Programs

Because branches can dramatically affect pipeline performance, we should look at their behavior to get some ideas about how the penalties of branches and jumps might be reduced. We already know the branch frequencies for our programs from Chapter 3. Figure 4.25 reviews the overall frequency of control-flow operations for three of the machines and gives the breakdown between branches and jumps.

We will replace this data with more extensive measurements of DLX branch behavior.

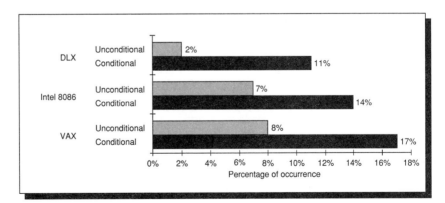

FIGURE 4.25 The frequency of instructions (branches, jumps, calls, and returns) that may change the PC. These data represent the average over the programs measured in Chapter 4. Instructions are divided into two classes: branches, which are conditional (including loop branches), and those that are unconditional (jumps, calls, and returns). The 360 is omitted because the ordinary unconditional branches are not separated from the conditional branches. Emer and Clark [1984] reported that 38% of the instructions executed in their measurements of the VAX were instructions that could change the PC. They measured that 67% of these instructions actually cause a branch in control flow. Their data were taken on a timesharing workload and reflect many uses; their measurement of branch frequency is much higher than the one in this chart.

All of the machines show a conditional branch frequency of 11%–17%, while the frequency of unconditional branches varies between 2% and 8%. An obvious question is: How many of the branches are taken? Knowing the breakdown between taken and untaken branches is important because this will affect strategies for reducing the branch penalties. For the VAX, Clark and Levy [1984] measured simple conditional branches to be taken with a frequency of just about 50%. Other branches, which occur much less often, have different ratios. Most bit-testing branches are not taken, and loop branches are taken with about 90% probability.

For DLX, we measured the branch behavior in Chapter 3 and summarized it in Figure 3.12 (page 105). That data showed 53% of the conditional branches are taken. Finally, 75% of the branches executed are forward-going branches. With this data in mind, let's look at ways to reduce branch penalties.

Reducing Pipeline Branch Penalties

There are several methods for dealing with the pipeline stalls due to branch delay, and four simple compile-time schemes are discussed in this section. In these schemes the predictions are static—they are fixed for each branch during the entire execution, and the predictions are compile-time guesses. After discussing these schemes, we examine compile-time branch prediction since these schemes all rely on such technology. In the next chapter, we look both at more powerful compile-time schemes (such as loop unrolling) that reduce the frequency of loop branches, and at dynamic hardware-based prediction schemes.

The simplest scheme to handle branches is to *freeze* or *flush* the pipeline, holding any instructions after the branch until the branch destination is known. The attractiveness of this solution lies primarily in its simplicity. It is the solution used earlier in the pipeline shown in Figure 4.22.

Untaken branch instruction	IF	ID	EX	MEM	WB				
Instruction *i*+1		IF	ID	EX	MEM	WB			
Instruction *i*+2			IF	ID	EX	MEM	WB		
Instruction *i*+3				IF	ID	EX	MEM	WB	
Instruction *i*+4					IF	ID	EX	MEM	WB

Taken branch instruction	IF	ID	EX	MEM	WB				
Instruction *i*+1		IF	IF	ID	EX	MEM	WB		
Instruction *i*+2			*stall*	IF	ID	EX	MEM	WB	
Instruction *i*+3				*stall*	IF	ID	EX	MEM	WB
Instruction *i*+4					*stall*	IF	ID	EX	MEM

FIGURE 4.26   The predict-not-taken scheme and the pipeline sequence when the branch is untaken (on the top) and taken (on the bottom). When the branch is untaken, determined during ID, we have fetched the fall-through and just continue. If the branch is taken during ID, we restart the fetch at the branch target. This causes all instructions following the branch to stall one clock cycle.

A better and only slightly more complex scheme is to predict the branch as not taken, simply allowing the hardware to continue as if the branch were not executed. Here, care must be taken not to change the machine state until the branch outcome is definitely known. The complexity that arises from this—that is, knowing when the state might be changed by an instruction and how to "back out" a change—might cause us to reconsider the simpler solution of flushing the pipeline. In the DLX pipeline, this *predict-not-taken* or *predict-untaken* scheme is implemented by continuing to fetch instructions as if the branch were a normal instruction. The pipeline looks as if nothing out of the ordinary is happening. If the branch is taken, however, we need to turn the fetched instructions into noops(simply by clearing the IF/ID register) and restart the fetch. Figure 4.26 shows both situations.

An alternative scheme is to predict the branch as taken. As soon as the branch is decoded and the target address is computed, we assume the branch to be taken and begin fetching and executing at the target. Because in our DLX pipeline we don't know the target address any earlier than we know the branch outcome, there is no advantage in this approach in this case. If the branch condition were dependent on the immediately preceding instruction, then a data hazard stall would occur for the register that is in the branch condition, and we would know the target address first. In such cases, predict-taken could be beneficial. Additionally, in some machines—especially those with implicitly-set condition codes or more powerful (and hence slower) branch conditions—the branch target is known before the branch outcome, and a predict-taken scheme makes sense.

A fourth scheme in use in some machines is called delayed branch. This technique is also used in many microprogrammed control units. In a *delayed branch*, the execution cycle with a branch delay of length n is:

```
branch instruction
sequential successor₁
sequential successor₂
........
sequential successorₙ
branch target if taken
```

The sequential successors are in the *branch-delay slots*. The job of the software is to make the successor instructions valid and useful. A number of optimizations are used. Figure   27 shows the three ways in which the branch delay can be scheduled. Figure 4.28 shows the different constraints for each of these branch-scheduling schemes, as well as situations in which they win.

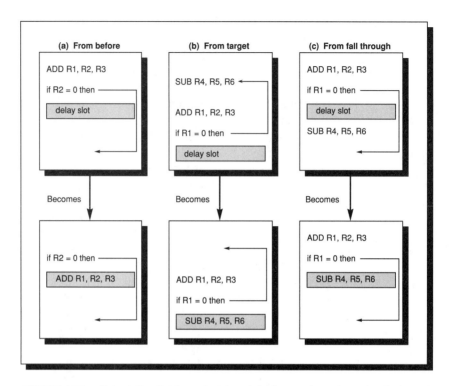

FIGURE 4.27   Scheduling the branch-delay slot. The top picture in each pair shows the code before scheduling; the bottom picture shows the scheduled code. In (a) the delay slot is scheduled with an independent instruction from before the branch. This is the best choice. Strategies (b) and (c) are used when (a) is not possible. In the code sequences for (b) and (c), the use of R1 in the branch condition prevents the ADD instruction (whose destination is R1) from being moved after the branch. In (b) the branch-delay slot is scheduled from the target of the branch; usually the target instruction will need to be copied because it can be reached by another path. Strategy (b) is preferred when the branch is taken with high probability, such as a loop branch. Finally, the branch may be scheduled from the not-taken fall-through, as in (c). To make this optimization legal for (b) or (c), it must be "OK" to execute the SUB instruction when the branch goes in the unexpected direction. By "OK" we mean that the work is wasted, but the program will still execute correctly. This is the case, for example, if R4 were a temporary register unused when the branch goes in the unexpected direction.

Scheduling strategy	Requirements	Improves performance when?
(a) From before branch	Branch must not depend on the rescheduled instructions.	Always.
(b) From target	Must be OK to execute rescheduled instructions if branch is not taken. May need to duplicate instructions.	When branch is taken. May enlarge program if instructions are duplicated.
(c) From fall-through	Must be OK to execute instructions if branch is taken.	When branch is not taken.

FIGURE 4.28   Delayed-branch–scheduling schemes and their requirements. The origin of the instruction being scheduled into the delay slot determines the scheduling strategy. The compiler must enforce the requirements when looking for instructions to schedule the delay slot. When the slots cannot be scheduled, they are filled with no-op instructions. In strategy (b), if the branch target is also accessible from another point in the program—as it would be if it were the head of a loop—the target instructions must be copied and not just moved.

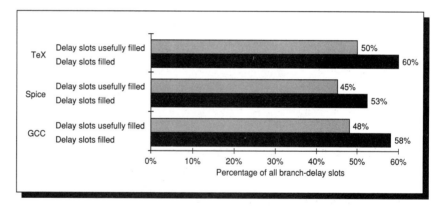

FIGURE 4.29   Frequency with which a single branch-delay slot is filled and how often the instruction is useful to the computation. The solid bar shows the percentage of the branch-delay slots occupied by some instruction other than a no-op. The difference between 100% and the dark column represents those branches that are followed by a no-op. The shaded bar shows how often those instructions do useful work. The difference between the shaded and solid bars is the percentage of instructions executed in a branch delay but not contributing to the computation. These instructions occur because optimization (b) is only useful when the branch is taken. If optimization (c) were used, it would also contribute to this difference, since it is only useful when the branch is not taken.

The limitations on delayed-branch scheduling arise from (1) the restrictions on the instructions that are scheduled into the delay slots and (2) our ability to predict at compile time whether a branch is likely to be taken or not. Figure 4.29 shows the effectiveness of the branch scheduling in DLX with a single branch-delay slot using a simple branch-scheduling algorithm. It shows that slightly more than half the branch-delay slots are filled, and most of the filled slots do useful work. On average, about 80% of the filled delay slots contribute to the computation. This number seems surprising, as branches are only taken about 53% of the time. The success rate is high because about one-half of the branch delays are being filled with an instruction from before the branch (strategy (a)), which is useful whether the branch is taken or untaken.

When the scheduler in Figure 4.29 cannot use strategy (a)—moving an instruction from before the branch to fill the branch-delay slot—it uses only strategy (b)—moving it from the target. For simplicity reasons, the schedule does not use strategy (c). In total, nearly half the branch-delay slots are dynamically useful, eliminating one-half the branch stalls. Looking at Figure 4.29, we see that the primary limitation is the number of empty slots—those filled with noops. It is unlikely that the ratio of useful slots to filled slots, about 80%, can be improved, because this would require much better accuracy in predicting branches. In the exercises, we consider an extension of the delayed-branch idea that tries to fill more slots.

There is a small additional hardware cost for delayed branches. Because of the delayed effect of branches, multiple PCs (one plus the length of the delay) are needed to correctly restore the state when an interrupt occurs. Consider when the interrupt occurs after a taken-branch instruction is completed, but before all the instructions in the delay slots and the branch target are completed. In this case, the PC's of the delay slots and the PC of the branch target must be saved, since they are not sequential.

Performance of Branch Schemes

What is the effective performance of each of these schemes? The effective pipeline speedup with branch penalties assuming an ideal CPI of 1 is:

$$\text{Pipeline speedup} = \frac{\text{Pipeline depth}}{1 + \text{Pipeline stall cycles from branches}}$$

Because

$$\text{Pipeline stall cycles from branches} = \text{Branch frequency} \times \text{Branch penalty}$$

we obtain:

$$\text{Pipeline speedup} = \frac{\text{Pipeline depth}}{1 + \text{Branch frequency} \times \text{Branch penalty}}$$

Using the DLX measurements in this section, Figure 4.30 shows several hardware options for dealing with branches, along with their performances (assuming a base CPI of 1).

Scheduling scheme	Branch penalty	Effective CPI	Pipeline speedup over unpipelined machine	Pipeline speedup over stall pipeline on branch
Stall pipeline	3	1.42	3.5	1.0
Predict taken	1	1.14	4.4	1.26
Predict not taken	1	1.09	4.5	1.29
Delayed branch	0.5	1.07	4.6	1.31

FIGURE 4.30 Overall costs of a variety of branch schemes with the DLX pipeline. These data are for our DLX pipeline using the measured control-instruction frequency of 14% and the measurements of delay-slot filling from Figure 4.29. In addition, we know that 65% of the control instructions actually change the PC (taken branches plus unconditional changes). Shown are both the resultant CPI and the speedup over an unpipelined machine, which we assume would have a CPI of 5 without any branch penalties. The last column of the table gives the speedup over a scheme that always stalls on branches.

Remember that the numbers in this section are **dramatically** affected by the length of the pipeline delay and the base CPI. A longer pipeline delay will cause an increase in the penalty and a larger percentage of wasted time. A delay of only one clock cycle is small–the R4000 pipeline, which we examine in Section 4.8, has a branch delay of three cycles. With a low CPI, the delay must be kept small, while a higher base CPI would reduce the relative penalty from branches.

Static Branch Prediction: Using Compiler Technology

Delayed branches are a technique that exposes a pipeline hazard so that the compiler can reduce the penalty associated with the hazard. As we saw, the effectiveness of this technique depends on whether we correctly guess which way a branch will go. Being able to accurately predict a branch at compile time is also helpful for scheduling data hazards. Consider the following code segment:

```
        LW      R1,0(R2)
        SUB     R1,R1,R3
        BEQZ    R1,L
        OR      R4,R5,R6
        . . . .
L:      ADD     R7,R8,R9
```

The dependence of the SUB and BEQZ on the LW instruction means that a stall will be needed after the LW. Suppose we knew that this branch was almost always taken and that the value of R7 was not needed on the fall-through path, then we could increase the speed of the program by moving the instruction ADD R7,R8,R9 to the position after the LW. Correspondingly, if we knew the branch was usually not taken, then we could contemplate moving the OR instruction. In addition, we can also use the information to better schedule any branch delay, since choosing how to schedule the delay depends on knowing the branch behavior.

To perform these optimizations, we need to predict the branch statically when we compile the program. In the next chapter, we will examine the use of dynamic prediction based on run-time program behavior. We will also look at a variety of compile-time methods for scheduling code; these techniques require static branch prediction and thus the ideas in this section are critical.

There are two basic methods we can use to statically predict branches: by examination of the program structure and by the use of profile information collected from earlier runs of the program. Using the program structure is straightforward: as a starting point, we could assume that backwards-going branches are taken, and forwards-going branches are untaken. Figure 4.31 shows how well such a scheme works. This scheme is not very effective for most programs. Beyond this simple technique it is difficult to make a better guess simply based on program structure.

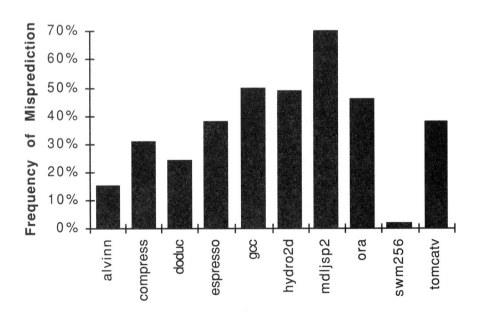

FIGURE 4.31   **The accuracy of branch prediction based on the branch direction varies greatly from about 98% to as low of 30%.** The simple scheme predicts backwards branches as taken and forwards branches as untaken.

The alternative technique is to predict branches based on profile information collected from earlier runs. The key observation that makes this worthwhile is that the behavior of branches is often bimodally distributed, that is, an individual branch is often highly biased towards taken or untaken. Figure 4.32 shows the success of branch prediction using this strategy. The same input data was used for runs and for collecting the profile; other studies have shown that changing the input so that the profile is for a different run leads to only a small change in the accuracy of profile-based prediction.

While Figures 4.31 and 4.32 tell us the accuracy of these schemes, the wide range of frequency of branches in these programs, from under 1% to over 16%, means that the overall frequency of a mispredicted branch varies widely. Figure 4.33 shows the number of instructions executed between mispredicted branches for both a profile-based and a direction-based predictor.

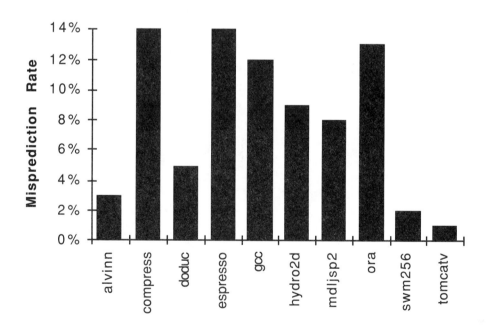

FIGURE 4.32 Accuracy of a profile-based predictor varies widely depending on the type of program. These programs were compiled for a MIPS R3000 using the standard MIPS compilers. The profile and actual run are identical. The data were collected by David Wall as part of a study we describe in detail in the next chapter.

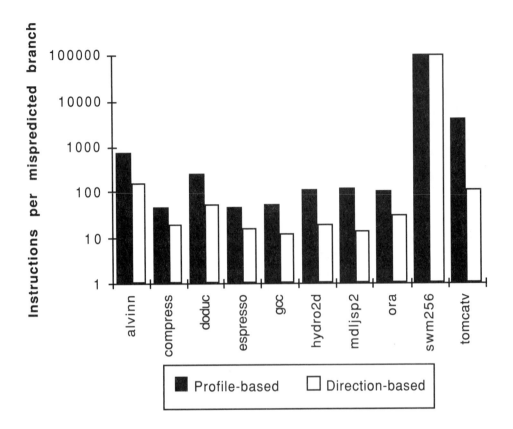

FIGURE 4.33   Accuracy of a profile-based predictor as measured from the number of instructions executed between mispredicted branches. The wide variation arises because programs such as swm256 have both low branch frequency (0.5%) and highly predictable branches, while gcc has 30 times as many branches that are six times less predictable.

Summary: Performance of the DLX Integer Pipeline

We close this section on hazard detection and elimination by showing the total distribution of idle clock cycles for our benchmarks when run on the DLX integer pipeline with software for pipeline scheduling. Figure 4.34 shows the distribution of clock cycles lost to load and branch delays, which is obtained by combining the separate measurements shown in Figures 4.17 (page 192) and 4.30 (page 205).

We will add additional benchmarks to this data in the final version.

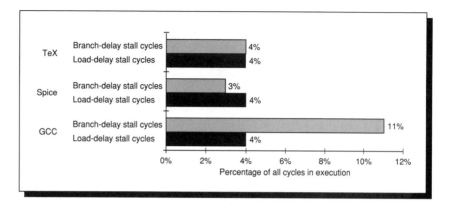

FIGURE 4.34 Percentage of the clock cycles spent on delays versus executing instructions. This assumes a perfect memory system; the clock-cycle count and instruction count would be identical if there were no integer pipeline stalls. This graph says that from 7% to 15% of the clock cycles are stalls; the remaining 85% to 93% are clock cycles that issue instructions. The Spice clock cycles do not include stalls in the FP pipeline, which will be shown at the end of Section 6.6. The pipeline scheduler fills load delays before branch delays, and this affects the distribution of delay cycles.

For the GCC and TeX programs, the effective CPI (ignoring any stalls except those from pipeline hazards) on this pipelined version of DLX is 1.1. Compare this to the CPI for the complete unpipelined, hardwired version of DLX described in Section 4.1, which would be close 5. Ignoring all other sources of stalls and assuming that the clock rates will be the same, the performance improvement from pipelining is about 4.5 times.

4.6 | What Makes Pipelining Hard to Implement

Now that we understand how to detect and resolve hazards, we can deal with some complications that we have avoided so far. The first part of this section deals with the challenges of interrupts and exceptions. In the second part of this section, we discuss some of the challenges raised by different instruction sets.

Dealing with Interrupts

Interrupts are harder to handle in a pipelined machine because the overlapping of instructions makes it more difficult to know whether an instruction can safely change the state of the machine. In a pipelined machine, an instruction is executed piece by piece and is not completed for several clock cycles. Unfortunately, other instructions in the pipeline can raise interrupts that may force the machine to abort the instructions in the pipeline before they complete

As in unpipelined implementations, the most difficult interrupts have two properties: (1) they occur within instructions (that is, in the middle of the instruction execution corresponding to EX or MEM), and (2) they must be restartable. In our DLX pipeline, for example, a virtual memory page fault resulting from a data fetch cannot occur until sometime in the MEM cycle of the instruction. By the time that fault is seen, several other instructions will be in execution. A page fault must be restartable and requires the intervention of another process, such as the operating system. Thus, the pipeline must be safely shut down and the state saved so that the instruction can be restarted in the correct state. This is usually implemented by saving the PC of the instruction to restart at. If the restarted instruction is not a branch then we will continue to fetch the sequential successors and begin their execution in the normal fashion. If the restarted instruction is a branch, then we will reevaluate the branch condition and begin fetching from either the target or the fall-through. When an interrupt occurs, we can take the following steps to save the pipeline state safely:

1.   Force a trap instruction into the pipeline on the next IF.

2.   Until the trap is taken, turn off all writes for the faulting instruction and for all instructions that follow in the pipeline; this can be done by placing zeros into the pipeline latches of all instructions in the pipeline, starting with the interrupting instruction, but not those that precede the interrupting instruction. This prevents any state changes for instructions that will not be completed before the interrupt is handled.

3.   After the interrupt-handling routine in the operating system receives control, it immediately saves the PC of the faulting instruction. This value will be used to return from the interrupt later.

When we use delayed branches, it is no longer possible to re-create the state of the machine with a single PC because the instructions in the pipeline may not be sequentially related. In particular, when the instruction that causes the interrupt is in a branch-delay slot, and the branch is taken, then the instructions to restart are those in the slot plus the instruction at the branch target. The branch itself has completed execution and is not restarted. The addresses of the instructions in the branch-delay slot and the target are not sequential. So we need to save and restore as many PCs as the length of the branch delay plus one. This is done in the third step above.

After the interrupt has been handled, special instructions return the machine from the interrupt by reloading the PCs and restarting the instruction stream (using RFE in DLX). If the pipeline can be stopped so that the instructions just before the faulting instruction are completed and those after it can be restarted from scratch, the pipeline is said to have *precise interrupts*. Ideally, the faulting instruction would not have changed the state, and correctly handling some interrupts requires that the faulting instruction have no effects. For other interrupts, such as floating-point exceptions, the faulting instruction on some machines writes its result before the interrupt can be handled. In such cases, the hardware must be prepared to retrieve the source operands, even if the destination is identical to one of the source operands. Because floating point operations may run for many cycles, it is highly likely that some other instruction may have written the source operands (as we will see in the next section, floating point operations often complete out of order). To overcome this, many recent high performance machines have introduced two modes of operation. One mode has precise interrupts and the other does not. Of course, the precise interrupt mode is slower, since it allows less overlap among floating point instructions. In some machines, the precise mode is much slower (>10 times) and thus useful only for debugging of codes.

Supporting precise interrupts is a requirement in many systems, while in others it is valuable because it simplifies the operating system interface. At a minimum, any machine with demand paging or IEEE arithmetic trap handlers must make its interrupts precise, either in the hardware or with some software support.

Interrupts in DLX

Figure 4.35 shows the DLX pipeline stages and which "problem" interrupts might occur in each stage. With pipelining, multiple interrupts may occur in the same clock cycle because there are multiple instructions in execution. For example, consider this instruction sequence:

LW	IF	ID	EX	MEM	WB
ADD		IF	ID	EX	MEM	WB

This pair of instructions can cause a data page fault and an arithmetic interrupt at the same time, since the LW is in MEM while the ADD is in EX. This case can be handled by dealing with only the data page fault and then restarting the execution. The second interrupt will reoccur (but not the first, if the software is correct), and when the second interrupt occurs, it can be handled independently.

Pipeline stage	Problem interrupts occurring
IF	Page fault on instruction fetch; misaligned memory access; memory-protection violation
ID	Undefined or illegal opcode
EX	Arithmetic interrupt
MEM	Page fault on data fetch; misaligned memory access; memory-protection violation
WB	None

FIGURE 4.35 Interrupts that may occur in the DLX pipeline. Interrupts raised from instruction or data-memory access account for six out of seven cases.

In reality, the situation is not as straightforward as this simple example. Interrupts may occur out of order; that is, an instruction may cause an interrupt before an earlier instruction causes one. Consider again the above sequence of instructions LW followed by ADD. The LW can get a data page fault, seen when the instruction is in MEM, and the ADD can get an instruction page fault, seen when the ADD instruction is in IF. The instruction page fault will actually occur first, even though it is caused by a later instruction! This situation can be resolved in two ways. To explain the alternatives, let's call the instruction in the position of the LW "instruction *i*", and the instruction in the position of the ADD "instruction *i*+1."

The first approach is completely precise and is the simplest to understand for the user of the architecture. The hardware posts all interrupts caused by a given instruction in a status vector associated with that instruction. The interrupt status vector is carried along as the instruction goes down the pipeline. When an instruction enters WB (or is about to leave MEM), the interrupt status vector is checked. If any interrupts are posted, they are handled in the order in which they would occur in time—the interrupt corresponding to the earliest pipestage is handled first. This guarantees that all interrupts will be seen on instruction *i* before any are seen on *i*+1. Of course, any action taken on behalf of instruction *i* may be invalid, but because no state is changed until WB, this is not a problem in the DLX pipeline. Nevertheless, pipeline control may want to disable any actions on behalf of an instruction *i* (and its successors) as soon as the interrupt is recognized. For pipelines that could update the machine state earlier than WB, this disabling is required.

The second approach is to handle an interrupt as soon as it appears. This could be regarded as slightly less precise because interrupts occur in an order different from the order they would occur in if there were no pipelining. Figure 4.36 shows two interrupts occurring in the DLX pipeline. Because the interrupt at instruction *i*+1 is handled when it appears, the pipeline must be stopped immediately without completing any instructions that have yet to change state. For the DLX pipeline, this will be *i*–2, *i*–1, *i*, and *i*+1, assuming the interrupt is recognized at the end of the IF stage of the ADD instruction. The pipeline is then restarted with instruction *i*–2. Because the instruction causing the interrupt can be any of *i*–2, *i*–1, *i*, or *i*+1, the operating system must determine which instruction faulted. This is easy to figure out if the type of interrupt and its corresponding pipe stage are known. For example, only *i*+1 (the ADD instruction) could get an instruction page fault at this point, and only *i*–2 could get a data page fault. After handling the fault for *i*+1 and restarting at *i*–2, the data page fault will be encountered on instruction *i*, which will cause *i*, ..., *i*+3 to be interrupted. The data page fault can then be handled.

Instruction i–3		IF	ID	EX	MEM	WB				
Instruction i–2			IF	ID	EX	MEM	*WB*			
Instruction i–1				IF	ID	EX	*MEM*	*WB*		
Instruction i (LW)					IF	ID	*EX*	*MEM*	*WB*	
Instruction i+1 (ADD)						**IF**	*ID*	*EX*	*MEM*	*WB*
Instruction i+2							*IF*	*ID*	*EX*	*MEM*	*WB*

Instruction i–3		IF	ID	EX	MEM	WB				
Instruction i–2			IF	ID	EX	MEM	WB			
Instruction i–1				IF	ID	EX	MEM	WB		
Instruction i (LW)					IF	ID	EX	**MEM**	*WB*	
Instruction i+1 (ADD)						IF	ID	*EX*	*MEM*	*WB*
Instruction i+2							IF	*ID*	*EX*	*MEM*	*WB*
Instruction i+3								*IF*	*ID*	*EX*	*MEM*
Instruction i+4									IF	ID	EX

FIGURE 4.36 The actions taken for interrupts occurring at different points in the pipeline and handled immediately. This shows the instructions interrupted when an instruction page fault occurs in instruction i+1 (in the top diagram), and a data page fault in instruction i in the bottom diagram. The pipe stages in bold are the cycles during which the interrupt is recognized. The pipe stages in italics are the instructions that will not be completed due to the interrupt, and will need to be restarted. Because the earliest effect of the interrupt is on the pipe stage after it occurs, instructions that are in the WB stage when the interrupt occurs will complete, while those that have not yet reached WB will be stopped and restarted.

Instruction Set Complications

In DLX, no instruction has more than one result and our DLX pipeline writes that result only at the end of an instruction's execution. When an instruction is guaranteed to complete it is called *committed*.In the DLX integer pipeline, all instructions are committed when they reach the MEM/WB stage and no instruction updates state before that stage. Thus, precise interrupts are straightforward. Some machines have instructions that change the state in the middle of the instruction execution before the instruction and its predecessors are guaranteed to complete. For example, autoincrement addressing modes on the VAX cause the update of registers in the middle of an instruction execution. In such a case, if the instruction is aborted because of an interrupt, it will leave the machine state altered. Restarting the instruction stream after such an imprecise interrupt is difficult. Alternatively, we could avoid updating the state before the instruction commits, but this may be difficult or costly, since there may be dependences on the updated state (consider a VAX instruction that autoincrements the same register multiple times). Thus, to maintain a precise interrupt model, most machines with such instructions have the ability to back out any state changes made before the instruction is committed. If an interrupt occurs, the machine uses this ability to reset the state of the machine to its value before the interrupted instruction started. In the next section, we will see that the more powerful DLX floating point pipeline can introduce similar problems, and the next chapter is full of such difficulties!.

A related source of difficulties arises from instructions that update memory state during execution, such as the string copy operations on the VAX. To make it possible to interrupt and restart these instructions, the instructions are defined to use the general purpose registers as working registers thus allowing the state of the partially completed instruction to be recorded in the registers, saved on an interrupt, and restored after the interrupt. In the VAX an additional bit of state records when an instruction has started updating the memory state, so that when the pipeline is restarted, the machine knows whether to restart the instruction from the beginning or from the middle of the instruction. The 80x86 string instructions also use the registers as working storage, allowing restart of such an instruction.

A different set of difficulties arises from odd bits of state that may create additional pipeline hazards or may require extra hardware to save and restore. Condition codes are a good example of this. Many machines set the condition codes implicitly as part of the instruction. This approach has advantages, since condition codes decouple the evaluation of the condition from the actual branch. However, implicitly-set condition codes can cause difficulties in making branches fast. They limit the effectiveness of branch scheduling because most operations will modify the condition code, making it hard to schedule instructions between the setting of the condition code and the branch. Furthermore, in machines with condition codes, the processor must decide when the branch condition is fixed. This involves finding out when the condition code has been set for the last time prior to the branch. On the VAX, most instructions set the condition code, so that an implementation will have to stall if it tries to determine the branch condition early. Alternatively, the branch condition can be evaluated by the branch late in the pipeline, but this still leads to a long branch delay. On the 80x86, many, but not all, instructions set the condition codes. Figure 4.37 shows how the situation differs on the DLX, the VAX, and the 80x86 for the following C code sequence, assuming that b and d are initially in registers R2 and R3 (and should not be destroyed):

```
a = b + d;
if (b==0) ...
```

DLX	VAX	Intel 80x86
`ADD R1,R2,R3`	`ADDL3 a,R2,R3`	`MOV R1,R2`
`...`	`...`	`ADD R1,R2`
`SW  a,R1`	`CL   R2,0`	`MOV  a,R1`
`...`	`BEQL label`	`...`
`BEQZ R2,label`		`JZ label`

FIGURE 4.37 Code sequence for the above two statements. Because the ADD computes the sum of b and d, and the branch condition depends only on an explicit compare (on R2) is needed on the VAX and 360. On DLX, the branch depends only on R2 and can be arbitrarily far away from it. (In addition, the SW could be moved into the branch-delay slot.) On the VAX and the 80x86, all ALU operations and moves set the condition codes, so that a compare must be right before the branch.

Provided there is lots of hardware to spare, **all** the instructions before the branch in the pipeline can be examined to decide when the branch is determined. Of course, architectures with explicitly-set condition codes avoid this difficulty. However, pipeline control must still track the last instruction that sets the condition code to know when the branch condition is decided. In effect, the condition code must be treated as an operand that requires hazard detection for RAW hazards with branches, just as DLX must do on the registers.

A final thorny area in pipelining is multicycle operations. Imagine trying to pipeline a sequence of VAX instructions such as this:

```
MOVL R1,R2
ADDL3 42(R1),56(R1)+,@(R1)
SUBL2 R2,R3
MOVC3 @(R1)[R2],74(R2),R3
```

These instructions differ radically in the number of clock cycles they will require, from as low as one up to hundreds of clock cycles. They also require different numbers of data memory accesses, from zero to possibly hundreds. The data hazards are very complex and occur both between and within instructions. The simple solution of making all instructions execute for the same number of clock cycles is unacceptable because it introduces an enormous number of hazards and bypass conditions, and makes an immensely long pipeline. Pipelining the VAX at the instruction level is difficult, but a clever solution was found by the VAX 8800 designers. They pipeline the microinstruction execution; because the microinstructions are simple (they look a lot like DLX), the pipeline control is much easier. While it is not clear that this approach can achieve quite as low a CPI as an instruction-level pipeline for the VAX, it is much simpler, possibly leading to a shorter clock cycle.

In comparison, load/store machines have simple operations with similar amounts of work and pipeline more easily. If architects realize the relationship between instruction set design and pipelining, they can design architectures for more efficient pipelining. In the next section we will see how the DLX pipeline deals with long-running instructions, specifically floating point operations.

<table>
<tr><td>**4.7**</td><td>**Extending the DLX Pipeline to Handle Multicycle Operations**</td></tr>
</table>

We now want to explore how our DLX pipeline can be extended to handle floating-point operations. This section concentrates on the basic approach and the design alternatives, closing with some performance measurements of a DLX floating-point pipeline.

It is impractical to require that all DLX floating-point operations complete in one clock cycle, or even in two. Doing so would mean either accepting a slow clock or using enormous amounts of logic in the floating-point units, or both. Instead, the floating-point pipeline will allow for a longer latency for operations. This is easier to grasp if we imagine the floating-point instructions as having the same pipeline as the integer instructions, with two important changes. First, the EX cycle may be repeated as many times as needed to complete the operation—the number of repetitions can vary for different operations. Second, there may be multiple floating-point functional units. A stall will occur if the instruction to be issued will either cause a structural hazard for the functional unit it uses or cause a data hazard.

For this section, let's assume that there are four separate functional units in our DLX implementation:

1. The main integer unit

2. FP and integer multiplier

3. FP adder

4. FP and integer divider

The integer unit handles all loads and stores to either register set, all the integer operations (except multiply and divide), and branches. If we also assume that the execution stages of the other functional units are not pipelined, then Figure 4.38 shows the resulting pipeline structure. Because EX is not pipelined, no other instruction using the functional unit may issue until the previous instruction leaves EX. Moreover, if an instruction cannot proceed to the EX stage, the entire pipeline behind that instruction will be stalled. In the next chapter, we will deal with schemes that allow the pipeline to progress when there are more functional units or when the functional units are pipelined.

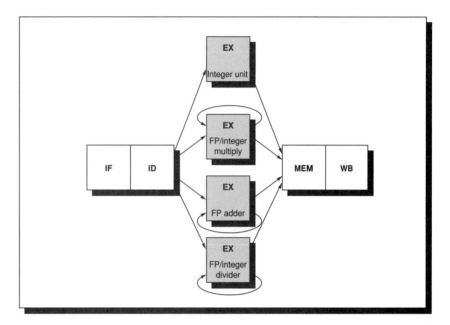

FIGURE 4.38 The DLX pipeline with three additional unpipelined, floating-point, functional units. Because only one instruction issues on every clock cycle, all instructions go through the standard pipeline for integer operations. The floating-point operations simply loop when they reach the EX stage. After they have finished the EX stage, they proceed to MEM and WB to complete execution.

In reality, the intermediate results are probably not cycled around the EX unit as Figure 4.38 suggests; instead, the EX pipeline stage has some number of clock delays larger than 1. We can generalize the structure of the FP pipeline shown in Figure 4.38 to allow pipelining of some stages and multiple ongoing operations. To describe such a pipeline, we must define both the latency of the functional units and also the *initiation rate* or *repeat rate*. This is the rate at which new operations of a given type may be started. For example, consider the following latencies and repeat rates:

Functional Unit	Latency	Repeat Rate
Integer ALU	1	1
Data memory	1	1
FP Add	2	1
FP Multiply (also integer multiply)	6	3
FP Divide (also integer divide)	15	15

This example pipeline structure allows up to two outstanding FP adds, two outstanding FP/integer multiplies, and one FP divide. Figure 4.39 shows how this pipeline can be drawn, by extending Figure 4.38. The repeat rate is shown in Figure 4.39 by adding additional pipeline stages, which will be separated by an additional pipeline register: EX1/EX2. The pipeline stages that take multiple clock cycles are further subdivided to show the latency of those stages. Because they are not complete stages, only one operation may be active.

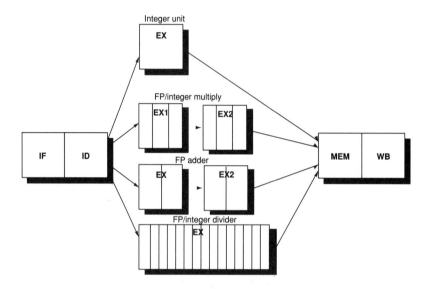

FIGURE 4.39   A pipeline that supports multiple outstanding loads. The two stage structure of the FP multiply and FP add units shows that there can be two outstanding operations in these stages. The finer division of the pipeline stages show the latency of each stage.

The structure of the pipeline in Figure 4.39 requires the introduction of the EX1/EX2 registers and the modification of the connections to the ID/EX and EX/MEM registers. ID/EX must be modified to will feed either an EX or an EX1 pipestage, and EX/MEM will be connected either to an EX or EX2 pipestage. Because an operation in a pipestage may not complete in one clock, there is a question of where to store the control information associated with that pipestage, while the instruction is in the pipestage, but has not yet completed the last pipestage. Because only one operation can be in this pipestage (or any of its substages), we need only one register. There are two possible solutions: introduce an intermediate register, which tracks the result, or use the normal pipeline register, but track that the contents as pending until the operation has completed. The latter works because there is only one operation in these substages at a time and hence only one pending result; we choose to add a pending bit for simplicity in the discussions that follow.

Hazards and Forwarding in Longer Latency Pipelines

There are a number of different aspects to the hazard detection and forwarding for a pipeline like that in Figure 4.39:

1. Because the units are not fully pipelined, structural hazards can occur. These will need to be detected and issuing instructions will need to be stalled.

2. Because the instructions have varying running times, the number of register writes required in a cycle can be larger than 1.

3. WAW hazards are possible, since instructions no longer reach WB in order. Note that WAR hazards are not possible, since the register reads always occur in ID.

4. Instructions can complete in a different order than they were issued, causing problems with interrupts; we deal with this in the next subsection.

First, let's examine the second and third problems before describing the overall solution for hazard detection.

If we assume the FP register file has one write port, sequences of FP operations, as well as a FP load together with FP operations, can cause conflicts for the register write port. Consider the pipeline sequence shown in Figure 4.40: In clock cycle 10, all three instructions will reach WB and want to write the register file. With only a single register file write port, the machine must serialize the instruction completion. This single register port represents a structural hazard. We could increase the number of write ports to solve this, but that solution may be unattractive, since the additional write ports would be used only rarely. This is because the maximum steady state number of write ports needed is 1. Instead we choose to detect and enforce access to the write port as a structural hazard.

Instruction	Clock cycle number									
	1	**2**	**3**	**4**	**5**	**6**	**7**	**8**	**9**	**10**
MULTD F0,F4,F6	IF	ID	$EX1_1$	$EX1_2$	$EX1_3$	$EX2_1$	$EX2_2$	$EX2_3$	MEM	WB
...		IF	ID	EX	MEM	WB				
ADDD F2,F4,F6			IF	ID	$EX1_1$	$EX1_2$	$EX2_1$	$EX2_2$	MEM	WB
...				IF	ID	EX	MEM	WB		
...					IF	ID	EX	MEM	WB	
LD F8,0(R2)						IF	ID	EX	MEM	WB

FIGURE 4.40   Three instructions want to perform a write back to the FP register file simultaneously, as shown in color in clock cycle 10. This is *not* the worst case, since earlier multiplies, divides, and adds in the FP unit could also finish on the same clock.

There are two different ways to avoid this hazard. The first is to track the use of the write port in the ID stage and to stall an instruction before it issues, just as we would for any other structural hazard. Tracking the use of the write port can be done with a shift register that indicates when already-issued instructions will use the register file. If the instruction in ID needs to use the register file at the same time as an instruction in EX, EX1, or EX2, the instruction in ID is stalled for a cycle. On each clock the reservation register is shifted one bit. This implementation has the advantage that it maintains the property that we stall instructions only in the ID stage. The cost is the addition of the shift register and write conflict logic. We will assume this scheme throughout this section.

An alternative scheme is to stall a conflicting instruction when it tries to enter the MEM stage. If we wait to stall the conflicting instructions until they want to enter the MEM stage, we can choose to stall either instruction. A simple, though sometimes suboptimal, heuristic is to give priority to the unit with the longest latency, since that is the one most likely to be the cause of the bottleneck and to stall the other (or others). The advantage of this scheme is that it does not require us to detect the conflict until the entrance of the MEM stage, where it is easy to see. The disadvantage is that it complicates pipeline control, as stalls can now arise from two places. Notice that stalling before entering MEM will cause the EX or EX2 stage to be occupied, possibly forcing the stall to trickle back in the pipeline.

Our other problem is the possibility of WAW hazards. To see that these exist, consider the example in Figure 4.40. If the LD instruction were issued one cycle earlier and had a destination of F2, then it would create a WAW hazard, because it would write F2 one cycle earlier than the ADDD. Note that this hazard only occurs when the result of the ADDD is overwritten *without* any instruction ever using it! If there were a use of F2 between the ADDD and the LD, the pipeline would need to be stalled for a RAW hazard, and the LD would not issue until the ADDD was completed. We could argue that, for our pipeline, WAW hazards only occur when a useless instruction is executed, but we must still detect them and make sure that the result of the LD appears in F2 when we are done. (As we will see in Section 4.9, such sequences sometimes *do* occur in reasonable code.)

There are two possible ways to handle this WAW hazard. The first approach is to delay the issue of the load instruction until the ADDD enters MEM. The second approach is to stamp out the result of the add by detecting the hazard and changing the control so that the add does not write its result. Then, the LD can issue right away. Because this hazard is rare, either scheme will work fine—you can pick whatever is simpler to implement. In either case, the hazard can be detected during ID when the LD is issuing. Then stalling the LD or making the ADDD a no-op is easy. The difficult situation is to detect that the LD might finish before the ADDD, because that requires knowing the length of the pipeline and the current position of the ADDD. Luckily, this code sequence (two writes with no intervening read) will be very rare, so we can use a simple solution: if an instruction in ID wants to write the same register as an instruction in EX1 or EX2, do not issue the instruction to EX. In the next chapter, we will see how additional hardware can eliminate these hazards. First, let's put together the pieces for implementing the hazard and issue logic in our FP pipeline.

In detecting the possible hazards, we must consider hazards among FP instructions, as well as hazards between an FP instruction and an integer instruction. Except for FP loads/stores and FP-integer register moves, the FP and integer registers are distinct, and all integer instructions operate on the integer registers, while the floating-point operations operate only on their own registers. Thus, we need only consider FP loads/stores and FP register moves in detecting hazards between FP and integer instructions. This simplification of pipeline control is an additional advantage of having separate register files for integer and floating-point data. (The main advantages are a doubling of the number of registers, without making either set larger and an increase in bandwidth without adding more ports to either set.) Assuming that the pipeline does all hazard detection in ID, there are three checks that must be performed, before an instruction can issue:

1. *Check for structural hazards*—Wait until the required functional unit is not busy and the register write port is available when it will be needed.

2. *Check for a RAW data hazard*—Wait until the source registers are not listed as pending destinations in either the ID/EX (which corresponds to the instruction issued on the last cycle), EX1/EX2, or EX/MEM registers.

3. *Check for a WAW data hazard*–Determine if the instruction in EX1, or EX2 has the same register destination as this instruction. If so, stall the issue of the instruction in ID.

Although the hazard detection is slightly more complex with the multicycle FP operations, the concepts are the same as for the DLX integer pipeline. The same is true for the forwarding logic. The forwarding can be implemented by checking if the destination register in the EX/MEM or MEM/WB registers is one of the source registers of the floating-point instruction; if so, the appropriate input multiplexer will have to be enable so as to choose the forwarded data. In the exercises, you will have the opportunity to specify the logic for the RAW and WAW hazard detection as well as for forwarding. Multicycle FP operations also introduce new problems for our interrupt mechanisms.

Maintaining Precise Interrupts

Another problem caused by these long-running instructions can be illustrated with the following sequence of code:

```
DIVF    F0,F2,F4
ADDF    F10,F10,F8
SUBF    F12,F12,F14
```

This code sequence looks straightforward; there are no dependences. A problem arises, however, because an instruction issued early may complete after an instruction issued later. In this example, we can expect ADDF and SUBF to complete *before* the DIVF completes. This is called *out-of-order completion* and is common in pipelines with long-running operations. Because hazard detection will prevent any dependence among instructions from being violated, why is out-of-order completion a problem? Suppose that the SUBF causes a floating-point–arithmetic interrupt at a point where the ADDF has completed but the DIVF has not. The result will be an imprecise interrupt, something we are trying to avoid. It may appear that this could be handled by letting the floating-point pipeline drain, as we do for the integer pipeline. But the interrupt may be in a position where this is not possible. For example, if the DIVF decided to take a floating-point–arithmetic interrupt after the add completed, we could not have a precise interrupt at the hardware level. In fact, because the ADDF destroys one of its operands, we could not restore the state to what it was before the DIVF, even with software help.

This problem arises because instructions are completing in a different order from the order in which they were issued. There are four possible approaches to dealing with out-of-order completion. The first is to ignore the problem and settle for imprecise interrupts. This approach was used in the 1960s and early 1970s. It is still used in some supercomputers, where certain classes of interrupts are not allowed or are handled by the hardware without stopping the pipeline. It is difficult to use this approach in most machines built today, due to features such as virtual memory and the IEEE floating-point standard, which essentially require precise interrupts through a combination of hardware and software. As mentioned earlier, some recent machines have solved this problem by introducing two modes of execution: a fast, but possibly imprecise mode and a slower, precise mode.

A second approach is to buffer the results of an operation until all the operations that were issued earlier are complete. Some machines actually use this solution, but it becomes expensive when the difference in running times among operations is long, since the number of results to buffer can become large. Furthermore, results from the queue must be bypassed to continue issuing instructions while waiting for the longer instruction. This requires a large number of comparators and a very large multiplexer. There are two viable variations on this basic approach. The first is a *history file*, used in the CYBER 180/990. The history file keeps track of the original values of registers. When an interrupt occurs and the state must be rolled back earlier than some instruction that completed out of order, the original value of the register can be restored from the history file. A similar technique is used for autoincrement and autodecrement addressing on machines like VAXes. Another approach, the *future file*, proposed by J. Smith and Plezkun [1988], keeps the newer value of a register; when all earlier instructions have completed, the main register file is updated from the future file. On an interrupt, the main register file has the precise values for the interrupted state. In the next chapter, we will see extensions of this idea.

A third technique in use is to allow the interrupts to become somewhat imprecise, but to keep enough information so that the trap-handling routines can create a precise sequence for the interrupt. This means knowing what operations were in the pipeline and their PCs. Then, after handling the interrupt, the software finishes any instructions that precede the latest instruction completed, and the sequence can restart. Consider the following worst-case code sequence:

Instruction$_1$—a long-running instruction that eventually interrupts execution

Instruction$_2$, ... , Instruction$_{n-1}$—a series of instructions that are not completed

Instruction$_n$—an instruction that is finished

Given the PCs of all the instructions in the pipeline and the interrupt return PC, the software can find the state of instruction$_1$ and instruction$_n$. Because instruction$_n$ has completed, we will want to restart execution at instruction$_{n+1}$. After handling the interrupt, the software must simulate the execution of instruction$_1$, ... , instruction$_{n-1}$. Then we can return from the interrupt and restart at instruction$_{n+1}$. The complexity of executing these instructions properly by the handler is the major difficulty of this scheme. There is an important simplification for simple DLX-like pipelines: If instruction$_2$, ... , instruction$_n$ are all integer instructions, then we know that if instruction$_n$ has completed, all of instruction$_2$, ... , instruction$_{n-1}$ have also completed. Thus, only floating-point operations need to be handled. To make this scheme tractable the number of floating-point instructions that can be overlapped in execution can be limited. For example, if we only overlap two instructions, then only the interrupting instruction need be completed by software. This restriction may reduce the potential throughput if the FP pipelines are deep or if there is a significant number of FP functional units. This approach is used in the SPARC architecture to allow overlap of floating-point and integer operations.

The final technique is a hybrid scheme that allows the instruction issue to continue only if it is certain that all the instructions before the issuing instruction will complete without causing an interrupt. This guarantees that when an interrupt occurs, no instructions after the interrupting one will be completed, and all of the instructions before the interrupting one can be completed. This sometimes means stalling the machine to maintain precise interrupts. To make this scheme work, the floating-point functional units must determine if an interrupt is possible early in the EX stage (in the first three clock cycles in the DLX pipeline), so as to prevent further instructions from completing. This scheme is used in the MIPS R2000/3000 and R4000 architectures and is discussed further in Appendix A.

Performance of a DLX FP Pipeline

To look at the FP pipeline performance of DLX, we need to specify the latency and issue restrictions for the FP operations. We have chosen to use the pipeline structure of the MIPS R2010/3010 FP unit. While this unit has some structural hazards, it tends to have low-latency FP operations compared to similar FP units with small device counts. The latencies and issue restrictions for DP floating-point operations are shown by the pipeline structure given in Figure 4.42.

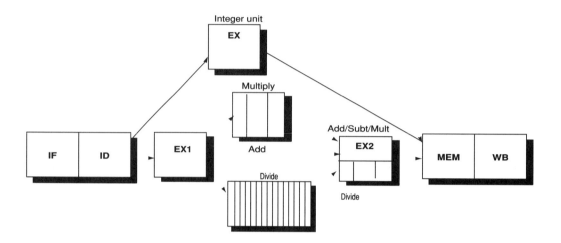

FIGURE 4.41   The FP pipeline on the MIPS R2010/3010 FP unit includes shared logic for the first and last cycle of every FP operation. All FP operations use the common EX1 and EX2 stages, so no overlap is possible in those stages. FP adds and subtracts take only those two stages. In addition, FP multiply has a three-cycle unpipelined execution stage between these two, for a total of 5 cycles; this three-cycle intermediate stage can overlap with the EX1 and EX2 stages of another instruction. Divide has a 15-cycle, nonoverlapped stage between the EX1 and EX2 stages. Divide also takes three cycles in the EX2 stage, rather than just one; this originates from the added complexity of correctly rounding divides. Further motivation for this pipeline design is discussed further in Appendix A .

Figure 4.42 gives the breakdown of integer and floating-point stalls for Spice. There are four classes of stalls: load delays, branch delays, floating-point structural delays, and floating-point data hazards. The compiler tries to schedule both load and FP delays before it schedules branch delays. Interestingly, about 27% of the time in Spice is spent waiting for a floating-point result. Because the structural hazards are small, further pipelining of the floating-point unit would not gain much. In fact, the impact might easily be negative if the floating-point pipeline latency became longer.

Note to the reader: The final version will have data for other FP SPEC programs in Figure 4.42.

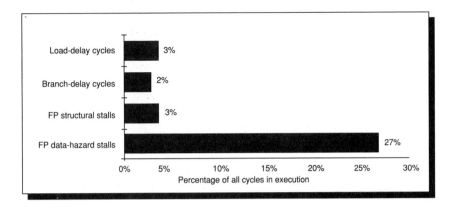

FIGURE 4.42 Percentage of clock cycles in Spice that are pipeline stalls assuming the pipeline structure of Figure 4.41. This again assumes a perfect memory system with no memory-system stalls. In total, 35% of the clock cycles in Spice are stalls, and without any stalls, Spice would run about 50% faster. The percentage of stalls differs from Figure 4.29 (page 203) because this cycle count includes all the FP stalls, while the previous graph includes only the integer stalls.

4.8 Putting It All Together: The MIPS R4000 Pipeline

In this section we look at the pipeline structure and performance of the MIPS R4000 processor family. The MIPS-3 instruction set, which the R4000 implements, is a 64-bit instruction set similar to DLX. The R4000 uses a deeper pipeline than our DLX model both for integer and FP programs. This deeper pipeline allows it to achieve higher clock rates (100 –200 MHz) by decomposing the five-stage integer pipeline into eight stages. Because cache access is particularly time critical, most of the extra pipeline stages come from decomposing the memory access. This type of deeper pipelining is sometimes called *superpipelining*.

Figure 4.43 shows the eight-stage pipeline structure. The function of each stage is as follows:

- IF–first half of instruction fetch; PC selection actually happens here, together with initiation of instruction cache access.

- IS–second half of instruction fetch, complete instruction cache access.

- RF–instruction decode and register fetch, hazard checking and also instruction cache hit detection.

- EX–execution, which includes effective address calculation, ALU operation, and branch target computation and condition evaluation.

- DF–data fetch, first half of data cache access.

- DS–second half of data fetch, compete of data cache access.

- TC–tag check, determine whether the data cache access hit.

- WB–write back for loads and register-register operations.

Instruction number	Clock number								
	1	2	3	4	5	6	7	8	9
Instruction *i*	IF	IS	RF	EX	DF	DS	TC	WB	
Instruction *i*+1		IF	IS	RF	EX	DF	DS	TC	WB
Instruction *i*+2			IF	IS	RF	EX	DF	DS	TC
Instruction *i*+3				IF	IS	RF	EX	DF	DS
Instruction *i*+4					IF	IS	RF	EX	DF

FIGURE 4.43   The structure of the R4000 primary pipeline. The pipelining of the instruction and data caches increases the pipeline depth to eight stages.

In addition to substantially increasing the amount of forwarding required, this longer latency pipeline increases both the load and branch delays. As Figure 4.44, shows the load delay becomes two instructions rather than 1. The branch delay also increases to a total of three cycles, as shown in Figure 4.45. Because the MIPS architecture has a single cycle delayed branch, one of these cycles is used to execute the branch delay slot and the other two are idle. The instruction set provides a branch likely instruction, which we describe in the exercise and which helps in filling branch delays. Pipeline interlocks enforce both the two cycle branch stall penalty and any data hazard stall that arises from use of a load result.

Instruction number	Clock number								
	1	2	3	4	5	6	7	8	9
Load instruction	IF	IS	RF	EX	DF	DS	TC	WB	
other instruction		IF	IS	RF	EX	DF	DS	TC	WB
other instruction			IF	IS	RF	EX	DF	DS	TC
First use				IF	IS	RF	EX	DF	DS
Second use					IF	IS	RF	EX	DF
Third use						IF	IS	RF	EX

FIGURE 4.44   Load delays in the R4000 pipeline are two clocks. Normal forwarding paths can be used after two cycles; after four cycles the result is fetched from the register file.

Instruction number	Clock number								
	1	2	3	4	5	6	7	8	9
Branch instruction	IF	IS	RF	EX	DF	DS	TC	WB	
delay slot		IF	IS	RF	EX	DF	DS	TC	WB
stall			stall	stall	stall	stall	stall	stall	stall
stall				stall	stall	stall	stall	stall	stall
Branch successor					IF	IS	RF	EX	DF

FIGURE 4.45 **Branch delays in the R4000 pipeline are a total of three clock cycles.** The first cycle is a delayed branch slot and the other two cycles are idle.

In addition to the increase in stalls for loads and branches, the deeper pipeline increases the number of levels of forwarding that are required. In our DLX five-stage pipeline, forwarding between two register-register ALU instructions could happen from the ALU/MEM or the MEM/WB registers. In the R4000 pipeline, there are four possible sources for an ALU bypass: EX/DF, DF/DS, DS/TC, and TC/WB. The exercises ask you to explore all the possible forwarding conditions for the DLX instruction set using an R4000-style pipeline.

The Floating Point Pipeline

The floating point unit consists of three functional units: a floating point divider, a floating point multiplier, and a floating point adder. As in the R3000, the adder logic is used on the final step of a multiply or divide. Double-precision FP operations can take from 2 cycles (for a negate) up to 112 cycles for a square root. In addition, the various units have different initiation rates. The floating point functional unit can be thought of as having 8 different stages:

Stage	Functional unit	Description
A	FP adder	Mantissa ADD stage
D	FP divider	Divide pipeline stage
E	FP multiplier	Exception test stage
M	FP multiplier	First stage of multiplier
N	FP multiplier	Second stage of multiplier
R	FP adder	Rounding stage
S	FP adder	Operand shift stage
U		Unpack FP numbers

There is a single copy of each of these stages, and various instructions may use a stage zero or more times and in different orders. Figure 4.46 shows the latency, initiation rate, and pipeline stages used by the most common double-precision FP operations. The latency is the number of clock cycles that must pass before the result of this instruction can be used without a stall; this assumes full forwarding. Likewise, the initiation rate is the number of cycles that must pass before the same instruction can issue without a structural hazard and resultant stall.

FP Instruction	Latency	Initiation Rate	Pipestages
Add, Subtract	4	3	U,S+A,A+R,R+S
Multiply	8	4	U,E+M,M,M,M,N,N+A,R
Divide	36	35	U,A,R,D^{28},D+A,D+R,D+R,D+A,D+R,A,R
Square root	112	111	U,E,(A+R)^{108},A,R
Negate	2	1	U,S
Absolute value	2	1	U,S
FP compare	3	2	U,A,R

FIGURE 4.46   The latency and initiation rate for the FP operations both depend on the FP unit stages that a given operation must use. The pipestages are shown in the order in which they are used for any operation. The notation S+A indicates a clock cycle in which both the S and A stages are used. The notation D28 indicates that the D stage is used 28 times in a row.

The latency in Figure 4.46 tell us how close together two dependent instructions may be, while the initiation rate tells us how close two operations of the same type may be. From the information in Figure 4.46, we can also determine whether a sequence of different, independent FP operations can issue without stalling. If the timing of the sequence is such that a conflict occurs for a shared pipeline stage, then a stall will be needed. Figures 4.47, 4.48, 4.49, and 4.50 show four common possible two-instruction sequences: a multiply followed by add, an add followed by a multiply, a divide followed by add, and an add followed by a divide. The figures show all the interesting starting positions for the second instruction and whether that second instruction will issue or stall for each position. Of course, there could be three instructions active, in which case the possibilities for stalls are much higher and the figures more complex.

Operation	Issue/Stall	Clock cycle												
		0	1	2	3	4	5	6	7	8	9	10	11	12
Mult	Issue	U	M	M	M	M	N	N+A	R					
A	Issue		U	S+A	A+R	R+S								
d	Issue			U	S+A	A+R	R+S							
d	Issue				U	S+A	A+R	R+S						
	Stall					U	S+A	A+R	R+S					
	Stall						U	S+A	A+R	R+S				
	Issue							U	S+A	A+R	R+S			
	Issue								U	S+A	A+R	R+S		

FIGURE 4.47 **A FP multiply issued at clock 0 is followed by a single FP add issued between clocks 1 and 7.** The second column indicates whether an instruction of the specified type stalls when it is issued *n* cycles later, where *n* is the clock cycle number in which the U stage of the second instruction occurs. The stage or stages that cause a stall are highlighted in color. In this case, the add will stall if it is used 4 or 5 cycles after the multiply; otherwise, it issues without stalling. Notice that the add will be stalled for two cycles if it issues in cycle 4 and one otherwise.

Operation	Issue/Stall	Clock cycle												
		0	1	2	3	4	5	6	7	8	9	10	11	12
Add	Issue	U	S+A	A+R	R+S									
M	Issue		U	M	M	M	M	N	N+A	R				
u	Issue			U	M	M	M	M	N	N+A	R			

FIGURE 4.48 **A multiply issuing after an add can always precede without stalling, since the shorter instruction clears the shared pipeline stages before the longer instruction reaches them.**

Operation	Issue/Stall	Clock cycle												
		0	1	2	3	4	5	6	7	8	9	10	11	12
Divide	Issue	D	D	D	D	D	D+A	D+R	D+A	D+R	A	R		
A	Issue		U	S+A	A+R	R+S								
d	Issue			U	S+A	A+R	R+S							
d	Stall				U	S+A	A+R	R+S						
	Stall					U	S+A	A+R	R+S					
	Stall						U	S+A	A+R	R+S				
	Stall							U	S+A	A+R	R+S			
	Stall								U	S+A	A+R	R+S		
	Stall									U	S+A	A+R	R+S	
	Issue										U	S+A	A+R	R+S
	Issue											U	S+A	A+R
	Issue												U	S+A

FIGURE 4.49   An FP divide can cause a stall for an add that starts near the end of the divide. The divide starts much earlier but completes in cycle 10. Since the divide makes heavy use of the rounding hardware needed by the add, it stalls the add. Notice the add starting in cycle 3 will be stalled until cycle 9. If the add started right after the divide it would not conflict, since the add could complete before the divide needed the shared stages, just as we saw in Figure 4.48 for a multiply and add.

Operation	Issue/Stall	Clock cycle												
		0	1	2	3	4	5	6	7	8	9	10	11	12
Add	Issue	U	S+A	A+R	R+S									
D	Stall		U	A	R	D	D	D	D	D	D	D	D	D
i	Issue			U	A	R	D	D	D	D	D	D	D	D
v	Issue				U	M	M	M	M	N	N+A	R		

FIGURE 4.50   A double-precision add is followed by a double-precision divide. If the divide starts one cycle after the add it stalls, but after that there is not conflict.

Performance of the R4000 Pipeline

In this section we examine the stalls that occur for the SPEC92 benchmarks when running on the R4000 pipeline structure. There are four major causes of pipeline stalls or losses:

1. Load stalls: delays arising from the use of a load result one or two cycles after the load.

2. Branch stalls: two-cycle stall on every branch plus some fraction of unfilled branch delay slots.

3. FP result stalls: stalls that arise due to RAW hazards for an FP operand.

4. FP structural stalls: delays that arise because of issue restrictions in the FP pipeline.

Figure 4.51 shows the pipeline CPI breakdown for the R4000 pipeline for 10 of the SPEC benchmarks. Figure 4.52 shows the same data but in tabular form.

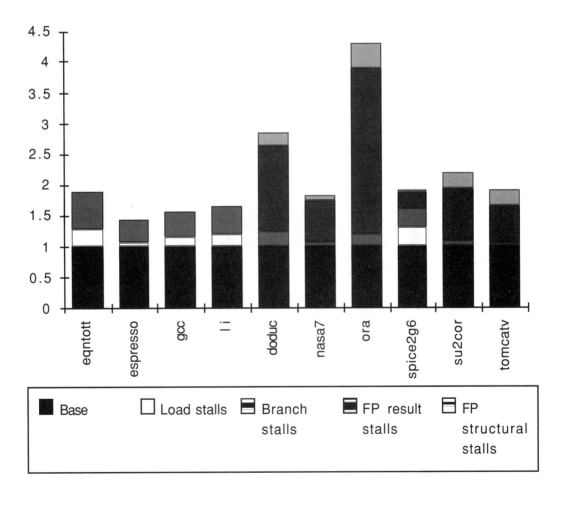

FIGURE 4.51   The pipeline CPI for 10 of the SPEC92 benchmarks, assuming a perfect cache. The pipeline CPI varies from 1.4 to 2.8. The leftmost four programs are integer programs, and branch delays are the major CPI contributor for these. The rightmost six programs are FP, and FP result stalls are the major contributor for these..

Benchmark	Pipeline CPI	Load stalls	Branch stalls	FP result stalls	FP structural stalls
eqntott	1.88	0.27	0.61	0.00	0.00
espresso	1.42	0.07	0.35	0.00	0.00
gcc	1.56	0.13	0.43	0.00	0.00
li	1.64	0.18	0.46	0.00	0.00
doduc	2.84	0.01	0.22	1.39	0.22
nasa7	1.83	0.00	0.08	0.65	0.10
ora	4.30	0.00	0.19	2.69	0.42
spice2g6	1.91	0.30	0.29	0.26	0.06
su2cor	2.18	0.02	0.07	0.84	0.26
tomcatv	1.90	0.00	0.05	0.60	0.25
Mean	2.15	0.10	0.27	0.64	0.13

FIGURE 4.52 **The total pipeline CPI and the contributions of the four major sources of stalls are shown.**

From the data in Figure 4.51 and 4.52, we can see the penalty of the deeper pipelining. The longer branch delay compared to the five-stage DLX-style pipeline substantially increases the cycles spent on branches, especially for the integer programs with the higher branch frequency. An interesting result for the FP programs is that the latency of the FP functional units leads to more stalls than the partial pipelining. Thus, reducing the latency of FP operations should be the first target, rather than more pipelining. Of course, such a change would increase the structural stalls, since many potential structural stalls are hidden behind data hazards.

4.9 | Fallacies and Pitfalls

Fallacy: Instruction set design has little impact on pipelining.

This is perhaps the most prominent misconception about pipelining and one that was widely held until recently. Many of the difficulties of pipelining arise because of instruction set complications. Here are some examples, many of which are mentioned in the chapter:

- Variable instruction lengths and running times can lead to imbalance among pipeline stages causing other stages to back up. They also severely complicate hazard detection and the maintenance of precise interrupts. Of course, there are exceptions to every rule. For example, caches cause instruction running times to vary when they miss; however, the performance advantages of caches make the added complexity acceptable. To minimize the complexity, most machines freeze the pipeline on a cache miss. Other machines try to continue running parts of the pipeline; though this is complex, it may overcome some of the performance losses from cache misses.

- Sophisticated addressing modes can lead to different sorts of problems. Addressing modes that update registers, such as post-autoincrement, complicate hazard detection. They also slightly increase the complexity of instruction restart. Other addressing modes that require multiple memory accesses substantially complicate pipeline control and make it difficult to keep the pipeline flowing smoothly.

- Architectures that allow writes into the instruction space (self-modifying code) can cause trouble for pipelining (as well as for cache designs). For example, if an instruction in the pipeline can modify another instruction, we must constantly check if the address being written to by an instruction corresponds to the address of an instruction further on in the pipeline. If so, the pipeline must be flushed or the instruction in the pipeline somehow updated.

- Implicitly-set condition codes increase the difficulty of finding when a branch has been decided and the difficulty of scheduling branch delays. The former problem occurs when the condition-code setting is not uniform, making it difficult to decide which instruction assigns the condition code last. The latter problem occurs when the setting of the condition code is not under program control. This makes it hard to find instructions that can be scheduled between the condition evaluation and the branch. Many newer architectures avoid condition codes or set them explicitly under program control to eliminate the pipelining difficulties.

As a simple example, suppose the DLX instruction format were more complex, so that a separate, decode pipe stage were required before register fetch. This would increase the branch delay to two clock cycles. At best, the second branch-delay slot would be wasted at least as often as the first. Gross [1983] found that a second delay slot was only used half as often as the first. This would lead to a performance penalty for the second delay slot of more than 0.1 clock cycles per instruction.

Pitfall: Unexpected execution sequences may cause unexpected hazards.

At first glance, WAW hazards look like they should never occur because no compiler would ever generate two writes to the same register without an intervening read. But they can occur when the sequence is unexpected. For example, the first write might be in the delay slot of a taken branch when the scheduler thought the branch would not be taken. Here is the code sequence that could cause this:

```
                   BNEZ    R1,foo
                   DIVD    F0,F2,F4 ; moved into delay slot
                                    ; from fall-through

                   . . . . .

                   . . . . .
        foo:       LD      F0,qrs
```

If the branch is taken, then before the DIVD can complete, the LD will reach WB, causing a WAW hazard. The hardware must detect this and may stall the issue of the LD. Another way this can happen is if the second write is in a trap routine. This occurs when an instruction that traps and is writing results continues and completes after an instruction that writes the same register in the trap handler. The hardware must detect and prevent this as well.

Pitfall: Extensive pipelining can impact other aspects of a design, leading to overall lower cost/performance.

The best example of this phenomenon comes from two implementations of the VAX, the 8600 and the 8700. When the 8600 was initially delivered, it had a cycle time of 80 nS. Subsequently, a redesigned version, called the 8650, with a 55-nS clock was introduced. The 8700 has a much simpler pipeline that operates at the microinstruction level. The 8700 CPU is much smaller and has a faster clock rate, 45 nS. The overall outcome is that the 8650 has a CPI advantage of about 20%, but the 8700 has a clock rate that is about 20% faster. Thus, the 8700 achieves the same performance with much less hardware.

Fallacy: Increasing the depth of pipelining always increases performance.

Two factors combine to limit the performance improvement gained by pipelining. Limited ILP in the code means that increasing the pipeline depth will eventually increase the CPI, due to dependences that require stalls. Second, clock skew and latch overhead combine to limit the decrease in clock period obtained by further pipelining. Figure 4.53 shows the tradeoff between pipeline depth and performance for the first 14 of the Livermore Loops (see Chapter 2, page 43). The performance flattens out when the pipeline depth reaches 4 and actually drops when the execution portion is pipelined 16 deep. Although this study is limited to a small set of FP programs, the tradeoff of increasing CPI versus increasing clock rate by more pipelining arises constantly.

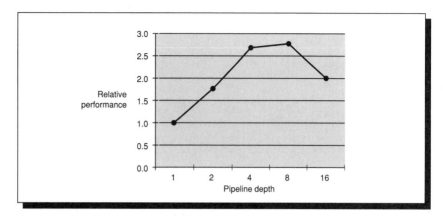

FIGURE 4.53 The depth of pipelining versus the speedup obtained. This data is based on Table 2 in Kunkel and Smith [1986]. The x-axis shows the number of stages in the EX portion of the floating-point pipeline. A single-stage pipeline corresponds to 32 levels of logic, which might be appropriate for a single FP operation.

Pitfall: Evaluating a scheduler on the basis of unoptimized code.

Unoptimized code—containing redundant loads, stores, and other operations that might be eliminated by an optimizer—is much easier to schedule than "tight" optimized code. In GCC running on a DECstation 3100, the frequency of idle clock cycles increases by 18% from the unoptimized and scheduled code to the optimized and scheduled code. TeX shows a 20% increase for the same measurement. To fairly evaluate a scheduler you must use optimized code, since in the real system you will derive good performance from other optimizations in addition to scheduling.

4.10 | Concluding Remarks

Pipelining has been and is likely to continue to be one of the most important techniques for enhancing the performance of processors. Improving performance via pipelining was the key focus of many early computer designers in the late 1950s through the mid 1960s. In the late 1960s through the late 1970s, the attention of computer architects was focused on other things including the dramatic improvements cost, size, and reliability that were achieved by the introduction of integrated circuit technology. In this period pipelining played a secondary role in many designs. Since pipelining was not a primary focus many instruction sets designed in this period made pipelining overly difficult and reduced its payoff. The VAX architecture is perhaps the best example.

In the late 1970s and early 1980s several researchers realized that instruction set complexity and implementation ease, particularly ease of pipelining were related. The RISC movement led to a dramatic simplification in instruction sets that allowed rapid progress in the development of pipelining techniques. As we will see in the next chapter, these techniques have become extremely sophisticated. The implementation complexity that many designs now achieve would have been extremely difficult with the more complex architectures of the 1970s.

In this chapter, we introduced the basic ideas in pipelining and looked at some simple compiler strategies for enhancing performance. The pipelined microprocessors of the 1980s relied on these strategies with the R4000-style machine representing one of the most advanced of the "simple" pipeline organizations. To further improve performance in this decade most microprocessors have introduced schemes such as hardware-based pipeline scheduling, dynamic branch prediction, the ability to issue more than one instruction in a cycle, and the use of more powerful compiler technology. These more advanced techniques are the subject of the next chapter.

4.11 | Historical Perspective and References

This section describes some of the major advances in pipelining and ends with some of the recent literature on high-performance pipelining.

The first general-purpose pipelined machine is considered to be Stretch, the IBM 7030. Stretch followed on the IBM 704 and had a goal of being 100 times faster than the 704. The goals were a stretch from the state of the art at that time—hence the nickname. The plan was to obtain a factor of 1.6 from overlapping fetch, decode, and execute, using a 4-stage pipeline. Bloch [1959] and Bucholtz [1962] describe the design and engineering tradeoffs, including the use of ALU bypasses. The CDC 6600 developed in the early 1960s also introduced several enhancements in pipelining; these innovations and the history of that design are discussed in the next chapter.

A series of general pipelining descriptions that appeared in the late 1970s and early 1980s provided most of the terminology and described most of the basic techniques used in simple pipelines. These surveys include Keller [1975], Ramamoorthy and Li [1977], Chen [1980], and Kogge's book [1981], devoted entirely to pipelining. Davidson and his colleagues [1971, 1975] developed the concept of pipeline reservation tables as a design methodology for multicycle pipelines with feedback (also described in Kogge [1981]). Many designers use a variation of these concepts, as we did in Sections 4.2 and 4.3.

The RISC machines were originally designed with ease of implementation and pipelining in mind. Several of the early RISC papers attempt to quantify the performance advantages of the simplification in instruction set. The best analysis, however, is a comparison of a VAX and MIPS implementation published by

Bhandarkar and Clark in 1991. After long arguments about the implementation benefits of RISC, this paper convinced even the most skeptical designers of the advantages of the RISC instruction set architecture.

The RISC machines refined the notion of compiler-scheduled pipelines in the early 1980s, though earlier work on this topic is described at the end of the next chapter. The concepts of delayed branches and delayed loads—common in microprogramming—were extended into the high-level architecture. The Stanford MIPS architecture made the pipeline structure purposely visible to the compiler and allowed multiple operations per instruction. Simple schemes for scheduling the pipeline in the compiler were described by Sites [1979] for the Cray, by Hennessy and Gross [1983], (and in Gross's thesis [1983]) and by Gibbons and Muchnik [1986]. More advanced techniques will be described in the next chapter. Rymarczyk [1982] describes the interlock conditions that programmers should be aware of for a 360-like machine; this paper also shows the complex interaction between pipelining and an instruction set not designed to be pipelined. Static branch prediction by profiling has been explored by McFarling and Hennessy [1986] and by Fisher and Fruenberger [1992].

J. E. Smith and his colleagues have written a number of papers examining instruction issue, interrupt handling, and pipeline depth for high-speed scalar machines. Kunkel and Smith [1986] evaluate the impact of pipeline overhead and dependences on the choice of optimal pipeline depth; they also have an excellent discussion of latch design and its impact on pipelining. Smith and Plezkun [1988] evaluate a variety of techniques for preserving precise interrupts, including the future file concept mentioned in Section 6.6. Weiss and Smith [1984] evaluate a variety of hardware pipeline scheduling and instruction-issue techniques.

The MIPS R4000 in addition to being one of the first deeply pipelined microprocessors, was the first true 64-bit architecture. It is described in Riordan at al [1990].

References

AGERWALA, T. AND J. COCKE [1987]. "High performance reduced instruction set processors," IBM Tech. Rep. (March).

BHANDARKAR, D. AND D.W. CLARK [1991] "Performance from architecture: comparing a RISC and a CISC with similar hardware organizations," Proc. Fourth Conf. on Architectural Support for Programming Languages and Operating Systems, IEEE/ACM (April), Palo Alto, 310-319.

BLOCH, E. [1959]. "The engineering design of the Stretch computer," *Proc. Fall Joint Computer Conf.,* 48–59.

BUCHOLTZ, W. [1962]. *Planning a Computer System: Project Stretch,* McGraw-Hill, New York.

CHEN, T. C. [1980]. "Overlap and parallel processing" in *Introduction to Computer Architecture,* H. Stone, ed., Science Research Associates, Chicago, 427–486.

CLARK, D. W. [1987]. "Pipelining and performance in the VAX 8800 processor," *Proc. Second Conf. on Architectural Support for Programming Languages and Operating Systems,* IEEE/ACM (March), Palo Alto, Calif., 173–177.

DAVIDSON, E. S. [1971]. "The design and control of pipelined function generators," *Proc. Conf. on Systems, Networks, and Computers,* IEEE (January), Oaxtepec, Mexico, 19–21.

DAVIDSON, E. S., A. T. THOMAS, L. E. SHAR, AND J. H. PATEL [1975]. "Effective control for pipelined processors," *COMPCON, IEEE* (March), San Francisco, 181–184.

DEROSA, J., R. GLACKEMEYER, AND T. KNIGHT [1985]. "Design and implementation of the VAX 8600 pipeline," *Computer* 18:5 (May) 38–48.

DIGITAL EQUIPMENT CORPORATION [1987]. *Digital Technical J.* 4 (March), Hudson, Mass. (This entire issue is devoted to the VAX 8800 processor.)

EARLE, J. G. [1965]. "Latched carry-save adder," *IBM Technical Disclosure Bull.* 7 (March) 909–910.

EMER, J. S. AND D. W CLARK [1984]. "A characterization of processor performance in the VAX-11/780," *Proc. 11th Symposium on Computer Architecture* (June), Ann Arbor, Mich., 301–310.

GIBBONS, P. B. AND S. S. MUCHNIK [1986]. "Efficient Instruction Scheduling for a Pipelined Processor," *SIGPLAN '86 Symposium on Compiler Construction, ACM* (June), Palo Alto, CA, 11-16.

GROSS, T. R. [1983]. *Code Optimization of Pipeline Constraints,* Ph.D. Thesis (December), Computer Systems Lab., Stanford Univ.

HENNESSY, J. L. AND T. R. GROSS [1983]. "Postpass code optimization of pipeline constraints," *ACM Trans. on Programming Languages and Systems* 5:3 (July) 422-448

IBM [1990]. "The IBM RISC System/6000 processor," collection of papers, *IBM Jour. of Research and Development* 34:1, (January), 119 pages.

KELLER R. M. [1975]. "Look-ahead processors," *ACM Computing Surveys* 7:4 (December) 177–195.

KOGGE, P. M. [1981]. *The Architecture of Pipelined Computers,* McGraw-Hill, New York.

KUNKEL, S. R. AND J. E. SMITH [1986]. "Optimal pipelining in supercomputers," *Proc. 13th Symposium on Computer Architecture* (June), Tokyo, 404–414.

RAMAMOORTHY, C. V. AND H. F. LI [1977]. "Pipeline architecture," *ACM Computing Surveys* 9:1 (March) 61–102.

RYMARCZYK, J. [1982]. "Coding guidelines for pipelined processors," *Proc. Symposium on Architectural Support for Programming Languages and Operating Systems,* IEEE/ACM (March), Palo Alto, Calif., 12–19.

SITES, R. [1979]. *Instruction Ordering for the CRAY-1 Computer,* Tech. Rep. 78-CS-023 (July), Dept. of Computer Science, Univ. of Calif., San Diego.

SMITH, J. E. AND A. R. PLEZKUN [1988]. "Implementing precise interrupts in pipelined processors," *IEEE Trans. on Computers* 37:5 (May) 562–573.

TROIANI, M., S. S. CHING, N. N. QUAYNOR, J. E. BLOEM, AND F. C. COLON OSORIO [1985]. "The VAX 8600 I Box, a pipelined implementation of the VAX architecture," *Digital Technical J.* 1 (August) 4–19.

EXERCISES

Exercises 4.1–4.6 For these problem, we will explore a pipeline for a register-memory architecture. The architecture has two instruction formats: a register–register format and a register–memory format. There is a single memory addressing mode (offset + base register).

There is a set of ALU operations with format:

ALUop Rdest, $Rsrc_1$, $Rsrc_2$

or

ALUop Rdest, $Rsrc_1$, MEM

Where the ALUop is one of the following: Add, Subtract, And, Or, Load ($Rsrc_1$ ignored), Store. Rsrc or Rdest are registers. MEM is a base register and offset pair.

Branches use a full compare of two registers and are PC-relative. Assume that this machine is pipelined so that a new instruction is started every clock cycle. The following pipeline structure—similar to that used in the VAX 8800 micropipeline—is used:

IF	RF	ALU1	MEM	ALU2	WB				
	IF	RF	ALU1	MEM	ALU2	WB			
		IF	RF	ALU1	MEM	ALU2	WB		
			IF	RF	ALU1	MEM	ALU2	WB	
				IF	RF	ALU1	MEM	ALU2	WB
					IF	RF	ALU1	MEM	ALU2	WB

The first ALU stage is used for effective address calculation for memory references and branches. The second ALU cycle is used for operations and branch comparison. RF is both a decode and register-fetch cycle.

4.1 [12] <4.2> Find the number of adders needed, counting any adder or incrementer; show a combination of instructions and pipe stages that justify this answer. You need only give one combination that maximizes the adder count. Assume that when a register read and a register write of the same register occur in the same clock the write data is forwarded.

4.2 [13] <4.2> Find the number of register read and write ports and memory read and write ports required. Show that your answer is correct by showing a combination of instructions and pipeline stage indicating the instruction and the number of read ports and write ports required for that instruction.

4.3 [15] <4.4> Determine any *data forwarding* for any ALUs that will be needed. Assume that there are separate ALUs for the ALU1 and ALU2 pipe stages. Put in all forwarding of ALU to ALU needed to avoid or reduce stalls. Show the relationship between the two instructions involved in forwarding using the format of the table in Figure 4.20 but ignoring the last column.

4.4 [20] <4.4> Show any other data-forwarding requirements for the units using the same format as Figure 4.20, again ignoring the last column. Remember to forward to and from memory references.

4.5 [15] <4.4> Show all the remaining hazards using a table like that in Figure4.19, but listing the length of hazard in place of the last column.

4.6 [15] <4.5> Show all control hazard types by example and state the length of the stall. Use a format like Figure 4.22 labeling each example.

4.7 [12] <4.1–4.5> A machine is called "underpipelined" if additional levels of pipelining can be added without changing the pipeline-stall behavior appreciably. Suppose that the DLX integer pipeline was changed to four stages by merging ID and EX and lengthening the clock cycle by 50%. How much faster would the conventional DLX pipeline be versus the underpipelined DLX on integer code only? Make sure you include the effect of any change in pipeline stalls using the data in Figure 4.34 (page 209).

4.8 [15] <4.4> Add the forwarding entries for stores and for the zero detect unit (for branches) to the table in Figure 4.20.

4.9 [20] <4.4,4.8> Create a table showing the forwarding logic for the R4000 pipeline using the same format as Figure 4.20. Assume the same DLX instructions we considered in Figure 4.20.

4.10 [15] <4.4,4.8> Create a table showing the R4000 hazard detection using the same format as Figure 4.19. Assume the instruction set is the same DLX subset we considered in Section 4.4.

4.11 [15] <4.5> Suppose the branch frequencies (as percentages of all instructions) are as follows:

Conditional branches	20%
Jumps and calls	5%
Conditional branches	60% are taken

We are examining a four-deep pipeline where the branch is resolved at the end of the second cycle for unconditional branches, and at the end of the third cycle for conditional branches. Assuming that only the first pipe stage can always be done independent of whether the branch goes and ignoring other pipeline stalls, how much faster would the machine be without any branch hazards?

4.12 [20] <4.5> Several designers have proposed the concept of canceling branches (also called squashing or nullifying), as a way to improve the performance of delayed branches. The idea is to allow the branch to indicate that the instruction in the delay slot should be aborted if the branch is mispredicted. The advantage of canceling branches is that the delay slot can **always** be filled, because the branch can abort the contents of the delay slot if mispredicted. The compiler need not worry about whether the instruction is OK to execute when the branch is mispredicted. The R4000 includes a version of this instruction that cancels if the branch is untaken; the instruction is called *branch likely*.

A simple version of canceling branches cancels if the branch is not taken; assume this type of canceling branch. Use the data in Figure 4.25 (page 199) for branch frequency. Assume that 27% of the branch-delay slots are filled using strategy (a) of Figure 4.27 (page 202) with standard delayed branches, and that the rest of the slots are filled using canceling branches and strategy (b). Using the taken/not taken data from Figure 3.12 on page 105, show the performance of this scheme with canceling branches using the same format as the graph in Figure 4.29 (page 203). How much faster would a machine with canceling branches run, assuming there is no clock-speed penalty compared to a machine with only delayed branches? Use Figure 4.34 (page 209) to find the number of load and branch-delay stalls.

Exercises 4.13–4.15 Suppose that we have the following pipeline layout:

Stage	Function
1	Instruction fetch
2	Operand decode
3	Execution or memory access (branch resolution)

All data dependences are between the register written in Stage 3 of instruction i and a register read in Stage 2 of instruction $i + 1$, before instruction i has completed. The probability of such an interlock occurring is $1/p$.

We are considering a change in the machine organization that would write back the result of an instruction during an effective 4th pipe stage. This would decrease the length of the clock cycle by d (i.e., if the length of the clock cycle was T, it is now T–d). The probability of a dependence between instruction i and instruction $i+2$ is p^{-2}. (Assume that the value of p^{-1} excludes instructions that would interlock on $i+2$.) The branch would also be resolved during the fourth stage.

4.13 [20] <4.4> Considering only the data hazard, find the lower bound on d that makes this a profitable change. Assume that each result has exactly one use and that the basic clock cycle has length T.

4.14 [15] <4.4> Suppose that the probability of an interlock between i and $i+n$ were 0.3 – 0.1n for $1 \le n \le 3$. What increase in the clock rate is needed so that this change improves performance?

4.15 [20] <4.4> Now assume that we have used forwarding to eliminate the extra hazard introduced by the change. That is, for all *data* hazards the pipeline length is *effectively* 3. This design may still not be worthwhile because of the impact of control hazards coming from a four-stage versus a three-stage pipeline. Assume that only Stage 1 of the pipeline can be safely executed before we decide whether a branch goes or not. We want to know what the impact of branch hazards can be before this longer pipeline does not yield high performance. Find an upper bound on the percent of conditional branches in programs in terms of the ratio of d to the original clock-cycle time, so that the longer pipeline has better performance. What if d is a 10% reduction, what is the maximum percentage of conditional branches, before we lose with this longer pipeline? Assume the taken-branch frequency for conditional branches is 60%.

4.16 [20] <4.4,4.7> Construct a table like that in Figure 4.19 that shows the structural stalls for the DLX FP pipeline.

4.17 [20] <4.4,4.7> Construct a table like that in Figure 4.19 that shows the data hazard stalls for the DLX FP pipeline. Consider both integer-FP and FP-FP interactions.

4.18 [20] <4.4,4.7> Construct the forwarding table for the DLX FP pipeline as we did in Figure 4.20. Consider both FP to FP forwarding and forwarding of FP loads to the FP units.

4.19 [25] <4.4,4.7> Suppose DLX had only one register set. Construct the forwarding table for the FP and integer instructions using the format of Figure 4.20.

4.20 [15] Construct a table like Figure 4.19 to check for WAW stalls in the DLX FP pipeline.

4.21 [35] <4.2.–4.7> Change the DLX instruction simulator to be pipelined. Measure the frequency of empty branch-delay slots, the frequency of load delays, and the frequency of FP stalls for a variety of integer and FP programs. Also, measure the frequency of forwarding operations. Determine what the performance impact of eliminating forwarding and stalling would be.

4.22 [35] <4.7> Using a DLX simulator, create a DLX pipeline simulator. Explore the impact of lengthening the FP pipelines, assuming both fully pipelined and unpipelined FP units. How does clustering of FP operations affect the results? Which FP units are most susceptible to changes in the FP pipeline length?

4.23 [40] <4.3–4.5> Write an instruction scheduler for DLX that works on DLX assembly language. Evaluate your scheduler using either profiles of programs or with a pipeline simulator. If the DLX C compiler does optimization, evaluate your scheduler's performance both with and without optimization.

"Who's first?"

"America."

"Who's second?"

"Sir, there is no second."

> Dialog between two observers of the sailing race later to be entitled "The America's Cup" and run on a yearly basis.

> This quote was the inspiration for John Cocke's naming of the IBM research machine "America". This machine was the precursor to the RS/6000 series and the first superscalar machine.

5

Advanced Pipelining and Instruction Level Parallelism

5.1 | Instruction Level Parallelism: Concepts and Challenges

In the last chapter we saw how pipelining can overlap the execution of instructions when they are independent of one another. This potential overlap among instructions is called *instruction level parallelism* (ILP) since the instructions involved can be evaluated in parallel. In this chapter, we look at a wide range of techniques for extending the pipelining ideas by increasing the amount of parallelism exploited among instructions. We start by looking at techniques that reduce the impact of data and control hazards and then turn to the topic of increasing the ability of the processor to exploit parallelism. We then discuss the compiler technology used to increase the ILP and examine the results of a study of available ILP. The Putting It All Together section covers an IBM Power-2 implementation, one of the highest performing machine using advanced pipelining as of 1994. Before discussing these topics and techniques, we need to define some commonly used terms and discuss what features of both programs and machines limit the amount of parallelism that can be exploited among instructions. We conclude this section by looking at simple compiler techniques for enhancing the exploitation of pipeline parallelism by a compiler.

To begin, recall the equation from the last chapter:

$$\text{Pipeline CPI} = \text{Ideal Pipeline CPI} + \text{Structural Stalls} + \text{RAW stalls} + \text{WAR stalls} + \text{WAW stalls} + \text{Control Stalls}$$

The *ideal pipeline CPI* is the maximum throughput attainable by the implementation. By reducing each of the terms of the right-hand side, we minimize the overall pipeline CPI, and thus increase the instruction throughput per clock. While the focus of the last chapter was on reducing the RAW stalls and the Control Stalls, in this chapter we will see that the techniques we introduce to further reduce the RAW and control stalls, as well as reduce the ideal CPI, can increase the importance of dealing with structural, WAR, and WAW stalls. This equation also allows us to characterize the various techniques we examine in this chapter by what component of the overall CPI a technique reduces. Figure 5.1 shows some of the techniques we examine and how they affect the contributions to the CPI.

Technique	Reduces	Section
Loop unrolling	Control stalls	5.1
Basic pipeline scheduling	RAW stalls	5.1 (also Chapter 4)
Dynamic scheduling with scoreboarding	RAW stalls	5.2
Dynamic scheduling with register renaming	WAR and WAW stalls	5.2
Dynamic branch prediction	Control stalls	5.3
Issuing multiple instructions per cycle	Ideal CPI	5.4
Compiler dependence analysis	Ideal CPI and data stalls	5.5
Software pipelining and trace scheduling	Ideal CPI and data stalls	
Speculation	All data and control stalls	5.6
Dynamic memory disambiguation	RAW stalls involving memory	5.2, 5.6

FIGURE 5.1   The major techniques examined in this chapter are shown together with the component of the CPI equation that the technique affects.

Before we examine these techniques in detail, we need to define the concepts on which these techniques are built and which, in the end, determine the limits on how much parallelism can be exploited.

ILP: Data Dependence and Hazards

All of the techniques in this chapter exploit parallelism among instruction sequences. As we stated above, this type of parallelism is called instruction level parallelism or ILP. The amount of parallelism available within a basic block (a straight-line code sequence with no branches in except to the entry and no branches out except at the exit) is quite small. For example, in Chapter 3 we saw that the average dynamic branch frequency in integer programs was about 16%, meaning that about five instructions execute between a pair of branches. Since these five instructions are likely to depend upon one another, the amount of overlap we can exploit within a basic block is likely to be much less than five. To obtain substantial performance enhancements, we must exploit ILP across multiple basic blocks.

The simplest and most common way to increase the amount of parallelism available among instructions is to exploit parallelism among iterations of a loop. This type of parallelism is often called *loop level parallelism*. Here is a simple example of a loop, which adds two 1000-element vectors, that is completely parallel:

```
for (i=1; i<=1000; i=i+1)
        x[i] = x[i] + y[i];
```

Every iteration of the loop can overlap with any other iteration, though within each loop iteration there is little opportunity for overlap.

There are a number of techniques we will examine for converting such loop level parallelism into instruction level parallelism. Basically, such techniques work by unrolling the loop either statically using the compiler or dynamically in the hardware. We will look at a detailed example of loop unrolling later in this section.

An important alternative method for exploiting loop level parallelism is the use of vector instructions. Essentially, a vector instruction operates on a sequence of data items. For example, the above code sequence could execute in four instructions on a typical vector machine: two instructions to load the vectors x and y from memory, one instruction to add the two vectors, and an instruction to store the result vector back. Of course, these instructions would be pipelined and have relatively long latencies, but these latencies may be overlapped. Vector instructions and the operation of vector machines are described in detail in Appendix V[1]. Although the development of the vector ideas preceded most of the techniques we examine in this chapter for exploiting parallelism, machines that exploit ILP are replacing the vector-based machines; the reasons for this technology shift are discussed in more detail later in this chapter and in the historical perspectives at the end of the chapter.

Dependences

To define exactly what we mean by loop level and instruction level parallelism, and to quantify the amount of such parallelism available, we need to define what it means for instructions and loops to be parallel. We start by explaining what it

---

[1]   point to the vector appendix

means for a pair of instructions to be parallel. If two instructions are *parallel*, they can execute simultaneously in a pipeline without causing any stalls, assuming the pipeline has sufficient resources (and hence no structural hazards exist).

Hence, two instructions that are dependent are not parallel. There are three different types of dependences: data dependences, name dependences, and control dependences. An instruction j is *data dependent* on instruction i if either of the following holds:

- instruction i produces a result that is used by instruction j, or

- instruction j is data dependent on instruction k, and instruction k is data dependent on instruction i.

The second condition simply states that one instruction is dependent on another if there exists a chain of dependences of the first type between the two instructions. This dependence chain can be as long as the entire program.

If two instructions are data dependent they cannot execute simultaneously or completely overlapped. The dependence implies that there would be a chain of one or more RAW hazards between the two instructions. Executing the instructions simultaneously will cause a machine with pipeline interlocks to detect a hazard and stall reducing or eliminating the overlap. In a machine without interlocks that relies on compiler scheduling, the compiler cannot schedule dependent instructions in such a way that they completely overlap, since the program will not execute correctly. The presence of a data dependence in an instruction sequence reflects a data dependence in the source code from which the instruction sequence was generated. The effect of the original data dependence must be preserved.

Dependences are a property of programs. Whether or not a given dependence results in an actual hazard being detected and whether or not that hazard actually causes a stall are properties of the pipeline organization. Indeed, many of the techniques in this chapter deal with avoiding hazards or circumventing the need to stall the pipeline when a hazard occurs, while preserving the dependence. The importance of the data dependences is that they set an upper bound on how much parallelism can possibly be exploited. The presence of a data dependence also means that the results must be calculated in a specific order, since a later instruction depends on the result of the former.

A data value may flow between instructions either through registers or through memory locations. When the data flow occurs in a register, detecting the dependence is reasonably straightforward since the register names are fixed in the instructions (although it gets more complicated when branches intervene). Dependences that flow through memory locations are more difficult to detect since two addresses may refer to the same location, but look different (e.g., 100(R4) and 20(R6) may be identical). In addition, the effective address of a load or store may change from one execution of the instruction to another (so that 20(R40) and 20(R4) will be different), further complicating the detection of a dependence. In this chapter, we examine both hardware and software techniques for detecting data dependences that involve memory locations. The compiler techniques for detecting such dependences are critical in uncovering loop level parallelism, as we will see shortly.

The second type of dependence is a *name dependence*. A name dependence occurs when two instructions use the same name (either register or memory location), but there is not a flow of data between the instructions. There are two types of name dependences between an instruction i that precedes instruction j in program order:

1. An *antidependence* between instruction i and instruction j occurs when instruction j writes a register or memory location that instruction i reads from and instruction i is executed first. An antidependence corresponds to a WAR hazard and the hazard detection for WAR hazards forces the ordering of an antidependent instruction pair.

2. An *output dependence* occurs when instruction i and instruction j write the same register or memory location. The ordering between the instructions must be preserved. Output dependences are preserved by detecting WAW hazards.

Both antidependences and output dependences are name dependences, as opposed to true data dependences, since there is no value being transmitted between the instructions. This means that instructions involved in a name dependence can execute simultaneously or be reordered, if the name (register number or memory location) used in the instructions is changed so the instructions do not conflict. This renaming can be more easily done for register operands and is called *register renaming* . Register renaming can be done either statically by a compiler or dynamically by the hardware.

Example

What are the name dependences in the following code sequence, and how can they be eliminated?

```
ADD    R1,R2,R3
SUB    R2,R3,R4
AND    R5,R1,R2
OR     R1,R3,R4
```

Answer

There is an antidependence with register R2, which could create a WAR hazard, between the ADD and the SUB. This can be eliminated by renaming the destination of the SUB as R6 and changing all the instructions that use the value of the subtract to use the value from R6 (in this case there is only the last operand in the AND instruction). The use of R1 in the OR instruction creates both an output dependence with the ADD instruction and an antidependence with the AND instruction. Both dependences can be eliminated by changing the destination of either the ADD or the OR instructions. In the former case, any instructions that use the result of the ADD instruction before the OR instruction writes R1 must be changed (just the second operand of the AND instruction, in this case). Alternatively, all uses of the result of the OR can change to use a different register. An alternative to renaming in the compiler is hardware register renaming, which can be used in situations where branches occur that may be difficult or impossible for a compiler to do; the next section discusses this technique extensively.

The last type of dependence is a control dependence. A *control dependence* determines the ordering of an instruction with respect to a branch instruction so that the non-branch instruction is executed only when it should be. Every instruction in the program is control dependent on some set of branches, and, in general, these control dependences must be preserved. One of the simplest examples of a control dependence is the dependence of the statements in "then" part of an if-statement on the branch. For example, in the code segment:

```
if p1 {
        S1;
};
if p2 {
        S2;
}
```

S1 is control dependent on p1 and S2 is control dependent on p2 but not on p1.
    There are two constraints on control dependences:

1. An instruction that is control dependent on a branch cannot be moved before the branch so that its execution is no longer controlled by the branch. For example, we cannot take an instruction from the then portion of an if-statement and move it before the if-statement.

2. An instruction that is not control dependent on a branch cannot be moved to after the branch so that its execution is controlled by the branch. For example, we cannot take a statement before the if-statement and move it into the then portion.

The following example illustrates these two constraints.

Example

What are the control dependences in the following code sequence assuming branches are not delayed:

```
            ADD    R1,R2,R3
            BEQZ   R12,skipnext
            SUB    R4,R5,R6
skipnext:   OR     R7,R1,R9
            MULT   R13,R1,R4
```

Answer

The SUB instruction is control dependent on the BEQZ, since changing the ordering of these instructions changes the computation. If the SUB is moved before the branch, the result of the MULT will not be the same when the branch is taken. Likewise, the ADD instruction cannot be moved after the branch, since that would change the outcome of the MULT when the branch was not taken. The OR instruction is not control dependent on the branch, since the OR instruction is executed independently of whether the branch is taken or not. Since the OR instruction is nether data dependent on any earlier instruction in the sequence above, nor control dependent on the branch, the OR instruction can be moved before the branch without changing the values computed by the sequence. This assumes, of course, that the OR instruction has no side effects (such as causing an exception). When we want to reorder instructions with such potential side effects, additional compiler analysis or hardware support, which are discussed in sections 5.5 and 5.6, are required.

Control dependence is preserved by two properties in simple pipelines, such as that of Chapter 4. First, instructions execute in order. This ensures that an instruction that occurs before a branch is executed before the branch; thus, the ADD instruction in the above sequence will execute before the branch. Second, the detection of control or branch hazards ensures that an instruction that is control dependent on a branch is not executed until the branch direction is known. The control hazard hardware would ensure that the SUB instruction would not execute until the machine determines that the branch instruction is not taken.

Although preserving control dependence is a useful and simple way to help preserve program correctness, the control dependence in itself is not the fundamental performance limit. We may be willing to execute instructions that should not have been executed, thereby violating the control dependences, if we can do so without affecting the correctness of the program. Control dependence is not the critical property that must be preserved. Instead, the two properties critical to program correctness, and normally preserved by control dependence, are the *exception behavior* and the *data flow*.

Preserving the *exception behavior* means that any changes in the ordering of instruction execution must not change how exceptions are raised in the program. Often this is relaxed to mean that the reordering of instruction execution must not cause any new exceptions in the program. A simple example shows how maintaining the control dependences can prevent such situations. Consider the code sequence:

```
        BEQZ   R2,L1
        LW     R1,0(R2)
   L1:
```

In this case, if we ignore the control dependence and move the load instruction before the branch, the load instruction may cause a memory protection exception. Notice that there is no data dependence that prevents us from interchanging the BEQZ and the LW, it is only the control dependence. A similar situation could arise with an FP instruction that could raise an exception. In either case, if the branch is taken, such an exception would not occur if the instruction were not hoisted above the branch. To allow us to reorder the instructions, we would like to just ignore the exception, if the branch is untaken. In Section 5.6, we will look at two techniques, speculation and conditional instructions, that allow us to overcome this exception problem.

The second property preserved by maintenance of control dependences is the data flow. The *data flow* is the actual flow of data among instructions that produce results and those that consume them. Branches make the data flow dynamic, since they allow the source of data for a given instruction to come from many points. Consider the following code fragment:

```
        ADD      R1,R2,R3
        BEQZ     R4,L
        SUB      R1,R5,R6
   L:   OR       R7,R1,R8
```

In this example, the value of R1 used by the OR instruction depends on whether the branch is taken or not. Data dependence alone is not sufficient to preserve correctness, since it deals only with the static ordering of reads and writes. Thus while the OR instruction is data dependent on both the ADD and SUB instructions, this is insufficient for correct execution. Instead, when the instructions execute, the data flow must be preserved: if the branch is not taken then the value of R1 computed by the SUB should be used by the OR , and if the branch is taken the value of R1 computed by the ADD should be used by the OR. Moving the SUB before the branch does not affect the static dependence, but it will certainly affect the data flow and thus result in incorrect execution. By preserving the control dependence of the SUB on the branch, we prevent an illegal change to the data flow. Speculation and conditional instructions, which help with the exception problem, also allow us to change the control dependence while still maintaining the data flow, as we will see in Section 5.6.

Sometimes we can determine that violating the control dependence cannot affect either the exception behavior or the data flow. Consider the slightly modified code sequence from earlier:

```
          ADD    R1,R2,R3
          BEQZ   R12,skipnext
          SUB    R4,R5,R6
          ADD    R5,R4,R9
skipnext: OR     R7,R8,R9
```

Suppose we knew that the register destination of the SUB instruction (R4) was unused after the instruction labeled skipnext. (The property of whether a value will used by an upcoming instruction is called liveness and we will define it more formally shortly.) If R4 were unused, then changing the value of R4 just before the branch would not affect the data flow. Thus, if R4 were unused and the SUB instruction could not generate an exception, we could move the SUB instruction before the branch, since the program result could not be affected by this change. If the branch is taken the SUB instruction will execute and will be useless, but it will not affect the program results. This type of code scheduling is sometimes called *speculation,* since the compiler is basically betting on the branch outcome; in this case that the branch is usually not taken. More ambitious compiler speculation mechanisms are discussed in Section 5.5.

Delayed branches, which we saw in the previous chapter, can be used to reduce the stalls arising from branches and sometimes make use of speculation in scheduling branch delays.

Example

Show that the rules for scheduling branch delay slots in the last chapter reflect the requirement that the control and data dependences of the program must be preserved when they affect execution. Remember that there are three locations from which to choose an instruction to schedule into the branch delay slot: (1) from before the branch, (2) from the path that starts at the branch target, and (3) from the path starting with the sequential successor of the branch (the untaken path). In any case, the instruction placed into the branch delay slot will execute whether or not the branch is taken.

Answer

If the instruction is chosen from before the branch, there is no control dependence change, since the instruction will execute independent of the branch outcome in either case. The only requirement is that the data dependences (including any between the scheduled instruction and the branch condition) be maintained.

If the instruction is chosen from either the taken or untaken path, the selected instruction is control dependent on the branch. Hence, the selected instruction must not affect any register in use, nor can it generate an exception. These conditions make the change unobservable, even though the control dependence has been altered.

Control dependence is preserved by implementing control hazard detection that causes control stalls. Control stalls can be eliminated or reduced by a variety of hardware and software techniques. Delayed branches, for example, can reduce the stalls arising from control hazards. Other techniques for reducing the control hazard stalls include loop unrolling, converting branches into conditionally executed instructions, and compiler and hardware speculation. This chapter examines most of these techniques.

Loop Level Parallelism: Concepts and Techniques

Loop level parallelism is normally analyzed at the source level or close to it, while most analysis of ILP is done once instructions have been generated by the compiler. Loop level analysis involves determining what dependences exist among the operands in the loop across the iterations of the loop. For now, we will consider only data dependences, which arise when an operand is written at some point and read at a later point. We'll discuss name dependences shortly. The analysis of loop level parallelism focuses on determining whether data accesses in later iterations are data dependent on data values produced in earlier iterations.

Example

Consider a loop like this one:

```
for (i=1; i<=100; i=i+1) {
    A[i+1] = A[i] + C[i]; /* S1 */
    B[i+1] = B[i] + A[i+1]; }/* S2 */
}
```

Assume, that A, B, and C are distinct, nonoverlapping arrays. (In practice, the arrays may sometimes be the same or may overlap. Because the arrays may be passed as parameters to a procedure, which includes this loop, determining whether arrays overlap or are identical requires sophisticated, interprocedural analysis of the program.) What are the data dependences among the statements in the loop?

Answer

There are two different dependences:

1. S1 uses a value computed by S1 in an earlier iteration, since iteration *i* computes *A[i+1]* which is read in iteration *i+1*. The same is true of S2 for *B[i]* and *B[i+1]*.

2. S2 uses the value, *A[i+1]*, computed by S1 in the same iteration.

These two dependences are different and have different effects. To see how they differ, let's assume that only one of these dependences exists at a time. Consider the dependence of statement S1 on an earlier iteration of S1. This dependence is a *loop-carried dependence*, meaning that the dependence exists between different iterations of the loop. Furthermore, since the statement S1 is dependent on itself, successive iterations of statement S1 must execute in order.

The second dependence above (S2 depending on S1) is not loop-carried. Thus, if this were the only dependence, multiple iterations of the loop could execute in parallel, as long as each pair of statements in an iteration were kept in order. Techniques for exploiting loop level parallelism with pipelining are explored in this chapter.

There is a third type of data dependence that arises in loops, as shown in the following example.

Consider a loop like this one:

Example

```
for (i=1; i<=100; i=i+1) {
    A[i] = A[i] + B[i];      /* S1 */
    B[i+1] = C[i] + D[i];    /* S2 */
}
```

Answer

What are the dependences between S1 and S2?

Statement S1 uses the value assigned in the previous iteration by statement S2, so there is a loop-carried dependence between S2 and S1.

Despite this loop-carried dependence, this loop can be made parallel. Unlike the earlier loop this dependence is not circular: neither statement depends on itself and while S1 depends on S2, S2 does not depend on S1. A loop is parallel unless there is a cycle in the dependences.

Although there are no circular dependences in the above loop, it must be transformed into a different structure to expose the parallelism. Two observations are critical to this transformation:

1. There is no dependence from S1 to S2. If there were then there would be a cycle in the dependences and the loop would not be parallel. Since this other dependence is absent, interchanging the two statements will not affect the execution of S2.

2. On the first iteration of the loop, statement S1 depends on the value of B[1] computed prior to initiating the loop.

These two observations allow us to replace the loop above with the following code sequence:

```
A[1] = A[1] + B[1];
for (i=1; i<=99; i=i+1) {
    B[i+1] = C[i] + D[i];
    A[i+1] = A[i+1] + B[i+1];
}
B[101] = C[100] + D[100];
```

The dependence between the two statements is no longer loop-carried, so that iterations of the loop may be overlapped, provided the statements in each iteration are kept in order. There are a variety of such transformations that restructure loops to expose parallelism.

The key focus of the rest of this chapter is on techniques that exploit instruction level parallelism. The data dependences in a compiled program act as a limit on how much ILP can be exploited. The challenge is to approach that limit by trying to minimize the actual hazards and associated stalls that arise. The techniques we examine become ever more sophisticated in an attempt to exploit all the available parallelism while maintaining the true data dependences in the code. Both the compiler and the hardware have a role to play: the compiler tries to eliminate or minimize dependences, while the hardware tries to prevent dependences from becoming stalls.

Basic Pipeline Scheduling and Loop Unrolling

To keep a pipeline full, parallelism among instructions must be exploited by finding sequences of unrelated instructions that can be overlapped in the pipeline. To avoid a pipeline stall, a dependent instruction must be separated from the source instruction by a distance in clock cycles equal to the pipeline latency of that source instruction. A compiler's ability to perform this scheduling depends both on the amount of ILP available in the program and on the latencies of the functional units in the pipeline. Throughout this chapter we will assume the latencies shown in Figure 5.2, unless different latencies are explicitly stated. We assume that branches have a delay of one clock cycle so that the instruction following the branch cannot be determined for one clock cycle after the branch. We assume that the functional units are fully pipelined or replicated (as many times as the pipeline depth), so that an operation of any type can be issued on every clock cycle and there are no structural hazards.

Instruction producing result	Instruction using result	Latency in clock cycles
FP ALU op	Another FP ALU op	3
FP ALU op	Store double	2
Load double	FP ALU op	1
Load double	Store double	0

FIGURE 5.2   Latencies of operations used in this section and others. The first column shows the originating instruction type. The second column is the type of the consuming instruction. The last column is the separation in clock cycles to avoid a stall. These numbers are similar to the average latencies we would see on an FP unit, like the one we described for DLX in Figure 6.29 (page 289).[2] The latency of a floating point load to a store is zero, since the result of the load can be bypassed without stalling the store.

---

2.   This is the old references--should be a newer number in chapter 4 somewhere.

In this short section, we look at how the compiler can increase the amount of available ILP by unrolling loops. To illustrate these techniques, we will use a simple loop that adds a scalar value to a vector in memory; this is a parallel loop since there are no loop-carried dependences. We assume that initially R1 is the address of the last element in the vector (i.e., the element with the highest address), and F2 contains the scalar value to increment each element by. The DLX code, not accounting for the pipeline, looks like this:

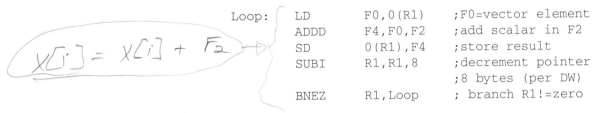

```
Loop:   LD      F0,0(R1)    ;F0=vector element
        ADDD    F4,F0,F2    ;add scalar in F2
        SD      0(R1),F4    ;store result
        SUBI    R1,R1,8     ;decrement pointer
                            ;8 bytes (per DW)
        BNEZ    R1,Loop     ; branch R1!=zero
```

$$X[i] = X[i] + F2$$

For simplicity, we assume the array starts at location 0. If it were located elsewhere, the loop would require one additional integer instruction to perform the comparison with R1.

Let's start by seeing how well this loop will run when it is scheduled on a simple pipeline for DLX with the latencies from Figure 5.2.

Example

Show how the loop would look on DLX, both scheduled and unscheduled, including any stalls or idle clock cycles. Schedule for both delays from floating point operations and for the delayed branch.

Answer

Without any scheduling the loop will execute as follows:

```
                                          Clock cycle issued
Loop:   LD      F0,0(R1)                          1
        stall                                     2
        ADDD    F4,F0,F2                          3
        stall                                     4
        stall                                     5
        SD      0(R1),F4                          6
        SUBI    R1,R1,#8                          7
        BNEZ    R1,LOOP                           8
  (nop) stall                                     9
```

This requires 9 clock cycles per iteration: one stall for the LD, two for the ADDD, and one for the delayed branch. We can schedule the loop to obtain

```
Loop:      LD      F0,0(R1)
           stall
           ADDD    F4,F0,F2
           SUBI    R1,R1,#8
           BNEZ    R1,LOOP      ; delayed branch
           SD      8(R1),F4     ; altered when
                                ;interchanged with SD
```

Execution time has been reduced from 9 clock cycles to 6.

Notice that to schedule the delayed branch, the compiler had to determine that it could swap the SUBI and SD by changing the address the SD stored to: The address was 0(R1) and is now 8(R1). This is not trivial, since most compilers would see that the SD instruction depends on the SUBI and would refuse to interchange them. A smarter compiler could figure out the relationship and perform the interchange. The dependence chain from the LD, to the ADDD, and then to the SD determines the clock cycle count for this loop.

In the above example, we complete one loop iteration and store back one vector element every 6 clock cycles, but the actual work of operating on the vector element takes just 3 (the load, add, and store) of those 6 clock cycles. The remaining 3 clock cycles consist of loop overhead—the SUBI and BNEZ—and a stall. To eliminate these 3 clock cycles we need to get more operations within the loop relative to the number of overhead instructions. A simple scheme for increasing the number of instructions relative to the branch and overhead instructions is *loop unrolling*. This is done by simply replicating the loop body multiple times, and adjusting the loop termination code.

Loop unrolling can also be used to improve the scheduling. In this case, we can eliminate the load delay stall, by creating additional independent instructions within the loop body. The compiler can then schedule these instructions into the load delay slot. If we simply replicated the instructions when we unrolled the loop, the resulting name dependences could prevent us from effectively scheduling the loop. Thus, we will want to use different registers for each iteration, increasing the required register count.

Example   Show our loop unrolled so that there are four copies of the loop body, assuming R1 is initially a multiple of 4. Eliminate any obviously redundant computations, and do not reuse any of the registers.

Answer   Here is the result after merging the SUBI instructions and dropping the unnecessary BNEZ operations that are duplicated during unrolling.

```
Loop:    LD      F0,0(R1)
         ADDD    F4,F0,F2
         SD      0(R1),F4 ;drop SUBI & BNEZ
         LD      F6,-8(R1)
         ADDD    F8,F6,F2
         SD      -8(R1),F8 ;drop SUBI & BNEZ
         LD      F10,-16(R1)
         ADDD    F12,F10,F2
         SD      -16(R1),F12 ;drop SUBI & BNEZ
         LD      F14,-24(R1)
         ADDD    F16,F14,F2
         SD      -24(R1),F16
         SUBI    R1,R1,#32
         BNEZ    R1,LOOP
```

We have eliminated three branches and three decrements of R1. The addresses on the loads and stores have been compensated to allow the SUBI instructions on R1 to be merged. Without scheduling, every operation is followed by a dependent operation, and thus will cause a stall. This loop will run in 27 clock cycles—each LD takes 2 clock cycles, each ADDD 3, the branch 2, and all other instructions 1—or 6.8 clock cycles for each of the four elements. Although this unrolled version is currently slower than the scheduled version of the original loop, this will change when we schedule the unrolled loop. Loop unrolling is normally done early in the compilation process, so that redundant computations can be exposed and eliminated by the optimizer.

In real programs we do not usually know the upper bound on the loop. Suppose it is n, and we would like to unroll the loop to make k copies of the body. Instead of a single unrolled loop, we generate a pair of loops. The first executes (n mod k) times and has a body that is the original loop. The unrolled version of the loop is surrounded by an outer loop that iterates (n div k) times.

In the above example, unrolling improves the performance of this loop by eliminating overhead instructions, although it increases code size substantially. What will happen to the performance increase when the loop is scheduled on DLX?

Example | Show the unrolled loop in the previous example after it has been scheduled on DLX.

Answer

```
Loop:   LD     F0,0(R1)
        LD     F6,-8(R1)
        LD     F10,-16(R1)
        LD     F14,-24(R1)
        ADDD   F4,F0,F2
        ADDD   F8,F6,F2
        ADDD   F12,F10,F2
        ADDD   F16,F14,F2
        SD     0(R1),F4
        SD     -8(R1),F8
        SD     -16(R1),F12
        SUBI   R1,R1,#32
        BNEZ   R1,LOOP
        SD     8(R1),F16; 8-32 = -24
```

The execution time of the unrolled loop has dropped to a total of 14 clock cycles, or 3.5 clock cycles per element, compared to 6.8 per element before scheduling and compared to 6 cycles when scheduled but not unrolled.

The gain from scheduling on the unrolled loop is even larger than on the original loop. This is because unrolling the loop exposes more computation that can be scheduled to minimize the stalls; the code above has no stalls. Scheduling the loop in this fashion necessitates realizing that the loads and stores are independent and can be interchanged. Data dependence analysis allows us to determine whether the loads and stores are independent; we will look at techniques for dependence analysis in Section 5.5.

Loop unrolling is a simple but useful method for increasing the size of straight-line code fragments that can be scheduled effectively. This transformation is useful in a variety of machines from simple pipelines like those in DLX to the pipelines described in Section 5.4 that issue more than one instruction per cycle. The next section examines techniques that use hardware to dynamically schedule the pipeline and reduce RAW stalls as we did with the compiler techniques described above.

5.2 | Overcoming Data Hazards with Dynamic Scheduling

In Chapter 4 we assumed that our pipeline fetches an instruction and issues it, unless there is a data dependence between an instruction already in the pipeline and the fetched instruction that cannot be hidden with bypassing or forwarding. Forwarding logic reduces the effective pipeline latency so that the certain dependences do not result in hazards. If there is a data dependence that cannot be hidden, then the hazard detection hardware stalls the pipeline (starting with the instruction that uses the result). No new instructions are fetched or issued until the dependence is cleared. We also examined compiler techniques for scheduling the instructions so as to separate dependent instructions and minimize the number of actual hazards and resultant stalls. This approach, which has been called *static scheduling*, while first used in the 1960s, became popular in the 1980s as pipelining became widespread.

Several early machines used another approach, called *dynamic scheduling*, whereby the hardware rearranges the instruction execution to reduce the stalls. Dynamic scheduling offers several advantages: it enables handling some cases when dependences are unknown at compile time (e.g., because they may involve a memory reference), and it simplifies the compiler. It also allows code that was compiled with one pipeline in mind to run efficiently on a different pipeline. As we will see, these advantages are gained at a significant increase in hardware complexity.

While a dynamically scheduled machine cannot remove true data dependences, it tries to avoid stalling when dependences are present. In contrast, static pipeline scheduling, like that we have already seen, tries to minimize stalls by separating dependent instructions so that they will not lead to hazards. Of course, static scheduling can also be used on code destined to run on a machine with a dynamically scheduled pipeline. We will examine two different schemes, with the second one extending the ideas of the first to attack WAW and WAR hazards as well as RAW stalls.

Dynamic Scheduling: The Idea

A major limitation of the pipelining techniques we have used so far is that they all use in-order instruction issue: if an instruction is stalled in the pipeline, no later instructions can proceed. Thus, if there is a dependence among two closely spaced instructions in the pipeline, a stall will result. If there are multiple functional units, these units could lie idle. If instruction j depends on a long-running instruction i, currently in execution in the pipeline, then all instructions after j must be stalled until i is finished and j can execute. For example, consider this code:

```
DIVD   F0,F2,F4
ADDD   F10,F0,F8
SUBD   F8,F8,F14
```

The SUBD instruction cannot execute because the dependence of ADDD on DIVD causes the pipeline to stall; yet SUBD is not data dependent on anything in the pipeline. This is a performance limitation that can be eliminated by not requiring instructions to execute in order.

In the DLX pipeline developed in the last chapter, both structural and data hazards were checked during instruction decode (ID): When an instruction could execute properly, it was issued from ID. To allow us to begin executing the SUBD in the above example, we must separate the issue process into two parts: checking the structural hazards and waiting for the absence of a data hazard. We can still check for structural hazards when we issue the instruction; thus, we still use in-order instruction issue. However, we want the instructions to begin execution as soon as their data operands are available. Thus, the pipeline will do *out-of-order execution*, which implies *out-of-order completion*.

Out-of-order completion creates major complications in handling exceptions. In the dynamically scheduled machines addressed in this section, exceptions are imprecise, since instructions may complete before an instruction issued earlier raises an exception. Thus, it is difficult to restart after an interrupt. Rather than address these problems in this section, we will discuss a solution for precise exceptions in the context of a machine with speculation in Section 5.6. The approach discussed in Section 5.6 can be used to solve the simpler problem that arises in these dynamically scheduled machines. For floating point exceptions other solutions may be possible, as discussed in Appendix A.

In introducing out-of-order execution, we have essentially split the ID pipe-stage into two stages:

1. Issue—decode instructions, check for structural hazards

2. Read operands—wait until no data hazards, then read operands

The EX stage then follows just as in the DLX pipeline. As in the DLX floating point pipeline, execution may take multiple cycles, depending on the operation. Thus, we may need to distinguish when an instruction *begins execution* and when it *completes execution*; between the two times, the instruction is *in execution*. This allows multiple instructions to be in execution at the same time. In addition to these changes to the pipeline structure, we will also change the functional unit design by varying the number of units, the latency of operations, and the functional unit pipelining, so as to better explore these more advanced pipelining techniques.

Dynamic Scheduling with a Scoreboard

In a dynamically scheduled pipeline, all instructions pass through the issue stage in order (in-order issue); however, they can be stalled or bypass each other in the second stage (read operands), and thus enter execution out of order. *Scoreboarding*; is a technique for allowing instructions to execute out of order when there are sufficient resources and no data dependences; it is named after the CDC 6600 scoreboard, which developed this capability.

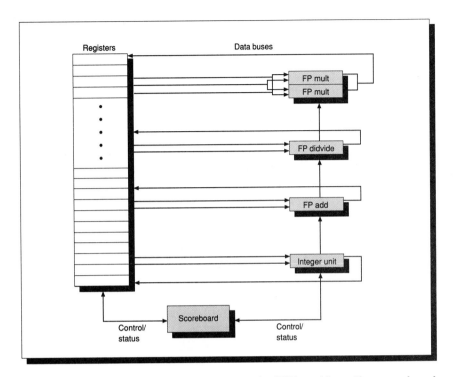

FIGURE 5.3 This shows the basic structure of a DLX machine with a scoreboard. The scoreboard's function is to control instruction execution (vertical control lines). All data flows between the register file and the functional units over the buses (the horizontal lines, called trunks in the CDC 6600). There are two FP multipliers, an FP divider, an FP adder, and an integer unit. One set of buses (two inputs and one output) serves a group of functional units. The details of the scoreboard are shown in Figures 5.4-5.7 *Change this figure so the line labeled control/status goes to the boxes but up the right-hand-side rather than through the boxes.*

Before we see how scoreboarding could be used in the DLX pipeline, it is important to observe that WAR hazards, which did not exist in the DLX floating-point or integer pipelines, may arise when instructions execute out of order. In the above example, the SUBD destination is F8, which is a source for the ADDD. Hence, there is an antidependence between the ADDD and the SUBD: If the pipeline executes the SUBD before the ADDD, it will violate the antidependence. This WAR can be avoided by two rules: (1) read registers only during Read Operands, and (2) queue both the ADDD operation **and** copies of its operands. To avoid violating output dependences, WAW hazards (e.g., as would occur if the destination of the SUBD were F10) must still be detected. WAW hazards can be eliminated by stalling the issue of an instruction whose destination is the same as one already in the pipeline.

The goal of a scoreboard is to maintain an execution rate of one instruction per clock cycle (when there are no structural hazards) by executing an instruction as early as possible. Thus, when the next instruction to execute is stalled, other instructions can be issued and executed if they do not depend on any active or stalled instruction. The scoreboard takes full responsibility for instruction issue and execution, including all hazard detection. Taking advantage of out-of-order execution requires multiple instructions to be in their EX stage simultaneously. This can be achieved with either multiple functional units or with pipelined functional units or with both. Since these two capabilities—pipelined functional units and multiple functional units—are essentially equivalent for the purposes of pipeline control, we will assume the machine has multiple functional units.

The CDC 6600 had 16 separate functional units, including 4 floating-point units, 5 units for memory references, and 7 units for integer operations. On DLX, scoreboards make sense primarily on the floating-point unit since the latency of the other functional units is very small. Let's assume that there are two multipliers, one adder, one divide unit, and a single integer unit for all memory references, branches, and integer operations. Although this example is much smaller than the CDC 6600, it is sufficiently powerful to demonstrate the principles without having a mass of detail or needing very long examples. Because both DLX and the CDC 6600 are load/store architectures, the techniques are nearly identical for the two machines. Figure 5.3 shows what the machine looks like.

Every instruction goes through the scoreboard, where a record of the data dependences is constructed; this step corresponds to instruction issue and replaces part of the ID step in the DLX pipeline. The scoreboard then determines when the instruction can read its operands and begin execution. If the scoreboard decides the instruction cannot execute immediately, it monitors every change in the hardware and decides when the instruction can execute. The scoreboard also controls when an instruction can write its result into the destination register. Thus, all hazard detection and resolution is centralized in the scoreboard. We will see a picture of the scoreboard later (Figure 5.4 on page 267), but first we need to understand the steps in the issue and execution segment of the pipeline.

Each instruction undergoes four steps in executing. (Since we are concentrating on the FP operations, we will not consider a step for memory access.) Let's first examine the steps informally and then look in detail at how the scoreboard keeps the necessary information that determines when to progress from one step to the next. The four steps, which replace the ID, EX, and WB steps in the standard DLX pipeline, are as follows:

1. Issue—If a functional unit for the instruction is free and no other active instruction has the same destination register, the scoreboard issues the instruction to the functional unit and updates its internal data structure. By ensuring that no other active functional unit wants to write its result into the destination register, we guarantee that WAW hazards cannot be present. If a structural or WAW haz-

ard exists, then the instruction issue stalls, and no further instructions will issue until these hazards are cleared. This step replaces a portion of the ID step in the DLX pipeline.

2. Read operands—The scoreboard monitors the availability of the source operands. A source operand is available if no earlier issued active instruction is going to write it, or if the register containing the operand is being written by a currently active functional unit. When the source operands are available, the scoreboard tells the functional unit to proceed to read the operands from the registers and begin execution. The scoreboard resolves RAW hazards dynamically in this step, and instructions may be sent into execution out of order. This step, together with Issue, completes the function of the ID step in the simple DLX pipeline.

3. Execution—The functional unit begins execution upon receiving operands. When the result is ready, it notifies the scoreboard that it has completed execution. This step replaces the EX step in the DLX pipeline and takes multiple cycles in the DLX FP pipeline.

4. Write result—Once the scoreboard is aware that the functional unit has completed execution, the scoreboard checks for WAR hazards. A WAR hazard exists if there is a code sequence like our earlier example with ADDD and SUBD. In that example we had the code

```
DIVD  F0,F2,F4
ADDD  F10,F0,F8
SUBD  F8,F8,F14
```

ADDD has a source operand F8, which is the same register as the destination of SUBD. But ADDD actually depends on an earlier instruction. The scoreboard will still stall the SUBD in its write result stage until ADDD reads its operands. In general, then, a completing instruction cannot be allowed to write its results when

- there is an instruction that has not read its operands that precedes (i.e., in order of issue) the competing instruction, and

- one of the operands is the same register as the result of the completing instruction.

If this WAR hazard does not exist, or when it clears, the scoreboard tells the functional unit to store its result to the destination register. This step replaces the WB step in the simple DLX pipeline.

At first glance, it might appear that the scoreboard will have difficulty separating RAW and WAR hazards. Exercise 5.6 will help you understand how the scoreboard distinguishes these two cases and thus knows when to stall a instruction that is ready to write its results, so as to prevent a WAR hazard.

Because the operands for an instruction are read only when both operands are available in the register file, this scoreboard does not take advantage of forwarding. Instead registers are only read when they are both available. This is not as large a penalty as you might initially think, since unlike our simple pipeline of Chapter 4, instructions will write their result into the register file as soon as they complete execution (assuming no WAR hazards), rather than wait for a statically assigned write slot that may be several cycles away. The effect of this is to reduce the pipeline latency and the benefits of forwarding. To eliminate the remaining cycle that arises since the write result and read operand stages cannot overlap we need additional buffering. Such buffering is provided in Tomasulo's scheme, which we discuss shortly.

Based on its own data structure, the scoreboard controls the instruction progression from one step to the next by communicating with the functional units. There is a small complication, however. There are only a limited number of source operand buses and result buses to the register file, which represents a structural hazard. The scoreboard must guarantee that the number of functional units allowed to proceed into steps 2 and 4 do not exceed the number of buses available. We will not go into further detail on this, other than to mention that the CDC 6600 solved this problem by grouping the 16 functional units together into four groups and supplying a set of buses, called *data trunks*, for each group. Only one unit in a group could read its operands or write its result during a clock.

Now let's look at the detailed data structure maintained by a DLX scoreboard with five functional units. Figure 5.4 (page 267) shows what the scoreboard's information looks like part way through the execution of this simple sequence of instructions:

```
LD      F6,34(R2)
LD      F2,45(R3)
MULTD   F0,F2,F4
SUBD    F8,F6,F2
DIVD    F10,F0,F6
ADDD    F6,F8,F2
```

There are three parts to the scoreboard:

1. Instruction status—Indicates which of the four steps the instruction is in.

2. Functional unit status—Indicates the state of the functional unit (FU). There are nine fields for each functional unit:

    Busy—Indicates whether the unit is busy or not

    Op—Operation to perform in the unit (e.g., add or subtract)

    Fi—Destination register

    Fj, Fk—Source-register numbers

Qj, Qk—Functional units producing source registers Fj, Fk

Rj, Rk—Flags indicating when Fj, Fk are ready

3. Register result status—Indicates which functional unit will write each register, if an active instruction has the register as its destination. This field is set to blank whenever there are no pending instructions that will write that register.

Instruction status				
Instruction	**Issue**	**Read operands**	**Execution complete**	**Write result**
LD F6,34(R2)	√	√	√	√
LD F2,45(R3)	√	√	√	
MULTD F0,F2,F4	√			
SUBD F8,F6,F2	√			
DIVD F10,F0,F6	√			
ADDD F6,F8,F2				

Functional unit status									
Name	**Busy**	**Op**	**Fi**	**Fj**	**Fk**	**Qj**	**Qk**	**Rj**	**Rk**
Integer	Yes	Load	F2	R3				No	
Mult1	Yes	Mult	F0	F2	F4	Integer		No	Yes
Mult2	No								
Add	Yes	Sub	F8	F6	F2		Integer	Yes	No
Divide	Yes	Div	F10	F0	F6	Mult1		No	Yes

Register result status									
	F0	**F2**	**F4**	**F6**	**F8**	**F10**	**F12**	**...**	**F30**
FU	Mult1	Integer			Add	Divide			

FIGURE 5.4 Components of the scoreboard. Each instruction that has issued or is pending issue has an entry in the instruction-status table. There is one entry in the functional-unit–status table for each functional unit. Once an instruction issues, the record of its operands is kept in the functional-unit–status table. Finally, the register-result table indicates which unit will produce each pending result; the number of entries is equal to the number of registers. The instruction-status register says that (1) the first LD has completed and written its result, and (2) the second LD has completed execution but has not yet written its result. The MULTD, SUBD, and DIVD have all issued but are stalled, waiting for their operands. The functional-unit status says that the first multiply unit is waiting for the integer unit, the add unit is waiting for the integer unit, and the divide unit is waiting for the first multiply unit. The ADDD instruction is stalled due to a structural hazard; it will clear when the SUBD completes. If an entry in one of these scoreboard tables is not being used, it is left blank. For example, the Rk field is not used on a load, and the Mult2 unit is unused, hence its fields have no meaning. Also, once an operand has been read, the Rj and Rk fields are set to No. Fields that are not in use or are idle (such as entries in the Functional Unit Status or Result table) are left blank to simplify the tables. For example the Fk field is not used on a load, and the Mult2 unit is unused; the fields are blank in both cases.

Now let's look at how the code sequence begun in Figure 5.4 continues execution. After that, we will be able to examine in detail the conditions that the scoreboard uses to control execution.

Example

Assume the following EX cycle latencies (chosen to illustrate the behavior and not representative) for the floating-point functional units: Add is 2 clock cycles, multiply is 10 clock cycles, and divide is 40 clock cycles. Using the code segment in Figure 5.4 and beginning with the point indicated by the instruction status in Figure 5.4, show what the status tables look like when MULTD and DIVD are each ready to go to the write-result state.

Answer

There are RAW data hazards from the second LD to MULTD and SUBD, from MULTD to DIVD, and from SUBD to ADDD. There is a WAR data hazard between DIVD and ADDD. Finally, there is a structural hazard on the add functional unit for ADDD. What the tables look like when MULTD and DIVD are ready to write their results are shown in Figures 5.5 and 5.6, respectively.

Instruction status				
Instruction	**Issue**	**Read operands**	**Execution complete**	**Write result**
LD F6,34(R2)	√	√	√	√
LD F2,45(R3)	√	√	√	√
MULTD F0,F2,F4	√	√	√	
SUBD F8,F6,F2	√	√	√	√
DIVD F10,F0,F6	√			
ADDD F6,F8,F2	√	√	√	

Functional unit status										
Name	**Busy**	**Op**	**Fi**	**Fj**	**Fk**	**Qj**	**Qk**	**Rj**	**Rk**
Integer	No								
Mult1	Yes	Mult	F0	F2	F4			No	No
Mult2	No								
Add	Yes	Add	F6	F8	F2			No	No
Divide	Yes	Div	F10	F0	F6	Mult1		No	Yes

Register result status									
	F0	**F2**	**F4**	**F6**	**F8**	**F10**	**F12**	**...**	**F30**
FU no.	Mult1			Add		Divide			

FIGURE 5.5   Scoreboard tables just before the MULTD goes to write result. The DIVD has not yet read either of its operands, since it has a dependence on the result of the multiply. The ADDD has read its operands and is in execution, although it was forced to wait until the SUBD finished to get the functional unit. ADDD cannot proceed to write result because of the WAR hazard on F6, which is used by the DIVD.

Instruction status				
Instruction	**Issue**	**Read operands**	**Execution complete**	**Write result**
LD F6,34(R2)	√	√	√	√
LD F2,45(R3)	√	√	√	√
MULTD F0,F2,F4	√	√	√	√
SUBD F8,F6,F2	√	√	√	√
DIVD F10,F0,F6	√	√	√	
ADDD F6,F8,F2	√	√	√	√

Functional unit status									
Name	**Busy**	**Op**	**Fi**	**Fj**	**Fk**	**Qj**	**Qk**	**Rj**	**Rk**
Integer	No								
Mult1	No								
Mult2	No								
Add	No								
Divide	Yes	Div	F10	F0	F6			No	No

Register Result status								
	F0	**F2**	**F4**	**F6**	**F8**	**F10**	**F12**	**...**	**F30**
FU no.						Divide			

FIGURE 5.6 **Scoreboard tables just before the** DIVD **goes to write result.** ADDD **was able to complete as soon as** DIVD **passed through read operands and got a copy of F6**. Only the DIVD remains to finish.

Instruction status	**Wait until**	**Bookkeeping**
Issue	Not busy (FU) and not result(D)	Busy(FU)← yes; Op(FU)← op; Fi(FU)← `D'; Fj(FU)← `S1'; Fk(FU)← `S2'; Qj← Result('S1'); Qk← Result(`S2'); Rj← not Qj; Rk← not Qk; Result('D')← FU;
Read operands	Rj and Rk	Rj← No; Rk← No
Execution complete	Functional unit done	
Write result	$\forall f$((Fj(f)≠Fi(FU) or Rj(f)=No) & (Fk(f) ≠Fi(FU) or Rk(f)=No))	$\forall f$(if Qj(f)=FU then Rj(f)← Yes); $\forall f$(if Qk(f)=FU then Rj(f)← Yes); Result(Fi(FU))← 0; Busy(FU)← No

FIGURE 5.7 **Required checks and bookkeeping actions for each step in instruction execution.** FU stands for the functional unit used by the instruction, D is the destination register name, S1 and S2 are the source register names, and op is the operation to be done. To access the scoreboard entry named F_j for functional unit FU we use the notation F_j(FU). Result(D) is the value of the result register field for register D. The test on the write-result case prevents the write when there is a WAR hazard, which exists if another instruction has this instruction's destination (Fi(FU)) as a source (either Fj(f) or Fk(f)), and if some other instruction has written the register (Rj=Yes or Rk=Yes). The notation 'Ri" is used to mean the name of register Ri rather than the contents of register Ri.

Now we can see how the scoreboard works in detail by looking at what has to happen for the scoreboard to allow each instruction to proceed. Figure 5.7 shows what the scoreboard requires for each instruction to advance and the bookkeeping action necessary when the instruction does advance. The scoreboard, like a number of other structures that we examine in this chapter, records operand specifier information, such as register numbers. For example, we must record the source registers when an instruction is issued. This introduces a potential ambiguity into our hardware description, since we usually use a register name on the right-hand-side of an assignment to stand for the *value* in the register rather than the *name* of the register. To avoid this ambiguity, we place the register name in quotes whenever the context could be ambiguous and we want to refer to the name rather than the register contents. For example, Fj(FU) ← `S1` causes the register name designated by S1 to be placed in Fj(FU), as opposed to the contents of the register S1.

The costs and benefits of scoreboarding are an interesting question. The CDC 6600 designers measured a performance improvement of 1.7 for FORTRAN programs and 2.5 for hand-coded assembly language. However, this was measured in the days before software pipeline scheduling, semiconductor main memory, and caches (which lower memory-access time). The scoreboard on the CDC 6600 had about as much logic as one of the functional units, which is surprisingly low. The main cost was in the large number of buses—about four times as many as would be required if the machine only executed instructions in order (or if it only initiated one instruction per Execute cycle). The recently increasing interest in dynamic scheduling is motivated by attempts to issue more instructions per clock (so the cost of more buses must be paid anyway) and ideas like speculation (explored in Section 5.6) that naturally build on dynamic scheduling.

A scoreboard uses the available ILP to minimize the number of stalls arising from the program's true data dependences. In eliminating stalls, a scoreboard is limited by several factors:

1. The amount of parallelism available among the instructions: this determines whether independent instructions can be found to execute. If each instruction depends on its predecessor, no dynamic scheduling scheme can reduce stalls. If the instructions in the pipeline simultaneously must be chosen from the same basic block (as was true in the 6600), this limit is likely to be quite severe.

2. The number of scoreboard entries: this determines how far ahead the pipeline can look for independent instructions. The set of instructions examined as candidates for potential execution is called the *window*. The size of the scoreboard determines the size of the window. In this section, we assume a window does not extend beyond a branch, so the window (and the scoreboard) always contain straightline code from a single basic block. Section 5.6 deals with speculation, which allows the window to extend beyond a branch.

3. The number and types of functional units: this determines the importance of structural hazards, which can increase when dynamic scheduling is used.

4. The presence of antidependences and output dependences that lead to WAR and WAW stalls.

This entire chapter focuses on techniques that attack the problem of exposing and better utilizing available ILP. The second and third factors can be attacked by increasing the size of the scoreboard and the number of functional units; however, these changes have cost implications and may also affect cycle time. WAW and WAR hazards become more important in dynamically scheduled machines, because the pipeline exposes more name dependences. WAW hazards also become more important if we use dynamic scheduling with a branch prediction scheme that allows multiple iterations of a loop to overlap.

The next section looks at a technique called *register renaming* that dynamically eliminates name dependences so as to avoid WAR and WAW hazards. Register renaming does this by replacing the register names (such as those kept in the scoreboard) with the names of a larger set of virtual registers. The register renaming scheme also is the basis for implementing forwarding.

Another Dynamic Scheduling Approach— the Tomasulo Approach

Another approach to allow execution to proceed in the presence of hazards was used by the IBM 360/91 floating-point unit. This scheme was invented by Robert Tomasulo and is named after him. Tomasulo's scheme combines key elements of the scoreboarding scheme with the introduction of register renaming. There are many variations on this scheme, though the key concept of renaming registers to avoid WAR and WAW hazards is the most common characteristic.

The IBM 360/91 was completed about three years after the CDC 6600, just before caches appeared in commercial machines. IBM's goal was to achieve high floating-point performance from an instruction set and from compilers designed for the entire 360 computer family, rather than specialized for the high-end machines. The 360 architecture had only four double-precision floating-point registers, which limits the effectiveness of compiler scheduling; this fact was another motivation for the Tomasulo approach. Lastly, the IBM 360/91 had long memory accesses and long floating-point delays, which Tomasulo's algorithm was designed to overcome. At the end of the section, we will see that Tomasulo's algorithm can also support the overlapped execution of multiple iterations of a loop.

We explain the algorithm, which focuses on the floating-point unit, in the context of a pipelined, floating-point unit for DLX. The primary difference between DLX and the 360 is the presence of register–memory instructions in the latter machine. Because Tomasulo's algorithm uses a load functional unit, no significant changes are needed to add register–memory addressing modes; the primary addition is another bus. The IBM 360/91 also had pipelined functional units, rather than multiple functional units. The only difference between these is that a pipelined unit can start at most one operation per clock cycle. Since there are really no fundamental differences, we describe the algorithm as if there were multiple functional units. The IBM 360/91 could accommodate three operations for the floating-point adder and two for the floating-point multiplier. In addition, up to six floating-point loads, or memory references, and up to three floating-point stores could be outstanding. Load data buffers and store data buffers are used for this function. Although we will not discuss the load and store units, we do need to include the buffers for operands.

Tomasulo's scheme shares many ideas with the scoreboard scheme, so we assume the reader understands the scoreboard thoroughly. In fact, Tomasulo's algorithm is largely just the addition of register renaming to a scoreboarding scheme, though there are some significant implementation differences in the Tomasulo and scoreboard scheme. In the last section, we saw how a compiler could rename registers to avoid WAW and WAR hazards. In Tomasulo's scheme this functionality is provided by the *reservation stations* , which buffer the operands of instructions waiting to issue, and by the issue logic. The basic idea is that a reservation station fetches and buffers an operand as soon as it is available, eliminating the need to get the operand from a register. In addition, pending instructions designate the reservation station that will provide their input. Finally, when successive writes to a register appear, only the last one is actually used to update the register. As instructions are issued the register specifiers for pending operands are renamed to the names of the reservation stations. This combination of issue logic and reservation stations provides renaming and eliminates WAW and WARE hazards. Since there can be more reservation stations than real registers, this technique can eliminate hazards that could not be eliminated by a compiler. As we explore the components of this scheme, we will return to this topic of register renaming and see exactly how the renaming occurs and how it eliminates hazards.

In addition to the use of register renaming, there are two other significant differences in the organization of Tomasulo's scheme and scoreboarding. First, hazard detection and execution control are distributed: the reservation stations at each functional unit control when an instruction can begin execution at that unit. This function is centralized in the scoreboard. Second, results are passed directly to functional units from the reservation stations where they are buffered, rather than going through the registers. This is done with a common result bus that allows all units waiting for an operand to be loaded simultaneously (on the 360/91 this is called the *common data bus,* or CDB). In comparison, the scoreboard writes results into registers, where waiting functional units may have to contend for them. The number of result buses in either the scoreboard or in Tomasulo's scheme can be varied. In the actual implementations, the CDC 6600 had multiple completion buses (two in the floating-point unit), while the IBM 360/91 had only one.

Figure 5.8 shows the basic structure of a Tomasulo-based floating-point unit for DLX; none of the execution control tables are shown. The reservation stations hold instructions that have been issued and are awaiting execution at a functional unit, the operands for that instruction if they have already been computed or the source of the operands otherwise, as well as the information needed to control the instruction once it has begun execution at the unit. The load buffers and store buffers hold data or addresses coming from and going to memory. The floating-point registers are connected by a pair of buses to the functional units and by a single bus to the store buffers. All results from the functional units and from memory are sent on the common data bus, which goes everywhere except to the load buffer. All the buffers and reservation stations have tag fields, employed by hazard control.

Before we describe the details of the reservation stations and the algorithm, let's look at the steps an instruction goes through—just as we did for the scoreboard. Since operands are transmitted differently than in a scoreboard, there are only three steps:

1. Issue—Get an instruction from the floating-point operation queue. If the operation is a floating-point operation, issue it if there is an empty reservation station, and send the operands to the reservation station if they are in the registers. If the operation is a load or store, it can issue if there is an available buffer. If there is not an empty reservation station or an empty buffer, then there is a structural hazard and the instruction stalls until a station or buffer is freed. This step also performs the process of renaming registers.

2. Execute—If one or more of the operands is not yet available, monitor the CDB while waiting for the register to be computed. When an operand becomes available it is placed into the corresponding reservation station. When both operands are available, execute the operation. This step checks for RAW hazards.

3. Write result—When the result is available, write it on the CDB and from there into the registers and any functional units waiting for this result.

Although these steps are fundamentally similar to those in the scoreboard, there are three important differences. First, there is no checking for WAW and WAR hazards—these are eliminated when the register operands are renamed during issue. Second, the CDB is used to broadcast results rather than waiting on the registers. Third, the loads and stores are treated as basic functional units.

The data structures used to detect and eliminate hazards are attached to the reservation stations, the register file, and the load and store buffers. Although different information is attached to different objects, everything except the load buffers contains a tag field per entry. These tags are essentially names for an extended set of virtual registers used in renaming. register renaming In this example, the tag field is a four-bit quantity that denotes one of the five reservation stations or one of the six load buffers; as we will see this produces the equivalent of nine registers that can be designated as result registers (as opposed to the four double precision registers that the 360 architecture contains). (In a machine with more real registers, we would want renaming to provide an even larger set of virtual registers.) The tag field describes which reservation station contains the instruction that will produce a result needed as a source operand. Once an instruction has issued and is waiting for a result, it refers to the operand by the reservation station number, rather than by the number of the destination register written by the instruction producing the value. Unused values, such as zero, indicate that the operand is already available in the registers. Because there are more reservation stations than actual register numbers, WAW and WAR hazards can be reduced by renaming results using reservation station numbers. Although in Tomasulo's scheme the reservation stations are used as the extended virtual registers, other approaches could use a register set with additional registers or a structure like the reorder buffer, which we will see in Section 5.6.

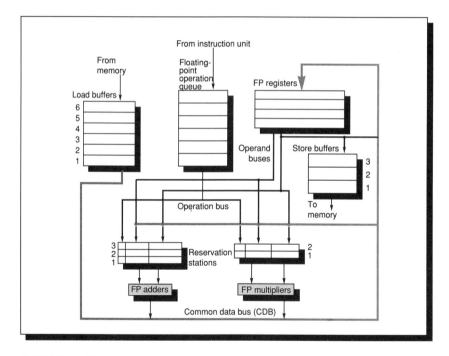

FIGURE 5.8   The basic structure of a DLX FP unit using Tomasulo's algorithm. Floating-point operations are sent from the instruction unit into a queue when they are issued. The reservation stations include the operation and the actual operands, as well as information used for detecting and resolving hazards. There are load buffers to hold the results of outstanding loads and store buffers to hold the addresses of outstanding stores waiting for their operands. All results from either the FP units or the load unit are put on the common data bus (CDB), which goes to the FP register file as well as the reservation stations and store buffers. The FP adders implement addition and subtraction, while the FP multipliers do multiplication and division.

In describing the operation of this scheme, scoreboard terminology is used wherever this will not lead to confusion. The terminology used by the IBM 360/91 is also shown. It is important to remember that the tags in the Tomasulo scheme refer to the buffer or unit that will produce a result; the register names are discarded when an instruction issues to a reservation station.

Each reservation station has six fields:

Op—The operation to perform on source operands S1 and S2.

Qj, Qk—The reservation stations that will produce the corresponding source operand; a value of zero indicates that the source operand is already available in Vi or Vj, or is unnecessary. (The IBM 360/91 calls these SINKunit and SOURCEunit.)

Vj, Vk—The value of the source operands. These are called SINK and SOURCE on the IBM 360/91. Note that only one of the V field or the Q field is valid for each operand.

Busy—Indicates that this reservation station and its accompanying functional unit are occupied.

The register file and store buffer each have a field, Qi:

Qi—The number of the reservation station that contains the operation whose result should be stored into this register or into memory. If the value of Qi is blank, no currently active instruction is computing a result destined for this register or buffer. For a register, this means the value is simply the register contents.

The load and store buffers each require a busy field, indicating when a buffer is available due to completion of a load or store assigned there; the register field will have a blank Qi field when it is not busy. The store buffer also has a field V, which holds the value to be stored.

Before we examine the algorithm in detail, let's see what the information tables look like for the following code sequence:

```
1. LD     F6,34(R2)
2. LD     F2,45(R3)
3. MULTD  F0,F2,F4
4. SUBD   F8,F6,F2
5. DIVD   F10,F0,F6
6. ADDD   F6,F8,F2
```

We saw what the scoreboard looked like for this program when only the first load had written its result. Figure 5.9 depicts the reservation stations, load and store buffers, and the register tags. The numbers appended to the names add, mult, and load stand for the tag for that reservation station—Add1 is the tag for the result from the first add unit. In addition we have included a central table called "Instruction status." This table is included only to help the reader understand the algorithm; it is **not** actually a part of the hardware. Instead, the state of each operation that has issued is kept in a reservation station.

There are two important differences from scoreboards that are immediately observable in these tables. First, the value of an operand is stored in the reservation station in one of the V fields as soon as it is available; it is not read from the register file nor from a reservation station once the instruction has issued. Second, the ADDD instruction, blocked in the scoreboard by a WAR hazard, has issued.

Instruction status			
Instruction	**Issue**	**Execute**	**Write result**
LD F6,34(R2)	√	√	√
LD F2,45(R3)	√	√	
MULTD F0,F2,F4	√		
SUBD F8,F6,F2	√		
DIVD F10,F0,F6	√		
ADDD F6,F8,F2	√		

Reservation stations						
Name	**Busy**	**Op**	**Vj**	**Vk**	**Qj**	**Qk**
Add1	Yes	SUB	Mem[34+Regs[R2]]			Load2
Add2	Yes	ADD			Add1	Load2
Add3	No					
Mult1	Yes	MULT		Regs[F4]	Load2	
Mult2	Yes	DIV		Mem[34+Regs[R2]]	Mult1	

Register status									
Field	**F0**	**F2**	**F4**	**F6**	**F8**	**F10**	**F12**	**...**	**F30**
Qi	Mult1	Load2		Add2	Add1	Mult2			

FIGURE 5.9   Reservation stations and register tags. All of the instructions have issued, but only the first load instruction has completed and written its result to the CDB. The instruction-status table is not actually present, but the equivalent information is distributed throughout the hardware. The Vj and Vk fields show the value of an operand in our hardware description language. The load and store buffers are not shown. Load buffer 2 is the only busy load buffer and it is performing on behalf of instruction 2 in the sequence—loading from memory address R3 + 45. Remember that an operand is specified by either a Q field or a V field at any time.

The major advantages of the Tomasulo scheme are (1) the distribution of the hazard detection logic, and (2) the elimination of stalls for WAW and WAR hazards. The first advantage arises from the distributed reservation stations and the use of the CDB. If multiple instructions are waiting on a single result, and each instruction already has its other operand, then the instructions can be released simultaneously by the broadcast on the CDB. In the scoreboard the waiting instructions must all read their results from the registers when register buses are available.

WAW and WAR hazards are eliminated by renaming registers using the reservation stations, and by the process of storing operands into the reservation station as soon as they are available. For example, in our code sequence in Figure 5.9 we have issued both the DIVD and the ADDD, even though there is a WAR hazard involving F6. The hazard is eliminated in one of two ways. If the instruction providing the value for the DIVD has completed, then Vk will store the result, allowing DIVD to execute independent of the ADDD (this is the case shown). On the other hand, if the LD had not completed, then Qk would point to the Load1 reservation station, and the DIVD instruction would be independent of the ADDD. Thus, in either case, the ADDD can issue and begin executing. Any uses of the result of the MULTD result would point to the reservation station, allowing the ADDD to complete and store its value into the registers without affecting the DIVD. We'll see an example of the elimination of a WAW hazard shortly. But let's first look at how our earlier example continues execution.

Example

Assume the same latencies for the floating-point functional units as we did for Figure 5.6: Add is 2 clock cycles, multiply is 10 clock cycles, and divide is 40 clock cycles. With the same code segment, show what the status tables look like when the MULTD is ready to write its result.

Answer

The result is shown in the three tables in Figure 5.10. Unlike the example with the scoreboard, ADDD has completed since the operands of DIVD are copied, thereby overcoming the WAR hazard.

Instruction status			
Instruction	**Issue**	**Execute**	**Write result**
LD F6,34(R2)	√	√	√
LD F2,45(R3)	√	√	√
MULTD FO,F2,F4	√	√	
SUBD F8,F6,F2	√	√	√
DIVD F10,FO,F6	√		
ADDD F6,F8,F2	√	√	√

Reservation stations						
Name	**Busy**	**Op**	**Vj**	**Vk**	**Qj**	**Qk**
Add1	No					
Add2	No					
Add3	No					
Mult1	Yes	MULT	Mem[45+Regs[R3]]	Regs[F4]		
Mult2	Yes	DIV		Mem[34+Regs[R2]]	Mult1	

Register status									
Field	**F0**	**F2**	**F4**	**F6**	**F8**	**F10**	**F12**	**...**	**F30**
Qi	Mult1					Mult2			

FIGURE 5.10   Multiply and divide are the only instructions not finished. This is different from the scoreboard case, because the elimination of WAR hazards allowed the ADD to finish right after the SUBD on which it depended.

Figure 5.11 gives the steps that each instruction must go through. Load and stores are only slightly special. A load can execute as soon as it is available. When execution is completed and the CDB is available, a load puts its result on the CDB like any functional unit. Stores receive their values from the CDB or from the register file and execute autonomously; when they are done they turn the busy field off to indicate availability, just like a load buffer or reservation station.

Instruction status	Wait until	Action or bookkeeping

Issue	Station or buffer empty	```if (Register['S1'].Qi ≠0)```
		   ```{RS[r].Qj← Register['S1'].Qi}```
		```else {RS[r].Vj← S1}; RS[r].Qj← 0};```
		```if (Register[S2].Qi≠0)```
		   ```{RS[r].Qk← Register[S2].Qi};```
		```else {RS[r].Vk← S2; RS[r].Qk← 0}```
		```RS[r].Busy← yes;```
		```Register['D'].Qi=r;```

Execute	(RS[r].Qj=0) and (RS[r].Qk=0)	None—operands are in Vj and Vk

Write result	Execution completed at *r*
	and CDB available
		```∀x(if (Register[x].Qi=r) {Fx← result;```
		   ```Register[x].Qi← 0});```
		```∀x(if (RS[x].Qj=r) {RS[x].Vj← result;```
		   ```RS[x].Qj ← 0});```
		```∀x(if (RS[x].Qk=r) {RS[x].Vk← result;```
		   ```RS[x].Qk ← 0});```
		```∀x(if (Store[x].Qi=r) {Store[x].V← result;```
		   ```Store[x].Qi ← 0});```
		```RS[r].Busy← No```

FIGURE 5.11 Steps in the algorithm and what is required for each step. For the issuing instruction, D is the destination, S1 and S2 are the source register numbers, and *r* is the reservation station or buffer that D is assigned to. RS is the reservation-station data structure. The value returned by a reservation station or by the load unit is called the "result." Register is the register data structure, while Store is the store-buffer data structure. Recall that 'Ri' means the name of register Ri, rather than the contents of Ri. When an instruction is issued, the destination register has its Qi field set to the number of the buffer or reservation station to which the instruction is issued. If the operands are available in the registers, they are stored in the V fields. Otherwise, the Q fields are set to indicate the reservation station that will produce the values needed as source operands. The instruction waits at the reservation station until both its operands are available, indicated by zero in the Q fields. The Q fields are set to zero either when this instruction is issued, or when an instruction on which this instruction depends completes and does its write back. When an instruction has finished execution and the CDB is available, it can do its write back. All the buffers, registers, and reservation stations whose value of Qj or Qk is the same as the completing reservation station update their values from the CDB and mark the Q fields to indicate that values have been received. Thus, the CDB can broadcast its result to many destinations in a single clock cycle, and if the waiting instructions have their operands, they can all begin execution on the next clock cycle.

To understand the full power of eliminating WAW and WAR hazards through dynamic renaming of registers, we must look at a loop. Consider the following simple sequence for multiplying the elements of a vector by a scalar in F2:

```
Loop:    LD      F0,0(R1)
         MULTD   F4,F0,F2
         SD      0(R1),F4
         SUBI    R1,R1,#8
         BNEZ    R1,Loop    ; branches if R1≠0
```

If we predict that branches are taken, using reservation stations will allow multiple executions of this loop to proceed at once. This advantage is gained without unrolling the loop—in effect, the loop is unrolled dynamically by the hardware. In the 360 architecture, the presence of only 4 FP registers would severely limit the use of unrolling, since we would generate many WAW and WAR hazards. As we saw earlier on page 259, when we unroll a loop and schedule it to avoid interlocks, many more registers are required. Tomasulo's algorithm supports the overlapped execution of multiple copies of the same loop with only a small number of registers used by the program. The reservations stations extend the real register set via the renaming process.

Let's assume we have issued all the instructions in two successive iterations of the loop, but none of the floating-point loads/stores or operations has completed. The reservation stations, register-status tables, and load and store buffers at this point are shown in Figure 5.12. (The integer ALU operation is ignored, and it is assumed the branch was predicted as taken.) Once the system reaches this state, two copies of the loop could be sustained with a CPI close to 1.0 provided the multiplies could complete in four clock cycles. If we ignore the loop overhead, which is not reduced in this scheme, the performance level achieved matches what we would obtain with compiler unrolling and scheduling, assuming we had enough registers.

An additional element that is critical to making Tomasulo's algorithm work is shown in this example. The load instruction from the second loop iteration could easily complete before the store from the first iteration, although the normal sequential order is different. The load and store can safely be done in a different order, provided the load and store access different addresses. This is checked by examining the addresses in the store buffer whenever a load is issued. If the load address matches the store-buffer address, we must stop and wait until the store buffer gets a value; we can then access it or get the value from memory. This dynamic disambiguation of addresses is an alternative to the techniques that a compiler would use when interchanging a load and store.

This dynamic scheme can yield very high performance, provided the cost of branches can be kept small, an issue we address in the next section. The major drawback of this approach is the complexity of the Tomasulo scheme, which requires a large amount of hardware. In particular, there are many associative stores that must run at high speed, as well as complex control logic. Lastly, the performance gain is limited by the single completion bus (CDB). While additional CDBs can be added, each CDB must interact with all the pipeline hardware, including the reservation stations. In particular, the associative tag-matching hardware would need to be duplicated at each station for each CDB.

In Tomasulo's scheme two different techniques are combined: the renaming of registers to a larger virtual set of registers and buffering of source operands from the register file. Source operand buffering resolves WAR hazards that arise when the operand is available in the registers. As we will see later, it is also possible to eliminate WAR hazards by renaming of a register together with buffering of a result until no outstanding references to the earlier version of the register remain; this approach will be used when we discuss hardware speculation.

Tomasulo's scheme is appealing if the designer is forced to pipeline an architecture that is difficult to schedule code for or has a shortage of registers. On the other hand, the advantages of the Tomasulo approach versus compiler scheduling for a efficient single issue pipeline are probably less than the costs of implementation. But, as machines become more aggressive in their issue capability and designers are concerned with the performance of difficult to schedule code (such as most nonnumeric code), techniques such as register renaming and dynamic scheduling will become more important. Later in this chapter, we will see that they are one important component of most schemes for incorporating hardware speculation.

The key components for enhancing ILP in Tomasulo's algorithm are dynamic scheduling, register renaming, and dynamic memory disambiguation. It is difficult to assess the value of these features independently. When we examine the studies of ILP in Section 5.7, we will look at how these features affect the amount of parallelism discovered.

Corresponding to the dynamic hardware techniques for scheduling around data dependences are dynamic techniques for handling branches efficiently. These techniques are used for two purposes: to predict whether a branch will be taken, and to find the target more quickly. *Hardware branch prediction*, the name for these techniques, is the next topic we discuss.

Instruction status				
Instruction	**From iteration**	**Issue**	**Execute**	**Write result**
LD F0,0(R1)	1	√	√	
MULTD F4,F0,F2	1	√		
SD 0(R1),F4	1	√		
LD F0,0(R1)	2	√	√	
MULTD F4,F0,F2	2	√		
SD 0(R1),F4	2	√		

Reservation stations						
Name	**Busy**	**Fm**	**Vj**	**Vk**	**Qj**	**Qk**
Add1	No					
Add2	No					
Add3	No					
Mult1	Yes	MULT		Regs[F2]	Load1	
Mult2	Yes	MULT		Regs[F2]	Load2	

Register status									
Field	**F0**	**F2**	**F4**	**F6**	**F8**	**F10**	**F12**	**...**	**F30**
Qi	Load2		Mult2						

Load buffers			
Field	**Load 1**	**Load 2**	**Load 3**
Address	Regs[R1]	Regs[R1]-8	
Busy	Yes	Yes	No

Store buffers			
Field	**Store 1**	**Store 2**	**Store 3**
Qi	Mult1	Mult2	
Busy	Yes	Yes	No
Address	(Regs[R1]	Regs[R1]-8	

FIGURE 5.12   Two active iterations of the loop with no instruction having yet completed. Load and store buffers are included, with addresses to be loaded from and stored to. The loads are in the load buffer; entries in the multiplier reservation stations indicate that the outstanding loads are the sources. The store buffers indicate that the multiply destination is their value to store.

5.3 | Reducing Branch Penalties with Dynamic Hardware Prediction

The previous section describes techniques for overcoming data hazards. The frequency of branches and jumps demands that we also attack the potential stalls arising from control dependences. Indeed, as the amount of ILP we attempt to exploit grows, control dependences rapidly become the limiting factor. While schemes in this section are helpful in machines that try to maintain one instruction issue per clock, they are *crucial* to any machine that tries to issue more than one instruction per clock for two reasons. First, branches will arrive *n* times faster in an *n* issue machine and providing an instruction stream will probably require that we predict the outcome of branches. Second, the relative impact of the control stalls with the lower ideal CPI of a multiple issue machine will be larger.

In the last chapter, we examined a variety of static schemes for dealing with branches; these schemes are static since the action taken does not depend on the dynamic behavior of the branch. We also examined the delayed branch scheme, which allows software to optimize the branch behavior by scheduling it at compile-time. This section focuses on using hardware to dynamically predict the outcome of a branch—the prediction will change if the branch changes its behavior while the program is running. We start with a simple branch prediction scheme and then examine approaches that increase the accuracy of our branch prediction mechanisms. After that, we look at more elaborate schemes that try to find the instruction following a branch even earlier. The goal of all these mechanisms is to allow the machine to resolve the outcome of a branch early, thus prevent control dependences from causing stalls. The effectiveness of a branch prediction scheme depends not only on the accuracy, but also on the cost of a branch when the prediction is correct and when the prediction is incorrect. These branch penalties depend on the structure of the pipeline, the type of predictor, and the strategies used for recovering from misprediction. Later in this chapter we will look at some typical examples.

Basic Branch Prediction and Branch Prediction Buffers

The simplest dynamic branch-prediction scheme is a *branch-prediction buffer* or *branch history table*. A branch-prediction buffer is a small memory indexed by the lower portion of the address of the branch instruction. The memory contains a bit that says whether the branch was recently taken or not. This is the simplest sort of buffer; it has no tags and is useful only to reduce the branch delay when it is longer than the time to compute the possible target PCs. We don't know, in fact, if the prediction is correct—it may have been put there by another branch that has the same low-order address bits. But this doesn't matter. The prediction is a hint that is assumed to be correct, and fetching begins in the predicted direction. If the hint turns out to be wrong, the prediction bit is inverted. Of course, this buffer is effectively a cache where every access is a hit, and, as we will see, the performance of the buffer depends on both how often the prediction is for the branch of interest and how accurate the prediction is when it matches. We can use all the caching techniques to improve the accuracy of finding the prediction matching this branch, as we will see shortly. Before we do that, it is useful to make a small, but important, improvement in the accuracy of the branch prediction scheme.

This simple one-bit prediction scheme has a performance shortcoming: If a branch is almost always taken, then when it is not taken, we will likely predict incorrectly twice, rather than once, as the following example shows.

Example

Consider a loop branch whose behavior is taken nine times sequentially, then not taken once. What is the prediction accuracy for this branch assuming the prediction bit for this branch remains in the prediction buffer?

Answer

The steady state prediction behavior will be to mispredict on the first and last loop iterations. Mispredicting the last iteration is inevitable since the prediction bit will say taken (the branch has been taken 9 times in a row at that point). The misprediction on the first iteration happens because the bit is flipped on prior execution of the last iteration of the loop, since the branch was not taken on that iteration. Thus, the prediction accuracy for this branch that is taken 90% of the time is only 80% (2 incorrect predictions and 8 correct ones). In general, for branches whose behavior is typical of loops–a branch is taken many times in a row and then not taken once–a one-bit predictor will mispredict at twice that the branch is not taken. Ideally, the accuracy of the predictor would match the taken branch frequency for these highly regular branches.

To remedy this, 2-bit prediction schemes are often used. In a 2-bit scheme, a prediction must miss twice before it is changed. Figure 5.13 shows the finite-state machine for the 2-bit prediction scheme.

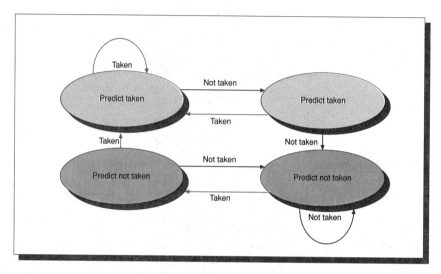

FIGURE 5.13   This shows the states in a 2-bit prediction scheme. By using two bits rather than one, a branch that strongly favors taken or not taken—as many branches do—will be mispredicted only once. The two bits are used to encode the four states in the system.

The 2-bit scheme is actually a specialization of a more general scheme that has an n-bit counter for each entry in the prediction buffer. With an n-bit counter, the counter can take on values between 0 and 2^n-1. The prediction scheme is then:

- If the counter is greater than or equal to 2^{n-1} (the halfway point) then the branch is predicted as taken. If the branch is predicted correct the counter is incremented (unless it has reached its maximum value); if the prediction is incorrect, the counter is decremented.

- If the counter is less than 2^{n-1} (the halfway point) then the branch is predicted as not taken. If the branch is predicted correctly, the counter is decremented (unless it has reached 0); if the prediction is incorrect, the counter is incremented.

Studies of n-bit predictors have shown that the 2-bit predictors do almost as well, and thus most systems rely on 2-bit branch predictors rather than the more general n-bit predictors.

A branch-prediction buffer can be implemented as a small, special "cache" accessed with the instruction address during the IF pipe stage, or as a pair of bits attached to each block in the instruction cache and fetched with the instruction. If the instruction is decoded as a branch and if the branch is predicted as taken, fetching begins from the target as soon as the PC is known. Otherwise, fetching and sequential executing continue. If the prediction turns out to be wrong, the prediction bits are changed as shown in Figure 5.13. While this scheme is useful for most pipelines, the DLX pipeline finds out both whether the branch is taken and what the target of the branch is at roughly the same time assuming there is no a hazard is accessing the register specified in the conditional branch. (Remember that this is true for the DLX pipeline because the branch does a compare of a register against zero during the ID stage which is when the effective address is also computed.) Thus, this scheme does not help for the simple DLX pipeline; we will explore a scheme that can work for DLX a little later. First, let's see how well a prediction buffer works with a longer pipeline.

As we mentioned, the accuracy of a 2-bit prediction scheme is affected by how often the prediction for each branch is correct and by how often the entry in the prediction buffer matches the branch being executed. When the entry does not match, the prediction is used anyway because no better information is available. Even if the entry was for another branch, the guess could be a lucky one. Since on average the number of bits predicting taken will be equal to the taken frequency, we can compute the probability of a lucky guess. Using the branch taken frequency from Chapter 3 for DLX (53% taken), the probability of a correct guess can be computed as follows:

% lucky guess $=$ % predict taken $\times$ % taken + % predict not taken $\times$ % not taken

% lucky guess $= 0.53 \times 0.53 + 0.47 \times 0.47$

% lucky guess $= 0.50 = 50\%$

Example

Assume that the 2-bit prediction scheme has an accuracy of about 90% when the entry in the buffer is the branch entry and assume a hit rate of 90%. If the probability of being lucky is 50%, what is the overall prediction accuracy?

Answer

The overall prediction accuracy is given by

Accuracy = (% predicted correctly $\times$ % matching prediction) +
(% lucky guess) $\times$ (1 – % matching prediction)
Accuracy = (90% $\times$ 90%) + (50% $\times$ 10%) = 86%

What kind of accuracy can be expected from a branch prediction buffer using 2-bits per entry on real applications? For the SPEC-89 benchmarks a branch prediction buffer with 4096 entries results in a prediction accuracy ranging from over 99% to 82%, or a *misprediction rate* of 1% to 18%, as shown in Figure 5.14. To show the differences more clearly, we plot misprediction frequency rather than prediction frequency. A 4K-entry buffer, like that used for these results, is considered very large; smaller buffers would have worse results.

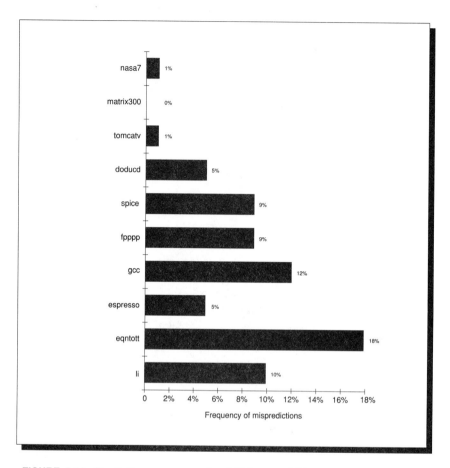

FIGURE 5.14   Prediction accuracy of a 4,096 entry 2-bit prediction buffer for the SPEC89 benchmarks. The misprediction rate for the integer benchmarks (gcc, espresso, eqntott, and li) is substantially higher (average of 11%) than for the FP programs (average of 4%). Even omitting the FP kernels (nasa7, matrix300, and tomcatv) still yields a higher accuracy for the FP benchmarks (than for the integer benchmarks. This data, as well as the rest of the data in this section, is taken from a branch prediction study done using the IBP Power architecture and optimized code for that system.

Knowing just the prediction accuracy, as shown in Figure 5.14, is not enough to determine the performance impact of branches, even given the branch costs and penalties for misprediction. We also need to take into account the branch frequency, since the importance of accurate prediction is larger in programs with higher branch frequency. For example, the integer programs–li, eqntott, espresso, and gcc–have higher branch frequencies than the more easily predicted FP programs.

As we try to exploit more ILP, the accuracy of our branch prediction becomes critical. As we can see in Figure 5.14, the accuracy of the predictors for integer programs, which typically also have higher branch frequencies, is lower than for the loop-intensive scientific programs. We can attack this problem in two ways: by increasing the size of the buffer and by increasing the accuracy of the scheme we use for each prediction. A buffer with 4K entries is already quite large and, as Figure 5.15 shows, performs quite comparably to an infinite buffer. The data in Figure 5.15 make it clear that the hit rate of the buffer is not the limiting factor. As we mentioned above, increasing the number of bits per predictor also has little impact.

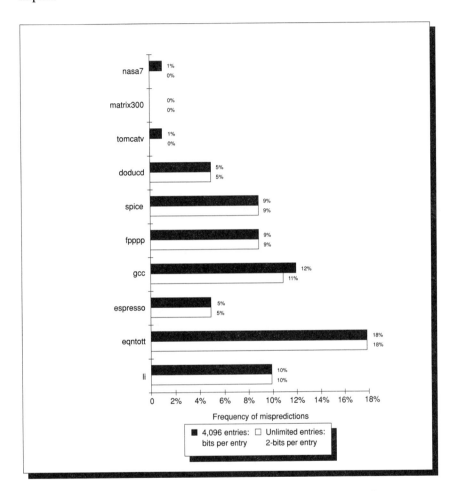

FIGURE 5.15 **Prediction accuracy of a 4,096 entry 2-bit prediction buffer versus an infinite buffer for the SPEC89 benchmarks.**

These 2-bit predictor schemes use the recent behavior of a branch to predict the future behavior of that branch. It may be possible to improve the prediction accuracy, if we also look at the recent behavior of *other* branches rather than just the branch we are trying to predict. Consider a small code fragment from the

SPEC92 benchmark eqntott (the worst case for the 2-bit predictor):

```
if (aa==2)
        aa=0;
if (bb==2)
        bb=0;
if (aa!=bb) {
```

Here is the DLX code that we would typically generate for this code fragment assuming that aa and bb are assigned to registers R1 and R2:

```
        SUBI   R3,R1,#2
        BNEZ   R3,L1      ; branch b1 (aa!=2)
        ADD    R1,R0,R0   ; aa==0
L1:     SUBI   R3,R1,#2
        BNEZ   R3,L2      ;branch b2(bb!=2)
        ADD    R2,R0,R0   ; bb==0
L2:     SUB    R3,R1,R2   ; R3=aa-bb
        BEQZ   R3,L3      ; branch b3 (aa==bb)
```

Let's label these branches b1, b2, and b3. The key observation is that the behavior of branch b3 is correlated with the behavior of branches b1 and b2. Clearly, if branches b1 and b2 are both not taken (i.e., the if-conditions both evaluate to true and aa and bb are both assigned 0), then b3 will be taken, since aa and bb are clearly equal. A predictor that uses only the behavior of a single branch to predict the outcome of that branch can never capture this behavior.

Branch predictors that use the behavior of other branches to make a prediction are called *correlating predictors* or *two-level predictors*. To see how such predictors work, let's choose a simple hypothetical case. Consider the following simplified code fragment (chosen for illustrative purposes):

```
if (d==0)
        d=1;
if (d==1)
```

Here is the typical code sequence generated for this fragment, assuming that d is assigned to R1:

```
        BNEZ   R1,L1      ; branch b1 (d!=0)
        ADDI   R1,R0,#1   ; d==0, so d=1
L1:     SUBI   R3,R1,#1
        BNEZ   R3,L2      ;branch b2(d!=1)
        . . .
```

L2:

The branches corresponding to the two if-statements are labeled b1 and b2. The possible execution sequences for an execution of this fragment, assuming d has values 0, 1, and 2, are:

Initial value of d	d==0 ?	b1	Value of d before b2	d==1 ?	b2
0	yes	not taken	1	yes	not taken
1	no	taken	1	yes	not taken
2	no	taken	2	no	taken

From this table, we see that if b1 is not taken then b2 will be not taken. A correlating predictor can take advantage of this, but our standard predictor cannot. Rather than consider all possible branch paths, consider a sequence where d is 2 on one iteration and 0 on the next. A one-bit predictor initialized to not-taken has the following behavior (T=taken, NT=not taken):

Iteration	b1 prediction	b1 action	new b1 prediction	b2 prediction	b2 action	new b2 prediction
First	NT	T	T	NT	T	T
Second	T	NT	NT	T	NT	NT

In this case, *all* the branches are mispredicted!

Alternatively, consider a predictor that uses one-bit of correlation. The easiest way to think of this is that every branch has two separate prediction bits: one prediction assuming the last branch executed was not taken and another prediction that is used if the last branch executed was taken. Note that, in general, the last branch executed is *not* the same instruction as the branch being predicted, though this can occur in simple loops consisting of a single basic block (since there are no branches in the loops).

We write the pair of prediction bits together with the first bit being the behavior of the last branch executed in the program and the second bit being the predicted behavior of the given branch. The four possible combinations are then:

T/NT means that the prediction is not taken if the last branch executed was taken.

T/T means that the prediction is taken if the last branch executed was taken.

NT/NT means that the prediction is not taken if the last branch executed was not taken.

NT/T means that the prediction is taken if the last branch executed was not taken.

Here is the action of the one-bit predictor with one-bit of correlation, when initialized to NT/NT (the prediction used is in color):

Iteration	b1 prediction	b1 action	new b1 prediction	b2 prediction	b2action	new b2 prediction
First	NT/NT	T	NT/T	T/NT	T	T/T
Second	T/NT	NT	T/NT	NT/NT	NT	NT/NT

In this case, both branches are predicted correctly on the second iteration. The correct prediction of b1 is luck (since b1 is not obviously correlated with the previous prediction of b2), but the correct prediction of b2 shows the advantage of correlating predictors. Even if we had initialized the predictors to taken, the predictor for b2 would correctly predict the case when b1 is not taken, on every execution of b2 after one incorrect prediction.

The predictor is called a (1,1) predictor since it uses the behavior of the last branch to choose from among a pair of 1-bit per branch predictors. In the general case an (m,n) predictor uses the behavior of the last m branches to choose from 2^m branch predictors, each of which is a n-bit predictor for a single branch. The attraction of this type of correlating branch predictor is that it can yield higher prediction rates than the 2-bit scheme and requires only a trivial amount of additional hardware. The simplicity of the hardware comes from a simple observation: the global history of the most recent m branches can be recorded in an m-bit shift register, where each bit records whether the branch was taken or not taken. The branch prediction buffer can then be indexed using a concatenation of the low-order bits from the branch address with the m-bit global history. For example, Figure 5.16 shows a (2,2) predictor and how the prediction is accessed.

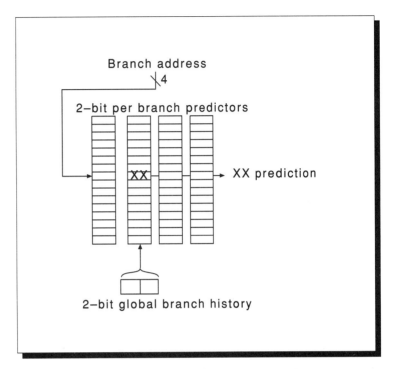

Branch address

2-bit per branch predictors

XX → XX prediction

2-bit global branch history

FIGURE 5.16 A (2,2) branch prediction buffer uses a 2-bit global history to choose from among 4 predictors for each branch address. Each predictor is in turn a 2-bit predictor for that particular branch. The branch prediction buffer shown here has a total of 64 entries; the branch address is used to choose 4 of these entries and the global history is used to choose 1 of the 4. The 2-bit global history can be implemented as a shifter register that simply shifts in the behavior of a branch as soon as it is known.

There is one subtle effect in this implementation: because the prediction buffer is not a cache, the counters indexed by a single value of the global predictor may in fact correspond to different branches at some point in time; this is no different from our earlier observation, that the prediction may not correspond to the current branch. In Figure 5.16 we draw the buffer as a two-dimensional object to ease understanding. In reality, the buffer can simply be implemented as a linear memory array that is 2-bits wide; the indexing is done by concatenating the global history bits and the number of required bits from the branch address. For the example in Figure 5.16, a (2,2) buffer with 64 total entries, the four low order address bits of the branch (word address) and the two global bits form a 6-bit index that can be used to index the 64 counters.

How much better do the correlating branch predictors work compared to the standard 2-bit scheme? To compare them fairly, we must compare predictors that use the same number of state bits. The number of bits in a (m,n) predictor is

$2^m \times n \times$ number of prediction entries selected by the branch address

Example

A two bit predictor with no global history is simply a (0,2) predictor.
How many bits are in the branch (0,2) branch predictor, we examined earlier?
How many bits are in the branch predictor shown in Figure 5.16?

Answer

The earlier predictor had 4K entries selected by the branch address. Thus the total number of bits is

$$2^0 \times 2 \times 4K = 8K.$$

The predictor in Figure 5.16 has

$$2^2 \times 2 \times 16 = 128 \text{ bits.}$$

To compare the performance of a correlating predictor with our simple 2-bit predictor, whose performance we examined in Figure 5.14, we need to determine how many entries we should assume for the correlating predictor.

Example

How many branch-selected entries are in a (2,2) predictor that has a total of 8K bits in the prediction buffer?

Answer

We know that

$$2^2 \times 2 \times \text{number of prediction entries selected by the branch} = 8K$$

Hence

Number of prediction entries selected by the branch $= 8K$

Figure 5.17 compares the performance of the earlier 2-bit simple predictor with 4K entries and a (2,2) predictor with 1K entries. As you can see, this predictor not only outperforms a simple 2-bit predictor with the same total number of state bits, it often outperforms a 2-bit predictor with an unlimited number of entries. There are a wide spectrum of correlating predictors with the (0,2) and (2,2) predictors being among the most interesting. The exercises ask you to explore the performance of a third extreme: a predictor that does not rely on the branch address. For example, (12,2) predictor that has a total of 8K bits does not use the branch address in indexing the predictor, but instead relies solely on the global branch history. Surprisingly, this degenerate case can outperform a non correlating 2-bit predictor, if enough global history is used and the table is large enough!

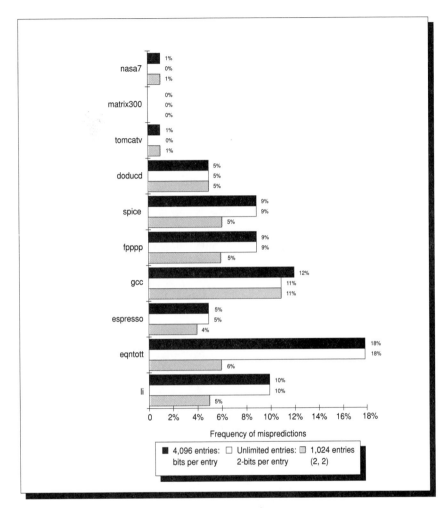

FIGURE 5.17   Comparison of a 2-bit predictors. A non correlating predictor for 4,096 bits is first, followed by a non correlating 2-bit predictor with unlimited entries, and lastly, a 2-bit predictor with 2-bits of global history and a total of 1,024 entries.

Further Reducing Control Stalls: Branch Target Buffers

To reduce the branch penalty on DLX, we need to know from what address to fetch by the end of IF. This means we must know whether the as-yet-undecoded instruction is a branch and, if so, what the next PC should be. If the instruction is a branch and we know what the next PC should be, we can have a branch penalty of zero. A branch-prediction cache that stores the predicted address for the next instruction after a branch is called a *branch-target buffer*.

For the standard DLX pipeline, a branch prediction buffer would be accessed during the ID cycle, so that at the end of ID we know the branch target address (since it is computed during ID), the fall through address (computed during IF), and the prediction. Thus, by the end of ID we know enough to fetch the next predicted instruction. For a branch target buffer, we access the buffer during the IF stage using the instruction address of a possible branch to index the buffer. If we get a hit, then we know the predicted instruction address at the end of the IF cycle, which is one cycle earlier than for a branch prediction buffer.

Because we are predicting the next instruction address and will send it out **before** decoding the instruction, we **must** know whether the fetched instruction is predicted as a taken branch. We also want to know whether the address in the target buffer is for a taken or not-taken prediction, so that we can reduce the time to find a mispredicted branch. Figure 5.18 shows what the branch-target buffer looks like. If the PC of the fetched instruction matches a PC in the buffer, then the corresponding predicted PC is used as the next PC. In Chapter 6 we will discuss caches in much more detail; we will see that the hardware for this branch-target buffer is essentially identical to the hardware for a cache.

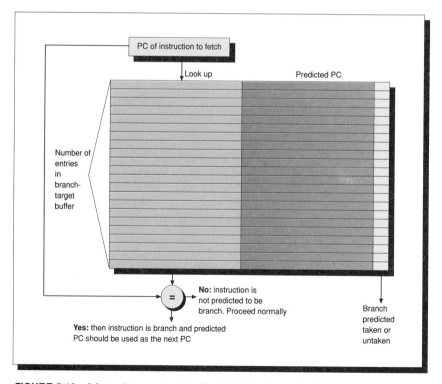

FIGURE 5.18   A branch-target buffer. The PC of the instruction being fetched is matched against a set of instruction addresses stored in the first column; these represent the addresses of known branches. If the PC matches one of these entries, then the instruction being fetched is a branch. If it is a branch, then the second field, predicted PC, contains the prediction for the next PC after the branch. Fetching begins immediately at that address. The third field just tracks whether the branch was predicted taken or untaken and helps keep the misprediction penalty small. *This figure can be made smaller, by removing some of the middle.*

If a matching entry is found in the branch-target buffer, fetching begins immediately at the predicted PC. Note that (unlike a branch-prediction buffer) the entry must be for this instruction, because the predicted PC will be sent out before it is known whether this instruction is even a branch. If we did not check whether the entry matched this PC, then the wrong PC would be sent out for instructions that were not branches, resulting in a slower machine. In the simplest case both predicted-taken and predicted-untaken branches are stored in the branch target buffer, but it is possible to store only predicted-taken branches, since an untaken branch follows the same strategy (fetch the next sequential instruction) as a non-branch. Complications arise when we are using a two-bit predictor since this requires that we store information for both taken and untaken branches. This alternative is explored further in the exercises.

Figure 5.19 shows the steps followed when using a branch-target buffer and when these steps occur in the pipeline. From this we can see that there will be no branch delay if a branch-prediction entry is found in the buffer and is correct. Otherwise, there will be a penalty of at least one clock cycle. In practice, there could be a penalty of two clock cycles because the branch target buffer must be updated. We could assume that the instruction following a branch or at the branch target is not a branch, and do the update during that instruction time. However, this does complicate the control. Instead, we will take a two-clock-cycle penalty when the branch is not correctly predicted or when we get a miss in the buffer. Dealing with the mispredictions and misses is a significant challenge, since we typically will have to halt instruction fetch while we rewrite the buffer entry. Thus, we would like to make this process fast to minimize the penalty.

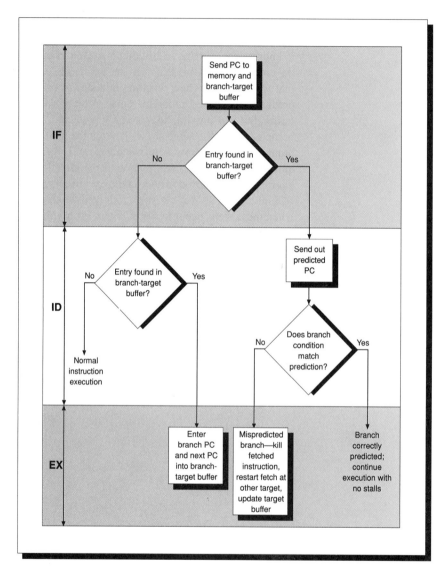

FIGURE 5.19   The steps involved in handling an instruction with a branch-target buffer. If the PC of an instruction is found in the buffer, then the instruction must be a branch, and fetching immediately begins from the predicted PC in ID. If the entry is not found and it subsequently turns out to be a branch, it is entered in the buffer along with the target, which is known at the end of ID. If the instruction is a branch, is found, and is correctly predicted, then execution proceeds with no delays. If the prediction is incorrect, we suffer a one-clock-cycle delay fetching the wrong instruction and restart the fetch one clock cycle later. If the branch is not found in the buffer and the instruction turns out to be a branch, we will have proceeded as if the instruction were a branch and can turn this into an assume-not-taken strategy; the penalty will differ depending on whether the branch is actually taken or not.

To evaluate how well a branch-target buffer works, we first must determine what the penalties are in all possible cases. Figure 5.20 contains this information.

Instruction in buffer	Prediction	Actual branch	Penalty cycles
Yes	Taken	Taken	0
Yes	Taken	Not taken	2
Yes	Not taken	Not taken	0
Yes	Not taken	Taken	2
No		Taken	2
No		Not taken	1

FIGURE 5.20 Penalties for all possible combinations of whether the branch is in the buffer, how it is predicted, and what it actually does. There is no branch penalty if everything is correctly predicted and the branch is found in the target buffer. If the branch is not correctly predicted, the penalty is equal to one clock cycle to update the buffer with the correct information (during which an instruction cannot be fetched) and one clock cycle, if needed, to restart fetching the next correct instruction for the branch. If the branch is not found and not taken, the penalty is only one clock cycle because the pipeline assumes not taken when it is not aware that the instruction is a branch. Other mismatches cost two clock cycles, since we must restart the fetch and update the buffer.

Example

Determine the total branch penalty for a branch target buffer assuming the penalty cycles for individual cases from Figure 5.20. Make the same assumptions about prediction accuracy and hit rate that we did when evaluating a branch prediction buffer in the example on page 283.

Answer

The assumptions we used in the earlier example were:

- prediction accuracy is 90%,

- hit rate in the buffer is 90%

Using a 60% taken branch frequency, yields the following:

Branch penalty = % buffer hit rate × % incorrect predictions × 2
             + (1 − % buffer hit rate × taken branches × 2
             + (1 − % buffer hit rate × untaken branches × 1

Branch penalty = (90% × 10% × 2)
             + (10% × 60% × 2)
             + (10% × 40% × 1)

Branch penalty = 0.18 + 0.12 + 0.04 = 0.34 clock cycles

This compares with a branch penalty for delayed branches, which we evaluated in Section 4.4[3] of the last chapter, of about 0.5 clock cycles per branch. Remember, though, that the improvement from dynamic branch prediction will grow as the branch delay grows; in addition, better predictors will yield a larger performance advantage.

One variation on the branch target buffer is to store one or more *target instructions*, instead of, or in addition to the predicted *target address*. This variation has two potential advantages. First, it allows the branch target buffer access to take longer than the time between successive instruction fetches. This could allow a larger branch target buffer. Second, buffering the actual target instructions allows us to perform an optimization called *branch folding*. Branch folding can be used to obtain zero-cycle unconditional branches, and sometimes zero-cycle conditional branches. Consider a branch target buffer that buffers instructions from the predicted path and is being accessed with the address of an unconditional branch. The only function of the unconditional branch is to change the PC. Thus, when the branch target buffer signals a hit and indicates that the branch is unconditional, the pipeline can simply substitute the instruction from the branch target buffer in place of the instruction that is returned from the cache (which is the unconditional branch). In some cases, it may be possible to eliminate the cost of a conditional branch, when the condition codes are preset; we will see how this scheme can be used in the IBM Power-2 machine in the Putting It All Together Section.

Another method that designers have studied and will probably include in future machines is a technique for predicting indirect jumps, that is, jumps whose destination address varies at run-time. While high-level-language programs will generate such jumps for indirect procedure calls, select or case statements and Fortran computed gotos, the vast majority of the indirect jumps come from procedure returns. For example, for the SPEC benchmarks procedure returns account for 85% of the indirect jumps on average. Thus, focusing on procedure returns seems appropriate.

Though procedure returns can be predicted with a branch target buffer, the accuracy of such a prediction technique can be low if the procedure is called from multiple sites and the calls from one site are not clustered in time. To overcome this problem, the concept of a small buffer of return addresses operating as a stack has been proposed. This structure caches the most recent return addresses: pushing a return addresses on the stack at a call and popping one off at a return. If the cache is sufficiently large (i.e., as large as the maximum call depth), it will predict the returns perfectly. Figure 5.21 shows the performance of such a return buffer with 1-16 elements for a number of the SPEC benchmarks. We will use this type of return predictor when we examine the studies of ILP in Section 5.7.

---

3.   this is to the section that used to be in chapter 6 and was 6.4.

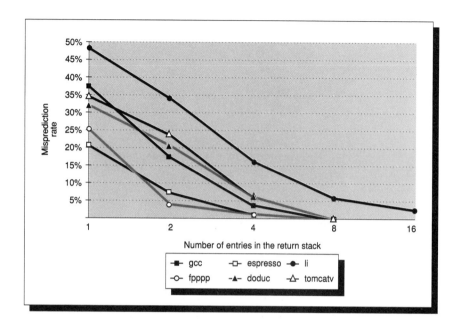

FIGURE 5.21 Prediction accuracy for a return address buffer operated as a stack.
The accuracy is the fraction of return addresses predicted correctly. Since call depths are typically not large, with some exceptions, a modest buffer works well. On average returns account for 81% of the indirect jumps in these six benchmarks.

Branch-prediction schemes are limited both by prediction accuracy and by the penalty for misprediction. As we have seen, typical prediction schemes achieve prediction accuracy in the range of 80-95% depending on the type of program and the size of the buffer. In addition to trying to increase the accuracy of the predictor, we can try to reduce the penalty for misprediction. This is done by fetching from both the predicted and unpredicted direction. This requires that the memory system be dual ported, have an interleaved cache, or fetch from one path and then the other (as we will see the IBM Power-2 does). While this adds cost to the system, it may be the only way to reduce branch penalties below a certain point. Another alternative that some machines have used is to cache addresses or instructions from multiple paths in the target buffer.

We have seen a variety of software-based static schemes and hardware-based dynamic schemes for trying to boost the performance of our pipelined machine. These schemes attack both the data dependences (the previous sections) and the control dependences (this section). Our focus to date has been on sustaining the throughput of the pipeline at one instruction per clock. In the next section we will look at techniques that attempt to exploit more parallelism by issuing multiple instructions in a clock cycle.

5.4 Taking Advantage of More ILP with Multiple Issue

Machines are being produced with the potential for very many parallel operations on the instruction level...Far greater extremes in instruction level parallelism are on the horizon.

> J. Fisher (1981) This paper describing trace scheduling
> is the first to use the term "instruction level parallelism."

The techniques of the previous two sections can be used to eliminate data and control stalls and achieve an ideal CPI of 1. To improve performance further we would like to decrease the CPI to less than one. But the CPI cannot be reduced below one if we issue only one instruction every clock cycle. The goal of the *multiple issue machines* discussed in this section is to allow multiple instructions to issue in a clock cycle. Multiple issue machines come in two flavors: *superscalar* machines and *VLIW* (Very Long Instruction Word) machines. Superscalar machines issue varying numbers of instructions per clock and may be either statically scheduled by the compiler or dynamically scheduled using techniques based on scoreboarding and Tomasulo's algorithm. In this section, we examine simple versions of both a statically scheduled superscalar and a dynamically scheduled superscalar. VLIWs, in contrast, issue a fixed number of instructions formatted either as one large instruction or as a fixed instruction packet. VLIW machines are inherently statically scheduled by the compiler. Section 5.5 explores compiler technology useful for scheduling both VLIWs and superscalars.

To explain and compare the techniques in this section we will assume the pipeline latencies we used earlier in Section 5.1 (Figure 5.2) and the same example code segment, which adds a scalar to a vector in memory:

```
Loop:   LD      F0,0(R1)    ;F0=vector element
        ADDD    F4,F0,F2    ;add scalar in F2
        SD      0(R1),F4    ;store result
        SUBI    R1,R1,#8    ;decrement pointer
                            ;8 bytes (per DW)
        BNEZ    R1,LOOP     ; branch R1!=zero
```

We begin by looking at a simple superscalar machine.

A Superscalar Version of DLX

Machines that issue a variable number of instructions per clock cycle are called *superscalar machines*. In a typical superscalar machine, the hardware might issue from 1 to 8 instructions in a clock cycle. Usually, these instructions must be independent and will have to satisfy some constraints, such as no more than one memory reference issued per clock. If some instruction in the instruction stream is dependent or doesn't meet the issue criteria, only the instructions preceding that one in sequence will be issued, hence the variability in issue rate. In contrast, in VLIWs, the compiler has complete responsibility for creating a package of instructions that can be simultaneously issued, and the hardware does not dynamically make any decisions about multiple issue.

What would the DLX machine look like as a superscalar? Let's assume two instructions can be issued per clock cycle. One of the instructions can be a load, store, branch, or integer ALU operation, and the other can be any floating-point operation. As we will see, issue of an integer operation in parallel with a floating-point operation is much simpler and less demanding than arbitrary dual issue. This configuration is, in fact, very close to the organization used in the HP 7100 processor.

Issuing two instructions per cycle will require fetching and decoding 64 bits of instructions. To keep the decoding simple, we could require that the instructions be paired and aligned on a 64-bit boundary, with the integer portion appearing first. The alternative is to examine the instructions and possibly swap them when they are sent to the integer or FP datapath; however, this introduces additional requirements for hazard detection. In either case, the second instruction can be issued only if the first instruction can be issued. Remember that the hardware makes this decision dynamically, issuing only the first instruction if the conditions are not met. Figure 5.22 shows how the instructions look as they go into the pipeline in pairs. This table does not address how the floating-point operations extend the EX cycle, but it is no different in the superscalar case than it was for the ordinary DLX pipeline; the concepts of Section 3.Y[4] apply directly.

With this pipeline, we have substantially boosted the rate at which we can issue floating-point instructions. To make this worthwhile, however, we need either pipelined floating-point units or multiple independent units. Otherwise, the floating-point datapath will quickly become the bottleneck, and the advantages gained by dual issue will be small

---

4.   cross reference to section in chapter 3, concerning multicyclle and FP pipelining

Instruction type	Pipe	Stages						
Integer instruction	IF	ID	EX	MEM	WB			
FP instruction	IF	ID	EX	MEM	WB			
Integer instruction		IF	ID	EX	MEM	WB		
FP instruction		IF	ID	EX	MEM	WB		
Integer instruction			IF	ID	EX	MEM	WB	
FP instruction			IF	ID	EX	MEM	WB	
Integer instruction				IF	ID	EX	MEM	WB
FP instruction				IF	ID	EX	MEM	WB

FIGURE 5.22   Superscalar pipeline in operation. The integer and floating-point instructions are issued at the same time, and each executes at its own pace through the pipeline. This scheme will only improve the performance of programs with a fair fraction of floating point operations.

By issuing an integer and a floating-point operation in parallel, the need for additional hardware, beyond the usual hazard detection logic, is minimized—integer and floating-point operations use different register sets and different functional units on load/store architectures. Furthermore, enforcing the issue restriction as a structural hazard (which it is since only specific pairs of instructions can issue), requires only looking at the opcodes. The only difficulties that arise are when the integer instruction is a floating-point load, store, or move. This creates contention for the floating-point register ports and may also create a new RAW hazard when the floating-point operation that could be issued in the same clock cycle, is dependent on the first instruction of the pair.

The register port problem could be solved by requiring the FP loads and stores issue by themselves, which treats the case of an FP load, store, or move that is paired with an FP operation as a structural hazard. This is easy to implement, but has substantial performance drawbacks. This hazard could instead be eliminated by providing two additional ports, a read and a write, on the floating-point register file.

When the fetched instruction pair consists of an FP load and an FP operation that is dependent on it, we must detect the hazard and avoid issuing the FP operation. Except for this case, other possible hazards are essentially the same as for our single-issue pipeline. We will, however, need some additional bypass paths to prevent unnecessary stalls.

There is another difficulty that may limit the effectiveness of a superscalar pipeline. In our simple DLX pipeline, loads had a latency of one clock cycle, which prevented one instruction from using the result without stalling. In the superscalar pipeline, the result of a load instruction cannot be used on the *same* clock cycle or on the *next* clock cycle. This means that the next three instructions cannot use the load result without stalling. The branch delay also becomes three instructions, since a branch must be the first instruction of a pair. To effectively exploit the parallelism available in a superscalar machine, more ambitious compiler or hardware scheduling techniques, as well as more complex instruction decoding, will need to be implemented. Let's examine how compiler scheduling works before looking at hardware techniques.

Let's see how well loop unrolling and scheduling work on a superscalar version of DLX with the delays in clock cycles from Figure 5.2 on page 256.

Example

Below is the loop we unrolled and scheduled earlier in Section 5.1. How would it be scheduled on a superscalar pipeline for DLX?

```
Loop:    LD      F0,0(R1)      ;F0=vector element
         ADDD    F4,F0,F2      ;add scalar in F2
         SD      0(R1),F4      ;store result
         SUBI    R1,R1,#8      ;decrement pointer
                               ;8 bytes (per DW)
         BNEZ    R1,Loop       ; branch R1!=zero
```

Answer

To schedule it without any delays, we will need to unroll it to make five copies of the body. After unrolling the loop will contain five of each of LD, ADDD and SD, and one SUBI and one BNEZ. The unrolled and scheduled code is shown in Figure 5.23.

	Integer instruction		FP instruction	Clock cycle
Loop:	LD	F0,0(R1)		1
	LD	F6,-8(R1)		2
	LD	F10,-16(R1)	ADDD F4,F0,F2	3
	LD	F14,-24(R1)	ADDD F8,F6,F2	4
	LD	F18,-32(R1)	ADDD F12,F10,F2	5
	SD	0(R1),F4	ADDD F16,F14,F2	6
	SD	-8(R1),F8	ADDD F20,F18,F2	7
	SD	-16(R1),F12		8
	SD	-24(R1),F16		9
	SUBI	R1,R1,#40		10
	BNEZ	R1,LOOP		11
	SD	-32(R1),F20		12

FIGURE 5.23 The unrolled and scheduled code as it would look on a superscalar DLX.

This unrolled superscalar loop now runs in 12 clock cycles per iteration, or 2.4 clock cycles per element, versus 3.5 for the scheduled and unrolled loop on the ordinary DLX pipeline. In this example, the performance of the superscalar DLX is limited by the balance between integer and floating-point computation. Every floating-point instruction is issued together with an integer instruction, but there are not enough floating-point instructions to keep the floating-point pipeline full. When scheduled, the original loop ran in 6 clock cycles per iteration. We have improved on that by a factor of 2.5, but more than half of which came from loop unrolling, which took us from 6 to 3.5 (a factor of 1.7), while superscalar execution gave us a factor of 1.5 improvement.

Ideally, our superscalar machine will pick up two instructions and issue them both if the first is an integer and the second is a floating-point instruction. If they do not fit this pattern, which can be quickly detected, then they are issued sequentially. This points to two of the major advantages of a superscalar machine, compared to a VLIW machine. First, there is little impact on code density, since the machine detects whether the next instruction can issue, and we do not need to lay out the instructions to match the issue capability. Second, even unscheduled programs, or those compiled for older implementations, can be run. Of course, such programs may not run well; one way to overcome this is to use dynamic scheduling.

Multiple Instruction Issue with Dynamic Scheduling

Multiple instruction issue can also be applied to dynamically scheduled machines. We could start with either the scoreboard scheme or Tomasulo's algorithm. Let's assume we want to extend Tomasulo's algorithm to support issuing two instructions per clock cycle, one integer and one floating point. We do not want to issue instructions to the reservation stations out of order, since this makes the bookkeeping extremely complex. Rather, by employing separate data structures for the integer and floating-point registers, we can simultaneously issue a floating-point instruction and an integer instruction to their respective reservation stations, as long as the two issued instructions do not access the same register set.

Unfortunately, this approach bars issuing two instructions with a dependence in the same clock cycle, such as a floating point load (an integer instruction) and a floating point add. Of course, we cannot execute these two instructions in the same clock, but we would like to issue them to the reservations stations where they will later be serialized. In the superscalar machine of the previous section, the compiler is responsible for finding independent instructions to issue. If a hardware scheduling scheme cannot find a way to issue two dependent instructions in the same clock, there will be little advantage to a hardware scheduled scheme versus a compiler based scheme.

Luckily, there are two approaches that can be used to achieve dual issue. The first is to pipeline the instruction-issue stage so that it runs twice as fast as the basic clock rate. This permits updating the tables before processing the next instruction; then the two instructions can begin execution on the same clock cycle.

The second approach is based on the observation that with the issue restrictions assumed, it will only be FP loads and moves from the GP to the FP registers that will create dependences among instructions that we can issue together. To see why this is true, remember that we can only issue two instructions together if the first is an integer instruction and the second is an FP instruction. The FP instruction could only depend on the integer instruction, if the integer instruction set an FP register that was used by the FP instruction. The only integer instructions that cam set an FP register are FP loads and moves to the FP registers. If we had a more complex set of issue capabilities, there would be additional possible dependences that we would need to handle. In this approach, the dependences are issued constraints are examined in parallel.

The need for reservation tables for loads and moves can be eliminated by using queues for the result of a load or a move. Queues can also be used to allow stores to issue early and wait for their operands, just as did in Tomasulo's algorithm. Since dynamic scheduling is most effective for data moves, while static scheduling is highly effective in register–register code sequences, we could use static scheduling to eliminate reservation stations completely and rely only on the queues for loads and stores. This style of machine organization has been called a *decoupled architecture*. The Power-2 machine, which we discuss in Section 5.8, uses queues for loads and stores so as to decouple the integer unit, which operates in-order, from the FP unit, which allows out-of-order execution.

A machine that dynamically schedules loads and stores may cause loads and stores to be reordered. This may result in violating a data dependence through memory, and thus requires some detection hardware for this potential hazard. We can detect such hazards with the same scheme we used for the single-issue version of Tomasulo's algorithm: we dynamically check whether the memory source address specified by a load is the same as the target address of an outstanding, uncompleted store. If there is such a match, we can stall the load instruction until the store completes. Since the address of the store has already been computed and resides in the store buffer, we can use an associative check (possibly with only a subset of the address bits), to determine whether a load conflicts with a store in the buffer. There is also the possibility of WAW and WAR hazards through memory, which must be prevented, although they are much less likely than a true data dependence. In contrast to the dynamic techniques for detecting memory dependences, the next section discusses compiler-based approaches.

For simplicity, let us assume that we have pipelined the instruction issue logic so that we can issue two operations that are dependent but use different functional units, assuming the integer instruction appears first and the FP instruction second. Let's see how this would work with the same code sequence we used earlier.

Example

Consider the execution of our simple loop on a DLX pipeline extended with Tomasulo's algorithm and with multiple issue. Assume that both a floating-point and an integer operation can be issued on every clock cycle, even if they are related, provided the integer instruction is the first instruction. The number of cycles of latency per instruction is the same. Assume that issue and write results take one cycle each, and that there is dynamic branch-prediction hardware. Create a table showing when each instruction issues, begins execution, and writes its result, for the first two iterations of the loop. Here is the original loop:

```
Loop:      LD    F0,0(R1)
           ADDD  F4,F0,F2
           SD    0(R1),F4
           SUBI  R1,R1,#8
           BNEZ  R1,LOOP
```

Answer

The loop will be dynamically unwound and, whenever possible, instructions will be issued in pairs. The result is shown in Figure 5.24. The loop runs in $4 + \dfrac{7}{n}$ clock cycles per result for n iterations. For large n this approaches 4 clock cycles per result.

Iteration number	Instructions	Issues at clock-cycle number	Executes at clock-cycle number	Writes result at clock-cycle number
1	LD F0,0(R1)	1	2	4
1	ADDD F4,F0,F2	1	5	8
1	SD 0(R1),F4	2	9	
1	SUBI R1,R1,#8	3	4	5
1	BNEZ R1,LOOP	4	5	
2	LD F0,0(R1)	5	6	8
2	ADDD F4,F0,F2	5	9	12
2	SD 0(R1),F4	6	13	
2	SUBI R1,R1,#8	7	8	9
2	BNEZ R1,LOOP	8	9	

FIGURE 5.24   The time of issue, execution, and writing result for a dual-issue version of our Tomasulo pipeline. The write-result stage does not apply to either stores or branches, since they do not write any registers.

The number of dual issues is small because there is only one floating-point operation per iteration. The relative number of dual-issued instructions would be helped by the compiler partially unwinding the loop to reduce the instruction count by eliminating loop overhead. With that transformation, the loop would run as fast as on a superscalar machine. We will return to this transformation in the exercises. Alternatively, if the machine was "wider", that is could issue more integer operations per cycle, larger improvements would be possible.

The VLIW Approach

With a VLIW we can reduce the amount of hardware needed to implement a multiple issue machine., and the potential savings in hardware increases as we increase the issue width. For example, our two-issue superscalar machine requires that we examine the opcodes of two instructions, the six register specifiers, and that we dynamically determine whether one or two instructions can issue and dispatch them to the appropriate functional units. While the hardware required for a two issue machine is modest and we could extend the mechanisms to handle three or four instructions (or more if the issue restrictions were chosen carefully), it becomes increasingly difficult to determine whether a significant number of instructions can all issue simultaneously without knowing both the order of the instructions before they are fetched and also what dependencies might exist among them.

An alternative is an LIW (*Long Instruction Word*) or VLIW (*Very Long Instruction Word*) architecture. VLIWs use multiple, independent functional units. Rather than attempting to issue multiple, independent instructions to the units, a VLIW packages the multiple operations into one very long instruction, hence the name. Since the burden for choosing the instructions to be issued simultaneously falls on the compiler, the hardware needed in a superscalar to make these issue decisions in unneeded. Since this advantage of a VLIW increases as the maximum issue rte grows, we focus on a wider issue machine.

A VLIW instruction might include two integer operations, two floating-point operations, two memory references, and a branch. An instruction would have a set of fields for each functional unit—perhaps 16 to 24 bits per unit, yielding an instruction length of between 112 and 168 bits. To keep the functional units busy there must be enough parallelism in a straight-line code sequence to fill the available operation slots. This parallelism is uncovered by unrolling loops and scheduling code across basic blocks using a global scheduling technique. In addition to eliminating branches by unrolling loops, global scheduling techniques allow the movement of instructions across branch points. In the next section, we will discuss *trace scheduling*, one of these techniques developed specifically for VLIWs; the references also provide pointers to other approaches. For now, let's assume we have a technique to generate long, straight-line code sequences for building up VLIW instructions and examine how well these machines operate.

Example

Suppose we have a VLIW that could issue two memory references, two FP operations, and one integer operation or branch in every clock cycle. Show an unrolled version of the vector sum loop for such a machine. Unroll as many times as necessary to eliminate any stalls. Ignore the branch-delay slot.

Answer

The code is shown in Figure 5.25. The loop has been unrolled to make seven copies of the body, which eliminates all stalls (i.e., completely empty issue cycles), and runs in 9 cycles. This yields a running rate of 7 results in 9 cycles, or 1.28 cycles per result.

Memory reference 1	Memory reference 2	FP operation 1	FP operation 2	Integer operation / branch
LD F0,0(R1)	LD F6,-8(R1)			
LD F10,-16(R1)	LD F14,-24(R1)			
LD F18,-32(R1)	LD F22,-40(R1)	ADDD F4,F0,F2	ADDD F8,F6,F2	
LD F26,-48(R1)		ADDD F12,F10,F2	ADDD F16,F14,F2	
		ADDD F20,F18,F2	ADDD F24,F22,F2	
SD 0(R1),F4	SD -8(R1),F8	ADDD F28,F26,F2		
SD -16(R1),F12	SD -24(R1),F16			
SD -32(R1),F20	SD -40(R1),F24			SUBI R1,R1,#48
SD -0(R1),F28				BNEZ R1,LOOP

FIGURE 5.25   VLIW instructions; that occupy the inner loop and replace the unrolled sequence. This code takes nine cycles assuming no branch delay; normally the branch would also be scheduled. The issue rate is 23 operations in 9 clock cycles, or 2.5 operations per cycle. The efficiency, the percentage of available slots that contained an operation, is about 60%. To achieve this issue rate requires a larger number of registers than DLX would normally use in this loop. The VLIW code sequence above requires at least 8 FP registers, while the same code sequence for the base DLX machine can use as little as 2 FP registers or as many as 5 when unrolled and scheduled; in the superscalar example in Figure 5.23, 6 registers were needed.

Limitations in Multiple Issue Machines

What are the limitations of a multiple issue approach? If we can issue 5 operations per clock cycle, why not 50? The difficulty in expanding the issue rate comes from three areas:

1. inherent limitations in ILP,

2. difficulties in building the underlying hardware, and

3. limitations specific to either a superscalar or VLIW implementation.

Limits on available ILP are the simplest and most fundamental. For example, in a statically scheduled machine, unless loops are unrolled very large numbers of times, there may not be enough operations to fill the available instruction issue slots. At first glance, it might appear that 5 instructions that could execute in parallel would be sufficient to keep our example VLIW completely busy. This, however, is not the case. Several of these functional units—the memory, the branch, and the floating-point units—will be pipelined and have a multicycle latency, requiring a larger number of operations that can execute in parallel to prevent stalls. For example, if the floating-point pipeline has a latency of five clocks, and we want to schedule the FP pipeline without stalling there must be eight FP operations that are independent of the most recently issued FP operation. In general, we need to find a number of independent operations roughly equal to the average pipeline depth times the number of functional units. This means that roughly 15 to 20 operations could be needed to keep a multiple issue machine with 5 functional units busy.

The second cost, the hardware resources for a multiple issue machine, arises from the hardware needed both to issue and to execute multiple instructions per cycle. The hardware for executing multiple operations per cycle seems quite straightforward: duplicating the floating-point and integer functional units is easy and cost scales linearly. However, there is a large increase in the memory- and register-file bandwidth. For example, even with a split floating-point and integer register file, our VLIW machine will require 7 read ports and 3 write ports on the integer register file and 5 read ports and 3 write ports on the floating-point register file. This bandwidth cannot be supported without an increase in the silicon area of the register file and possible degradation of clock speed. Our 5-unit VLIW also has 2 data memory ports, which are substantially more expensive than register ports. If we wanted to expand the number of issues further, we would need to continue adding memory ports. Adding only arithmetic units would not help, since the machine would be starved for memory bandwidth. As the number of data memory ports grows, so does the complexity of the memory system. To allow multiple memory accesses in parallel, we could break the memory into banks containing different addresses with the hope that the operations in a single instruction do not have conflicting accesses, or the memory may be truly dual ported, which is substantially more expensive. Yet another approach is used in the IBM Power-2 design: the memory is accessed twice per clock cycle, but even with an aggressive memory system, this approach may be too slow for a high speed machine. These memory system alternatives are discussed in more detail in the next chapter. The complexity and access time penalties of a multiported memory hierarchy are probably the most serious hardware limitations faced by any type of multiple issue machine, whether VLIW or superscalar.

The hardware needed to support instruction issue varies significantly depending on the multiple issue approach. At one end of the spectrum are the dynamically scheduled superscalar machines that have a substantial amount of hardware involved in implementing either scoreboarding or Tomasulo's algorithm. In addition to the silicon that such mechanisms consume, dynamic scheduling substantially complicates the design making it more difficult to achieve high clock rates, as well as significantly increasing the task of verifying the design. At the other end of the spectrum are VLIWs, which require little or no additional hardware for instruction issue and scheduling, since that function is handled completely by the compiler. Between these two extremes lie most existing superscalar machines, which use a combination of static scheduling by the compiler with the hardware making the decision of how many of the next n instructions to issue. Depending on what restrictions are made on the order of instructions and what types of dependences must be detected among the issue candidates, statically scheduled superscalars will have issue logic either closer to that of a VLIW or more like that of a dynamically scheduled machine. Much of the challenge in designing multiple issue machines lies in assessing the costs and performance advantages of a wide spectrum of possible hardware mechanisms versus the compiler-driven alternatives.

Finally, there are problems that are specific to either the superscalar or VLIW model. We have already discussed the major challenge for a superscalar machine, namely the instruction issue logic. For the VLIW model, there are both technical one logistical problems. The technical problems are the increase in code size and the limitations of lock-step operation. There are two different elements that combine to increase code size substantially for a VLIW. First, generating enough operations in a straight-line code fragment requires ambitiously unrolling loops, which increases code size. Second, whenever instructions are not full, the unused functional units translate to wasted bits in the instruction encoding. In Figure 5.25, we saw that only about 60% of the functional units were used; almost half of each instruction was empty. To combat this problem, clever encodings are sometimes used. For example, there may be only one large immediate field for use by any functional unit. Another technique is to compress the instructions in main memory and expand them when they are read into the cache or are decoded. Because a VLIW is statically scheduled and operates lock-step, a stall in any functional unit pipeline must cause the entire machine to stall, since all the functional units must be kept synchronized. While we may be able to schedule the deterministic functional units so as not to stall, predicting which data accesses will encounter a cache stall and scheduling them is very difficult. Hence, a cache miss must cause the entire machine to stall. As the issue rate and number of memory references becomes large, this lock-step structure makes it difficult to use a data cache, thereby increasing memory complexity and latency.

Binary code compatibility is the major logistical problem for VLIWs. In a VLIW, different number of issues and functional unit latencies require different versions of the code. Thus, migrating between successive implementations is more difficult than it may be for a superscalar design. Of course, obtaining improved performance from a new superscalar design may require recompilation. Nonetheless, the ability to run old binary files is a practical advantage for the superscalar approach. One possible solution to this problem, and the problem of binary code compatibility in general, is object-code translation or emulation. This technology is developing quickly and could play a significant role in future migration schemes.

The major challenge for all multiple issue machines is to try to exploit large amounts of ILP. When the parallelism comes from unrolling simple loops in FP programs, the original loop probably could have been run efficiently on a vector machine (described in Appendix ???[5]). It is not clear that a multiple issue machine is preferred over a vector machine for such applications; the costs are similar, and the vector machine is typically the same speed or faster. The potential advantages of a multiple issue machine versus a vector machine are two-fold. First, the potential to extract some amount of parallelism from less regularly structured code, and, second, the ability to use a less expensive memory system. For these reasons it appears clear that multiple issue approaches will be the primary method for taking advantage of instruction-level parallelism and vectors will primarily be an extension to the these machines.

5.5 | Compiler Support for Exploiting ILP

In this section we discuss compiler technology for increasing the amount of parallelism that we can exploit in a program. We begin by examining techniques to detect dependences and to eliminate name dependences.

Detecting and Eliminating Dependences

Finding the data dependences in a program is an important part of three tasks: (1) good scheduling of code, (2) determining which loops might contain parallelism, and (3) eliminating name dependences. The complexity of dependence analysis arises because of the presence of arrays (and pointers in languages like C). Since scalar variable references explicitly refer to a name, they can usually be analyzed quite easily, with aliasing due to pointers and reference parameters causing some complications and uncertainty in the analysis.

---

5.   vector appendix

Our analysis needs to find all dependences and determine whether there is a cycle in the dependences, since that is what prevents us from running the loop in parallel. Consider the following example:

```
for (i=1;i<=100;i=i+1) {
      A[i] = B[i] + C[i]
      D[i] = A[i] * E[i]
}
```

Because the dependence involving A is not loop-carried, we can unroll the loop and find parallelism; we just cannot interchange the two references to A. If a loop has loop-carried dependences, but no circular dependences (recall the example in Section 5.1), we can transform the loop to eliminate the dependence and then unrolling will uncover parallelism. In many parallel loops, the amount of parallelism is limited only by the number of unrollings, which is limited only by the number of loop iterations. Of course, in practice, to take advantage of that much parallelism would require many functional units and an enormous number of registers. The absence of a loop-carried dependence simply tells us that we have a large amount of parallelism available.

The code fragment above also illustrates another opportunity for improvement. The second reference to A need not be translated to a load instruction, since we know that the value is computed and stored by the previous statement; hence, the second reference to A can simply be a reference to the register into which A was computed. Performing this optimization requires knowing that the two references are always to the same memory address and that there are no intervening access to the same location. Normally data dependence analysis only tells that one reference *may* depend on another; a more complex analysis is required to determine that two references *must be* to the exact same address. In the example, above a simple version of this analysis suffices, since the two references are in the same basic block.

Often loop-carried dependences are in the form of a *recurrence*:

```
for (i=2;i<=100,i=i+1) {
      Y[i] = Y[i-1] + Y[i];
}
```

Detecting a recurrence can be important for two reasons: some architectures (especially vector machines) have special support for executing recurrences, and some recurrences can be the source of a reasonable amount of parallelism. To see how the latter can be true, consider this loop:

```
for (i=6;i<=100;i=i+1) {
      Y[i] = Y[i-5] + Y[i];
}
```

On the iteration j, the loop references element j–5. The loop is said to have a dependence of *distance* 5. The previous loop had a dependence distance of 1. The larger the distance the more potential parallelism that can be obtained by unrolling the loop. For example, if we unroll the first loop, with a dependence distance of 1, successive statements are dependent on one another; there is still some parallelism among the individual instructions, but not much. If we unroll the loop that has a dependence distance of 5, there is a sequence of five instructions that have no dependences, and thus much more ILP. Although many loops with loop-carried dependences have a dependence distance of 1, cases with larger distances do arise, and the longer distance may well provide enough parallelism to keep a machine busy.

How does the compiler detect dependences in general? Nearly all dependence analysis algorithms work on the assumption that array references are *affine*. In simplest terms, a one-dimensional array index is affine if it can be written in the form: $a \times i + b$, where a and b are constants, and i is the loop index variable. The index of a multidimensional array is affine if the index in each dimension is affine.

Determining whether there is a dependence between two references to the same array in a loop is thus equivalent to determining whether two affine functions can have the same value for different indices between the bounds of the loop. For example, suppose we have stored to an array element with index value $a \times i + b$, and loaded from the same array with index value $c \times i + d$, where i is the for-loop index variable that runs from m to n. A dependence exists if two conditions hold:

1. There are two iteration indices, j and k, both within the limits of the for loop. That is $m \leq j, k \leq n$.

2. The loop stores into an array element indexed by $a \times j + b$ and later fetches from that **same** array element when it is indexed by $c \times k + d$. That is, $a \times j + b = c \times k + d$.

In general, we cannot determine whether a dependence exists at compile time. For example, the values of a, b, c, and d may not be known (they could be values in other arrays), making it impossible to tell if a dependence exists. In other cases, the dependence testing may be very expensive but decidable at compile-time. For example, the accesses may depend on the iteration indices of multiply nested loops. Many programs, however, contain primarily simple indices where a, b, c, and d are all constants. For these cases, it is possible to devise reasonable tests for dependence.

As an example, a simple and sufficient test for the absence of a dependence is the *greatest common divisor*, or GCD test. It is based on the observation that if a loop-carried dependence exists, then GCD (c,a) must **divide** $(d–b)$. (Remember that an integer, x, *divides* another integer, y, if there is no remainder when we do the division $\frac{y}{x}$ and get an integer quotient.) The GCD test is sufficient to guarantee that no dependence exists (as you can show in the exercises); however, there are cases where the GCD test succeeds, but no dependence exists. This can arise, for example, because the GCD test does not take the loop bounds into account.

Example

Use the GCD test to determine whether dependences exist in the following loop:

```
for (i=1; i<=100; i=i+1) {
        X[2*i+3] = X[2*i] * 5.0;
        }
```

Answer

Given the values $a=2$, $b=3$, $c=2$, and $d=0$, then $GCD(a,c) = 2$, and $d-b = -3$. Since 2 does not divide -3, no dependence is possible.

In general, determining whether a dependence actually exists is NP-complete. In practice, however, many common cases can be analyzed precisely at low cost. Recently, approaches using a hierarchy of exact tests increasing in generality and cost, have been shown to be both accurate and efficient. (A test is exact if it precisely determines whether a dependence exists. Although the general case is NP-complete, there exist exact tests for restricted situations that are much cheaper.)

In addition to detecting the presence of a dependence, a compiler wants to classify the types of dependence. This allows a compiler to recognize name dependences and eliminate them at compile-time by renaming and copying.

Example

The following loop has multiple types of dependences. Find all the true dependences, output dependences, and antidependences, and eliminate the output dependences and antidependences by renaming.

```
for (i=1; i<=100; i=i+1) {
        Y[i] = X[i] / c; /*S1*/
        X[i] = X[i] + c; /*S2*/
        Z[i] = Y[i] + c; /*S3*/
        Y[i] = c - Y[i]; /*S4*/
        }
```

Answer

The following dependences exist among the four statements:

1. There are true dependences from S1 to S3 and from S1 to S4 because of Y[i]. These are not loop carried, so they do not prevent the loop from being considered parallel. These dependences will force S3 and S4 to wait for S1 to complete.

2. There is an antidependence from S1 to S2.

3. There is an output dependence from S1 to S4.

The following version of the loop eliminates these false (or pseudo) dependences.

```
for (i=1; i=i+1; i<=100) {
        /* Y renamed to T to remove
           output dependence*/
        T[i] = X[i] / c ;
        /* X renamed to X1 to remove
           antidependence*/
        X1[i] = X[i] + c;
        Z[i] = T[i] + c;
        Y[i] = c - T[i];
}
```

After the loop the variable X has been renamed X1. In code that follows the loop, the compiler can simply replace the name X by X1. In this case, renaming does not require an actual copy operation but can be done by substituting names or by register allocation. In other cases, however, renaming will require copying.

Dependence analysis is a critical technology for exploiting parallelism. At the instruction level it provides information needed to interchange memory references when scheduling, as well as to determine the benefits of unrolling a loop. For detecting loop level parallelism, dependence analysis is the basic tool. Effectively compiling programs to either vector machines or multiprocessors depends critically on this analysis. In addition, it is useful in scheduling instructions to determine whether memory references are potentially dependent. The major drawback of dependence analysis is that it applies only under a limited set of circumstances, namely among references within a single loop nest and using affine index functions. Thus, there are a wide variety of situations in which dependence analysis cannot tell us what we might want to know, including:

- when objects are referenced via pointers rather than array indices,

- when array indexing is indirect through another array, which happens with many representations of sparse arrays,

- a dependence may exist for some value of the inputs, but does not exist in actuality when the code is run since the inputs never take on certain values,

- when an optimization depends on knowing more than just the possibility of a dependence, but needs to know on which write a read of a variable depends.

The rapid progress in dependence analysis algorithms has led us to a situation where we are often limited by the lack of applicability of the analysis rather than a shortcoming in dependence analysis per se.

Software Pipelining: Symbolic Loop Unrolling

We have already seen that one compiler technique, loop unrolling, is useful to uncover parallelism among instructions, by creating longer sequences of straight-line code. There are two other important techniques that have been developed for this purpose: software pipelining and trace scheduling.

Software pipelining is a technique for reorganizing loops such that each iteration in the software-pipelined code is made from instructions chosen from different iterations of the original loop. This is most easily understood by looking at the scheduled code for the superscalar version of DLX, which appeared in Figure 5.23 on page 303. The scheduler essentially interleaves instructions from different loop iterations, so as to separate the dependent instructions that occur within a single loop iteration. A software-pipelined loop interleaves instructions from different iterations without unrolling the loop, as illustrated in Figure 5.26. This technique is the software counterpart to what Tomasulo's algorithm does in hardware. The software-pipelined loop for the earlier example would contain one load, one add, and one store, each from a different iteration. There is also some startup code that is needed before the loop begins as well as code to finish-up after the loop is completed. We will ignore these in this discussion, for simplicity; the topic is addressed in the exercises.

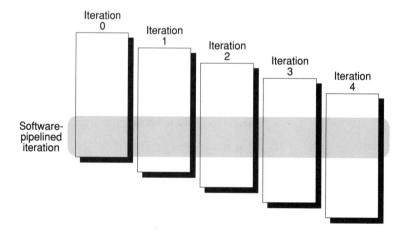

FIGURE 5.26   A software-pipelined loop chooses consists on instructions from different loop iterations, thus separating the dependent instructions with one iteration of the original loop. The start-up and finish-up code will correspond to the portions above and below the software pipelined iteration.

Example

Show a software-pipelined version of this loop, which increments all the elements of an array whose starting address is in R1 by the contents of F2:

```
Loop:      LD    F0,0(R1)
           ADDD  F4,F0,F2
           SD    0(R1),F4
           SUBI  R1,R1,#8
           BNEZ  R1,LOOP
```

You may omit the start-up and clean-up code.

Answer

Ignoring the start-up and finishing code, we have:

```
Loop:      SD    0(R1),F4      ;stores into M[i]
           ADDD  F4,F0,F2      ;adds to M[i-1]
           LD    F0,-16(R1)    ;loads M[i-2]
           BNEZ  R1,LOOP
           SUBI  R1,R1,#8      ;sub in delay slot
```

This loop can be run at a rate of 5 cycles per result, ignoring the start-up and clean-up portions. Because the load fetches two array elements beyond the element count, the loop should run for two fewer iterations. This would be accomplished by decrementing R1 by 16 prior to the loop. Notice that the reuse of registers (e.g. F4, F0, and R1) requires the hardware to avoid generating WAR hazards and stalling the loop. This should not be a problem in this case, since no data dependent stalls should occur.

Register management in software pipelined loops can be tricky. The example above is not too hard since the registers that are written on one loop iteration are read on the next. In other cases, we may need to increase the number of iterations between when we issue an instruction and when the result is used. This occurs when there are a small number of instructions in the loop body and the latencies are large. In such cases, a combination of software pipelining and loop unrolling are needed. An example of this is shown in the exercises.

Software pipelining can be thought of as symbolic loop unrolling. Indeed, some of the algorithms for software pipelining use loop unrolling to figure out how to software pipeline the loop. The major advantage of software pipelining over straight loop unrolling is that software pipelining consumes less code space. Software pipelining and loop unrolling, in addition to yielding a better scheduled inner loop, each reduce a different type of overhead. Loop unrolling reduces the overhead of the loop—the branch and counter-update code. Software pipelining reduces the time when the loop is not running at peak speed to once per loop at the beginning and end. If we unroll a loop that does 100 iterations a constant number of times, say 4, we pay the overhead 100/4 = 25 times—every time the inner unrolled loop is initiated. Figure 5.27 shows this behavior graphically. Because these techniques attack two different types of overhead, the best performance can come from doing both.

The other technique used to generate additional parallelism is *trace scheduling*. Trace scheduling extends loop unrolling with a technique for finding parallelism across conditional branches other than loop branches. Trace scheduling is useful for machines with very large number of issues per clock where loop unrolling may not be sufficient by itself to uncover enough ILP to keep the machine busy. Trace scheduling is a combination of two separate processes. The first process, called *trace selection*, tries to find a likely sequence of basic blocks whose operations will be put together into a smaller number of instructions; this sequence is called a *trace*. Loop unrolling is used to generate long traces, since loop branches are taken with high probability. Additionally, by using static branch prediction, other conditional branches are also chosen as taken or not taken, so that the resultant trace is a straightline sequence resulting from concatenating many basic blocks. Once a trace is selected, the second process, called *trace compaction*, tries to squeeze the trace into a small number of wide instructions. Trace compaction attempts to move operations as early as it can in a sequence (trace), packing the operations into as few wide instructions (or issue packets) as possible.

Trace compaction is global code scheduling. There are two different limitations, which arise in any global code scheduling scheme, that must be handled: data dependences, which force a partial order on operations, and branch points, which create places across which code cannot be easily moved. In essence, the code wants to be compacted into the shortest possible sequence that preserves the data and control dependences. Data dependences are overcome by unrolling and using dependence analysis to determine if two references refer to the same address. Control dependences are also reduced by unrolling. The major advantage of trace scheduling over simpler pipeline-scheduling techniques is that it provides a scheme for reducing the effect of control dependences by moving code across conditional nonloop branches using the predicted behavior of the branch. Figure 5.28 shows a code fragment, which may be thought of as an iteration of an unrolled loop, and the trace selected.

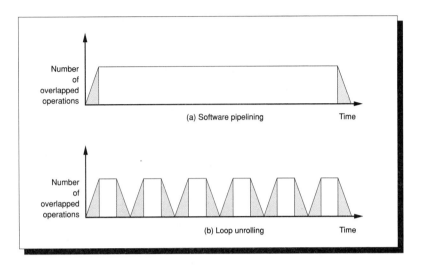

FIGURE 5.27 **This shows the execution pattern for (a) a software-pipelined loop and (b) an unrolled loop.** The shaded areas are the times when the loop is not running with maximum overlap or parallelism among instructions. This occurs once at loop beginning and once at the end for the software-pipelined loop. For the unrolled loop it occurs $\frac{m}{n}$ times if the loop has a total of m iterations and is unrolled n times. Each block represents an unroll of n iterations. Increasing the number of unrollings will reduce the start-up and clean-up overhead. *Note: edit the figure to shorten the width of the rectangle in the top figure to about 2/3 of its current length.*

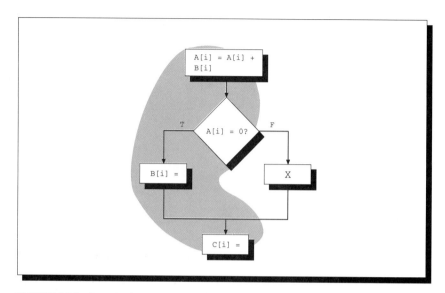

FIGURE 5.28   A code fragment and the trace selected shaded with gray. This trace would be selected first, if the probability of the true branch being taken were much higher than the probability of the false branch being taken. The branch from the decision (A[i]=0) to X is a branch out of the trace, and the branch from X to the assignment to C is a branch into the trace. These branches are what make compacting the trace difficult. *Note: in the top box the text must appear on one line: OK to widen box to do this (A[i]=A[i]+B[i] should be ONE line.*

Once the trace is selected as shown in Figure 5.28, it must be compacted so as to fill the machine's resources. Compacting the trace involves moving the assignments to variables B and C up to the block before the branch decision. Any global scheduling scheme, including trace scheduling, performs such movement under a set of constraints. In trace scheduling, branches are viewed as jumps into or out of the selected trace, which is assumed to the most probable path. When code is moved across such trace entry and exit points, additional bookkeeping code may be needed on the entry or exit point. The key assumption is that the selected trace is the most probable event, otherwise, the cost of the bookkeeping code may be excessive.

What is involved in moving the assignments to B and C? The computation of and assignment to B is control dependent on the branch, while the computation of C is not. Moving these statements can only be done if they either do not change the control and data dependences or if the effect of the change is not visible and thus does not affect program execution. To see what's involved, let's look at a typical code generation sequence for the flow chart in Figure 5.28. Assuming that the addresses forA, B, C are in R1, R2, and R3, respectively, here is such a sequence:

```
        LW     R4,0(R1)    ;load A[i]
        ADDI   R4,R4,...   ; Add to A[i]
        SW     0(R1),R4    ; Store A[i]
        ...
        BNEZ   R4,elsepart ; Test A[i]
        ...                ; then part
        SW     0(R2),...   ; Stores to B[i]
        j      join        ; jump over else
elsepart: ...              ; else part
        X                  ; code for X
        ...
join:   ...                ; after if
        SW     0(R3),...   ; store C[i]
```

Let's first consider the problem of moving the assignment to B to before the BNEZ instruction. Since B is control dependent on that branch before it is moved but not after, we must ensure the execution of the statement cannot cause any exception, since that exception would not have been raised in the original program if the else part of the statement were selected. The movement of B must also not affect the data flow. To define the requirements clearly, we need the concept of a *live* variable;. A variable, Z, is live at a statement if there is an execution path from that statement to a use of Z without an intervening assignment to Z. Intuitively, a variable is live at a statement if inserting an assignment to that variable at the statement could change the semantics of the program.

Returning to our example, there are two possible ways that moving B could change the data flow in this program:

1. B is referenced in the code for X (the else part) before it is assigned.

2. B is live at the end of the if-statement and is not assigned to within X.

In both cases moving the assignment to B will cause some instruction, *i*, (either in X or later in the program) to become data dependent on the moved version of instructions rather than on an earlier assignment to B that occurs before the loop and on which *i* originally depended. Since this would change the result of the program, B cannot be moved if either of the above conditions is true. One could imagine more clever schemes: for example, in the first case, we could make a shadow copy of B before the if-statement and use that shadow copy in X. Such schemes are generally not used, both because they are complex to implement and because they will slow down the program if the trace selected is not optimal and the operations end up requiring additional instructions to execute.

To move the assignment to C up to before the first branch requires that it be moved over the join point of the else case into the trace (a trace entry). This makes the instructions for C control dependent on the branch and means that they will not execute if the else path , which is not on the trace, is chosen. Hence, instructions that were data dependent on the assignment to C, and which execute after this code fragment, will be affected. To ensure the correct value is computed for such instructions, a copy is made of the instructions that compute and assign to C on the branch into the trace, that is, at the end of X on the else path. We can move C from the then-case of the branch across the branch condition, if it does not affect any data flow into the branch condition. If C is moved to before the if-test, the copy of C in the else branch can be eliminated.

Loop unrolling, trace scheduling, and software pipelining all aim at trying to increase the amount of ILP that can be exploited by a machine issuing more than one instruction on every clock cycle. The effectiveness of each of these techniques and their suitability for various architectural approaches are among the hottest topics being actively pursued by researchers and designers of high speed processors.

5.6 | Hardware Support for Extracting More Parallelism

Techniques such as loop unrolling and trace scheduling can be used to increase the amount of parallelism available when the behavior of branches is fairly predictable at compile-time. When the behavior of branches is not well known, compiler techniques alone may not be able to uncover much ILP. This section introduces two techniques that can help overcome such limitations. The first is an extension of the instruction set to include *predicated* or *conditional instructions*. Such instructions can be used to eliminate branches and to assist in allowing the compiler to move instructions past branches. As we will see, predicated or conditional instructions enhance the amount of ILP, but still have significant limitations. To exploit more parallelism, designers have explored an idea called *speculation*, which allows the execution of an instruction before the processor knows that the instruction should execute (i.e. it avoids control dependence stalls). Other techniques, proposed, but not in use, are discussed in the historical perspectives.

Predicated or Conditional Instructions

The concept behind predicated instructions is quite simple: an instruction refers to a condition, which is evaluated as part of the instruction execution. If the condition is true, the instruction is executed normally; if the condition is false, the execution continues as if the instruction was a no-op. Many newer architectures include some form of conditional instructions. The most common example of such an instruction is conditional move, which moves a value from one register to another if the condition is true. Such an instruction can be used to completely eliminate the branch in simple code sequences.

Example

Answer

Consider the following code:

```
if (A=0) {S=T;};
```

Assuming that registers R1, R2, and R3 hold the values of A, S, and T, respectively, show the code for this statement with the branch and with the conditional move.

The straightforward code using a branch for this statement is:

```
        BEQZ   R1,L
        MOV    R2,R3
    L:
```

Using a conditional move that performs the move only if the third operand is equal zero, we can implement this statement in one instruction:

```
        CMOVZ R2,R3,R1
```

The predicated instruction allows us to convert the control dependence present in the branch-based code sequence to a data dependence. (This transformation is also used for vector machines, where it is called *if-conversion*.) For a pipelined machine, this moves the place where the dependence must be resolved from near the front of the pipeline, where it is resolved for branches, to the end of the pipeline where the register write occurs.

One use for conditional move is to implement the absolute value function: A = abs (B), which is implemented as if (B<0) {A=-B) else {A=B}. This if-statement can be implemented as a pair of conditional moves, or as one unconditional move (A=B) and one conditional move (A=–B).

Predicated instructions can also be used to improve scheduling in superscalar or VLIW processors. Here is an example code sequence for a two-issue superscalar that can issue a combination of one memory reference and one ALU operation, or a branch by itself, every cycle:

```
        LW R1,40(R2)          add  R3,R4,R5
                              add  R6,R3,R7

        BEQZ  R10,L
        LW    R8,20(R10)
        LW    R9,0(R8)
```

This sequence wastes a memory operation slot in the second cycle and will incur a data dependence stall if the branch is not taken, since the secondLW after the branch depends on the prior load. If a conditional version ofLW is available, then the LW immediately following the branch (LW R8,20(R10)) can be moved up to the second issue slot. This improves the execution time by several cycles since it eliminates one instruction issue slot and reduces the pipeline stall for the last instruction in the sequence.

To use a conditional instruction successfully in examples like this, the instruction semantics must define the instruction to have no effect if the condition is not satisfied. This means that the instruction cannot write the result destination nor cause any exceptions if the condition is not satisfied. The property of not causing exceptions is quite critical, as the example above shows: if register R10 contains zero, the instruction LW R8,20(R10) executed unconditionally is likely to cause a protection exception, and this exception should not occur. It is this property that prevents a compiler from simply moving the load of R8 across the branch. Of course, if the condition is satisfied, the LW may still cause an exception (e.g., a page fault), and the hardware must take the exception when it knows that the controlling condition is true.

Conditional instructions are certainly helpful for implementing short alternative control flows. Nonetheless, the usefulness of conditional instructions is significantly limited by several factors:

- Conditional instructions that are annulled (i.e. whose conditions are false) still take execution time. Therefore, moving an instruction across a branch and making it conditional will slow the program down whenever the moved instruction would not have been normally executed. An important exception to this occurs when the cycles used by the moved instruction when it is not performed, would have been idle anyway (as in the superscalar example above). Moving an instruction across a branch is essentially speculating on the outcome of the branch. Conditional instructions make this easier but do not eliminate the execution time taken by an incorrect guess.

- Conditional instructions are most useful when the condition can be evaluated early. If the condition and branch cannot be separated (because of data dependences in determining the condition), then a conditional instruction will help less, though it may still be useful since it delays the point when the condition must be known till nearer the end of the pipeline.

- The use of conditional instructions is limited when the control flow involves more than a simple alternative sequence. For example, moving an instruction across multiple branches requires making it conditional on both branches, which requires two conditions to be specified, an unlikely capability, or requires additional instructions to compute the "and" of the conditions.

- Conditional instructions may have some speed penalty compared to unconditional instructions. This may show up as a higher cycle count for such instructions or a slower clock rate overall. If conditional instructions are more expensive they will need to be used judiciously.

For these reasons, many architectures have included a few simple conditional instructions (with conditional move being the most frequent), but few architectures include conditional versions for the majority of the instructions. Figure 5.29 shows the conditional operations available in a variety of recent architectures.

Alpha	HP PA	MIPS	Power PC	SPARC
Conditional move	Any register-register instruction can nullify the following instruction, making it conditional.	Conditional move	Conditional move	Conditional move

FIGURE 5.29 Conditional instructions available in five different RISC architectures. Unless stated otherwise the conditional move is available for both integer and FP registers with the condition being specified in the same manner as for a conditional branch instruction.

Speculation

Hardware supported speculation allows an instruction to execute before a branch on which that instruction depends has been resolved. This reduces the penalties that arise from enforcing the control dependences of the program. To understand why speculation is useful, consider the following simple code segment that traverses a linked list and increments each element in the list:

```
for (p=head; p <> nil; *p=*p.next) {
        *p.value = *p.value+1;
}
```

Unlike the for-loops we encountered in the earlier section, unrolling this loop will not increase the amount of ILP available. Instead, each unrolled iteration will contain an if-statement and loop exit. Here is the DLX code for the loop, assuming the value of head is in R4, which is used to hold p, and that each list entry consists of the value field followed by the link. The test has been placed at the bottom so that there is only one branch per loop iteration.

```
              J       looptest
    start:    LW      R5,0(R4)
              ADDI    R5,R5,#1
              SW      0(R4),R5
              LW      R4,4(R4)
    looptest: BNEZ R4,start
```

We can see that loop unrolling does not help, by looking at the loop unrolled once:

```
                    J       looptest
          start:    LW      R5, 0(R4)
                    ADDI    R5,R5,#1
                    SW      0(R4),R5
                    LW      R4,4(R4)
                    BEQZ    R4, end
                    LW      R5, 0(R4)
                    ADDI    R5,R5,#1
                    SW      0(R4),R5
                    LW      R4,4(R4)
          looptest: BNEZ    R4
          end:
```

Even with branch prediction we cannot overlap instructions from two different loop iterations, and conditional instructions won't help much either. There are several difficulties in extracting parallelism in the unrolled loop:

- The first instruction in the loop iteration (LW R5, 0(R4)) is control dependent on both branches. Thus, the instruction cannot execute successfully (and safely) until we know the branch outcomes.

- The second and third instructions in a loop iteration are data dependent on the first instruction of the loop.

- The fourth instruction in each loop iteration (LW R4,4(R4)) is control dependent on both branches and antidependent on theSW immediately preceding.

- The last instruction of the loop iteration depends on the fourth.

Together these conditions mean that we cannot overlap any instructions between successive loop iterations! There is a small opportunity for overlap by register renaming either in hardware or in software when the loop is unrolled, so that the second load is no longer antidependent on theSW and can be moved earlier.

Alternatively, by speculating that the branch will not be taken we can try to overlap successive loop iterations. Indeed, this is exactly what a trace scheduling compiler does. When the branches are predictable at compile-time and the compiler can find instructions that it can safely move past branch points, a compiler based solution is ideal. These two conditions are the key limitations on exploiting ILP statically with the compiler. Consider the unrolled loop above. The branch is simply not very predictable, since the frequency with which it is taken depends on the length of the list being traversed. In addition, we cannot safely move the load instructions across the branch, since if the contents of R4 are nil, then the load word instruction that uses R4 as the base register is guaranteed to fail and will typically generate a protection exception. Many systems make the value nil point to an unusable page and then trap the access; while this is a good general scheme for detecting nil pointers, it is not much help here, since we may regularly trigger this exception and the cost of the exception plus undoing the speculation will be large.

To overcome these difficulties a machine can include hardware support for speculation. This technique allows the machine to execute an instruction that may be control dependent and to avoid any consequences of the instruction (including exceptions) if it should not have been taken. Thus speculation, like conditional instructions, overcomes the two difficulties that can arise when executing instructions early: the possibility of an exception and the undesired state change caused by the instruction. In addition, speculation can execute an instruction before the branch *condition* is evaluated, which is not true for a conditional instruction. Of course, supporting speculation in hardware is complex and requires substantial hardware resources.

One approach that has been well explored in a variety of research projects and is in use in varying degrees in machines that have been or are being designed is to combine dynamic scheduling with speculation. The 360/91 did this to a certain extent since it could use branch prediction to fetch instructions and assign them to reservation stations. Speculation involves going further and actually executing the instructions as well as executing other instructions dependent on the speculated instructions. Just as with Tomasulo's algorithm, we explain hardware speculation in the context of the floating point unit, but the ideas are easily applicable to the integer unit.

The hardware that implements Tomasulo's algorithm can be extended to support speculation. To do so, we must separate the bypassing of results among instructions, which is needed to execute an instruction speculatively, from the actual completion of an instruction. By making this separation, we can allow an instruction to execute and to bypass its results to other instructions, without allowing the instruction to perform any updates that cannot be undone, until we know that the instruction is no longer speculative. Using the bypass is like performing a speculative register read, since we do not know whether that instruction providing the source register value is providing the correct result until the instruction is no longer speculative. When an instruction is no longer speculative, we allow it to update the register file or memory; we call this additional step in the instruction execution sequence *instruction commit*.

The key idea behind implementing speculation is to allow instructions to execute out-of-order but to force them to commit *in order* and to prevent any irrevocable action (such as updating state or taking an exception) until an instruction commits. In the simple single-issue DLX pipeline we could ensure that instructions committed in order and only after any exceptions for that instruction had been detected simply by moving writes to the end of the pipeline. When we add speculation, we need to separate the process of instruction commit, since it may occur much later than in the DLX pipeline. Adding this commit phase to the instruction execution sequence requires some changes to the sequence as well as an additional set of hardware buffers that hold the results of instructions that have finished execution but have not committed. This hardware buffer, which we call the *reorder buffer*, is also used to pass results among instructions that may be speculated.

The reorder buffer provides additional virtual registers in the same way as the reservations stations in Tomasulo's algorithm extend the register set. The reorder buffer holds the result of an instruction between the time the operation associated with the instruction completes and the time the instruction commits. Hence, the reorder buffer is a source of operands for instructions, just as the reservation stations provide operands in Tomasulo's algorithm. The key difference is that in Tomasulo's algorithm, once an instruction writes its result, any subsequently issued instructions will find the result in the register file. With speculation, the register file is not updated until the instruction commits (and we know definitively that the instruction should execute); thus, the reorder buffer supplies operands in the interval between completion of execution and instruction commit. The reorder buffer is not unlike the store buffer in Tomasulo's algorithm and we integrate the function of the store buffer into the reorder buffer for simplicity. Since the reorder buffer is responsible for holding results until they are stored into the registers, it also replaces the function of the load buffers.

Each entry in the reorder buffer contains three fields: the instruction type, the destination field, and the value field. The instruction type field indicates whether the instruction is a branch (and has no destination result), a store (which has a memory address destination), or a register operation (ALU operation or load, which have register destinations). The destination field supplies the register number (for loads and ALU operations) or the memory address (for stores), where the instruction result should be written. The value field is used to hold the value of the instruction result until the instruction commits. Figure 5.30 shows the hardware structure of the machine including the reorder buffer. The reorder buffer completely replaces the load and store buffers. Although the renaming function of the reservation stations is replaced by the reorder buffer, we still need a place to buffer operations (and operands) between the time they issue and when they begin execution and this function is still provided by the reservation stations. Since every instruction has a position in the reorder buffer until it commits (and the results are posted to the register file), we tag a result using the reorder buffer entry number rather than using the reservation station number. This requires that the reorder buffer assigned for an instruction must be tracked in the reservation stations.

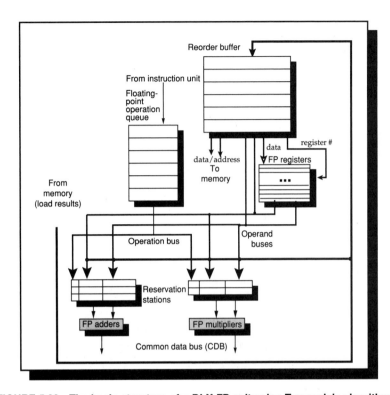

FIGURE 5.30 The basic structure of a DLX FP unit using Tomasulo's algorithm and extended to handle speculation. Comparing this to Figure 5.8 which implemented Tomasulo's algorithm, the major changes are the addition of the reorder buffer and the elimination of the load and store buffers (their functions are subsumed by the reorder buffer). This mechanism can be extended to multiple issue by making the CDB (Common Data Bus) wider to allow for multiple completions per clock.

Here are the four steps involved in instruction execution:

1. Issue—Get an instruction from the floating-point operation queue. Issue the instruction if there is an empty reservation station and an empty slot in the reorder buffer; send the operands to the reservation station if they are in the registers or the reorder buffer; and update the control entries to indicate the buffers are in use. The number of the reorder buffer allocated for the result is also sent to the reservation station, so that the number can be used to tag the result when it is placed on the CDB. If either all reservations are full or the reorder buffer is full then instruction issue is stalled until both have available entries.

2. Execute—If one or more of the operands is not yet available, monitor the CDB (Common Data Bus) while waiting for the register to be computed. This

step checks for RAW hazards. When both operands are available at a reservation station, execute the operation.

3. Write result—When the result is available, write it on the CDB (with the reorder buffer tag sent when the instruction issued) and from the CDB into the reorder buffer as well as to any reservation stations waiting for this result. (It is also possible to read results from the reorder buffer, rather than from the CDB, just as the scoreboard read results from the registers rather than from a completion bus. The tradeoffs are similar to those that exist in a central scoreboard scheme versus a broadcast scheme using a CDB.) Mark the reservation station as available.

4. Commit–When an instruction reaches the head of the reorder buffer and its result is present in the buffer, update the register with the result (or perform a memory write if the operation is a store) and remove the instruction from the reorder buffer.

Once an instruction commits, its entry in the reorder buffer is reclaimed and the register or memory destination is updated, eliminating the need for the reorder buffer entry. To avoid changing the reorder buffer numbers as instructions commit, we implement the reorder buffer as a circular queue, so that positions in the reorder buffer change only when an instruction is committed. If the reorder buffer fills, we simply stop issuing instructions until an entry is made free. Now, let's examine how this scheme would work with the same example we used for Tomasulo's algorithm.

Example   Assume the same latencies for the floating-point functional units as in earlier examples: Add is 2 clock cycles, multiply is 10 clock cycles, and divide is 40 clock cycles. Here is the code segment we used earlier, show what the status tables look like when the MULTD is ready to go to commit.

```
LD     F6,34(R2)
LD     F2,45(R3)
MULTD  F0,F2,F4
SUBD   F8,F6,F2
DIVD   F10,F0,F6
ADDD   F6,F8,F2
```

Answer   The result is shown in the three tables in Figure 5.31. Note that although the SUBD and ADDD instructions have completed they do not commit until the MULTD commits, because instruction commit is kept in order so as to preserve precise exceptions and allow backing-out of an incorrect speculation. Note that all tags in the Qj and Qk fields as well as in the register status fields have been replaced with reorder buffer numbers, and the Dest field designates the reorder buffer number that is the destination for the result.

Reservation stations							
Name	**Busy**	**Op**	**Vj**	**Vk**	**Qj**	**Qk**	**Dest**
Add1	No						
Add2	No						
Add3	No						
Mult1	No	MULT	Mem[45+Regs[R3]]	Regs[F4]			#3
Mult2	Yes	DIV		Mem[34+Regs[R2]]	#3		#5

Reorder Buffer						
Entry	**Busy**	**Instruction**		**State**	**Destination**	**Value**
1	No	LD	F6,34(R2)	Commit	F6	Mem[34+Regs[F2]]
2	No	LD	F6,45(R3)	Commit	F2	Mem[45+Regs[R3]]
3	No	MULTD	F0,F2,F4	Write result	F0	#2 x Regs[F4]
4	Yes	SUBD	F8,F6,F2	Write Result	F8	#1 − #2
5	Yes	DIVD	F10,F0,F6	Execute	F10	
6	Yes	ADDD	F6,F8,F2	Write result	F6	#4 + #2

Register status									
Field	**F0**	**F2**	**F4**	**F6**	**F8**	**F10**	**F12**	**...**	**F30**
Reorder #	3			6	4	5			
Busy	Yes	No	No	Yes	Yes	Yes	No	...	No

FIGURE 5.31 **Only the two LD instructions have committed, though several others have completed execution.** The SUBD and ADDD instructions will not commit until the MULTD instruction commits, though the results of the instructions are available and can be used as sources for other instructions. The value column indicates the value being held, the format #X is used to refer to a value field of reorder buffer entry X.

The above example illustrates the key important difference between a machine with speculation and a machine with dynamic scheduling. Compare the contents of Figure 5.31 to Figure 5.10, which shows the same code sequence in operation on a machine with Tomasulo's algorithm. The key difference is that in the example above, no instruction after the earliest uncompleted instruction (MULTD above) is allowed to complete. In contrast, in Figure 5.10 the SUBD and ADDD instructions have also completed.

One implication of this difference is that the machine with the reorder buffer can dynamically execute code while maintaining a precise interrupt model. For example, if the MULTD instruction caused an interrupt, we could simply wait till it reached the head of the reorder buffer and take the interrupt, flushing any other pending instructions. Because instruction commit happens in order, this yields a perfectly precise exception. By contrast, in the example using Tomasulo's algorithm, the SUBD and ADDD instructions could both complete before the MULTD raised the exception. The result is that the registers F8 and F6 (destinations of the SUBD and ADDD instructions) could be overwritten, and the interrupt would be imprecise. Some users and architects have decided that imprecise floating point exceptions are acceptable in high performance machines, since the program will likely terminate; see Appendix A for further discussion of this topic. Other types of exceptions, such as page faults, are much more difficult to accommodate if they are imprecise since the program must transparently resume execution after handling such an exception. The use of a reorder buffer with in-order instruction commit provides precise exceptions, in addition to supporting speculative execution, as the next example shows.

Example   Consider the code example used earlier for Tomasulo's algorithm and shown in Figure 5.12 in execution:

```
Loop:   LD      F0,0(R1)
        MULTD   F4,F0,F2
        SD      0(R1),F4
        SUBI    R1,R1,#8
        BNEZ    R1,Loop; branches if R1≠0
```

Assume that we have issued all the instructions in the loop twice. Let's also assume that the LD and MULTD from the first iteration have committed and all other instructions have completed execution. (The Tomasulo example assumed that neither LD instruction had completed.) In an implementation that uses dynamic scheduling for both the integer and floating point units, the store would wait in the reorder buffer for both the effective address (0+R1 in this example) and the value (F4 in this example); however, since we are only considering the floating point resources, assume the effective address for the store is computed by the time the instruction is issued.

Answer   The result is shown in the three tables in Figure 5.32.

Reservation stations							
Name	**Busy**	**Op**	**Vj**	**Vk**	**Qj**	**Qk**	**Dest**
Mult1	No	MULT	Mem[0+Regs[R1]]	Regs[F2]	#1		#2
Mult2	No	MULT	Mem[0+Regs[R1]]	Regs[F2]	#6		#7

Reorder Buffer					
Entry	**Busy**	**Instruction**	**State**	**Destination**	**Value**
1	No	LD F0,0(R1)	Commit	F0	Mem[0+Regs[R1]]
2	No	MULTD F4,F0,F2	Commit	F4	Regs[F0] x Regs[F2]
3	Yes	SD 0(R1),F4	Write result	0+Reg[R1]	#2
4	Yes	SUBI R1,R1,#8	Write result	R1	R1–8
5	Yes	BNEZ R1,Loop	Write result		
6	Yes	LD F0,0(R1)	Write result	F0	Mem[#2+R1]
7	Yes	MULTD F4,F0,F2	Write result	F4	#6 x Regs[F2]
8	Yes	SD 0(R1),F4	Write Result	0+Reg[R1]	#8
9	Yes	SUBI R1,R1,#8	Write result	R1	#4 – 8
10	Yes	BNEZ R1,Loop	Write result		

Register status									
Field	**F0**	**F2**	**F4**	**F6**	**F8**	**F10**	**F12**	**...**	**F30**
Reorder #	6		7						
Busy	Yes	No	Yes	No	No	No	No	...	No

FIGURE 5.32 Only the two LD instructions have committed, though several others have completed execution. The SUBD and ADDD instructions will not commit until the MULTD instruction commits, though the results of the instructions are available and can be used as sources for other instructions.

Because neither the register values nor any memory values are actually written until an instruction commits, the machine can easily undo its speculative actions when a branch is found to be mispredicted. Suppose that in the above example (Figure 5.32), the branch BNEZ is not taken the first time. The instructions prior to the branch will simply commit when each reaches the head of the reorder buffer; when the branch reaches the head of that buffer, the buffer is simply cleared and the machine begins fetching instructions from the other path.

Exceptions are handled by not recognizing the exception until it is ready to commit. If a speculated instruction raises an exception, the exception is recorded in the reorder buffer. If a branch misprediction arises and the instruction should not have been executed, the exception is flushed along with the instruction when the reorder buffer is cleared. If the instruction reaches the head of the reorder buffer, then we know it is no longer speculative and the exception should really be taken.

Figure 5.33 shows the steps of execution for an instruction, as well as the conditions that must be satisfied to proceed to the step and the actions taken. Of course, in practice, we might want the misprediction case to be handled more efficiently. This can be accommodated by clearing the contents of the reorder buffer that are after the branch and fetching the instructions from the alternative path, as soon as the misprediction is detected, rather than waiting until the branch reaches the head of the reorder buffer. In speculative machines, performance is more sensitive to the branch prediction mechanisms, since the impact of a misprediction will be higher. Thus, all the aspects of handling branches–prediction accuracy, misprediction detection, and misprediction recovery–increase in importance.

Instruction status	Wait until	Action or bookkeeping

Issue	Station and reorder buffer both available	```if (Register['S1'].Busy)```
		``` {RS[r].Qj← Register['S1'].Reorder}```
		```else {RS[r].Vj← S1; RS[r].Qj← 0};```
		```if (Register['S2'].Busy)```
		``` {RS[r].Qk← Register[S2].Reorder}```
		```else {RS[r].Vk← S2; RS[r].Qk← 0};```
		```RS[r].Busy← yes; Rs[r].Dest← b;```
		```Register['D'].Qi=b; Register['D'].Busy=true;```
		```Reorder[b].Dest← 'D';```

Execute	(RS[r].Qj=0) and (RS[r].Qk=0)	None—operands are in Vj and Vk

Write result	Execution completed at *r* with buffer number b (= RS[r].Reorder)and CDB available, value is result	```∀x(if (RS[x].Qj=b) {RS[x].Vj← result;```
		``` RS[x].Qj ← 0});```
		```∀x(if (RS[x].Qk=b) {RS[x].Vk← result;```
		``` RS[x].Qk ← 0});```
		```RS[r].Busy← No;```
		```Reorder[b].Value← result;```

Commit	Instruction is at the head of the reorder buffer (entry h) and instruction has completed Write result.	```if Reorder[h].Instruction=Store```
		``` {Mem[Reorder[h].Dest]← Reorder[h].Value;}```
		```else {Regs[Reorder[h].Dest]← Reorder[h].Value;}```
		```Register[Reorder[h]].Busy← No;```
		```Reorder[h].Busy← No;```

FIGURE 5.33   Steps in the algorithm and what is required for each step.   For the issuing instruction D is the destination, S1 and S2 are the sources, and r is the reservation station allocated and b is the assigned reorder buffer entry. RS is the reservation-station data structure. The value returned by a reservation station is called the result. Register is the register data structure, while Reorder is the reorder buffer data structure. Recall that 'Ri' stands for the name of register Ri rather than its value,

Although this explanation of speculative execution has focused on floating point, the techniques easily extend to the integer registers and functional units. Indeed, speculation may be more useful in integer programs since such programs tend to have code where the branch behavior is less predictable. Additionally, these techniques can be extended to work in a multiple issue machine by allowing multiple instructions to issue and commit every clock. Indeed, speculation is probably most interesting in such machines, since less ambitious techniques can probably exploit sufficient ILP within basic blocks when assisted by a compiler using unrolling.

A speculative machine can be extended to multiple issue (see the exercises) using the same techniques we employed when extending a Tomasulo-based machine in Section 5.4. The same techniques for solving the instruction issue unit can be used: we process multiple instructions per clock assigning reservation stations and reorder buffers to the instructions. The challenge here is in deciding what instructions can issue and in performing the renaming within the allowable clock period. We also need to widen the CDB to allow multiple instructions to complete with a clock cycle. The challenge lies in monitoring the multiple completion buses for operands without impacting the clock cycle. In Section 5.7 we will examine the importance of speculation on the amount of ILP that can be extracted.

The alternative to hardware-based speculation is compiler-based speculation. Such approaches are useful when branches cannot be eliminated by techniques such as loop unrolling but are statically predictable, so that the compiler can choose how to speculate. Conditional instructions are a simple form of compiler speculation. Supporting more powerful compiler-based speculation can be done using techniques similar to the reorder buffer; several such approaches have been proposed (see the historical perspectives). Whether speculation will be supported primarily in hardware or primarily in software is point of current debate.

Of course, all the techniques described in the last chapter and in this one cannot take advantage of more parallelism than is provided by the application. The question of how parallelism is available has been hotly debated and is the topic of the next section.

5.7 | Studies of ILP

Exploiting ILP to increase performance began with the first pipelined machines in the 1960s. In the 1980s and 1990s, these techniques were key to achieving rapid performance improvements. The question of how much ILP exists is critical to our long term ability to enhance performance at a rate that exceeds the increase in speed of the base integrated circuit technology. On a shorter scale, the critical question of what is needed to exploit more ILP is crucial to both computer designers and compiler writers. The data in this section also provides us with a way to examine the value of ideas that we have introduced in this chapter, including memory disambiguation, register renaming, and speculation.

In this section we review one of the studies done of these questions. The historical section describes several studies, including the source for the data in this section. All these studies of available parallelism operate by making a set of assumptions and seeing how much parallelism is available under those assumptions. The data we examine here is from a study that makes the fewest assumptions; in fact, the ultimate hardware model is completely unrealizable. Nonetheless, all such studies assume a certain level of compiler technology and some of these assumptions could affect the results despite the use of incredibly ambitious hardware. In the future, advances in compiler technology together with significantly new and different hardware techniques may be able to overcome some limitations assumed in these studies; however, it is unlikely that such advances *when coupled with realistic hardware* will overcome these limits in the near future. Instead, developing new hardware and software techniques to overcome the limits seen in these studies will continue to be one of the most important challenges in computer design.

The Hardware Model

To see what the limits of ILP might be, we first need to define an ideal machine. An ideal machine is one where all artificial constraints on ILP are removed. The only limits on ILP in such a machine are true data dependences either through registers or memory.

The assumptions made for a perfect machine are as follows:

1. Register renaming–there are an infinite number of virtual registers available and all WAW and WAR hazards are avoided.

2. Branch prediction–branch prediction is perfect. All conditional branches are predicted exactly.

3. Jump prediction–all jumps (including jump register used for return and computed jumps) are perfectly predicted. When combined with perfect branch prediction, this is equivalent to having a machine with perfect speculation and an unbounded buffer of instructions available for execution.

4. Memory-address alias analysis–all memory addresses are known exactly and a store can be moved before a load provided that the addresses are not identical.

Initially, we examine a machine that can issue an unlimited number of instructions at once looking arbitrarily far ahead in the computation. For all the machine models we examine there are no restrictions on what types of instructions can execute in a cycle. For the unlimited issue case, this means there may be an unlimited number of loads or stores issuing in one clock cycle. In addition, all functional unit latencies are assumed to be 1 cycle, so that any sequence of dependent instructions can issue on successive cycles. Latencies longer than one cycle would decrease the number of issues per cycle, although not the number of instructions under execution at any point. (The instructions in execution at any point are often referred to as *in-flight*.) Of course, this machine is completely unrealizable. For example, the IBM Power-2, which we look at the end of the chapter, is one of the highest performance superscalar machine to date. Power-2 issues up to six instructions per clock (with significant restrictions on the instruction types), supports limited renaming, has multicycle latencies, uses branch prediction, but has no support for speculation. After looking at the parallelism available for the perfect machine, we will examine the impact of restricting various features.

To measure the available parallelism, the programs were compiled and optimized with the standard MIPS optimizing compilers. The programs were instrumented and executed to produce a trace of the instruction and data references. Every instruction in the trace is then scheduled as early as possible, limited only by the data dependences. Since a trace is used, perfect branch prediction and perfect alias analysis are easy to do. With these mechanisms, instructions may be scheduled much earlier than they would otherwise, moving across large numbers of instructions on which they are not data dependent, including branches, since branches are perfectly predicted.

Figure 5.34 shows the average amount of parallelism available for six of the SPEC92 benchmarks. Throughout this section the parallelism is measured by the average instruction issue rate (remember that all instructions have a one cycle latency). Three of these benchmarks (fpppp, doduc, and tomcatv) are floating point intensive while the other three are integer programs. Two of the floating point benchmarks (fpppp and tomcatv) have extensive parallelism, which could be exploited by a vector machine or by a multiprocessor. Doduc has extensive parallelism, but the parallelism does not occur in simple parallel loops as it does in fpppp and tomcatv. The program li is a LISP interpreter which has many short dependences.

In the next few sections, we restrict various aspects of this machine to show what the effects of various assumptions are before looking at some ambitious but realizable machines.

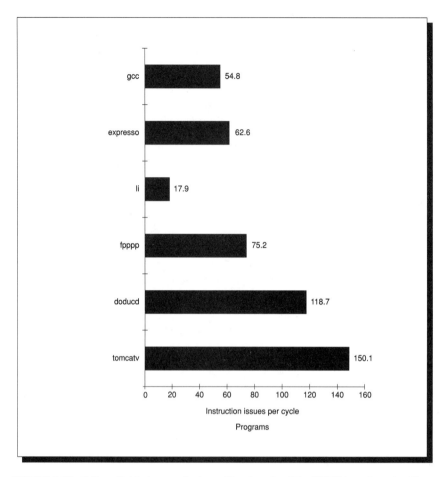

FIGURE 5.34   ILP available in a perfect machine for six of the SPEC benchmarks. The first three programs are integer programs, while the last three are floating point programs. The floating point programs are loop-intensive and have large amounts of loop level parallelism.

This and the subsequent graphs in this section should be kept small--they are currently too large. There should be two to a page (at least!).

Limitations on the window size and maximum issue count

To build a machine that even comes close to perfect branch prediction and perfect alias analysis requires extensive dynamic analysis, since static compile-time schemes cannot be perfect. Of course, most realistic dynamic schemes will not be perfect, but the use of dynamic schemes will provide the ability to uncover parallelism that cannot be analyzed by static, compile-time analysis. Thus, a dynamic machine might be able to more closely match the amount of parallelism uncovered by our ideal machine.

How close could a real dynamically scheduled, speculative machine come to the ideal machine? To gain insight into this question, consider what the perfect machine must do:

1. Examine a set of instructions–the machine may have to look arbitrarily far ahead to find a set of instructions to issue.

2. Rename all register uses to avoid RAW and WAW hazards.

3. Determine which instructions can issue and which must wait because of a register dependence.

3. Determine if any memory dependences exist and prevent dependent instructions from issuing.

5. Predict all branches.

6. Provide enough replicated functional units to allow the instructions to issue.

Obviously, this analysis is quite complicated. For example, to determine whether n instructions have any register dependences among them assuming all instruction are register-register requires comparisons.

$$2n - 2 + 2n - 4 + ... + 2 = 2\sum_{1}^{n-1} n = 2\frac{(n-1)(n-2)}{2} = n^2 - 3n + 2$$

To detect dependences among the next 2000 instructions (the default size we assume in several figures) requires almost *four million* comparisons! Even examining only 50 instructions requires 2,352 comparisons. This obviously limits the number of instructions that can be considered for issue at once. The set of instructions examined for simultaneous execution is called the *window*. Since each instruction in the window must be kept in the processor and the number of comparisons required to execute any instruction in the window grows quadratically, real window sizes are likely to be small. To date, the window size has been in the range of 4 to 8; future machines may have windows as large as 32 (which requires about 900 comparisons), but probably not larger. The window size limits the number of instructions considered for issue and thus implicitly, the maximum number of instructions that may issue. In addition to the cost in dependence checking and renaming hardware, real machines will have a limited number of functional units available and limited copies of each functional unit. Thus, the maximum number of instructions that may issue in a real machine might be smaller than the window size.

Issuing large numbers of instructions will almost certainly lengthen the clock cycle. For example, in the early 1990s, the machines with the most powerful multiple issue capabilities typically had clock cycles that were 1.5 to 3 times longer than the machines with the simplest pipelines that were designed to emphasize a high clock rate. This does not mean the multiple issue machines had lower performance, since they "typically" had CPIs that were 2 to 3 times lower. We will see such a comparison in the next section when we examine the performance of the Power-2 design.

Figures 5.35 and 5.36 show the effects of restricting the size of the window from which instruction can issue ; the *only* difference in the two graphs is the format–the data are identical. As we can see in Figure 5.35, the amount of parallelism uncovered falls sharply with decreasing window size. Even a window of 32, which would be ambitious in 1995 technology, achieves about one-fifth of the average issue rate of an infinite window. As we can see in Figure 5.36, the integer programs do not contain nearly as much parallelism as the floating point programs. This is to be expected. Looking at how the parallelism drops off in Figure 5.36 makes it clear that the parallelism in the floating point cases is coming from loop level parallelism. The fact that the amount of parallelism at low window sizes is not that different among the floating point and integer programs, implies a structure where there are non-loop-carried dependences within loop bodies, but few loop-carried dependences in programs such as tomcatv. At small window sizes, the machines simply cannot see the instructions in the next loop iteration that could be issued in parallel with instructions from the current iteration. This is an example of where better compiler technology could uncover higher amounts ILP, since it can find the loop level parallelism and schedule the code to take advantage of it, even with small window sizes. Software pipelining, for example, could do this.

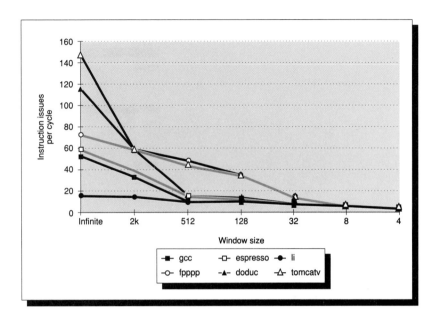

FIGURE 5.35 The effects of reducing the size of the window. The window is the group of instructions from which an instruction can issue.

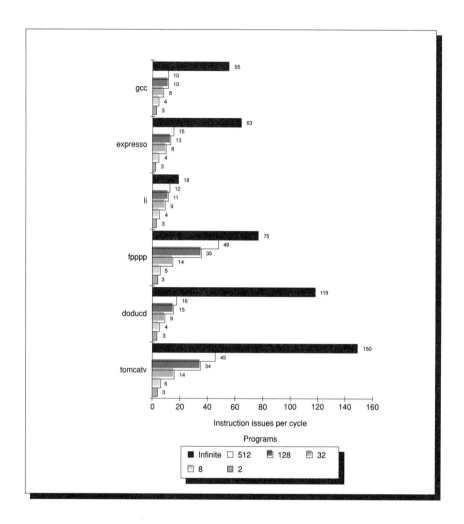

FIGURE 5.36   The effect of window size shown by each application by plotting the average number of instruction issues per clock cycle. The most interesting observation is that at modest window sizes, the amount of parallelism found in the integer and floating point programs is similar.

We know that large window sizes are impractical and the data in Figures 5.35 and 5.36 tell us that issue rates will be considerably reduced with realistic windows, we will assume a base window size of 2K entries and a maximum issue capability of 64 instructions. As we will see in the next few sections, when the rest of the machine is not perfect, a 2K window and a 64 issue limitation do not constrain the machine.

The Effects of Realistic Branch and Jump Prediction

Our ideal machine assumes that branches can be perfectly predicted: the outcome of any branch in the program is known before the first instruction is executed! Of course, no real machine can ever achieve this. Figures 5.37 and 5.38 show the effects of more realistic prediction schemes in two different formats. We need to predict jumps as well as branches. We assume separate predictor is used for used jumps: except when prediction is perfect, we use a pair of 2K entries, one organized as a circular buffer for predicting returns and one organized as a standard predictor and used for computed jumps (as in case statement or computed gotos). These jump predictors are nearly perfect, though the jump predictors are important primarily with the most accurate branch predictors, since the branch frequency is higher and the accuracy of the branch predictors dominates.

The five levels of branch and jump prediction shown in these figures are:

1. Perfect–all branches and jumps are perfectly predicted at the start of execution.

2. Selective history predictor–the prediction scheme using a correlating 2-bit predictor and a non correlating 2-bit predictor together with a selector, which chooses the best predictor for each branch. The prediction buffer contains 2^{13} (8K) entries each consisting of three 2-bit fields, two of which are predictor and the third is a selector. The correlating predictor is indexed using the exclusive-or of the branch address and the global branch history. The non correlating predictor is the standard 2-bit predictor indexed by the branch address. The selector table is also indexed by the branch address and specifies whether the correlating or non correlating predictor should be used. The selector is incremented or decremented just as we would for a standard 2-bit predictor. This predictor, which uses a total of 48K bits, outperforms both the correlating and non correlating predictors, achieving an accuracy of at least 97% for these six SPEC benchmarks.

3. Standard 2-bit predictor with 512 2-bit entries. In addition, we assume a 16-entry buffer to predict returns.

4. Static–a static predictor uses the profile history of the program and predicts that the branch is always taken or always not taken based on the profile, as we discussed in the last chapter.

5. None–no branch prediction is used, though jumps are still predicted. Parallelism is largely limited to within a basic block.

Since we do charge additional cycles for a mispredicted or unpredicted branch, the effect of varying the branch prediction is to vary the amount of parallelism that can be exploited across basic blocks by speculation.

Figure 5.38 shows that the branch behavior of two of the floating point loops is much simpler than the other programs, allowing significant amounts of parallelism to be exploited with realistic prediction schemes. In contrast, for all the integer programs and for doduc, the FP benchmarks with the least loop-level parallelism, even the difference between perfect branch prediction and the ambitious selective predictor is dramatic. Like the window size data, these figures tells us that to achieve significant amounts of parallelism in integer programs, the machine must select and execute instructions that are widely separated. When branch prediction is not highly accurate, the mispredicted branches become a barrier to finding the parallelism.

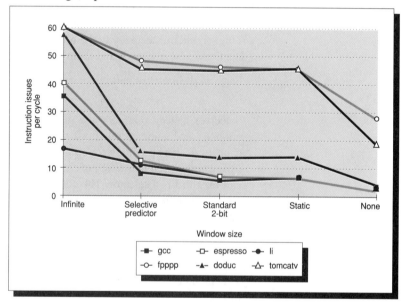

FIGURE 5.37   The effect of branch prediction schemes. This graph shows the impact of going from a perfect model of branch prediction (all branches predicted correctly arbitrarily far ahead) to various dynamic predictors (infinite and 2K entries) to compile-time, profile-based prediction, and finally to using no predictor.

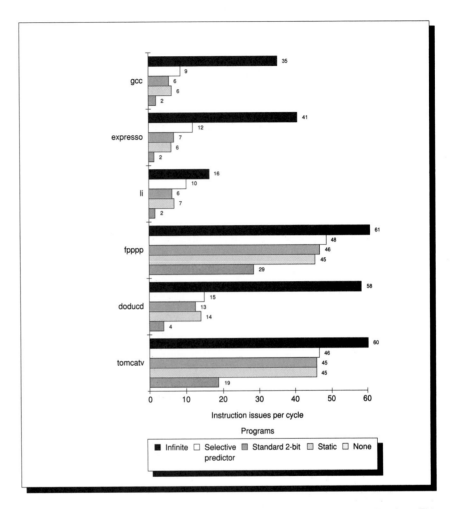

FIGURE 5.38 The effect of branch prediction schemes sorted by application. This graph highlights the differences between the programs with extensive loop level parallelism (tomcatv and fpppp) and those without the integer programs and doduc).

As we have seen branch prediction is critical, even with a window size of 2K instructions and an issue limit of 64. For the rest of the studies, in addition to the window and issue limit, we assume as a base an ambitious predictor that uses two-levels of prediction and a total of 8K entries. This predictor, which requires more than 150Kbits of storage, slightly outperforms the selective predictor described above (by about 0.5-1%). We also assume a pair of 2K jump and return predictors, as described above.

The Effects of Finite Registers

Our ideal machine eliminates all name dependences among register references using an infinite set of virtual registers. While several machines have used register renaming for this purpose, most have only a few extra virtual registers. For example, the IBM Power-1 implementation provides 22 extra FP registers in addition to the 32 FP registers provided for in the architecture. Figure 5.39 and 5.40 show the effect of reducing the number of registers available for renaming, again using the same data in two different forms. The x-axis in both graphs indicates how many additional registers are available; both the FP and GP registers are increased by the number shown.

At first, the results in these tables might seem somewhat surprising: you might expect that name dependences should only slightly reduce the parallelism available. Remember though, exploiting large amounts of parallelism requires evaluating many independent threads of execution. Thus, many registers are needed to hold live variables from these threads. Figure 5.39 shows that the impact of having only a finite number of registers is significant, if extensive parallelism exists. Although these graphs show a large impact on the floating point programs, the impact on the integer programs is small primarily because the limitations in window size and branch prediction have limited the ILP substantially, making renaming less valuable. In addition, notice that the reduction in available parallelism is significant even if just 32 registers are available for renaming, which is still more than the number of registers available on any existing machine.

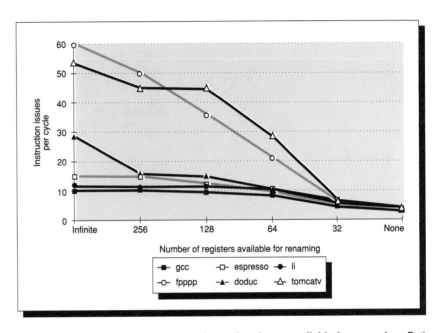

FIGURE 5.39   The effect of finite numbers of registers available for renaming. Both the number of FP registers and the number of GP registers are increased by the number shown on the x-axis. The effect is most dramatic on the integer programs, although having only 32 extra GP and 32 extra FP registers has a significant impact on all the programs .

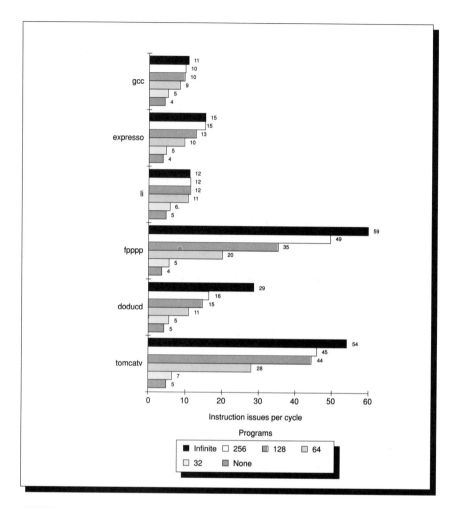

FIGURE 5.40   The reduction in available parallelism is significant when fewer than an unbounded number of renaming registers are available. For the integer programs, the impact of having more than 64 registers is not seen here. To use more than 64 registers requires uncovering lots of parallelism, which for the integer programs requires essentially perfect branch prediction.

While register renaming is obviously critical to performance, an infinite number of registers is obviously not practical. Thus, for the next section, we assume that there are 256 registers available for renaming–far more than any anticipated machine has.

The Effects of Imperfect Alias Analysis

Our optimal model assumes that it can perfectly analyze all memory dependences, as well as eliminate all register name dependences. Of course, perfect alias analysis is not possible in practice: the analysis cannot be perfect at compile-time, and it requires a potentially unbounded number of comparisons at run-time. Figures 5.41 and 5.42 show the impact of three other models of memory alias analysis, in addition to perfect analysis. The three models are:

1. Global/stack perfect–this model does perfect predictions for global and stack references and assumes all heap references conflict. This represents an idealized version of the best compiler-based analysis schemes currently available.

2. Inspection–this model examines the accesses to see if they can be determined not to interfere at compile-time. For example, if an access uses R10 as a base register with an offset of 20, then another access that uses R10 as a base register with an offset of 100 cannot interfere. This analysis is similar to that performed by many existing commercial compilers, though newer compilers can do better through the use of dependence analysis, at least for loop-oriented programs.

3. None–all memory references are assumed to conflict.

As one might expect, for the Fortran programs (where no heap references exist), there is no difference between perfect and global/stack perfect analysis. The global/stack perfect analysis is optimistic, since no compiler could ever find all dependences exactly. The fact that perfect analysis of global and stack references is still a factor of two better than inspection, indicates that either sophisticated compiler analysis or dynamic analysis on the fly will be required to obtain much parallelism.

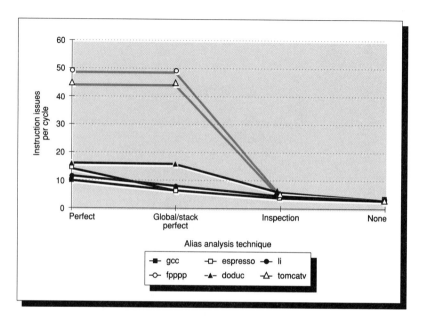

FIGURE 5.41   The effect of various alias analysis techniques on the amount of ILP.
Anything less than perfect analysis has a dramatic impact of the amount of parallelism found
in the integer programs, while global /stack analysis is perfect (and unrealizable) for the Fortran programs.

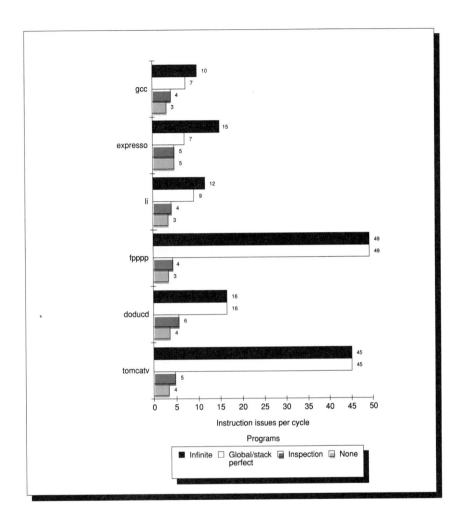

FIGURE 5.42 **The effect of varying level of alias analysis is shown on individual programs.**

ILP for Realizable Machines

In this section we look at the performance of machines with realistic levels of hardware support in all dimensions. In particular we assume the following fixed attributes:

1. A selective predictor with 1K entries and a 16-entry return predictor.

2. Perfect disambiguation of memory references done dynamically—this is ambitious but perhaps attainable for small window sizes.

3. Register renaming with 64 additional registers.

Figures 5.43 and 5.44 show the result for this configuration as we vary the window size. This configuration is still substantially more complex and expensive than existing or planned implementations. Nonetheless, it gives a useful upper bound on what such implementations might yield. The data in these figures is likely to be very optimistic for another reason: the simulated machine assumes that there are no issue restrictions. Up to as many instructions as the window size may issue and they may all be memory references—no one would even contemplate this capability in a single processor at this time. Unfortunately, it is quite difficult to bound the performance of a machine with reasonable issue restrictions; not only is the space of possibilities quite large, but the existence of issue restrictions requires that the parallelism be evaluated with an accurate instruction scheduler, making the cost of studying machines with large numbers of issues very expensive.

In addition, remember that in interpreting these results, cache misses and non-unit latencies have not been taken into account, and both these effects will have significant impact (see the exercises).

Figure 5.43 shows the parallelism versus window size. The most startling observation is that with the realistic machine constraints listed above, the effect of the window size for the integer programs is not so severe as for FP programs. This points at the key difference between these two types of programs: the availability of loop-level parallelism in two of the FP programs, means that the amount of ILP that can be exploited is higher, but that for integer programs other factors—such as branch prediction, register renaming, and less parallelism to start with—are all important limitations.

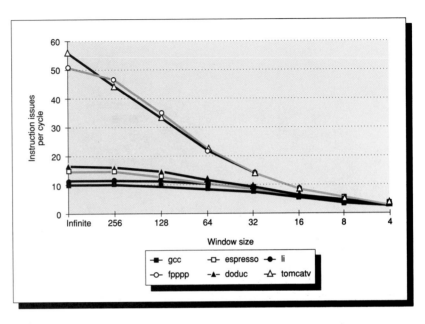

FIGURE 5.43 The amount of parallelism available for a wide variety of window sizes and a fixed implementation .

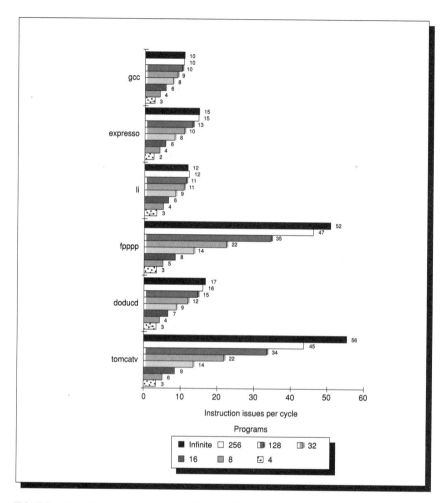

FIGURE 5.44   The amount of parallelism available versus the window size, for a variety of integer and floating point programs.

Given the difficulty of increasing the instruction rates with realistic hardware designs, designers face a challenge in deciding how best to use the limited resources available on a integrated circuit. One of the most interesting tradeoffs is between simpler machines with larger caches and higher clock rates versus more emphasis on instruction-level parallelism with a slower clock and smaller caches.

The following example illustrates the challenges.

Consider the following three hypothetical, but not atypical, machines, which we run with the SPEC gcc benchmark:

1. A simple DLX pipe running with a clock rate of 300 MHz and achieving a pipeline CPI of 1.1. This machine has a cache system that yields 0.03 misses per instruction.

2. A deeply pipelined version of DLX with slightly smaller caches and a 400MHz clock rate. The pipeline CPI of the machine is 1.5, and the smaller caches yield 0.035 misses per instruction on average.

3. A speculative superscalar with a 32-entry window. It achieves 75% of the ideal issue rate measured for this window size. (Use the data in Figure 5.44). This machine has the smallest caches, which leads to 0.05 misses per instruction. This machine has a 200MHz clock.

Assume that the main memory time (which sets the miss penalty) is 200 nS. Determine the relative performance of these three machines.

First, we use the miss penalty and miss rate information to compute the contribution to CPI from cache misses for each configuration. We do this with the following formula:

$$\text{Cache CPI} = \text{misses per instruction} \times \text{miss penalty}$$

We need to compute the miss penalties for each system:

$$\text{Miss penalty} = \frac{\text{memory access time}}{\text{clock cycle}}$$

The clock cycle times for the machines are 3.3 nS, 2.5 nS, and 5 nS, respectively. Hence, the miss penalties are:

$$\text{Miss penalty}_1 = \frac{200 \text{ ns}}{3.3 \text{ ns}} = 61 \text{ cycles}$$

$$\text{Miss penalty}_2 = \frac{200 \text{ ns}}{2.5 \text{ ns}} = 80 \text{ cycles}$$

$$\text{Miss penalty}_3 = \frac{200 \text{ ns}}{5 \text{ ns}} = 40 \text{ cycles}$$

Applying this for each cache:

Cache $CPI_1 = 0.03 \times 61 = 1.83$

Cache $CPI_2 = 0.035 \times 80 = 2.8$

Cache $CPI_3 = 0.05 \times 40 = 2.0$

We know the pipeline CPI contribution for everything but machine 3; its pipeline CPI is given by:

$$\text{Pipeline } CPI_3 = \frac{1}{\text{issue rate}} = \frac{1}{8 \times 0.75} = \frac{1}{6} = 0.167$$

Now we can find the CPI for each machine by adding the pipeline and cache CPI contributions.

$CPI_1 = 1.1 + 1.83 = 2.93$

$CPI_2 = 1.5 + 2.8 = 4.3$

$CPI_3 = 0.167 + 2.0 = 2.167$

Since this is the same architecture we can compare instruction execution rates to determine relative performance:

$$\text{Instruction execution rate} = \frac{CR}{CPI}$$

$$\text{Instruction execution rate}_1 = \frac{300 \text{ MHz}}{2.93} = 102 \text{ mips}$$

$$\text{Instruction execution rate}_2 = \frac{400 \text{ MHz}}{4.3} = 93 \text{ mips}$$

$$\text{Instruction execution rate}_3 = \frac{200 \text{ MHz}}{2.167} = 92 \text{ mips}$$

So the simplest design is the fastest. Of course, the designer building either system 2 or system 3 will probably be alarmed by the large fraction of the system performance lost to cache misses. In the next chapter we'll see the most common solution to this problem: adding another level of caches.

Before we move to the next chapter, let's see how some of the advanced ideas in this chapter are put to use in a real machine.

5.8 | Putting it All Together: The IBM Power2

As of the middle of 1994, the IBM Power2 machine is one of the most advanced superscalar processor in existence. It is capable of issuing up to six instructions per clock including two memory references and two floating point operations. It uses a combination of static and dynamic scheduling that includes register renaming. Power2 implements a version of the PowerPC architecture described in Appendix C, excluding the 64-bit integer and addressing instructions. In addition, Power 2 adds quadword floating point loads and stores; these operations load or store a pair of 64-bit floating point registers and are useful for vector-like numeric codes. This section describes the Power-2 implementation and looks at some typical performance characteristics.

Power 2 is implemented in eight custom chips containing over 23 million transistors and mounted on an IBM ceramic MultiChip Module (MCM), a technology that allows the chips to be placed close together and allows large numbers of short interconnections on multiple levels of the ceramic substrate. The eight chips and their interconnections are shown in Figure 5.45. To understand how the Power2 processor operates, let's look at the function of each of the major units shown in Figure 5.45.

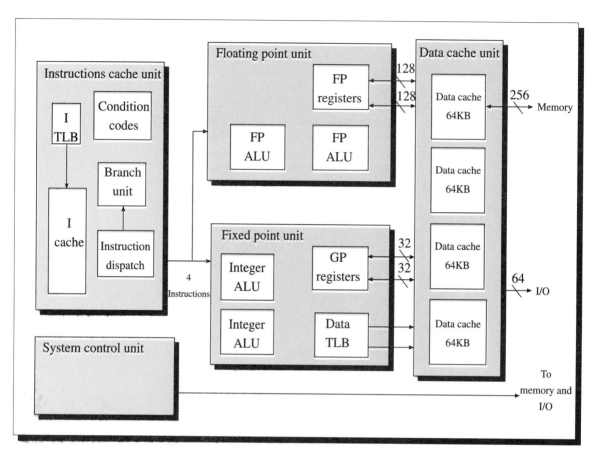

FIGURE 5.45   The basic structure of the Power-2 design consists of 5 major units organized as 8 chips: the data cache unit is 4 separate 64KB parts. The system control unit primarily handles I/O. The instruction cache unit can deliver four instructions every clock. The data cache units can deliver two separate memory references: 32-bits each if it is an integer or either 64 bits or 128 bits each if a float.

Instruction Cache Unit

The Instruction Cache Unit (ICU)–contains both the instruction TLB and cache (see Chapter 6), as well as the branch unit and the condition codes. The ICU has a 16-entry prefetch buffer that holds instructions fetched from the on-chip instruction cache. The ICU fetches up to eight instructions from the cache (assuming there is space in the prefetch buffer) and can dispatch up to six instructions per clock. Four of the six instructions can go to the fixed and floating point units, while two instructions can be handled within the ICU. The instructions executed inside the ICU include instructions that change the condition codes as well as branches. Up to two branches per cycle may be issued or a combination of a condition code instruction and a branch. Two branches can be issued only if the first branch is an untaken conditional branch.

The ICU takes one clock cycle (effectively the first stage of the pipeline for all instruction types) to fetch the instructions. In the same clock it issues instructions to the internal branch unit or the fixed point unit (FXU). Floating point instructions take another cycle to issue to the floating point pipeline (FPU). All instruction issue is in order to the respective functional units; however, instructions may change order once they reach the floating point unit, and integer instructions can execute out-of-order with respect to floating point instructions. Figure 5.46 shows the ICU pipeline structure with the dispatch to the FXU and FPU.

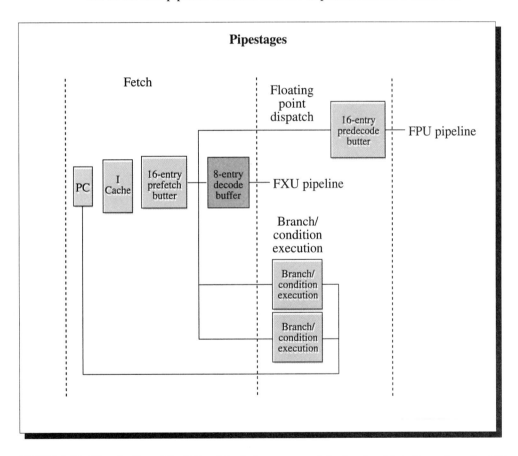

FIGURE 5.46 The pipeline of the ICU unit includes a one-cycle instruction fetch. The units on the ICU are shown shaded in color, while the fixed point decode buffer, shown in gray, resides on the fixed point unit (FXU). Floating point instructions take an extra cycle to dispatch (called the S cycle in Power-2 documentation) to a 16-entry predecode buffer residing on the floating point unit (and shown unshaded).

Branches use a scheme similar to that in the earlier Power-1 implementation. The condition code registers reside in the ICU. When a branch is decoded, the condition code can be checked and the appropriate action taken on the next clock cycle, assuming the condition codes have already been set. Thus, in the best situation, branches complete one pipe cycle after they are fetched. To assist in reducing the penalty on taken branches when the condition code is not ready, there is an eight instruction buffer that is filled from the target address of a branch starting when the branch is decoded (this is in addition to the normal prefetch buffer that will hold the instructions sequentially following the branch). The first four instructions in this buffer are completely decoded so that as soon as the branch outcome is known instructions from either the normal prefetch/decode buffer or from the target buffer can be issued. This combination allows the Power-2 to have a zero cycle untaken branch and a one cycle taken branch even when a compare immediately precedes a branch.

Fixed Point Unit

Figure 5.47 shows the pipeline of the fixed point unit (FXU), which handles integer instructions and loads/stores. This unit can initiate execution of up to two instructions per clock as long as the instructions are independent. The pipeline flow is similar to a standard pipeline in Chapter 4. The two ALUs are somewhat different and instructions are dispatched to the required ALU. The functions of the two ALUs are:

1. A 2-input 32-bit ALU and shifter.

2. A 3- input adder, shifter, and 36-bit integer multiply/divide unit.

Integer instructions, including loads and stores, are taken from the FXU decode buffer and executed in-order. After effective address computation, loads and stores use the TLB to translate memory addresses and then the data cache unit (off-chip). For integer loads, the data returns from the data cache unit and is placed in the integer registers. Floating point loads/stores are coordinated with the Floating Point Unit (FPU), as we will see shortly. The fixed point unit also contains a set of queues used for pending stores, which are not shown in Figure 5.46. The FP and Fixed store queues accept effective addresses from the ALU and buffer them until the data to be stored is available and the data cache is free. Loads are given priority over stores and all load addresses are checked for a conflict against a pending store address in the store queues.

Pipestages

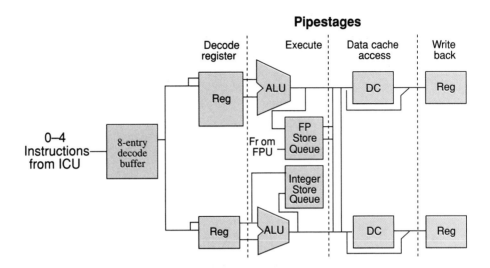

FIGURE 5.47   The fixed point pipeline showing the major functional units. After a one cycle fetch from the instruction cache, instructions arrive in an 8-entry buffer on the FXU. Up to two instructions are decoded (in order) and dispatched to the two integer pipelines. The D-TLB units translates up to two addresses per clock and operates in parallel with the data cache; it is not shown in this figure. The D cache is shown in color to indicate that it resides in a separate chip. (the Data Cache Units). The FP and integer store buffers are buffers that sit between the ALU output and the D-cache inputs. They hold computed addresses until the data to be stored is available and the data cache is free. Since Power-2 can perform two FP stores per clock, there are dual paths to the D-cache chips from the FP store queue. The data to be stored for an FP store comes from the FP unit. *Note that when this is printed text doesn't fit in boxes--needs to be fixed.*

In general, the FXU issues instruction pairs only when the instructions are not dependent. If the instructions are dependent then only the first is executed. The one exception is that the three-input adder allows dual issue of instruction pairs of the form:

```
ADD    R3,R1,R2;    ADD    R5,R3,R4
```

These two instructions are sent to one ALU, but occupy both the issue slots of the FXU.

The integer multiplier takes two cycles, while divide takes 13 to 14 in most cases. Because integer instructions issue and complete in order, the integer unit will stall if it receives an instruction while a divide is still executing.

Floating Point Unit

The Floating Point Unit (FPU) pipeline is shown in Figure 5.48. It contains two full floating point ALUs, organized as a multiplier followed by an adder, and each implementing add, multiply, multiply-add, divide, and square root. The FPU executes instructions out-of-order both with respect to integer instructions and within the floating point stream. The individual queues for each functional unit allow instructions to be selected dynamically from the individual queues for loads, stores, and FP arithmetic operations. During the second pipeline stage within the FPU, all registers are renamed to a set of 54 virtual registers (this is 22 extra FP registers) so as to reduce name dependence hazards.

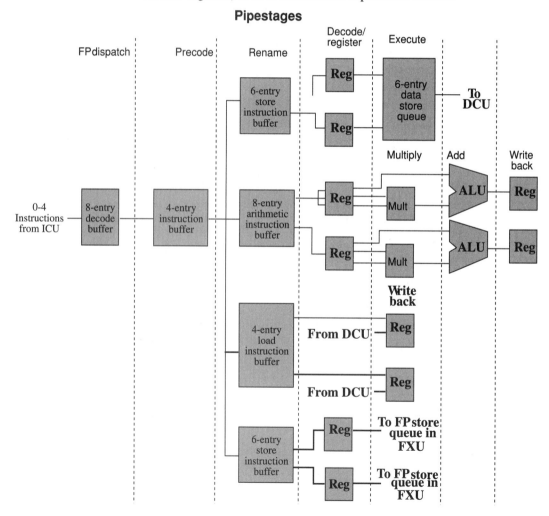

FIGURE 5.48   The pipeline of the floating point unit can issue up to four instructions per cycle consisting of up to two load or stores and two FP operations. The floating point pipeline includes a stage of predecode and a stage for re-naming, followed by the instruction-dependent stages. For FP stores, the data is sent from the registers to the FP store queues on the FXU, as soon as it is available.

Floating point loads work by having the FXU and FPU both receive the instruction and decode it. The FXU does the effective address calculation and initiates the data cache access. When the data cache access completes, the data is latched into a temporary register on the FPU and stored into the register file on the subsequent clock cycle. The execution clock cycle for loads is determined by the FXU, which keeps instructions in order; the FPU is passive, merely waiting for the data and storing it.

Stores are more complex since they involve more coordination between the FXU and FPU. The store address is computed in the FXU, but the data is computed in the FPU and may be delayed while waiting for its result. When the register source of a store is available, the data is placed into the store queue, freeing up the register. When the entry at the head of the store queue has its data available, it signals the FXU which sends the address from the entry at the head of the FP store address queue to the DCU while the FPU sends the data from the store queue. Since stores are kept in order within these queues and stores only occur from the head of the queue, store order is preserved. Up to two memory reference instructions can be completed every clock cycle; together with the capability of a quadword load/store to the floating point registers, the Power-2 can transfer 32 bytes per clock cycle between the FP registers and the data cache.

A Simple Power-2 Code Example

How well does the Power-2 implementation perform? Let's first look at a code example, and then examine the SPEC92 numbers. Let's use our simple example from Section 5.1 used in the superscalar examples. The source code looks like:

```
for (i=1; i<=100; i=i+1) {
        x[i] = a + x[i];
}
```

The Power-2 architecture provides auto incrementing loads, so a straightforward version of the code, assuming the initial base address is in R2, the end of the array is precomputed in R3, and the value of a is in F0, looks like:

```
                 J          loopentry
loop:            LD         F4,0(R2) ; load
                 ADDD       F8,F0,F4
                 SD         0(R2+),F8; store&increment
                 CMP        R2,R3
loopentry:       BNEQ       loop
```

We can unwind the loop to expose additional optimization opportunities; here is the unwound loop:

```
            J       loopentry
loop:       LD      F4,0(R2)  ; load
            ADDD    F8,F0,F4
            SD      0(R2+),F8 ; store&increment
            LD      F4,0(R2)  ; load
            ADDD    F8,F0,F4
            SD      0(R2+),F8 ; store&increment
            LD      F4,0(R2)  ; load
            ADDD    F8,F0,F4
            SD      0(R2+),F8 ; store&increment
            LD      F4,0(R2)  ; load
            ADDD    F8,F0,F4
            SD      0(R2+),F8 ; store&increment
            CMP     R2,R3
loopentry:  BNEQ    loop
```

Since renaming is implemented in the hardware, there is no need to rename the registers on each loop iteration. But, the unwound loop makes it clear that we can use the quadword load/store instructions:

```
            J       loopentry
loop:       LQ      F4,0(R2)  ; load quad
            ADDD    F8,F0,F4  ; add 1/2 quad
            ADDD    F10,F0,F6 ; add other half
            SQ      F8,0(R2+) ; store&increment
            LQ      F4,0(R2)  ; load
            ADDD    F8,F0,F4  ; add 1/2 quad
            ADDD    F10,F0,F6 ; add other half
            SQ      F8,0(R2+) ; store&increment
            CMP     R2,R3
loopentry:  BNEQ    loop
```

Once this loop reaches steady state, each iteration takes only two clock cycles, since there are four memory references and four FP operations. Since the un-rolled loop is equivalent to four copies of the original loop, we achieve a rate of 2 iterations of the original loop per clock. At the Power-2 clock rate of 71.5 MHz, this is equivalent to 143 MFLOPS for this loop. If the inner loop made use of the multiply-add capability, but didn't require any additional memory bandwidth, this performance could be doubled!

Comparative Performance

Figure 5.49 shows the performance of the IBM RS/6000 Model 990, which uses a Power-2 chip set running at 71.5 MHz versus the DEC 7000/Model 610, which uses a 200 MHz Alpha chip. The Power-2 implementation has one of the lowest clock rates among its contemporaries. In comparison, the Alpha pipeline is a simple two-issue static superscalar that emphasizes a high clock rate. Although the Alpha chip has a clock rate that is almost three times higher, the Power-2 design is faster for most of the benchmarks. Remember though, the implementations are not identical in cost (there are more custom chips in a Power-2 design, the Alpha design has a large secondary cache), the implementation technologies are not identical, nor is the power consumption. Thus, cost performance may be different. Perhaps, the most interesting observation is the similarity in performance given the radically different approaches.

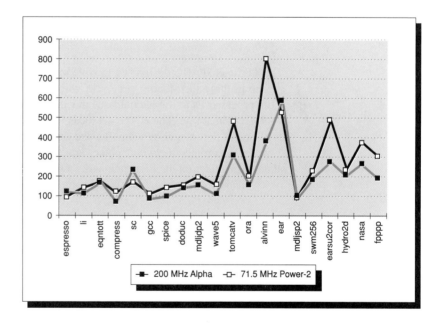

FIGURE 5.49 The performance of the Power-2 versus the Alpha design. Overall, the Power-2 performance is about 1.09 times higher on the integer benchmarks and about 1.35 times higher on the FP benchmarks.

5.9 | Fallacies and Pitfalls

Fallacy: Machines with lower CPIs will always be faster.

Although a lower CPI is certainly better, sophisticated pipelines, like the Power-2, typically have lower clock rates than machines with simple pipelines. In applications with limited ILP or where the parallelism cannot be exploited by the hardware resources, the faster clock rate often wins. Comparing the low CPI Power-2 against the high CPI Decchip 21064 (Alpha), shows that on a few benchmarks the fast clock rate of Alpha leads to better performance (see Figure 5.49). Of course, this fallacy is nothing more than a restatement of a Pitfall from Chapter 2 about comparing machines using only one part of the performance equation.

Pitfall: Emphasizing a reduction in CPI by increasing in issue rate while sacrificing clock rate can lead to lower performance.

The TI SuperSPARC design is a flexible multiple issue machine capable of issuing up to three instructions per cycle with a clock rate of 60MHz. The HP PA 7100 processor is a simple dual issue machine (integer and FP combination) with a 99MHz clock rate. The HP processor is faster on all the SPEC benchmarks except two of the integer benchmarks and one FP benchmark, as shown in Figure 5.50.2. On average, the two machines are close on integer, but the HP machine is about 50% faster on the FP benchmarks. Of course, differences in compiler technology as well as the processor could contribute to the performance differences.

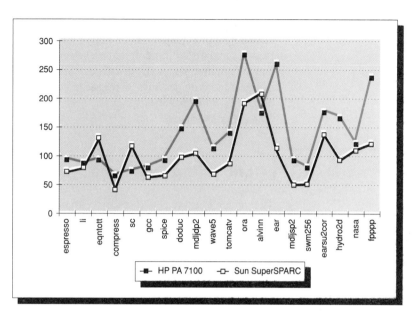

FIGURE 5.50 **The performance of a 99MHz HP PA7100 processor versus a 60 MHz SuperSPARC.**

The potential of multiple issue techniques has caused many designers to focus on reducing CPI while possibly not focusing adequately on the trade-off in cycle time incurred when implementing these sophisticated techniques. This inclination arises at least partially because it is easier with good simulation tools to evaluate the impact of enhancements that affect CPI than it is to evaluate the cycle time impact. There are two factors that lead to this outcome. First, it is difficult to know the clock rate impact of an approach until the design is well underway, and then it may be too late to make large changes in the organization. Second, the design simulation tools available for determining and improving CPI are generally better than those available for determining and improving cycle time. In understanding the complex interaction between cycle time and various organizational approaches, the experience of the designers seems to be one of the most valuable factors.

Pitfall: Improving only one aspect of a multiple issue machine and expecting overall performance improvement.

This is simply a restatement of Amdahl's law. A designer might simply look at a design, see a poor branch prediction mechanism and improve it, expecting to see significant performance improvements. The difficulty is that many factors limit the performance of multiple issue techniques and improving one aspect of a machine often exposes some other aspect that previously did not limit performance. We can see examples of this in the data on ILP. For example, looking just at the effect of branch prediction in Figure 5.38 on page 345, we can see that going from a standard 2-bit predictor to a selective predictor significantly improves the parallelism in espresso (from an issue rate of 7 to an issue rate of 12). However, if the machine provides only 32 registers for renaming, the amount of parallelism is limited to 5 issues per clock cycle, even with a branch prediction scheme better than either alternative.

5.10 | Concluding Remarks

The tremendous interest in multiple issue organizations came about because of an interest in improving performance without affecting the standard uniprocessor programming model. While taking advantage of ILP is conceptually simple, the design problems are amazingly complex in practice and it is extremely difficult to achieve the performance one might expect from a simple first-level analysis.

The tradeoffs between increasing clock speed and decreasing CPI though multiple issue are extremely hard to quantify. Although one might expect that it is possible to build an advanced multiple issue machine with a high clock rate, a factor of two in clock rate has consistently separated the highest clock rate processors and the most sophisticated multiple issue machines. It is simply too early to tell whether this difference is due to fundamental implementation tradeoffs, or to the difficulty of dealing with the complexities in multiple issue machines, or simply a lack of experience in implementing such machines. One insight that is clear is that the peak to sustained performance ratios for multiple issue machines are often quite large and typically grow as the issue rate grows. Thus, increasing the clock rate by a constant factor is almost always a better choice than increasing the issue width by the same factor, though often the clock rate increase may rely largely on deeper pipelining, substantially narrowing the advantage. On the other hand, a simple two-way superscalar that issues FP instructions in parallel with integer instructions can probably be built with little impact on clock rate and should perform better on FP applications and suffer little or no degradation on integer applications. Whether approaches based primarily on faster clock rates, simpler hardware, and more static scheduling or approaches using more sophisticated hardware to achieve lower CPI will win out is difficult to say and may depend on the benchmarks. At the present, both approaches seem capable of delivering similar performance.

What will happen to multiple issue machines in the long-term? The basic trends in integrated circuit technology lead to an important insight: the number of devices available on a chip will grow faster than the device speed. This means that designs that obtain performance with more transistors rather than just raw gate speed are a more promising direction. Three other factors limit how far we can exploit this trend, however. One is the increasing delay of interconnections compared to gates, which means that bigger designs will have longer cycle times. The second factor is the diminishing returns seen when trying to exploit ILP. The last factor is the potential impact of increased complexity on either the clock rate or the design time. Combined, these effects may serve as effective limits to how much performance can be gained by exploiting ILP within a single processor.

The alternative to trying to continue to push uniprocessors to exploit ILP is to look towards multiprocessors, the topic of Chapter 9. Looking towards multiprocessors to take advantage of parallelism overcomes a fundamental problem in ILP machines: building a cost-effective memory system. A multiprocessor memory system is inherently multiported and, as we will see, can even be distributed in a larger machine. Using multiprocessors to exploit parallelism encounters two difficulties. First, it is likely that the software model will need to change. Second MP approaches may have difficulty in exploiting fine-grained, low-level parallelism. While it appears clear that using a large number of processors requires new programming approaches, using smaller number of processors efficiently could be based on compiler approaches. Exploiting the type of fine-grained parallelism that a compiler can easily uncover can be quite difficult in a multiprocessor, since the processors are relatively far apart. To date, computer architects do not know how to design processors that can effectively exploit ILP in a multiprocessor configuration. Existing high performance designs are either tightly integrated uniprocessors or loosely coupled multiprocessors. Early in the next century, it should be possible to place two fully configured processors on a single die. Perhaps this capability will inspire the design of a new type of architecture that allows processors to be more tightly coupled than before, but also separates them sufficiently that the design can be partitioned and that each processor can individually achieve very high performance.

5.11 | Historical Perspective and References

This section describes some of the major advances in compiler technology and advanced pipelining and ends with some of the recent literature on multiple issue machines. The basic concepts–data dependence and its limitation in exploiting parallelism–are old ideas that were studied in the 1960s. Ideas such as dataflow computation derived from observations that programs were limited by data dependence. Loop unrolling is a similarly old idea, practiced by early computer programmers on machines with very expensive branches.

The Introduction of Dynamic Scheduling

In 1964 CDC delivered the first CDC 6600. The CDC 6600 was unique in many ways. In addition to introducing scoreboarding, the CDC 6600 was the first machine to make extensive use of multiple functional units. It also had peripheral processors that used a timeshared pipeline. The interaction between pipelining and instruction set design was understood, and the instruction set was kept simple to promote pipelining. The CDC 6600 also used an advanced packaging technology. Thornton [1964] describes the pipeline and I/O processor architecture, including the concept of out-of-order instruction execution. Thornton's book [1970] provides an excellent description of the entire machine, from technology to architecture, and includes a foreword by Cray. (Unfortunately, this book is currently out of print.) The CDC 6600 also has an instruction scheduler for the Fortran compilers, described by Thornton [1967].

The IBM 360/91 introduced many new concepts, including tagging of data, register renaming, dynamic detection of memory hazards, and generalized forwarding. Tomasulo's algorithm is described in his 1967 paper. Anderson, Sparacio, and Tomasulo [1967] describe other aspects of the machine, including the use of branch prediction.

Branch Prediction Schemes

Basic dynamic hardware branch-prediction schemes are described by J. E. Smith [1981] and by A. Smith and Lee [1984]. Ditzel [1987] describes a novel branch-target buffer for CRISP, which implements branch folding. McFarling and Hennessy [1986] did a quantitative comparison of a variety of compile-time and run-time branch-prediction schemes. The first implementation of a correlating predictor was in the IBM Power-1 and is described by Pan, So, and Rameh in 1992. Yeh and Patt [1992,1993] have written several papers on multilevel predictors that use branch histories for each branch. McFarling's competitive prediction scheme is described in 1993 technical report.

The Development of Multiple Issue Machines

The concept of multiple issue designs has been around for a while, though most early machines followed an LIW or VLIW design approach. Charlesworth [1981] reports on the Floating Point Systems AP-120B, one of the first wide-instruction machines containing multiple operations per instruction. Floating Point Systems applied the concept of software pipelining in both a compiler and by hand-writing assembly language libraries to use the machine efficiently. Since the machine was an attached processor, many of the difficulties of implementing multiple issue in general-purpose machines, e.g. virtual memory and exception handling, could be ignored. The Stanford MIPS processor had the ability to place two operations in a single instruction, though this capability was dropped in commercial variants of the architecture, primarily for performance reasons. Along with his colleagues at Yale, Fisher [1983] proposed creating a machine with a very wide instruction (512 bits), and named this type of machine a VLIW. Code was generated for the machine using trace scheduling, which Fisher [1981] had developed originally for generating horizontal microcode. The implementation of trace scheduling for the Yale machine is described by Fisher, et. al. [1984] and by Ellis [1986]. The Multiflow machine (see Colwell et. al. [1987]) was based on the concepts developed at Yale, although many important refinements were made to increase the practicality of the approach. Among these was a controllable store buffer that provided support for a form of speculation. Although more than 100 Multiflow machines were sold, a variety of problems, including the difficulties of introducing a new instruction set from a small company and the competition provided from RISC microprocessors that changed the economics in the minicomputer market, led to failure of Multiflow as a company. Around the same time, Cydrome was founded to build a VLIW style machine [see Rau et. al.] 1989, which was also unsuccessful commercially. Dehnert, Hsu, and Bratt [1989] explain the architecture and performance of the Cydrome Cydra 5, a machine with a wide instruction word that provides dynamic register renaming and additional support for software pipelining. The Cydra 5 is a unique blend of hardware and software, including conditional instructions, aimed at extracting ILP. Cydrome relied on more hardware than the Multiflow machine and achieved competitive performance primarily on vector-style codes. In the end, Cydrome suffered from similar problems as Multiflow and was not a commercial success. Both Multiflow and Cydrome, though unsuccessful as commercial entities, produced a number of people with extensive experience in exploiting ILP as well as advanced compiler technology; many of those people have gone on to incorporate their experience and the pieces of the technology in newer machines. Recently, Fisher and Rau [1993] edited a comprehensive collection of papers covering the hardware and software of these two important machines.

Rau had also developed a scheduling technique called *polycyclic scheduling*, which is a basis for most software pipelining schemes (see Rau, Glaeser, and Picard 1982). Rau's work built on earlier work by Davidson and his colleagues on the design of optimal hardware schedulers for pipelined machines. Other LIW machines have included the Apollo DN 10000 and the Intel i860, both of which could dual issue FP and integer operations.

One of the interesting approaches used in early VLIW machines, such as the AP 120B and i860, was the idea of a pipeline organization that requires operations to be "pushed through" a functional unit and the results to be caught at the end of the pipeline. In such machines, operations advance only when another operation pushes them from behind (in sequence). Furthermore, an instruction specifies the destination for an instruction issued earlier that will be pushed out of the pipeline when this new operation is pushed in. Such an approach has the advantage that it does not specify a result destination when an operation first issues but only when the result register is actually written. This eliminates the need to detect WAW and WAR hazards in the hardware. The disadvantage is that it increases code size since no-ops may be needed to push results out when there is a dependence on an operation that is still in the pipeline. and no other operations of that type are immediately needed. Instead of the "push-and-catch" approach used in these two machines, almost all designers have chosen to use *self-draining pipelines* that specify the destination in the issuing instruction and in which an issued instruction will complete without further action. The advantages in code density and simplifications in code generation seems to outweigh the advantages of the more unusual structure.

The earliest proposal for a superscalar machine that dynamically makes issue decisions was by John Cocke; he described the key ideas in several talks in the mid-1980's, and coined the name superscalar. This original design was named America and is described by Agerwala and Cocke [1987]. The IBM Power-1 architecture (the RS/6000 line) is based on these ideas (see Bakoglu et al. [1989]).

J. E. Smith and his colleagues at Wisconsin [1984] proposed the decoupled approach that included multiple issue with limited dynamic pipeline scheduling. A key feature of this machine is the use of queues to maintain order among a class of instructions (such as memory references) while allowing it to slip behind or ahead of another class of instructions. The Astronautics ZS-1 described by Smith et al. [1987] embodies this approach with queues to connect the load/store unit and the operation units. The Power-2 design uses queues in a similar fashion. J. E. Smith [1989] also describes the advantages of dynamic scheduling and compares that approach to static scheduling.

The concept of speculation has its roots in the original 360/91, which performed a very limited form of speculation. Patt and his colleagues have described an approach, called HPSm, that is an extension of Tomasulo's algorithm [Hwu and Patt 1986] and supports speculative-like execution. Other researchers, including S. Weiss and J.E. Smith [1984] and Sohi and Vajapayem [1987], explored speculative techniques as a way of boosting issue rates and of maintaining precise interrupts in the presence of dynamic scheduling.

The use of speculation as a technique in multiple issue machines was evaluated by Smith, Johnson, and Horowitz [1989]; their goal was to study available ILP in nonscientific code using speculation and multiple issue. In a subsequent book, Johnson [1992] describes the design of a speculative superscalar machine.

What is surprising about the development of multiple issue machines is that many of these machines have not been successful. Recent superscalars with modest issue capabilities (e.g. the DEC 21064 or HP 7100) have shown that the techniques can be used together with aggressive clock rates to build very fast machines, and designs like the Power-2 and TFP [Hsu 1993] processor show that very high issue rate machines can be successful in the FP domain.

Compiler Technology

Loop-level parallelism and dependence analysis was developed by primarily by D. Kuck and his colleagues at the University of Illinois in the 1970s. They also coined the commonly used terminology of antidependence and output dependence and developed several standard dependence tests including the GCD and Banerjee tests. The latter test was named after Uptal Banerjee and comes in a variety of flavors. Recent work on dependence analysis has focused on using a variety of exact tests ending with an algorithm called Fourier-Motzkin, which is a linear programming algorithm. D. Maydan and W. Pugh both showed that the sequences of exact tests were a practical solution.

In the area of uncovering and scheduling ILP, much of the early work was connected to the development of VLIW machines, described earlier. Lam [1988] developed algorithms for software pipelining and evaluated their use on Warp, a wide-instruction-word machine designed for special-purpose applications. Weiss and J. E. Smith [1987] compare software pipelining versus loop unrolling as techniques for scheduling code on a pipelined machine. Recently several groups have been looking at techniques for scheduling code for machines with conditional and speculative execution, but without full support for dynamic hardware scheduling. For example, Smith, Lam, and Horowitz [1992] created a concept called boosting that contains a hardware facility for supporting speculation but relies on compiler scheduling of speculated instructions. The sentinel concept, developed by Hwu and his colleagues [Malke et al.] is a more general form of this idea.

Studies of ILP

A series of early papers, including Tjaden and Flynn [1970] and Riseman and Foster [1972], concluded that only small amounts of parallelism could be available at the instruction level without investing an enormous amount of hardware. These papers dampened the appeal of multiple instruction issue for more than ten years. Nicolau and Fisher [1984] published a paper based on their work with trace scheduling and asserting the presence of large amounts of potential ILP in scientific programs.

Since then there have been many studies of the available ILP. Such studies have been criticized since they presume some level of both hardware support and compiler technology. Nonetheless, the studies are useful to set expectations as well as to understand the sources of the limitations. Wall has participated in several such strategies including Jouppi and Wall [1989], Wall [1991], and Wall [1993]. While the early studies were criticized as being conservative (e.g., they didn't include speculation), the latest study is by far the most ambitious study of ILP to date and the basis for the data in Section 5.8. Sohi and Vajapeyam [1989] give measurements of available parallelism for wide-instruction-word machines.

Smith, Johnson, and Horowitz [1991] also used a speculative superscalar machine to study ILP limits. At the time of their study, they anticipated that the machine they specified was an upper bound on reasonable designs. Recent and upcoming machines, however, are likely to be at least as ambitious as their machine. Most recently, Lam and Wilson [1993] have looked at the limitations imposed by speculation and shown that additional gains are possible by allowing machines to speculate in multiple directions, which requires more than one PC. Such ideas represent one possible alternative for future processor architectures, since they represent a hybrid organization between a conventional uniprocessor and a conventional multiprocessor.

Recent Advanced Microprocessors

Much debate has be had over the merits of multiple issue (superscalar) versus deeper pipelining (superpipelined). Jouppi and Wall [1989] examine the performance differences between superpipelined and simple superscalar systems, concluding that their performance is similar, but that superpipelined machines may require less hardware to achieve the same performance. In practice, many factors including the implementation technology, the memory hierarchy, the skill of the designers, and the type of applications benchmarked all play a role in determining which approach is best. The chart in Figure 5.11.1 shows some of the most interesting recent processors, their characteristics and suggested references.

Machine	Year First Shipped	Characteristics	References
MIPS R4000	1991	Superpipelined, single issue machine.	Hot Chips, Compcon
IBM Power-1	1991	Four issues per clock; smaller simpler than Power-2.	IBM J. Res & Dev.
HP 7100	1992	Static two-issue (FP/integer); off-chip cache	Hot Chips 1992; Micro June 1993
DEC Alpha (21064)	1992	Two issues per clock one from each of FP, integer, load/store, and branch; superpipelined	Hot Chips Digital Technical Journal
SuperSPARC	1993	Three issues per clock; on-chip caches.	Hot Chips [1992]
IBM Power-2	1994	Six issues: up to two FP, 2 load/store, and 2 branches (see Section 5.8).	Weiss and Smith [1994]
MIPS TFP	1994	Four issue: up to 2 load/store, 2 FP, 2 integer per clock.	Hsu [1993], Hot Chips
Intel Pentium	1994	Two-issue superscalar with up to memory accesses/clock.	Alpert [1993], Hot Chips

FIGURE 5.51 Recent high performance processors and their characteristics and suggested references.

References

AGERWALA, T. AND J. COCKE [1987]. "High performance reduced instruction set processors," IBM Tech. Rep. (March).

ANDERSON, D. W., F. J. SPARACIO, AND R. M. TOMASULO [1967]. "The IBM 360 Model 91: Machine philosophy and instruction handling," *IBM J. of Research and Development* 11:1 (January) 8–24.

BAKOGLU, H. B., G. F. GROHOSKI, L. E. THATCHER, J. A. KAHLE, C. R. MOORE, D. P. TUTTLE, W. E. MAULE, W. R. HARDELL, D. A. HICKS, M. NGUYEN PHU, R. K. MONTOYE, W. T. GLOVER , AND S. DHAWAN [1989]. "IBM second-generation RISC machine organization," Proc. Int'l Conf. on Computer Design, IEEE (October) Rye, N.Y., 138–142.

CHARLESWORTH, A. E. [1981]. "An approach to scientific array processing: The architecture design of the AP-120B/FPS-164 family," *Computer* 14:12 (December) 12–30.

COLWELL, R. P., R. P. NIX, J. J. O'DONNELL, D. B. PAPWORTH, AND P K. RODMAN [1987]. "A VLIW architecture for a trace scheduling compiler," *Proc. Second Conf. on Architectural Support for Programming Languages and Operating Systems,* IEEE/ACM (March), Palo Alto, Calif., 180–192.

DEHNERT, J. C., P. Y.-T. HSU, AND J. P. BRATT [1989]. "Overlapped loop support on the Cydra 5," *Proc. Third Conf. on Architectural Support for Programming Languages and Operating Systems* (April), IEEE/ACM, Boston, 26–39.

DITZEL, D. R. AND H. R. McLELLAN [1987]. "Branch folding in the CRISP microprocessor: Reducing the branch delay to zero," *Proc. 14th Symposium on Computer Architecture* (June), Pittsburgh, 2–7.

ELLIS, J. R [1986]. *Bulldog: A Compiler for VLIW Architectures,* The MIT Press,1986.

FISHER, J. A. [1981]. "Trace Scheduling: A Technique for Global Microcode Compaction," *IEEE Trans. on Computers* 30:7 (July), 478-490.

FISHER, J. A. [1983]. "Very long instruction word architectures and ELI-512," *Proc. Tenth Symposium on Computer Architecture* (June), Stockholm, Sweden., 140-150.

FISHER J. A., J. R. ELLIS, J. C. RUTTENBERG, AND A. NICOLAU [1984]. "Parallel processing: A smart compiler and a dumb machine," *Proc. SIGPLAN Conf. on Compiler Construction* (June), Palo Alto, CA, 11-16.

FISHER J. A. AND B.R. RAU, *Journal of Supercomputing xx:1 (January),* Kluwer.

FOSTER, C. C. AND E. M. RISEMAN [1972]. "Percolation of code to enhance parallel dispatching and execution," *IEEE Trans. on Computers* C-21:12 (December) 1411–1415.

HWU, W.-M. AND Y. PATT [1986]. "HPSm, a high performance restricted data flow architecture having minimum functionality," *Proc. 13th Symposium on Computer Architecture* (June), Tokyo, 297–307.

IBM [1990]. "The IBM RISC System/6000 processor," collection of papers, *IBM Jour. of Research and Development* 34:1, (January), 119 pages.

JOUPPI, N. P. AND D. W. WALL [1989]. "Available instruction level parallelism for superscalar and superpipelined machines," *Proc. Third Conf. on Architectural Support for Programming Languages and Operating Systems,* IEEE/ACM (April), Boston, 272–282.

KUNKEL, S. R. AND J. E. SMITH [1986]. "Optimal pipelining in supercomputers," *Proc. 13th Symposium on Computer Architecture* (June), Tokyo, 404–414.

LAM, M. [1988]. "Software pipelining: An effective scheduling technique for VLIW machines," *SIGPLAN Conf. on Programming Language Design and Implementation,* ACM (June), Atlanta, Ga., 318–328.

McFarling, S. [1993] "Combining branch predictors," *WRL Technical Note TN-36 (June),* Digital Western Research Laboratory, Palo Alto, CA.

McFarling, S. and J. Hennessy [1986]. "Reducing the cost of branches," *Proc. 13th Symposium on Computer Architecture* (June), Tokyo, 396–403.

Nicolau, A. and J. A. Fisher [1984]. "Measuring the parallelism available for very long instruction work architectures," *IEEE Trans. on Computers* C-33:11 (November) 968–976.

Rau, B.R., Glaeser, C.D., and Picard, R.L. [1982]. "Efficient code generation for horizontal architectures: Compiler techniques and architectural support," *Proc. 9th Symposium on Computer Architecture* (April), 131-139.

Rau, B.R., Yen, D.W.L., Yen, W., and Towle, R.A. [1989] "The Cydra 5 departmental supercomputer: Design philosophies, decisions, and trade-offs," *IEEE Computers* 22:1 (January) 12-34.

Riseman, E.M. and C.C. Foster [1972]. "Percolation of code to enhance parallel dispatching and execution," *IEEE Trans. on Computers* C-21:12 (December) 1411–1415.

Smith, A. and J. Lee [1984]. "Branch prediction strategies and branch target buffer design," *Computer* 17:1 (January) 6–22.

Smith, J. E. [1981]. "A study of branch prediction strategies," *Proc. Eighth Symposium on Computer Architecture* (May), Minneapolis, 135–148.

Smith, J. E. [1984]. "Decoupled access/execute computer architectures," *ACM Trans. on Computer Systems* 2:4 (November), 289–308.

Smith, J. E. [1989]. "Dynamic instruction scheduling and the Astronautics ZS-1," *Computer* 22:7 (July) 21–35.

Smith, J. E., G. E. Dermer, B. D. Vanderwarn, S. D. Klinger, C. M. Rozewski, D. L. Fowler, K. R. Scidmore, J. P. Laudon [1987]. "The ZS-1 central processor," *Proc. Second Conf. on Architectural Support for Programming Languages and Operating Systems,* IEEE/ACM (March), Palo Alto, Calif., 199–204.

Smith, M. D., M. Johnson, and M. A. Horowitz [1989]. "Limits on multiple instruction issue," *Proc. Third Conf. on Architectural Support for Programming Languages and Operating Systems,* IEEE/ACM (April), Boston, Mass., 290–302.

Sohi , G. S., and S. Vajapeyam [1989]. "Tradeoffs in instruction format design for horizontal architectures," *Proc. Third Conf. on Architectural Support for Programming Languages and Operating Systems,* IEEE/ACM (April), Boston, Mass. 15–25.

Thornton, J. E. [1964]. "Parallel operation in the Control Data 6600," *Proc. Fall Joint Computer Conf.* 26, 33–40.

Thornton, J. E. [1970]. *Design of a Computer, the Control Data 6600,* Scott, Foresman, Glenview, Ill.

Tjaden, G. S. and M. J. Flynn [1970]. "Detection and parallel execution of independent instructions," *IEEE Trans. on Computers* C-19:10 (October) 889–895.

Tomasulo, R. M. [1967]. "An efficient algorithm for exploiting multiple arithmetic units," *IBM J. of Research and Development* 11:1 (January) 25–33.

Weiss, S. and J. E. Smith [1984]. "Instruction issue logic for pipelined supercomputers," *Proc. 11th Symposium on Computer Architecture* (June), Ann Arbor, Mich., 110–118.

Weiss, S. and J. E. Smith [1987]. "A study of scalar compilation techniques for pipelined supercomputers," *Proc. Second Conf. on Architectural Support for Programming Languages and Operating Systems* (March), IEEE/ACM, Palo Alto, Calif., 105–109.

Weiss, S. and J. E. Smith [1994]. *Inside IBM Power and PowerPC,* Morgan Kaufmann, San Francisco, CA.

Lam, M.S... and R.P. Wilson [1992]. "Limits of Control Flow on Parallelism," *Proc. 19th Symposium on Computer Architecture* (May), Gold Coast, Austrailia, 46-57.

YEH, T.. AND Y. N. PATT [1992]. "Alternative Implementations of Two-Level Adaptive Branch Prediction," *Proc. 19th Symposium on Computer Architecture* (May), Gold Coast, Austrailia, 124-134.

YEH, T.. AND Y. N. PATT [1993]. "A Comparison of Dynamic Branch Predictors that Use Two Levels of Branch History," *Proc. 20th Symposium on Computer Architecture* (May), San Diego, 257-266.

EXERCISES

5.1 [15] <5.1> List all the dependences (output, anti, and true) in the following code fragment. Indicate whether the true dependences are loop-carried or not. Show why the loop is not parallel.

```
for (i=2;i<100;i=i+1) {
        a[i] = b[i] + a[i];    /* S1 */
        c[i-1] = a[i] + d[i];  /* S2 */
        a[i-1] = 2 * b[i];     /* S3 */
        b[i+1] = 2 * b[i];     /* S4 */
}
```

5.2 [15] <5.1> Here is an unusual loop. First, list the dependences and then rewrite the loop so that it is parallel.

```
for (i=1;i<100;i=i+1) {
        a[i] = b[i] + c[i];    /* S1 */
        b[i] = a[i] + d[i];    /* S2 */
        a[i+1] = a[i] + e[i];  /* S3 */
}
```

5.3 [10] <5.1> For the following code fragment, list the control dependences. For each control dependence, tell whether the statement can be scheduled before the if-statement. Assume that all data references are shown, that all values are defined before use, and that only b mad c are used again after this segment. You may ignore any possible exceptions.

```
if (a>c) {
        d = d + 5;
        a = b + d + e;}
else {
        e = e + 2;
        f = f + 2;
        c = c + f;
}
b = a + f;
```

5.4 [15] <5.1> Assume the pipeline latencies from Figure 5.2, unroll the following loop as many times as necessary to schedule it without any delays, collapsing the loop overhead instructions. Show the schedule. The loop computes Y[i] = a * X[i] + Y[i], the key step in a Gaussian elimination.

```
loop:   LD      F0,0(R1)
        MULTD   F0,F0,F2
        LD      F4,0(R2)
        ADDD    F0,F0,F4
        SD      0(R2),F0
        SUBI    R1,R1,8
        SUBI    R2,R2,8
        BNEQZ   R1,loop
```

5.5 [15] <5.1> Assume the pipeline latencies from Figure 5.2. Unroll the following loop a sufficient number of times to schedule it without any delays. Show the schedule after eliminating any redundant overhead instructions. The loop is a dot product (assuming F2 is initially 0) and contains a recurrence. Despite the fact that the loop is not parallel, it can be scheduled with no delays.

```
loop:   LD      F0,0(R1)
        LD      F4,0(R2)
        MULTD   F0,F0,F4
        ADDD    F2,F0,F2
        SUBI    R1,R1,8
        SUBI    R2,R2,8
        BNEQZ   R1,loop
```

5.6 [20] <5.2> It is critical that the scoreboard be able to distinguish RAW and WAR hazards, since a WAR hazard requires stalling the instruction doing the writing until the instruction reading an operand initiates execution, while a RAW hazard requires delaying the reading instruction until the writing instruction finishes–just the opposite. For example, consider the sequence:

```
        MULTD   F0,F6,F4
        SUBD    F8,F0,F2
        ADDD    F2,F10,F2
```

The SUBD depends on the MULTD (a RAW hazard) and the MULTD must be allowed to complete before the SUBD; if the MULTD is stalled for the SUBD, the machine will deadlock. This sequence contains a WAR hazard between the ADDD and the SUBD, and the ADDD cannot be allowed to complete until the SUBD begins execution. The difficulty lies in distinguishing the RAW hazard between MULTD and SUBD, and the WAR hazard between the SUBD and ADDD.

Describe how the scoreboard avoids this problem and show the scoreboard values for the above sequence assuming the ADDD is the only instruction that has completed execution. (Hint: Think about how the third class of hazards are prevented and what this implies about active instruction sequences.)

5.7 [12] <5.3> A shortcoming of the scoreboard approach occurs when multiple functional units that share input buses are waiting for a single result. The units cannot start simultaneously, but must serialize. This is not true in Tomasulo's algorithm. Give a code sequence that uses no more than 10 instructions and shows this problem. Use the FP latencies from Figure 5.2 (page 256) and the same functional units in both examples. Indicate where the

Tomasulo approach can continue, but the scoreboard approach must stall.

5.8 [15] <5.3> Tomasulo's algorithm also has a disadvantage versus the scoreboard: only one result can complete per clock, due to the CDB. Using the FP latencies from Figure 6.29 (page 289) and the same functional units in both cases, find a code sequence of no more than 10 instructions where scoreboard does not stall, but Tomasulo's algorithm must. Indicate where this occurs in your sequence.

5.9 [45] <5.3> One benefit of a dynamically scheduled machine is its ability to tolerate changes in latency or issue capability without requiring recompilation. This was a primary motivation behind the 360/91 implementation. The purpose of this programming assignment is to evaluate this effect. Implement a version of Tomasulo's algorithm for DLX to issue one instruction per clock; your implementation should also be capable of in-order issue. Assume the following counts of functional units and the following latencies:

Unit	Count	Latency
Integer	6.	7.
Branch	8.	9.
Load/Store	10.	11.
FP Add	12.	13.
FP Mult	14.	15.
FP Divide	16.	17.

Where a one cycle latency means that the unit and the result are available for the next instruction. Assume the machine takes a one cycle stall for branches, in addition to any data dependent stalls. Choose 5-10 small FP benchmarks (with loops) to run; compare the performance with and without dynamic scheduling. Try scheduling the loops by hand and see how close you can get with the statically scheduled machine to the dynamically scheduled results.

Change the machine to the following configuration:

Unit	Count	Latency
Integer	18.	19.
Branch	20.	21.
Load/Store	22.	23.
FP Add	24.	25.
FP Mult	26.	27.
FP Divide	28.	29.

Rerun the loops and compare the performance of the dynamically scheduled machine and the statically scheduled machine.

5.10 [15] <5.4> Suppose we have a deeply pipelined machine, for which we implement a branch-target buffer for the conditional branches only. Assume that the misprediction penalty is always 4 cycles and the buffer miss penalty is always 3 cycles. Assume 90% hit rate and 90% accuracy, and the branch statistics in Figure 4.xx (page XYZ).[6] How much faster is the machine with the branch-target buffer versus a machine that has a fixed 2-cycle branch penalty? Assume a base CPI without branch stalls of 1.

5.11 [10] <5.4> Determine the improvement from branch folding for unconditional branches. Assume a 90% hit rate, a base CPI of 1, and the data in Figure 4.xx (page XYZ),[7] how much improvement is gained by this enhancement versus a machine whose effective CPI is 1.1.

5.11.5 [30] <5.4> Implement a simulator to evaluate the performance of a branch prediction buffer that does not store branches that are predicted as untaken. Consider the following prediction schemes: a 1-bit predictor storing only predicted taken branches, a 2-bit predictor storing all the branches, a scheme with a target buffer that stores only predicted taken branches and a 2-bit prediction buffer. Explore different sizes for the buffers keeping the total number of bits (assuming 32 bit addresses) the same for all schemes. Determine what the branch penalties are using Figure 5.20 as a guideline. How do the different schemes compare both in prediction accuracy and in branch cost?

5.12 [30] <5.4> Implement a simulator to evaluate various branch prediction schemes. You can use the instruction portion of a set of cache traces to simulate the branch prediction buffer. Pick a set of table sizes (e.g., 1Kbits, 2Kbits, 8Kbits, and 16Kbits). Determine the performance of both (0,2) and (2,2) predictors for the various table sizes. Also compare the performance of the degenerate predictor that uses no branch address information for these table sizes. Determine how large must the table be for the degenerate predictor to perform as well as a (0,2) predictor with 256 entries.

Exercises 5.13–5.24 For these problems we will look at how a common vector loop runs on a variety of pipelined versions of DLX. The loop is the so-called SAXPY loop (discussed extensively in Chapter 7), and the central operation in Gaussian elimination The loop implements the vector operation Y = a*X+Y for a vector of length 100. Here is the DLX code for the loop:

```
foo:    LD      F2,0(R1)        ;load X(i)
        MULTD   F4,F2,F0        ;multiply a*X(i)
        LD      F6,0(R2)        ;load Y(i)
        ADDD    F6,F4,F6        ;add a*X(i) + Y(i)
        SD      0(R2),F6        ;store Y(i)
        ADDI    R1,R1,#8        ;increment X index
        ADDI    R2,R2,#8        ;increment Y index
        SGTI    R3,R1,done      ;test if done
        BEQZ    R3,foo          ; loop if not done
```

---

6.   This is a reference to old figure 6.18, which now appears in chapter 4.

7.   also a cross reference to old 6.18

For these problems, assume that the integer operations issue and complete in one clock cycle and that their results are fully bypassed. Ignore the branch delay. You will use the FP latencies shown in Figure 6.29 (page 289)[8] unless stated otherwise. Assume the FP units are not pipelined unless the problem states otherwise.

5.13 [20] <5.1> For this problem use the pipeline constraints shown in Figure 6.29 (page 289)[9]. and assume a single issue pipeline. Show the number of stall cycles for each instruction and what clock cycle the instruction begins execution (i.e., enters its first EX cycle) on the first iteration of the loop. How many clock cycles does each loop iteration take?

5.14 [22] <5.1> Unroll the DLX code for SAXPY to make four copies of the body and schedule it for the standard DLX pipeline. Assume the FP latencies of Figure 6.29.[10] When unwinding, you should optimize the code as we did in Section 5.1`. Significant reordering of the code will be needed to maximize performance. What is the speedup over the original loop?

5.15 [22] <5.2> Using the DLX code for SAXPY above, show the state of the scoreboard tables (as in Figure 5.4) when the SGTI instruction reaches Write result. Assume that issue and read operands each take a cycle. Assume that there are three integer functional units and they take only a single execution cycle (including loads and stores). Assume the functional unit count described in Section 5.3 with the FP latencies of Figure 6.29.[11] The branch should not be included in the scoreboard.

5.16 [22] <5.2> Use the DLX code for SAXPY above and the latencies of Figure 6.29[12]. Assuming Tomasulo's algorithm for the hardware with the functional units described in Section 5.3 show the state of the reservation stations and register-status tables (as in Figure 5.9) when the SGTI writes its result on the CDB. Make the same assumptions about latencies and functional units as the previous exercise.

5.17 [22] <5.2> Using the DLX code for SAXPY above, assume a scoreboard with the functional units described in the algorithm for the hardware, plus three integer functional units (also used for load/store). Assume the following latencies in clock cycles:

FP multiply	10
FP add	6
FP load/store	2
All integer operations	1

Show the state of the scoreboard (as in Figure 5.4) when the branch issues for the second

8.   this is the old figure number--figure is now in chapter 4

9.   old reference--figure now in chapter 4

10. old reference now in Chap 4

11. old reference--now in chapter 4

12. same old reference again

time. Assume the branch was correctly predicted taken and took one cycle. How many clock cycles does each loop iteration take? You may ignore any register port/bus conflicts.

5.18 [25] <5.2> Use the DLX code for SAXPY above. Assume Tomasulo's algorithm for the hardware using the functional-unit count shown in Section 5.3 Assume the following latencies in clock cycles:

FP multiply	10
FP add	6
FP load/store	2
All integer operations	1

Show the state of the reservation stations and register status tables (as in Figure 5.9) when the branch is executed for the second time. Assume the branch was correctly predicted as taken. How many clock cycles does each loop iteration take?

5.19 [25] <5.4> Assume a superscalar architecture that can issue any two independent operations in a clock cycle (including two integer operations). Unwind the DLX code for SAXPY to make four copies of the body and schedule it assuming the FP latencies of Figure 6.29[13]. Assume one fully-pipelined copy of each functional unit (e.g., FP adder, FP multiplier). How many clock cycles will each iteration on the original code take? When unwinding, you should optimize the code as in Section 6.8. What is the speedup versus the original code?

5.20 [25] <5.4> In a superpipelined machine, rather than have multiple functional units, we would fully pipeline all the units. Suppose we designed a superpipelined DLX that had twice the clock rate of our standard DLX pipeline and could issue any two unrelated instructions in the same time that the normal DLX pipeline issued one operation. If the second instruction is dependent on the first, only the first will issue. Unroll the DLX SAXPY code to make four copies of the loop body and schedule it for this superpipelined machine assuming the FP latencies of Figure 6.29[14]. How many clock cycles does each loop iteration take? Remember that these clock cycles are half as long as those on a standard DLX pipeline or a superscalar DLX.

5.21 [20] <5.4> Start with the SAXPY code and the machine used in Figure 5.22. Unroll the SAXPY loop to make four copies of the body, performing simple optimizations (as in Section 5.1). Fill in a table like Figure 5.23 for the unrolled loop. How many clock cycles does each loop iteration take?

5.22 [20] <5.4> Using the SAXPY code from above, show the tables for a dynamically scheduled machine using reservation tables (as in Figure 5.9) at the time the first branch commits. Assume the following latencies in clock cycles:

FP multiply	10
FP add	6

---

13.   old reference now in chapter 4
14.   old reference now in chapter 4

FP load/store	2
All integer operations	1
Branch	5

5.23 [22] <5.2> Using the DLX code for SAXPY above, assume a speculative machine with the functional unit organization used in Section 5.6 and a single integer functional unit. Assume the following latencies in clock cycles:

FP multiply	10
FP add	6
FP load/store	2
All integer operations	1

Show the state of the machine (as in Figure 5.28) when the branch issues for the second time. Assume the branch was correctly predicted taken and took one cycle. How many clock cycles does each loop iteration take?

5.24 [22] <5.2> Using the DLX code for SAXPY above, assume a speculative machine that can issue one load/store, one integer operation, and one FP operation. Assume the following latencies in clock cycles:

FP multiply	10
FP add	6
FP load/store	2
All integer operations	1

Show the state of the machine (as in Figure 5.28) when the branch issues for the second time. Assume the branch was correctly predicted taken and took one cycle. How many clock cycles does each loop iteration take?

5.25 [15] <5.5> Here is a simple code fragment:

```
for (i=2;i+=2;i<=100)
    a[i] = a[50*i+1];
```

To use the GCD test this loop must first be "normalized"—written so that the index starts at 1 and increments by 1 on every iteration. Write a normalized version of the loop (change the indices as needed), then use the GCD test to see if there is a dependence.

5.26 [15] <5.1, 5.5> Here is another loop:

```
for (i=2,i+=2; i<=100)
    a[i] = a[i-1];
```

Normalize the loop and use the GCD test to detect a dependence. Is there a loop-carried, true dependence in this loop?

5.27 [25] <5.5> Show that if for two array elements A(a*i +b) and A(c*i+d) there is a true dependence, then GCD(c,a) divides (d–b).

5.28 [15] <5.5> Show the start-up and finish-up code for the software pipelined loop shown on page 317 in Section 5.5. Remember that the software pipelined loop is executed two fewer times than the original loop . This determines what code must go in the start-up and finish-up sequences.

5.29 [20] <5.5> Consider the loop that we software pipelined on page 317 in Section 5.5. Suppose the latency of the ADDD was five cycles. The software pipelined loop now has a stall. Show how this loop can be written using both software pipelining and loop unrolling to eliminate any stalls. The loop should be unrolled as few times as possible (once is enough).

Exercises 5.30-5.31 Consider our speculative machine from Section 5.6: Since the reorder buffer contains a value field, you might think that the value field of the reservation stations could be eliminated.

5.30 [15] <5.6> Show an example where this is the case and an example where the value field of the reservations station is still needed. How many value fields are needed in each reservation station?

5.31 [15] <5.6> Find a modification to the rules for instruction commit that allows elimination of the value fields in the reservation station? What are the negative side effects of such a change?

5.32 [20] <5.6> Our implementation of speculation uses a reorder buffer and introduces the concept of instruction commit, delaying commit and the irrevocable updating of the registers until we know an instruction will complete. There are two other possible implementation techniques, both originally developed as a method for preserving precise interrupts when issuing out of order. One idea introduces a future file that keeps future values of a register; this idea is similar to the reorder buffer. An alternative is to keep a history buffer that records values of registers that have been speculatively over-written.

Design a speculative machine like the one in Section 5.6 but using a history buffer. Show the state of the machine, including the contents of the history buffer, for the example in Figure 5.32. Show the changes needed to Figure 5.33 for a history buffer implementation. Describe exactly how and when entries in the history buffer are read and written, including what happens on an incorrect speculation.

Exercises 5.33-5.34 These exercises involve a programming assignment to evaluate what types of parallelism might be expected in more modest, and more realistic, machines than those studied in Section 5.7. These studies can be done using traces available with this text or obtained from other tracing programs. To simplify the task, make the following assumptions:

- Assume perfect branch and jump prediction: hence you can use the trace as the input to the window, without having to consider branch effects–the trace is perfect.

- Assume there are 64 spare integer and 64 spare floating point registers; this is easily implemented by just stalling the issue of the machine whenever there are more live registers required.

- Assume a window size of 64 instructions (the same for alias detection). Use greedy scheduling of instructions in the window. That is, at any clock cycle, pick for execution the first n instructions in the window that meet the issue constraints.

5.33 [30] <5.8> Determine the effect of limited instruction issue by performing the following experiments:

- vary the issue count from 4-16 instructions per clock,

- assuming 8 issues per clock: determine what the effect of restricting the machine to 2 memory references is.

5.34 [30] <5.8> Determine the impact of latency in instructions. Assume the following latency models for a machine that issue up to 16 instructions per clock:

- Model 1: all latencies are one clock,

- Model 2: Load latency and branch latency are one clock; all FP latencies are two clocks.

- Model 3: Load and branch latency is 2 clocks; all FP latencies are five clocks.

Remember that with limited issue and a greedy scheduler, the impact of latency effects will be worse.

Exercises 5.35-5.37 For these exercises use the SAXPY loop from Exercise 5.12 and the description of the Power-2 structure and pipeline from Section 5.8.

5.35 [20] <5.8> Without unrolling the code in Exercise 5.12, change it to Power-2 code and determine how the code will run in the steady state. Show the steady state in a table that indicates when each instruction in the loop body is started and when it finishes. Make sure you include enough information in the table to support your result, including recording any assumptions you find necessary.

5.36 [15] <5.8> Unroll the SAXPY code from Exercise 5.12 and generate code for the IBM Power-2 using the description of the machine in Section 5.8 and the instruction set description in Appendix E. Make sure you take advantage of the quadword memory instructions and the multiply-add instruction if these are appropriate.

5.37 [20] <5.8> Using the code from Exercise 5.35, determine the performance in the steady-state on the Power-2 design. Make a table or figure showing when each instruction becomes and completes execution. State any assumptions you use.

5.38 [Discussion] <5.3,5.6> Dynamic instruction scheduling requires a considerable investment in hardware. In return, this capability allows the hardware to run programs that could not be run at full speed with only compile-time, static scheduling. What tradeoffs should be taken into account in trying to decide between a dynamically and a statically scheduled scheme? What sort of situations in both hardware technology and program characteristics are likely to favor one approach or the other? Most speculative schemes rely on dynamic scheduling; how does speculation affect the arguments in favor of dynamic scheduling?

5.39 [Discussion] <5.3> There is a subtle problem that must be considered when implementing Tomasulo's algorithm. It might be called the "two ships passing in the night problem." What happens if an instruction is being passed to a reservation station during the same clock period as one of its operands is going onto the common data bus? Before an instruction is in a reservation station, the operands are fetched from the register file; but once it is in the station, the operands are always obtained from the CDB. Since the instruction and its operand tag are in transit to the reservation station, the tag cannot be matched against the tag on the CDB. So there is a possibility that the instruction will then sit in the reservation station forever waiting for its operand, which it just missed. How might this problem be solved? You might consider subdividing one of the steps in the algorithm into multiple parts. (This intriguing problem is courtesy of J. E. Smith.)

5.40 [Discussion] <5.4-5.6> Discuss the advantages and disadvantages of a superscalar implementation, a superpipelined implementation, and a VLIW approach in the context of DLX. What levels of ILP favor each approach. What other concerns would you consider in choosing which type of machine to build? How does speculation affect the results?

Ideally one would desire an indefinitely large memory capacity such that any particular . . . word would be immediately available. . . . We are . . . forced to recognize the possibility of constructing a hierarchy of memories, each of which has greater capacity than the preceding but which is less quickly accessible.

A. W. Burks, H. H. Goldstine, and J. von Neumann,
*Preliminary Discussion of the Logical Design
of an Electronic Computing Instrument* (1946)

6 Memory-Hierarchy Design

6.1 Introduction

Computer pioneers correctly predicted that programmers would want unlimited amounts of fast memory. An economical solution to that desire is a *memory hierarchy*, which takes advantage of locality and cost-performance of memory technologies. The *principle of locality*, presented in the first chapter, says that most programs do not access all code or data uniformly (see Section 1.?, pages ??-??)[1]. This principle, plus the guideline that smaller hardware is faster, lead to the hierarchy based on memories of different speeds and sizes. Since fast memory is expensive, a memory hierarchy is organized into several levels—each smaller, faster, and more expensive per byte than the level below. The goal is to provide a memory system with cost almost as low as the lowest level of memory and speed almost as fast as the highest level. The levels of the hierarchy usually subset one another; all data in one level is also found in the level below, and all data in that lower level is found in the one below it, and so on until we reach the bottom of the hierarchy. Chapter 1 gives us a formula to evaluate the effectiveness of a level of the memory hierarchy:

---

[1] This is a cross reference to 1/e sections 8.1 and 8.2 which will be moved to 2/e Chapter 1 (not yet moved in the Beta edition).

$$\text{Average memory access time} = \text{Hit time} + \text{Miss rate} \times \text{Miss penalty}$$

where *Hit time* is the time to hit in the cache, *Miss rate* is the faction of accesses that are not in the cache, and *Miss penalty* is the additional time to service the miss. Recall that a *block* is the minimum unit of information that can be present in the cache (*bit* the cache) or not (*miss* the cache).

This chapter uses this formula to evaluate about a half-dozen examples that demonstrate how the principle of locality can improve performance while keeping the memory system affordable. The common principles allow us to pose four questions about **any** level of the hierarchy :

Q1: Where can a block be placed in the upper level? (*Block placement*)

Q2: How is a block found if it is in the upper level? (*Block identification*)

Q3: Which block should be replaced on a miss? (*Block replacement*)

Q4: What happens on a write? (*Write strategy*)

The answers to these questions help us understand the different tradeoffs of memories at different levels of a hierarchy, hence we ask these four questions at each level.

All these strategies map addresses from a larger memory to a smaller but faster memory. As part of address mapping, the memory hierarchy is usually given the responsibility of address checking; protection schemes for scrutinizing addresses are also covered in this chapter.

To put these abstract ideas in practice, throughout the chapter we show examples from the four levels of the memory hierarchy in a computer using the Alpha AXP 21064 microprocessor. Towards the end of the chapter we evaluate the impact of these levels on performance using the SPEC92 benchmark programs.

6.2 | The ABCs of Caches

Cache: a safe place for hiding or storing things.

Webster's New World Dictionary of the American Language,
Second College Edition (1976)

Cache is the name generally given to the first level of the memory hierarchy encountered once the address leaves the CPU. Since the principle of locality applies at many levels, and taking advantage of locality to improve performance is so popular, the term cache is now applied whenever commonly occurring items may be reused; examples include *file caches*, *name caches*, and so on. We start our description of caches by answering the four common questions for the first level of the memory hierarchy; you'll see similar answers to these questions for all levels of caches.

Q1: Where can a block be placed in a cache?

Figure 6.1 shows the restrictions on where a block is placed create three categories of cache organization:

- If each block has only one place it can appear in the cache, the cache is said to be *direct mapped*. The mapping is usually:

$$(block\ address)\mathrm{mod}(number\ of\ blocks\ in\ cache)$$

- If a block can be placed anywhere in the cache, the cache is said to be *fully associative*.

- If a block can be placed in a restricted set of places in the cache, the cache is said to be *set associative*. A *set* is a group of two or more blocks in the cache. A block is first mapped onto a set, and then the block can be placed anywhere within the set. The set is usually chosen by *bit selection*; that is,

$$(block\ address)\mathrm{mod}(number\ of\ sets\ in\ cache)$$

- If there are *n* blocks in a set, the cache placement is called *n-way set associative*.

The range of caches from direct mapped to fully associative is really a continuum of levels of set associativity: Direct mapped is simply one-way set associative and a fully associative cache with *m* blocks could be called *m*-way set associative; alternatively, direct mapped can be thought of as having *m sets* and fully associative as having one *set*. The vast majority of processor caches today are either direct mapped or 2-way set associative, for reasons we shall see shortly.

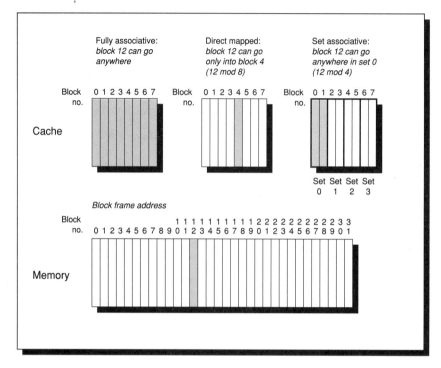

FIGURE 6.1   The cache has 8 block-frames, while memory has 32 blocks. The set-as-sociative organization has 4 sets with 2 blocks per set, called two-way set associative. (Real caches contain hundreds of block-frames and real memories contain hundreds of thousands of blocks.) Assume that there is nothing in the cache and that the block address in question identifies lower-level block 12. The three options for caches are shown left to right. In fully associative, block 12 from the lower level can go into any of the 8 block-frames of the cache. With direct mapped, block 12 can only be placed into block-frame 4 (12 modulo 8). Set as-sociative, which has some of both features, allows the block to be placed anywhere in set 0 (12 modulo 4). With two blocks per set, this means block 12 can be placed either in block 0 or block 1 of the cache.

Q2: How is a block found if it is in the cache?

Caches have an address tag on each block-frame that gives the block address. The tag of every cache block that might contain the desired information is checked to see if it matches the block address from the CPU. As a rule, all possi-ble tags are searched in parallel because speed is of the essence.

There must be a way to know that a cache block does not have valid informa-tion. The most common procedure is to add a *valid bit* to the tag to say whether or not this entry contains a valid address. If the bit is not set, there cannot be a match on this address.

FIGURE 6.2   The three portions of an address in a set-associative or direct-mapped cache. The tag is used to check all the blocks in the set and the index is used to select the set. The block offset is the address of the desired data within the block.

Before proceeding to the next question, let's explore the relationship of a CPU address to the cache. Figure 6.2 shows how an address is divided. The first division is between the *block address* and the *block offset*. The block frame address can be further divided into the *tag* field and the *index* field. The block-offset field selects the desired data from the block, the index field selects the set, and the tag field is compared for a hit. While the comparison could be made on more of the address than the tag, there is no need:

- Checking the index would be redundant, since it was used to select the set to be checked (an address stored in set 0, for example, must have 0 in the index field or it couldn't be stored in set 0).

- The offset is unnecessary in the comparison since the entire block is present or not and hence all block offsets must match.

If the total cache size is kept the same, increasing associativity increases the number of blocks per set, thereby decreasing the size of the index and increasing the size of the tag. That is, the tag/index boundary in Figure 6.2 moves to the right with increasing associativity, with the end case of fully associative caches having no index field.

Q3: Which block should be replaced on a cache miss?

When a miss occurs, the cache controller must select a block to be replaced with the desired data. A benefit of direct-mapped placement is that hardware decisions are simplified. In fact, so simple that there is no choice for this question: Only one block-frame is checked for a hit, and only that block can be replaced. With fully associative or set-associative placement, there are several blocks to choose from on a miss. There are two primary strategies employed for selecting which block to replace:

- *Random*—To spread allocation uniformly, candidate blocks are randomly selected. Some systems generate pseudo-random block numbers to get reproducible behavior, which is particularly useful during hardware debugging.

- *Least-recently used* (LRU)—To reduce the chance of throwing out information that will be needed soon, accesses to blocks are recorded. The block replaced is the one that has been unused for the longest time. This makes use of a corollary of locality: If recently used blocks are likely to be used again, then the best candidate for disposal is the **least** recently used.

A virtue of random is that it is simple to build in hardware. As the number of blocks to keep track of increases, LRU becomes increasingly expensive and is frequently only approximated. Figure 6.3 shows the difference in miss rates between LRU and random replacement.

Associativity:	2-way		4-way		8-way	
Size	LRU	Random	LRU	Random	LRU	Random
16 KB	5.18%	5.69%	4.67%	5.29%	4.39%	4.96%
64 KB	1.88%	2.01%	1.54%	1.66%	1.39%	1.53%
256 KB	1.15%	1.17%	1.13%	1.13%	1.12%	1.12%

FIGURE 6.3   Miss rates comparing least-recently used versus random replacement for several sizes and associativities. This data was collected for a block size of 16 bytes using one of the VAX traces containing user and operating system code. There is little difference between LRU and random for larger size caches in this trace. Although not included in the table, a first-in first-out order does worse than random or LRU.

Q4: What happens on a write?

Reads dominate processor cache accesses. All instruction accesses are reads, and most instructions don't write to memory. Figure 4.34 (page 181[2]) in Chapter 3 suggests a mix of 9% stores and 17% loads for DLX programs, making writes about 7% of the overall memory traffic and about 35% of the data cache traffic. Making the common case fast means optimizing caches for reads, especially since processors traditionally wait for reads to complete but need not wait for writes. Amdahl's Law (Chapter 1, page 8) reminds us, however, that high-performance designs cannot neglect the speed of writes.

Fortunately, the common case is also the easy case to make fast. The block can be read at the same time that the tag is read and compared, so the block read begins as soon as the block address is available. If the read is a hit, the requested part of the block is passed on to the CPU immediately. If it is a miss, there is no benefit—but also no harm; just don't write the register.

---

[2] Need to be referenced

Such is not the case for writes. Modifying a block cannot begin until the tag is checked to see if the address is a hit. Because tag checking cannot occur in parallel, then, writes normally take longer than reads. The processor specifies the size of the write, usually between 1 and 8 bytes; only that portion of a block can be changed.

Thus, it is the write policies that distinguish many cache designs. There are two basic options when writing to the cache:

- *Write through* (or *store through*)—The information is written to both the block in the cache **and** to the block in the lower-level memory.

- *Write back* (also called *copy back* or *store in*)—The information is written only to the block in the cache. The modified cache block is written to main memory only when it is replaced.

To reduce the frequency of writing back blocks on replacement, a feature called the *dirty bit* is commonly used. This status bit indicates whether is *dirty*–modified while in the cache–or *clean*–not modified. If it is clean, the block is not written on a miss, since the lower level has the same information as the cache.

Both write back and write through have their advantages. With write back, writes occur at the speed of the cache memory, and multiple writes within a block require only one write to the lower-level memory. Since some writes don't go to memory, write back uses less memory bandwidth, making write back attractive in multiprocessors. With write through, read misses never result in writes to the lower level, and write through is easier to implement than write back. Write through also has the advantage that the next lower level has the most current copy of the data. This is important for I/O and for multiprocessors, which we examine in Chapters 7 and 9. (I/O and multiprocessors are fickle: they want write back for processor caches to reduce the memory traffic per processor and write through to keep the cache consistent with lower levels of the memory hierarchy.)

When the CPU must wait for writes to complete during write through, the CPU is said to *write stall*. A common optimization to reduce write stalls is a *write buffer*, which allows the processor to continue as soon as the data is written to the buffer, thereby overlapping processor execution with memory updating. As we shall see shortly, write stalls can occur even with write buffers.

There are two common options on a write miss:

- *Write allocate* (also called *fetch on write*)—The block is loaded, followed by the write-hit actions above. This is similar to a read miss.

- *No write allocate* (also called *write around*)—The block is modified in the lower level and not loaded into the cache.

Although either write-miss policy could be used with write through or write back, write-back caches generally use write allocate (hoping that subsequent writes to that block will be captured by the cache) and write-through caches often use no write allocate (since subsequent writes to that block will still have to go to memory).

An Example: The Alpha AXP 21064 Data Cache and Instruction Cache

To give substance to these ideas, Figure 6.4 shows the organization of the data cache in the Alpha AXP 21064 microprocessor that is found in the DEC 3000 Model 800 workstation. The cache contains 8192 bytes of data in 32-byte blocks with direct-mapped placement, write through with a four block write buffer, and no write allocate on a write miss.

Let's trace a cache hit through the steps of a hit as labeled in Figure 6.4. (The four steps are shown in color as circled numbers.) As we shall see (Figure 6.41 on page 465), the 21064 microprocessor presents a 34-bit physical address to the cache for tag comparison. The address coming into the cache is divided into two fields: the 29-bit block address and 5-bit block offset. The block address is further divided into an address tag and cache index. Step 1 shows this division.

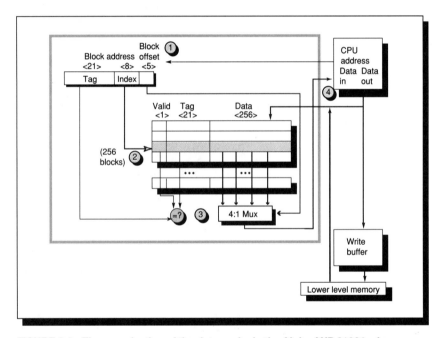

FIGURE 6.4   The organization of the data cache in the Alpha AXP 21064 microprocessor. The 8-KB cache is direct mapped with 32-byte blocks. It has 256 blocks selected by the 8-bit index. The four steps of a read hit, shown as circled numbers in order of occurrence, label this organization. Although we show a 4:1 multiplexor to select the desired 8 bytes, in reality the data RAM is organized 8 bytes wide and the multiplexor is unnecessary: two bits of the block offset join the index to supply the RAM address to select the proper 8 bytes. See Figure 6.7. (The line from memory to the cache is used on a miss to load the cache.)

The cache index selects the tag to be tested to see if the desired block is in the cache. The size of the index depends on cache size, block size, and set associativity. The 21064 cache is direct mapped, so set associativity is set to one, and we calculate the index as follows:

$$2^{\text{index}} = \frac{\text{Cache size}}{\text{Block size} \times \text{Set associativity}} = \frac{8192}{32 \times 1} = 256 = 2^8$$

Hence the index is 8 bits wide, and the tag is 29 – 8 or 21 bits wide.

Index selection is step 2 in Figure 6.4. Remember that direct mapping allows the data to be read and sent to the CPU in parallel with the tag being read.

After reading the tag from the cache, it is compared to the tag portion of the block address from the CPU. This is step 3 in the figure. To be sure the tag contains valid information, the valid bit must be set or else the results of the comparison are ignored.

Assuming the tag does match, the final step is to signal the CPU to load the data from the cache.

The 21064 allows two clock cycles for these four steps, so the instructions in the following two clock cycles would stall if they tried to use the result of the load.

Handling writes is more complicated than handling reads in the 21064, as it is in any cache. If the word to be written is in the cache, the first three steps are the same. After the tag comparison indicates a hit, the data is written. (Section 6.5 shows how the 21064 avoids the extra time on write hits that this description implies.)

Since this is a write-through cache, the write process isn't yet over. The data is also sent to a write buffer that can contain up to four 32-byte blocks. If the write buffer is empty, the data and the full address are written in the buffer, and the write is finished from the CPU's perspective; the CPU continues working while the write buffer prepares to write the word to memory. If the buffer contains other modified blocks, the addresses are checked to see if the address of this new block is equal to the address of the valid write buffer entry; if so, the new data is merged into that entry, called *write merging*. Without this optimization, four stores to sequential addresses would fill the buffer, even though these four words easily fit within a single 32-byte block of the write buffer when merged. Figure 6.6 shows a write buffer with and without write merging. If the buffer is full and there is no address match, the cache (and CPU) must wait until the buffer has an empty entry.

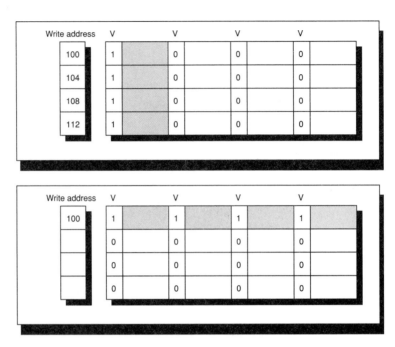

FIGURE 6.5   To illustrate write merging, the write buffer on top does not use it while the write buffer on the bottom does. Each buffer has four entries, and each entry holds four words. The address for each entry is on the left, with valid bits(V) indicating whether or not the next sequential four bytes are occupied in this entry. The four writes are merged into a single buffer entry with write merging; without it, all four entries are used.

So far we assumed the common case of a cache hit. What happens on a miss? On a read miss, the cache sends a stall signal to the CPU telling it to wait, and 32 bytes are read from the next level of the hierarchy. The path to the next lower level is 16 bytes wide in the DEC 3000 model 800 workstation, one of the several models that use the 21064. That takes 5 clock cycles per transfer, or 10 clock cycles for all 32 bytes. Since the data cache is direct mapped, there is no choice on which block to replace. Replacing a block means updating the data, the address tag, and the valid bit. On a write miss, the CPU writes "around" the cache to lower-level memory and does not affect the cache; that is, the 21064 follows the no-write-allocate rule.

Hit or miss, the *data* cache cannot supply all the memory needs of the processor. When a load or store instruction is executed, the pipelined processor will simultaneously request both a data word **and** an instruction word. Hence a single cache would present a structural hazard for loads and stores, leading to stalls. One simple way to conquer this problem is to divide it; one cache is dedicated to instructions and another to data. Separate caches are found in most recent processors, including the Alpha AXP 21064. It has an 8 KB instruction cache that is nearly identical to its 8 KB data cache in Figure 6.4.

The CPU knows whether it is issuing an instruction address or a data address, so there can be separate ports for both, thereby doubling the bandwidth between the memory hierarchy and the CPU. Separate caches also offer the opportunity of optimizing each cache separately: different capacities, block sizes, and associativities may lead to better performance. (In contrast to instruction caches and data caches of the 21064, the terms *unified* or *mixed* are applied to caches that can contain either instructions or data.)

Figure 6.6 shows that instruction caches have lower miss rates than data caches. Separating instructions and data removes misses due to conflicts between instruction blocks and data blocks, but the split also fixes the cache space devoted to each type. Which is more important to miss rates? A fair comparison of separate instruction and data caches to unified caches requires the total cache size to be the same. For example, a separate 1-KB instruction cache and 1-KB data cache should be compared to a 2-KB unified cache. Calculating the average miss rate with separate instruction and data caches necessitates knowing the percentage of memory references to each cache. For the SPEC92 programs running on the DECstation 5000, the split is about 75% instruction references to 25% data references. Splitting affects performance beyond what is indicated by the change in miss rates, as this example illustrates.

Size	Instruction Cache	Data Cache	Unified Cache
1 KB	3.06%	24.61%	13.34%
2 KB	2.26%	20.57%	9.78%
4 KB	1.78%	15.94%	7.24%
8 KB	1.10%	10.19%	4.57%
16 KB	0.64%	6.47%	2.87%
32 KB	0.39%	4.82%	1.99%
64 KB	0.15%	3.77%	1.35%
128 KB	0.02%	2.88%	0.95%

FIGURE 6.6   Miss rates for instruction- data, and unified caches of different sizes. The data are for a direct mapped cache with 32-byte blocks for an average of SPEC92 benchmarks on the DECstation 5000 (Gee, Hill, Pnevmatikatos, Smith [1993].) The percentage of instruction references is about 75%.

Example

Which has the lower miss rate: a 16-KB instruction cache with a 16-KB data cache or a 32-KB unified cache? Which has the lowest average memory access time? Assume a hit takes 1 clock cycle and a miss costs 10 clock cycles and a load or store hit takes 1 extra clock cycle on a unified cache since there is only one cache port to satisfy two simultaneous requests. What is the average memory access time in each case? Assume write-through caches with a write buffer and ignore stalls due to the write buffer.

Answer   As stated above, 75% of the memory accesses are instruction references. Thus, the overall miss rate for the split caches is

$$(75\% \times 0.64\%) + (25\% \times 6.47\%) = 2.10\%$$

A 32-KB unified cache has a slightly lower miss rate of 1.99%.

The average memory access time formula can be divided into instruction and data accesses:

Average memory access time =
$$\%\text{instructions} \times (\text{Read Hit time} + \text{Read Miss rate} \times \text{Miss penalty})$$
$$= \%\text{data} \times (\text{Write Hit time} + \text{Write Miss rate} \times \text{Miss penalty})$$

So the time for each organization is:

Average memory access time$_{\text{split}}$ $= 75\% \times (1 + 0.64\% \times 10) + 25\% \times (1 + 6.47\% \times 10)$
$= (75\% \times 1.064) + (25\% \times 1.647) = 0.798 + 0.412 = 1.21$
Average memory access time$_{\text{unified}}$ $= 75\% \times (1 + 1.99\% \times 10) + 25\% \times (2 + 1.99\% \times 10)$
$= (75\% \times 1.1990 + (25\% \times 2.199) = 0.899 + 0.550 = 1.45$

Hence the split caches in this example–which offer two memory ports per clock cycle thereby avoiding the structural hazard–have a better average memory access time than the single ported unified cache even though their effective miss rate is higher.

Cache Performance

CPU time can be divided into the clock cycles the CPU spends executing the program and the clock cycles the CPU spends waiting for the memory system. Thus,

$$\text{CPUtime} = (\text{CPUexecution clock cycles} + \text{Memory stall clock cycles}) \times \text{Clock cycle time}$$

To simplify evaluation of cache alternatives, sometimes designers assume that all memory stalls are due to cache misses. This is true for many machines; on machines where this is not true, the memory hierarchy typically dominates other reasons for stalls. We use this simplifying assumption here, but it is important to account for **all** memory stalls when calculating final performance!

The formula above raises the question whether the clock cycles for a cache hit should be considered part of CPU-execution clock cycles or part of memory-stall clock cycles. Although either convention is defensible, the most widely accepted is to include hit clock cycles in CPU-execution clock cycles.

Memory-stall clock cycles can then be defined in terms of the number of memory accesses per program, miss penalty (in clock cycles), and miss rate for reads and writes:

Memory stall clock cycles = Reads × Read miss rate × Read miss penalty
+ Writes × Write miss rate × Write miss penalty

We often simplify the complete formula by combining the reads and writes and finding the average miss rates and miss penalty for reads **and** writes:

Memory stall clock cycles = Memory accesses × Miss rate × Miss penalty

This formula is an approximation since the miss rates and miss penalties are often different for reads and writes.

Factoring instruction count (IC) from execution time and memory stall cycles, we now get a CPU-time formula that includes memory accesses per instruction, miss rate, and miss penalty:

$$\text{CPUtime} = \text{IC} \times \left(\text{CPI}_{\text{execution}} + \frac{\text{Memory accesses}}{\text{Instruction}} \times \text{Miss rate} \times \text{Miss penalty} \right) \times \text{Clock cycle time}$$

Some designers prefer measuring miss rate as *misses per instruction* rather than misses per memory reference:

$$\frac{\text{Misses}}{\text{Instruction}} = \frac{\text{Memory accesses}}{\text{Instruction}} \times \text{Miss rate}$$

The advantage of this measure is that it is independent of the hardware implementation. For example, the 21064 instruction prefetch unit can make repeated references to a single word (see Section 6.11), which can artificially reduce the miss rate if measured as misses per memory reference rather than per instruction executed. The drawback is that misses per instruction is architecture dependent; for example, the average number of memory accesses per instruction will be very different for an 80x86 than it will be for DLX. Thus misses per instruction is most popular with architects working with a single computer family. They then use this version of the CPU-time formula:

$$\text{CPUtime} = \text{IC} \times \left(\text{CPI}_{\text{execution}} + \frac{\text{Memory stall clock cycles}}{\text{Instruction}} \right) \times \text{Clock cycle time}$$

We can now explore the consequences of caches on performance.

Example   Let's use a machine similar to the Alpha AXP as a first example. Assume the cache miss penalty is 10 clock cycles, and all instructions normally take 2.0 clock cycles (ignoring memory stalls). Assume the miss rate is 10%, and there is an average of 1.33 memory references per instruction. What is the impact on performance when behavior of the cache is included?

Answer

$$\text{CPUtime} = \text{IC} \times \left(\text{CPI}_{\text{execution}} + \frac{\text{Memory stall clock cycles}}{\text{Instruction}} \right) \times \text{Clock cycle time}$$

The performance, including cache misses, is

$$\begin{aligned} \text{CPUtime}_{\text{with cache}} &= \text{IC} \times (2.0 + (1.33 \times 10\% \times 10)) \times \text{Clock cycle time} \\ &= \text{IC} \times 3.33 \times \text{Clock cycle time} \end{aligned}$$

The clock cycle time and instruction count are the same, with or without a cache, so CPU time increases with CPI with from 2.0 for a "perfect cache" to 3.33 with a cache that can miss. Hence, the impact of including the memory hierarchy in the CPI calculations to stretch the CPU time by a factor of 1.67. (Of course, with out any memory hierarchy at all the CPI would increase to 2.0 + 10 × 1.33 or 15.3: a factor of 7.6!)

As this example illustrates, cache behavior can have enormous impact on performance. Furthermore, cache misses have a double-barreled impact on a CPU with a low CPI and a fast clock:

1. The lower the $\text{CPI}_{\text{execution}}$, the higher the **relative** impact of a fixed number of cache miss clock cycles.

2. When calculating CPI, the cache miss penalty is measured in **CPU** clock cycles for a miss. Therefore, even if memory hierarchies for two computers are identical, the CPU with the higher clock rate has a larger number of clock cycles per miss and hence the memory portion of CPI is higher.

The importance of the cache for CPUs with low CPI and high clock rates is thus greater; and, consequently, greater is the danger of neglecting cache behavior in assessing performance of such machines.

While minimizing average memory-access time is a reasonable goal and we will use it in much of this chapter, keep in mind that the final goal is to reduce CPU execution time. The next example shows how these two can differ.

Example

What is the impact of two different cache organizations on the performance of a CPU? Assume that the CPI with a perfect cache is 2.0 with a clock cycle time of 2 ns, that there are 1.3 memory references per instruction, and that the size of both caches is 64 KB and both have a block size of 32 bytes. One cache is direct mapped and the other is two-way set associative. Figure 6.7 shows that for set associative caches we must add a multiplexor to select between the blocks in the set depending on the tag match. Since the speed of the CPU is tied directly to the speed of a cache hit, assume the CPU clock cycle time must be stretched 1.08 times to accommodate the selection multiplexor of the set-associative cache. To the first approximation, the cache miss penalty is 50 ns for either cache organization. (In practice it must be rounded up or down to an integer number of clock cycles.) First, calculate the average memory-access time, and then CPU performance. Assume the hit time is one clock cycle.

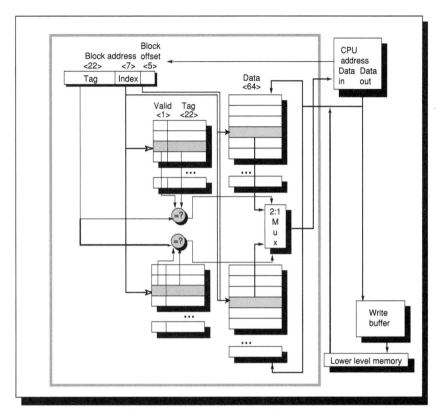

FIGURE 6.7 **A two-way set associative version of Figure 6.4, showing the extra multiplexor in the path.** Unlike the prior figure, the data portion of the cache is drawn more realistically, with the two leftmost bits of the block offset combined with the index to address the desired 64-bit word to send the CPU.

Answer Assume that the miss rate of a direct-mapped 64-KB cache is 1.4% and the miss rate for a two-way set-associative cache of the same size is 1.0%. Average memory-access time is

$$\text{Average memory access time} = \text{Hit time} + \text{Miss rate} \times \text{Miss penalty}$$

Thus, the time for each organization is

$$\text{Average memory access time}_{1\text{-way}} = 2.0 + (.014 \times 50) = 2.70ns$$
$$\text{Average memory access time}_{2\text{-way}} = 2.0 \times 1.08 \neq (.010 \times 50) = 2.66ns$$

The average memory-access time is better for the two-way–set-associative cache.

CPU performance is

$$CPUtime = IC \times \left(CPI_{Execution} + \frac{Misses}{Instruction} \times Miss\ penalty \right) \times Clock\ cycle\ time$$

$$= IC \times \left(\begin{array}{l} (CPI_{Execution} \times Clock\ cycle\ time) + \\ \left(\frac{Memory\ accesses}{Instruction} \times Miss\ rate \times Miss\ penalty \times Clock\ cycle\ time \right) \end{array} \right)$$

Substituting 50 ns for (Miss penalty * Clock cycle time), the performance of each cache organization is

$$CPUtime_{1\text{-way}} = IC \times (2.0 \times 2 + (1.3 \times 0.014 \times 50)) = 4.91 \times IC$$
$$CPUtime_{2\text{-way}} = IC \times (2.0 \times 2 \times 1.08 + (1.3 \times 0.010 \times 50)) = 4.97 \times IC$$

and relative performance is

$$\frac{CPUtime_{2\text{-way}}}{CPUtime_{1\text{-way}}} = \frac{4.97 \times Instruction\ count}{4.91 \times Instruction\ count} = \frac{4.97}{4.91} = 1.01$$

In contrast to the results of average memory access-time comparison, the direct-mapped cache leads to slightly better average performance because the clock cycle is stretched for **all** instructions for the two-way case, even if there are fewer misses. Since CPU time is our bottom-line evaluation (and direct mapped is simpler to build), the preferred cache is direct mapped in this example. (See the fallacy on page 490 for more on this kind of trade-off.)

Improving Cache Performance

The increasing gap between CPU and main memory speeds has attracted the attention of many architects. The next three sections cover a plethora of techniques for improving cache performance: subblock placement, write buffer optimizations, out-of-order fetching, multi-level caches, and so on. The average memory access time formula gives us the directions on how to improve caches as well as a framework to present cache optimizations:

Average memory access time = Hit time + Miss rate × Miss penalty

The next three sections present several important techniques in each of these three categories:

1. Reduce the miss rate,

2. Reduce the miss penalty, or

3. Reduce the time to hit in the cache.

Figure 6.28 on page 444 concludes with a summary of the implementation complexity and the performance benefits of the 15 techniques presented in Sections 6.3 to 6.5.

6.3 | Reducing Cache Misses

The first machine with a cache was announced in 1968, and researchers wasted no time studying variations of this basic concept. A bibliographic search for the years 1989 to 1993 revealed more than 1500 research papers on the subject of caches. Your authors' job was to survey all 1500 papers, decide what is and is not worthwhile, transliterate the results into a common terminology, reduce the results to their essence, write in a fashion that the reader finds intriguing, and provide just the right amount of detail!

Most of these papers have concentrated on reducing the miss rate, so that is where we start our exploration. To gain better insights into the causes of misses, we start with a model that sorts all misses into three simple categories:

- *Compulsory*—The first access to a block is not in the cache, so the block must be brought into the cache. These are also called *cold start misses* or *first reference misses*.

- *Capacity*—If the cache cannot contain all the blocks needed during execution of a program, capacity misses will occur due to blocks being discarded and later retrieved.

- *Conflict*—If the block-placement strategy is set associative or direct mapped, conflict misses (in addition to compulsory and capacity misses) will occur because a block can be discarded and later retrieved if too many blocks map to its set. These are also called *collision misses* or *interference misses*.

Figure 6.8 shows the relative frequency of cache misses, broken down by the "three Cs." To show the benefit of associativity, conflict misses are divided into misses caused by each decrease in associativity. Here are the four divisions:

8-way: conflict misses due to going from fully associative (no conflicts) to 8-way associative

4-way: conflict misses due to going from 8-way associative to 4-way associative

2-way: conflict misses due to going from 4-way associative to 2-way associative

1-way: conflict misses due to going from 2-way associative to 1-way associative (direct mapped)

Figure 6.9 (page 408) presents the same data graphically. The top graph shows absolute miss rates; the bottom graph plots percentage of all the misses by type of miss as a function of cache size. As we can see from the figures, the compulsory miss rate of the SPEC92 programs is very small.

Having identified the three Cs, what can a computer designer do about them? Conceptually, conflicts are the easiest: Fully associative placement avoids all conflict misses. Full associativity is expensive in hardware, however, and may slow the processor clock rate (see the example above or the fallacy on page 490), leading to lower overall performance.

There is little to be done about capacity except to enlarge the cache. If the upper-level memory is much smaller than what is needed for a program, and a significant percentage of the time is spent moving data between two levels in the hierarchy, the memory hierarchy is said to *thrash*. Because so many replacements are required, thrashing means the machine runs close to the speed of the lower-level memory, or maybe even slower due to the miss overhead.

Another approach to improving the three Cs is to make blocks larger to reduce the number of compulsory misses, but as we shall see it can increase other kinds of misses.

The three C's give insight into the cause of misses, but this simple model has its limits. For example, increasing cache size reduces conflict misses as well as capacity misses, since a larger cache spreads out references to more blocks. Thus, a miss might move from one category to the other as parameters change. The three C's also ignore replacement policy, since it is difficult to model and since, in general, it is of less significance. In specific circumstances the replacement policy can actually lead to anomalous behavior, such as poorer miss rates for larger associativity, which is directly contradictory to the three C's model.

Cache size	Degree associative	Total miss rate	Miss-rate components (relative percent) *(Sum = 100% of total miss rate)*					
			Compulsory		Capacity		Conflict	
1 KB	1-way	0.133	0.002	1%	0.080	60%	0.052	39%
1 KB	2-way	0.105	0.002	2%	0.080	76%	0.023	22%
1 KB	4-way	0.095	0.002	2%	0.080	84%	0.013	14%
1 KB	8-way	0.087	0.002	2%	0.080	92%	0.005	6%
2 KB	1-way	0.098	0.002	2%	0.044	45%	0.052	53%
2 KB	2-way	0.076	0.002	2%	0.044	58%	0.030	39%
2 KB	4-way	0.064	0.002	3%	0.044	69%	0.018	28%
2 KB	8-way	0.054	0.002	4%	0.044	82%	0.008	14%
4 KB	1-way	0.072	0.002	3%	0.031	43%	0.039	54%
4 KB	2-way	0.057	0.002	3%	0.031	55%	0.024	42%
4 KB	4-way	0.049	0.002	4%	0.031	64%	0.016	32%
4 KB	8-way	0.039	0.002	5%	0.031	80%	0.006	15%
8 KB	1-way	0.046	0.002	4%	0.023	51%	0.021	45%
8 KB	2-way	0.038	0.002	5%	0.023	61%	0.013	34%
8 KB	4-way	0.035	0.002	5%	0.023	66%	0.010	28%
8 KB	8-way	0.029	0.002	6%	0.023	79%	0.004	15%
16 KB	1-way	0.029	0.002	7%	0.015	52%	0.012	42%
16 KB	2-way	0.022	0.002	9%	0.015	68%	0.005	23%
16 KB	4-way	0.020	0.002	10%	0.015	74%	0.003	17%
16 KB	8-way	0.018	0.002	10%	0.015	80%	0.002	9%
32 KB	1-way	0.020	0.002	10%	0.010	52%	0.008	38%
32 KB	2-way	0.014	0.002	14%	0.010	74%	0.002	12%
32 KB	4-way	0.013	0.002	15%	0.010	79%	0.001	6%
32 KB	8-way	0.013	0.002	15%	0.010	81%	0.001	4%
64 KB	1-way	0.014	0.002	14%	0.007	50%	0.005	36%
64 KB	2-way	0.010	0.002	20%	0.007	70%	0.001	10%
64 KB	4-way	0.009	0.002	21%	0.007	75%	0.000	3%
64 KB	8-way	0.009	0.002	22%	0.007	78%	0.000	0%
128 KB	1-way	0.010	0.002	20%	0.004	40%	0.004	40%
128 KB	2-way	0.007	0.002	29%	0.004	58%	0.001	14%
128 KB	4-way	0.006	0.002	31%	0.004	61%	0.001	8%
128 KB	8-way	0.006	0.002	31%	0.004	62%	0.000	7%

FIGURE 6.8   Total miss rate for each size cache and percentage of each according to the "three Cs." Compulsory misses are independent of cache size, while capacity misses decrease as capacity increases. Gee et al [1993] calculated the average miss rate for the SPEC92 benchmark suite with 32-byte blocks and LRU replacement on a DECstation 5000. Figure 6.9 (page 408) shows the same information graphically. The compulsory rate was calculated as the miss rate of a fully associative 1 MB cache. Note that the 2:1 cache rule of thumb (inside front cover) is supported by the statistics in this table: a direct-mapped cache of size N has about the same miss rate as a 2-way–set-associative cache of size N/2.

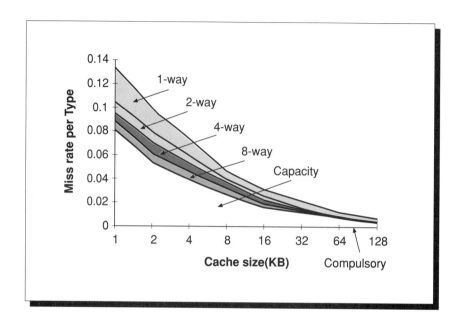

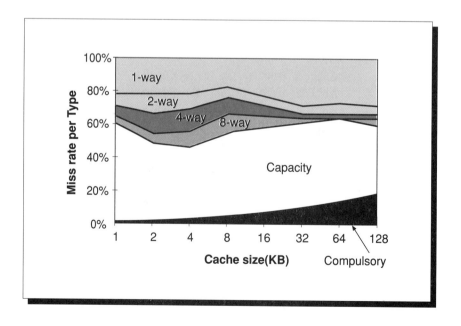

FIGURE 6.9 Total miss rate (top) and distribution of miss rate (bottom) for each size cache according to three Cs for the data in Figure 6.8 (page 407). The top diagram is the actual miss rates, while the bottom diagram is scaled to the

Alas, many of the techniques that reduce miss rates also increase hit time or miss penalty. The desirability of reducing miss rates using the seven techniques presented in the rest of this section must be balanced against the goal of making the whole system fast. This first examples shows the importance of a balanced perspective.

First Miss Rate Reduction Technique: Larger Block Size

This simplest way to reduce miss rate is to increase the block size. Figure 6.10 shows the tradeoff of block size versus miss rate for a set of programs and cache sizes. Larger block sizes may reduce compulsory misses. This reduction occurs because the principle of locality has two components: locality due to reuse over time, called *temporal locality,* and locality due to proximity, called *spatial locality.* Larger blocks take advantage of spatial locality.

At the same time, larger blocks increase the miss penalty; since they reduce the number of blocks in the cache, larger blocks may increase increasing conflict misses and even capacity misses if the cache is small. Clearly there is little reason to increase the block size to such a size that it **increases** the miss rate, but there is also no benefit to reducing miss rate if it increases the average memory access time; the increase in miss penalty may outweigh the decrease in miss rate.

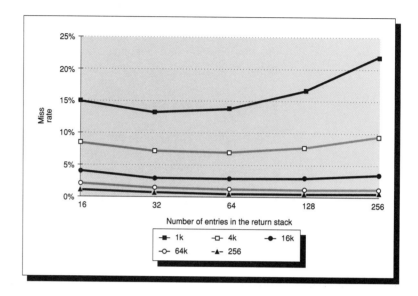

FIGURE 6.10   Miss rate versus block size for five different sized caches. Each line represents a cache of different size. Figure 6.11 shows the data used to plot these lines. This graph is based on the same measurements found in Figure 6.9.

Block Size	Cache Size				
	1K	4K	16K	64K	256K
16	15.05%	8.57%	3.94%	2.04%	1.09%
32	13.34%	7.24%	2.87%	1.35%	0.70%
64	13.76%	7.00%	2.64%	1.06%	0.51%
128	16.64%	7.78%	2.77%	1.02%	0.49%
256	22.01%	9.51%	3.29%	1.15%	0.49%

FIGURE 6.11   Actual Miss rate versus block size for five different sized caches in Figure 6.10 . Note that for a 1-KB cache, 64-byte, 128-byte, and 256-byte blocks have a higher miss rate than 32-byte blocks. In this example, the cache would have to be 256 KB in order for a 256 byte block to decrease misses.

Example

Figure 6.11 shows the actual miss rates plotted in Figure 6.10. Assume the memory system takes 4 clock cycles of overhead and then delivers 16 bytes every 2 clock cycles. Thus it can supply 16 bytes in 6 clock cycles, 32 bytes in 8 clock cycles, and so on. Which block size has the minimum average memory access time for each cache size in Figure 6.11?

Answer

Average memory-access time is

$$\text{Average memory access time} = \text{Hit time} + \text{Miss rate} \times \text{Miss penalty}$$

If we assume the hit time is one clock cycle independent of block size, then the average memory access time for a 16 byte block in a 1 K byte cache is

$$\text{Average memory access time} = 1 + (15.05\% \times 6) = 1.903 \text{ clock cycles}$$

and for a 256 byte block in a 256 K byte cache the average memory access time is

$$\text{Average memory access time} = 1 + (0.49\% \times 36) = 1.176 \text{ clock cycles}$$

Block Size	Miss Penalty	Cache Size				
		1K	4K	16K	64K	256K
16	6	<u>1.903</u>	<u>1.514</u>	1.236	1.122	1.065
32	8	2.067	1.579	<u>1.230</u>	<u>1.108</u>	<u>1.056</u>
64	12	2.651	1.840	1.317	1.127	1.061
128	20	4.328	2.556	1.554	1.204	1.098
256	36	8.924	4.424	2.184	1.414	1.176

FIGURE 6.12   Average Memory Access Time versus block size for five different sized caches in Figure 6.10. The smallest average time per cache size is shown in color.

Figure 6.12 shows the average memory access time for all block and cache sizes between those two extremes. The entries in color show the fastest block size for a given cache size: 16 bytes for 1 KB and 4 KB caches and 32 bytes for the larger caches. These sizes are in fact the popular block sizes for most processor caches today.

As in all of these techniques, the cache designer is trying to minimize both the miss rate and the miss penalty. The selection of block size depends on both the latency **and** bandwidth of the lower level memory: high latency and high bandwidth encourages large block size since the cache gets many more bytes per miss for a small increase in miss penalty. Conversely, low latency and low bandwidth encourages smaller block sizes since there is little time saved from a larger block–twice the miss penalty for a small block may be close to penalty of a block twice the size–and the larger number of small blocks may reduce conflict misses.

After seeing the positive and negative impact of larger block size on compulsory and capacity misses, we next look at the potential of higher associativity to reduce conflict misses.

Second Miss Rate Reduction Technique: Higher Associativity

Figures 6.8 and 6.9 above show how miss rates improve with higher associativity. There are two general rules of thumb that can be gleaned from these figures. The first is that 8-way set associative is for practical purposes as effective in reducing misses for these sized caches as fully associative. The second observations, called the *2:1 cache rule of thumb* and found on the front inside cover, is that a direct-mapped cache of size N has about the same miss rate as a 2-way, set-associative cache of size N/2.

Like many of these examples, improving one aspect of the average memory access time comes at the expense of another. Increasing block size reduced miss rate while increasing miss penalty, and greater associativity can come at the cost of increased hit time. Hill [1988] found about a 10% difference in hit times for TTL or ECL board-level caches and 2% difference for custom CMOS caches for direct mapped caches versus two-way set associative caches. Hence the pressure of a fast processor clock cycle encourages design of simple cache designs, as the following example suggests.

Example   Assume that going to higher associativity would increase the clock cycle as suggested below:

$$\text{Clock cycle time}_{2\text{-way}} = 1.10 \times \text{Clock cycle time}_{1\text{-way}}$$
$$\text{Clock cycle time}_{4\text{-way}} = 1.12 \times \text{Clock cycle time}_{1\text{-way}}$$
$$\text{Clock cycle time}_{8\text{-way}} = 1.14 \times \text{Clock cycle time}_{1\text{-way}}$$

Assume that the hit time is 1 clock cycle, that the miss penalty for the direct mapped case is 10 clock cycles, and that the miss penalty need not be rounded to an integral number of clock cycles. Using Figure 6.8 for miss rates, for which cache sizes are each of these three statements true?

$$\text{Average memory access time}_{8\text{-way}} < \text{Average memory access time}_{4\text{-way}}$$
$$\text{Average memory access time}_{4\text{-way}} < \text{Average memory access time}_{2\text{-way}}$$
$$\text{Average memory access time}_{2\text{-way}} < \text{Average memory access time}_{1\text{-way}}$$

Answer | Average memory-access time for each associativity is:

$$\text{Average memory access time}_{8\text{-way}} = \text{Hit time}_{8\text{-way}} + \text{Miss rate}_{8\text{-way}} \times \text{Miss penalty}_{1\text{-way}}$$
$$= 1.14 + \text{Miss rate}_{8\text{-way}} \times 10$$
$$\text{Average memory access time}_{4\text{-way}} = 1.12 + \text{Miss rate}_{4\text{-way}} \times 10$$
$$\text{Average memory access time}_{2\text{-way}} = 1.10 + \text{Miss rate}_{2\text{-way}} \times 10$$
$$\text{Average memory access time}_{1\text{-way}} = 1.00 + \text{Miss rate}_{1\text{-way}} \times 10$$

The miss penalty is the same time in each case, so we leave it as 10 clock cycles. For example, the average memory-access time for a 1 KB, direct mapped cache is

$$\text{Average memory access time}_{1\text{-way}} = 1.00 + (0.133 \times 10) = 2.330$$

and the time for a 128 KB, 8-way set associative cache is

$$\text{Average memory access time}_{8\text{-way}} = 1.14 + (0.006 \times 10) = 1.200$$

Using these formulas and the miss rates from Figure 6.8, Figure 6.13 shows the average memory access time for each cache and associativity. The figure shows that the formulas in this example hold for caches less than 8 KB but do not for caches greater than 8 KB. At exactly 8 KB, the average memory access time of 8-way is less than 4-way and 4-way is less than 2-way, but 2-way cache is not less than 1-way.

Cache Size (KB)	Associativity			
	1-way	2-way	4-way	8-way
1	2.33	2.15	2.07	2.01
2	1.98	1.86	1.76	1.68
4	1.72	1.67	1.61	1.53
8	1.46	1.48	1.47	1.43
16	1.29	1.32	1.32	1.32
32	1.20	1.24	1.25	1.27
64	1.14	1.20	1.21	1.23
128	1.10	1.17	1.18	1.20

FIGURE 6.13   Average memory access time using miss rates in Figure 6.8 for parameters in the example. Color means that this time is lower than the number to the left ; that is, high associativity reduces average memory access time.

Note that we did not account for the slower clock rate on the rest of the program in this example, thereby understating the advantage of direct mapped cache.

Third Miss Rate Reduction Technique: Victim Caches

Larger block size and higher associativity are two classic techniques to reduce miss rates that have been considered by architects since the earliest caches. Starting with this subsection, we see more recent inventions to reduce miss rate without affecting the clock cycle time nor the miss penalty.

Higher associativity reduces conflict misses, but it may degrade hit time and processor clock rate. One solution that reduces conflict misses without impairing clock rate is to add a small, fully associative cache between a cache and its refill path. Figure 6.14 shows the organization. This *victim cache* contains only blocks that are discarded from a cache due to a miss, and are checked on a miss to see if they have the desired data before going to the next lower level memory. If it is found there, the victim block and cache block are swapped. Jouppi [1990] found that victim caches of 1 to 5 entries are effective at reducing conflict misses, especially for small, direct-mapped, data caches. Depending on a the program, a 4 entry victim cache removed 20% to 95% of the conflict misses in a 4 KB direct mapped data cache.

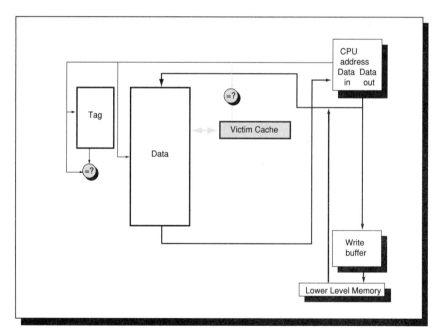

FIGURE 6.14   Placement of victim cache in the memory hierarchy.

Fourth Miss Rate Reduction Technique: Pseudo-Associative Caches

Another approach to getting the miss rate of set-associative caches and the hit speed of direct mapped is called *pseudo-associative* or *column associative*. A cache access proceeds just as in the direct mapped cache for a hit. On a miss, however, before going to the next lower level of the memory hierarchy, another cache entry is checked to see if it matches there. A simple way is to invert the most significant bit of the index field to find the other block in the "pseudo set."

Pseudo-associative caches then have one fast and one slow hit time–corresponding to a regular hit and a pseudo hit–in addition to the miss penalty. Figure 6.15 shows the relative times. The danger is if many of the fast hit times of the direct mapped cache became slow hit times in the pseudo-associative cache, then the performance would be degraded by this optimization. Hence it is important to be able to indicate for each set which block should be the fast hit and which should be the slow one; one way is simply to swap the contents of the blocks.

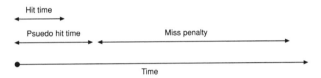

FIGURE 6.15   Relationship between a regular hit time, pseudo hit time, and miss penalty.

Let's do an example to see how well pseudo-associativity works.

Example

Assume that it takes 2 extra cycles to find the entry in the alternative location if it is not found in the direct mapped location. Using the parameters from the previous example, which of direct mapped, 2-way set associative, and pseudo-associative organizations is fastest for 2 KB and 128 KB sizes?

Answer

The average memory access time for pseudo-associative caches starts with the standard formula:

$$\text{Average memory access time}_{\text{pseudo}} = \text{Hit time}_{\text{pseudo}} + \text{Miss rate}_{\text{pseudo}} \times \text{Miss penalty}_{\text{pseudo}}$$

Let's start with the last part of the equation. The miss penalty is the same no matter what we do to hits, so that is unchanged by this scheme. To determine the miss rate we need to see when misses occur. As long as we invert the most significant bit of the index to find the other block, the two blocks in the "pseudo set" are selected using the same index that would be used in a 2-way set associative cache and hence have the same miss rates. Thus the last part of the equation is:

$$\text{Miss rate}_{\text{pseudo}} \times \text{Miss penalty}_{\text{pseudo}} = \text{Miss rate}_{\text{2-way}} \times \text{Miss penalty}_{\text{1-way}}$$

Returning to the beginning of the equation, the hit time for a pseudo associative cache is the time to hit in a direct mapped cache plus the fraction of accesses that are found in the pseudo associative search times the extra time it takes to find the hit:

$$\text{Hit time}_{\text{pseudo}} = \text{Hit time}_{\text{1-way}} + \text{Alternate Hit rate}_{\text{pseudo}} \times 2$$

The hit rate for the pseudo associative search is the difference between the hits that would occur in a two-way set associative cache and the number of hits in a direct mapped cache:

$$\begin{aligned}
\text{Alternate Hit rate}_{\text{pseudo}} &= \text{Hit rate}_{\text{2-way}} - \text{Hit rate}_{\text{1=way}} \\
&= (1 - \text{Miss rate}_{\text{2-way}}) - (1 - \text{Miss rate}_{\text{1-way}}) \\
&= \text{Miss rate}_{\text{1-way}} - \text{Miss rate}_{\text{2-way}}
\end{aligned}$$

Putting the pieces back together:

$$\begin{aligned}
\text{Average memory access time}_{\text{pseudo}} = \text{Hit time}_{\text{1-way}} &+ (\text{Miss rate}_{\text{1-way}} - \text{Miss rate}_{\text{2-way}}) \times 2 \\
&+ \text{Miss rate}_{\text{2-way}} \times \text{Miss penalty}_{\text{1-way}}
\end{aligned}$$

Figure 6.8 supplies the values we need to plug into our formulas

$$\begin{aligned}
\text{Average memory access time}_{\text{pseudo 2KB}} &= 1 + (0.098 - 0.076) \times 2 + (0.076 \times 10) \\
&= 1 + (0.022 \times 2) + 0.760 = 1 + 0.044 + 0.760 \\
&= 1.804 \\
\text{Average memory access time}_{\text{pseudo 128KB}} &= 1 + (0.010 - 0.007) \times 2 + (0.007 \times 10) \\
&= 1 + (0.003 \times 2) + 0.700 = 1 + 0.006 + 0.070 \\
&= 1.076
\end{aligned}$$

From Figure 6.13 in the last example we know these results for 2 KB caches:

$$\text{Average memory access time}_{\text{1-way}} = 1.98 \text{ clock cycles}$$
$$\text{Average memory access time}_{\text{2-way}} = 1.86 \text{ clock cycles}$$

For 128 KB caches the times are:

$$\text{Average memory access time}_{\text{1-way}} = 1.10 \text{ clock cycles}$$
$$\text{Average memory access time}_{\text{2-way}} = 1.17 \text{ clock cycles}$$

The pseudo-associative cache is fastest for both cache sizes.

Although an attractive idea on paper, variable hit times can complicate a pipelined CPU design. Hence the authors expect the most likely use of pseudo associativity is with caches further from the processor (see the description of second level caches in the next section).

Fifth Miss Rate Reduction Technique: Hardware Prefetching of Instructions and Data

Victim caches and pseudo associativity both promise to improve miss rates without affecting the processor clock rate. A third way is to prefetch items before they are requested by the processor. Both instructions and data can be prefetched.

Instruction prefetch is frequently done in hardware outside of the cache. For example, the Alpha AXP 21064 microprocessor fetches two blocks on a miss: the requested block and the next consecutive block. The requested block is placed in the instruction cache when it returns, and the prefetched block is placed into the instruction stream buffer. If the requested block is present in the instruction stream buffer, the original cache request is canceled, the block is read from the stream buffer, and the next prefetch request is issued. There is never more than one 32 byte block in the 21064 instruction stream buffer. Jouppi [1990] found that a single instruction stream buffer would catch 15% to 25% of the misses from a 4 KB direct mapped instruction cache with 16 byte blocks. With 4 blocks in the instruction stream buffer the hit rate improves to about 50%, and to 72% with 16 blocks.

A similar approach can be applied to data accesses. Jouppi found that a single data stream buffer caught about 25% of the misses from the 4KB direct mapped cache. Instead of having a single stream, there could be multiple stream buffers beyond the data cache each prefetching at different addresses. Jouppi found that 4 data stream buffers increased the data hit rate to 43%. Palacharla and Kessler [1994] looked at a set of scientific programs and considered stream buffers that could handle either instructions or data. They found that 8 stream buffers could capture 50% to 70% of all misses from a processor with two 64 KB 4-way set associative caches, one for instructions and the other for data.

Example   What is the effective miss rate of the Alpha AXP 21064 using instruction prefetching? How much bigger an instruction cache would be needed in the Alpha AXP 21064 to match the average access time if prefetching were removed?

Answer   We assume it takes 1 extra clock cycle if the instruction is misses the cache but is found in the prefetch buffer. Here is our revised formula:

$$\text{Average memory access time}_{\text{prefetch}} = \text{Hit time} + \text{Miss rate} \times \text{Prefetch Hit rate} \times 1$$
$$+ \text{Miss rate} \times (1 - \text{Prefetch Hit rate}) \times \text{Miss penalty}$$

Let's assume the prefetch hit rate is 25%. Figure 6.6 on page 399 gives the miss rate for an 8 KB instruction cache as 1.10%. Using the parameters from the example on page 401, the hit time is 2 clock cycles, miss penalty is 10 clock cycles:

$$\text{Average memory access time}_{\text{prefetch}} = 2 + (1.10\% \times 25\% \times 1) + (1.10\% \times (1-25\%) \times 10)$$
$$= 2 + 0.00275 + 0.083 = 2.086$$

To find the effective miss rate with the equivalent performance, we start with the original formula and solve for the miss rate:

$$\text{Average memory access time} = \text{Hit time} + \text{Miss rate} \times \text{Miss penalty}$$

$$\text{Miss rate} = \frac{\text{Average memory access time} - \text{Hit time}}{\text{Miss penalty}}$$

$$\text{Miss rate} = \frac{2.0862}{10} = \frac{0.086}{10} = 0.86\%$$

Our calculation suggests that the effective miss rate of prefetching with an 8 KB cache is 0.86%. Figure 6.6 on page 399 gives the miss rate of 16 KB instruction cache as 0.64%, so 8 KB with prefetching is midway between the 1.10% and 0.64% miss rates of the 8 KB and 16 KB caches.

Prefetching relies on utilizing memory bandwidth that otherwise would be unused, and should not interfere with demand misses. Help from compilers can reduce useless prefetching.

Sixth Miss Rate Reduction Technique: Compiler Controlled Prefetching

An alternative to hardware prefetching is for the compiler to insert prefetch instructions to request the data before it is needed. There are several flavors of prefetch:

- *Register prefetch* will load the value into a register.

- *Cache prefetch* loads data only into the cache and not the register.

Either of these can be *faulting* or *non-faulting*; that is, the address does or does not cause an exception for virtual address faults and protection violations. Using this terminology, a normal load instruction could be considered a "faulting, register prefetch instruction." Non-faulting prefetches simply stop if they would normally result in an exception. The most effective prefetch are "semantically invisible" to a program: they don't change the contents of registers or memory and they cannot cause virtual memory faults. This section assumes non-faulting cache prefetch.

Prefetching makes sense only if the processor can proceed while the prefetched data is being fetched; that is, the caches continues to supply instructions and data while waiting for the prefetched data to return. Such a nimble cache is called a *non-blocking* cache or *lockup free* cache; we'll discuss it in more detail later.

Like hardware controlled prefetching, the goal is to overlap execution with the prefetching of data. If the miss penalty is small, the compiler just unrolls the loop (if any) once or twice and it schedules the prefetches with the execution. If the miss penalty is large, it uses software pipelining (page ??[3] in Chapter 5) to prefetch data for a future iteration.

Issuing prefetch instructions incurs an instruction overhead, however, so care must be taken to ensure that such overheads do not exceed the benefits. By concentrating on references that are likely to be cache misses, programs can avoiding unnecessary prefetches while improving average memory access time significantly.

Example

For the code below, determine which accesses are likely to cause data cache misses, then insert prefetch instructions to reduce misses, and calculate the number of prefetch instructions executed and the misses that are prefetched.

```
for (i = 0; i < 3; i = i+1)
    for (j = 0; j < 100; j = j+1)
        a[i][j] = b[j][0] * b[j+1][0];
```

Answer

The first step is for the compiler to determine which accesses are likely to cause cache misses; otherwise we will waste time on issuing prefetch instructions for data that would be hits. Let's assume we have an 8 KB direct mapped data cache with 16 byte blocks, it is a write back cache that does write allocate, and that each element of a and b are 8 bytes long as they are double precision floating point arrays with 3 rows and 100 columns for a and 3 rows and 101 columns for b. Let's also assume they are not in the cache at the start of the program.

Elements of a are written in the order that they are stored in memory, so a will benefit from spatial locality: the even values of j will miss and the odd values will hit. Since a has 3 rows and 100 columns, its accesses will lead to $\frac{3 \times 100}{2}$ or 150 misses. The array b does not benefit from spatial locality since the accesses are not in the order it is stored. The array b does benefit from temporal locality twice: the same elements are accessed for each iteration of i and each iteration of j uses the same value of b as the last iteration. Ignoring potential conflict misses, the misses due to b will be for b[j][0] accesses when $i = 0$ (and also the first access to b[j+1][0] when $j = 0$). Since j goes from 0 to 99 when $i = 0$, accesses to b lead to $100 + 1$ or 101 misses. Thus this loop will miss the data cache approximately $150 + 101$ or 251 times.

---

3.   Xref 2/e to Chapter 5 section on software pipelining.

To simplify our optimization, we will not worry about prefetching the first accesses of the loop nor in suppressing the prefetches at the end of the loop: if these were **faulting** prefetches, we could not take this luxury. Given our analysis of misses, we split the loop so the first loop will prefetch b as well as a, and the second loop will just prefetch a, since b will have already been prefetched. Let's assume that the miss penalty is so long we need to prefetch at least 7 iterations in advance.

```
for (j = 0; j < 100; j = j+1) {




    a[0][j] = b[j][0] * b[j+1][0];};
for (i = 1; i < 3; i = i+1)
    for (j = 0; j < 100; j = j+1) {



    a[i][j] = b[j][0] *b[j+1][0];}
```

This revised code prefetches the a[i][7] through a[i][99] and b[7][0] through b[99][0], reducing the number of non-prefetched misses to

$$\frac{3 \times 7}{2} + 8 = 11 + 8 = 19$$

The cost of avoiding 232 cache misses is executing 400 prefetch instructions.

Example

Calculate the time saved in the example above. Ignore instruction cache misses and assume there are no conflict or capacity misses in the data cache. Here are the key loop times ignoring cache misses: the original loop takes 7 clock cycles per iteration, the first prefetch loop takes 9 clock cycles per iteration, and the second loop takes 8 clock cycles per iteration (including the overhead of the outer for loop). A miss takes 20 clock cycles.

Answer

The original loop takes $3 \times 100 \times 7$ or 2100 clock cycles plus cache delays of 251 $\times 20$ or 5020 clock cycles, giving a total of 7120 clock cycles. The first prefetch loop takes 100×9 or 900 clock cycles plus 11*20 or 220 clock cycles for cache misses, giving a total of 1120. The second prefetch loop takes $2 \times 100 \times 8$ or 1600 clock cycles plus 8×20 or 160 clock cycles for cache misses, or 1760 clock cycles. The prefetch code is then 7120/(1120+1760) or about 2.5 times faster.

Seventh Miss Rate Reduction Technique: Compiler Optimizations

Thus far our techniques to reduce misses have required changes or additions to the hardware: larger blocks, higher associativity, pseudo associativity, hardware prefetching, or prefetch instructions. This final technique reduces miss rates without any hardware changes. This magical reduction comes from optimized software–the hardware designer's favorite solution.

The increasing performance gap between processors and main memory has inspired compiler writers to scrutinize the memory hierarchy to see if compile time optimizations can improve performance. Once again research is split between improvements in instruction misses and improvements in data misses.

Code can easily be rearranged without affecting correctness; for example, reordering the procedures of a program might reduce instruction miss rates by reducing conflict misses, but it must not cause bugs. McFarling [1989] looked at using profiling information to determine likely conflicts between groups of instructions, and reordered the instructions to reduce misses by 50% for a 2 KB direct mapped instruction cache with 4 byte blocks, and by 75% in a 8 KB cache. McFarling got the best performance when it was possible to prevent some instructions from ever entering the cache, but even without that feature, optimized programs on a direct-mapped cache had lower miss rates than unoptimized programs on an 8-way set-associative cache of the same size.

Data has even fewer restrictions on location than code. The goal of such transformations is to try to improve the spatial and temporal locality of the data. For example, array calculations can be changed to operate on all the data in a cache block rather than blindly striding through arrays in the order the programmer happened to place the loop. To give a feeling of this type of optimization, we will show four examples, transforming the C code by hand to reduce cache misses. Figure 6.16 shows the performance improvement in using these optimizations on a subset of the SPEC92 floating point benchmarks.

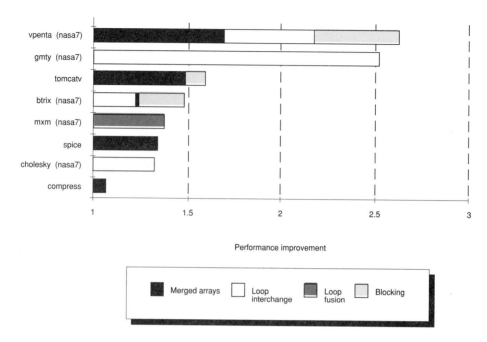

FIGURE 6.16 Lebeck and Wood [1994] performed the four optimizations in this section by hand on three SPEC92 programs. and five separate portions of the NASA7 benchmark.

Merging Arrays. This first technique reducing misses by improving spatial locality. Some programs reference multiple arrays in the same dimension with the same indices at the same time. The danger is that these accesses will interfere with each other, leading to conflict misses. This danger is removed by combining these independent matrices into a single compound array so that a single cache block can contain the desired elements.

```
/* Before */
int val[SIZE];
int key[SIZE];

/* After */
struct merge {
    int val;
    int key;
};
struct merge merged_array[SIZE];
```

An interesting characteristic of this example is that the proper coding practice of using an array of records would achieve the same benefits as this optimization.

Loop Interchange. Some programs have nested loops that access data in memory in non-sequential order. Simply exchanging the nesting of the loops can make the code access the data in the order it is stored. Like the prior example, this technique reduces misses by improving spatial locality; reordering maximizes use of data in a cache block before it is discarded.

```
/* Before */
for (k = 0; k < 100; k = k+1)
    for (j = 0; j < 100; j = j+1)
        for (i = 0; i < 5000; i = i+1)
            x[i][j] = 2 * x[i][j];

/* After */
for (k = 0; k < 100; k = k+1)
    for (i = 0; i < 5000; i = i+1)
        for (j = 0; j < 100; j = j+1)
            x[i][j] = 2 * x[i][j];
```

The original code would skip through memory in strides of 100 words, while the revised versions accesses all the words in the cache block before going to the next one. This optimization is improves cache performance without affecting the number of instructions executed, unlike the prior example.

Loop Fusion. Some programs have separate sections of code that access the same arrays with the same loops, performing different computations on the common data. By "fusing" the code into a single loop, the data that is fetched into the cache can be used repeatedly before being swapped out. Hence in contrast to our first two techniques, the target of this optimization is reducing misses via improved temporal locality.

```
/* Before */
for (i = 0; i < N; i = i+1)
    for (j = 0; j < N; j = j+1)
        a[i][j] = 1/b[i][j] * c[i][j];

for (i = 0; i < N; i = i+1)
    for (j = 0; j < N; j = j+1)
        d[i][j] = a[i][j] + c[i][j];
```

```
/* After */
for (i = 0; i < N; i = i+1)
   for (j = 0; j < N; j = j+1)
   {
        a[i][j] = 1/b[i][j] * c[i][j];
        d[i][j] = a[i][j] + c[i][j];
   }
```

The original code would take all the misses to access arrays a and c twice, once in the first loop and then again in the second. In the fused loop, the second statement freeloads on the cache accesses of the first statement.

Blocking. This optimization, perhaps the most famous of the cache optimizations, again tries to reduce misses via improved temporal locality. We are again dealing with multiple arrays, with some arrays are accessed by rows and some by columns. Storing the arrays in row by row (*row major order*) or in column by column (*column major order*) does not solve the problem because both rows and columns are used in every iteration of the loop. Such orthogonal accesses mean the other transformations we have seen are not helpful.

Instead of operating on entire rows or columns of an array, blocked algorithms operate on submatrices or *blocks*. The goal is to maximize accesses to the data loaded into the cache before the data are replaced. The code example below, which performs matrix multiplication, helps motivate the optimization:

```
/* Before */
for (i = 0; i < N; i = i+1)
   for (j = 0; j < N; j = j+1)
      {r = 0;
       for (k = 0; k < N; k = k+1) {
          r = r + y[i][k]*z[k][j]; };
       x[i][j] = r;
      };
```

The two inner loops read all N by N elements of z, access the same N elements in a row of y repeatedly, and write one row of N elements of x. Figure 6.17 illustrates the accesses to the three arrays, with a dark shade indicating a recent access, a light shade indicating an older access, and white meaning not accessed.

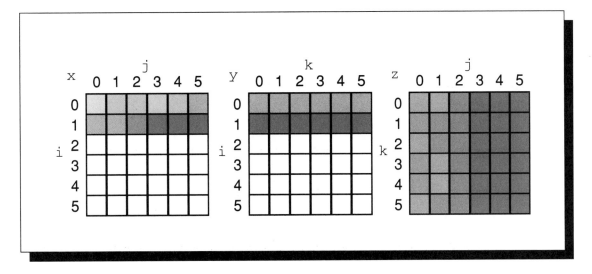

FIGURE 6.17   The age of accesses to the arrays x, y, and z indicated by color: white means never touched, light means older access and dark means newer accesses.   The variables i, j, and k are shown along the rows or columns used to access the arrays.

The number of capacity misses clearly depends on the size of the cache and N. If it can hold all three N by N matrices, then all is well provided there are no cache conflicts. If the cache can hold one N by N matrix and one row of N, then at least the i-th row of y and the array z may stay in the cache. Less than that and misses may occur for both x and z. In the worst case, there would be $2N^3 + N^2$ words read from memory for N^3 operations.

To ensure that the elements being accessed can fit in the cache, the original code is changed to compute on a submatrix of size B by B by having the two inner loops compute in steps of size B rather than going from beginning to end of x and z. B is called the *blocking factor.*

```
/* After */
for (jj = 0; jj < N; jj = jj+B)
for (kk = 0; kk < N; kk = kk+B)
for (i = 0; i < N; i = i+1)
     for (j = jj; min(jj+B-1,N);
                    j = j+1)
     {r = 0;
      for (k = kk; k < min(kk+B-1,N);
                    k = k+1) {
       r = r + y[i][k]*z[k][j]; };
      x[i][j] = r;
     };
```

Figure 6.18 illustrates the accesses to the three arrays using blocking. Looking only at capacity misses, the total number of memory words accessed is $2N^3/B + N^2$, which is an improvement by about a factor of B.

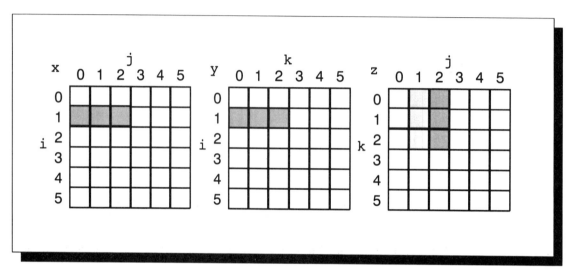

FIGURE 6.18   The age of accesses to the arrays   x , y, and z. Note in contrast to Figure 6.17 the smaller number of elements accessed.

(Although we have been aimed at reducing cache misses, blocking can also be used to help register allocation. By taking a small blocking size such that the block can be held in registers, we can minimize the number of loads and stores in program.)

Traditionally blocking has been aimed at reducing capacity misses, under the simplifying assumption that conflict misses are either not significant or can be removed by more associative caches. Since blocking reduces the number of words that are active in a cache at a given time, choosing a blocking size smaller than capacity can also reduce conflict misses. Figure 6.19 gives a qualitative view of this tradeoff.

These last two subsections have concentrated on the potential benefit of cache-aware compilers and programs. Given that increasing gap in processor speed and memory access times, this benefit will only increase in importance over time.

Now that we have spent 24 pages on techniques that reduce cache misses, it is time to look a reducing the next component of average memory access time.

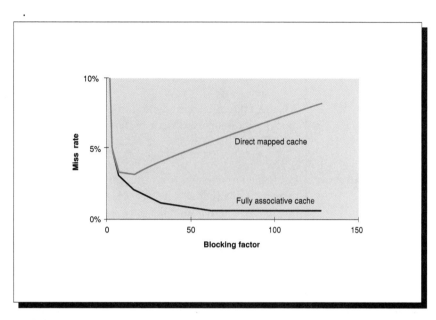

FIGURE 6.19 The impact of conflict misses in caches that aren't fully associative on block size. For example, Lam, Rothberg, and Wolf [1991] found one case where a blocking factor of 24 had a fifth the number of misses of a blocking factor of 48 despite both fitting into the cache.

6.4 | Reducing Cache Miss Penalty

Reducing cache misses has been the traditional focus of cache research, but the cache performance formula assures us that improvements in miss penalty can be just as beneficial as improvements in miss rate. Moreover, technology trends have improved the speed of processors faster than DRAMs, making the relative cost of miss penalties increase over time. We give five optimizations here to address this problem. Perhaps the most interesting optimization is the final one, which adds another cache to reduce miss penalty.

First Miss Penalty Reduction Technique: Giving Priority to Read Misses over Writes

With a write-through cache the most important improvement is a write buffer (page 395) of the proper size (see the fallacy on page 490 in Section 6.12). Write buffers, however, do complicate things in that they might hold the updated value of a location needed on a read miss.

Example

Look at this code sequence:

```
SW 512(R0),R3   ; M[512] ← R3    (cache index 0)
LW R1,1024(R0)  ; R1 ← M[1024]   (cache index 0)
LW R2,512(R0)   ; R2 ← M[512]    (cache index 0)
```

Assume a direct-mapped, write-through cache that maps 512 and 1024 to the same block, and a four-word write buffer. Will the value in R2 always be equal to the value in R3?

Answer

Using the terminology from Chapter 5, this is a Read After Write data hazard in memory. Let's follow a cache access to see the danger. The data in R3 is placed into the write buffer after the store. The following load uses the same cache index and is therefore a miss. The second load instruction tries to put the value in location 512 into register R2; this also results in a miss. If the write buffer hasn't completed writing to location 512 in memory, the read of location 512 will put the old, wrong value into the cache block, and then into R2. Without proper precautions, R3 would not be equal to R2!

The simplest way out of this dilemma is for the read miss to wait until the write buffer is empty. A write buffer of a few words in a write-through cache will almost always have data in the buffer on a miss, thereby increasing the read miss penalty. The designers of the MIPS M/1000 estimated that waiting for a four-word buffer to empty would have increased the average read miss penalty by 50%. The alternative is to check the contents of the write buffer on a read miss, and if there are no conflicts and the memory system is available, let the read miss continue.

The cost of writes in a write-back cache can also be reduced. Suppose a read miss will replace a dirty block. Instead of writing the dirty block to memory, and then doing the read, we could copy the dirty block to a buffer, then do the read, and **then** do the write. This way the read, for which the CPU is probably waiting, will finish sooner. Similar to the situation above, if a read miss occurs the CPU can either stall until the buffer is empty or check the addresses of the words in the buffer for conflicts.

Second Miss Penalty Reduction Technique: Subblock Placement for Reduced Miss Penalty

The first scheme to reduce miss penalty fetches full blocks from memory, which can be costly for large blocks. *Subblock placement* was invented originally to reduce tag storage for caches, but more recently it has been used to reduce the long miss penalty of large blocks. There is a valid bit on units smaller than the full block, called *subblocks*. Only a single subblock need be read on a miss. The valid bits specify some parts of the block as valid and some parts as invalid, so a match of the tag doesn't mean the word is necessarily in the cache, as the valid bit for that word must also be on. Figure 6.20 gives an example. Note that for caches with subblock placement, a block can no longer be defined as the minimum unit transferred between cache and memory. For such caches a block is defined as the unit of information associated with an address tag. Figure 6.20 shows the reduction in tag storage; if the valid bits had to be replaced by full tags, there would be much more memory dedicated to tags.

Subblock placement also provides another option on a write miss: the block is allocated in the cache and the appropriate subblock is written, but the rest of the subblocks are left empty; see page 451.

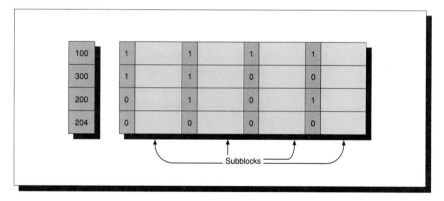

FIGURE 6.20 In this example there are four subblocks per block. In the first block (top) all the valid bits are on, equivalent to the valid bit being on for a block in a normal cache. In the last block (bottom), the opposite is true; no valid bits are on. In the second block, locations 300 and 301 are valid and will be hits, while locations 302 and 303 will be misses. For the third block, locations 201 and 203 are hits. If, instead of this organization, there were 16 blocks the size of the subblock, 16 tags would be needed instead of 4.

Third Miss Penalty Reduction Technique: Early Restart And Critical Word First

The first two techniques require extra hardware to reduce miss penalty, but this third technique does not. It is based on the observation that the CPU needs just one word of the block at a time. This strategy is impatience: Don't wait for the full block to be loaded before sending the requested word and restarting the CPU. Here are two specific strategies:

- *Early restart*—As soon as the requested word of the block arrives, send it to the CPU and let the CPU continue execution.

- *Critical Word First*—Request the missed word first from memory and send it to the CPU as soon as it arrives; let the CPU continue execution while filling the rest of the words in the block. Critical-word-first fetch is also called *wrapped* fetch and *requested word first*.

Generally these techniques only benefit designs with very large cache blocks, since the benefit is low unless blocks are large.

Example

Let's assume a machine has a 32 byte cache block and the memory system takes 5 clock cycles to fetch bytes over a 16-byte wide path to memory, as in the case of the Alpha AXP 21064. Calculate the average miss penalty for critical word first with early restart, assuming that there will be no other accesses to the other half of the block until it is completely fetched. Then calculate assuming the following instruction reads data from the other half of the block.

Answer

Since we can assume that the accesses either half of the cache block are equally likely, the average miss penalty is (5+10)/2 or 7.5 clock cycles for critical word first. For back to back reads of both halves of the cache block, only 1 cycle is saved since the pipeline will only move one instruction further until it must stall on the missing data.

As this example illustrates, the benefits of critical word first and early restart depend on the size of the block and the likelihood of another access to the portion of the block that has not yet been fetched.

The next technique takes overlap between the CPU and cache miss penalty even further to reduce the average miss penalty.

Fourth Miss Penalty Reduction Technique: Non-Blocking Caches to Reduce Stalls on Cache Misses

Early restart still waits for the requested word to arrive before the CPU can continue execution. For pipelined machines that allow out-of-order completion using a scoreboard or Tomasulo-style control (Section 6.7 of Chapter 6), the CPU need not stall on a cache miss. For example, the CPU could continue fetching instructions from the instruction cache while waiting for the data cache to return the missing data. A *non-blocking cache* or *lockup-free cache* escalates the potential benefits of such a scheme by allowing the data cache to continue to supply cache hits during a miss. This "hit under miss" optimization reduces the effective miss penalty by being helpful during a miss instead of ignoring the requests of the CPU. A subtle and complex option is that the cache may further lower the effective miss penalty if it can overlap multiple **misses**: a "hit under multiple miss" or "miss under miss" optimization. The second option is beneficial only if the memory system can service multiple misses (see page 451). Beware that hit under miss significantly increases the complexity of the cache controller as there can be multiple memory accesses.

Figure 6.21 shows the average time in clock cycles for cache misses for an 8 KB data cache as the number of outstanding misses is varied. Floating point programs benefit from increasing complexity, while integer programs get most of the benefit form a simple hit under miss scheme.

Program	Blocking Cache	Hit under 1 miss	Hit under 2 misses	Hit under 64 misses
alvinn	0.494	0.398	0.371	0.365
doduc	0.346	0.245	0.147	0.084
ear	0.094	0.067	0.050	0.048
fpppp	0.434	0.234	0.119	0.062
hydro2d	0.708	0.466	0.246	0.189
mdljdp2	0.314	0.231	0.193	0.167
mdljsp2	0.154	0.088	0.057	0.046
nasa7	1.865	1.452	0.753	0.519
ora	1.000	1.000	1.000	1.000
su2cor	1.266	1.055	0.437	0.093
swm256	0.297	0.110	0.070	0.067
spice2g6	1.092	0.958	0.903	0.891
tomcatv	1.140	0.714	0.310	0.066
wave5	0.277	0.194	0.132	0.107
FPaverage	0.677	0.515	0.342	0.265
compress	0.453	0.354	0.349	0.348
eqntott	0.108	0.078	0.073	0.073
espresso	0.209	0.176	0.170	0.169
xlisp	0.211	0.185	0.176	0.176
Intaverage	0.245	0.198	0.192	0.192

FIGURE 6.21   Average memory access time for data accesses in clock cycles for an 8 KB data cache as the number of outstanding misses is varied for 18 SPEC92 programs. The last column allows one miss for every register in the machine. This data was for a direct mapped cache with 32 byte blocks and a 16 clock cycle miss penalty. This data was generated using the VLIW Multiflow Compiler which scheduled loads away from use (Farkas and Jouppi [1994]).

Example

Assume the miss penalty is 16 clock cycles. Assume that going to 2-way set associativity would shrink average floating point miss rates by a factor of 0.93 and integer miss rates by a factor of 0.82. Using the results in Figure 6.21, which is more important for these two types of programs: 2-way set associativity or hit under one miss?

Answer

Since the miss time is the product of the miss rate and the miss penalty, shrinking the miss rate by a factor of 0.93 or 0.85 just shrinks the overall time. Hence the times are

$$\text{Set Assoc Miss time}_{FP} = 0.677 \times 0.93 = 0.630$$
$$\text{Set Assoc Miss time}_{Int} = 0.245 \times 0.82 = 0.201$$

The average hit under one miss time was 0.515 for floating point and 0.198 for integer, so hit under miss was more effective than 2-way set associativity for both cases, although it is very close for integer programs.

Fifth Miss Penalty Reduction Technique: Second Level Caches

The first four techniques to reduces miss penalty all concentrate on the interface between the CPU and the cache. This final technique concentrates on the interface between the cache and main memory.

The performance gap between processors and memory leads the architect to this question: Should I make the cache faster to keep pace with the speed of CPUs, or make the cache larger to overcome the widening gap between the CPU and main memory? One answer is: Both. By adding another level of cache between the original cache and memory, the first-level cache can be small enough to match the clock cycle time of the fast CPU while the second-level cache can be large enough to capture many accesses that would go to main memory, thereby lessening the effective miss penalty.

While the concept of adding another level in the hierarchy is straightforward, it complicates performance analysis. Definitions for a second level of cache are not always straightforward. Let's start with the definition of *average memory-access time* for a two-level cache. Using the subscripts L1 and L2 to refer respectively to a first-level and a second-level cache, the original formula is

$$\text{Average memory access time} = \text{Hit time}_{L1} + \text{Miss rate}_{L1} \times \text{Miss penalty}_{L1}$$

and

$$\text{Miss penalty}_{L1} = \text{Hit time}_{L2} + \text{Miss rate}_{L2} \times \text{Miss penalty}_{L2}$$

so

$$\text{Average memory access time} = \text{Hit time}_{L1} + \text{Miss rate}_{L1}$$

$$\times (\text{Hit time}_{L2} + \text{Miss rate}_{L2} \times \text{Miss penalty}_{L2})$$

In this formula, the success of the second-level miss rate is measured on the left-overs from the first-level cache. To avoid ambiguity, these terms are adopted here for a two-level cache system:

- *Local miss rate*—The number of misses in the cache divided by the total number of memory accesses to this cache; this is Miss rate$_{L2}$ above.

- *Global miss rate*—The number of misses in the cache divided by the total number of memory accesses generated by the CPU; using the terms above, the global miss rate is Miss rate$_{L1}$ × Miss rate$_{L2}$.

Example

Suppose that in 1000 memory references there are 40 misses in the first-level cache and 20 misses in the second-level cache. What are the various miss rates?

Answer

The miss rate (either local or global) for the first-level cache is 40/1000 or 4%. The local miss rate for the second-level cache is 20/40 or 50%. The global miss rate of the second-level cache is 20/1000 or 2%.

Figures 6.22 and 6.23 show how miss rates and relative execution time change with the size of a second-level cache for one design. From these figures we can gain two insights. The first is that the global cache miss rate is very similar to the single cache miss rate, provided that the second level cache is much larger than the first level cache. Hence our intuition and knowledge about the first level caches apply. The second insight is that the **local** cache is rate is **not** a good measure of secondary caches; it is a function of the miss rate of the first level cache, and hence can vary by changing the first level cache. Thus, the global cache miss rate should be used when evaluating second level caches.

With these definitions in place, we can consider the parameters of second-level caches. The foremost difference between the two levels is that the speed of the first-level cache affects the clock rate of the CPU, while the speed of the second-level cache only affects the miss penalty of the first-level cache. Thus, we can consider many alternatives in the second-level cache that would be ill chosen for the first-level cache. There is but one question for the design of the second-level cache: Will it lower the average memory-access–time portion of the CPI and how much does it cost?

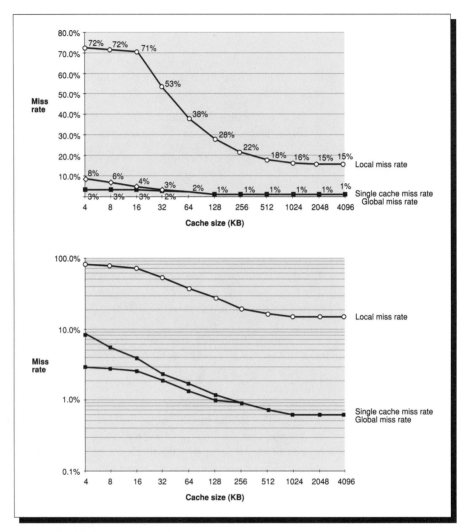

FIGURE 6.22   Miss rates versus cache size. The top graph shows the results plotted on a linear scale as we have done with earlier figures, while the bottom graph shows the results plotted on a log scale. As miss rates shrink the log scale makes the differences easier to follow. The miss rate of a single-level cache versus size is plotted against the local miss rate and global miss rate of a second-level cache using a 32-KB first-level cache. Second-level caches **smaller** than the 32-KB first level make little sense, as reflected in the high miss rates.. After 256 KB the single cache and global miss rates are virtually identical. Przybylski [1990] used four traces from the VAX system and four user programs from the MIPS R2000 that were randomly interleaved to duplicate the effect of process switches.

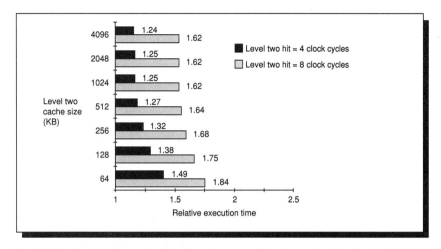

FIGURE 6.23 Relative execution time by second-level–cache size. Przybylski [1990] collected these data using a 32-KB, first-level, write-back cache, varying the size of the second-level cache. The two bars are for different clock cycles for a level two cache hit. The reference execution time of 1.00 is for a 4096-KB, second-level cache with a one–clock-cycle latency on a second-level hit. This data was collected the same way as in Figure 6.22.

The initial decision is the size of a second-level cache. Since everything in the first-level cache is likely to be in the second-level cache, the second-level cache should be bigger then the first. If second-level caches are just a little bigger, the local miss rate will be high. This observation inspires design of huge second-level caches—the size of main memory in older computers! Large size means that the second-level cache may have practically no capacity misses, leaving a few compulsory and conflict misses for our attention. One question is whether set associativity makes more sense for second-level caches.

Example

Given the data below, what is the impact of second-level–cache associativity on the miss penalty?

- Two-way set associativity increases hit time by 10% of a CPU clock cycle

- Hit time$_{L2}$ for direct mapped = 4 clock cycles

- Local miss rate$_{L2}$ for direct mapped = 25%

- Local miss rate$_{L2}$ for two-way set associative = 20%

- Miss penalty$_{L2}$ = 30 clock cycles

Answer   For a direct-mapped, second-level cache, the first-level cache miss penalty is

$$\text{Miss penalty}_{1\text{ way L1}} = 4 + 25\% \times 30 = 11.5 \text{ clock cycles}$$

Adding the cost of associativity increases the hit cost only 0.1 clock cycles, making the new first-level–cache miss penalty

$$\text{Miss penalty}_{2\text{ way L1}} = 4.1 + 20\% \times 30 = 10.1 \text{ clock cycles}$$

In reality, second-level caches are almost always synchronized with the first-level cache and CPU. Accordingly, the second-level hit time must be an integral number of clock cycles. If we are lucky, we can shave the second-level hit time to four cycles; if not, we can round up to five cycles. Either choice is an improvement over the direct-mapped, second-level cache:

$$\text{Miss penalty}_{2\text{ way L1}} = 4 + 20\% \times 30 = 10.0 \text{ clock cycles}$$

$$\text{Miss penalty}_{2\text{ way L1}} = 5 + 20\% \times 30 = 11.0 \text{ clock cycles}$$

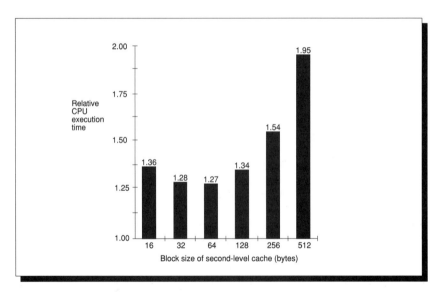

FIGURE 6.24   Relative execution time by block size for a two-level cache. Przybylski [1990] collected these data using a 512-KB second-level cache. This data was collected the same way as in Figure 6.22.

Now we can reduce the miss penalty by reducing the miss **rate** of the second level caches using techniques from section 6.3. Higher associativity or pseudo-associativity (page 415) are worth considering because they have small impact on the second-level hit time and because so much of the average access time is due to misses in the second level cache. Although the larger size of the second level cache eliminates conflict misses by distributing data over more blocks, it also eliminates most of the capacity misses; thus the **percentage** of conflict misses is still significant in direct mapped second level caches.

Another approach to reducing misses is increasing block size in second level caches. Increasing block size can increase conflict misses with small caches since there may not be enough places to put data, therefore increasing miss rate. Because this is not an issue in large, second-level caches, and because memory-access time is relatively longer, block sizes of 32 bytes and 64 bytes are popular. Figure 6.24 shows the variation in execution time as the second-level block size changes.

Another consideration concerns whether all data in the first-level cache is always in the second-level cache. If so, the second-level cache is said to have the *multilevel inclusion property*. Inclusion is desirable because consistency between I/O and caches (or between caches in a multiprocessor) can be determined just by checking the second-level cache.

The drawback to this natural inclusion is that the lower average memory-access times can suggest smaller blocks for the smaller first-level cache and larger blocks for the larger second-level cache. Inclusion can still be maintained in this case with more work on a second-level miss: The second-level cache must invalidate all first-level blocks that map onto the second-level block to be replaced, causing a slightly higher first-level miss rate. Inclusion escalates in complexity when combined with performance optimizations, such as a non-blocking secondary cache.

Finally, although a novice might design the first and second level caches independently, the designer of the first level cache has a simpler job given a second level cache to back up the first. It is less of a gamble to use a write through , for example, if there is a write back cache at the next level to act as a backstop for repeated writes.

Summarizing the second level cache considerations, the essence of cache design is balancing fast hits and few misses. Most optimizations that help one hurt the other. For second level caches, there are many fewer hits than in the first level cache, so the emphasis shifts to fewer misses. This insight leads to larger caches with higher associativity and somewhat larger blocks.

6.5 | Reducing Hit Time

Now that we have examined ways to improve cache performance by reducing misses (in Section 6.3) and by reducing miss penalty (this section), we are ready to reduce the third component of the average memory access time.

Hit time is critical because it affects the clock rate of the processor; on many machines today the cache access time limits the clock cycle rate, even for machines that take multiple clock cycles to access the cache. Hence a fast hit time is multiplied in importance beyond the average memory-access time formula because it helps everything. This section gives two general techniques and then two optimizations for write hits.

First Hit Time Reduction Technique: Small and Simple Caches

A time consuming portion of a cache hit is using the index portion of the address to read the tag memory and then compare it to the address. Our guideline from Chapter 1 suggests that smaller hardware is faster, and a small cache certainly helps the hit time. It is also critical to keep the cache small enough to fit on the same chip as the processor to avoid the time penalty of going off-chip. Some designs strike a compromise by keeping the tags on-chip and the data off-chip, promising a fast tag check yet providing the greater capacity of separate memory chips. The second guideline is to keep the cache simple, such as using direct mapping (see page 412). A main benefit of direct mapped caches is that the designer can overlap the tag check with the transmission of the data. This effectively reduces hit time. Hence the pressure of a fast clock cycle encourages small and simple cache designs for first level caches.

Second Hit Time Reduction Technique: Avoiding Address Translation during Indexing of the Cache

Even a small and simple cache must cope with the translation of a virtual address from the CPU to a physical address to access memory. As described below in Section 6.7, processors treat main memory as just another level of the memory hierarchy, and thus the address of the virtual memory that exists on disk must be mapped onto the main memory.

Our guideline from Chapter 1 of making the common case fast suggests that we use virtual addresses for the cache, since hits are much more common than misses. Such caches are termed *virtual caches*, with *physical cache* used to identify the traditional cache which uses physical addresses. Virtual addressing eliminates address translation time from a cache hit. Then why doesn't everyone build virtually addressed caches? One reason is that every time a process is switched, the virtual addresses refer to different physical addresses, requiring the cache to be flushed. Figure 6.25 shows the impact on miss rates of this flushing. One solution is to increase the width of the cache-address tag with a *process-identifier tag* (PID). If the operating system assigns these tags to processes, it only need flush the cache when a PID is recycled; that is, the process ID distinguishes whether or not the data in the cache is for this program. Figure 6.25 shows the improvement in miss rates by using PIDs to avoid cache flushes.

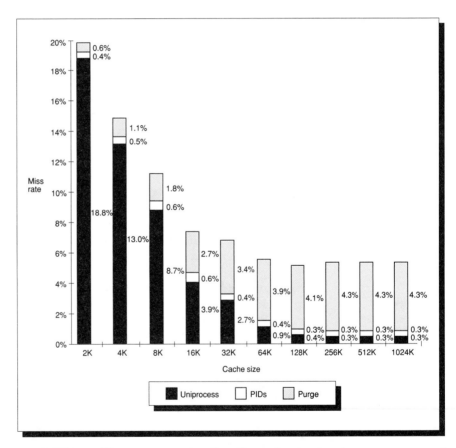

FIGURE 6.25   Miss rate versus virtually-addressed cache size of a program measured three ways: without process switches (uniprocess), with process switches using a process- identifier tag (PIDs), and with process switches but without PIDs (purge). PIDs increase the uniprocess absolute miss rate by 0.3 to 0.6 and save 0.6 to 4.3 over purging. Agarwal [1987] collected these statistics for the Ultrix operating system running on a VAX, assuming direct-mapped caches with a block size of 16 bytes.

Another reason why virtual caches are not more popular is that operating systems and user programs may use two different virtual addresses for the same physical address. These duplicate addresses, called *synonyms* or *aliases*, could result in two copies of the same data in a virtual cache; if one is modified, the other will have the wrong value. With a physical cache this wouldn't happen, since the accesses would first be translated to the same physical cache block. Hardware solutions, called *anti-aliasing*, guarantee every cache block a unique physical address, but software can make this much easier by forcing aliases to share some address bits. The version of UNIX from Sun Microsystems, for example, requires all aliases to be identical in the last 18 bits of their addresses; this restriction is called *page coloring*. Thus, a direct-mapped cache that is 2^{18} (256K) bytes or smaller can never have duplicate physical addresses for blocks. The difficulties of I/O and the operating system lead most designers to find alternative solutions to virtual caches. (Of course, the best software solution from the hardware designer's perspective is to do away with aliases!)

The final area of concern with virtual addresses is I/O. I/O typically uses physical addresses and thus would require mapping to virtual addresses to interact with a virtual cache. (The impact of I/O on caches is further discussed below in Section 6.10)

One technique to get fast hits is to break address translation and cache access into separate pipeline stages, giving fast cycle time and slow hits. This increases the number of pipeline stages for a memory access, leading to greater penalty on mispredicted branches and more clock cycles between the issue of the load and the use of the data (see page 5-?).[4]

One alternative to get the best of both virtual and physical caches is to use the page offset–the part unaffected by address translation–to index the cache while sending the virtual part to be translated. This alternative allows the comparison to be with physical addresses and yet overlap the time to read the tags with address translation. The limitation of this alternative is that a direct-mapped cache can be no bigger than the page size. This is an advantage of the 8 KB caches of the Alpha AXP 21064; the minimum page size is 8 KB, so the 8 bit index can be taken from the physical part of the address.

One way to keep the index small enough to be taken from the physical part of the address and still have a large cache is to use high associativity. Recall that the size of the index is controlled by this formula:

$$2^{\text{index}} = \frac{\text{Cache size}}{\text{Block size} \times \text{Set associativity}}$$

4.   2/e Xref to Chapter 5 talking about cost of increasing length of pipeline.

The IBM 3033 cache, as an extreme example, is 16-way set associative, even though studies show there is little benefit to miss rates above 4-way set associativity. This high associativity allows a 64 KB cache to be addressed with a physical index despite the limitation of 4 KB pages in the IBM architecture. Figure 6.26 shows the relationship of index to page offset.

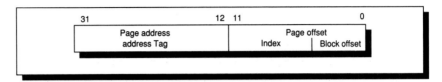

FIGURE 6.26   Relationship of index field and page offset in the IBM 3033 cache. The 4 KB page means the last 12 bits of the address are not translated, and hence can used to index the cache.

Another approach to trying to get the best of both worlds is to get the index from some combination of the virtual address and page offset yet to keep the comparison with the physical address. This scheme may be have few systems implications while keeping tag comparison fast, provided the operating system restricts aliasing problems by coloring pages as it likely would for a virtually addressed cache.

An alternative to higher associativity is for the operating system to implement page coloring by guaranteeing that the last few bits of the virtual and physical page address are identical. Such cooperating allows a larger index than first with the page offset and still compares physical addresses.

Keeping caches small and simple and techniques to avoid delays of address translation will make both read hits and write hits faster. The next two subsections concentrate only on writes.

Third Hit Time Reduction Technique: Pipelining Writes for Fast Write Hits

Write hits usually take longer than read hits because the tag must be checked before writing the data: otherwise the wrong address would be written. One technique, used by the Alpha AXP 21064 and other machines, pipelines the writes. Figure 6.27 shows the hardware organization of pipelined writes. First, tags and data are split so that they can be addressed independently. As usual, the cache compares the tag with the current write address. The difference is that the data memory access during this comparison uses the address and data from the **previous** write. Thus the logical pipeline is between writes and ignores read hits—the second stage of the write occurs during the first stage of the next write or during a cache miss. Therefore, writes can be performed back to back at one per clock cycle because the CPU does not have to wait for the tag check before writing.

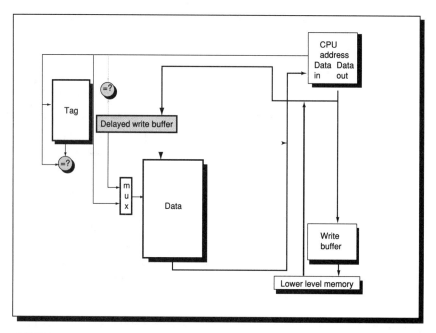

FIGURE 6.27   The hardware organization of pipelined writes. It is possible to find the desired data in the delayed write buffer. In that case, either the write buffer supplies the newer data or the write buffer could complete and then the new data is read from the cache.

Fourth Hit Time Reduction Technique: Subblock for Fast Write Hits in Write Through Caches

Pipelining writes allows write hits to take a single clock cycle. This second technique gives the same benefit without requiring the buffer and multiplexing seen in Figure 6.27. Subblock placement can reduce tag storage, miss penalty (see page 429), and it can help with write hits. Assuming the subblock is one word, this technique helps write hits by **always** writing the word (no matter what happens with the tag match), turning the valid bit on, and then sending the word to memory. Let's look at the possible cases to see why this trick works:

- *Tag match and valid bit already set.* Writing the block was the proper action, and nothing was lost by setting the valid bit on again.

- *Tag match and valid bit not set.* The tag match means that this is the proper block; writing the data into the subblock makes it appropriate to turn the valid bit on.

- *Tag mismatch.* This is a miss and will modify the data portion of the block. As this is a write-through cache, however, no harm was done; memory still has an up-to-date copy of the old value. Only the tag to the address of the write and the tag bits of the other subblock need be changed because the valid bit for this subblock has already been set. If the subblock size is one word and the store instruction is writing one word, then the write is complete. When the block is larger than a word or if the instruction is a byte or halfword store, then memory is requested to send the missing part of the block (write allocate).

This trick isn't possible with a write-back cache because the only valid copy of the data may be in the block, and it could be overwritten before checking the tag. This trick would also work with caches whose block size is one word.

Cache Optimization Summary

The techniques mentioned in Sections 6.3 to 6.5 to improve individually miss rate, miss penalty, and hit time generally impact the other components of average memory access equation as well as the complexity of the memory hierarchy. Figure 6.28 summarizes these techniques and estimates the impact on complexity, with + meaning that the technique improves the factor, – means it hurts that factor, and blank means it has no impact. Note that few techniques help more than one category, and none help all three.

Technique	Miss Rate	Miss Penalty	Hit Time	Hardware Complexity	Comment
Larger Block Size	+	–		0	Trivial
Higher Associativity	+		–	1	
Victim Caches	+			2	
Pseudo-Associative Caches	+			2	
Hardware Prefetching of Instructions and Data	+			2	Data is harder to prefetch
Compiler Controlled Prefetching	+			3	Needs non-block-ing cache too
Compiler Techniques to Reduce Cache Misses	+			0	Software is challenge
Giving Priority to Read Misses over Writes		+		1	Trivial for uniprocessor
Subblock Placement		+	+	1	Write through + 1 word subblock help writes
Early Restart And Critical Word First		+		2	
Non-Blocking Caches		+		3	
Second Level Caches		+		2	Costly hardware; harder if block size $L1 \neq L2$
Small and Simple Caches	–		+	0	Trivial
Avoiding Address Translation during Indexing of the Cache			+	2	Trivial if small cache
Pipelining Writes for Fast Write Hits			+	1	

FIGURE 6.28   Summary of cache optimizations and impact on the three aspects of cache performance and on cache complexity. + means that the technique improves the factor, – means it hurts that factor, and blank means it has no impact. The complexity measure is subjective, with 0 being the easiest and 3 being a challenge.

6.6 | The ABCs of Main Memory

> *... the one single development that put computers on their feet was the invention of a reliable form of memory, namely, the core memory. ... Its cost was reasonable, it was reliable and, because it was reliable, it could in due course be made large.*

> Maurice Wilkes, *Memoirs of a Computer Pioneer* (1985, p. 209)

Main memory is the next level down in the hierarchy. Main memory satisfies the demands of caches and serves as the I/O interface, as it is the destination of input as well as the source for output. Performance measures of main memory emphasize both latency and bandwidth. Traditionally, main memory latency (which affects the cache miss penalty) is the primary concern of the cache, while main-memory bandwidth is the primary concern of I/O. With the popularity of second-level caches and their larger block sizes, main memory bandwidth becomes important to caches as well. In fact, cache designers may take advantage of the high memory bandwidth by increasing block size. The relationship of main memory and I/O is discussed in Chapter 7.

Memory latency is traditionally quoted using two measures—access time and cycle time. *Access time* is the time between when a read is requested and when the desired word arrives, while *cycle time* is the minimum time between requests to memory. One reason that cycle time is greater than access time is that the memory needs the address lines to be stable between accesses.

As early DRAMs grew in capacity, the cost of a package with all the necessary address lines were an issue. The solution was to multiplex the address lines, thereby cutting the number of address pins in half. One half of the address is sent first, called the *row-access strobe* or *RAS*. It is followed by the other half of the address, sent during the *column-access strobe* or *CAS*. These names come from the internal chip organization, for the memory is organized as a rectangular matrix addressed by rows and columns.

An additional requirement of DRAMs derives from the property signified by its first letter, D, for dynamic. DRAMs use only a single transistor to store a bit, but reading that bit can disturb the information. To prevent loss of information, each bit must be "refreshed" periodically. Fortunately, all the bits in a row can be refreshed simultaneously just by reading that row. Hence every DRAM in the memory system must access every row within a certain time window, such as 8 milliseconds.

This requirement means that the memory system is occasionally unavailable because it is sending a signal telling every chip to *refresh*. The time for a refresh is typically a full memory access (RAS and CAS) for each row of the DRAM. Since the memory matrix in a DRAM is conceptually square, the number of steps in a refresh is usually the square root of the DRAM capacity. DRAM designers try to keep time spent refreshing to be less than 5% of the total time. Memory controllers include hardware to periodically refresh the DRAMs.

In contrast to DRAMs are SRAMs—the first letter standing for "static." The dynamic nature of the circuits in DRAM require data to be written back after being read, hence the difference between the access time and the cycle time as well as the need to refresh. SRAMs use four to six transistors per bit to prevent the information from being disturbed when read. Thus, unlike DRAMs, there is no difference between access time and cycle time and there is no need to refresh SRAM. In DRAM designs the emphasis is on capacity, while SRAM designs are concerned with both speed **and** capacity. (Because of this concern, SRAM address lines are not multiplexed.) For memories designed in comparable technologies, the capacity of DRAMs is roughly 4 to 8 times that of SRAMs, and the cycle time and cost of SRAMs is 8 to 16 times faster than DRAMs.

The main memory of virtually every computer sold since 1975 is composed of semiconductor DRAMs (and virtually all caches use SRAM); the exception that proves the rule is Cray supercomputers such as the C-90, which use SRAM for main memory.

Amdahl suggested a rule of thumb that memory capacity should grow linearly with CPU speed to keep a balanced system (see Section 1.4), and CPU designers rely on DRAMs to supply that demand: they expect a four-fold improvement in capacity every three years in the base technology, or 60% per year. Unfortunately, the performance of DRAMs is growing at a much slower rate. Figure 6.29 shows a performance improvement in row-access time of about 22% per generation, or 7% per year. As noted in Chapter 1, CPU performance improved 50% per year since 1987, and 18% to 35% per year prior to 1987. Figure 6.30 plots CPU performance projections against the steady 7% performance improvement in DRAM speeds.

Year of introduction	Chip size	Row access (RAS)		Column access (CAS)	Cycle time
		Slowest DRAM	Fastest DRAM		
1980	64 Kbit	180 ns	150 ns	75 ns	250 ns
1983	256 Kbit	150 ns	120 ns	50 ns	220 ns
1986	1 Mbit	120 ns	100 ns	25 ns	190 ns
1989	4 Mbit	100 ns	80 ns	20 ns	165 ns
1992	16 Mbit	80 ns	60 ns	15 ns	120 ns
1995?	64 Mbit	≈65 ns	≈45 ns	≈10 ns	≈100 ns

FIGURE 6.29 Times of fast and slow DRAMs with each generation. The improvement by a factor of two in column access accompanied the switch from NMOS DRAMs to CMOS DRAMs. With three years per generation, the performance improvement of row access time is about 7% per year. Data in the last row represent predicted performance for 64-Mbit DRAMs, which were not available at the time of this edition.

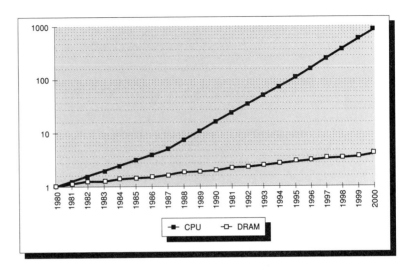

FIGURE 6.30 **Starting with 1980 performance as a baseline, the performance of DRAMs and CPUs are plotted over time.** The DRAM baseline is 64 KB in 1980, with three years to the next generation with a 7% per year performance improvement. The CPU line assumes a 25% improvement per year until 1987 and a 50% improvement thereafter. Note that the vertical axis must be on a logarithmic scale to record the size of the CPU–DRAM performance gap. Note that microprocessors in 1980 were often designed without caches, while in 1995 they usually come with **two** levels of caches. further evidence of the gap.

The CPU–DRAM performance gap is clearly a problem today—Amdahl's Law warns us what will happen if we ignore one portion of the computation while trying to speed up the rest. The previous sections describe what can be done with cache organization to reduce this performance gap, but simply making caches larger or adding more levels of caches may not be a cost-effective way to eliminate the gap. Innovative organizations of main memory are needed as well. In the next section we examine techniques for organizing memory to improve bandwidth, concluding with techniques especially for DRAMs.

6.7 | Organizations for Improving Main Memory Performance

Although caches are interested in low latency memory, it is generally easier to improve memory bandwidth with new organizations than it is to reduce latency. Caches benefit from bandwidth improvement by allowing each cache-block size to increase without a large increase in the miss penalty.

Let's illustrate these organizations with the case of satisfying a cache miss. Assume the performance of the basic memory organization is

1 clock cycle to send the address

6 clock cycles for the access time per word

1 clock cycle to send a word of data

Given a cache block of four words, the miss penalty is $4 \times (1 + 6 + 1)$ or 32 clock cycles, with a memory bandwidth of one-half byte per clock cycle.

Figure 6.31 shows some of the options to faster memory systems. These generic solutions are the basis of the next subsection which assume generic memory, either DRAM or SRAM. DRAM specific solutions form the last subsection.

The simplest approach to increasing memory bandwidth, then, is to make the memory wider; we examine this first.

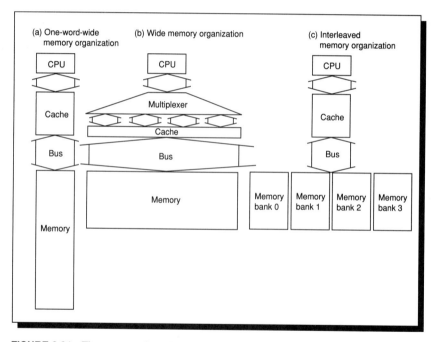

FIGURE 6.31   Three examples of bus width, memory width, and memory interleaving to achieve higher memory bandwidth. (a) is the simplest design, with everything the width of one word; (b) shows a wider memory, bus, and cache; while (c) shows a narrow bus and cache with an interleaved memory.

First Technique for Higher Bandwidth: Wider Main Memory

First-level caches are often organized with a physical width of one word because most CPU accesses are that size. Systems without second level caches often design main memory to match the width of the cache. Doubling or quadrupling the width of the cache and the memory will therefore double or quadruple the memory bandwidth. With a main memory width of two words, the miss penalty in our example would drop from 4×8 or 32 clock cycles to 2×8 or 16 clock cycles. At four words wide the miss penalty is just 1×8 clock cycles. The bandwidth is then one byte per clock cycle at two words wide and two bytes per clock cycle when the memory is four words wide.

There is cost in the wider connection between the CPU and memory, typically called a memory *bus*. CPUs will still access the cache a word at a time, so there now needs to be a multiplexer between the cache and the CPU—and that multiplexer may be on the critical timing path. Second level caches can help since the multiplexing can be between first and second level caches, which is not on the critical path. Another drawback is that since main memory is traditionally expandable by the customer, the minimum increment is doubled or quadrupled when the width is doubled or quadrupled. Finally, memories with error correction have difficulties with writes to a portion of the protected block (e.g., a write of a byte); the rest of the data must be read so that the new error correction code can be calculated and stored when the data is written. If the error correction is done over the full width, the wider memory will increase the frequency of such "read-modify-write" sequences because more writes become partial block writes. Many designs of wider memory have separate error correction every 32 bits since most writes are that size.

One example of wide main memory is the Alpha AXP 21064 whose second-level cache, memory bus, and memory are all 256 bits wide. To allow customers to purchase small amounts memory without sacrificing width, DEC sells older generations of DRAM for small memories as well as current DRAMs for the larger memory systems; see Section 6.11.

Second Technique for Higher Bandwidth: Simple Interleaved Memory

Increasing width is one way to improve bandwidth, but another is to take advantage of the potential parallelism of having many DRAMs in a memory system. Memory chips can be organized in banks to read or write multiple words at a time rather than a single word. In general, the purpose of interleaved memory is to try to take advantage of the potential memory bandwidth of **all** the DRAMs in the system; in contrast, most systems activate only the DRAMs containing the needed words.

The banks are often one word wide so that the width of the bus and the cache need not change, but sending addresses to several banks permits them all to read simultaneously. Figure 6.31 shows this organization. For example, sending an address to four banks (with access times shown on page 446) yields a miss penalty of $1 + 6 + 4 \times 1$ or 11 clock cycles, giving a bandwidth of about 1.5 bytes per clock cycle. Banks are also valuable on writes. While back-to-back writes would normally have to wait for earlier writes to finish, banks allow one clock cycle for each write, provided the writes are not destined to the same bank. Such a memory organization is especially important for write through.

The mapping of addresses to banks affects the behavior of the memory system. The example above assumes the addresses of the four banks are interleaved at the word level—bank 0 has all words whose address modulo 4 is 0, bank 1 has all words whose address modulo 4 is 1, and so on. Figure 6.32 shows this interleaving. This mapping is referred to as the *interleaving factor*; *interleaved memory* normally means banks of memory that are word interleaved. This optimizes sequential memory accesses. A cache-read miss is an ideal match to word-interleaved memory, as the words in a block are read sequentially. Write-back caches make writes as well as reads sequential, getting even more efficiency from word interleaved memory.

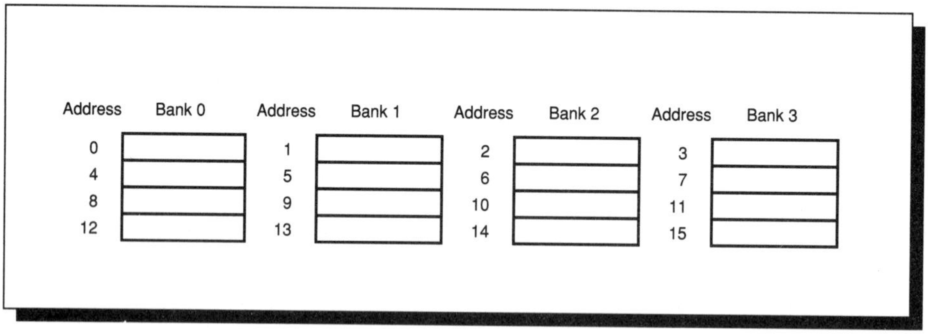

FIGURE 6.32   Four-way interleaved memory.

Example

What can interleaving and a wide memory buy? Consider the following description of a machine and its cache performance:

Block size = 1 word

Memory bus width = 1 word

Miss rate = 15%

Memory accesses per instruction = 1.2

Cache miss penalty = 8 cycles (as above)

Average cycles per instruction (ignoring cache misses) = 2

If we change the block size to two words, the miss rate falls to 10%, and a four-word block has a miss rate of 5%. What is the improvement in performance of interleaving two ways and four ways versus doubling the width of memory and the bus, assuming the access times on page 446?

Answer The CPI for the base machine using one-word blocks is

$$2 + (1.2 \times 15\% \times 8) = 3.44$$

Since the clock cycle time and instruction count won't change in this example, we can calculate performance improvement by just comparing CPI.

Increasing the block size to two words gives the following options:

32-bit bus and memory, no interleaving $= 2 + (1.2 \times 10\% \times 2 \times 8) = 3.92$

32-bit bus and memory, interleaving $= 2 + (1.2 \times 10\% \times (1 + 6 + 2)) = 3.08$

64-bit bus and memory, no interleaving $= 2 + (1.2 \times 10\% \times 1 \times 8) = 2.96$

Thus, doubling the block size slows down the straightforward implementation (3.92 versus 3.44), while interleaving or wider memory is 1.12 or 1.16 times faster, respectively. If we increase the block size to four, the following is obtained:

32-bit bus and memory, no interleaving $= 2 + (1.2 \times 5\% \times 4 \times 8) = 3.92$

32-bit bus and memory, interleaving $= 2 + (1.2 \times 5\% \times (1 + 6 + 4)) = 2.66$

64-bit bus and memory, no interleaving $= 2 + (1.2 \times 5\% \times 2 \times 8) = 2.96$

Again, the larger block hurts performance for the simple case, although the interleaved 32-bit memory is now fastest—1.29 times faster versus 1.16 for the wider memory and bus.

This subsection shows that interleaved memory is logically a wide memory, except that accesses to banks are staged over time to share internal resources–the bus in this example.

Third Technique for Higher Bandwidth: Independent Memory Banks

The original motivation for memory banks was higher memory bandwidth by interleaving sequential accesses. This hardware is not much more difficult since the banks can share address lines with a memory controller, enabling each bank to use the data portion of the memory bus. A generalization of interleaving is to allow multiple independent accesses, where multiple memory controllers allow banks (or sets of word-interleaved banks) to operate independently. Each banks need separate address lines and possibly separate data bus. For example, an input device may use one controller and its memory, the cache read may use another, and a cache write may use a third. Non-blocking caches (page 430) allow the

CPU to proceed beyond a cache miss, potentially allowing multiple cache misses to be serviced simultaneously. Such a design only makes sense with memory banks; otherwise the multiple reads will be serviced by a single memory port and get no benefit of overlap. Multiprocessors that share a common memory provide further motivation for memory banks (see Chapter 9).

Thus memory bank has potentially two conflicting definitions. We use the term *super bank* to mean all memory active on one block transfer and the term *bank* for the portion within a bank that is interleaved. Figure 6.33 shows this relationship.

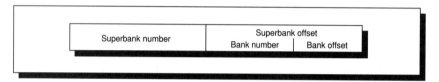

FIGURE 6.33   The relationship of "superbanks" and banks.

How many bank s should be included? One metric, used in vector computers (Appendix B), is as follows:

$$\text{number of bank s} \geq \text{number of clock cycles to access word in bank}$$

The goal is to make sure that the memory system can deliver information from a new bank each clock cycle for sequential accesses. To see why this formula holds, imagine there were fewer bank s than clock cycles to access a word in a bank; say, 8 banks with an access time of 10 clock cycles. After 10 clock cycles the CPU could get a word from bank 0, and then bank 0 would begin fetching the next desired word as the CPU received the following 7 words from the other 7 banks. At clock cycle 18 the CPU would be at the door of bank 0, waiting for it to supply the next word. The CPU would have to wait until clock cycle 20 for the word to appear. Hence we want more bank s than clock cycles to access a bank .

We well discuss conflicts on accesses to bank s for non-sequential accesses in the next subsection. For now, we note that having many banks reduces the chance of these bank   conflicts.

Ironically, as capacity per memory chip increases, there are fewer chips in the same-sized memory system, making multiple banks much more expensive. For example, a 64-MB main memory takes 512 memory chips of 1 M x 1 bits, easily organized into 16 banks of 32 memory chips. But it takes only 32 64-M x 1-bit memory chips for 64 MB, making one bank the limit. Even though the Amdahl/ Case rule of thumb for balanced computer systems recommends increasing memory capacity with increasing CPU performance, many manufacturers will want to have a small memory option in the baseline model. This shrinking number of DRAMs is the main disadvantage of interleaved memory banks. DRAMs organized with wider paths, such as 16-M by 4 bit or 8-M by 8-bits, will postpone this weakness.

A second disadvantage of memory banks is again the difficulty of main memory expansion. Either the memory system must support multiple generations of DRAM, as in the DEC 300 model 800 which uses the Alpha AXP 21064, or the minimum increment will be to double main memory.

Fourth Technique for Higher Bandwidth: Avoiding Memory Bank Conflicts

If the memory system is being designed to support multiple independent requests–as in the case of miss under miss caches, multiprocessors (See Chapter 9), or vector computers (see Appendix B)–the effectiveness of the system will depend on the frequency that independent requests will go to different banks. Sequential accesses, or more generally accesses that differ by an odd number, work well with traditional interleaving. The problem is when this difference between addresses is an even number. One solution, used by larger computers, is to statistically reduce the chances by having many banks; the NEC SX/3, for instance, has up to 128 banks.

The problem with such a solution is that data memory references are not random, and may go to the same bank no matter how many banks are provided. Suppose we have 128 memory banks, interleaved on a word basis, and execute this code:

```
int x[256][512];
    for (j = 0; j < 512; j = j+1)
        for (i = 0; i < 256; i = i+1)
            x[i][j] = 2 * x[i][j];
```

Since the 512 is an even multiple of 128, all the elements of a column will be in the same memory bank and code will stall on data cache misses no matter how sophisticated a CPU or memory system.

There are both software and hardware solutions to this problem. The compiler could do the loop interchange optimization (see page 6-53?[5]) to avoid accessing the same bank. A simpler solution would be for the programmer or the compiler to expand the size of the array so that it is not a power of two, thereby forcing the addresses above go to different banks.

---

5.   2/e Xref to compiler optimizations in miss rate section

Before describing a hardware solution, let's review how addressing of banks works. The mapping of an address to a location in a memory bank can be expressed as two problems:

$$\text{bank number} = \text{address } \mathbf{mod} \text{ number of banks}$$

$$\text{address within bank} = \text{address} \text{ / number of banks}$$

Traditional memory systems keep the number of banks a power of two to make this calculation trivial.

One hardware solution to reduce the number of bank conflicts is to have a prime number of banks! Such a number would seem to demand that each memory access be lengthened by the time to calculate the modulo and the division mentioned above. There are several hardware schemes to calculate modulo quickly, especially if the prime number of memory banks is one less than a power of 2 (see Exercise 6.9?). It turns out that the division can be replaced by the following simple calculation:

$$\text{address within bank} = \text{address } \mathbf{mod} \text{ number of words in bank}$$

Since the number of words in a bank is very likely a power of 2, we have replaced division by a prime number by bit selection.

The proof of this simplification is based on the *Chinese Remainder Theorem*. This 2000 year old observation states that as long as two sets of integers a_i and b_i follow these rules:

$$b_i = x \bmod a_i, 0 \leq b_i < a_i, 0 \leq x < a_0 \times a_1 \times a_2 \times \dots$$

and that a_i and a_j are co-prime if $i \neq j$, then the integer x has only one solution (two integers are *co-prime* if neither divides evenly into the other). The Chinese Remainder Theorem guarantees that there is no ambiguity with this mapping of address to banks because the following conditions hold:

bank number = address **mod** number of banks ($b_0 = x \bmod a_0$);

address within bank = address **mod** number of words in bank ($b_1 = x \bmod a_1$);

bank number is less than number of banks ($0 \leq b_0 \leq a_0$);

address within a bank is less than the number of words in bank ($0 \leq b_1 < a_1$);

address is less than the number of banks multiplied by the number of words in a bank ($0 \leq x < a_0 \times a_1$);

the number of banks and the number of words in a bank are co-prime (a_0 and a_1 are co-prime);

The first two conditions above are simply the definition of the mapping. The next three conditions are trivially true because a N word address goes from 0 to N-1. The last condition is true since the number of banks is a prime number greater than 2 and the number of words in a bank is a power of 2.

Figure 6.34 shows three memory modules, each with 8 words, showing with the traditional sequentially interleaved mapping of addresses on the left and the new mapping on the right.

	Sequentially Interleaved			Modulo Interleaved		
Bank Number:	0	1	2	0	1	2
Address within Bank:						
0	0	1	2	0	16	8
1	3	4	5	9	1	17
2	6	7	8	18	10	2
3	9	10	11	3	19	11
4	12	13	14	12	4	20
5	15	16	17	21	13	5
6	18	19	20	6	22	14
7	21	22	23	15	7	23

FIGURE 6.34   Three memory banks with sequentially interleaved addressing on the left, requiring a division as part of addressing of the word within a module, and the new mapping which requires only modulo to a power of 2. For example, address 5 is mapped the second word of memory bank 2 on the left and to the sixth word of memory bank 2 on the right.

Fifth Technique for Higher Bandwidth: DRAM-Specific Interleaving

Thus far we have seen four techniques that improve memory bandwidth: wider memory, interleaved memory, banked memory, and avoiding bank conflicts. These techniques work with any memory technology, and have been used or discussed since before DRAMs were invented. This section presents techniques that take advantage of the nature of DRAMs

As mentioned earlier, DRAM access is divided into row access and column access. DRAMs must buffer a row of bits inside the DRAM for the column access, and this row is usually the square root of the DRAM size—1024 bits for 1 Mbit, 2048 for 4 Mbits, and so on. To improve performance, all DRAMs come with timing signals that allow repeated accesses to the buffer without another row-access time. There are three versions for this optimization:

- *Nibble mode*—The DRAM can supply three extra bits from sequential locations for every RAS.

- *Page mode*—The buffer acts like a SRAM; by changing column address, random bits can be accessed in the buffer until the next row access or refresh time.

- *Static column*—Very similar to page mode, except that it's not necessary to toggle the column-access strobe line every time the column address changes.

Starting with the 1-Mbit DRAMs, most can perform any of the three options, with the optimization selected at the time the die is packaged by choosing which pads to wire up. These operations change the definition of cycle time for DRAMs. Figure 6.35 shows the traditional cycle time plus the fastest speed between accesses in the optimized mode.

The advantage of such optimizations is that they use the circuitry already on the DRAMs, adding little cost to the system while achieving almost a fourfold improvement in bandwidth. For example, nibble mode was designed to take advantage of the same program behavior as interleaved memory. The chip reads four bits at a time internally, supplying four bits externally in the time of four optimized cycles. Unless the bus transfer time is faster than the optimized cycle time, the cost of four-way interleaved memory is only more complicated timing control. Page mode and static column could also be used to get even higher interleaving with slightly more complex control. DRAMs also tend to have weak tristate buffers, implying traditional interleaving with more memory chips must include buffer chips for each memory bank.

Recently new breeds of DRAMs have been produced which further optimize the interface between the DRAM and CPU. One example is from RAMBUS. This company takes the standard DRAM core and provides a new interface, making a single chip act more likely a memory system than a memory component. RAMBUS has dropped RAS/CAS, replacing it with a bus that allows other accesses over the bus between the sending of the address and return of the data. (Such a bus is called a *packet-switched bus* or *split-transaction* bus, which is described in Chapters 7 and 8.) This bus allows a single chip to act as a memory bank. A chip can return a variable amount of data from a single request., and even perform its own refresh. RAMBUS offers a byte wide interface, and a clock signal so that the chip can be tightly synchronized to the CPU clock. Once the address pipeline is full, a single chip can deliver one byte every 2 ns.

Chip size	Row access		Column access	Cycle time	Optimized time nibble, page, static column
	Slowest DRAM	**Fastest DRAM**			
64 Kbits	180 ns	150 ns	75 ns	250 ns	150 ns
256 Kbits	150 ns	120 ns	50 ns	220 ns	100 ns
1 Mbits	120 ns	100 ns	25 ns	190 ns	50 ns
4 Mbits	100 ns	80 ns	20 ns	165 ns	40 ns
16 Mbits	80 ns	60 ns	15 ns	120 ns	30 ns
64 Mbits	≈65 ns	≈45 ns	≈10 ns	≈100 ns	≈20 ns

FIGURE 6.35 DRAM cycle time for the optimized accesses. This is Figure 6.29 (page 446) with a column added to show the optimized cycle time for the three modes. Starting with the 1-Mbit DRAM, optimized cycle time is about four times faster than unoptimized cycle time. It is so much faster that page mode was renamed *fast page mode*. The optimized cycle time is the same no matter which of the 3 optimized modes is selected.

Most main memory systems use techniques such as page mode to reduce the CPU–DRAM performance gap. Unlike traditional interleaved memories, there are no disadvantages using such a mode as DRAMs scale upward in capacity. On the other hand, the new breed of DRAMs such as RAMBUS might cost a premium of, say, 20% per megabyte over traditional DRAMs to provide the greater bandwidth. The marketplace will determine whether the more radical DRAMs such as RAMBUS will become popular for main memory, or whether the price premium restricts them to niche markets.

One example niche market is computer graphics, where a DRAM with a fast serial output line is used to drive displays. This special DRAM is called a Video RAM or VRAM; RAMBUS may challenge VRAMs in this market.

6.8 | Virtual Memory

… a system has been devised to make the core drum combination appear to the programmer as a single level store, the requisite transfers taking place automatically.

Kilburn et al. [1962]

At any instant in time computers are running multiple processes, each with its own address space. (Processes are described in the next section.) It would be too expensive to dedicate a full-address-space worth of memory for each process, especially since many processes use only a small part of their address space. Hence, there must be a means of sharing a smaller amount of physical memory among many processes. One way to do this, *virtual memory*, divides physical memory into blocks and allocates them to different processes. Inherent in such an approach must be a *protection* scheme that restricts a process to the blocks belonging only to that process. Most forms of virtual memory also reduce the time to start a program, since not all code and data need be in physical memory before a program can begin.

While virtual memory is essential for current computers, sharing is not the reason virtual memory was invented. If a program became too large for physical memory, it used to be up to the programmer to make it fit. Programmers divided programs into pieces and then identified the pieces that were mutually exclusive. These *overlays* were loaded or unloaded under user program control during execution, with the programmer ensuring that the program never tried to access more physical main memory in the machine. As one can well imagine, this responsibility eroded programmer productivity. Virtual memory, invented to relieve programmers of this burden, automatically managed the two levels of the memory hierarchy represented by main memory and secondary storage. Figure 6.36 shows the problem.

In addition to sharing protected memory space and automatically managing the memory hierarchy, virtual memory also simplifies loading the program for execution. Called *relocation*, this procedure allows the same program to run in any location in physical memory. The program in Figure 6.36 can be placed anywhere in physical memory or disk just by changing the mapping between them. (Prior to the popularity of virtual memory, machines would include a relocation register just for that purpose.) An alternative to a hardware solution would be software that changed all addresses in a program each time it was run.

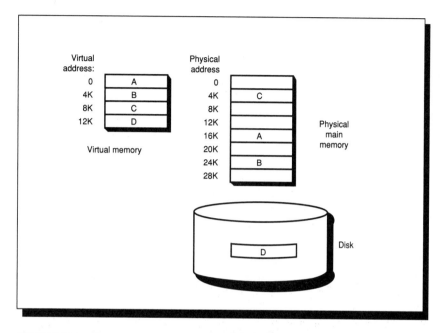

FIGURE 6.36   The logical program in its contiguous virtual address space is shown at the top. Three of the blocks are located in physical memory and one is located on disk.

Several general memory-hierarchy terms from Chapter 1[6] apply to virtual memory, while some other terms are different. *Page* or *segment* is used for block, and *page fault*, or *address fault*, is used for miss. With virtual memory, the CPU produces *virtual addresses* that are translated by a combination of hardware and software to *physical addresses*, which can be used to access main memory. This process is called *memory mapping* or *address translation*. Today, the two memory hierarchy levels controlled by virtual memory are DRAMs and magnetic disks. Figure 6.37 shows a typical range of memory hierarchy parameters for virtual memory.

---

6.   1/e Xref to definition of cache terms; will be moved from 8.3 of 1/e to chapter 1 2/e (not yet done in Beta edition)

Parameter	First Level Cache	Virtual Memory
Block (page) size	4 – 32 bytes	4096 – 16,384 bytes
Hit time	1 – 2	10 – 100 clock cycles
Miss penalty	8 – 66 clock cycles	700,000 – 6,000,000 clock cycles
(Access time)	(6–50 clock cycles)	(500,000–4,000,000 clock cycles)
(Transfer time)	(2–16 clock cycles)	(200,000–2,000,000 clock cycles)
Miss rate	0.5% – 20%	0.00001%– 0.001%
Data Memory Size	0.004 MB – 0.125 MB	16 MB – 8192 MB

FIGURE 6.37   Typical ranges of parameters for caches and virtual memory. Virtual memory parameters represent increases of 10 to 100,000 times. over cache parameters

There are further differences between caches and virtual memory beyond those quantitative ones mentioned in Figure 6.37:

- Replacement on cache misses is primarily controlled by hardware, while virtual memory replacement is primarily controlled by the operating system; the longer miss penalty means its more important to make a really good decision and also that the operating system can afford to get involved and spend more time deciding what to replace.

- The size of the processor address determines the size of virtual memory, but the cache size is normally independent of the processor address size.

- In addition to acting as the lower-level backing store for main memory in the hierarchy, secondary storage is also used for the file system that is not normally part of the address space; most of secondary storage is in fact taken up by the file system.

Virtual memory also encompasses several related techniques. Virtual memory systems can be categorized into two classes: those with fixed-size blocks, called *pages*, and those with variable size blocks, called *segments*. Pages are fixed at 4096 to 16384 bytes, while segment size varies. The largest segment supported on any machine ranges from 2^{16} bytes up to 2^{32} bytes; the smallest segment is one byte. Figure 6.38 shows how the two approaches might divide code and data.

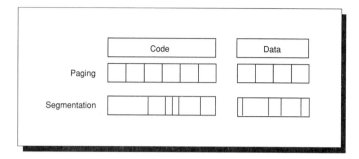

FIGURE 6.38   Example of how paging and segmentation divide a program.

The decision to use paged virtual memory versus segmented virtual memory affects the CPU. Paged addressing has a single, fixed-size address divided into page number and offset within a page, analogous to cache addressing. A single address does not work for segmented addresses; the variable size of segments requires one word for a segment number and one word for an offset within a segment, for a total of two words. An unsegmented address space is simpler for the compiler.

The pros and cons of these two approaches have been well documented in operating systems textbooks; Figure 6.39 summarizes the arguments. Because of the replacement problem (the third line of the figure), few machines today use pure segmentation. Some machines use a hybrid approach, called *paged segments*, in which a segment is an integral number of pages. This simplifies replacement because memory need not be contiguous, and the full segments need not be in main memory. A more recent hybrid is for a machine to offer multiple page sizes, with the larger sizes being powers of two times the smallest page size. The Alpha AXP 21064, for example, allows 8 KB, 64 KB ($2^3 \times 8$ KB), 512 KB ($2^7 \times 8$ KB), and 4096 KB ($2^9 \times 8$ KB) to act as a single page.

We are now ready to answer the four memory-hierarchy questions for virtual memory.

Q1: Where can a block be placed in main memory?

The miss penalty for virtual memory involves access to a rotating magnetic storage device and is therefore quite high. Given the choice of lower miss rates or a simpler placement algorithm, operating systems designers always pick lower miss rates because of the exorbitant cost of a miss. Thus, operating systems allow blocks to be placed anywhere in main memory. According to the terminology in Figure 6.1 (page 392), this strategy would be labeled fully associative.

Q2: How is a block found if it is in main memory?

Both paging and segmentation rely on a data structure that is indexed by the page or segment number. This data structure contains the physical address of the block. For segmentation, the offset is added to the segment's physical address to obtain the final virtual address. For paging, the offset is simply concatenated to this physical page address (see Figure 6.40, page 463).

	Page	**Segment**
Words per address	One	Two (segment and offset)
Programmer visible?	Invisible to application programmer	May be visible to application programmer
Replacing a block	Trivial (all blocks are the same size)	Hard (must find contiguous, variable-size, unused portion of main memory)
Memory use inefficiency	Internal fragmentation (unused portion of page)	*External fragmentation* (unused pieces of main memory)
Efficient disk traffic	Yes (adjust page size to balance access time and transfer time)	Not always (small segments may transfer just a few bytes)

FIGURE 6.39   Paging versus segmentation. Both can waste memory, depending on the block size and how well the segments fit together in main memory. Programming languages with unrestricted pointers require both the segment and the address to be passed. A hybrid approach, called *paged segments*, shoots for the best of both worlds: segments are composed of pages, so replacing a block is easy, yet a segment may be treated as a logical unit.

This data structure, containing the physical page addresses, usually takes the form of a *page table*. Indexed by the virtual page number, the size of the table is the number of pages in the virtual-address space. Given a 28-bit virtual address, 4 KB pages, and 4 bytes per page-table entry, the size of the page table would be 256 KB. To reduce the size of this data structure, some machines apply a hashing function to the virtual address so that the data structure need only be the size of the number of **physical** pages in main memory; this number could be much smaller than the number of virtual pages. Such a structure is called an *inverted page table*. Using the example above, a 64-MB physical memory would only need 64 KB (4*64 MB/4 KB) for an inverted page table.

To reduce address translation time, computers use a cache dedicated to these address translations, called a translation-lookaside buffer, or simply translation buffer. They are described in more detail shortly.

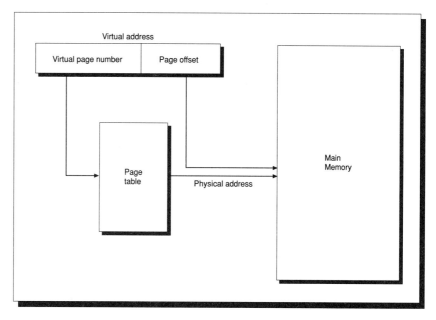

FIGURE 6.40   The mapping of a virtual address to a physical address via a page table.

Q3: Which block should be replaced on a virtual memory miss?

As mentioned above, the overriding operating system guideline is minimizing page faults. Consistent with this, guideline, almost all operating systems try to replace the least-recently used (LRU) block, because that is the one least likely to be needed. To help the operating system estimate LRU, many machines provide a *use bit* or *reference bit*, which is set whenever a page is accessed. The operating system periodically clears the use bits and later records them so it can determine which pages were touched during a particular time period. By keeping track in this way, the operating system can select a page that is among the least-recently referenced.

Q4: What happens on a write?

The level below main memory contains rotating magnetic disks that take millions of clock cycles to access. Because of the great discrepancy in access time, no one has yet built a virtual memory operating system that can write through main memory straight to disk on every store by the CPU. (This remark should not be interpreted as an opportunity to become famous by being the first to build one!) Thus, the write strategy is always write back. Since the cost of an unnecessary access to the next-lower level is so high, virtual memory systems include a dirty bit so that the only blocks written to disk are those that have been altered since they were loaded from the disk.

Techniques for Fast Address Translation

Page tables are usually so large that they are stored in main memory, and sometimes paged themselves. This means that every memory access logically takes at least twice as long, with one memory access to obtain the physical address and a second access to get the data. This cost is far too dear.

One remedy is to remember the last translation, so that the mapping process is skipped if the current address refers to the same page as the last one. A more general solution is to again rely on the principle of locality; if the accesses have locality, then the *address translations* for the accesses must also have locality. By keeping these address translations in a special cache, a memory access rarely requires a second access to translate the data. This special address translation cache is referred to as a *translation-lookaside buffer* or TLB, also called a *translation buffer*, or TB.

A TLB entry is like a cache entry where the tag holds portions of the virtual address and the data portion holds a physical page-frame number, protection field, valid bit, and usually a use bit and dirty bit. To change the physical page-frame number or protection of an entry in the page table, the operating system must make sure the old entry is not in the TLB; otherwise, the system won't behave properly. Note that this dirty bit means the corresponding **page** is dirty, not that the address translation in the TLB is dirty nor that a particular block in the data cache is dirty.

Figure 6.41 shows the Alpha AXP 21064 data TLB organization, with each step of a translation labeled. The TLB uses fully associative placement; thus, the translation begins (steps 1 and 2) by sending the virtual address to all tags. Of course, the tag must be marked valid to allow a match. At the same time, the type of memory access is checked for a violation (also in step 2) against protection information in the TLB.

For reasons similar to those in the cache case, there is no need to include the 13 bits of the Alpha AXP 21064 page offset in the TLB. The matching tag sends the corresponding physical address through the 32:1 multiplexer (step 3). The page offset is then combined with the physical page frame to form a full 34-bit physical address (step 4).

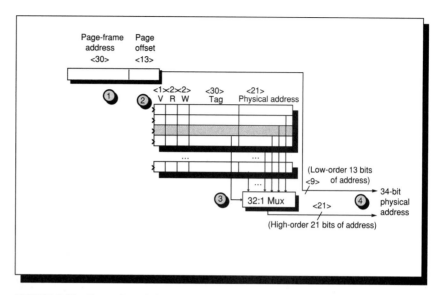

FIGURE 6.41   Operation of the Alpha AXP 21064 TLB during address translation. The four steps of a TLB hit are shown as circled numbers. Note that there is no specific reference, use bit, or dirty bit. Hence, a page-replacement algorithm such as LRU must rely on disabling reads and writes occasionally to record reads and writes to pages to measure usage and whether or not pages are dirty. The advantage of these omissions is that the TLB need not be written for most memory accesses.

As mentioned on page 438, one architectural challenge stems from the difficulty of combining caches with virtual memory. Small caches can restrict the index to the page offset so that the index can proceed immediately. While the cache address tags are being read, the virtual portion of the address (the page-frame address) is sent to the TLB to be translated. The address comparison is then between the physical address from the TLB and the cache tag, hence the cache index is virtual but the tags are physical.

Address translation can easily be on the critical path determining the clock cycle of the processor, since even in the simplest cache the TLB values must be read and compared. Thus the TLB is usually smaller and faster than the cache-address-tag memory, so that simultaneous TLB reading does not stretch the cache hit time. For example, in the Alpha AXP 21064, the data TLB has 32 blocks and the data cache has 256 blocks. Because of its critical nature, TLB access is sometimes pipelined.

Selecting a Page Size

The most obvious architectural parameter is the page size. Choosing the page is a question of balancing forces that favor a larger page size versus those favoring a smaller size. The following favor a larger size:

- The size of the page table is inversely proportional to the page size; memory (or other resources used for the memory map) can therefore be saved by making the pages bigger.

- As mentioned on page 440 in Section 6.5, a larger page size simplifies fast cache hit times.

- Transferring larger pages to or from secondary storage, possibly over a network, is more efficient than transferring smaller pages.

- The number of TLB entries are restricted, so a larger page size means that more memory can be mapped efficiently thereby reducing the number of TLB misses.

It this final reason that recent microprocessors have decided to support multiple page sizes; for some programs and TLB/memory organizations, TLB misses can be as significant on CPI as the cache misses.

The main motivation for a smaller page size is conserving storage. A small page size will result in less wasted storage when a contiguous region of virtual memory is not equal in size to a multiple of the page size. The term for this unused memory in a page is *internal fragmentation*. Assuming that each process has three primary segments (text, heap, and stack), the average wasted storage per process will be 1.5 times the page size. This is negligible for machines with megabytes of memory and page sizes in the range of 4 KB to 8 KB. Of course, when the page sizes become very large (more than 32 KB), lots of storage (both main and secondary) may be wasted, as well as I/O bandwidth. A final concern is process start-up time; many processes are small, so larger page sizes would lengthen the time to invoke a process.

6.9 | Protection and Examples of Virtual Memory

The invention of multiprogramming led to new demands for protection and sharing among programs. These are closely tied to virtual memory in computers today, and so we cover the topic here along with two examples of virtual memory.

Multiprogramming leads to the concept of a *process*. Metaphorically, a process is a program's breathing air and living space; that is, a running program plus any state needed to continue running it. Timesharing means sharing the CPU and memory with several users at the same time, giving the illusions that all users have their own machines. Thus, at any instant it must be possible to switch from one process to another. This is called a *process switch* or *context switch*.

A process must operate correctly whether it executes continuously from start to finish or is interrupted repeatedly and switched with other processes. The responsibility for maintaining correct process behavior is shared by the computer designer, who must ensure that the CPU portion of the process state can be saved and restored, and the operating system designer, who must guarantee that processes do not interfere with each others' computations. The safest way to protect the state of one process from another would be to copy the current information to disk. But a process switch would then take seconds—far too long for a timesharing environment. This problem is solved by operating systems partitioning main memory so that several different processes have their state in memory at the same time. This means that the operating system designer needs help from the computer designer to provide protection so that one process cannot modify another. Besides protection, the computers also provide for sharing of code and data between processes, to allow communication between processes or to save memory by reducing the number of copies of identical information.

Protecting Processes

The simplest protection mechanism is a pair of registers that checks every address to be sure that it falls between the two limits, traditionally called *base* and *bound*. An address is valid if

$$\text{Base} \leq \text{Address} \leq \text{Bound}$$

In some systems the address is considered an unsigned number that is always added to the base, so the limit test is just

$$(\text{Base} + \text{Address}) \leq \text{Bound}$$

If user processes are allowed to change the base and bounds registers, then users can't be protected from each other. The operating system, however, must be able to change the registers so that it can switch processes. Hence, the computer designer has three more responsibilities in helping the operating system designer protect processes from each other:

1. Provide at least two modes, indicating whether the running process is a user process or an operating system process. This latter process is sometimes called a *kernel* process, a *supervisor* process, or an *executive* process.

2. Provide a portion of the CPU state that a user process can use but not write. This includes the base/bound registers, a user/supervisor mode bit(s), and the exception enable/disable bit. Users are prevented from writing this state because the operating system cannot control user processes if users can change the address-range checks, give themselves supervisor privileges, or disable exceptions.

3. Provide mechanisms whereby the CPU can go from user mode to supervisor mode and vice versa. The first direction is typically accomplished by a *system call*, implemented as a special instruction that transfers control to a dedicated location in supervisor code space. The PC from the point of the system call is saved, and the CPU is placed in supervisor mode. The return to user mode is like a subroutine return that restores the previous user/supervisor mode.

Base and bound constitute the minimum protection system, while virtual memory offers a more fine-grained alternative to this simple model. As we have seen, the CPU address must go through a mapping from virtual to physical address. This mapping provides the opportunity for the hardware to check further for errors in the program or to protect processes from each other. The simplest way of doing this is to add writes by user processors permission flags to each page or segment. For example, since few programs today intentionally modify their own code, an operating system can detect accidental writes to code by offering read-only protection to pages. This page-level protection can be extended by adding user/kernel protection to prevent a user program from trying to access pages that belong to the kernel. As long as the CPU provides a read/write signal and a user/kernel signal, it is easy for the address translation hardware to detect stray memory accesses before they can do damage. Such reckless behavior simply interrupts the CPU and invokes the operating system. Processes are protected from one another by having their own page tables, each pointing to distinct pages of memory. Obviously, user programs must be prevented from modifying their page tables or protection would be circumvented.

Protection can be escalated, depending on the apprehension of the computer designer or the purchaser. Rings added to the CPU-protection structure expand memory-access protection from two levels (user and kernel) to many more. Like a military classification system of top secret, secret, classified, and unclassified, concentric *rings* of security levels allow the most trusted to access anything, the second most trusted to access everything except the innermost level, and so on down to "civilian" programs which are the least trusted and, hence, have the most limited range of accesses. There may also be restrictions on what pieces of memory can contain code–execute protection–and even on the entrance point between the levels. The Intel Pentium protection structure, which uses rings, is described later in this section. It is not clear today whether rings are an improvement in practice over the simple system of user and kernel modes.

As the designer's apprehension escalates to en trepidation, these simple rings may not suffice. The freedom given a program in the inner sanctum calls for a new classification system. Instead of a military model, the analogy of this next model is to keys and locks: A program can't unlock access to the data unless it has the key. For these keys, or *capabilities*, to be useful, the hardware and operating system must be able to explicitly pass them from one program to another without allowing a program itself to forge them. Such checking requires a great deal of hardware support if execution time for checking is to be kept under control.

A Paged Virtual Memory Example:
The Alpha AXP Memory Management and the 21064 TLB

The Alpha AXP architecture uses a combination of segmentation and paging, providing protection while minimizing page-table size. The 64-bit address space is first divided into three segments: *seg0* (bit 63 = 0), *kseg* (bits 63 and 62 = 10_{two}), and *seg1* (bits 63 and 62 = 11_{two}). kseg is reserved for the operating system kernel, and has uniform protection for the whole space and does not use memory management. User processes use seg0 and seg1, which are mapped into pages with individual protection. Figure 6.42 shows the layout of seg0 and seg1. seg0 grows from address 0 upward while seg1 grows downward to 0. Many systems today use some such combination of predivided segments and paging. The approach provides many advantages: segmentation divides the address space and conserves page-table space, while paging provides virtual memory, relocation, and protection.

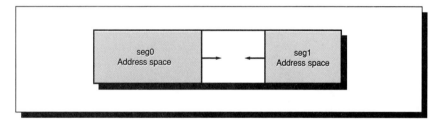

FIGURE 6.42   The organization of seg0 and seg1 in the Alpha. Operating systems put the text and heap areas into seg0 and a downward growing stack into seg1.

Even with this division, the size of page tables for the 64-bit address space is alarming. Hence the Alpha uses a three-level hierarchical page table to map the address space to keep the size reasonable. The addresses for each of these page tables come from three "level" fields, labeled level1, level2, and level3. Figure 6.43 shows address translation in the Alpha AXP. Address translation starts with adding the level1 address field to the Page Table Base Register and then reading memory from this location to get the base of the second level page table. The level address field is in turn added to this newly fetched address, and memory is accessed again to determine the base of the third page table. The level3 address field is added to this base address, and memory is read using this sum to (finally) get the physical address of the page being referenced. This address is concatenated with the page offset to get the full physical address. Each page table in the Alpha AXP architecture is constrained to fit within a single page, so all page table addresses are physical addresses that need no further translation.

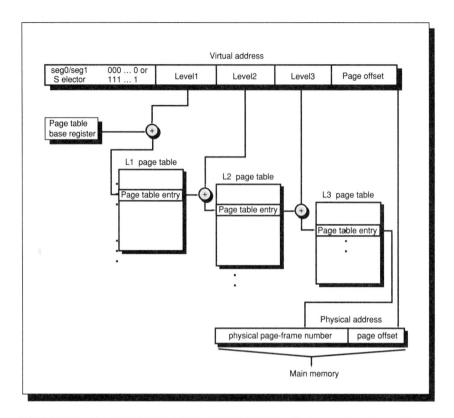

FIGURE 6.43   The mapping of a Alpha virtual address. Each page table is exactly one page long, so each level field is n bits wide where 2^n = page size/8. The Alpha AXP architecture document allows the page size to grow from 8 KB in the current implementations to 16 KB, 32 KB, or 64 KB in the future. The virtual address for each page size grows from the current 43 bits to 47, 51, or 55 bits and the maximum physical address grows from the current 41 bits to 45, 47, or 48 bits. The 21064 uses 8 KB pages, but it implements just 34 bits of the maximum 41 bits physical address possible in this scheme.

The Alpha uses a 64-bit *Page Table Entry (PTE)* in each of these page tables. The first 32-bits contain the physical page frame number, and the other half includes the following protection fields:

User Write Enable–allows user programs to write data within this page;

Kernel Write Enable–allows the kernel to write data within this page;

User Read Enable–allows user programs to read data within this page;

Kernel Read Enable–allows the kernel to read data within this page;

Valid–says that the page frame number is valid for hardware translation.

In addition, the PTE has fields reserved for systems software to use as it pleases.

Since the Alpha goes through three levels of tables on a TLB miss, there are three potential places to check protection restrictions. The Alpha obeys only the third level PTE, checking the first two only to be sure the Valid bit is set.

Note that there is no specific reference bit, use bit, or dirty bit. Hence, a page-replacement algorithm such as LRU must rely on disabling reads and writes occasionally to record reads and writes to pages to measure usage and whether or not pages are dirty. The advantage of these omissions is that the TLB need not be written for most memory accesses.

Since the PTEs are 8 bytes long, the page tables are exactly one page long, and the Alpha AXP 21064 has 8 KB pages, each page table has 1024 PTEs. Each of the three level fields are 10 bits long and the page offset is 13 bits, which leaves $64 - (3*10 + 13)$ or 21 bits to be defined. If this is a seg0 address the most significant bit is a 0, and for seg1 the two most significant bits are 11_{two}. Alpha requires that all bits from the most significant bit of the level1 field through the most significant bit of the 64 bit address be identical. For seg0 these 22 bits are all zeros and for seg1 they are all ones. This means the 21064 virtual addresses are really 43 bits long instead of the full 64 bits found in registers. The physical addresses would appear to be $32 + 13$ or 45 bits, but Alpha AXP architecture requires that the physical address be smaller than virtual address. The 21064 saves space on the chip by further limiting the physical address to 34 bits.

The maximum virtual address and physical address is then tied to the page size. The architecture document allows for the Alpha to expand the minimum page size from 8 KB up to 64 KB, thereby increasing the virtual address to $3 \times 13 + 16$ or 55 bits and the maximum physical address to $32+16$ or 48 bits; it will be interesting to see whether or not operating systems accommodate such expansion plans over the life of the Alpha.

While we have explained translation of legal addresses, what prevents the user from creating illegal address translations and getting into mischief? The page tables themselves are protected from being written by user programs. Thus, the user can try any virtual address, but by controlling the page-table entries the operating system controls what physical memory is accessed. Sharing of memory between processes is accomplished by having a page-table entry in each address space point to the same physical-memory page.

The first implementation of this architecture was the Alpha AXP 21064, which employs two TLBs to reduce address-translation time, one for instruction accesses and another for data accesses. Figure 6.44 shows the key parameters of each TLB. The Alpha allows the operating system to tell the TLB that contiguous sequences of pages can act as one: the options are 8, 64, and 512 times the minimum page size. Thus the variable page size of a PTE mapping makes the match more challenging, as the size of the space being mapped in the PTE also must be checked to determine the match. Figure 6.41 above describes the data TLB.

Block size	1 PTE (8 bytes)
Hit time	1 clock cycle
Miss penalty (average)	?? clock cycles
TLB size	Instruction: 8 PTE for 8 KB pages, 4 PTE for 4M pages (96 bytes total) Data: 32 PTE for 8 KB, 64K, 512K, or 4M pages (256 bytes total)
Block selection	Random, but not last used
Write strategy	(Not applicable)
Block placement	Fully Associative

FIGURE 6.44   Memory hierarchy parameters of the Alpha AXP 21064 TLB.

Memory management in the Alpha 21064 is typical of most computers today, relying on page level address translation and correct operation of the operating system to provide safety to multiple processes sharing the computer. The primary difference is that Alpha has extended the virtual address beyond 32 bits. In the next section we see a protection scheme for individuals who want to trust the operating system as little as possible.

A Segmented Virtual Memory Example: Protection in the Intel Pentium

The second system is the most dangerous system a man ever designs... . The general tendency is to over-design the second system, using all the ideas and frills that were cautiously sidetracked on the first one.

F. P. Brooks, Jr., *The Mythical Man-Month* (1975)

The original 8086 used segments for addressing, yet it provided nothing for virtual memory or for protection. Segments had base registers but no bound registers and no access checks; and before a segment register could be loaded the corresponding segment had to be in physical memory. Intel's dedication to virtual memory and protection is evident in subsequent models, with a few fields extended to support larger addresses. This protection scheme is elaborate, with many details carefully architected to try to avoid security loopholes. The next few pages highlight a few of the Intel safeguards; if you find the reading difficult, imagine the difficulty of implementing them!

The first enhancement is to double the traditional two-level protection model: the Pentium has four levels of protection. The innermost level (0) corresponds to Alpha kernel mode and the outermost level (3) corresponds to Alpha user mode.

The Pentium has separate stacks for each level to avoid security breaches between the levels. There are also data structures analogous to Alpha page tables that contain the physical addresses for segments, as well as a list of checks to be made on translated addresses.

The Intel designers did not stop there. The Pentium divides the address space, allowing both the operating system and the user access to the full space. The Pentium user can call an operating system routine in this space and even pass parameters to it while retaining full protection. This safe call is not a trivial action, since the stack for the operating system is different from the user's stack. Moreover, the Pentium allows the operating system to maintain the protection level of the **called** routine for the parameters that are passed to it. This potential loophole in protection is prevented by not allowing the user process to ask the operating system to access something indirectly that it would not have been able to access itself. (Such security loopholes are called *Trojan horses*.)

The Intel designers were guided by the principle of trusting the operating system as little as possible, while supporting sharing and protection. As an example of the use of such protected sharing, suppose a payroll program writes checks and also updates the year-to-date information on total salary and benefits payments. Thus, we want to give the program the ability to **read** the salary and year-to-date information and **modify** the year-to-date information but not the salary. We shall see the mechanism to support such features shortly. In the rest of this section, we will look at the big picture of the Pentium protection and examine its motivation.

Adding Bounds Checking and Memory Mapping

The first step in enhancing the Intel processor was getting the segmented addressing to check bounds as well as supply a base. Rather than a base address, as in the 8086, segment registers in the Pentium contain an index to a virtual memory data structure called a *descriptor table*. Descriptor tables play the role of page tables in the Alpha. On the Pentium the equivalent of a page-table entry is a *segment descriptor*. It contains fields found in PTEs:

A *present bit*—equivalent to the PTE valid bit, used to indicate this is a valid translation;

A *base field*—equivalent to a page-frame address, containing the physical address of the first byte of the segment;

An *access bit*—like the reference bit or use bit in some architectures that is helpful for replacement algorithms;

An *attributes field*—specifies the valid operations and protection levels for operations that use this segment.

There is also a *limit field*, not found in paged systems, which establishes the upper bound of valid offsets for this segment. Figure 6.45 shows examples of Pentium segment descriptors.

Pentium provides an optional paging system in addition to this segmented addressing, where the upper portion of the 32-bit address selects the segment descriptor and the middle portion is used as an index into the page table selected by the descriptor. We describe below the protection system which does not rely on paging .

Adding Sharing and Protection

To provide for protected sharing, half of the address space is shared by all processes and half is unique to each process, called *global address space* and *local address space*, respectively. Each half is given a descriptor table with the appropriate name. A descriptor pointing to a shared segment is placed in the global-descriptor table, while a descriptor for a private segment is placed in the local-descriptor table.

A program loads a Pentium segment register with an index to the table **and** a bit saying which table it desires. The operation is checked according to the attributes in the descriptor, the physical address being formed by adding the offset in the CPU to the base in the descriptor, provided the offset is less than the limit field. Every segment descriptor has a separate two-bit field to give the legal access level of this segment. A violation occurs only if the program tries to use a segment with a lower protection level in the segment descriptor.

We can now show how to invoke the payroll program mentioned above to update the year-to-date information without allowing it to update salaries. The program could be given a descriptor to the information that has the writable field clear, meaning it can read but not write the data. A trusted program can then be supplied that will only write the year-to-date information and is given a descriptor with the writable field set (Figure 6.45). The payroll program invokes the trusted code using a code-segment descriptor with the conforming field set. This means the called program takes on the privilege level of the code being called rather than the privilege level of the caller. Hence, the payroll program can read the salaries and call a trusted program to update the year-to-date totals, yet the payroll program cannot modify the salaries. If a Trojan horse exists in this system, to be effective it must be located in the trusted code whose only job is to update the year-to-date information. The argument for this style of protection is that limiting the scope of the vulnerability enhances security.

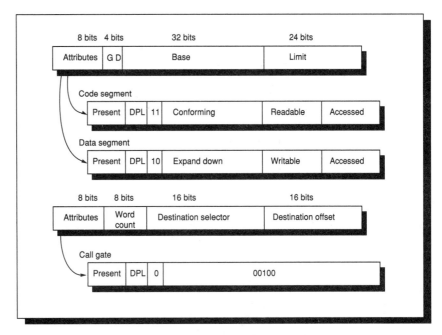

FIGURE 6.45   The Pentium segment descriptors are distinguished by bits in the attributes field. *Base*, *limit, present*, *readable*, and *writable* are all self-explanatory. D gives the default addressing size of the instructions: 16 bits or 32 bit. G gives the granularity of the segment limit: 0 means in bytes and 1 means in 4 KB pages. G is set to 1 when paging it turned on to set the size of the page tables. DPL means *descriptor privilege level*—this is checked against the code privilege level to see if the access will be allowed. *Conforming* says the code takes on the privilege level of the code being called rather than the privilege level of the caller; it is used for library routines. The *expand-down field* flips the check to let the base field be the high-water mark and the limit field be the low-water mark. As one might expect, this is used for stack segments that grow down. *Word count* controls the number of words copied from the current stack to the new stack on a call gate. The other two fields of the call-gate descriptor, *destination selector* and *destination offset*, select the descriptor of the destination of the call and the offset into it. There are many more than these three segment descriptors in the Pentium.

Adding Safe Calls from User to OS Gates and Inheriting Protection Level for Parameters

Allowing the user to jump into the operating system is a bold step. How, then, can a hardware designer increase the chances of a safe system without trusting the operating system or any other piece of code? The Pentium approach is to restrict where the user can enter a piece of code, to safely place parameters on the proper stack, and to make sure the user parameters don't get the protection level of the called code.

To restrict entry into others' code, the Pentium provides a special segment descriptor, or *call gate*, identified by a bit in the attributes field. Unlike other descriptors, call gates are full physical addresses of an object in memory; the offset supplied by the CPU is ignored. As stated above, their purpose is to prevent the user from randomly jumping anywhere into a protected or more-privileged code segment. In our programming example, this means the only place the payroll program can invoke the trusted code is at the proper boundary. This is needed to make conforming segments work as intended.

What happens if caller and callee are "mutually suspicious," so that neither trusts the other? The solution is found in the word-count field in the bottom descriptor in Figure 6.45. When a call instruction invokes a call-gate descriptor, the descriptor copies the number of words specified in the descriptor from the local stack onto the stack corresponding to the level of this segment. This allows the user to pass parameters by first pushing them onto the local stack. The hardware then safely transfers them onto the correct stack. A return from a call gate will pop the parameters off both stacks and copy any return values to the proper stack. Note that this model is incompatible with the current practice of passing parameters in registers.

This still leaves open the potential loophole of having the operating system use the user's address, passed as parameters, with the operating system's security level, instead of with the user's level. The Pentium solves this problem by dedicating two bits in every CPU segment register to the *requested protection level*. When an operating system routine is invoked, it can execute an instruction that sets this two-bit field in all address parameters with the protection level of the user that called the routine. Thus, when these address parameters are loaded into the segment registers, they will set the requested protection level to the proper value. The Pentium hardware then uses the requested protection level to prevent any foolishness: No segment can be accessed from the system routine using those parameters if it has a more-privileged protection level than requested.

Summary: Protection on the Alpha Versus the Pentium

If the Pentium protection model looks harder to build than the Alpha model, that's because it is. This effort must be especially frustrating for the Pentium engineers, since few customers use the elaborate protection mechanism. Also, the fact that the protection model is a mismatch for the simple paging protection of UNIX means it will be used only by someone writing an operating system specially for this computer. NT from Microsoft is the best candidate, but only time will tell whether the performance cost of such protection is justified for a personal-computer operating system. Two questions remain: Will the considerable protection-engineering effort, which must be borne by each generation of the 80x86 family, be put to good use, and will it prove any safer in practice than its paging system?

6.10 | Cross-Cutting Issues in the Design of Memory Hierarchies

This section describes four topics discussed in other chapters that are fundamental to memory hierarchy design.

Superscalar CPU and Number of Ports to the Cache

One complexity of the advanced designs of Chapter 5[7] is that multiple instructions can be issued within a single clock cycle. Clearly, if there is not sufficient peak bandwidth from the cache to match the peak demands of the instructions, there is little benefit to designing such parallelism in the processor. As mentioned above, similar reasoning applies to CPUs that want to continue executing instructions on a cache miss: clearly the memory hierarchy must also be non-blocking or the CPU benefits little.

For example, the IBM RS/6000 Power 2 model 900 (pages 5-113? to 5-121?[8]) can issue up to 6 instructions per clock cycle, and its data cache can supply two 128-bit accesses per clock cycle. The RS/6000 does this by making the instruction cache and data cache wide and by making two reads to the data cache each clock cycle, certainly likely to be the critical path in the 71.5 MHz machine.

Speculative Execution and the Memory System

Inherent in CPUs that support speculative execution or conditional instructions is the possibility of generating invalid addresses that would not occur without speculative execution. Not only would this be incorrect behavior, if exceptions were taken, the benefits of speculative execution would be swamped by false exception overhead. Hence the memory system must identify speculatively-executed instructions and conditionally-executed instructions and suppress the corresponding exception.

By similar reasoning we cannot such instructions to cause the cache to stall on a miss, for again unnecessary stalls could overwhelm the benefits of speculation. Hence these CPUs must be matched with non-blocking caches (see page 430).

---

7.   Cross reference to the section on superscalar or multiple issue instructions in the 2/e new chapter.

8.   2/e Xref to Chapter 5 P.I.A.T. on Power 2 IBM machine

Compiler Optimization: Instruction Level Parallelism vs. Reducing Cache Misses

Sometimes the compiler must choose between improving instruction level parallelism and improving cache performance. For example, the code below:

```
for (i = 0; i < 512; i = i+1)
    for (j = 1; j < 512; j = j+1)
        x[i][j] = 2 * x[i][j-1];
```

accesses the data in the order it is stored, thereby minimizing cache misses. Unfortunately, the dependency limits parallel execution. Unrolling the loop shows this dependency:

```
for (i = 0; i < 512; i = i+1)
    for (j = 1; j < 512; j = j+4){
        x[i][j]   = 2 * x[i][j-1];
        x[i][j+1] = 2 * x[i][j];
        x[i][j+2] = 2 * x[i][j+1];
        x[i][j+3] = 2 * x[i][j+2];
    };
```

Each of the last three statements has a RAW dependency on the prior statement. We can improve parallelism by interchanging the two loops:

```
for (j = 1; j < 512; j = j+1)
    for (i = 0; i < 512; i = i+1)
        x[i][j] = 2 * x[i][j-1];
```

Unrolling the loop shows this parallelism:

```
for (j = 1; j < 512; j = j+1)
    for (i = 0; i < 512; i = i+4) {
        x[i][j]   = 2 * x[i][j-1];
        x[i+1][j] = 2 * x[i+1][j-1];
        x[i+2][j] = 2 * x[i+2][j-1];
        x[i+3][j] = 2 * x[i+3][j-1];
    };
```

Now all four statements in the loop are independent! Alas, increasing parallelism leads to accesses that hop through memory, reducing spatial locality and cache hit rates.

I/O and Consistency of Cached Data

Because of caches, data can be found in memory or in the cache. As long as the CPU is the sole device changing or reading the data and the cache stands between the CPU and memory, there is little danger in the CPU seeing the old or *stale* copy. I/O devices mean the opportunity exists for other devices to cause copies to be inconsistent or for other devices to read the stale copies. Figure 6.46 illustrates the problem. This is generally referred to as the *cache-coherency* problem.

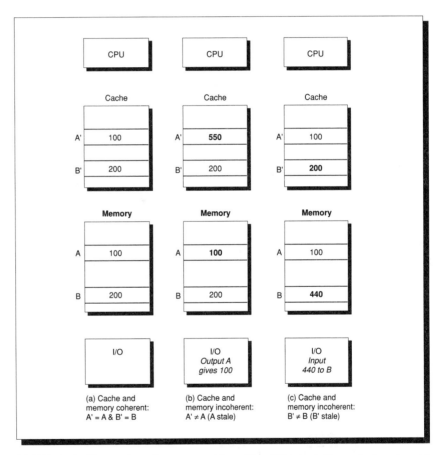

FIGURE 6.46 The cache-coherency problem. A' and B' refer to the cached copies of A and B in memory. (a) shows cache and main memory in a coherent state. In (b) we assume a write-back cache when the CPU writes 550 into A. Now A' has the value but the value in memory has the old, stale value of 100. If an output used the value of A from memory, it would get the stale data. In (c) the I/O system inputs 440 into the memory copy of B, so now B' in the cache has the old, stale data.

The question is this: Where does the I/O occur in the computer—between the I/O device and the cache or between the I/O device and main memory? If input puts data into the cache and output reads data from the cache, both I/O and the CPU see the same data, and the problem is solved. The difficulty in this approach is that it interferes with the CPU. I/O competing with the CPU for cache access will cause the CPU to stall for I/O. Input will also interfere with the cache by displacing some information with the new data that is unlikely to be accessed by the CPU soon. For example, on a page fault the CPU may need to access a few words in a page, but a program is not likely to access every word of the page if it were loaded into the cache. Given the integration of caches onto the same integrated circuit, it is also difficult for that interface to be visible.

The goal for the I/O system in a computer with a cache is to prevent the stale-data problem while interfering with the CPU as little as possible. Many systems, therefore, prefer that I/O occur directly to main memory, acting as an I/O buffer. If a write-through cache is used, then memory has an up-to-date copy of the information, and there is no stale-data issue for output. (This is a reason many machines use write through.) Input requires some extra work. The software solution is to guarantee that no blocks of the I/O buffer designated for input are in the cache. In one approach, a buffer page is marked as non-cacheable; the operating system always inputs to such a page. In another approach, the operating system flushes the buffer addresses from the cache after the input occurs. A hardware solution is to check the I/O addresses on input to see if they are in the cache; to avoid slowing down the cache to check addresses, sometimes a duplicate set of tags are used to allow checking of I/O addresses in parallel with processor cache accesses. If there is a match of I/O addresses in the cache, the cache entries are invalidated to avoid stale data. All these approaches can also be used for output with write-back caches. More about this is found in Chapter 7 on Input/Output.

The cache-coherency problem applies to multiprocessors as well as I/O. Unlike I/O, where multiple data copies is a rare event—one to be avoided whenever possible—a program running on multiple processors will want to have copies of the same data in several caches. Performance of a multiprocessor program depends on the performance of the system when sharing data. The protocols to maintain coherency for multiple processors are called *cache-coherency protocols,* and are described in Chapter 9 on Multiprocessors.

6.11 | Putting It All Together: The Alpha AXP 21064 Memory Hierarchy

Thus far we have given glimpses of the Alpha AXP 21064 memory hierarchy; this section unveils the full design and shows the performance of its components for the SPEC92 programs. Figure 6.47 gives the overall picture of this design.

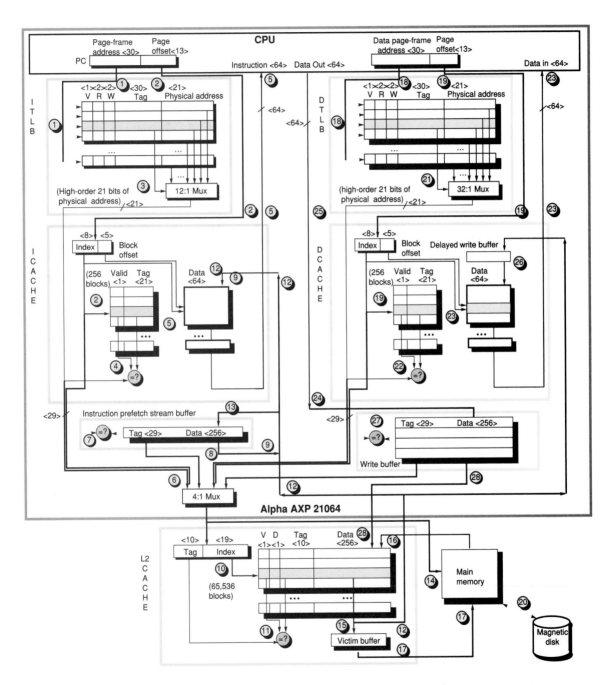

FIGURE 6.47   The overall picture of the Alpha AXP 21064 memory hierarchy. Individual components can be seen in greater detail in Figures 6.4 (page 396), 6.27 (page 442), and 6.41 (page 465).

Let's really start at the beginning, when the Alpha is turned on. Hardware on the chip loads the instruction cache from an external PROM. This initialization allows the 8 KB instruction cache to omit a valid bit, for there are always valid instructions in the cache; they just might not be the ones your program is interested in. The hardware does clear the valid bits in the data cache. The PC is set to the kseg segment so that the instruction addresses are not translated, thereby avoiding the TLB.

One of the first steps is to update the instruction TLB with valid Page Table Entries (PTEs) for this process. Kernel code updates the TLB with the contents of the appropriate page table entry for each page to be mapped. The instruction TLB has eight entries for 8 KB pages and four for 4 MB pages. (The 4 MB pages are used by large programs such as the operating system or data bases which will likely touch most of their code.) A miss in the TLB invokes the Privileged Architecture Library ("PALcode") software which updates the TLB. PAL code is simply machine language routines with some implementation-specific extensions to allow access to low level hardware, such as the TLB. PAL code runs with exceptions disabled and instruction accesses are not checked for memory management violations, allowing PALcode to fill the TLB.

Once the operating system is ready to begin executing a user process, it sets the PC to the appropriate address in segment seg0.

We are now ready to follow memory hierarchy in action: Figure 6.47 is labeled with the steps of this narrative. The page frame portion of this address is sent to the TLB (step 1), while the 8-bit index from the page offset is sent to the direct-mapped 8 KB (256 32-byte block) instruction cache (step 2). The fully associative TLB simultaneously searches all 12 entries to find a match between the address and a valid PTE (step 3). In addition to translating the address, the TLB checks to see if the PTE demands that this access result in an exception. An exception might occur if either this access violates the protection on the page or if the page is not in main memory. If there is not exception, and if the translated physical address matches the tag in the instruction cache (step 4), then the proper 8 bytes of the 32 byte block are furnished to the CPU using the lower bits of the page offset (step 5), and the instruction stream access is done.

A miss, on the other hand, simultaneously starts an access to the second level cache (step 6) and checks the prefetch instruction stream buffer (step 7). If the desired instruction is found in the stream buffer (step 8), the critical 8 bytes are sent to the CPU, the full 32 byte block of the stream buffer is written into the instruction cache (step 9), and the request to the second level cache is canceled. Steps 6 to 9 take just a single clock cycle.

If the instruction is not in the prefetch stream buffer, the second level cache continues trying to fetch the block. The 21064 microprocessor is designed to work with direct -mapped, second level caches from 128 KB to 8 MB with a miss penalty between 3 and 16 clock cycles. For this section we use the memory system of the DEC 3000 model 800 Alpha AXP. It has a 2 MB (65,536 32-byte block) second level cache, so the 29-bit block address is divided into a 10-bit tag and a 19-bit index (step 10). The cache reads the tag from that index and if it matches (step 11), the cache returns the critical 16 bytes in the first 5 clock cycles and the other 16 bytes in the next 5 clock cycles (step 12). The path between the first and second level cache is 128 bits wide (16 bytes). At the same time, a request is made for the next sequential 32 byte block, which is loaded into the instruction stream buffer in the next 10 clock cycles (step 13).

The instruction stream does not rely on the TLB for address translation. It simply increments the physical address of the miss by 32 bytes, checking to make that the new address is within the same page. If the incremented address crosses a page boundary, then the prefetch is suppressed.

If the instruction is not found in the secondary cache, the translated physical address is sent to memory (step 14). The DEC 3000 model 800 divides memory into 4 Memory Mother Boards (MMB), each of which contains 2 to 8 SIMMs (Single Inline Memory Modules). The SIMMs come with 8 DRAMs for data plus 2 DRAMS for error protection per side, and the options are single or double sided SIMMs using 1 Mbit , 4 Mbit, or 16 Mbit DRAMs. Hence the memory capacity of the model 800 is 8 MB ($4 \times 2 \times 8 \times 1 \times 1/8$) to 1024 MB ($4 \times 8 \times 8 \times 16 \times 2/8$), always organized 256 bits wide. The average time to transfer 32 bytes from memory to the secondary cache is 36 clock cycles after the processor makes the request. The second level cache loads this data 16 bytes at a time.

Since the second level cache is a write back cache, any miss can lead to the old block being written back to memory. The 21064 places this "victim" block into a victim buffer to get out of the way of new data (step 15). The new data is loaded into the cache as soon as it arrives (step 16), and then the old data is written from the victim buffer (step 17). There is a single block in the victim buffer, so a second miss would need to stall until the victim buffer empties.

Suppose this initial instruction is a load. It will send the page frame of its data address to the data TLB (step 18) at the same time as the 8-bit index from the page offset is sent to the data cache (step 19). The Data TLB is a fully associative cache containing 32 PTEs, each of which represents page sizes from 8 KB to 4 MB. A TLB miss will trap to PALcode to load the valid PTE for this address. In the worst case, the page is not in memory, and the operating system gets the page from disk (step 20). Since millions of instructions could execute during a page fault, the operating system will swap in another process if there is something waiting to run.

Assuming that we have a valid PTE in the data TLB (step 21), the cache tag and the physical page frame are compared (step 22), with a match sending the desired 8 bytes from the 32-byte block to the CPU (step 23). A miss goes to the second level cache, which proceeds exactly like an instruction miss.

Suppose the instruction is a store instead of a load. The page frame portion of the data address is again sent to the data TLB and the data cache (steps 18 and 19), which checks for protection violations as well as translates the address. The physical address is then sent to the data cache (steps 21 and 22). Since the data cache uses write through, the store data is simultaneously sent to the write buffer (step 24) and the data cache (step 25). As explained on page 441 the 21064 pipe-lines write hits. The data address of this store is checked for a match and at the same time the data from the previous write hit is written to the cache (step 26). If address check was a hit, then the data from this store is then placed write pipeline buffer. On a miss, the data is just sent to the write buffer since the data cache does not allocate on a write miss.

The write buffer takes over now. It has four entries, each containing a whole cache block. If the buffer is full, then the CPU must stall until a block is written to the second level cache. If the buffer is not full, the CPU continues and the ad-dress of the word is presented to the write buffer (step 27). It checks to see if the word matches any block already in the buffer so that a sequence of writes can be stitched together into a full block, thereby optimizing the write bandwidth be-tween the first and second level cache.

All writes are eventually passed on to the second level cache. If a write is a hit, then the data is written to the cache (step 28). Since the second level cache uses write back, it cannot   pipeline writes: a full 32-byte block write takes 5 clock cy-cles to check the address and 10 clock cycles to write the data. A write of 16 bytes or less takes 5 clock cycles to check the address and 5 clock cycles to write the data. In either case the cache marks the block as dirty.

If the access to the second level cache is a miss, the victim block is checked to see if it is dirty; if so, it is placed in the victim buffer as before (step 15). If the new data is a full block, then the data is simply written and marked dirty. A par-tial block write results in an access to main memory since the second level cache policy is to allocate on a write miss.

Performance of the 21064 Memory Hierarchy

How well does the 21064 work? The bottom line in this evaluation is the per-centage of time lost while the CPU is waiting for the memory hierarchy. The ma-jor components are the instruction and data caches, instruction and data TLBs, and the secondary cache. Figure 6.48 shows the percentage of the execution time due to the memory hierarchy for the SPEC92 programs and three commercial programs. The three commercial programs tax the memory much more heavily, with secondary cache misses alone responsible for 20% to 28% of the execution time.

Figure 6.48 also shows the miss rates for each component. The SPECint92 programs have about a 2% instruction miss rate, a 13% data cache miss rate, and a 0.6% second level cache miss rate. For SPECfp92 the averages are 1%, 21%, and 0.3%, respectively. The commercial workloads really exercise the memory hierarchy, the averages of the three miss rates being 6%, 32%, and 10%.

Program	CPI			Total	Instr	Other	Total	Miss Rates				
	I cache	D cache	L2	Cache	issue	stalls	CPI	ITB	I cache	DTB	D cache	L2
TPC-B (db1)	0.57	0.53	0.74	1.84	0.79	1.67	4.30	?	8.10%	?	41.00%	7.40%
TPC-B (db2)	0.58	0.48	0.75	1.81	0.76	1.73	4.30	?	8.30%	?	34.00%	6.20%
AlphaSort	0.09	0.24	0.50	0.83	0.70	1.28	2.81	?	1.30%	?	22.00%	17.40%
AvgComm	0.41	0.42	0.66	1.49	0.75	1.56	3.80	?	5.90%	?	32.33%	10.33%
Espresso	0.06	0.13	0.01	0.20	0.74	0.57	1.51	?	0.84%	?	9.00%	0.33%
Li	0.14	0.17	0.00	0.31	0.75	0.96	2.02	?	2.04%	?	9.00%	0.21%
Eqntott	0.02	0.16	0.01	0.19	0.79	0.41	1.39	?	0.22%	?	11.00%	0.55%
Compress	0.03	0.30	0.04	0.37	0.77	0.52	1.66	?	0.48%	?	20.00%	1.19%
Sc	0.20	0.18	0.04	0.42	0.78	0.85	2.05	?	2.79%	?	12.00%	0.93%
Gcc	0.33	0.25	0.02	0.60	0.77	1.14	2.51	?	4.67%	?	17.00%	0.46%
AvgSPECint92	0.13	0.20	0.02	0.35	0.77	0.74	1.86	?	1.84%	?	13.00%	0.61%
Spice	0.01	0.68	0.02	0.71	0.83	0.99	2.53	?	0.21%	?	36.00%	0.43%
Doduc	0.16	0.26	0.00	0.42	0.77	1.58	2.77	?	2.30%	?	14.00%	0.11%
Mdljp2	0.00	0.31	0.01	0.32	0.83	2.18	3.33	?	0.06%	?	28.00%	0.21%
Wave5	0.04	0.39	0.04	0.47	0.68	0.84	1.99	?	0.57%	?	24.00%	0.89%
Tomcatv	0.00	0.42	0.04	0.46	0.67	0.79	1.92	?	0.06%	?	20.00%	0.89%
Ora	0.00	0.10	0.00	0.10	0.72	1.25	2.07	?	0.05%	?	7.00%	0.10%
Alvinn	0.03	0.49	0.00	0.52	0.62	0.25	1.39	?	0.38%	?	18.00%	0.01%
Ear	0.01	0.15	0.00	0.16	0.65	0.24	1.05	?	0.11%	?	9.00%	0.01%
Mdljsp2	0.00	0.09	0.00	0.09	0.80	1.67	2.56	?	0.05%	?	5.00%	0.11%
Swm256	0.00	0.24	0.01	0.25	0.68	0.37	1.30	?	0.02%	?	13.00%	0.32%
Su2cor	0.03	0.74	0.01	0.78	0.66	0.71	2.15	?	0.41%	?	43.00%	0.16%
Hydro2d	0.01	0.54	0.01	0.56	0.69	1.23	2.48	?	0.09%	?	32.00%	0.32%
Nasa7	0.01	0.68	0.02	0.71	0.68	0.64	2.03	?	0.19%	?	37.00%	0.25%
Fpppp	0.52	0.17	0.00	0.69	0.70	0.97	2.36	?	7.42%	?	7.00%	0.01%
AvgSPECfp92	0.06	0.38	0.01	0.45	0.71	0.98	2.14	?	0.85%	?	20.93%	0.27%

FIGURE 6.48 **Percentage of execution time due to memory latency and miss rates for 3 commercial programs and the SPEC92 benchmarks (see Chapter 2) running on the Alpha AXP 21064 in the DEC 3000 model 800.** The first two commercial programs are pieces of the TP1 benchmark and the last is a sort of 100-byte records in a 100 MB database. (We will have a machine in the final edition that includes all cache measurements.)

6.12 | Fallacies and Pitfalls

As the most naturally quantitative of the computer architecture disciplines, memory hierarchy would seem to be less vulnerable to fallacies and pitfalls. Yet the authors were limited here not by lack of warnings, but by lack of space.

Pitfall: Too small an address space.

Just five years after DEC and Carnegie-Mellon University collaborated to design the new PDP-11 computer family, it was apparent that their creation had a fatal flaw. An architecture announced by IBM six years **before** the PDP-11 was still thriving, with minor modifications, 25 years later. And the DEC VAX, criticized for including unnecessary functions, has sold 100,000 units since the PDP-11 went out of production. Why?

The fatal flaw of the PDP-11 was the size of its addresses as compared to the IBM 360 and the VAX. Address size limits the program length, since the size of a program and the amount of data needed by the program must be less than $2^{\text{address size}}$. The reason the address size is so hard to change is that it determines the minimum width of anything that can contain an address: PC, register, memory word, and effective-address arithmetic. If there is no plan to expand the address from the start, then the chances of successfully changing address size are so slim that it normally means the end of that computer family. Bell and Strecker [1976] put it like this:

There is only one mistake that can be made in computer design that is difficult to recover from—not having enough address bits for memory addressing and memory management. The PDP-11 followed the unbroken tradition of nearly every known computer. [p. 2]

A partial list of successful machines that eventually starved to death for lack of address bits includes the PDP-8, PDP-10, PDP-11, Intel 8080, Intel 8086, Intel 80186, Intel 80286, AMI 6502, Zilog Z80, CRAY-1, and CRAY X-MP. A few companies already offer computers with 64-bit flat addresses, and the authors expect that the rest of the industry will offer 64-bit address machines before the third edition of this book!

Fallacy: Predicting cache performance of one program from another.
Figure 6.49 shows the instruction miss rates and data miss rates for three programs from the SPEC92 benchmark suite as cache size varies. Depending on the program, the data miss rate for a direct mapped 4 KB cache is either 28%, 12%, or 8%, and the instruction miss rate for a direct mapped 1 KB cache is either 10%, 3%, or 0%. Clearly it is not safe to generalize cache performance from one of these programs to another.

Nor is it safe to generalize cache measurements from one architecture to another. Figure 6.48 for the DEC Alpha with 8 KB caches running gcc gets miss rates of 17% for data and 4.67% for instructions yet the DEC MIPS machine running the same program measured in Figure 6.50 suggest 10% for data and 4% for instructions.

Pitfall: Simulating enough instructions to get accurate performance measures of the memory hierarchy.

There are really two pitfalls here. One is trying to predict performance of a large cache using a small trace, and the other is that a program's locality behavior is not constant over the run of the entire program. Figure 6.50 shows the cumulative average memory access time for four programs over the execution of billions of instructions. For these programs, the average memory access times for the first billion instructions executed is very different from their average memory access times for the second billion. While two of the programs need execute half of the total number of instructions to get a good estimate of the average memory access time, SOR needs to get to the three-quarters mark and TV needs to finish completely before the accurate measure appears.

The first edition of this book included another example of this pitfall. The compulsory miss ratios were erroneously high (e.g., 1%) due to tracing too few memory accesses. A program with an infinite cache miss ratio of 1% running on a machine accessing memory ten million memory times per second would touch hundreds megabytes of new memory every minute:

$$\frac{10,000,000 \text{ accesses}}{\text{second}} \times \frac{0.01 \text{ misses}}{\text{access}} \times \frac{32 \text{ bytes}}{\text{miss}} \times \frac{60 \text{ seconds}}{\text{minute}} = \frac{192,000,000 \text{ bytes}}{\text{minute}}$$

Data on typical page faults rates and process sizes do not support the conclusion that memory is touched at this rate.

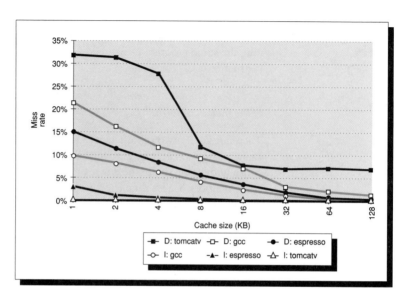

FIGURE 6.49   Instruction and data miss rates for direct mapped caches with 32 byte blocks for running for DEC 5000 as cache size varies from 1 KB to 128 KB. from the programs espresso, gcc, and tomcatv form the SPEC92 benchmark suite.

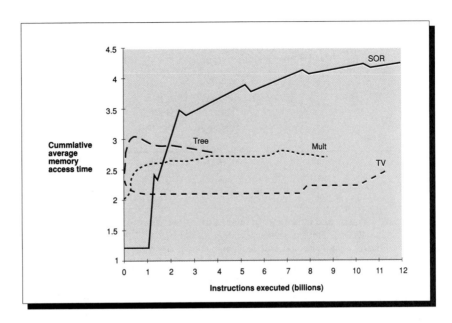

FIGURE 6.50 Average memory access times for four programs over execution time of billions of instructions. The assumed memory hierarchy was a 4 KB instruction cache and 4 KB data cache with 16 byte blocks, and a 512 KB second level cache with 128 byte blocks using the Titan RISC instruction set. The first level data cache is write through with a four entry write buffer and the second level cache is write back. This is miss penalty for the first level cache to second level cache is 12 clock cycles and the miss penalty from the second level cache to main memory is 200 clock cycles. SOR is a Fortran program for successive over-relaxation, Tree is a Scheme program that builds and searches a tree, mult is a multiprogrammed workload consisting of 6 smaller programs, and TV is Pascal program for timing verification of VLSI circuits. (This figure taken from Figure 3-5 on page 276 of the paper by Borg, Kessler, and Wall [1990]).

Pitfall: Ignoring the impact of the operating system on the performance of the memory hierarchy.

Figure 6.51 shows the memory stall time due to the operating system spent on three large workloads. About 25% of the stall time is either spent in misses in the operating system or is due to misses in the application programs due to interference with the operating system.

Workload	Misses		Time						
	% in Appl	% in OC	% time due to Appl. misses		% time due directly to OS misses				% time OS misses
			inherent Appl. misses	OS conflicts w. Appl.	OS instr misses	data misses for Migration	data misses in block operations	rest of OS misses	& Appl. conflicts
Pmake	47%	53%	14.1%	4.8%	10.9%	1.0%	6.2%	2.9%	25.8%
Multipgm	53%	47%	21.6%	3.4%	9.2%	4.2%	4.7%	3.4%	24.9%
Oracle	73%	27%	25.7%	10.2%	10.6%	2.6%	0.6%	2.8%	26.8%

FIGURE 6.51 Misses and time spent in misses for applications and operating system. Collected on Silicon Graphics POWER station 4D/340, a multiprocessor with four 33 MHz R3000 CPUs running three application workloads under a Unix System V : Pmake: a parallel compile of 56 files; Multipgm: the parallel numeric program MP3D running with currently with Pmake and five screen edit session; and Oracle: running a restricted version of the TP-1 benchmark using the Oracle database. Each CPU has a 64 KB instruction cache and a two-level data cache of with 64 KB in the first level and 256 KB in the second level; all caches are direct mapped with 16 bye blocks. Data is taken from paper by Torrellas, Gupta, and Hennessy [1992].

Fallacy: Given the hardware resources, the computer designer who selects a set-associative cache over a direct-mapped cache of the same size will get a faster computer.

The question here is whether the extra logic of the set-associative cache affects the hit time, and therefore possibly the CPU clock rate. Direct-mapped caches also allow the data read to be sent to the CPU and used even before hit/miss is determined, particularly useful with a pipelined CPU. As mentioned earlier, Hill found about a 10% difference in hit times for TTL or ECL board-level caches and 2% difference for custom CMOS caches, with an absolute change in the miss rates of less than 1% for large caches. Since a direct-mapped cache hit can be accessed faster and hit time typically sets the clock cycle time of the processor, a CPU with a direct-mapped cache can be as fast as or faster than a CPU with a two-way–set-associative cache of the same size. Przybylski, Horowitz, and Hennessy [1988] show several examples of such tradeoffs.

Pitfall: Basing the size of the write buffer on the speed of memory and the average mix of writes.

This seems like a reasonable approach:

$$\text{Write buffer size} = \frac{\text{Memory references}}{\text{Clock cycle}} \times \text{Write percentage} \times \text{Clock cycles to write memory}$$

If there is one memory reference per clock cycle, 10% of the memory references are writes, and writing a word of memory takes 10 cycles, then a one-word buffer is added ($1 \times 10\% \times 10 = 1$). Calculating for the Alpha AXP 21064,

$$\text{Write buffer size} = \frac{1.36 \text{ memory references}}{2.0 \text{ clock cycles}} \times 0.1 \text{ writes} \times \frac{15 \text{ clock cycles}}{\text{Write}} = 1.0$$

Thus, a one-word buffer seems sufficient.

The pitfall is that when writes come close together, the CPU must stall until the prior write is completed. Hence the calculation above says that a one word buffer would be utilized 100% of the time. Queuing theory tells us if utilization is close to 100%, then writes will be in the queue for the write buffer most of the time and the CPU will stall.

The proper question to ask is how large a buffer is needed to keep utilization low so that the buffer rarely fills, thereby keeping CPU write stalls time low. The impact of write-buffer size can be established by simulation or estimated with a queuing model.

6.13 | Concluding Remarks

The difficulty of building a memory system to keep pace with faster CPUs is underscored by the fact that the raw material for main memory is the same as that found in the cheapest computer. It is the principle of locality that saves us here—its soundness is demonstrated at all levels of the memory hierarchy in current computers, from disks to TLBs. Figure 6.52 summarizes the attributes of the memory-hierarchy examples described in this chapter.

Yet the design decisions at these levels interact, and the architect must take the whole system view to make wise decisions. The challenge for the memory-hierarchy designer is in choosing parameters that work well together, not in inventing new techniques. The increasingly fast CPUs are spending a larger fraction of time waiting for memory, which has led to new inventions that have increased the number of choices: variable page size, pseudo-associative caches, and cache aware compilers weren't found in the 1st edition of this book. Fortunately, there tends to be a technological "sweet spot" in balancing cost, performance, and complexity: missing the target wastes performance, hardware, design time, debug time, or possibly all four. Architects hit the target by careful, quantitative analysis.

	TLB	First-level cache	Second-level cache	Virtual memory
Block size	4 – 8 bytes (1 PTE)	4 – 32 bytes	32 – 256 bytes	4096 – 16,384 bytes
Hit time	1 clock cycle	1 – 2 clock cycles	4 – 10 clock cycles	10–100 clock cycles
Miss penalty	10 – 30 clock cycles	8 – 66 clock cycles	30 – 200 clock cycles	700,000 – 6,000,000 clock cycles
Miss rate (local)	0.1% – 2%	0.5% – 20%	15% – 30%	0.00001% – 0.001%
Size	32 – 8192 bytes (8 – 1024 PTEs)	1 KB – 128 KB	256 KB – 16 MB	16 MB – 8192 MB
Backing store	First-level cache	Second-level cache	Page-mode DRAM	Disks
Q1: block placement	Fully associative or Set associative	Direct mapped	Direct mapped or Set associative	Fully associative
Q2: block identification	Tag/ block	Tag/ block	Tag/ block	Table
Q3: block replacement	Random	N.A. (Direct mapped)	Random	≈ LRU
Q4: write strategy	Flush on a write to page table	Write through or write back	Write back	Write back

FIGURE 6.52 Summary of the memory-hierarchy examples in this chapter.

6.14 | Historical Perspective and References

While the pioneers of computing knew of the need for a memory hierarchy and coined the term, the automatic management of two levels was first proposed by Kilburn, et al. [1962] and demonstrated with the Atlas computer at the University of Manchester. This was the year **before** the IBM 360 was announced. While IBM planned for its introduction with the next generation (System/370), the operating system wasn't up to the challenge in 1970. Virtual memory was announced for the 370 family in 1972, and it was for this machine that the term "translation-lookaside buffer" was coined (see Case and Padegs [1978]). The only computers today without virtual memory are a few supercomputers and older personal computers.

Both the Atlas and the IBM 360 provided protection on pages, and the GE 635 was the first system to provide paged segmentation. The Intel 80286, the first 80x86 to have the protection mechanisms described on pages ?? to ??[9], was inspired by the Multics protection software that ran on the GE 635. Over time machines evolved more elaborate mechanisms. The most elaborate mechanism was *capabilities*, which reached its highest interest in the late 1970s and early 1980s [Fabry 1974 and Wulf, Levin, and Harbison 1981]. Wilkes [1982], one of the early workers on capabilities, had this to say about capabilities:

Anyone who has been concerned with an implementation of the type just described [capability system], or has tried to explain one to others, is likely to feel that complexity has got out of hand. It is particularly disappointing that the attractive idea of capabilities being tickets that can be freely handed around has become lost ....

Compared with a conventional computer system, there will inevitably be a cost to be met in providing a system in which the domains of protection are small and frequently changed. This cost will manifest itself in terms of additional hardware, decreased runtime speed, and increased memory occupancy. It is at present an open question whether, by adoption of the capability approach, the cost can be reduced to reasonable proportions.

Today there is little interest in capabilities either from the operating systems or the computer architecture communities, although there is growing interest in protection and security.

Bell and Strecker [1976] reflected on the PDP-11 and identified a small address space as the only architectural mistake that is difficult to recover from. At the time of the creation of PDP-11, core memories were increasing at a very slow rate, and the competition from 100 other minicomputer companies meant that DEC might not have a cost-competitive product if every address had to go through the 16-bit datapath twice. Hence, the architect's decision to add just 4 more address bits than the predecessor of the PDP-11. The architects of the IBM 360 were aware of the importance of address size and planned for the architecture to extend to 32 bits of address. Only 24 bits were used in the IBM 360, however, because the low-end 360 models would have been even slower with the larger addresses in 1964. Unfortunately, the architects didn't reveal their plans to the software people, and the expansion effort was foiled by programmers who stored extra information in the upper eight "unused" address bits. Virtually every machine since then, including the Alpha AXP, will check to make sure the unused bits stay unused, and trap if the bits have the wrong value.

A few years after the Atlas paper, Wilkes published the first paper describing the concept of a cache [1965]:

---

9.   2/e Xref to the Intel Pentium description.

The use is discussed of a fast core memory of, say, 32,000 words as slave to a slower core memory of, say, one million words in such a way that in practical cases the effective access time is nearer that of the fast memory than that of the slow memory. [p. 270]

This two-page paper describes a direct-mapped cache. While this is the first publication on caches, the first implementation was probably a direct-mapped instruction cache built at the University of Cambridge. It was based on tunnel diode memory, the fastest form of memory available at the time. Wilkes states that G. Scarott suggested the idea of a cache memory.

Subsequent to that publication, IBM started a project that led to the first commercial machine with a cache, the IBM 360/85 [Liptay 1968]. Gibson [1967] describes how to measure program behavior as memory traffic as well as miss rate and shows how the miss rate varies between programs. Using a sample of 20 programs (each with 3,000,000 references!), Gibson also relied on average memory-access time to compare systems with and without caches. This was over 25 years ago, and yet many used miss rates until recently.

Conti, Gibson, and Pitkowsky [1968] describe the resulting performance of the 360/85. The 360/91 outperforms the 360/85 on only 3 of the 11 programs in the paper, even though the 360/85 has a slower clock cycle time (80 ns versus 60 ns), smaller memory interleaving (4 versus 16), and a slower main memory (1.04 µsec versus 0.75 µsec). This paper was also the first to use the term "cache." Strecker [1976] published the first comparative cache-design paper examining caches for the PDP-11. Smith [1982] later published a thorough survey paper, using the terms "spatial locality" and "temporal locality"; this paper has served as a reference for many computer designers. While most studies have relied on simulations, Clark [1983] used a hardware monitor to record cache misses of the VAX-11/780 over several days. Hill [1987] proposed the three Cs used in Section 8.4 to explain cache misses. One of the first papers on non-blocking caches is by Kroft [1983].

This chapter relies on the measurements of SPEC92 benchmarks collected by Gee, Hill, Pnevmatikatos, and Smith [1993] for DEC 5000s. There are several other papers used in this chapter that typically cited in the captions of the figures that use the data: Borg, Kessler, and Wall [1990], Farkas and Jouppi [1994], Jouppi [1990], Lam, Rothberg, and Wolf [1991], Mowry, Lam, and Gupta [1992], ?? & Wood[1994], and Torrellas, Gupta, and Hennessy [1992]. Readers interested in more on prime number of memory modules should read Gao [1993]; those interested in more on pseudo-associative caches should see Agarwal and Pudar [1993]. Caches remain an active area of research.

The Alpha AXP architecture is described in detail by Sites [1993], and the best source of data on implementations is the *Digital Technical Journal* issue no.4 of 1992, which is dedicated to articles on Alpha.

References

This section adds a square bullet next to publications that are tutorial in nature and review a topic from this chapter in more depth.

AGARWAL, A. [1987]. *Analysis of Cache Performance for Operating Systems and Multiprogramming*, Ph.D. Thesis, Stanford Univ., Tech. Rep. No. CSL-TR-87-332 (May).

AGARWAL, A.; PUDAR, S.D. [1993] "Column-associative caches: a technique for reducing the miss rate of direct-mapped caches," 20th Annual International Symposium on Computer Architecture ISCA '20, San Diego, CA, USA, 16-19 May 1993 .Computer Architecture News, May 1993, vol.21, (no.2):179-90.

BAER, J.-L. AND W.-H. WANG [1988]. "On the inclusion property for multi-level cache hierarchies," *Proc. 15th Annual Symposium on Computer Architecture* (May–June), Honolulu, 73–80.

BELL , C. G. AND W. D. STRECKER [1976]. "Computer structures: What have we learned from the PDP-11?," *Proc. Third Annual Symposium on Computer Architecture* (January), Pittsburgh, Penn., 1–14.

BORG, A.; KESSLER, R.E.; WALL, D.W.[1990] Generation and analysis of very long address traces.. Proceedings. The 17th Annual International Symposium on Computer Architecture (Cat. No.90CH2887-8). (Proceedings. The 17th Annual International Symposium on Computer Architecture (Cat. No.90CH2887-8),Seattle, WA, USA, 28-31 May 1990). Los Alamitos, CA, USA: IEEE Computer. Soc. Press, . p. 270-9.

CASE, R.P. AND A. PADEGS [1978]. "The architecture of the IBM System/370," *Communications of the ACM* 21:1, 73–96. Also appears in D. P. Siewiorek, C. G. Bell, and A. Newell, *Computer Structures: Principles and Examples* (1982), McGraw-Hill, New York, 830–855.

CLARK, D. W. [1983]. "Cache performance of the VAX-11/780," *ACM Trans. on Computer Systems* 1:1, 24–37.

CONTI, C., D. H. GIBSON, AND S. H. PITOWSKY [1968]. "Structural aspects of the System/360 Model 85, part I: General organization," *IBM Systems J.* 7:1, 2–14.

CRAWFORD, J. H AND P. P. GELSINGER [1987]. *Programming the 80386*, Sybex, Alameda, Calif.

FABRY, R. S. [1974]. "Capability based addressing," *Comm. ACM* 17:7 (July) 403–412.

FARKAS, K.I. AND JOUPPI, N.P.[1994] Complexity/Performance Tradeoffs with Non-Blocking Loads. IN: Proceedings. The 21st Annual International Symposium on Computer Architecture , Chicago IL, USA, (April 1994).

GAO, Q.S. The Chinese remainder theorem and the prime memory system. (20th Annual International Symposium on Computer Architecture ISCA '20, San Diego, CA,USA, 16-19 May 1993).Computer Architecture News, May 1993, vol.21, (no.2):337-40.

GEE, J.D.; HILL, M.D.; PNEVMATIKATOS, D.N.; SMITH, A.J. [1993] Cache performance of the SPEC92 benchmark suite. IEEE Micro, Aug. 1993, vol.13, (no.4):17-27.

■   HANDY, J.{1993] *The cache memory book*. Boston : Academic Press.

HILL, M. D. [1987]. *Aspects of Cache Memory and Instruction Buffer Performance*, Ph. D. Thesis, Univ. of California at Berkeley Computer Science Division, Tech. Rep. UCB/CSD 87/381 (November).

■   HILL, M. D. [1988]. "A case for direct mapped caches," *Computer* 21:12 (December) 25–40.

JOUPPI, N.P.[1990] Improving direct-mapped cache performance by the addition of a small fully-associative cache and prefetch buffers. IN: Proceedings. The 17th Annual International Symposium on Computer Architecture (Cat. No.90CH2887-8). (Proceedings. The 17th Annual International Symposium on Computer Architecture (Cat. No.90CH2887-8), Seattle, WA, USA, 28-31 May 1990). Los Alamitos, CA, USA: IEEE Computer. Soc. Press, 1990. p. 364-73.

KILBURN, T., D. B. G. EDWARDS, M. J. LANIGAN, F. H. SUMNER [1962]. "One-level storage system," *IRE Transactions on Electronic Computers* EC-11 (April) 223–235. Also appears in D. P. Siewiorek, C. G. Bell, and A. Newell, *Computer Structures: Principles and Examples* (1982), McGraw-Hill, New York, 135–148.

KROFT, D. [1981]. "Lockup-free instruction fetch/prefetch cache organization," *Proc. Eighth Annual Symposium on Computer Architecture* (May 12–14), Minneapolis, Minn., 81–87.

LAM, M.S.; ROTHBERG, E.E.; WOLF, M.E. [1991] "The cache performance and optimizations of blocked algorithms." (Fourth International Conference on Architectural Support for Programming Languages and Operating Systems, Santa Clara, CA, USA, 8-11 April 1991).SIGPLAN Notices, April 1991, vol.26, (no.4):63-74.

LEBECK AND Wood, D. [1994] "Compiler Optimization for SPEC92", *IEEE Micro,* September.

LIPTAY, J. S. [1968]. "Structural aspects of the System/360 Model 85, part II: The cache," *IBM Systems J.* 7:1, 15–21.

MCFARLING, S. [1989]. "Program optimization for instruction caches," *Proc. Third International Conf. on Architectural Support for Programming Languages and Operating Systems* (April 3–6), Boston, Mass., 183–191.

MOWRY, T.C.; LAM, S.; GUPTA, A.[1992] "Design and evaluation of a compiler algorithm for prefetching," Fifth International Conference on Architectural Support for Programming Languages and Operating Systems (ASPLOS-V), Boston, MA, USA, 12-15 Oct.1992. SIGPLAN Notices, Sept. 1992, vol.27, (no.9):62-73.

PALACHARLA, S.; KESSLER, R.E.[1994] "Evaluating stream buffers as a secondary cache replacement. " *Proceedings the 21st Annual International Symposium on Computer Architecture*, Chicago, IL, USA, 18-21 April 1994). Los Alamitos, CA, USA: IEEE Comput. Soc. Press, 1994. p. 24-33.

PRZYBYLSKI, S. A. [1990]. *Cache Design: A Performance-Directed Approach,* Morgan Kaufmann Publishers, San Mateo, Calif.

PRZYBYLSKI, S. A., M. HOROWITZ, AND J. L. HENNESSY [1988]. "Performance tradeoffs in cache design," *Proc. 15th Annual Symposium on Computer Architecture* (May–June), Honolulu, Hawaii, 290–298.

SAAVEDRA-BARRERA, RAFAEL HECTOR. CPU performance evaluation and execution time prediction using narrow spectrum benchmarking, Ph.D. dissertation, University of California, Berkeley, May 1992.

SAMPLES, A. D. AND P. N. HILFINGER [1988]. "Code reorganization for instruction caches," Tech. Rep. UCB/CSD 88/447 (October), Univ. of Calif., Berkeley.

SITES, R.L. (editor), [1992] *Alpha architecture reference manual,* Burlington, MA : Digital Press.

SMITH, A. J. [1982]. "Cache memories," *Computing Surveys* 14:3 (September) 473–530.

STRECKER, W. D. [1976]. "Cache memories for the PDP-11?," *Proc. Third Annual Symposium on Computer Architecture* (January), Pittsburgh, Penn., 155–158.

TORRELLAS, J.; GUPTA, A.; HENNESSY, J. [1992] "Characterizing the caching and synchronization performance of a multiprocessor operating system," (Fifth International Conference on Architectural Support for Programming Languages and Operating Systems (ASPLOS-V), Boston, MA, USA, 12-15 Oct. 1992).SIGPLAN Notices, Sept. 1992, vol.27, (no.9):162-74.

WANG, W.-H., J.-L. BAER, AND H. M. LEVY [1989]. "Organization and performance of a two-level virtual-real cache hierarchy," *Proc. 16th Annual Symposium on Computer Architecture* (May 28–June 1), Jerusalem, Israel , 140–148.

WILKES, M. [1965]. "Slave memories and dynamic storage allocation," *IEEE Trans. Electronic Computers* EC-14:2 (April) 270–271.

■ WILKES, M. V. [1982]. "Hardware support for memory protection: Capability implementations," *Proc. Symposium on Architectural Support for Programming Languages and Operating Systems* (March 1–3), Palo Alto, Calif., 107–116.

WULF, W. A., R. LEVIN AND S. P. HARBISON [1981]. *Hydra/C.mmp: An Experimental Computer System,* McGraw-Hill, New York.

EXERCISES

A bullet is placed next to the authors' favorite exercises, meaning that these exercises have the best ratio of student time invested to insight gained, or they are fun to do.

● **6.1** [15/15/12/12] <2.2,8.4> Let's try to show how you can make *unfair* benchmarks. Here are two machines with the same processor and main memory but different cache organizations. Assume the miss time is 10 times a cache-hit time for both machines. Assume writing a 32-bit word takes 5 times as long as a cache hit (for the write-through cache), and that writing a whole 32-byte block takes 10 times as long as a cache-read hit (for the write-back cache). The caches are unified; that is, they contain both instructions and data.

> **Cache A**: 128 sets, 2 elements per set, each block is 32 bytes, and it uses write through and no write allocate.

> **Cache B**: 256 sets, 1 element per set, each block is 32 bytes, and it uses write back and does allocate on write misses.

  a.   [15] Describe a program that makes machine A run as much faster as possible than machine B. (Be sure to state any further assumptions you need, if any.)

  b.   [15] Describe a program that makes machine B run as much faster as possible than machine A. (Be sure to state any further assumptions you need, if any.)

  c.   [12] Approximately how much faster is the program in Part a on machine A than machine B?

  d.   [12] Approximately how much faster is the program in Part b on machine B than machine A?

● **6.2** [25] Run a program to evaluate the behavior of a memory system. The key is having accurate timing and then having the program stride through memory to invoke different levels of the hierarchy. Below is the code in C for UNIX systems. The first part is a procedure that uses a standard UNIX utility to get an accurate measure of the user CPU time; this procedure may need to change to work on some systems. The second part is a nest loop to read and write memory at different strides and cache sizes. To get accurate cache timing, this code is repeated many times. The third part is times the nested loop overhead only so that it can be subtracted form overall measured times to see how long the accesses were. The last part is prints the time per access as the size and stride varies. You may need to change CACHE_MAX depending on the question you are answering and the size of memory on the system you are measuring. The code below was taken from a program written by Andrea Dusseau of U.C. Berkeley, and was based on a detailed description found Saavedra-Barrera [1992].

```
#include <stdio.h>
#include <sys/times.h>
#include <sys/types.h>
#include <time.h>
#define CACHE_MIN (1024) /\ smallest cache */
#define CACHE_MAX (1024*1024) /* largest cache */
#define SAMPLE 10 /* to get a larger time sample */
#define CLK_TCK 60 /* number clock ticks per second */
int x[CACHE_MAX]; /* array going to stride through */

double get_seconds() { /* routine to read time */
   struct tms rusage;
   times(&rusage); /* UNIX utility: time in clock ticks */
   return (double) (rusage.tms_utime)/CLK_TCK;
}
void main() {
int register i, index, stride, limit, temp;
int steps, tsteps, csize;
double sec0, sec; /* timing variables */

for (csize=CACHE_MIN; csize <= CACHE_MAX; csize=csize*2)
   for (stride=1; stride <= csize/2; stride=stride*2) {
      sec = 0; /* initialize timer */
      limit = csize-stride+1; /* cache size this loop */

      steps = 0;
      do { /* repeat until collect 1 second */
      sec0 = get_seconds(); /* start timer */
      for (i=SAMPLE*stride;i!=0;i=i-1) /* larger sample */
        for (index=0; index < limit; index=index+stride)
            x[index] = x[index] + 1; /* cache access */
      steps = steps + 1; /* count while loop iterations */
      sec = sec + (get_seconds() - sec0);/* end timer */
      } while (sec < 1.0); /* until collect 1 second */

      /* Repeat empty loop to subtract loop overhead */
      tsteps = 0; /* used to match no. while iterations */
      do { /* repeat until same no. iterations as above */
      sec0 = get_seconds(); /* start timer */
      for (i=SAMPLE*stride;i!=0;i=i-1) /* larger sample */
        for (index=0; index < limit; index=index+stride)
            temp = temp + index; /* dummy code */
      tsteps = tsteps + 1; /* count while iterations */
      sec = sec - (get_seconds() - sec0);/* - overhead */
      } while (tsteps<steps); /* until = no. iterations */
```

```
    printf("Size:%7d Stride:%7d read+write:%14.0f ns\n",
        csize*sizeof(int), stride*sizeof(int), (double)
    sec*1e3/(steps*SAMPLE*stride*((limit-1)/stride+1)));
}; /* end of both outer for loops */
}
```

Assume sizes of memory hierarchy components are all powers of 2., and answer these questions below.

a. [15] Plot the experimental results with elapsed time on the Y-axis and the memory stride on the X-axis as you vary `stride`. Use logarithmic scales for both axes, and draw a line for each cache size.

b. [10] How many levels of cache are there?

c. [12] What is the size of the first level cache? Block size? Hint: Assume the size of the page is much large than the size of a block in a secondary cache (if any), and the size of a second-level cache block is greater than or equal to the size of a block in a first-level cache.

d [12] What is the size of the second level cache (if any)? Block size?

e. [12] What is the associativity of the first level cache? Second-level cache?

f. [12] What is the page size?

g [12] How many entries are in the TLB?

h. [12] What is the miss penalty for the first level cache? Second level?

i. [12] What is the time for a page fault to secondary memory? Hint: a page fault to magnetic disk should be measured in milliseconds.

j. [12] What is the miss penalty for the TLB?

k. [12] Is there anything else you have discovered about the memory hierarchy from these measurements?

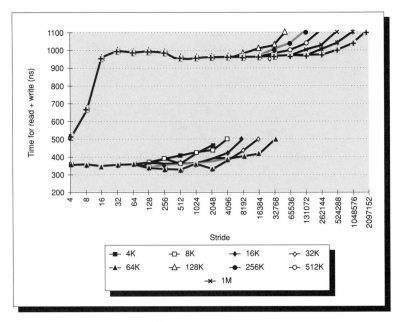

FIGURE 6.53   Results of running program in Exercise 6.2 on a SPARCstation 1.

● 6.2.5 [10/10/10] Figure 6.53 shows the output from running the program in Exercise 6.5 on a SPARCstation 1, which has single unified cache.

a.   [10] What is the size of the cache?

b   [10] What is the block size of the cache?

c   [10] What is the miss penalty for the first level cache?

6.3 [15/15] <8.4> You purchased an Acme computer with the following features:

1.   90% of all memory accesses are found in the cache;

2.   Each cache block is two words, and the whole block is read on any miss;

3.   The processor sends references to its cache at the rate of 10^8 words per second;

4.   25% of the references of (3) are writes;

5.   Assume that the memory system can support 10^8 words per second, reads or writes;

6.   The bus reads or writes a single word at a time (the memory system cannot read or write two words at once);

7.   Assume at any one time, 30% of the blocks in the cache have been modified;

8.   The cache uses write allocate on a write miss.

You are considering adding a peripheral to the system, and you want to know how much of the memory system bandwidth is already used. Calculate the percentage of memory system bandwidth used on the average in the two cases below. Be sure to state your assumptions.

a. [15] The cache is write through.

b. [15] The cache is write back.

6.4 [20] <6.5> One difference between a write through cache and write back cache can be in the time it takes to write. During the first cycle, we detect whether a hit will occur, and during the second (assuming a hit) we actually write the data. Let's assume that 50% of the blocks are dirty for a write-back cache. For this question, assume that the write buffer for write through will never stall the CPU (no penalty). Assume a cache read hit takes 1 clock cycle, the cache miss penalty is 10 clock cycles, and a block write from the cache to main memory takes 10 clock cycles. Finally, assume the instruction-cache miss rate is 2% and the data-cache miss rate is 4%.

a. [15] Using statistics for loads and stores from DLX in Figure C.4 in Appendix C[10], estimate the performance of a write-through cache with a two-cycle write versus a write-back cache with a two-cycle write for each of the programs.

b. [15] Do the same comparison, but this time assume the write through cache pipelines the writes, as described on page 441, so that a write hit takes just one clock cycle.

6.5 [20] <6.3> Improve on compiler prefetch example found on page 417: Try to eliminate both the number of extraneous prefetches and the number of non-prefetched cache misses. Calculate the performance of this refined version using the parameters above.

6.6 [15/12] <6.3> The example evaluation of a pseudo-associative cache on page 415 assumed that on a hit to the slower block that the hardware swapped the contents with the corresponding fast block so that subsequent hits on this address would all be to the fast block. Assume that if we don't swap, a hit in the slower block takes just one extra clock cycle instead of two extra clock cycles.

a. [15] Write the average memory access time formula for this case defined in terms of direct mapped and two-way set associative parameters, similar to what is found on page 415.

b. [12] Recalculate the two cases found in the example. Which pseudo-associative scheme is faster for this cache data?

6.7 [20] <6.3> If the base CPI with a perfect memory system is 1.5, what is the CPI for these cache organizations? Use Figure 6.8 (page 407):

a. Direct-mapped, 16-KB unified cache using write back.

b. Two-way–set-associative, 16-KB unified cache using write back.

c. Direct-mapped, 32-KB unified cache using write back.

---

10.   1/e Xref; must update

Assume the memory latency is 10 clocks, the transfer rate is 4 bytes per clock cycle and that 50% of the transfers are dirty. There are 16 bytes per block and 20% of the instructions are data-transfer instructions. The caches fetch words of the block in address order and the CPUs stall until all words of the block arrive. There is no write buffer. Add to the assumptions above a TLB that takes 20 clock cycles on a TLB miss. A TLB does not slow down a cache hit. For the TLB, make the simplifying assumption that 1% of all references aren't found in TLB, either when addresses come directly from the CPU or when addresses come from cache misses. What is the impact on performance of the TLB if the cache above is physical or virtual?

6.8 [10] <6.2> What is the formula for average access time for a three-level cache?

6.9[20] <6.2> The section on avoiding bank conflicts by having a prime number of memory banks mentioned that there were techniques for fast modulo arithmetic, especially when the prime number can be represented as $2^N - 1$. The idea is that by understanding the laws of modulo arithmetic we can simplify the program. The key insights are

1. Modulo arithmetic obeys the laws of distribution:

(a modulo c) + (b modulo c) = (a + b) modulo c
(a modulo c) $\times$ (b modulo c) = (a $\times$ b) modulo c

2. A binary number a is expressed as:

$a_i \times 2^i + ... + a_2 \times 2^2 + a_1 \times 2^1 + a_0 \times 2^0$ modulo 7 =
$((a_0 + a_3 + ... + a_i) \times 1 + (a_1 + a_4 + ... + a_{i+1}) \times 2 + (a_2 + a_5 + ... + a_{i+2}) \times 4)$modulo

3. The sequence2^0modulo 2^N–1, 2^1modulo 2^N–1, 2^2modulo 2^N–1, ... is a repeating pattern $2^0, 2^1, 2^2$ and so on for powers of 2 less than .2^N For example, if 2^N–1 = 7, then

2^0 modulo 7 = 1
2^0 modulo 7 = 2
2^0 modulo 7 = 4
2^0 modulo 7 = 1
2^0 modulo 7 = 2
2^0 modulo 7 = 4

4. Thus the binary number can be divided into a sum of components multiplied by each modulo result. Once again, if 2^N–1 = 7, then we can represent a modulo 7 as:

$a_i \times 2^i + ... + a_2 \times 2^2 + a_1 \times 2^1 + a_0 \times 2^0$ modulo 7 =
$((a_0 + a_3 + ... + a_i) \times 1 + (a_1 + a_4 + ... + a_{i+1}) \times 2 + (a_2 + a_5 + ... + a_{i+2}) \times 4)$modulo 7

5. Since these multiplications are just binary shifts, this is a fast calculation.

6. The address is now small enough, find the modulo by looking it up in a read-only memory (ROM) to get the bank number.

Finally, we are ready for the questions.

a. [15] Given 2^N–1 memory banks, what is the approximate reduction in size of an address that is M bits wide as a result of the intermediate result in step 4 above? Give the general formula, and then show the specific case of N=3 and M=32.

b.   [15] Draw the block structure of the hardware that would pick the correct bank out of 7 banks given a 32 bit byte address. Assume that each bank is 8 bytes wide. What is the size of the adders and ROM used in this organization?

6.10 [15/25/15/15] <6.6> The Intel i860 had its caches on chip and its die size is 1.2 cm*1.2 cm. It has a 2-way–set-associative, 4-KB instruction cache and a 2-way–set-associative, 8-KB data cache using write through or write back. Both caches use 32-byte blocks. There are no write buffers or process identifiers to reduce cache flushing. The i860 also includes a 64-entry, 4-way–set-associative TLB to map its 4-KB pages. Address translation occurs before the caches are accessed. The Cypress 7C601 CPU chip size was 0.8 cm by 0.7 cm and has no on-board cache—a cache controller chip (7C604) and two 16K * 16 cache chips (7C157) are offered to form a 64-KB unified cache. The controller includes a TLB with 64 entries managed fully associatively with 4096 process identifiers to reduce flushing. It supports 32-byte blocks with direct-mapped placement, and either write through or write back. There is a one-block write buffer for write back and a four-word write buffer for write through. The chip sizes are 1.0 cm by 0.9 cm for the 7C604 and 0.8 cm by 0.7 cm. for the 7C157.

a.   [15] Using the cost model of Chapter 2, what is the cost of the Cypress chip set versus the Intel chip? (Use Figure 2.11 on page 62 to determine chip costs by finding the closest die size in that table to the Intel and Cypress die area.)

b.   [25] Use the DLX cache traces and cache simulator to determine the average memory-access time for each cache organization. Assume a miss takes 6 clocks latency plus 1 clock for each 32-bit word. Assume both systems run at the same clock rate and use write allocate.

c.   [15] What is the comparative cost/performance of these chips using average memory-access time as the measure?

d.   [15] What is the percent increase in cost of a color workstation that uses the more expensive chips?

6.11 [25/10/15] <6.6> The CRAY X-MP instruction buffers can be thought of as an instruction-only cache. The total size is 1 KB, broken into 4 blocks of 256 bytes per block. The cache is fully associative and uses a first-in/first-out replacement policy. The access time on a miss is 10 clock cycles, with the transfer time of 64 bytes every clock cycle. The X-MP takes 1 clock cycle on a hit. Use the cache simulator to determine:

a.   [25] Instruction miss rate

b.   [10] Average instruction memory-access time measured in clock cycles

c.   [15] What does the CPI of the CRAY X-MP have to be for the portion due to instruction cache misses to be 10% or less?

6.12 [25] <6.6> Traces from a single process give too-high estimates for caches used in a multiprocess environment. Write a program that merges the uniprocess DLX traces into a single reference stream. Use the process-switch statistics in Figure 8.25 (page 439) as the average process-switch rate with an exponential distribution about that mean. (Use number of clock cycles rather than instructions, and assume the CPI of DLX is 1.5.) Use the cache simulator on the original traces and the merged trace. What is the miss rate for each assuming a 64-KB direct-mapped cache with 16-byte blocks? (There is a process-identified tag in the cache tag so that the cache doesn't have to be flushed on each switch.)

6.13 [25] <6.6> One approach to reducing misses is to prefetch the next block. A simple but effective strategy, found in the Alpha 21064, is when block i is referenced to make sure block $i+1$ is in the cache, and if not, to prefetch it. Do you think prefetching is more or less effective with increasing block size? Why? Is it more or less effective with increasing cache size? Why? Use statistics from the cache simulator and the traces to support your conclusion.

6.14 [20/25] <6.6> Smith and Goodman [1983] found that for a **small-instruction** cache, a cache using direct mapping could consistently outperform one using fully associative with LRU replacement.

a.   [20] Explain why this would be possible. (Hint: you can't explain this with the 3C model because it ignores replacement policy.)

b.   [25] Use the cache simulator to see if their results hold for the traces.

6.15 [30] <6.8> Use the cache simulator and traces to calculate the effectiveness of a 4-bank versus 8-bank interleaved memory. Assume each word transfer takes one clock on the bus and a random access is 8 clocks. Measure the bank conflicts and memory bandwidth for these cases:

a.   No cache and no write buffer.

b.   A 64-KB, direct-mapped, write-though cache with four-word blocks.

c.   A 64-KB, direct-mapped, write-back cache with four-word blocks.

d.   A 64-KB, direct-mapped, write-though cache with four-word blocks but the "interleaving" comes from a page-mode DRAM.

e.   A 64-KB, direct-mapped, write-though cache with four-word blocks but the "interleaving" comes from a page mode DRAM.

6.16 [25] <6.?> Use the traces to calculate the effectiveness of early restart and out-of-order fetch. What is the distribution of first accesses to a block as block size increases from 2 words to 64 words by factors of two for:

a.   A 64-KB, instruction-only cache?

b.   A 64-KB, data-only cache?

c.   A 128-KB unified cache?
Assume direct-mapped placement.

6.17 [30] <6.2> Use the cache simulator and traces with a program you write yourself to compare the effectiveness schemes for fast writes:

a.   1-word buffer and the CPU stalls on a data-read cache miss with a write-through cache.

b. 4-word buffer and the CPU stalls on a data-read cache miss with a write-through cache.

c. 4-word buffer and the CPU stalls on a data-read cache miss only if there is a potential conflict in the addresses with a write-through cache.

d. A write-back cache that writes dirty data first and then loads the missed block.

e. A write-back cache with a one-block write buffer that loads the miss data first and then stalls the CPU on a clean miss if the write buffer is not empty.

f. A write-back cache with a one-block write buffer that loads the miss data first and then stalls the CPU on a clean miss only if the write buffer is not empty and there is a potential conflict in the addresses.

Assume a 64-KB, direct-mapped cache for data and a 64-KB, direct-mapped cache for instructions with a block size of 32 bytes. The CPI of the CPU is 1.5 with a perfect memory system and it takes 14 clocks on a cache miss and 7 clocks to write a single word to memory.

6.18 [25] <6.?> Using the UNIX pipe facility, connect the output of one copy of the cache simulator to the input of another. Use this pair to see at what cache size is the global miss rate of a second-level cache approximately the same as a single-level cache of the same capacity for the traces provided.

6.19 [Discussion] <6.2.1> Some people have argued that with increasing capacity of memory storage per chip, virtual memory is an idea whose time has passed, and they expect to see it dropped from future computers. Find reasons for and against this argument.

6.20 [Discussion] <6.2.1> So far, few computer systems take advantage of the extra security available with gates and rings found in a machine like the Intel Pentium. Construct some scenario whereby the computer industry would switch over to this model of protection.

6.21 [Discussion] <8.3> Many times a new technology has been invented that is expected to make a major change to the memory hierarchy. For the sake of this question, let's suppose that biological computer technology becomes a reality. Suppose biological memory technology has an unusual characteristic: It is as fast as the fastest semiconductor DRAMs, and it can be randomly accessed; but it only costs as much as magnetic-disk memory. It has the further advantage of not being any slower no matter how big it is. The only drawback is that you can only Write it Once, but you can Read it Many times. Thus it is called a "WORM" memory. Because of the way it is manufactured, the WORM- memory module can be easily replaced. See if you can come up with several new ideas to take advantage of WORMs to build better computers using "bio-technology."

I/O certainly has been lagging in the last decade.

Seymour Cray, Public Lecture (1976)

Also, I/O needs a lot of work.

David Kuck, Keynote Address,
15th Annual Symposium on Computer Architecture (1988)

7 Storage Systems

7.1 | Introduction

Input/output has been the orphan of computer architecture. Historically neglected by CPU enthusiasts, the prejudice against I/O is institutionalized in the most widely used performance measure, CPU time (page 35). Whether a computer has the best or the worst I/O system in the world cannot be measured by CPU time, which by definition ignores I/O. The second class citizenship of I/O is even apparent in the label "peripheral" applied to I/O devices.

This attitude is contradicted by common sense. A computer without I/O devices is like a car without wheels—you can't get very far without them. And while CPU time is interesting, response time—the time between when the user types a command and when she gets results—is surely a better measure of performance. The customer who pays for a computer cares about response time, even if the CPU designer doesn't. Finally, as rapid improvements in CPU performance compress traditional classes of computers together, it is I/O that serves to distinguish them:

- The difference between a mainframe computer and a minicomputer is that a mainframe can support many more terminals and disks.

- The difference between a minicomputer and a workstation is that a workstation has a screen, a keyboard, and a mouse.

- The difference between a file server and a workstation is that a file server has disks and tape units but no screen, keyboard, or mouse.

- The difference between a workstation and a personal computer is that workstations are always connected together on a network.

It may come to pass that computers from high-end workstations to low-end supercomputers will use the same "super-microprocessors." Differences in cost and performance would be determined only by the memory and I/O systems (and the number of processors).

I/O's revenge is at hand. Suppose we have a difference between CPU time and response time of 10%, and we speed up the CPU by a factor of 10, while neglecting I/O. Amdahl's Law tells us that we will get a speedup of only 5 times, with half the potential of the CPU wasted. Similarly, making the CPU 100 times faster without improving the I/O would obtain a speedup of only 10 times, squandering 90% of the potential. If, as predicted in Chapter 1, performance of CPUs improves at 50% to 100% per year, and I/O does not improve, every task will become I/O bound. There would be no reason to buy faster CPUs—and no jobs for CPU designers.

While this single chapter cannot fully vindicate I/O, it may at least atone for some of the sins of the past and restore some balance.

Are CPUs Ever Idle?

Some suggest that the prejudice is well founded. I/O speed doesn't matter, they argue, since there is always another process to run while one process waits for a peripheral.

There are several points to make in reply. First, this is an argument that performance is measured as throughput—more tasks per hour—rather than as response time. Plainly, if users didn't care about response time, interactive software never would have been invented, and there would be no workstations today. (The next section gives experimental evidence on the importance of response time.) It may also be expensive to rely on processes while waiting for I/O, since main memory must be larger or else the paging traffic from process switching would actually increase I/O. Furthermore, with desktop computing there is only one person per CPU, and thus fewer processes than in timesharing; many times the only waiting process is the human being! And some applications, such as transaction processing (Section 7.3), place strict limits on response time as part of the performance analysis.

But let's accept the argument at face value and explore it further. Suppose the difference between response time and CPU time today is 10%, and a CPU that is ten times faster can be achieved without changing I/O performance. A process will then spend 50% of its time waiting for I/O, and two processes will have to be perfectly aligned to avoid CPU stalls while waiting for I/O. Any further CPU improvement will only increase CPU idle time.

Thus, I/O throughput can limit system throughput, just as I/O response time limits system response time. Let's see how to predict performance for the whole system.

7.2 | Predicting System Performance

System performance is limited by the slowest part of the path between CPU and I/O devices. The performance of a system can be limited by the speed of any of these pieces of the path, shown in Figure 7.1:

- The CPU

- The cache memory

- The main memory

- The memory–I/O bus

- The I/O controller or I/O channel

- The I/O device

- The speed of the I/O software

- The efficiency of the software's use of the I/O device

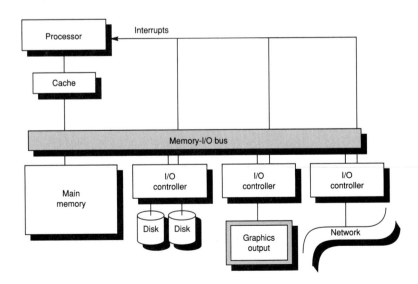

FIGURE 7.1   Typical collection of I/O devices on a computer.

If the system is not balanced, the high performance of some components may be lost due to the low performance of one link in the chain. The art of I/O design is to configure a system such that the speeds of all components are matched.

In earlier chapters we have assumed that the fastest CPU is the single object of our desire, but CPU performance is not the same as system performance. For example, suppose we have two workloads, A and B. Both workloads take 10 seconds to run. Workload A does so little I/O that it is not worth mentioning. Workload B keeps I/O devices busy four seconds, and this time is completely overlapped with CPU activities. Suppose the CPU is replaced by a newer model with five times the performance. Intuitively, we realize that workload A takes two seconds—fully five times faster—but workload B is I/O bound and cannot take less than four seconds. Figure 7.2 illustrates our intuition.

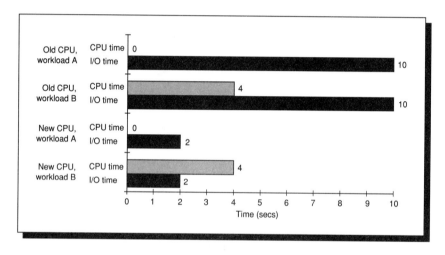

FIGURE 7.2 The overlapped execution of the two workloads with the original CPU and then a CPU with five times the performance. We can see that the elapsed time for workload A is indeed 1/5 of the time with the new CPU, but it is limited to four seconds in workload B because I/O speed is not improved.

Determining the performance of such cases requires a new formula. The elapsed execution time of a workload can be broken into three pieces

$$\text{Time}_{\text{workload}} = \text{Time}_{\text{CPU}} + \text{Time}_{\text{I/O}} - \text{Time}_{\text{overlap}}$$

where Time_{CPU} means the time the CPU is busy, $\text{Time}_{\text{I/O}}$ means the time the I/O system is busy, and $\text{Time}_{\text{overlap}}$ means the time both the CPU and the I/O system are busy. Using workload B with the old CPU in Figure 7.2 as an example, the times in seconds are:

10 for Time$_{workload}$,

10 for Time$_{CPU}$,

4 for Time$_{I/O}$, and

4 for Time$_{overlap}$.

Assuming we speed up only the CPU, one way to calculate the time to execute the workload is:

$$Time_{workload} = \frac{Time_{CPU}}{Speedup_{CPU}} + Time_{I/O} - \frac{Time_{overlap}}{Speedup_{CPU}}$$

Since the CPU time is shrunk, it stands to reason that the overlap time is also shrunk. The system speedup when we want to improve I/O is equivalent

$$Time_{workload} = Time_{CPU} + \frac{Time_{I/O}}{Speedup_{I/O}} - \frac{Time_{overlap}}{Speedup_{I/O}}$$

Let's try an example before explaining a limitation of these formulas.

Example   One workload takes 50 seconds to run, with the CPU being busy 30 seconds and the I/O being busy 30 seconds. How much time will the workload take if we replace the CPU with one that has four times the performance?

Answer   The total elapsed time is 50 seconds, yet the sum of CPU time and I/O time is 60 seconds. Thus the overlap time must be 10 seconds. Plugging into the formula:

$$Time_{workload} = \frac{Time_{CPU}}{Speedup_{CPU}} + Time_{I/O} - \frac{Time_{overlap}}{Speedup_{CPU}} = \frac{30}{4} + 30 - \frac{10}{4} = 35$$

This example uncovers a complication with this formula: How much of the time that the workload is busy on the faster CPU is overlapped with I/O? Figure 7.3 (page 512) shows three options. Depending on the resulting overlap after speedup, the time for the workload varies from 30 to 37.5 seconds.

In reality we can't know which is correct without measuring the workload on the faster CPU to see what overlap occurs. The formulas above assume option (c) in Figure 7.3; the overlap scales by the same speedup as the CPU, so we will call it Time$_{scaled}$ (rather than Time$_{workload}$). Maximum overlap assumes that as much of the overlap as possible is maintained, but that the new overlap cannot be larger than the original overlap or the CPU time after speedup. Minimum overlap assumes that as much of the overlap as possible is eliminated, but that the overlap time will not shrink by more than the time removed from the CPU or I/O time. If we introduce the abbreviations New$_{cpu}$ = Time$_{cpu}$ / Speedup$_{cpu}$ and New$_{I/O}$ = Time$_{I/O}$ / Speedup$_{I/O}$, the time of the workload for maximum overlap (Time$_{best}$) and minimum overlap (Time$_{worst}$) can be written as:

$$Time_{best} = New_{CPU} + Time_{I/O} - \text{Minimum } (Time_{overlap}, New_{CPU})$$

$$Time_{worst} = New_{CPU} + Time_{I/O} - \text{Maximum } (0, Time_{overlap} - (Time_{CPU} - New_{CPU}))$$

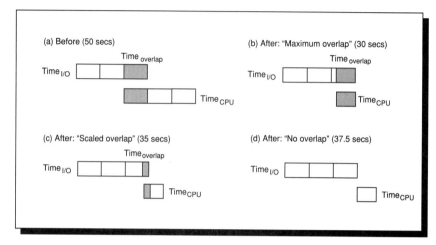

FIGURE 7.3   The original overlap in the example above (a) and three interpretations of overlap after speedup. Each block represents 10 seconds, except that the block for the new CPU time is 7.5 seconds. The overlapped portions of $Time_{CPU}$ and $Time_{I/O}$ are shaded. (b) shows the new $Time_{CPU}$ overlapping completely with I/O, giving a time of the workload of 30 seconds. (c) shows the overlap of the $Time_{CPU}$ is scaled with $Speedup_{CPU}$, giving a total of 35 seconds, with 2.5 seconds of overlapped execution. (d) shows no overlap with I/O, so the total is 37.5 seconds.

Example

Answer

Calculate the three time predictions for workload B in Figure 7.2

$$Time_{best} = \frac{10}{5} + 4 - \text{Minimum}\left(\frac{10}{5}, 4\right) = 2 + 4 - 2 = 4$$

$$Time_{scaled} = \frac{10}{5} + 4 - \frac{4}{5} = 2 + 4 - 0.8 = 5.2$$

$$Time_{worst} = \frac{10}{5} + 4 - \text{Maximum } (0, 4 - (10 - \frac{10}{5})) = 2 + 4 - 0 = 6$$

Sometimes changes will be made to both the CPU and the I/O system. The formulas become:

$$Time_{scaled} = New_{CPU} + New_{I/O} - \frac{Time_{overlap}}{\text{Maximum}(Speedup_{CPU}, Speedup_{I/O})}$$

$$Time_{best} = New_{CPU} + New_{I/O} - \text{Minimum}(Time_{overlap}, New_{CPU}, New_{I/O})$$

$$Time_{worst} = New_{CPU} + New_{I/O} - \text{Max } (0, Time_{overlap} - \text{Max } (Time_{CPU} - New_{CPU}, Time_{I/O} - New_{I/O}.))$$

The formula for scaled overlap says that the overlap period is reduced by the larger of the two speedups. The formula for maximum overlap (Time$_{best}$) says that as much overlap as possible is retained, but the new overlap cannot be larger than the original overlap or the CPU or I/O time after speedup. Finally, the formula for minimum overlap (Time$_{worst}$) says that the overlap is reduced by the larger of the time removed from the CPU time and the time removed from the I/O time (but that the overlap time cannot be less than 0). Figure 7.4 shows the three examples of speedup where both the I/O and CPU are improved.

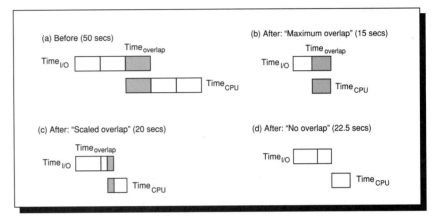

FIGURE 7.4   Time for workload in Figure 7.3(a) with Speedup$_{CPU}$ = 4 and Speedup$_{I/O}$ = 2.

Let's look at a detailed example showing speedup of both the CPU and I/O.

Example

Suppose a workload on the current systems takes 64 seconds. The CPU is busy the whole time, and the channels connecting the I/O devices to the CPU are busy 36 seconds. The computer manager is considering two upgrade options: either a single CPU that has twice the performance, or two CPUs that have twice the throughput and twice as many channels. The time of the actual I/O devices is so small it can be ignored. For the dual CPU option assume that the workload can be evenly spread between the CPUs and channels. What is the performance improvement for each option?

Answer

Since there is no change to the I/O system with the single faster CPU, time for the workload assuming scaled overlap is then simply

$$\text{Time}_{scaled} = \frac{\text{Time}_{CPU}}{\text{Speedup}_{CPU}} + \text{Time}_{I/O} - \frac{\text{Time}_{overlap}}{\text{Speedup}_{CPU}}$$

$$= \frac{64}{2} + 36 - \frac{36}{2} = 32 + 36 - 18 = 50$$

For the dual CPU with more channels,

$$\text{Time}_{\text{scaled}} =$$

$$\frac{\text{Time}_{\text{CPU}}}{\text{Speedup}_{\text{CPU}}} + \frac{\text{Time}_{\text{I/O}}}{\text{Speedup}_{\text{I/O}}} - \frac{\text{Time}_{\text{overlap}}}{\text{Maximum}(\text{Speedup}_{\text{CPU}}, \text{Speedup}_{\text{I/O}})}$$

$$= \frac{64}{2} + \frac{36}{2} - \frac{36}{\text{Maximum}(2, 2)} = 32 + 18 - 18 = 32$$

Assuming scaled overlap, the dual CPU is more than 50% faster. Using best-case scaling, the dual CPU is 13% faster, while worst-case scaling suggests it is 39% faster.

As these examples demonstrate, we need improvement in I/O performance to match the improvement in CPU performance if we are to achieve faster computer systems. We can now examine metrics of I/O devices to understand how to improve their performance and thus the whole system.

7.3 | I/O Performance Measures

I/O performance has measures that have no counterparts in CPU design. One of these is diversity: Which I/O devices can connect to the computer system? Another is capacity: How many I/O devices can connect to a computer system?

In addition to these unique measures, the traditional measures of performance, response time and throughput also apply to I/O. (I/O throughput is sometimes called "I/O bandwidth" and response time is sometimes called "latency.") The next two figures offer insight into how response time and throughput trade off against each other. Figure 7.5 shows the simple producer-server model. The producer creates tasks to be performed and places them in the queue; the server takes tasks from the queue and performs them.

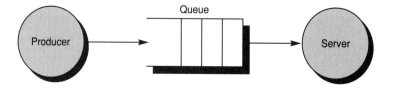

FIGURE 7.5   The traditional producer-server model of response time and throughput. Response time begins when a task is placed in the queue and ends when it is completed by the server. Throughput is the number of tasks completed by the server in unit time.

Response time is defined as the time a task takes from the moment it is placed in the queue until the server finishes the task. Throughput is simply the average number of tasks completed by the server over a time period. To get the highest possible throughput, the server should never be idle, and thus the queue should never be empty. Response time, on the other hand, counts time spent in the queue and is therefore minimized by the queue being empty.

Another measure of I/O performance is the interference of I/O with CPU execution. Transferring data may interfere with the execution of another process. There is also overhead due to handling I/O interrupts. Our concern here is how many more clock cycles a process will take because of I/O for another process.

Throughput Versus Response Time

Figure 7.6 shows throughput versus response time (or latency), for a typical I/O system. The knee of the curve is the area where a little more throughput results in much longer response time or, conversely, a little shorter response time results in much lower throughput.

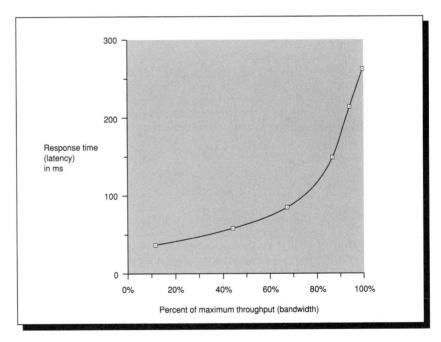

FIGURE 7.6   Throughput versus response time. Latency is normally reported as response time. Note that absolute minimum response time achieves only 11% of the throughput while the response time for 100% throughput takes seven times the minimum response time. Chen [1989] collected these data for an array of magnetic disks.

Life would be simpler if improving performance always meant improvements in both response time and throughput. Adding more servers, as in Figure 7.7, increases throughput: By spreading data across two disks instead of one, tasks may be serviced in parallel. Alas, this does not help response time, unless the workload is held constant and the time in the queues is reduced because of more resources.

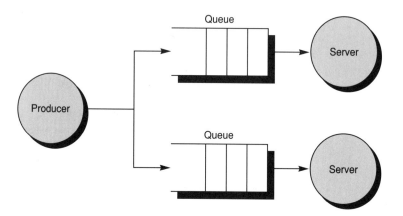

FIGURE 7.7   The single-producer, single-server model of Figure 7.5 is extended with another server and queue. This increases I/O system throughput and takes less time to service producer tasks. Increasing the number of servers is a common technique in I/O systems. There is a potential imbalance problem with two queues; unless data is placed perfectly in the queues, sometimes one server will be idle with an empty queue while the other server is busy with many tasks in its queue.

How does the architect balance these conflicting demands? If the computer is interacting with human beings, Figure 7.8 suggests an answer. This figure presents the results of two studies of interactive environments, one keyboard oriented and one graphical. An interaction or *transaction* with a computer is divided into three parts:

1. *Entry time*: The time for the user to enter the command. In the graphics system in Figure 7.8 it took 0.25 seconds on average to enter the command versus 4.0 seconds for the conventional system.

2. *System response time*: The time between when the user enters the command and the complete response is displayed.

3. *Think time*: The time from the reception of the response until the user begins to enter the next command.

The sum of these three parts is called the *transaction time*. Several studies report that user productivity is inversely proportional to transaction time; transactions per hour measures the work completed per hour by the user.

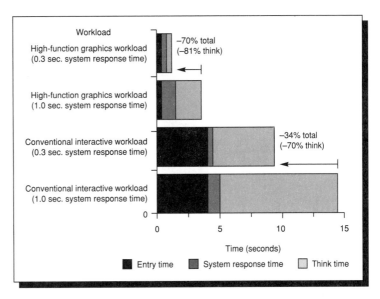

FIGURE 7.8 A user transaction with an interactive computer divided into entry time, system response time, and user think time for a conventional system and graphics system. The entry times are the same independent of system response time. The entry time was 4 seconds for the conventional system and 0.25 seconds for the graphics system. (From Brady [1986].)

The results in Figure 7.8 show that reduction in response time actually decreases transaction time by more than just the response time reduction: Cutting system response time by 0.7 seconds saves 4.9 seconds (34%) from the conventional transaction and 2.0 seconds (70%) from the graphics transaction. This implausible result is explained by human nature; people need less time to think when given a faster response.

Whether these results are explained as a better match to the human attention span or getting people "on a roll," several studies report this behavior. In fact, as computer responses drop below a second, productivity seems to make a more than linear jump. Figure 7.9 (page 518) compares transactions per hour (the inverse of transaction time) of a novice, an average engineer, and an expert performing physical design tasks at graphics displays. System response time magnified talent: a novice with subsecond response time was as productive as an experienced professional with slower response, and the experienced engineer in turn could outperform the expert with a similar advantage in response time. In all cases the number of transactions per hour jumps more than linearly with subsecond response time.

Since humans may be able to get much more work done per day with better response time, it is possible to attach an economic benefit to the customer of lowering response time into the subsecond range [IBM 1982], thereby helping the architect decide how to tip the balance between response time and throughput.

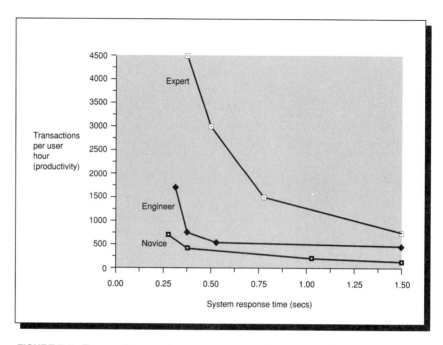

FIGURE 7.9   Transactions per hour versus computer response time for a novice, experienced engineer, and expert doing physical design on a graphics system. Transactions per hour is a measure of productivity. (From IBM [1982].)

Examples of Measurements of I/O Performance—
Magnetic Disks

Benchmarks are needed to evaluate I/O performance, just as they are needed to evaluate CPU performance. We begin with benchmarks for magnetic disks. Three traditional applications of disks are with large-scale scientific problems, transaction processing, and file systems.

Supercomputer I/O Benchmarks

Supercomputer I/O is dominated by accesses to large files on magnetic disks. For example, Bucher and Hayes [1980] benchmarked supercomputer I/O using 8-MB sequential file transfers. Many supercomputer installations run batch jobs, each of which may last for hours. In these situations, I/O consists of one large read followed by writes to snapshot the state of the computation should the computer crash. As a result, supercomputer I/O in many cases consists of more output than input. Some models of Cray Research computers have such limited main memory that programmers must break their programs into overlays and swap them to disk (see Section 8.5 of Chapter 8), which also causes large sequential transfers. Thus, the overriding supercomputer I/O measure is data throughput: number of bytes per second that can be transferred between supercomputer main memory and disks during large transfers.

Transaction Processing I/O Benchmarks

In contrast, *transaction processing* (TP) is chiefly concerned with *I/O rate*: the number of disk accesses per second, as opposed to *data rate*, measured as bytes of data per second. TP generally involves changes to a large body of shared information from many terminals, with the TP system guaranteeing proper behavior on a failure. If, for example, a bank's computer fails when a customer withdraws money, the TP system would guarantee that the account is debited if the customer received the money and that the account is unchanged if the money was not received. Airline reservations systems as well as banks are traditional customers for TP.

Two dozen members of the TP community conspired to form a benchmark for the industry and, to avoid the wrath of their legal departments, published the report anonymously [1985]. This benchmark, called DebitCredit, simulates bank tellers and has as its bottom line the number of debit/credit transactions per second (TPS); in 1990, the TPS for high-end machines is about 300. The DebitCredit performs the operation of a customer depositing or withdrawing money. The performance measurement is the peak TPS, with 95% of the transactions having less than a one-second response time. The DebitCredit computes the cost per TPS, based on the five-year cost of the computer-system hardware and software. Disk I/O for DebitCredit is random reads and writes of 100-byte records along with occasional sequential writes.

Depending on how cleverly the transaction-processing system is designed, each transaction results in between two and ten disk I/Os and takes between 5,000 and 20,000 CPU instructions per disk I/O. The variation largely depends on the efficiency of the transaction processing software, although in part it depends on the extent to which disk accesses can be avoided by keeping information in main memory. The benchmark requires that for TPS to increase, the number of tellers and the size of the account file must also increase. Figure 7.10 shows this unusual relationship in which more TPS requires more users.

TPS	Number of ATMs	Account-file size
10	1,000	0.1 GB
100	10,000	1.0 GB
1,000	100,000	10.0 GB
10,000	1,000,000	100.0 GB

FIGURE 7.10 Relationship among TPS, tellers, and account-file size. The DebitCredit benchmark requires that the computer system handle more tellers and larger account files before it can claim a higher transaction-per-second milestone. The benchmark is supposed to include "terminal handling" overhead, but this metric is sometimes ignored.

This is to ensure that the benchmark really measures disk I/O; otherwise a large main memory dedicated to a database cache with a small number of accounts would unfairly yield a very high TPS. (Another perspective is the number of accounts must grow since a person is not likely to use the bank more frequently just because the bank has a faster computer!)

File System I/O Benchmarks

File systems, for which disks are mainly used in timesharing systems, have a different access pattern. Ousterhout et al. [1985] measured a UNIX file system and found that 80% of accesses to files of less than 10 KB and 90% of **all** file accesses were sequential. The distribution by type of file access was 67% reads, 27% writes, and 6% read-write accesses. In 1988, Howard et al. [1988] proposed a file-system benchmark that is becoming popular. Their paper describes five phases of the benchmark, using 70 files with a total size of 200 KB:

MakeDir—Constructs a target subtree that is identical in structure to the source subtree.

Copy—Copies every file from the source subtree to the target subtree.

ScanDir—Recursively traverses the target subtree and examines the status of every file in it. It does not actually read the contents of any file.

ReadAll—Scans every byte of every file in the target subtree once.

Make—Compiles and links all the files in the target subtree. [p. 55]

The file-system measurements of Howard et al. [1988], like those of Ousterhout et al. [1985], found the ratio of disk reads to writes to be about 2:1. This benchmark reflects that measure.

7.4 | Types of I/O Devices

Now that we have covered measurements of I/O performance, let's describe the devices themselves. While the computing model has changed little since 1950, I/O devices have become rich and diverse. Three characteristics are useful in organizing this disparate conglomeration:

- *Behavior*—input (read once), output (write only, cannot be read), or storage (can be reread and usually rewritten)

- *Partner*—either a human or a machine is at the other end of the I/O device, either feeding data on input or reading data on output

- *Data rate*—the peak rate at which data can be transferred between the I/O device and the main memory or CPU

Using these characteristics, a keyboard is an input device used by a human with a peak data rate of about 10 bytes per second. Figure 7.11 shows some of the I/O devices connected to computers.

The advantage of designing I/O devices for humans is that the performance target is fixed. Figure 7.12 shows the I/O performance of people.

Device	Behavior	Partner	Data rate (KB/sec)
Keyboard	Input	Human	0.01
Mouse	Input	Human	0.02
Voice input	Input	Human	0.02
Scanner	Input	Human	200.00
Voice output	Output	Human	0.60
Line printer	Output	Human	1.00
Laser printer	Output	Human	100.00
Graphics display	Output	Human	30,000.00
(CPU to frame buffer)	Output	Human	200.00
Network-terminal	Input or output	Machine	0.05
Network-LAN	Input or output	Machine	200.00
Optical disk	Storage	Machine	500.00
Magnetic tape	Storage	Machine	2,000.00
Magnetic disk	Storage	Machine	2,000.00

FIGURE 7.11 Examples of I/O devices categorized by behavior, partner, and data rate. This is the raw data rate of the device rather than the rate an application would see. Storage devices can be further distinguished by whether they support sequential access (e.g., tapes) or random access (e.g., disks). Note that networks can act either as input or output devices but, unlike storage, cannot reread the same information.

Human organ	I/O rate (KB/sec)	I/O latency (ms)
Ear	8.000–60.000	10
Eye—reading text	0.030–0.375	10
Eye—pattern recognition	125.000	10
Hand—typing	0.010–0.020	100
Voice	0.003–0.015	100

FIGURE 7.12 Peak I/O rates for people. Input via seeing patterns is our highest I/O rate; hence the popularity of graphic output devices. Maberly [1966] says the average reading speed is 28 bytes per second and the maximum is 375 bytes per second. The telephone company sets a 170-ms limit to the time between when an operator pushes a button to accept a call until a voice path must be established. The phone company transmits voice at 8 KB per second. (None of these parameters are expected to change, unless anabolic steroids become a breakfast supplement!)

To put the data rates of each device into perspective, Figure 7.13 shows the relative peak memory bandwidth needed to support each device, assuming a computer had exactly one of each device transferring at its peak rate.

Rather than discuss the characteristics of all I/O devices, we will concentrate on the three devices with the highest data rates: magnetic disks, graphics displays, and local area networks. These are also the devices that have the highest leverage on user productivity. In this chapter we are not talking about floppy disks, but the original "hard" disks. These magnetic disks are what IBM calls *DASDs*, for *Direct-Access Storage Devices*.

Magnetic Disks

I think Silicon Valley was misnamed. If you look back at the dollars shipped in products in the last decade there has been more revenue from magnetic disks than from silicon. They ought to rename the place Iron Oxide Valley.

Al Hoagland, one of the pioneers of magnetic disks (1982)

In spite of repeated attacks by new technologies, magnetic disks have dominated secondary storage since 1965. Magnetic disks play two roles in computer systems:

- Long-term, nonvolatile storage for files, even when no programs are running

- A level of the memory hierarchy below main memory used for virtual memory during program execution (see Section 8.5 in Chapter 8)

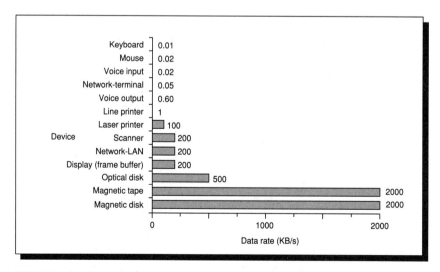

FIGURE 7.13   I/O devices sorted from lowest data rate to highest. The data rate for the graphics display is from the CPU to the frame buffer because the CPU isn't involved in the transfer from the frame buffer to the display (see Graphics Displays subsection below).

As descriptions of magnetic disks can be found in countless books, we will only list the key characteristics with the terms illustrated in Figure 7.14. A magnetic disk consists of a collection of platters (1 to 20), rotating on a spindle at about 3600 revolutions per minute (RPM). These platters are metal disks covered with magnetic recording material on both sides. Disk diameters vary by a factor of five, from 14 to 2.5 inches. Traditionally, the widest disks have the highest performance, and the smallest disks have the lowest cost per disk drive.

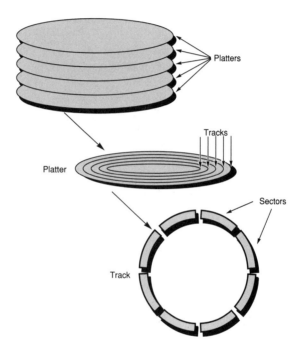

FIGURE 7.14   Disks are organized into platters, tracks, and sectors. Both sides of a platter are coated so that information can be stored on both surfaces.

Each disk surface is divided into concentric circles, designated *tracks*. There are typically 500 to 2000 tracks per surface. Each track in turn is divided into *sectors* that contain the information; each track might have 32 sectors. The sector is the smallest unit that can be read or written. The sequence recorded on the magnetic media is a sector number, a gap, the information for that sector including error correction code, a gap, the sector number of the next sector, and so on. Traditionally all tracks have the same number of sectors; the outer tracks, which are longer, record information at a lower density than the inner tracks. Recording more sectors on the outer tracks than on the inner tracks, called *constant bit den-*

sity, is becoming more widespread with the advent of intelligent interface standards such as SCSI (see Section 7.5). IBM mainframe disks allow users to select the size of the sectors, while almost all other systems fix the size of the sector.

To read and write information into a sector, a movable *arm* containing a *read/write head* is located over each surface. Bits are recorded using a run-length limited code, which improves the recording density of the magnetic media. The arms for each surface are connected together and move in conjunction, so that every arm is over the same track of every surface. The term *cylinder* is used to refer to all the tracks under the arms at a given point on all surfaces.

To read or write a sector, the disk controller sends a command to move the arm over the proper track. This operation is called a *seek,* and the time to move the arm to the desired track is called *seek time.* Average seek time is the subject of considerable misunderstanding. Disk manufacturers report minimum seek time, maximum seek time, and average seek time in the manuals. The first two are easy to measure, but average was open to wide interpretation. The industry decided to calculate average seek time as the sum of the time for all possible seeks divided by the number of possible seeks. Average seek times are advertised to be 12 ms to 20 ms, but depending on the application and operating system the actual average seek time may be only 25% to 33% of the advertised number, due to locality of disk references. Section 7.10 has a detailed example.

The time for the requested sector to rotate under the head is the *rotation latency* or *rotational delay.* Most disks rotate at 3600 RPM, and an average latency to the desired information is halfway around the disk; the average rotation time for most disks is therefore

$$\text{Average rotation time} = \frac{0.5}{3600 \text{ RPM}} = 0.0083 \text{ sec} = 8.3 \text{ ms}$$

The next component of a disk access, *transfer time,* is the time to transfer a block of bits, typically a sector, under the read-write head. This is a function of the block size, rotation speed, recording density of a track, and speed of the electronics connecting disk to computer. Transfer rates in 1990 are typically 1 to 4 MB per second.

In addition to the disk drive, there is usually also a device called a *disk controller.* Between the disk controller and main memory is a hierarchy of controllers and data paths, whose complexity varies with the cost of the computer (see Section 7.9). Since the transfer time is often a small portion of a full disk access, the controller in higher performance systems disconnects the data paths from the disks while they are seeking so that other disks can transfer their data to memory.

Thus, the final component of disk-access time is *controller time,* which is the overhead the controller imposes in performing an I/O access. When referring to performance of a disk in a computer system, the time spent waiting for a disk to become free (*queueing delay*) is added to this time.

Example

What is the average time to read or write a 512-byte sector for a typical disk today? The advertised average seek time is 20 ms, the transfer rate is 1MB/sec, and the controller overhead is 2 ms. Assume the disk is idle so that there is no queuing delay.

Answer

Average disk access is equal to average seek time + average rotational delay + transfer time + controller overhead. Using the calculated, average seek time, the answer is

$$20 \text{ ms} + 8.3 \text{ ms} + \frac{0.5 \text{ KB}}{1.0 \text{ MB/sec}} + 2 \text{ ms} = 20 + 8.3 + 0.5 + 2 = 30.8 \text{ ms}$$

Assuming the measured, average seek time is 25% of the calculated number, the answer is

$$5 \text{ ms} + 8.3 \text{ ms} + 0.5 \text{ ms} + 2 \text{ ms} = 15.8 \text{ ms}$$

Figure 7.15 shows characteristics of magnetic disks for four manufacturers. Large-diameter drives have many more megabytes to amortize the cost of electronics, so the traditional wisdom was that they had the lowest cost per megabyte. But this advantage is offset for the small drives by the much higher sales volume, which lowers manufacturing costs: 1990 OEM prices are $2 to $3

Characteristics	IBM 3380	Fujitsu M2361A	Imprimis Wren IV	Conner CP3100
Disk diameter (inches)	14	10.5	5.25	3.5
Formatted data capacity (MB)	7500	600	344	100
MTTF (hours)	52,000	20,000	40,000	30,000
Number of arms/box	4	1	1	1
Maximum I/Os/second/arm	50	40	35	30
Typical I/Os/second/arm	30	24	28	20
Maximum I/Os/second/box	200	40	35	30
Typical I/Os/second/box	120	24	28	20
Transfer rate (MB/sec)	3	2.5	1.5	1
Power/box (W)	1,650	640	35	10
MB/W	1.1	0.9	9.8	10.0
Volume (cu. ft.)	24	3.4	0.1	.03
MB/cu. ft.	310	180	3440	3330

FIGURE 7.15 Characteristics of magnetic disks from four manufacturers. Comparison of IBM 3380 disk model AK4 for mainframe computers, Fujitsu M2361A "Super Eagle" disk for minicomputers, Imprimis Wren IV disk for workstations, and Conner Peripherals CP3100 disk for personal computers. Maximum I/Os/second signifies maximum number of average seeks and average rotates for a single sector access. (Table from Katz, Patterson, and Gibson [1990].)

per megabyte, almost independent of width. The small drives also have advantages in power and volume. The price of a megabyte of disk storage in 1990 is 10 to 30 times cheaper than the price of a megabyte of DRAM in a system.

The Future of Magnetic Disks

The disk industry has concentrated on improving the capacity of disks. Improvement in capacity is customarily expressed as *areal density*, measured in bits per square inch:

$$\text{Areal density} = \frac{\text{Tracks}}{\text{Inch}} \text{ on a disk surface} * \frac{\text{Bits}}{\text{Inch}} \text{ on a track}$$

Areal density can be predicted according to the *maximum areal density* (MAD) formula:

$$\text{MAD} = 10^{(\text{year}-1971)/10} \text{ million bits per square inch}$$

Thus, storage density improves by a factor of 10 every decade, doubling density every three years.

Cost per megabyte has dropped consistently at 20% to 25% per year, with smaller drives playing the larger role in this improvement. Because it is easier to

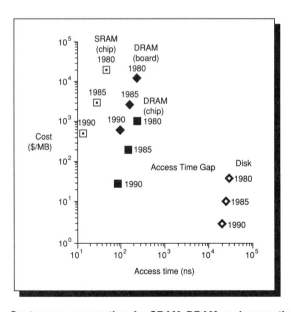

FIGURE 7.16   Cost versus access time for SRAM, DRAM, and magnetic disk in 1980, 1985, and 1990. (Note the difference in cost between a DRAM chip and DRAM chips packaged on a board and ready to plug into a computer.) The two-order-of-magnitude gap in cost and access times between semiconductor memory and rotating magnetic disk has inspired a host of competing technologies to try to fill it. So far, such attempts have been made obsolete before production by improvements in magnetic disks, DRAMs, or both.

spin the smaller mass, smaller diameter disks save power as well as volume. Smaller drives also have fewer cylinders so the seek distances are shorter. In 1990, 5.25-inch or 3.5-inch drives are probably the leading technology, while the future may see even smaller drives. We can expect significant savings in volume and power, but little in speed. Increasing density (bits per inch on a track) has improved transfer times, and there has been some small improvement in seek speed. Rotation speeds have been steady at 3600 RPM for a decade, but some manufacturers plan to go to 5400 RPM in the early 1990s.

As mentioned earlier, magnetic disks have been challenged many times for supremacy of secondary storage. One reason has been the fabled *Access Time Gap* as shown in Figure 7.16. Many a scientist has tried to invent a technology to fill that gap. Let's look at some of the recent attempts.

Using DRAMs as Disks

A current challenger to disks for dominance of secondary storage is *solid state disks* (SSDs), built from DRAMs with a battery to make the system nonvolatile; and *expanded storage* (ES), a large memory that allows only block transfers to or from main memory. ES acts like a software-controlled cache (the CPU stalls during the block transfer) while SSD involves the operating system just like a transfer from magnetic disks. The advantages of SSD and ES are trivial seek times, higher potential transfer rate, and possibly higher reliability. Unlike just a larger main memory, SSDs and ESs are autonomous: They require special commands to access their storage, and thus are "safe" from some software errors that write over main memory. The block-access nature of SSD and ES allows error correction to be spread over more words, which means lower cost or greater error recovery. For example, IBM's ES uses the greater error recovery to allow it to be constructed from less reliable (and less expensive) DRAMs without sacrificing product availability. SSDs, unlike main memory and ES, may be shared by multiple CPUs because they function as separate units. Placing DRAMs in an I/O device rather than memory is also one way to get around the address-space limits of the current 32-bit computers. The disadvantage of SSD and ES is cost, which is at least ten times per megabyte the cost of magnetic disks.

Optical Disks

Another challenger to magnetic disks is *optical compact disks* or CDs. The *CD/ROM* is removable and inexpensive to manufacture, but it is a read-only media. The newer CD/writable is also removable, but has a high cost per megabyte and low performance. A common misperception about *write-once optical disks* is that once they are written, the information cannot be destroyed; in fact, write once means one reliable write and then a "fuzzy" bitwise ORing of the previous and new data.

So far, magnetic disk challengers have never had a product to market at the right time. By the time a new product ships, disks have made advances as predicted by MAD formula, and costs have dropped accordingly. Optical disks, however, may have the potential to compete with new tape technologies for archival storage.

Disk Arrays

One other future candidate for optimizing storage is not a new technology, but a new organization of disk storage—arrays of small and inexpensive disks. The argument for arrays is that since price per megabyte is independent of disk size, potential throughput can be increased by having many disk drives and, hence, many disk arms. Simply spreading data over multiple disks automatically forces accesses to several disks. (While arrays improve throughput, latency is not necessarily improved.) The drawback to arrays is that with more devices, reliability drops: N devices generally have $1/N$ the reliability of a single device.

Reliability and Availability

This brings us to two terms that are often confused—reliability and availability. The term reliability is commonly used incorrectly to mean availability; if something breaks, but the user can still use the system, it seems as if the system still "works," and hence it seems more reliable. Here is the proper distinction:

Reliability—is anything broken?

Availability—is the system still available to the user?

Adding hardware can therefore improve availability (for example, ECC on memory), but it cannot improve reliability (the DRAM is still broken). Reliability can only be improved by bettering environmental conditions, by building from more reliable components, or by building with fewer components. Another term, *data integrity*, refers to always reporting when information is lost when a failure occurs; this is very important to some applications.

So, while a disk array can never be more reliable than a smaller number of larger disks when each disk has the same failure rate, availability can be improved by adding redundant disks. That is, if a single disk fails, the lost information can be reconstructed from redundant information. The only danger is in getting another disk failure between the time a disk fails and the time it is replaced (termed *mean time to repair* or MTTR). Since the *mean time to failure* (MTTF) of disks is three to five years, and the MTTR is measured in hours, redundancy can make the availability of 100 disks much higher than that of a single disk.

Since disk failures are self-identifying, information can be reconstructed from just parity: The good disks plus the parity disk can be used to calculate the information that is on the failed disk. Hence, the cost of higher availability is $1/N$, where N is the number of disks protected by parity. Just as direct-mapped associative placement in caches can be considered a special case of set-associative placement (see Section 8.4), the *mirroring* or *shadowing* of disks can be considered the special case of one data disk and one parity disk ($N=1$). Parity can be accomplished by duplicating the data, so mirrored disks have the advantage of simplifying parity calculation. Duplicating data also means that the controller can improve read performance by reading from the disk of the pair that has the shortest seek distance, although this optimization is at the cost of write performance because the arms of the pair of disks are no longer always over the same track. Of course, the redundancy of $N = 1$ has the highest overhead for increasing disk availability.

The higher throughput, measured either as megabytes per second or as I/Os per second, and the ability to recover from failures make disk arrays attractive. When combined with the advantages of smaller volume and lower power of small-diameter drives, redundant arrays of small or inexpensive drives may play a larger role in future disk systems. The current drawback is the added complexity of a controller for disk arrays.

Graphics Displays

Through computer displays I have landed an airplane on the deck of a moving carrier, observed a nuclear particle hit a potential well, flown in a rocket at nearly the speed of light and watched a computer reveal its innermost workings.

Ivan Sutherland (the "father" of computer graphics), quoted in
"Computer Software for Graphics," *Scientific American* (1984)

While magnetic disks may dominate throughput and cost of I/O devices, the most fascinating I/O device is the graphics display. Based on television technology, a *raster cathode ray tube* (CRT) *display* scans an image out one line at a time, 30 to 60 times per second. At this *refresh rate* the human eye doesn't notice a "flicker" on the screen. The image is composed of a matrix of picture elements, or *pixels*, which can be represented as a matrix of bits, called a *bit map*. Depending on size of screen and resolution, the display matrix consists of 340*512 to 1560*1280 pixels. For black and white displays, often 0 is black and 1 is white. For displays that support over 100 different shades of black and white, sometimes called *grayscale* displays, 8 bits per pixel are required. A color display might use 8 bits for each of the three primary colors (red, blue, and green), for 24 bits per pixel.

The hardware support for graphics consists mainly of a *raster refresh buffer*, or *frame buffer*, to store the bit map. The image to be represented on screen is stored into the frame buffer, and the bit pattern per pixel is read out to the graphics display at the refresh rate. Figure 7.17 (page 530) shows a frame buffer with four bits per pixel and Figure 7.18 (page 530) shows how the buffer is connected to the bus.

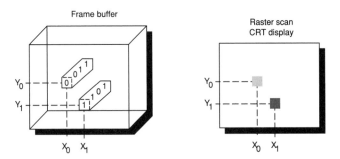

FIGURE 7.17   Each coordinate in the frame buffer on the left determines the shade of the corresponding coordinate for the raster scan CRT display on the right. Pixel (x_0,y_0) contains the bit pattern 0011, which is a lighter shade of gray on the screen than the bit pattern 1101 in pixel (x_1,y_1).

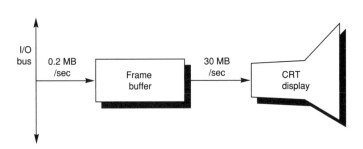

FIGURE 7.18   The frame buffer is connected to both the I/O bus and the display. Because of the high data rate from the buffer to the display, the frame buffer is frequently dual ported.

The goal of the bit map is to faithfully represent what is on the screen. As the computer switches from one image to another, the screen may look "splotchy" during the change. Here are two ways of dealing with this:

■ Change the frame buffer only during the "vertical blanking interval." This is the time the gun in the raster CRT display takes to go back to the upper-left-hand corner before starting to paint the pixels of the next image. This takes 1 to 2 ms of every 16 ms at the 60-Hz refresh rate each time the screen is painted.

- If the vertical blanking interval is not long enough, the frame buffer can be double buffered, so that one is read while the other is being written. This way, images in sequence (as in animation) are drawn in alternate frame buffers. Double buffering, of course, doubles the cost of the memory in the frame buffer.

From the point of view of the CPU, graphics is logically output only. But the frame buffer is capable of being read as well as written, permitting operations to be performed directly on the screen images. These operations are called *bit blts*, for bit block transfer. Bit blts are commonly used for operations such as moving a window or changing the shape of the cursor. A current debate in graphics architecture is whether reading the frame buffer is limited to the operating system or should user programs be able to read it as well.

Cost of Computer Graphics

The CRT monitor itself is based on television technology and is sensitive to consumer demand. Today prices vary from $100 for a black-and-white monitor to $15,000 for a large studio color monitor, not including memory. The amount of memory in a frame buffer depends directly on the size of the screen and the bits per pixel:

$$340*512*1 \text{ bits} = 21.5 \text{ KB}$$

$$1280*1024*24 \text{ bits} = 3840 \text{ KB}$$

(By the way, this bottom dimension is the proposed size for high-definition television.) Note that the memory cost is doubled if double buffering is used.

To reduce costs of a color frame buffer, many systems use a two-level representation that takes advantage of the fact that few pictures need the full pallet of possible colors (see Figure 7.19 on page 532).

The intermediate level contains the full color width of, say, 24 bits and a large collection of the possible colors that can appear on the screen—256 different colors, for example. While this collection is large, it is still much smaller than 2^{24}. This intermediary table has been variously named a *color map*, *color table*, or *video look-up table*. Each pixel need have only enough bits to indicate a color in the color map. As a simple example, Figure 7.19 uses a 4-word color map, which means the frame buffer needs only 2 bits per pixel. The savings for a full-sized color display with a 256-color map is

$$1280*1024*24 - (1280*1024*8 + 256*24)$$

$$= 3,840 \text{ KB} - (1280 \text{ KB} + .75 \text{ KB}) \approx 2560 \text{ KB}$$

This amounts to a threefold reduction in memory size. In 1990 a 256- by 24-bit color map and an analog interface to a color CRT fit in a single chip.

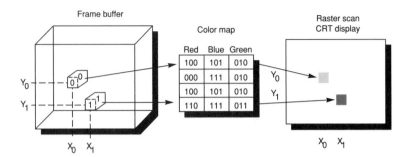

FIGURE 7.19   An example of a color map to reduce the cost of the frame buffer. Suppose only nine bits per color are needed. Rather than store the full nine bits per pixel in the frame buffer, just enough bits per pixel are stored to index the table containing the unique colors in a picture. Only the color map has the nine bits for the colors in the display. Near photographic color pictures can be produced with about 125 colors using the right shades of the color spectrum; but at least 24 bits are needed to get the right shades! The color map is loaded by the application program, offering each picture its own palette of colors to chose from.

Performance Demands of Graphics Displays

The performance of graphics is determined by the frequency an application needs new images and by the quality of those images. The amount of information transferred from memory to the frame buffer depends on complexity of image, with a full color display requiring almost four megabytes. The transfer rate depends on the speed with which the image should be changed as well as the amount of information. Animation requires at least 15 changes per second for movement to appear smooth on a screen. For interactive graphics, the time to update the frame buffer measures the effectiveness of the application; for people to feel comfortable the total reaction time must be less than a second (see Figure 7.9, page 518). With a drawing system, the portion of the screen one is working on must change almost immediately, as human visual perception is on the order of 0.02 seconds. Figure 7.20 shows some sample graphics tasks and their performance requirements. Note that the frame buffer must have enough bandwidth to refresh the display **and** to allow the CPU to change the image being refreshed.

The high data rate—and the large market of graphics displays—has made a dual-ported DRAM chip popular. This chip has a serial I/O port and internal shift register that is connected to the display in a graphics application in addition to the traditional randomly addressed data port. This chip is so widely used in frame buffers that it is called a *video DRAM*.

Graphics tasks	Bandwidth requirements
Text editor—Scrolling text in window means moving all bits in half the frame buffer about 10 times per second.	0.8 MB/sec
VLSI design—Moving a portion of the design means moving all bits in half of a color frame buffer in less than 0.1 second.	6.3 MB/sec
Television commercial—Showing movie-quality images means changing 24 times per second.	90.0 MB/sec
Visualization of scientific data—About the same as a television commercial.	90.0 MB/sec

FIGURE 7.20 Graphics tasks and their performance requirements. VLSI design uses 8 bits of color while the television commercial and visualization use 24 bits. Bandwidth is measured at the frame buffer.

Future Directions in Graphics Displays

It is safe to predict that people will want better pictures in the future. They will want, for example, more lines on a screen and more bits per inch on a line to make sharper images, more bits per color to make more colorful images, and more bandwidth to allow animation.

To simplify the display of three-dimensional images, a z dimension per pixel can be added to the x and y coordinates. It says where the pixel is located from the viewer along a z axis (e.g., into the CRT). A 3D image starts with z set to the furthest possible location from the viewer and the color set to the background color. To get a proper 3D perspective, the z coordinate stored with the pixel in the frame buffer is checked before placing a color in a pixel. If the new color is closer, the old color is replaced and the z coordinate is updated; if it is further away, the new color is discarded. This scheme is called a *z buffer* approach to *hidden surface elimination*. It adds at least 8 bits per pixel, plus the performance cost of reading and comparing before writing a pixel. The Silicon Graphics 4D series of graphics workstations uses 16 bits for the z dimension in its pixels, meaning objects are assigned a 16-bit number to show how close they are to the viewer.

The increasing number of bits per DRAM chip reduces the number of chips needed in the frame buffer, as well as the number of chips that can simultaneously transfer bits to the screen. This is why video DRAMS are so popular. As capacity increases, the serial ports of video DRAMs will have to become faster and wider to match the demands of future graphics systems.

Networks

There is an old network saying: Bandwidth problems can be cured with money. Latency problems are harder because the speed of light is fixed—you can't bribe God.

David Clark, M.I.T.

Networks are the backbone of current computer systems; a new machine without an optional network interface would be ridiculed. By connecting computers electronically, networked computers have these advantages:

- *Communication*—Information is exchanged between computers at high speeds.

- *Resource sharing*—Rather than each machine having its own I/O devices, devices can be shared by computers on the network.

- *Nonlocal access*—By connecting I/O devices over long distances, users need not be near the computer they are using.

Figure 7.21 shows the characteristics of networks. These characteristics are illustrated below with three examples.

Distance	0.01 to 10,000 kilometers
Speed	0.001 MB/sec to 100 MB/sec
Topology	Bus, ring, star, tree
Shared lines	None (point-to-point) or shared (multidrop)

FIGURE 7.21　Range of network characteristics.

The RS232 standard provides a 0.3- to 19.2-Kbits-per-second *terminal network*. A central computer connects to many terminals over slow but cheap dedicated wires. These point-to-point connections form a star from the central computer, with each terminal ranging from 10 to 100 meters in distance from the computer.

The *local area network*, or LAN, is what is commonly meant today when people mention a network, and *Ethernet* is what most people mean when they mention a LAN. (Ethernet has in fact become such a common term that it is often used as a generic term for LAN.) The Ethernet is essentially a 10,000 Kbits-per-second bus that has no central control. Messages or *packets* are sent over the Ethernet in blocks that vary from 128 bytes to 1530 bytes and take 0.1 ms and 1.5 ms to send, respectively. Since there is no central control, all nodes "listen" to see if there is a message for that node. Without a central arbiter to decide who gets the bus, a computer first listens to make sure it doesn't send a message while another message is on the network. If the network is idle the node tries to send. Of course, some other node may decide to send at the same instant. Luckily, the computer can detect any resulting collisions by listening to what is sent. (Mixed messages will sound like garbage.) To avoid repeated head-on collisions, each node whose packet was trashed backs off a random time before resending. If Ethernets do not have high utilization, this simple approach to arbitration works well. Many LANs become overloaded through poor capacity planning, and response time and throughput can degrade rapidly at higher utilization.

The success of LANs has led to multiples of them at a single site. Connecting computers to separate Ethernets becomes necessary at a certain point because there is a limit to the number of nodes that can be active on a bus if effective communication speeds are to be achieved; one limit is 1024 nodes per Ethernet. There is also a physical limit to the distance of an Ethernet, usually about 1 kilometer. To allow Ethernets to work together, two kinds of devices have been created:

- A *bridge* connects two Ethernets. There are still two independent buses that can simultaneously send messages, but the bridge acts as a filter, allowing only those messages from nodes on one bus to nodes on the other bus to cross over the bridge.

- A *gateway* typically connects several Ethernets. It receives a message, looks up the destination address in a table, and then routes the message over the appropriate network to the proper node. This *routing table* can be changed during execution to reflect the state of the networks. Some use the term *router* instead of gateway since it is closer to the function performed.

When Ethernets are connected together with gateways they form an *Internet*.

Long-haul networks cover distances of 10 to 10,000 kilometers. The first and most famous long-haul network was the ARPANET (named after its funding agency, the Advanced Research Projects Agency of the U.S. government). It transferred at 50 Kbits per second and used point-to-point dedicated lines leased from telephone companies. The host computer talked to an *interface message processor* (IMP), which communicated over the telephone lines. The IMP took information and broke it into 1-Kbit packets. At each hop the packet was stored and then forwarded to the proper IMP according to the address in the packet. The destination IMP reassembled the packets into a message and then gave it to the host. *Fragmentation and reassembly*, as it was called, was done to reduce the latency due to the *store and forward delay*. Most networks today use this *packet switched* approach, where packets are individually routed from source to destination. Figure 7.22 (page 536) summarizes the performance, distance, and costs of these various networks.

While these networks have been presented here as alternatives, a computer system is really a hierarchy of networks, as Figure 7.23 (page 536) shows. To deal with this hierarchy of networks connecting machines that communicate differently, there must be a standard software interface to handle messages. These are called *protocols*, and are typically layered to interface with different levels of software in computer systems. The overhead of these protocols can eat up a significant portion of the network bandwidth.

Just as with disks in Figure 7.6 (page 515), there is a tradeoff of latency and throughput in networks. Small messages give the lowest latency in most networks, but they also result in lower network bandwidth; similarly, a network can achieve higher bandwidth at the cost of longer latency.

Network	Performance (Kbits / sec)	Distance (km)	Cable cost	Connect to network cost	Connector to computer cost
RS232	19	0.1	$0.25 /foot	$1–$5 / connector	$5 /serial port chip
Ethernet	10,000	1.0	$1–$5 /foot	$100 / transceiver	$50 /Ethernet interface chip
Arpanet	50	10,000.0	$10,000/ month	$50,000– $100,000/ IMP	$5,000–$10,000 /IMP connection

FIGURE 7.22   The performance, maximum distance, and costs of three example networks. An Internet is simply multiple Ethernets and a bridge, which costs about $2,000 to $5,000, or a gateway, which costs about $20,000 to $50,000.

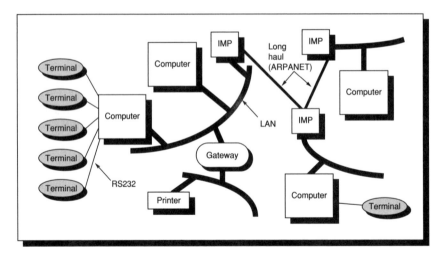

FIGURE 7.23   A computer system today participates in a hierarchy of networks. Ideally, the user is not aware of what network is being used in performing tasks. The gateway routes packets to a particular network, a network routes packets to a particular host computer, and the host computer routes packets to a particular process.

7.5 | Buses—Connecting I/O Devices to CPU/Memory

In a computer system, the various subsystems must have interfaces to one another; for instance, the memory and CPU need to communicate, as well as the CPU and I/O devices. This is commonly done with a *bus*. The bus serves as a shared communication link between the subsystems. The two major advantages of the bus organization are low cost and versatility. By defining a single interconnection scheme, new devices can easily be added, and peripherals may even be ported between computer systems that use a common bus. The cost is low, since a single set of wires is shared multiple ways.

The major disadvantage of a bus is that it creates a communication bottleneck, possibly limiting the maximum I/O throughput. When I/O must pass through a central bus this bandwidth limitation is as real as—and sometimes more severe than—memory bandwidth. In commercial systems, where I/O is very frequent, and in supercomputers, where the necessary I/O rates are very high because the CPU performance is high, designing a bus system capable of meeting the demands of the processor is a major challenge.

One reason bus design is so difficult is that the maximum bus speed is largely limited by physical factors: the length of the bus and the number of devices (and, hence, bus loading). These physical limits prevent arbitrary bus speedup. The desire for high I/O rates (low latency) and high I/O throughput can also lead to conflicting design requirements.

Buses are traditionally classified as *CPU–memory buses* or *I/O buses*. I/O buses may be lengthy, may have many types of devices connected to them, have a wide range in the data bandwidth of the devices connected to them (see Figure 7.1 on page 509), and normally follow a bus standard. CPU–memory buses, on the other hand, are short, generally high speed, and matched to the memory system to maximize memory–CPU bandwidth. During the design phase, the designer of a CPU–memory bus knows all the types of devices that must connect together, while the I/O bus designer must accept devices varying in latency and bandwidth capabilities. To lower costs, some computers have a single bus for both memory and I/O devices.

Let's consider a typical bus transaction. A *bus transaction* includes two parts: sending the address and receiving or sending the data. Bus transactions are usually defined by what they do to memory: A *read* transaction transfers data *from* memory (to either the CPU or an I/O device), and a *write* transaction writes data to the memory. In a read transaction, the address is first sent down the bus to the memory, together with the appropriate control signals indicating a read. The memory responds by returning the data on the bus with the appropriate control signals. A write transaction requires that the CPU or I/O device send both address and data and requires no return of data. Usually the CPU must wait between sending the address and receiving the data on a read, but the CPU often does not wait on writes.

The design of a bus presents several options, as Figure 7.24 (page 539) shows. Like the rest of the computer system, decisions will depend on cost and performance goals. The first three options in the figure are clear choices—separate address and data lines, wider data lines, and multiple-word transfers all give higher performance at more cost.

The next item in the table concerns the number of *bus masters*. These are devices that can initiate a read or write transaction; the CPU, for instance, is always a bus master. A bus has multiple masters when there are multiple CPUs or when I/O devices can initiate a bus transaction. If there are multiple masters, an arbitration scheme is required among the masters to decide who gets the bus next. Arbitration is often a fixed priority, as is the case with daisy-chained devices or an approximately fair scheme that randomly chooses which master gets the bus.

With multiple masters a bus can offer higher bandwidth by going to packets, as opposed to holding the bus for the full transaction. This technique is designated *split transactions*. (Some systems call this ability *connect/disconnect* or a *pipelined bus*.) The read transaction is broken into a read-request transaction that contains the address, and a memory-reply transaction that contains the data. Each transaction must now be tagged so that the CPU and memory can tell what is what. Split transactions make the bus available for other masters while the memory reads the words from the requested address. It also normally means that the CPU must arbitrate for the bus to send the data and the memory must arbitrate for the bus to return the data. Thus, a split-transaction bus has higher bandwidth, but it usually has higher latency than a bus that is held during the complete transaction.

The final item, clocking, concerns whether a bus is synchronous or asynchronous. If a bus is *synchronous* it includes a clock in the control lines and a fixed protocol for address and data relative to the clock. Since little or no logic is needed to decide what to do next, these buses can be both fast and inexpensive. However, they have two major disadvantages. Everything on the bus must run at the same clock rate, and because of clock-skew problems, synchronous buses cannot be long. CPU–memory buses are typically synchronous.

An *asynchronous* bus, on the other hand, is not clocked. Instead, self-timed, handshaking protocols are used between bus sender and receiver. This scheme makes it much easier to accommodate a wide variety of devices and to lengthen the bus without worrying about clock skew or synchronization problems. If a synchronous bus can be used, it is usually faster than an asynchronous bus because of the overhead of synchronizing the bus for each transaction. The choice of synchronous versus asynchronous bus has implications not only for data bandwidth but also for an I/O system's capacity in terms of physical distance and

Option	High performance	Low cost
Bus width	Separate address and data lines	Multiplex address and data lines
Data width	Wider is faster (e.g., 32 bits)	Narrower is cheaper (e.g., 8 bits)
Transfer size	Multiple words has less bus overhead	Single-word transfer is simpler
Bus masters	Multiple (requires arbitration)	Single master (no arbitration)
Split transaction?	Yes—separate Request and Reply packets gets higher bandwidth (needs multiple masters)	No—continuous connection is cheaper and has lower latency
Clocking	Synchronous	Asynchronous

FIGURE 7.24   The main options for a bus. The advantage of separate address and data buses is primarily on writes.

number of devices that can be connected to the bus; asynchronous buses scale better with technological changes. I/O buses are typically asynchronous. Figure 7.25 suggests the relationship of when to use one over the other.

Bus Standards

The number and variety of I/O devices are not fixed on most computer systems, permitting customers to tailor computers to their needs. As the interface to which devices are connected, the I/O bus can also be considered an expansion bus for adding I/O devices over time. Standards that let the computer designer and I/O-device designer work independently, therefore, play a large role in determining the choice of buses. As long as both the computer-system designer and the I/O-device designer meet the requirements, any I/O device can connect to any computer. In fact, an I/O bus standard is the document that defines how to connect them.

Machines sometimes grow to be so popular that their I/O buses become de facto standards; examples are the PDP-11 Unibus and the IBM PC-AT Bus. Once many I/O devices have been built for the popular machine, other computer designers will build their I/O interface so that those devices can plug into their machines as well. Sometimes standards also come from an explicit standards effort on the part of I/O device makers. The *intelligent peripheral interface* (IPI) and Ether-

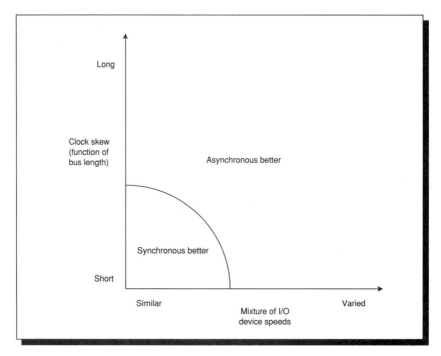

FIGURE 7.25   Preferred bus type as a function of length/clock skew and variation in I/O device speed. Synchronous is best when the distance is short and the I/O devices on the bus all transfer at similar speeds.

net are examples of standards from cooperation of manufacturers. If standards are successful, they are eventually blessed by a sanctioning body like ANSI or IEEE. Occasionally, a bus standard comes top-down directly from a standards committee—the FutureBus is one example.

Figure 7.26 summarizes characteristics of several bus standards. Note that the bandwidth entries in the figure are not listed as single numbers for the CPU–memory buses (VME, FutureBus, and Multibus II). Because of the bus overhead, the size of the transfer affects bandwidth significantly. Since the bus usually transfers to or from memory, the speed of the memory also affects the bandwidth. For example, with infinite transfer size and infinitely fast (0 ns) memory, Future-Bus is 240% faster than VME, but FutureBus is only about 20% faster than VME for single-word transfers from a 150-ns memory.

	VME bus	FutureBus	Multibus II	IPI	SCSI
Bus width (signals)	128	96	96	16	8
Address/data multiplexed?	Not multi-plexed	Multiplexed	Multiplexed	N/A	N/A
Data width (primary)	16 to 32 bits	32 bits	32 bits	16 bits	8 bits
Transfer size	Single or multiple	Single or multi-ple	Single or multiple	Single or multiple	Single or multiple
Number of bus masters	Multiple	Multiple	Multiple	Single	Multiple
Split transaction?	No	Optional	Optional	Optional	Optional
Clocking	Asynchronous	Asynchronous	Synchronous	Asynchronous	Either
Bandwidth, 0-ns access memory, single word	25.0 MB/sec	37.0 MB/sec	20.0 MB/sec	25.0 MB/sec	5.0 MB/sec or 1.5 MB/sec
Bandwidth, 150-ns access memory, single word	12.9 MB/sec	15.5 MB/sec	10.0 MB/sec	25.0 MB/sec	5.0 MB/sec or 1.5 MB/sec
Bandwidth, 0-ns access memory, multiple words (infinite block length)	27.9 MB/sec	95.2 MB/sec	40.0 MB/sec	25.0 MB/sec	5.0 MB/sec or 1.5 MB/sec
Bandwidth, 150-ns access memory, multiple words (infinite block length)	13.6 MB/sec	20.8 MB/sec	13.3 MB/sec	25.0 MB/sec	5.0 MB/sec or 1.5 MB/sec
Maximum number of devices	21	20	21	8	7
Maximum bus length	0.5 meter	0.5 meter	0.5 meter	50 meters	25 meters
Standard	IEEE 1014	IEEE 896.1	ANSI/IEEE 1296	ANSI X3.129	ANSI X3.131

FIGURE 7.26 Information on five bus standards. The first three were defined originally as CPU–memory buses and the last two as I/O buses. For the CPU–memory buses the bandwidth calculations assume a fully loaded bus and are given for both single-word transfers and block transfers of unlimited length; measurements are shown both ignoring memory latency and assuming 150-ns access time. Bandwidth assumes the average distance of a transfer is one-third of the backplane length. (Data in the first three columns is from Borrill [1986].) The bandwidth for the I/O buses is given as their maximum data-transfer rate. The SCSI standard offers either asynchronous or synchronous I/O; the asynchronous version transfers at 1.5 MB/sec and the synchronous at 5 MB/sec.

7.6 | Interfacing to the CPU

Having described I/O devices and looked at some of the issues of the connecting bus, we are ready to discuss the CPU end of the interface. The first question is how the physical connection of the I/O bus should be made. The two choices are connecting it to memory or to the cache. In the following section we will discuss the pros and cons of connecting an I/O bus directly to the cache; in this section we examine the more usual case in which the I/O bus is connected to the main memory bus. Figure 7.27 shows a typical organization. In low-cost systems, the I/O bus **is** the memory bus; this means an I/O command on the bus could interfere with a CPU instruction fetch, for example.

Once the physical interface is chosen, the question becomes how does the CPU address an I/O device that it needs to send or receive data. The most common practice is called *memory-mapped* I/O. In this scheme, portions of the address space are assigned to I/O devices. Reads and writes to those addresses may cause data to be transferred; some portion of the I/O space may also be set aside for device control, so commands to the device are just accesses to those memory-mapped addresses. The alternative practice is to use dedicated I/O opcodes in the CPU. In this case, the CPU sends a signal that this address is for I/O devices. Examples of computers with I/O instructions are the Intel 80x86 and the IBM 370 computers. No matter which addressing scheme is selected, each I/O device has registers to provide status and control information. Either through loads and stores

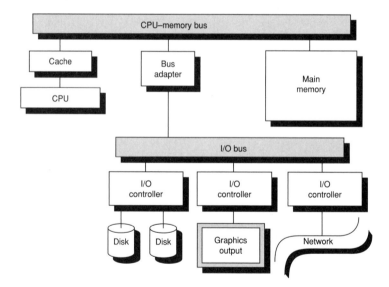

FIGURE 7.27   A typical interface of I/O devices and an I/O bus to the CPU–memory bus.

in memory-mapped I/O or through special instructions, the CPU sets flags to determine the operation the I/O device will perform.

I/O is rarely a single operation. For example, the DEC LP11 line printer has two I/O device registers: one for status information and one for data to be printed. The status register contains a *done bit*, set by the printer when it has printed a character, and an *error bit*, indicating that the printer is jammed or out of paper. Each byte of data to be printed is put into the data register; the CPU must then wait until the printer sets the done bit before it can place another character in the buffer.

This simple interface, in which the CPU periodically checks status bits to see if it is time for the next I/O operation, is called *polling*. As one might expect, the fact that CPUs are so much faster than I/O devices means polling may waste a lot of CPU time. This was recognized long ago, leading to the invention of interrupts to notify the CPU when it is time to do something for the I/O device. *Interrupt-driven* I/O, used by most systems for at least some devices, allows the CPU to work on some other process while waiting on the I/O device. For example, the LP11 has a mode that allows it to interrupt the CPU whenever the done bit or error bit is set. In general-purpose applications, interrupt driven I/O is the key to multitasking operating systems and good response times.

The drawback to interrupts is the operating system overhead on each event. In real-time applications with hundreds of I/O events per second, this overhead can be intolerable. One hybrid solution for real-time systems is to use a clock to periodically interrupt the CPU, at which time the CPU polls all I/O devices.

Delegating I/O Responsibility from the CPU

Interrupt-driven I/O relieves the CPU from waiting for every I/O event, but there are still many CPU cycles spent in transferring data. Transferring a disk block of 2048 words, for instance, would require at least 2048 loads and 2048 stores, as well as the overhead for the interrupt. Since I/O events so often involve block transfers, *direct memory access* (DMA) hardware is added to many computer systems to allow transfers of numbers of words without intervention by the CPU.

DMA is a specialized processor that transfers data between memory and an I/O device, while the CPU goes on with other tasks. Thus, it is external to the CPU and must act as a master on the bus. The CPU first sets up the DMA registers, which contain a memory address and number of bytes to be transferred. Once the DMA transfer is complete, the controller interrupts the CPU. There may be multiple DMA devices in a computer system; for example, DMA is frequently part of the controller for an I/O device.

Increasing the intelligence of the DMA device can further unburden the CPU. Devices called *I/O processors*, (or *I/O controllers*, or *channel controllers*) operate from either fixed programs or from programs downloaded by the operating system. The operating system typically sets up a queue of *I/O control blocks* that contain information such as data location (source and destination) and data size. The I/O processor then takes items from the queue, doing everything requested and sending a single interrupt when the task specified in the I/O control blocks is complete. Whereas the LP11 line printer would cause 4800 interrupts to print a 60-line by 80-character page, an I/O processor could save 4799 of those interrupts.

I/O processors can be compared to multiprocessors in that they facilitate several processes executing simultaneously in the computer system. I/O processors are less general than CPUs, however, since they have dedicated tasks, and thus parallelism is also much more limited. Also, an I/O processor doesn't normally change information, as a CPU does, but just moves information from one place to another.

7.7 | Interfacing to an Operating System

In a manner analogous to the way compilers use an instruction set (see Section 3.7 of Chapter 3), operating systems control what I/O techniques implemented by the hardware will actually be used. For example, many I/O controllers used in early UNIX systems were 16-bit microprocessors. To avoid problems with 16-bit addresses in controllers, UNIX was changed to limit the maximum I/O transfer to 63 KB or less; at the time of this book's publication, that limit is still in effect. Thus, a new I/O controller designed to efficiently transfer 1-MB files would never see more than 63 KB at a time under UNIX, no matter how large the files.

Caches Cause Problems for Operating Systems—Stale Data

The prevalence of caches in computer systems has added to the responsibilities of the operating system. Caches imply the possibility of two copies of the data—one each for cache and main memory—while virtual memory can result in three copies—for cache, memory and disk. This brings up the possibility of *stale data*: the CPU or I/O system could modify one copy without updating the other copies (see Section 8.8 in Chapter 8). Either the operating system or the hardware must make sure that the CPU reads the most recently input data and that I/O outputs the correct data, in the presence of caches and virtual memory. Whether the stale-data problem arises depends in part on where the I/O is connected to the computer. If it is connected to the CPU cache, as shown in Figure 7.28 (page 545), there is no stale-data problem; all I/O devices and the CPU see the most accurate version in the cache, and existing mechanisms in the memory hierarchy ensure that other copies of the data will be updated. The side effect is lost CPU performance, since I/O will replace blocks in the cache with data that are unlikely to be needed by the process running in the CPU at the time of the transfer. In other words, all I/O data goes through the cache but little of it is referenced. This arrangement also requires arbitration between CPU and I/O to decide who accesses the cache. If I/O is connected to memory, as in Figure 7.27 (page 542), then it doesn't interfere with CPU, provided the CPU has a cache. In this situation, however, the stale-data problem occurs. Alternatively, I/O can just invalidate data—either all data that might match (no tag check) or only data that matches.

There are two parts to the stale-data problem:

1. The I/O system sees stale data on output because memory is not up to date.

2 The CPU sees stale data in the cache on input after the I/O system has updated memory.

The first dilemma is how to output correct data if there is a cache and I/O is connected to memory. A write-through cache solves this by ensuring that memory will have the same data as the cache. A write-back cache requires the operating system to flush output addresses to make sure they are not in the cache. This takes time, even if the data is not in the cache, since address checks are sequential. Alternatively, the hardware can check cache tags during output to see if they are in a write-back cache, and only interact with the cache if the output tries to read data that is in the cache.

The second problem is ensuring that the cache won't have stale data after input. The operating system can guarantee that the input data area can't possibly be

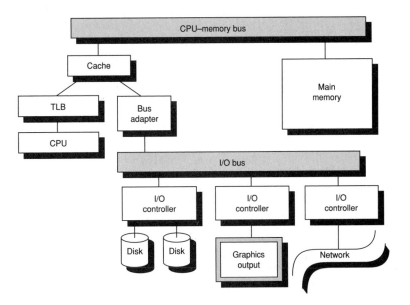

FIGURE 7.28   Example of I/O connected directly to the cache.

in the cache. If it can't guarantee this, the operating system flushes input addresses to make sure they are not in the cache. Again, this takes time, whether or not the input addresses are in the cache. As before, extra hardware can be added to check tags during an input and invalidate the data if there is a conflict. These problems are basically the same as cache coherency in a multiprocessor, discussed in Section 8.8 of Chapter 8; I/O can be thought of as a second dedicated processor in a multiprocessor.

DMA and Virtual Memory

Given the use of virtual memory, there is the matter of whether DMA should transfer using virtual addresses or physical addresses. Here are some problems with DMA using physically mapped I/O:

- Transferring a buffer that is larger than one page will cause problems, since the pages in the buffer will not usually be mapped to sequential pages in physical memory.

- Suppose DMA is ongoing between memory and a frame buffer, and the operating system removes some of the pages from memory (or relocates them). The DMA would then be transferring data to or from the wrong page of memory.

One answer to these questions is *virtual DMA*. It allows the DMA to use virtual addresses that are mapped to physical addresses during the DMA. Thus, a buffer must be sequential in virtual memory but the pages can be scattered in physical memory. The operating system could update the address tables of a DMA if a process is moved using virtual DMA, or the operating system could "lock" the pages in memory until the DMA is complete. Figure 7.29 (page 547) shows address-translation registers added to the DMA device.

Caches Helping Operating Systems— File or Disk Caches

While the invention of caches made the life of the operating systems designer more difficult, operating systems designers' concern for performance led them to cache-like optimizations, using main memory as a "cache" for disk traffic to improve I/O performance. The impact of using main memory as a buffer or cache for file or disk accesses is demonstrated in Figure 7.30 (page 547). It shows the change in disk I/Os for a cacheless system measured as miss rate (see Section 8.2 in Chapter 8). File caches or disk caches change the number of disk I/Os and the mix of reads and writes; depending on cache size and write policy, between 50% to 70% of all disk accesses could become writes with such caches. Without file or disk caches, between 15% and 33% of all accesses are writes, depending on the environment.

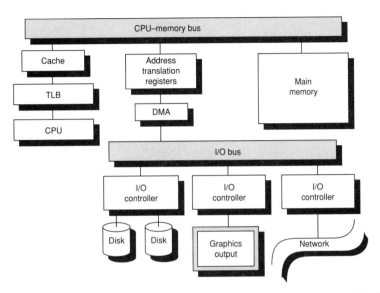

FIGURE 7.29   Virtual DMA requires a register for each page to be transferred in the DMA controller, showing the protection bits and the physical page corresponding to each virtual page.

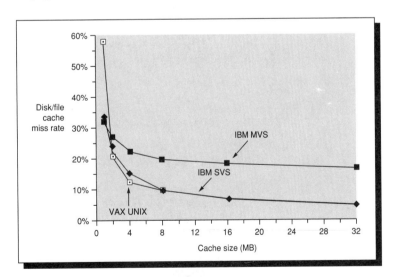

FIGURE 7.30   The effectiveness of a file cache or disk cache on reducing disk I/Os versus cache size. Ousterhout et al. [1985] collected the VAX UNIX data on VAX-11/785s with 8 MB to 16 MB of main memory, running 4.2 BSD UNIX using a 16-KB block size. Smith [1985] collected the IBM SVS and IBM MVS traces on IBM 370/168 using a one-track block size (which varied from 7294 bytes to 19254 bytes, depending on the disk). The difference between a file cache and a disk cache is that the file cache uses logical block numbers while a disk cache uses addresses that have been mapped to the physical sector and track on a disk. This difference is similar to the difference between a virtually addressed and a physically addressed cache (see Section 8.8 in Chapter 8).

7.8 | Designing an I/O System

The art of I/O is finding a design that meets goals for cost and variety of devices while avoiding bottlenecks to I/O performance. This means that components must be balanced between main memory and the I/O device because performance—and hence effective cost/performance—can only be as good as the weakest link in the I/O chain. The architect must also plan for expansion so that customers can tailor the I/O to their applications. This expansibility, both in numbers and types of I/O devices, has its costs in longer backplanes, larger power supplies to support I/O devices, and larger cabinets.

In designing an I/O system, analyze performance, cost, and capacity using varying I/O connection schemes and different numbers of I/O devices of each type. Here is a series of six steps to follow in designing an I/O system. The answers in each step may be dictated by market requirements or simply by cost/performance goals.

1. List the different types of I/O devices to be connected to the machine, or a list of standard buses that the machine will support.

2. List the physical requirements for each I/O device. This includes volume, power, connectors, bus slots, expansion cabinets, and so on.

3. List the cost of each I/O device, including the portion of cost of any controller needed for this device.

4. Record the CPU resource demands of each I/O device. This should include:

   Clock cycles for instructions used to initiate an I/O, to support operation of an I/O device (such as handling interrupts), and complete I/O

   CPU clock stalls due to waiting for I/O to finish using the memory, bus, or cache

   CPU clock cycles to recover from an I/O activity, such as a cache flush

5. List the memory and I/O bus resource demands of each I/O device. Even when the CPU is not using memory, the bandwidth of main memory and the I/O bus are limited.

6. The final step is establishing performance of the different ways to organize these I/O devices. Performance can only be properly evaluated with simulation, though it may be estimated using queuing theory.

You then select the best organization, given your performance and cost goals.

Cost and performance goals affect the selection of the I/O scheme and physical design. Performance can be measured either as megabytes per second or I/Os per second, depending on the needs of the application. For high performance, the only limits should be speed of I/O devices, number of I/O devices, and speed of memory and CPU. For low cost, the only expenses should be those for the I/O devices themselves and for cabling to the CPU. Cost/performance design, of course, tries for the best of both worlds.

To make these ideas clearer, let's go through several examples.

Example

First, let's look at the impact on the CPU of reading a disk page directly into the cache. Make the following assumptions:

Each page is 8 KB and the cache-block size is 16 bytes.

The addresses corresponding to the new page are **not** in the cache.

The CPU will not access any of the data in the new page.

90% of the blocks that were displaced from the cache will be read in again, and each will cause a miss.

The cache uses write back, and 50% of the blocks are dirty on average.

The I/O system buffers a full cache block before writing to the cache (this is called a *speed-matching buffer*, matching transfer bandwidth of the I/O system and memory).

The accesses and misses are spread uniformly to all cache blocks.

There is no other interference between the CPU and I/O for the cache slots.

There are 15,000 misses every one million clock cycles when there is **no** I/O.

The miss penalty is 15 clock cycles, plus 15 more cycles to write the block if it was dirty.

Assuming one page is brought in every one million clock cycles, what is the impact on performance?

Answer

Each page fills 8192/16 or 512 blocks. I/O transfers do not cause cache misses on their own because entire cache blocks are transferred. However, they do displace blocks already in the cache. If half of the displaced blocks are dirty it takes 256*15 clock cycles to write them back to memory. There are also misses from 90% of the blocks displaced in the cache because they are referenced later, adding another 90%*512, or 461 misses. Since this data was placed into the cache from the I/O system, all these blocks are dirty and will need to be written back when replaced. Thus, the total is 256*15 + 461*30 more clock cycles than the original 1,000,000 + 15,000*15. This turns into a 1% decrease in performance:

$$\frac{256 * 15 + 461 * 30}{1000000 + 15000 * 15} = \frac{17670}{1225000} = 0.014$$

Now let's look at the cost/performance of different I/O organizations. A simple way to perform this analysis is to look at maximum throughput assuming that resources can be used at 100% of their maximum rate without side effects from interference. A later example takes a more realistic view.

Example

Given the following performance and cost information:

a 50-MIPS CPU costing $50,000

an 8-byte-wide memory with a 200-ns cycle time

80 MB/sec I/O bus with room for 20 SCSI buses and controllers

SCSI buses that can transfer 4 MB/sec and support up to 7 disks per bus (these are also called SCSI *strings*)

a $2500 SCSI controller that adds 2 milliseconds (ms) of overhead to perform a disk I/O

an operating system that uses 10,000 CPU instructions for a disk I/O

a choice of a large disk containing 4 GB or a small disk containing 1 GB, each costing $3 per MB

both disks rotate at 3600 RPM, have a 12-ms average seek time, and can transfer 2MB/sec

the storage capacity must be 100 GB, and

the average I/O size is 8 KB

Evaluate the cost per I/O per second (IOPS) of using small or large drives. Assume that every disk I/O requires an average seek and average rotational delay. Use the optimistic assumption that all devices can be used at 100% of capacity and that the workload is evenly divided between all disks.

Answer

I/O performance is limited by the weakest link in the chain, so we evaluate the maximum performance of each link in the I/O chain for each organization to determine the maximum performance of that organization.

Let's start by calculating the maximum number of IOPS for the CPU, main memory, and I/O bus. The CPU I/O performance is determined by the speed of the CPU and the number of instructions to perform a disk I/O:

$$\text{Maximum IOPS for CPU} = \frac{50 \text{ MIPS}}{10000 \text{ instructions per I/O}} = 5000$$

The maximum performance of the memory system is determined by the memory cycle time, the width of the memory, and the size of the I/O transfers:

$$\text{Maximum IOPS for main memory} = \frac{(1/200 \text{ ns}) * 8}{8 \text{ KB per I/O}} \approx 5000$$

The I/O bus maximum performance is limited by the bus bandwidth and the size of the I/O:

$$\text{Maximum IOPS for the I/O bus} = \frac{80 \text{ MB/sec}}{8 \text{ KB per I/O}} \approx 10000$$

Thus, no matter which disk is selected, the CPU and main memory limits the maximum performance to no more than 5000 IOPS.

Now its time to look at the performance of the next link in the I/O chain, the SCSI controllers. The time to transfer 8 KB over the SCSI bus is

$$\text{SCSI bus transfer time} = \frac{8 \text{ KB}}{4 \text{ MB/sec}} = 2 \text{ ms}$$

Adding the 2-ms SCSI controller overhead means 4 ms per I/O, making the maximum rate per controller

$$\text{Maximum IOPS per SCSI controller} = \frac{1}{4 \text{ ms}} = 250 \text{ IOPS}$$

All the organizations will use several controllers, so 250 IOPS is not the limit for the whole system.

The final link in the chain is the disks themselves. The time for an average disk I/O is

$$\text{I/O time} = 12 \text{ ms} + \frac{0.5}{3600 \text{ RPM}} + \frac{8 \text{ KB}}{2 \text{ MB/sec}} = 12 + 8.3 + 4 = 24.3 \text{ ms}$$

so the disk performance is

$$\text{Maximum IOPS (using average seeks) per disk} = \frac{1}{24.3 \text{ ms}} \approx 41 \text{ IOPS}$$

The number of disks in each organization depends on the size of each disk: 100 GB can be either 25 4-GB disks or 100 1-GB disks. The maximum number of I/Os for all the disks is:

$$\text{Maximum IOPS for 25 4-GB disks} = 25 * 41 = 1025$$

$$\text{Maximum IOPS for 100 1-GB disks} = 100 * 41 = 4100$$

Thus, provided there are enough SCSI strings, the disks become the new limit to maximum performance: 1025 IOPS for the 4-GB disks and 4100 for the 1-GB disks.

While we have determined the performance of each link of the I/O chain, we still have to determine how many SCSI buses and controllers to use and how many disks to connect to each controller, as this may further limit maximum performance. The I/O bus is limited to 20 SCSI controllers and the SCSI standard limits disks to 7 per SCSI string. The minimum number of controllers is for the 4-GB disks

$$\text{Minimum number of SCSI strings for 25 4-GB disks} = \frac{25}{7} \text{ or } 4$$

and for 1-GB disks

$$\text{Minimum number of SCSI strings for 100 1-GB disks} = \frac{100}{7} \text{ or } 15$$

We can calculate the maximum IOPS for each configuration:

$$\text{Maximum IOPS for 4 SCSI strings} = 4 * 250 = 1000 \text{ IOPS}$$

$$\text{Maximum IOPS for 15 SCSI strings} = 15 * 250 = 3750 \text{ IOPS}$$

The maximum performance of this number of controllers is slightly lower than the disk I/O throughput, so let's also calculate the number of controllers so they don't become a bottleneck. One way is to find the number of disks they can support per string:

$$\text{Number of disks per SCSI string at full bandwidth} = \frac{250}{41} = 6.1 \text{ or } 6$$

and then calculate the number of strings:

$$\text{Number of SCSI strings for full bandwidth 4-GB disks} = \frac{25}{6} = 4.1 \text{ or } 5$$

$$\text{Number of SCSI strings for full bandwidth 1-GB disks} = \frac{100}{6} = 16.7 \text{ or } 17$$

This establishes the performance of four organizations: 25 4-GB disks with 4 or 5 SCSI strings and 100 1-GB disks with 15 to 17 SCSI strings. The maximum performance of each option is limited by the bottleneck (in boldface):

4-GB disks, 4 strings   = Min(5000,5000,10000,1025,**1000**) = 1000 IOPS

4-GB disks, 5 strings   = Min(5000,5000,10000,**1025**,1250) = 1025 IOPS

1-GB disks, 15 strings = Min(5000,5000,10000,4100,**3750**) = 3750 IOPS

1-GB disks, 17 strings = Min(5000,5000,10000,**4100**,4250) = 4100 IOPS

We can now calculate the cost for each organization:

4-GB disks, 4 strings   = $50,000 + 4*$2,500 + 25 * (4096*$3)   = $367,200

4-GB disks, 5 strings   = $50,000 + 5*$2,500 + 25 * (4096*$3)   = $369,700

1-GB disks, 15 strings = $50,000 + 15*$2,500 + 100 * (1024*$3) = $394,700

1-GB disks, 17 strings = $50,000 + 17*$2,500 + 100 * (1024*$3) = $399,700

Finally, the cost per IOPS for each of the four configurations is $367, $361, $105, and $97, respectively. Calculating maximum number of average I/Os per second assuming 100% utilization of the critical resources, the best cost/performance is the organization with the small disks and the largest number of controllers. The small disks have 3.4 to 3.8 times better cost/performance than the large disks in this example. The only drawback is that the larger number of disks will affect system availability unless some form of redundancy is added (see pages 520–521).

This above example assumed that resources can be used 100%. It is instructive to see what is the bottleneck in each organization.

Example

For the organizations in the last example, calculate the percentage of utilization of each resource in the computer system.

Answer

Figure 7.31 gives the answer.

Resource	4-GB disks, 4 strings	4-GB disks, 5 strings	1-GB disks, 15 strings	1-GB disks, 17 strings
CPU	20%	21%	75%	82%
Memory	20%	21%	75%	82%
I/O bus	10%	10%	38%	41%
SCSI buses	100%	82%	100%	96%
Disks	98%	100%	91%	100%

FIGURE 7.31 The percentage of utilization of each resource given the four organizations in the previous example. Either the SCSI buses or the disks are the bottleneck.

In reality buses cannot deliver close to 100% of bandwidth without severe increase in latency and reduction in throughput due to contention. A variety of rules of thumb have been evolved to guide I/O designs:

No I/O bus should be utilized more than 75% to 80%;

No disk string should be utilized more than 40%;

No disk arm should be seeking more than 60% of the time.

Example

Recalculate performance in the example above using these rules of thumb, and show the utilization of each component. Are there other organizations that follow these guidelines and improve performance?

Answer

Figure 7.31 shows that the I/O bus is far below the suggested guidelines, so we concentrate on the utilization of seek and SCSI bus. The utilization of seek time per disk is

$$\frac{\text{Time of average seek}}{\text{Time between I/Os}} = \frac{12}{\dfrac{1}{41 \text{ IOPS}}} = \frac{12}{24} = 50\%$$

which is below the rule of thumb. The biggest impact is on the SCSI bus:

$$\text{Suggested IOPS per SCSI string} = \frac{1}{4 \text{ ms}} * 40\% = 100 \text{ IOPS}.$$

With this data we can recalculate IOPS for each organization:

4-GB disks, 4 strings   = Min(5000,5000,7500,1025,**400**)   = 400 IOPS

4-GB disks, 5 strings   = Min(5000,5000,7500,1025,**500**)   = 500 IOPS

1-GB disks, 15 strings = Min(5000,5000,7500,4100,**1500**) = 1500 IOPS

1-GB disks, 17 strings = Min(5000,5000,7500,4100,**1700**) = 1700 IOPS

Under these assumptions, the small disks have about 3.0 to 4.2 times the performance of the large disks.

Clearly, the string bandwidth is the bottleneck now. The number of disks per string that would not exceed the guideline is

$$\text{Number of disks per SCSI string at full bandwidth} = \frac{100}{41} = 2.4 \text{ or } 2$$

and the ideal number of strings is

$$\text{Number of SCSI strings for full bandwidth 4-GB disks} = \frac{25}{2} = 12.5 \text{ or } 13$$

$$\text{Number of SCSI strings for full bandwidth 1-GB disks} = \frac{100}{2} = 50$$

This suggestion is fine for 4-GB disks, but the I/O bus is limited to 20 SCSI controllers and strings so that becomes the limit for 1-GB disks:

4-GB disks, 13 strings = Min(5000,5000,7500,**1025**,1300) =1025 IOPS

1-GB disks, 20 strings = Min(5000,5000,7500,4100,**2000**) =2000 IOPS

We can now calculate the cost for each organization:

4-GB disks, 13 strings = $50,000 + 13*$2,500 + 25 * (4096*$3) = $389,700

1-GB disks, 20 strings = $50,000 + 20*$2,500 + 100 * (1024*$3) = $407,200

In this case the small disks cost 5% more yet have about twice the performance of the large disks. The utilization of each resource is shown in Figure 7.25 (page 540). It shows that following the rule of thumb of 40% string utilization sets the performance limit in all but one case.

Resource	4-GB disks, 4 strings	4-GB disks, 5 strings	1-GB disks, 15 strings	1-GB disks, 17 strings	4-GB disks, 13 strings	1-GB disks, 20 strings
CPU	8%	10%	30%	34%	21%	40%
Memory	8%	10%	30%	34%	21%	40%
I/O bus	5%	7%	20%	23%	14%	27%
SCSI buses	40%	40%	40%	40%	32%	40%
Disks	39%	49%	37%	41%	100%	49%
Seek utilization	19%	24%	18%	20%	49%	24%
IOPS	400	500	1500	1700	1025	2000

FIGURE 7.32 The percentage of utilization of each resource given the six organizations in this example, which tries to limit utilization of key resources to the rules of thumb given above.

7.9 | Putting It All Together: The IBM 3990 Storage Subsystem

If computer architects were polled to select the leading company in I/O design, IBM would win hands down. A good deal of IBM's mainframe business is commercial applications, known to be I/O intensive. While there are graphic devices and networks that can be connected to an IBM mainframe, IBM's reputation comes from disk performance. It is on this aspect that we concentrate in this section.

The IBM 360/370 I/O architecture has evolved over a period of 25 years. Initially, the I/O system was general purpose, and no special attention was paid to any particular device. As it became clear that magnetic disks were the chief consumers of I/O, the IBM 360 was tailored to support fast disk I/O. IBM's dominant philosophy is to choose latency over throughput whenever it makes a difference. IBM almost never uses a large buffer outside the CPU; their goal is to set up a clear path from main memory to the I/O device so that when a device is ready, nothing can get in the way. Perhaps IBM followed a corollary to the quote on page 526: you can buy bandwidth, but you need to design for latency. As a secondary philosophy, the CPU is unburdened as much as possible to allow the CPU to continue with computation while others perform the desired I/O activities.

The example for this section is the high-end IBM 3090 CPU and the 3990 Storage Subsystem. The IBM 3090, models 3090/100 to 3090/600, can contain one to six CPUs. This 18.5-ns-clock-cycle machine has a 16-way interleaved memory that can transfer eight bytes every clock cycle on each of two (3090/100) or four (3090/600) buses. Each 3090 processor has a 64-KB, 4-way–set-associative, write-back cache, and the cache supports pipelined access taking two cycles. Each CPU is rated about 30 IBM MIPS (see page 78), giving at most 180 MIPS to the IBM 3090/600. Surveys of IBM mainframe installations suggest a rule of thumb of about 4 GB of disk storage per MIPS of CPU power (see Section 7.12).

It is only fair warning to say that IBM terminology may not be self-evident, although the ideas are not difficult. Remember that this I/O architecture has evolved since 1964. While there may well be ideas that IBM wouldn't include if they were to start anew, they are able to make this scheme work, and make it work well.

The 3990 I/O Subsystem Data-Transfer Hierarchy and Control Hierarchy

The I/O subsystem is divided into two hierarchies:

1. Control—This hierarchy of controllers negotiates a path through a maze of possible connections between the memory and the I/O device and controls the timing of the transfer.

2. Data—This hierarchy of connections is the path over which data flows between memory and the I/O device.

After going over each of the hierarchies, we trace a disk read to help understand the function of each component.

For simplicity, we begin by discussing the data-transfer hierarchy, shown in Figure 7.33 (page 557). This figure shows one section of the hierarchy that contains up to 64 large IBM disks; using 64 of the recently announced IBM 3390 disks, this piece could connect to over one trillion bytes of storage! Yet this piece represents only one-sixth of the capacity of the IBM 3090/600 CPU. This ability to expand from a small I/O system to hundreds of disks and terabytes of storage is what gives IBM mainframes their reputation in the I/O world.

The best-known member of the data hierarchy is the *channel*. The channel is nothing more than 50 wires that connect two levels on the I/O hierarchy together. Only 18 of the 50 wires are used for transferring data (8 data plus 1 parity in each direction), while the rest are for control information. For years the maximum data rate was 3 MB per second, but it recently was raised to 4.5 MB per second. Up to 48 channels can be connected to a 3090/100 CPU, and up to 96 channels to a

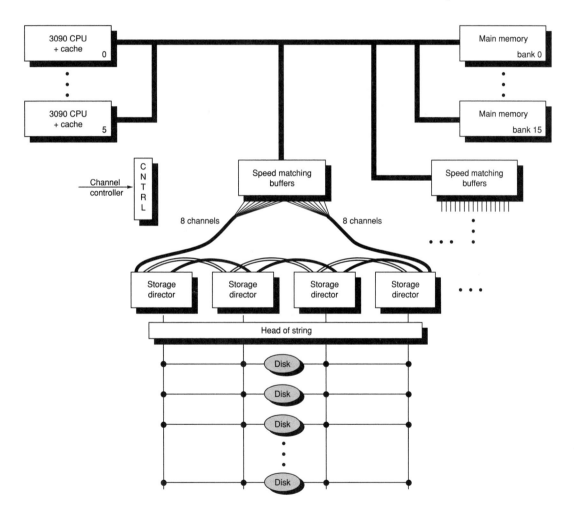

FIGURE 7.33   The data-transfer hierarchy in the IBM 3990 I/O Subsystem. Note that all the channels are connected to all the storage directors. The disks at the bottom represent the quad-ported IBM 3380 disk drives, with the maximum of 64 disks. The collection of disks on the same path to the head-of-string controller is called a *string* .

3090/600. Because they are "multiprogrammed," channels can actually service several disks. For historical reasons, IBM calls this *block multiplexing*.

Channels are connected to the 3090 main memory via two *speed-matching buffers*, which funnel all the channels into a single port to main memory. Such buffers simply match the bandwidth of the I/O device to the bandwidth of the memory system. There are two 8-byte buffers per channel.

The next level down the data hierarchy is the *storage director*. This is an intermediary device that allows the many channels to talk to many different I/O devices. Four to sixteen channels go to the storage director depending on the model, and two or four paths come out the bottom to the disks. These are called *two-path strings* or *four-path strings* in IBM parlance. Thus, each storage director can talk to any of the disks using one of the strings. At the top of each string is the *head of string*, and all communication between disks and control units must pass through it.

At the bottom of the datapath hierarchy are the disk devices themselves. To increase availability, disk devices like the IBM 3380 provide four paths to connect to the storage director; if one path fails, the device can still be connected.

The redundant paths from main memory to the I/O device not only improve availability, but also can improve performance. Since the IBM philosophy is to avoid large buffers, the path from the I/O device to main memory must remain connected until the transfer is complete. If there were a single hierarchical path from devices to the speed-matching buffer, only one I/O device in a subtree could transfer at a time. Instead, the multiple paths allow multiple devices to transfer simultaneously through the storage director and into memory.

The task of setting up the datapath connection is that of the control hierarchy. Figure 7.34 shows both the control and data hierarchies of the 3990 I/O subsystem. The new device is the I/O processor. The 3090 channel controller and I/O processor are load/store machines similar to DLX, except that there is no memory hierarchy. In the next subsection we see how the two hierarchies work together to read a disk sector.

Tracing a Disk Read in the IBM 3990 I/O Subsystem

The 12 steps below trace a sector read from an IBM 3380 disk. Each of the 12 steps is labeled on a drawing of the full hierarchy in Figure 7.34 (page 559).

1. The user sets up a data structure in memory containing the operations that should occur during this I/O event. This data structure is termed an *I/O control block*, or IOCB, which also points to a list of channel control words (CCWs). This list is called a *channel program*. Normally, the operating system provides the channel program, but some users write their own. The operating system checks the IOCB for protection violations before the I/O can continue.

2. The CPU executes a START SUBCHANNEL instruction. The actual request is defined in the channel program. A channel program to read a record might look like Figure 7.35.

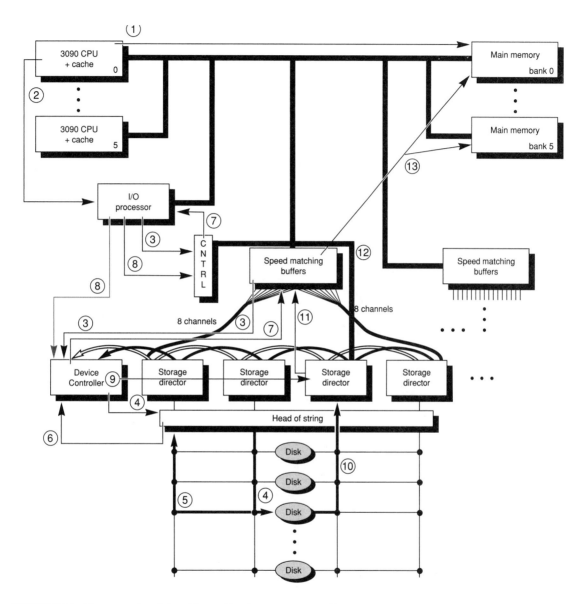

FIGURE 7.34 The control and data hierarchies in the IBM 3990 I/O subsystem labeled with the 12 steps to read a sector from disk. The only new box over Figure 7.33 (page 557) is the I/O processor.

Location	CCW	Comment
CCW1:	Define Extent	Transfers a 16-byte parameter to the storage director. The channel sees this as a write data transfer.
CCW2:	Locate Record	Transfers a 16-byte parameter to the storage director as above. The parameter identifies the operation (read in this case) plus seek, sector number, and record ID. The channel again sees this as a write data transfer.
CCW3:	Read Data	Transfers the desired disk data to the channel and then to the main memory.

FIGURE 7.35 A channel program to perform a disk read, consisting of three channel command words (CCWs). The operating system checks for virtual memory access violations of CCWs by simulating them to check for violations. These instructions are linked so that only one START SUBCHANNEL instruction is needed.

3. The I/O processor uses the control wires of one of the channels to tell the storage director which disk is to be accessed and the disk address to be read. The channel is then released.

4. The storage director sends a SEEK command to the head-of-string controller and the head-of-string controller connects to the desired disk, telling it to seek to the appropriate track, and then disconnects. The disconnect occurs between CCW2 and CCW3 in Figure 7.35.

Upon completion of these first four steps of the read, the arm on the disk seeks the correct track on the correct IBM 3380 disk drive. Other I/O operations can use the control and data hierarchy while this disk is seeking and the data is rotating under the read head. The I/O processor thus acts like a multiprogrammed system, working on other requests while waiting for an I/O event to complete.

An interesting question arises: When there are multiple uses for a single disk, what prevents another seek from screwing up the works before the original request can continue with the I/O event in progress? The answer is the disk appears busy to the programs in the 3090 between the time a Start SubChannel instruction starts a channel program (step 2) and the end of that channel program. An attempt to execute another Start SubChannel instruction would receive busy status from the channel or from the disk device.

After both the seek completes and the disk rotates to the desired point relative to the read head, the disk reconnects to a channel. To determine the rotational position of the 3380 disk, IBM provides rotational positional sensing (RPS), a feature that gives early warning when the data will rotate under the read head. IBM essentially extends the seek time to include some of the rotation time, thereby tying up the datapath as little as possible. Then the I/O can continue:

5. When the disk completes the seek and rotates to the correct position, it contacts the head-of-string controller.

6. The head-of-string controller looks for a free storage director to send the signal that the disk is on the right track.

7. The storage director looks for a free channel so that it can use the control wires to tell the I/O processor that the disk is on the right track.

8. The I/O processor simultaneously contacts the storage director and I/O device (the IBM 3380 disk) to give the OK to transfer data, and tells the channel controller where to put the information in main memory when it arrives at the channel.

There is now a direct path between the I/O device and memory and the transfer can begin:

9. When the disk is ready to transfer, it sends the data at 3 megabytes per second over a bit-serial line to the storage director.

10. The storage director collects 16 bytes in one of two buffers and sends the information on to the channel controller.

11. The channel controller has a pair of 16-byte buffers per storage director and sends 16 bytes over a 3-MB or 4.5-MB per second, 8-bit-wide datapath to the speed-matching buffers.

12. The speed-matching buffers take the information coming in from all channels. There are two 8-byte buffers per channel that send 8 bytes at a time to the appropriate locations in main memory.

Since nothing is free in computer design, one might expect there to be a cost in anticipating the rotational delay using RPS. Sometimes a free path cannot be established in the time available due to other I/O activity, resulting in an *RPS miss*. An RPS miss means the 3990 I/O Subsystem must either:

■ Wait another full rotation—16.7 ms—before the data is back under the head, or

■ Break down the hierarchical datapath and start all over again!

Lots of RPS misses can ruin response times.

As mentioned above, the IBM I/O system evolved over many years, and Figure 7.36 shows the change in response time for a few of those changes. The first improvement concerns the path for data after reconnection. Before the System/370-XA, the data path through the channels and storage director (steps 5 through 12) had to be the same as the path taken to request the seek (steps 1 through 4). The 370-XA allows the path after reconnection to be different, and this option is called *dynamic path reconnection* (DPR). This change reduced the time waiting for the channel path and the time waiting for disks (queueing delay), yielding a reduction in the total average response time of 17%. The second change in Figure

7.36 involved a new disk design. Improvements to the microcode control of the 3380D made slight improvements in seek time plus removed a restriction that disk arms that were on the same internal path were prevented from operating at the same time. IBM calls this option *Device Level Select* (DLS). This change reduced internal path delays to 0. This had little impact since there was not much time waiting on internal delays because customers intentionally placed data on disks trying to avoid internal path delays. This second change reduced response time another 9%. The final change was addition of a 32-MB write-through disk cache to a 3380D, called the IBM 3880-23. The disk cache reduced average rotational latency, seek time, and queueing delays, giving another 41% reduction in response time.

One indication of the effectiveness of DPR is the number of disk devices connected to a string. Studies of IBM systems using DPR, which average 16 disk devices per string versus 12 without DPR, suggest dynamic reconnect allows a higher I/O rate with comparable response time [Henly and McNutt 1989].

Summary of the IBM 3990 I/O Subsystem

Goals for I/O systems consist of supporting the following:

- Low cost

- A variety of types of I/O devices

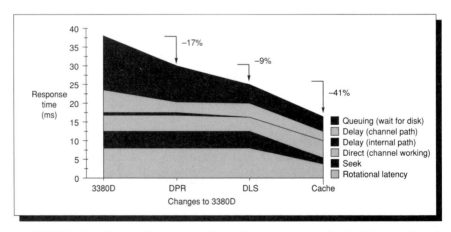

FIGURE 7.36   Changes in response time with improvements in 3380D broken into six categories [Friesenborg and Wicks 1985]. Queueing delay refers to the time when the program waits for another program to finish with the disk. Channel-path delay is the time the operation waits due to the channel path and storage director being busy with another task. Internal-path delay is similar to channel-path delay except it refers to internal paths in the 3380D. Direct means the time the channel path is busy with the operation. Seek time and rotational latency are the standard definitions. Robinson and Blount [1986] report in the study of the 3880-23 that the read hit rate for the 32-MB write-through cache in some large systems averages about 90%, with reads accounting for 92% of the disk accesses.

- A large number of I/O devices at a time

- High performance

- Low latency

Substantial expendability and lower latency are hard to get at the same time. IBM channel-based systems achieve the third and fourth goals by utilizing hierarchical data paths to connect a large number of devices. The many devices and parallel paths allow simultaneous transfers and, thus, high throughput. By avoiding large buffers and providing enough extra paths to minimize delay from congestion, channels offer low-latency I/O as well. To maximize use of the hierarchy, IBM uses rotational positional sensing to extend the time that other tasks can use the hierarchy during an I/O operation.

Therefore, a key to performance of the IBM I/O subsystem is the number of rotational positional misses and congestion on the channel paths. A rule of thumb is that the single-path channels should be no more than 30% utilized and the quad-path channels should be no more than 60% utilized, or too many rotational positional misses will result. This I/O architecture dominates the industry, yet it would be interesting to see what, if anything, IBM would do differently if given a clean slate.

7.10 | Fallacies and Pitfalls

Fallacy: I/O plays a small role in supercomputer design

The goal of the Illiac IV was to be the world's fastest computer. It may not have achieved that goal, but it showed I/O as the Achilles' Heel of high-performance machines. In some tasks, more time was spent in loading data than in computing. Amdahl's Law demonstrated the importance of high performance in all the parts of a high-speed computer. (In fact, Amdahl made his comment in reaction to claims for performance through parallelism made on behalf of the Illiac IV.) The Illiac IV had a very fast transfer rate (60 MB/sec), but very small, fixed-head disks (12-MB capacity). Since they were not large enough, more storage was provided on a separate computer. This led to two ways of measuring I/O overhead:

Warm start—Assuming the data is on the fast, small disks, I/O overhead is the time to load the Illiac IV memory from those disks.

Cold start—Assuming the data is in on the other computer, I/O overhead must include the time to first transfer the data to the Illiac IV fast disks.

Figure 7.37 shows ten applications written for the Illiac IV in 1979. Assuming warm starts, the supercomputer was busy 78% of the time and waiting for I/O 22% of the time; assuming cold starts, it was busy 59% of the time and waiting for I/O 41% of the time.

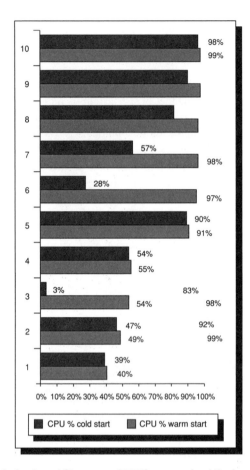

FIGURE 7.37   Feierback and Stevenson [1979] summarized the important Illiac IV applications and the percentage of time spent computing versus waiting for I/O. The arithmetic means of the 10 programs are 78% computing for warm start and 59% computing for cold start.

Pitfall: Moving functions from the CPU to the I/O processor to improve performance.

There are many examples of this pitfall, although I/O processors can enhance performance. A problem inherent with a family of computers is that the migration of an I/O feature usually changes the instruction set architecture or system architecture in a programmer-visible way, causing all future machines to have to live with a decision that made sense in the past. If CPUs are improved in cost/performance more rapidly than the I/O processor (and this will likely be the case) then moving the function may result in a slower machine in the next CPU.

The most telling example comes from the IBM 360. It was decided that the performance of the ISAM system, an early database system, would improve if some of the record searching occurred in the disk controller itself. A key field was associated with each record, and the device searched each key as the disk rotated until it found a match. It would then transfer the desired record. For the disk to find the key, there had to be an extra gap in the track. This scheme is applicable to searches through indices as well as data.

The speed a track can be searched is limited by the speed of the disk and of the number of keys that can be packed on a track. On an IBM 3330 disk the key is typically 10 characters, but the total gap between records is equivalent to 191 characters if there were a key. (The gap is only 135 characters if there is no key, since there is no need for an extra gap for the key.) If we assume the data is also 10 characters and the track has nothing else on it, then a 13165-byte track can contain

$$\frac{13165}{191 + 10 + 10} = 62 \text{ key-data records}$$

This performance is

$$\frac{16.7 \text{ ms (1 revolution)}}{62} \approx .25 \text{ ms/key search}$$

In place of this scheme, we could put several key-data pairs in a single block and have smaller inter-record gaps. Assuming there are 15 key-data pairs per block and the track has nothing else on it, then

$$\frac{13165}{135 + 15 * (10 + 10)} = \frac{13165}{135 + 300} = 30 \text{ \textbf{blocks} of key-data pairs}$$

The revised performance is then

$$\frac{16.7 \text{ ms (1 revolution)}}{30 * 15} \approx .04 \text{ ms/key search}$$

Yet as CPUs got faster, the CPU time for a search was trivial. While the strategy made early machines faster, programs that use the search-key operation in the I/O processor run six times slower on today's machines!

Fallacy: Comparing the price of media versus the price of the packaged system.

This happens most frequently when new memory technologies are compared to magnetic disks. For example, comparing the DRAM-chip price to magnetic-disk packaged price in Figure 7.16 (page 526) suggests the difference is less than a factor of 10, but its much greater when the price of packaging DRAM is included. A common mistake with removable media is to compare the media cost not including the drive to read the media. For example, optical media costs only $1 per MB in 1990, but including the cost of the optical drive may bring the price closer to $6 per MB.

Fallacy: The time of an average seek of a disk in a computer system is the time for a seek of one-third the number of cylinders.

This fallacy comes from confusing the way manufacturers market disks with the expected performance and with the false assumption that seek times are linear in distance. The 1/3 distance rule of thumb comes from calculating the distance of a seek from one random location to another random location, not including the current cylinder and assuming there are a large number of cylinders. In the past, manufacturers listed the seek of this distance to offer a consistent basis for comparison. (As mentioned on page 516, today they calculate the "average" by timing all seeks and dividing by the number.) Assuming (incorrectly) that seek time is linear in distance, and using the manufacturers reported minimum and "average" seek times, a common technique to predict seek time is:

$$\text{Time}_{\text{seek}} = \text{Time}_{\text{minimum}} + \frac{\text{Distance}}{\text{Distance}_{\text{average}}} * (\text{Time}_{\text{average}} - \text{Time}_{\text{minimum}})$$

The fallacy concerning seek time is twofold. First, seek time is **not** linear with distance; the arm must accelerate to overcome inertia, reach its maximum traveling speed, decelerate as it reaches the requested position, and then wait to allow the arm to stop vibrating (settle time). Moreover, in recent disks sometimes the arm must pause to control vibrations. Figure 7.38 (page 567) plots time versus seek distance for an example disk. It also shows the error in the simple seek-time formula above. For short seeks, the acceleration phase plays a larger role than the maximum traveling speed, and this phase is typically modeled as the square root of the distance. Figure 7.39 (page 567) shows accurate formulas used to model the seek time versus distance for two disks.

The second problem is the average in the product specification would only be true if there was no locality to disk activity. Fortunately, there is both temporal and spatial locality (page 403 in Chapter 8): disk blocks get used more than once and disk blocks near the current cylinder are more likely to be used than those farther away. For example, Figure 7.40 (page 568) shows sample measurements of seek distances for two workloads: a UNIX timesharing workload and a business-processing workload. Notice the high percentage of disk accesses to the same cylinder, labeled distance 0 in the graphs, in both workloads.

Thus, this fallacy couldn't be more misleading. The Exercises debunk this fallacy in more detail.

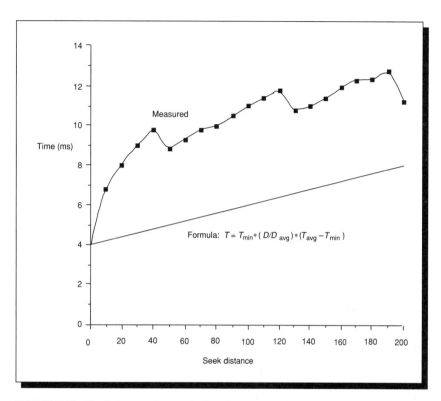

FIGURE 7.38   Seek time versus seek distance for the first 200 cylinders. The Imprimis Sabre 97209 contains 1.2 GB using 1635 cylinders and has the IPI-2 interface [Imprimis 1989]. This is an 8-inch disk. Note that longer seeks can take less time than shorter seeks. For example, a 40-cylinder seek takes almost 10 ms, while a 50-cylinder seek takes less than 9 ms.

IBM 3380D Range for formula		Formulas	IBM 3380J Range for formula		Formulas
$\geq$	$\leq$		$\geq$	$\leq$	
1	50	$11.9 + \sqrt{\text{Distance}} - \dfrac{\text{Distance}}{50}$	1	50	$12.48 + \sqrt{\text{Distance}} - \dfrac{\text{Distance}}{20}$
51	100	$8.1 + 0.044 * (\text{Distance}-50)$	51	130	$7.28 + 0.0320 * (\text{Distance}-50)$
101	500	$10.3 + 0.025 * (\text{Distance}-100)$	131	500	$10.08 + 0.0166 * (\text{Distance}-130)$
501	884	$20.4 + 0.017 * (\text{Distance}-500)$	501	884	$16.00 + 0.0114 * (\text{Distance}-500)$

FIGURE 7.39   Formulas for seek time in ms for two IBM disks. Thisquen [1988] measured these disks and proposed these formulas to model them. The two columns on the left show the range of seek distances in cylinders to which each formula applies. Each disk has 885 cylinders, so the maximum seek is 884.

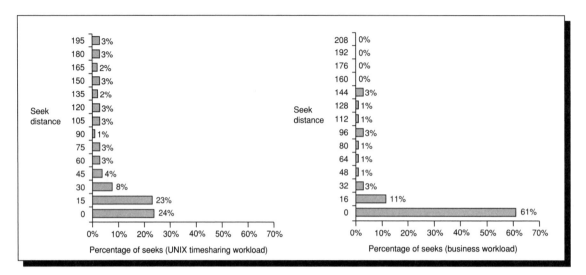

FIGURE 7.40   Sample measurements of seek distances for two systems. The left measurements were taken on a UNIX timesharing system. The right measurements were taken from a business processing application in which the disk seek activity was scheduled. Seek distance of 0 means the access was made to the same cylinder. The rest of the numbers show the collective percentage for distances up between numbers on the y axis. For example, 11% for the bar labeled 16 in the business graph means that the percentage of seeks between 1 and 16 cylinders was 11%. The UNIX measurements stopped at 200 cylinders, but this captured 85% of the accesses. The total was 1000 cylinders. The business measurements tracked all 816 cylinders of the disks. The only seek distances with 1% or greater of the seeks that are not in the graph are 224 with 4% and 304, 336, 512, and 624 each having 1%. This total is 94%, with the difference being small but nonzero distances in other categories. The measurements are courtesy of Dave Anderson of Imprimis.

7.11 | Concluding Remarks

I/O systems are judged by the variety of I/O devices, the maximum number of I/O devices, cost, and performance, measured both in latency and in throughput. These common goals lead to widely varying schemes, with some relying extensively on buffering and some avoiding buffering at all costs. If one is clearly better than the other, it is not obvious today. Perhaps this situation is like the instruction set debates of the 1980s, and the strengths and weaknesses of the alternatives will become apparent in the 1990s.

According to Amdahl's Law, ignorance of I/O will lead to wasted performance as CPUs get faster. Disk performance is growing at 4% to 6% per year, while CPUs are growing at a much faster rate. The future demands for I/O include better algorithms, better organizations, and more caching in a struggle to keep pace.

7.12 | Historical Perspective and References

The forerunner of today's workstations was the Alto developed at Xerox Palo Alto Research Center in 1974 [Thacker et al. 1982]. This machine reversed traditional wisdom, making instruction set interpretation take back seat to the display: the display used half the memory bandwidth of the Alto. In addition to the bit-mapped display, this historic machine had the first Ethernet [Metcalfe and Boggs 1976] and the first laser printer. It also had a mouse, invented earlier by Doug Engelbart of SRI, and a removable cartridge disk. The 16-bit CPU implemented an instruction set similar to the Data General Nova and offered writable control store (see Chapter 5, Section 5.8). In fact, a single microprogrammable engine drove the graphics display, mouse, disks, network, and, when there was nothing else to do, interpreted the instruction set.

The attraction of a personal computer is that you don't have to share it with anyone. This means response time is predictable, unlike timesharing systems. Early experiments in the importance of fast response time were performed by Doherty and Kelisky [1979]. They showed that if computer-system response time increased a second that user think time did also. Thadhani [1981] showed a jump in productivity as computer response times dropped to a second and another jump as they dropped to a half-second. His results inspired a flock of studies, and they supported his observations [IBM 1982]. In fact, some studies were started to disprove his results! Brady [1986] proposed differentiating entry time from think time (since entry time was becoming significant when the two were lumped together) and provided a cognitive model to explain the more than linear relationship between computer response time and user think time.

The ubiquitous microprocessor has inspired not only personal computers in the 1970s, but the current trend to moving controller functions into I/O devices in the late 1980s and 1990s. For example, microcoded routines in a central CPU made sense for the Alto in 1975, but technological changes soon made separate microprogrammable controller I/O devices economical. These were then replaced by the application-specific integrated circuits. I/O devices continued this trend by moving controllers into the devices themselves. These are called *intelligent devices*, and some bus standards (e.g., IPI and SCSI) have been created just for these devices. Intelligent devices can relax the timing constraints by handling many of the low-level tasks and queuing the results. For example, many SCSI-compatible disk drives include a track buffer on the disk itself, supporting read ahead and connect/disconnect. Thus, on a SCSI string some disks can be seeking and others loading their track buffer while one is transferring data from its buffer over the SCSI bus.

Speaking of buses, the first multivendor bus may have been the PDP-11 Unibus in 1970. DEC encouraged other companies to build devices that would plug into their bus, and many companies did. A more recent example is SCSI, which stands for *small computer systems interface*. This bus, originally called SASI, was invented by Shugart and was later standardized by the IEEE. Sometimes buses are developed in academia; the *NuBus* was developed by Steve Ward and his colleagues at MIT and used by several companies. Alas, this open- door policy on buses is in contrast to companies with proprietary buses using patented interfaces, thereby preventing competition from plug-compatible vendors. This practice also raises costs and lowers availability of I/O devices that plug into proprietary buses, since such devices must have an interface designed just for that bus. Levy [1978] has a nice survey on issues in buses.

We must also give a few references to specific I/O devices. Readers interested in the ARPANET should see Kahn [1972]. As mentioned in one of the section quotes, the father of computer graphics is Ivan Sutherland, who received the ACM Turing Award in 1988. Sutherland's Sketchpad system [1963] set the standard for today's interfaces and displays. See Foley and Van Dam [1982] and Newman and Sproull [1979] for more on computer graphics. Scranton, Thompson, and Hunter [1983] were among the first to report the myths concerning seek times and distances for magnetic disks.

Comments on the future of disks can be found in several sources. Goldstein [1987] projects the capacity and I/O rates for IBM mainframe installations in 1995, suggesting that the ratio is no less than 3.7 GB per IBM mainframe MIPS today, and that will grow to 4.5 GB per MIPS in 1995. Frank [1987] speculated on the physical recording density, proposing the MAD formula on disk growth that we used in Section 7.4. Katz, Patterson, and Gibson [1990] survey current high-performance disks and I/O systems and speculate about future systems. The possibility of achieving higher-performance I/O systems using collections of disks is found in papers by Kim [1986], Salem and Garcia-Molina [1986], and Patterson, Gibson, and Katz [1987].

Looking backward rather than forward, the first machine to extend interrupts from detecting arithmetic abnormalities to detecting asynchronous I/O events is credited as the NBS DYSEAC in 1954 [Leiner and Alexander 1954]. The following year the first machine with DMA was operational, the IBM SAGE. Just as today's DMA, the SAGE had address counters that performed block transfers in parallel with CPU operations. The first I/O channel may have been on the IBM 709 in 1957 [Bashe et al. 1981 and 1986]. Smotherman [1989] explores the history of I/O in more depth.

References

ANON ET AL. [1985]. "A measure of transaction processing power," Tandem Tech. Rep. TR 85.2. Also appeared in *Datamation*, April 1, 1985.

BASHE, C. J., W. BUCHHOLZ, G .V. HAWKINS, J .L. INGRAM, AND N. ROCHESTER [1981]. "The architecture of IBM's early computers," *IBM J. of Research and Development* 25:5 (September) 363–375.

BASHE, C. J., L. R. JOHNSON, J. H. PALMER, AND E. W. PUGH [1986]. *IBM's Early Computers*, MIT Press, Cambridge, Mass.

BORRILL, P. L. [1986]. "32-bit buses–An objective comparison," *Proc. Buscon 1986 West,* San Jose, Calif., 138–145.

BRADY, J. T. [1986]. "A theory of productivity in the creative process," *IEEE CG&A* (May) 25–34.

BUCHER, I. V. AND A. H. HAYES [1980]. "I/O Performance measurement on Cray-1 and CDC 7000 computers," *Proc. Computer Performance Evaluation Users Group, 16th Meeting*, NBS 500-65, 245–254.

CHEN, P. [1989]. *An Evaluation of Redundant Arrays of Inexpensive Disks Using an Amdahl 5890*, M. S. Thesis, Computer Science Division, Tech. Rep. UCB/CSD 89/506.

DOHERTY, W. J. AND R. P. KELISKY [1979]. "Managing VM/CMS systems for user effectiveness," *IBM Systems J.* 18:1, 143–166.

FEIERBACK, G AND D. STEVENSON [1979]. "The Illiac-IV," in *Infotech State of the Art Report on Supercomptuers*, Maidenhead, England. This data also appears in D. P. Siewiorek, C. G. Bell, and A. Newell, *Computer Structures: Principles and Examples* (1982), McGraw-Hill, New York, 268–269.

FOLEY, J. D. AND A. VAN DAM [1982]. *Fundamentals of Interactive Computer Graphics*, Addison-Wesley, Reading, Mass.

FRANK, P. D. [1987]. "Advances in Head Technology," presentation at *Challenges in Winchester Technology* (December 15), Santa Clara Univ.

FRIESENBORG, S. E. AND R. J. WICKS [1985]. "DASD expectations: The 3380, 3380-23, and MVS/XA," Tech. Bulletin GG22-9363-02 (July 10), Washington Systems Center.

GOLDSTEIN, S. [1987]. "Storage performance—an eight year outlook," Tech. Rep. TR 03.308-1 (October), Santa Teresa Laboratory, IBM, San Jose, Calif.

HENLY, M. AND B. McNUTT [1989]. "DASD I/O characteristics: A comparison of MVS to VM," Tech. Rep. TR 02.1550 (May), IBM, General Products Division, San Jose, Calif.

HOWARD, J. H. ET AL. [1988]. "Scale and performance in a distributed file system," *ACM Trans. on Computer Systems* 6:1, 51–81.

IBM [1982]. *The Economic Value of Rapid Response Time*, GE20-0752-0 White Plains, N.Y., 11–82.

IMPRIMIS [1989]. "Imprimis Product Specification, 97209 Sabre Disk Drive IPI-2 Interface 1.2 GB," Document No. 64402302 (May).

KAHN, R. E. [1972]. "Resource-sharing computer communication networks," *Proc. IEEE* 60:11 (November) 1397-1407.

KATZ, R. H., D. A. PATTERSON, AND G. A. GIBSON [1990]. "Disk system architectures for high performance computing," *Proc. IEEE* 78:2 (February).

KIM, M. Y. [1986]. "Synchronized disk interleaving," *IEEE Trans. on Computers* C-35:11 (November).

LEINER, A. L. [1954]. "System specifications for the DYSEAC," *J. ACM* 1:2 (April) 57–81.

LEINER, A. L. AND S. N. ALEXANDER [1954]. "System organization of the DYSEAC," *IRE Trans. of Electronic Computers* EC-3:1 (March) 1–10.

LEVY, J. V. [1978]. "Buses: The skeleton of computer structures," in *Computer Engineering: A DEC View of Hardware Systems Design*, C. G. Bell, J. C. Mudge, and J. E. McNamara, eds., Digital Press, Bedford, Mass.

MABERLY, N. C. [1966]. *Mastering Speed Reading*, New American Library, Inc., New York.

METCALFE, R. M. AND D. R. BOGGS [1976]. "Ethernet: Distributed packet switching for local computer networks," *Comm. ACM* 19:7 (July) 395–404.

NEWMAN, W. N. AND R. F. SPROULL [1979]. *Principles of Interactive Computer Graphics*, 2nd ed., McGraw-Hill, New York.

OUSTERHOUT, J. K. ET AL. [1985]. "A trace-driven analysis of the UNIX 4.2 BSD file system," *Proc. Tenth ACM Symposium on Operating Systems Principles*, Orcas Island, Wash., 15–24.

PATTERSON, D. A., G. A. GIBSON, AND R. H. KATZ [1987]. "A case for redundant arrays of inexpensive disks (RAID)," Tech. Rep. UCB/CSD 87/391, Univ. of Calif. Also appeared in *ACM SIGMOD Conf. Proc.*, Chicago, Illinois, June 1–3, 1988, 109–116.

ROBINSON, B. AND L. BLOUNT [1986]. "The VM/HPO 3880-23 performance results," IBM Tech. Bulletin, GG66-0247-00 (April), Washington Systems Center, Gathersburg, Md.

SALEM, K. AND H. GARCIA-MOLINA [1986]. "Disk striping," *IEEE 1986 Int'l Conf. on Data Engineering.*

SCRANTON, R. A., D. A. THOMPSON, AND D. W. HUNTER [1983]. "The access time myth," Tech. Rep. RC 10197 (45223) (September 21), IBM, Yorktown Heights, N.Y.

SMITH, A. J. [1985]. "Disk cache—miss ratio analysis and design considerations," *ACM Trans. on Computer Systems* 3:3 (August) 161–203.

SMOTHERMAN , M. [1989]. "A sequencing-based taxonomy of I/O systems and review of historical machines," *Computer Architecture News* 17:5 (September) 5–15.

SUTHERLAND, I. E. [1963]. "Sketchpad: A man-machine graphical communication system," *Spring Joint Computer Conf.* 329.

THACKER, C. P., E. M. MCCREIGHT, B. W. LAMPSON, R. F. SPROULL, AND D. R. BOGGS [1982]. "Alto: A personal computer," in *Computer Structures: Principles and Examples*, D. P. Siewiorek, C. G. Bell, and A. Newell, eds., McGraw-Hill, New York, 549–572.

THADHANI, A. J. [1981]. "Interactive user productivity," *IBM Systems J.* 20:4, 407–423.

THISQUEN, J. [1988]. "Seek time measurements," *Amdahl Peripheral Products Division Tech. Rep.* (May).

E X E R C I S E S

7.1 <7.10> [10/25/10] Using the formulas in Figure 7.39 (page 567):

a. [10] Calculate the seek time for moving the arm one-third of the cylinders for both disks.

b. [25] Write a program to calculate the "average" seek time by estimating the time for all possible seeks using these formulas and then dividing by the number of seeks.

c. [10] How close does (a) approximate (b)?

7.2 <7.10> [15/20] Using the formulas in Figure 7.39 (page 567) and the statistics in Figure 7.40 (page 568), calculate the average seek distance and the average seek time on the IBM 3380J. Use the midpoint of a range as the seek distance. For example, use 98 as the seek distance for the entry representing 91–105 in Figure 7.40. For the business workload, just ignore the missing 5% of the seeks. For the UNIX workload, assume the missing 15% of the seeks have an average distance of 300 cylinders.

a. [15] If you were misled by the fallacy, you might calculate the average distance as 884/3. What is the measured distance for each workload?

b. [20] The time to seek 884/3 cylinders on the IBM 3380J is about 12.8 ms. What is average seek time for each workload on the IBM 3380J using the measurements?

7.3 <1.4,8.4,7.4> [20/10/Discussion] Assume the improvements in density of DRAMs and magnetic disks continue as predicted in Figure 1.5 (page 17). Assuming that the improvement in cost per megabyte tracks the density improvements and that 1990 is the start of the 4-megabit DRAM generation, when will the cost per megabyte of DRAM equal the cost per megabyte of magnetic disk given:

- The cost difference in 1990 is that DRAM is 10 times more expensive.

- The cost difference in 1990 is that DRAM is 30 times more expensive.

a. [20] Which generation of DRAM chip—measured in bits per chip—will reach equity for each cost difference assumption? What year will that occur?

b. [10] What will be the difference in cost in the previous generation?

c. [Discussion] Do you think the cost difference in the previous generation is sufficient to prevent disks being replaced by DRAMs?

7.4 <7.2> [12/12/12] Assume a workload takes 100 seconds total, with the CPU taking 70 seconds and I/O taking 50 seconds.

a. [12] Assume that the floating-point unit is responsible for 25 seconds of the CPU time. You are considering a floating-point accelerator that goes five times faster. What is the time of the workload for maximum overlap, scaled overlap, and no overlap?

b. [12] Assume that seek and rotational delay of magnetic disks are responsible for 10 seconds of the I/O time. You are considering replacing the magnetic disks with solid state disks that will remove all the seek and rotational delay. What is the time of the workload for maximum overlap, scaled overlap, and no overlap?

c. [12] What is the time of the workload for scaled overlap if you make both changes?

7.5–7.9 Transaction-processing performance. The I/O bus and memory system of a computer are capable of sustaining 100 MB/sec without interfering with the performance of an 80-MIPS CPU (costing $50,000). Here are the assumptions about the software:

- Each transaction requires 2 disk reads plus 2 disk writes.

- The operating system uses 15,000 instructions for each disk read or write.

- The database software executes 40,000 instructions to process a transaction.

- The transfer size is 100 bytes.

You have a choice of two different types of disks:

- A 2.5-inch disk that stores 100 MB and costs $500.

- A 3.5-inch disk that stores 250 MB and costs $1250.

- Either disk in the system can support on average 30 disk reads or writes per second.

Answer the questions below using the TP-1 benchmark in Section 7.3. Assume that the requests are spread evenly to all the disks, that there is no waiting time due to busy disks, and that the account file must be large enough to handle 1000 TPS according to the benchmark ground rules.

7.5 <7.3,7.4> [20] How many TP-1 transactions per second are possible with each disk organization, assuming that each uses the minimum number of disks to hold the account file?

7.6 <7.3,7.4> [15] What is the system cost per transaction per second of each alternative for TP-1?

7.7 <7.3,7.4> [15] How fast a CPU makes the 100 MB/sec I/O bus a bottleneck for TP-1? (Assume that you can continue to add disks.)

7.8 <7.3,7.4> [15] As manager of MTP (Mega TP), you are deciding whether to spend your development money building a faster CPU or improve the performance of the software. The database group says they can reduce a transaction to 1 disk read and 1 disk write and cut the database instructions per transaction to 30,000. The hardware group can build a faster CPU that sells for the same amount of the slower CPU with the same development budget. (Assume you can add as many disks as needed to get higher performance.) How much faster does the CPU have to be to match the performance gain of the software improvement?

7.9 <7.3,7.4> [15/15] The MTP I/O group was listening at the door during the software presentation. They argue that advancing technology will allow CPUs to get faster without significant investment, but that the cost of the system will be dominated by disks if they don't develop new faster 2.5-inch disks. Assume the next CPU is 100% faster at the same cost and that the new disks have the same capacity as the old ones.

a. [15] Given the new CPU and the old software, what will be the cost of a system with enough old 2.5-inch disks so that they do not limit the TPS of the system ?

b. [15] Now assume you have as many new disks as you had old 2.5 inch disks in the original design. How fast must the new disks be (I/Os per second) to achieve the same TPS rate with the new CPU as the system in part a? What will the system cost?

7.10 <7.4> [20/20/20] Assume that we have the following two magnetic-disk configurations: a single disk and an array of four disks. Each disk has 20 surfaces, 885 tracks per surface with 16 sectors/track, each sector holds 1K bytes, and it revolves at 3600 RPM. Using the seek-time formula, for the IBM 3380D in Figure 7.39 (page 567). The time to switch between surfaces is the same as to move the arm one track. In the disk array all the spindles are synchronized—sector 0 in every disk rotates under the head at the exact same time— and the arms on all four disks are always over the same track. The data is "striped" across all 4 disks, so four consecutive sectors on a single disk system will be spread one sector per disk in the array. The delay of the disk controller is 2 ms per transaction, either for a single disk or for the array. Assume the performance of the I/O system is limited only by the disks and that there is a path to each disk in the array. Compare the performance in both I/Os per second and megabytes per second of these two disk organizations assuming the following request patterns:

a. [20] Random reads of 4 KB of sequential sectors. Assume the 4 KB are aligned under the same arm on each disk in the array.

b. [20] Reads of 4 KB of sequential sectors where the average seek distance is 10 tracks. Assume the 4 KB are aligned under the same arm on each disk in the array.

c. [20] Random reads of 1 MB of sequential sectors. (If it matters, assume the disk controller allows the sectors to arrive in any order.)

7.11 [20] <7.4> Assume that we have one disk defined as in Exercise 7.9. Assume that we read the next sector after any read and that *all* read requests are one sector in length. We store the extra sectors that were read ahead in a *disk cache*. Assume that the probability of receiving a request for the sector we read ahead at some time in the future (before it must be discarded because the disk-cache buffer fills) is 0.1. Assume that we must still pay the controller overhead on a disk-cache read hit, and the transfer time for the disk cache is 250 ns per word. Is the read-ahead strategy faster? (Hint: Solve the problem in the steady state by assuming that the disk cache contains the appropriate information and a request has just missed.)

7.12–7.14 Assume the following information about our DLX machine:

Loads 2 cycles

Stores 2 cycles

All other instructions are 1 cycle. Use the summary instruction mix information in Figure C.4 in Appendix C on DLX for GCC.

Here are the cache statistics for a write-through cache:

- Each cache block is four words, and the whole block is read on any miss.

- Cache miss takes 13 cycles.

- Write through takes 6 cycles to complete, and there is no write buffer.

Here are the cache statistics for a write-back cache:

- Each cache block is four words, and the whole block is read on any miss.

- Cache miss takes 13 cycles for a clean block and 21 cycles for a dirty block.

- Assume that on a miss, 30% of the time the block is dirty.

Assume that the bus

- is only busy during transfers,

- transfers on average 1 word / clock cycle, and

- must read or write a single word at a time (it is not faster to read or write two at once).

7.12 [20/10/20/20] <7.4,7.5,7.6> Assume that DMA I/O can take place simultaneously with CPU cache hits. Also assume that the operating system can guarantee that there will be no stale-data problem in the cache due to I/O. The sector size is 1 KB.

a.   [20] Assume the cache miss rate is 5%. On the average, what percentage of the bus is used for each cache write policy? This measured is called the *traffic ratio* in cache studies.

b.   [10] If the bus can be loaded up to 80% of capacity without suffering severe performance penalties, how much memory bandwidth is available for I/O for each cache write policy? The cache miss rate is still 5%.

c.   [20] Assume that a disk sector read takes 1000 clock cycles to initiate a read, 100,000 clock cycles to find the data on the disk, and 1000 clock cycles for the DMA to transfer the data to memory. How many disk reads can occur per million instructions executed for each write policy? How does this change if the cache miss rate is cut in half?

d.   [20] Now you can have any number of disks. Assuming ideal scheduling of disk accesses, what is the maximum number of sector reads that can occur per million instructions executed?

7.13 [20/20] <7.4,7.5> Most machines today have a separate frame buffer to update the screen to avoid slowing down the memory system. An interesting issue is the percentage of the memory bandwidth that would be used if there were no frame buffer. Assume that all accesses to the memory are the size of a full cache block and they all take the time of a cache miss. The refresh rate is 60 Hz. Using the information in Section 7.4, calculate the memory traffic for the following graphics devices:

1.   A 340 by 540 black-and-white display.

2.   A 1280 by 1024 color display with 24 bits of color.

3.   A 1280 by 1024 color display using a 256-word color map.

Assume the clock rate of the CPU is 60 MHz.

a.   [20] What percentage of the memory/bus bandwidth do each of the three displays consume?

b.   [20] Suppose instead of the bus and main memory being 32 bits wide that both are 512 bits wide. How long should a memory access take now using the wider bus? What percentage of memory bandwidth is now used by each display?

7.14 [20] <7.4,7.9> The IBM 3990 I/O Subsystem storage director can have a large cache for reads and writes. Assume the cache costs the same as four 3380D disks. What hit rate must the cache achieve to get the same performance as four more 3380D disks? (See Figure 7.15 (page 525) for 3380 performance.) Assume the cache could support 5000 I/Os per second if everything hit the cache.

7.15 [50] <7.3, 7.4> Take your favorite computer and write three programs that achieve the following:

1. Maximum bandwidth to and from disks

2. Maximum bandwidth to a frame buffer

3. Maximum bandwidth to and from the local area network

What is the percentage of the bandwidth that you achieve compared to what the I/O device manufacturer claims? Also record CPU utilization in each case for the programs running separately. Next run all three together and see what percentage of maximum bandwidth you achieve for three I/O devices as well as the CPU utilization. Try to determine why one gets a larger percentage than the others.

7.16 [40] <7.2> The system speedup formulas are limited to one or two types of devices. Derive simple to use formulas for unlimited numbers of devices, using as many different assumptions on overlap that you can handle.

7.17 [Discussion] <7.2> What are arguments for predicting system performance using maximum overlap, scaled overlap, and nonoverlap? Construct scenarios where each one seems most likely and other scenarios where each interpretation is nonsensical.

7.18 [Discussion] <7.11> What are the advantages and disadvantages of a minimal buffer I/O system like that used by IBM versus a maximal buffer I/O system on I/O system cost/performance?

"The Medium is the Message" because it is the medium that shapes
and controls the search and form of human associations and
actions.

Marshall McLuhan,
Understanding Media (1964)

*The marvels—of film, radio, and television—are marvels of one-
way communication, which is not communication at all.*

Milton Mayer,
Citation (year)

8

Interconnect Technology

Notes to reviewers: This is a new Chapter for Computer Architecture: A Quantitative Approach, Second Edition (2/e). This chapter comes after the I/O chapter and before a new chapter on shared bus multiprocessors. CA:AQA is used as a first level graduate text in architecture. This is the alpha draft, so its not polished. Don't worry about page breaks.

I am interested in feedback on mistakes, answers to my specific notes to reviewers placed in the paper, what is unclear or confusing, wrong or missing terms, wrong figure number, awkward sentences, inconsistencies, ... I'm also interested in what should be left out, what important topics are missing, or other general comments. If some sections are too dry, it would be great to suggest examples or figures that could spruce them up. Finally, there is concern whether this chapter is quantitative enough to match the style of the rest of the book. Suggestions of more quantitative examples are especially welcome.

8.1 Introduction

Thus far we have covered the components of a single computer, which has been the traditional focus of computer architecture. In this chapter we see how to connect computers together, forming a community of computers. Figure 8.1 shows the generic components of this community: computer nodes, hardware and software interfaces, links to the interconnection, and the interconnection. Interconnections are also called *networks* or *communication subnets*, and nodes are sometimes called *end systems* or *hosts*. This topic is vast, with whole books written about portions of this figure. The goal of this chapter is to help the reader understand the architectural implications of interconnect technology, providing introductory explanations of the key ideas and then references to more detailed descriptions.

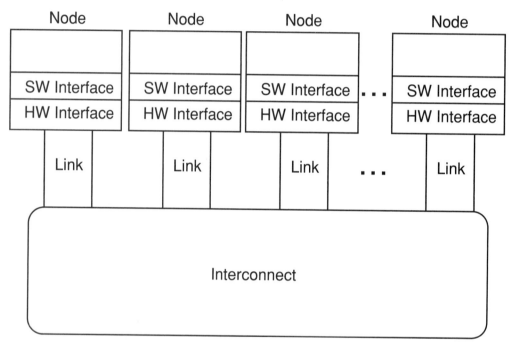

FIGURE 8.1   Drawing of the generic interconnection.

Let's start with the generic types of interconnections. Depending on the number of nodes and their proximity, these interconnections are given different names:

- *Massively Parallel Processor (MPP) network:* This interconnect can connect thousands of nodes, and the maximum distance is typically less than 25 meters. The nodes are typically found in a row of adjacent boxes.

- *Local Area Network (LAN):* This device connects hundreds to thousands computers and the distance is up to a few kilometers. Unlike the MPP network, the LAN connects computers distributed throughout a building.

■ *Wide Area Network (WAN)*: Also called *long haul networks*, they connect computers distributed throughout the world. WANs include thousands of computers and the maximum distance is thousands of kilometers.

The connection of two or more interconnections is called *internetworking*, relying on software standards to convert information from one kind of network to another.

These three interconnections have been designed and sustained by three different cultures–MPP community, workstation community, and telecommunications community–each using their own dialects and their own favorite approaches to the goal of how to best interconnect autonomous computers. This common goal led us to try to treat them in a single chapter.

This chapter gives a common framework for evaluating all interconnects, using a common set of terms to describe the three basic alternatives. To contrast these general classes, we will use three popular examples to demonstrate alternative solutions to common issues:

1. The example MPP network is found in the Connection Machine 5 from Thinking Machines Corporation, first shipped in 1991. Designed to connect up to 16,384 nodes, the largest built thus far holds 2048 nodes. The interconnect is laid out as a tree with the nodes as leaves of the tree; two leaves may be up to 25(?) meters apart. The peak transfer speed to a single node is 20 MB/second.

2. The example LAN is the Ethernet. This interconnect is so common that Ethernet has almost become like Kleenex, with the name being more widely used than the generic name (LAN). It is also the oldest of these three interconnect examples, having been in the field since 1978. Each cable can be up to 0.5 kilometers long, although there are simple devices to concatenate up to five segments giving a total length of 2.5 km. There may be up to 254 nodes on an Ethernet. The peak transfer speed to a single device is 1.25 MB/second (10 Mbit/second); new standards being developed will increase bandwidth to 12.5 MB/sec

3. The example WAN is ATM (Asynchronous Transfer Mode). This WAN is a new interconnect that began to be put in place in 1994, with initial systems running at just under 20 MB/second (155 Mbit/second); there are plans for ATM to be able to transfer at 300 MB/second and even higher rates.

Figure 8.33 in Section 8.10 of this chapter gives several other examples of each of these three types of interconnections. As we shall see, some components are common to each type and some are quite different.

The following four sections describe concerns in the design of an interconnection: implementation issues, performance measures, architectural issues, and practical issues. We use the three examples above throughout these sections to illustrate these tradeoffs. No matter the class of interconnect, its use involves software. This software can be as simple as a store instruction for an MPP interconnect or as complicated as an operating system routine that must offer safe communication to untrustworthy computers located anywhere in the world over an unreliable WAN. The hardware/software interface of interconnections is described in Section 8.6.

8.2 | Implementation Issues

The cost and performance of an interconnection involves the length of the interconnection and its links, the number of lines in the interconnection, the clock rate, and the medium itself. The length affects the cost of communicating at a high clock rate, as the longer the length generally the more expensive it is to run at a high clock rate. Shorter lengths also make it easier to assign more lines to the interconnection, as the power to drive many wires from a chip is less if the lines are short. Shorter lines are also cheaper than long lines, both to purchase and to install. Long cables are also susceptible to cross-talk and to clock skew. The medium can vary in cost from a few cents for copper traces on a printed circuit card to hundreds of dollars optical fiber with electrical-to-optical interfaces. Figure 8.2 shows the decisions made by our three examples on these implementation issues.

Interconnect	MPP	LAN	WAN
Example	CM-5	Ethernet	ATM
Maximum length between nodes	25 meters	500 meters; can connect 5 with repeaters	copper: 100 meters optical: 1000 meters
Number data lines	4	1	1
Clock Rate	40 MHz	10 MHz	155.5 MHz or higher
Shared vs. Switch	Switch	Shared	Switch
Maximum number of nodes	2048	254	> 10,000
Media Material	Copper	Twisted pair copper wire or Coaxial cable	Twisted pair copper wire or optical fiber

FIGURE 8.2   Implementation parameters for three interconnects.

One important issue is whether all nodes share access to the interconnect (called shared medium) or whether each does has a dedicated link to a central switch. Figure 8.3 shows the potential bandwidth improvement of switches.

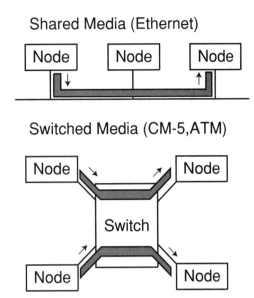

FIGURE 8.3   Shared medium vs. Switch. All nodes on the Ethernet must share the 1.25 MB/sec interconnection, but switches like ATM can support multiple 20 MB/sec transfers simultaneously.

The Ethernet, our example Local Area Network (LAN), shares a single medium so that communication between pairs of nodes occurs sequentially over this shared resource. Shared media LANs are similar to the I/O buses of the last chapter. The long length of LANs precludes the large number of parallel lines that is typically found in a bus. Thus Ethernet uses serial transmission, originally over coaxial cable and today over unshielded twisted pair copper wire (the same as low cost wire found in telephone lines). Serial lines have the advantage of not having to deal with the problems of synchronizing signals on parallel lines. Imperfections in the copper wires or integrated circuit pad drivers can cause skew in the arrival of signals, limiting the clock rate, and the length and number of the parallel lines. These factors can conspire to allow a serial line to have a higher clock rate *and* longer distance than a set of parallel lines. Ethernet is quite an old technology, but new standards propose to run 10 times faster than the original standard, giving it both a higher clock rate and much longer distance than buses.

In contrast to Ethernet, both the CM-5 and ATM use switches to connect pairs of nodes that wish to communicate. Switches allow multiple pairs of nodes to communicate simultaneously, giving these interconnections much higher potential bandwidth than the speed of a single link to a node. Switches also allow the interconnect to scale to a very large number of nodes. Switches are called *data switching exchanges, multistage interconnection networks,* or even *Interface Message Processors (IMPs).* The CM-5 uses many small switches that are distributed throughout the machine, while ATM uses large, centralized switches. Section 8.4 shows the organization of each switch. Depending on the distance of the node to the switch, these ATM cables are either copper wire or optical fiber, with the optical interfaces being considerably more expensive.

Switches allow communication to be from one end of the line to the other end, without intermediate nodes to interfere with these signals. Such *point-to-point* communication is faster than a line shared between many nodes. Since every node of a shared line will see every message, even if it is just to check to see whether or not the message is for this node, this style of communication is sometimes called *broadcast* to contrast it with point-to-point. The shared media makes it easy to broadcast a message to every node, and even to broadcast to subsets of nodes, called *multicasting.*

8.3 | Performance Measures

There is an old network saying: Bandwidth problems can be cured with money. Latency problems are harder because the speed of light is fixed—you can't bribe God.

David Clark, M.I.T.

God's unwillingness to intercede on the part of interconnection designers likely explains why bandwidth is used to motivate new interconnection designs. This practice is so common that the bandwidth is included in the names of some interconnections: 10 megabit Ethernet, 155 megabit ATM, and so on. Alas, concentrating on a single figure of merit can lead designers astray, for improving bandwidth at the cost of much higher latency may lead to an interconnection that is no faster for real workloads. Moreover, the bandwidth number chosen is usually the peak bandwidth which often cannot be achieved in practice, potentially making this single measure even more misleading; hence it shares many of the problems that MIPS or MFLOPS have as a measure of processor performance (see pages 40 to 44 of Chapter 2). For example, this bandwidth measure is typically the peak speed of the interconnection medium as opposed to measured bandwidth taking into account the links to the interconnection, the hardware and software interfaces, and information lost due to interference or congestion.

A fuller set of performance measures are the bandwidth and latency of the interconnection and the bandwidth and latency of the interface between the node and the interconnection. Figure 8.4 labels the generic drawing of an interconnection with these performance measures identified. To avoid confusion between the latency of the network and the latency of the network interface, we use the term *overhead* to describe the latency of the interface.

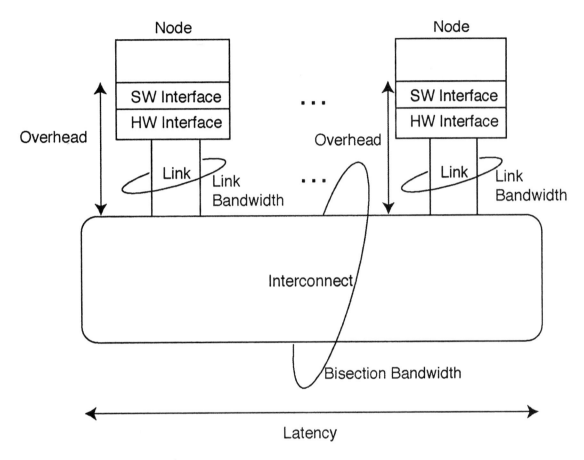

FIGURE 8.4 The performance metrics for interconnections. The interconnect will be described in greater detail in Sections 8.4 and 8.7, and the software interface is described in Section 8.6, The hardware interface to the interconnect is usually a first-in-first-out queue for outgoing messages and one for incoming messages plus flag registers that are set to send a message or checked to see if a message has arrived on the incoming queue. Many hardware interfaces can interrupt the processors when a messages arrives.

As we shall see in section 8.4, the bandwidth of some interconnections varies depending on where you measure. To avoid confusion, the *bisection bandwidth* is used. This measure is calculated by dividing the interconnect into two parts, each with half the nodes. You then sum the bandwidth of the lines that cross that imaginary dividing line. Since some interconnections are not symmetric, the question arises as to where to draw the imaginary line when bisecting the interconnect. Bisection bandwidth is a worst case metric, so the answer is to choose the division that pessimizes interconnection performance; stated alternatively, calculate all possible bisection bandwidths and pick the smallest. Figure 8.5 shows the performance numbers for each of the example interconnections.

Interconnect	MPP	LAN	WAN
Example	CM-5	Ethernet	ATM
(Bisection) Interconnect Bandwidth (measured)	N x 5 MB/sec, where N is number of nodes	1.125 MB/sec	N x 10 MB/sec, where N is number of nodes
Interface/Link Bandwidth (measured)	20 MB/sec	1.125 MB/sec	10 MB/sec
Interconnect Latency	5 μsecs	15 μsecs	50 μsecs to 10,000 μsecs, depending on distance
HW Overhead to or from interconnect	0.5 μsec	6 μsecs	6 μsecs
SW Overhead to interconnect	1.6 μsecs	TCP/IP: 200 μsecs	TCP/IP: 207 μsecs
SW Overhead from interconnect	12.4 μsecs	TCP/IP: 241 μsecs	TCP/IP: 360 μsecs

FIGURE 8.5 **Performance parameters for three interconnects.** The Ethernet and ATM measures were taken on a SPARCstation 10 running Solaris 2.3 and using a SynOptics 16-way switch for ATM. The TCP/IP software overheads is explained in Section 8.6. The CM-5 receive software overhead shown assumes that is message interrupts upon arrival; polling based software drops this figure to just 3 microseconds. THe bisection bandwidth of the CM-5 is not N x 20 MB/sec because the interconnect is a restricted fat tree which has limited bandwidth near the bottom of the tree.

The use of a switch has considerable impact on these examples. The shared media of the Ethernet means the bisection bandwidth of the interconnect is no higher than the link bandwidth, while the CM-5 and ATM can scale the bisection bandwidth with the number of nodes. Thus the largest CM-5 has 1000 times the bisection bandwidth of the Ethernet.

The latency of the interconnection is a function of the distance–since God can't be bribed–and the delay through the intermediary switches (if any). The CM-5 latency is 5 microseconds for its largest MPP, but ATM can vary by a factor of 1000 depending on the number of intermediate switches and the distance–from inside a building to across a continent.

The overhead to place a message into the interconnect can be divided into a hardware component and a software component. The hardware overheads are the smallest component and similar in length for our examples; it is the software overhead that varies dramatically. The MPP can quickly check to be sure that the communication is legitimate, using a low overhead software interface. The LAN and WAN must invoke the operating system and elaborate layers of software to ensure safe communication, and these are responsible for the huge overheads. Section 8.6 describes these software layers in more detail.

Example

Calculate and compare the time to send the smallest message from one machine to another for the three example interconnections.

Answer

A simple model of communication is the time to send a zero length message plus the size of the message divided by the bandwidth of the interconnection. The one-way time using the parameters in this figure is the hardware and software overheads to send and receive messages plus the latency of the interconnection:

Using the values for these parameters from Figure 8.5 gives this lower bound,

$$\text{MinTime}_{\text{1-way}} = \text{SW Overhead}_{\text{send}} + \text{HW Overhead}_{\text{send}}$$
$$+ \text{Latency}_{\text{interconnection}} + \text{HW Overhead}_{\text{receive}} + \text{SW Overhead}_{\text{receive}}$$

not including the time to send the data:

$$\text{MinTime}_{\text{CMS}} = 1.6 + 0.5 + 5 + 0.5 + 12.4 = 20 \; \mu\text{sec}$$
$$\text{MinTime}_{\text{Ethernet}} = 200 + 6 + 15 + 6 + 214 = 468 \; \mu\text{sec}$$
$$\text{MinTime}_{\text{ATM}} = 207 + 6 + 50 + 6 + 360 = 629 \; \mu\text{sec}$$

Let's examine the difference between peak bandwidth and delivered bandwidth.

Example

Figure 8.6 shows the size of Network File System (NFS) messages for 239 machines at Berkeley collected over a period of several days. NFS sends messages to the file system at a server over a network. These files that can be up to 2 GB in size, and can be read or written as part of the message sent to the server. Plot the delivered bandwidth of an interconnect as you vary the peak bandwidth and minimum time for a one-way transmission varies from 1 microsecond to 1000 microseconds by factors of 10.

Range	Messages	% Total Msgs	Cumulative %	Bytes in Msgs	% Total Bytes	Cumulative %
0	0	0.0%	0.0%	0	0.0%	0.0%
32	771,060	6.8%	6.8%	33,817,052	0.8%	0.8%
64	56,923	0.5%	7.3%	4,101,088	0.1%	0.9%
96	4,082,014	35.8%	43.1%	428,346,316	9.8%	10.7%
128	5,574,092	48.9%	92.1%	779,600,736	17.9%	28.6%
160	328,439	2.9%	94.9%	54,860,484	1.3%	29.9%
192	16,313	0.1%	95.1%	3,316,416	0.1%	30.0%
224	4,820	0.0%	95.1%	1,135,380	0.0%	30.0%
256	24,766	0.2%	95.4%	9,150,720	0.2%	30.2%
512	32,159	0.3%	95.6%	25,494,920	0.6%	30.8%
1024	69,834	0.6%	96.2%	79,578,564	1.8%	32.6%
1536	8,842	0.1%	96.3%	15,762,180	0.4%	33.0%
2048	9,170	0.1%	96.4%	20,621,760	0.5%	33.4%
2560	20,206	0.2%	96.6%	56,319,740	1.3%	34.7%
3072	13,549	0.1%	96.7%	43,184,992	1.0%	35.7%
3584	4,200	0.0%	96.7%	16,152,228	0.4%	36.1%
4096	67,808	0.6%	97.3%	285,606,596	6.6%	42.7%
5120	6,143	0.1%	97.4%	35,434,680	0.8%	43.5%
6144	5,858	0.1%	97.4%	37,934,684	0.9%	44.3%
7168	4,140	0.0%	97.5%	31,769,300	0.7%	45.1%
8192	287,577	2.5%	100.0%	2,390,688,480	54.9%	100.0%
8368	0	0.0%	100.0%	0	0.0%	100.0%
TOTAL	11,387,913	100.0%		4,352,876,316	100.0%	

FIGURE 8.6   The size of NFS messages for a 7 day session in the Computer Science Department at U.C. Berkeley.
This was the traffic to the Auspex file server which served 239 clients over many Ethernets. Each row shows sizes from leftmost column to one byte less than the next row, with the second column showing the number of messages of those sizes and the fifth column showing the number of bytes sent of these sizes. For example, there are 771,060 messages from 32 bytes through 63 bytes long, and these messages sent a total of 33,817,052 data bytes.

Answer   Using the message sizes in Figure 8.6, Figure 8.7 shows the delivered bandwidth versus peak bandwidth as one-way message time is varied. Clearly a 10X improvement in startup latency can be much more important than a 10X improvement in peak bandwidth.

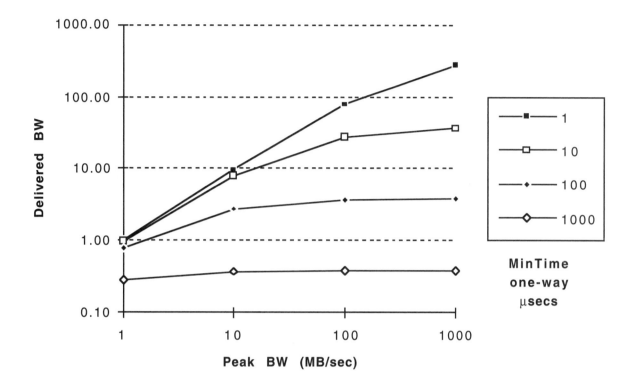

FIGURE 8.7 Using the message sizes in Figure 8.6, this figure shows the delivered bandwidth versus the peak bandwidth assuming a simple message time of startup overhead + message size/peak bandwidth.

8.4 Architectural Issues

Having covered implementation issues and how to measure interconnection performance, we are now ready for five architectural issues. Figure 8.8 shows how these issues were resolved for our three interconnections. The most visible is the topology of the interconnection, which is our first topic.

Interconnect	MPP	LAN	WAN
Example	CM-5	Ethernet	ATM
Topology	"Fat" tree	Line	Variable, constructed from multistage switches
Connection v. Connectionless	Connectionless	Connectionless	Connection based
Data Transfer Size	Variable: 4 to 20 bytes	Variable: 0 to 1500 bytes	Fixed: 48 bytes
Store and Forward vs. Cut Through	Cut Through	Not Applicable	Store and Forward
Congestion control	At source: Flow control via back pressure	At source: listen for Ethernet to be idle	TBD: rate based via choke packets is leading candidate

FIGURE 8.8   Architectural parameters for three interconnects.

Topology

The simplest way to connect nodes is to have a common set of lines shared by all nodes; Ethernet uses this simplest approach as do buses. A straightforward alternative is to have a dedicated communication link between every node. Between the low cost and performance of shared lines and the high cost and performance of this fully connected alternative are a set of interconnections that constitute a wide range of trade-offs in cost-performance. They all involve switches to reduce the number of dedicated lines to connect nodes while allowing some pairs of nodes to communicate simultaneously.

Illustrations can help in understanding the pros and cons of these topologies. Interconnections are normally drawn as graphs, with each arc of the graph representing a link of the communication interconnection, with a node shown as a black square. The shared lines of a bus are drawn as follows:

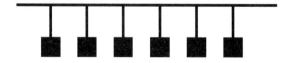

In this section all links are bi-directional; that is, information can flow in either direction.

The first improvement over shared lines is an interconnection that connects a sequence of nodes together (the switch is shown as a colored circle):

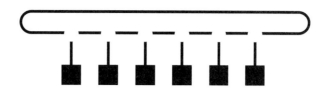

This topology is called a *ring*. Since some nodes are not directly connected, some messages will have to hop along intermediate nodes until they arrive at the final destination. Unlike shared lines, a ring is capable of many simultaneous transfers; the first node can send to the second at the same time as the third node can send to the fourth. The bisection bandwidth of a ring is twice that of the shared lines, since two lines cross any division that bisects the graph.

(One variation of rings used in local area networks is called *token rings*. In this case a single slot or *token* is passed around the ring to determine which node is allowed to send a message: a node can send only when it gets the token. Rather than use the ring to increase bandwidth of the interconnect as in this example, the ring is used to circulate a token to arbitrate which node gets to use the interconnect. In this section we will evaluate the ring as a topology with more bandwidth rather than one that may be simpler to arbitrate than a long bus.)

Question for reviewer: LAN ring vs. MPP ring sound OK?

At the other extreme from a ring is a fully connected interconnection, where every node has a bi-directional link to every other node. For fully connected interconnections the bisection bandwidth is $(N/2)^2$, where N is the number of nodes.

The tremendous improvement in performance of fully connected interconnections is offset by the tremendous increase in cost, typically going up with the square of the number of nodes. This inspires designers to invent new topologies that are between the cost of rings and the performance of fully connected interconnections. The evaluation of success depends in large part on the nature of the communication on the interconnection.

The number of different topologies that have been discussed in publications would be difficult to count, but the number that have been used commercially is just a handful, with MPP designers being the most visible and imaginative. Figure 8.9 illustrates three popular topologies for MPPs. Real machines frequently add extra links to these simple topologies to improve performance and reliability. Figure 8.10 summarizes these different topologies using bisection bandwidth and the number of links for 64 nodes.

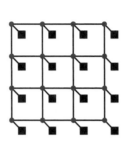   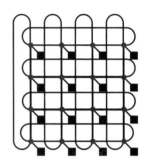

a. 2D grid or mesh of 16 nodes   b. 2D torus of 16 nodes

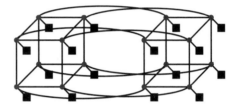

c. N-cube tree of 16 nodes ($16 = 2^4$ so N = 4)

FIGURE 8.9   Network topologies that have appeared in commercial MPPs. The colored circles represent switches and the black squares represent nodes. Even though a switch has many links, generally only one goes to the node. Frequently these basic topologies have been supplemented with extra arcs to improve performance and reliability. For example, the switches in the left and right columns of the 2D grid are connected together using the unused ports on each switch to form the 2D torus. The Boolean N-cube topology is an N-dimensional interconnect with 2^N nodes, requiring N ports per switch (plus one for the processor) and thus N nearest neighbor nodes.

Evaluation Category		Bus	Ring	2D Torus	6-cube	Fully connected
Performance	**Bisection bandwidth**	1	2	16	32	1024
Cost	**Ports per switch**	n.a.	3	5	7	64
	Total number of lines	1	128	192	256	2080

FIGURE 8.10   Relative cost and performance of several interconnects for 64 nodes. Note that any network topology that scales the bisection bandwidth linearly must scale the number of interconnection lines faster than linearly. Figure 8.12a on page 597 is an example of a fully connected network.

Example

Let's examine the difference between the bisection bandwidths of each topology in Figure 8.10 for 64 nodes. Assume all-to-all communication: each node does a single transfer to every other node. We simplify the communication cost model for this example: it takes one time unit to go from switch to switch and there is no cost in or out of the processor. Assuming every link of every interconnect is the same speed and that a node can send as many messages as it wants at a time, how long does it take for complete communication?

Answer

For each node to send a message to every other node, we need to send 64 x 63 or 4032 messages. Here are the cases in order of difficulty of explanation:

Bus: transfers are done sequentially, so it takes 4032 time units.

Fully connected: all transfers are done in parallel, taking just the 1 time unit.

Ring: This is easiest to see step by step. The first step is that each node sends a message to the node with the next higher address, with node 63 sending to node 0. This takes one step for all 64 transfers to the nearest neighbor. The second step send to the node address + 2 modulo 64. Since this goes through 2 links it takes 2 time units. It would seem that this would continue until we send to the node address + 63 modulo 64 taking 63 time units, but remember that these are bi-directional links. Hence sending from node 1 to node 1 + 63 modulo 64 = 0 takes just one time unit because there is a link connecting them together. Then the calculation for the ring is:

$$\text{Time}_{\text{Ring}} = 1 + 2 + \ldots + 31 + 32 + 31 + \ldots + 2 + 1$$

$$= \frac{31 \times 32}{2} + 32 + \frac{31 \times 32}{2} = 496 + 32 + 496$$

$$= 1024$$

2D Torus: There are 8 rows and 8 columns in our torus of 64 nodes. Remember that the top and bottom rows of a torus are just one link away as are the leftmost and rightmost columns. This allows us to treat the communication similarly to how we did the ring, in that there are no special cases at the edges. Let's first calculate the time to send a message to all the nodes in the same row. This time is the same as a ring with just 8 nodes:

$$\text{Time}_{\text{Row}} = 1 + 2 + 3 + 4 + 3 + 2 + 1$$

$$= \frac{3 \times 4}{2} + 4 + \frac{3 \times 4}{2} = 6 + 4 + 6$$

$$= 16$$

To send a message to all the elements in the row below, all 8 messages must first take 1 time unit to get to that row. The time for the 8 messages to get to the proper node within that is the same as the time to send a message to all elements of a row:

$$\text{Time}_{\text{Row below}} = 8 \times 1 + \text{Time}_{\text{Row}}$$

This can be generalized as the time it takes to send 8 messages to each row plus the time to distribute the messages within a row:

$$\text{Time}_{\text{2D}} = \text{Time}_{\text{Row}} + (8 \times 1 + \text{Time}_{\text{Row}}) + (8 \times 2 + \text{Time}^{\text{Row}}) + \ldots$$

$$+ (8 \times 4 + \text{Time}_{\text{Row}}) + \ldots + (8 \times 1 + \text{Time}_{\text{Row}})$$

$$= \text{Time}_{\text{Row}} + 8 \times (1 + 2 + 3 + 4 + 3 + 2 + 1 + \text{Time}_{\text{Row}})$$

$$= \text{Time}_{\text{Row}} + 8 \times \left(\frac{3 \times 4}{2} + 4 + \frac{3 \times 4}{2} + \text{Time}_{\text{Row}} \right)$$

$$= \text{Time}_{\text{Row}} + 8 \times (16 + \text{Time}_{\text{Row}})$$

$$= 16 + 8 \times (16 + 16) = 16 + 8 \times 32 = 16 + 256$$

$$= 272$$

This is only sending one message at a time per node, even though each node has multiple links. The communication pattern suggested above first uses vertical links and then uses horizontal links, using only half the potential interconnection bandwidth. By carefully selecting pairs of communications that have the same number of vertical hops as the other has horizontal hops and vice versa, the time for complete communication can be cut approximately in half.

6-cube: Rather than indicate the sequence, let's derive it from the time to send the total number of messages. Each node can first send to its nearest neighbors. These 64 x 6 or 384 messages take 2 time units since a message can be on a link only in one direction. Sending to the neighbors one step removed takes 4 time units and results in another 384 messages. The total 4032 messages will take 4032/384 or 11 steps. The calculation is then:

$$\text{Time}_{\text{6-cube}} = 2 \times (1 + 2 + 3 + \ldots + 10 + 11)$$

$$= 2 \times \left(\frac{11 \times 12}{2} \right) = 11 \times 12$$

$$= 132$$

Figure 8.11 summarizes the calculations from this example.

Evaluation Category	Bus	Ring	2D Torus	6-cube	Fully connected
Time all-to-all	4032	1024	272	11	1
Time North & East	112	9	2	2	1

FIGURE 8.11 **Summary of the communication times for all-to-all and for nearest northern and eastern neighbors calculated in the surrounding examples.**

Example

A common communication pattern in scientific codes is to consider the nodes as elements of a two dimensional array and then have communication to the nearest neighbor in a given direction. (This is sometimes called NEWS communication standing for North, East, West, and South, the directions on the compass). Place an 8 by 8 array on the 64 nodes in each topology and assuming every link of every interconnect is the same speed. How long does it take for each node to send one message to its northern neighbor and one to its eastern neighbor? Ignore nodes that have no northern or eastern neighbors.

Answer

In this case we want to send 2 x (64 − 8) or 112 messages. Here are the cases, again in order of difficulty of explanation:

Bus: The placement of the 8 by 8 array makes no difference for the bus, since all nodes are equally distant. The 112 transfers are done sequentially, taking 112 time units.

Fully connected: Again the nodes are equally distant; all transfers are done in parallel, taking just the 1 time unit.

Ring: Here the nodes are differing distances. Assume the first row of the array is placed on nodes 0 to 7, the second row on nodes 8 to 15, and so on. It takes just one time unit to send to the eastern neighbor, for this is a send from node N to node N+1. The northern neighbor is exactly 8 nodes away in this scheme, so it takes 8 time units for each node to send to their northern neighbors. The ring total is 9 time units.

2D Torus: There are 8 rows and 8 columns in our grid of 64 nodes, which is a perfect match to the NEWS communication. It takes just 2 time units to send to the northern and eastern neighbors.

6-cube: It is possible to place the array so that it will take just 2 time units for this communication pattern, as in the case of the 2D grid.

Figure 8.11 summarizes the calculations from this example.

Multistage Interconnection

Thus far the interconnect topologies have assumed that there is one switch per computer and then varied the topologies to get different cost and performance. An alternative to placing a computer at every node in a interconnection is to leave only the switch at intermediate nodes. The switches are smaller than processor-memory-switch nodes, and thus may be packed more densely, thereby lessening distance and increasing performance. Such interconnections are frequently called *multistage interconnections* to reflect the multiple steps that a message may travel. Types of multistage interconnections are as numerous as single stage interconnections; Figure 8.12 illustrates two of the popular multistage organizations, with the path from node P0 to node P6 highlighted in each topology. A fully connected or *crossbar* interconnection allows any node to communicate with any other node in one pass through the interconnection. An *Omega* interconnection uses less hardware than the crossbar interconnection ($2N \log_2 N$ vs. N^2 switches), but contention can occur between messages, depending on the pattern of communication. For example, the Omega interconnection in Figure 8.12 cannot send a message from P0 to P6 at the same time as a message from P1 to P7. Of course, if two nodes try to send to the same destination–both P0 and P1 send to P6–there will be contention for that link, even in the crossbar.

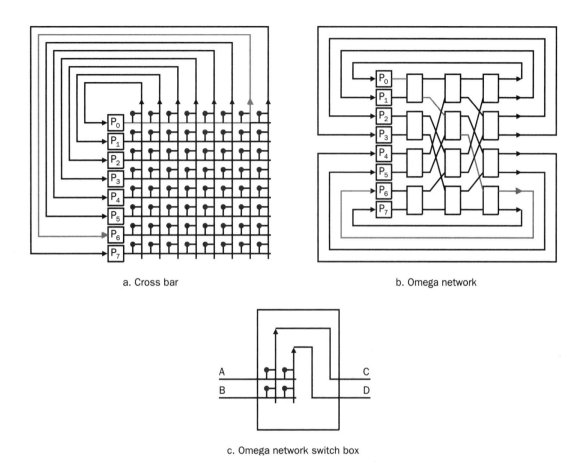

a. Cross bar

b. Omega network

c. Omega network switch box

FIGURE 8.12 Popular multistage network topologies for 8 nodes. The switches in these drawings are simpler than in earlier drawings because the links are unidirectional; data comes in at the bottom and exits out the right link. The switch box in (c) can pass A to C and B to D or B to C and A to D. The crossbar uses n^2 switches, where n is the number of processors while the Omega network uses n/2 log2 n of the large switch boxes, each of which is logically composed of 4 of the smaller switches. In this case the crossbar uses 64 switches versus 12 switch boxes or 48 switches in the Omega network. The crossbar, however, can support any combination of messages between processors while the Omega network cannot.

The CM-5 uses a multistage interconnection based on a tree with bandwidth added higher in the tree to match the requirements of common communications patterns. This topology, commonly called a *fat tree*, is shown in Figure 8.13. This figure shows that there are multiple paths between any two nodes; for example, between node 0 and node 8 there are four paths. By randomly assigning messages to different paths, the CM-5 ensures that communication can take advantage of the full bandwidth of the fat tree topology.

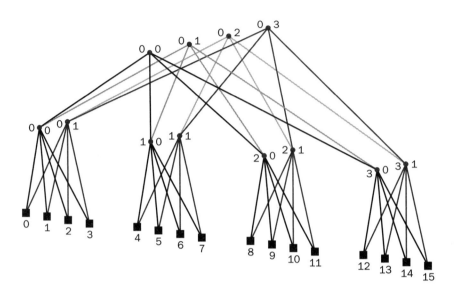

FIGURE 8.13   The CM-5 data network fat-tree topology for 16 nodes The colored circles are switches and the squares at the bottom are processor-memory nodes. Some lines are in color just to try to make the fat tree easier to understand. In the CM-5 fat-tree implementation, the switches have 4 downward connections and 2 or 4 upward connections; in this figure the switches have 2 upward connections . The switches are like the Figure 8.4.4a, in that there are paths between all ports without contention. This three dimensional view shows the increase in bandwidth over a simple tree as you move up from the nodes at the bottom.

This simple analysis of all the interconnections in this section ignores one important practical consideration in the construction of an interconnection: these three-dimensional drawings must be mapped onto chips and boards which are essentially two-dimensional media. The bottom line is that topologies that appear elegant when sketched on the blackboard may look awkward when constructed from chips, cables, boards, and boxes. Another consideration is to pick topologies that allow simple message routing, thereby simplifying hardware and minimizing latency per switch.

To put these topologies in perspective, Figure 8.14 lists those used in commercial MPPs.

Institution	Name	Number of Nodes	Basic Topology	Data Bits/ Link	Network Clock Rate	Peak BW/ Link (MB/ sec)	Bisection (MB/sec)	Year
Thinking Machines	CM-2	1024 to 4096	12-cube	1	7 MHz	1	1,024	1987
nCube	nCube/ten	1 to 1024	10-cube	1	10 MHz	1.2	640	1987
Intel	iPSC/2	16 to 128	7-cube	1	16 MHz	2	345	1988
Maspar	MP-1216	32 to 512	2D grid + multistage Omega	1	25 MHz	3	1,300	1989
Intel	Delta	540	2D grid	16	40 MHz	40	640	1991
Thinking Machines	CM-5	32 to 2048	Multistage fat tree	4	40 MHz	20	10,240	1991
Meiko	CS-2	32 to 1024	Multistage fat tree	8	70 MHz	50	50,000	1992
Intel	Paragon	4 to 1024	2D grid	16	100MHz	200	6,400	1992
Cray Research	T3D	16 to 1024	3D Torus	16	150 MHz	300	19,200	1993

FIGURE 8.14   Characteristics of interconnections of some commercial MPPs. The bisection bandwidth is given for the largest machine. The 2D grid of the Intel Delta is 16 rows by 35 columns. The fat tree topology of the CM-5 is restricted in the lower two levels, hence the lower bandwidth in the bisection. Note that the Cray T3D has two processors per node and the Intel Paragon has two to as many as four processors per node.

Connection-Oriented vs. Connectionless Communication

Before computers came on the scene, the telecommunications industry allowed voice to be sent around the world. An operator would set up a *connection* between the caller and the receiver, and once the connection was established, conversation could continue for hours. To share transmission lines over long distances, the telecommunications industry uses switches to multiplex several conversations on the same lines. Since voice has a relatively low bandwidth, the solution was to divide the bandwidth of the transmission line into a fixed number of slots, with each slot assigned to a conversation. This technique is called *time division multiplexing*.

While a good match for voice, using time division multiplexing to sharing lines is inefficient for sending data. The problem is that the time slot is dedicated to the conversation whether or not there is anything being said. Hence the long distance lines are "busy" based on the number of conversations, and not on the amount of information being sent at a particular time. An alternative style of communication is called *connectionless*, where every package of information must have an address. Each package is routed to the destination by looking at its address, making the postal system a good example of connectionless communication.

Closely related to the ideas of connection versus connectionless communication are the terms *circuit switching* and *packet switching*. Circuit switching is the traditional way to offer a connection-based service. A circuit is established from source to destination to carry the conversation. The alternative to circuit switched transmission is to divide the information into *packets* or *frames*, with each packet including the destination of the packet plus a portion of the information. This *packet switched* approach allows the information to use all the bandwidth of the shared medium, and is the traditional way to support connectionless communication.

This packet format typically includes fields for the length of the data and error detection fields in addition to the address and data. Figure 8.15 shows the packet formats for three examples.

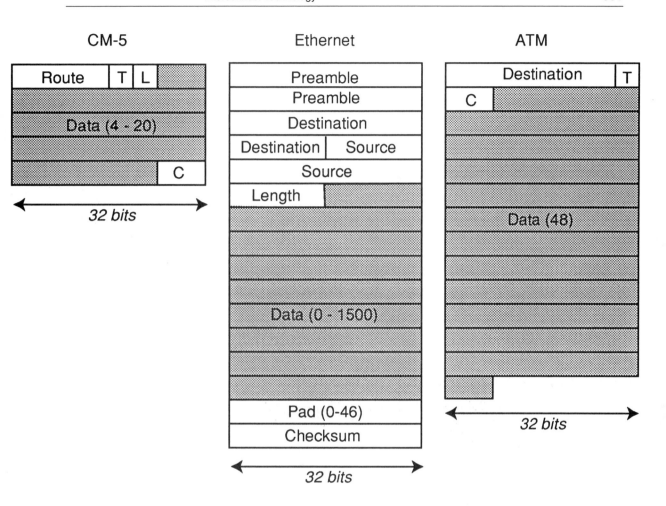

FIGURE 8.15   Packet format for CM-5, Ethernet, and ATM. ATM uses cells instead of packets, so this is the ATM cell format. The width of each drawing is 32 bits .All three formats have destination addressing fields, although the CM-5 destination is given as directions on how many levels to go up the 4-ary tree and then the path down to the destination. All three also have a checksum field (C) to catch transmission errors, although the ATM checksum field is calculated only over the header; ATM relies on higher-level protocols to catch errors in the data. Both CM-5 and the Ethernet have a length field (L) since the packets hold a variable amount of data, with the former counted in 32-bit words and the later in bytes . The CM-5 and ATM headers have a type field T that gives the type of packet. The remaining Ethernet fields are a preamble to synchronize the receiver's clock with the sender's clock, the source address, and a pad field to make sure the smallest packet is 64 bytes (including the header). (Buses can offer packets as well , using the name *split-phase transaction* buses instead of packet switching.)

Going back to our examples, both Ethernet and MPPs offer connectionless service using packets. ATM uses cell-based routing to offer a connection based service, which as we shall see in Section 8.9 has similar benefits to packet switching while supporting connections.

Question for Reviewer; Some simple example? (either no queuing theory or very simple queuing theory)

Transfer Size

In general, the larger the size of the transfer, the higher the delivered bandwidth of the interconnection. On the other hand, larger transfer sizes also have higher latency. To offer the best of both worlds, many interconnections support a range of transfer sizes allowing the situation to determine the size. Figure 8.16 shows the sizes for our three examples.

Interconnect	MPP	LAN	WAN
Example	**CM-5**	**Ethernet**	**ATM**
Data Transfer Size	Variable: 4 to 20 bytes	Variable: 0 to 1500 bytes	Fixed: 48 bytes
Header Size	4 bytes	26 bytes	5 bytes

FIGURE 8.16 Performance parameters for three interconnects. The ATM packet is not a power of 2 as a compromise between two adversaries in the standards committee, one who wanted 32 byes and the other 64. More recent versions of the CM-5 have expanded the maximum data size from 20 bytes to 76 bytes.

Example

Assume the software overhead to send a zero length data packet is 468 microseconds (see the example on page 587) and that an unloaded network can transmit at 90% of the peak 10 Mbit/sec rating. Plot the delivered bandwidth as the data transfer size varies from 32 bytes to 1500.

Answer

Figure 8.17 shows delivered bandwidth vs. packet size. The delivered bandwidth improves by a factor of 13 as the packet size increases from 32 bytes to 1500 bytes.

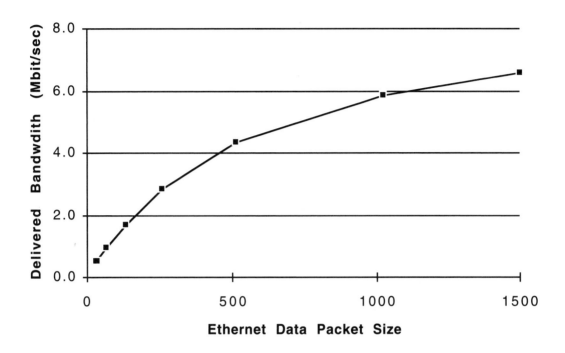

FIGURE 8.17 Delivered bandwidth as Ethernet packets varies in size assume the minimum time for one-way communication given in example. Like Figure 8.7, this figure shows the delivered bandwidth versus the peak bandwidth assuming a simple message time of startup overhead + message size/peak bandwidth. Note this figure includes the 26 byte Ethernet header but does not count the header as delivered information when calculating the delivered bandwidth.

Note that ATM has a fixed transfer size, in contrast to our other examples. There are two reasons for this decision. First, a fixed transfer size is easier for the hardware interfaces than variable sized transfers. The second reason is that when a short message is behind a long message, a node may need to wait for an entire transfer to complete. For applications that are time sensitive, such as when transmitting voice or video, the large transfer size may result in transmission delays that are too long for the application. ATM is intended for transferring voice and video as well as data, which led to the small, fixed transfer size.

Example

On an unloaded interconnection, what is the worst case delay if a node must wait for one full size Ethernet packet versus an ATM transfer?

Answer

Figure 8.16 shows that the maximum transfer size of the Ethernet is 1500 bytes of data plus 26 bytes of header. With a transfer rate of 1.25 MB/sec, the delay is

$$\frac{1526 \text{ bytes}}{1.25 \text{ MB/sec}} = \frac{1526}{1.25}\mu\text{secs} = 1220.8\mu\text{secs}$$

The ATM data transfer size is 48 bytes plus a 5 byte header. With a transfer rate of 19.5 MB/sec (155 Mbit/sec), the delay is

$$\frac{53 \text{ bytes}}{19.5 \text{ MB/sec}} = \frac{53}{19.5}\mu\text{secs} = 2.7\mu\text{secs}$$

The large transfer size and relatively low bandwidth of Ethernet versus ATM can add milliseconds of delay when the interconnection is busy. On loaded networks the calculation is more complicated, so ATM offers special guarantees to deliver voice and video when interconnections are loaded.

Congestion Control

One advantage of circuit switched networks is that once the circuit is established, there is sufficient bandwidth to deliver all the information that can be sent along that circuit. Thus interconnection bandwidth is reserved as circuits are established rather than consumed as data is sent, and if the network is full, no more circuits can be established. You may have encountered this blockage when trying to place a long distance phone call on a popular holiday, as the telephone system will tell you that "all circuits are busy" and to please call back at a later time.

Packet switched networks do not reserve interconnect bandwidth in advance, and so the interconnection can become clogged with too many packets. Just as with rush hour traffic, a traffic jam of packets will increase latency and may lower the bandwidth of the interconnect. Packets will take longer to arrive and fewer packets per second will be delivered by the interconnect, just as is the case for the poor rush-hour commuters.

Intermediate switches have buffers to store packets on their way to their final destination, so these intermediate switches can hold packets that must wait for earlier packets to be delivered to clear their paths. There is even the computer equivalent of gridlock: *deadlock* is achieved when packets in the interconnect can make no forward progress no matter what sequence of events happens. Avoiding this ultimate congestion is addressed in the next chapter.

The basic solution to congestion is to prevent new packets from entering the interconnect until traffic is reduced. Using our automobile analogy, this is the role of the metering lights on freeway on-ramps that control the rate of cars entering the freeway. There are three basic schemes used for congestion control in computer interconnect, each with its own weaknesses: packet discarding, flow control, and choke packets.

The simplest and most callous is *packet discarding*. If a packet arrives at a switch and there is no room in the buffer, the packet is discarded. This scheme relies on higher level software that handles errors in transmission to resend lost packets; we'll see such protocols in Section 8.6.

The second scheme is to rely on *flow control* between pairs of receivers and senders. The basic idea is to use feedback to tell the sender when it is allowed to send the next packet. One version of feedback is via separate wires between adjacent senders and receivers that tell the sender to stop immediately when the receiver cannot accept another message. This *back-pressure* feedback is rapidly sent back to the original sender over dedicated lines, causing all links between the two end points to be frozen until the receiver can make room for the next message. A more sophisticated variation of feedback is for the ultimate receiver to give the original sender the right to send N packets before getting permission to send more. The collection of N packets is typically called a *window*, with the window's size determining the minimum frequency of communication from receiver to sender. The goal of the window is to send enough packets to overlap the latency of the interconnection with the overhead to send and receive a packet.

This brings us to a point of confusion on terminology in many papers and textbooks. Note that flow control describes just two end systems of the interconnection, and not the total interconnection between all end systems. *Congestion control* refers to schemes that reduce traffic when the collective traffic of all end systems is too large for the interconnection to handle. Hence flow control helps congestion control, but it is not a universal solution.

The third scheme is based on *choke packets*. In this scheme the observation is that you only want to limit traffic when the interconnection is congested. The idea is for each switch to see how busy it is, entering a warning state when it passes a threshold. Each packet received by the switch in a warning state will be sent back to the source via a choke packet which includes the intended destination. The source is then expected to reduce traffic to that destination by a fixed percentage. Since it will likely have already sent many packets along that path, it waits for all the packets in transit to be returned before taking choke packets seriously.

Our three interconnection examples use different schemes for congestion control. Congestion control is simple with a shared medium since "congestion" occurs when more than one node ties to use the LAN. An Ethernet node first listens to make sure it doesn't send a message while another message is on the network. If the interconnection is idle, the node tries to send. Of course, some other node may decide to send at the same instant. Luckily, the network interface can detect any resulting collisions by listening to what is sent. (Mixed messages will sound like garbage.) Listening to avoid and detect collisions is called *carrier sensing*. To avoid repeated head-on collisions, each node whose packet was bashed waits (or "backs off") a random time before resending. Subsequent collisions result in exponentially increasing time between attempts by nodes to retransmit. While this approach is not fair–some subsequent node may transmit while those that collided are waiting–it does control congestion. If Ethernets do not have high utilization, this simple approach works well.

The CM-5 uses back-pressure flow control; a node must test to see if there is room in its output queue before sending a packet. The output queue in turn can send only if there is room on the switch to receive its packet. This continues until the receiver's input queue is checked. By dedicating wires for back pressure between senders and receivers in this multistage switch, the fullness of a buffer along the path is quickly reflected back to senders to throttle traffic at the sources. To reduce the chances of such congestion, the CM-5 switches use randomization techniques to evenly spread the message load across the possible paths.

As we shall see in Section 8.8 ATM is still an evolving standard, with congestion control still a topic of hot debate. The likely winner at the time of this writing is rate based flow control using choke packets. The send rate moves up slowly, sending more and more packets until it is told by the receiver to cut back. The frequency that rates change are a function of the round trip time for a packet between sender and receiver.

Question for Reviewer; Some simple example? (either no queuing theory or very simple queuing theory)

Store and Forward vs. Cut Through/Worm Hole

Most switches use a *store-and-forward* policy; each switch waits for the full packet to arrive in the switch before it is sent on to the next switch. The alternative is the switch examines the header, decides where to send the message, and then starts forwarding it immediately. This alternative is called either *cut through* routing or *worm hole* routing. In worm hole routing when the head of the message is blocked the message stays strung out over the network, potentially blocking other messages. Cut through routing lets the tail continue when the head is blocked, accordioning the whole message into a single switch. Clearly cut-through routing requires a buffer large enough to hold the largest packet while worm hole routing needs only buffer the piece of the packet that is sent between switches. The CM-5 uses worm-hole routing, with each switch buffer being just four bits per port.

The advantage of either scheme is that latency reduces from a function of the number of intermediate switches *multiplied* by the size of the packet to the time for the first part of the packet to negotiate the switches *plus* the packet size divided by the interconnect bandwidth.

Example	Compare efficiency of store and forward versus worm-hole routing for a 128 node machine using a CM-5 interconnection sending a 16 byte payload. Assume each switch takes 0.25 microseconds and that the transfer rates is 20 MB/s.
Answer	Each switch in the CM-5 is one node of the 4-ary fat tree. The CM-5 interconnection for 128 nodes is 4-levels high, so a message goes through 7 intermediate switches. Each CM-5 packet has 4 bytes of header information, so the length of this packet is 20 bytes. The time to transfer 20 bytes over one CM-5 link is:

$$\frac{20}{20 \text{ MB/s}} = 1 \mu\text{sec}$$

Then the time for store and forward is

$$\text{switches} \times (\text{switch delay} + \text{transfer time}) = 7 \times (0.25 + 1) = 8.75 \mu\text{secs}$$

while worm-hole routing is

$$(\text{switches} \times \text{switch delay}) + \text{transfer time} = (7 \times 0.25) + 1 = 2.75 \mu\text{secs}$$

For this example, worm-hole routing improves latency by a factor of 3.

8.5 | Practical Issues

There are three practical issues in addition to the technical issues described so far that are important considerations for some interconnections: standardization, fault tolerance, and "hot" insertion. Figure 8.18 shows the decisions on these practical issues for our examples.

Interconnect	MPP	LAN	WAN
Example	CM-5	Ethernet	ATM
Standard vs. Proprietary	Proprietary	Standard: IEEE 802.3	Standard: ATM Forum, CCITT
Fault tolerance	No	Yes	Yes
Hot Insert	No	Yes	Yes

FIGURE 8.18   Implementation parameters for three interconnects.

Standardization

The first practical issue is whether or not the interconnection follows a standard. Advantages of successful standards include low cost and stability: the customer has many vendors to choose from which both keeps price close to cost due to competition and makes the viability of the interconnection independent of the viability of a single company. Components designed to be used in a standard interconnection may also have a larger market, and this higher volume can lower costs of the vendor, further benefiting the customer. Finally, a standard allows many companies to build products with interfaces to the standard, so the customer does not have to wait for a single company to develop interfaces to all the products the customer might be interested in.

One drawback of standards is that it takes a long time for committees to agree on the definition of standards, which is a problem when technology is changing quickly. Another problem is when to standardize: on one hand designers would like to have a standard before anything is built, but on the other hand it would be better if something is built before standardization to avoid legislating useless features or omitting important ones. Standards can also suppress innovation, since the interfaces are determined by the standard.

Figure 8.18 shows that the example MPP interconnection is proprietary while LAN and WAN use standards. WANs involve many types of companies as well as having to connect many brands of computers, so it is difficult to imagine a proprietary WAN ever being successful. The ubiquitous nature of the Ethernet shows the popularity of standards for LANs as well as WANs, and it seems unlikely that many customers would tie the viability of their LAN to the viability of a single company.

Since an MPP is really a single brand of computer from a single company, the customer is already betting on a single company, removing one of the main reasons for interconnect standards. Thus the few MPPs that used standard interconnections did so to take advantage of the lower cost of components developed for these standards.

Fault Tolerance

The second practical issue refers to whether or not the interconnection relies on all the nodes being operational for the interconnection to work properly. Since software failures are generally much more frequent than hardware failures, the question is whether a software crash on a single node can prevent the rest of the nodes from communicating.

Clearly WANs would be useless if they demanded that thousands of computers spread across a continent were continuously available, and so they all tolerate the failures of individual nodes. LANs connect dozens to hundreds of computers together, and again it would be impractical to require that no computer ever fail. All successful LANs normally survive node failures.

While some MPPs have the ability to work around failed nodes and switches, its not clear that MPP operating systems support this feature. The close cooperation of the software on an MPP during communication also makes it unlikely that the interconnection would be useful if a single node crashed.

Example

Figure 8.19 shows the number of failures of 58 workstations on a local area network for a period of just over one year. Suppose that one local area network is based on an MPP network which requires all machines to be operational for the interconnection to send data; if a node crashes it cannot accept messages so the interconnection becomes choked with data waiting to be delivered. An alternative is the traditional local area network, which can operate in the presence of node failures; the interconnection simply discards messages for a node that decides not to accept them. Assuming that you need to have both your workstation and the connecting LAN to get your work done, how much greater are your chances of being prevented from getting your work done using MPP LAN versus traditional LANs? Assume the down time for a crash is less than 30 minutes. Calculate using the 1-hour intervals.

Answer

Assuming the numbers for Figure 8.19, The percentage of hours that you can't get your work done using the MPP network is

$$\frac{\text{Intervals with failures}}{\text{Total Intervals}} = \frac{\text{Total Intervals} - \text{Intervals no failures}}{\text{Total Intervals}}$$

$$= \frac{8974 - 8605}{8974} = \frac{369}{8974} = 4.1\%$$

The percentage of hours that you can't get you can't get your work done using the traditional network is just the time your workstation has crashed. Assuming that these failures are equally distributed among workstations, the percentage is:

$$\frac{\text{Failures/Machines}}{\text{Total Intervals}} = \frac{654/58}{8974} = \frac{11.28}{8974} = 0.13\%$$

Hence you would have been more than 30 times more likely to be prevented from getting your work done with the MPP LAN than the traditional LAN using the failure statistics in Figure 8.19.

Failed Machines	1-hour intervals with no. failures	Total failures per 1-hour interval	1-day intervals with no. failure	Total failures per 1-day interval
0	8605	0	184	0
1	264	264	105	105
2	50	100	35	70
3	25	75	11	33
4	10	40	6	24
5	7	35	9	45
6	3	18	6	36
7	1	7	4	28
8	1	8	4	32
9	2	18	2	18
10	2	20		
11	1	11	2	22
12			1	12
17	1	17		
20	1	20		
21	1	21	1	21
31			1	31
38			1	38
58			1	58
Total	8974	654	373	573

FIGURE 8.19   Measurement of reboots of 58 DECstation 5000s running Ultrix over a 373 day period. These reboots are divided into time tine intervals of one hour and one day. The first column is used to sort the intervals according to the number of machines that failed in that interval. The second column shows the number of 1-hour intervals with that many failures and the fourth columns shows the number of 1-day intervals. The third and fifth columns are just the product of the number of failed machines and the number of intervals. The last row shows the total number of each column: there number of failures don't agree because multiple reboots of the same machine in the same interval do not result in separate entries. (This data was collected by Randy Wang of U.C. Berkeley.)

Hot Insert

This last practical issue is tied to the previous point: if the interconnection can survive a failure, can it also continue operation while a new node is added to the interconnection? If not, the interconnection would need to be disabled each time a new node is added. Disabling is impractical for both WANs and LANs, but generally not an important issue for traditional MPPs markets.

One potential MPP market that would care is systems aimed at high availability, such as those used for commercial banking. In this environment customers want to replace a failed component without taking the system off-line, so the system must tolerate the failure and then allow the failed component to be replaced and put back into service.

Question for reviewers: Drop this last paragraph?

8.6 | The Hardware/Software Interface of Interconnections: The Internet Protocol Family

Undoubtedly one of the most important inventions in the communications community has been internetworking. It allows computers on independent and incompatible networks to communicate reliably and efficiently. For example, it is vastly less expensive to send electronic mail than to make a coast-to-coast telephone call and leave a message on an answering machine. This dramatic cost improvement is achieved using the same long haul communication lines as the telephone call, which makes the improvement even more impressive.

The enabling technologies for internetworking are software standards that allow reliable communication without demanding reliable networks. The underlying principle of these successful standards is to compose the standards as a hierarchy of layers, giving each layer responsibility for a portion of the overall communication task. Each computer, network, and switch implements its layer of the standards, relying on the other components to faithfully fulfill their responsibilities. These layered software standards are called *protocol families* or *protocol suites*. They enable applications to work with any interconnection without extra work by the application programmer.

The most popular internetworking standard is *TCP/IP*, which stands for *Transmission Control Protocol/Internet Protocol*. This protocol family is the basis of the humbly named *Internet*, which connects tens of millions of people around the world. This popularity means TCP/IP is used even when communicating locally across compatible networks; for example, the network file system NFS uses IP even though it is very likely to be communicating across a homogenous LAN such as Ethernet.

We use TCP/IP as our protocol family example; other protocol families follow similar lines. This section gives an overview of protocol families and details of TCP/IP, followed by an example of sending a file from Stanford to Berkeley over the Internet. Section 8.11 gives the history of TCP/IP.

An Introduction to Protocol Families

The goal of a family of protocols is to simplify the standard by dividing responsibilities hierarchically among layers, with each layer offering services needed by the layer above. The application program is at the top and the physical communication medium which sends the bits is at the bottom. Just as abstract data types simplify the programmer's task by shielding the programmer from details of the implementation of the data type, this layered standard should make the standard easier to understand.

The key to protocol families is that communication occurs logically at the same level of the protocol, called *peer-to-peer*, but it is implemented via services of the lower level. As an analogy, imagine that General A needs to send a message to General B on the battlefield. General A writes the message, puts it in an envelope addressed to General B, and gives it to a colonel with orders to deliver it. This colonel puts it in an envelope and writes the name of the corresponding colonel who reports to General B, and gives it to a major with instructions for delivery. The major does the same thing and gives it to a captain, who gives it to a lieutenant, who gives it to a sergeant. The sergeant takes the envelope from the lieutenant, puts it into a envelope with the name of a sergeant that is in General B's division, and finds a private with orders to take the large envelope. The private borrows a motorcycle and delivers the envelope to the sergeant. Once it arrives it is passed up the chain of command, with each person removing an outer envelope with their name on it and passing on the inner envelop to their superior. As far as General B can tell, the note is from another general. Neither general knows who was involved in transmitting the envelope nor how it was transported from one division to the other.

Protocol families are closer to this analogy than you might think, as Figure 8.20 shows. The original message is given a header and possibly a trailer to be sent by the lower level protocol. The next lower protocol in turn adds its own header to the message, possibly breaking it up into smaller messages if it is too large for this layer. This division of the message and prepending of headers continues until the messages descends to the physical transmission medium. The message is then sent to the destination. Each level of the protocol family on the receiving end will check the message at its level and peel off its headers and trailers, passing it on to the next higher level. This nesting of protocol layers for a specific message is often referred to as a *protocol stack*, reflecting the last-in-first-out nature of the addition and removal of headers.

As in our analogy, the danger in this layered approach is adding considerable latency to message delivery. Clearly one way to reduce overhead is to reduce the number of layers. But keep in mind that protocol families are used to define a standard, not to force how the standard is implemented. Just as there are many ways to implement an instruction set architecture, there are many ways to implement a protocol family.

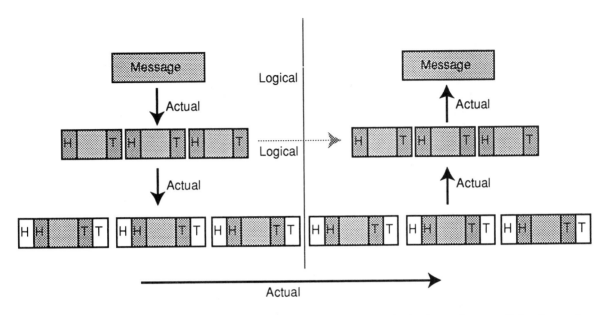

FIGURE 8.20 A generic protocol stack with two layers. Note that communication is peer-to-peer, with headers and trailers for the peer added at each sending layer and removed by each receiving layer. Each layer is intended to offer services to the one above to shield it from details that it does not have a need to know.

Our protocol stack example is TCP/IP. Let's assume that the bottom or physical protocol layer is Ethernet. The next level up is the Internet Protocol or IP layer; the official term for an IP packet is *datagram*. It is the job of the IP layer to route the datagram to the destination machine, which may involve many intermediate machines or switches. IP makes a best effort to deliver the packets, but does not guarantee delivery nor content of datagrams. The TCP layer above IP makes that guarantee of reliable delivery and prevents corruption of datagrams.

Following the model is Figure 8.20, assume an application program wants to send a message to a machine that happens to be connected by an Ethernet. It starts with TCP. The largest number of bytes that can be sent at one time with TCP is 64 KB. Since the data may well be much larger than 64KB, its is up to TCP divide it into smaller segments and to reassemble them in proper order upon arrival. TCP adds a 20 byte header (Figure 8.21) to every datagram, and passes them down to IP. The IP layer above the physical layer adds a 20 byte header, also shown in Figure 8.21. The data sent down from the IP level to the Ethernet would be sent in packets with the format shown in Figure 8.15 on page 601. We will explain the use of the highlighted fields of Figure 8.21 in our example, but note that the TCP packet appears inside the data portion of the IP datagram, just as Figure 8.20 suggests. (The other fields are described in the caption of Figure 8.21.)

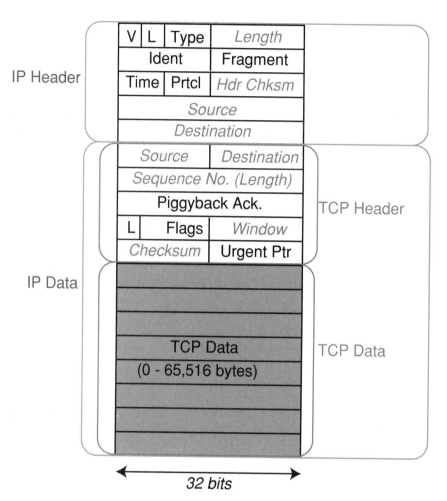

FIGURE 8.21   The headers for IP and TCP. The fields using italicizes text in color will be explained in t he example. This drawings are 32 bits wide. The standard headers for both are 20 bytes, but both allow the headers to optionally be expanded for rarely transmitted information. Both headers have a length of header field (L) to accommodate the optional fields, as well as Source and Destination fields. The length field of the whole datagram is in a separate Length field in IP while TCP combines the length of the datagram with the sequence number of the datagram by giving the sequence number in bytes. IP provides checksum error detection for the header while TCP provides it for the whole packet. The *piggyback acknowl-edgment field* of TCP is an optimization. Since some applications send data back and forth over the same connection, it seems wasteful to send a datagram containing only an acknowledgment. This piggyback field allows a datagram carrying data to also carry the acknowledgment for a previous transmission, "piggybacking" on top of a data transmission. The *Ur-gent Pointer field* of TCP gives the address within the datagram of an important byte, such as a break character. This point-er allows the application software to skip over data so that the user doesn't have to wait for all prior data to be processed before seeing a character that tells the software to stop. The *Identifier field* and *Fragment field* of IP allow intermediary ma-chines to break the original datagram into many smaller datagrams. A unique identifier is associated with the original data-gram and placed in every fragment, with the fragment field saying which piece is which. The *Time-to-Live field* allows a datagram to be killed off after going through a maximum number of intermediate switches no matter where it is in the net-

work. Knowing the maximum number of hops that it will take for a datagram to arrive–if it ever arrives–simplifies the protocol software. The *Protocol field* identifies which possible upper layer protocol sent the IP datagram; in our case it is TCP. The V (for *version*) and *Type fields* allow there to be different versions of the IP protocol software to be used in the network. Explicit version numbering is included so that software can be upgraded gracefully machine by machine, without shutting down the entire network.

An Example: Sending a file from Stanford to Berkeley

Question for reviewer: too much detail about TCP/IP headers and/or FTP example for this text?

Let's show TCP/IP in action by transferring a file from the machine named mojave.stanford.edu at Stanford University to the machine mammoth.berkeley.edu at the University of California at Berkeley, a distance of about 75 km. The first step is turning the machine names into Internet addresses. Internet addresses are 32 bits long, and are traditionally represented as four decimal numbers separated by decimal points. For example, 36.22.0.120 represents the binary number

$$00100100\ 00010110\ 00000000\ 01111000_{two}$$

Internet addresses are divided into a network number and a node or *host* number on that network.

To transfer a file we could use the FTP program. After logging into the remote machine, FTP would invoke TCP to transfer the file. FTP would first use TCP to set up a connection between Stanford and Berkeley by sending IP datagrams. A *connection* is a reliable communication channel that delivers every piece of data intact and in the proper order. TCP uses the Checksum field to be sure that the datagram has not been corrupted and the Sequence Number field to be sure the datagrams are assembled into the proper order when they arrive. Once the connection is established, TCP sends data through that connection, relying on lower level protocols to deliver the datagrams. The connection that was established is shown in Figure 8.22.

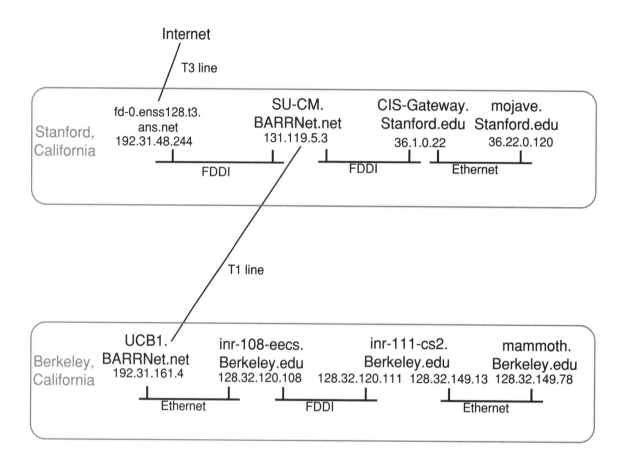

FIGURE 8.22 The connection established between mojave.stanford.edu and mammoth.berkeley.edu. FDDI is a 100 Mbit/sec LAN, while a T1 line is a 1.5 Mbit/sec telecommunications line and a T3 is a 45 Mbit/sec telecommunications line. Note that inr-111-cs2.Berkeley.edu is a router with two Internet addresses, one for each port.

The connection from mojave.Stanford.edu goes over a Ethernet to a machine named CIS-Gateway.Stanford.edu, which connects Center for Integrated Systems to the Stanford campus network. On this campus network is SU-CM.BARRNET.NET, which is Stanford's connection to the Wide Area Network called BARRNet, which stands for Bay Area Research network. It connects research institutions in the San Francisco Bay Area to each other and to the Internet. The next step of the connection is to cross the bay to Berkeley. This line from Stanford is a leased telephone line that transfers 1.5 Mbit/s, called a *T1 line*. At the other end is another machine belonging to BARRNet, but located on the Berkeley campus, called UCB1.BARRNet.net. The next step for the connection goes from BARRNet over an Ethernet to the inr-108-eecs.Berkeley.edu. This machine routes messages from all over the Berkeley campus to the BARRNet. Mammoth is not connected directly to this machine, so the connection goes over the FDDI network to another router called inr-111-cs2.Berkeley.edu, which goes over another Ethernet to mammoth.

With the path completed, TCP then picks the proper size for the datagrams to transfer the file. This consists of the sending TCP program asking the receiving TCP program how large a packet it can buffer. There is also a decision for an IP datagram, trying to pick is the best to the maximum transfer size to reduce the unpacking and repacking of data into different sized packets to match the underlying protocols. This size is set by the systems administrator for each machine, with the traditional default size being 536 bytes.

Once the connection is established, TCP sends the first piece of the file, prepended with the TCP header. Note that the TCP source and destination in Figure 8.21 are only 16 bits long, clearly not enough for the Internet address. The reason that Internet addresses aren't used is that the next lower level protocol will provide the Internet addresses, so there is no need to include them here. There might be multiple connections between two machines, however; for example, one sending mail and one sending a file. Hence the source and destination addresses refer to a *port number* which identifies the desired connection between the two machines. The next field of the TCP header is the segment number, used to be sure that datagrams are placed in proper order when they arrive. The other important field is the Checksum, which is used to find transmission errors in the data or the header.

TCP passes down this first datagram to IP, which adds its own 20 byte header (Figure 8.21). This header includes the Internet addresses for source and destination, the length of the datagram, and eventually a checksum for the IP header, since the TCP checksum obviously cannot include the header from a lower level protocol.

The next step is for mojave.stanford.edu is to send the IP datagram over the Ethernet to CIS-Gateway. The Ethernet software will lookup the Ethernet addresses for mojave and CIS-Gateway to place them in the Ethernet header shown in Figure 8.15 on page 601. (There is no relationship between the 48-bit Ethernet address and the 32-bit Internet address.) It puts in the length, the standard preamble, and then calculates another checksum. The Ethernet packet is then sent to CIS-Gateway. Figure 8.23 shows the protocol stacks used in first part of this transfer.

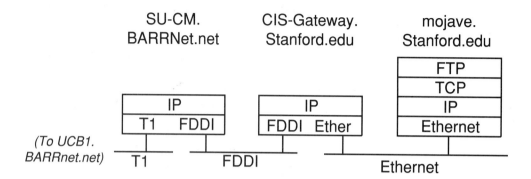

FIGURE 8.23   The protocol stacks used at Stanford University in the FTP example along the path of Figure 8.22.

When the Ethernet packet arrives at the CIS-Gateway, software strips off its header and trailer, making sure that the checksum agrees with the contents of the packet. The remaining IP datagram is then passed up to the IP layer. It checks the destination and then sends it down to another layer of software to onto the FDDI LAN to SU-CM. It translates the FDDI packet and puts it onto the T1 line to send it to UCB.BARRNet.net.

After hops through two more intermediary machines at Berkeley, each replacing the packet header and trailer at the layer below IP, the datagram finally arrives at the IP layer on mammoth.berkeley.edu. The IP software peels off the IP header and hands the first datagram to the TCP layer. TCP checks the TCP header to see which connection is involved and then compares the data tot he checksum to be sure there are no transmission errors. It then peels of its header and saves this the first piece of data.

It would seem that the next step would be to send an acknowledgment back down the connection to tell TCP on mojave to send the next datagram. This would be exceedingly slow, as we would have to wait a whole round trip time between successive datagrams. The optimization is that TCP is allowed to send a sequence of datagrams before waiting for permission to send more. The number of datagrams that can be sent without waiting for approval is called the *window*. The window field in the TCP header in Figure 8.21 tells how many bytes may be sent beyond the byte being acknowledged by this datagram. TCP will adjust the size of the window depending on the success of the IP layer in sending datagrams; the more reliable it is, the larger TCP makes the window. Since the window slides forward as the data arrives and is acknowledged, this technique is called a *sliding window protocol*.

The rest of the file is transferred a piece at time from TCP via IP and the underlying interconnections until it is fully assembled on mammoth.berkeley.edu.

Clearly the speed of transfer is limited by the weakest link in the chain, so the upper bound must be 1.5 Mbit/sec given the use of T1 lines. A 1.75 MB file transferred in 34 seconds, giving a rate of 0.42 Mbits/sec. The likely reason for the lower bandwidth is the sharing of the T1 line with other Internet traffic.

8.7 | Cross Cutting Issues for Interconnections

This section describes ?? topics discussed in other chapters that are fundamental to interconnections.

Efficient Interface to Memory Hierarchy vs. Interconnection

Traditional evaluations of processor performance, such as SPECint and SPECfp, encourage the memory hierarchy to be closely integrated with the processor as the efficiency of the memory hierarchy translates directly into processor performance. Hence microprocessors today have the first level caches on chip along with buffers for writes, and they usually have second level caches immediately next to the chip. Benchmarks such as SPECint and SPECfp do not reward good interfaces to interconnections, and hence in many machines make the access time to the interconnection delayed by the full memory hierarchy: writes must lumber their way through full write buffers and reads must go through the cycles of first and second level cache misses before reaching the interconnection. This can result in newer systems having the same latency to interconnections as older machines. For example, the 40 MHz SPARCstation 2 takes 250(?) ns to access the S-bus but the more recent 50 MHz SPARCstation 10 takes 400(?) ns to access the S-bus. One of the main reasons for the extra delay is the second level cache in the newer machines.

Where to draw the hardware/software dividing line for interconnection functions

The choice of hardware vs. software support for interconnections has many of the same tradeoffs of as other parts of a computer. Examples of features implemented in hardware in some systems and in software with others are message routing, message error detection, and retransmission.

Early MPPs would involve each processor along a path to route a message from switch to switch. This software overhead dominated switch latency, and thus all recent MPPs have hardware routing. Hardware routing in turn affects the complexity of the topologies of the interconnection, since hardware simplicity demands a simple routing algorithm. For some interconnections the path through the switches is picked in advance, so that the hardware merely examines a few bits to see how to route the packet through a given switch. In others the destination address of the packet uniquely determines the path through the switch.

Another example of the hardware/software implementation decision is reliable delivery of messages. TCP will check to make sure that messages are delivered reliably by including check sums, yet LANs like Ethernet will also include check sums in hardware to determine whether packets have reliably been delivered. Some interconnection interfaces will hold onto a packet until it has been acknowledged by the receiving hardware, retransmitting in case of failure. These same functions are provided in software by TCP. Reliable delivery is one area where there is considerable duplication of effort between the hardware and software rather than a clear division of responsibilities.

Question for reviewer: do you have suggestions for more cross cutting issues? The idea is to feature topics that cut across several chapters, covering them here.

8.8 | Putting It All Together: An ATM Network of Workstations

Ethernet has been extraordinarily successful; the 10 Mbit/sec standard proposed in 1978 is used everywhere today, with many classes of computers including Ethernet as a standard interface. Given that computers are more than 100 times faster than they were in 1978 and the shared interconnection is no faster, engineers have had to invent temporary solutions until a faster interconnect could take Ethernet's place. One solution has to use more Ethernets to connect machines, and connect these smaller Ethernets with devices that can take traffic from one Ethernet and pass it on to another as needed. These devices allow individual Ethernets to operate in parallel, thereby increasing the interconnection bandwidth of a collection of computers. Figure 8.24 shows the potential parallelism. Depending on how they pass traffic and what kinds of interconnections they can put together, these devices are named differently:

- *bridges*: these devices connect LANs together, passing traffic from one side to another depending on the addresses in the packet. Bridges operate at the Ethernet protocol level, and usually simpler and cheaper than routers.

- *routers* or *gateways*: these devices connect LANs to WANs or WANs to WANs and will resolve incompatible addressing. Generally slower than bridges, they operate at the IP protocol level. Routers divide the interconnect into separate smaller subnets, which simplifies manageability and improves security.

Since these devices were not planned for as part of the Ethernet standard, their ad hoc nature has added to the difficulty and cost of maintaining LANs.

Single Ethernet: 1 packet at a time

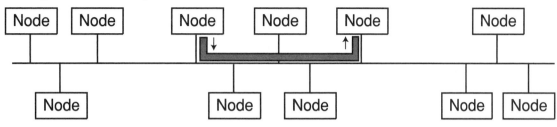

Multiple Ethernets: Multiple packets at a time

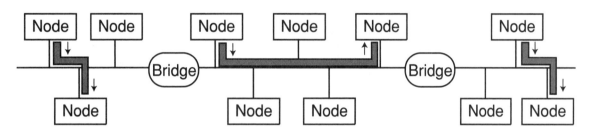

FIGURE 8.24   **The potential increased bandwidth of using many Ethernets and bridges.**

It is long past time to replace the Ethernet, and there have been several unsuccessful candidates. The most recent has been FDDI, which stands for Fiber Distributed Data Interface. This optical-based interconnection was specified at 100 Mbit/sec and could use much longer cables than Ethernet. Unfortunately, the FDDI committee took a very long time to agree on the standard and the resulting interfaces were are expensive. It also shared the Ethernet weakness that all machines shared the interconnection medium, with only one packet on the medium at a time, and FDDI still needed bridges and routers. FDDI is currently used as a "backbone" network, which simply means connecting LANs together via routers rather than connecting desktop computers.

The failure of FDDI on the desktop has led the LAN community to look elsewhere, and at the time of this writing there are three promising candidates. The first candidate is one of two competing standards that offer a 100 Mbit/sec version of the Ethernet. The second builds on the trend towards smaller networks connected by bridges by making switches a part of the standard. *Switched Ethernet* simply includes fast, multiport bridges so that the bandwidth to a single machine is no higher, but the collective bandwidth of the LAN is much higher.

Question for reviewer: Leave this gradual introduction to ATM above, or move to Historical Perspective or elsewhere?

The third option is borrowed from the telecommunications industry. Given the desirability of using switches and the need to efficiently interface to WANs, why not use ATM as a LAN? In addition to have the scalable bandwidth of switched Ethernet, ATM is defined independently from the physical medium, which allows the system to be upgraded gracefully to higher speed interconnections. Unlike Ethernet, several data rates are included in the standard.

It is ATM that we discuss in this section. ATM is still evolving as a standard, so we will describe the subset of ATM that seems likely today to be popular for LAN. Section 8.11 tells more about ATM and gives references for the interested reader. The hope of ATM is that it will allow much higher performance communication while avoiding the hodgepodge of devices needed to connect segments of LANs together or to connect LANs to WANs, since the same underlying technology can be used from top to bottom.

Our example is 16 SPARCstation 10 workstations connected via a SynOptics Lattiscell ATM switch. Figure 8.25 shows details of the organization. The SPARCstation 10 uses a 50 MHz SuperSPARC microprocessor which consists of a superscalar CPU and instruction and data caches on a single chip. This chip interfaces to a 1 MB second level cache which stands between the microprocessor and the 40 MHz M-bus. The M-bus connects to memory and to a bus interface to the 20 MHz S-bus, Sun's I/O bus.

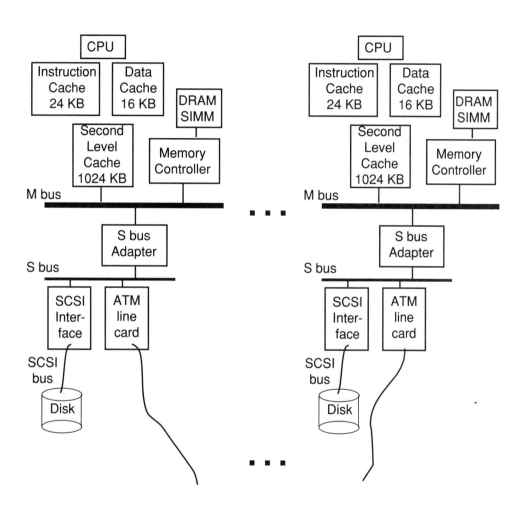

FIGURE 8.25 The organization of the SPARCstation-10 and the ATM switch.

It is on the S-bus that we find the ATM *line card*, which interfaces to the ATM switch. Each machine has a line card which is connected to the 16-by-16 ATM switch. Figure 8.26 gives details of those components. Depending on the distance to the switch, the media can either be unshielded twisted pair copper wire or optical fibers. The latter option requires expensive electrical-to-optical interfaces, but stretches the distance between the line card and switch from tens of meters to kilometers. The ATM switch itself is a multistage switch similar to the Omega switch in Figure 8.12 (page 597), with an internal bandwidth that is twice the demand of the sixteen 155 Mbit/sec ports.

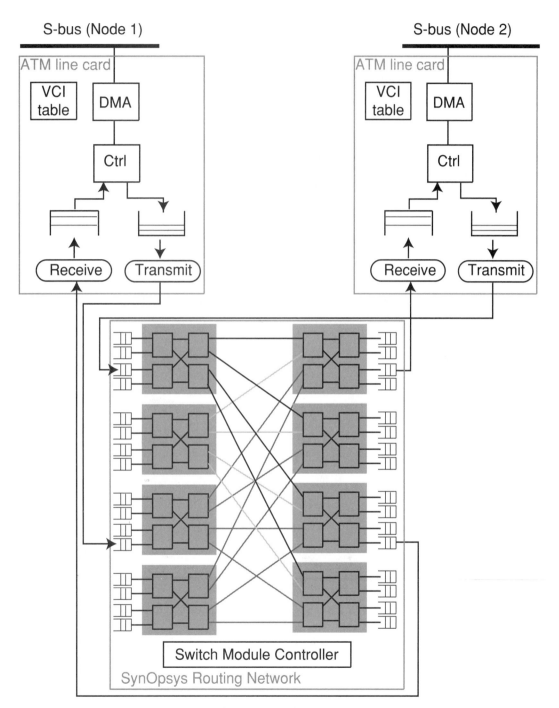

FIGURE 8.26 ATM line card s and 16-by-16 LattisCell ATM switch from Synoptics . The switch connection is called a Delta connection, which is a relative of the Omega switch. The switch also has a copy network that is identical to the routing network to support multicast ; it is placed before the router The switch module finds the outgoing destination port of the switch by indexing into a table using the incoming VCI port number.

Let's use FTP as our example, as we did in the prior section. The transfer proceeds down the TCP and IP layers until it reaches ATM. At the top of the ATM software is the ATM Adaptation Layer. Figure 8.27 show this relationship between layers and Figure 8.3 shows AAL-5. For this example we are going to assume that the connections have already been established between machines, so that we do not need to establish a connection.

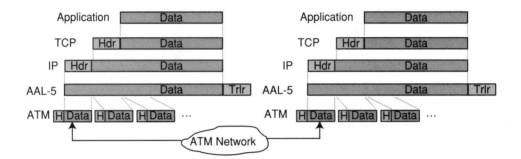

FIGURE 8.27   show this relationship between TPC, IP, and AAL-5. The ATM Forum hopes that over time adaptation layers such as AAL-5 will replace protocol suites such as TCP/IP.

AAL-5

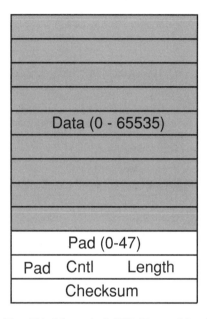

FIGURE 8.28 The AAL-5 format of ATM. The evolving ATM standard has at least five proposals for AALs, but in our view AAL-5 is the most likely winner for LANs when shipping datagrams. Lower level protocols set bits in packets to show the end of the transfer. The Pad field ensures that the data payload plus the AAL-5 trailer is a multiple of 48 bytes, the data size of an ATM cell. The Control field (Cntl) is reserved for future use. Length and Checksum fields are self-explanatory.

Question for reviewer: I'm not clear on this point. Is the AAL-5 trailer included or not in the modulo 48 bytes? Must it be included in the max. of 64KB, or is it an extra 48B beyond a 64KB data payload?

Question for reviewer: Should we skip AAL-5 figure & description?

The next layer of ATM software breaks up the data payload into the 48-byte units transferred in each ATM cell. Figure 8.29 shows the details of the ATM header. Unlike Ethernet, ATM is based on connections being set up in advance before data can be transmitted between two machines. These connections are called *virtual channels*, with the *Virtual Channel Identifier* (VCI) used to pick the proper connection for each ATM cell. The ATM switch uses the VCI to send the cell to the proper output port. The header also provides a *Virtual Path Identifier* (VPI); *virtual paths* simply represent bundles of virtual channels, and may be used by ATM switches to route many channels at once rather than having to route them individually. The Payload Type Indicator field is used by AAL-5 to mark the end of a packet.

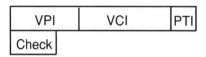

FIGURE 8.29   The ATM header format. The VPI field is 12 bits, VCI is 16 bits, PTI field is 4 bits, and the Checksum field is 8 bits. The main use of the Payload Type Indicator field is to mark the end of the AAL-5 packet. This is the format of the ATM Network to Network Interface.

Note that ATM uses a fixed sized unit of transmission to simplify the design of switches and interfaces. These units are called *cells* rather than packets because ATM is a connection based interconnection, and the cell selects the connection rather than including the destination address in every cell.

Once all the cells that comprise the AAL-5 message are delivered to the appropriate machine, they are assembled in proper order and then passed to the AAL-5 layer software. The layer then checks the data and passes it up to the IP software, proceeding then as our prior example.

Performance of SPARCStations and ATM

To put this design in context, this section measures compares performance of one of the initial ATM switches to an Ethernet LAN. Since Ethernet and its software are mature and ATM is an emerging technology, we would expect ATM software overheads improve much more rapidly than Ethernet in the future.

Figure 8.30 shows the latency of different components of the ATM local area network and Figure 8.31 shows the TCP bandwidth as the size of the TCP packets are increased for Ethernet and ATM. Sending larger packets amortizes the overhead of TCP, IP, and the ATM driver.

This figure understates the ATM bandwidth since the switch can support many simultaneous transfers while multiple transfers must share the single 10Mbit/sec peak speed of the Ethernet. Using 8 KB TCP packets, the SynOptics ATM switch supports multiple connections that each run at 78 Mbit/sec.

This example ATM for LAN actually has a higher software overhead to launch a message. Amdahl's Law tells us that ATM vendors will need to improve the time to send and receive a small message as well as large messages if many applications are to benefit from this potential improvement.

	Time	CPU Clock Cycles	Instructions
HW Latency			
CPU to Sbus	0.8 μsecs	4.0	≈ 45
ATM Interface to Switch	5 μsecs	250	≈ 275
ATM Switch	53 μsecs	2,650	≈ 3,000
SW Latency			
Send (TCP/IP/Driver)	207 μsecs	10,350	≈ 13,000
Receive (TCP/IP/Driver)	360 μsecs	18,000	≈ 22,500

FIGURE 8.30   Hardware and software latencies for the SPARCstation-10 and Syn-Optics ATM interfaces and switch. The processor has a 50 MHz clock and the superscalar processor executes at about 0.9 CPI. (Measurements taken by Kim Keeton of U.C. Berkeley.)

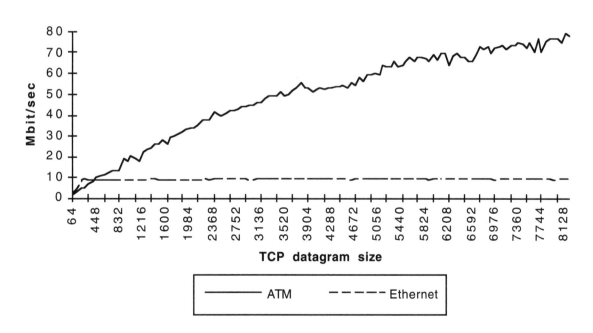

FIGURE 8.31   TCP Bandwidth of ATM vs. Ethernet between two machines as datagram size varies from 64 bytes to 8K bytes.

Question for reviewer: Was this too low level a Putting It All Together section? Not enough big picture? Do we need to show some application running on Ethernet vs. ATM (as in Fallacies and Pitfalls?)

8.9 | Fallacies and Pitfalls

Interconnections are filled with myths and hazards; this section has just a few warnings, so proceed carefully.

Fallacy: Most messages are large.

Many interconnect designers assume this is the case, including optimizations that improve interconnect bandwidth for large messages. Figure 8.6 on page 588 shows the size of Network File System (NFS) messages for 239 machines at Berkeley collected over a period of one week. The maximum NSF message size is 8KB, with 95% of the messages being 190 bytes long or less. Another study of the traffic on the Berkeley network that connects many local area networks together found that the average size was 210 bytes.

Fallacy: Delivered performance tracks peak bandwidth.

Many messages are small, so if the higher bandwidth interconnect does not reduce the startup overhead to send a message by a commensurate amount, then Amdahl's Law tells us that there will be little benefit. Measurements from Figure 8.5 on page 586 show the one way time for the smallest packet on an unloaded Ethernet to be 456 microseconds versus the 626 microseconds for ATM from Figure 8.30. We model the time as the fixed overhead for each interconnection plus the time to transfer. Our ATM measurements suggest a peak rate of 78 Mbit/sec using TCP/IP for the SynOptics ATM Switch and 9 Mbit/sec for Ethernet. Figure 8.32 shows the overhead time, transmission time, and total time for to send all the NSF messages from Figure 8.6 over Ethernet and ATM. The peak link speed of ATM is 15 times faster and the measured link speed for 8 KB datagrams is almost 9 times faster, but the higher overheads offsets the benefits so that ATM would transmit these messages only 1.2 times faster.

Size	No. Messages	Overhead (secs)		No. Data Bytes	Transmission (secs)		Total Time (secs)	
		ATM	Ethernet		ATM	Ethernet	ATM	Ethernet
32	771,060	483	352	33,817,052	4	48	487	399
64	56,923	36	26	4,101,088	0	5	36	31
96	4,082,014	2,555	1,861	428,346,316	46	475	2,601	2,336
128	5,574,092	3,489	2,542	779,600,736	83	822	3,572	3,364
160	328,439	206	150	54,860,484	6	56	211	206
192	16,313	10	7	3,316,416	0	3	11	11
224	4,820	3	2	1,135,380	0	1	3	3
256	24,766	16	11	9,150,720	1	9	16	20
512	32,159	20	15	25,494,920	3	23	23	38
1024	69,834	44	32	70,578,564	8	72	52	104
1536	8,842	6	4	15,762,180	2	14	7	18
2048	9,170	6	4	20,621,760	2	19	8	23
2560	20,206	13	9	56,319,740	6	51	18	60
3072	13,549	8	6	43,184,992	4	39	13	45
3584	4,200	3	2	16,152,228	2	14	4	16
4096	67,808	42	31	285,606,596	29	255	72	286
5120	6,143	4	3	35,434,680	4	32	7	34
6144	5,858	4	3	37,934,684	4	34	8	37
7168	4,140	3	2	31,769,300	3	28	6	30
8192	287,577	180	131	2,390,688,480	245	2,132	425	2,263
Total	11,387,913	7,129	5,193	4,352,876,316	452	4,132	7,581	9,325

FIGURE 8.32   Using the messages in Figure 8.6, this figure shows the total time on Ethernet and ATM, calculating the total overhead and transmission time separately. Note that the size of the headers needs to be added to the data bytes to calculate transmission time.

Pitfall: Ignoring software overhead when determining message overhead.

Low software overhead requires cooperation with the operating system as well as with the communication libraries. As an example, the Thinking Machines Software on the CM-5 has an software overhead of 20 μsecs to send a message and a hardware overhead of 0.5 μsecs. The Intel Paragon reduced the hardware overhead to just 0.2 μsecs, but the initial release of software has a software overhead of 250 μsecs. Latter releases reduced this overhead to 50 μsecs, which still dominates the hardware overhead.

Pitfall: Adding functions to interconnection system that violate the end-to-end argument.

This argument is against providing features at a lower level that only partially satisfy the communication demand that can only accomplished at the highest level. Saltzer, Reed, and Clark [1984] give the end-to-end argument as:

The function in question can completely and correctly be specified only with the knowledge and help of the application standing at the endpoints of the communication system. Therefore, providing that questioned function as a feature of the communication system itself is not possible. (page 278)

Their example of the pitfall was a network at MIT that used several gateways, each of which added a checksum from one gateway to the next. The programmers of the application assumed the checksum guaranteed accuracy, incorrectly assuming that the message was protected while stored in the memory of each gateway. One gateway developed a transient failure that swapped one pair of bytes per million bytes transferred through the gateway. Over time the sources of one operating system were repeatedly passed through the gateway, thereby corrupting the sources. The only solution was to correct the infected source files by comparing to paper listings and repairing the code by hand. Had the checksums been calculated and checked by the application running on the end systems, safety would have been assured.

Pitfall: Ignoring packetization delay when calculating communication performance.

The header formats of packets must be created for each packet as well as the data. Several of the formats require calculating a checksum, which requires reading every the byte of data. Even the "low" latency of Ethernet can become high if the packet must be buffed for 1.2 milliseconds to create the proper message.

Question for reviewer: other suggestions for fallacies or pitfalls?

8.10 | Concluding Remarks

Figure 8.33 summarizes a variety of hardware interconnections, including the examples from this chapter plus a few others. While we couldn't have the Internet without the telecommunication media, it is the protocol suites such as TCP/IP that make electronic communication practical. More than any other area of computer science and engineering, these protocols embrace the concept that failures are the norm and so the system must operate reliably in the presence of failures.

Interconnection hardware and software blend telecommunications with data communications, calling into question whether they should remain as separate academic disciplines or just be combined as single field called communications. This merger has led to dramatic improvement in cost/performance of communications, enabling millions of people around the world to find others with common interests. As the quotes at the beginning of this chapter suggest, the authors believe this revolution in two-way communication will change the form of human associations and actions.

Question for reviewer: Know any of the missing values, or which ones there are wrong?

	MPP			LAN			WAN
	CM-5	Intel Parago	Cray T3D	Ethernet	100 Mb Ethernet	Switched Ethernet	ATM
Length (meters)	25	?	10.3	500/2500	200	?	100/1000
Number data lines	4	16	16	1	1	1	1
Clock Rate (MHz)	40	100 MHz	150 MHz	10	100	10	155/622...
Switch?	Yes	Yes	Yes	No	No	Yes	Yes
Nodes	≤2048	≤1024	≤1024	254	254	254	10000
Material	copper	copper	copper	copper	copper	copper	copper/fiber
Bisection BW (MB/s)	xNode	$20xN^{1/2}$	$300xN^{2/3}$	1.25	12.5	1.25xNodes	10xNodes
Peak Link BW	20	200	300	1.25	12.5	1.25	12
Measured Link BW	20	150	100	1.12	??	??	10
Latency (μsecs)	5	2	0.1	15	??	??	50
HW Overhead (μsecs)	0.5	0.2	0.1	6	6	6	6
SW Overhead (μsecs)	7	23	0.1	210	210	210	280
Topology	Fat Tree	2D Mesh	3D torus	Line	Line	Star	Star
Connectionless?	Yes	Yes	Yes	Yes	Yes	Yes	No
Store & Forward?	No	No	No	No	No	No	Yes
Congestion Control	Backpre	Backpressure	Backpressure	Carrier Sens	??	??	TBD
Standard	No	No	No	IEEE 802.3	??	??	ATM Forum
Fault Tolerance	No	No	No	Yes	Yes	Yes	Yes
Hot Insert?	No	No	No	Yes	Yes	Yes	Yes

FIGURE 8.33   Several examples of MPP, LAN, and WAN interconnections.

8.11 | Historical Perspective and References

Note to reviewers: This is a pretty short history. Know some interesting history to add? How about important references?

This chapter has taken the unusual perspective that computers inside a cabinet of an MPP and computers on a intercontinental WAN share many of the same concerns. While this observation may be true, their histories are very different.

The earliest of the interconnections are WANs. The forerunner of the Internet is the ARPANET, which in 1969 connected computer science departments across the country that had research grants funded by ARPA. It was originally envisioned as using reliable communications at lower levels; it was the practical experience with failures of underlying technology that led to the failure tolerant TCP/IP, which is the basis for the Internet today. Kahn [1972] is an early reference on the ideas of ARPANET.

ARPA's success with wide area networks led directly to the most popular local area networks. The researchers at Xerox Palo Alto Research Center had all been funded by ARPA while working at universities, and so they all knew the value of networking. This group invented the forerunner of today's workstations [Thacker et al. 1982] and Ethernets in 1974 [Metcalfe and Boggs1976]. This first Ethernet provided a 3 Mbit/sec interconnection which seemed like an unlimited amount of communication bandwidth with computers of that era, relying on the interconnect technology developed for the cable television industry. The announcement by Digital Equipment Corporation, Intel, and Xerox of a standard for 10 Mbit/sec Ethernet was critical to the commercial success of Ethernet. This announcement short-circuited a lengthy IEEE standards effort, which eventually did publish IEEE 802.3 as an standard for Ethernets.

The final component of interconnects are found in massively parallel processors (MPPs). One forerunner of today's MPPs is the Cosmic Cube [Seitz 1985], which used the Ethernet interface chips to connect 8086 computers in a hypercube. MPP interconnections have improved considerably since then, with messages routed automatically through intermediate switches to their final destinations at high bandwidths and with low latency. Considerable research has gone into the benefits over different topologies in both construction and program behavior. Whether it is fads or changes in technology is hard to say, but topologies certainly become very popular and then disappear. The hypercube, widely popular in the 1980s, have disappeared from MPPs of the 1990s.

Today we are seeing increasing attention paid to interconnection, with competing proposals as to who will be the winners of the next generation of interconnections. Today there are two competing proposals for a 100 Mbit/sec successor to the 10 Mbit/sec Ethernet standard: 100BaseT gets the bandwidth via multiple unshielded twisted pairs and 100VG uses a different protocol to support Ethernet and Token-ring networks. Adding switches to Ethernet are also becoming popular. The ATM Forum is hoping to leverage the technology developed for next generation of telecommunications systems as the successor to the next generation of LANs. Time will tell us who wins and who loses.

References

ANTHONY ALLES, *ATM in Private Networking*, Interop '93 Tutorial, 1993.

ATM FORUM, *ATM user-network interface specification : version 3.1.*, Englewood Cliffs, N.J. : PTR Prentice Hall, 1994.

COMER, DOUGLAS. *Internetworking with TCP/IP,* 2nd ed. Englewood Cliffs, N.J. : Prentice Hall, 1993.

KAHN, R. E. [1972]. "Resource-sharing computer communication networks," *Proc. IEEE* 60:11 (November) 1397-1407.

METCALFE, R.M. "Computer/network interface design: lessons from Arpanet and Ethernet. *IEEE Journal on Selected Areas in Communications*, Feb. 1993, vol.11,(no.2):173-80.

METCALFE, R. M. AND D. R. BOGGS [1976]. "Ethernet: Distributed packet switching for local computer networks," *Comm. ACM* 19:7 (July) 395–404.

PARTRIDGE, CRAIG, *Gigabit networking*. Reading, Mass. : Addison-Wesley,1994.

SALTZER, J.H.; REED, D.P.; CLARK, D.D. "End-to-end arguments in system design." ACM *Transactions on Computer Systems*, Nov. 1984, vol.2, (no.4):277-88.

SEITZ, C.L. "The Cosmic Cube (concurrent computing).,"*Communications of the ACM*, Jan. 1985, vol.28, (no.1):22-33.

TANENBAUM, ANDREW S., Computer networks   2nd ed. Englewood Cliffs, N.J.   : Prentice-Hall, 1988.

THACKER, C. P., E. M. MCCREIGHT, B. W. LAMPSON, R. F. SPROULL, AND D. R. BOGGS [1982]. "Alto: A personal computer," in *Computer Structures: Principles and Examples*, D. P. Siewiorek, C. G. Bell, and A. Newell, eds., McGraw-Hill, New York, 549–572.

WALRAND, JEAN. *Communication networks : a first course.* Homewood, IL   Aksen Associates : Irwin, 1991.

EXERCISES

Reviewers: suggestions of Exercises would be very helpful!

8.1 Is Electronic communication always fastest? Calculate the time to sending 100 GB using twenty 8 mm tapes and an overnight delivery service versus sending 100 GB by FTP over the Internet. Make the following four assumptions:

1) The tapes are picked up at 4 PM Pacific time and delivered 2500 miles away at 10 AM Eastern time (7AM Pacific time).

2) On one route the slowest link is a T1 line, which transfers at 1.5 Mbit/sec.

3) On another route the slowest link is a 10 Mbit/sec Ethernet.

4)   You can use 50% of the slowest link between the two sites.

Will the all the bytes sent either Internet route arrive before the overnight delivery person arrives?

8.2 What is the bandwidth of overnight delivery? Making the same assumptions as Exercise 8.1, calculate the average bandwidth of overnight delivery service for a 100 GB package.

8.3 Is you have access to a UNIX system, use "ping" to explore the internet. First read the manual page. Then use ping without option flags to be sure you can reach the following sites. It should say that "X is alive". Depending on your system you may be able to see the path by setting the flags to verbose mode (-v) and trace route mode (-R) to see the path between your machine and the example machine. Alternatively, you may need to use the program "traceroute" to see the path. If so, try its manual page. You may want to use the UNIX command "script" to make a record of your session. Here are the targets:

a)   Find another machine on the same local area network;

b)   Find another machine on your campus that is not on the same local area network;

c)   Trace the route to another machine off campus. For example, if you have a friend you send email too, try tracing that route.

d)   One of the more interesting sites is the McMurdo NASA Government station in Antarctica. Try ping to mcmvax.mcmurdo.gov.

8.4 Redo cut-through routing calculation for ATM of different sizes: 64, 256, and 1024 nodes.

8.5 Calculate the time to performance a broadcast (from-one-to-all) on each of the topologies in Figure 8.10 on page 592 making the same assumptions as the two examples on pages 593–595.

8.6 Compare the interconnection latency of a crossbar, Omega network, and fat tree with 8 nodes. Use Figure 8.12 on page 597 and add a fat tree similar to Figure 8.4. on page 585 as a third option. Assume that each switch costs a unit time delay. Assume the fat tree randomly picks a path, so give the best case and worst case for each example. How long will take it to send a message from Node P0 to P6? How long will it take P1 and P7 to also communicate?

8.7 One interesting measure of the latency and bandwidth of an interconnection is to calculate the size of a message needed to achieve one-half of the peak bandwidth. This half-way point is sometimes referred to as $n_{1/2}$, taken from the vector processing. Using Figure 8.31 on page 629, estimate $n_{1/2}$, for TCP/IP message using ATM and the Ethernet.

8.8 Use FTP to transfer a file from a remote site and then between local sites on the same LAN. What is the difference in bandwidth for each transfer? Try the transfer at different ties of day or days of the week. Is WAN or LAN bandwidth time sensitive?

8.9 Draw the topology of a 6-cube similar to the drawing of the 4-cube in Figure 8.9 on page 592.

The turning away from the conventional organization came in the middle 1960's, when the law of diminishing returns began to take effect in the effort to increase the operational speed of a computer . . . . Electronic circuits are ultimately limited in their speed of operation by the speed of light . . . and many of the circuits were already operating in the nanosecond range.

Bouknight et al. [1972]

. . . sequential computers are approaching a fundamental physical limit on their potential computational power. Such a limit is the speed of light . . .

A. L. DeCegama, *The Technology of Parallel Processing, Volume I* (1989)

. . . today's machines . . . are nearing an impasse as technologies approach the speed of light. Even if the components of a sequential processor could be made to work this fast, the best that could be expected is no more than a few million instructions per second.

Mitchell [1989]

9 Multiprocessors

9.1 Introduction

We begin this chapter with a taxonomy so that the reader can appreciate both the breadth of design alternatives for multiprocessors as well as the context that has led to the development of the dominant form of multiprocessors. We briefly describe the alternatives and the rationale behind them; a longer description of how these different models were born (and often died) can be found in the historical perspectives at the chapter end.

The idea of using multiple processors both to increase performance as well as improve reliability is an old idea dating back to the earliest electronic computers. About 30 years ago, Flynn proposed a simple model of categorizing all computers that is still useful today. He looked at the parallelism in the instruction and data streams called for by the instructions at the most constrained component of the machine, and placed all computers in one of four categories:

1. *Single instruction stream, single data stream* (SISD, the uniprocessor)

2. *Single instruction stream, multiple data streams* (SIMD)

3. *Multiple instruction streams, single data stream* (MISD)

4. *Multiple instruction streams, multiple data streams* (MIMD)

This is a coarse model, as some machines are hybrids of these categories. Nonetheless, it is useful to put a framework on the design space.

Many of the early multiprocessors were SIMD, and we discuss their advantages and disadvantages in the historical perspectives. In the last few years, however, MIMD has emerged as the clear architecture of choice for general-purpose multiprocessors. Two factors are primarily responsible for the rise of the MIMD machines:

1. An MIMD offers flexibility: with the correct hardware and software support, an MIMD can function as single-user machine focusing on high performance for one application, as a multiprogrammed machine running many tasks simultaneously, or as some combination of these functions.

2. An MIMD can build on the cost-performance advantages of off-the-shelf microprocessors. In fact, nearly all multiprocessors being built today use the same microprocessors found in workstations and small, single processor servers.

Existing MIMD machines fall into two classes, depending on the number of processors involved, which in turn dictates a memory organization and interconnect strategy.

The first group is small-scale, shared memory machines that have at most a few dozen processors (less than 32). For multiprocessors with small processor counts, it is possible for the processors to share a single centralized memory and to interconnect the processors and memory by a bus. With large caches, the bus and the single memory can satisfy the memory demands of a handful of processors. Since there is a single main memory with a uniform access time, these machines are sometimes called *UMAs* for *Uniform Memory Access*. This type of small-scale shared memory architecture is by far the most popular organization at the current time. Figure 9.1 shows what these machines look like. The architecture of such multiprocessors is the topic of Section 9.3.

The second group of machines are large-scale machines with distributed memory. To support larger processor counts, memory must be distributed with the processors rather than centralized, otherwise, the memory system would be unable to support the bandwidth demands of a larger number of processors. Of course, a high bandwidth interconnect, which we saw examples of in Chapter 8, is also required. Figure 9.2 shows what these machines look like.

As processor counts increase, a distributed memory model with a higher bandwidth interconnect is unavoidable. With the rapid increase in processor performance and the associated increase in a processor's memory bandwidth requirements, the scale of machine for which distributed memory is required continues to decrease in number, just as the number of processors supportable on a shared bus with a single memory has decreased as processors have gotten faster.

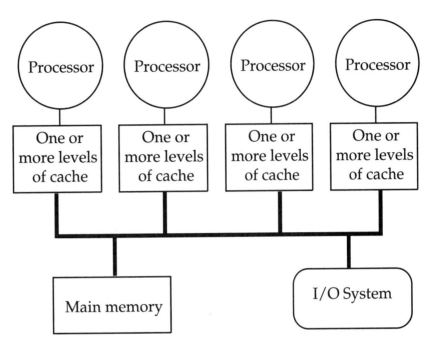

FIGURE 9.1   Basic structure of a small-scale shared memory multiprocessor. Multiple processor-cache subsystems share the same physical memory, typically connected by a bus.

Distributing the memory among the nodes has two major benefits. First, it is a cost-effective way to scale the memory bandwidth, if many of the accesses are to the local memory in the node. Second, it reduces the latency for accesses to the local memory. These two advantages are further decreasing the processor count at which a distributed memory architecture makes sense.

Typically I/O, as well as memory, is distributed among the nodes, and the nodes may actually contain a small number (2-8) of processors interconnected with a different technology. While this *clustering* of multiple processors per memory and network interface may be quite useful from a cost-efficiency viewpoint, it is not fundamental to how these machines work, so we will focus on the one processor per node style of machine throughout this chapter. The major architectural differences that distinguish the distributed memory machines are how communication is performed and what the logical model of memory is.

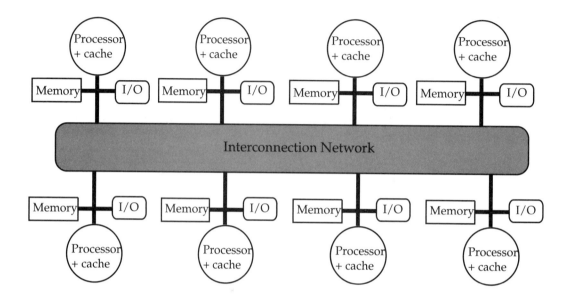

FIGURE 9.2   The basic architecture of a distributed memory machine consists of individual nodes containing a processor, some memory, typically some I/O, and an interface to an interconnection network that connects all the nodes. Individual nodes may contain a small number of processors, which may be interconnected by a small or some other interconnection technology, which is often less scalable than the global interconnection network.

Models for Communication and Memory Architecture

As discussed above, any large-scale multiprocessor must use multiple memories that are physically distributed with the processors. There are two alternative organizations for the addressing of these memories and with these two alternative methods for communicating data among processors. The physically separate memories can be addressed as one logical address space, meaning that a memory reference can be made by any processor to any memory location, assuming it has the correct access rights. These machines are called *distributed shared memory* (*DSM*), *scalable shared-memory* architectures, or sometimes *NUMAs, Non-Uniform Memory Access*, since the access time depends on the location of a data word in memory.

Alternatively, the address space can consist of multiple private address spaces that are logically disjoint and that cannot be accessed (in hardware) by another processor. In such an instance, each processor-memory module is essentially a separate computer, hence these machines have been called *multicomputers*.

With each of these organizations for the address space, there is an associated communication mechanism. For a machine with a single address space, that address space can be used to communicate data via load and store operations. Hence, the name *shared memory* for such machines. For a machine with multiple address spaces, communication of data must use another mechanism: passing messages among the processors; hence, these machine are often called *message passing machines*.

Each of these communication mechanisms has its own advantages. For shared memory communication these include:

- Compatibility with the well-understood mechanisms in use in both uniprocessors and small-scale multiprocessors, both of which use shared memory communication.

- Ease of programming when the communication patterns among processors are complex or vary dynamically during execution. Similar advantages simplify compiler construction.

- Lower latency for communication and better use of bandwidth when communicating small items.

- The ability to use hardware controlled caching to reduce the frequency of remote communication by allowing caching of all data, both shared and private.

The major advantages for message passing communication include:

- The hardware can be simpler, especially by comparison with a shared memory model that supports scalable cache coherency.

- Communication patterns are explicit, forcing programmers (or compilers) to pay attention to communications, which typically has a high cost associated with it.

Of course, the desired communication model can be created on top of a hardware model that supports either of these mechanisms. Supporting message passing on top of shared memory is considerably easier, assuming that the machine has adequate communication bandwidth. The major difficulties arise from dealing with messages that may be misaligned and of arbitrary length in a memory system that is normally oriented towards transferring aligned, blocks of data organized as cache blocks. These difficulties can be overcome either with small performance penalties in software or with essentially no penalties using a small amount of hardware support.

Supporting shared memory efficiently on top of message passing is much more difficult. Without explicit hardware support for shared memory, all shared memory references will need to involve the operating system to provide address translation and memory protection, as well as to translate memory references into messages sends and receives. Since loads and stores usually move small amounts of data, the high overhead of handling these communications in software makes it essentially impossible to use a machine with only software support as a shared memory machine.

In evaluating any communication mechanism, three performance characteristics are critical:

1. Bandwidth: ideally the communication bandwidth will be limited by processor, memory, and interconnection bandwidths, rather than by some aspect of the communication mechanism. The overhead of communication (e.g., how long is the processor tied up) affects this directly.

2. Latency: ideally the latency is as low as possible. Software and hardware overheads to initiate and complete communication are critical in determining this.

3. Latency hiding: how well can the mechanism hide latency by overlapping communication with computation or with other communication.

Each of these performance measures is affected by the communication characteristics. In particular, the latency and bandwidth may vary with the size of the data item. In general, mechanisms that perform well with smaller as well as larger data communication requests will be more flexible and efficient.

It is the memory model and communication mechanisms that distinguish these machines, since they all use distributed memory. Historically, distributed memory machines originally were built with message passing, since it was clearly simpler and many designers and researchers did not believe that a single address space could be built with distributed memory. More recently shared-memory communication has begun to be supported in virtually every machine being designed. Although centralized memory machines using a bus interconnect still dominate in terms of market size, long term technical trends favor distributing memory even in moderate scale machines; we'll discuss these issues in more detail at the end of this chapter. As we will see in Section 9.4, possibly the most significant outstanding issue in distributed shared memory machines is the question of caching and cache coherency.

Challenges of Parallel Processing

Two important challenges, both explainable with Amdahl's Law, make the efficient use of parallel processing challenging. The first has to do with limited parallelism available in programs and the second arises from the relatively high cost of communications. Limitations in available parallelism make it difficult to achieve good speed-ups in parallel machines, as our first example shows.

Example

Suppose you want to achieve a speedup of 80 with 100 processors. What fraction of the original computation can be sequential?

Answer

Amdahl's Law is

$$\text{Speedup} = \frac{1}{\dfrac{\text{Fraction}_{\text{enhanced}}}{\text{Speedup}_{\text{enhanced}}} + (1 - \text{Fraction}_{\text{enhanced}})}$$

For simplicity in this example, assume that the program operates in only two modes: parallel with all processors fully used or serial with only one processor in use. With this simplification, the speedup in enhanced mode is simply the number of processors, while the fraction of enhanced mode is the time spent in parallel mode. Substituting into the equation above:

$$80 = \frac{1}{\dfrac{\text{Fraction}_{\text{parallel}}}{100} + (1 - \text{Fraction}_{\text{parallel}})}$$

Simplifying this equation yields

$$0.8 \times \text{Fraction}_{\text{parallel}} + 80 \times (1 - \text{Fraction}_{\text{parallel}}) = 1$$

$$80 - 79.2 \times \text{Fraction}_{\text{parallel}} = 1$$

$$\text{Fraction}_{\text{parallel}} = 0.9975$$

Thus, to achieve a speedup of 80 with 100 processors, only 0.25% of original computation can be sequential. Of course, to achieve linear speedup (speedup of n with n processors), the entire program must be parallel with no serial portions. In practice, programs do not just operate in parallel and sequential mode, but often use less than the full complement of the processors. Exercise 9.8 asks you to extend Amdahl's Law to deal with such a case.

The second major challenge involves the large latency of remote access in any parallel machine. In existing machines, communication of data between processors may cost anywhere from 40 cycles to over 1,000 cycles depending on the communication mechanism, the type of interconnection network, and the scale of the machine. Figure 9.3 shows the typical round-trip delays to retrieve a word from a remote memory for several different parallel machines.

Machine	Communication mechanism	Interconnection network	Processor count	Typical remote memory access time
SPARCCenter	Shared memory	bus	≤ 20	1 μs
SGI Challenge	Shared memory	bus	≤ 32	1 μs
T3D	Shared memory	3-d mesh	64-1024	1 μs
Convex Explempar	Shared memory	cross-bar/ring	8-64	2 μs
KSR-1	Shared memory	bus/ring	32-??	2–6 μs
CM-5	Message passing	fat tree	64-1024	10 μs
Intel Paragon	Message passing	2-d mesh	32-2048	10-30 μs
IBM SP-1	Message passing	Multistage switch	32-256	30-100 μs

FIGURE 9.3   Typical remote access times to retrieve a word from a remote memory. In the case of shared memory, this is the remote load time. For a message passing machine, we use the time to send a message and reply to the message.

The effect of long communication delays should be obvious. Let's consider a simple example.

Example   Suppose we have an application running on a SGI Challenge, which has a 1μs time to handle a cache miss. Assume that processors are stalled on a remote request. The cycle time of the processors in a Challenge is 6.67 nS. If the base CPI assuming all local references is 2.0, how much faster is the machine if all references are local versus 1% of the references being remote?

Answer   The effective CPI for the machine with 1% remote references is:

$$\text{CPI} = \text{Base CPI} + \text{Remote Request Rate} \times \text{Remote Request Cost}$$

$$= 2.0 + 1\% \times \text{Remote Request Cost}$$

The Remote Request Cost is

$$\frac{\text{remote access cost}}{\text{cycle time}} = \frac{1000 \text{ nS}}{6.67 \text{ nS}} = 150 \text{ cycles}$$

Hence, we can compute the CPI:

$$\text{CPI} = 2.0 + 1\% \times 150 = 3.5$$

The machine with locally references is $\frac{3.5}{2.0} = 1.75$ times faster. In practice, the situation could be quite a bit worse, since contention caused by many references trying to use the global interconnect can lead to increased delays.

There are many ways to try to reduce or hide the long latency of remote communication. We can try to reduce the frequency of remote accesses with either hardware mechanisms, such as caching shared data, or software mechanisms. We can try to tolerate the latency by using prefetch, which we examined in Chapter 6. The rest of the chapter discusses many of these techniques. For example, Section 9.3 discusses bus-based multiprocessors and snoopy cache coherence for them, while the section following that extends the ideas to machines using scalable interconnects. Section 9.6 talks about latency hiding techniques, while Section 9.6 discusses synchronization. Before we wade into those topics, it is helpful for the reader to have some understanding of the characteristics of parallel applications, both for better comprehension of the results we show using some of these applications and for a greater understanding in general.

9.2 | Characteristics of Application Domains and Their Implications

This section briefly describes the characteristics of three different domains of multiprocessor workloads: parallel programs, operating systems and multiprogramming workloads, and a transaction processing application. This section describes the structure of the applications and provides some general quantitative information about their behavior from the viewpoint of a shared memory machine. Later, we will see additional performance measurements using these applications.

Parallel Applications

Our parallel applications workload consists of four applications and two computational kernels. The kernels are an FFT and an LU decomposition, which were chosen since they represent commonly used techniques in a wide variety of applications and have performance characteristics typical of many parallel scientific applications. The three applications that we use in this chapter are Barnes, Ocean, and VolRend. We briefly describe each of these applications and kernels and characterize their basic behavior in terms of parallelism and communication.

Note: The final version will have a characterization of basic communication (sharing) versus processor count.

The Fast Fourier Transform (FFT) is the key kernel in applications that use spectral methods, which arise in fields ranging from signal processing to fluid flow to climate modeling. The FFT application we study here is a complex one-dimensional version of a common parallel algorithm for FFT. It has an execution time for n data points of $n \log n$ and parallelism proportional to n. The algorithm uses a high radix (equal to $\sqrt{\text{number of data data points}}$) that optimizes communication by minimizing the number of passes required. There are two primary data structures: the array of data being transformed and the roots of unity matrix, which is precomputed and only read during the execution; both arrays are organized as square matrices with each side being the radix. The six steps in the algorithm are:

1. Transpose data matrix.

2. Perform 1-D FFT on each row of data matrix.

3. Apply roots of unity to data matrix.

4. Transpose data matrix.

5. Perform 1-D FFT on each row of data matrix.

6. Transpose data matrix.

Both the data matrix and the roots of unity matrix are partitioned among processors in contiguous chunks of rows, so that each processor's partition falls in its local address space. The first row of the roots of unity matrix is accessed heavily by all processors, and is therefore replicated at the beginning of the program.

The only communication is in the transpose phases, which require all-to-all communication of large amounts of data. Contiguous subcolumns in the rows assigned to a processor are grouped into blocks, which are transposed and placed into the proper location of the destination matrix. Every processor transposes one block locally, and sends one block to each of the other processors in the system. Although there is no reuse of individual words in the transpose, with long cache blocks it makes sense to block the transpose to take advantage of the spatial locality, afforded by long blocks in the source matrix. The cache block size is used as a runtime parameter to decide how to block the communication effectively.

LU is an LU factorization of a dense matrix and is representative of many dense linear algebra computations, such as QR factorization, Cholesky factorization, and eigenvalue methods. For a matrix of size $n \times n$ the running time is n^3 and the parallelism is proportional to n^2. Dense LU factorization can be performed efficiently by blocking the algorithm, which leads to highly efficient cache behavior and low communication. After blocking the algorithm, the dominant computation is a dense, matrix multiply that occurs in the innermost loop. Two details are important for reducing interprocessor communication: the blocks of the matrix are assigned to processors using a 2-D tiling, and the dense matrix multiplication is performed by the processor that owns the destination block. The block size is chosen to be large enough to keep the cache miss rate low, and small enough both to reduce the time spent in the less parallel parts of the computation. Relatively small block sizes (B=8 or B=16) tend to satisfy both criteria. During the reduction, the blocks are communicated in a regular and predictable fashion.

A natural way to code the blocked LU factorization of a 2-D matrix in a shared address space is to use a 2-D array to represent the matrix. Since blocks are allocated in a tiled decomposition, and a block is not contiguous in the address space in a 2-D array, this makes it very difficult to allocate blocks in the local memories of the processors that own them. The solution is to ensure that blocks assigned to a processor are allocated locally and contiguously by using a 4-D array (with the first two dimensions specifying the block number in the 2-D grid of blocks, and the next two specifying the element in the block).

Barnes is an implementation of the Barnes-Hut n-body algorithm solving a problem in galaxy evolution. N-body codes simulate the interaction among a large number of bodies that have forces interacting among them. In this instance the bodies represent collections of objects and the force is gravity. To reduce the computational time required to model the individual interactions among the bodies, which would grow as n^2, n-body algorithms take advantage of the fact that the forces drop off with distance (gravity, for example, drops off as $1 / n^2$). The Barnes-Hut algorithm takes advantage of this property by treating a collection of bodies that are "far away" from another body as a single point at the center of mass of the collection and with mass equal to the collection. If the body is far enough from any body in the collection, then the error introduced will be negligible. This algorithm yields an n log n running time with parallelism proportional to n.

The Barnes-Hut algorithm uses a octree (each node has up to eight children) to represent the eight cubes in a portion of space. Because the density of space varies and the leaves represent individual bodies, the depth of the tree varies. The tree is traversed once per body to compute the net force acting on that body. The force-calculation algorithm for a body starts at the root of the tree. For every cell it visits, the algorithm determines if the center of mass of the cell is "far enough away" from the body. If so, the entire subtree under that cell is approximated by a single particle at the center of mass of the cell, and the force this center of mass exerts on the body computed. On the other hand, if the center of mass is not far enough away, the cell must be "opened" and each of its subcells visited. The distance between the body and the cell together with the error tolerances determine which cell must be opened. This force calculation phase dominates the execution time.

Obtaining effective parallel performance on the Barnes-Hut is challenging because the distribution of bodies is nonuniform and changes over time making the partitioning the work among the processors and maintenance of good locality of reference difficult. We are helped by two properties: the system evolves slowly and since gravitational forces fall off quickly, each cell requires touching a small number of other cells that were used on the last time step with high probability. The tree can be partitioned by allocating each processor a subtree. Many of the access need to compute the force on a body in the subtree will be to other bodies in the subtree. Since the amount of work associated with a subtree varies (cells in dense portions of space will need to access more cells), the size of the subtree allocated to a processor is based on some measure of the work it has to do (e.g., how many other cells does it need to visit), rather than just on the number of nodes in the subtree. By partitioning the octree representation, we can obtain good load balance and good locality of reference, while keeping the partitioning cost low. This partitioning scheme also results in good locality of reference, although the resulting data references will tend to be for small amounts of data and will be unstructured. Thus, this scheme requires an efficient implementation of shared memory communication.

Ocean simulates the influence of eddy and boundary currents on large-scale flow in the ocean. It uses a Red-Black Gauss-Seidel multigrid technique to solve a set of elliptical partial differential equations. Red-black Gauss-Seidel is an iteration technique that colors the points in the grid so as to consistently update each point based on previous values of the adjacent neighbors. Multigrid methods solve finite difference equations by iteration using a set of hierarchical grids. Each grid in the hierarchy has fewer points of the grid below, and is an approximation to the lower grid. The finer grids increase accuracy and thus the rate of convergence, while also increasing the execution time. Which level of grids is used for a given iteration is determined by the rate of change of the data values. The coarsest grid that satisfies the error bounds is chosen for each step. When the iteration converges at the finest level, a solution has been reached. Each iteration has n^2 work for an $n \times n$ grid and the same amount of parallelism.

The arrays representing each grid are dynamically allocated and sized to the particular problem. The entire ocean basin is partitioned into square (as close as possible) subgrids that are allocated from the address space of individual processors and assigned to those processors. There are five steps present in a time iteration, since data is exchanged between these, all the processors present synchronize at the end of each step before proceeding to the next. Communication occurs when the boundary points of a subgrid are accessed by the adjacent subgrid in nearest neighbor fashion.

VolRend is an application that does parallel volume rendering. Volume visualization techniques are becoming of key importance in the analysis and understanding of complex data. This application, which renders volumes using optimized ray tracing techniques, is a parallel version of the fastest known sequential algorithm for volume rendering.

The volume to be rendered is represented by a cube of voxels (or volume elements). The outermost loop of the computation is over a series of frames or images. Successive frames correspond to changing angles between the viewer and the volume being rendered. For each frame, rays are cast from the viewing position into the volume data through every pixel in the image plane corresponding to that frame. Rays pass straight through the volume unless they encounter too much opacity and are terminated early. Finally, ray samples are composed to produce an image or frame.

The value for each voxel is computed based on its neighboring voxels. An octree data structure is used to find the first interesting (non-transparent) voxel in a ray's path efficiently, and to determine whether the neighboring voxels around a sample point are interesting. The data for the runs used here are taken from an image of the human head that has 256×256×113 voxels, or about 30MB of data.

The most important and heavily referenced data structure, the voxel data set, is accessed in a read-only fashion. Thus, if the entire voxel data set were replicated in the local memory of every processing node, there would be essentially no communication during rendering; however, such replication would imply either unreasonable amounts of local memory per processor or that large data sets cannot be run. In our shared address space implementation, the data set is not replicated at all in main memory but only to some extent in the caches. Because of this, communication is generated when accessing voxel data, since caches are finite and the voxel data get replaced in them. All communication is, however, read-only since the data set is not changed.

The rays are statically assigned to the processors initially. After a processor has processed its statically assigned rays, it steals rays from other processors if it is idle. Stealing introduces additional synchronization and communication, and is the main source of performance loss if the number of rays stolen by a processor is large compared to the number statically assigned to it. For this data set, stealing is not significant.

While the data size and running time are proportional to the number of voxels (i.e., the volume), the parallelism is only proportional to the area, since the surface area determines the number of parallel rays. Fortunately, the dimensions tend to be significantly larger than the number of processors, and allocating a few rays per processor results in significant work, and small load balancing problems.

Multiprogramming and OS Workload

This is planned for the final version.

Transaction Processing Workload

This is planned for the final version.

9.3 | Small-Scale Shared Memory Architectures

As we saw in Chapter 6, the use of large, multilevel caches can substantially reduce the memory bandwidth demands of a processor. If the main memory bandwidth demands of a single processor are reduced, multiple processors may be able to share the same memory. Starting in the 1980s, this observation combined with the emerging dominance of the microprocessor, motivated many designers to create small-scale multiprocessors where several processors shared a single physical memory connected by a shared bus. Because of the small size of the processors and the significant reduction in bus bandwidth achieved by large caches, such machines are extremely cost-effective, provided that a sufficient amount of memory bandwidth exists. Early designs of such machines were able to place an entire CPU and cache subsystem on a board, which then plugged into the bus backplane. More recently designs have placed up to four processors per board. Figure 9.4 shows a simple diagram of such a machine.

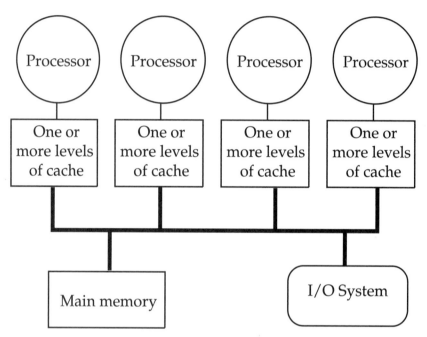

FIGURE 9.4   Basic structure of a small-scale shared memory multiprocessor. Multiple processor-cache subsystems share the same physical memory, typically connected by a bus.

In such a machine, the caches may hold both *shared* and *private* data. Private data is data that is used by a single processor, while shared data is used by multiple processors, essentially providing communication among the processors. When a private item is cached, its location is migrated to the cache reducing the average access time as well as the memory bandwidth required. Since no other processor uses the data, this process is identical to that in a uniprocessor. When shared data is cached, the shared value is replicated, since it may be held in multiple caches. In addition to the reduction in access latency and required memory bandwidth, this replication also provides a reduction in contention that may exist for shared data items that are being read by multiple processor simultaneously. Caching of shared data, however, introduces a new problem: cache coherency.

Multiprocessor Cache Coherency: The Basics

As we saw in Chapter 6, the introduction of caches caused a coherency problem for I/O operations, since the view of memory through the cache could be different from the view of memory obtained through the I/O subsystem. In the case of multiprocessors, the same problem exists, since the view of memory held by two different processors is through their individual caches. Figure 9.5 illustrates the problem. This is generally referred to as the *cache coherency* problem.

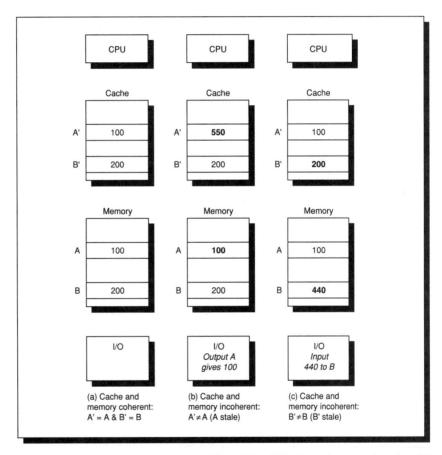

FIGURE 9.5 The cache-coherency problem. A' and B' refer to the cached copies of A and B in memory. (a) shows cache and main memory in a coherent state. In (b) we assume a write-back cache when the CPU writes 550 into A. Now A' has the new value but the value in memory has the old, stale value of 100. If an output used the value of A from memory, it would get the stale data. In (c) the I/O system inputs 440 into the memory copy of B, so now B' in the cache has the old, stale data.

The coherency problem for multiprocessors and I/O, while similar in origin, has different characteristics that affect the appropriate solution. Unlike I/O, where multiple data copies is a rare event—one to be avoided whenever possible—a program running on multiple processors will want to have copies of the same data in several caches, since the performance of a multiprocessor program depends on the performance of the system when sharing data, and cache access will be cheaper than memory accesses. Thus, rather than try to solve the problem by avoiding it in software, small-scale multiprocessors adopt a hardware solution to the problem by introducing a protocol to maintain coherent caches.

The protocols to maintain coherency for multiple processors are called *cache-coherency protocols*. There are two classes of protocols in use:

- *Directory based*—The information about one block of physical memory is kept in just one location called the *directory*; we focus on this approach in the next section on scalable shared memory.

- *Snooping*—Every cache that has a copy of the data from a block of physical memory also has a copy of the information about it and no centralized record is kept. The caches are usually on a shared-memory bus, and all cache controllers monitor or *snoop* on the bus to determine whether or not they have a copy of the shared block.

Snooping protocols became popular with multiprocessors using microprocessors and caches attached to a single shared memory because they can use a preexisting physical connection: the bus to memory to interrogate the status of the caches.

Informally, the coherency problem is to ensure that any read of a data item returns the most recently written value of that data item. This definition is not quite correct because we do not require that a read instantaneously see the value written for the data by some other processor. If, for example, a write on one processor precedes a read of the same location on another processor by a very small time, it may be impossible to ensure that the read returns the value of the data written, since the written data may not even have left the processor at that point. The issue of exactly when a written value must be seen by a reader is defined by a *memory consistency model*—a topic that we discuss in Section 9.5. For simplicity, and because we cannot explain the problem in full detail at this point, assume that we require that a value written by a write be seen by a read occurring sometime after the write and that writes by a given processor are always seen in order. We will rely on this assumption until we reach Section 9.5

With this simple definition of memory consistency, we can guarantee coherency by ensuring two properties:

1. A read by a processor that follows a write by another processor to the same location will see the written value if the read and write are sufficiently separated.

2. Writes to the same location are serialized: that is, two writes to the same location will be seen as occurring in the same order as they occur within the processor doing the writing.

The first property is obviously related to the notion of what it means to have a coherent view of memory: if a processor could continuously read an old data value, we would clearly say that memory was incoherent.

The need for write serialization is more subtle, but equally important. Suppose we did not serialize writes, then processor P1 could write a data location followed by P2 writing the same location. Serializing the writes ensures two important outcomes for this sequence of writes. First, it ensures that every processor will see the write done by P2 at some point. If we did not serialize the writes, it might be the case that some processor could see the write of P2 first and then see the write of P1, maintaining the value written by P1 indefinitely. A more subtle problem arises in maintaining a reasonable model of program order and memory coherency for the user: suppose a third processor is constantly reading the same location written by processors P1 and P2; it should see the value written by P1 and then the value written by P2. It is possible it never sees the value written by P1, because the write by P2 arrives before the read. If it ever sees the value written by P1 it must see the value written by P2 on a later read. Likewise, any other processor that can observe the values written by both P1 and P2, should observe the identical behavior. The simplest way to enforce these properties is to serialize writes, so that all writes to the same location are seen in the same order; this property is called *write serialization*. As we will see in Section 9.5, the question of when a processor must see a value written by another processor is complex and has significant performance implication, especially in larger machines.

Alternative Protocols

There are two ways to maintain the coherency described above. One method is to ensure that a processor has exclusive access to a data item before it writes that item. This style of protocol is called a *write invalidate protocol*, because it invalidates other copies on a write. It is by far the most common protocol, both for snoopy and directory schemes. Exclusive access ensures that no other readable or writable copies of an item exist when the write occurs: all other cached copies of the item are invalidated. To see how this ensures coherency, consider a write followed by a read by another processor: since the write requires exclusive access, any copy held by the reading processor must be invalidated (hence the protocol name). Thus, when the read occurs, it will miss in the cache and be forced to fetch a new copy of the data. For a write, we can require that the processor have a valid copy of the data in its cache before writing it. Thus, if two processors attempt to write the same data simultaneously, one of them wins the race (we'll see how we decide who wins shortly) causing the other processor's copy to be invalidated. For the other processor to complete its write, it must obtain a new copy of the data, which must now contain the updated value.

The alternative to an invalidate protocol is to update all the cached copies of a data item when that item is written. This type of protocol is called a *write update* or *write broadcast* protocol. To keep the bandwidth requirements of this protocol under control it is useful to track whether or not a word in the cache is shared, that is, is contained in other caches. If it is not, then there is no need to broadcast or update any other caches.

The performance differences between write update and write invalidate protocols arise from three characteristics:

1. Multiple writes to the same word with no intervening reads require multiple write broadcasts in an update protocol, but only one initial invalidation in a write invalidate protocol.

2. With multiword cache blocks, each word written in a cache block requires a write broadcast in an update protocol, while only the first write to any word in the block needs to generate an invalidate in an invalidation protocol. An invalidation protocol works on cache blocks, while an update protocol must work on individual words (or bytes, when bytes are written).

3. The delay between writing a word in one processor and reading the written value in another processor is usually less in a write update scheme, since the written data will immediately be broadcast to the reader (assuming that the reading processor has a copy of the data). By comparison, in an invalidation protocol, the reader will be invalidated first, then later read the data and be stalled until a copy can be read and returned to the processor.

These two schemes are analogous, in many ways, to the write through and write back schemes. Just as write back schemes require less memory bandwidth, since they take advantage of block operations, write invalidate normally requires less traffic than write broadcast, since multiple writes to the same cache block do not require multiple broadcasts of the write. With write through the memory is updated almost immediately after a write (possibly with some write buffer delay). Similarly in write broadcast, other copies are updated as soon as possible. The most important performance differences between invalidate and update schemes occur because of application characteristics and the choice of block size; we will discuss these issues shortly. First, let's look at how these schemes are implemented.

Basic Implementation Techniques

The key to implementing either an invalidate or an update scheme in a small scale machine is the use of the bus to perform these operations. To perform an update or invalidate the processor simply acquires bus access and broadcasts the address to be invalidated or updated on the bus. All processors continuously snoop on the bus watching the addresses. The processors check whether the address on the bus is in their cache. If so, the corresponding data in the cache is either invalidated or updated, depending on the protocol. The serialization of access enforced by the bus also forces serialization of writes, since when two processors compete to write the same location, one must obtain bus access before the other. The first processor to obtain bus access will cause the other processor's copy to be updated or invalidated. In either case, the writes will be strictly serialized. One implication of this scheme is that a write to a shared data item cannot complete until it obtains bus access.

In addition to invalidating or updating outstanding copies of a cache block that is being written into, we also need to locate a data item when a cache miss occurs. In a write through cache, it is easy to find the recent value of a data item, since all written data are always sent to the memory, from which the most recent value of a data item can always be fetched. (Write buffers can lead to some additional complexities, which are discussed in Section 9.5.)

For a write back cache, however, the problem of finding the most recent data value is harder, since the most recent value of a data item can be in a cache rather than in memory. The same snooping scheme is used as with writes: Each processor snoops an address placed on the bus. If a processor finds that it has a dirty copy of a cache block, then it provides that cache block in response to the read request and causes the memory access to be aborted. Since write back caches generate lower requirements for memory bandwidth, they are greatly preferable in a multiprocessor, despite the slight increase in complexity. Since using write-back caches is only slightly more complex and is greatly preferable from a performance viewpoint, we focus on implementation with write-back caches.

The normal cache tags can be used to implement the process of snooping. Furthermore, the valid bit makes invalidation is easy to implement. Read misses, whether generated by an invalidation or some other event, are also straightforward since they simply rely on the snooping capability. For writes, we'd like to know whether any other copies of the block are cached, since if there are no other cached copies, then the write need not be sent to the bus, which reduces both the time taken by the write and the required bandwidth.

To track whether or not a cache block is shared we can add an extra state bit associated with each cache block, just as we have a valid bit and a dirty bit. By adding a bit indicating whether the block is shared, we can decide whether a write must generate an invalidate, in an invalidation protocol, or a broadcast, in an update protocol. When a write to a block in the shared state occurs in an invalidate protocol, the cache generates an invalidation on the bus and marks the block as private. No further invalidation will be sent by that processor for that block. The processor with the sole copy of a cache block is normally called the *owner* of the cache block.

In an update protocol, if a block is in the shared state, then every write to that block must be broadcast. In the case of an invalidation protocol, the cache state is changed from shared to unshared (or private) when the invalidation is sent; later if another processor requests this cache the state must be made shared again.

Since our snooping cache also sees any misses, it knows when that cache block has been requested by another processor and the state should be made shared.

Since every bus transaction checks cache-address tags, this could potentially interfere with CPU cache accesses. This potential interference is reduced by one of two techniques: duplicating the tags or employing a multilevel cache with *inclusion*, whereby the levels closer to the CPU are a subset of those further away. If the tags are duplicated, then the CPU and the snoop activity may proceed in parallel. Of course, if the cache misses, it will need to arbitrate for and update both sets of tags. Likewise, if the snoop finds a matching tag entry, it will need to arbitrate for and access both sets of cache tags (to perform an invalidate or to update the shared bit), as well as possibly the cache data array to retrieve a copy of a block. Thus, with duplicate tags the processor only needs to be stalled when it does a cache access at the same time that a snoop has detected a copy in the cache. Furthermore, snooping activity is only delayed when the cache is dealing with a miss.

If the CPU uses a multilevel cache with the inclusion property, then every entry in the primary cache is also in the secondary cache. Thus, the snoop activity can be directed to the second level cache, while most of the processor's activity will be directed to the primary cache. If the snoop gets a hit in the secondary cache, then it must arbitrate for the primary cache to update the state and possibly retrieve the data, which will usually require a stall of the processor. Since many multiprocessors will want to use a multilevel cache to decrease the bandwidth demands of the individual processors, this solution has been adopted in many designs. Sometimes, it may even be useful to duplicate the tags of the secondary cache to further decrease contention between the CPU and the snooping activity. We discuss the inclusion property in more detail in Section 9.8.

As you might imagine, there are many variations on cache coherency, depending on whether the scheme is invalidate-based or update-based, whether the cache is write-back or write-through, when updates occur, and if and how ownership is recorded. Figure 9.7 summarizes several snooping cache-coherency protocols and shows some machines that have used or are using that protocol.

Name	Protocol Type	Memory-write policy	Unique feature	Machines using
Write Once	Write invalidate	Write back after first write	First snoopy protocol described.	
Synapse N+1	Write invalidate	Write back	Explicit state where memory is the owner.	Synapse machines; first cache-coherent machines.
Berkeley	Write invalidate	Write back	Owned shared state	Berkeley SPUR machine.
Illinois	Write invalidate	Write back	Clean private state; can supply data from any cache with a clean copy	SGI Power and Challenge series
"Firefly"	Write broadcast	Write back for private, Write through for shared	Memory updated on broadcast	SPARCCenter 2000

FIGURE 9.6 Six snooping protocols summarized. Archibald and Baer [1986] use these names to describe the six protocols, and Eggers [1989] summarizes the similarities and differences as shown above. The Firefly protocol was named for the experimental DEC Firefly multiprocessor, in which it appeared.

An Example Protocol and Its Implementation

A bus based coherency protocol is usually implemented by incorporating a finite state controller in each node. This controller responds to requests from the processor and from the bus, changing the state of the selected cache block, as well as using the bus to access data or invalidate it. Figure 9.7 shows the requests generated by the processor-cache module as well as those coming from the bus. For simplicity, the protocol we explain does not distinguish between a write hit and a write miss to a shared data item: in both cases, we treat such an access as a write miss. When the write miss is placed on the bus, any processors with copies of the data will invalidate it. In a write-back cache, if the data is exclusive in just one cache, that cache will also write back the data. This simplification reduces the number of different bus transactions, and simplifies the controller, as we will see shortly.

Request	Source	Function
Read hit	Processor	Read data in cache
Write hit	Processor	Write data in cache
Read miss	Bus	Request data from cache or memory
Write miss	Bus	Request data from cache or memory; perform any needed invalidates

FIGURE 9.7 The cache coherency mechanisms receives requests from both the processor and the bus and responds to these based on the type of request and the state of the cache block specified in the request.

Figure 9.8 (page 661) shows a finite-state transition diagram for a write-invalidation protocol for a cache using write-back. The three states of the protocol are duplicated to represent transitions based on CPU requests (in the top half), as opposed to transitions based on bus requests (in the bottom half). Italics are used to distinguish the bus actions, as opposed to the conditions on which a transition depends. The state in each node represents the state of the selected cache block.

All of the states in this cache protocol would be needed in a uniprocessor cache, where they would correspond to the invalid, valid (and clean), and dirty states. The transactions in the bottom half of Figure 9.8 are needed only for coherency. All of the state changes in the top half of Figure 9.8 would be needed in a write-back uniprocessor cache; the only difference in a multiprocessor is that we must send a write miss when the processor has a hit for a cache block in the Shared state that it wishes to write.

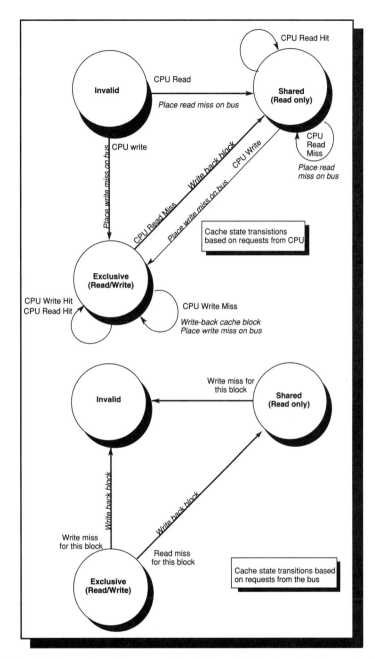

FIGURE 9.8   A write-invalidate, cache-coherency protocol for a write-back cache. The cache states are shown in circles (with the allowed access in parenthesis), the stimulus shown on the transition arcs in normal type, and any bus actions shown on the transition arc in italics. The upper part of the diagram shows state transitions based on actions of the CPU associated with this cache; the lower part shows transitions based on operations on the bus. Whenever a bus transaction occurs, all caches take the action dictated by the bottom half of the diagram. The protocol assumes that memory provides data on a read miss to a block that is clean in all caches. This protocol is somewhat simpler than those in use in existing multiprocessors.

In reality, there is only one finite-state machine per cache, with stimuli coming either from the attached CPU or from the bus. Figure 9.9 actually shows how the state transitions from the bottom half of Figure 9.8 are combined with those in the top half of Figure 9.8 to form a single state diagram for the caches.

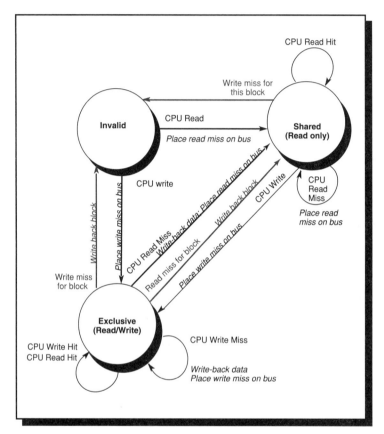

FIGURE 9.9 The cache coherency state diagram with the state transitions induced by the local processor shown in black and by the bus activities shown in color. As in Figure 9.8, the activities on a transition are shown in italics.

To understand why this protocol works, observe that any valid cache block is either in the Shared state in multiple caches or in the Exclusive state in exactly one cache. Any transition to the Exclusive state (which is required for a processor to write to the block) causes a write miss to be placed on the bus causing all caches to make the block invalid; in addition, if some other cache had the block in Exclusive state it generates a write-back, which supplies the block containing the desired address. Finally, if a read miss occurs on the bus to a block in the Exclusive state, the owning cache also makes it state Shared, forcing a subsequent write to require exclusive ownership. The actions in color, which handle read and write misses on the bus, are essentially the snooping component of the protocol. On other property that is preserved in this protocol, and most other protocols, is any memory block in the Shared state is always up-to-date in the memory. This simplifies the implementation, as we will see shortly.

As stated earlier, this coherency protocol is actually simpler than those used in practice. There are two major simplifications compared to the protocols in most machines. First, in our protocol all transitions to the Exclusive state generate a write miss on the bus, and we assume that the requesting cache always fills the block with the contents returned. This simplifies the detailed implementation. Most real protocols distinguish between a write miss and a write hit, which can occur when the cache block is initially in the Shared state. Such misses are called *ownership* or *upgrade* misses, since they involve changing the state of the block, but do not actually require a data fetch. To support such state changes, a protocols uses an *invalidate operation*, in addition to a write miss. With such operations, however, the actual implementation becomes more complex.

The second major difference is that most machines distinguish between a cache block that is really shared and one that exists in the clean state in exactly one cache. This addition of a "clean private" state eliminates the need to generate a bus transaction on a write to such a block. Other enhancements in use in existing multiprocessors include allowing other caches to supply data on a miss to a shared block and distinguishing between write misses and write hits to a block in a Shared state, since the latter only requires establishing ownership and not actually retrieving the data.

Implementing the Protocol

There is one very important, but subtle, requirement that must be ensured in implementing the finite state controller. To ensure write serialization, a write cannot alter the cache until the write miss has successfully been placed on the bus. The tricky part is that two processors may have the same block in their caches in the shared state and try to write the block at the same time. If both caches were able to transition to the Exclusive state at the same time, the writes would not be serialized. Clearly, the requirement to broadcast the write miss on the bus will lead to one processor obtaining access before the other. What happens to the processor that doesn't get to the bus first? Since it has not yet obtained the bus, its write operation is not completed. When it places its write miss on the bus, the processor that wrote first will return the updated block, into which the second processor will write. The access are serialized by this two step process.

Because of this two-step process, the finite state diagram in Figure 9.9 does not correctly represent the actual controller. The finite state diagram in that figure also does not deal with the case of a write miss to an Exclusive block, which requires two bus actions. Figure 9.10 shows the actual finite state diagram for implementing coherency under the assumption that a bus transaction is atomic, once the bus is acquired. This simply means that the bus is not split transaction and once it is acquired any requests are processed before another processor can acquire the bus; we discuss the complexities of a split transaction bus shortly. In the

simplest implementation, the finite state machine in Figure 9.10 is simply replicated for each block in the cache. Since there is no interaction among operations
on different cache blocks, this replication of the controller actually works. Replicating the controller is not actually necessary, but before we see why, let's look
make sure we understand how the finite state controller in Figure 9.10 operates.

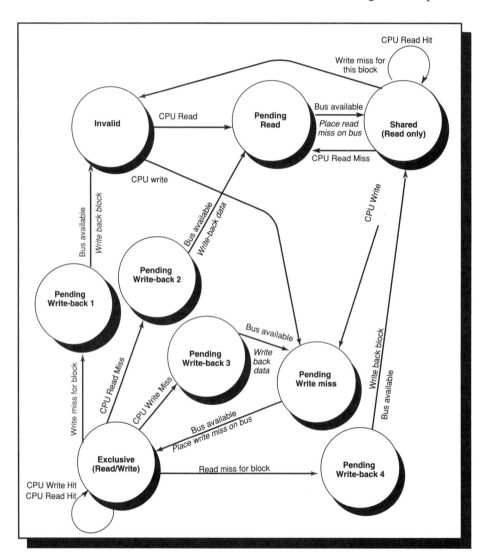

**FIGURE 9.10   A finite state controller for a simple cache coherency scheme with a write-back
cache.** The engine that implements this controller must be reentrant. The diagram assumes the processor stalls until a request is completed, but other transactions must be handled. This controller also
assumes that a transition to a new state that involves a bus access does not complete until the bus
access is completed. Notice that if we did not require a processor to generate a write miss when it
transitioned from the Shared to Exclusive state, it might not obtain the latest value of a cache block,
since some other processor may have updated that block. In a protocol using ownership or upgrade
transitions, we will need to be able to transition out of the pending write state and restart an access,
if a conflicting write obtains the bus first.

To understand how the finite state machine in Figure 9.10 operates, we first examine the function of the states in the machine, then we show why replicating the machine works. The additional states are all transient: the controller will leave those states when the bus is available. Four of the states are pending write-back states that arise because in a write-back cache when a block is replaced (or invalidated) it must be written back to the memory. Four events can cause such a write back:

1. A write miss on the bus by another processor for this block .

2. A CPU read miss that forces the Exclusive block to be replaced.

3. A CPU write miss that forces the Exclusive block to be replaced.

4. A read miss on the bus by another processor for this block.

In each of the cases, the next state differs, hence there are four separate pending write-back states with four different successor states.

Logically replicating the controller for each cache block allows correct operation if two conditions hold (in addition to our base assumption that the processor blocks till a cache access completes):

1. An operation on the bus for a block and a pending operation for a different block are noninterfering.

2. The controller in Figure 9.10 correctly deals with the cases when a pending operation and a bus operation are for the same block.

The first condition is certainly true. To see why the second condition is true consider each of the pending states and what happens if a conflicting access occurs:

- Pending write-back 1: The cache is writing back the data to eliminate it anyway, so a read or write miss for the block has no new effect. Notice, however, that the pending cache *must* use the bus cycle generated by the read or write miss to complete the write-back. Otherwise, there will be no response to the miss, since the pending cache still has the only copy of the cache block. When it sees that the address of a miss matches the address of the block it is waiting to write back, it recognizes that the bus is available, writes the data, and transitions its state. This applies to all the pending write-back states.

- Pending write-back 2, 3: The cache is eliminating a block in the Exclusive state, so another miss for that block simply allows the write-back to occur immediately. If the read or write miss on the bus is for the new block that the processor is trying to share, there is no interaction, since the processor does not yet have a copy of the block.

- Pending write-back 4: In this case the processor is surrendering an Exclusive block and simply completes the write-back.

- Pending Read, Pending Write: The processor does not yet have a copy of the block that it is waiting for, so a read or write miss for that block has no effect. Since the waiting cache still needs to place a miss on the bus and fetch the block, it is guaranteed to get a new copy.

With these additional states and our assumptions that the bus operates atomically, that misses always cause the state to be updated, and that the processor blocks till an access completes, our coherency implementation is both deadlock-free and correct. If some fairness is guarantee is made for bus access, then this controller is also free of *livelock*. Livelock occurs when some portion of a computation cannot make progress, though other portions can. If one processor could be denied the bus indefinitely, then that processor could never make progress in its computation. Some guarantee of fairness on bus access prevents this.

There is still, however, one more critical implementation detail related to the bus transactions and what happens when a miss is processed. The key difference between the cache coherence case and the standard uniprocessor case occurs when the block is Exclusive in some cache, which because it is a write-back cache, the memory copy is stale. In this case, the coherency unit will retrieve the block (called an *intervention*) and generate a write back. Since the memory does not know the state of the block, it will attempt to respond to the request as well. Since the data has been updated, the cache and processor will each attempt to drive the bus with different values. To prevent this, a line is added to the bus (often called the Shared line) to coordinate the response. When the processor detects that it has a copy in the Exclusive state, it signals the memory on this line and the memory aborts the transaction. When the write-back occurs, the memory gets the data and updates its copy. Since it is difficult to bound the amount of time that it can take to snoop the local cache copy, this line is usually implemented as a wired-or with each processor holding its input low until it knows it does not have the block in exclusive state. The memory waits for the line to go high, indicating that no cache has the copy in the Exclusive state, before putting data on the bus.

Since we use a nonsplit transaction bus, we have assumed one other simplification in this controller: we treat a bus access as an atomic (uninterruptible) operation that takes place during a transition between states. For example, when a cache miss occurs and the bus is available, the miss is placed on the bus. We assume that the bus transaction occurs atomically and that the data requested is returned before the controller advances to the next state. If the bus does not implement split transactions, this simplification merely eliminates a state for each bus request. The function of this state would be to wait for the memory or a processor to respond to a read or write miss. This simplification does not change the operation of the controller, since the bus is not relinquished to any other processor when it is responding to a read or write request.

Dealing with a Split Transaction Bus

If the bus had a split transaction capability than we could not assume that a response would occur immediately. In fact, implementing a split transaction with coherency is significantly more complex. One complication arises from the fact that we must number and track bus transactions, so that a controller knows when a bus action is a response to its request. Another complication is dealing with races that can arise because two operations for the same cache block could potentially be outstanding simultaneously. An example illustrates this complication best. What happens when two processors try to write a word in the same cache block? Without split transactions, one of the operations reaches the bus first and the other must change the state of the block to invalid and try the operation again. Only one of the transactions is outstanding on the bus at any point.

Suppose the bus is split transaction and suppose that no cache has a copy of the block, when both P1 and P2 try to write a word in the block. Then the following sequence of events could occur:

1. P1 places a write miss for the block on the bus. Since P2 has the data in the Invalid state nothing occurs.

2. P2 places its write miss on the bus; again, since no copy exists, no state changes are needed.

3. The memory responds to P1's request. P1 places the block in the Exclusive state and writes the word into the block.

4. The memory responds to P2's request. P2 places the block in the Exclusive state and writes the word into the block.

Disaster! Two caches now have the same block in the Exclusive state and memory will be inconsistent.

How can this race be avoided? The simplest way is to use the bus broadcast capability. All coherency controllers track all bus accesses. In a split transaction bus, the transactions must be tagged with the processor identity (or a transaction number), so that a processor can identify a reply to its request. Every controller can keep track of the memory address of any outstanding bus requests, since it can see the request and the corresponding reply on the bus. When the local processor generates a miss, the controller does not place the miss request on the bus until there are no outstanding requests for the same cache block. This will force P2 in the above example to wait for P1's access to complete, allowing P1 to place the data in the Exclusive state (and write the word into the block). The miss request from P2 will then cause P1 to do a write-back and move the block to the Invalid state.

These race conditions are what makes implementing coherency even more tricky as the interconnection mechanism becomes more sophisticated. As we will see in Section 9.4, such problems are slightly worse in a directory-based system that does not have a broadcast mechanism like a bus that can order all accesses. Before we see how these difficulties are resolved in directory based schemes, lets look at some performance data for snoopy protocols.

Performance of Snoopy Coherence Protocols

In a bus-based multiprocessor using an invalidation protocol, several different phenomena are at work. In particular, the overall cache performance is a combination of the behavior of ordinary cache miss traffic and the traffic caused by communication, which results in invalidation and subsequent cache misses. Changing the processor count, cache size, and block size can affect these two components of the miss rate in different ways, leading to overall system behavior that is some combination of the two effects. Let's consider increasing processor count first.

Performance for Parallel Workloads

In this section, we use a simulator to study the performance of our five parallel programs. For these measurements, the problem sizes are as follows:

- Barnes-Hut: 16K bodies run for six time steps (the accuracy control is set to 1.0, a typical, realistic value),

- FFT: 1 million, complex data points,

- LU: a 512×512 matrix is used with 16×16 blocks,

- Ocean: a 130×130 grid with a typical error tolerance,

- Volrend: a 256×256×113 voxel image of a human head is used.

Figure 9.11 shows the miss rates for our five applications, as we increase the number of processors from one to sixteen, while keeping the problem size constant. We can see the competing effects of ordinary uniprocessor cache misses (which we will call capacity misses, for short) versus coherency misses as the processor count increases. As we increase the number of processors, the total amount of cache increases, causing the capacity misses to drop. In contrast, increasing the processor count usually causes the amount of communication to increase, in turn, causing the coherency misses to rise. The magnitude of these two effects differs by application.

In FFT, the capacity miss rate drops (from nearly 7% to just over 5%) but the coherency miss rate increases (from about 1% to about 2.7%), leading to a constant overall miss rate. In Ocean, there are a combination of effects, including some that relate to the partitioning of the grid and how grid boundaries map to cache blocks. For a typical grid code the communication-generated misses are proportional to the boundary of each portion of the grid, while the capacity misses are proportional to the area of the grid. Thus, increasing the total amount of cache, while keeping the total problem size fixed will have a more significant effect on the capacity miss rate, at least until each subgrid fits within an individual processor's cache. The significant jump in miss rate between one and two processors occurs because of conflicts that arise from the way in which the grids are mapped to the caches. This conflict is present for direct-mapped and two-way set associative caches, but fades at higher associativities. Such conflicts are not unusual in array-based applications. In addition the coherency misses initially fall as we add processors due to a large number of misses that are write ownerships misses to data that is potentially, but not actually, shared. As the subgrids begin to fit in the aggregate cache (around 16 processors), this effect lessens.

In the other three applications, the increase in processor count has little effect on the miss rate, sometimes causing a slight increase and sometimes causing a slight decrease. To see how the coherency misses cause this effect, consider Figure 9.12, which plots the fraction of the miss rate due to coherency traffic. This includes read and writes misses that require communication as well as write hits that are treated as ownership misses. For all the applications, the coherency traffic rises as we increase the processor count.

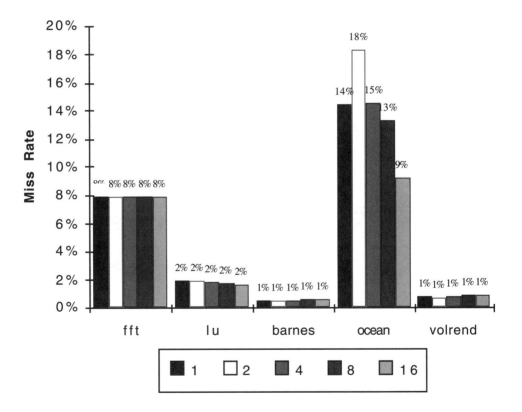

FIGURE 9.11 **This miss rates can vary in nonobvious ways as the processor count is increased from 1 to 16 processors.** The cache size is 64KB, 2-way set associative, with 32B blocks. This includes all misses: for shared and unshared data, as well as write upgrades, which count as write misses. With the exception of Volrend, the misses in these applications are generated by accesses to data that is potentially shared. In all except Ocean, this data is heavily shared, while in Ocean only the boundaries of the subgrids are actually shared, though the entire grid is treated as a shared data object. Of course, since the boundaries change as we increase the processor count (for a fixed size problem), different amounts of the grid become shared. The analmous increase in miss rate for Ocean in moving from 1 to 2 processors arises because of conflict misses in accessing the subgrids.

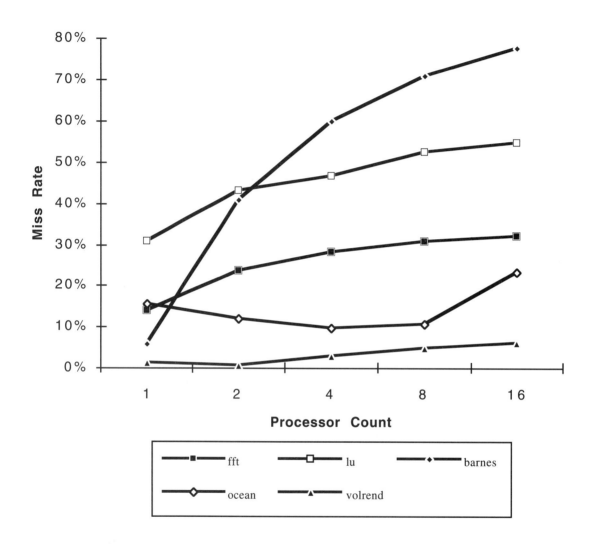

FIGURE 9.12   The fraction of the cache misses caused by coherency transactions typically rises when a fixed size problem is run on an increasing number of processors. The absolute number of coherency misses is increasing in all these benchmarks, including Ocean. In Ocean, however, it is difficult to separate out these misses from others, since the amount of sharing of the grid varies with processor count.. The number of invalidations generated increases significantly. .In FFT the miss rate arising from coherency misses increases from nothing to almost 7%.

How significant are these miss rates in limiting speedup for a bus based machine? The following example gives us some insight.

Example

Suppose we have a 100MHz superscalar processor that issues a data memory reference every clock, when it is not stalled. Assume that cache misses take 50 cycles, during which the bus is unavailable. What is the maximum speed-up achievable with any number of processors for the FFT kernel? Assume that adding a processor adds additional contention for the bus, but ignore other effects and assume the miss rate is flat after 16 processors.

Answer

This example will use basic queuing theory techniques to bound the speed-up. We will introduce the basic techniques in the revised version of the chapter on storage.

Increasing the cache size will have a beneficial affect on performance, since it will reduce the frequency of costly cache misses. Figure 9.13 shows the change in miss rate as cache size is increased. Two effects can lead to a miss rate that does not decrease (at least as quickly as we might expect) as cache size increases: inherent communication and plateaus in miss rate. Inherent communication leads to a certain frequency of coherency misses that are not affected by increasing cache size. Thus, if the cache size is increased while maintaining a fixed problem size, the coherency miss rate eventually limits the decrease in cache miss rate. As Figure 9.14 shows this effect is at work in Ocean. As the caches become large enough to hold each local subgrid, the coherency portion of the miss rate starts to climb.

A less important effect is a temporary plateau in the miss rate that arises when the application has some fraction of its data present in cache but some significant portion of the data set does not fit in the cache or in caches that are slightly bigger. This effect is at work between 64KB and 256KB for FFT. Beyond that cache size, a decrease in the miss rate is seen, as some other major data structure begins to reside in the cache. At very large cache sizes, FFT becomes limited by coherency misses and has a miss rate of 2% to 3%, depending on the block size. These plateaus are common in programs that deal with large arrays.

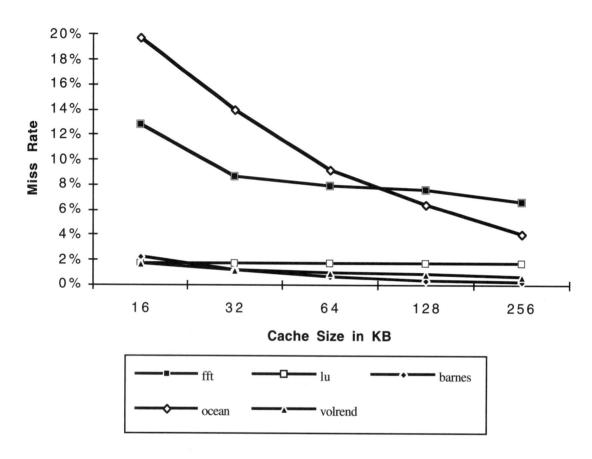

FIGURE 9.13   **The miss rate drops as the cache size is increased, unless the miss rate is dominated by coherency misses. The block size is 32B and the cache is 2-way set-associative.** The processor count is fixed at 16 processors.

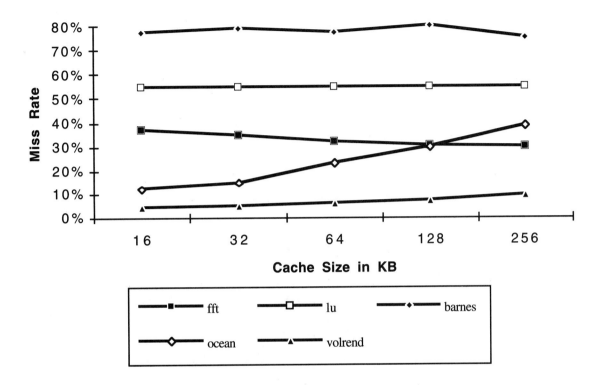

FIGURE 9.14 Fraction of the misses due to communication of shared data as the cache size is increased.

Increasing the block size is another way to decrease the miss rate in a cache. In uniprocessors, large block sizes are often optimal with large caches. In multiprocessors, two new effects come into play: a reduction is spatial locality for shared data and an effect called *false sharing*. Several studies have shown that shared data has lower spatial locality than unshared data. This means that for shared data, fetching larger blocks will be less effective than in a uniprocessor, because the probability that the block will be replaced before it is used is higher.

The second effect, false sharing, arises from the use of an invalidation-based coherency algorithm. False sharing occurs when a block is invalidated (and a subsequent reference causes a miss) because some word in the block, other than the one being read, is written into. If the word written into is actually used by the processor that received the invalidate, than the reference was a true sharing reference and would have caused a miss independent of the block size or position of words. If, however, the word being written and the word read are different and the invalidation does not cause a new value to be communicated, but only causes an extra cache miss, then it is a false sharing miss. The block appears to be shared, but is not in reality, and the miss would not occur if the block size was a single word.

Example

Assume words x1 and x2 are in one cache block that is cached clean in the caches of P1 and P2, which have previously read x1 and x2. Assuming the following sequence of events, identify each miss as a true sharing miss, a false sharing miss, or a hit. Any miss that would occur if the block size were one word is designated a true sharing miss.

Time	P1	P2
1	Write x1	
2		Read x2
3	Write x1	
4		Write x2
5	Read x2	

Answer

Here are classifications:

1. This is a true sharing miss, since x1 was read by P2 and needs to be invalidated.

2. This is a false sharing miss since x2 was invalidated by the write of x1 in P1, but that value of x1 is not used in P2.

3. This is a false sharing miss, since the block containing x1 is marked shared due to the read in P2, but P2 did not read x1.

4. This is a false sharing miss for the same reason as #3.

5. This is a true sharing miss, since the value being read was written by P2.

Figure 9.15 shows the miss rates as the block size is increased. The miss rate of some programs does not decrease at all, because it is already small, and because spatial locality is limited. In other programs, especially Ocean and FFT, the miss rates drops more slowly than what we might expect based on observations from uniprocessor cache analysis.

Figure 9.16 shows the fraction of misses due to communication activity as the block size grows. FFT communicates data in large blocks and the communication adapts to the block size (it is a parameter to the code); hence, this application makes effective use of large blocks. In Ocean, there are competing effects that favor different block size. In particular, consider the accesses to the boundary of each subgrid, in one direction the accesses match the array layout, taking advantage of large blocks, while in the other dimension, they do not match. These two effects largely cancel each other out leading to an overall decrease in the coherency misses as well as the capacity misses. In the Fallacies and Pitfalls section, we will examine the behavior of Ocean when memory is not carefully allocated.

Although the drop in miss rates with longer blocks, may lead you to believe that choosing a longer block size is the best decision, the bottleneck in bus-based multiprocessors is often the limited memory and bus bandwidth. Figure 9.17 shows the growth in bus traffic as the block size is increased. The growth in traffic is most serious in the programs that have a high miss rate (although the relative growth is largest for Volrend). The growth in traffic can actually lead to performance slowdowns due to bus contention.

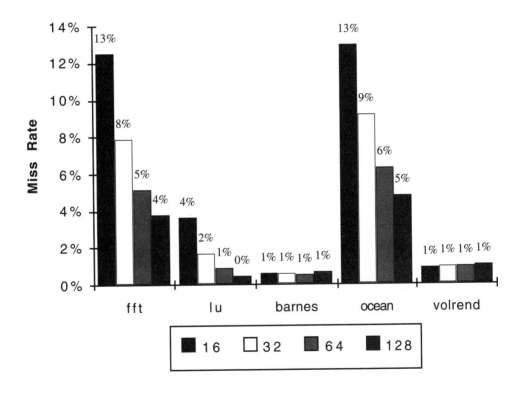

FIGURE 9.15 The miss rate drops as the block size is increased. All these results are for a 64K cache with 32B blocks and 2-way set associativity.

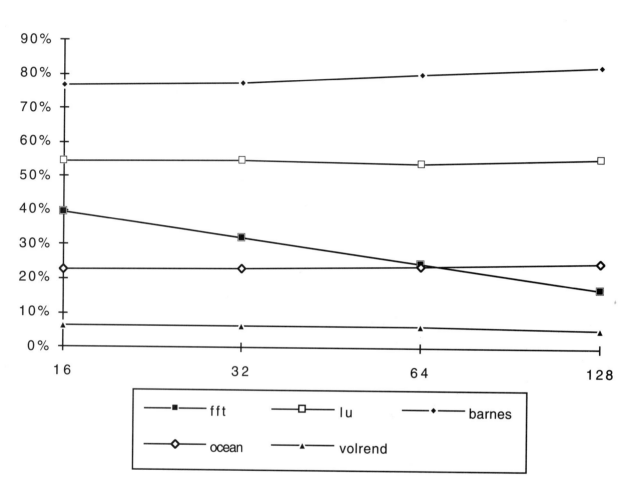

FIGURE 9.16 Fraction of misses from communication as block size increases. Due to a combination of false sharing and lower spatial locality in the shared data, the miss rates for communicated data are often level or increase as the block size is increased. Since communication is very structured and block-oriented, FFT continues to improve even with longer blocks.

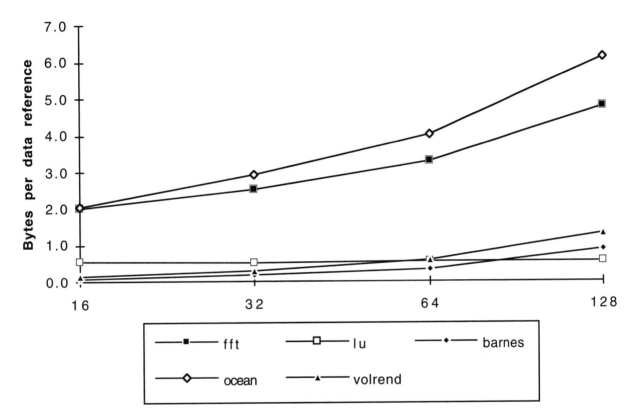

FIGURE 9.17 Bus traffic climbs steadily as the block size is increased. For Volrend the increase is actually more than a factor of 10, although the low miss rate keeps the absolute traffic small. The factor of 3 increase in traffic for Ocean is the best argument against larger block sizes. Remember that our protocol treats ownership misses the same as other misses, slightly increasing the penalty for large cache blocks: in both Ocean and FFT this effect accounts for less than 10% of the traffic.

Performance of Multiprogramming and OS Workloads

This is planned for the final version.

Performance of a Transaction Processing Workload

This is planned for the final version.

9.4 | **Larger-Scale Shared Memory Architectures**

*Multis are a new class of computers based on multiple microprocessors. The small size, low cost, and high performance of microprocessors allow design and construction of computer structures that offer significant advantages in manufacture, price-performance ratio, and reliability over traditional computer families....
Multis are likely to be the basis for the next, the fifth, generation of computers.*

Bell [1985, 463]

There are two different ways we could choose to build a scalable machine supporting shared memory. The simplest way is to exclude cache coherency, focusing instead on a scalable memory system. Several companies have built this style of machine; the current best known example is the Cray T3D. In such machines, memory is distributed into the nodes and all nodes are interconnected by a network. Access can be either local or remote: A controller inside each node decides, on the basis of the address, whether the data resides in the local memory or in a remote memory. In the latter case, a message is sent to the controller in the remote memory to access the data.

To prevent coherency problems, shared data is marked as uncacheable. Of course, software can still explicitly cache the value of shared data, by copying the data from the shared portion of the address space to the local private portion of the address space that is cached. Coherency is then controlled by software. The advantage of such a mechanism is that little hardware support is required, though support for features such as block copy may be useful, since remote accesses fetch only single words (or double words) rather than cache blocks. There are two major disadvantages of this approach.

First, compiler mechanisms for software cache coherency are currently very limited. The techniques that currently exist apply primarily to programs with well-structured loop-level parallelism, and these techniques have significant overhead arising from explicitly copying data. For irregular problems or problems involving dynamic data structures and pointers (including operating systems, for example), compiler-based software cache coherency is currently impractical. The basic difficulty is that software-based coherency algorithms must be conservative, resulting in excess coherency overhead. Due to the complexity of the possible interactions, asking programmers to deal with coherency is inappropriate.

Second, the advantage of being able to fetch and use multiple words in a single cache block for close to the cost of fetching one word is essentially lost. Support for a block copy mechanism can help, but such mechanisms are often either costly to use (since they often require OS intervention) or expensive to implement since special-purpose hardware support and a buffer are needed.

These disadvantages are magnified by the large latency of access to remote memory versus a local cache. For example, on the Cray T3D a local cache access has a latency of two cycles and is pipelined, while a remote access takes about 150 cycles. Of course techniques such as prefetching can be used to reduce the impact of longer accesses but hiding frequent long latency accesses with prefetching will be difficult and require extensive hardware overhead. Section 9.6 and 9.8 discuss latency hiding ideas applicable to shared memory machines either with or without cache coherency.

For small-scale multiprocessors, cache-coherency is an accepted fact. For larger-scale architectures, there are new challenges to extending the cache-coherent shared-memory model. Although the bus could certainly be replaced with a more scalable interconnection network and we could certainly distribute the memory so that the memory bandwidth could also be scaled, this leaves the lack of salability of the broadcast-oriented snoopy coherency scheme unsolved. One might think that the source of the problem is the use of a bus, but even if we replaced the bus by a scalable interconnect, we could not scale the machine beyond a limited number of processors, since the coherency protocol is inherently broadcast-oriented. The protocol requires every cache to snoop on every potentially shared miss and every write to a cache block that is shared must be serialized. The absence of any centralized data structure that tracks the state of the caches is both the fundamental advantage of a snoopy-based scheme, since it allows it to be inexpensive, as well as its Achilles' heal when it comes to scalability. For example, with 64 processors and a block size of 64 bytes, the total bus bandwidth demands for the five parallel programs range from 470 MB/sec (for LU) to 11.5 GB/sec (for Ocean), assuming a processor that issues a data reference every 20 ns, which is what a 200MHz R4000 or DEC Alpha might generate. In comparison, the Silicon Graphics Challenge bus, the highest bandwidth bus-based multiprocessor in existence, provides 1.2GB of bandwidth.

The alternative to a snoopy protocol is to provide a directory that tracks the state of the caches. The logically-single directory keeps the state of every block that may be cached. Information in the directory usually includes which caches have copies of the block, whether it is dirty, and so on. Existing directory implementations associate the directory information with each memory block and place the directory near the memory. There are also protocols that have been proposed that place some of the information at the caches. The advantage of keeping all the directory information at the memory is that it yields a much simpler protocol, since all the information about the state of a cache block is in one location. The disadvantage is the directory structure is proportional to the memory size, rather than the cache size. This is not a problem for machines with less than about a hundred processors, since the directory overhead will be tolerable. For larger machines, we need methods to allow the directory structure to be efficiently scaled. Several such schemes have been proposed.

To prevent the directory from becoming the bottleneck, directory entries can be distributed along with the memory, so that different directory access can go to different locations, just as different memory requests go to different memories. A distributed directory retains the characteristic that the sharing status of a block is always in a single known location This property is what allows the coherence protocol to avoid broadcast. Figure 9.18 shows how our distributed memory machine looks with the directories added to each node.

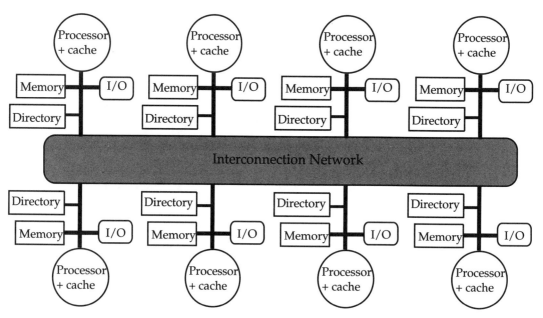

FIGURE 9.18   A directory is added to each node to implement cache coherency in a distributed memory machine. Each directory is responsible for tracking the caches that share the memory addresses of the portion of memory in the node. The directory may communicate with the processor and memory over a common bus, as shown, or it may have a separate port to memory, or it may be part of a central node controller through which all intranode and internode communications pass. In some machines the directory may be part of a centralized node controller that implements all transfers among the components of the node, as well as to or from the interconnection network.

Directory-based Cache Coherence Protocols: The Basics

A directory scheme can be used to implement either a broadcast or an invalidation protocol. Since all existing machines use either exclusively invalidation or use invalidation as the primary scheme, we focus on an invalidation protocol. Just as with a snoopy protocol, there are two primary operations that the protocol must implement: handling a read miss and handling a write to a shared, clean cache block. (Handling a write miss to a shared block is a simple combination of these two.)

Just as in the snoopy cache, the directory must track the state of each cache block. In a simple protocol, these states could be:

- *shared*: one or more processors have the block cached, and the value in memory is up-to-date (as well as in all the caches),

- *uncached*: no processor has a copy of the cache block,

- *exclusive*: exactly one processor has a copy of the cache block and it has written the block, so the memory copy is out-of-date. The processor is called the *owner* of the block.

In addition to tracking the state of each cache block, we must track the processors that have copies of the block when it is shared, since they will need to be invalidated on a write. The simplest way to do this is to keep a bit vector for each memory block. When the block is shared, each bit of the vector indicates whether the corresponding processor has a copy of that block. We can also use the bit vector to keep track of the owner of the block when it is exclusive. For efficiency reasons, we also track the state of each cache block at the individual caches. The states and transitions for the state machine at each cache are identical to what we used for the snoopy cache, though the actions on a transition are slightly different. We make the same simplifying assumptions that we made in the case of the snoopy cache: attempts to write nonexclusive data always generate write misses, and the processors block until an access completes. Of course, the most important simplification–that the interconnect could perform atomic broadcast–is not true and this means that all requests must be followed by explicit responses. Similarly, although a write hit to a shared block is treated as a write miss, the directory cannot interrogate all processors to find the cache block.

For simplicity, we describe a protocol that assumes that all data can be shared. For efficiency, one might want to partition the address space into private and shared regions and not implement coherency actions for the private regions. While this may improve performance, it has drawbacks; for example, passing a pointer to data in the private area to another processor will not work correctly.

Before we see the protocol state diagrams, it is useful to examine a catalog of the message types that may be sent between the processors and the directories. Figure 9.19 shows the type of messages sent among nodes in the processor. The *local* node is the node where a request originates. The *home* node is the node where the memory location of an address resides. The physical address space is statically distributed, so the node that contains the memory and directory for a given physical address is known. For example, the high-order bits may provide the node number, while the low-order bits provide the offset within the memory on that node.

The *remote* node is the node that has a copy of a cache block, whether exclusive or shared. The local node may also be the home node, or the home node may also be the remote node. In either case, the protocol is the same, though internode messages can be replaced by intranode transactions, which should be faster.

In this section, we assume a simple model of memory consistency. To minimize the type of messages and the complexity of the protocol, we make an assumption that messages will be received and acted upon in the same order they are sent. This assumption may not be true in practice and can result in additional complications, some of which we address in Section 9.5 when we discuss memory consistency models. In this section, we use this assumption to ensure that invalidates sent by a processor will be honored immediately.

Message type	Source	Destination	Message contents	Purpose
Read miss	Local processor	Home directory	P, A	Processor P reads data at address A; send data and make P a read sharer.
Write miss	Local processor	Home directory	P, A	Processor P writes data at address A; send data and make P the exclusive owner.
Invalidate	Home directory	Remote caches	A	Invalidate a shared copy at address A.
Fetch	Home directory	Remote cache	A	Fetch the block at address A and send it to its home directory
Fetch/invalidate	Home directory	Remote cache	A	Fetch the block at address A and send it to its home directory; invalidate the block in the cache.
Data value reply	Home directory	Local cache	Data	Return a data value either from the home memory.
Data write-back	Remote cache	Home directory	A, Data	Write-back a data value for address A.

FIGURE 9.19   The possible messages sent among nodes to maintain coherency. Data value replies are used to send a value from the home node when the block is up-to-date in the home node in the shared state and to send a value that has been written back to the home directory to the requesting node. Data value writebacks occur for two reasons: when a block is replaced and must be written back and also when the state of a block is changed from exclusive to shared. Writing back the data value whenever the block becomes shared simplifies the number of states in the protocol, since any dirty block must be exclusive and any shared block is always available in the home memory.

An Example Directory Protocol

The basic states of a cache block in a directory-based protocol are exactly like those in a snoopy protocol and the states in the directory are also analogous, to those we showed earlier. Thus, we can start with simple state diagrams that show the state transitions for an individual cache block and for the directory entry corresponding to each block in memory. As in the snoopy case, these state transition diagrams do not represent all the details of a coherency protocol; however, the actual controller is highly dependent on a number of details of the machine (message delivery properties, buffering structures, etc.), so we explain the gnarl issues involved in implementing these state transition diagrams.

Figure 9.20 shows the protocol actions to which an individual cache responds. We use the same notion as in the last section with requests coming from outside the node in color, and actions in italics. The state transitions for an individual cache are caused by read misses, write misses, invalidates, and data fetch requests and these operations are all shown in Figure 9.20. An individual cache also generates read and write miss messages that are sent to the home directory. Read and writes misses require data value replies and these events will wait for replies before changing state.

As we did for the snoopy controller, we assume an attempt to write a shared cache block is treated as a miss; in practice, such a transaction can be treated as an ownership request or upgrade request and can deliver ownership without requiring that the cache block be fetched. The operation of the state transition diagram in Figure 9.20 is essentially the same as it is for the snoopy case: the states are identical, and the stimulus is almost identical. The write miss operation, which was broadcast on the bus in the snoopy scheme, is replaced by the data fetch and invalidate operations that are selectively sent by the directory controller. Like the snoopy protocol, any cache block must be in the Exclusive state when it is written and any shared block must be up-to-date in memory.

This state transition diagram is a simplification, just as it was in the snoopy cache case. In directory case, it is a larger simplification, since our assumption that bus transactions are atomic, no longer applies. This directory protocol is also simpler than that used in most machines. In particular, when a read or write miss occurs for a block that is exclusive, the block is first sent back to the directory at the home node, from there it is stored into the home memory and also sent to the original requesting node. Many protocols forward the data from the owner node to the requesting node directly (as well as performing the write-back to the home). While the protocol we examine here is simpler to explain, it has some implementation difficulties that a forwarding style protocol does not have. Before we explore the detailed implementation where the challenges can be seen, we need to understand how the directory operates.

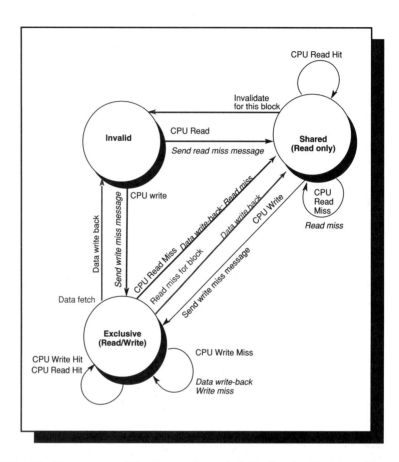

FIGURE 9.20   The state transition diagram for an individual cache block in a directory based system. The states are identical to those in the snoopy case, and the transactions are very similar with explicit invalidate and write-back requests replacing the write misses that were formerly broadcast on the bus.

A message sent to a directory causes two different types of actions: updates of the directory state and additional messages sent to satisfy the request. The states in the directory represent the three standard states for a block, but for all the copies of a memory block rather then for a single cache block. The memory block may be uncached, cached in multiple nodes and readable (Shared), or cached exclusively and writable in exactly one node. In addition to the state of each block, the directory must track the set of processors that have a copy of a block; we use a set called *Sharers* to perform this function. In small scale machines ($\leq$ 128 nodes), this set is typically kept as a bit vector. In larger machines, other techniques, which we discuss in the exercises, are needed. Directory requests will need to update the set Sharers and also use the set to perform invalidations.

Figure 9.21 shows the actions taken at the directory in response to messages received. The directory receives four different requests: read miss, write miss, and data write-back. The messages sent in response by the directory are shown in italics, while the updating of the set Sharers is shown in bold italics. Since all the stimulus messages are external, all actions are shown in color. Our simplified protocol assumes that some actions are atomic, such as requesting a value and sending it to another node; a more detailed implementation cannot use this assumption.

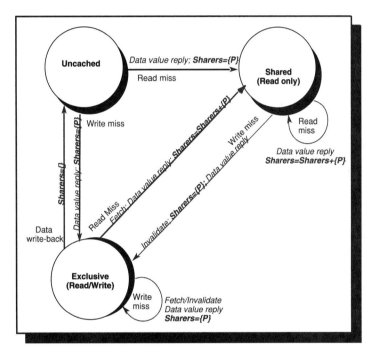

FIGURE 9.21   The state transition diagram for the directory has the same states and structure as the transition diagram for an individual cache, All actions are in color since they all are externally caused. Italics indicates the action taken the directory in response to the request. Bold italics indicate an action that updates the sharing set, Sharers, as opposed to sending a message.

To understand these directory operations, let's examine the requests received and actions taken state by state. When a block is in the Uncached state, the copy in memory is the current value, and the only possible requests for that block are:

■ Read miss: the requesting processor is sent back the data from memory and the requestor the only sharing node. The state of the block is made Shared.

- Write miss: the requesting processor is sent the value and becomes the Sharing node. The block is made Exclusive to indicate that the only valid copy is cached. Sharers indicates the identity of the owner.

When the block is Shared, the memory value is up-to-date, and the same two requests can occur:

- Read miss: the requesting processor is sent back the data from memory and the requesting processor is added to the sharing set.

- Write miss: the requesting processor is sent the value. All processors in the set Sharers are sent invalidate messages, and the Sharers set is to contain the identity of the requesting processor. The state of the block is made Exclusive.

When the block is Exclusive, the current value of the block is held in the cache of the processor identified by the set Sharers (the owner), and there are three possible directory requests:

- Read miss: the owner processor is sent a data fetch message, which causes the state of the block in the owner's cache to transition to Shared and causes the owner to send the data to the directory , where it is written to memory and sent back to the requesting processor. The identity of the requesting processor is added to the set Sharers, which still contains the identity of the processor that was the owner (since it still has a readable copy).

- Data write-back: the owner processor is replacing the block and hence must write it back. This makes the memory copy up-to-date (the home directory essentially becomes the owner), the block is now uncached, and the Sharer set is empty.

- Write miss: the block has a new owner. A message is sent to the old owner causing the cache to send the value of the block to the directory from which it is send to the requesting processor, which becomes the new owner. Sharers is set to the identity of the new owner, and state of the block is made Exclusive.

Implementing the Directory Protocol

Note to reviewer: this section shows why this protocol works with no additional complications, when the network has infinite bandwidth.

It's complex, but typical of the situation that exists in real machines. We could try to move it to an exercise and guide the reader through it, or we could leave it here. Comments are requested.

The complexity of a directory protocol comes from the lack of atomicity in transactions. Several of the operations that are atomic in a bus-based snoopy protocol cannot be atomic in a directory based machine. This causes most of the complexities in translating these state transition diagrams into actual finite state controllers. There are two assumptions about the interconnection network that significantly simplify the implementation. First, we assume that the network provides *in order delivery* of all messages. This means that two messages sent from a single node to another node arrive in the order they were sent. No assumptions are made about messages originating from, or destined to, different nodes. Second, we assume the network has unlimited bandwidth. This second assumption means that a message can always be accepted into the network. This reduces the possibility for deadlock and allows us to treat some nonatomic actions as atomic. Of course, we also assume that the network delivers all messages within a finite time. While the first assumption, in-order transmission, is quite reasonable and is, in fact, true in many machines, the second assumption, unlimited bandwidth, may not be, though in practice the network need only be capable of receiving a finite number of messages, since we still assume that processors block on misses. Later, we will discuss what has to change to eliminate the assumption that a message can always be accepted, while still preventing deadlock.

We also assume that the coherency controller is duplicated for each cache block (to avoid having to deal with unrelated transactions) and that a state transition only completes when a message has been a transmitted and a data value reply received, when needed. This last assumption simply means that we do not allow the CPU to continue and read or write a cache block, until the read or read miss is satisfied by a data value reply message. This simply eliminates a transition state that waits for the block to arrive. Because, we are assuming unlimited bandwidth, we also assume that a outcoming message is always transmitted before the next incoming message is accepted.

Under these assumptions, the state transition diagram of Figure 9.20 can be used for the coherency controller at the cache, if the controller simply throws away any incoming transactions, other than the data value reply, while waiting for a read or write miss. The reasoning behind this depends on looking at each possible case that can arise while the cache is waiting for a response from the directory. Cases where the cache is transitioning the block to invalid, either from the Shared or Exclusive state do not matter, since any incoming signals for this block do not affect the block once it is invalid. Hence, we need only consider cases where the processor is transitioning to the Shared or Exclusive state. There are two such cases:

- CPU Read miss from either Invalid or Exclusive: the directory will not reply until the block is available. Furthermore, since any write back of an Exclusive entry for this block has been done, the controller can ignore any requests.

- CPU Write miss: any required write-back is done first and the processor is stalled. Since it cannot hold a block exclusive in this cache entry, it can ignore requests for this block, until the write miss is satisfied from the directory.

The directory case is more complex to explain, since multiple cache controllers may send a message for the same block close to the same time. These operations must be serialized. Unlike the snoopy case where every controller sees every request on the bus at the same time, the individual caches only know what has happened when they are notified by the directory. Because the directory serializes the messages when it receives them and because all write misses for a given cache block go the same directory, writes will be serialized by the home directory.

Thus, the directory controller's main problem is to deal with the distributed representation of the cache state. Since the directory must wait for the completion of certain operations, such as sending invalidates and fetching a cache block, before transitioning state, most potential races are eliminated. Because we assume unlimited bandwidth, the directory can always complete a transaction before accepting the next incoming message. For this reason, the state transition diagram in Figure 9.21 can be used as an implementation. To see why, we must consider cases where the directory and the local cache do not agree on the state of a block. The cache can only have a block in a less restricted state than the directory believes the block is in, because transitioning to Exclusive from Invalid or Shared, or to Shared from Invalid, requires a message to the directory and a reply. Thus, the only cases to consider are:

- Local cache state is Invalid, directory state is Exclusive: the cache controller must have performed a data write back of the block (see Figure 9.20). Hence the directory will shortly obtain the block. Furthermore no invalidation is needed, since the block has been replaced.

- Local cache state is Invalid, directory state is Shared: the directory will send an Invalidate, which may be ignored, since the block has been replaced.

- Local cache state is Shared, directory state is Exclusive: the write back has already been done and the block has been replaced, so a Fetch/Invalidate, which could be sent by the directory, can be ignored.

Implementing the Protocol with a Finite Bandwidth Network

Note to reviewers: this next section discusses how the protocol is implemented when the network has finite bandwidth. Finite bandwidth introduces both deadlock and livelock problems that are extremely complex. This section outlines an implementation strategy and shows that it works.

But, it is complex. There are three alternatives:

1. Keep it with any improvements you can suggest.

2. Keep the strategy (basically the first page of the discussion) and move the rest to an exercise.

3. Move it all to an extended exercise that would explain the strategy and let the reader argue why it suffices.

Your comment and suggestions are requested.

What happens when the network does not have unlimited bandwidth? The major implication of this is that a cache or directory controller may be unable to complete a message send. This could lead to deadlock.

Example

Show how two processors can deadlock by requesting a block from each other at the same time.

Answer

1. Processor P1 has a write miss for block X, which is exclusive in the cache of processor P2. The directory sends a fetch/invalidate to P2.

2. P2 has a write miss for block Y, which is exclusive in the cache of processor P1. The directory sends a fetch/invalidate to P1.

Because no more buffers are available, P2 cannot receive the fetch/invalidate for X. Similarly, P1 cannot receive the fetch/invalidate for Y. Both processors are now deadlocked, since they are waiting on each other. Furthermore, the directory controllers for X and Y are also deadlocked, since they are each waiting for a response.

One solution to this problem is to guarantee that there are always buffers to accept messages. While this is possible for a small machine with processors that block on a cache miss, it may not be very practical, even in a small machine, since a single write could generate many invalidate messages. There is an alternative strategy, which most systems use. It has four parts:

1. A separate network (physical or virtual) is used for requests and replies, where a reply is any message that a controller waits for in transitioning between states.

2. Every request that expects a reply, allocates space to accept the reply when it returns. If no space is available, the request waits.

3. Any controller can reject (usually with a *negative acknowledge* or *NAK*) any request, but it can never NAK a reply.

4. Any request that receives a NAK in response is simply retried.

To understand why this is sufficient to prevent deadlock, let's first consider our example above. Because a write miss is a request that requires a reply, the space to accept the reply is preallocated. Hence both nodes will have space for the reply. Since the networks are separate a reply can be received even if no more space is available for requests. Since the requests are for two different blocks, the separate coherence controllers handle the requests. If the accesses are for the same address, then they are serialized at the directory and no problem exists.

The short version would conclude about here with a sentence or two and then a pointer to an exercise.

To see that there are no deadlocks more generally, we must ensure that all replies can be accepted, and that every request is eventually serviced. Since a cache controller or directory controller can have at most one request needing a reply outstanding, it can always accept the reply when it returns. To see that every request is eventually serviced, we need only show that any request could be completed. Since every request starts with a read or write miss at a cache, it is sufficient to show that any read or write miss is eventually serviced. Since the write miss case includes the actions for a read miss as a subset, we focus on showing the write misses are serviced. There are two cases that cover the third case: the block is currently Shared and the block is Exclusive in some other cache. Let's consider the case where the block is Shared:

- The CPU attempts to do a write and generates a write miss that is sent to the directory. At this point the processor is stalled.

- The write miss is sent to the directory controller for this memory block. Note that although one cache controller handles all the requests for a given cache block, regardless of its memory contents, there is a controller for every memory block, thus the only conflict at the directory controller is when two requests arrive for the same block. This is critical to the deadlock-free operation of the controller, and needs to be addressed in an implementation using a single controller.

- Now consider what happens at the directory controller: suppose the write miss is the next thing to arrive at the directory controller. The controller sends out the invalidates, which can always be accepted if the controller for this block is idle. If the controller is not idle, then the processor must be stalled. Since the processor is stalled, it must have generated a read or write miss. If it generated a read miss, then it has either displaced this block, or does not have a copy. If it does not have a copy, then it has sent a read miss and cannot continue until the read miss is processed by the directory (the read miss will not be handled until the write miss is). If the controller has replaced the block, then we need not worry about it. If the controller is idle, then an invalidate occurs, and the copy is eliminated.

The case where the block is Exclusive is somewhat trickier. Our analysis begins when the write miss arrives at the directory controller for processing. There are two cases to consider:

- The directory controller sends a fetch/invalidate message to the processor where it arrives to find the cache controller idle and in the Exclusive state. The controller sends a data write-back and makes its state invalid. This reply arrives at the directory controller, which can always accept the reply. The directory controller sends back the data to the requesting processor, which can always accept the reply, and then restart execution.

- The directory controller sends a fetch/invalidate message to the processor where it arrives to find the cache controller has had a read or write miss that caused the block to be replaced. In this case, the cache controller has already sent the block to the directory with a data write-back and made the data unavailable. Since this is exactly the effect of the fetch/invalidate message, the protocol operates correctly.

We have shown that our coherency mechanism operates correctly when controllers are replicated and when responses can be NAKed and retried. Both of these assumptions generate some problems in the implementation.

The next paragraphs can stay unless the entire section above is eliminated.

First, let's consider how these controllers, which we have assumed are replicated, can be built without actually replicating them. On the side of the cache controllers, because the processors stall, the actual implementation is quite similar to what was needed for the snoopy controller. We can simply add the transient states just as we did for the snoopy case and note that a transaction for a different cache block can be handled while the current processor-generated operation is pending. Since a processor blocks on a request, at most one pending operation need be dealt with.

On the side of the directory controller, things are more complicated. The difficulty arises from the way we handle the retrieval and return of a block. In particular, because a directory retrieves an Exclusive block and returns it to the requesting node, the directory must accommodate other transactions while waiting for the block to return. Otherwise, integrating the directory controllers in a single node will lead to the possibility of deadlock. Because of this situation, the directory controller must be reenterant, that is, it must be capable of suspending its execution while waiting for a reply and accept another transaction. The only place this must occur is in response to read or write misses, while waiting for a response from the owner. This leads to three important observations:

1. The state of the controller need only be saved and restored while either a fetch or a fetch/invalidate operation is outstanding.

2. The implementation can bound the number of outstanding transactions being handled in the directory, by simply NAKing read or write miss requests that could cause the number of outstanding requests to be exceeded.

3. If instead of returning the data through the directory, the owner node forwards the data directly to the requester (as well as returning it to the directory), we can eliminate the need for the directory to handle more than one outstanding request. This motivation, in addition to the reduction of latency, are the reasons for using the forwarding style of protocol. The forwarding style protocol has a introduces another type of problem that we discuss in the exercises.

The major remaining implementation difficulty is to implement NAKs. One alternative is for each processor to keep track of its outstanding transaction, so it knows, when the NAK is received, what the requested transaction was. The alternative is to bundle the original request into the NAK, so that the controller receiving the NAK can determine what the original request was. Because every request allocates a slot to receive a reply and a NAK is a reply, NAKs can always be received. Now that we have seen how to build directory-based machines, let's examine the performance of such a machine.

Performance of Directory-based Coherency Protocols

The performance of a directory-based machine depends on the factors that influence the performance of bus-based machines (e.g., cache size, processor count, and block size), as well as the distribution of misses and frequency of remote dirty misses. To give an idea of he performance impact of these factors, we use a simple example of a directory based machine. Figure 9.22 shows the parameters we assume for our simple machine. It assumes that the time to first word for a local memory access is 25 cycles and that the path to local memory is 8 bytes wide while the network interconnect is 2 bytes wide. This model ignores the effects of contention, which are probably not too serious in the parallel benchmarks we examine, but could be in other programs.

Characteristic	# processor cycles
Processor cycles between data access	1
Cache hit	1
Cache miss to local memory	$25 + \dfrac{\text{block size in bytes}}{8}$
Cache miss to home directory	$75 + \dfrac{\text{block size in bytes}}{2}$
Cache miss to remotely cached data	$100 + \dfrac{\text{block size in bytes}}{2}$

FIGURE 9.22   Characteristics of the example directory-based machine.

Performance for Parallel Workloads

In this section we start by examining the performance as we increase the processor count. We assume perfect speed-up when all cache accesses are hits.

Since the machine is larger and has longer latencies, we assume a larger cache (128KB) and a block size of 64 bytes. As Figure 9.23 shows the miss rates with these sizes are fairly low and not affected much by changes in processor count with the exception of Ocean, where the miss rate rises at 64 processors. This occurs because of mapping conflicts that occur when the grid becomes small and because of a rise in the coherency misses.

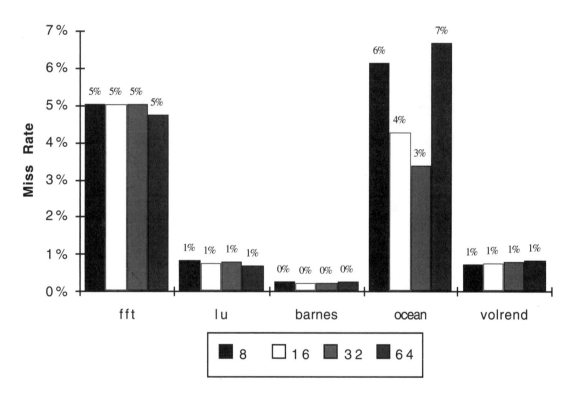

FIGURE 9.23   The miss rate is often steady as processors are added for these benchmarks. Ocean, due to its grid structure, has an initially decreasing miss rate, which rises when there are 64 processors.

Figure 9.24 shows how the miss rates change as the cache size is increased, assuming a 64 processor execution and 64-byte blocks. These miss rates decrease at rates that we might expect, though the dampening effect caused by slow reduction in coherency misses is present.

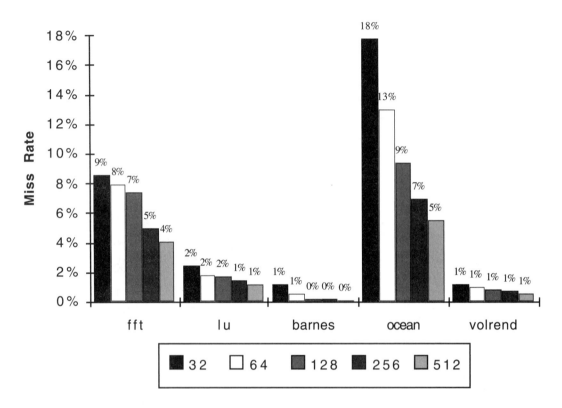

FIGURE 9.24 Miss rates decrease as cache sizes grow. Steady decreases are seen in all miss rates as larger caches allow the handling of more private as well as shared references.

Finally, we examine the effect of changing the block size in Figure 9.25. Increases in block size lower the miss rate, even for large blocks, though the performance benefits for going to the largest blocks are small.

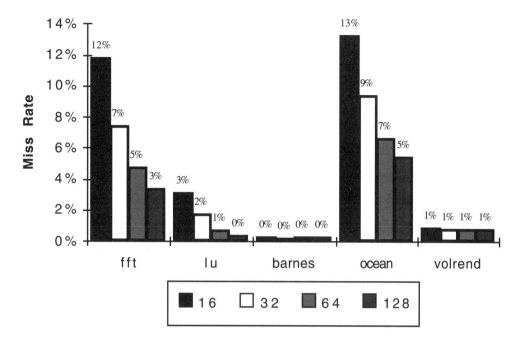

FIGURE 9.25 Miss rate versus block size assuming a 128KB cache and 64 processors in total.

9.5 | Synchronization

There are three aspects to implementing synchronization in a shared memory multiprocessor. First, we need a uninterruptible instruction capable of atomically retrieving and changing a value. Several different options are explored for this in the first section. Second, we need to build user level synchronization operations using the basic hardware primitives. We will see how very efficient spin locks can be built using a basic hardware operation and the coherence mechanism. Third, in larger-scale machines synchronization can become a performance bottleneck, since it can introduce contention and because latency is potentially greater in such a machine. We will see how contention can arise in implementing some common user-level synchronization operations and examine more powerful hardware-supported synchronization primitives that can reduce contention, as well as latency.

Basic Hardware Primitives

The key ability we require in any multiprocessor is the ability to atomically update a memory location. Without such a capability, the cost of building basic synchronization primitives will be too high and will increase as the processor count increases. There are a number of alternative formulations of the atomic synchronization operation, all of which provide the ability to atomically read and update a location together with some way to tell if the update was successful. Let's start with one such operation and show how it can provide basic synchronization.

One typical operation for building synchronization operations is the atomic exchange that interchanges a value in a register for a value in memory. To use this as a synchronization operation, we can perform an exchange using a register that contains the value 1 and a memory location, where the value 0 is used to indicate that the synchronization variable is free and a 1 is used to indicate that the synchronization variable is locked and unavailable. A processor tries to set the synchronization variable by doing an exchange of 1 with the memory location. When the exchange completes, the value obtained from the exchange is 1 if some other processor had already claimed access and 0 otherwise. In the latter case, the value is also changed to be 1, preventing any competing exchange from also retrieving a 1. For example, consider two processors that each try to do the exchange simultaneously: this race is broken since exactly one of the processors will perform the exchange first, returning 0, and the second processor will return 1 when it does the exchange. The key to using the exchange (or swap) primitive to implement synchronization is that the operation is atomic: the exchange is indivisible.

There are a number of other atomic primitives that can be used to implement synchronization. They all have the key property that they change a memory value in a manner that we can tell whether or not the operation executed atomically. One operation present in many older machines is a test-and-set, that tests a value and sets it if the value passes the test. For example, we could define an operation that tested for 0 and set the value to 1, which is similar to how we used atomic exchange. Another atomic synchronization primitive is fetch-and-increment: it returns the value of a memory location and atomically increments it. By using the value 0 to indicate that the synchronization variable is unclaimed, we can use fetch-and-increment, just as we used exchange. There are other uses of operations like fetch-and-increment, which we will see shortly.

A slightly different approach to providing atomic operations has been used in some recent machines. Implementing a single atomic memory operation introduces some challenges, since it requires both a memory read and a write in a single, uninterruptible instruction. An alternative is to have a pair of instructions where the second instruction returns a value from which it can be deduced whether the pair of instructions was executed in an atomic fashion. The pair of instructions includes a special load called a *load linked* or *load locked* and a special store called a *store conditional*. These instructions are used in sequence: if the address specified by the load linked is changed before the sore conditional occurs, then the store conditional fails and is aborted. If the processor is interrupted between the two instructions, then the store conditional also fails. The store conditional is defined to return a value indicating whether or not the store was successful. Since the load linked returns the initial value and the store conditional returns 1 if it succeeds and 0 otherwise, the following sequence implements an atomic exchange on the memory location specified by the contents of R1:

```
try:        mov         R3,R4   ;mov exchange value
            ll          R2,0(R1) ;load linked
            sc          R3,0(R1) ;store
            beqz        R3,try  ;branch store fails
            mov         R4,R2   ;put load value in R4
```

At the end of this sequence the contents of R4 and the memory location specified by R1 have been atomically exchanged.

Another advantage of the load linked/store conditional mechanism is that it can be used to build other synchronization primitives. For example, here is an atomic fetch and increment:

```
try:        ll          R2,0(R1) ;load linked
            addi        R2,R2,#1 ;increment
            mov         R3,R2   ;save value
            sc          R2,0(R1) ;store
            beqz        R2,try  ;branch store fails
```

Since the store conditional will fail after either another reference to the load linked address or any exception, care must be taken in choosing what goes between the two instructions. In particular, only register-register instructions can safely be permitted. In addition, the number of instructions between the load linked and the store conditional should be small to minimize the probability that an unrelated event causes the store to fall frequently.

Implementing Locks Using Coherency

Once we have an atomic operation, we can use the coherency mechanisms of a multiprocessor to implement *spin locks*: locks that processor continuously try to acquire, spinning around a loop trying to get the lock. The simplest implementation, which we would use if there were no cache coherency, would keep the lock variables in memory. A processor could continually try to acquire the lock using an atomic operation, say exchange, and test whether the exchange returned the lock as free. To release the lock, the processor simply stores the value 0 to the lock. Here is the code sequence to lock the spin-lock whose address is in R1 using an atomic exchange:

```
            li      R2,#1
lockit:     exch    R2,0(R1) ;atomic exchange
            bnez    R2,lockit ;already locked?
```

If our machine supports cache coherency, we can cache the locks using the coherency mechanism to maintain the lock value coherently. This has two advantages. First, it allows an implementation where the process of "spinning" (trying to test and acquire the lock in a tight loop) could be done on a local cached copy rather than requiring a global memory access on each attempt to acquire the loop. The second advantage comes from the observation that there is often locality in lock accesses, that is, the processor that used the lock last will use it again. In such cases, the lock value may reside in the cache of the processor, greatly reducing the time to acquire the lock.

To obtain the first advantage: being able to spin on a local cached copy rather than generating a memory request for each attempt to acquire the lock, mandates a change in our simple spin procedure. Each attempt to exchange in the loop directly above is a write operation. If multiple processors are attempting to get the lock, each will generate the write. Most of these writes will lead to write misses, since each write by a processor generates an invalidate of any copies of the lock in other caches.

Thus, we should modify our spin lock procedure so that it spins by doing reads on a local copy of the lock, until it successfully sees that the lock is available, then it attempts to acquire the lock, by doing a swap operation. Figure 9.26 shows this procedure assuming that 0 means unlocked and 1 means locked. A processor first reads the lock variable to test its state. A processor keeps reading and testing until the value indicates that the lock is unlocked. The processor then races against all other processes that were similarly "spin waiting" to see who can lock the variable first. All processes use a swap instruction that reads the old value and stores a 1 into the lock variable. The single winner will see the 0, and the losers will see a 1 that was placed there by the winner. (The losers will continue to set the variable to the locked value, but that doesn't matter.) The winning processor executes the code after the lock and then stores a 0 into the lock variable when it exits, starting the race all over again.

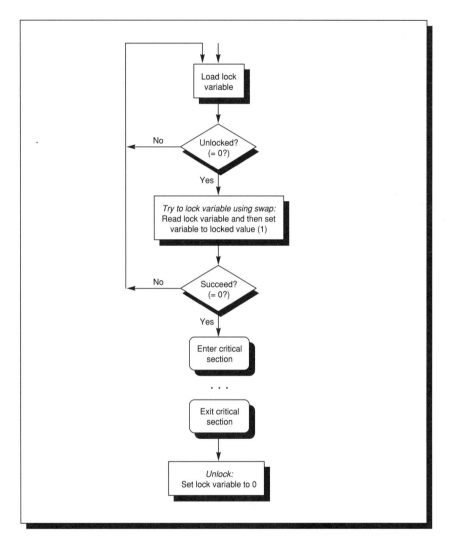

FIGURE 9.26   Steps to acquire a lock to synchronize processes and then to release the lock on exit from the key section of code.

Step	Processor P0	Processor P1	Processor P2	Coherency state of lock	Bus/directory activity
1	Has lock	Spins, testing if lock = 0	Spins, testing if lock = 0	Shared	None
2	Set lock to 0	(Invalidate received)	(Invalidate received)	Exclusive	Write invalidate of lock variable from P0
3		Cache miss	Cache miss	Shared	Bus/directory services P2 cache miss; write back from P0.
4		(Waits while bus/directory busy)	Lock = 0	Shared	Cache miss for P2 satisfied
5		Lock = 0	Executes swap, gets cache miss.	Shared	Cache miss for P1 satisfied
6		Executes swap, gets cache miss.	Completes swap: returns 0 and sets Lock =1.	Exclusive	Bus/directory services P2 cache miss; generates invalidate.
7		Swap completes and returns 1.	Enter critical section	Shared	Bus/directory services P2 cache miss; generates write-back.
8		Spins, testing if lock = 0			None

FIGURE 9.27 Cache-coherency steps and bus traffic for three processors, P0, P1, and P2. This figure assumes write-invalidate coherency. P0 starts with the lock (step 1). P0 exits and unlocks the lock (step 2). P1 and P2 race to see which reads the unlocked value during the swap (steps 3-5). P2 wins and enters the critical section (steps 6 and 7), while P1's attempt fails so it starts spin waiting (steps 7 and 8). In a real system, these events will take many more than eight clock ticks, since acquiring the bus and replying to misses takes much longer.

Let's examine how the "spin lock" scheme of Figure 9.26 works with cache coherency. Figure 9.27 shows the bus and cache operations for multiple processes trying to lock a variable using an atomic swap. Once the processor with the lock stores a 0 into the lock, all other caches are invalidated and must fetch the new value to update their copy of the lock. One such cache gets the copy of the unlocked value (0) first and performs the swap. When the cache miss of other processors is satisfied, they find that the variable is already locked, so they must return to testing and spinning.

This example, shows another advantage of the load linked/store conditional primitives: the read and write operation are explicitly separated. The load linked need not cause any bus traffic. This allows the following simple code sequence, which has the same characteristics as the optimized version using exchange (R1 has the address of the lock):

```
lockit:    ll      R2,0(R1) ;load linked
           bnez    R2,lockit ;not available-spin
           addi    R2,R2,1;get locked value
           sc      R2,0(R1) ;store
           beqz    R2,try  ;branch if store fails
```

The first branch forms the spinning loop, while the second branch resolves races when two processors see the lock available simultaneously.

Notice that with write-broadcast cache coherency, the caches would update their copy rather than first invalidate and then load from memory. This would improve both the time to get the lock, as well as reduce the bus traffic. This advantage in handling synchronization is a primary reason why some designers have included support for write broadcast protocols in processors. While our spin lock scheme is simple and compelling, it has difficulty scaling up to handle many processors because of the communication traffic generated when the lock is released. The next sections discuss these problems in more detail, as well as techniques to overcome these problems in larger machines.

Synchronization Performance Challenges

To understand why the simple spin lock scheme of the previous section does not scale well, imagine a large machine with all processors contending for the same lock. The directory will act as a point of serialization for all n processors, leading to lots of contention, as well as traffic. The following example shows how bad things can be.

Example   Suppose there are 20 processors on a bus that each try to lock a variable simultaneously. Assume that each bus cycle is 50 clocks. You can ignore the time of the actual read or write of a lock held in the cache as well as the time the lock is held (they won't matter much!). Determine the number of bus transactions required for all 20 processors to acquire the lock, assuming they are all spinning when the lock is released at time 0. About how long will it take to process the 20 requests. Assume the bus is totally fair so that every pending request is serviced before a new request and that the processors are equally fast.

Answer   The following table shows the sequence of events from the time of the release to the time for the next release:

Event	Duration
Read miss by all waiting processors to fetch lock	1000
Write miss by releasing processor and invalidates	50
Read miss by all waiting processors	1000
Write miss by all waiting processors , one successful lock, and invalidation of all lock copies	1000
Total time for one processor to acquire and release lock	3,050 cycles

Of course, the number of processors contending for the lock drops by one each time the lock is acquired, which reduces the average cost to 1,525 cycles. Thus, for 20 lock-unlock pairs, it will take over 30,000 cycles for the processors to pass through the lock. Furthermore, the average processor will spend half this time idle, simply trying to get the lock. The number of bus transactions involved is over 400!

The difficulty in this situation arises from contention for the lock and serialization of lock access, as well as the latency of the bus access. The fairness property of the bus actually makes things worse, since it delays the processor that claims the lock, but for any bus arbitration scheme some worst case scenario can exist. The root of the problem is the contention and the fact that the lock access is serialized. The key advantages of spin locks, namely that they have low overhead in terms of bus or network cycles and offer good performance when locks are reused by the same processor, are both lost in this example. We will consider alternative implementations in the next section, but before we do that, let's consider the use of spin locks to implement another common high level synchronization primitive.

One common synchronization operation in programs with parallel loops is a *barrier*. A barrier forces all processes to wait until all the processes reach the barrier and then releases all of the processes. A typical implementation of a barrier can be done with two spin locks: one used to protect a counter that tallies the processes arriving at the barrier and one used to hold the processes until the last process arrives at the barrier. To implement a barrier we usually use the ability to spin on a variable until it satisfies a test; we use the notation `spin(condition)` to indicate this. The following is a typical implementation, assuming that lock and unlock provide basic spin locks and the total is the number of processes that must reach the barrier:

```
lock (counterlock);
count++;
if (count==0) release=0;
if (count==total) {
        unlock (counterlock);
        count=0;
        release=1;
}
else {
        unlock(counterlock);
        spin (release=1);
}
```

The lock counterlock protects the counter so that it can be atomically incremented. The variable count keeps the tally of how many processes have reached the barrier. The variable release is used to hold the processes until the last one reaches the barrier.

In practice, another complication often makes the barrier implementation more complex. Frequently, a barrier is used within a loop, so that processes once released from the barrier would do some work and then reach the barrier again. Assume that one of the processes never actually leaves the barrier (it stays at the spin operation), which could happen if the OS scheduled another processes for example. Now it is possible that one process races ahead and gets to the barrier again before the last processes has left. The fast process traps that last slow processes in the barrier by resetting the flag release. Now all the processes will wait infinitely at the next instance of this barrier, since one processes is trapped at the last instance, and the number of processes can never reach the value of total. The important observation, is that the programmer did nothing wrong, the implementer of the barrier made some assumptions about forward progress that in practice cannot be assumed. The solution to this is to count the processes as they exit the barrier (just as we did on entry) and not to allow any process to reenter and reinitialize the barrier until all processes have left the prior instance of this barrier. This increases the latency of the barrier and the contention, which as we can see in the next example, are already large.

Example

Suppose there are 20 processors on a bus that each try to execute a barrier simultaneously. Assume that each bus cycle is 50 clocks. You can ignore the time of the actual read or write of a lock held in the cache as the time to execute other non synchronization operations in the barrier implementation (they won't matter much!). Determine the number of bus transactions required for all 20 processors to barrier and be released from the barrier, and about how long will it take for the 20 processors to get past the barrier. Assume the bus is totally fair so that every pending request is serviced before a new request and that the processors are equally fast. Don't worry about counting the processors out of the barrier.

Answer | The following table shows the sequence of events for one processor to traverse the barrier, assuming that the first process to grab the bus does not have the lock:

Event	Duration for one processor	Duration for 20 processors
Time for each processor to grab lock, increment, and release lock	1,525	30,500
Time to execute release	50	50
Time for each processor to get the release flag	50	1,000
Total		31,550

Our barrier operation takes a little longer than the 20 processor lock and unlock sequence. The number of bus transactions is about 440.

As we can see from these examples, synchronization performance can be much worse when there is contention among multiple processes. When there is no contention, we primarily are concerned about the latency of a synchronization primitive, that is, how long it takes an individual process to complete a synchronization operation. Our basic spin lock operation can do this in two bus cycles: one to initially read the lock and one to write it. We could improve this to a single bus cycle by a variety of methods: for example, we could simply spin on the swap operation. If the lock were almost always free, this could be better, but if the lock were not free, it would lead to lots of bus traffic, since each attempt to lock the variable would lead to a bus cycle. In practice, the latency of our spin lock is not quite as bad as we have seen in this example, since the write miss for a data item present in the cache is treated as an upgrade and will be much cheaper than a true read miss.

The more serious problem in these examples is the serialization of each process' attempt to complete the synchronization. This serialization is a problem when there is contention, since it greatly increases the time to complete the synchronization operation. For example, if the time to complete all 20 lock and unlock operations depended only on the latency in the uncontended case, then it would take 2,000 rather than 40,000 cycles to complete the synchronization operations. The use of a bus interconnect exacerbates this problem, but serialization could be just as serious in a directory based machine, where the latency would be larger, even if more overlap occurred.

Synchronization Mechanisms for Larger-Scale Machines

What we would like are synchronization primitives that have low latency in uncontended cases and minimize serialization in the case where contention is significant. We show two examples of hardware-supported primitives that can be used to accomplish these goals. Although these primitives may reduce latency, their goal is to minimize serialization, while preserving low latency. The first primitive deals with locks, while the second is useful for barriers and a number of other user-level operations that require counting or supplying distinct indices.

The major problem with our lock implementation it that it introduces a large amount of unneeded contention. For example, when the lock is released all processors generate both a read and a write miss, though at most one processor can successfully get the lock in the unlocked state. This happens on each of the 20 lock/unlock sequences. We can improve this situation by explicitly handing the lock from one waiting processor to the next. Rather than simply allowing a processor to compete every time the lock is released, we keep a list of the waiting processors and hand the lock to them explicitly, when their turn comes. This sort of mechanism has been called a *queueing lock* and is closely related to the QOLB primitive supported in the SCI bus protocol.

How does a queuing lock work? On the first miss to the lock variable, the miss is sent to a synchronization controller, which may be integrated with the memory controller (in a bus-based system) or the directory controller. If the lock is free, it is simply returned to the processor. If the lock is unavailable, the controller creates a record of the node's request (such as a bit in a vector) and sends the processor back a locked version of the lock variable. When the lock is freed, the controller selects a processor to go ahead from the list of waiting processors. It can then either update the lock variable in the selected processor's cache or invalidate the copy, causing the processor to miss and fetch an available copy of the lock.

Example

How many bus transaction and how long does it take to have 20 processors lock and unlock the variable using a queuing lock that updates the lock on a miss. Make the other assumptions about the system the same as before.

Answer

Each processor misses once on the lock initially and once to free the lock, so it takes only 40 bus cycles. The first 20 initial misses take 1,000 cycles, followed by a 50 cycle delay for each of the 20 releases. This is a total of 2,050 cycles–significantly better than the case with conventional coherency-based spin-locks.

There are a couple of key insights in implementing such a queuing lock capability. First, we need to be able to distinguish the initial access to the lock, so we can perform the queuing operation, and also the lock release, so we can provide the lock to another processor. The queue of waiting processes can be implemented by a variety of mechanisms. In a directory-based machine, this queue is akin to the sharing set and similar hardware can be used to implement the directory and queuing lock operations.

Queuing locks can be used to improve the performance of our barrier operation (see the exercises), but a larger improvement can be obtained by introducing a primitive that reduces the amount of time needed to increment the barrier count, thus reducing the serialization at this bottleneck. One primitive that has been introduced for this and other user-level operations is *fetch-and-increment*. Fetch-and-increment atomically fetches a variable and increments its value. The returned value can be either the incremented or fetched value. Using fetch-and-increment we can dramatically improve our barrier implementation.

Example

Write the code for a barrier using fetch-and-op. Making the same assumptions as our earlier example and also assuming that a fetch-and-op takes 50 clock cycles, determine the time for 20 processors to barrier. How many bus cycles are required?

Answer

Here's the code, we assume for simplicity that `release` and `counterlock` are both initialized to 0 and that the barrier is not reentered without reinitializing both variables.

```
fetch_and_increment (counterlock);
if (count==total) {
    release=1;
}
else {
    spin (release=1);
}
```

This implementation requires 20 fetch-and-increment operations and 20 caches misses for the release operation. This is a total time of 2,000 cycles and 40 bus/interconnect operations versus an earlier implementation that took over 15 times longer and 10 times more bus operations to complete the barrier. Even this implementation can be improved by reducing the serialization in releasing the processors once they have all reached the barrier. This can be done by broadcasting the release on a bus or by distributing the release in parallel on a larger machines using a generalized interconnect.

As we have seen, synchronization problems can become quite acute in larger-scale machines. When the challenges posed by synchronization are combined with the challenges posed by long memory latency and potential load imbalance in computations, we can see why getting efficient usage of large-scale parallel machines is very challenging. Later, in the Putting It All Together section we will examine the costs of synchronization on a existing bus-based multiprocessor for some real applications.

9.6 | Models of Memory Consistency

Cache coherency ensures that multiple processors see a consistent view of memory. It does not answer the question of *how* consistent the view of memory must be. By this we mean: when must a processor see a value that has been updated by another processor? Since processors communicate through shared variables (both those for data values and those used for synchronization), the question boils down to: in what order must a processor observe the data writes of another processor? Of course, as we discussed earlier, we also must ensure that reads and writes appear atomic.

Though the question of "how consistent?" seems like a simple question, it is remarkably complicated, as we can see with a simple example. Here are two code segments from processes P1 and P2 shown side by side:

```
P1:    A = 0;              P2:    B = 0;
       .....                      .....
       A = 1;                     B = 1;
L1:    if (B == 0) ...     L2:    if (A == 0) ...
```

Assume the processes are running on different processors, and that locations A and B are originally cached by both processors with the initial value of 0. If writes always take immediate effect and are immediately seen by other processors, it will be impossible for *both* if statements (labeled L1 and L2) to evaluate their conditions as true, since reaching the if statement means that either A or B must have been assigned the value 1. But suppose the write invalidate is delayed, and the processor is allowed to continue during this delay, then it is possible that both P1 and P2 have not seen the invalidations for B and A (respectively) *before* they attempt to read the values. The question is should this behavior be allowed, and, if so, under what conditions?

The most straightforward model for memory consistency is called *sequential consistency*. Sequential consistency requires that the result of any execution be the same as if the accesses of each processor were kept in order and the accesses among different processors were interleaved in some possible order. This eliminates the possibility of some nonobvious execution in the above example, since the assignments must be completed before the if-statements are initiated. The simplest way to implement sequential consistency is to require a processor to delay the completion of any memory access until all the invalidations caused by that access are completed; of course, it is equally simple to delay the next memory access, until the previous one is completed. Although this model presents a simple programming paradigm, it reduces potential performance, especially in a machine with a large number of processors, or long interconnect delays, as we can see in the next example.

Example

Suppose we have a processor where a remote request takes 10 cycles to issue and 50 cycles to complete. How long does a write miss stall the processor, if there are four sharing processors for the block being written on a sequentially consistent machine? Assume that the invalidates must be explicitly acknowledged before the directory controller knows they are completed. Suppose we could continue after handling the write miss without waiting for the invalidates, how long would the write take?

Answer

The case where we don't wait for the invalidates is easy: it simply requires a 50 cycle stall. The directory controller will be tied up longer, but not the processor. When we wait for invalidates, the following delays occur:

   50 cycles for the initial miss and reply

   10 cycles of serialization for the first three invalidates

   50 cycles of latency for the last invalidate and acknowledge

The total delay seen by the write is: 50+10+10+10+50=130 cycles or roughly 2.6 times more delay than when we do not have to wait for the invalidates.

To provide better performance, designers have developed less restrictive models that allow for faster hardware. Such models do affect how the programmer sees the machine, so before we discuss these less restrictive models, let's look at what the programmer expects.

The Programmer's View

While the sequential consistency model has a performance disadvantage, it has the advantage of simplicity from the viewpoint of the programmer. The challenge is to develop a programming model that is simple to explain and yet allows a high performance implementation. One such programming model that allows us to have a more efficient implementation is to assume that programs are *synchronized*. A program is synchronized if all access to shared data are ordered by synchronization operations. A data reference is ordered by a synchronization operation if: in every possible execution, a write of a variable by one processor and a read of that variable by another are separated by a pair of synchronization operations, one executed after the write by the writing processor and one executed before the read by the reading processor. As a simple example, consider a variable being read and updated by two different processors. Each processor will surround the read and update with a lock and an unlock to both ensure mutual exclusion for the update and to ensure that the read is consistent. Clearly, every write is now separated from a read by the other processor by a pair of synchronization operations: one unlock (after the write) and one lock (before the read).

We call the synchronization operation corresponding to the unlock a *release*, since it releases a potentially blocked processor, and the synchronization operation corresponding to a lock an *acquire*, since it acquires the right to read the variable. We will use the terminology acquire and release since it applies to a wide set of synchronization structures not just locks and unlocks.

Thus, a program is synchronized if in every execution sequence containing a write by a processor and a subsequent read by another processor of the same data has the following structure:

```
write (x)
...
release (s)
...
acquire (s)
...
read(x)
```

It is easy to see that if all such execution sequences look like this, the program is synchronized in the sense that accesses to shared data are always ordered by synchronization. Notice that if a program is synchronized it cannot have *data races:* that is it cannot have unordered reads and writes to the same data by different processors.

It is a broadly accepted observation that most programs are synchronized. This is true primarily because if the accesses were unsynchronized, the behavior of the program would be quite difficult to determine since the speed of execution would determine which processor won a data race and thus affect the results of the program. Programmers could attempt to guarantee ordering by constructing their own synchronization mechanisms, but such attempts can lead to buggy programs and may not be supported architecturally, meaning that they may not work in future generations of the machine. Thus, most programs will be synchronized using the standard synchronization operations that can be classified as releases or acquires, or sometimes as both, as, for example, in the case of a barrier.

The major use of unsynchronized accesses is in programs that want to avoid synchronization cost and are willing to accept an inconsistent view of memory. For example, in a stochastic program, we may be willing to have a read return an old value of a data item, since the program will still converge on the correct answer. In such cases, we do not care about having a consistent view of memory and we do not need to specify exactly what the architecture or implementation provides.

Relaxed Models for Memory Consistency

Since most programs are synchronized and since a sequential consistency model imposes major inefficiencies, we would like to define more relaxed model that allows higher performance implementations and still preserves a simple programming model for synchronized programs. In fact, there are a number of relaxed models that all maintain the property that the execution semantics of a synchronized program is the same under the model as it would be under a sequential consistency model. The relaxed models vary both in how tightly they constrain the set of possible execution sequences, and thus, how many constraints they impose on the implementation.

To understand the variations among the relaxed models and the possible implications for an implementation, it is simplest if we define the models in terms of what orderings among reads and writes performed by a single processor are preserved by each model. There are four such orderings (abbreviating a read as R and write as W):

1.   R → R: a read followed by a read.

2.   R → W: a read followed by a write, which is always preserved if the operations are to the same address, since this is an antidependence.

3.   W → R: a write followed by a read, which is always preserved i they are to the same address, since this is a true dependence.

4.   W → W: a write followed by a write, which is always preserved if they are to the same address, since this is an output dependence.

If there is a dependence among the read and write, then uniprocessor program semantics demands that the operations be ordered. When there is no dependence, the memory consistency model determines what orders must be preserved. A sequential consistency model requires that all four orderings be preserved and is thus equivalent to assuming a single centralized memory module that serializes all processor operations. When an order is relaxed, it simply means that we allow an operation executed later by the processor to complete first. For example, relaxing the ordering W → R means we allow a read that is later than a write to complete, before the write has completed. Remember that a write does not complete until all its invalidations complete, so letting the read occur after the writ miss has been handled but before the invalidations are done does not preserve the ordering.

The first model we examine relaxes the ordering between a write and a read (to a different address). Such models allow the buffering of writes with bypassing by reads, which occurs whenever the processor allows a read to proceed before it guarantees that an earlier write by that processor has been seen by all the other processors. This model allows a machine to hide some of the latency of a write operation. Furthermore, by relaxing only this one ordering, many applications, even those that are unsynchronized, operate correctly. Both the processor consistency and total store ordering (TSO) models match this model, and many machines have implicitly selected this model.

If we also allow nonconflicting writes to potentially complete out of order, by relaxing the W → W ordering, we arrive at a model that has been called partial store ordering (PSO). From an implementation viewpoint, it allows pipelining or overlapping of write operations, rather than forcing one operation to complete before another. This increases the amount of write latency that a machine can hide.

The third major class of relaxed models eliminates the $R \rightarrow R$ and $R \rightarrow W$ orderings, in addition to the other two orders. This model, which is called *weak ordering*, does not preserve ordering among references, except for:

- A read or write is completed before any synchronizaton operation that is executed by the processor after the read or write.

- A synchronization operation is always completed before any reads or writes that occur after the operation.

Thus, if S is a synchronization access, the orderings preserved are $S \rightarrow R$, $S \rightarrow W$, $R \rightarrow S$, and $W \rightarrow S$. This model allows us to reorder any memory references except that we may not move a reference across a synchronization operation.

From an implementation viewpoint, this has two important implication. First, the completion of a write operation, which entails the receipt of any required invalidations, only needs to delay the processor at a synchronization point. Under ideal circumstances this allows the latency of the write operation to be completely hidden. Second, if the processor provides nonblocking loads then the latency of a load miss can be hidden by allowing reads or writes that follow the load that misses to be executed.

The most relaxed model is an extension of weak ordering. The model, called *release consistency*, distinguishes between synchronization operations that are used to acquire access to a shared variable (denoted A) and those that release a object to allow another processor to acquire access (denoted Z). Release consistency is based on the observation that in synchronized programs, an acquire operation must proceed a use of shared data and a release operation must follow any updates to shared data and also proceed the time of the next acquire. This allows us to slightly relax the ordering by observing that a read or write that proceeds an acquire need not complete before the acquire and also that a read or write that follows a release need not wait for the release. Thus, the orderings that are preserved are: $A \rightarrow R$, $A \rightarrow W$, $R \rightarrow Z$, and $W \rightarrow Z$. Hence, there are four orderings required under weak ordering that are *not* imposed: $R \rightarrow A$, $W \rightarrow A$, $Z \rightarrow R$, and $Z \rightarrow W$. While most synchronization operations are either an acquire or a release (an acquire normally reads a synchronization variable and atomically updates it, while a release usually just write it), some operations, such as a barrier, act as both an acquire and a release and cause the ordering to be equivalent to weak ordering.

Implementation and Performance Potential of Relaxed Models

Relaxed models of consistency can usually be implemented with little or no additional hardware. Most of the complexity lies in implementing memory or interconnect systems that can take advantage of a relaxed model. For example, if the memory or interconnect does not allow multiple outstanding writes from a processor, then the benefits of the more ambitious relaxed models will be small. In this section, we describe a straightforward implementation of processor consistency, and release consistency. Our directory protocols already implement a version of version of sequential consistency, since the processor stalls until an operation is complete and the directory first invalidates all sharers before responding to a write miss.

Processor consistency (or TSO) is typically implemented by allowing read misses to bypass pending writes. A write buffer that can support a check to determine whether any pending write in the buffer is to the same address as a read miss, together with a memory and interconnection system that can support two outstanding references per node is sufficient to implement this scheme. Qualitatively, the advantage of processor consistency over sequential consistency is that it allows the latency of write misses to be hidden.

Release consistency allows additional write latency to be hidden, and if the processor supports nonblocking reads, allows the read latency to also be hidden. To allow write latency to be hidden as much as possible, the processor must allow multiple outstanding writes with read misses able to bypass writes. To maximize performance we need to allow writes to complete and clear the write buffer as early as possible; this also allows any dependent reads to go forward. This requires allowing a write to complete as soon as data is available and before all pending invalidations are completed (since our consistency model allows this). To implement this, either the directory or the original requester can keep track of the invalidation count. After each invalidation is acknowledged, the pending invalidation count is decreased. Since we must ensure that all pending invalidates complete before we allow a release to complete, we simply check the pending invalidation counts when a release is executed. The release is held up until all such invalidations complete.

To hide read latency we must have a machine that has nonblocking reads, otherwise, when the processor blocks, little progress will be made. If reads are nonblocking we can simply allow them to execute, knowing that the data dependences will preserve correct execution.

Note: The final edition will contain some measurements of the benefits of relaxed models for typical configurations.

At the present time, most machines being built support some sort of weak consistency model, varying from processor consistency to release consistency. Many of these machines will support sequential consistency as an option. Since synchronization is highly machine specific and error prone, the expectation is that most programmers will use standard synchronization libraries and will write synchronized programs, making the choice of a weak consistency model invisible to the programmer and yielding higher performance. Yet to be developed, are ideas of how to deal with nondeterministic programs that do not rely on getting the latest values. One possibility is that programmers will not need to rely on when variables are updated in such programs, the other possibility is that machine-specific models of update behavior will be needed and used. In any event, as latencies increase, the importance of choosing a consistency model that delivers both a convenient programming model and high performance is increasing.

9.7 | Cross Cutting Issues

Since multiprocessors redefine many system characteristics, they introduce interesting design problems across the spectrum. In this section, we give four examples: benchmarking and performance measurement, two examples involving memory systems, and an example of the interaction between compilers and the memory consistency model.

Performance Measurement of Parallel Machines

One of the most controversial issues has been how to measure the performance of parallel machines. Of course, the straightforward answer is to measure a benchmark as supplied and to examine wall-clock time. Measureing wall clock time obviously makes sense since in a parallel processor, measuring CPU time can be misleading because the processors may be idle but unavailable for other uses.

Users and designers are often interested in knowing not just how well a machine performs with a certain, fixed number of processors, but also how the performance scales as additional processors are added. In many cases, it makes sense to scale the application or benchmark, since if the benchmark is smaller, effects arising from limited parallelism and increases in communication can lead to results that are pessimistic when the expectation is that more processors will be used to solve larger problems. Thus, it is often useful to measure the speed-up as processors are added both for a fixed-size problem and for a scaled version of the problem, providing an unscaled and scaled version of the speed-up curves. The choice of how to measure the uniprocessor algorithm is also important to avoid anomalous results, since using the parallel version of the benchmark may understate the uniprocessor performance, and thus overstate the speed-up. This is discussed with an example in the Fallacies and Pitfalls.

Once we have decided to measure scaled speed-up, the question is *how* to scale the application. Let's assume we have determined that running a benchmark of size n on p processors makes sense. The question is how to scale the benchmark to run on $m \times p$ processors. There are two obvious ways to scale the problem: by keeping the amount of memory used per processor constant, which is scaled *memory-constrained scaling*, and keeping the total execution time in the ideal case constant, which is called *time-constrained* scaling. Memory-constrained scaling means that the problem is scaled so that the amount of memory required per processor is constant. Thus, with $m \times p$ processors, we would run a problem of size $m \times n$. With time-constrained scaling, we scale the problem so that the execution time is the same. For example, suppose the running time of the application with data size n is proportional to n^2, then with time-constrained scaling, the problem to run is the problem whose ideal running time on $m \times p$ processors is $n^2 \times m$. The problem with this ideal running time has size $\sqrt{m} \times n$.

Example

Suppose we have a problem whose execution time for a problem of size n *is* n^3. Suppose the actual running time on a 10 processor machine were 1 hour. Under the time constrained and memory constrained scaling models, find the size of the problem to run and the effective running time for a 100 processor machine

Answer

For the time constrained problem, the running time is the ideal running time is the same: 1 hour. The problem size is $\sqrt[3]{10} \times n$. For memory constrained scaling the size of the problem is $10n$ and the ideal execution time is $\dfrac{10^3}{10}$ or 100 hours!

Since most users will be reluctant to run a problem on an order of magnitude more processors for 100 times longer, this size problem is probably not too interesting for comparison.

In addition to the scaling methodology, there are question as to how the program should be scaled when increasing the problem size affects the quality of the result. Since many parallel programs are simulations of physical phenomena, changing the problem size changes the quality of the result, and we must change the application to deal with this effect. As a simple example consider the effect of time to convergence for solving differential equation. This time typically increases as the problem size increases. This means that a smaller problem will take the same execution time. For example suppose the number of iterations grows as the log of the problem size, then for a problem whose ideal running time is linear, execution time scaling for a problem of size n running on 10 processors would allow us to run a problem of size $\log 10 \times n$ or about $2.3n$, rather than $10n$. In practice, scaling to deal with error requires a good understanding of the application and may involve other factors, such as error tolerances (e.g., it affects the cell-opening criteria in Barnes-Hut). In turn, such effects often significantly affect the communication or parallelism properties of the application as well as the choice of problem size.

Scaled speed-up is not the same as unscaled (or true) speed-up. The danger of confusing the two has led to erroneous claims, an example of which is discussed in the Fallacies and Pitfalls. Certainly, scaled speed-up has a role, but only when the scaling methodology is sound and the results are clearly reported as using a scaled version of the application.

Inclusion and its implementation

Many multiprocessors will want to use multilevel cache hierarchies to reduce both the demand on the global interconnect and the latency of cache misses. If the cache also provide multilevel inclusion, i.e. every level of cache hierarchy is a subset of the level further away, then we can use the multilevel structure to reduce the contention between coherency traffic and processor traffic as we explained earlier. Thus, most multiprocessors with multilevel caches enforce the inclusion property. This restriction is also called the subset property, since each cache is a subset of the cache below it in the hierarchy.

At first glance, preserving the multilevel inclusion property seems trivial. Consider a two-level example: any miss in L1 either hits in L2 or generates a miss in L2 causing it to be brought into both L1 and L2. Likewise, any invalidate the hits in L2 must be sent to L1, where it will cause the block to be invalidated, if it exists.

The catch is what happens when the block size of L1 and L2 are different. Choosing different block sizes is quite reasonable, since L2 will be much larger and have a much longer latency component in its miss penalty. What happens to our "automatic" enforcement of inclusion, when the block sizes differ? A block in L2 represents multiple blocks in L1, and a miss in L2 causes words to be replaced that may exist in L1 breaking the inclusion property. For example, if the block size of L2 is four times that of L1, then a miss in L2 will replace the equivalent of four L1 blocks. Let's consider a detailed example.

Example

Assume that L2 has a block size four times that of L1. Show how a miss for an address that causes a replacement in L1 and L2, can lead to violation of the inclusion property.

Answer

Assume L1 and L2 are direct mapped and that the block size of L2 is b. Assume L1 contains blocks with starting addresses x and $x+b$. Since L2 is larger and has a block size of $4b$, it contains the L1 blocks x, $x+b$, $x+2b$, and $x+3b$ in a single L2 cache block. Suppose the processor, generates a reference to block y that maps to the block containing x in both caches and hence misses. Since L2 missed, it fetches $4b$ words and replaces the block containing x, $x+b$, $x+2b$, and $x+3b$, while L1 takes b words and replaces the block containing x. Since L1 still contains $x+b$, but L2 does not, the inclusion property no longer holds.

To maintain inclusion with multiple block sizes, we must probe the higher levels of the hierarchy when a replacement is done at the lower level to ensure that any words replaced in the lower level are invalidated in the high-level caches. Most systems chose this solution rather than the alternative of not relying on inclusion and snooping high level caches. In the Exercises we explore inclusion further and show that similar problems exist if the associativity of the levels is different.

Nonblocking Caches and Prefetching

We saw the idea of nonblocking or lockup-free caches in Chapter 6 where the concept was used to reduce cache misses by overlapping them with execution and by pipelining misses. There are additional benefits in the multiprocessor case. The first is that the miss penalties are likely to be larger, meaning there is more to latency to hide, and the opportunity for pipelining misses is also probably larger, since the memory and interconnect system can often handle multiple outstanding memory references. Thus, nonblocking caches can reduce the stall time for misses.

Nonblocking caches are required to take advantage of weak consistency models. For example, to implement a model like processor consistency requires that writes be nonblocking for reads so that a processor can continue as soon as it establishes ownership of a block. Relaxed consistency models allow further reordering of misses, but nonblocking caches are required to take full advantage of this flexibility.

Lastly, nonblocking support is critical to implementing prefetching. Prefetching, which we also discussed in Chapter 6, is even more important in multiprocessors than in uniprocessors, for these reasons: more bandwidth is available to support prefetching and memory latencies are larger. In Chapter 6, we described why it was important that prefetches not affect the semantics of the program that way they could be inserted anywhere without causing problems. In a multiprocessor, another property becomes very important: we would like that prefetches are kept coherent. By this we mean, that when a value is prefetched, it is kept coherent as long as it remains in memory. This is exactly the property that cache coherency gives us for other variables. A prefetch that brings a data value closer and guarantees that on the actual use the most recent value of the data item is obtained is called *nonbinding*, since the data value is not bound to a local copy, which would be incoherent. By contrast, a prefetch that moves a data value into a general-purpose register is binding, since the register value is a new variable, as opposed to a cache block, which is a coherent copy of a variable.

Why is nonbinding prefetch critical? Consider, a simple, but typical, example: a data value written by one processor and used by another. In this case, the consumer would like to prefetch the value as early as possible, but suppose the producing process is delayed for some reason, then the prefetch may fetch the old value of the data item. A binding prefetch would deliver that data item to the processor, as if it were the new value. A nonbinding prefetch would maintain the coherency. If the value of that location were written after the prefetch, the prefetched copy would be invalidated (or updated in a broadcast protocol). Because of the long memory latencies, a prefetch may need to be placed a hundred or more instructions earlier than the data use, if we aim to hide the entire latency. This makes the nonbinding property vital to ensure correct usage of the prefetch.

Implementing prefetch requires the same sort of support that a lock-up free cache needs, since there are multiple outstanding memory accesses. This causes several complications:

1. A local node will need to keep track of the multiple outstanding accesses, since the replies may return in a different order than they were sent in. This can be handled by adding tags to the requests, or by incorporating the address of the memory block in the reply.

2. Before issuing a request, the node must ensure that it has not already issued a request for the same block, since two requests for the same block could lead to incorrect operation of the protocol. In particular, if the node issues a write miss to a block, while it has such a write miss outstanding both our snoopy protocol and directory protocol fail to operate properly, as you can show in the exercises.

3. Our implementation of the directory and snoopy controllers assumes that the processor stalls on a miss. This allows the engine to simply wait for a reply when it has generated a request. With a nonblocking cache, this is not possible and the actual implementation must deal with additional processor requests. We discuss this complication in more detail in the exercises.

Compiler Optimization and Consistency Model

Another reason for defining a model for memory consistency is to specify the range of legal compiler optimizations that can be performed on shared data. In explicitly parallel programs, unless the synchronization points are clearly defined and the programs are synchronized, the compiler could not interchange a read and a write of two different shared data items, since such transformations might affect the semantics of the program. This prevents even relatively simple optimizations, such as register allocation of shared data, since such a process will usually interchange reads and writes. In implicitly parallelized programs, e.g. those written in HPF, programs must be synchronized and the synchronization points are known, so this issue does not arise.

Using Virtual Memory Support to Build Shared Memory

Suppose we wanted to support a shared address space among a group of workstations connected to a network. One approach is to use the virtual memory mechanism and OS support to provide shared memory. This approach was first explored more than 10 years ago and has been called Distributed Virtual Memory (DVM) or Virtual Shared Memory (VSM). The key observation that this idea builds on is that the virtual memory hardware has the ability to control access to portions of the address space both for reading and writing. By using the hardware to check and intercept accesses and the operating system to ensure coherency, we can create a coherent, shared address space across the distributed memory of multiple processors.

In DVM, pages become the units of coherency, rather than cache blocks. The OS can allow pages to be replicated in read-only fashion using the virtual memory support to protect the pages from writing. When a processor attempts to write such a page, it will be trapped. The operating system on that processor can then send messages to the OS on each node that shares the page requesting that the page be invalidated. Just as in a directory system, each page has a home node and the operating system running in that node is responsible for tracking who has copies of the page.

The mechanisms are quite similar to those at work in coherent distributed shared memory. The key differences are that the unit of coherency is a page and that software is used to implement the coherency algorithms. It is exactly these two differences that lead to the major performance differences. A page is considerably bigger than a cache line and the possibilities for poor usage of a page and for false sharing are very high. This leads to much less stable performance and sometimes even lower performance than a uniprocessor. Because the coherency algorithms are implemented in software, they have much higher overhead.

The result of this combination is that distributed virtual memory has become an acceptable substitute for loosely-coupled message passing, but it is not competitive with schemes that have hardware supported, coherent memory. Thus, most programs written for coherent shared memory, cannot be run efficiently on virtual shared memory. Several factors could change this. Better implementations and small amounts of hardware support could reduce the overhead in the operating system. The disadvantages of using a page as the unit of coherency may be more difficult to overcome. One possibility is the use of smaller or multiple page sizes, so that the system could control coherency at a smaller granularity. The concept of software supported shared memory remains at important and active area of research and the technology may play an important role either in improving the hardware mechanisms or in extending them to larger or more distributed machines.

9.8 | Putting It All Together

In this section we examine the design and performance of the Silicon Graphics Challenge multiprocessor. The Challenge is a bus-based design with a wide, high speed bus, capable of holding up to 36 MIPS R4400 processors with 4 processors on a board and up to 16 GB of 8-way interleaved memory. The Power Challenge design uses the much higher performance TFP processors but with the same bus, memory, and I/O system; with 2 processors per board, a Power Challenge can hold up to 18 processors. Our discussion will focus on the bus, coherency hardware, and synchronization support, and our measurements use a 150 MHz R4400-based Challenge system.

The Challenge System Bus (POWERpath-2)

The core of the Challenge design is a wide (256 data bits; 40 address bits), 50 MHz bus (using reduced voltage swing) called POWERpath-2. This bus interconnects all the major system components and provides support for coherency. Figure 9.28 shows a diagram of the system configuration.

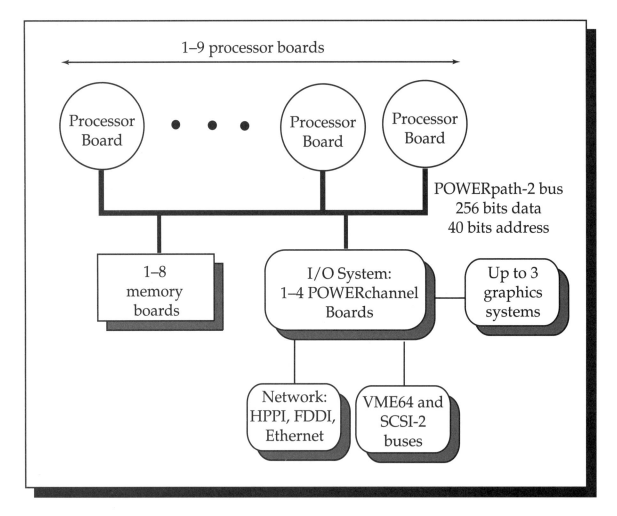

1–9 processor boards

Processor Board

• • •

Processor Board

Processor Board

POWERpath-2 bus
256 bits data
40 bits address

1–8 memory boards

I/O System:
1–4 POWERchannel Boards

Up to 3 graphics systems

Network:
HPPI, FDDI, Ethernet

VME64 and SCSI-2 buses

FIGURE 9.28   The Challenge system structure relies on a fast wide bus to interconnect the system and to allow expansion. Each processor board holds 4 R4400 processor or 2 TFP processors. Each memory board holds up to 2GB. In the largest configuration (48 bus slots), the maximum system has 9 CPU boards (26 R4400s or 18 TFPs), 8 memory boards (16 GB), 5 VME64 buses (with up to 20 more in an extension box), 32 SCSI-2 channels, 8 Ethernets, 4 HPPI channels, 4 FDDI connections, and up to 3 graphics subsystems. This configuration allows 32GB of disk in the main cabinet and up to 3 Terabytes with expansion cabinets.

The POWERpath-2 implements a write invalidate coherency scheme using four states: the three states we saw in Section 9. 3 and an additional state representing a block that is clean but exclusive in one cache. The basic coherency protocol is a slight extension over the three state protocol we examined in detail.

When a block is read that is not shared by any cache, it is placed in the Clean Exclusive state. Additional reads misses of the same block transfer the block to the shared state. A write miss causes the block to be transferred to the Exclusive (Dirty Exclusive) state. The major advantage of this protocol is that there is no need to generate a write miss when a block is upgraded from Clean Exclusive to Dirty Exclusive. Although this is unlikely to be a large effect for accesses to shared data (since such data will often be in some processor's cache), it does improve the performance of accesses to private data that are not shared. In particular, such data behaves as if the machine were a uniprocessor, where a cache miss would not be needed to write a block already resident in the cache. Implementing the Clean Exclusive state is straightforward, since the processor sees any attempt to read or write the block and can change the state accordingly.

The POWERpath-2 bus supports split transactions and can have up to eight pending reads outstanding. All pending reads are tracked at each processor board, and resource identifiers are assigned to reads as they arrive. The resource identifiers are than used to tag results, so that processors know when a response to their request is on the bus. If all eight resources are occupied a read must wait for one to become free. To prevent the problem we discussed earlier concerning coherency on a split transaction bus, a processor board will not issue an invalidate (or write miss) for the same address as any pending read. If a processor board receives a read miss for an address on which there is an outstanding read, it can "piggyback" on the earlier read: it need not generate a new request, but simply uses the data when the response to the first request occurs.

Each read request has an inhibit line used to indicate that a read request should not be responded to my memory. Since snoops can take variable amounts of time, depending on the state of the processor and the block, this signal is critical to implementing coherency. When a processor receives a snoop request, it asserts the inhibit line until it completes its snoop. If the snoop finds a clean block, the processor drops the inhibit line. If all the processors drop the inhibit line, the memory will respond, since it knows that all the processor copies are clean. If a processor finds a dirty copy of the block, it requests the bus and places the data on the bus, after which is drops the inhibit line. Both the requesting processor and the memory receive the data and write it. In this latter case, since there are separate tags for snoooping and retrieving a value from the first or second level cache takes much longer than detecting the presence of the data, this solution of letting memory respond when its copy is valid is considerably faster than always intervening.

A bus transaction consists of five cycles that are executed simultaneously by the bus controllers on each board. These five cycles are arbitration, resolution, address, decode, and acknowledge. To reduce the latency when the bus is idle, the bus controllers use a two cycle idle loop that can respond to a request for arbitration immediately. The data and address buses are separately arbitrated. Write requests use both buses, while invalidate and read requests need only the address bus. Since the buses are separately arbitrated and assigned, the bus can simultaneously carry a new read request and a response to an earlier request. Under normal situations, the memory system responds to a read request, two bus cycles after it is generated, and reads are granted higher priority than writes.

To obtain high bandwidth from memory, each memory board provides a 576-bit path to the DRAMs (512 bits of data and 64 bits of ECC) allowing a single memory cycle to provide the data for 2 bus transfers. With two-way interleaving a single memory board can support the full bandwidth of 1.2 GB/second. To respond to a request for a 128 byte cache block, requires four bus transfers and one access to each half of the interleaved memory bank. The total time to satisfy a read miss with no contention is 22 bus cycles:

1. The initial read request is one bus transaction or 5 bus clock cycles.

2. The latency till memory is ready to transfer is 12 bus clock cycles.

3. The reply transfers four 512-bit words in one reply transaction, taking 5 bus clock cycles.

The latency of the access from the processor viewpoint is 20 bus clock cycles (which is 40 processor clock cycles), since the memory access can start when the address is received. The ability to start a bus transaction on any clock is needed to allow the reply transaction to start immediately after the data is available. Since the bus is split transaction, other requests and replies can occur during the memory access time.

The 20 cycle latency, which is the bus and memory system component of a cache miss, translates to 400 nS. The total latency of a miss is close to 1 μS, with the additional time coming from the initial miss detection and handling and the cache reload and restart. The initial miss detection consists of three steps: detecting a miss in the primary on-chip cache, initiating a secondary (off-chip) cache access and detecting a miss in the secondary cache, driving the complete address off-chip through the system bus (which differs from the secondary cache bus). This process takes about 30 100 MHz processor clocks, or about 300 nS. The R4000 is stalled until the entire cache line is reloaded. The memory interface is 64-bits and operates at the external bus timing of 50MHz. Reloading the 128-byte cache line takes 16 clock cycles. Additional clock cycles are used to reload the primary cache and to restart the pipeline bringing the total for the reload and restart to about 30 cycles or 300 ns. Thus, the total miss penalty for a secondary cache miss is 300+400+300 ns = 1 μS or 100 processor clocks for a 100MHz R4000. This number is considerably larger a uniprocessor memory access, as we discuss in the Fallacies and Pitfalls section. The next section discusses performance.

Performance of a Challenge System

The five parallel benchmarks were run on a 16-processor Challenge system using 150 MHz R4400, which have a miss penalty of approximately 125 processor clocks, due to relative growth is the memory access component of the miss rate.

The following section contains results for some of our benchmarks, but not all. The Beta version will contain full data sets and additional discussion. These numbers are also relative speed-up; true speed-up will be included.

Figure 9.9.2 shows the speed-up for our applications running on up to 16 processors. The speed-ups for 16 processors vary from 10.5 to 15. To understand what's behind the speed-ups we can break up the execution time.

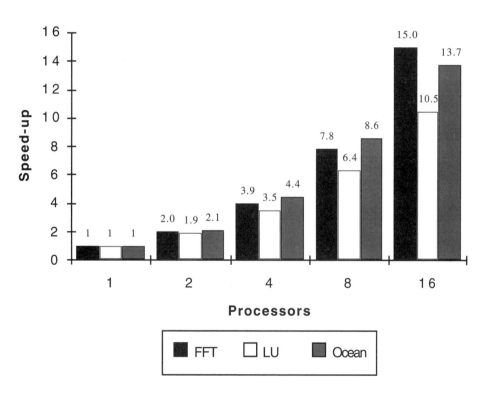

FIGURE 9.29 **The speed-ups for the parallel benchmarks are shown versus processor count for a 150MHz R4400 Challenge system.**

We plan to analyze the performance of each benchmark breaking the execution time into: the ideal execution time, the memory overhead, the synchronization time, and the parallel overhead (imperfect parallelization).

An interesting question is whether we should examine the benchmarks individually or whether the right model is to examine the three components. Organizing the graphs by benchmark is probably more informative, but we are seeking input.

9.9 | Fallacies and Pitfalls

Given the lack of maturity in our understanding of parallel computing, there are many hidden pitfalls that will be uncovered either by careful designers or by unfortunate ones. Given the large amount of "hype" often surrounding multiprocessors, especially at the high-end, common fallacies abound. We have included a selection of these. In choosing the Pitfalls, we were restrained by the fact that there are many opportunities in this part of computer design, since our understanding is still quite limited.

Pitfall: Measuring performance of multiprocessors by linear speedup versus execution time.

"Mortar shot" graphs—plotting performance versus number of processors showing linear speedup, a plateau, and then a falling off—have long been used to judge the success of parallel processors. While scalability is one facet of a parallel program, it is not a direct measure of performance. The first question is the power of the processors being scaled: A program that linearly improves performance to equal 100 Intel 8080s may be slower than the sequential version on a workstation. Be especially careful of floating-point–intensive programs, as processing elements without hardware assist may scale wonderfully but have poor collective performance.

Comparing execution times is only fair if you are comparing the best algorithms on each machine. (Of course, you can't subtract time for idle processors when evaluating a multiprocessor, so CPU time is inappropriate for multiprocessors.) Comparing the identical code on two machines may seem fair, but it is not; the parallel program may be slower on a uniprocessor than a sequential version. Sometimes, developing a parallel program will lead to algorithmic improvements, so that comparing the previously best-known sequential program with the parallel code—which seems fair—will not compare equivalent algorithms. To reflect this issue, sometimes the terms *relative speedup* (same program) and *true speedup* (best programs) are used. Results that suggest *super-linear* performance, when a program on n processors is more than n times faster than the equivalent uniprocessor, may indicate that the comparison is unfair, although there are rare instances where "real" superlinear speedups have been encountered.

Fallacy: Amdahl's Law doesn't apply to parallel computers.

In 1987, the head of a research organization claimed that Amdahl's Law (see Section 1.3) had been broken by a MIMD machine. This hardly meant, however, that the law has been overturned for parallel computers; the neglected portion of the program will still limit performance. To try to understand the basis of the media reports, let's see what Amdahl [1967] originally said:

A fairly obvious conclusion which can be drawn at this point is that the effort expended on achieving high parallel processing rates is wasted unless it is accompanied by achievements in sequential processing rates of very nearly the same magnitude. [page 483]

One interpretation of the law was that since portions of every program must be sequential, there is a limit to the useful economic number of processors—say 100. By showing linear speedup with 1000 processors, this interpretation of Amdahl's Law was disproved.

The basis for the statement that Amdahl's Law had been "overcome" was the use of scaled speed-up. The approach of the researchers was to change the input to the benchmark, so that rather than going 1000 times faster, they essentially computed 1000 times more work in comparable time. For their algorithm the sequential portion of the program was constant independent of the size of the input, and the rest was fully parallel—hence, linear speedup with 1000 processors.

We have already described the dangers of relating scaled speed-up as true speed-up, as well as the care that must be taken when scaling benchmarks.

Fallacy: Multiprocessors are "free."

This fallacy has two different interpretations, both of which are erroneous. The first is: given that modern microprocessor contain support for snoopy caches, we can build small scale, bus-based multiprocessors for no additional cost in dollars (other than the microprocessor cost) or performance. Many designers believed this to be true and even tried to build machines to prove it. To understand why this doesn't work, you need to compare a design with no multiprocessing extensability against a design that allows for a moderate level of multiprocessing (say 2-4 processors). The 2-4 processor design requires some sort of bus and a coherency controller that is more complicated than the simple memory controller required for the uniprocessor design. Furthermore, the memory access time is always faster in the uniprocessor case, since the processor can be directly connected to memory with no intervening bus. Thus, the strictly uniprocessor solution will typically have better performance and lower cost than the one-processor configuration of even a very small multiprocessor.

Note to reviewers: should we make the se two points stronger. The above one by comparing two machines (uni and MP), or is it obvious. The point below is diffi-

cult to "prove" but a quote could show that designers really believed this would be possible. Comments?

It also became popular in the 1980s to believe that the multiprocessor design was free in the sense that an MP could be quickly constructed from state-of-the-art microprocessors and then quickly updated using newer processors as they became available. This viewpoint ignores the complexity of cache coherency and the challenge of designing high bandwidth, low latency memory systems, which for modern processors is extremely difficult. The next two fallacies are closely related to this one.

Fallacy: Scalability is free.

The goal of scalable parallel computing has been a focus of much of the research and a significant segment of the high-end machine development since the mid-1980s. Until recently, it was widely held that one could build for scalability and then simply offer the machine at any point on the scale from a small number of processors to a large number. The difficulty with this view is that machines that scale to larger processor counts require substantially more investment (both dollars and design time) in the interprocessor communication network, as well as in aspects such as reliability and reconfigurability.

As an example, consider the CM-5, it provides an interconnection network capable of scaling to thousands of processors, where it can deliver a bisection bandwidth of XXX GB/sec. At a more typical 32 to 64 processor configuration, however, the bisection bandwidth is only 160–320 MB/sec, which is less than what most bus-based systems provide. Furthermore, the cost per CPU is higher than in a bus-based system in this range.

The cost of scalability can be seen even in more limited design ranges: such as very small MP systems (2-8 processors) versus bus-based systems that scale to 16-32 processors. While a fast 64-bit bus, might be adequate for a small machine with less than 4 processors, a larger number of processors requires a wider, higher bandwidth bus (e.g., the 256-bit Challenge bus). The user who buys the large system pays for the cost of this high performance bus. The SPARCCenter 20 design addresses this by using a two bus design (with narrower buses). In a small system, only one bus is needed, while a larger system can include two buses. The interleaved to allow transfer to be done simultaneously on both buses.

Fallacy: Using a bus is the best way to build a small scale multiprocessor.

This fallacy points out how things are changing and how buses may have a reduced role due to local memory overhead. Will be quantitative using realistic numbers.

Pitfall: Not developing the software to take advantage of, or optimize, for a multiprocessor architecture.

There is a long history of software lagging behind on massively parallel machines, possibly because the software problems are much harder. Rather than discuss these problems, we choose to examples from mainstream, bus-based multiprocessors. The first having to do with not being able to take advantage of architectural capability, and the second arising from the need to optimize the software for a multiprocessor.

The SUN SPARCCenter is a bus-based machine with one or two buses. Memory is distributed on the boards with the processors, so that the architecture has the ability to have fast local access and use the bus to access remote memory, as for coherency operations. The SUN operating system, however, was not able to deal with the NUMA aspect of memory, including such issues as controlling where memory was allocated (local versus global). If memory pages were allocated randomly, then successive runs of the same application could have substantially different performance. To avoid this problem, the SPARCCenter design was changed so that all memory accesses go over the bus, even those destined for the local memory on the same board as the processor. This results in a uniform memory access time, but eliminates the possibility of taking advantage of the lower access time for local memory.

Our second example shows the subtle kinds of problems that can arise when software designed for a uniprocessor is adapted to a multiprocessor environment. The SGI operating system protects the page table data structure with a lock on the page table entry. In a uniprocessor this does not represent a performance problem. In a multiprocessor situation, it can become a major performance bottleneck for some programs. Consider a program that uses a large number of pages that are initialized at start-up (which UNIX does for statically allocated pages). Suppose the program is parallelized so that multiple processes allocate the pages. Since page allocation requires the use of the page table data structure, which is locked whenever in use, even a multithreaded kernel will be serialized if the processes all try to allocate their pages at once (which is exactly what we might expect at initialization time!). This serialization eliminates parallelism in initialization and significantly impacts overall parallel performance. This performance bottleneck is even more intrusive: suppose we split the program apart into separate processes and run them, one per process, trying to use ,multiprogramming to overcome the problem. (This is exactly what the user did, since he reasonably believed that the performance problem was in his application.) Unfortunately, the lock still serializes all the processes–so even the multiprogramming performance is poor. Although the solution to this problem is relatively straightforward, this pitfall indicates the kind of subtle, but significant, performance bugs that can arise when software runs on multiprocessors.

Fallacy: Data distribution plays no role in a shared memory machine.

Use quantitative data to show how distribution for FFT or Ocean makes a significant difference for large problems.

9.10 | Concluding Remarks—Evolution Versus Revolution in Computer Architecture

This will be extensively rewritten; we will include the evolution/revolution point and show how that has supported the move to DSM. We'll end by discussion future directions and conclude by describing the current directions in MPPs and networks of workstations.

Practically since the first working computer, architects have been striving for the El Dorado of computer design: To compose a powerful computer by simply connecting many existing smaller ones. The user orders as many CPUs as he can afford and gets a commensurate amount of performance. Other advantages of MIMD may be highest absolute performance, faster than the largest uniprocessor, and highest reliability/availability (page 520) via redundancy.

For decades, computer designers have been looking for the missing piece of the puzzle that allows this speedup to happen, as if by magic. People are heard making statements that begin "Now that computers have dropped to such a low price..." or "This new interconnection scheme will overcome the scaling problem, so..." or "As this new programming language becomes widespread...," and end with "MIMDs will (finally) dominate computing."

With so many attempts to use parallelism, there are a few terms that are useful to know when discussing MIMDs. The principal division is that which delineates how information is shared. *Shared-memory* processors offer the programmer a single memory address that all processors can access; cache-coherent multiprocessors are shared-memory machines (see Sections 8.8 and 9.8). Processes communicate through shared variables in memory, with loads and stores capable of accessing any memory location. Synchronization must be available to coordinate processes. An alternative model to sharing data is where processes communicate by sending messages. As an extreme example, processes on different workstations communicate by sending messages over a local area network. This communication distinction is so fundamental that Bell suggests the term *multiprocessor* be limited to MIMDs that can communicate via shared memory, while MIMDs that can only communicate via explicit message passing should be called *multicomputers*. Since a portion of a shared memory could be used for messages, most multiprocessors can efficiently execute message-passing software. A multicomputer might be able to simulate shared memory by sending a message for every load or store, but presumably this would run excruciatingly slowly. Thus, Bell's distinction is based on the underlying hardware and program execution model, reflected in the performance of shared-memory communication, as opposed to the software that might run on a machine. Message-passing docents question the *scalability* of multiprocessors, while shared-memory advocates question the programmability of multicomputers. The next section examines this debate further.

The good news is that after many assaults, MIMD has established a beach-head. Today it is generally agreed that a multiprocessor may be more effective for a timesharing workload than a SISD. No single program takes less CPU time, but more independent tasks can be completed per hour—a throughput versus latency argument. Not only are start-up companies like Encore and Sequent selling small-scale multiprocessors, but the high-end machines from IBM, DEC, and Cray Research are multiprocessors. This means multiprocessors now embody a significant market, responsible for a majority of the mainframes and virtually all supercomputers. The only disappointment to computer architects is that shared memory is practically irrelevant for user programs run on the machine, with the operating system being the only benefactor. The development of a multiprocessor's operating system, particularly its resource manager, is simplified by shared memory.

The bad news is that it remains to be seen how many important applications run faster on MIMDs. The difficulty has not lain in the prices of SISDs, in flaws in topologies of interconnection networks, or in programming languages; but in the lack of applications software that have been reprogrammed to take advantage of many processors to complete important tasks sooner. Since it has been even harder to find applications that can take advantage of many processors, the challenge is greater for large scale MIMDs. When the positive gains from timesharing are combined with the scarcity of highly parallel applications, we can appreciate the predicament facing computer architects designing large-scale MIMDs that do not support timesharing.

But why is this so? Why should it be so much harder to develop MIMD programs than sequential programs? One reason is that it is hard to write MIMD programs that achieve close to linear speedup as the number of processors dedicated to the task increases. As an analogy, think of the communication overhead for a task done by one person versus the overhead for a task done by a committee, especially as the size of the group increases. While n people may have the potential to finish any task n times faster, the communication overhead for the group can prevent it from achieving this; this becomes especially hard as n increases. (Imagine the change in communication overhead going from 10 people to 1,000 people to 1,000,000.) Another reason for the difficulty in writing parallel programs is how much the programmer must know about the hardware. On a uniprocessor, the high-level language programmer writes his program ignoring the underlying machine organization—that's the job of the compiler. For a multiprocessor today, the programmer had better know the underlying hardware and organization if he is to write fast and scalable programs. This intimacy also makes portable parallel programs rare. Though this second obstacle may lessen over time, it is now the biggest challenge facing computer science. Finally, from Chapter 1 comes Amdahl's Law (page 8) to remind us that even small parts of a program must be parallelized to reach the full potential. Thus, coming close to linear speedup involves inventing new algorithms that are inherently parallel.

The Roads to El Dorado

Figure 9.30 shows the state of the industry, plotting number of processors versus performance of an individual processor. The massive parallelism question is whether taking the high road or the low road in Figure 9.30 will get us to El Dorado. Currently we don't know enough about parallel programming and applications to be able to quantitatively trade-off number of processors versus performance per processor to achieve the best cost/performance.

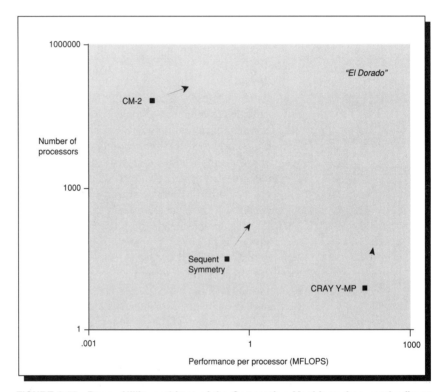

FIGURE 9.30   Danny Hillis, architect of the Connection Machines, has used a figure similar to this to illustrate the multiprocessor industry. (Hillis's x axis was processor width rather than processor performance.) Processor performance on this graph is approximated by the MFLOPS rating of a single processor for the DAXPY procedure of the Linpack benchmark for a 1000 x 1000 matrix. Generally, it is easier for programmers when moving to the right , while moving up is easier for the hardware designer because there is more hardware replication. The massive parallelism question is, "Which is the quickest path to the upper right corner?" The computer design question is, "Which has the best cost/performance or is more scalable for equivalent cost/performance?"

It is interesting to note that very different changes are required to improve performance depending on whether you take the low road or the high road in this figure. Since most programs are written in high-level languages, moving along the horizontal direction (increasing performance per processor) is almost entirely a matter of improving the hardware. The applications are unchanged, with compilers adapting them to the more powerful processor. Hence, increasing processor performance versus number of processors is easier for the applications software. Improving performance by moving in the vertical direction (increasing parallelism), on the other hand, may involve significant changes to applications, since programming ten processors may be very different from programming a thousand, and different yet again from programming a million. (But going from 100 to 101 is probably not different.) An advantage of the vertical path to performance is that the hardware may be simply replicated—the processors in particular, but also the hardware of the interconnection switch. Hence, increasing number of processors versus processor performance results in more hardware replication. An advantage of the low road is that it is much more likely that there will be a market at the various points along the way to El Dorado. In addition, those who take the high road must grapple with Amdahl's Law. Reading conference and journal articles from the last 20 years can leave one discouraged; so much effort has been expended with so little impact. Optimistically speaking, these papers act as gravel and, when placed logically together, form the foundation for the next generation of computers. From a more pessimistic point of view, if 90% of the ideas disappeared no one would notice.

One reason for this could be called the "von Neumann syndrome." By hoping to invent a new model of computation that will revolutionize computing, researchers are striving to become known as the von Neumann of the 21st century. Another reason is taste: researchers often select problems that no one else cares about. Even if important problems are selected, there is frequently a lack of experimental evidence to convincingly demonstrate the value of the solution. Moreover, when important problems are selected and the solutions are demonstrated, the proposed solutions may be too expensive relative to their benefit. Sometimes this expense is measured as straightforward cost/performance—the performance enhancement does not merit the added cost. More often the expense of innovation is that it is too disruptive to computer users. Figure 9.31 shows what we mean by the *evolution-revolution spectrum* of computer architecture innovation. To the left are ideas that are invisible to the user (presumably excepting better cost, better performance, or both). This is the evolutionary end of the spectrum. At the other end are revolutionary architecture ideas. Those are the ideas that require new applications from programmers who must learn new programming languages and models of computation, and must invent new data structures and algorithms.

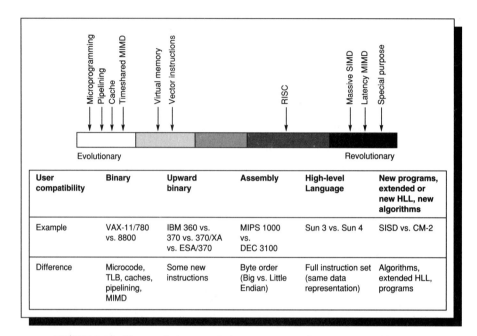

FIGURE 9.31   The evolution-revolution spectrum of computer architecture. The first four columns are distinguished from the last column in that applications and operating systems can be ported from other computers rather than written from scratch. For example, RISC is listed in the middle of the spectrum because user compatibility is only at the level of high-level languages, while microprogramming allows binary compatibility, and latency-oriented MIMDs require changes to algorithms and extending HLLs. Time-shared MIMD means MIMDs justified by running many independent programs at once, while latency MIMD means MIMDs intended to run a single program faster.

Revolutionary ideas are easier to publish than evolutionary ideas, but to be adopted they must have a much higher payoff. Caches are an example of an evolutionary improvement. Within five years after the first publication about caches almost every computer company was designing a machine with a cache. The RISC ideas were nearer to the middle of the spectrum, for it took closer to ten years for most companies to have a RISC product. An example of a revolutionary computer architecture is the Connection Machine. Every program that runs efficiently on that machine was either substantially modified or written especially for it, and programmers need to learn a new style of programming for it. Thinking Machines was founded in 1983, but only a few companies offer that style of machine.

There **is** value in projects that do not affect the computer industry because of lessons that they document for future efforts. The sin is not in having a novel architecture that is not a commercial success; the sin is in not quantitatively evaluating the strengths and weaknesses of the novel ideas. The next section mentions several machines whose primary contribution is documentation of the machine and experience using it.

When contemplating the future—and when inventing your own contributions to the field—remember the evolution-revolution spectrum. Also keep in mind the laws and principles of computer architecture found in the early chapters; these will surely guide computers of the future, just as they have guided computers of the past.

9.11 | Historical Perspective and References

For over a decade prophets have voiced the contention that the organization of a single computer has reached its limits and that truly significant advances can be made only by interconnection of a multiplicity of computers in such a manner as to permit cooperative solution.... Demonstration is made of the continued validity of the single processor approach...

Amdahl [1967, 483]

The cost of a general multiprocessor is, however, very high and further design options were considered which would decrease the cost without seriously degrading the power or efficiency of the system. The options consist of recentralizing one of the three major components.... Centralizing the [control unit] gives rise to the basic organization of [an]... array processor such as the Illiac IV.

Bouknight et al. [1972]

This has not been updated: it will be extensively revised to discuss history and more recent developments, especially for DSM.. A lot has happened since 1990!

We also plan to include references/developments in the software area. These would include: High Performance Fortran and Fortran 90 discussions, some discussion of compiler technology and references, and a discussion of OS activities (e.g. scheduling, page replication/migration, and memory allocation).

Your suggestions for further additions/deletions would be welcome.

SIMD Computers—Single Instruction Stream, Multiple Data Streams

The SIMD model was one of the earliest models of parallel computing dating back to the first large-scale multiprocessor, the ILLIAC IV, described in the historical section. The key idea in that machine, as in more recent SIMD machines, is to have a single instruction that operates on many data items at once using many functional units.

The virtues of SIMD are that all the parallel execution units are synchronized and that they all respond to a single instruction from a single PC. From a programmer's perspective, this is close to the already familiar SISD. The original motivation for SIMD was to amortize the cost of the control unit over dozens of execution units. Additionally, there may be some savings in code size, since there is only one copy of the program.

Real SIMD computers need to have a mixture of SISD and SIMD instructions. There is a SISD host computer to perform operations such as branches or address calculation that do not need parallel operation. The SIMD instructions are broadcast to all the execution units, each of which has its own set of registers. For flexibility, individual execution units can be disabled during a SIMD instruction. In addition, massively parallel SIMD machines rely on interconnection or communication networks to exchange data between processing elements.

SIMD works best in dealing with arrays in for-loops. Hence, to have the opportunity for massive parallelism in SIMD there must be massive amounts of data, or *data parallelism*. SIMD is at its weakest in case statements, where each execution unit must perform a different operation on its data, depending on what data it has. The execution units with the wrong data are disabled so that the proper units can continue. Such situations essentially run at $1/n$th performance, where n is the number of cases.

The basic tradeoff in SIMD machines is performance of a processor versus number of processors. Recent machines emphasize a large degree of parallelism over performance of the individual processors. The Connection Machine 2, for example, offers 65,536 single bit-wide processors while the ILLIAC IV had 64 64-bit processors.

The SIMD model is rapidly fading as a general-purpose multiprocessor architecture. The primary reasons are two. First, it is too inflexible. A number of important problems cannot use such a style of machine and the architecture does not scale down in a competitive fashion, that is, small scale SIMD machines often have worse cost-performance compared to the alternatives. Second, SIMD cannot take advantage of the tremendous performance and cost advantages of microprocessor technology. Instead of leveraging this low-cost technology, designers of SIMD machines must build custom processors for their machines.

While SIMD computers are likely to fade from the scene as general-purpose alternatives, this style of architecture will continue to have a role in special-purpose designs. Many special-purpose tasks are highly data parallel and require a limited set of functional units. Thus, designers can build in support for certain operations as well as hardwire interconnection paths among functional units. Such organizations are often called array processors, and are useful for tasks like image and signal processing.

The quotes at the chapter opening give the classic arguments for abandoning the current form of computing, and Amdahl [1967] gives the classic reply. Arguments for the advantages of parallel execution can be traced back to 19th century [Menabrea 1842]! Yet the effectiveness of the multiprocessor for reducing latency of individual important programs is still being determined.

The earliest ideas on SIMD-style computers are from Unger [1958] and Slotnick, Borck, and McReynolds [1962]. Slotnick's Solomon design formed the basis of the Illiac IV, perhaps the most infamous of the supercomputer projects. While successful in pushing several technologies useful in later projects, it failed as a computer. Costs escalated from the 8 million estimate in 1966 to 31 million by 1972, despite constructing only a quarter of the planned machine. Actual performance was at best 15 MFLOPS versus initial predictions of 1000 MFLOPS for the full system (see Hord [1982]). Delivered to NASA Ames Research 1972, the computer took three more years of engineering before it was usable. These events slowed investigation of SIMD, with Danny Hillis [1985] resuscitating this style in the Connection Machine: The cost of a program memory for each of 65,636 1-bit processors was prohibitive, and SIMD was the solution.

It is difficult to distinguish the first multiprocessor. The first computer from the Eckert-Mauchly Corporation, for example, had duplicate units to improve availability. Holland [1959] gave early arguments for multiple processors. After several laboratory attempts at multiprocessors, the 1980s first saw successful commercial multiprocessors. Bell [1985] suggests the key was that the smaller size of the microprocessor allowed the memory bus to replace the interconnection network hardware, and that portable operating systems meant multiprocessor projects no longer required the invention of a new operating system. This is the paper in which he defines the terms "multiprocessor" and "multicomputer." Two of the best-documented multiprocessor projects are the C.mmp [Wulf and Bell 1972 and Wulf and Habrison 1978] and Cm* [Swan et al. 1977 and Gehringer, Siewiorek, and Segall 1987]. Recent commercial multiprocessors include the Encore Multimax [Wilson 1987] and the Sequent Symmetry [Lovett and Thakkar 1988]. The Cosmic Cube is an early multicomputer [Seitz 1985]. Recent commercial multicomputers are the Intel Hypercube and the Transputer-based machines [Whitby-Strevens 1985]. Attempts at building a scalable shared-memory multiprocessor include the IBM RP3 [Pfister, Brantley, George, Harvey, Kleinfekder, McAuliffe, Melton, Norton, and Weiss 1985], the NYU Ultracomputer [Schwartz 1980 and Elder, Gottlieb, Kruskal, McAuliffe, Randolph, Snir, Teller, and Wilson 1985], and the University of Illinois Cedar project [Gajksi, Kuck, Lawrie, and Sameh 1983].

There is unbounded information on multiprocessors and multicomputers: Conferences, journal papers, and even books seem to be appearing faster than any single person can absorb the ideas. One good source is the International Conference on Parallel Processing, which has met annually since 1972. Two recent books on parallel computing have been written by Almasi and Gottlieb [1989] and Hockney and Jesshope [1988]. Eugene Miya of NASA Ames has collected an on-line bibliography of parallel-processing papers that contains more than 10,000 entries. To highlight a few papers, he sends out electronic requests every

January to ask which papers every serious student in the field should read. After collecting the ballots, he picks the ten papers most frequently recommended and publishes that list. Here is an alphabetical list of the winners: Andrews and Schneider [1983]; Batcher [1974]; Dewitt, Finkel, and Solomon [1984]; Kuhn and Padua [1981]; Lipovski and Tripathi [1977]; Russell [1978]; Seitz [1985]; Swan, Fuller, and Siewiorek [1977]; Treleaven, Brownbridge, and Hopkins [1982]; and Wulf and Bell [1972].

Special-purpose computers predate the stored-program computer. Brodersen [1989] gives a history of signal processing and its evolution to programmable devices. H. T. Kung [1982] coined the term "systolic array" and has been one of the leading proponents of this style of computer design. Recent research has been in the direction of making programmable systolic-array elements and providing a programming environment to simplify the programming task.

It's hard to predict the future, yet Gordon Bell has made two predictions for 1995. The first is that a computer capable of sustaining a TeraFLOPS—one million MFLOPS—will be constructed by 1995, either using a multicomputer with 4K to 32K nodes or a Connection Machine with several million processing elements [Bell 1989]. To put this prediction in perspective, each year the Gordon Bell Prize acknowledges advances in parallelism, including the fastest real program (highest MFLOPS). In 1988, the winner achieved 400 MFLOPS using a CRAY X-MP with four processors and 16 megawords and in 1989 the winner used an eight-processor Cray Y-MP to run at 1680 MFLOPS. Machines and programs will have to improve by a factor of three each year for the fastest program to achieve 1 TFLOPS in 1995.

The second Bell prediction concerns the number of data streams in super-computers shipped in 1995. Danny Hillis believes that while supercomputers with a small number of data streams may be best sellers, the biggest machines will be machines with many data streams, and these will perform the bulk of the computations. Bell bet Hillis that in the last quarter of calendar year 1995 more sustained MFLOPS will be shipped in machines using few data streams (≤ 100) rather than many data streams (≥ 1000). This bet concerns only supercomputers, defined as machines costing more than 1,000,000 and used for scientific applications. Sustained MFLOPS is defined for this bet as the number of floating-point operations per **month**, so availability of machines affects their rating. The loser must write and publish an article explaining why his prediction failed; your authors will act as judge and jury.

References

ALMASI, G. S. AND A. GOTTLIEB [1989]. Highly Parallel Computing, Benjamin/Cummings, Redwood City, Calif.

AMDAHL, G. M. [1967]. "Validity of the single processor approach to achieving large scale computing capabilities," *Proc. AFIPS Spring Joint Computer Conf.* 30, Atlantic City, N. J. (April) 483–485.

ANDREWS, G. R. AND F. B. SCHNEIDER [1983]. "Concept and notations for concurrent programming," *Computing Surveys* 15:1 (March) 3–43.

BATCHER, K. E. [1974]. "STARAN parallel processor system hardware," *Proc. AFIPS National Computer Conference*, 405–410.

BELL, C. G. [1985]. "Multis: A new class of multiprocessor computers," *Science* 228 (April 26) 462–467.

BELL, C. G. [1989]. "The future of high performance computers in science and engineering," *Comm. ACM* 32:9 (September) 1091–1101.

BOUKNIGHT, W. J, S. A. DENEBERG, D. E. MCINTYRE, J. M. RANDALL, A. H. SAMEH, AND D. L. SLOTNICK [1972]. "The Illiac IV system," *Proc. IEEE* 60:4, 369–379. Also appears in D. P. Siewiorek, C. G. Bell, and A. Newell, *Computer Structures: Principles and Examples* (1982), 306–316.

BRODERSEN, R. W. [1989]. "Evolution of VLSI signal-processing circuits," *Proc. Decennial Caltech Conf. on VLSI* (March) 43–46, The MIT Press, Pasadena, Calif.

DEWITT, D. J., R. FINKEL, AND M. SOLOMON [1984]. "The CRYSTAL multicomputer: Design and implementation experience, Computer Sciences Tech. Rep. No. 553, University of Wisconsin-Madison, September.

ELDER, J., A. GOTTLIEB, C. K. KRUSKAL, K. P. MCAULIFFE, L. RANDOLPH, M. SNIR, P. TELLER, AND J. WILSON [1985]. "Issues related to MIMD shared-memory computers: The NYU Ultracomputer approach," *Proc. 12th Int'l Symposium on Computer Architecture* (June), Boston, Mass., 126–135.

FLYNN, M. J. [1966]. "Very high-speed computing systems," *Proc. IEEE* 54:12 (December) 1901–1909.

GAJSKI, D., D. KUCK, D. LAWRIE, AND A. SAMEH [1983]. "CEDAR—A large scale multiprocessor," *Proc. Int'l Conf. on Parallel Processing* (August) 524–529.

GEHRINGER, E. F., D. P. SIEWIOREK, AND Z. SEGALL [1987]. *Parallel Processing: The Cm* Experience*, Digital Press, Bedford, Mass.

HILLIS, W. D. [1985]. *The Connection Machine,* The MIT Press, Cambridge, Mass.

HOCKNEY, R. W. AND C. R. JESSHOPE [1988]. *Parallel Computers-2, Architectures, Programming and Algorithms,* Adam Hilger Ltd., Bristol, England and Philadelphia.

HOLLAND, J. H. [1959]. "A universal computer capable of executing an arbitrary number of subprograms simultaneously," *Proc. East Joint Computer Conf.* 16, 108–113.

HORD, R. M. [1982]. *The Illiac-IV, The First Supercomputer,* Computer Science Press, Rockville, Md.

KUHN, R. H. AND D. A. PADUA, EDS. [1981]. *Tutorial on Parallel Processing*, IEEE.

KUNG, H. T. [1982]. "Why systolic architectures?," *IEEE Computer* 15:1, 37–46.

LIPOVSKI , A. G. AND A. TRIPATHI [1977]. "A reconfigurable varistructure array processor," *Proc. 1977 Int'l Conf. of Parallel Processing* (August), 165–174.

LOVETT, T. AND S. THAKKAR [1988]. "The Symmetry multiprocessor system," *Proc. 1988 Int'l Conf. of Parallel Processing*, University Park, Pennsylvania, 303–310.

MENABREA, L. F. [1842]. "Sketch of the analytical engine invented by Charles Babbage," Bibiothèque Universelle de Genève (October).

MITCHELL, D. [1989]. "The Transputer: The time is now," *Computer Design*, RISC supplement, 40–41 (November).

PFISTER, G. F., W. C. BRANTLEY, D. A. GEORGE, S. L. HARVEY, W. J. KLEINFEKDER, K. P. MCAULIFFE, E. A. MELTON, V. A. NORTON, AND J. WEISS [1985]. "The IBM research parallel processor prototype (RP3): Introduction and architecture," *Proc. 12th Int'l Symposium on Computer Architecture* (June), Boston, Mass., 764–771.

RUSSELL, R. M. [1978]. "The Cray-1 computer system," *Comm. ACM* 21:1 (January) 63–72.

SEITZ, C. [1985]. "The Cosmic Cube," *Comm. ACM* 28:1 (January) 22–31.

SLOTNICK, D. L., W. C. BORCK, AND R. C. MCREYNOLDS [1962]. "The Solomon computer," *Proc. Fall Joint Computer Conf.* (December), Philadelphia, 97–107.

SWAN, R. J., A. BECHTOLSHEIM, K. W. LAI, AND J. K. OUSTERHOUT [1977]. "The implementation of the Cm* multi-microprocessor," *Proc. AFIPS National Computing Conf.*, 645–654.

SWAN, R. J., S. H. FULLER, AND D. P. SIEWIOREK [1977]. "Cm*—A modular, multi-microprocessor," *Proc. AFIPS National Computer Conf.* 46, 637–644.

SWARTZ, J. T. [1980]. "Ultracomputers," *ACM Transactions on Programming Languages and Systems* 4:2, 484–521

TRELEAVEN, P. C., D. R. BROWNBRIDGE, AND R. P. HOPKINS [1982]. "Data-driven and demand-driven computer architectures," *Computing Surveys*, 14:1 (March) 93–143.

UNGER, S. H. [1958]. "A computer oriented towards spatial problems," *Proc. Institute of Radio Engineers* 46:10 (October) 1744–1750.

VON NEUMANN, J. [1945]. "First draft of a report on the EDVAC." Reprinted in W. Aspray and A. Burks, eds., *Papers of John von Neumann on Computing and Computer Theory* (1987), 17–82, The MIT Press, Cambridge, Mass.

WHITBY-STREVENS C. [1985]. "The transputer," *Proc. 12th Int'l Symposium on Computer Architecture*, Boston, Mass. (June) 292–300.

WILSON, A. W., JR. [1987]. "Hierarchical cache/bus architecture for shared memory multiprocessors," *Proc. 14th Int'l Symposium on Computer Architecture* (June), Pittsburg, Penn., 244–252.

WULF, W. AND C. G. BELL [1972]. "C.mmp—A multi-mini-processor," *Proc. AFIPS Fall Joint Computing Conf.* 41, part 2, 765–777.

WULF, W. AND S. P. HARBISON [1978]. "Reflections in a pool of processors—An experience report on C.mmp/Hydra," *Proc. AFIPS 1978 National Computing Conf.* 48 (June), Anaheim, Calif. 939–951.

EXERCISES

Not updated as yet; near the bottom you can find one-line descriptions of new exercises. Additional suggestions are welcome!

9.1 [Discussion] <9.4> The weakness of SIMD for case statements, as well as the failure of the first machine to popularize SIMD, prevented exploration of SIMD designs while MIMD was still an open frontier. MIMD also has the advantage of riding the wave of improvements in SISD processors. Now that MIMD programming has not succumbed easily to assaults of computer scientists, the issue arises whether the simpler programming model of SIMD might lead it to victory over MIMD for large numbers of processors. It looks as if MIMD programs for thousands of processors will consist of thousands of copies of one program rather than thousands of different programs. Thus, the direction is toward a single **program** with multiple data streams, independent of whether the machine itself is SIMD or MIMD. What trends favor MIMD over SIMD, and vice versa? Be sure to consider utilization of memory and processors (including communication and synchronization).

9.2 [Discussion] <9.3–9.5> It might take approximately 100 clocks to communicate in a massively parallel SIMD or MIMD machine. What hardware techniques might reduce this time? How can you change the architecture or the programming model to make a computer more immune to such delays?

9.3 [Discussion] <9.4,9.8> What must happen before latency-oriented MIMD machines become commonplace?

9.4 [Discussion] <9.6> When do special-purpose processors make sense economically?

9.5 [Discussion] <9.8> Construct a scenario whereby a truly revolutionary architecture—pick your favorite candidate—will play a significant role. Significant is defined as 10% of the computers sold, 10% of the users, 10% of the money spent on computers, or 10% of some other figure of merit.

9.6 [30] <9.2> The CM-2 uses 64K 1-bit processors in SIMD mode. Bit-serial operations can easily be simulated 32 bits one step by a 32-bit-wide SISD, at least for logical operations. The CM-2 takes about 500 ns for such operations. If you have access to a fast SISD, calculate how long add and logical and take on 64K 1-bit numbers.

9.7 [30] <9.2> Similar to the question above, a popular use of the CM-2 is to operate on 32-bit data using multiple steps with the 64K 1-bit processors. The CM-2 takes about 16 microseconds for a 32-bit and or add. Simulate this activity on a fast SISD; calculate how long it takes to add and logical and 64K 32-bit numbers.

9.8–9.12 <2.2,9.4> **If you have access to a few different multiprocessors or multicomputers, performance comparison is the basis of some projects.**

9.8 [50] <2.2,9.4> One argument for super-linear speedup (pages 585–586) is that time spent servicing interrupts or switching contexts is reduced when you have many processors, since only one need service interrupts and there are more processors to be shared by users. Measure the time spent on a workload in handling interrupts or context switching on a uniprocessor versus a multiprocessor. This workload may be a mix of independent jobs for a multiprogramming environment or a single large job. Does the argument hold?

9.9 [50] <2.2,9.4> A multiprocessor or multicomputer is typically marketed using programs that can scale performance linearly with the number of processors. The project would be to port programs written for one machine to the others and measure their absolute performance and how it changes as you change the number of processors. What changes need to be made to improve performance of the ported programs on each machine? What is the ratio of processor performance according to each program?

9.10 [50] <2.2,9.4> Instead of trying to create fair benchmarks, invent programs that make one multiprocessor or multicomputer look terrible compared to the others, and also programs that always make one look better than the others. It would be an interesting result if you couldn't find a program that made one multiprocessor or multicomputer look worse than the others. What are the key performance characteristics of each organization?

9.11 [50] <2.2,9.4> Multiprocessors and multicomputers usually show performance increases as you increase the number of processors, with the ideal being *n* times speedup for *n* processors. The goal of this biased benchmark is to make a program that gets worse performance as you add processors. For example, this means that 1 processor on the multiprocessor or multicomputer runs the program fastest, 2 is slower, 4 is slower than 2, and so on. What are the key performance characteristics for each organization that give inverse linear speedup?

9.12 [50] <9.4> Networked workstations can be considered multicomputers, albeit with slow communication relative to computation. Port multicomputer benchmarks to a network using remote procedure calls for communication. How well do the benchmarks scale on the network versus the multicomputer? What are the practical differences between networked workstations and a commercial multicomputer?

Suppose we have an application that runs in three modes: all processors used, half the processors in use, and serial mode. Assume 0.02% of the time is serial mode, and there are 100 processors in total. Find the maximum time that can be spent in the mode when half the processors are used, if our goal is a speedup of 80, as in the previous example. What speedup is achieved if this half-efficiency mode is not available?

Exercise: add clean private state to our coherency protocol.

Exercise : distributed shared memory wit bus.

Add clean write ownership state

In the exercises we explore an optimized version of this protocol that sends all the invalidates and then receives acknowledgments, which allows more overlap and thus a lower latency.

the convex machine

scalable directories

race problem in forwarding protocols

multiple context

prove inclusion: associativity and inclusion

block copy: exercise and programming

COMA

hierarchy

multiple outstanding misses from anode: reads/writes, directory/snoop

lock-up free and its complications

broadcast protocol for syn variables:

    lock/unlock

    barrier examples

use queueing locks for barriers

another synchronization primitive: loop index distribution? add to parallel task queue?

barriers: counting out as well as in with/without fetch and op

barriers: signalling to reduce release contention or broadcast on a bus

write programs such that results are same as sequentially consistent for each of following models: PC, PSO, WO, RC.

exercise using data for write upgrades versus write misses

invalidate versus update

performance with two way caches: contention etc.

replacement issues: There is one other type of occurrence that, while not requiring any additions to the coherency controller, is typical of the type of problems that arise when state is distributed. To satisfy a cache miss, the cache controller may replace a block that is Exclusive or Shared with another block. Because such a replacement happens without the knowledge of the directory, the controller may receive an Invalidate, Data Fetch, or Data Fetch/Invalidate message for a block that has been replaced. In such cases, the local coherency controller can ignore the action, since it no longer has the block. If the directory had the value, then the local node has already sent it.

prove that for synchronized programs, a relaxed consistency model allows only the same results as sequential consistency.

The Fast drives out the Slow even if the Fast is wrong.

W. Kahan

by David Goldberg

(Xerox Palo Alto Research Center)

# Computer Arithmetic

A.1 | Introduction

A tremendous variety of algorithms have been proposed for use in floating-point accelerators. However, actual floating-point chips are usually based on refinements and variations of just a few basic algorithms. In this appendix, we focus on those basic algorithms. In addition to choosing algorithms for addition, subtraction, multiplication and division, the computer architect must make other choices. What precisions should be implemented? How should exceptions be handled? This appendix will give you the background for making these and other decisions.

Our discussion of floating point will focus almost exclusively on the IEEE floating-point standard (IEEE 754) because of its rapidly increasing acceptance. Although floating-point arithmetic involves manipulating exponents and shifting fractions, the bulk of the time in floating-point operations is spent operating on fractions using integer algorithms (but not necessarily sharing the hardware that implements integer instructions). Thus, after our discussion of floating point, we will take a more detailed look at integer algorithms.

Some good references on computer arithmetic, in order from least to most detailed, are Chapter 4 of *Computer Organization and Design*, Chapter 7 of Hamacher, Vranesic, and Zaky [1984], Gosling [1980], and Scott [1985].

A.2 | Basic Techniques of Integer Arithmetic

Readers who have studied computer arithmetic before will find most of this section to be review.

Ripple-Carry Addition

Adders are usually implemented by combining multiple copies of simple components. The natural components for addition are *half adders* and *full adders*. The half adder takes two bits a and b as input and produces a sum bit s and a carry bit c_{out} as output. Mathematically, $s = (a + b) \bmod 2$, and $c_{out} = \lfloor (a + b)/2 \rfloor$, where $\lfloor \ \rfloor$ is the floor function. As logic equations, $s = a\bar{b} + \bar{a}b$ and $c_{out} = ab$, where ab means $a \wedge b$ and $a + b$ means $a \vee b$. The half adder is also called a (2,2) adder, since it takes two inputs and produces two outputs. The full adder is a (3,2) adder and is defined by $s = (a + b + c) \bmod 2$, $c_{out} = \lfloor (a + b + c)/2 \rfloor$, or the logic equations

A.2.1
$$s = a\bar{b}\bar{c} + \bar{a}b\bar{c} + \bar{a}\bar{b}c + abc$$

A.2.2
$$c_{out} = ab + ac + bc$$

The principal problem in constructing an adder for *n*-bit numbers out of smaller pieces is propagating the carries from one piece to the next. The most obvious way to solve this is with a *ripple-carry adder*, consisting of *n* full adders, as illustrated in Figure 32. (In the figures in this appendix the least significant bit is always on the right.) The inputs to the adder are $a_{n-1}a_{n-2}\cdots a_0$ and $b_{n-1}b_{n-2}\cdots b_0$, where $a_{n-1}a_{n-2}\cdots a_0$ represents the number $a_{n-1}2^{n-1} + a_{n-2}2^{n-2} + \cdots + a_0$. The c_{i+1} output of the *i*th adder is fed into the c_{i+1} input of the next adder (the $(i + 1)$-th adder) with the lower order carry-in c_0 set to 0. Since the low-order carry-in is wired

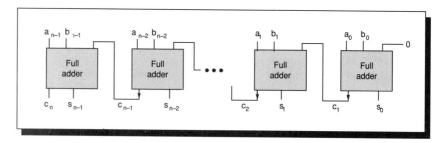

FIGURE A.1 Ripple-carry adder, consisting of n full adders. The carry-out of one full adder is connected to the carry-in of the adder for the next most significant bit. The carries ripple from the least significant bit (on the right) to the most significant bit (on the left).

to zero, the low-order adder could be a half adder. Later, however, we will see that setting the low-order carry-in bit to 1 is useful for performing subtraction.

In general, the time a circuit takes to produce an output is proportional to the maximum number of logic levels through which a signal travels. However, determining the exact relationship between logic levels and timings is highly technology dependent. Therefore, when comparing adders we will simply compare the number of logic levels in each one. How many levels are there for a ripple-carry adder? It takes two levels to compute c_1 from a_0 and b_0. Then two more levels to compute c_2 from c_1, a_1 and b_1, and so on up to c_n. So there are a total of $2n$ levels. Typical values of n are 32 for integer arithmetic and 53 for double-precision floating point. The ripple-carry adder is the slowest adder, but also the cheapest. It can be built with only n simple cells, connected in a simple, regular way.

Because the ripple-carry adder is relatively slow compared to the designs discussed in Section A.8, one might wonder why it is used at all. In technologies like CMOS, even though ripple adders take time $O(n)$, the constant factor is very small. In such cases short ripple adders are often used as building blocks in larger adders.

Radix-2 Multiplication and Division

The simplest multiplier computes the product of two unsigned numbers, one bit at a time, as illustrated in Figure 33(a) (page A-4). The numbers to be multiplied are $a_{n-1}a_{n-2}\cdots a_0$ and $b_{n-1}b_{n-2}\cdots b_0$, and they are placed in registers A and B, respectively. Register P is initially zero. Each multiply step has two parts.

Multiply Step   (*i*)   If the least significant bit of A is 1, then register B, containing $b_{n-1}b_{n-2}\cdots b_0$, is added to P; otherwise $00\cdots00$ is added to P. The sum is placed back into P.

(*ii*)   Registers P and A are shifted right, with the low-order bit of P being moved into register A and the rightmost bit of A, which is not used in the rest of the algorithm, being shifted out.

After n steps, the product appears in registers P and A, with A holding the lower-order bits.

The simplest divider also operates on unsigned numbers and produces the quotient bits one at a time. A hardware divider is shown in Figure 33(b). To compute a/b, put a in the A register, b in the B register, 0 in the P register, and then perform n divides steps. Each divide step consists of four parts.:

Divide Step   (*i*)   Shift the register pair (P, A) one bit left.

(*ii*)   Subtract the content of register B (which is $b_{n-1}b_{n-2}\cdots b_0$) from register P, putting the result back into P.

(*iii*)   If the result of step 2 is negative, set the low-order bit of A to 0, otherwise to 1.

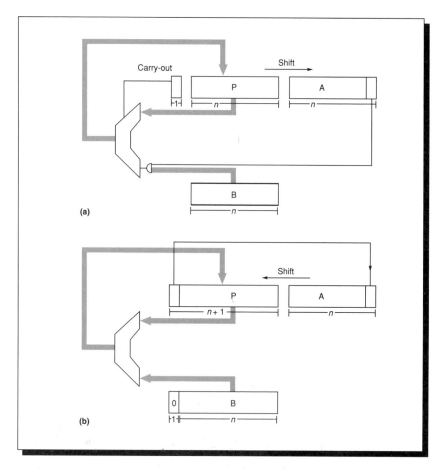

FIGURE A.2   Block diagram of (a) simple multiplier and (b) divider for n-bit unsigned integers. Each multiplication step consists of adding the contents of P to either B or 0 (depending on the low-order bit of A), replacing P with the sum, and then shifting both P and A one bit right. Each division step involves first shifting P and A one bit left, subtracting B from P, and if the difference is nonnegative, putting it into P. If the difference is nonnegative, the low-order bit of A is set to 1.

(*iv*) If the result of step 2 is negative, restore the old value of P by adding the contents of register B back into P.

After repeating this process *n* times, the A register will contain the quotient, and the P register will contain the remainder. This algorithm is the binary version of the paper-and-pencil method; a numerical example is illustrated in Figure 34(a) (page A-6).

Notice that the two block diagrams in Figure 33 are very similar. The main difference is that the register pair (P, A) shifts right when multiplying and left when dividing. By allowing these registers to shift bidirectionally, the same hardware can be shared between multiplication and division.

The division algorithm illustrated in Figure 34(a) (page A-6) is called *restoring*, because if subtraction by b yields a negative result, the P register is restored by adding b back in. The restoring algorithm has a variant which skips the restoring step, and instead works with the resulting negative numbers. Each step of this *nonrestoring* algorithm has three parts:

Nonrestoring   If P is negative,

Divide Step

      (*i-a*) Shift the register pair (P, A) one bit left,

      (*ii-a*) Add the contents of register B to P.

Else,

      (*i-b*) Shift the register pair (P, A) one bit left.

      (*ii-b*) Subtract the contents of register B from P.

(*iii*) If P is negative, set the low-order bit of A to 0, otherwise set it to 1.

After repeating this n times, the quotient is in A. If P is nonnegative, it is the remainder. Otherwise, it needs to be restored (i.e., add b), and then it will be the remainder. A numerical example is given in Figure 34(b). Since (*i-a*) and (*i-b*) are the same, you might be tempted to perform this common step first, and then test the sign of P. That doesn't work, since the sign bit can be lost when shifting.

The explanation for why the nonrestoring algorithm works is this. Let r_k be the contents of the (P, A) register pair at step k, ignoring the quotient bits (which are simply sharing the unused bits of register A). In Figure 34(a), initially A contains 14, so $r_0 = 14$. At the end of the first step $r_1 = 28$, and so on. In the restoring algorithm, part (*i*) computes $2r_k$ and then part (ii) $2r_k - 2^n b$ ($2^n b$ since b is subtracted from the left half). If $2r_k - 2^n b \geq 0$, both algorithms end the step with identical values in (P, A). If $2r_k - 2^n b < 0$, then the restoring algorithm restores this to $2r_k$, and the next step begins by computing $r_{res} = 2(2r_k) - 2^n b$. In the nonrestoring algorithm, $2r_k - 2^n b$ is kept as a negative number, and in the next step $r_{nonres} = 2(2r_k - 2^n b) + 2^n b = 4r_k - 2^n b = r_{res}$. Thus (P, A) has the same bits in either algorithm.

If a and b are unsigned n-bit numbers, hence in the range $0 \leq a,b \leq 2^n - 1$, then the multiplier in Figure 33 will work if register P is n bits long. However, for division, P must be extended to $n + 1$ bits in order to detect the sign of P. Thus the adder must also have $n + 1$ bits.

Why would anyone implement restoring division, which uses the same hardware as nonrestoring division (the control is slightly different) but involves an extra addition? In fact, the usual implementation for restoring division doesn't literally perform an add in step (*iv*). Rather, the sign resulting from the subtraction is tested at the output of the adder, and only if the sum is nonnegative is it loaded back into the P register.

```
        P      A
      00000   1110    Divide 14 = 1110 by 3 = 11. B always contains 0011
      00001   110     step 1(i): shift
     -00011           step 1(ii): subtract
     -00010   1100    step 1(iii): result is negative, set quotient bit to 0
      00001   1100    step 1(iv): restore
      00011   100     step 2(i): shift
     -00011           step 2(ii): subtract
      00000   1001    step 2(iii): result is nonnegative, set quotient bit to 1
      00001   001     step 3(i): shift
     -00011           step 3(ii): subtract
     -00010   0010    step 3(iii): result is negative, set quotient bit 0
      00001   0010    step 3(iv): restore
      00010   010     step 4(i): shift
     -00011           step 4(ii): subtract
     -00001   0100    step 4(iii): result is negative, set quotient bit to 0
      00010   0100    step 4(iv): restore. The quotient is 0100 and the remainder is 00010.
(a)
```

```
      00000   1110    Divide 14 = 1110 by 3 = 11. B always contains 0011
      00001   110     step 1(i-b): shift
     +11101           step 1(ii-b): subtract b (add 2's complement)
      11110   1100    step 1(iii): P is negative, so set quotient bit 0
      11101   100     step 2(i-a): shift
     +00011           step 2(ii-a): add b
      00000   1001    step 2(iii): P is nonnegative, so set quotient bit to 1
      00001   001     step 3(i-b): shift
     +11101           step 3(ii-b): subtract b
      11110   0010    step 3(iii): P is negative, so set quotient bit to 0
      11100   010     step 4(i-a): shift
     +00011           step 4(ii-a): add b
      11111   0100    step 4(iii): P is negative, so set quotient bit to 0
     +00011           remainder is negative, so do final restore step
      00010           The quotient is 0100  and the remainder is 00010
(b)
```

FIGURE A.3   Numerical example of (a) restoring division and (b) nonrestoring division.

As a final point, before beginning to divide, the hardware must check to see if the divisor is zero.

Signed Numbers

There are four methods commonly used to represent signed n-bit numbers: *sign magnitude, two's complement, one's complement,* and *biased.* In the sign-magnitude system, the high-order bit is the sign bit, and the low-order $n - 1$ bits are the magnitude of the number. In the two's complement system, a number and its negative add up to 2^n. In one's complement, the negative of a number is obtained by complementing each bit (or alternatively, the number and its negative add up to $2^n - 1$). In each of these three systems, nonnegative numbers are represented in the usual way. In a biased system, nonnegative numbers do not have their usual representation. Instead, all numbers are represented by first adding them to the bias, and then encoding this sum as an ordinary unsigned number. Thus a negative number k can be encoded as long as $k + \text{bias} \geq 0$. A typical value for the bias is 2^{n-1}.

Example

Using 4-bit numbers ($n = 4$), if $k = 3$ (or in binary, $k = 0011_2$), how is $-k$ expressed in each of these formats?

Answer

In signed magnitude, the leftmost bit in $k = 0011_2$ is the sign bit, so flip it to 1: $-k = 1011_2$. In two's complement, $k + 1101_2 = 2^n = 16$. So $-k = 1101_2$. In one's complement, the bits of $k = 0011_2$ are flipped, so $-k = 1100_2$. For a biased system, assuming a bias of $2^{n-1} = 8$, k is represented as $k + \text{bias} = 1011_2$, and $-k$ as $-k + \text{bias} = 0101_2$.

The most widely used system for representing integers, two's complement, is the system we will use here. One reason for the popularity of two's complement is that it makes signed addition easy: Simply discard the carry-out from the high-order bit. To add $5 + -2$, for example, add 0101_2 and 1110_2 to obtain 0011_2, resulting in the correct value of 3. A useful formula for the value of a two's complement number $a_{n-1}a_{n-2}\cdots a_1a_0$ is

A.2.3

$$-a_{n-1}2^{n-1} + a_{n-2}2^{n-2} + \cdots + a_1 2^1 + a_0$$

As an illustration of this formula, the value of 1101_2 as a 4-bit two's complement number is $-1\cdot2^3 + 1\cdot2^2 + 0\cdot2^1 + 1\cdot2^0 = -8 + 4 + 1 = -3$, confirming the result of the example above.

Overflow occurs when the result of the operation does not fit in the representation being used. For example, if unsigned numbers are being represented using four bits, then $6 = 0110_2$, and $11 = 1011_2$. Their sum (17) overflows because its binary equivalent (10001_2) doesn't fit into four bits. For unsigned numbers, detecting overflow is easy; it occurs exactly when there is a carry-out of the most significant bit. For two's complement, things are trickier: Overflow occurs exactly when the carry into the high-order bit is different from the (to be discarded) carry-out of the high-order bit. In the example of $5 + -2$ above, a 1 is carried both into and out of the leftmost bit, avoiding overflow.

Negating a two's complement number involves complementing each bit and then adding 1. For instance, to negate 0011_2, complement it to get 1100_2 and then add 1 to get 1101_2. Thus, to implement $a - b$ using an adder, simply feed a and into the adder, and set the low-order, carry-in bit to 1. This explains why the rightmost adder in Figure 32 is a full adder.

Multiplying two's complement numbers is not quite as simple as adding them. The obvious approach is to convert both operands to be nonnegative, do an unsigned multiplication, and then (if the original operands were of opposite signs) negate the result. Although this is conceptually simple, it requires extra time and hardware. Here is a better approach: Suppose that we are multiplying a times b using the hardware shown in Figure 33(a) (page A-4). Register A is loaded with the number a; B is loaded with b. Since the contents of register B is always b, we will use B and b interchangeably. If B is potentially negative but A is nonnegative, the only change needed to convert the unsigned multiplication algorithm into a two's complement one is to ensure that when P is shifted, it is shifted arithmetically; that is, the bit shifted into the high-order bit of P should be the sign bit of P. Note that our n-bit–wide adder will now be adding n-bit two's complement numbers between -2^{n-1} and $2^{n-1} - 1$.

Next, suppose a is negative. The method for handling this case is called *Booth recoding*. Booth recoding is a very basic technique in computer arithmetic and will play a key role in Section A.9. The algorithm on page A-3 computes $a \times b$ by examining the bits of a from least significant to most significant. For example, if $a = 7 = 0111_2$, then part (i) will successively add B, add B, add B, and add 0. Booth recoding "recodes" the number 7 as $8 - 1 = 1000_2 - 0001_2 .= 100\bar{1}$, where $\bar{1}$ represents -1. This gives an alternate way to compute $a \times b$, namely successively subtract B, add 0, add 0 and add B. This is more complicated than the unsigned algorithm on page A-3, since it uses both addition and subtraction. The advantage shows up for negative values of a. For example, take $a = -4 = 1100_2$. Think of 1100_2 as the unsigned number 12, and write it as $12 = 16 - 4 = 10000_2 - 0100_2$. If the multiplication algorithm is only iterated n times ($n = 4$ in this case), the 10000_2 term is ignored, and we end up subtracting $0100_2 = 4$ times the multiplier—exactly the right answer. This suggests that multiplying using a recoded form of a will work equally well for both positive and negative numbers. And indeed, to deal with negative values of a, all that is required is to sometimes subtract b from P, instead of either adding b or 0 to P. Here are the precise rules: If the initial content of A is $a_{n-1} \cdots a_0$, then at the ith multiply step, the low-order bit of register A is a_i, and step (i) in the multiplication algorithm becomes

I.   If $a_i = 0$ and $a_{i-1} = 0$ then add 0 to P.

```
   P      A
 0000   1010      Put −6 = 1010 into A, −5 = 1011 into B.

 0000   1010      step 1(i): a₀ = a₋₁ = 0, so from rule I add 0.

 0000   0101      step 1(ii): shift.

+ 0101            step 2(i): a₁ = 1, a₀ = 0. Rule III says subtract b (or add -b).

 0101   0101

 0010   1010      step 2(ii): shift.

+ 1011            step 3(i): a₂ = 0, a₁ = 1. Rule II says add b (1011).

 1101   1010

 1110   1101      step 3(ii): shift. (Arithmetic shift—load 1 into leftmost bit.)

+ 0101            step 4(i): a₃ = 1, a₂ = 0. Rule III says subtract b.

 0011   1101

 0001   1110      step 4(ii): shift. Final result is 00011110 = 30.
```

FIGURE A.4 Numerical example of Booth recoding. Multiplication of a = –6 by b = –5 to get 30.

II. If $a_i = 0$ and $a_{i-1} = 1$ then add B to P.

III. If $a_i = 1$ and $a_{i-1} = 0$ then subtract B from P.

IV. If $a_i = 1$ and $a_{i-1} = 1$ then add 0 to P.

For the first step, when $i = 0$, take a_{i-1} to be 0.

Example   When multiplying –6 times –5, what is the sequence of values in the (P, A) register pair?

Answer   See Figure 35

The four cases above can be restated as saying that in the ith step you should add $(a_{i-1} - a_i)$B to P. With this observation, it is easy to verify that these rules work, because the result of all the additions is

$$\sum_{i=0}^{n-1} b(a_{i-1} - a_i)2^i = b(-a_{n-1}2^{n-1} + a_{n-2}2^{n-2} + \cdots + a_12 + a_0) + ba_{-1}$$

Using Equation A.2.3 (page A-7) together with $a_{-1} = 0$, the right hand side is seen to be the value of b×a as a two's complement number.

The simplest way to implement the rules for Booth recoding is to extend the A register one bit to the right so that this new bit will contain a_{i-1}. Unlike the naive method of inverting any negative operands, this technique doesn't require extra steps or any special casing for negative operands. It has only a slightly more control logic. If the multiplier is being shared with a divider, there will already be the capability for subtracting b, rather than adding it. To summarize, a simple method for handling two's complement multiplication is to pay attention to the sign of P when shifting it right, and to save the most recently shifted off bit of A to use in deciding whether to add or subtract b from P.

Booth recoding is usually the best method for designing multiplication hardware that operates on signed numbers. For hardware that doesn't directly implement it, however, performing Booth recoding in software or microcode is usually too slow, due to the conditional tests and branches. If the hardware supports arithmetic shifts (so that negative b is handled correctly), then the following method can be used. Treat the multiplier a as if it were an unsigned number, and perform the first $n-1$ multiply steps using the algorithm on page A-3. If $a < 0$ (in which case there will be a 1 in the low-order bit of the A register at this point), then subtract b from P; otherwise ($a \geq 0$) neither add nor subtract. In either case, do a final shift (for a total of n shifts). This works because it amounts to multiplying b by $-a_{n-1}2^{n-1} + \cdots + a_1 2 + a_0$, which is the value of $a_{n-1}\cdots a_0$ as a two's complement number by Equation A.2.3. If the hardware doesn't support arithmetic shift, then converting the operands to be nonnegative is probably the best approach.

Two final remarks: A good way to test a signed-multiply routine is to try $-2^{n-1} \times -2^{n-1}$, since this is the only case that produces a $2n-1$ bit result. Unlike multiplication, division is usually performed in hardware by converting the operands to be nonnegative and then doing an unsigned divide; because division is substantially slower (and less frequent) than multiplication, the extra time used to manipulate the signs has less impact than it does on multiplication.

Systems Issues

When designing an instruction set, there are a number of issues related to integer arithmetic that need to be resolved. Several of them are discussed here.

First, what should be done about integer overflow? This situation is complicated by the fact that detecting overflow is different depending on whether the operands are signed or unsigned integers. Consider signed arithmetic first. There are three approaches: Set a bit on overflow, trap on overflow, or do nothing on overflow. In the last case, software has to check whether or not an overflow occurred. The most convenient solution for the programmer is to have an enable bit. If this bit is turned on, then overflow causes a trap. If it is turned off, then overflow sets a bit (or alternatively, have two different add instructions). The advantage of this approach is that both trapping and nontrapping operations require only one instruction. Furthermore, as we will see in Section A.7, this is analogous to how the IEEE floating-point standard handles floating-point overflow. Figure 36 shows how some common machines treat overflow.

Machine	Trap on signed overflow?	Trap on unsigned overflow?	Set bit on signed overflow?	Set bit on unsigned overflow?
VAX	If enable is on	No	Yes. Add sets V bit.	Yes. Add sets C bit.
IBM 370	If enable is on	No	Yes. Add sets cond code.	Yes. Logical add sets cond code.
Intel 8086	No	No	Yes. Add sets V bit.	Yes. Add sets C bit.
MIPS R3000	There are 2 add instructions: one always traps, the other never does.	No	No. Software must deduce it from sign of operands and result.	
SPARC	No	No	Addcc sets V bit. Add does not.	Addcc sets C bit. Add does not.

FIGURE A.5   Summary of how various machines handle integer overflow. Both the 8086 and SPARC have an instruction that traps if the V bit is set, so the cost of trapping on overflow is one extra instruction.

What about unsigned addition? Notice that none of the architectures in Figure 36 trap on unsigned overflow. The reason for this is that the primary use of unsigned arithmetic is in manipulating addresses. It is convenient to be able to subtract from an unsigned address by adding. For example, when $n = 4$, we can subtract 2 from the unsigned address $10 = 1010_2$ by adding $14 = 1110_2$. This generates an overflow, but we would not want a trap to be generated.

A second issue concerns multiplication. Should the result of multiplying two n-bit numbers be a $2n$-bit result, or should multiplication just return the low-order n bits, signaling overflow if the result doesn't fit in n bits? An argument in favor of an n-bit result is that in virtually all high-level languages, multiplication is an operation whose arguments are integer variables and whose result is an integer variable of the same type. Therefore, compilers won't generate code that utilizes a double-precision result. An argument in favor of a $2n$-bit result is that it can be used by an assembly language routine to speed up multiplication of multiple-precision integers substantially (by about a factor of 3).

A third issue concerns machines that want to execute one instruction every cycle. It is rarely practical to perform a multiplication or division in the same amount of time that an addition or register–register move takes. There are three possible approaches to this problem. The first is to have a single-cycle *multiply-step* instruction. This might do one step of the Booth algorithm. The second approach is to do integer multiplication in the floating-point unit and have it be part of the floating-point instruction set. (This is what DLX does.) The third approach is to have an autonomous unit in the CPU do the multiplication. In this case, the result can either be guaranteed to be delivered in a fixed number of cycles—and the compiler charged with waiting the proper amount of time—or there can be an interlock. The same comments apply to division as well. As examples, the SPARC has a multiply-step instruction but no divide-step instruction, and the

MIPS R3000 has an autonomous unit that does multiplication and division (but see Section E-6 for new extensions to the SPARC for arithmetic). The designers of the HP Precision Architecture did an especially thorough job of analyzing the frequency of the operands for multiplication and division, and based their multiply and divide steps accordingly. (See Magenheimer et al. [1988] for details.)

The final issue involves the computation of integer division and remainder for negative numbers. For example, what is −5 DIV 3 and −5 MOD 3? When computing x DIV y and x MOD y, negative values of x occur frequently enough to be worth some careful consideration (on the other hand, negative values of y are quite rare). If there are built-in hardware instructions for these operations, they should correspond to what high level languages specify. Unfortunately, there is no agreement among existing programming languages. See Figure 37.

Language	Division	Remainder
FORTRAN	−5/3 = −1	MOD(−5, 3) = −2
Pascal	−5 DIV 3 = −1	−5 MOD 3 = 1
Ada	−5/3 = −1	−5 MOD 3 = 1 −5 REM 3 = −2
C	−5/3 undefined	−5 % 3 undefined
Modula-3	−5 DIV 3 = −2	−5 MOD 3 = 1

FIGURE A.6   Examples of integer division and integer remainder in various programming languages.

There is one definition for these expressions that stands out as clearly superior. Namely x DIV $y = \lfloor x/y \rfloor$, so that 5 DIV 3 = 1, −5 DIV 3 = −2. And MOD should satisfy x = (x DIV y) × y + x MOD y, so that x MOD y ≥ 0. Thus 5 MOD 3 = 2, and −5 MOD 3 = 1. Some of the many advantages of this definition are:

1. A calculation to compute an index into a hash table of size N can use MOD N and be guaranteed to produce a valid index in the range from 0 to $N − 1$.

2. In graphics, when converting from one coordinate system to another, there is no "glitch" near 0. For example to convert from a value x expressed in a system that uses 100 dots per inch to a value y on a bitmapped display with 70 dots per inch, the formula $y = (70 \times x)$ DIV 100 maps one or two x coordinates into each y coordinate. But if DIV were defined as in Pascal to be x/y rounded to 0, then 0 would have three different points (−1, 0, 1) mapped into it.

3. x MOD 2^k is the same as performing a bitwise AND with a mask of k bits, and x DIV 2^k is the same as doing a k-bit arithmetic right shift.

Finally, a potential pitfall worth mentioning concerns multiple-precision addition. Many instruction sets offer a variant of the add instruction that adds three operands: two *n*-bit numbers together with a third single-bit number. This third number is the carry from the previous addition. Since the multiple-precision number will typically be stored in an array, it is important to be able to increment the array pointer without destroying the carry bit.

A.3 | Floating Point

Introduction

Many applications require numbers that aren't integers. There are a number of ways that non-integers can be represented. One is to use *fixed point*; that is, use integer arithmetic and simply imagine the binary point somewhere other than just to the right of the least significant digit. Adding two such numbers can be done with an integer add, whereas multiplication requires some extra shifting. Other representations that have been proposed involve storing the logarithm of a number and doing multiplication by adding the logarithms, or using a pair of integers (a,b) to represent the fraction a/b. However, there is only one non-integer representation that has gained widespread use, and that is the floating-point representation. In this system, a computer word is divided into two parts, an exponent and a significand. As an example, an exponent of -3 and significand of 1.5 might represent the number $1.5 \times 2^{-3} = 0.1875$. The advantages of standardizing a particular representation are obvious. Numerical analysts can build up high-quality software libraries, computer designers can develop techniques for implementing high-performance hardware, and hardware vendors can build standard accelerators. Given the predominance of the floating-point representation, it appears unlikely that any other representation will come into widespread use.

The semantics of floating-point instructions are not as clear cut as the semantics of the rest of the instruction set, and in the past the behavior of floating-point operations varied considerably from one computer family to the next. The variations involved such things as the number of bits allocated to the exponent and significand, the range of exponents, how rounding was carried out, and the actions taken on exceptional conditions like underflow and overflow. Computer architecture books used to dispense advice on how to deal with all these details, but fortunately this is no longer necessary. That's because the computer industry is rapidly converging on the format specified by IEEE standard 754-1985 (also an international standard, IEC 559). The advantages of using a standard variant of floating point are similar to those for using floating point over other non-integer representations. In this chapter we will discuss only the IEEE version of floating point. IEEE arithmetic differs from many previous arithmetics in the following major ways:

1. When rounding a "halfway" result to the nearest floating-point number, it picks the one which is even.

2. It includes the *special values* NaN, ∞, and −∞

3. It uses *denormal* numbers to represent the result of computations whose value is less than $1.0 \times 2^{E_{min}}$.

4. It rounds to nearest by default, but also has three other rounding modes.

5. It has sophisticated facilities for handling exceptions.

To elaborate on (1), note that when operating on two floating-point numbers, the result is usually a number that cannot be exactly represented as another floating-point number. For example, in a floating-point system using base 10 and two significant digits, $6.1 \times 0.5 = 3.05$. This needs to be rounded to two digits. Should it be rounded to 3.0 or 3.1? In the IEEE standard, such halfway cases are rounded to the number whose low-order digit is even. That is, 3.05 rounds to 3.0, not 3.1. The standard actually has four *rounding modes*. The default is *round to nearest*, which rounds ties to an even number as just explained. The other modes are round toward 0, round toward +∞ and round toward −∞.

We will elaborate on the other differences in following sections. For further reading see IEEE [1985], Cody et al. [1984], and Goldberg [1991].

Special Values and Denormals

Probably the most notable feature of the standard is that by default a computation continues in the face of exceptional conditions, such as dividing by zero or taking the square root of a negative number. For example, the result of taking the square root of a negative number is a *NaN* (*Not a Number*), a bit pattern that does not represent an ordinary number. As an example of how NaNs might be useful, consider the code for a zero finder that takes a function F as an argument and evaluates F at various points to determine a zero for it. If the zero finder accidentally probes outside the valid values for F, F may well cause an exception. Writing a zero finder that deals with this case is highly language and operating-system dependent, because it relies on how the operating system reacts to exceptions and how this reaction is mapped back into the programming language. In IEEE arithmetic it is easy to write a zero finder that handles this situation and runs on many different systems. After each evaluation of F, it simply checks to see if F has returned a NaN; if so, it knows it has probed outside the domain of F.

In IEEE arithmetic, if the input to an operation is a NaN, the output is NaN (e.g. 3 + NaN = NaN). Because of this rule, writing floating-point subroutines that can accept NaN as an argument rarely requires any special case checks. For example, suppose that arccos is computed in terms of arctan, using the formula $\arccos x = 2 \arctan(\sqrt{(1-x)/(1+x)})$. If arctan handles an argument of NaN properly, arccos will automatically do so too. That's because if x is a NaN, $1 + x$, $1 - x$, $(1 + x)/(1 - x)$ and $\sqrt{(1 - x) / (1 + x)}$ will also be NaNs. No checking for NaNs is required.

While the result of $\sqrt{-1}$ is a NaN, the result of $1/0$ is not a NaN, but $+\infty$, which is another special value. The standard defines arithmetic on infinities (there is both $+\infty$ and $-\infty$) using rules such as $1/\infty = 0$. The formula arccos $x = 2 \arctan(\sqrt{(1 - x) / (1 + x)})$ illustrates how infinity arithmetic can be used. Since $\arctan x$ asymptotically approaches $\pi/2$ as x approaches ∞, it is natural to define $\arctan(\infty) = \pi/2$, in which case arccos(-1) will automatically be computed correctly as $2 \arctan(\infty) = \pi$.

The final kind of special values in the standard are *denormal* numbers. In many floating-point systems if E_{min} is the smallest exponent, a number less than $1.0 \times 2^{E_{min}}$ cannot be represented, and a floating-point operation that results in a number less than this is simply flushed to zero. In the IEEE standard, on the other hand, numbers less than $1.0 \times 2^{E_{min}}$ are represented using significands less than 1. This is called *gradual underflow*. Thus, as numbers decrease in magnitude below $2^{E_{min}}$, they gradually lose their significance and are only represented by zero when all their significance has been shifted out. For example, in base 10 with 4 significant figures, let $x = 1.234 \times 10^{E_{min}}$. Then $x/10$ will be rounded to $0.123 \times 10^{E_{min}}$, having lost a digit of precision. Similarly $x/100$ rounds to $0.012 \times 10^{E_{min}}$, and $x/1000$ to $0.001 \times 10^{E_{min}}$, while $x/10000$ is finally small enough to be rounded to zero. Denormals make dealing with small numbers more predictable by maintaining familiar properties such as $x = y \Leftrightarrow x - y = 0$. For example, in a flush-to-zero system (again in base 10 with 4 significant digits), if $x = 1.256 \times 10^{E_{min}}$, and $y = 1.234 \times 10^{E_{min}}$, then $x - y = 0.022 \times 10^{E_{min}}$, which flushes to zero. So even though $x \neq y$, the computed value of $x - y = 0$. This never happens with gradual underflow. In this example, $x - y = 0.02 \times 10^{E_{min}}$ is a denormal number, and so the computation of $x - y$ is exact.

Representation of Floating-Point Numbers

Let us consider how to represent single precision numbers in IEEE arithmetic. Single-precision numbers are stored in 32 bits: 1 for the sign, 8 for the exponent, and 23 for the fraction. The exponent is a signed number represented using the bias method (see the subsection *Signed Numbers*, page A-6) with a bias of 127. The term *biased exponent* refers to the unsigned number contained in bits one through nine and *unbiased exponent* (or just exponent) means the actual power to which two is to be raised. The fraction represents a number less than one, but the *significand* of the floating-point number is one plus the fraction part. In other words, if e is the biased exponent (value of the exponent field) and f is the value of the fraction field, the number being represented is $1.f \times 2^{e-127}$.

Example

Answer

What single-precision number does the following 32-bit word represent?

1 10000001 01000000000000000000000

Considered as an unsigned number, the exponent field is 129, making the value of the exponent $129 - 127 = 2$. The fraction part is $.01_2 = .25$, making the significand 1.25. Thus, this bit pattern represents the number $-1.25 \times 2^2 = -5$.

The fractional part of a floating-point number (.25 in the example above) must not be confused with the significand, which is one plus the fractional part. The leading 1 in the significand $1.f$ does not appear in the representation; that is, the leading bit is implicit. When performing arithmetic on IEEE format numbers, the fraction part is usually *unpacked*, which is to say the implicit one is made explicit.

Figure 38 summarizes the parameters for single (and other) precisions. It shows the range of exponents for single precision to be -126 to 127; accordingly, the biased exponent ranges from 1 to 254. The biased exponents of 0 and 255 are used to represent special values. This is summarized in Table A.8. When the biased exponent is 255, a zero fraction field represents infinity, and a nonzero fraction field represents a NaN. Thus, there is an entire family of NaNs. When the biased exponent and the fraction field are zero, then the number represented is zero. Because ordinary numbers always have a significand greater than or equal to 1—and are thus never zero—a special convention such as this is required to represent zero. Denormalized numbers are implemented by having a word with a zero exponent field represent the number $0.f \times 2^{E_{min}}$.

	Single	**Single extended**	**Double**	**Double extended**
p (bits of precision)	24	≥ 32	53	≥ 64
E_{max}	127	≥ 1023	1023	≥ 16383
E_{min}	-126	≤ -1022	-1022	≤ -16382
Exponent bias	127		1023	

FIGURE A.7   Format parameters for the IEEE 754 floating-point standard. The first row gives the number of bits in the significand. The blank boxes are unspecified parameters.

Exponent	Fraction	Represents
$e = E_{min} - 1$	$f = 0$	± 0
$e = E_{min} - 1$	$f \neq 0$	$0.f \times 2^{E_{min}}$
$E_{min} \leq e \leq E_{max}$	—	$1.f \times 2^e$
$e = E_{max} + 1$	$f = 0$	$\pm \infty$
$e = E_{max} + 1$	$f \neq 0$	NaN

FIGURE A.8   Representation of Special Values. When the exponent of a number falls outside the range $E_{min} \leq e \leq E_{max}$, then that number has a special interpretation as indicated in the table.

The primary reason why the IEEE standard, like most other floating-point formats, uses biased exponents is that it means nonnegative numbers are ordered in the same way as integers. That is, the magnitude of floating-point numbers can be compared using an integer comparator. Another (related) advantage is that zero is represented by a word of all zeros. The down side of biased exponents is that adding them is slightly awkward, because it requires that the bias be subtracted from their sum.

A.4 | Floating-Point Multiplication

The simplest floating-point operation is multiplication, so we discuss it first. A binary floating-point number x is represented as a significand and an exponent, $x = s \cdot 2^e$. The formula

$$(s_1 \cdot 2^{e_1}) \cdot (s_2 \cdot 2^{e_2}) = (s_1 \cdot s_2) \cdot 2^{e_1 + e_2}$$

shows that a floating-point multiply algorithm has several parts. The first part multiplies the significands using ordinary integer multiplication. Because floating-point numbers are stored in sign-magnitude form, the multiplier need only deal with unsigned numbers (although we have seen that Booth recoding handles signed two's complement numbers painlessly). The second part rounds the result. If the significands are unsigned p-bit numbers (e.g. $p = 24$ for single precision), then the product can have as many as $2p$ bits and must be rounded to a p-bit number. The third part computes the new exponent. Because exponents are stored with a bias, this involves subtracting the bias from the sum of the biased exponents.

Example

How does the multiplication of the single precision numbers

$$1\ \ 10000010\ \ 000...\ =\ -1\ \bullet\ 2^3$$

$$0\ \ 10000011\ \ 000...\ =\ \ \ 1\ \bullet\ 2^4$$

proceed in binary?

Answer

When unpacked, the significands are both 1.0, their product is 1.0, and so the result is of the form

$$1\ \ ????????\ \ 000...$$

To compute the exponent, use the formula

$$\text{biased exp }(e_1 + e_2) = \text{biased exp}(e_1) + \text{biased exp}(e_2) - \text{bias}$$

From Figure 38, the bias is $127 = 01111111_2$, so in two's complement -127 is 10000001_2. Thus the biased exponent of the product is

$$
\begin{array}{r}
10000010 \\
10000011 \\
+\ 10000001 \\
\hline
10000110 \\
\end{array}
$$

Since this is 134 decimal, it represents an exponent of $134 - \text{bias} = 134 - 127 = 7$, as expected.

The interesting part of floating-point multiplication is rounding. Some of the different cases that can occur are illustrated in Figure 40. Since the cases are similar in all bases, the figure uses human-friendly base 10, rather than base 2.

In the figure $p = 3$, so the final result must be rounded to three significant digits. The three most significant digits are in boldface. The fourth most significant digit (marked r) is the *round* digit.

If the round digit is less than 5, then the bold digits represent the rounded result. If the round digit is greater than 5, (as in (a)), then 1 must be added to the least significant bold digit. If the round digit is exactly 5 (as in (b)), then additional digits must be examined to decide between truncation or incrementing by one. It is only necessary to know if any digits past 5 are nonzero. In the algorithm below, this will be recorded in a *sticky bit*. Comparing (a) and (b) in the figure shows that there are two possible positions for the round digit (relative to the least significant digit of the product). Case (c) illustrates that when adding 1 to the least significant bold digit, there may be a carry-out. When this happens, the final result must be 10.0.

a)
        1.23
     $\times$ 6.78   r = 9 > 5 so round up
     08.33**94**   rounds to 8.34
          r

b)
        2.83
     $\times$ 4.47   r =5 and a following digit != 0 so round up
     12.65**01**   rounds to 1.27 $\times$ 10
          r

c)
        1.28
     $\times$ 7.81   r = 6 > 5 so round up
     09.99**68**   rounds to 1.00 $\times$ 10
          r

FIGURE A.9   Examples of rounding a multiplication. Using base 10 and $p = 3$, parts (a) and (b) illustrate that the result of a multiplication can have either $2p - 1$ or $2p$ digits, and hence the position where a 1 is added when rounding up (marked with r) can vary. Part (c) shows that rounding up can cause a carry-out.

There is a straightforward method of handling rounding using the multiplier of Figure 33 (page A-4) together with an extra sticky bit. If p is the number of bits in the significand, then the A, B, and P registers should be p bits wide. Multiply the two significands to obtain a $2p$-bit product in the (P, A) registers (see Figure 41). During the multiplication, the first $p - 2$ times a bit is shifted into the A register, OR it into the sticky bit. This will be used in halfway cases. Let s represent the sticky bit, g (for guard) the most significant bit of A, and r (for round) the second most significant bit of A. There are two cases:

1. The high-order bit of P is 0. Shift P left 1 bit, shifting in the g bit from A. Shifting the rest of A is not necessary.

2. The high-order bit of P is 1. Set $s := s \vee r$ and $r := g$, and add 1 to the exponent.

Now if $r = 0$, P is the correctly rounded product. If $r = 1$ and $s = 1$, then P + 1 is the product (where by P + 1 we mean adding 1 to the least significant bit of P). If $r = 1$ and $s = 0$, we are in a halfway case, and round up according to the least significant bit of P. As an example, apply the decimal version of these rules to Figure 40(b). After the multiplication, P = 126 and A = 501, with $g = 5$, $r = 0$, $s = 1$. Since the high order digit of P is nonzero, case (2) applies and $r := g$, so that $r = 5$, just as in Figure 40. Since $r = 5$, we could be in a halfway case, but $s = 1$ indicates that the result is in fact slightly over 1/2, so add 1 to P to obtain the correctly rounded product.

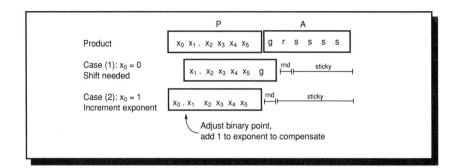

FIGURE A.10   The two cases of the floating-point multiply algorithm. The top line shows the contents of the P and A registers after multiplying the significands, with $p = 6$. In case (1), the leading bit is 0, and so the P register must be shifted. In case (2), the leading bit is 1, no shift is required, but both the exponent and the round and sticky bits must be adjusted.

The precise rules for rounding depend on the rounding mode and are given in Figure 42. Note that P is nonnegative, i.e. it contains the magnitude of the result. A good discussion of more efficient ways to implement rounding is in Santoro, Bewick, and Horowitz [1989].

Rounding mode	sign of result ≥ 0	sign of result < 0
$-\infty$		$+1$ if $r \vee s$
$+\infty$	$+1$ if $r \vee s$	
0		
Nearest	$+1$ if $r \wedge p_0$ or $r \wedge s$	$+1$ if $r \wedge p_0$ or $r \wedge s$

FIGURE A.11   Rules for implementing the IEEE rounding modes. Let S be the magnitude of the preliminary result. Blank boxes mean that the p most significant bits of S are the actual result bits. If the condition in the box is true, add 1 to the pth most significant bit of S. The symbols r and s represent the round and sticky bits, while p_0 is the pth most significant bit of S.

Example

In binary with $p = 4$, show how the multiplication algorithm computes the product $-5 \cdot 10$ in each of the four rounding modes

Answer | In binary, -5 is $-1.010_2 \times 2^2$, and $10 = 1.010_2 \times 2^3$. Applying the integer multiplication algorithm to the significands gives 01100100_2, so $P = 0110_2$, $A = 0100_2$, $g = 0$, $r = 1$, and $s = 0$. The high order bit of P is 0, so case (1) applies. Thus P becomes 1100_2, and since the result is negative, table A.10 gives

round to $-\infty$	1101_2	add 1 since $r \vee s = 1 \vee 0 = \text{TRUE}$
round to $+\infty$	1100_2	
round to 0	1100_2	
round to nearest	1100_2	no add since $r \wedge p_0 = 1 \wedge 0 = \text{FALSE}$
		$r \wedge s = 1 \wedge 0 = \text{FALSE}$

The exponent is $2 + 3 = 5$, so the result is $-1.100 \times 2^5 = -48$, except when rounding to $-\infty$, in which case it is $-1.101_2 \times 2^5 = -52$.

Overflow occurs when the rounded result is too large to be represented. In single precision, this occurs when the result has an exponent of 128 or higher. If e_1 and e_2 are the two biased exponents, then $1 \leq e_i \leq 254$, and the exponent calculation $e_1 + e_2 - 127$ gives numbers between $1 + 1 - 127$ and $254 + 254 - 127$, or between -125 and 381. This range of numbers can be represented using 9 bits. So one way to detect overflow is to perform the exponent calculations in a 9-bit adder (see exercise A.12). Remember that you must check for overflow *after* rounding, and the example in Figure 40(c) show that this can make a difference.

Denormals

Checking for underflow is somewhat more complex because of denormals. In single precision, if the result has an exponent less than -126, that does not necessarily indicate underflow, because the result might be a denormal number. For example the product of (1×2^{-64}) with (1×2^{-65}) is 1×2^{-129}, and -129 is below the legal exponent limit. But this result is a valid denormal number, namely 0.125×2^{-126}. In general, when the unbiased exponent of a product dips below -126, the resulting product must be shifted right and the exponent incremented until the exponent reaches -126. If this process causes the entire significand to be shifted out, then underflow has occurred. The precise definition of underflow is somewhat subtle—see section A.7 for details.

Denormal numbers present a major stumbling block to implementing floating-point multiplication, because they require performing a variable right shift in the multiplier, which wouldn't otherwise be needed. This right shift is required when the output is denormal, and also when one of the inputs to a multiplication is denormal, even if the product is a normalized number. Thus, high-performance, floating-point multipliers often do not handle denormalized numbers, but instead trap, letting software handle them. There are a few practical codes that frequently underflow, even when working properly, and these programs usually run quite a bit slower on systems that require denormals to be processed by a trap handler.

One procedure followed by some floating-point units is to have the multiplier deliver denormalized outputs in *wrapped* form. That is, the fraction part is normalized, and the exponent is wrapped around to a large positive number. This is exactly the result when following the multiplication algorithm for normalized numbers given above. Since the addition unit must have a barrel shifter, it is usually straightforward to provide a way to convert wrapped numbers into their correct denormalized form by passing them through the adder. However, if a trap handler has to intervene in order to send wrapped numbers into the adder, multiplication will still be slowed down substantially.

Precision of Multiplication

In the discussion of integer multiplication, we mentioned that designers must decide whether to deliver the low-order word of the product or the entire product. A similar issue arises in floating-point multiplication, where the exact product can be rounded to the precision of the operands or to the next higher precision. In the case of integer multiplication, none of the standard high-level languages contains a construct that would generate a "single times single gets double" instruction. The situation is different for floating point. Not only do many languages allow assigning the product of two single-precision variables to a double-precision one, but the construction can also be exploited by numerical algorithms. The best-known case is using iterative refinement to solve linear systems of equations.

A.5 Floating-Point Addition

Typically, a floating-point operation takes two inputs with p bits of precision, and returns a p-bit result. The ideal algorithm would compute this by first performing the operation exactly, and then rounding the result to p bits (using the current rounding mode). The multiplication algorithm presented in the previous section follows this strategy. Even though hardware implementing IEEE arithmetic must return the same result as the ideal algorithm, it doesn't need to actually perform the ideal algorithm. And in fact for addition, there are better ways to proceed. To see this, consider some examples.

First, the sum of the binary 6-bit numbers 1.10011_2 and $1.110001_2 \cdot 2^{-5}$. When the summands are shifted so they have the same exponent, this is

```
  1.10011
+  .0000110001
```

Using a 6-bit adder (and discarding the low order bits of the second addend) gives

```
    1.10011
+    .00001
    1.10100
```

The first discarded bit is 1. This isn't enough to decide whether to round up. The rest of the discarded bits, 0001 need to be examined. Or actually, we just need to record whether any of these bits are nonzero, storing this fact in a sticky bit just as in the multiplication algorithm. So for adding two p-bit numbers, a p-bit adder is sufficient, as long as the first discarded bit (round) and the OR of the rest of the bits (sticky) are kept. Then table A.10 can be used to determine if a round-up is necessary, just as with multiplication. In the example above, sticky is 1 so a round-up is necessary, the final sum being 1.10101_2.

Here's another example:

```
    1.11011
+    .0101001
```

A 6-bit adder gives

```
    1.11011
+    .01010
  10.00101
```

Because of the carry-out on the left, the round bit isn't the first discarded bit, but rather is the low order bit of the sum (1). The discarded bits, 01 are OR'ed together to make sticky. Because round and sticky are both 1, the high order 6 bits of the sum, 10.0010_2, must be rounded up for the final answer of 10.0011_2.

Next consider subtraction, and the following example.

```
    1.00000
-    .00000101111
```

The simplest way of computing this is to convert $-.0000100101_2$ to its two's complement form, so the difference becomes a sum

```
    1.00000
+  1.11111010001
```

Computing this sum in a six-bit adder gives

```
    1.00000
+  1.11111
    0.11111
```

Because the top bits canceled, the first discarded bit (the guard bit) is needed to fill in the least significant bit of the sum, which becomes 0.111110_2, and the second discarded bit becomes the round bit. This is analogous to case 1 in the multiplication algorithm. The round bit of 1 isn't enough to decide whether to round up. Instead, we need to OR all the remaining bits (0001) into a sticky bit. In this case, sticky is 1, so the final result must be rounded up to 0.111111. This example shows that if subtraction causes the most significant bit to cancel, then one guard bit is needed. It is natural to ask whether two guard bits are needed for the case when the *two* most significant bits cancel. The answer is no, because if x and y are so close that the top two bits of $x - y$ cancel, then $x - y$ will be exact, so guard bits aren't needed at all.

To summarize, addition is more complex than multiplication because, depending on the signs of the operands, it may actually be a subtraction. If it is an addition there can be carry-out on the left (second example) whereas if it is subtraction there can be cancellation (the third example) In each case, the position of the round bit is different. However, we don't need to compute the exact sum and then round, but rather can infer it from the sum of the high order p bits together with the round and sticky bits.

Here is an algorithm for adding two binary floating-point numbers a_1 and a_2. The notations e_i and s_i are used for the exponent and significand of the addends a_i. This means that the floating-point inputs have been unpacked and that s_i has an explicit leading bit.

1. If $e_1 < e_2$, swap the operands. This ensures that the difference of the exponents satisfies $d = e_1 - e_2 \geq 0$. Tentatively set the exponent of the result to e_1.

2. If the signs of a_1 and a_2 differ, replace s_2 by its two's complement.

3. Place s_2 in a p-bit register and shift it $d = e_1 - e_2$ places to the right (shifting in 1's if s_2 was complemented in previous step). From the $d - 2$ bits shifted out, set g to the most significant bit, r to the next most significant bit, and set sticky to the OR of the rest.

4. Compute a preliminary significand $S = s_1 + s_2$ by adding s_1 to the p-bit register containing s_2. If the signs of a_1 and a_2 are different, the most significant bit of S is 1, and there was no carry-out then S is negative, so replace S with its two's complement. This can only happen when $d = 0$.

5. Shift S as follows. If the signs of a_1 and a_2 are the same and there was a carry-out in step 4, shift S right by one, filling in the high order position with 1 (the carry-out). Otherwise shift it left until it is normalized. When left shifting, on the first shift fill in the low order position with the g bit, after that shift in zeros. Adjust the exponent of the result accordingly.

6. Adjust r and s. If S was shifted right in step 5, set $r :=$ low order bit of S before shifting, and $s := g$ OR r OR s. If there was no shift, set $r := g$, $s := r$ OR s. If there was a single left shift, don't change r and s. If there were two or more

left shifts, $r := 0$, $s := 0$. (In the last case, two or more shifts can only happen when a_1 and a_2 have opposite signs and the same exponent, in which case the computation $s_1 + s_2$ in step 4 will be exact).

7. Round S using Table A.10, namely if a table entry is non-empty, add 1 to the low order bit of S. If rounding causes carry-out, shift S right and adjust the exponent. This is the significand of the result.

8. Compute the sign of the result. If a_1 and a_2 have the same sign, this is the sign of the result. If a_1 and a_2 have different signs, then the sign of the result depends on which of a_1, a_2 is negative, whether there was a swap in step 1 and whether S was replaced by its two's complement in step 4. See Figure 43.

swap	compl	sgn(a_1)	sgn(a_2)	sgn(result)
yes		+	-	-
yes		-	+	+
no	no	+	-	+
no	no	-	+	-
no	yes	+	-	-
no	yes	-	+	+

FIGURE A.12 Rules for computing the sign of a sum when the addends have different signs. The *swap* column refers to swapping the operands in step 1, while the *compl* column refers to performing a two's complement in step 4. Blank boxes are "don't care".

Example

Use the algorithm to compute the sum $(-1.001_2 \cdot 2^{-2}) + (-1.111_2 \cdot 2^0)$

Answer

$s_1 = 1.001$, $e_1 = -2$, $s_2 = 1.111$, $e_2 = 0$

1. $e_1 < e_2$, so swap. $d = 2$. Tentative exp $= 0$.

2. signs of both operands negative, don't negate s_2.

3. shift s_2 (1.001 after swap) right by 2, giving $s_2 = .0100$ $g = 0$, $r = 1$, $s = 0$.

4. 1.111
   + .010
   _____
   (1)0.001 $S = 0.001$, with a carry-out.

5. carry-out, so shift S right, $S = 1.000$, exp $=$ exp $+ 1$, so exp $= 1$.

6. r = low order bit of sum = 1, $s = g \vee r \vee s = 0 \vee 1 \vee 0 = 1$.

7. r AND s = TRUE, so Figure 42 says round up, $S = S + 1$ or $S = 1.001$.

8. both signs negative, so sign of result is negative. Final answer: $-S \times 2^{\exp} = -1.001_2 \times 2^1$.

Example

Use the algorithm to compute the sum $(-1.010_2) + 1.100_2$

Answer

$s_1 = 1.010$, $e_1 = 0$, $s_2 = 1.100$, $e_2 = 0$

1. no swap, $d = 0$, tentative exp = 0

2. signs differ, replace s_2 with 0.100

3. $d = 0$, so no shift. $r = g = s = 0$.

4. $\begin{array}{r} \texttt{1.010} \\ + \texttt{0.100} \\ \hline \texttt{1.110} \end{array}$ signs are different, most sig bit is 1, no carry-out, so must two's complement sum, giving $S = 0.010$

5. shift left twice, so $S = 1.000$, exp = exp – 2, or exp = –2

6. two left shifts, so $r = g = s = 0$.

7. no addition required for rounding

8. answer is sign $\times S \times 2^{\exp}$ or sign $\times 1.000 \times 2^{-2}$. Get sign from table A.11. Since complement but no swap, and sgn(a_1) is –, the sign of sum is +. Thus answer = $1.000_2 \times 2^{-2}$.

Speeding Up Addition

Let us estimate how long it takes to perform the algorithm above. Step 2 may require an addition, step 4 requires one or two additions, and step 7 may require an addition. If it takes T time units to perform a p-bit add (where $p = 24$ for single precision, 53 for double), then it appears the algorithm will take at least $4T$ time units. But that is too pessimistic. If step 4 requires an add, then a_1 and a_2 have the same exponent and different signs. But in that case the difference is exact, and so no round-up is required in step 7. Thus only three additions will ever occur. Similarly, it appears that a variable shift may be required both in step 3 and step 5. But if $|e_1 - e_2| \leq 1$, then step 3 requires a right shift of at most one place, so only step 5 needs a variable shift. And if $|e_1 - e_2| > 1$, then step 3 needs a variable shift, but step 5 will require a left shift of at most one place. So only a single variable shift will be performed. Still, the algorithm requires three sequential adds, which in the case of a 53 bit double precision significand, can be rather time consuming. There are a number of techniques that can speed up addition. One is to use pipelining. The "Putting it All Together" section gives examples of how some commercial chips pipeline addition. Another method (used on the Intel 860 [Kohn 1989]) is to perform two additions in parallel. This is sketched next.

There are three cases to consider. First, suppose that both operands have the same sign. We want to combine the addition operations from steps 4 and 7. The position of the high-order bit of the sum is not known ahead of time, because the addition in step 4 may or may not cause a carry-out. Both possibilities are accounted for by having two adders. The first adder assumes the add in step 4 will not result in a carry-out. Thus the values of r and s can be computed before the add is actually done. If r and s indicate a round-up is necessary, the first adder will compute $S = s_1 + s_2 + 1$, where the notation +1 means adding 1 at the position of the least significant bit of s_1. This can be done with a regular adder by setting the low-order carry-in bit to 1. If r and s indicate no round-up, the adder computes $S = s_1 + s_2$ as usual. One extra detail: when $r = 1$, $s = 0$ you will also need to know the low order bit of the sum, which can also be computed in advance very quickly. The second adder covers the possibility that there will be carry-out. The values of r and s, and the position where the round-up 1 is added are different from above, but again can be quickly computed in advance. It is not known whether there will be a carry-out until after the add is actually done, but that doesn't matter. By doing both adds in parallel, one is guaranteed to have the correct answer.

The next case is when a_1 and a_2 have opposite signs, but the same exponent. The sum $a_1 + a_2$ is exact in this case (no round-up is necessary), but the sign isn't known until the add is completed. So don't compute the two's complement (which requires an add) in step 2, but instead compute $\bar{s}_1 + s_2 + 1$ and $s_1 + \bar{s}_2 + 1$ in parallel. The first sum has the result of simultaneously complementing s_1 and computing the sum, resulting in $s_2 - s_1$. The second sum computes $s_1 - s_2$. One of these will be non-negative, and hence the correct final answer. Once again, all the additions are done in one step using two adders operating in parallel.

The last case, when a_1 and a_2 have opposite signs and different exponents, is more complex. If $|e_1 - e_2| > 1$, the location of the leading bit of the difference is in one of two locations, so there are two cases just as in addition. When $|e_1 - e_2| = 1$, cancellation is possible and the leading bit could be almost anywhere. However, only if the leading bit of the difference is in the same position as the leading bit of s_1 could a round-up be necessary. So one adder assumes a roundup, the other assumes no roundup. Thus the addition of step 4 and the rounding of step 7 can be combined. However, there is still the problem of the addition in step 2! To eliminate this addition, consider the following diagram of step 4:

```
           |--- p ---|
    s1     1.xxxxxxx
    s2   -       1yyzzzzz
```

If the bits marked z are all 0, then the high order p bits of $S = s_1 - s_2$ can be computed as $s_1 + \bar{s}_2 + 1$. If at least one of the z bits is 1, use $s_1 + \bar{s}_2$. So $s_1 - s_2$ can be computed with one addition. However, we still don't know g and r for the two's complement of s_2, which are needed for rounding in step 7.

To compute $s_1 - s_2$ and get the proper g and r bits, combine steps 2 and 4 as follows. Don't complement s_2 in step 2. Extend the adder used for computing S two bits to the right (call the extended sum S'). If the preliminary sticky (computed in step 3) is 1 compute $S' = s'_1 + \bar{s}'_2$, where s'_1 has two 0 bits tacked onto the right, and s'_2 has preliminary g and r appended. If $s = 0$, compute $s'_1 + \bar{s}'_2 + 1$. Now the low two order bits of S' have the correct values of g and r (s was already computed properly in step 3). Finally, this modification can be combined with the modification that combines the addition from step 4 and 7 to provide the final result using just one addition.

There are a few more details that need to be considered, see Santaro et al [1989] and exercise A.17. Although the Santaro paper is aimed at multiplication, much of the discussion applies to addition as well. Also relevant is exercise A.19, which contains an alternate method for adding signed magnitude numbers.

Denormalized Numbers

Unlike multiplication, for addition very little changes in the above description if one of the inputs is a denormal number. There must be a test to see if the exponent field is 0. If it is, then when unpacking the significand there will not be a leading 1. By setting the biased exponent to 1 when unpacking a denormal, the algorithm works unchanged.

In order to deal with denormalized outputs, step 5 must be modified slightly. Shift S until it is normalized, or until the exponent becomes $E_{\min}$ (that is, the biased exponent becomes 1). If the exponent is $E_{\min}$, and if after rounding, the high-order bit of S is 1, then the result is a normalized number and should be packed in the usual way, by omitting the 1. If, on the other hand, the high-order bit is 0, the result is denormal, and when the result is unpacked the exponent field must be set to 0. Section A.7 discusses the exact rules for detecting underflow.

Incidentally, detecting overflow is very easy. It can only happen if step 5 involves a shift right, and if the biased exponent at that point is bumped up to 255 in single precision (or 2047 for double precision), or if this occurs after rounding.

A.6 | Division and Remainder

Iterative Division

We earlier discussed an algorithm for integer division. Converting it into a floating-point division algorithm is similar to converting the integer multiplication algorithm into floating point. The formula

$$(s_1 \bullet 2^{e_1}) / (s_2 \bullet 2^{e_2}) = (s_1/s_2) \bullet 2^{e_1-e_2}$$

show that if the divider computes s_1/s_2, then the final answer will be this quotient multiplied by $2^{e_1-e_2}$. Referring to Figure 33(b) (page A-4), the alignment of operands is slightly different from integer division. Load s_2 into b and s_1 into P. The A register is not needed to hold the operands. Then the integer algorithm for division (with the one small change of skipping the very first left shift) can be used, and the result will be of the form $q_0.q_1\cdots$. To round, simply compute two additional quotient bits (guard and round) and use the remainder as the sticky bit. The guard digit is necessary because the first quotient bit might be zero. However, since the numerator and denominator are both normalized, it is not possible for the two most significant quotient bits to be zero. This algorithm produces one quotient bit on each step.

There is a different approach to division which converges to the quotient at a quadratic rather than linear rate. An actual machine that uses this algorithm will be discussed in Section A.10. First, we will describe the two main iterative algorithms and then discuss the pros and cons of iteration compared to the direct algorithms. There is a general technique for constructing iterative algorithms, called *Newton's iteration*, shown in Figure 44. First, cast the problem in the form of finding the zero of a function. Then, starting from a guess for the zero, approximate the function by its tangent at that guess and form a new guess based on where the tangent has a zero. If x_i is a guess at a zero, then the tangent line has the equation

$$y - f(x_i) = f'(x_i)(x - x_i)$$

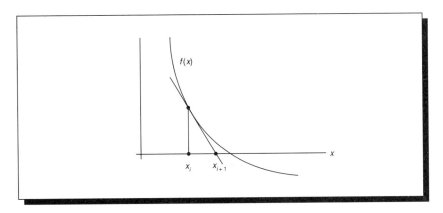

FIGURE A.13 Newton's iteration for zero finding. If xi is an estimate for a zero of f, then xi+1 is a better estimate. To compute x_{i+1}, find the intersection of the x axis with the tangent line to f at $f(x_i)$.

This equation has a zero at

A.6.1
$$x = x_{i+1} = x_i - \frac{f(x_i)}{f'(x_i)}$$

To recast division as finding the zero of a function, consider $f(x) = 1/x - b$. Since the zero of this function is at $1/b$, applying Newton's iteration to it will give an iterative method of computing $1/b$ from b. Using $f'(x) = -1/x^2$, Equation A.6.1 becomes

A.6.2
$$x_{i+1} = x_i - \frac{1/x_i - b}{-1/x_i^2} = x_i + x_i - x_i b = x_i(2 - x_i b)$$

Thus, we could implement computation of a/b using the following method:

1. Scale b to lie in the range $1 \le b < 2$ and get an approximate value of $1/b$ (call it x_0) using a table lookup.

2. Iterate $x_{i+1} = x_i(2 - x_i b)$ until reaching an x_n that is accurate enough.

3. Compute ax and reverse the scaling done in step 1.

Here are some more details. How many times will step 2 have to be iterated? To say that x_i is accurate to p bits means that $|(x_i - 1/b)/(1/b)| = 2^{-p}$, and a simple algebraic manipulation shows that when this is so, then $(x_{i+1} - 1/b)/(1/b) = 2^{-2p}$. Thus the number of correct bits doubles at each step. Newton's iteration is **self-correcting** in the sense that making an error in x_i doesn't really matter. That is, it treats x_i as a guess at $1/b$ and returns x_{i+1} as an improvement on it (roughly doubling the digits). One thing that would cause x_i to be in error is rounding error. More importantly, however, in the early iterations we can take advantage of the fact that we don't expect many correct bits by performing the multiplication in reduced precision, thus gaining speed without sacrificing accuracy. Some other applications of Newton's iteration are discussed in exercise A.20.

The second iterative division method is sometimes called *Goldschmidt's algorithm*. It is based on the idea that to compute a/b, you should multiply the numerator and denominator by a number r with $rb \approx 1$. In more detail, let $x_0 = a$ and $y_0 = b$. At each step compute $x_{i+1} = r_i x_i$ and $y_{i+1} = r_i y_i$. Then the quotient $x_{i+1}/y_{i+1} = x_i/y_i = a/b$ is constant. If we pick r_i so that $y_i \to 1$, then $x_i \to a/b$, so the x_i converge to the answer we want. This same idea can be used to compute other functions. For example, to compute the square root of a, let $x_0 = a$ and $y_0 = a$, and at each step compute $x_{i+1} = r_i^2 x_i$, $y_{i+1} = r_i y_i$. Then $x_{i+1}/y_{i+1}^2 = x_i/y_i^2 = 1/a$, so if the r_i are chosen to drive $x_i \to 1$, then $y_i \to \sqrt{a}$. This technique is used to compute square roots on the TI 8847.

Returning to Goldschmidt's division algorithm, set $x_0 = a$ and $y_0 = b$, and write $b = 1 - \delta$, where $|\delta| < 1$. If we pick $r_0 = 1 + \delta$, then $y_1 = r_0 y_0 = 1 - \delta^2$. We next pick $r_1 = 1 + \delta^2$, so that $y_2 = r_1 y_1 = 1 - \delta^4$, and so on. Since $|\delta| < 1$, $y_i \rightarrow 1$. With this choice of r_i, the x_i will be computed as $x_{i+1} = r_i x_i = (1 + \delta^{2^i})x_i = (1 + (1 - b)^{2^i})x_i$, or

A.6.3

$$x_{i+1} = a\,[1 + (1 - b)]\,[1 + (1 - b)^2]\,[1 + (1 - b)^4] \cdots [1 + (1 - b)^{2^i}]$$

There appear to be two problems with this algorithm. First, convergence is slow when b is not near 1 (that is, δ is not near 0); and second, the formula isn't self-correcting—since the quotient is being computed as a product of independent terms, error in one of them won't get corrected. To deal with slow convergence, if you want to compute a/b, look up an approximate inverse to b (call it b'), and run the algorithm on ab'/bb'. This will converge rapidly since $bb' \approx 1$.

To deal with the self-correction problem, the computation should be run with a few bits of extra precision to compensate for rounding errors. However, Goldschmidt's algorithm does have a weak form of self-correction, in that the precise value of the r_i does not matter. Thus, in the first few iterations, you can choose r_i to be a truncation of $1 + \delta^{2^i}$ which may make these iterations run faster without affecting the speed of convergence. If r_i is truncated, then y_i is no longer exactly $1 - \delta^{2^i}$, so Equation A.6.3 can no longer be used, but it is easy to organize the computation so that it does not depend on the precise value of r_i. With these changes, Goldschmidt's algorithm is as follows (the notes in brackets show the connection with our earlier formulas).

1. Scale a and b so that $1 \le b < 2$.

2. Look up an approximation to $1/b$ (call it b') in a table.

3. Set $x_0 = ab'$ and $y_0 = bb'$.

4. Iterate until x_i is close enough to a/b :

   $r \approx 2 - y$ [if $y_i = 1 + \delta_i$, then $r \approx 1 - \delta_i$]

   $y = y \times r$ [$y_{i+1} = y_i \times r \approx 1 - \delta_i^2$]

   $x_{i+1} = x_i \times r$ [$x_{i+1} = x_i \times r$]

The two iteration methods are related. Suppose in Newton's method that we unroll the iteration and compute each term x_{i+1} directly in terms of b, instead of recursively in terms of x_i. By carrying out this calculation, we discover that (see problem A.22)

$$x_{i+1} = x_0(2 - x_0 b)\,[(1 + (x_0 b - 1)^2]\,[1 + (x_0 b - 1)^4] \ldots [1 + (x_0 b - 1)^{2^i}]$$

This formula is of a very similar form to Equation A.6.3. In fact they are identical if a, b in A.6.3 are replaced with ax_0, bx_0 and $a = 1$. Thus if the iterations were done to infinite precision, the two methods would yield exactly the same sequence x.

The advantage of iteration is that it doesn't require special divide hardware, but can instead use the multiplier (which, however, requires extra control). Further, on each step, it delivers twice as many digits as in the previous step—unlike ordinary division, which produces a fixed number of digits at every step. There are two disadvantages with inverting by iteration. The first is that the IEEE standard requires division to be correctly rounded, but iteration only delivers a result that is close to the correctly rounded answer. In the case of Newton's iteration, which computes $1/b$ instead of a/b directly, there is an additional problem. Even if $1/b$ was correctly rounded, there is no guarantee that a/b will be. An example in decimal with $p = 2$. is $a = 13$, $b = 51$. Then $a/b = .2549...$ which rounds to $.25$. But $1/b = .0196...$ which rounds to $.020$, and then $a \times .020 = .26$, which is off by one. The second disadvantage is that iteration does not give a remainder. This is especially troublesome if the floating-point divide hardware is being used to perform integer division, since a remainder operation is present in almost every high-level language.

Traditional folklore has held that the way to get a correctly rounded result from iteration is to compute $1/b$ to slightly more than $2p$ bits, compute a/b to slightly more than $2p$ bits, and then round to p bits. However, there is a faster way, which apparently was first implemented on the TI 8847. In this method, a/b is computed to about six extra bits of precision, giving a preliminary quotient q. By comparing qb with a (again with only six extra bits), it is possible to quickly decide whether q is correctly rounded or whether it needs to be bumped up or down by 1 in the least significant place. This algorithm is explored further in exercise A.21.

One factor to take into account when deciding on division algorithms is the relative speed of division and multiplication. Since division is more complex than multiplication, it will run more slowly. A common rule of thumb is that division algorithms should try to achieve a speed that is about one-third that of multiplication. One argument in favor of this rule is that there are real programs (such as some versions of Spice) where the ratio of division to multiplication is 1:3. Another place where a factor of three arises is in the standard iterative method for computing square root. This method involves one division per iteration, but can be replaced by one using three multiplications. This is discussed in exercise A.20.

Floating-Point Remainder

For nonnegative integers, integer division and remainder satisfy

$$a = (a\ \text{DIV}\ b)b + a\ \text{REM}\ b,\ \ 0 \le a\ \text{REM}\ b < b$$

A floating-point remainder x REM y can be similarly defined as $x = \text{INT}(x/y)y + x$ REM y. How should x/y be converted to an integer? The IEEE remainder function uses the round-to-even rule. That is, pick $n = \text{INT}(x/y)$ so that $|x/y - n| \le 1/2$. If two different n satisfy this relation, pick the even one. Then REM is defined to be $x - yn$. Unlike integers where $0 \le a$ REM $b < b$, for floating-point numbers $|x$ REM

$y| \leq y/2$. Although this defines REM precisely, it is not a practical operational definition, because n can be huge. In single precision, n could be as large as $2/2 = 2 \approx 10$.

There is a natural way to compute REM if a direct division algorithm is used. Proceed as if you were computing x/y. If $x = s_1 2^{e_1}$ and $y = s_2 2^{e_2}$ and the divider is as in Figure 33(b) (page A-4), then load s_1 into P and s_2 into B. After $e_1 - e_2$ division steps, the P register will hold a number r of the form $x - yn$ satisfying $0 \leq r < y$. The IEEE remainder is then either r or $r - y$. It is only necessary to keep track of the last quotient bit produced, which is needed in order to resolve halfway cases. Unfortunately, $e_1 - e_2$ can be a lot of steps, and floating-point units typically have a maximum amount of time they are allowed to spend on one instruction. Thus, it is usually not possible to implement REM directly. None of the chips discussed in Section A.10 implement REM, but they could by providing a remainder-step instruction—this is what is done on the Intel 8087 family. A remainder step takes as arguments two numbers x and y, and performs divide steps until either the remainder is in P, or else n steps have been performed, where n is a small number, such as the number of steps required for division in the highest supported precision. The REM driver calls the REM-step instruction $\lfloor (e_1 - e_2)/n \rfloor$ times, initially using x as the numerator, but then replacing it with the remainder from the previous REM step.

One place that REM can be used is for computing trigonometric functions. To simplify things, imagine that we are working in base 10 with 5 significant figures, and consider computing $\sin x$. Suppose that $x = 7$. Then we can reduce by $\pi = 3.1416$ and compute $\sin(7) = \sin(7 - 2 \times 3.1416) = \sin(0.7168)$ instead. But suppose we want to compute $\sin(2.0 \times 10^5)$. Then $2 \times 10^5 / 3.1416 = 63661.8$, which in our 5-place system comes out to be 63662. Since multiplying 3.1416 times 63662 gives 200000.5392, which rounds to 2.0000×10^5, argument reduction reduces 2×10^5 to 0, which is not even close to being correct. The problem is that our 5-place system does not have the precision to do correct argument reduction. Suppose we had the REM operator. Then we could compute 2×10^5 REM 3.1416 and get $-.5392$. However, this is still not correct because we used 3.1416, which is an approximation for π. The value of 2×10^5 REM π is $-.071513$.

Traditionally, there have been two approaches to computing periodic functions with large arguments. The first is to return an error for their value when x is large. The second is to store π to a very large number of places and do exact argument reduction. The REM operator is not much help in either of these situations. There is a third approach that has been used in some math libraries, such as the Berkeley UNIX 4.3bsd release. In these libraries, π is computed to the nearest floating-point number. Let's call this machine π, and denote it by π'. Then when computing $\sin x$, reduce x using x REM π'. As we saw in the above example, x REM π' is quite different from x REM π when x is large, so that computing $\sin x$ as $\sin(x \, \text{REM} \, \pi')$ will not give the exact value of $\sin x$. However, computing trigonometric functions in this fashion has the property that all familiar identities (such as $\sin^2 x + \cos^2 x = 1$) are true to within a few rounding errors. Thus, using REM together with machine $\pi'p$ provides a simple method of computing trigonometric functions that is accurate for small arguments and still may be useful for large arguments.

When REM is used for argument reduction, it is very handy if it also returns the low order bits of n (where x REM $y = x - ny$). This is because a practical implementation will reduce by something smaller than 2π. For example, it might use $\pi/2$, exploiting identities such as $\sin(x - \pi/2) = -\cos x$, $\sin(x - \pi) = -\sin x$. Then the low bits of n are needed to choose the correct identity.

A.7 | More on Floating-Point Arithmetic

Fused Multiply-Add

Probably the most common use of floating-point units is to perform matrix operations, and the most frequent matrix operation is the multiplication of a matrix times a matrix (or vector), which boils down to computing an inner product, $x_1 \cdot y_1 + x_2 \cdot y_2 + \ldots + x_n \cdot y_n$. Computing this requires a series of multiply-add combinations.

Motivated by this, the IBM RS/6000 introduced a single instruction that computes $ab + c$, the *fused multiply-add*. Although this requires being able to read three operands in a single instructions, it has the potential for improving the performance of computing inner products.

The fused multiply-add computes $ab + c$ exactly and then rounds. Although rounding only once increases the accuracy of inner products somewhat, that is not its primary motivation. There are two main advantages of rounding once. First, as we saw in the previous sections, rounding is expensive to implement because it may require an addition. By rounding only once, an addition operation has been eliminated. Second, the extra accuracy of fused multiply-add can be used to compute correctly rounded division and square root when these are not available directly in hardware. Fused multiply-add can also be used to implement efficient multiple floating-point precision packages.

The implementation of division using fused multiply-add has many details, but the main idea is simple. Consider again the example from section A.6 (page A-28), which was computing a/b with $a = 13$, $b = 51$. Then $1/b$ rounds to $b' = .020$, and ab' rounds to $q' = .26$, which is not the correctly rounded quotient. Applying fused multiply-add twice will correctly adjust the result, via the formulas

$$r = a - bq'$$
$$q'' = q' + rb'$$

Computing to two digits accuracy, $bq' = 51 \times .26$ rounds to 13, and so $r = a - bq'$ would be zero, giving no adjustment. But using fused multiply-add gives $r = a -$

$bq' = 13 - 51 \times .26 = -.26$, and then $q'' = q' + rb' = .26 - .0052 = .2548$ which rounds to the correct quotient, .25. More details can be found in the papers [Montoye 1990] and [Markstein 1990].

Precisions

The standard specifies four precisions: *single*, *single extended*, *double*, and *double extended*. The properties of these precisions are summarized in Figure 38 (page A-16). Implementations are not required to have all four precisions, but are encouraged to support either the combination of single and single extended or all of single, double, and double extended. Because of the widespread use of double precision in scientific computing, double precision is almost always implemented. Thus the computer designer usually only has to decide whether to support double extended, and if so, how many bits it should have.

The Motorola 68882 and Intel 387 coprocessors implement extended precision using the smallest allowable size of 80 bits (64 bits of significand). However, most of the more recently designed, high-performance floating-point chips do not implement 80-bit extended precision. One reason is that the 80-bit width of extended precision is awkward for 64-bit buses and registers. Some new architectures, such as SPARC V8 and PA-RISC specify a 128 bit extended (or *quad*) precision. They have established a *de facto* convention for quad which has 15 bits of exponent and 113 bits of significand.

Although most high level language do not provide access to extended precision, it is very useful to writers of mathematical software. As an example, consider writing a library routine to compute the length of a vector in the plane $\sqrt{x^2 + y^2}$. If x is larger than $2^{E_{max}/2}$, then computing this in the obvious way will overflow. This means that either the allowable exponent range for this subroutine will be cut in half, or a more complex algorithm using scaling will have to be employed. But if extended precision is available, then the simple algorithm will work. Computing the length of a vector is a simple task, and it is not difficult to come up with an algorithm that doesn't overflow. However, there are more complex problems for which extended precision means the difference between a simple, fast algorithm and a much more complex one. One of the best examples of this is binary/decimal conversion. An efficient algorithm for binary-to-decimal conversion that makes essential use of extended precision is very readably presented in Coonen [1984]. This algorithm is also briefly sketched in Goldberg [1991]. Computing accurate values for transcendental functions is another example of a problem that is made much easier if extended precision is present.

One very important fact about precision concerns *double rounding*. To illustrate in decimal, suppose that we want to compute 1.9×0.66, and that single precision is two digits, while extended precision is three digits. The exact result of the product is 1.254. Rounded to extended precision, the result is 1.25. When further rounded to single precision, we get 1.2. However, the result of 1.9×0.66 correctly rounded to single precision is 1.3. Thus, rounding twice may not produce the same result as rounding once. Suppose you want to build hardware that only does double-precision arithmetic. Can you simulate single precision by computing first in double precision and then rounding to single? The above example suggests that you can't. However, double rounding is not always dangerous. In fact, the following rule is true (this is not easy to prove, but see exercise A.25).

> *If x and y have p-bit significands, and $x + y$ is computed exactly and then rounded to q places, a second rounding to p places will not change the answer if $p \leq (q - 1)/2$. This is true not only for addition, but also for multiplication, division, and square root.*

In our example above, $q = 3$, and $p = 2$, so $2 \leq (3 - 1)/2$ is not true. On the other hand, for IEEE arithmetic, double precision has $p = 53$, and single precision is $p = 24 \leq (q - 1)/2 = 26$. Thus, single precision can be implemented by computing in double precision (that is, computing the answer exactly and then rounding to double) and then rounding to single precision.

Exceptions

The IEEE standard defines five exceptions: underflow, overflow, divide by zero, inexact, and invalid. By default, when these exceptions occur, they merely set a flag and the computation continues. The flags are *sticky*, meaning that once set they remain set until explicitly cleared. The standard strongly encourages implementations to provide a trap-enable bit for each exception. When an exception with an enabled trap handler occurs, a user trap handler is called, and the value of the associated exception flag is undefined. In section A.3 we mentioned that $\sqrt{-3}$ has the value NaN and 1/0 is ∞. These are examples of operations that raise an exception. By default computing $\sqrt{-3}$ sets the invalid flag and returns the value NaN. Similarly 1/0 sets the divide-by-zero flag and returns ∞.

The underflow, overflow, and divide-by-zero exceptions are found in most other systems. The *invalid exception* is for things like $\sqrt{-1}$, 0/0 or $\infty - \infty$, which don't have any natural value as a floating-point number or as $\pm\infty$. The *inexact exception* is peculiar to IEEE arithmetic and occurs when either the result of an operation must be rounded or when it overflows. In fact, since 1/0 and an operation that overflows both deliver ∞, the exception flags must be consulted to distinguish between them. The inexact exception is an unusual "exception," in that it is not really an exceptional condition because it occurs so frequently. Thus, enabling a trap handler for inexact will most likely have a severe impact on performance. Enabling a trap handler doesn't affect whether an operation is exceptional except in the case of underflow. This is discussed below.

The IEEE standard assumes that when a trap occurs, it is possible to identify the operation that trapped and its operands. On machines with pipelining, or machines with multiple arithmetic units, when an exception occurs, it may not be enough to simply have the trap handler examine the program counter. Hardware support may be necessary in order to identify exactly which operation trapped. Another problem is illustrated by the following program fragment.

```
r1 = r2 / r3
r2 = r4 + r5
```

These two instructions might well be executed in parallel. If the divide traps, its argument r2 could already have been overwritten by the addition, especially since addition is almost always faster than division. Computer systems that support trapping in the IEEE standard must provide some way to save the value of r2, either in hardware or by having the compiler avoid such a situation in the first place. This kind of problem is not peculiar to floating-point. In the sequence

```
r1 = 0(r2)
r2 = r3
```

it would be efficient to execute r2=r3 while waiting for memory. But if accessing 0(r2) causes a page fault, r2 might no longer be available for restarting the instruction r1=0(r2).

One approach to this problem, used in the MIPS R3010, is to identify instructions that may cause an exception early in the instruction cycle. For example, an addition can overflow only if one of the operands has an exponent of E_{max}, and so on. This early check is conservative: It might flag an operation that doesn't actually cause an exception. However, if such false positives are rare, then this technique will have excellent performance. When an instruction is tagged as being possibly exceptional, special code in a trap handler can compute it without destroying any state. Remember that all these problems occur only when trap handlers are enabled. Otherwise, setting the exception flags during normal processing is straightforward.

Underflow

We have alluded several times to the fact that detection of underflow is more complex than for the other exceptions. The IEEE standard specifies that if user trap handlers are enabled, the system must trap if the result is denormal. On the other hand, if trap handlers are disabled, then the underflow flag is set only if there is a loss of accuracy—that is, if the result must be rounded. The rationale for this is that if no accuracy is lost on an underflow, there is no point in setting a warning flag. But if a trap handler is enabled, the user might be trying to simulate flush-to-zero and should therefore be notified whenever a result dips below $1.0 \times 2^{E_{min}}$.

So if there is no trap handler, the underflow exception is signaled only when the result is denormal and inexact. But the definition of denormal and inexact are both subject to multiple interpretations. First consider inexact. Normally, inexact means there was a result that couldn't be represented exactly and had to be rounded. Consider the example (in a base 2 floating-point system with 3-bit significands) of $(1.11_2 \times 2^{-2}) \times (1.11_2 \times 2^{E\text{min}}) = 0.110001_2 \times 2^{E\text{min}}$, with round to nearest in effect. The delivered result is $0.11_2 \times 2^{E\text{min}}$, which had to be rounded, causing inexact to be signaled. But is it correct to also signal underflow? Gradual underflow loses significance because the exponent range is bounded. If the exponent range were unbounded, the delivered result would be $1.10_2 \times 2^{E\text{min}-1}$, exactly the same answer obtained with gradual underflow. The fact that denormalized numbers have fewer bits in their significand than normalized numbers therefore doesn't make any difference in this case. The commentary to the standard [Cody et al. 1984] encourages this as the criterion for setting the underflow flag. That is, it should be set whenever the delivered result is different from what would be delivered in a system with the same fraction size, but with a very large exponent range. However, owing to the difficulty of implementing this scheme, the standard allows setting the underflow flag whenever the result is denormal and different from the infinitely precise result

There are also two possible definitions of what is means for a result to be denormal. Consider the example of $1.11_2 \times 2^{-2}$ multiplied by $1.11_2 \times 2^{E\text{min}}$. The exact product is $0.110001_2 \times 2^{E\text{min}}$. If the rounding mode is round toward plus infinity, the rounded result is the normal number $1.00_2 \times 2^{E\text{min}}$. Should underflow be signaled? Signaling underflow means that one is using the *before rounding* rule, because the result was denormal before rounding. Not signaling underflow means that one is using the *after rounding* rule, because the result is normalized after rounding. The IEEE standard provides for choosing either rule; however, the one chosen must be used consistently for all operations.

To illustrate these rules, consider floating-point addition. When the result of an addition (or subtraction) is denormal, it is always exact. Thus the underflow flag never needs to be set for addition. That's because if traps are not enabled, then no exception is raised. And if traps are enabled, the value of the underflow flag is undefined, so again it doesn't need to be set.

There is one final subtlety that should be mentioned concerning underflow. When there is no underflow trap handler, the result of an operation on p-bit numbers that causes an underflow is a denormal number with $p - 1$ or fewer bits of precision. When traps are enabled, the trap handler is provided with the result of the operation rounded to p bits and with the exponent wrapped around. Now there is a potential double-rounding problem. If the trap handler wants to return the denormal result, it can't just round its argument, because that might lead to a double-rounding error. Thus, the trap handler must be passed at least one extra bit of information if it is to be able to deliver the correctly rounded result.

A.8 | Speeding Up Integer Addition

The previous section showed that there are many steps that go into implementing floating-point operations. However, each floating-point operation eventually reduces to an integer operation. Thus, increasing the speed of integer operations will also lead to faster floating point.

Integer addition is the simplest operation and the most important. Even for programs that don't do explicit arithmetic, addition must be performed to increment the program counter and to do address calculations. Despite the simplicity of addition, there isn't a single best way to perform high-speed addition. We will discuss three techniques that are in current use: carry lookahead, carry skip, and carry select.

Carry Lookahead

An n-bit adder is just a combinational circuit. It can therefore be written by a logic formula whose form is a sum of products and can be computed by a circuit with two levels of logic. How does one figure out what this circuit looks like? From Equation A.2.1 the formula for the ith sum can be written as

A.8.1
$$s_i = a_i + b_i + c_i + a_i b_i c_i$$

where c_i is both the carry-in to the i-th adder and the carry-out from the $(i-1)$-st adder.

The problem with this formula is that although we know the values of a_i and b_i—they are inputs to the circuit—we don't know c_i. So our goal is to write c_i in terms of a_i and b_i. To accomplish this, we first rewrite Equation A.2.2 (page A-2) as

A.8.2
$$c_i = g_{i-1} + p_{i-1}c_{i-1}, \quad g_{i-1} = a_{i-1}b_{i-1}, \quad p_{i-1} = a_{i-1} + b_{i-1}$$

Here is the reason for the symbols p and g: If g_{i-1} is true, then c_i is certainly true, so a carry is *generated*. Thus, g is for generate. If p_{i-1} is true, then if c_{i-1} is true, it is *propagated* to c_i. Start with Equation A.8.1 and use Equation A.8.2 to replace c_i with $g_{i-1} + p_{i-1}c_{i-1}$. Then, use Equation A.8.2 with $i-1$ in place of i, to replace c_{i-1} with c_{i-2}, and so on. This gives the result

A.8.3
$$c_{i+1} = g_i + p_i g_{i-1} + p_i p_{i-1} g_{i-2} + \cdots + p_i p_{i-1} \cdots p_1 g_0 + p_i p_{i-1} \cdots p_1 p_0 c_0$$

An adder that computes carries using Equation A.8.3 is called a *carry-lookahead adder,* or CLA adder. A CLA adder requires one logic level to form p and g, two levels to form the carries, and two for the sum, for a grand total of five logic levels. This is a vast improvement over the $2n$ levels required for the ripple-carry adder.

Unfortunately, as is evident from Equation A.8.3 or from Figure 45, a carry-lookahead adder on n bits requires a fan-in of $n + 1$ at the OR gate as well as at the rightmost AND gate. Also, the p_{n-1} signal must drive n AND gates. In addition, the rather irregular structure and many long wires of Figure 45 make it impractical to build a full carry-lookahead adder when n is large.

However, we can use the carry-lookahead idea to build an adder that has about $\log_2 n$ logic levels (substantially less than the $2n$ required by a ripple-carry adder), and yet has a simple, regular structure. The idea is to build up the p's and g's in steps. We have already seen that

$$c_1 = g_0 + c_0 p_0$$

This says there is a carry-out of the 0th position (c_1) if there is either a carry generated in the 0th position, or if there is a carry into the 0th position and the carry propagates. Similarly,

$$c_2 = G_{01} + P_{01} c_0$$

G_{01} means there is a carry generated out of the block consisting of the first two bits. P_{01} means that a carry propagates through this block. P and G have the following logic equations:

$$G_{01} = g_1 + p_1 g_0$$

$$P_{01} = p_1 p_0$$

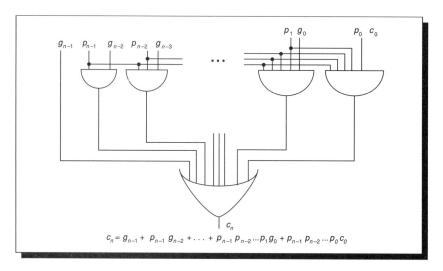

FIGURE A.14   Pure carry-lookahead circuit for computing the carry-out cn of an n-bit adder.

More generally, for any j with $i < j$, $j + 1 < k$, we have the recursive relations

A.8.4
$$c_{k+1} = G_{ik} + P_{ik}c_i$$

A.8.5
$$G_{ik} = G_{j+1,k} + P_{j+1,k}G_{ij}$$

A.8.6
$$P_{ik} = P_{ij}P_{j+1,k}$$

Equation A.8.5 says that a carry is generated out of the block consisting of bits i through k inclusive if it is generated in the high-order part of the block $(j+1, k)$ or if it is generated in the low-order (i,j) part of the block and then propagated through the high part. These equations will also hold for $i \leq j < k$ if we set $G_{ii} = g_i$ and $P_{ii} = p_i$.

Example

Express P_{03} and G_{03} in terms of p's and g's.

Answer

Using A.8.6, $P_{03} = P_{01}P_{23} = P_{00}P_{11}P_{22}P_{33}$. Since $P_{ii} = p_i$, $P_{03} = p_0p_1p_2p_3$. For G_{03}, Equation A.8.5 says $G_{03} = G_{23} + P_{23}G_{01} = (G_{33} + P_{33}G_{22}) + (P_{22}P_{33})(G_{11} + P_{11}G_{00}) = g_3 + p_3g_2 + p_3p_2g_1 + p_3p_2p_1g_0$.

With these preliminaries out of the way, we can now show the design of a practical CLA adder. The adder consists of two parts. The first part computes various values of P and G from p_i and g_i, using Equations A.8.5 and A.8.6; the second part uses these P and G values to compute all the carries via Equation A.8.4. The first part of the design is in Figure 46. At the top of the diagram, input numbers $a_7 \cdots a_0$ and $b_7 \cdots b_0$ are converted to p's and g's using cells of type 1. Then various P's and G's are generated by combining cells of type 2 in a binary-tree structure. The second part of the design is shown in Figure 47. By feeding c_0 in at the bottom of this tree, all the carry bits come out the top. Each cell must know a pair of (P,G) values in order to do the conversion, and the value it needs is written inside the cells. Now compare Figure 46 and Figure 47. There is a one-to-one correspondence between cells, and the value of (P,G) needed by the carry-generating cells is exactly the value known by the corresponding (P,G) generating cells. The combined cell is shown in Figure 48. The numbers to be added flow into the top and downward through the tree, combining with c_0 at the bottom and flowing back up the tree to form the carries. Note that there is one thing missing from Figure 48: a small piece of extra logic to compute c_8 for the carry-out of the adder.

The bits in a CLA must pass through about $\log_2 n$ logic levels, compared with $2n$ for a ripple-carry adder. This is a substantial speed improvement, especially for a large n. Whereas the ripple-carry adder had n cells, however, the CLA adder has $2n$ cells, although in our layout they will take $n \log n$ space. The point is that a small investment in size pays off in a dramatic improvement in speed.

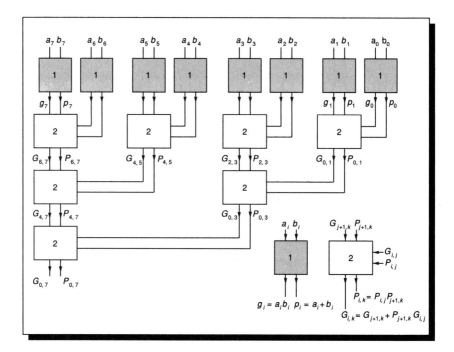

FIGURE A.15   First part of carry-lookahead tree. As signals flow from the top to the bottom, various values of P and G are computed.

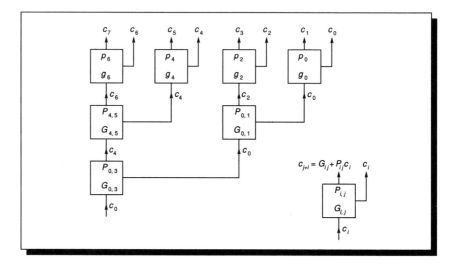

FIGURE A.16   Second part of carry-lookahead tree. Signals flow from the bottom to the top, combining with P and G to form the carries.

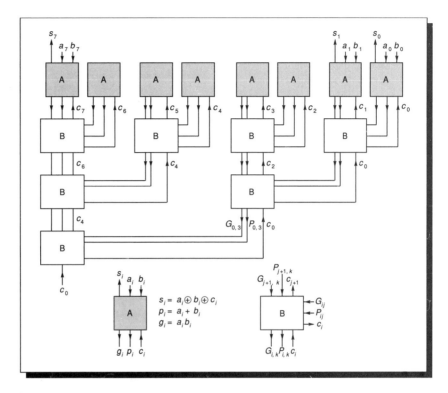

FIGURE A.17 Complete carry-lookahead tree adder. This is the combination of Figures 46 and 47. The numbers to be added enter at the top, flow to the bottom to combine with c_0, and then flow back up to compute the sum bits.

There are a number of technology-dependent modifications that can improve CLA adders. For example, if each node of the tree has three inputs instead of two, then the height of the tree will decrease from $\log_2 n$ to $\log_3 n$. Of course, the cells will be more complex and thus might operate more slowly, negating the advantage of the decreased height. For technologies where rippling works well, a hybrid design might be better. This is illustrated in Figure 49. Carries ripple between adders at the top level, while the "B" boxes are the same as in Figure 48. This design will be faster if the time to ripple between four adders is faster than the time it takes to traverse a level of "B" boxes.

Carry-Skip Adders

A *carry-skip adder* sits midway between a ripple-carry adder and a carry-lookahead adder, both in terms of speed and cost. (A carry-skip adder is not called a CSA, as that name is reserved for carry-save adders.) The motivation for this adder comes from examining the equations for P and G. For example,

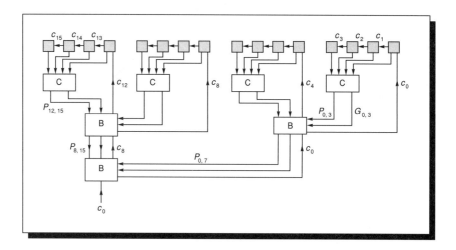

FIGURE A.18   Combination of CLA adder and ripple-carry adder. In the top row, carries ripple within each group of four boxes.

$$P_{03} \;=\; p_0 p_1 p_2 p_3$$

$$G_{03} \;=\; g_3 + p_3 g_2 + p_3 p_2 g_1 + p_3 p_2 p_1 g_0$$

Computing P is much simpler than computing G, and a carry-skip adder only computes the P's. Such an adder is illustrated in Figure 50. Carries begin rippling simultaneously through each block. If any block generates a carry, then the carry-out of a block will be true, even though the carry-in to the block may not be correct yet. If at the start of each add operation the carry-in to each block is zero, then no spurious carry-outs will be generated. Thus, the carry-out of each block can thus be thought of as if it were the G signal. Once the carry-out from the least significant block is generated, it not only feeds into the next block, but is also fed through the AND gate with the P signal from that next block. If the carry-out and P signals are both true, then the carry **skips** the second block and is ready to feed into the third block, and so on. The carry-skip adder is only practical if the carry-in signals can be easily cleared at the start of each operation—for example by precharging in CMOS.

To analyze the speed of a carry-skip adder, let's assume that it takes one time unit for a signal to pass through two logic levels. Then it will take k time units for a carry to ripple across a block of size $k,$ and it will take one time unit for a carry to skip a block. The longest signal path in the carry-skip adder starts with a carry being generated at the 0th position. Then it takes k time units to ripple through the first block, $n/k - 2$ time units to skip blocks, and k more to ripple through the last block. To be specific: If we have a 20-bit adder broken into groups of 4 bits, it will take $4 + (20/4 - 2) + 4 = 11$ time units to perform an add. Some experimentation reveals that there are more efficient ways to divide 20 bits into blocks. For example consider five blocks with the least significant 2 bits in the first block, the next 6 bits in the second block, followed by blocks of size 5, 4, and 3. Then the add time is reduced to 8 time units. This illustrates an important general principle. For a carry-skip adder, making the interior blocks larger will speed up the adder. In fact, the same idea of varying the block sizes can sometimes speed up other adder designs as well. Because of the large amount of rippling, a carry-skip adder is most appropriate for technologies where rippling is fast

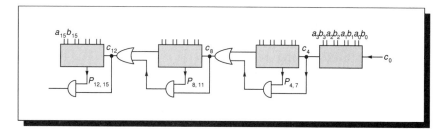

FIGURE A.19   Carry-skip adder.

Carry-Select Adder

A *carry-select adder* works on the following principle: Two additions are performed in parallel, one assuming the carry-in is zero and the other assuming the carry-in is one. When the carry-in is finally known, the correct sum (which has been precomputed) is simply selected. An example of such a design is shown in Figure 51. An 8-bit adder is divided into two halves, and the carry-out from the lower half is used to select the sum bits from the upper half. If each block is computing its sum using rippling (a linear-time algorithm), then the design in Figure 51 is twice as fast at 50% more cost. However, note that the c_4 signal must drive many muxes, which may be very slow in some technologies. Instead of dividing the adder into halves, it could be divided into quarters for a still further speedup. This is illustrated in Figure 52. If it takes k time units for a block to add k-bit numbers, and if it takes one time unit to compute the mux input from the two carry-out signals, then for optimal operation each block should be one bit wider than the next, as shown in Figure 52. Therefore, as in the carry-skip adder, the best design involves variable-sized blocks.

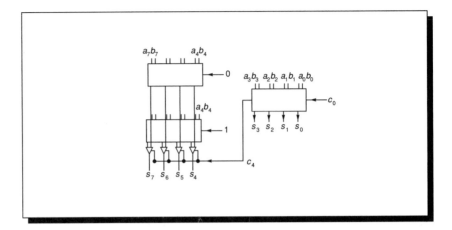

FIGURE A.20   Simple carry-select adder. At the same time that the sum of the low-order four bits are being computed, the high-order bits are being computed twice in parallel: once assuming that $c_4 = 0$, and once assuming $c_4 = 1$.

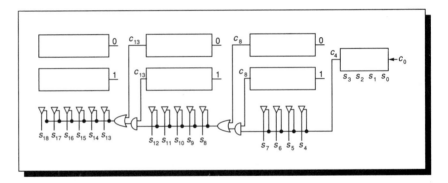

FIGURE A.21   Carry-select adder. As soon as the carry-out of the rightmost block is known, it is used to select the other sum bits.

	Time	**Space**
Ripple	$O(n)$	$O(n)$
CLA	$O(\log n)$	$O(n \log n)$
Carry skip	$O(\sqrt{n})$	$O(n)$
Carry select	$O(\sqrt{n})$	$O(n)$

FIGURE A.22   Asymptotic time and space requirements for four different types of adders.

As a summary of this section, the asymptotic time and space requirements for the different adders are given in Figure 53 (see problem A.27). These different adders shouldn't be thought of as disjoint choices, but rather as building blocks to be used in constructing an adder. The utility of these different building blocks is highly dependent on the technology used. For example, the carry-select adder works well when a signal can drive many muxes, and the carry-skip adder is attractive in technologies where signals can be cleared at the start of each operation. Knowing the asymptotic behavior of adders is useful in understanding them, but relying too much on that behavior is a pitfall. The reason is that asymptotic behavior is only important as n grows very large. But n for an adder is the bits of precision, and double precision today is the same as it was twenty years ago—about 53 bits. Although it is true that as computers get faster, computations get longer—and thus have more rounding error, which in turn requires more precision—this effect grows very slowly with time.

A.9 | Speeding Up Integer Multiplication and Division

The multiplication and division algorithms presented in Section A.2 are fairly slow, producing one bit per cycle (although that cycle might be a fraction of the CPU instruction cycle time). In this section we discuss various techniques for higher performance multiplication and division.

Shifting Over Zeros

Shifting over zeros is a technique that is not currently used much, but is instructive to consider. It is distinguished by the fact that its execution time is operand dependent. Its lack of use is primarily attributable to its failure to offer enough speedup over bit-at-a-time algorithms. In addition, pipelining, synchronization with the CPU, and good compiler optimization are difficult with algorithms that run in variable time. In multiplication, the idea behind shifting over zeros is to add logic that detects when the low-order bit of the A register is zero (see Figure 33(a)) and, if so, skip the addition step and proceed directly to the shift step—hence the term *shifting over zeros*. This technique becomes more useful if the number of zeros in the A operand can be increased.

What about shifting for division? In nonrestoring division, an ALU operation (either an addition or subtraction) is performed at every step, so that there appears to be no opportunity for skipping an operation. But think about division this way: To compute a/b, subtract multiples of b from a, and then report how many subtractions were done. At each stage of the subtraction process the remainder must fit into the P register of Figure 33(b) (page A-4). In the case when the remainder is a small positive number, you normally subtract b; but suppose instead you only shifted the remainder and subtracted b the next time. As long as the remainder was sufficiently small (its high-order bit 0), after shifting it still would fit into the p register, and no information would be lost. However, this method does require changing the way we keep track of the number of times b has been subtracted from a. This idea usually goes under the name of *SRT division*, for Sweeney, Robertson, and Tocher, who independently proposed algorithms of this nature. The main extra complication of SRT division is that the quotient bits cannot be determined immediately from the sign of p at each step, as it can be in ordinary nonrestoring division.

More precisely, to divide a by b where a and b are n-bit numbers, load a and b into the A and B registers, respectively, of Figure 33 (page A-4).

SRT Division   1.   If B has k leading zeros when expressed using n bits, shift all the registers left k bits. After this shift, since b has $n + 1$ bits, its most significant bit will be 0, and its second-most-significant bit will be 1.

2.   For $i = 0, n - 1$ do

(a) If the top three bits of P are equal, set $q_i = 0$ and shift (P, A) one bit left.

(b) If the top three bits of p are not all equal and p is negative, set $q_i = -1$ (also written as $\bar{1}$), shift (P, A) one bit left, and add B.

(c) Otherwise set $q_i = 1$, shift (P, A) one bit left, and subtract B

Endloop

3.   If the final remainder is negative, correct the remainder by adding B, and correct the quotient by subtracting 1 from q_0. Finally, the remainder must be shifted k bits right, where k is the initial shift.

A numerical example is given in Figure 54. Although we are discussing integer division, it helps in explaining the algorithm to imagine the binary point just left of the most significant bit. This changes example A.22 from $01000_2/0011_2$ to $0.1000_2/.0011_2$. Since the binary point is changed in both the numerator and denominator, the quotient is not affected. The (P, A) register pair holds the remainder, and is a two's complement number. For example if P contains 11110_2 and A = 0, then the remainder is $1.1110_2 = -1/8$. If r is the value of the remainder, then $-1 \leq r < 1$.

Given these preliminaries, we can now analyze the SRT division algorithm. The first step of the algorithm shifts b so that $b \geq 1/2$. The rule for which ALU operation to perform is this: If $-1/4 \leq r < 1/4$ (true whenever the top three bits of P are equal), then compute $2r$ by shifting (P, A) left one bit; else if $r < 0$ (and hence $r < -1/4$, since otherwise it would have been eliminated by the first condition), then compute $2r + b$ by shifting and then adding, else $r \geq 1/4$ and subtract b from $2r$. Using $b \geq 1/2$, it is easy to check that these rules keep $-1/2 \leq r < 1/2$. For nonrestoring division, we only have $|r| \leq b$, and we need P to be $n + 1$ bits wide. But for SRT division, the bound on r is tighter, namely $-1/2 \leq r < 1/2$. Thus, we can save a bit by eliminating the high-order bit of P (and b and the adder). In particular, the test for equality of the top three bits of P becomes a test on just two bits.

```
     P        A
   00000    1000        Divide 8 = 1000 by 3 = 0011. B contains 0011.
   00010    0000        Step 1: B had 2 leading 0s, so shift left by 2. B now contains 1100.
                        Step 2.1: Top three bits are equal. This is case (a), so
   00100    0000            set q0 = 0 and shift.
                        Step 2.2: Top 3 bits not equal and P >= 0 is case (c), so
   01000    0001            set q1 = 1 and shift.
 + 10100                    Subtract B.
   11100    0001        Step 2.3: Top bits equal is case (a), so
   11000    0010            set q2 = 0 and shift.
                        Step 2.4: Top 3 bits unequal is case (b), so
    1000    010̄1            set q3 = −1 and shift.
 + 01100                    Add B.
   11100                Step 3. Remainder is negative so restore it and subtract 1 from q.
 + 01100
   01000                Must undo the shift in step 1, so right shift by 2 to get true remainder.
                            Remainder = 10, quotient = 0101 − 1 = 0010.
```

FIGURE A.23 SRT division of $1000_2/0011_2$. The quotient bits are shown in bold, using the notation $\overline{1}$ for −1.

The algorithm might change slightly in an implementation of SRT division. After each ALU operation, the P register can be shifted as many places as necessary to make either $r \geq 1/4$ or $r < -1/4$. By shifting k places, k quotient bits are set equal to zero all at once. For this reason SRT division is sometimes described as one that keeps the remainder normalized to $|r| \geq 1/4$.

Notice that the value of the quotient bit computed in a given step is based on which operation is performed in that step (which in turn depends on the result of the operation from the previous step). This is in contrast to nonrestoring division, where the quotient bit computed in ith step depends on the result of the operation in the same step. This difference is reflected in the fact that when the final remainder is negative, the last quotient bit must be adjusted in SRT division, but not in nonrestoring division. However, the key fact about the quotient bits in SRT division is that they can include $\overline{1}$. Although Figure 54 show the quotient bits being stored in the low order bits of A, an actual implementation can't do this because you can't fit the three values −1, 0, 1 into one bit. Furthermore, the quotient must be converted to ordinary two's complement in a full adder. A common way to do this is to accumulate the positive quotient bits in one register and the negative quotient bits in another, and then subtract the two registers after all the bits are known. Because there is more than one way to write a number in terms of the digits −1, 0, 1, SRT division is said to use a *redundant* quotient representation.

The differences between SRT division and ordinary nonrestoring division can be summarized as follows:

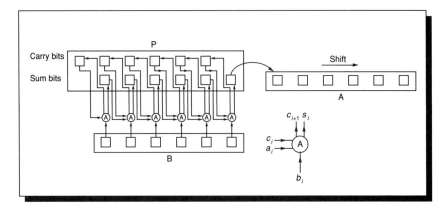

FIGURE A.24   Carry-save multiplier. Each circle represents a (3,2) adder working independently. At each step, the only bit of P that needs to be shifted is the low-order sum bit.

1. ALU decision rule: In nonrestoring division, it is determined by the sign of P; in SRT, it is determined by the two most significant bits of P.

2. Quotient determination: In nonrestoring division, it is immediate from the signs of P; in SRT, it must be computed in a full n-bit adder.

3. Speed: SRT division will be faster on operands that produce zero quotient bits.

The simple version of the SRT division algorithm given above does not offer enough of a speedup to be practical in most cases. However, later on in this section we will study variants of SRT division that are quite practical.

Speeding Up Multiplication with a Single Adder

As mentioned before, shifting-over zero techniques are not used much in current hardware. We now discuss some methods that are in widespread use. Methods that increase the speed of multiplication can be divided into two classes: those that use a single adder and those that use multiple adders. Let's first discuss techniques that use a single adder.

In the discussion of addition we noted that, because of carry propagation, it is not practical to perform addition with two levels of logic. Using the cells of Figure 48, adding two 64-bit numbers will require a trip through seven cells to compute the P's and G's, and seven more to compute the carry bits, which will require at least 28 logic levels. In the simple multiplier of Figure 33, each multiplication step passes through this adder. The amount of computation in each step can be dramatically reduced by using *carry-save adders* (CSA). A carry-save adder is simply a collection of n independent full adders. A multiplier using such an adder is illustrated in Figure 55. Each circle marked "A" is a single-bit full adder, and each box represents one bit of a register. Each addition operation results in a pair of bits, stored in the sum and carry parts of P. Since each add is independent, only two logic levels are involved in the add—a vast improvement over 28.

To operate the multiplier in Figure 55, load the sum and carry bits of P with zero and perform the first ALU operation. (If Booth recoding is used, it might be a subtraction rather than an addition.) Then shift the low-order sum bit of P into A, as well as shifting A itself. The $n - 1$ high-order bits of P don't need to be shifted because on the next cycle the sum bits are fed into the next lower order adder. Each addition step is substantially increased in speed, since each add cell is working independently of the others, and no carry is propagated. There are two drawbacks to carry-save adders. First, they require more hardware because there must be a copy of register P to hold the carry outputs of the adder. Second, after the last step, the high-order word of the result must be fed into an ordinary adder to combine the sum and carry parts. One way to accomplish this is by feeding the output of P into the adder used to perform the addition operation. Multiplying with a carry-save adder is sometimes called redundant multiplication because P is represented using two registers. Since there are many ways to represent P as the sum of two registers, this representation is redundant. The term *carry-propagate adder* (CPA) is used to denote an adder that is not a CSA. A propagate adder may propagate its carries using ripples, carry lookahead, or some other method.

Another way to speed up multiplication without using extra adders is to examine k low-order bits of A at each step, rather than just one bit. This is often called *higher-radix multiplication*. As an example, suppose that $k = 2$. If the pair of bits is 00, add 0 to P, and if it is 01, add B. If it is 10, simply shift b one bit left before adding it to P. Unfortunately, if the pair is 11, it appears we would have to compute $b + 2b$. But this can be avoided by using a higher-radix version of Booth recoding. Imagine A as a base 4 number: When the digit 3 appears, change it to and add 1 to the next higher digit to compensate. An extra benefit of using this scheme is that just like ordinary Booth recoding, it works for negative as well as positive integers (cf. sec A-2).

The precise rules for radix 4 Booth recoding are given in Figure 56. At the i-th multiply step, the low order two bits of the A register contain a_{2i} and a_{2i+1}. These two bits, together with the bit just shifted out (a_{2i-1}) are used to select the multiple of b that must be added to the P register. A numerical example is given in Figure 57. Another name for this multiplication technique is *overlapping triplets*, since it looks at 3 bits to determine what multiple of b to use, whereas ordinary Booth recoding looks at 2 bits.

Besides having more complex control logic, overlapping triplets also requires that the P register be one bit wider to accommodate the possibility of $2b$ or $-2b$ being added to it. It is possible to use a radix-8 (or even higher) version of Booth recoding. In that case, however, it will be necessary to use the multiple 3B as a potential summand. Radix-8 multipliers normally compute 3B once and for all at the beginning of a multiplication operation.

Low order bits of A		Last bit shifted out	Multiple
$2i + 1$	$2i$	$2i - 1$	
0	0	0	0
0	0	1	$+b$
0	1	0	$+b$
0	1	1	$+2b$
1	0	0	$-2b$
1	0	1	$-b$
1	1	0	$-b$
1	1	1	0

FIGURE A.25   Multiples of b to use for radix-4 Booth recoding. For example, if the two low-order bits of the A register are both 1, and the last bit to be shifted out of the A register was 0, then the correct multiple is $-b$, obtained from the second to last row of the table.

```
     P       A   L
   00000    1001        Multiply –7 = 1001 times –5 = 1011. B contains 1011.
 + 11011                Low order bits of A are 0, 1, L=0 so add B.
   11011    1001
   11110    1110  0     Shift right by two bits, shifting in 1s on the left.
 + 01010                Low order bits of A are 1, 0, L=0 so add –2b.
   01000    1110  0
   00010    0011  1     Shift right by two bits.
                        Product is 25 = 0100011.
```

FIGURE A.26   Multiplication of –7 times –5 using radix 4 Booth recoding. The column labeled L contains the last bit shifted out the right end of A.

Faster Multiplication with Many Adders

If the space for many adders is available, then multiplication speed can be improved. Figure 58 shows a simple array multiplier for multiplying two 5-bit numbers, using three CSAs and one propagate adder. Part (a) is a block diagram of the kind we will use throughout this section. Parts (b) and (c) show the adder in more detail. All the inputs to the adder are shown in (b); the actual adders with their interconnections are shown in (c). Each row of adders in (c) corresponds to a box in (a). The picture is "twisted" so that bits of the same significance are in the same column. In an actual implementation, the array would most likely be laid out as a square instead.

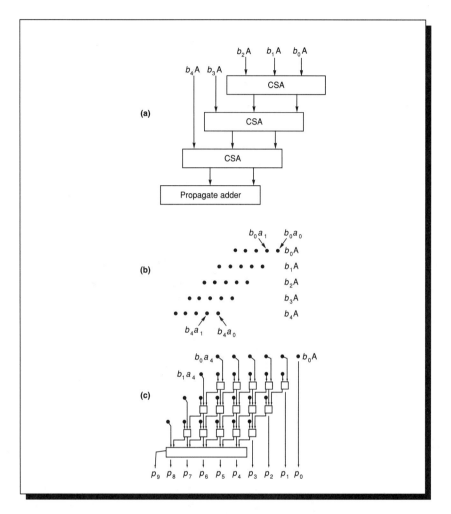

FIGURE A.27   An array multiplier. The 5 bit number in A is multiplied by $b_4b_3b_2b_1b_0$. Part (a) shows the block diagram; (b) the inputs to the array; and in (c) the array is expanded to show all the adders.

The array multiplier in Figure 58 performs the same number of additions as the design in Figure 55, so its latency is not dramatically different from that of a single carry-save adder. However, with the hardware in Figure 58, multiplication can be pipelined, increasing the total throughput. On the other hand, although this level of pipelining is sometimes used in array processors, it is not used in any of the single-chip, floating-point accelerators discussed in Section A.10. Pipelining is discussed in general in Chapter 6 and by Kogge [1981] in the context of multipliers.

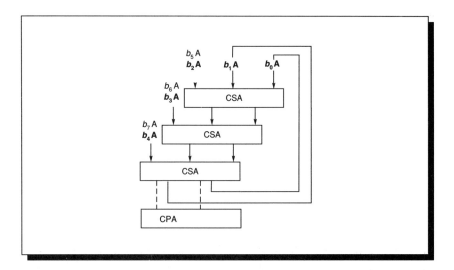

FIGURE A.28 Multipass array multiplier. Multiplies two 8-bit numbers with about half the hardware that would be used in a one-pass design like that of Figure 58. At the end of the second pass, the bits flow into the CPA.

With the technology of 1990, it is not possible to fit an array large enough to multiply two double-precision numbers on a single chip and have space left over for the other arithmetic operations. Thus, a popular design is to use a two-pass arrangement such as the one shown in Figure 58 (page A-54). The first pass through the array "retires" five bits of B. Then the result of this first pass is fed back into the top to be combined with the next three summands. The result of this second pass is then fed into a CPA. This design, however, loses the ability to be pipelined.

If arrays require as many addition steps as the much cheaper arrangements in Figures 33 and 55, why are they so popular? First of all, using an array has a smaller latency than using a single adder—because the array is a combinational circuit, the signals flow through it directly without being clocked. Although the two-pass adder of Figure 59 would normally still use a clock, the cycle time for passing through k arrays can be less than k times the clock that would be needed for designs like the ones in Figures 33 or 55. Secondly, the array is amenable to various schemes for further speedup. One of them is shown in Figure 60 (page A-56). The idea of this design is that two adds proceed in parallel or, to put it another way, each stream passes through only half the adders. Thus, it runs at almost twice the speed of the multiplier in Figure 58. This *even/odd* multiplier is popular in VLSI because of its regular structure. Arrays can also be speeded up using asynchronous logic. One of the reasons why the multiplier of Figure 33 (page A-4) needs a clock is to keep the output of the adder from feeding back into the input of the adder before the output has fully stabilized. Thus, if the array in

Figure 59 is long enough so that no signal can propagate from the top through the bottom in the time it takes for the first adder to stabilize, it may be possible to avoid clocks altogether. Williams et al. [1987] discusses a design using this idea, although it is for dividers instead of for multipliers.

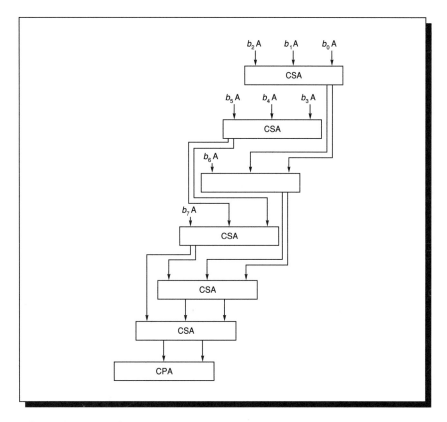

FIGURE A.29   Even/odd array. The first two adders work in parallel. Their results are fed into the third and fourth adders, which also work in parallel, and so on.

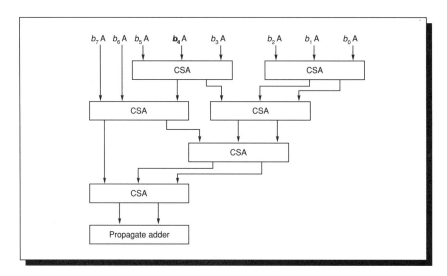

FIGURE A.30   Wallace-tree multiplier. An example of a multiply tree that computes a product in 0(log n) steps.

The techniques of the previous paragraph still have a multiply time of $O(n)$, but the time can be reduced to $\log n$ using a tree. The simplest tree would combine pairs of summands $b_0 A \cdots b_{n-1} A$, cutting the number of summands from n to $n/2$. Then these $n/2$ numbers would be added in pairs again, reducing to $n/4$, and so on, and resulting in a single sum after $\log n$ steps. However, this simple binary-tree idea doesn't map into full (3,2) adders, which reduce three inputs to two rather than reducing two inputs to one. A tree that does use full adders, known as a *Wallace tree*, is shown in Figure 61. When computer arithmetic units were built out of MSI parts, a Wallace tree was the design of choice for high-speed multipliers. There is, however, a problem with implementing them in VLSI. If you try to fill in all the adders and paths for the Wallace tree of Figure 61 (page A-57), you will discover that it does not have the nice, regular structure of Figure 58. This is why VLSI designers have often chosen to use other $\log n$ designs such as the *binary-tree multiplier*, which is discussed next.

The problem with adding summands in a binary tree is that of coming up with a (2,1) adder that combines two digits and produces a single-sum digit. Because of carries, this isn't possible using binary notation, but it can be done with some other representation. We will use the *signed-digit representation* 1, , and 0, which we used previously to understand Booth's algorithm. This representation has two costs. First, it takes two bits to represent each signed digit. Second, the algorithm for adding two signed-digit numbers a_i and b_i is complex and requires examining $a_i a_{i-1} a_{i-2}$ and $b_i b_{i-1} b_{i-2}$. Although this means you must look two bits back, in binary addition you might have to look an arbitrary number of bits back (because of carries).

$$
\begin{array}{cccccc}
1 & 1 & \bar{1} & 0 & 1\ x & \bar{1}\ x \\
+1 & +\bar{1} & +\bar{1} & +0 & +0\ y & +0\ y \\
\hline
1\,0 & 0\,0 & \bar{1}\,0 & 0\,0 & 1\,\bar{1}\quad \text{if } x \ge 0 \text{ and } y \ge 0 & 0\,\bar{1}\quad \text{if } x \ge 0 \text{ and } y \ge 0 \\
& & & & 0\,1\quad \text{otherwise} & \bar{1}\,1\quad \text{otherwise}
\end{array}
$$

FIGURE A.31 Signed-digit addition table. The leftmost sum shows that when computing 1 + 1, the sum bit is 0 and the carry bit is 1.

We can describe the algorithm for adding two signed-digit numbers as follows. First, compute sum and carry bits s_i and c_{i+1} using the table in Figure 62. Then compute the final sum as $s_i + c_i$. The tables are set up so that this final sum does not generate a carry.

Example

What is the sum of the signed-digit numbers $1\bar{1}0_2$ and 001_2 ?

Answer

The two low-order bits sum to $0 + 1 = 1\bar{1}$, the next pair sums to $\bar{1} + 0 = 0\bar{1}$, and the high-order pair sums to $1 + 0 = 01$, so the sum is $1\bar{1} + 0\bar{1}0 + 0100 = 10\bar{1}_2$.

This, then, defines a (2,1) adder. With this in hand, we can use a straightforward binary tree to perform multiplication. In the first step it adds $b_0A + b_1A$ in parallel with $b_2A + b_3A, \cdots, b_{n-2}A + b_{n-1}A$. The next step adds the results of these sums in pairs, and so on. Although the final sum must be run through a carry-propagate adder to convert it from signed-digit form to two's complement, this final add step is necessary in any multiplier using CSAs.

To summarize, both Wallace trees and signed-digit trees are $\log n$ multipliers. The Wallace tree uses the fewer gates but is harder to lay out. The signed-digit tree has a more regular structure, but requires two bits to represent each digit and has more complicated add logic. As with adders, it is possible to combine different multiply techniques. For example, Booth recoding and arrays can be combined. In Figure 58 (page A-54) instead of having each input be b_iA, we could have it be $b_ib_{i-1}A$, and in order to avoid having to compute the multiple $3b$, we can use Booth recoding.

Faster Division with One Adder

The two techniques for speeding up multiplication with a single adder were carry-save adders and higher-radix multiplication. There is a difficulty when trying to utilize these approaches to speed up nonrestoring division. If the adder in Figure 33(b) is replaced with a carry-save adder, then P will be replaced with two registers, one for the sum bits and one for the carry bits. At the end of each cycle, the sign of P is uncertain (since P is the unevaluated sum of the two registers), yet it is the sign of P that is used to compute the quotient digit and decide on the next ALU operation. When a higher radix is used, the problem is deciding what value to subtract from P. In the paper-and-pencil method, you have to guess the quotient digit. In binary division there are only two possibilities; we were able to finesse the problem by initially guessing one and then adjusting the guess based on the sign of P. This doesn't work in higher radices because there are more than two possible quotient digits, rendering quotient selection potentially quite complicated: You would have to compute all the multiples of b and compare them to P.

Both the carry-save technique and higher-radix division can be made to work if we use a redundant quotient representation. Recall from our discussion of SRT division (page A-48) that by allowing the quotient digits to be -1, 0, or 1, there is often a choice of which one to pick. The idea in the previous algorithm was to choose zero whenever possible because that meant an ALU operation could be skipped. In carry-save division, the idea is that because the remainder (P register) is not known exactly (being stored in carry-save form), the exact quotient digit is also not known. But thanks to the redundant representation, the remainder doesn't have to be known precisely in order to pick a quotient digit. This is illustrated in Figure 63, where the x axis represents r_i, the contents of the (P, A) register pair after i steps. The line labeled $q_i = 1$ shows the value that r_{i+1} would be if we choose $q_i = 1$, and similarly for the lines $q_i = 0$ and $q_i = -1$. We can choose any value for q_i, as long as $r_{i+1} = 2r_i - q_i b$ satisfies $|r_{i+1}| \le b$. The allowable ranges are shown in the right half of Figure 63. Thus we only need to know r precisely enough to decide in which range in Figure 63 it lies.

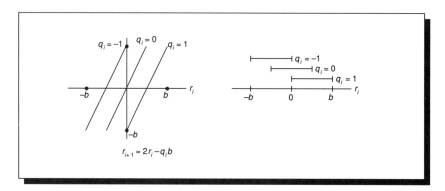

FIGURE A.32   Quotient selection for radix-2 division. The x axis represents the i th remainder, which is the quantity in the (P, A) register pair. The y axis shows the value of the remainder after one additional divide step. Each bar on the right-hand graph gives the range of r_i values for which it is permissible to select the associated value of q_i.

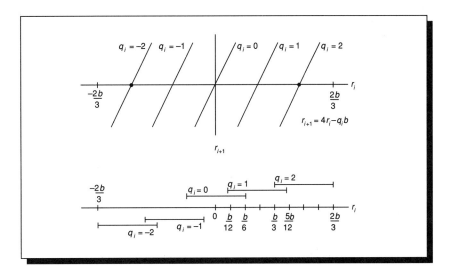

FIGURE A.33   Quotient selection for radix-4 division.

This is the basis for using carry-save adders. Look at the high-order bits of the carry-save adder and sum them in a propagate adder. Then use this approximation of r to compute q_i, usually by means of a lookup table. The same technique works for higher-radix division (whether or not a carry-save adder is used). The high-order bits P can be used to index a table that gives one of the allowable quotient digits.

The design challenge when building a high-speed SRT divider is figuring out how many bits of P and B need to be examined. For example, suppose that we take a radix of 4, use quotient digits of 2, 1, 0, , , but have a propagate adder. How many bits of P and B need to be examined? Deciding this involves two steps. For ordinary radix-2 nonrestoring division, because at each stage $|r| \leq b$, the P buffer won't overflow. But for radix 4, $r_{i+1} = 4r_i - q_i b$ is computed at each stage, and if r_i is near b, then $4r_i$ will be near $4b$, and even the largest quotient digit will not bring r back to the range $|r_{i+1}| \leq b$. In other words, the remainder might grow without bound. However, restricting $|r_i| \leq 2b/3$ makes it easy to check that r_i will stay bounded.

After figuring out the bound that r_i must satisfy, we can draw the diagram in Figure 64, which is analogous to Figure 63. For example, the diagram show that if r_i is between $(1/12)b$ and $(5/12)b$, we can pick $q = 1$, and so on. Or to put it another way, if r/b is between 1/12 and 5/12, we can pick $q = 1$. Suppose the divider examines 5 bits of P (including the sign bit) and 4 bits of b (ignoring the sign, since it is always nonnegative). The interesting case is when the high bits of P are $00011xxx\cdots$, while the high bits of b are $1001xxx\cdots$. To simplify calculation, imagine the binary point at the left end of each register. Since we truncated, r (the value of P concatenated with A) could have a value from 0.0011_2 to 0.0100_2, and b could have a value from $.1001_2$ to $.1010_2$. Thus r/b could be as small as $0.0011_2/.1010_2$ or as large as $0.0100_2/.1001_2$. But $0.0011_2/.1010_2 = 3/10 < 1/3$ would require a quotient bit of 1, while $0.0100_2/.1001_2 = 4/9 > 5/12$ would require a quotient bit of 2. In other words, 5 bits of P and 4 bits of b aren't enough to pick a quotient bit. It turns out that 6 bits of P and 4 bits of b are enough. This can be verified by writing a simple program that checks all the cases. The output of such a program is shown in Figure 65.

b	Range of P		q	b	Range of P		q
8	−13	−7	−2	12	−18	−10	−2
8	−6	−3	−1	12	−10	−4	−1
8	−2	1	0	12	−4	3	0
8	2	5	1	12	3	9	1
8	6	12	2	12	9	17	2
9	−14	−8	−2	13	−19	−11	−2
9	−7	−3	−1	13	−10	−4	−1
9	−3	2	0	13	−4	3	0
9	2	6	1	13	3	9	1
9	7	13	2	13	10	18	2
10	−15	−9	−2	14	−21	−11	−2
10	−8	−3	−1	14	−11	−4	−1
10	−3	2	0	14	−4	3	0
10	2	7	1	14	3	10	1
10	8	14	2	14	10	20	2
11	−17	−9	−2	15	−22	−12	−2
11	−9	−3	−1	15	−12	−4	−1
11	−3	2	0	15	−5	4	0
11	2	8	1	15	3	11	1
11	8	16	2	15	11	21	2

FIGURE A.34   Quotient digits for radix-4 SRT division with a propagate adder. The top row says that if the high-order 4 bits of b are $1000_2 = 8$, and if the top 6 bits of P are between $110011_2 = -13$ and $111001_2 = -7$, then -2 is a valid quotient digit.

```
      P          A
000000000 10010101    Divide 149 by 5. B contains 00000101.
000010010 10100000    step 1:    B had 5 leading 0s, so shift left by 5. B now
                                 contains 10100000, so use b = 10 column of table.
                      step 2.1:  Top 6 bits of P are 2, so
001001010 10000000               shift left by 2. From table, can pick q to be
                      step 2.2:  0 or 1. Choose q0 = 0.
100101010 00000002               Top 6 bits of P are 9, so shift left 2. q1  = 2.
+ 011000000                      Subtract 2b.
111101010    000020   step 2.3:  Top bits = -3, so
110101000    000202              shift left 2. Can pick 0 or 1 for q,
                                 pick q2 = 0.
                      step 2.4:  Top bits = -11, so
010100000    02022̄               shift left 2. q3 = -2.
+ 101000000                      Add 2b.
111100000             step 3:    Remainder is negative, so restore
+ 010100000                      by adding b and subtract 1 from q.
010000000             Answer:    q = 020 (-2) - 1 = 29.
                                 To get remainder, undo shift in step 1 so
                                 remainder = 010000000 >> 5 = 4.
```

FIGURE A.35   **Example of radix-4 SRT division.** Division of 149 by 5.

Example

Using 8 bit registers, compute 149/5 using radix 4 SRT division.

Answer

Follow the SRT algorithm on page A-47, but replace the quotient selection rule in step 2 with one that uses Figure 65. See Figure 66.

Although these are simple cases, all SRT analyses proceed in the same way. First compute the range of r_i, then plot r_i against r_{i+1} to find the quotient ranges, and finally write a program to compute how many bits are necessary. (It is sometimes also possible to compute the required number of bits analytically.) There various details that need to be considered in building a practical SRT divider. For example, the quotient lookup table has a fairly regular structure which means it is usually cheaper to encode it as a PLA rather than in ROM. For more details about SRT division, see [Burgess 1994].

A.10 Putting It All Together

In this section, we will compare the Weitek 3364, the MIPS R3010, and the Texas Instruments 8847 (see Figures 67 and A.37, pages A-65–A-64). In many ways, these are ideal chips to compare. They each implement the IEEE standard for addition, subtraction, multiplication, and division on a single chip. All were introduced in 1988 and run with a cycle time of about 40 nanoseconds. However, as we will see, they use quite different algorithms. The Weitek chip is well described in Birman et al. [1990], the MIPS chip is described in less detail in Rowen, Johnson, and Ries [1988], and details of the TI chip can be found in Darley [1989].

	MIPS R3010	Weitek 3364	TI 8847
Clock cycle time (ns)	40	50	30
Size (mil^2)	114,857	147,600	156,180
Transistors	75,000	165,000	180,000
Pins	84	168	207
Power (watts)	3.5	1.5	1.5
Cycles/add	2	2	2
Cycles/mult	5	2	3
Cycles/divide	19	17	11
Cycles/sq root	–	30	14

FIGURE A.36 Summary of the three floating-point chips discussed in this section. The cycle times are for production parts available in June 1989. The cycle counts are for double-precision operations.

There are a number of things that these three chips have in common. They perform addition and multiplication in parallel, and they implement neither extended precision nor a remainder step operation (recall from section A.6 that it is easy to implement the IEEE remainder function in software if a remainder step instruction is available). The designers of these chips probably decided not to provide extended precision because the most influential users are those who run portable codes, which can't rely on extended precision. However, as we have seen, extended precision can make for faster and simpler math libraries.

A summary of the three chips is given in Figures 67 (page A-65) and A.37. Note that a higher transistor count generally leads to smaller cycle counts. Comparing the cycles/op numbers needs to be done carefully because the figures for the MIPS chip are those for a complete system (R3000/3010 pair), while the Weitek and TI numbers are for standalone chips, and are usually larger when used in a complete system.

The MIPS chip has the fewest transistors of the three. This is reflected in the fact that it is the only chip of the three that does not have any pipelining or hardware square root. Further, the multiplication and addition operations are not completely independent because they share the carry-propagate adder that performs

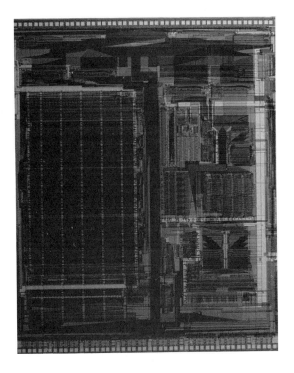

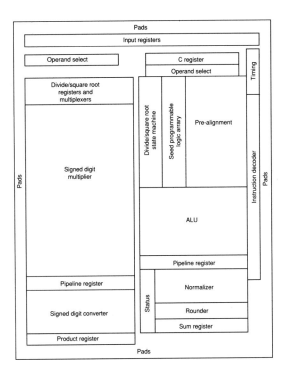

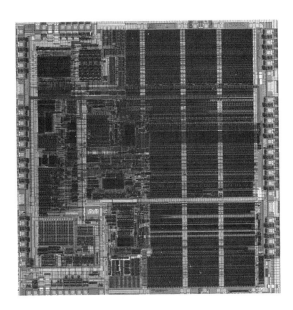

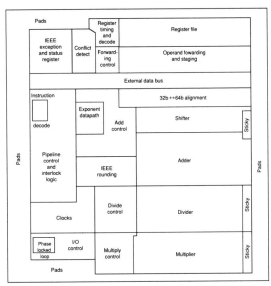

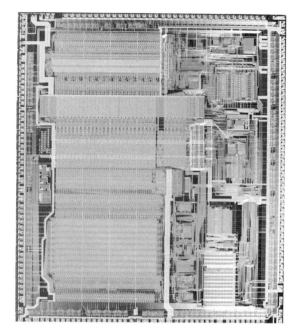
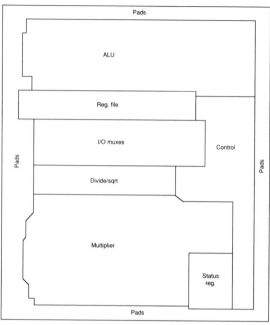

FIGURE A.37   Chip layout. In the left-hand column are the photomicrographs; the right-hand column shows the corresponding floor plans.

the final rounding (as well as the rounding logic). Addition on the R3010 uses a mixture of ripple, CLA, and carry select. A carry-select adder is used in the fashion of Figure 51 (page A-46). Within each half, carries are propagated using a hybrid ripple-CLA scheme of the type indicated in Figure 49. However, this is further tuned by varying the size of each block, rather than having each fixed at four bits (as they are in Figure 49 on page A-44). The multiplier is midway between the designs of Figures 33 (page A-4) and 58 (page A-54). It has an array just large enough so that output can be fed back into the input without having to be clocked. Also, it uses radix-4 Booth recoding and the even-odd technique of Figure 60 (page A-56). The R3010 can do a divide and multiply in parallel (like the Weitek chip but unlike the TI chip). The divider is a radix-4 SRT method with quotient digits −2, −1, 0, 1, and 2, and is similar to that described in Taylor [1985]. Double-precision division is about four times slower than multiplication. The R3010 shows that for chips using an $O(n)$ multiplier, an SRT divider can operate fast enough to keep a reasonable ratio between multiply and divide.

The Weitek 3364 has independent add, multiply, and divide units, and also uses radix-4 SRT division. However, the add and multiply operations on the Weitek chip are pipelined. The three addition stages are (1) exponent compare, (2) add followed by shift (or vice versa), and (3) final rounding. Stages (1) and (3) take only a half-cycle, allowing the whole operation to be done in two cycles, even though there are three pipeline stages. The multiplier uses an array of the style of Figure 59 but uses radix-8 Booth recoding, which means it must compute 3 times the multiplier. The three multiplier pipeline stages are (1) compute $3b$, (2) pass through array, and (3) final carry-propagation add and round. Single precision passes through the array once, double precision twice. Like addition, the latency is two cycles. The Weitek chip uses an interesting addition algorithm. It is a variant on the carry-skip adder pictured in Figure 50 (page A-45). However P_{ij}, which is the logical AND of many terms, is computed by rippling, performing one AND per ripple. Thus, while the carries propagate left within a block, the value of P_{ij} is propagating right within the next block, and the block sizes are chosen so that both waves complete at the same time. Unlike the MIPS chip, the 3364 has hardware square root, which shares the divide hardware. The ratio of double-precision multiply to divide is 2:17. The large disparity between multiply and divide is due to the fact that multiplication uses radix-8 Booth recoding, while division uses a radix-4 method. In the MIPS R3010, multiplication and division use the same radix. The notable feature of the TI 8847 is that it does division by iteration (using the Goldschmidt algorithm discussed in Section A.6). This improves the speed of division (the ratio of multiply to divide is 3:11), but means that multiplication and division cannot be done in parallel as on the other two chips. Addition has a two-stage pipeline. Exponent compare, fraction shift, and fraction addition are done in the first stage, normalization and rounding in the second stage. Multiplication uses a binary tree of signed-digit adders and has a three-stage pipeline. The first stage passes through the array retiring half the bits, the second stage passes through the array a second time, and the third stage converts from signed-digit form to two's complement. Since there is only one array, a new multiply operation can only be initiated in every other cycle. However, by slowing down the clock, two passes through the array can be made in a single cycle. In this case, a new multiplication can be initiated in each cycle. The 8847 adder uses a carry-select algorithm rather than carry lookahead. As mentioned in Section A.6, the TI carries 60 bits of precision in order to do correctly rounded division.

These three chips illustrate the different tradeoffs made by designers with similar constraints. One of the most interesting things about these chips is the diversity of their algorithms. Each uses a different add algorithm, as well as a different multiply algorithm. In fact, Booth recoding is the only technique that is universally used by all the chips.

A.11 | Fallacies and Pitfalls

Fallacy: Underflows rarely occur in actual floating-point application code.

Although most codes rarely underflow, there are actual codes that underflow frequently. SDRWAVE [Kahaner 1988], which solves a one-dimensional wave equation, is one such example. This program underflows quite frequently, even when functioning properly. Measurements on one machine show that adding hardware support for gradual underflow would cause SDRWAVE to run about 50% faster.

Fallacy: Conversions between integer and floating point are rare.

In fact, in Spice they are as frequent as divides. The assumption that conversions are rare leads to a mistake in the SPARC instruction set, which does not provide an instruction to move from integer registers to floating-point registers.

Pitfall: Don't increase the speed of a floating-point unit without increasing its memory bandwidth.

A typical use of a floating-point unit is to add two vectors to produce a third vector. If these vectors consist of double-precision numbers, then each floating-point add will use three operands of 64 bits each, or 24 bytes of memory. The memory bandwidth requirements are even greater if the floating-point unit can perform addition and multiplication in parallel (as most do).

Pitfall: $-x$ is not the same as $0 - x$.

This is a fine point in the IEEE standard that has tripped up some designers. Because floating-point numbers use the sign/magnitude system, there are two zeros, $+0$ and -0. The standard says that $0 - 0 = +0$, whereas $-(0) = -0$. Thus $-x$ is not the same as $0 - x$ when $x = 0$.

A.12 | Historical Perspective and References

The earliest computers used fixed point rather than floating point. In "Preliminary Discussion of the Logical Design of an Electronic Computing Instrument," Burks, Goldstine, and von Neumann [1946] put it like this:

There appear to be two major purposes in a "floating" decimal point system both of which arise from the fact that the number of digits in a word is a constant fixed by design considerations for each particular machine. The first of these purposes is to retain in a sum or product as many significant digits as possible and the second of these is to free the human operator from the burden of estimating and inserting into a problem "scale factors" — multiplicative constants which serve to keep numbers within the limits of the machine.

There is, of course, no denying the fact that human time is consumed in arranging for the introduction of suitable scale factors. We only argue that the time so consumed is a very small percentage of the total time we will spend in preparing an interesting problem for our machine. The first advantage of the floating point is, we feel, somewhat illusory. In order to have such a floating point, one must waste memory capacity which could otherwise be used for carrying more digits per word. It would therefore seem to us not at all clear whether the modest advantages of a floating binary point offset the loss of memory capacity and the increased complexity of the arithmetic and control circuits.

This enables us to see things from the perspective of early computer designers, who believed that saving computer time and memory were more important than saving programmer time.

The original papers introducing the Wallace tree, Booth recoding, SRT division, overlapped triplets, and so on, are reprinted in Swartzlander [1990]. A good explanation of an early machine (the IBM 360/91) that used a pipelined Wallace tree, Booth recoding, and iterative division is in Anderson et al. [1967]. A discussion of the average time for single-bit SRT division is in Freiman [1961]; this is one of the few interesting historical papers that does not appear in Swartzlander.

The standard book of Mead and Conway [1980] discouraged the use of CLAs as not being cost effective in VLSI. Brent and Kung [1982] was an important paper that helped combat that view. An example of a detailed layout for CLAs can be found in Ngai and Irwin [1985] or in Weste and Eshraghian [1985], and a more theoretical treatment is given by Leighton [1992]. Takagi, Yasuura, and Yajima [1985] provides a detailed description of a signed-digit–tree multiplier.

Before the ascendancy of IEEE arithmetic, many different floating-point formats were in use. Three important ones were used by the IBM/370, the DEC VAX, and the Cray. Here is a brief summary of these older formats. The VAX format is closest to the IEEE standard. Its single-precision format (F format) is like IEEE single precision in that it has a hidden bit, 8 bits of exponent, and 23 bits of fraction. However, it does not have a sticky bit, which causes it to round halfway cases up instead of to even. The VAX has a slightly different exponent range than IEEE single: E_{min} is -128 rather than -126 as in IEEE, and E_{max} is 126 instead of 127. The main differences between VAX and IEEE are the lack of special values and gradual underflow. The VAX has a reserved operand, but it works like a signaling NaN: it traps whenever it is referenced. Originally, the VAX's double precision (D format) also had 8 bits of exponent. However, as this is too small for many applications, a G format was added; like the IEEE standard, this format has 11 bits of exponent. The VAX also has an H format, which is 128 bits long.

The IBM/370 floating-point format uses base 16 rather than base 2. This means it cannot use a hidden bit. In single precision, it has 7 bits of exponent and 24 bits (6 hex digits) of fraction. Thus, the largest representable number is $16^{2^7} = 2^{4 \times 2^7} = 2^{2^9}$, compared with 2^{2^8} for IEEE. However, a number that is normalized in the hexadecimal sense only needs to have a nonzero leading digit. When interpreted in binary, the three most significant bits could be zero. Thus, there are potentially fewer than 24 bits of significance. The reason for using the higher base was to minimize the amount of shifting required when adding floating-point numbers. However, this is less significant in current machines, where the floating-point add time is usually fixed independent of the operands. Another difference between 370 arithmetic and IEEE arithmetic is that the 370 has neither a round digit nor a sticky digit, which effectively means that it truncates rather than rounds. Thus, in many computations, the result will systematically be too small. Unlike the VAX and IEEE arithmetic, every bit pattern is a valid number. Thus, library routines must establish conventions for what to return in case of errors. In the IBM FORTRAN library, for example, $\sqrt{-4}$ returns 2!

Arithmetic on Cray computers is interesting because it is driven by a motivation for the highest possible floating-point performance. It has a 15-bit exponent field and a 48-bit fraction field. Addition on Cray computers does not have a guard digit, and multiplication is even less accurate than addition. Thinking of multiplication as a sum of p numbers, each $2p$ bits long, what Cray computers do is to drop the low-order bits of each summand. Thus, analyzing the exact error characteristics of the multiply operation is not easy. Reciprocals are computed using iteration, and division of a by b is done by multiplying a times $1/b$. The errors in multiplication and reciprocation combine to make the last three bits of a divide operation unreliable. At least Cray computers serve to keep numerical analysts on their toes!

The IEEE standardization process began in 1977, inspired mainly by W. Kahan, and is based partly on Kahan's work with the IBM 7094 at the University of Toronto [Kahan 1968]. The standardization process was a lengthy affair, with gradual underflow causing the most controversy. (According to Cleve Moler, visitors to the U.S. were advised that the sights not to be missed were Las Vegas, the Grand Canyon, and the IEEE standards committee meeting.) The standard was finally approved in 1985. The Intel 8087 was the first major commercial IEEE implementation and appeared in 1981, before the standard was finalized. It contains features that were eliminated in the final standard, such as projective bits. According to Kahan, the length of double-extended precision was based on what could be implemented in the 8087. Although the IEEE standard was not based on any existing floating-point system, most of its features were present in some other system. For example the CDC 6600 reserved special bit patterns for INDEFINITE and INFINITY, while the idea of denormal numbers appears in Goldberg [1967] as well as in Kahan [1968]. Kahan was awarded the 1989 Turing prize in recognition of his work on floating point.

References

ANDERSON, S. F., J. G. EARLE, R. E. GOLDSCHMIDT, AND D. M. POWERS [1967]. "The IBM System/ 360 Model 91: Floating-point execution unit," *IBM J. Research and Development* 11, 34–53. Reprinted in [Swartzlander 1990].

   Good description of an early high-performance floating-point unit that used a pipelined Wallace-tree multiplier and iterative division.

BELL, C. G. AND A. NEWELL [1971]. *Computer Structures: Readings and Examples,* McGraw-Hill, New York.

BIRMAN, M., A. SAMUELS, G. CHU, T CHUK, L. HU, J. MCLEOD, J. BARNES [1990]. "Developing the WRL3170/3171 Sparc Floating-Point Coprocessors," *IEEE Micro* 10:1, 55–64.

   These chips have the same floating-point core as the Weitek 3364, and this paper has a fairly detailed description of that floating-point design.

BRENT, R. P. AND H. T. KUNG [1982] "A regular layout for parallel adders," *IEEE Trans. on Computers* C-31, 260–264.

   This is the paper that popularized CLA adders in VLSI.

BURGESS, N. AND T. WILLIAMS [1994] "Choices of operand truncation in the SRT division algorithm," *IEEE Trans. on Computers*, to appear.

   Analyzes how many bits of divisor and remainder need to be examined in SRT division.

BURKS, A. W., H. H. GOLDSTINE, AND J. VON NEUMANN [1946]. *Preliminary Discussion of the Logical Design of an Electronic Computing Instrument.*

CODY, W. J., J. T. COONEN, D. M. GAY, K. HANSON, D. HOUGH, W. KAHAN, R. KARPINSKI, J. PALMER, F. N. RIS, AND D. STEVENSON [1984]. "A proposed radix- and word-length-independent standard for floating-point arithmetic," *IEEE Micro* 4:4, 86–100.

   Contains a draft of the 854 standard, which is more general than 754. The significance of this article is that it contains commentary on the standard, most of which is equally relevant to 754. However, beware that there are some differences between this draft and the final standard.

COONEN, J. [1984]. *Contributions to a Proposed Standard for Binary Floating-Point Arithmetic,* Ph.D. Thesis, Univ. of Calif., Berkeley.

   The only detailed discussion of how rounding modes can be used to implement efficient binary decimal conversion.

DARLEY, H. M., *et. al.* [1989]. "Floating point/integer processor with divide and square root functions," *U.S. Patent 4,878,190,* Oct 31, 1989.

Pretty readable as patents go. Gives a high-level view of the TI 8847 chip, but doesn't have all the details of the division algorithm.

DEMMEL, J. W. AND X. LI [1993]. "Faster numerical algorithms via exception handling," *Proc. Eleventh IEEE Symposium on Computer Arithmetic,* 234–241.

A good discussion of how the features unique to IEEE floating-point can improve the performance of an important software library.

FREIMAN, C. V. [1961]. "Statistical analysis of certain binary division algorithms," *Proc. IRE* 49:1, 91–103.

Contains an analysis of the performance of shifting-over-zeros SRT division algorithm.

GOLDBERG, D. [1991]. "What every computer scientist should know about floating-point arithmetic," *Computing Surveys.* 23:1, 5–48.

Contains an in-depth tutorial on the IEEE standard from the software point of view.

GOLDBERG, I. B. [1967]. "27 bits are not enough for 8-digit accuracy," *Comm. ACM* 10:2, 105–106.

This paper proposes using hidden bits and gradual underflow.

GOSLING, J. B. [1980]. *Design of Arithmetic Units for Digital Computers,* Springer-Verlag New York, Inc., New York.

A concise, well-written book, although it focuses on MSI designs.

HAMACHER, V. C., Z. G. VRANESIC, AND S. G. ZAKY [1984]. *Computer Organization,* 2nd ed., McGraw-Hill, New York.

Introductory computer architecture book with a good chapter on computer arithmetic.

HWANG, K. [1979]. *Computer Arithmetic: Principles, Architecture, and Design,* Wiley, New York.

This book contains the widest range of topics of the computer arithmetic books.

IEEE [1985]. "IEEE standard for binary floating-point arithmetic," *SIGPLAN Notices* 22:2, 9–25.

IEEE 754 is reprinted here.

KAHAN, W. [1968]. "7094-II system support for numerical analysis," *SHARE Secretarial Distribution* SSD-159.

This system had many features that were incorporated into the IEEE floating-point standard.

KAHANER, D. K. [1988]. "Benchmarks for 'real' programs," *SIAM News* (November).

The benchmark presented in this article turns out to cause many underflows.

KNUTH, D. [1981]. *The Art of Computer Programming,* vol II, 2nd ed., Addison-Wesley, Reading, Mass.

Has a section on the distribution of floating-point numbers.

KOGGE, P. [1981]. *The Architecture of Pipelined Computers,* McGraw-Hill, New York.

Has brief discussion of pipelined multipliers.

KOHN, L. AND S.-W. FU, [1989]. "A 1,000,000 transistor microprocessor," *IEEE Int'l Solid-State Circuits Conf.,* 54–55.

There are several articles about the i860, but this one contains the most details about its floating-point algorithms.

KOREN, I. [1989]. *Computer Arithmetic Algorithms,* Prentice Hall, Englewood Cliffs, New Jersey.

LEIGHTON, F. T. [1992]. *Introduction to parallel algorithms and architectures: arrays, trees, hypercubes,* Morgan Kaufmann, San Mateo, California.

This is an excellent book, with emphasis on the complexity analysis of algorithms. Section 1.2.1 has a nice discussion of carry lookahead addition on a tree.

MAGENHEIMER, D. J., L. PETERS, K. W. PETTIS, AND D. ZURAS [1988]. "Integer multiplication and division on the HP Precision Architecture," *IEEE Trans. on Computers* 37:8, 980–990.

Rationale for the integer- and divide-step instructions in the Precision architecture.

MARKSTEIN, P. W. [1990]. "Computation of elementary functions on the IBM RISC System/6000 processor," *IBM Journal of Research and Development* 34:1, 111–119.

Explains how to use fused muliply-add to compute correctly rounded division and square root.

MEAD, C. AND L. CONWAY [1980]. *Introduction to VLSI Systems,* Addison-Wesley, Reading, Mass.

Montoye, R. K., E. Hokenek, and S. L. Runyon [1990]. "Design of the IBM RISC System/6000 floating-point execution" *IBM Journal of Reserach and Development* 34:1, 59 – 70.

Describes one implementation of fused multiply-add.

NGAI, T-F. AND M. J. IRWIN [1985]. "Regular, area-time efficient carry-lookahead adders," *Proc. Seventh IEEE Symposium on Computer Arithmetic,* 9–15.

Describes a CLA adder like that of Figure 45, where the bits flow up and then come back down.

PENG, V., S. SAMUDRALA, AND M. GAVRIELOV [1987]. "On the implementation of shifters, multipliers, and dividers in VLSI floating point units," *Proc. Eighth IEEE Symposium on Computer Arithmetic,* 95–102.

Highly recommended survey of different techniques actually used in VLSI designs.

ROWEN, C., M. JOHNSON, AND P. RIES [1988]. "The MIPS R3010 floating-point coprocessor," *IEEE Micro* 53–62 (June).

SANTORO, M. R., G. BEWICK, AND M. A. HOROWITZ [1989]. "Rounding algorithms for IEEE multipliers," *Proc. Ninth IEEE Symposium on Computer Arithmetic,* 176–183.

A very readable discussion of how to efficiently implement rounding for floating-point multiplication.

SCOTT, N. R. [1985]. *Computer Number Systems and Arithmetic,* Prentice-Hall, Englewood Cliffs, N.J.

SWARTZLANDER, E., ED. [1990]. *Computer Arithmetic,* IEEE Computer Society Press, Los Alamitos, CA.

A collection of historical papers in two volumes.

TAKAGI, N., H. YASUURA, AND S. YAJIMA [1985]."High-speed VLSI multiplication algorithm with a redundant binary addition tree," *IEEE Trans. on Computers* C-34:9, 789–796.

A discussion of the binary-tree signed multiplier that was the basis for the design used in the TI 8847.

TAYLOR, G. S. [1981]. "Compatible hardware for division and square root," *Proc. Fifth IEEE Symposium on Computer Arithmetic,* 127–134.

Good discussion of a radix-4 SRT division algorithm.

TAYLOR, G. S. [1985]. "Radix 16 SRT dividers with overlapped quotient selection stages," *Proc. Seventh IEEE Symposium on Computer Arithmetic,* 64–71.

Describes a very sophisticated high-radix division algorithm.

WESTE, N. AND K. ESHRAGHIAN [1985]. *Principles of CMOS VLSI Design,* Addison-Wesley, Reading, Mass.

This textbook has a section on the layouts of various kinds of adders.

WILLIAMS, T. E., M. HOROWITZ, R. L. ALVERSON, AND T. S. YANG [1987]. "A self-timed chip for division," *Advanced Research in VLSI, Proc. 1987 Stanford Conf.,* The MIT Press, Cambridge, Mass.

Describes a divider that tries to get the speed of a combinational design without using the area that would be required by one.

E X E R C I S E S

A.1 [12] <A.2> Using *n* bits, what is the largest and smallest integer that can be represented in the two's complement system?

A.2 <A.2> In the subsection *Signed Numbers* (p. A-6), it was stated that two's complement overflows when the carry into the high order bit position is different from the carry-out from that position.

a.   [20] Give examples of pairs of integers for all four combinations of carry-in and carry-out. Verify the rule stated above.

b.   [25] Explain why the rule is always true.

A.3 [12] <A.2> Using 4-bit binary numbers, multiply -8×-8 using Booth recoding.

A.4 [15] <A.2> Equations A.2.1 and A.2.2 are for adding two *n*-bit numbers. Derive similar equations for subtraction, where there will be a borrow instead of a carry.

A.5 [25] <A.2> On a machine that doesn't detect integer overflow in hardware, show how you would detect overflow on a signed addition operation in software.

A.6 [15/15/20] <A.3> Represent the following numbers as single-precision and double-precision IEEE floating-point numbers.

a.   [15] 10

b.   [15] 10.5

c.   [20] 0.1

A.7 <A.3> Below is a list of floating-point numbers. In single precision, write down each number in binary, in decimal, and give its representation in IEEE arithmetic.

a.   [12] The largest number less than 1.

b.   [12] The largest number.

c.   [12] The smallest positive normalized number.

d.   [12] The largest denormal number.

e.   [12] The smallest positive number.

A.8 [15] <A.3> Is the ordering of nonnegative floating-point numbers the same as integers when denormalized numbers are also considered? What if the denormalized numbers are represented using the wrapped representation mentioned in Section A.4?

A.9 [20] <A.3> Write a program that prints out the bit patterns used to represent floating-point numbers on your favorite computer. What bit pattern is used for NaN?

A.10 [15] <A.4> Using $p = 4$, show how the binary floating-point multiply algorithm computes the product of 1.875×1.875.

A.11 <A.4> Concerning the addition of exponents in floating-point multiply:

a. [12] What would the hardware that implements the addition of exponents look like?

b. [10] If the bias in single precision was 129 instead of 127, would addition be harder or easier to implement?

A.12 <A.4> In the discussion of overflow detection for floating-point multiplication, it was stated that (for single precision) you can detect an overflowed exponent by performing exponent addition in a 9-bit adder .

a. [15] Give the exact rule for detecting overflow.

b. [12] Would overflow detection be any easier if you used a 10-bit adder instead?

A.13 <A.4> Regarding Figure 40(c).

a. [15] Construct two single precision floating-point numbers whose product doesn't overflow until the final rounding step.

b. [10] Is there any rounding mode where this phenomenon cannot occur?

A.14 [15] <A.4> Give an example of a product with a denormal operand but a normalized output. How large was the final shifting step? What is the maximum possible shift that can occur when the inputs are double precision numbers?

A.15 [15] <A.5> Use the floating-point addition algorithm on page A-24 to compute $1.010_2 - .1001_2$ (in 4-bit precsion) .

A.16 <A.5> In certain situations, you can be sure that $a + b$ is exactly representable as a floating-point number, that is, no roundup is necessary.

a. [10] If a, b have the same exponent and different signs, explain why $a + b$ is exact. This was used in the subsection *Speeding Up Addition* on page A-27.

b. [15] Give an example where the exponents differ by 1, and $a + b$ is not exact.

c. [20] If $a \geq b \geq 0$, and the top two bits of a cancel when computing $a - b$, explain why the result is exact (this fact is mentioned on p. A-23).

d. [20] If $a \geq b \geq 0$, and the exponents differ by 1, show that $a - b$ is exact unless the high order bit of $a - b$ is in the same position as that of a (mentioned in *Speeding Up Addition*, p. A-27).

e. [20] If the result of $a - b$ or $a + b$ is denormal, show that the result is exact (mentioned in the subsection *Underflow*, page A-38).

A.17 <A.5> Fast floating-point addition (using parallel adders) for $p = 5$.

a. [15] Step through the fast addition algorithm for $a + b$ where $a = 1.0111_2$ and $b = .11011_2$.

b. [20] Suppose the rounding mode is towards $+\infty$. What complication arises in the above example for the adder that assumes a carry-out? Suggest a solution.

A.18 [12] <A.4/A.5> How would you use two parallel adders to avoid the final round-up addition in floating-point multiplication?

A.19 [30/10] <A.5> This problem presents a way to reduce the number of addition steps in floating-point addition from three to two using only a single adder.

a. [30] Let A and B be integers of opposite signs, with a and b be their magnitudes. Show that the following rules for manipulating the unsigned numbers a and b gives $A + B$

1. Complement one of the operands.

2. Using end around carry to add the complemented operand and the other (uncomplemented) one.

3. If there was a carry-out, the sign of the result is the sign associated with the uncomplemented operand.

4. Otherwise, if there was no carry-out, complement the result, and give it the sign of the complemented operand.

b. [10] Use the above to show how steps 2 and 4 in the floating-point addition algorithm can be perfomed using only a single addition.

A.20 [20/15/20/15/20/15] <A.6> Iterative square root.

a. [20] Use Newton's method to derive an iterative algorithm for square root. The formula will involve a division.

b. [15] What is the fastest way you can think of to divide a floating-point number by 2?

c. [20] If division is slow, then the iterative square root routine will also be slow. Use Newton's method on $f(x) = 1/x^2 - a$ to derive a method that doesn't use any divisions.

d. [15] Assume that the ratio division by 2 : floating-point add : floating-point multiply is 1:2:4. What ratios of multiplication time to divide time makes each iteration step in the method of Part c faster than each iteration in the method of Part a?

e. [20] When using the method of Part a, how many bits need to be in the initial guess in order to get double-precision accuracy after 3 iterations? (You may ignore rounding error.)

f. [15] Suppose that when Spice runs on the TI 8847, it spends 16.7% of its time in the square root routine (this percentage has been measured on other machines). Using the values in Figure 63 and assuming 3 iterations, how much slower would Spice run if square root was implemented in software using the method of Part a?

A.21 [10/20/15/15/15] <A.6> Correctly rounded iterative division. Let a and b be floating-point numbers with p-bit significands ($p = 53$ in double precision). Let q be the exact quotient $q = a/b$, $1 \leq q < 2$. Suppose that $\overline{q}$ is the result of an iteration process, that $\overline{q}$ has a few extra bits of precision, and that $0 < q - \overline{q} < 2^{-p}$. For the following, it is important that $\overline{q} < q$, even when q can be exactly represented as a floating-point number.

a. [10] If x is a floating-point number, and $1 \leq x < 2$, what is the next representable number after x?

b. [20] Show how to compute q' from $\overline{q}$, where q' has $p + 1$ bits of precision and $|q - q'| < 2^{-p}$.

c. [15] Assuming round to nearest, show that the correctly rounded quotient is either q', $q' - 2^{-p}$, or $q' + 2^{-p}$.

d. [15] Give rules for computing the correctly rounded quotient from q' based on the low-order bit of q' and the sign of $a - bq'$.

e. [15] Solve Part c for the other three rounding modes.

A.22 [15] <A.6>. Verify the formula on the top of page A-32. [Hint: If $x_n = x_0(2 - x_0b) \times \prod_{i=1,n} [1 + (1 - x_0b)^{2^i}]$, then $2 - x_nb = 2 - x_0b(2 - x_0b) \prod[1 + (1 - x_0b)^{2^i}] = 2 - [1 - (1 - x_0b)^2] \prod[1 + (1 - x_0b)^{2^i}]$.]

A.23 [15] <A.7> In the subsection *Underflow* (page A-38), the product $(1.11 \times 2^{-2}) \times (1.11 \times 2^{E_{min}})$ was given as an example that may or may not signal underflow, depending on whether the before or after rounding tests is used. This example required round to $+\infty$ mode. Find an example using round-to-nearest.

A.24 [15] <A.7> Our example that showed that double rounding can give a different answer from rounding once used the round-to-even rule. If halfway cases are rounded up, is double rounding still dangerous?

A.25 <A.7> Some of the cases of the italicized statement in the *Precision* subsection (page A-36) aren't hard to demonstrate.

a. [10] Show that for multiplication of p-bit numbers, rounding to q places followed by rounding to p places is the same as rounding immediately to p places if $q \geq 2p$.

b. [20] If a and b are p-bit numbers with the same sign, show that rounding $a + b$ to q places followed by a rounding to p places is the same as rounding immediately to p places if $q \geq 2p + 1$.

c. [20] Do part (b) when a and b have opposite signs.

A.26 [Discussion] <A.7>In the MIPS approach to exception handling, you need a test for determining whether two floating-point operands could cause an exception. This should be fast and also not have too many false positives. Can you come up with a practical test? The performance cost of your design will depend on the distribution of floating-point numbers. This is discussed in Knuth [1981] and the Hamming paper in Swartzlander [1990].

A.27 [20/10] <A.8> Carry-skip adders.

a.   [20] Assuming that time is proportional to logic levels, what (fixed) block size gives the fastest addition for an adder of some fixed total length?

b.   [10] Explain why the carry-skip adder takes time $\sqrt{n}$.

A.28 [10/15/20] <A.8> Complete the details of the block diagrams for the following adders.

a.   [10] In Figure 46, show how to implement the "1" and "2" boxes in terms of AND and OR gates.

b.   [15] In Figure 49, what signals need to flow from the adder cells in the top row into the "C" cells? Write the logic equations for the "C" box.

c.   [20] Show how to extend the block diagram in A.16 so it will produce the carry-out bit c_8.

A.29 [15] <A.9> For ordinary Booth recoding, the multiple of b used in the ith step is simply $a_{i-1} - a_i$. Can you find a similar formula for radix-4 Booth recoding (overlapped triplets)?

A.30 [20] <A.9> Expand Figure 60 in the fashion of A.26, showing the individual adders.

A.31 [25] <A.9> Write out the analogue of Figure 56 for radix-8 Booth recoding.

A.32 [15] <A.9> The text discussed radix-4 SRT division with quotient digits of -2, $-1, 0, 1, 2$. Suppose that 3 and -3 are also allowed as quotient digits. What relation replaces $|r_i| \leq 2b/3$?

A.33 <A.9> Concerning the SRT division table, Figure 65:

a.   [25] Write a program to generate the results of Figure 65.

b.   [20] Note that Figure 65 has a certain symmetry with respect to positive and negative values of P. Can you come up with a method that only stores the values for positive P?.

c.   [30] Suppose a carry-save adder is used instead of a propagate adder. The input to the quotient lookup table will be k bits of divisor, and l bits of remainder, where the remainder bits are computed by summing the top l bits of the sum and carry registers. What are k and l? Write a program to generate the analogue of Figure 65.

A.34 [20] <A.6,A.9> The discussion of the remainder-step instruction assumed that division was done using a bit-at-a-time algorithm. What would have to change if division was implemented using a higher-radix method?

A.35 [25] <A.9> In the array of Figure 59, the fact that an array can be pipelined is not exploited. Can you come up with a design that feeds the output of the bottom CSA into the bottom CSAs instead of the top one, and that will run faster than the arrangement of Figure 59?

I'm certainly not inventing vector machines. There are three kinds that I know of existing today. They are represented by the Illiac-IV, the (CDC) Star machine, and the TI (ASC) machine. Those three were all pioneering machines. . . . One of the problems of being a pioneer is you always make mistakes and I never, never want to be a pioneer. It's always best to come second when you can look at the mistakes the pioneers made.

Seymour Cray, Public Lecture at Lawrence Livermore Laboratories
on the Introduction of the CRAY-1 (1976)

B | Vector Processors

| **Why Vector Machines?**

In Chapters 4 and 5 we looked at pipelining in detail and saw that pipeline scheduling, issuing multiple instructions per clock cycle, and more deeply pipelining a processor could significantly the performance of a machine. Yet there are limits on the performance improvement that pipelining can achieve. These limits are set by two primary factors:

- Clock cycle time—The clock cycle time can be decreased by making the pipelines deeper, but a deeper pipeline will increase the pipeline dependences and result in a higher CPI. At some point, each increase in pipeline depth has a corresponding increase in CPI. As we saw in an example in Section 4.9, very deep pipelining can slow down a processor.

- Instruction fetch and decode rate—This limitation, sometimes called the *Flynn bottleneck* (based on Flynn [1966]), prevents fetching and issuing of more than a few instructions per clock cycle.

The dual limitations imposed by deeper pipelines and issuing multiple instructions can be viewed from the standpoint of either clock rate or CPI: It is just as difficult to schedule a pipeline that is n times deeper as it is to schedule a machine that issues n instructions per clock cycle.

High-speed, pipelined machines are particularly useful for large scientific and engineering applications. A high-speed pipelined machine will usually use a cache to avoid forcing memory reference instructions to have very long latency. However, big, long-running, scientific programs often have very large active data sets that are often accessed with low locality, yielding poor performance from the memory hierarchy. The resulting impact is a decrease in cache performance. This problem could be overcome by not caching these structures if it were possible to determine the memory-access patterns and pipeline the accesses efficiently. Compiler assistance may help address this problem in the future .

Vector machines provide high-level operations that work on *vectors*—linear arrays of numbers. A typical vector operation might add two 64-entry, floating-point vectors to obtain a single 64-entry vector result. The vector instruction is equivalent to an entire loop, with each iteration computing one of the 64 elements of the result, updating the indices, and branching back to the beginning.

Vector operations have several important properties that solve most of the problems mentioned above:

- The computation of each result is independent of the computation of previous results, allowing a very deep pipeline *without* generating any data hazards. Essentially, the absence of data hazards was determined by the compiler or programmer when they decided that a vector instruction could be used.

- A single vector instruction specifies a great deal of work—it is equivalent to executing an entire loop. Thus, the instruction bandwidth requirement is reduced, and the Flynn bottleneck is considerably mitigated.

- Vector instructions that access memory have a known access pattern. If the vector's elements are all adjacent, then fetching the vector from a set of heavily interleaved memory banks works very well. The high latency of initiating a main memory access versus accessing a cache is amortized because a single access is initiated for the entire vector rather than to a single word. Thus, the cost of the latency to main memory is seen only once for the entire vector, rather than once for each word of the vector.

- Because an entire loop is replaced by a vector instruction whose behavior is predetermined, control hazards that would normally arise from the loop branch are nonexistent.

For these reasons, vector operations can be made faster than a sequence of scalar operations on the same number of data items, and designers are motivated to include vector units if the applications domain can use them frequently.

As mentioned above, vector machines pipeline the operations on the individual elements of a vector. The pipeline includes not only the arithmetic operations (multiplication, addition, and so on), but also memory accesses and effective address calculations. In addition, most high-end vector machines allow multiple vector operations to be done at the same time, creating parallelism among the operations on different elements. In this appendix, we focus on vector machines that gain performance by pipelining and instruction overlap.

B.2 | Basic Vector Architecture

A vector machine typically consists of an ordinary pipelined scalar unit plus a vector unit. All functional units within the vector unit have a latency of several clock cycles. This allows a shorter clock cycle time and is compatible with long-running, vector operations that can be deeply pipelined without generating hazards. Most vector machines allow the vectors to be dealt with as floating-point numbers (FP), as integers, or as logical data, though we will focus on floating point. The scalar unit is basically no different from the type of advanced pipelined CPU discussed in Chapter 5.

There are two primary types of vector architectures: vector-register machines and memory–memory vector machines. In a *vector-register machine*, all vector operations—except load and store—are among the vector registers. These machines are the vector counterpart of a load/store architecture. All major vector machines being shipped in 1994 use a vector-register architecture; these include the Cray Research machines (CRAY-1, CRAY-2, X-MP, and Y-MP), the Japanese supercomputers (NEC SX/2, Fujitsu VP200, and the Hitachi S820), and the mini-supercomputers (Convex C-1 and C-2). In a *memory–memory vector machine* all vector operations are memory to memory. The first vector machines were of this type, as were CDC's machines. From this point on we will focus on vector-register architectures only; we will briefly return to memory–memory vector architectures at the end of the chapter (Section B.8) to discuss why they have not been as successful as vector-register architectures.

We begin with a vector-register machine consisting of the primary components shown in Figure B.1 (page B-3). This machine, which is loosely based on the CRAY-1, is the foundation for discussion throughout most of this chapter. We will call it DLXV; its integer portion is DLX, and its vector portion is the logical vector extension of DLX. The rest of this section examines how the basic architecture of DLXV relates to other machines.

The primary components of the instruction set architecture of DLXV are:

- Vector registers—Each vector register is a fixed-length bank holding a single vector. DLXV has eight vector registers, and each vector register holds 64 doublewords. Each vector register must have at least two read ports and one write port in DLXV. This will allow a high degree of overlap among vector operations to different vector registers. (The CRAY-1 manages to implement the register file with only a single port per register using some clever implementation techniques.)

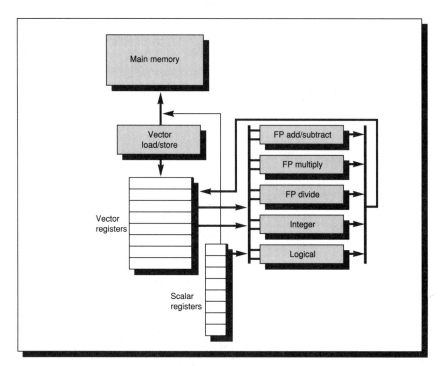

FIGURE B.68   The basic structure of a vector-register architecture, DLXV. This machine has a scalar architecture just like DLX. There are also eight 64-element vector registers, and all the functional units are vector functional units. Special vector operations and vector loads and stores are defined. We show vector units for logical and integer operations. These are included so that DLXV looks like a standard vector machine, which usually includes these units. However, we will not be discussing these units except in the Exercises. In Section B.6 we add chaining, which will require additional interconnect capability.

- Vector functional units—Each unit is fully pipelined and can start a new operation on every clock cycle. A control unit is needed to detect hazards, both on conflicts for the functional units (structural hazards) and on conflicts for register accesses (data hazards). DLXV has five functional units, as shown in Figure B.1. For simplicity, we will focus exclusively on the floating-point functional units.

- Vector load/store unit—A vector memory unit that loads or stores a vector to or from memory. The DLXV vector loads and stores are fully pipelined, so that words can be moved between the vector registers and memory with a bandwidth of one word per clock cycle, after an initial latency.

- set of scalar registers—These can also provide data as input to the vector functional units, as well as compute addresses to pass to the vector load/store unit. These are the normal 32 general-purpose registers and 32 floating-point registers of DLX.

Figure B.2 shows the characteristics of some typical vector machines, including the size and count of the registers, the number and types of functional units, and the number of load/store units.

In DLXV, the vector operation has the same name as the DLX name with the letter "V" appended. These are double-precision, floating-point, vector operations. (We have omitted single-precision FP operations and integer and logical operations for simplicity.) Thus, ADDV is an add of two double-precision vectors. The vector operations take as their input either a pair of vector registers (ADDV) or a vector register and a scalar register designated by appending "SV" (ADDSV). In the latter case, the value in the scalar register is used as the input for all operations—the operation ADDSV will add the contents of a scalar register to each element in a vector register. Vector operations always have a vector destination register. The names LV and SV denote vector load and vector store, and load or store an entire vector of double-precision data. One operand is the

Machine	Year announced	Vector registers	Elements per vector register (64-bit elements)	Vector functional units	Vector load / store units
CRAY-1	1976	8	64	6: add, multiply, reciprocal, integer add, logical, shift	1
CRAY X-MP CRAY Y-MP	1983 1988	8	64	8: FP add, FP multiply, FP reciprocal, integer add, 2 logical, shift, population count/parity	2 loads 1 store
CRAY-2	1985	8	64	5: FP add, FP multiply, FP reciprocal/sqrt, integer (add shift, population count), logical	1
Fujitsu VP100/200	1982	8–256	32–1024	3: FP or integer add/logical, multiply, divide	2
Hitachi S810/820	1983	32	256	4: 2 integer add/logical, 1 multiply-add and 1 multiply/divide–add unit	4
Convex C-1	1985	8	128	4: multiply, add, divide, integer/logical	1
NEC SX/2	1984	8 + 8192	256 variable	16: 4 integer add/logical, 4 FP multiply/divide, 4 FP add, 4 shift	8
DLXV	1990	8	64	5: multiply, divide, add, integer add, logical	1

FIGURE B.69 Characteristics of several vector-register architectures. The vector functional units include all operation units used by the vector instructions. The functional units are floating point unless stated otherwise. If the machine is a multiprocessor, the entries correspond to the characteristics of one processor. Each vector load/store unit represents the ability to do an independent, overlapped transfer to or from the vector registers. The Fujitsu VP200's vector registers are configurable: The size and count of the 8K 64-bit entries may be varied inversely to one another (e.g., 8 registers each 1K elements long, or 128 registers each 64 elements long). The NEC SX/2 has 8 fixed registers of length 256, plus 8K of configurable 64-bit registers. The reciprocal unit on the CRAY machines is used to do division (and square root on the CRAY-2). Add pipelines perform floating-point add and subtract. The multiply/divide–add unit on the Hitachi S810/200 performs an FP multiply or divide followed by an add or subtract (while the multiply-add unit performs a multiply followed by an add or subtract). Note that most machines use the vector FP multiply and divide units for vector integer multiply and divide, just like DLX, and several of the machines use the same units for FP scalar and FP vector operations.

vector register to be loaded or stored; the other operand, which is a DLX general-purpose register, is the starting address of the vector in memory. Figure B.3 lists the DLXV vector instructions. In addition to the vector registers, we need two additional special-purpose registers: the vector-length and vector-mask registers. We will discuss these registers and their purpose in Sections B.3 and B.6, respectively.

Vector instruction	Operands	Function
ADDV	V1,V2,V3	Add elements of V2 and V3, then put each result in V1.
ADDSV	V1,F0,V2	Add F0 to each element of V2, then put each result in V1.
SUBV	V1,V2,V3	Subtract elements of V3 from V2, then put each result in V1.
SUBVS	V1,V2,F0	Subtract F0 from elements of V2, then put each result in V1.
SUBSV	V1,F0,V2	Subtract elements of V2 from F0, then put each result in V1.
MULTV	V1,V2,V3	Multiply elements of V2 and V3, then put each result in V1.
MULTSV	V1,F0,V2	Multiply F0 by each element of V2, then put each result in V1.
DIVV	V1,V2,V3	Divide elements of V2 by V3, then put each result in V1.
DIVVS	V1,V2,F0	Divide elements of V2 by F0, then put each result in V1.
DIVSV	V1,F0,V2	Divide F0 by elements of V2, then put each result in V1.
LV	V1,R1	Load vector register V1 from memory starting at address R1.
SV	R1,V1	Store vector register V1 into memory starting at address R1.
LVWS	V1,(R1,R2)	Load V1 from address at R1 with stride in R2, i.e., R1+i*R2.
SVWS	(R1,R2),V1	Store V1 from address at R1 with stride in R2, i.e., R1+i*R2.
LVI	V1,(R1+V2)	Load V1 with vector whose elements are at R1+V2(i), i.e., V2 is an index.
SVI	(R1+V2),V1	Store V1 with vector whose elements are at R1+V2(i), i.e., V2 is an index.
CVI	V1,R1	Create an index vector by storing the values 0,1*R1,2*R1,...,63*R1 into V1.
S__V	V1,V2	Compare (EQ, NE, GT, LT, GE, LE) the elements in V1 and V2. If condition is true
S__SV	F0,V1	put a 1 in the corresponding bit vector; otherwise put 0. Put resulting bit vector in vector-mask register (VM). The instruction S__SV performs the same compare but using a scalar value as one operand.
POP	R1,VM	Count the 1s in the vector-mask register and store count in R1.
CVM		Set the vector-mask register to all 1s.
MOVI2S	VLR,R1	Move contents of R1 to the vector-length register.
MOVS2I	R1,VLR	Move the contents of the vector-length register to R1.
MOVF2S	VM,F0	Move contents of F0 to the vector-mask register.
MOVS2F	F0,VM	Move contents of vector-mask register to F0.

FIGURE B.70   The DLXV vector instructions. Only the double-precision FP operations are shown. In addition to the vector registers there are two special registers VLR (discussed in Section B.3) and VM (discussed in Section B.6). The operations with stride are explained in Section B.3, and the use of the index creation and indexed load/store operations are explained in Section B.6.

A vector machine is best understood by looking at a vector loop on DLXV. Let's take a typical vector problem, which will be used throughout this chapter:

$$Y = a * X + Y$$

X and Y are vectors, initially resident in memory, and a is a scalar. This is the so-called SAXPY or DAXPY (Single-precision or Double-precision A*X Plus Y) loop that forms the inner loop of the Linpack benchmark. Linpack is a collection of linear algebra routines; the Gaussian elimination portion of Linpack is the segment used as a benchmark. SAXPY represents a small piece of the program, though it takes most of the time in the benchmark.

For now, let us assume that the number of elements, or length, of a vector register (64) matches the length of the vector operation we are interested in. (This restriction will be lifted shortly.)

Example

Show the code for DLX and DLXV for the DAXPY loop. Assume that the starting addresses of X and Y are in Rx and Ry, respectively.

Answer

Here is the DLX code.

```
        LD      F0,a
        ADDI    R4,Rx,#512   ;last address to load
loop:
        LD      F2,0(Rx)     ;load X(i)
        MULTD   F2,F0,F2     ;a*X(i)
        LD      F4,0(Ry)     ;load Y(i)
        ADDD    F4,F2,F4     ;a*X(i) + Y(i)
        SD      F4,0(Ry)     ;store into Y(i)
        ADDI    Rx,Rx,#8     ;increment index to X
        ADDI    Ry,Ry,#8     ;increment index to Y
        SUB     R20,R4,Rx    ;compute bound
        BNZ     R20,loop     ;check if done
```

Here is the code for DLXV for DAXPY.

```
        LD      F0,a         ;load scalar a
        LV      V1,Rx        ;load vector X
        MULTSV  V2,F0,V1     ;vector-scalar multiply
        LV      V3,Ry        ;load vector Y
        ADDV    V4,V2,V3     ;add
        SV      Ry,V4        ;store the result
```

There are some interesting comparisons between the two code segments in the example above. The most dramatic is that the vector machine greatly reduces the dynamic instruction bandwidth, executing only 6 instructions versus almost 600 for DLX. This reduction occurs both because the vector operations work on 64 elements, and because the overhead instructions that constitute nearly half the loop on DLX are not present in the DLXV code.

Another important difference is the frequency of pipeline interlocks. In the straightforward DLX code every ADDD must wait for a MULTD, and every SD must wait for the ADDD. On the vector machine, each vector instruction operates on all the vector elements independently. Thus, pipeline stalls are required only once per vector operation, rather than once per vector element. In this example, the pipeline-stall frequency on DLX will be about 64 times higher than it is on DLXV. The pipeline stalls can be eliminated on DLX by using software pipelining or loop unrolling (as we saw in Chapter 5, Section 5.1). However, the large difference in instruction bandwidth cannot be reduced.

Vector Start-up Time and Initiation Rate

Let's investigate the running time of this vector code on DLXV. The running time of each vector operation in the loop has two components—the *start-up time* and the *initiation rate*. The start-up time comes from the pipelining latency of the vector operation and is principally determined by how deep the pipeline is for the functional unit used. For example, a latency of 10 clock cycles means both that the operation takes 10 clock cycles and that the pipeline is 10 deep. (In discussions of the performance of vector operations, clock cycles are customarily used as the metric.) The initiation rate is the time per result once a vector instruction is running; this rate is usually one per clock cycle for individual operations, though some supercomputers have vector operations that can produce 2 or more results per clock, and others have units that may not be fully pipelined. The *completion rate* must at least equal the initiation rate—otherwise there is no place to put results. Hence, the time to complete a single vector operation of length n is:

$$\text{Start-up time} + n * \text{Initiation rate}$$

Example   Suppose the start-up time for a vector multiply is 10 clock cycles. After start-up the initiation rate is one per clock cycle. What is the number of clock cycles per result (i.e., one element of the vector) for a 64-element vector?

Answer

$$\text{Clock cycles per result} = \frac{\text{Total time}}{\text{Vector length}}$$

$$= \frac{\text{Start-up time} + 64 * \text{Initiation rate}}{64}$$

$$= \frac{10 + 64}{64} = 1.16 \text{ clock cycles}$$

Figure B.4 shows the effect of start-up time and initiation rate on vector performance. The effect of increasing start-up time on a slow-running vector is small, while the same increase in start-up time on a system with an initiation rate of one per clock decreases performance by a factor of nearly two.

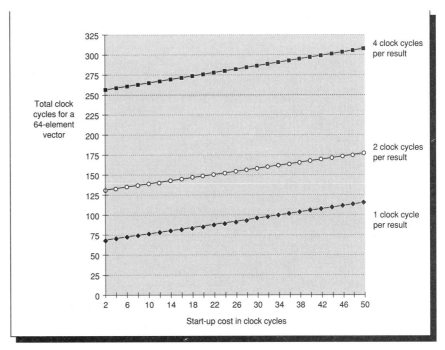

FIGURE B.71   Total running time increases with start-up cost from 2 to 50 clock cycles per operation on the x axis. The impact of start-up time is much greater for fast-running than for slow-running vectors. The operation running at one clock cycle per result increases its run time by 75%, while the operation running at four clock cycles per result increases by less than 20%.

What determines the start-up and initiation rates? Let's first consider the operations that do not involve a memory access. For register–register operations the start-up time (in clock cycles) is equal to the depth of the functional unit pipeline, since this is the time to get the first result. In the earlier example, the depth of 10 gave a start-up time of 10 clock cycles. In the next few sections, we will see that there are other costs involved that increase the start-up time. The initiation rate is determined by how often the corresponding vector functional unit can accept an operand. If it is fully pipelined, then it can start an operation on new operands every clock cycle, yielding an initiation rate of one per clock (as in the earlier example).

Start-up time for an operation comprises the total latency for the functional unit implementing that operation. If the initiation rate is to be kept at 1 clock per result, then

$$\text{Pipeline depth} = \left\lceil \frac{\text{Total functional unit time}}{\text{Clock cycle time}} \right\rceil$$

For example, if an operation takes 10 clock cycles, it must be pipelined 10 deep to achieve an initiation rate of one per clock. Pipeline depth, then, is determined by the complexity of the operation and the clock cycle time of the machine. The pipeline depths of functional units vary widely—from 2 to 20 stages is not uncommon—though the most heavily used units have start-up times of 4 to 8 clocks.

For DLXV, we will choose the same pipeline depths as the CRAY-1. All functional units are fully pipelined. Pipeline depths are six clock cycles for floating-point add and seven clock cycles for floating-point multiply. If a vector computation depends on an uncompleted computation and will need to be stalled, it adds an extra 4-clock-cycle start-up penalty. This penalty is typical on vector machines and arises due to the lack of bypassing: the penalty is the time to write and then read the operands and is only seen when there is a dependence. Thus, back-to-back dependent vector operations will see the full latency of a vector operation. On DLXV, as on most vector machines, independent vector operations using different functional units can issue without any penalty or delay. Independent vector operations may also be fully overlapped, and each instruction issue only takes one clock. Thus, when the operations are independent and different, DLXV can overlap vector operations, just as DLX can overlap integer and floating-point operations.

Because DLXV is fully pipelined, the initiation rate for a vector instruction is always 1. However, a sequence of vector operations will not be able to run at that rate, due to start-up costs. The term *sustained rate* is applied to this situation and refers to the time per element for a collection of related vector operations. Here an element is not the result of a single vector operation, but one result of a series of vector operations. The time per element, then, is the time required for each operation to produce an element. For example, in the SAXPY loop, the sustained rate will be the time to compute and store one element of the result vector Y.

Example   For a vector length of 64 on DLXV and the following two vector instructions, what is the sustained rate for the sequence, and the effective number of floating-point operations per clock for the sequence?

```
MULTV  V1,V2,V3
ADDV   V4,V5,V6
```

Answer   Let's look at the start and completion times of these independent operations (remember that the start-up times are 7 cycles for multiply and 6 cycles for add):

Operation	Start	Complete
MULTV	0	$7 + 64 = 71$
ADDV	1	$1 + 6 + 64 = 71$

The sustained rate is one element per clock—remember that sustained rate requires all vector operations to produce a result. The sequence executes 128 FLOPs (FLoating-point OPerations) in 71 clock cycles, for a rate of 1.8 FLOPs per clock. A vector machine can sustain a throughput of more than one operation per clock cycle by issuing independent vector operations to different vector functional units.

The behavior of the load/store vector unit is significantly more complicated. The start-up time for a load is the time to get the first word from memory into a register. If the rest of the vector can be supplied without stalling, then the vector initiation rate is equal to the rate at which new words are fetched or stored. Typically, penalties for start-ups on load/store units are higher than for functional units—up to 50 clock cycles on some machines. For DLXV we will assume a low start-up time of 12 clock cycles, since the CRAY-1 and CRAY X-MP have load/store start-up times of between 9 and 17 clock cycles. For stores, we will not usually care about the start-up time, since stores do not directly produce results. However, when an instruction must wait for a store to complete (as a load might have to with only one memory pipeline), the load may see part or all of the 12-cycle latency of a store. Figure B.5 summarizes the start-up penalties for DLXV vector operations.

Operation	Start-up penalty
Vector add	6
Vector multiply	7
Vector divide	20
Vector load	12

FIGURE B.72   Start-up penalties on DLXV. These are the start-up penalties in clock cycles for DLXV vector operations. When a vector instruction depends on another vector instruction that has not completed at the time the second vector instruction issues, the start-up penalty is increased by 4 clock cycles.

To maintain an initiation rate of one word fetched or stored per clock, the memory system must be capable of producing or accepting this much data. This is usually done by creating multiple *memory banks*. Each memory bank is like a small, separate memory that can access different addresses in parallel with other banks. The words are then transferred from the memory at the maximum rate (one per clock in DLXV).

There are two possible implementation techniques for memory banks. One approach is to synchronize all the banks and to access them in parallel, latching the result in each bank. Once the result is latched, the next access can begin while the words are transferred. An alternative implementation technique uses independent bank phasing. On the first access, all the banks are accessed in parallel, and then the words are transferred one at a time from the banks. Once a bank has transmitted or stored its data, it begins the next access immediately. The first approach (synchronized accesses) requires more latches, but has simpler control than an approach that uses independent bank phasing. The concept of memory banks is similar to but not identical to interleaving, as we will see in Figure B.6. We discuss interleaving extensively in Chapter 6.

Assuming each bank is one double-precision-word wide, if an initiation rate of one per clock is to be maintained, the following must hold:

Number of memory banks ≥ Memory-bank access time in clock cycles

To see why this is true, start by considering the first access by each bank. After a time equal to the memory-access time, all the memory banks will have fetched a double-precision word, and the words can begin returning to the vector registers. (This requires, of course, that the accesses be aligned on doubleword boundaries.) Words are sent serially from the banks, starting with the bank fetching from the lowest address. If the banks are synchronized, the next accesses start immediately; if the banks are phased, then the next access begins after an element is transmitted from the bank. In either case, a bank begins its next access at a byte address that is (8 * number of banks) higher than the last byte address. Because the memory-access time in clock cycles is less than the number of memory banks and because the words are transferred from the banks in round-robin order at a rate of one transfer per clock cycle, a bank will complete the next access before its turn to transmit data comes again. To simplify addressing, the number of memory banks is usually made a power of two. As we will see shortly, designers will probably want to have more than the minimum number of required banks so as to minimize memory stalls.

| **Example** | Suppose we want to fetch a vector of 64 elements starting at byte address of 136, and a memory access takes 6 clocks. How many memory banks must we have? With what addresses are the banks accessed? When will the various elements arrive at the CPU? |

Answer | Six clocks per access require at least 6 banks, but because we want the number of banks to be a power of two, we choose to have 8 banks. Figure B.6 shows what byte addresses each bank accesses within each time period. Remember that a bank begins a new access as soon as it has completed the old access.

Beginning at clock no.	0	1	2	Bank 3	4	5	6	7
0	192	136	144	152	160	168	176	184
6	256	200	208	216	224	232	240	248
14	320	264	272	280	288	296	304	312
22	384	328	336	344	352	360	368	376

FIGURE B.73   Memory addresses (in bytes) by bank number and time slot at which access begins. The exact time when a bank transmits its data is given by the address it accesses minus the starting address divided by 8 plus the memory latency (6 clocks). It is important to observe that Bank 0 accesses a word in the next block (i.e., it accesses 192 rather than 128 and then 256 rather than 192, and so on). If Bank 0 were to start at the lower address we would require an extra cycle to transmit the data, and we would transmit one value unnecessarily. While this problem is not severe for this example, if we had 64 banks, up to 63 unnecessary clock cycles and transfers could occur. The fact that Bank 0 does not access a word in the same block of 8 distinguishes this type of memory system from interleaved memory. Normally, interleaved memory systems combine the bank address and the base starting address by concatenation rather than addition. Also, inter-leaved memories are almost always implemented with synchronized access. Memory banks require address latches for each bank, which are not normally needed in a system with only interleaving.

Figure B.7 shows the timing for the first few sets of accesses for an 8–bank system with a 6–clock-cycle access latency. Two important observations about these two figures are these: First, notice that the exact address fetched by a bank is largely determined by the lower-order bits in the bank number; however, the initial access to a bank is always within 8 doublewords of the initial address. Second, notice that once the initial latency is overcome (6 clocks in this case), the pattern is to access a bank every n clock cycles, where n is the total number of banks ($n=8$ in this case).

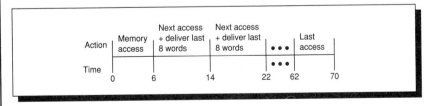

FIGURE B.74   Access timing for the first 64 double-precision words of the load. After the 6–clock-cycle initial latency, 8 double-precision words are returned every 8 clock cycles.

The number of banks in the memory system and the pipeline depth in the functional units are essentially counterparts, since they determine the initiation rates for operations using these units. The processor cannot access memory faster than the memory cycle time. Thus, if memory is built from DRAM, where cycle time is about twice the access time, the processor will usually need twice as many banks as the computations above would give. This characteristic of DRAM is discussed further in Chapter 6.

B.3 Two Real–World Issues: Vector Length and Stride

This section deals with two issues that transpire in real programs. These are what to do when the vector length in a program is not exactly 64, and how to deal with nonadjacent elements in vectors when a matrix is laid out in memory. First, let's deal with the issue of vector length.

Vector-Length Control

A vector-register machine has a natural vector length determined by the number of elements in each vector register. This length, which is 64 for DLXV, is unlikely to match the real vector length in a program. Moreover, in a real program the length of a particular vector operation is often unknown at compile time. In fact, a single piece of code may require different vector lengths. For example, consider this code:

```
        do 10 i = 1,n
10          Y(i) = a * X(i) + Y(i)
```

The size of all the vector operations depends on n, which may not even be known until run-time! The value of n might also be a parameter to the procedure and therefore be subject to change during execution.

The solution to these problems is to create a *vector-length register* (VLR). The VLR controls the length of any vector operation, including a vector load or store. The value in the VLR, however, cannot be any greater than the length of the vector registers. This solves our problem as long as the real length is less than the *maximum vector length* (MVL) defined by the machine.

What if the value of n is not known at compile time, and thus may be greater than MVL? To tackle this problem, a technique called *strip mining* is used. Strip mining is the generation of code such that each vector operation is done for a size less than or equal to the MVL. The strip-mined version of the SAXPY loop written in FORTRAN, the major language used for scientific applications, is shown with C-style comments:

```
      low = 1
      VL = (n mod MVL)  /*find the odd size piece*/
      do 1 j = 0,(n / MVL)  /*outer loop*/
          do 10 i = low,low+VL-1  /*runs for length VL*/
              Y(i) = a*X(i) + Y(i)  /*main operation*/
10        continue
          low = low+VL  /*start of next vector*/
          VL = MVL  /*reset the length to max*/
1     continue
```

The term n/MVL represents truncating integer division (which is what FOR-TRAN does) and is used throughout this section. The effect of this loop is to block the vector into segments which are then processed by the inner loop. The length of the first segment is (n mod MVL) and all subsequent segments are of length MVL. This is depicted in Figure B.8.

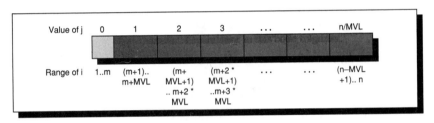

FIGURE B.75   A vector of arbitrary length processed with strip mining. All blocks but the first are of length MVL, utilizing the full power of the vector machine. In this figure, the variable *m* is used for the expression (n mod MVL).

The inner loop of the code above is vectorizable with length VL, which is equal to either (n mod MVL) or MVL. The VLR register must be set twice—once at each place where the variable VL in the code is assigned. With multiple vector operations executing in parallel, the hardware must copy the value of VLR when a vector operation issues, in case VLR is changed for a subsequent vector operation.

In the previous section, start-up overhead could be computed independently for each vector operation. With strip mining, a significant percentage of the start-up cost will be the strip-mining overhead itself; and, therefore, computing the start-up overhead will be more complex.

Let's see how significant these added overheads are. Consider a simple loop:

```
      do 10 i  = 1,n
10        A(i)  = B(i)
```

The compiler will generate two nested loops for this code, just as our earlier ex-ample does. The inner loop contains a sequence of two vector operations, LV (load vector) followed by SV (store vector). Each loop iteration of the original vector operation would require two clocks if there were no start-up penalties of any kind. The start-up penalties consist of two types: vector start-up overhead and strip-mining overhead. For DLXV the vector start-up overhead is 12 clock cycles for the vector load plus a 4-clock-cycle delay because the store depends on the load, for a total of 16 clock cycles. We can ignore the store latency, since nothing depends on it. Figure B.9 (page B-18) shows the impact of the vector start-up cost alone as the vector grows from length 1 to length 64. This start-up cost can decrease the throughput rate by a factor of as much as 9, depending on the vector length.

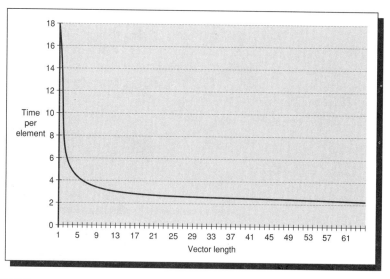

FIGURE B.76   The impact of just the vector start-up cost on a loop consisting of a vector assignment. For short vectors, the impact of the 16-cycle start-up cost is enormous, decreasing performance by up to nine times. The strip-mining overhead has not been included.

In Section B.4, we will see a unified performance model that incorporates all the start-up and overhead costs. First, let's examine how to implement vectors with nonsequential memory accesses.

Vector Stride

The second problem this section addresses is that the position in memory of adjacent elements in a vector may not be sequential. Consider the straightforward code for matrix multiply:

```
do 10 i = 1,100
    do 10 j = 1,100
        A(i,j) = 0.0
        do 10 k = 1,100
            A(i,j) = A(i,j)+B(i,k)*C(k,j)
```

10

At the statement labeled 10 we could vectorize the multiplication of each row of B with each column of C and strip-mine the inner loop with k as the index variable. To do so, we must consider how adjacent elements in B and adjacent elements in C are addressed. When an array is allocated memory it is linearized and must be laid out in either *row-major* or *column-major* order. Row-major order, used by most languages except FORTRAN, lays out the rows first, making elements B(i,j) and B(i,j+1) adjacent. Column-major order, used by FORTRAN, makes B(i,j) and B(i+1,j) adjacent. Figure B.10 illustrates these two alternatives. Let's look at the accesses to B and C in the inner loop of the matrix multiply. In FORTRAN, the accesses to the elements of B will be nonadjacent in memory, and each iteration will access an element that is separated by an entire row of the array. In this case, the elements of B that are accessed by iterations in the inner loop are separated by the row size times 8 (the number of bytes per entry) for a total of 800 bytes.

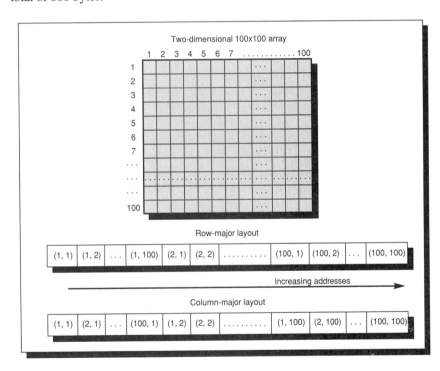

FIGURE B.77 Matrix for a two-dimensional array and corresponding layouts in one-dimensional storage. In row-major order, successive row elements are adjacent in storage, while in column-major order, successive column elements are adjacent. It is easy to imagine extending this to arrays with more dimensions.

This distance separating elements that are to be merged into a single vector is called the *stride*. In the current example, using column-major layout for the matrices means that matrix C has a stride of 1, or 1 doubleword (8 bytes), separating successive elements, and matrix B has a stride of 100, or 100 doublewords (800 bytes).

Once a vector is loaded into a vector register it acts as if it had logically adjacent elements. This enables a vector-register machine to handle strides greater than one, called *nonunit strides*, by making more general vector-load and vector-store operations. For example, if we could load a row of B into a vector register, we could then treat the row as logically adjacent.

Thus, it is desirable for the vector load and store operations to specify a stride in addition to a starting address. On a DLXV, where the addressable unit is a byte, the stride for our example would be 800. The value must be computed dynamically, since the size of the matrix may not be known at compile time, or—just like vector length—may change for different executions of the same statement. The vector stride, like the vector starting address, can be put in a general-purpose register, where it is used for the life of the vector operation. Then the DLXV instruction LVWS (Load Vector With Stride) can be used to fetch the vector into a vector register. Likewise, when a nonunit stride vector is being stored, SVWS (Store Vector With Stride) can be used. In some vector machines the loads and stores always have a stride value stored in a register, so there is only a single instruction.

Memory-unit complications can occur from supporting strides greater than one. Earlier, we saw that a vector-memory operation could proceed at full speed if the number of memory banks was at least as large as the memory-access time in clock cycles. However, once nonunit strides are introduced it becomes possible to request accesses from the same bank at a higher rate than the memory-access time. This situation is called *memory-bank conflict* and results in each load seeing a larger portion of the memory-access time. A memory-bank conflict occurs whenever the same bank is asked to do an access before it has completed another. Thus, a bank conflict, and hence a stall, will occur if:

$$\frac{\text{Least common multiple (Stride,Number of banks)}}{\text{Stride}} < \text{Memory-access latency}$$

Example Suppose we have 16 memory banks with an access time of 12 clocks. How long will it take to complete a 64-element vector load with a stride of 1? With a stride of 32?

Answer Since the number of banks is larger than the load latency, for a stride of 1, the load will take $12 + 64 = 76$ clock cycles, or 1.2 clocks per element. The worst possible stride is a value that is a multiple of the number of memory banks, as in this case with a stride of 32 and 16 memory banks. Every access to memory will collide with the previous one. This leads to an access time of 12 clock cycles per element and a total time for the vector load of 768 clock cycles.

Memory bank conflicts will not occur if the stride and number of banks are relatively prime with respect to each other and there are enough banks to avoid conflicts in the unit-stride case. Increasing the number of memory banks to a number greater than the minimum to prevent stalls with a stride of length 1 will decrease the stall frequency for some other strides. For example, with 64 banks, a stride of 32 will stall on every other access, rather than every access. If we originally had a stride of 8 and 16 banks, every other access would stall; while with 64 banks, a stride of 8 will stall on every eighth access. If we have multiple memory pipelines, we will also need more banks to prevent conflicts. In the 1990s, most vector supercomputers have at least 64 banks, and some have as many as 512.

B.4 | A Simple Model for Vector Performance

This section presents a model for understanding the performance of a vectorized loop. There are three key components of the running time of a strip-mined loop whose body is a sequence of vector instructions:

1. The time for each vector operation in the loop to process one element, ignoring the start-up costs, which we call $T_{element}$. The vector sequence often has a single result, in which case $T_{element}$ is the time to produce an element in that result. If the vector sequence produces multiple results, $T_{element}$ is the time to produce one element in each result. This time depends only on the execution of vector instructions. We will see an example shortly.

2. The overhead for each strip-mined block of vector instructions. This overhead consists of the cost of executing the scalar code for strip mining of each block, T_{loop}, plus the vector start-up cost for each block, T_{start}.

3. The overhead from computing the starting addresses and setting up the vector control. This occurs once for the entire vector operation. This time, T_{base}, consists solely of scalar overhead instructions.

These components can be used to state the total running time for a vector sequence operating on a vector of length n, which we will call T_n:

$$T_n = T_{base} + \left\lceil \frac{n}{MVL} \right\rceil * B(T_{loop} + T_{start}) + n * T_{element}$$

The values of T_{start} and T_{loop} are both compiler and machine dependent, while the value of $T_{element}$ depends mainly on the hardware. The exact vector sequence affects all three values; the effect on $T_{element}$ is probably the most pronounced, with T_{start} and T_{loop} less affected.

For simplicity, we will use constant values for T_{base} and for T_{loop} on DLXV. Based on a variety of measurements of CRAY-1 vector execution, the values chosen are 10 for T_{base} and 15 for T_{loop}. At first glance, you might think that these values, especially T_{loop}, are too small. The overhead in each loop requires: setting up the vector starting addresses and the strides, incrementing counters, and executing a loop branch. However, these scalar instructions can be overlapped with the vector instructions, minimizing the time spent on these overhead functions. The values of T_{base} and T_{loop} of course depend on the loop structure, but the dependence is slight compared to the connection between the vector code and the values of $T_{element}$ and T_{start}.

Example

What is the execution time for the vector operation A = B * s, where s is a scalar and the length of the vectors A and B is 200?

Answer

Here is the strip-mined DLXV code, assuming the addresses of A and B are initially in Ra and Rb, and s is in Fs:

```
        ADDI    R2,R0,#1600  ;no. bytes in vector
        ADD     R2,R2,Ra     ;end of A vector
        ADDI    R1,R0,#8     ;strip-mined length
        MOVI2S  VLR,R1       ;load vector length
        ADDI    R1,R0,#64    ;length in bytes
        ADDI    R3,R0,#64    ;vector length of other pieces
loop:   LV      V1,Rb        ;load B
        MULTVS  V2,V1,Fs     ;vector * scalar
        SV      Ra,V2        ;store A
        ADD     Ra,Ra,R1     ;next segment of A
        ADD     Rb,Rb,R1     ;next segment of B
        ADDI    R1,R0,#512   ;full vector length (bytes)
        MOVI2S  VLR,R3       ;set length to 64
        SUB     R4,R2,Ra     ;at the end of A?
        BNZ     R4,LOOP      ;if not, go back
```

From this code, we can see that: $T_{element} = 3$, for the load, multiply and store of each value of the vector. Furthermore, our assumptions for DLXV are $T_{loop} = 15$ and $T_{base} = 10$. Let's use our basic formula:

$$T_n = T_{base} + \left\lceil \frac{n}{MVL} \right\rceil * (T_{loop} + T_{start}) + n * T_{element}$$

$$T_{200} = 10 + (4) * (15 + T_{start}) + 200 * 3$$

$$T_{200} = 10 + 4 * (15 + T_{start}) + 600 = 670 + 4 * T_{start}$$

The value of T_{start} is the sum of

- The vector load start-up of 12 clock cycles,

- The 4–clock-cycle stall due to the dependence between the load and multiply,

- A 7–clock-cycle start-up for the multiply, plus

- A 4–clock-cycle stall due to the dependence between the multiply and store.

Thus, the value of T_{start} is given by:

$$T_{start} = 12 + 4 + 7 + 4 = 27$$

So, the overall value becomes

$$T_{200} = 670 + 4 * 27 = 778$$

The execution time per element with all start-up costs is then $\frac{778}{200} = 3.9$, compared with an ideal case of 3.

Figure B.11 shows the overhead and effective rates per element for the above example (A = B*s) with various vector lengths. Compared to the simpler model of start-up, illustrated in Figure B.9 on page B-18, we see that the overhead accounting for all sources is higher. In this example, the vector start-up cost, which is what is plotted in Figure B.9, accounts for only about half the total overhead per element.

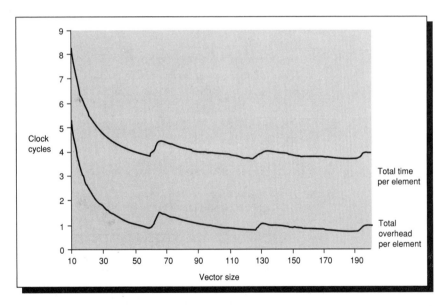

FIGURE B.78 **This shows the total execution time per element and the total overhead time per element, versus the vector length for the example on page B-22.** For short vectors the total start-up time is more than one-half of the total time, while for long vectors it reduces to about one-third of the total time. The sudden jumps occur when the vector length crosses a multiple of 64, forcing another iteration of the strip-mining code and execution of a set of vector instructions. These operations increase T_n by $T_{loop} + T_{start}$.

B.5 | Effectiveness of Compiler Vectorization

Two factors affect the success with which a program can be run in vector mode. The first factor is the structure of the program itself: do the loops have true data dependences, or can they be restructured so as not to have such dependences? This factor is influenced by the algorithms chosen and, to some extent, how they are coded. The second factor is the capability of the compiler. While no compiler can vectorize a loop where no parallelism among the loop iterations exists, there is tremendous variation in the ability of compilers to determine whether a loop can be vectorized.

As an indication of the level of vectorization that can be achieved in scientific programs, let's look at the vectorization levels observed for the Perfect Club benchmarks, discussed in Section 2.7 of Chapter 2. These benchmarks are large, real scientific applications. Figure B.12 (page B-24) shows the percentage of floating-point operations in each benchmark and the percentage executed in vector mode on the CRAY X-MP. The wide variation in level of vectorization has been observed by several studies of the performance of applications on vector machines. While better compilers might improve the level of vectorization in some of these programs, most will require rewriting to achieve significant increases in vectorization. For example, let's look at our version of the Spice benchmark in detail. In Spice with the input chosen we found that only 3.7% of the floating-point operations are executed in vector mode on the CRAY X-MP, and the vector version runs only 0.5% faster than the scalar version. Clearly, a new program or a significant rewrite will be needed to obtain the benefits of a vector machine on Spice.

Benchmark name	FP operations	FP operations executed in vector mode
ADM	23%	68%
DYFESM	26%	95%
FLO52	41%	100%
MDG	28%	27%
MG3D	31%	86%
OCEAN	28%	58%
QCD	14%	1%
SPICE	16%	7%
TRACK	9%	23%
TRFD	22%	10%

FIGURE B.79   Level of vectorization among the Perfect Club benchmarks when executed on the CRAY X-MP. The first column contains the percentage of operations that are floating point, while the second contains the percentage of FP operations executed in vector instructions. Note that this run of Spice with different inputs shows a higher vectorization ratio.

There is also tremendous variation in how well compilers do in vectorizing programs. As a summary of the state of vectorizing compilers, consider the data in Figure B.13, which shows the extent of vectorization for different machines using a test suite of 100 hand-written FORTRAN kernels. The kernels were designed to test vectorization capability and can all be vectorized by hand; we will see several examples of these loops in the exercises.

Machine	Compiler	Completely vectorized	Partially vectorized	Not vectorized
Ardent Titan-1	FORTRAN V1.0	62	6	32
CDC CYBER-205	VAST-2 V2.21	62	5	33
Convex C-series	FC5.0	69	5	26
CRAY X-MP	CFT77 V3.0	69	3	28
CRAY X-MP	CFT V1.15	50	1	49
CRAY-2	CFT2 V3.1a	27	1	72
ETA-10	FTN 77 V1.0	62	7	31
Hitachi S810/820	FORT77/HAP V20-2B	67	4	29
IBM 3090/VF	VS FORTRAN V2.4	52	4	44
NEC SX/2	FORTRAN77 / SX V.040	66	5	29
Stellar GS 1000	F77 prerelease	48	11	41

FIGURE B.80   Result of applying vectorizing compilers to the 100 FORTRAN test kernels. For each machine we indicate how many loops were completely vectorized, partially vectorized, and unvectorized. These loops were collected by Callahan, Dongarra, and Levine [1988]. The machines shown are those mentioned at some point in this chapter. Two different compilers for the CRAY X-MP show the large dependence on compiler technology.

B.6 | Enhancing Vector Performance

Three techniques for improving the performance of vector machines are discussed in this section. The first deals with making a sequence of dependent vector operations run faster. The other two deal with expanding the class of loops that can be run in vector mode. The first technique, chaining, originated in the CRAY-1, but is now supported on many vector machines. The techniques discussed in the second and third parts of this section are taken from a variety of machines and are, in general, more extensive than the capabilities provided on the CRAY-1 or CRAY X-MP architectures.

Chaining—The Concept of Forwarding Extended to Vector Registers

Consider the simple vector sequence

```
MULTV  V1,V2,V3
ADDV   V4,V1,V5
```

In DLXV as it currently stands these two instructions run in time equal to

$$T_{element} * \text{Vector length} + \text{Start-up time}_{ADDV} + \text{stall time} + \text{Start-up time}_{MULTV}$$

$$= 2 * \text{Vector length} + 6 + 4 + 7$$

$$= 2 * \text{Vector length} + 17$$

Because of the dependence, the MULTV must complete before the ADDV can begin. However, if the vector register, V1 in this case, is treated not as a single entity but as a group of individual registers, then the pipelining concept of forwarding can be extended to work on individual elements of a vector. This idea, which will allow the ADDV to start earlier in this example, is called *chaining*. Chaining allows a vector operation to start as soon as the individual elements of its vector source operand become available: The results from the first functional unit in the chain are forwarded to the second functional unit. (Of course, they must be different units to avoid using the same unit twice per clock!) In a chained sequence the initiation rate is equal to one per clock cycle if the functional units in the chained operations are all fully pipelined. Even though the operations depend on one another, chaining allows the operations to proceed in parallel on separate elements of the vector. A sustained rate (ignoring start-up) of two floating-point operations per clock cycle can be achieved, even though the operations are dependent!

The total running time for the above sequence becomes

$$\text{Vector length} + \text{Start-up time}_{ADDV} + \text{Start-up time}_{MULTV}$$

Figure B.14 shows the timing of a chained and an unchained version of the above pair of vector instructions with a vector length of 64. In Figure B.14, the total time for chained operation is 77 clock cycles. With 128 floating-point operations done in that time, 1.7 FLOPs per clock cycle are obtained, versus a total time of 145 clock cycles or 0.9 FLOPs per clock cycle for the unchained version.

We will see in Section B.7 that chaining plays a major role in boosting vector performance.

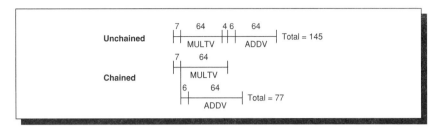

FIGURE B.81 Timings for a sequence of dependent vector operations ADDV and MULTV, both unchained and chained. The 4–clock-cycle delay comes from a stall for dependence, described earlier; the 6– and 7–clock-cycle delays are the latency of the adder and multiplier.

Conditionally Executed Statements and Sparse Matrices

In the last section, we saw that many programs only achieved low to moderate levels of vectorization. Because of Amdahl's Law, the speedup on such programs will be very limited. Two reasons why higher levels of vectorization are not achieved are the presence of conditionals (if statements) inside loops and the use of sparse matrices. Programs that contain if statements in loops cannot be run in vector mode using the techniques we have discussed so far because the if statements introduce control flow into a loop. Likewise, sparse matrices cannot be efficiently implemented using any of the capabilities we have seen so far; this is a major factor in the lack of vectorization for Spice. This section discusses techniques that allow programs with these structures to execute in vector mode. Let's start with conditional execution.

Consider the following loop:

```
do 100 i = 1, 64
      if (A(i) .ne. 0) then
            A(i) = A(i) - B(i)
      endif
100 continue
```

This loop cannot normally be vectorized because of the conditional execution of the body. However, if the inner loop could be run for the iterations for which A(i) $\neq 0$, then the subtraction could be vectorized.

Vector-mask control helps us do this. The *vector-mask control* takes a Boolean vector of length MVL. When the *vector-mask register* is loaded with the result of a vector test, any vector instructions to be executed operate only on the vector elements whose corresponding entries in the vector-mask register are 1. The entries in the destination vector register that correspond to a 0 in the mask register are unaffected by the vector operation. Clearing the vector-mask register sets it to all 1s, making subsequent vector instructions operate on all vector elements. The following code can now be used for the above loop, assuming that the starting addresses of A and B are in Ra and Rb respectively:

```
LV      V1,Ra       ;load vector A into V1
LV      V2,Rb       ;load vector B
LD      F0,#0       ;load FP zero into F0
SNESV   F0,V1       ;sets the VM to 1 if V1(i)≠F0
SUBV    V1,V1,V2    ;subtract under vector mask
CVM                 ;set the vector mask to all 1s
SV      Ra,V1       ;store the result in A
```

Most modern vector machines provide vector-mask control. The vector-mask capability described here is available on some machines, but others allow the use of the vector mask with only a small number of instructions.

Using a vector-mask register does, however, have disadvantages. First, execution time is not decreased, even though some elements in the vector are not operated on. Second, in some vector machines the vector mask serves only to disable the storing of the result into the destination register, and the actual operation still occurs. Thus, if the operation in the above example were a divide rather than a subtract and the test was on B rather than A, false floating-point exceptions might result since the operation was actually done. Machines that mask the operation as well as the result store avoid this problem.

Now, let's turn to sparse matrices; later we will show another method for handling conditional execution. We have dealt with vectors in which the elements are separated by a constant stride. If an application called for a sparse matrix, we might see code that looks like:

```
          do    100 i = 1,n
    100         A(K(i)) = A(K(i)) + C(M(i))
```

This code implements a sparse vector sum on the arrays A and C, using index vectors K and M to designate to the nonzero elements of A and C. (A and C must have the same number of nonzero elements—n of them.) Another common representation for sparse matrices uses a bit vector to say which elements exist and a dense vector for the nonzero elements (the CDC STAR-100 supported this format in hardware). Oten both representations exist in the same program. Sparse matrices are found in many codes, and there are many ways to implement them, depending on the data structure used in the program.

A mechanism for supporting sparse matrices is scatter-gather operations using index vectors. The goal of such operatons is to support moving between a dense representation (i.e. zeros are not included) and normal representation (i.e. the zeros are included) of a sparse matrix. A *gather* operation takes an *index vector*, and fetches the vector whose elements are at the addresses given by adding a base address to the offsets given in the index vector. The result is a nonsparse vector in a vector register. After these elements are operated on in dense form, the sparse vector can be stored in expanded form by a *scatter* store, using the same index vector. Hardware support for such operations is called *scatter-gather* and appeared on several machines. The instructions LVI (Load Vector Indexed) and SVI (Store Vector Indexed) provide these operations in DLXV. For example, assuming that Ra, Rc, Rk, and Rm contain the starting addresses of the vectors in the above sequence, the inner loop of the sequence can be coded with vector instructions such as:

```
LV    Vk,Rk          ;load K
LVI   Va,(Ra+Vk)     ;load A(K(I))
LV    Vm,Rm          ;load M
LVI   Vc,(Rc+Vm)     ;load C(M(I))
ADDV  Va,Va,Vc       ;add them
SVI   (Ra+Vk),Va     ;store A(K(I))
```

This technique allows code with sparse matrices to be run in vector mode. The source code above would **never** be automatically vectorized by a compiler because the compiler cannot know that the elements of K are distinct values, and thus that no dependences exist. Instead, a programmer directive would tell the compiler that it could run the loop in vector mode.

A scatter/gather capability is included on many of the newest supercomputers. Such operations rarely run at one element per clock, but they are still much faster than the alternative, which may be a scalar loop. If the sparsity properties of a matrix change, a new index vector must be computed. Many machines provide support for computing the index vector quickly. The CVI (Create Vector Index) instruction in DLXV creates an index vector given a stride (m), where the values in the index vector are $0,m,2*m,...,63*m$. Some machines provide an instruction to create a compressed index vector whose entries correspond to the positions with a 1 in the mask register. Other vector architectures provide a method to compress a vector. In DLXV, we define the CVI instruction to always create a compressed index vector using the vector mask. When the vector mask is all ones a standard index vector will be created.

The indexed loads/stores and the CVI instruction provide an alternative method to support conditional execution. Here is a vector sequence that implements the loop we saw on page B-28:

```
LV     V1,Ra          ;load vector A into V1
LD     F0,#0          ;load FP zero into F0
SNESV  F0,V1          ;sets the VM to 1 if V1(i)≠F0
CVI    V2,#8          ;generates indices in V2
POP    R1,VM          ;find the number of 1's in VM
MOVI2S VLR,R1         ;load vector length register
CVM
LVI    V3,(Ra+V2)     ;load the nonzero A elements
LVI    V4,(Rb+V2)     ;load corresponding B elements
SUBV   V3,V3,V4       ;do the subtract
SVI    (Ra+V2),V3     ;store A back
```

Whether the implementation using scatter/gather is better than the conditionally executed version depends on the frequency with which the condition holds and the cost of the operations. Ignoring chaining, the running time of the first version (on page XXX) is $5n + c_1$. The running time of the second version using indexed loads and stores with a running time of one element per clock is $4n + 4*f*n + c_2$, where f is the fraction of elements for which the condition is true (i.e., A ≠ 0). If we assume that the values of c_1 and c_2 are comparable, or that they are much smaller than n, we can find when this second technique is better.

$$\text{Time}_1 = 5n$$

$$\text{Time}_2 = 4n + 4*f*n$$

We want $\text{Time}_1 \geq \text{Time}_2$, so

$$5n \geq 4n + 4*f*n$$

$$\frac{1}{4} \geq f$$

That is, the second method is faster if less than one-quarter of the elements are nonzero. In many cases the frequency of execution is much lower. If the index vector can be reused, or if the number of vector statements within the if statement grows, the advantage of the scatter/gather approach will increase sharply.

Vector Reduction

As we saw in Section B.5, some loop structures are not easily vectorized. One common structure is a *reduction*—a loop that reduces an array to a single value by repeated application of an operation. This is a special case of a recurrence. A common example occurs in dot product:

```
          dot = 0.0
          do 10 i=1,64
10              dot = dot + A(i) * B(i)
```

This loop has an obvious loop-carried dependence (on `dot`) and cannot be vectorized in a straightforward fashion. The first thing a good vectorizing compiler would do is split the loop to separate out the vectorizable portion and the recurrence and perhaps rewrite the loop as:

```
          do 10 i=1,64
10              dot(i) = A(i) * B(i)
          do 20 i=2,64
20              dot(1) = dot(1) + dot(i)
```

The variable `dot` has been expanded into a vector; this transformation is called *scalar expansion*.

One simple scheme for compiling the loop with the recurrence is to add sequences of progressively shorter vectors—two 32-element vectors, then two 16-element vectors, and so on. This technique has been called *recursive doubling*. It is faster than doing all the operations in scalar mode. Many vector machines provide hardware assist for doing reductions, as we will see next.

Example

Show how the FORTRAN code would look for execution of the second loop in the code fragment above using recursive doubling.

Answer

Here is the code:

```
            len = 32
            do 100 j=1,6
                  do 10 i=1,len
  10                    dot(i) = dot(i) + dot(i+len)
                  len = len / 2
  100       continue
```

When the loop is done, the sum is in dot(1).

In some vector machines, the vector registers are addressable, and another technique, sometimes called partial sums, can be used. This is discussed in Exercise B.12. There is an important caveat in the use of vector techniques for reduction. To make reduction work, we are relying on the associativity of the operator being used for the reduction. Because of rounding and finite range, however, floating-point arithmetic is not strictly associative. For this reason, most compilers require the programmer to indicate whether associativity can be used to more efficiently compile reductions.

B.7 | Putting It All Together: Evaluating the Performance of Vector Processors

In this section we look at different measures of performance for vector machines and what they tell us about the machine. To determine the performance of a machine on a vector problem we must look at the start-up cost and the sustained rate. The simplest and best way to report the performance of a vector machine on a loop is to give the execution time of the vector loop. For vector loops people often give the MFLOPS (Millions FLoating point Operations Per Second) rating rather than execution time. We use the notation R_n for the MFLOPS rating on a vector of length n. Using the measurements T_n (time) or R_n (rate) is equivalent if the number of FLOPs is agreed upon (see Chapter 2, Section 2.2, for an extensive discussion on MFLOPS). In any event, either measurement should include the overhead.

In this section we examine the performance of DLXV on our SAXPY loop by looking at performance from different viewpoints. We will continue to compute the execution time of a vector loop using the equation developed in Section B.4. At the same time, we will look at different ways to measure performance using the computed time. The constant values for T_{loop} and T_{base} used in this section introduce some small amount of error, which will be ignored.

Measures of Vector Performance

Because vector length is so important in establishing the performance of a machine, length-related measures are often applied in addition to time and MFLOPs. These length-related measures tend to vary dramatically across different machines and are interesting to compare. (Remember, though, that **time** is always the measure of interest when comparing the relative speed of two machines.) Three of the most important length-related measures are:

R_∞—The MFLOPS rate on an infinite-length vector. Although this measure may be of interest when estimating peak performance, real problems do not have unlimited vector lengths, and the overhead penalties encountered in real problems will be larger. (R_n is the MFLOPS rate for a vector of length n.)

$N_{1/2}$—The vector length needed to reach one-half of R_∞. This is a good measure of the impact of overhead.

N_v—The vector length needed to make vector mode faster than scalar mode. This measures both overhead and the speed of scalars relative to vectors.

Let's look at these measures for our SAXPY problem running on DLXV. When chained, the inner loop of the SAXPY code looks like this (assuming that Rx and Ry hold starting addresses):

```
LV        V1,Rx        ;load the vector X
MULTSV    V2,S1,V1     ;vector*scalar-chained to LV X
LV        V3,Ry        ;vector load Y
ADDV      V4,V2,V3     ;sum aX + Y, chained to LV Y
SV        Ry,V4        ;store the vector Y
```

Recall our performance equation for the execution time of a vector loop with n elements, T_n:

$$T_n = T_{base} + \left\lceil \frac{n}{MVL} \right\rceil * (T_{loop} + T_{start}) + n * T_{element}$$

Since there are three memory references and only one memory pipeline, the value of $T_{element}$ must be at least 3, and chaining allows it to be exactly 3. If $T_{element}$ were a complete indication of performance, the loop would run at a MFLOPS rate of $\frac{2}{3} *$ clock rate (since there are 2 FLOPS per iteration). Thus, based only on the $T_{element}$ time, an 80-MHz DLXV would run this loop at 53 MFLOPS. But the Linpack benchmark, whose core is this computation, runs at only 13 MFLOPS (without some sophisticated compiler optimization we discuss in the Exercises) on an 80-MHz CRAY-1, DLXV's cousin! Let's see what accounts for the difference.

The Peak Performance of DLXV on SAXPY

First, we should determine what the peak performance, R_∞, really is, since we know it differs from the ideal 53-MFLOPS rate. Figure B.15 shows the timing within each block of strip-mined code.

Operation		Starts at clock number	Completes at clock number	Comment
LV	V1,Rx	0	$12 + 64 = 76$	Simple latency
MULTV	a,V1	$12 + 1 = 13$	$13 + 7 + 64 = 84$	Chained to LV
LV	V2,Ry	$76 + 1 = 77$	$77 + 12 + 64 = 153$	Starts after first LV done (memory contention)
ADDV	V3,V1,V2	$77 + 1 + 12 = 90$	$90 + 6 + 64 = 160$	Chained to MULTV and LV
SV	Ry,V3	$160 + 1 + 4 = 165$	$165 + 12 + 64 = 241$	Must wait on ADDV; not chained (memory contention)

FIGURE B.82   The SAXPY loop when chained in DLXV. There are three distinct types of delays: 4–clock-cycle delays when a nonchained dependence occurs, latency delays that occur when waiting for a result for the pipeline (6 for add, 7 for multiply, and 12 for memory access), and delays due to contention for the memory pipeline. The last cause is what makes the time per element at least 3 clocks.

From the data in Figure B.15 and the value of $T_{element}$, we know that

$$T_{start} = 241 - 64 * T_{element} = 241 - 192 = 49$$

This value is equal to the sum of the latencies of the functional units: $12 + 7 + 12 + 6 + 12 = 49$.

Using MVL = 64, $T_{loop} = 15$, $T_{base} = 10$, and $T_{element} = 3$ in the performance equation, the time for an n-element operation is

$$T_n = 10 + \left\lceil \frac{n}{64} \right\rceil * (15 + 49) + 3n$$

$$T_n = 10 + n + 64 + 3n = 4n + 74$$

The sustained rate is actually over 4 clock cycles per iteration, rather than the theoretical rate of 3 clocks per iteration, which ignores overhead. The major part of the difference is the cost of the overhead for each block of 64 elements. The basic start-up overhead, T_{base}, adds only $\frac{10}{n}$ to the time for each element. This overhead disappears with long vectors.

We can now compute R_∞ for an 80-MHz clock as

$$R_\infty = \lim_{n \to \infty} \left(\frac{\text{Operations per iteration} * \text{Clock rate}}{\text{Clock cycles per iteration}} \right)$$

The numerator is independent of n, hence

$$R_\infty = \frac{\text{Operations per iteration} * \text{Clock rate}}{\displaystyle \lim_{n \to \infty} (\text{Clock cycles per iteration})}$$

$$\lim_{n \to \infty} (\text{Clock cycles per iteration}) = \lim_{n \to \infty} \left(\frac{T_n}{n} \right) = \lim_{n \to \infty} \left(\frac{4n + 74}{n} \right) = 4$$

$$R_\infty = \frac{2 * 80\text{MHz}}{4} = 40 \text{ MFLOPS}$$

Sustained Performance of Linpack on DLXV

The Linpack benchmark is a Gaussian elimination on a 100x100 matrix. Thus, the vector element lengths range from 99 down to 1. A vector of length k is used k times. Thus, the average vector length is given by:

$$\frac{\displaystyle \sum_{i=1}^{99} i^2}{\displaystyle \sum_{i=1}^{99} i} = 66.3$$

Now we can obtain an accurate estimate of the performance of SAXPY using a vector length of 66.

$$T_{66} = 10 + 2 * (15 + 49) + 66 * 3 = 10 + 128 + 198 = 336$$

$$R_{66} = \frac{2 * 66 * 80}{336} \text{ MFLOPS} = 31.4 \text{ MFLOPS}$$

In reality, Linpack does not spend all its time in the inner loop. The benchmark's actual performance can be found by taking the weighted harmonic mean of the MFLOPS ratings inside the inner loop (31.4 MFLOPS) and outside that loop (about 0.5 MFLOPS). We can compute the weighting factors by knowing the percentage of the time inside the inner loop after vectorization.

The percentage in the inner loop after vectorization can be obtained using Amdahl's Law if we know the percentage in scalar and the speedup from vectorization. In scalar mode, about 75% of the execution time is spent in the inner loop, and the speedup from vectorization is about 5 times. With this information the percentage of time in the inner loop after vectorization can be computed:

$$\text{Total relative time after vectorization} = \frac{0.75}{5} + 0.25$$

$$= 0.15 + 0.25 = 0.40$$

$$\text{Percentage of time in inner loop after vectorization} = \frac{0.15}{0.40} = 3???.5\%$$

The remaining 62.5% of the time is spent outside the main loop. Thus, the overall MFLOPS rating is

$$\text{Percentage}_{inner} * \text{MFLOPS}_{inner} + \text{Percentage}_{other} * \text{MFLOPS}_{other}$$

$$= 3???.5\% * 31.4 + 62.5\% * 0.5 = 12.1 \text{ MFLOPS}$$

This is comparable to the rate at which the CRAY-1 runs this benchmark.

Example

What is $N_{1/2}$ for just the inner loop of SAXPY for DLXV with an 80-MHz clock?

Answer

Using R_{∞} as the peak rate, we want to know the vector length that will achieve about 20 MFLOPS. So,

$$\frac{\text{Clock cycles}}{\text{Iteration}} = \frac{\frac{\text{FLOPS}}{\text{Iteration}} * \frac{\text{Clocks}}{\text{Second}}}{\frac{\text{FLOPS}}{\text{Second}}}$$

$$= \frac{2 * 80 \text{ MHz}}{20 \text{ MFLOPS}} = 8$$

Hence, a rate of 20 MFLOPS means that a loop iteration completes every 8 clock cycles on average, or that $\frac{T_n}{n} = 8$. Using our equation and assuming that $n \le 64$,

$$T_n = 10 + 1 * 64 + 3 * n$$

Substituting for T_n in the first equation, we obtain

$$8n = 74 + 3 * n$$
$$5n = 74$$
$$n = 14.8$$

So $N_{1/2} = 15$; that is, a vector of length 15 gives approximately one-half the peak performance for the SAXPY loop on DLXV.

Example   What is the vector length, N_v, such that the vector operation runs faster than the scalar?

Answer   Again, we know that $N_v < 64$. The time to do one iteration in scalar mode can be estimated as $10 + 12 + 12 + 7 + 6 = 47$ clocks, where 10 is the estimate of the loop overhead, known to be somewhat less than the strip-mining loop overhead. In the last problem, we showed that this vector loop runs in vector mode in time $T_n = 74 + 3*n$ clock cycles for a vector of length ≤ 64. Therefore,

$$74 + 3n = 47n$$

$$n = \frac{74}{44}$$

$$N_v = 2$$

For the SAXPY loop, vector mode is faster than scalar as long as the vector has at least two elements. This number is surprisingly small, as we will see in the next section (Fallacies and Pitfalls).

SAXPY Performance on an Enhanced DLXV

SAXPY, like many vector problems, is memory limited. Consequently, performance could be improved by adding more memory-access pipelines. This is the major architectural difference between the CRAY X-MP and the CRAY-1. The CRAY X-MP has three memory pipelines, compared to the CRAY-1's single memory pipeline, and the X-MP has more flexible chaining. How does this affect performance?

Example   What would be the value of T_{66} for SAXPY on DLXV if we added two more memory pipelines?

Answer   Figure B.16 is a version of Figure B.15 (page B-33), adjusted for multiple memory pipelines.

Operation	Starts at clock number	Completes at clock number	Comment
LV V1,Rx	0	$12 + 64 = 76$	Simple latency
MULTV a,V1	$12 + 1 = 13$	$13 + 7 + 64 = 84$	Chained to LV
LV V2,Ry	2	$2 + 12 + 64 = 78$	Starts immediately
ADDV V3,V1,V2	$13 + 1 + 7 = 21$	$21 + 6 + 64 = 91$	Chained to MULTV and LV
SV Ry,V3	$21 + 1 + 6 = 28$	$28 + 12 + 64 = 104$	Chained to ADDV

FIGURE B.83   The SAXPY loop when chained in DLXV with three memory pipelines. The only delays are latency delays that occur when waiting for a result for the pipeline (6 for add, 7 for multiply, and 12 for each memory access).

With three memory pipelines, the performance is greatly improved. Here's our standard performance equation:

$$T_n = T_{base} + \left\lceil \frac{n}{MVL} \right\rceil * (T_{loop} + T_{start}) + n * T_{element}$$

With three memory pipelines the value of $T_{element}$ becomes 1, so that

$$T_{start} = 104 - 64 * T_{element} = 104 - 64 = 40$$

The reduction in stalls reduces the start-up penalty for each sequence. The values of T_{loop} and T_{base}, 15 and 10, remain the same. Therefore, for an average vector length of 66, we have:

$$T_{66} = T_{base} + \left\lceil \frac{66}{64} \right\rceil * (T_{loop} + T_{start}) + 66 * T_{element}$$

$$T_{66} = 10 + 2 * (15 + 40) + 66 * 1 = 186$$

With three memory pipelines, we have reduced the clock-cycle count for sustained performance from 336 to 186, a factor of 1.8. Note the effect of Amdahl's Law: We improved the theoretical peak rate, as measured by $T_{element}$, by a factor of 3, but only achieved an overall improvement of a factor of 1.8 in sustained performance. Because the speedup outside the inner loop is likely to be less than 1.8, the overall improvement in run time for the benchmark will also be less.

Another improvement could come from allowing the start-up of one loop iteration before another completes. This requires that one vector operation be allowed to begin using a functional unit, before another operation has completed. This complicates the instruction issue logic substantially, but has the advantage that the start-up overhead will only occur once, independent of the vector length. On a long vector the overhead per block ($T_{loop} + T_{start}$) can be completely amortized. In this way a machine with vector registers can have both low start-up overhead for short vectors and high peak performance for very long vectors.

Example

What would be the values of R_∞ and T_{66} for SAXPY on DLXV if we added two more memory pipelines and allowed the strip-mining and start-up overhead to be fully overlapped?

Answer

$$R_\infty = \lim_{n \to \infty} \left(\frac{\text{Operations per iteration} * \text{Clock rate}}{\text{Clock cycles per iteration}} \right)$$

$$\lim_{n \to \infty} (\text{Clock cycles per iteration}) = \lim_{n \to \infty} \left(\frac{T_n}{n} \right)$$

Since $T_n = n + 40 + 10 + 15 = n + 65$,

$$\lim_{n \to \infty} \left(\frac{T_n}{n} \right) = \lim_{n \to \infty} \left(\frac{n + 65}{n} \right) = 1$$

$$R_\infty = \frac{2 * 80 \text{ MHz}}{1} = 160 \text{ MFLOPS}$$

Thus, adding the extra memory pipelines and more flexible issue logic yields an improvement in peak performance of a factor of 4. However, $T_{66} = 131$, so for shorter vectors, the sustained performance improvement is about 40%.

In summary, we have examined several measures of vector performance. Theoretical peak performance can be calculated based purely on the value of $T_{element}$ as

$$\frac{\text{Number of FLOPS per iteration} * \text{Clock rate}}{T_{element}}$$

By including the loop overhead, we can calculate values for peak performance for an infinite-length vector (R_∞), and also for sustained performance R_n for a vector of length n, which is computed as:

$$R_n = \frac{\text{Number of FLOPS per iteration} * n * \text{Clock rate}}{T_n}$$

Using these measures we also can find $N_{1/2}$ and N_v, which give us another way of looking at the start-up overhead for vectors and the ratio of vector to scalar speed. A wide variety of measures of performance of vector machines are useful in understanding the wide range of performance that applications may see on a vector machine.

B.8 | Fallacies and Pitfalls

Pitfall: Concentrating on peak performance and ignoring start-up overhead.

Early vector machines such as the TI ASC and the CDC STAR-100 had long start-up times. For some vector problems, N_v could be greater than 100! Today, the Japanese supercomputers often have higher sustained rates than the Cray Research machines. But with start-up overheads that are 50–100% higher, the faster sustained rates often provide no real advantage. On the CYBER-205 the start-up overhead for SAXPY is 158 clock cycles, substantially increasing the break-even point. With a single vector unit, which contains 2 memory pipelines, the CYBER-205 can sustain a rate of 2 clocks per iteration. The time for SAXPY for a vector of length n is therefore roughly $158 + 2n$. If the clock rates of the CRAY-1 and the CYBER-205 were identical, the CRAY-1 would be faster until $n > 64$. Because the CRAY-1 clock is also faster (even though the 205 is newer), the crossover point is over 100. Comparing a four-vector-pipeline CYBER-205 (the maximum-size machine) to the CRAY X-MP that was delivered shortly after the 205, the 205 completes two results per clock cycle—twice as fast as the X-MP. However, vectors must be longer than about 200 for the CYBER-205 to be faster. The problem of start-up overhead has been the major difficulty for the memory–memory vector architectures.

Pitfall: Increasing vector performance, without comparable increases in scalar performance.

This is another area where Seymour Cray rewrote the rules. Many of the early vector machines had comparatively slow scalar units (as well as large start-up overheads). Even today, machines with higher peak vector performance, can be outperformed by a machine with lower vector performance but better scalar performance. Good scalar performance keeps down overhead costs (strip mining, for example) and reduces the impact of Amdahl's Law. A good example of this comes from comparing a fast scalar machine and a vector machine with lower scalar performance. The Livermore FORTRAN kernels are a collection of 24 scientific kernels with varying degrees of vectorization (see Chapter 2; Section 2.2). Figure B.17 shows the performance of two different machines on this benchmark. Despite the vector machine's higher peak performance, it's low scalar performance makes it slower than a fast scalar machine. The next fallacy is closely related.

Machine	Minimum rate for any loop	Maximum rate for any loop	Harmonic mean of all 24 loops
MIPS M/120-5	0.80 MFLOPS	3.89 MFLOPS	1.85 MFLOPS
Stardent-1500	0.41 MFLOPS	10.08 MFLOPS	1.72 MFLOPS

FIGURE B.84 Performance measurements for the Livermore FORTRAN kernels on two different machines. Both the MIPS M/120-5 and the Stardent-1500 (formerly the Ardent Titan-1) use a 16.7-MHz MIPS R2000 chip for the main CPU. The Stardent-1500 uses its vector unit for scalar FP and has about half the scalar performance (as measured by the minimum rate) of the MIPS M/120, which uses the MIPS R2010 FP chip. The vector machine is more than a factor of 2.5 times faster for a highly vectorizable loop (maximum rate). However, the lower scalar performance of the Stardent-1500 negates the higher vector performance when total performance is measured by the harmonic mean on all 24 loops.

*Fallacy: The scalar performance of the **best** supercomputers is low.*

The supercomputers from Cray Research have always had good scalar performance. Measurements of the CRAY Y-MP running (the nonvectorizable) Spice benchmark show this. When our Spice benchmark is run on the CRAY Y-MP in scalar mode it executes 665 million instructions, with a CPI of 4.1. By comparison, the DECstation 3100 executes 738 million instructions with a CPI of 2.1. Although the DECstation uses fewer cycles, the Y-MP uses fewer instructions and is much faster overall, since it has a clock cycle one-tenth as long.

Fallacy: You can get vector performance without providing memory bandwidth.

As we saw with the SAXPY loop, memory bandwidth is quite important. SAXPY requires 1.5 memory references per floating-point operation, and this ratio is typical of many scientific codes. Even if the floating-point operations took no time, a CRAY-1 could not increase the performance of the vector sequence used, since it is memory limited. Recently, the CRAY-1 performance on Linpack has jumped because the compiler used clever transformations to change the computation so that values could be kept in the vector registers. This lowered the number of memory references per FLOP and improved the performance by nearly a factor of 2! Thus, the memory bandwidth on the CRAY-1 became sufficient for a loop that formerly required more bandwidth.

B.9 | Concluding Remarks

In the late 1980s rapid performance increases in efficiently pipelined scalar machines lead to a dramatic closing of the gap between vector supercomputers, costing millions of dollars, and fast, pipelined, VLSI microprocessors costing less than $100,000. The basic reason for this was the rapidly decreasing CPI of the scalar machines.

For scientific programs, an interesting counterpart to CPI is clock cycles per FLOP, or CPF. We saw in this chapter that for vector machines this number was typically in the range of 2 (for a CRAY X-MP style machine) to 4 (for a CRAY-1 style machine). In Chapter 5, we saw that the pipelined machine varied from about 6 (for DLX) down to about 2.5 (for a superscalar DLX with no memory system losses running a SAXPY-type loop).

Recent trends in vector machine design have focused on high peak-vector performance and multiprocessing. Meanwhile, high-speed scalar machines concentrate on keeping the ratio of peak to sustained performance near one. Thus, if the peak rates advance comparably, the sustained rates of the scalar machines will advance more quickly, and the scalar machines will continue to close the CPF gap. These multiple-issue scalar machines can rival or exceed the performance of vector machines with comparable clock speeds, especially for levels of vectorization below 70%. Furthermore, the differences in clock rate are largely technology driven—the low-end, microprocessor-based vector machines have clock rates comparable to the pipelined machines using microprocessor technology. (In fact, they often use the same microprocessors!) In 1994, we saw two dramatic demonstrations that the gap between vector machines and superscalars may disappear in the future. First, microprocessors with clock rates exceeding those of the high-end Cray C-90 appeared. Second, microprocessors such as the MIPS R8000 (TFP) and the IBM Power-2 delivered CFP numbers competitive with vector machines, by issuing multiple memory references and FP operations per cycle. In the near future, it is likely that designers will be able to use the advances in silicon technology to achieve low CPF performance while also achieving a high clock rate. At that point it may be primarily the memory systems that distinguish vector machines from microprocessor-based superscalars. What is unclear is how many applications can justify the significantly larger cost of a vector-style memory system versus a cache-based memory system.

B.10 | Historical Perspective and References

The first vector machines were the CDC STAR-100 (see Hintz and Tate [1972]) and the TI ASC (see Watson [1972]), both announced in 1972. Both were memory–memory vector machines. They had relatively slow scalar units—the STAR used the same units for scalars and vectors—making the scalar pipeline extremely deep. Both machines had high start-up overhead and worked on vectors of several hundred to several thousand elements. The crossover between scalar and vector could be over 50 elements. It appears that not enough attention was paid to the role of Amdahl's Law on these two machines.

Cray, who worked on the 6600 and the 7600 at CDC, founded Cray Research and introduced the CRAY-1 in 1976 (see Russell [1978]). The CRAY-1 used a vector-register architecture to significantly lower start-up overhead. He also had efficient support for nonunit stride and invented chaining. Most importantly, the CRAY-1 was also the fastest scalar machine in the world at that time. This matching of good scalar and vector performance was probably the most significant factor in making the CRAY-1 a success. Some customers bought the machine primarily for its outstanding scalar performance. Many subsequent vector machines are based on the architecture of this first commercially successful vector machine. Baskett and Keller [1977] is a good evaluation of the CRAY-1.

In 1981, CDC started shipping the CYBER-205 (see Lincoln [1982]). The 205 had the same basic architecture as the STAR, but offered improved performance all around as well as expansibility of the vector unit with up to four vector pipelines, each with multiple functional units and a wide load/store pipe that provided multiple words per clock. The peak performance of the CYBER-205 greatly exceeded the performance of the CRAY-1. However, on real programs, the performance difference was much smaller.

The CDC STAR machine and its descendant, the CYBER-205, were memory–memory vector machines. To keep the hardware simple and support the high bandwidth requirements (up to 3 memory references per FLOP), these machines did not efficiently handle nonunit stride. While most loops have unit stride, a nonunit stride loop had poor performance on these machines because memory-to-memory data movements were required to gather together (and scatter back) the nonadjacent vector elements; these operations used special scatter-gather instructions. In addition, there was spacial support for sparse vectors that used a bit vector to represent the zeros and nonzeros and a dense vector of nonzero values. These more complex vector operations were slow because of the long memory latency and it was often faster to use scalar mode for sparse or nonunit stride operations.

Schneck [1987] described several of the early pipelined machines (e.g., Stretch) through the first vector machines including the 205 and CRAY-1. Dongarra [1986] did another good survey, focusing on more recent machines.

In 1983, Cray shipped the first CRAY X-MP (see Chen [1983]). With an improved clock rate (9.5 ns versus 12.5 on the CRAY-1), better chaining support, and multiple memory pipelines, this machine maintained the Cray Research lead in supercomputers. The CRAY-2, a completely new design configurable with up to four processors, was introduced later. It has a much faster clock than the X-MP, but also much deeper pipelines. The CRAY-2 lacks chaining, has an enormous memory latency, and has only one memory pipe per processor. In general, it is only faster than the CRAY X-MP on problems that require its very large main memory.

In 1983, the Japanese computer vendors entered the supercomputer marketplace, starting with the Fujitsu VP100 and VP200 (Miura and Uchida [1983]), and later expanding to include the Hitachi S810, and the NEC SX/2 (see Watanabe [1987]). These machines have proved to be close to the CRAY X-MP in performance. In general, these three machines have much higher peak performance than the CRAY X-MP, though because of large start-up overhead, their typical performance is often lower than the CRAY X-MP (see Figure 2.24 in Chapter 2). The CRAY X-MP favored a multiple-processor approach, first offering a two-processor version and later a four-processor machine. In contrast, the three Japanese machines had expandable vector capabilities. In 1988, Cray Research introduced the CRAY Y-MP—a bigger and faster version of the X-MP. The Y-MP allows up to 8 processors and lowers the cycle time to 6 ns. With a full complement of 8 processors, the Y-MP is generally the fastest supercomputer, though the single-processor Japanese supercomputers may be faster than a one-processor Y-MP. In late 1989 Cray Research was split into two companies, both aimed at building high-end machines available in the early 1990s. Seymour Cray continues to head the spin-off, which is now called Cray Computer Corporation.

In the early 1980s, CDC spun out a group, called ETA, to build a new supercomputer, the ETA-10, capable of 10 GigaFLOPs. The ETA machine delivered in the late 1980s (see Fazio [1987]) used low-temperature CMOS in a configuration with up to 10 processors. Each processor retained the memory–memory architecture based on the CYBER-205. Although the ETA-10 achieved enormous peak performance, its scalar speed was not comparable. In 1989 CDC, the first supercomputer vendor, closed ETA and left the supercomputer design business.

In 1986, IBM introduced the System/370 vector architecture (see Moore et al. [1987]) and its first implementation in the 3090 Vector Facility. The architecture extends the System/370 architecture with 171 vector instructions. The 3090/VF is integrated into the 3090 CPU. Unlike most other vector machines, the 3090/VF routes its vectors through the cache.

The 1980s also saw the arrival of smaller-scale vector machines, called mini-supercomputers. Priced at roughly one-tenth the cost of a supercomputer ($0.5 to $1 million versus $5 to $10 million), these machines caught on quickly. Although many companies joined the market, the two companies that have been most successful are Convex and Alliant. Convex started with a uniprocessor vector machine (C-1) and now offers a small multiprocessor (C-2); they emphasize Cray software capability. Alliant [1987] has concentrated more on the multiprocessor aspects; they build an eight-processor machine, with each processor offering vector capability.

The basis for modern vectorizing compiler technology and the notion of data dependence was developed by Kuck and his colleagues [1974] at the University of Illinois. Banerjee [1979] developed the test named after him. Padua and Wolf [1986] gave a good overview of vectorizing compiler technology.

Benchmark studies of various supercomputers including attempts to understand the performance differences have been undertaken by Lubeck, Moore and Mendez [1985], Bucher [1983], and Jordan [1987]. In Chapter 2, we discussed several benchmark suites aimed at scientific usage and often employed for supercomputer benchmarking, including Linpack, the Lawrence Livermore Laboratories FORTRAN kernels, and the Perfect Club suite.

In the late 1980s, graphics supercomputers arrived on the market from Stellar [Sporer, Moss, and Mathais 1988] and Ardent [Miranker, Rubenstein, and Sanguinetti 1988]. The Stellar machine used a timeshared pipeline to allow high-speed vector processing and efficient multitasking. This approach was used earlier in a machine designed by B. J. Smith [1981] called the HEP and built by Denelcor in the mid-1980s. This approach does not yield high-speed scalar performance, as evident in the scalar benchmarks of the Stellar machine. The Ardent machine combines a RISC processor (the MIPS R2000) with a custom vector unit. These vector machines, which cost about $100K, brought vector capabilities to a new potential market. In late 1989, Stellar and Ardent were merged to form Stardent, which eventually repositioned itself as a graphics software company.

In less than 20 years they have gone from unproven, new architectures to playing a significant role in the goal to provide engineers and scientists with ever larger amounts of computing power. The enormous price-performance advantages of microprocessor technology may bring this era to an end. Recently, both Cray and Convex announced and delivered large-scale multiprocessors (the T3D and Excalibar machines) based on microprocessors. By using advanced superscalar microprocessors, designers can build machines that exceed the peak performance of the fastest vector machines. The challenge, as we saw in Chapter 9, lies in programming these machines. As progress is made on this front, the role of vector machines in science and engineering may continue to decrease.

References

ALLIANT COMPUTER SYSTEMS CORP. [1987]. *Alliant FX/Series: Product Summary* (June), Acton, Mass.

BANERJEE, U. [1979]. *Speedup of Ordinary Programs*, Ph.D. Thesis, Dept. of Computer Science, Univ. of Illinois at Urbana-Champaign (October).

BASKETT, F. AND T. W. KELLER [1977]. "An Evaluation of the CRAY-1 Computer," in *High Speed Computer and Algorithm Organization*, Kuck, D. J., Lawrie, D. H. and A. H. Sameh, eds., Academic Press, 71-84.

BUCHER, I. Y. [1983]. "The computational speed of supercomputers," *Proc. SIGMETRICS Conf. on Measuring and Modeling of Computer Systems,* ACM (August) 151–165.

CALLAHAN, D., J. DONGARRA, AND D. LEVINE [1988]. "Vectorizing compilers: A test suite and results," *Supercomputing '88,* ACM/IEEE (November), Orlando, Fla., 98–105.

CHEN, S. [1983]. "Large-scale and high-speed multiprocessor system for scientific applications," *Proc. NATO Advanced Research Work on High Speed Computing* (June); also in K. Hwang, ed., "Supercomputers: Design and applications," *IEEE* (August) 1984.

DONGARRA, J. J. [1986]. "A survey of high performance computers," *COMPCON, IEEE* (March) 8–11.

FAZIO, D. [1987]. "It's really much more fun building a supercomputer than it is simply inventing one," *COMPCON, IEEE* (February) 102-105.

FLYNN, M. J. [1966]. "Very high-speed computing systems," *Proc. IEEE* 54:12 (December) 1901–1909.

HINTZ, R. G. AND D. P. TATE [1972]. "Control data STAR-100 processor design," *COMPCON, IEEE* (September) 1–4.

JORDAN, K. E. [1987]. "Performance comparison of large-scale scientific computers: Scalar mainframes, mainframes with vector facilities, and supercomputers," *Computer* 20:3 (March) 10–23.

KUCK, D., P. P. BUDNIK, S.-C. CHEN, D. H. LAWRIE, R. A. TOWLE, R. E. STREBENDT, E. W. DAVIS, JR., J. HAN, P. W. KRASKA, Y. MURAOKA [1974]. "Measurements of parallelism in ordinary FORTRAN programs," *Computer* 7:1 (January) 37–46.

LINCOLN, N. R. [1982]. "Technology and design trade offs in the creation of a modern supercomputer," *IEEE Trans. on Computers* C-31:5 (May) 363–376.

LUBECK, O., J. MOORE, AND R. MENDEZ [1985]. "A benchmark comparison of three supercomputers: Fujitsu VP-200, Hitachi S810/20, and CRAY X-MP/2," *Computer* 18:1 (January) 10–29.

MIRANKER, G. S., J. RUBENSTEIN, AND J. SANGUINETTI [1988]. "Squeezing a Cray-class supercomputer into a single-user package," *COMPCON, IEEE* (March) 452–456.

MIURA, K. AND K. UCHIDA [1983]. "FACOM vector processing system: VP100/200," *Proc. NATO Advanced Research Work on High Speed Computing* (June); also in K. Hwang, ed., "Supercomputers: Design and applications," *IEEE* (August 1984) 59–73.

MOORE, B., A. PADEGS, R. SMITH, AND W. BUCHOLZ [1987]. "Concepts of the System/370 vector architecture," *Proc. 14th Symposium on Computer Architecture* (June), ACM/IEEE, Pittsburgh, Pa., 282–292.

PADUA, D. AND M. WOLFE [1986]. "Advanced compiler optimizations for supercomputers," *Comm. ACM* 29:12 (December) 1184–1201.

RUSSELL, R. M. [1978]. "The CRAY-1 computer system," *Comm. of the ACM* 21:1 (January) 63–72.

SCHNECK, P. B. [1987]. *Supercomputer Architecture,* Kluwer Academic Publishers, Norwell, Mass.

SMITH, B. J. [1981]. "Architecture and applications of the HEP multiprocessor system," *Real-Time Signal Processing IV* 298 (August) 241–248.

SPORER, M., F. H. MOSS AND C. J. MATHAIS [1988]. "An introduction to the architecture of the Stellar Graphics supercomputer," *COMPCON, IEEE* (March) 464–46???.

WATANABE, T. [1987]. "Architecture and performance of the NEC supercomputer SX system," *Parallel Computing* 5, 247–255.

WATSON, W. J. [1972]. "The TI ASC–A highly modular and flexible super computer architecture," *Proc. AFIPS Fall Joint Computer Conf.*, 221–228.

EXERCISES

In these Exercises assume DLXV has a clock rate of 80 MHz and that $T_{base} = 10$ and $T_{loop} = 15$. Also assume that the store latency is always included in the running time.

B.1 [10] <B.1–B.2> Write a DLXV vector sequence that achieves the peak MFLOPS performance of the machine (use the functional unit and instruction description in Section B.2). Assuming an 80-MHz clock rate, what is the peak MFLOPS?

B.2 [20/15/15] <B.1–B.6> Consider the following vector code run on an 80-MHz version of DLXV for a fixed vector length of 64:

```
LV      V1,Ra
MULTV   V2,V1,V3
ADDV    V4,V1,V3
SV      Rb,V2
SV      Rc,V4
```

Ignore all strip-mining overhead, but assume that the store latency must be included in the time to perform the loop. The entire sequence produces 64 results.

a. [20] Assuming no chaining and a single memory pipeline, how many clock cycles per result (including both stores as one result) does this vector sequence require?

b. [15] If the vector sequence is chained, how many clock cycles per result does this sequence require?

c. [15] Suppose DLXV had three memory pipelines and chaining. If there were no bank conflicts in the accesses for the above loop, how many clock cycles are required per result for this sequence?

B.3 [20/20/15/15/20/20/20] <B.2–B.7> Consider the following FORTRAN code:

```
do 10 i=1,n
        A(i) = A(i) + B(i)
        B(i) = x * B(i)
10  continue
```

Use the techniques of Section B.7 to estimate performance throughout this exercise assuming an 80-MHz version of DLXV.

a. [20] Write the best DLXV vector code for the inner portion of the loop. Assume x is in F0 and the addresses of A and B are in Ra and Rb, respectively.

b. [20] Find the total time for this loop on DLXV (T_{100}). What is the MFLOP rating for the loop (R_{100})?

c. [15] Find R_{∞} for this loop.

d. [15] Find $N_{1/2}$ for this loop.

e. [20] Find N_v for this loop. Assume the scalar code has been pipeline scheduled so that each memory reference takes six cycles and each FP operation takes 3 cycles. Assume the scalar overhead is also T_{loop}.

f. [20] Assume DLXV has two memory pipelines. Write vector code that takes advantage of the second memory pipeline.

g. [20] Compute T_{100} and R_{100} for DLX with two memory pipelines.

B.4 [20/10] <B.3> Suppose we have a version of DLXV with eight memory banks (each a doubleword wide) and a memory-access time of eight cycles.

a. [20] If a load vector of length 64 is executed with a stride of 20 doublewords, how many cycles will the load take to complete?

b. [10] What percentage of the memory bandwidth do you achieve on a 64-element load at stride 20 versus stride 1?

B.5 [12/12/20] <B.4–B.7> Consider the following loop:

```
C = 0.0
do 10 i=1,64
        A(i) = A(i) + B(i)
        C = C + A(i)
10   continue
```

a. [12] Split the loop into two loops: one with no dependence and one with a dependence. Write these loops in FORTRAN—as a source-to-source transformation. This optimization is called *loop fission*.

b. [12] Write the DLXV vector code for the loop without a dependence.

c. [20] Write the DLXV code to evaluate the dependent loop using recursive doubling.

B.6 [20/15/20/20] <B.5–B.7> The compiled Linpack performance of the CRAY-1 (designed in 1976) was almost doubled by a better compiler in 1989. Let's look at a simple example of how this might occur. Consider the "SAXPY–like" loop (where k is a parameter to the procedure containing the loop):

```
do 10 i=1,64
        do 10 j=1,64
        Y(k,j) = a*X(i,j) + Y(k,j)
10   continue
```

a. [20] Write the **straightforward** code sequence for just the inner loop in DLXV vector instructions.

b. [15] Using the techniques of Section B.7, estimate the performance of this code on DLXV by finding T_{64} in clock cycles. You may assume that T_{base} applies once and T_{loop} of overhead is incurred for each iteration of the outer loop. What limits the performance?

c. [20] Rewrite the DLXV code to reduce the performance limitation; show the resulting inner loop in DLXV vector instructions. (Hint: think about what establishes $T_{element}$; can you affect it?) Find the total time for the resulting sequence.

d. [20] Estimate the performance of your new version using the techniques of Section B.7 and finding T_{64}.

B.7 [15/15/25] <B.6> Consider the following code.

```
      do 10 i=1,64
           if (B(i) .ne. 0) then
               A(i) = A(i) / B(i
   10  continue
```

Assume that the addresses of A and B are in Ra and Rb, respectively, and that F0 contains 0.

a. [15] Write the DLXV code for this loop using the vector-mask capability.

b. [15] Write the DLXV code for this loop using scatter/gather.

c. [25] Estimate the performance (T_{100} in clock cycles) of these two vector loops assuming a divide latency of 20 cycles. Assume that all vector instructions run at one result per clock, independent of the setting of the vector-mask register. Assume that 50% of the entries of B are 0. Considering hardware costs, which would you build if the above loop **was** typical?

B.8 [15/20/15/15] <B.1–B.7> In Figure 2.24 of Chapter 2 (page 75), we saw that the difference between peak and sustained performance could be large: For one problem, a Hitachi S810 had a peak speed twice as high as the CRAY X-MP, while for another more realistic problem the CRAY X-MP was twice as fast as the Hitachi machine. Let's examine why this might occur using two versions of DLXV and the following code sequences:

```
      C               Code sequence 1
           do 10 i=1,10000
               A(i+1) = x * A(i) + y * A(i)
   10  continue
```

```
      C               Code sequence 2
           do 10 i=1,100
               A(i+1) = x * A(i)
   10  continue
```

Assume there is a version of DLXV (call it DLXVII) that has two copies of every floating-point functional unit with full chaining among them. Assume that both DLXV and DLXVII have two load/store units. Because of the extra functional units and the increased complexity of assigning operations to units, all the overheads (T_{base}, T_{loop}, and the start-up overheads per vector operation) are doubled.

a. [15] Find the number of clock cycles for code sequence 1 on DLXV.

b. [20] Find the number of clock cycles on code sequence 1 for DLXVII. How does this compare to DLXV?

c. [15] Find the number of clock cycles on code sequence 2 for DLXV.

d. [15] Find the number of clock cycles on code sequence 2 for DLXVII. How does this compare to DLXV?

B.12 [25] <B.6> Because the difference between vector and scalar modes is so large on a supercomputer and the machines often cost tens of millions of dollars, programmers are frequently willing to go to extraordinary effort to achieve good performance. This often includes tricky assembly language programming. An interesting problem is to write a vectorizable sort for floating-point numbers—a task sometimes required in scientific code. Choose a sorting algorithm and write a version for DLXV that uses vector operations as much as possible. (Hint: One good choice is quicksort where the vector compares and compress/expand capability can be used.)

B.13 [25] <B.6> In some vector machines, the vector registers are addressable, and the operands to a vector operation may be two different parts of the same vector register. This allows another solution for the reduction shown on page XXX. The key idea in partial sums is to reduce the vector to m sums where m is the total latency through the vector functional unit including the operand read and write times. Assume that the DLXV vector registers are addressable (e.g., you can initiate a vector operation with the operand V1(16), indicating that the input operand began with element 16). Also, assume that the total latency for adds including operand read and write is eight cycles. Write a DLXV code sequence that reduces the contents of V1 to eight partial sums. It can be done with one vector operation.

B.14 [40] <B.2–B.6> Extend the DLX simulator to be a DLXV simulator including the ability to count clock cycles. Write some short benchmark programs in DLX and DLXV assembly language. Measure the speedup on DLXV, the percentage of vectorization, and usage of the functional units.

B.15 [50] <B.5> Modify the DLX compiler to include a dependence checker. Run some scientific code and loops through it and measure what percentage of the statements could be vectorized.

B.16 [Discussion] Some proponents of vector machines might argue that the vector processors have provided the best path to ever-increasing amounts of computer power by focusing their attention on boosting peak vector performance. Others would argue that the emphasis on peak performance is misplaced because an increasing percentage of the programs are dominated by nonvector performance. (Remember Amdahl's Law?) The proponents would respond that programmers should work to make their programs vectorizable. What do you think about this argument?

B.17 [Discussion] Consider the points raised in the Concluding Remarks (Section B.9). This topic—the relative advantages of pipelined scalar machines versus FP vector machines—is the source of much debate in the early 1990s. What advantages do you see for each side? What would you do in this situation?

B.18 [20] Here is a tricky piece of code with two-dimensional arrays. Does this loop have dependences? Can it be written so that there are Can these loops be written so they are parallel ? If so, how? Rewrite the **source** code so that it is clear that the loop can be vectorized, if possible.

```
      do 290 j = 2,n
         do 290 i = 2,j
      aa(i,j)=aa(i-1,j)*aa(i-1,j)+bb(i,j)
290      continue
```

B.19 Consider the following loop:

```
      do 10 i = 2,n
   A(i) = B
10         C(i) = A(i-1)
```

a.   [12] Show there is a loop-carried dependence in this code fragment.

b.   [15] Rewrite the code in Fortran so that it can be vectorized as two separate vector sequences.

Index

Y